ORGANIZATIONAL BEHAVIOUR

Visit the *Organizational Behaviour, Seventh Edition*, Companion Website at **www.pearsoned.co.uk/buchuc** to find valuable student learning material including:

- An audio summary of each chapter
- Video cases to contextualise your learning in the real world
- Multiple choice, fill in the blank and true/false questions with Grade Tracker function to test your learning and monitor your progress
- Interactive study guide with animations and activities
- Crossword puzzles to help test your understanding
- Flashcards to test your knowledge of key terms and definitions
- An online glossary to explain key terms

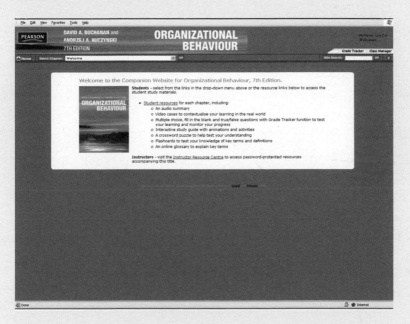

PEARSON

We work with leading authors to develop the
strongest educational materials in business and
management bringing cutting-edge thinking and best
learning practice to a global market.

Under a range of well-known imprints, including
Financial Times Prentice Hall, we craft high quality print and
electronic publications which help readers to understand
and apply their content, whether studying or at work.

To find out more about the complete range of our
publishing, please visit us on the World Wide Web at:
www.pearsoned.co.uk

ORGANIZATIONAL BEHAVIOUR

SEVENTH EDITION

David A. Buchanan
Cranfield University School of Management

Andrzej A. Huczynski
University of Glasgow School of Business and Management

**Financial Times
Prentice Hall
is an imprint of**

PEARSON

Harlow, England • London • New York • Boston • San Francisco • Toronto
Sydney • Tokyo • Singapore • Hong Kong • Seoul • Taipei • New Delhi
Cape Town • Madrid • Mexico City • Amsterdam • Munich • Paris • Milan

Pearson Education Limited
Edinburgh Gate
Harlow
Essex CM20 2JE
England

and Associated Companies throughout the world

Visit us on the World Wide Web at:
www.pearsoned.co.uk

First published by Prentice Hall International (UK) Ltd 1985
Second edition published by Prentice Hall International (UK) Ltd 1991
Third edition published by Prentice Hall Europe 1997
Fourth edition published by Pearson Education Ltd 2001
Fifth edition published by Pearson Education Ltd 2004
Sixth edition published by Pearson Education Ltd 2007
Seventh edition published by Pearson Education Ltd 2010

ISBN: 978-0-273-72822-1

British Library Cataloguing-in-Publication Data
A catalogue record for this book is available from the British Library

Library of Congress Cataloging-in-Publication Data
Buchanan, David A.
   Organizational behaviour / David A. Buchanan, Andrzej A. Huczynski. – 7th ed.
      p. cm.
   ISBN 978-0-273-72822-1 (pbk.)
   1. Organizational behavior.   I. Huczynski, Andrzej.   II. Title.
   HD58.7.H83 2010
   302.3'5–dc22
                                                                2009053037

10 9 8 7 6 5 4
14 13 12

Typeset in 9/12 pt Simbach by 35
Printed and bound by Rotolito Lombarda, Italy

Outline contents

Supporting resources

Visit **www.pearsoned.co.uk/buchuc** to find valuable online resources

Companion Website for students
- An audio summary of each chapter
- Video cases to contextualise your learning in the real word
- Multiple choice, fill in the blank and true/false questions with Grade Tracker function to test your learning and monitor your progress
- Interactive study guide with animations and activities
- Crossword puzzles to help test your understanding
- Flashcards to test your knowledge of key terms and definitions
- An online glossary to explain key terms

For instructors
- Complete Instructor's Manual, including 72 suggested lecture ideas based around chapters of the book
- PowerPoint slides that can be downloaded and used for presentations

For more information please contact your local Pearson Education sales representative or visit **www.pearsoned.co.uk/buchuc**

Full contents

Guided tour

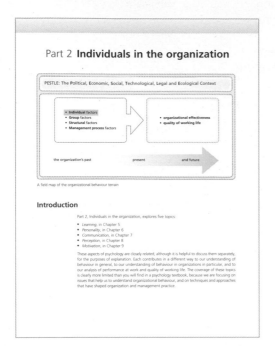

The book is divided into five **parts**, each with a **part map** and a full **introduction**, which makes the structure of the book more transparent and easier for you to navigate through.

Within each part, **Invitation to see** explores how work and organizations are presented in the media through images. This feature briefs you on how to analyse and 'decode' some of the messages within a photograph.

NEW! to this edition

Concluding each part opener, you'll find an insightful new feature: **What would you do? You're the employee**. Within this box you are presented with a dilemma that will help you relate Organizational Behaviour theory to practice by asking you to solve real-life problems.

A **Contents list** appears at the start of each chapter to help enable you to navigate the text easily.

Each chapter opener also contains a list of the main **key terms** and concepts that are defined, explained and illustrated throughout the chapter.

Learning outcomes to be achieved by the time you reach the end of the chapter appear at the beginning and are coupled with a **Recap** section at the end, which summarises the chapter content and can be used for reminder and revision.

NEW! to this edition!

Why did that happen? will place you in a decision-making role by asking you to help solve problems and justify your decisions.

Key terms, which were introduced at the start of the chapter, are highlighted in the text with a brief explanation in the margin where they first appear. These terms are also included in the **Glossary** at the end of the book.

Chapter 1 Explaining organizational behaviour

Key terms

organizational behaviour
organization
controlled performance
organizational dilemma
fundamental attribution error
organizational effectiveness
balanced scorecard
quality of working life

positivism
operational definition
variance theory
constructivism
process theory
evidence-based management
human resource management
employment cycle

Learning outcomes

When you have read this chapter, you should be able to define those key terms in your own words, and you should also be able to:

1. Explain the importance of an understanding of organizational behaviour.
2. Explain and illustrate the central dilemma of organizational design.
3. Understand the need for explanations of behaviour in organizations that take account of relationships between factors at different levels of analysis.
4. Understand the difference between positivist and constructivist perspectives, and their implications for the study of organizational behaviour.
5. Understand the difference between variance and process theories and their uses in understanding organizational behaviour.
6. Explain the development and limitations of evidence-based management.
7. Recognize the breadth of applications of organizational behaviour theory, in particular the contribution to human resource management practice.

---

6 Chapter 1 Explaining organizational behaviour

What is organizational behaviour?

Why did that happen?

It was a bad experience. You just ordered a soft drink and a sandwich. The person who served you was abrupt and unpleasant, did not smile, ignored you, did not make eye contact, and continued their conversation with a colleague, instead of maybe asking if you wanted something else. They slapped your change on the counter rather than put it in your hand, and turned away. You have used this café many times, but you have never been treated so rudely. You leave feeling angry, deciding never to return.

How can you explain the unusual behaviour of the person who served you?

Organizational behaviour: an interdisciplinary body of knowledge and field of research, concerned with how formal organizations, behaviour of people within organizations, and salient features of their context and environment, evolve and take shape, why all these things happen the way they do, and what purposes they serve.

This chapter explores how we can explain the behaviour of people in organizations. First, however, we have to define what organizational behaviour means.

Our margin definition is from Arndt Sorge and Malcolm Warner (1997, p.xii). The definition of a field of study identifies its scope, and the themes, questions, issues and problems that it seeks to address and to explain. It is important to note that this definition includes macro-organizational and micro-individual concerns – covering environmental and structural issues as well as individual and team factors. Chip Heath and Sim Sitkin (2001) distinguish between oB (or Big-B) and Ob (or Big-O) definitions of organizational behaviour. Big-B emphasizes interesting *behaviour*, such as stress or decision-making, and draws mainly on psychology. They argue that this approach misses out on what is distinctive about *organizations*. Stress, for example, occurs in many other social and domestic contexts. They prefer Ob – the Big-O definition – which emphasizes organizing, and pays attention to process, and to how factors at different levels of analysis (society, individual, group, organization) interact with each other.

Is this a dry, theoretical subject remote from day-to-day practical concerns? On the contrary. We live in an organized world. Look at the clothes you are wearing, the food that you eat, the computers that you use, the schools, colleges and universities where you study. What aspects of your life are not touched in some way by organizations of different kinds? Yes, of course, there are some, but not many. The study of organizational behaviour has direct practical implications for those who work in, manage, seek to subvert, or interact in other ways with organizations, whether they are small and local, or large and international.

You will see other similar labels: organization theory, industrial sociology, organizational psychology, organizational analysis, organization studies. Organization theory and industrial sociology tend to focus on macro-level studies of groups and organizations. Organizational psychology specializes in individual behaviour. Organizational analysis tends to emphasize practice rather than theory. Organization studies is a term which highlights the widening of the range of issues and perspectives that this field now embraces (Clegg *et al.*, 2006). These labels indicate subtle shifts in focus and emphasis rather than clearly defined boundaries. Organizational behaviour is widely recognized as the conventional 'umbrella' term, but some would argue with that view.

What is the explanation for your bad experience in that café? Well, we can blame the skills and the personality of the individual who served you. However, there are many other possibilities. Other explanations for your experience include:

* inadequate staff training;
* staff absences increasing working pressure;
* long hours, fatigue and poor work-life balance;
* equipment not working properly;

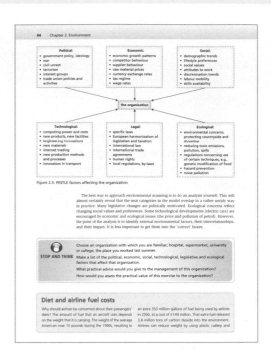

Cartoons, photos, tables and **diagrams** feature throughout the text to make it all the more engaging, digestible and readable.

You are frequently invited to **Stop and think** through contradictory and controversial points and arguments. You are also encouraged to apply ideas and analysis to your own experience and to challenge your own assumptions.

Throughout the text there are **portraits** of leading scholars who have contributed to our understanding of this subject.

Application and **illustration** of concepts, theories and frameworks are discussed throughout the text. These are clearly distinguishable from the text in colourful boxes and include recent management applications, international examples, examples of classic research and speculation about the future.

Recap and **Revision** provide a summary of the learning outcomes and offer a series of typical essay questions that can either be used for personal study or as tutorial revision aids.

The **Research assignment** gives you an opportunity to test your knowledge and to take your leaning further.

Springboard is a short annotated guide to further and more advanced learning.

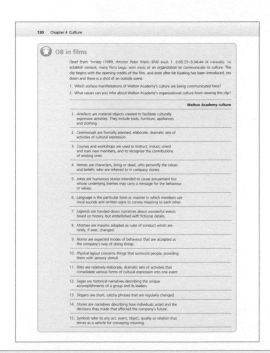

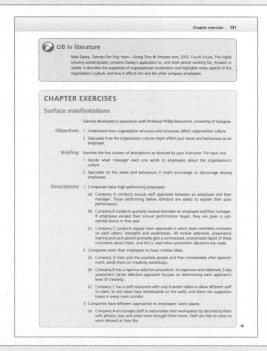

OB in films indentifies films, or television programmes that illustrate the wider relevance and application of the issues and ideas introduced in the chapter.

OB in literature suggests sources of creative writing to provide further illustration of concepts and themes from the chapter.

At the end of every chapter there are two **Chapter exercises**. One is designed for large classes and the other for smaller tutorial and seminar settings.

Online resources

Organizational Behaviour is supported by a free and fully interactive Companion Website available at **www.pearsoned.co.uk/buchuc** that contains a wealth of additional teaching and learning material.

For the lecturer

A range of password-protected teaching resources including:

- Complete, downloadable **Instructor's Manual** including 72 suggested lecture ideas based around chapters of the book.
- **PowerPoint slides** that can be downloaded and used for presentations.

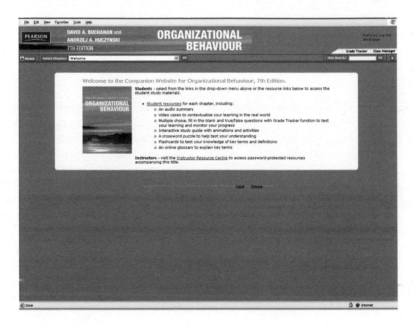

For the student

- An audio summary of each chapter
- Video cases to contextualize your learning in the real word
- Multiple choice, fill in the blank and true/false questions with Grade Tracker function to test your learning and monitor your progress
- Interactive study guide with animations and activities
- Crossword puzzles to help test your understanding
- Flashcards to test your knowledge of key terms and definitions
- An online glossary to explain key terms.

Acknowledgements

A large number of friends, colleagues and students have contributed their ideas, criticisms and advice to the development of this text. Our special thanks in this regard is therefore extended to Nadir Bheekhun, Phillip Beaumont, Lesley Buchanan, Lucy Gilmartin, Stuart Jack, Keith Macrosson, Gwénaëlle Madec, Bernard Mournian, Marc Poggia, Peder Schimmell, Adah Tole and Peter Yuille.

We would also like to thank the people at Pearson Education who have contributed to this edition. In particular: Gabrielle James Acquisitions Editor, Maggie Wells Deputy Design Manager, Angela Hawksbee Senior Production Controller, Emma Violet Editorial Assistant and Joy Cash Desk Editor.

Publisher's acknowledgements

The publisher would like to thank the following for their kind permission to reproduce their photographs:

(Key: b-bottom; c-centre; l-left; r-right; t-top)

Alamy Images: Bastian / © Caro 123, Chris Hennessy 102r, Ferenc Szelepcsenyi 541, © H. Mark Weidman Photography 73, © ICP 115, © Interfoto 697, Jacky Parker 419, Paul Doyle 686, Peter Jordan 479, Vince Bevan 295, © WorldFoto 145; © **Alan Bryman:** 41; **Alice Research Group, Carnegie Mellon University:** 632t; **The Ancient Art and Architecture Collection:** Ronald Sheridan 463; **Andrzej A. Huczynski:** 426b; **Archives of the History of American Psychology / The University of Akron:** 141, 144, 170b, 172, 189t, 241, 249, 252t, 273, 342l, 141, 144, 170b, 172, 189t, 241, 249, 252t, 273, 342l; **AT&T Archives and History Center:** 306tl, 306b, 307, 306tl, 306b, 307; **Bentley Historical Library / University of Michigan:** Charles Horton Cooley Collection 186t; **Bethlehem Steel Corporation:** 425, 426t; **Camera Press Ltd:** Fabian Bachrach 250t; **Center for the Study of Social Work Practice / Columbia University School of Social Work:** 156b; **Colin McDougall:** 216; **Copyright © News Group Newspapers Ltd:** 501; **Corbis:** © Bettmann 701, © Bill Varie 184, © Jagadeesh / Reuters 314bl, Ted Spiegel 222r, © Underwood & Underwood 429t; **Courtesy of Albert Bandura:** 151; **Courtesy of Alexandra Milgram:** From Obedience © 1965 Stanley Milgram 374r; **Courtesy of Arlie Russell Hoschchild:** 683; **Courtesy of Armstrong Healthcare ltd:** 394; **Courtesy of Barbara Tversky:** 637bl; **Courtesy of Bert Raven:** 696; **Courtesy of Brandeis University:** 268; **Courtesy of Bruce W. Tuckman:** 317; **Courtesy of Carl Ransom Rogers Memorial Library:** 187; **Courtesy of Charles Bryce Perrow:** 504; **Courtesy of Chris Argyris:** 156t; **Courtesy of David Clarence McClelland:** 189b; **Courtesy of Edwin Locke:** 275t; **Courtesy of Eric Kroll:** 374l; **Courtesy of Fred Luthans:** 149; **Courtesy of Frederick E. Fiedler:** 611; **Courtesy of Frederick Herzberg:** 279; **Courtesy of Geert Hofstede:** 122; **Courtesy of George Ritzer:** 438; **Courtesy of Hans Jürgen Eysenck:** 175; **Courtesy of Henry Mintzberg:** 498; **Courtesy of James G. March:** 632c; **Courtesy of Jeffrey Pfeffer:** 714; **Courtesy of Joanne Martin:** 113; **Courtesy of John Child:** 510b; **Courtesy of Kenneth Dean Benne:** 339; **Courtesy of Kenneth H. Blanchard:** 613b; **Courtesy of Kenneth Wayne Thomas:** 672; **Courtesy of Mrs F. Asch:** 373tl; **Courtesy of Mrs J. Evans:** 87b; **Courtesy of Paul Hersey:** 613t; **Courtesy of Philip G Zimbardo, Ph.D.:** 476; **Courtesy of Phillip Yetton:** 633bl; **Courtesy of R. Meredith Belbin:** 341l; **Courtesy of Richard Hackman:** 281t; **Courtesy of Steven Lukes:** 700; **Courtesy of the Ford Motor Company:** 431, 433; **Courtesy of Toyota (GB) Ltd:** 104; **Courtesy of University of

Michigan: 342r; **Courtesy of Victor Harold Vroom:** 274, 633t; **Courtesy of University of Oklahoma:** 365; **David A. Buchanan:** Courtesy of David Grayson 59; **Detroit Institute of Arts:** 435; **Dreamstime.com:** Luchschen 376, Pathathai Chungyam 688; **Merrelyn Emery:** Merrrelyn Emery; **Mary Evans Picture Library:** 170t, 712, 170t, 712; **Gary P. Latham / University of Toronto:** 275b; **Georgetown University website:** Linda Farwell Photography 213; **Getty Images:** AFP 546, B. Busco 347, Paula Bronstein 3, Mike Powell 685; **Harvard Business School Archives:** Baker Library 7, 305b, 313, 336, 509, 510t, 587, Baker Library 7, 305b, 313, 336, 509, 510t, 587; **Innocent Ltd:** 60, 106; **National Institute on Aging:** 179b; **Katz Pictures Ltd:** 566; **Larry Fink@Studio 55:** 400; **Library of Congress:** 147; **MIT:** MIT; **Motorola:** 102l; **MSOD:** 610t; **NASA:** 398, 646, EJA / NASA 300; **Courtesy of Edgar Henry Schein:** 101, 101; **Courtesy of Eric John Miller:** 87t; **Courtesy of Terrence E. Deal:** 119t; **Photolibrary.com:** RESO 271t; **Press Association Images:** STR / AP xxxi, Dave Weaver 220r, Hanusa / AP 527, Larry MacDougal 432, PA Archive 407, Richard Vogel / AP 530t; **Reuters:** China Daily 559, Mike Segar 250b, Str Old 222l; **Rex Features:** Action Press 443, Image Source 314t; **S C Williams Library / Stevens Institute of Technology:** 430, Frederick Winslow Taylor Collection 423; **Science & Society Picture Library:** NMPFT / Walter Nurnberg 429b; **The Advertising Archives:** 473; **The Linn Klimax System:** 284; **The Ohio State University:** 599; **The Tavistock Institute:** The Tavistock Institute; **University Archives, University of Pittsburgh:** 503; **University of Michigan:** 308, 607, 308, 607; **Valmet Automotive Inc:** 531; **Verena Geiges:** Leif Geiges Staufen. Reproduced by permission of Verena Geiges, Staufen 489; **www.lottolab.org:** R. Beau Lotto 245t, 245b; **Yale University Library / Manuscripts and Archives:** 644.

All other images © Pearson Education

Every effort has been made to trace the copyright holders and we apologise in advance for any unintentional omissions. We would be pleased to insert the appropriate acknowledgement in any subsequent edition of this publication.

We are grateful to the following for permission to reproduce copyright material:

Cartoons

Cartoon on page xxv © Sam Gross/Condé Nast Publications/www.cartoonbank.com; Cartoon on page 10 © Copyright 2000 United Feature Syndicate, Inc.; Cartoon on page 25 © Perry Barlow/Condé Nast Publications/www.cartoonbank.com; Cartoons on pages 52, 87, 109, 142, 178, 209, 283, 299, 326, 424, 500, 568 from www.CartoonStock.com; Cartoon on page 54 © Leo Cullum/Condé Nast Publications/www.cartoonbank.com; Cartoon on page 77 © Aaron Bacall/Condé Nast Publications/www.cartoonbank.com; Cartoons on pages 121, 319, 347, 401, 441, 474, 707 Copyright Grantland Enterprises; www.grantland.net; Cartoon on page 146 reproduced with the kind permission of King Features Syndicate; Cartoons on pages 174 and 616 Copyright P.C. Vey. Originally appeared in *Harvard Business Review*; Cartoon on page 202 reproduced with kind permission of the Zits Partnership and King Features Syndicate; Cartoon on page 242 artwork supplied by The Broadbent Partnership, London; Cartoon on page 243 © Charles Barsotti/Condé Nast Publications/www.cartoonbank. com; Cartoons on pages 248, 468 © Copyright 2001, 2003 United Features Syndicate, Inc.; Cartoon on page 269 © Tom Cheney/Condé Nast Publications/www.cartoonbank.com; Cartoon on page 364 from www.phdcomics.com; Cartoon on page 370 © Lee Lorenz/Condé Nast Publications/www.cartoonbank.com; Cartoons on pages 409, 654 Copyright Randy Glasbergen, www.glasbergen.com; Cartoon on page 493 © Copyright 2007 Scott Adams, Inc.; Cartoon on page 536 © Christopher Weyant/Condé Nast Publications/www.cartoonbank.com; Cartoons on pages 539, 632, 718 from The Joy of Tech by Nitrozac and Snaggy, www. joyoftech.com; Cartoon on page 583 from CALVIN AND HOBBES © 1989 Watterson. Dist. By UNIVERSAL UCLICK. Reprinted with permission. All rights reserved; Cartoon on page 600 from Roy Delgado. Originally appeared in *Harvard Business Review*; Cartoon on page 608 from Joseph Mirachi (Estate of); Cartoon on page 668 from CATHY © Cathy Guizewite. Reprinted with permission of UNIVERSAL PRESS SYNDICATE. All rights reserved; Cartoon on page 687 © Copyright 2000 United Feature Syndicate, Inc.

Figures

Figure 1.4 adapted from *Understanding the People and Performance Link: Unlocking the Black Box*, London: Chartered Institute of Personnel and Development (Purcell, J., Kinnie, N., Hutchinson, S., Rayton, B. and Stuart, J. 2003) p. 7, Reprinted by permission of the Chartered Institute of Personnel and Development; Figure 2.8 reprinted (with adaption) from *Organizational Dynamics*, Vol. 12, No. 2, Velasquez, M., Moberg, D.J. and Cavanagh, G.F., Organizational statesmanship and dirty politics: ethical guidelines for the organizational politician, p. 73, Copyright 1983, with permission from Elsevier; Figure 2.9 after *Exploring Corporate Strategy: Text and Cases*, 7th ed., Financial Times Prentice Hall (Johnson, G., Scholes, K. and Whittington, K. 2005) p. 189, Exhibit 4.7; Figure 3.2 after *Web 2.0 and HR: A Discussion Paper*, Chartered Institute for Personnel and Development (Martin, G., Reddington, M. and Kneafsey, M.B. 2008) p. 7, with the permission of the publisher, and the Chartered Institute of Personnel and Development, London (www.cipd.co.uk); Figure 4.1 from *Organizational Behaviour and Analysis: An Integrated Approach* 4th ed., Financial Times Prentice Hall (Rollinson, D. 2008) p. 592; Figure 4.3 Copyright © 1985, by The Regents of the University of California. Reprinted from the *California Management Review*. Vol. 27, No. 2. By permission of The Regents; Figure 4.4 from Organizational socialization: its content and consequences, *Journal of Applied Psychology*, 79(5), pp. 730–43 (Chao, G.T., O'Leary-Kelly, A.M., Wolf, S., Klein, H.J. and Gardner, P.D. 1994), Copyright © 1994 by the American Psychological Association. Reproduced with permission. The official citation that should be used in referencing this material is Chao, G.T., O'Leary-Kelly, A.M., Wolf, S., Klein, H.J. & Gardner, P.D. (1994). Organizational socialization: Its content and consequences. *Journal of Applied Psychology*, 79, 730–743. di: 10.1037/0021–9010.79.5.730; Figure 4.5 from Corporate culture; the last frontier of control? *Journal of Management Studies*, 23(3), pp. 287–97 (Ray, C.A. 1986); Figure 4.6 from *Organizational Behaviour: Individuals, Groups and Organization*, 2nd ed., Financial Times Prentice Hall (Brooks, I. 2003) p. 266; Figure 4.7 from GRIFFIN, RICKY W; PUSTAY, MICHAEL W., INTERNATIONAL BUSINESS, 5th Edition, © 2007, p. 102. Reprinted by permission of Pearson Education, Inc., Upper Saddle River, NJ.; Figure 6.8 from I.T. Robertson, 'Personality and personnel selection', in C.L. Cooper and D.M. Rousseau (eds), *Trends in Organizational Behaviour*, 1994, p. 8 Copyright 1994 © John Wiley & Sons Limited. Reproduced with permission; Figure on page 215 from *Gesture in Naples and Gesture in Classical Antiquity*, Indiana University Press (de Jourio, A., trans by Adam Kenton 2001) Cambridge University Press, reprinted by the permission of the Syndics of Cambridge University Library; Figure 9.3 reprinted by permission of Harvard Business Review. Figure on p. 75. From 'Inner work life: understanding the subtext of business performance' by Amabile, T.M. and Kramer, S.J., 85(5). Copyright © 2007 by the Harvard Business School Publishing Corporation, all rights reserved; Figure 9.4 Copyright © 1975, by The Regents of the University of California. Reprinted from the *California Management Review*, Vol. 17, No. 4. By permission of The Regents; Figure 10.1 modified from MCGRATH, GROUPS: INTERACTION AND PERFORMANCE, 1st Edition, © 1984, p. 61. Reprinted by permission of Pearson Education, Inc., Upper Saddle River, NJ.; Figure on page 306 from *Behaviour in Organizations*, 6/E by Greenberg/Baron, © 1997. Reprinted by permission of Pearson Education, Inc. Upper Saddle River, NJ.; Figure 10.3 after *New Patterns of Management*, McGraw-Hill (Likert, R. 1961) p. 105, © The McGraw Hill Companies, Inc.; Figure 10.4 from DAFT/MARCIC. *Management*, 6E. © 2009 South-Western, a part of Cengage Learning, Inc. Reproduced by permission. www.cengage.com/permissions; Figure 11.3 reprinted from *Group Processes* edited by L. Berkowitz, M.E. Shaw, Communications networks fourteen years later, pp. 351–61, Copyright 1978, with permission from Elsevier; Figure 11.4 from *Behaviour in Organizations*, 6/E, by Greenberg/Baron, © 1997. Reproduced by permission of Pearson Education, Inc., Upper Saddle River, NJ.; Figure 11.5 from *The Coming Shape of Organization*, Butterworth-Heinemann (Belbin, R. Meredith 1996) p. 122, Belbin Associates; Figure 11.6 from *Social Psychology*, 5th ed., Pearson Education Ltd (Hogg, M.A. and Vaughan, G.M. 2008) p. 314; Figure 11.7 from *A Primer on Organizational Behaviour*, 5th ed., (Bowditch, J.L. and Buono, A.F. 2001) p. 170, Copyright © 2001 John Wiley & Sons, Inc. Reproduced with the permission of John Wiley & Sons, Inc.; Figure 12.1 from Aronson *et al.*, SOCIAL PSYCHOLOGY, Figure 12.1 'Social Facilitation and Social Loafing', © 2010. Reproduced by permission of Pearson Education, Inc.; Figure 12.2 from *Managing Behaviour in Organizations*, 2nd ed., Prentice Hall (Greenberg, J. 1999) p. 158; Figure 12.4 reprinted from *Advances in Experimental Social Psychology*, Volume 15, Moreland, R.L. and Levine, J.M., Socialization in small groups: temporal changes in individual-group relations, pp. 137–92, Copyright 1982, with permission from Elsevier; Figure 12.5 from *Social Psychology*, 5th ed., Pearson Education Ltd. (Hogg, M.A. and Vaughan, G.M. 2008) p. 424; Figure on page 373 from Asche, S.E. 'Effects of group pressure upon the modification and distortion of judgements' in, *Groups, Leadership and Men*, pp. 177–90 (Guetzkow, H. (ed.) 1951); Figure 13.3 from Work teams: applications and effectiveness, *American Psychologist*, 45(2), pp. 120–33 (Figure on p. 122) (Sundstrom, E., De Meuse, K.P. and Futrell, D. 1990); Figure 14.2 from Mike Noon and Paul Blyton, *The Realities of Work*, published 1997, Palgrave, reproduced with permission of Palgrave Macmillan; Figure on page 457 from *Daily Telegraph, Appointments*, 31 December 1998, Reprinted by permission of Ward Executive Ltd.; Figure 15.4 from *Organizational Theory*, Prentice-Hall, Inc. (Robbins, S.P. 1990) p. 88; Figure 15.6 from *Management: An Introduction*, 3rd edn., Financial Times Prentice Hall (Boddy, D. 2005) p. 308 'The structure within a BAE factory'; Figure 15.7 from http://www.royalnavalmuseum.org/info_sheets_nav_rankings.htm, Trustees of the Royal Naval Museum; Figure 15.10 from Organizational Analysis, *Supplement to Manager, the British Journal of Administrative Management*, No. 18, March/April (Lysons, K. 1997); Figure on page 495 from http://media.popularmechanics.com/images/1206airbus_diagramTx.jpg; Figure 16.1 from *Creative Organization Theory*, Sage Publications, Inc. (Morgan, G. 1989) p. 66; Figure 16.2 from *Management and Technology*, HMSO (Woodward, J. 1958) p. 11, Crown Copyright material is reproduced with permission under the terms of the Click-Use License; Figure 16.4 from Perrow, Charles. *Organizational Analysis*. 1E. © 1970 Wadsworth, a part of Cengage Learning, Inc. Reproduced by permission. www.cengage.com/permissions; Figure 16.6 from ROBBINS, STEPHEN P.; JUDGE, TIMOTHY A., ORGANIZATIONAL BEHAVIOR, 12th Edition, © 2007. Reprinted by permission of Pearson Education, Inc., Upper Saddle River, NJ.; Figure on page 526 from Boeing 787 Dreamliner Engineering Chief Describes Partners Organization, *Design News* (May 15 2007), http://www.designnews.com/article/2659-Boeing_787_Dreamliner_Engineering_Chief_Describes_Partners_Organization.php, Used with permission of Design News Copyright © 2009. All rights reserved; Figure 17.8 adapted from *Human Resource Management: A Strategic Introduction*, 2nd ed., Blackwell (Mabey, C., Salaman, G. and Storey, J. 1998); Figure 17.15 reprinted by permission of *Harvard Business Review*. From 'The contribution revolution: Letting volunteers build your business' by Cook, S., 86(10). Copyright © 2008 by the Harvard Business School Publishing Corporation, all rights reserved; Figure 17.17 reprinted by permission of Harvard Business Review. From 'Which kind of collaboration is right for you?' by Pisano, G. and Verganti, R., 86(12). Copyright © 2008 by the Harvard Business School Publishing Corporation, all rights reserved; Figures on page 570 from Broussine, M. and Vince, R., 'Working with metaphor towards organizational change', in *Organizational Development: Metaphorical Explorations*, pp. 57–72 (Oswick, C. and Grant, D. (eds) 1996), Pearson Education Ltd; Figure 18.4 from *Reshaping Change: A Processual Approach*, Routledge (Dawson, P. 2003); Figure 19.2 reprinted by permission of H*arvard Business Review*. From "How to choose a leadership pattern" by Tannenbaum, R. and Schmidt, W.H., Vol. 37, March–April reprinted in May–June, 1973. Copyright © 1958 by the Harvard Business School Publishing Corporation, all rights reserved; Figure 19.3 from *Management of Organizational Behaviour: Utilizing Human Resources*, Prentice-Hall (Hersey, P. and Blanchard, K.H. 1988) Situational Leadership® is a registered trademark of the Center for Leadership Studies, © Copyright 2006 Reprinted with permission of the Center for Leadership Studies. Escondido, CA 92025. www.situational.com All Rights Reserved; Figure 20.2 reprinted (and adapted) from *Organizational Dynamics*, 28(4), Vroom, V.H., Leadership and the decision making process, pp. 82–94, Copyright 2000, with permission from Elsevier; Figure 21.4 reprinted from *Organizational Behaviour and Human Performance*, Vol. 16, T.H. Ruble and K. Thomas, Support for a two-dimensional model of conflict behaviour, p. 145, Copyright 1976, with permission from Elsevier; Figure 22.1 reuse of figure, p. 69 'Structural conditions producing the power . . .' from POWER IN ORGANIZATIONS by JEFFREY PFEFFER. Copyright © 1981 by Jeffery Pfeffer. Reprinted by permission of HarperCollins Publishers.

Tables

Table 2.1 from I. Ansoff, 'Measuring and managing for environmental turbulence: the Ansoff Associates approach', in Alexander Watson Haim (ed.), *The Portable Conference on Change Management*, HRSD Press Inc., 1997, pp. 67–83. Reprinted by permission of the Estate of H. Igor Ansoff; Table 2.2 reprinted (with adaption) from *Organizational Dynamics*, Vol. 12, No. 2, Velasquez, M., Moberg, D.J. and Cavanagh, G.F., Organizational states-manship and dirty politics: ethical guidelines for the organizational politician, p. 72, Copyright 1983, with permission from Elsevier; Table on page 91 adapted from Work sys-tems, quality of working life and attitudes of workers: an empirical study towards the effects of team and non-teamwork, *New Technology, Work and Employment* 16(3), pp. 191–203 (Steijn, B. 2001); Table 4.2 from p. 13 from *Cultures in Organizations: Three Perspectives* by Martin, J. (1992) by permission of Oxford University Press; Table 4.3 from *Organizational Behaviour: Improving Performance and Commitment in the Workplace* McGraw Hill (Colquitt, J.A., LePine, J.A. and Wesson, M.J. 2009) p. 557; Tables 4.6 and 4.7 from The business of international business is culture, *International Business Review*, 3(1), pp. 1–14 (p. 3 and p. 4) (Hofstede, G. 1994); Table 4.8 from HELLRIEGEL/SLOCUM. *Organizational Behaviour* (with Bind-in Competency Test Web Site Printed Access Card), 12E. © 2009 South-Western, a part of Cengage Learning, Inc. Reproduced by permission. www.cen-gage.com/permissions; Table 4.9 reprinted from *Organizational Dynamics*, 29(4), Javidan, M. and House, R.J., Cultural acumen for the global manager: lessons from the Project GLOBE, pp. 289–305, Copyright 2001, with permission from Elsevier; Table on pages 158–9 reprinted by permission of *Harvard Business Review*. From 'Is yours a learning organization?' by Garvin, D.A., Edmondson, A. and Gino, F., 86(3). Copyright © 2008 by the Harvard Business School Publishing Corporation, all rights reserved; Tables on page 191 and 192 from *Human Resource Management at Work*, 3rd ed., Chartered Institute of Personnel and Development (Marchington, M. and Wilkinson, A. 2005) with the permission of the pub-lisher, the Chartered Institute of Personnel and Development, London (www.cipd.co.uk); Table on page 200 from Born to lose, *The Times*, Times 2 Supplement, pp. 4–5 (Ahuja, A.), © *The Times*, 31 August 2006; Table on page 203 from *Focus*, p. 18 (May 1999); Table 10.1 from *Effective Behaviour in Organizations. Homewood, IL: Irwin (sixth edn).*, 6th ed., Irwin (Cohen, A.R., Fink, S.L., Gadon, H. and Willits, R.D. 1995) p. 142 © The McGraw-Hill Companies, Inc.; Table 10.3 reprinted by permission of *Harvard Business Review*. Table on p. 114 From 'Firing up the front line' by Katzenbach, J.R. and Santamaria, J.A., 77(3). Copyright © 1999 by the Harvard Business School Publishing Corporation, all rights reserved; Table on page 353 (Task 1) from Dodd-McCue, D., Journal of Management Education, 15(3), pp. 335–9, Copyright © 1991, OBTS Teaching Society for Management Educators. Reprinted by Permission of SAGE Publications.; Table on page 353 (Task 2) from A WHACK ON THE SIDE OF THE HEAD by Roger von Oech. Copyright © 1983, 1990, 1998 by Roger von Oech. By permission of GRAND CENTRAL PUBLISHING; Table on pages 354 (Task 3) adapted from Analytical or creative? A problem solving comparison, *The 1981 Annual Handbook for Group Facilitators*, pp. 24–6 (Pfeiffer), Copyright © 1981 Jossey-Bass Pfeiffer. Reproduced with permission of John Wiley & Sons, Inc.; Table 13.1 from Work teams: applications and effectiveness, *American Psychologist*, 45(2), pp. 120–33 (Table on p. 125) (Sundstrom, E., De Meuse, K.P. and Futrell, D. 1990); Table 13.4 reprinted by permission of SAGE Publications, London, Los Angeles, New Delhi and Singapore from, Clegg, S.R., Kornberger, M. and Pitsis, T., *Managing and Organizations*, Copyright (© Sage Publications 2008); Table 13.5 from The art of building a car: the Swedish experience re-examined, *New Technology, Work and Employment*, 6(2), pp. 85–90 (Table on p. 89) (Hammarstrom, O. and Lansbury, R.D. 1991); Table 14.4 from Paul S. Adler, The emanci-patory significance of Taylorism, in, *Readings in Organizational Science – Organizational Change in a Changing Context*, p. 9 (Cunha, M.P.E. and Marques, C.A. (eds) 1999), Instituto Superior de Psicologia Aplicada, Lisbon; Table on page 460 from *Bosses in British Business*, Routledge and Kegan Paul (Jervis, F.R. 1974) p. 87; Table 15.3 adapted from *Organizational Behavior: Concepts and Applications*, 3rd ed., Pearson Education, Inc. (Gray, J.L. and Starke, F.A. 1984) p. 412, Table 10.1; Table 16.4 adapted from *The Analysis of Organization*, John Wiley, Inc. (Litterer, J.A. 1973) p. 339, Reproduced by permission of the estate of Joseph A. Litterer.; Table 17.3 from *Strategy Synthesis: Text and Readings*, de Wit, B. and Meyer, R., Copyright 2005 International Thomson Business Press. Reproduced by permis-sion of Cengage Learning; Table 19.3 from Cast in a new light, *People Management*, 14(2), pp. 38–41 (Table on p. 41) (Alimo-Metcalfe, B. and Bradley, M. 2008); Table 20.8 from *A Diagnostic Approach to Organizational Behaviour*, 4th ed., Prentice-Hall, Inc. (Gordon, J.R. 1993) p. 253; Table on page 648 reprinted by permission of *Harvard Business Review*. Exhibit on p. 110 From 'What you don't know about making decisions' by Garvin, D.A. and Roberto, M.A., 79(8). Copyright © 2001 by the Harvard Business School Publishing Corporation, all rights reserved; Table 21.1 reprinted by permission of *Harvard Business Review*. Adapted exhibit on p. 115 From 'Can marketing and manufacturing coexist?' by Shapiro, B.S., 55(September–October). Copyright © 1977 by the Harvard Business School Publishing Corporation, all rights reserved; Table 21.2 adapted from *Managing Through Organization*, Hales, C., Copyright 1993 Routledge, Reproduced by permission of Cengage Learning; Table 21.3 from *Developing Management Skills for Europe*, Financial Times/Prentice Hall (Whetton, D., Cameron, K. and Woods, M. 2000) p. 345; Table 21.4 after Johnson & Johnson, JOINING TOGETHER, pp. 182–183, © 1975. Reproduced by permission of Pearson Education, Inc.; Table 22.4 reproduced by permission of SAGE Publications, London, Los Angeles, New Delhi and Singapore, from Buchanan, D.A. and Badham, R.J., *Power, Politics and Organizational Change: Winning the Turf Game*, Copyright (© Sage Publications 2008); Table 22.5 Reproduced by permission of SAGE Publications, London, Los Angeles, New Delhi and Singapore, adapted from Buchanan, D.A. and Badham, R.J., *Power, Politics and Organizational Change: Winning the Turf Game*, Copyright (© Sage Publications 2008); Table on page 712 reprinted (adapted) from Personality and Charisma in the U.S. Presidency: A Psychological Theory of Leader Effectiveness by Robert J. House, William D. Spangler and James Woycke published in *Administrative Science Quarterly*, vol. 36, September 1991 © Johnson Graduate School of Management, Cornell University; Table 22.2 after J. French and B. Raven, 'The bases of social power', in, *Studies in Social Power* (D. Cartwright (ed.) 1958), Research Center for Group Dynamics, Institute for Social Research, University of Michigan; Table 22.8 adapted from ROBBINS, STEPHEN P., JUDGE, TIMOTHY A., ORGANIZATIONAL BEHAVIOR, 12th Edition, © 2007, p. 483. Reprinted by permission of Pearson Education, Inc., Upper Saddle River, NJ. Table 22.9 reproduced by permission of SAGE Publications, London, Los Angeles, New Delhi and Singapore, from Buchanan, D.A. and Badham, R.J., *Power, Politics and Organizational Change: Winning the Turf Game*, Copyright (© Sage Publications 2008).

Text

Box on page 4 from Troubleshooter, *People Management*, 15 May 2008, pp. 50–1; Box on page 9 from Has it damaged me?: probably, *The Times*, 15 January 2009, Times 2, pp. 7–8 (Mone, M.), © *The Times*, 15 January 2009; Box on page 61 from *Annual Report 2004* (Royal Bank of Scotland 2004); Boxes on page 72, page 77, page 93 from *The Future Role of Trust in Work: The Key Success Factor for Mobile Technology*, Microsoft Corporation (Sørensen, C.

2004); Exercise on pages 97–8 from MARCIC. *Organizational Behavior*, 4E. © 1995 South-Western, a part of Cengage Learning, Inc. Reproduced by permission. www.cengage.com/permissions; Boxes on pages 108–9, 144 and 462 from *21 Dog Years: Doing Time @ Amazon.Com*. Fourth Estate (Daisey, M. 2002) – for US rights, adapted and reprinted with the permission of The Free Press, a Division of Simon & Schuster, Inc., from 21 DOG YEARS: Doing Time @ Amazon.com by Mike Daisey. Copyright © 2002 by Mike Daisey. All rights reserved; Exercise on pages 131–2 with thanks to Professor Phil Beaumont for his assistance in helping to develop this exercise; Exercise on pages 132–3 from WORKING ACROSS CULTURES by Martin J. Gannon. Copyright 2000 by Sage Publications Inc Books. Reproduced with permission of Sage Publications Inc Books in the format Textbook via Copyright Clearance Centre; Box on page 136 from Troubleshooter, *People Management*, 24 January 2008, p. 72; Box on page 159 from Carlsberg puts learning on tap, *People Management*, p. 8 (30 October 2008); Box on pages 176–7 from Sink or swim: which personality type are you?, *The Times*, Times 2, p. 5 (Ahuja, A.), © The Times, 1 March 2006; Exercise on pages 197–9 after The big five locator: a quick assessment tool for consultants and trainers, *The 1996 Annual: Volume 1 Training*, pp. 107–22 (Howard, P.J., Medina, P.L. and Howard, J.K. 1996), Copyright 1996 Pfeffier & Company. Reproduced with permission of John Wiley & Sons, Inc.; Box on page 208 (including Figure 7.2) from Charming the locals: A soldiers guide, *The Times*, p. 14 (Evans, M.), © The Times, 11 February 2008; Box on page 296 from Troubleshooter, *People Management*, 4 September 2008, pp. 46–7; Exercise on pages 354–5 adapted from *Management of Technology. The Technical Change Audit. Action for Results: 5: The Process Module*, Manpower Services Commission (Boddy, D. and Buchanan. D.A. 1987) pp. 32–5, Crown Copyright material is reproduced with permission under the terms of the Click-Use Licence; Exercise on pages 382–3 from *Organizational Behaviour and Management*, 3rd ed., Martin, J., Copyright 2005 Thomson. Reproduced by permission of Cengage Learning; Exercise on pages 383–4 adapted from GRIFFIN/MOORHEAD. *Organizational Behavior*, 9E. © 2010 South-Western, a part of Cengage Learning, Inc. Reproduced by permission. www.cengage.com/permissions; Box on page 427 from Controlling business?: agency and constraint in call centre working, *New Technology, Work and Employment*, 19(2), pp. 96–109 (Bcirnc, M., Riach, K. and Wilson, F. 2004); Exercise on pages 449–51 from *Organizational Behaviour and Management*, 3rd ed., Martin, J., Copyright 2005 Thomson. Reproduced by permission of Cengage Learning; Exercise on pages 556–7 reproduced by permission of SAGE Publications, London, Los Angeles, New Delhi and Singapore, from Mullern, T., 'Integrating team-based structure in the business process', in Pettigrew, A.M. and Fenton, E.M. (eds), *The Innovating Organisation*, Copyright (© Sage Publications 2000); Box on page 560 from Troubleshooter, *People Management*, 13 November 2008, p. 62; Box on pages 586–7 from Max headroom, *People Management*, 14(4), pp. 28–32 (McKeown, M. 2008), the article was developed from McKeown, M. (2008), *The Truth About Innovation*, London: Prentice Hall; Exercise on pages 627–8 from Marcic. *Organizational Behavior*, 3E. © 1992 South-Western, a part of Cengage Learning, Inc. Reproduced by permission. www.cengage.com/permissions; Exercise on pages 656–7 from SASHKIN, MARSHALL; MORRIS, WILLIAM C.; HELLRIEGE, DONALD, EXPERIMENTAL EXERCISES MANAGEMENT BOOK, © 1987, pp. 73–74, Reprinted by permission of Pearson Education, Inc., Upper Saddle River, NJ 07458; Exercise on pages 722–3 adapted from Barbuto, J.E., Power and the changing environment, in *Journal of Management Education*, 24(2), pp. 288–96, Copyright © 2000, OBTS Teaching Society for Management Educators, reprinted by permission of SAGE Publications.

In some instances we have been unable to trace the owners of copyright material, and we would appreciate any information that would enable us to do so.

Student briefing

What are the aims of this book?

Introduce the subject We aim to bring the study of human behaviour in organizations to students, undergraduate and postgraduate, who have little or no previous social science background.

Link to practice We aim to show readers how to translate organizational behaviour concepts, theories and techniques into practical work, organizational and management settings.

Recognize diversity We aim to stimulate awareness of the diverse social and cultural factors that affect behaviour in organizations; social science can be culture bound, as laws, norms and traditions vary from country to country, subculture to subculture.

Stimulate debate We aim to promote a challenging, critical perspective, observing that the 'correct' answers to organizational questions, and solutions to problems, rely on values, judgements and ideology, as well as on evidence; 'authorities' and 'received ideas' must be questioned.

Who are our readers?

Our target readership includes students who are new to the social sciences and to the study of organizational behaviour. This is a core subject on most business and management studies degree, diploma and masters programmes. Accountants, architects, bankers, computer scientists, doctors, engineers, hoteliers, teachers, nurses, surveyors and other subject specialists, who often have no background in social science, may all find themselves studying organizational behaviour as part of their professional examination schemes.

What approach do we adopt?

Social science perspective Our understanding of organizations derives from a broad range of social science disciplines. Most other texts adopt a managerial, psychological or sociological perspective. However, many other occupations benefit from an understanding of organizational behaviour. Not all students are going to be managers, psychologists or sociologists.

Self-contained chapters The understanding of one chapter does not rely on a prior reading of others. The material does not have to be read in the sequence in which it is presented. Ideas and theories are developed from the organizational context, to individual psychology, through social psychology, to organizational sociology, politics and management topics. Chapters cover both theory and practice, classic and contemporary.

Challenging ideas Many of the issues covered in this book are controversial, and competing views are explained. The aim is not to identify 'correct answers' or 'best practices', which are often simplistic and misleading. The aim is to raise further questions, to trigger discussion and debate, and to stimulate your critical thinking (see the Components of critical thinking box, and Stella Cottrell, 2005).

Flexible design This book works with either a two-semester or three-term, introductory-level programme. Short *Springboard* sections point to key sources for further project and assignment work. Organizational behaviour overlaps with other subjects such as human resource management, and this book is also useful for those modules.

Comparative analysis	One way to highlight the ways in which we behave in organizations is to compare our actions with those of others. Comparative studies have a long tradition in social science. As a student, you engage routinely in comparative analysis, on railways and aircraft, in buses, hotels, restaurants and hospitals, through exposure to different organizational settings. Is that management behaviour appropriate? Is that employee response effective? Does our theory help us to understand those behaviours, or not?

What aids to learning are included?

Learning outcomes	Chapters open with clear learning outcomes.
Key terms	Chapters open with a list of the key terms that are then explained. These are combined in the glossary.
Exercises	Chapters have two learning exercises for tutorial or seminar use; these can be used in a flexible way.
What would you do?	A problem or incident opens each part of the text, and you are asked to make, and to justify, your decision
Learning resources	The companion website for this textbook contains an additional set of resources relating to each chapter.
Home viewing	Each chapter lists a movie which illustrates the topic in a graphic, entertaining and memorable way.
OB in films	Chapters identify movie clips for classroom use illustrating specific issues, concepts, or arguments for analysis.
Stop and think	You are regularly invited to stop, to think through controversial and contradictory issues, to apply ideas and arguments to your own experience, to challenge your assumptions – individually or in class discussion.
OB in literature	Chapters identify a novel which illustrates aspects of the subject in a creative, literary manner.
Cartoons	We want to make the subject interesting and memorable by introducing novel, varied and unusual material where appropriate, such as cartoons, illustrations and research boxes, to change the pace, rhythm and appearance of the text, to make it more engaging and more readable.
Recap	Chapters close with a section summarizing the chapter content with respect to the learning outcomes.
Revision	Chapters close with sample examination questions, which can be used for personal study or as tutorial exercises.
Research assignment	Each chapter contains a short, focused, information-gathering project involving either a website search, library exercise or interviewing, or a combination of these methods.
Invitation to see	Each part of the text is prefaced with a photograph showing how work and organizations are portrayed visually; visual images are rarely neutral, and you are invited to 'decode' these pictures, identifying the range of both obvious and more subtle meanings which they promote.

What would you do?: This is designed to reveal the messy, complex, problematic nature of organization and management issues, often characterized by ambiguities and compromises. This is not the rational, logical, clinical, systematic, problem-solving process implied by some other textbooks. What went wrong? Why did that happen? How would you solve that problem? What would you advise? What happens next? You are put in the position of the employee, or a manager or an external consultant or 'troubleshooter'. These incidents illustrate the different kinds of problems that employees, supervisors, managers and team leaders have to deal with. They are also designed to increase your awareness of the pressures and constraints facing those who have to deal with such problems. We would also like you to use the concepts, theories, models and frameworks from your organizational behaviour course, and from this textbook, to help you to decide what you would do in each case.

"It sort of makes you stop and think, doesn't it."

Source: © Sam Gross/Condé Nast Publications/www.cartoonbank.com

Components of critical thinking

Alan Thomas argues that critical thinking is one aspect of effective management, and identifies four components of the critical thinking process:

1. Identifying and challenging assumptions about:

- the nature of management, its tasks, skills and purposes
- the nature of people and why they behave as they do
- the nature of organizations
- learning, knowing and acting
- values, goals and ends

2. Creating contextual awareness by understanding:

- how management has developed historically
- how management is conceived of in other societies
- the implications of different industrial, organizational, economic, political and cultural contexts for management
- the interrelation between organizations and society

3. Identifying alternatives by:

- becoming aware of the variety of ways in which managing and organizing can be undertaken

- inventing and imagining new ways of managing and organizing
- specifying new goals and priorities

4. Developing reflective scepticism by:

- adopting a questioning, quizzical attitude
- recognizing the limitations of much that passes for knowledge in the management field
- knowing how to evaluate knowledge claims
- developing a resistance to dogma and propaganda
- being able to distinguish systematic argument and reasoned judgement from sloppy thinking, simplistic formulae and sophistry

Thomas also observes that:

Critical thinking can be contrasted with its opposite, uncritical thinking. Uncritical thinking is the kind in which we accept common-sense assumptions at face value without systematically checking their validity, deny or ignore the significance of context for influencing beliefs and practices, fail to seek out and evaluate alternatives, and cling rigidly and unquestioningly to dogmas and authoritative pronouncements. Critical thinking is, then, not so much a step-by-step process as an attitude of mind, one which places emphasis on the need to ask 'why?'

From Thomas (2003).

Instructor briefing

What is our perspective?

Our aim is to provide you with a teaching resource, which includes a range of materials and ideas, that will enable you to design and to develop the courses that you want to deliver to the different student groups for which you are responsible. A single text and support materials cannot define the curriculum. We expect most instructors not to teach *to* this text, but *from* it, developing their own distinctive style and approach, incorporating their own topics and materials. This aim is accompanied by the goal of providing your students with a text that will also meet their needs in terms of content, interest, applicability and readability.

Challenge

We use a number of text features to encourage *an active and questioning approach* to the subject. We want to challenge your students by inviting them to confront real, practical and theoretical problems and issues for themselves. Students are invited regularly to stop reading and to consider controversial points, individually or in group discussion. We want to alert students to the significance of organizational behaviour in everyday life. The study of this subject cannot be confined to the lecture theatre and library. Eating a pizza in a restaurant, joining a queue at a cinema, returning a faulty product to a store, purchasing a train ticket, arguing with a colleague at work, taking a holiday job in a factory, reading a novel – are all experiences related to aspects of organizational behaviour.

Perspective

Some organizational behaviour texts offer a managerial perspective and give students little encouragement to question the material, or to consider other lines of reasoning and acting. In contrast, some texts offer a critical perspective, encouraging debate, but without always offering practical options. We aim to strike a balance. A perspective that encourages debate, challenge and criticism involves asking the following kinds of questions, when presented with a theory, an argument, evidence, or with a recommendation for action:

- Does this make sense, do I understand it, or is it confused and confusing?
- Is the supporting evidence compelling, or is it weak?
- Does a claim to 'novelty' survive comparison with previous thinking?
- Is the argument logical and coherent, or are there gaps and flaws?
- What biases and prejudices are revealed in this line of argument?
- Is a claim to 'neutrality' realistic, or does it conceal a hidden agenda?
- Are the arguments and judgements based convincingly on the evidence?
- Whose interests are served by this argument, and whose are damaged?
- Is the language of this argument designed to make it more appealing?

Where appropriate, we explore competing perspectives, from commentators who base their approaches on different assumptions and values. This approach is reinforced in the *Stop and think* boxes, and in the exercise and case materials at the end of each chapter. For a fuller treatment of a critical approach to understanding and researching organizational behaviour, see Mats Alvesson and Karen Lee Ashcraft (2009). For a highly regarded text written from a critical stance, see Paul Thompson and David McHugh (2002).

Historical backdrop

Management theorists generate a constant stream of new ideas and techniques. Managers tend to be fashion conscious, and are always interested in the latest thinking, which can create competitive advantage. Students (and textbook authors) also need to keep up with this flood of innovation. Armed with a knowledge of the history of the subject, however, one can often see in 'new' thinking and methods, aspects of familiar 'old' ideas. What appears to be new is often less a 'paradigm shift' in thinking, rather than a 'packaging shift'. Is the technique of 'job sculpting', invented in the late 1990s, really 'new' or just a reworking of 'job enrichment' from the 1960s? Is the 'McDonaldization' of work a contemporary trend, or the continuing expression of early twentieth-century management thinking? Is the currently fashionable concept of emotional intelligence a startling fresh development of relevance to management in the twenty-first century, or simply a restatement of ideas from the 1940s about personal and interpersonal awareness and sensitivity? It is, therefore, important to be aware of the findings and contributions of previous research.

Why recommend movies?

Voyeurism is a facet of our experience of cinema; we watch others dealing with their circumstances, their relationships, their problems. Films can thus influence attitudes and behaviours by telling us what is 'OK', desirable, acceptable, and what is not, by presenting role models which suggest, literally, how we should act. The people we see on the screen are often people like us, or people we would want to be, as well as those whom we would not wish to emulate. We are also, therefore, cast in a judgemental role: was that behaviour effective, appropriate, and one that I could use in similar circumstances?

As well as being entertaining, informative and persuasive, film also offers the viewer a vicarious experience which can be used in a number of related ways. First, it is common for the audience to consider how the settings, strategies and behaviours seen on the screen could be relevant to them. Second, vicarious experience is an invitation safely to explore unrealized possibilities: 'What would it be like to do this/to live like that?' Third, film can be inspirational: 'If I could do that.' Fictional narratives can contribute to our self-understanding and sense of identity. Feature films – and television programmes – can thus be an engaging way to illustrate aspects of organizational behaviour. The narratives on which films are based can also be valuable sources of theoretical insight, and may even be useful for testing theoretical ideas (Hassard and Buchanan, 2009).

Images of work, organization and management are often seen in movies (Boozer, 2002; Zaniello, 2003 and 2007; Bell, 2008). John Hassard and Ruth Holliday (1998) unkindly observe that textbooks like this offer a *sanitized* picture of organizational behaviour. Stephen Ackroyd and Paul Thompson (1999) similarly argue that orthodox texts overlook much evident *mis*-behaviour – 'soldiering', sabotage, pilfering, practical jokes. Gibson Burrell (1998, p.52) is uncompromising in his view of what organization theory neglects: 'there is little mention of sex, yet organizations are redolent with it; little mention of violence, yet organizations are stinking with it; little mention of pain, yet organizations rely upon it; little mention of the will to power, yet organizations would not exist without it'. The selective use of film as a teaching and learning tool can help to address these criticisms.

Hassard and Holliday note that film (and television) 'plays out sex, violence, emotion, power struggle, the personal consequences of success and failure, and *dis*organization upon its stage' (1998, p.1). The American Media Institute studied the portrayal of organizations in 200 episodes of 50 television programmes. Their analysis (Overell, 2002) showed that with fictional businesses portrayed on television:

- only 3 per cent engage in socially or economically productive activity;
- 45 per cent of management behaviours are portrayed as illegal;
- 55 per cent of company bosses commit illegal acts, such as fraud and murder.

Is this view sensationalized or realistic? To what extent do film and television reinforce or challenge popular stereotypes of work, authority, power, status and organization structure? It can be argued that popular media are at least partly responsible for creating, embellishing, and maintaining those stereotypes. Nelson Phillips (1995) argues that the use of narrative fiction, in film and also in novels, short stories, plays, songs and poems, is a way of strengthening the connection between organizational behaviour as an academic discipline, and the subjective experience of organizational membership. The advertising for some films suggests that stereotypes are challenged; *Philadelphia* for its portrayal of AIDS, *Disclosure* for the portrayal of female rape and sexual harassment at work. Hassard and Holliday argue, however, that the media reinforce conservative values, albeit in a stylized manner, rather than presenting fundamental challenges. Read their text and you will never again watch police and hospital television dramas without boring your companions with critical commentary on the traditional portrayal of hierarchy, group dynamics, sex role stereotyping, power relations, the role of authority figures and dysfunctional bureaucratic rules.

The action in numerous popular movies occurs in or revolves around fictional organizations such as Axis Chemicals (*Batman*), Oscorp Industries (*Spiderman*), Tyrell Corporation (*Blade Runner*), Benthic Petroleum (*The Abyss*), CompuTech (*The Stepford Wives*), Initech Corporation (*Office Space*), Ryan Entertainment (*Mulholland Drive*), Nakatomi Trading Company (*Die Hard*), Lacuna Inc (*Eternal Sunshine of the Spotless Mind*), Zap-Em (*Men in Black*) and Paper Street Soap Company (*Fight Club*). For further suggestions on movies that are suitable for management and organizational behaviour subjects, see the work of Joseph Champoux (2005, 2006, 2007), and the examples in Huczynski and Buchanan (2004, 2005).

Why recommend novels?

Most of the topics and themes in organizational behaviour are also addressed in powerful, insightful and entertaining ways in literature. To stimulate debate, considering and exploring ideas from unusual perspectives, chapters identify novels and other literature sources. We recognize that many students will not follow up these suggestions, but we wish nevertheless to reinforce the links between organizational behaviour and wider individual and social experience. Management courses based on novels have a long history. Novels have been written as didactic devices, illustrating points about, for example, quality management (*The Goal*, Goldratt and Cox, 1993) or employee exploitation (*Human Resources*, Kemske, 1996). Fiction, however, can also be used for instructional purposes. The allegorical novel *Watership Down* (Adams, 1973) provides a basis for discussing Henry Mintzberg's (1973) management roles. Other useful sources include Thompson and McGivern (1996), Czarniawska-Joerges and de Monthoux (1994), Knights and Willmott (1999), Denning (2004, 2005) and Gabriel (2004). Barbara Czarniawska (1998, 1999) describes organization theory as a 'literary genre', observing that narratives which unfold in the sequence, 'and then, and then', imply causality, and are therefore rich in theoretical insight.

Invitation to see: why analyze photographs?

Samantha Warren (2009) notes that visual research methods are well established in anthropology and sociology, but are rarely used in organization and management studies. But we live in a world saturated with visual imagery, from newspapers, magazines, street advertising, television and the internet. We are also presented with a range of other visual information; the appearance and dress of the people we meet, the design, layout, colours and decoration of their workplaces, the architecture of the buildings in which they work, the technology in use. Despite its volume, richness and complexity, we tend to take most of this visual information for granted, as part of the background tapestry in organizational and everyday life.

While we may smile or grimace at the occasional photograph, we rarely pause for long to dissect, analyse, interpret and debate the content of these visual images.

Why should we pay attention to these transient images? We see them once and rarely feel the need to refer to them again. Street advertisements and internet banners are displayed for brief periods before being updated. The photographs in magazines and newspapers are just illustrations, contextualized with a brief caption, and it is the accompanying text that matters. The images in television and street advertising are clearly contrived to attract our attention, and they cannot mislead us in that respect.

However, visual images are rarely, if ever, neutral. They are not 'just' illustrations. They usually tell a story, present a point of view, support an argument, perpetuate a myth, or maybe create, reinforce or challenge a stereotype. Images carry messages, sometimes obvious, sometimes subtle, sometimes clear, sometimes confusing. Visual imagery is thus a potentially valuable source of information which we often overlook. Visual research methods have been widely used in sociology and anthropology for many years (Bateson and Mead, 1942; Collier and Collier, 1986). There has been a recent growth of interest in the potential of visual methods in social science more generally, and in organizational behaviour (Prosser, 1998; Emmison and Smith, 2000; Buchanan, 2001; Mitchell, 2009).

We would like to encourage students to adopt a more critical perspective on visual images of organizational behaviour. You will find at the beginning of each Part of the book, a short section titled *Invitation to see*, displaying photographs showing aspects of work and organizations. Visual information constitutes data, in the same way that interviews and survey questionnaires provide data, and also therefore requires interpretation.

The aims of *Invitation to see* are to:

1. Encourage students to look at the organizational world, and the actors who populate it, in an entirely different way.

2. Demonstrate the value of visual data in offering insights into human and organizational behaviour.

3. Introduce and develop the concept of interpreting or 'decoding' visual images.

Photographs can be seen, read, interpreted or decoded, in three main ways.

Reality captured

Images can be seen as captured fragments of reality, frozen in time, indisputably accurate renditions of scenes and actors. This was the way in which photography was regarded when it was invented. The conclusion drawn by many commentators was that 'art is dead'. The artist could never hope to capture reality as accurately as a photograph, so why bother? This perspective is reflected in the saying, 'the camera doesn't lie'.

Reality fabricated

Photographs can instead be regarded as social and technological constructs, which reveal as much about the photographer as they do about the image. The photographer selects the scene, a camera, a lens (if it is that type of camera) and film, which in combination determine properties of the image, such as sharpness, contrast, grain and depth of field. More critically, the photographer selects the angle and framing of a shot, determining what is included, and also selects the moment to open the shutter and capture the image. Viewers see only what the photographer wants them to see. What is outside the frame, and the sequence of events before and after the shutter was fired, remain invisible. Digital photography has opened up a range of further possibilities to manipulate images after they have been captured. This perspective implies that 'the camera and the computer lie for the photographer'.

Multiple realities

How an image is interpreted by viewers, independent of the photographer's intent, is also significant. For the cover of this book, we wanted an image that had no direct association with organizations, factories, office buildings, managers, collaborative teams, aggressive animals, shoals of fish or any other typical organizational metaphor. There is a key question concerning whose interpretation of an image is correct, that of the photographer, or that of the viewer? Both points of view are equally valid and are of equal interest. As discussed in Chapter 2, the idea that texts can have many valid interpretations also applies to visual images. The viewer does not have to know the photographer's intent, which may be inferred from the image and its caption. Photographers cannot predict the interpretations which viewers will place on their work, but it is those interpretations that condition the viewer's response. This perspective implies that, 'what the camera produces is for us to determine'.

With *Invitation to see*, three questions are significant:

1. What are you being invited to see here? What did the *photographer* intend this image to convey? Does it tell a story, present a point of view, support an argument, perpetuate a myth, reinforce a stereotype, challenge a stereotype?

2. What does this image convey to *you*, personally? How do you interpret this? What do you think this means? Do you agree with what is being said here? Is the message inaccurate or misleading, perhaps insulting in some respect? Does this image carry meanings which the photographer may not have intended?

3. How do *others* interpret this image? Do they decode it in different ways? How can differences of interpretation of the same image be explained?

This photograph appeared in *The Times* (8 March 2003), with an article entitled 'Beauty in Epaulettes 2003', a Russian Army recruiting exercise in which contestants were assessed on their shooting as well as their appearance. The aim of one contestant was to raise the profile of women in the Spetsnaz, the Russian equivalent of the British SAS. This picture also appeared in the *Daily Telegraph* with the caption, 'Guns and poses: Russian female soldiers with Kalashnikov rifles prepare to compete in a shooting match during one of the rounds of the Beauty in Epaulettes contest which aims to attract more women into the Russian army.'

Source: STR/AP/Press Association Images

Russia's glamour brigade aims high

Here is one decoding of this image:

This photo shows two female Russian soldiers with guns. They are both laughing and smiling, clearly having fun. The male soldier in the background does not look quite so happy, but his comrade is standing too far back for us to see his expression. The ground around them is covered in snow. Perhaps the male soldier is cold, waiting for the photographer to finish? Perhaps it is his gun that one of the women is holding? Perhaps he is concerned that his role in the army – 'men's work' – is being invaded by women, posing a threat to his identity as a soldier? We are told that this photograph was taken at a shooting contest, in which these women were taking part, and is part of a campaign to attract more women into the Russian army. However, expecting to meet soldiers like these could attract more men into the army instead. Here is an attempt to shatter the stereotype of the Russian army as a male preserve?

What else does this image suggest?

Unfortunately, the other stereotype shown here is the 'dizzy blonde'. Would female soldiers on duty, particularly working with assault rifles, be allowed to wear lipstick and have their hair down? The woman on the right has an earring, which would almost certainly be prohibited while on duty. The main clue to what is probably happening here, however, lies in the way in which the woman at the front of the image is holding her rifle. Her right hand is carefully wrapped around the magazine which holds the ammunition, and not the pistol grip behind the trigger. This is the grasp of someone who has never held a rifle before. Both rifles have muzzle guards, so they are not ready to fire, or ready to compete in a shooting match. Are these 'Russian female soldiers', or are they models hired specially for this publicity shoot? Is the male soldier unhappy, perhaps even suspicious, because he wants his gun back before one of the 'dizzy blondes' has an accident?

It is therefore possible to reach different interpretations of this image. The message lies, in part, in the photograph, but also depends on the perceptions of the viewers. It is thus possible to see how this image can be seen as both contradicting and reinforcing a stereotype related to men's work and women's work, to blondes and soldiering. It is, of course, also possible to read too much into such an image. The key questions are, how do *you* read this image, what story does it tell *you*, what are *you* being invited to see here?

Film and copyright

The 'Home viewing' recommendations can be followed up by students who can watch these in their own time, perhaps in preparation for a tutorial discussion. If, as an instructor, you wish, for teaching purposes, to use a movie clip from our *OB cinema* recommendations, or a television programme recorded off-air, it is necessary first to confirm that you have appropriate copyright clearance. Regulations in this area are complex, are country-specific, vary with kinds of usage and are liable to change. In some instances, the regulations that apply may be specific to one organization, depending on the different ways in which films are used in teaching, and on the nature of the licence, or licences, that the institution holds. Before using film in the classroom, check with your local copyright administrator that you are operating within the law. In Britain, you may also find it helpful to check the terms and conditions of two organizations which supply licences:

Educational Licensing Authority
New Premier House
150 Southampton Row
London, WC1B 5AL
www.era.org.uk

Public Video Screening Licence
c/o Filmbank Distributors
98 Theobald's Road
London, WC1X 8WB
www.filmbank.co.uk

Part 1 The organizational context

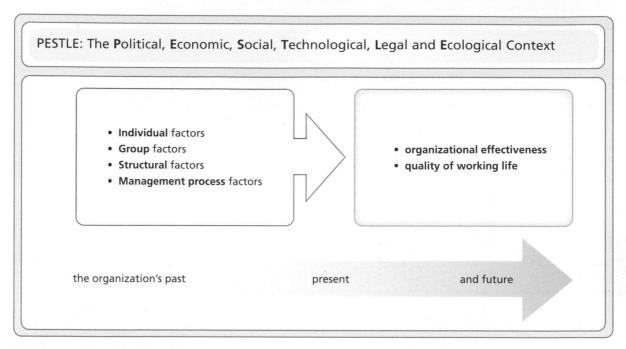

PESTLE: The **P**olitical, **E**conomic, **S**ocial, **T**echnological, **L**egal and **E**cological Context

- **Individual** factors
- **Group** factors
- **Structural** factors
- **Management process** factors

- **organizational effectiveness**
- **quality of working life**

the organization's past   present   and future

A field map of the organizational behaviour terrain

Introduction

Part 1, The organizational context, explores four topics:

1. Different ways to explain organizational behaviour, contrasting traditional variance explanations, with contemporary process explanations.
2. How the wider environment of the organization affects internal structures and working practices, including ethical behaviour and corporate social responsibility.
3. How developments in new technology, such as Web 2.0 applications, are changing the nature of work and organizations, and the role of choice in shaping the outcomes.
4. Aspects of organization culture, and different ways to understand this concept, and the links between culture to organizational change and performance.

The subject matter of organizational behaviour spans a number of levels of analysis – individual, group, organization and the wider environment, or context. Part 1 explores key aspects of the organizational context. These include the pace of social and technological change, and the pressures on management to be seen to be acting ethically and exercising corporate social responsibility. Organizations develop their own distinctive cultures, which are different from, while clearly linked to, the wider national cultures in which they operate.

A recurring theme in this text concerns the design of jobs, and the organization and experience of work. The organization of work reflects a number of influences, at different levels of analysis. We explain how the experience and organization of work is influenced by:

- *contextual* factors, in Chapter 2;
- *technological* factors, in Chapter 3;

- *psychological* factors, in Chapter 9;
- *social psychological* factors, in Chapter 13;
- *historical* factors, in Chapter 15;
- *power and political* factors, in Chapter 22.

Invitation to see

This image is similar to one used in *The Times* (7 November, 2009), with an article about climate change (original image unobtainable). The caption explained that the photograph showed workers in a chicken processing plant in China, noting that, 'Industrial farming methods are estimated to use ten calories of fossil fuels for each calorie of food produced'.

Source: Paula Bronstein/Getty Images

1. **Decoding**   Look at this image closely. Note in as much detail as possible what messages you feel that it is trying to convey. Does it tell a story, present a point of view, support an argument, perpetuate a myth, reinforce a stereotype, challenge a stereotype?

2. **Challenging**   To what extent do you agree with the messages, stories, points of view, arguments, myths, or stereotypes in this image? Is this image open to challenge, to criticism, or to interpretation and decoding in other ways, revealing other messages?

3. **Sharing**   Compare with colleagues your interpretation of this image. Explore explanations for differences in your respective decodings.

What would you do? You're the employee

You are 25 years old, and a member of 'Generation Y'. How would you advise this manager to address his problem?

Help me generate results from Generation Y staff. I'm the Managing Director of a small firm operating in a high-pressure environment. Despite high attrition in our industry, our team prides itself on good management practice as well as getting results. However, with new starters now having an average age of 25, I am finding that since I was young (I'm now 40), a lot has changed. Attitudes have been transformed – but not for the better. Not only are we having to work harder to attract our recruits, but we are finding that in their first few months we have to 'counsel' them to see the bigger picture.

For example, we have always motivated our team by offering a modest basic salary, plus performance-related bonuses. But, increasingly, we are finding that our recruits are perfectly content to earn just the basics.

The younger generation now have higher expectations. This is great, but all too often they seem to expect too much, too soon – without putting in the necessary work. As someone who climbed to the top through hard graft, I find this bewildering. How can I motivate our new starters and channel their energies in the right direction?

From 'Troubleshooter', People Management, *15 May 2008, pp.50–51.*

Chapter 1 Explaining organizational behaviour

Key terms

organizational behaviour

organization

controlled performance

organizational dilemma

fundamental attribution error

organizational effectiveness

balanced scorecard

quality of working life

positivism

operational definition

variance theory

constructivism

process theory

evidence-based management

human resource management

employment cycle

Learning outcomes

When you have read this chapter, you should be able to define those key terms in your own words, and you should also be able to:

1. Explain the importance of an understanding of organizational behaviour.

2. Explain and illustrate the central dilemma of organizational design.

3. Understand the need for explanations of behaviour in organizations that take account of relationships between factors at different levels of analysis.

4. Understand the difference between positivist and constructivist perspectives, and their implications for the study of organizational behaviour.

5. Understand the difference between variance and process theories and their uses in understanding organizational behaviour.

6. Explain the development and limitations of evidence-based management.

7. Recognize the breadth of applications of organizational behaviour theory, in particular the contribution to human resource management practice.

What is organizational behaviour?

Organizational behaviour an interdisciplinary body of knowledge and field of research, concerned with how formal organizations, behaviour of people within organizations, and salient features of their context and environment, evolve and take shape, why all these things happen the way they do, and what purposes they serve.

This chapter explores how we can explain the behaviour of people in organizations. First, however, we have to define what organizational behaviour means.

Our margin definition is from Arndt Sorge and Malcolm Warner (1997, p.xii). The definition of a field of study identifies its scope, and the themes, questions, issues and problems that it seeks to address and to explain. It is important to note that this definition includes macro-organizational and micro-individual concerns – covering environmental and structural issues as well as individual and team factors. Chip Heath and Sim Sitkin (2001) distinguish between oB (or Big-B) and Ob (or Big-O) definitions of organizational behaviour. Big-B emphasizes interesting *behaviour*, such as stress or decision-making, and draws mainly on psychology. They argue that this approach misses out on what is distinctive about *organizations*. Stress, for example, occurs in many other social and domestic contexts. They prefer Ob – the Big-O definition – which emphasizes *organizing*, and pays attention to process, and to how factors at different levels of analysis (society, individual, group, organization) interact with each other.

Is this a dry, theoretical subject remote from day-to-day practical concerns? On the contrary. We live in an organized world. Look at the clothes you are wearing, the food that you eat, the computers that you use, the schools, colleges and universities where you study. What aspects of your life are not touched in some way by organizations of different kinds? Yes, of course, there are some, but not many. The study of organizational behaviour has direct practical implications for those who work in, manage, seek to subvert, or interact in other ways with organizations, whether they are small and local, or large and international.

You will see other similar labels: organization theory, industrial sociology, organizational psychology, organizational analysis, organization studies. Organization theory and industrial sociology tend to focus on macro-level studies of groups and organizations. Organizational psychology specializes in individual behaviour. Organizational analysis tends to emphasize practice rather than theory. Organization studies is a term which highlights the widening of the range of issues and perspectives that this field now embraces (Clegg *et al.*, 2006). These labels indicate subtle shifts in focus and emphasis rather than clearly defined boundaries. Organizational behaviour is widely recognized as the conventional 'umbrella' term, but some would argue with that view.

What is the explanation for your bad experience in that café? Well, we can blame the skills and the personality of the individual who served you. However, there are many other possibilities. Other explanations for your experience include:

- inadequate staff training;
- staff absences increasing working pressure;
- long hours, fatigue and poor work-life balance;
- equipment not working properly;

- anxiety about anticipated organizational changes;
- domestic difficulties – family feuds, ill health;
- low motivation due to low pay;
- an autocratic supervisor;
- a dispute with colleagues created an uncomfortable working atmosphere;
- timing – you came in at the wrong moment.

Your experience could be explained by contextual, individual, group, structural, process and managerial factors, in and beyond the workplace. The explanation could come from any one of those factors. In many cases, a combination of factors will explain the behaviour in question. The customer walks away. As a member of that organization, you have to live with these issues. As a manager, you may be responsible for solving the problem.

Organizational behaviour enjoys a controversial relationship with management practice, and we will consider the practical applications of organizational behaviour theory. Most US and many British texts adopt a managerialist perspective. However, the focus on management is regarded by some commentators as unhelpful, for at least four reasons, concerning power inequalities, the subject agenda, multiple stakeholders and fashion victims.

Power inequalities: Management is an elite occupational group, with access to information and resources beyond those available to mere employees. Organizations typically display inequalities of reward and power. Why should a field of academic study support exclusively the affluent and powerful? A managerialist perspective can encourage an uncritical, unchallenging approach to management practice.

The agenda: A managerialist perspective focuses on a narrow range of issues of importance to managers, concerning management control and organizational performance. This pushes other topics off the agenda, such as issues that are significant to particular individuals and groups, theoretical analyses that have limited practical application, and arguments critical of the managerial role.

Multiple stakeholders: Management is only one group with a stake in the behaviour of organizations and their members. An understanding of this subject is of value to employees, groups subjected to discrimination, trade unions, customers, suppliers, investors and the wider community. Organizational behaviour is a subject of broad social and economic significance.

Fashion victims: Management is prone to pursue the latest in thinking and technique, in the interests of improving personal and organizational performance. A managerialist perspective, therefore, encourages a focus on fashion trends. Some fashions survive while others quickly fade. As some fads turn out to be old ideas freshly packaged, it is important to consider these developments in the context of the history of the subject, to reach an informed assessment.

In this text, we adopt a 'multiple-stakeholders-inclusive-agenda' view of organizational behaviour, developing a broad social science perspective. This does not mean that practical applications are ignored, but readers are encouraged to adopt a challenging, critical approach to research, theory and practice, rather than to accept a managerial or a social scientific point of view without question. Even 'authorities' get it wrong sometimes.

The term organizational behaviour was first used by Fritz Roethlisberger in the late 1950s, because it suggested a wider scope than human relations (Wood, 1995). The term behavioural sciences was first used to describe a Ford Foundation research programme at Harvard in 1950, and in 1957 the Human Relations Group at Harvard (previously the Mayo Group) became the Organizational Behaviour Group. Organizational behaviour was recognized as a subject at Harvard in 1962, with Roethlisberger as the first area head (Roethlisberger, 1977).

Fritz Jules
Roethlisberger
(1898–1974)

Organizational behaviour – a coherent subject area?

Management textbooks frequently state as fact that organizational behaviour is an inter-disciplinary field. It is not. It is in no way inter-disciplinary; multi-disciplinary perhaps, but not inter-disciplinary. OB is not a coherent field. It is a general area that encompasses thinking and research from numerous disciplines. It draws its material from psychology, sociology, anthropology, economics, the arts and humanities, law and medicine. Organizational behaviour is in reality a hodgepodge of various subjects; a collection of loosely related or even unrelated streams of scholarly and not-so-scholarly research. It is neither a discipline, nor is it a business function. And that makes it an anomalous area of management study.

From Wood (1995, p.3).

Organizations do not 'behave'. Only people can be said to behave. Organizational behaviour is shorthand for the activities and interactions of people in organizations. Organizations pervade our physical, social, cultural, political and economic environment, offering jobs, providing goods and services, creating our built environment, and contributing to the existence and fabric of whole communities. The products and services of McDonald's, Google, Nokia, Microsoft, Ford and Nintendo shape our existence and our daily experience. However, we tend to take organizations for granted precisely because they affect everything that we do. Familiarity can lead to an underestimation of their impact. With how many organizations have you interacted in some way *today*?

The study of organizations is multidisciplinary, drawing from psychology, social psychology, sociology, economics and political science, and to a lesser extent from history, geography, anthropology and medicine. The study of organizational behaviour has become a distinct discipline, with its own research traditions, academic journals and international networks. This is an area where the contributions of the different social and behavioural sciences can be integrated. The extent of that integration, however, is weak. 'Multidisciplinary' means drawing from different subjects. 'Interdisciplinary' suggests that different subjects collaborate with each other. Full interdisciplinary collaboration is rare.

STOP AND THINK   Why should the term, 'organization', be difficult to define? Consider the following list. Which of these are organizations, and which are not? Explain your decision in each case.

- A chemicals processing company
- The Jamieson family next door
- King's College Hospital
- The local street corner gang
- Clan Buchanan
- Your local squash club
- A terrorist cell
- A famine relief charity
- The Azande tribe
- A primary school

Organization a social arrangement for achieving controlled performance in pursuit of collective goals.

What is an **organization**? Why are you uncomfortable about calling some of the items on that list 'organizations'? Perhaps you considered size as a deciding factor? Or the provision of goods and services for sale? Or the offer of paid employment? If we define a term too widely, it becomes meaningless. Our margin definition is *one* way to define an organization.

This definition should help to explain why you perhaps found it awkward to describe a street corner gang as an organization, but not a hospital, a company, or a club. Let us examine this definition more closely.

Social arrangements

To say that organizations are social arrangements is simply to observe that they are groups of people who interact with each other as a consequence of their membership. However, all of the items on our list are social arrangements. This is not a distinctive feature.

Collective goals

Common membership implies shared objectives. Organizations are more likely to exist where individuals acting alone cannot achieve goals that are considered worth pursuing. Once again, all of the items on our list are social arrangements for the pursuit of collective goals, so this is not a distinctive feature either.

Controlled performance

Controlled performance setting standards, measuring performance, comparing actual with standard, and taking corrective action if necessary.

Organizations are concerned with controlled performance in the pursuit of goals. The performance of an organization as a whole determines its survival. The performance of a department determines the resources allocated to it. The performance of individuals determines pay and promotion prospects. Not any level of performance will do, however. We live in a world in which the resources available to us are not sufficient to meet all of our desires. We have to make the most efficient use of those scarce resources. Levels of performance, of individuals, departments and organizations are therefore tied to standards which determine what counts as inadequate, satisfactory or good.

A family is not an organization?

Michelle Mone, founder of the lingerie company *Ultimo*, explains:

> I wouldn't say that I'm a natural mother in terms of wanting to stay at home and pick the kids up from school, and I don't feel guilty about that. I still leave instructions. In the utility room there's one whiteboard for each child, saying what they need to do and where they need to go, how much the fees are for the dancing, the rugby.

My house is run like a business. My staff [nanny, gardener, housekeeper], the kids and my husband have key performance indicators and every Friday we get together with a flipchart and mark how the week has been. That sounds hard but it keeps everyone focused. Children love routine and this house is run like clockwork. I manage everything, but the kids and my husband aren't allowed to mark me.

> I have obsessive compulsive disorder and every night when I come in it takes me 17 minutes to go around the house and make sure everything is where it should be, all the white shirts together, all the black shirts together. The kids come home, hang up their uniforms, put on their pyjamas, get their homework done, and when they've done their tasks they're free to do what they want and have their friends round. It sounds regimented but it's a happy home as well.

From Mone (2009) © The Times, 15 January 2009

Performance has to be controlled, to ensure that it is good enough, or if not, that something is being done to improve it. An organization's members thus have to perform these control functions as well as the operating tasks required to fulfil their collective purpose. The need for controlled performance leads to a deliberate and ordered allocation of functions, or division of labour, between an organization's members.

Admission to membership of organizations is controlled, usually with reference to standards of performance; will the person be able to do the job? The price of failure to perform to standard is loss of membership. The need for controlled performance leads to the establishment of authority relationships. The controls only work where members comply with the orders of those responsible for performing the control functions.

To what extent are the Jamieson family, the Azande tribe, or the street gang, preoccupied with determining and monitoring performance standards and correcting deviations? To what extent does their existence depend on their ability to meet predetermined targets? To what extent do they allocate control functions to their members, programme their activities, and control their relationships with other members? The way in which you answer these questions may explain your readiness or reluctance to describe them as organizations.

It can be argued, therefore, that it is the *preoccupation with performance* and the *need for control* which distinguish organizations from other social arrangements.

STOP AND THINK

In what ways could the Jamieson family be concerned with performance and control?

How is membership of a street gang determined? What do you have to do to become a member? What behaviours lead to exclusion from gang membership?

Are organizations different from other social arrangements in degree only, and not different in kind? Are *all* social groupings not concerned with setting, monitoring and correcting standards of behaviour and performance, defined in different ways?

The way in which one defines a phenomenon determines ways of looking at and studying it. The study of organizational behaviour is characterized by the view that organizations should be studied from a range of different perspectives. In other words, it is pointless to dispute which is the 'correct' definition. The American management guru, Peter Drucker, presented another viewpoint, arguing that organizations are like symphony orchestras. Information technology, he argues, reduces the need for manual and clerical skills, and increases demand for 'knowledge workers'. Like musicians, Drucker sees knowledge workers exploring outlets for their creative talent, seeking interesting challenges, enjoying the stimulation of working with other specialists (Golzen, 1989).

Source: © Copyright 2000 United Feature Syndicate, Inc.

One author who has popularized the 'multiple perspectives' view of organizations is the Canadian academic Gareth Morgan. In *Images of Organizations* (2006), he offers eight metaphors which invite us to see organizations through a series of different lenses, as:

- machines;
- biological organisms;
- human brains;
- cultures or subcultures;
- political systems;
- psychic prisons;
- systems of change and transformation;
- instruments of domination.

Morgan presents these metaphors as ways of thinking about organizations, as approaches to the 'diagnostic reading' and 'critical evaluation' of organizational phenomena. The metaphor of 'organization as machine' suggests an analysis of its component elements and their interaction. The metaphor of the 'psychic prison' suggests an analysis of how an organization constrains and shapes the thinking and intellectual growth of its members. He suggests how, by using these different metaphors to understand their complex characteristics, it becomes possible to identify novel ways in which to design and manage organizations.

If we destroy this planet

If we eventually destroy this planet, the underlying cause will not lie with technology or weaponry. We will have destroyed it with ineffective organizations. The main limitation on human aspirations lies not in intellect nor in equipment, but in our ability to work together. The main cause of most man-made disasters (Bhopal, Chernobyl, Three Mile Island, *Challenger*) has been traced to organization and management factors.

Groups can achieve much more than individuals acting alone. Humans, like many other creatures on this planet, are social animals. We achieve psychological satisfaction and material gain from organized activity. Organizations, in their recruitment and other publicity materials, like you to think that they are 'one big happy family' working towards the same ends. Everyone is a team player, shooting at the same goals. Organizations, of course, do not have goals. People have goals. Collectively, the members of an organization may be making biscuits, treating patients or educating students, but individual members also pursue a variety of personal goals. Senior managers may decide on objectives and attempt to get others to agree with them by calling them the 'organization's mission' or 'corporate strategy'; but they are still the goals of the people who determined them in the first place.

Organizations can mean different things to those who use them and who work in them, because they are significant personal and social sources of:

- money, physical resources, other rewards;
- meaning, relevance, purpose, identity;
- order and stability;
- security, support and protection;
- status, prestige, self-esteem, self-confidence;
- power, authority, control.

Organizational dilemma how to reconcile inconsistency between individual needs and aspirations on the one hand, and the collective purpose of the organization on the other.

The goals pursued by individual members of an organization can be quite different from the collective purpose of their organized activity. This creates an organizational dilemma – how to design organizations that are effective in achieving overall objectives, while also meeting the needs of those who work for them. Mike Noon and Paul Blyton (2007; p.304) report the results of an international study which asked workers in manufacturing companies whether or not they agreed that managers and workers shared the same interests in their businesses. The percentages of workers who agreed to this were 24 per cent in The Netherlands, 36 per cent in Britain, and 42 per cent in Norway.

If we destroy this planet

Why did Joseph Hazelwood spend five summers collecting rubbish in Alaska? On 24 March 1989, the tanker *Exxon Valdez* hit a reef in Prince William Sound, leaking 11 million gallons of crude oil into the sea. This was the worst environmental disaster in American history, fouling 1,300 miles of coastline and damaging 23 species of wildlife. First reports blamed Captain Hazelwood; the *New York Times* headline read, 'Skipper Was Drunk'. He was pursued by journalists, received death threats, was fired by Exxon and was charged with criminal damage. *Time* magazine argued that the evidence showed a 'wider web of accountability':

1. There was no clear evidence to confirm that Hazelwood was drunk when the ship ran aground. Although he had a history of alcohol abuse, crewmates said he was sober.

2. Although Exxon officially banned alcohol from its ships, it supplied low alcohol beer to tanker crewmen. Hazelwood claimed to have drunk two bottles before 9.00 pm on the eve of the accident which took place while he was asleep at 12.10 am.

3. After the accident, Hazelwood adjusted the engines to keep the vessel stable against the reef, avoiding further spill and maybe saving lives; the coastguard praised his action.

4. Exxon had cut the *Valdez* crew, arguing that new technology made this possible, leaving fewer sailors working longer hours; fatigue may have contributed to the disaster.

5. The Second Mate, who should have been piloting, was exhausted and asleep. The 'pilotage endorsement' of the Third Mate, who had control of the vessel, was disputed.

6. The acting Helmsman had been promoted to Able Seaman one year earlier, from his job as Room Steward and waiter in the galley.

7. The coastguards failed to monitor the *Valdez* after it veered to avoid ice. They blamed this lapse on the weather, poor equipment, and the 'change of shift preoccupations of a watchman'. The coastguards argued that they were not required to track ships as far as the reef which the *Valdez* struck; the seamen said they depended on the coastguards.

Exxon paid $1 billion to the State of Alaska in 1991, and made compensation payments to 82 Eyak Indians in 1999. A study in 1999 showed that local people remained depressed and traumatized, with high rates of alcoholism and other social ills, and were still catching deformed salmon. Hazelwood said: 'I feel terrible about the effects of the spill, but I'm just an ordinary fellow caught up in an extraordinary situation – a situation which I had little control over.' His rubbish collection was a form of personal penance.

Based on Behar (1989); The Economist *(1999a);*
Whittell (1999).

Organizations can affect your body shape

The sun never sets on the golden arches. These gleaming symbols of the iconic fast food giant, McDonald's, can be found scattered across the surface of the earth. They seem to spread even further than the standards of ancient Rome, the cross of Christianity or the flag of imperial Britain. McDonald's is so ubiquitous that the film-maker Morgan Spurlock found that most children had difficulty recognizing the United States president and Jesus Christ, but they could instantly recognize Ronald McDonald. In the course of becoming the corporate power that it is today, McDonald's has transformed people's lives around the world in a way that emperors and governments have only dreamed of.

It might be argued that it has swept away thousands of small businesses throughout the world and replaced them with chain stores; that it has applied the standardized techniques of mass manufacture to the job of cooking food and serving people; that it has systematically rolled back the rights of workers; that is has hastened the introduction of monoculture factory farming; that it has aided the rapid decline in people's ability to prepare even the most basic food for themselves; and that it has even changed the shape of our bodies by encouraging obesity throughout Western nations. Whether or not we go that far, it is evident that the huge changes that McDonald's and other fast food restaurants have heralded reveal the kind of power that lies in the hands of the largest corporations. They have the power to change the landscape of business, the way we work, the way we eat and the way we live.

From Fleming and Spicer (2007, p.1).

Organizations are social arrangements in which people strive to achieve control over resources in order to produce goods and services efficiently. However, organizations are also political systems in which some individuals exert control over others. Power to define the collective purposes or goals of organizations is not evenly distributed. One of the main mechanisms of organizational control is hierarchy of authority. It is widely accepted (often with reluctance) that managers have the right to make the decisions while lower-level employees are obliged to comply or leave.

A concern with performance leads to rules and procedures, and to jobs that are simple and monotonous. These features simplify the tasks of planning, organizing and co-ordinating the efforts of large numbers of people. This efficiency drive, however, conflicts with the desire for freedom of expression, autonomy, creativity and self-development. It is difficult to design organizations that are efficient in using resources, and also in developing human potential. Many of the 'human' problems of organizations arise from conflicts between individual needs, and the constraints imposed in the interests of collective purpose. Attempts to control and co-ordinate human behaviour are thus often self-defeating.

That is a pessimistic view. Organizations are social arrangements, designed by people who can also change them. Organizations can be repressive and stifling, but they can also provide opportunities for self-fulfilment and expression. The point is, the individual and social consequences depend on how organizations are designed and run.

Happy cows give more milk

Clarence H. Eckles, in *Dairy Cattle and Milk Production* (Macmillan, New York, 1956, pp.332–33), identifies methods for maximizing milk production:

1. Cows become accustomed to a regular routine; disturbing this routine disturbs them and causes a decrease in milk production.

2. Attendants should come into close contact with the cows, and it is important that the best of relations exist between the cows and keepers.

3. The cows should not be afraid of the attendants.

4. Cows should never be hurried.

5. Chasing cows with dogs or driving them on the run should never be allowed.

6. In the barn, attendants must work quietly; loud shouting or quick movements upset cows and cause them to restrict production.

Based on Gray and Starke (1984, p.14).

A field map of the organizational behaviour terrain

How can behaviour in organizations be explained? To answer this question systematically, we will first develop a 'field map' of the organizational behaviour terrain; Figure 1.1. Organizations do not operate in a vacuum, but are influenced by their wider context, represented by the outer box on the map. One approach to understanding context influences is through 'PESTLE analysis', which explores the **P**olitical, **E**conomic, **S**ocial, **T**echnological, **L**egal and **E**cological issues affecting the organization and its members. The map shows that we want to explain two sets of outcomes; organizational effectiveness and quality of working life. There are five sets of factors which can explain those outcomes. These concern individual, group, structural, process and management factors. Finally, we cannot think of organizations as static entities. Organizations and their members have plans for the future which influence actions today. Past events shape current perceptions and actions. It is necessary to explain behaviours with reference to their location in time.

As well as helping to explain organizational behaviour, this model is an overview and a guide to the content of this book. You will find it reproduced at the beginning of each Part of the book, to help you to locate the separate topics in the wider context of the subject as a whole.

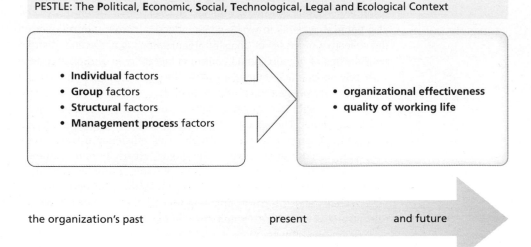

Figure 1.1: A field map of the organizational behaviour terrain

STOP AND THINK

The atmosphere just isn't the same any more, and the place is losing customers. Staff in the restaurant or bar that you use are less helpful and friendly than they used to be. The quality of service that you receive has declined sharply. Why?

Use the field map in Figure 1.1 as a source of possible explanations for this deterioration in performance. Can you blame the context, new technology, individuals, team working, organization structure, changes to the culture, or management style? Maybe the cause lies with a combination of these factors?

Fundamental attribution error
the tendency to emphasize explanations of the behaviour of others based on their personality or disposition, and to overlook the influence of wider social and contextual influences.

Remember the rude and unhelpful person serving in our café? Often in such circumstances we assume that the person is to blame, rather than take into account aspects of the context in which they find themselves. This tendency to blame the individual is known as the fundamental attribution error, a term first discussed by Lee Ross (1977).

In some circumstances, the individual may well be to blame, but not always. If we are not careful, the fundamental attribution error leads to false explanations for the behaviour of others. We must also be aware of how aspects of the social and organizational situation can affect people's behaviour, and of the influence of unseen and less obvious factors. To help overcome this attribution bias, Figure 1.1 includes individual factors, but also suggests a range of other possible explanations for the unhelpful behaviour of our shop assistant.

Context factors: Maybe the store is facing competition, sales have collapsed, the store is closing next month, and the loyal shop assistant is bitter about being made redundant (economic factors). Perhaps closure is threatened because the local population is falling, and reducing sales (social issues).

Individual factors: Maybe the shop assistant is not coping with the demands of the job because training has not been provided (learning deficit). Maybe this assistant is not suited to work that involves interaction with a demanding public (personality traits). Or perhaps the shop assistant finds the job boring and lacks challenge (motivation problem).

Group factors: Maybe the employees in this part of the organization have not formed a cohesive team (group formation issues). Maybe this shop assistant is excluded from the group for some reason (a newcomer, perhaps) and is unhappy (group structure problems). The informal norm for dealing with awkward customers like you is to be awkward in return, and this assistant is just 'playing by the rules' (group norms).

Structural factors: Perhaps the organization is bureaucratic and slow, and our assistant is anxiously waiting for a long-standing issue to be resolved. Maybe there is concern about the way in which work is allocated. Perhaps the unit manager cannot deal with problems without referring them to a regional manager, who doesn't understand local issues.

Process factors: Perhaps the shop assistant is suffering from 'initiative fatigue' from the many changes introduced in recent years (change problems). Maybe communication problems and conflict with another unit have not been resolved (organization development needs).

Management factors: Maybe the shop assistant is annoyed at the autocratic behaviour of the unit manager (inappropriate leadership style). Perhaps the shop assistant feels that management has made decisions without consulting employees who have useful information and ideas (management decision-making problems).

These are just some examples; maybe you can think of other individual, contextual, group, structural, process and management factors. This list of possible causes for your bad experience illustrates a number of features of explanations of organizational behaviour.

First, it is tempting to assume that the individual is at fault. However, this attribution of blame will often be incorrect. We need to look beyond the person, and consider factors at different levels of analysis: individual, group, organization, management – the wider context.

Second, it is also tempting to look for the main single cause of organizational behaviour. Behaviour can be influenced, however, by many factors which in combination, and over time, contribute to organizational effectiveness and the experience of work.

Third, while it is easy to address these factors separately, in practice they are often linked. Our employee's damaging behaviour could be the result of falling sales which jeopardize job security (context), and encourage an autocratic supervisory style (management), leading to changes in working practices (process), which affect existing jobs and lines of reporting (structure) and team memberships (group), resulting in increased anxiety and reduced job satisfaction (individual). These various links are not shown in Figure 1.1 because they can become complex (and would make the diagram untidy).

Fourth, we need to consider carefully the factors that we wish to explain. The term **organizational effectiveness** is controversial, because different stakeholders have different ideas about what counts as 'effective'. A stakeholder is anyone with an interest, or stake, in the organization.

> **Organizational effectiveness** a multi-dimensional concept defined differently by different stakeholders, including a range of quantitative and qualitative measures.

STOP AND THINK   Consider the institution in which you are currently studying. List the internal and external stakeholders. Identify how you think each stakeholder would define organizational effectiveness for this institution. Why the differences?

For commercial organizations, an obvious definition of effectiveness is 'profit', but this raises other problems. First, timescale has to be considered, as actions to improve short-term profits may damage long-term profitability. Second, some organizations forgo profit, at least in the short to medium term, in the interests of gaining market share, which contributes to corporate survival, growth and stability of operations and employment. Shareholders want a return on investment, customers want quality products or services at reasonable prices, managers want high-flying careers, most employees want decent pay, good working conditions, development and promotion opportunities, and job security. Environmental groups want organizations to conserving buildings and woodland, reduce carbon dioxide emissions and other forms of pollution, reduce traffic and noise levels, and so on. Organizational effectiveness is a slippery concept, and it has been difficult to demonstrate clearly the links between management practice on the one hand, and performance on the other.

One approach to establishing organizational effectiveness is the **balanced scorecard**. This involves determining a range of quantitative and qualitative performance measures, such as shareholder value, internal efficiencies, employee development and environmental concerns.

> **Balanced scorecard** an approach to defining organizational effectiveness using a combination of quantitative and qualitative measures to assess performance.

Quality of working life an individual's overall assessment of satisfaction with their job, working conditions, pay, colleagues, management style, organization culture, work-life balance, and training, development and career opportunities.

The phrase quality of working life has similar difficulties, as we each have different needs and expectations from work. A further problem is that quality of working life is linked both to organizational effectiveness, and also to most of the other factors on the left hand side of our map. It is difficult to talk about quality of working life without considering motivation, teamwork, organizational design, organization development and change, human resource policies and practices and management style.

What kind of model of organizational behaviour is this? The 'outputs' overlap with the 'inputs', and the causal arrow runs both ways. High motivation and group cohesiveness lead to organizational effectiveness, but good performance can increase motivation and teamwork. The 'outputs' can influence the 'inputs'. Can an 'effect' influence a 'cause'? Logically, this is the wrong way around. Is this a feature of social science explanations?

The problem with social science

What can social science offer to organizational behaviour? The contribution of social science to the sum of human knowledge in general is often regarded with scepticism. The natural sciences do not have this problem. What is the problem with social science?

We can put people on the moon, deliver music and movies to your computer, send video to mobile telephones on which you can watch television, genetically engineer disease-resistant crops, perform 'keyhole' surgery, and so on. Natural science has also given us technologies with which we can do enormous damage, to each other and to the planet. Textbooks in electrical engineering, naval architecture, quantum mechanics and cardio-vascular surgery tell the reader how things (including people) work, how to make things and how to fix them. Students from these disciplines often find psychology, sociology and organizational behaviour texts disappointing because they do not offer clear practical guidance. Social science often raises more questions than it answers, and draws attention to debates, conflicts, ambiguities and paradoxes, which are left unresolved. Natural science gives us material technology. Social science has not given us a convincing social engineering, of the kind which, say, would reduce car theft or eliminate football hooliganism. Nevertheless, managers expect organizational research to resolve organizational problems.

STOP AND THINK   You discover that one of your instructors has a novel way of enhancing student performance on her module. She always gives students poor grades for their first assignment, regardless of how good it is. This, she argues, stimulates higher levels of student performance in subsequent assignments.

This is an example of 'social engineering'. To what extent is this ethical?

The goals of science include description, explanation, prediction and control of events. These four goals represent increasing levels of sophistication. Social science, however, seems to struggle in all of these areas. Table 1.1 summarizes the problems.

However, these 'struggles' only arise if we expect social science to conform to natural science practice. If the study of people and organizations is a different kind of enterprise, then we need different procedures. Social science is just a different kind of science.

Description

Natural and social science can differ in what they are each attempting to describe. Natural science is describing an objective reality. Social science, in contrast, is often describing (or documenting) the ways in which people understand and interpret their circumstances. Objective reality is stable. People's perceptions change with experience.

Table 1.1: Goals of science and social science struggles

goals of science	practical implications	social science struggles
description	measurement	invisible and ambiguous variables people change over time
explanation	identify the time order of events establish causal links between variables	timing of events not always clear cannot always see interactions
prediction	generalizing from one setting to another	uniqueness, complexity and lack of comparability between settings
control	manipulation	ethical and legal constraints

The first goal of science, however, is description, and to achieve this, social science has only three methods; observation, asking questions and studying documents. Documents can include diaries, letters, company reports, committee minutes or publications. Physicists and chemists, for example, use only one of these methods – observation. Metals and chemicals do not respond well to interrogation, and do not publish autobiographies in the style that has become popular, for example, with corporate chief executives.

There are different modes of observation. The researcher can observe informal discussion in a cafeteria, join a selection interview panel, follow candidates through a training programme, or even take a job with an organization in order to experience personally what it is like to work there. Our understanding of the management role, for example, is based largely on observation, but this has obvious limitations. What can we say about someone's perceptions and motives merely by observing their behaviour? We could shadow somebody for a day or two, and make guesses. Eventually we will need to ask some probing questions.

Home viewing

The 'behind the scenes' activities of consultants who manipulate trial outcomes are shown in the movie *Runaway Jury* (director Gary Fleder, 2003). Gene Hackman stars as Rankin Fitch, a ruthless jury consultant who observes that, 'trials are too important to be left up to juries'. Identify the methods and tactics used in this movie to affect the trial outcome.

This may be fiction, but it reflects reality. Celebrity cases, like the one involving Michael Jackson for allegedly molesting a 13-year-old boy, are subject to intense study by specialists. Consultants are hired by both prosecution and defence to help choose jury members who are most likely to support their respective cases. In a case like Jackson's, consultants also try to identify the 'stealth jurors' who either want to influence the outcome of the trial, or to exploit media opportunities once the trial is over. Consultants construct psychological and social profiles of the jurors. They also observe each juror's reactions and gestures in the courtroom, in order to predict which presentation styles and arguments are most likely to influence them. So, 'each juror's current job, marital status, education, mannerisms, even their nervous tics, as observed in the courtroom, will be dissected by the army of pundits who will pontificate on the trial and its progress day after day on TV'. Michael Jackson was acquitted.

Based on Elsworth (2005).

How do we study phenomena that cannot be observed directly, such as learning (Chapter 5)? This is achieved through inference. As you read this book, we would like to think that you are learning about organizational behaviour. However, if we could open your head as you read, we would have difficulty finding anything that could be meaningfully described as 'the learning process' – but neurophysiology has made breakthroughs in understanding memory processes. The term 'learning' is a label for an invisible (to a social scientist) activity whose existence we can assume or infer.

Some changes must take place inside your head if learning is to occur. Neurophysiology can help to track down the processes involved, but it is not clear how an improved understanding of the neurology and biochemistry of learning would help us to design better job training programmes. The procedures for studying learning by inference are straightforward. We can examine your knowledge of this subject before you read this book, and repeat the test afterwards. If the second set of results is better than the first, then we can infer that learning has taken place. Your ability to perform a particular task has changed, and we can use that change to help us identify the conditions that caused it. We can proceed in this manner to study the effects of varying inputs to the learning process – characteristics of the teachers, learners, physical facilities, and the time and other resources devoted to the process. We can study variations in the delivery and study processes, in terms of methods, materials, and timing. Our understanding of the learning process and what affects it can thus develop systematically. From this knowledge, we can begin to suggest improvements.

Questions can be asked in person by the researcher in an interview, or through self-report questionnaires. The validity of responses, as a reflection of the 'truth', is questionable for at least three reasons.

First, our subjects may lie. People planning a bank robbery, or who resent the intrusion of a researcher, may give misleading replies. There are ways in which we can check the accuracy of what people tell us, but this is not always possible or convenient.

Second, our subjects may not know. The mental processes related to our motives typically operate without conscious effort. Few of us make the attempt to dig these processes out from our subconscious to examine them. Most of us struggle through life without the self-critical 'stop and think' that poses questions like, 'why am I here?', and 'what am I doing?'. The researcher gets the answers of which the person is aware, or which seem to be appropriate, rational, or 'correct' in the circumstances. The answers we get can simply be convenient inventions of the moment.

Third, our subjects may tell us what they think we want to hear. People rarely lie to researchers. They create problems by being helpful. Easier to give a simple answer than a complex history of intrigue and heartbreak. The socially acceptable answer is better than no answer at all. This does *not* mean that the answers we get are wrong; rather, we must be aware of the social context in which information is collected.

Explanation

A second goal of science is explanation. It is often possible to infer that one event has caused another even when the variables are not observable. If your test score is higher after reading this book than before, and if you have not been studying other materials, then we can infer that reading this book has caused your score to improve. The timing of events is not always easy to establish. We might assume, for instance, that satisfaction leads to higher job performance. However, we also know that good performance makes people more satisfied in their work. Which comes first? Which way does the causal arrow run?

The laws that govern human behaviour seem to be different from those that govern the behaviour of natural phenomena. Consider, for instance, the meteorological law, 'clouds mean rain'. This law holds good right around the planet. The cloud does not have to be told, either as a youngster or when it approaches hills, about the business of raining. Compare this situation with the social law, 'red means stop'. A society can choose to change this law, to 'blue means stop', because some people are red–green colour blind (and thus cause hideous accidents). The human driver can get it wrong by deliberately jumping the red light, or have a lapse of concentration and pass the red light accidentally. Clouds cannot vote to change the laws that affect them, nor can they break these laws, or get them wrong by accident.

We are not born with pre-programmed behavioural guides, although it appears that we are equipped from birth to learn certain behaviours, such as language (Pinker, 2002). We have to learn the rules of our particular society at a given time. There are strikingly different cultural rules concerning relatively trivial matters, such as how close people should stand to each other in social settings. We also have rules about how and when to shake hands and for how long the shake should last, about the styles of dress and address appropriate to different social occasions, about relationships between superior and subordinate, between men and women, between elderly and young. Even across the related cultures of Europe, and of the Pacific Rim, there are major differences in social rules, both between and within countries.

These observations have profound implications for the ways in which social science explains things, and we will explore the possibilities in more detail later in the chapter. It is important to recognize, however, that we cannot expect to discover laws governing human behaviour consistently across time and place. Social and cultural norms vary from country to country, and vary across subcultures in the same country. Our individual norms, attitudes and values also vary over time and with experience, and we are likely to answer that researcher's questions differently if approached a second time, some months later.

Prediction

A third goal of science is prediction. Social science can often explain events without being able to make precise predictions (Table 1.2). We may be able to predict the rate of suicide in a given society, or the incidence of stress-related disorders in an occupational group. However, we can rarely predict whether specific individuals will try to kill themselves, or suffer sleep and eating disorders. This limitation in our predictive ability is not necessarily critical. We are often more interested in the behaviour of groups than individuals, and more interested in tendencies and probabilities than in individual predictions and certainties.

There is a more fundamental problem. Researchers often communicate their findings to those who have been studied. Suppose you have never given much thought to the ultimate reality of human existence. One day, you read about an American psychologist, Abraham Maslow, who claims that we have a basic need for 'self-actualization', to develop our capabilities to their full potential. If this sounds like a good idea to you, and you act accordingly, then what he has said has become true, in your case. His claim has fulfilled itself. This may be because he has given you a new perspective on the human experience, or because he has given you a label to explain some aspect of your existing intellectual makeup.

Some predictions are thus self-fulfilling. The act of saying something will happen can either make that happen, or increase the likelihood of it happening. Equally, some predictions are intentionally self-defeating. Many of the disastrous predictions from economists, about currency exchange and interest rate movements, for example, are designed to trigger action to prevent those prophecies from coming true. In an organizational setting, one could predict that a particular management style will lead to the resignation of a number of valuable employees, in the hope that this will lead to a change in management style.

Table 1.2: We can explain – but we cannot confidently predict

we can explain staff turnover in a supermarket in terms of the repetitive and boring nature of the work	but we cannot predict which members of staff will leave, or when they will choose to do so
we can explain how different management styles encourage greater or lower levels of employee commitment and performance	but we cannot predict which managers will achieve the highest levels of commitment and performance in a given setting
we can explain the factors that contribute to group cohesiveness in an organization	but we cannot predict the level of cohesion and performance of particular groups
we can explain why some types of organization structure are more adaptable in the face of external change than others	but we cannot predict the performance improvements that will follow an organizational structure change

Control

A fourth goal of science is control, or the ability to change things. Social science findings can induce social change. Organizational research findings also prompt change. The natural scientist does not study the order of things in order to be critical, or to encourage that order to improve itself. It is hardly appropriate to evaluate, as good or bad, the observation that a gas expands when heated, or the number of components in a strand of DNA. Social scientists, on the other hand, are often motivated by a desire to change aspects of society and organizations. An understanding of how things currently work, and the strengths and weaknesses of those arrangements, is essential for that purpose. Such understanding, there-fore, is not necessarily a useful end in itself. Social science can be deliberately critical of the social and organizational order that it uncovers, because that order is only one of many that we are capable of creating.

An agenda for inducing social and organizational change is not the same as controlling or manipulating human behaviour, which many regard as unethical. As already indicated, we do not have a social technology, comparable to material technology, enabling us to manipulate other people anyway. Perhaps we should be grateful for this. However, Table 1.3 identifies a number of interventions that are designed to control aspects of employee behaviour.

It is important to recognize that our judgements and our recommendations are based not only on evidence, but also on values. Social science has been criticized as 'ideology in disguise'. However, if one studies organizations in order to change and improve them, then we cannot escape from that criticism. Suppose we study repetitive clerical work in an insurance company, or unskilled packing work in a factory. The employees are bored and unhappy, and our research identifies work redesign options. Managers claim that their work system is a cost-effective way of producing the goods and services their customers want. The tension between these positions cannot be resolved with reference only to empirical evidence.

Table 1.3: Interventions to control organizational behaviour

organizational intervention	attempts to control
staff training and development programmes (Chapter 5, Learning)	employee knowledge and skills
psychometric assessments (Chapter 6, Personality)	the types of people employed
employee communications (Chapter 7, Communication)	employee understanding of and compliance with management-inspired goals
job redesign (Chapter 9, Motivation)	employee motivation, commitment and performance
teambuilding (Part 3)	levels of team cohesion and performance
reorganization – structure change (Part 4)	ability of the organization to respond to external turbulence
organizational change (Chapter 18, Change)	speed of change and reduction of conflict and resistance
organization culture change (Chapter 4, Culture)	values, attitudes, beliefs and goals shared by management and employees
human resource management (Chapter 1, Explaining OB)	high employee performance
leadership style (Chapter 19, Leadership)	commitment to an overarching vision

Explaining organizational behaviour

Positivism a perspective which assumes that the world can be understood in terms of causal relationships between observable and measurable variables, and that these relationships can be studied objectively using controlled experiments.

We need to revisit our discussion of how social science deals with the task of explanation. The natural sciences are based on an approach known as positivism. Indeed, the term 'scientific' is often used to mean a positivist approach that is objective and rigorous, using observations and experiments to establish universal relationships.

Heat a bar of metal, and it expands. Eat more salt, and your blood pressure rises. The factor that causes a change is the *independent* variable. The effect to which it leads is the *dependent* variable. These are also known as the *causal* and *outcome* variables. Salt is the independent (causal) variable; blood pressure is the dependent (outcome) variable. Those variables can be measured, and those causal relationships are universal and unchanging. To measure something, you need an operational definition – a method for quantifying the variable.

Operational definition the method used to measure the incidence of a variable in practice.

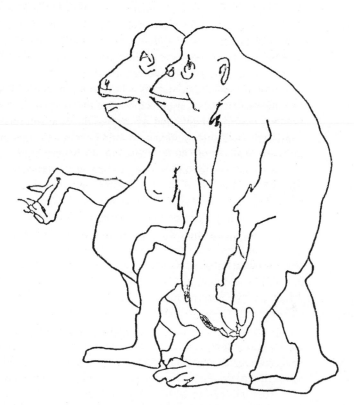

. . . and then he raises the issue of, 'how many angels can dance on the head of a pin?', and I say, you haven't operationalized the question sufficiently – are you talking about classical ballet, jazz, the two-step, country swing . . .

Variance theory an approach to explaining organizational behaviour based on universal relationships between independent and dependent variables which can be defined and measured precisely.

The operationalization of temperature and blood pressure involves thermometers and monitors. Questionnaires are often used as operational definitions of job satisfaction and management style. With those measures, we can answer questions about the effects of different management styles on employee satisfaction, and performance. That assumes that human behaviour can be explained with the methods used to study natural phenomena.

Our field map of the organizational behaviour terrain (Figure 1.1) can thus be read as a 'cause and effect' explanation. Manipulate the variables on the left, and alter the values of the organizational effectiveness and quality of working life variables on the right. Lawrence Mohr (1982) called this kind of explanation a variance theory. Do varying management styles lead to varying levels of satisfaction? Do varying personality traits lead to varying levels of job performance?

Constructivism
a perspective which argues that our social and organizational worlds have no ultimate objective truth or reality, but are instead determined by our shared experiences, meanings and interpretations.

Although positivism and variance theory have been successful in the natural sciences, many social scientists argue that this approach does not apply to social and organizational phenomena. Positivism assumes that there is an objective world 'out there' which can be observed, defined and measured. In contrast, **constructivism** argues that many aspects of that so-called objective reality are actually defined by us. In other words, 'reality' depends on how we perceive it, on how we *socially construct* it (Berger and Luckmann, 1966).

What does it mean to say that 'reality is *socially constructed*'? Suppose you want to measure aggression at student functions. In positivist mode, you first have to decide what counts as 'aggression'. Your *operational definition* could be an 'aggressiveness index' which you use to count the behaviours you observe that involve raised and angry voices, physical contact, pain and injury, and damage to property. This could reveal, for example, that some student functions are more aggressive than others, that aggressiveness is higher later in the evening, that female students are just as aggressive as male students, and so on.

Now, suppose you observe one male student shout at and punch another on the arm. The second student shouts angrily and pushes the first student away. A table is shaken, drinks are spilled, glasses are broken. Your 'aggressiveness index' just jumped by five or six points. In talking to the students, however, they describe their actions as friendly, fun and playful. The other members of their group agree. This *socially constructed* version of events, for actors and observers, involves friendship – the opposite of aggression. Your operational definition is false. What matters is how those involved interpret their own actions. Of course, in a different social or organizational setting, raised voices, physical violence, and damaged property will be understood as aggression. The interpretation of those behaviours is not consistent from one context to another. Temperatures of 45 degrees centigrade, or blood pressure readings of 180 over 90, will always be 'high', wherever you are.

Constructivism assumes that we are *self-interpreting* beings. We attach meaning and purpose to what we do. Chemical substances and metal bars do not attach meaning to their behaviour, nor do they give interviews or fill out questionnaires. So, human behaviour cannot be studied using methods that apply to natural objects and events. In constructivist mode, our starting point must lie with how others understand, interpret, and define their own actions, and not with operational definitions that we create for them. The organizational behaviour variables in which we are interested are going to mean different things, to different people, at different times, and in different places. Variance theory, therefore, is not going to get us very far. To understand organizational issues, we have to use **process theory** (Mohr, 1982; Langley, 2009).

Process theory an approach to explaining organizational behaviour based on narratives which show how many factors, combining and interacting over time in a particular context, are likely to produce the outcomes of interest.

Process theory, instead of correlating variables, shows how a sequence of events, in a particular context, lead to the outcomes in which we are interested. Those outcomes could concern individual satisfaction, organizational performance, the effectiveness of change, the resolution of conflict. The key point is that outcomes are often generated by *combinations* of factors *interacting* with each other over time. If eating salt raises your blood pressure, halving the amount of salt that you eat will reduce the pressure by a measurable amount. If leadership is necessary to the success of an organizational change initiative, it does not make sense to consider the implications of only half that leadership. Process theory is thus helpful when we want to understand complex and messy organizational phenomena:

- which are influenced by a number of different factors;
- which are difficult to define and measure, and which change with time and context;
- which combine and interact with each other;
- where the start and end points of the event sequence are not well defined;
- where the outcomes are also difficult to define and measure.

Variance theory offers *definitive* explanations in which causes and outcomes are related in unchanging ways. The values of the causal variables always predict the values of the outcome variables (this temperature, that volume). Process theories offer *probabilistic* explanations. We can say that combinations of explanatory factors are more likely to generate the outcomes of interest, but not in every case.

STOP AND THINK

Hospital managers are concerned that some patients with medical emergencies wait too long in the casualty department before they are diagnosed and treated.

The positivist wants to observe and record emergency patient numbers, waiting and treatment times, staffing levels, bed numbers and the availability of other resources.

The constructivist wants to talk to the doctors, nurses and ambulance crews, to find out how they feel about working here and where they believe the problems lie.

Which approach is more likely to resolve the waiting times problem, and why?

Positivism and *constructivism* are labels representing many shades of opinion (Burrell and Morgan, 1979; Deetz, 2000). While constructivism is now widely established, the study of organizational behaviour is still dominated by positivist methods and variance theories.

Table 1.4 summarizes the contrasting perspectives on which explanations for organizational behaviour can be based. For the purposes of explanation, this picture is oversimplified. Variance theorists use qualitative data and process theorists use quantitative data, when that is appropriate to the topic. Some positivist variance theorists rely on 'subjective' data from self-report questionnaires, which constructivists also use. Some process theorists use narrative frameworks to develop variance-based explanations involving sequences of events. In other words, theory and practice are rarely as tidy as textbook models can make them appear.

What are the implications for our field map of the organizational behaviour terrain? Seen from a *positivist* perspective, that model prompts the search for consistent causal links: this organization structure will improve effectiveness and adaptability, that approach to job design will enhance motivation and performance. The positivist is looking for method, for technique, for specific and codified universal solutions to organizational problems.

Seen from a *constructivist* perspective, the model prompts a range of other questions: how do we define and understand the term 'organization', and what does effectiveness mean to different stakeholder groups? What kind of work experiences are different individuals looking for, and how do they respond to their experience, and why? The constructivist argues

Table 1.4: Positivism versus constructivism

	Perspective	
	Positivism	**Constructivism**
Description	accepts mostly information that can be observed and quantified	accepts qualitative information, and relies on inference, studies meanings and interpretations
Explanation	uses variance theories	uses process theories
	relies mainly on observable quantitative data	relies mainly on qualitative data and self-interpretations
	seeks universal laws based on links between independent and dependent variables	develops explanatory narratives based on factors combining and interacting over time and in context
Prediction	based on knowledge of stable and consistent relationships between variables	based on shared understanding and awareness of multiple social and organizational realities
	predictions are deterministic	predictions are probabilistic
Control	aims to shape behaviour and achieve desired outcomes by manipulating explanatory variables	aims at social and organizational change through stimulating critical self-awareness

that explanations may apply only to a small part of the social and organizational world, and that explanations may have to change as the context changes, with time. The constructivist thus seeks to trigger new ideas and change by stimulating self-critical awareness.

This field map, or model, therefore, does not in any straightforward sense lay out causal links across the organizational behaviour terrain. It is simply one way of displaying a complex subject quickly and simply. We hope that it also gives you an overview of the subject, and helps you to organize the material in this book. It also serves as a reminder to consider the range of interacting factors that may explain what we observe, that it is often helpful to look beyond what may appear to be the main and obvious explanations.

Research and practice: evidence-based management

Do managers use organizational research to inform their plans and decision-making? Managers are more likely to be concerned with prediction and control, rather than with description and explanation. Given the problems facing social science in the areas of prediction and control, do the kinds of evidence and explanation that social science produces help managers in their task? Are academic research findings useful, irrelevant or misleading when applied to real world organizations and problems?

> When the late Peter Drucker was asked why managers fall for bad advice and fail to use sound evidence, he didn't mince words. 'Thinking is very hard work. And management fashions are a wonderful substitute for thinking.'
>
> *From Pfeffer and Sutton (2006, p.219).*

It is well known that there is a gap between academic research and organizational practice, and it is not difficult to explain why. Researchers publish their work in academic journals for other academics. Most managers do not read much, and few read academic journals. Many researchers follow lines of enquiry that do not focus on the problems that organizations and their managers are facing anyway – so even if managers did turn to those journals, they would not necessarily find anything of use to them. Research and practice also work on different timescales. A manager with a problem wants to solve it today; a researcher with a project could take two to three years to come up with some answers.

What does evidence-based management look like?

Here is what evidence-based management looks like. Let's call this example, a true story, 'Making Feedback People-Friendly'. The executive director of a health care system with twenty rural clinics notes that their performance differs tremendously across the array of metrics used. This variability has nothing to do with patient mix or employee characteristics. After interviewing clinic members who complain about the sheer number of metrics for which they are accountable (200+ indicators sent monthly, comparing each clinic to the 19 others), the director recalls a principle from a long-ago course in psychology: human decision makers can only process a limited amount of information at any one time. With input from clinic staff, a redesigned feedback system takes shape. The new system uses three performance categories – care quality, cost, and employee satisfaction – and provides a summary measure for each of the three. Over the next year, through provision of feedback in a more interpretable form, the health system's performance improves across the board, with low-performing units showing the greatest improvement.

In this example a *principle* (human beings can process only a limited amount of information) is translated into *practice* (provide feedback on a small set of critical performance indicators using terms people readily understand).

From Rousseau (2006, p.256).

Evidence, of course, is not the only ingredient that influences our decisions. Experience and judgement also play a role. Problems are likely to arise when decisions are based on habit, bias, and false assumptions. Jeffrey Pfeffer and Robert Sutton (2006) are particularly critical of 'pay performance' schemes designed to motivate people to higher levels of achievement.

Pay for performance is popular in education, and at the time of writing, the British government is considering a scheme to pay hospital surgeons depending on their success in their operating theatres. These schemes assume that (a) job performance depends on motivation, (b) performance can be measured in a consistent and reliable way, (c) employees are motivated by financial incentives, and (d) employees work alone, and are not dependent on the contributions of others. These assumptions are false. You may hate your job, but work harder in order to get a good reference. Performance in many jobs can have several different dimensions (consider waiting in a restaurant, for example), and some of those are subjective (courtesy to customers). The emphasis on financial rewards overlooks the importance that most of us attach to intrinsic rewards (the nature of the work). The surgeon in an operating theatre depends heavily on co-operation from many colleagues, all of whose efforts can affect the patient's wellbeing. Paying some members of staff more than others is divisive if the scheme is seen as unfair, and that will lower everyone's performance.

Evidence-based management systematically using the best available research evidence to inform decisions about how to manage people and organizations.

Pfeffer and Sutton note that, while pay for performance schemes are popular, there is no evidence that they work – except where those assumptions are correct – and there is evidence that these schemes actually lower performance. Managers aware of the evidence would avoid the costs of such schemes, and find better ways to motivate staff (see Chapter 9).

This line of reasoning, inspired by evidence-based medicine, has led to the growth of an **evidence-based management** movement. There is an Evidence-Based Management Collaborative, based at Carnegie Mellon University; EBMgt has a Wikipedia entry.

"I don't listen to the evidence. I like to make up my own mind."

Source: © Perry Barlow/Condé Nast Publications/www.cartoonbank.com

The similarities between medicine and management have been exaggerated. While medicine may confidently advise, 'take pill, cure headache', there are few if any such generic solutions to organizational problems. There is no such thing as 'best practice' because this depends on local circumstances. Management interventions thus vary widely according to the context. Usually, a number of initiatives or solutions are implemented simultaneously. It is rare to see a single intervention aimed at a single organizational problem. Medical and managerial decisions differ in other significant respects, too; doctors treating headaches do not have to consider the impact of their decisions on organization politics.

The problem is, organizational researchers cannot often say, 'if this is your problem, here is your solution'. So what role do research and evidence have? Anita McGahan (2007, p.748) argues that academic research contributes to management practice in five other ways, by:

1. generating counterintuitive insights;
2. demonstrating that fundamental business practices are changing in an important business activity, routine or practice;
3. showing that a widely used management practice violates important principles;
4. suggesting a specific theory to explain an interesting and current situation;
5. identifying an iconic problem, phenomenon, or activity that opens new areas of academic enquiry and management practice.

Organizational research can shape practice not just through developing specific solutions to particular problems, but in helping to transform, in creative and constructive ways, how problems are understood and defined in the first place, and also how they are approached. We can rarely say, 'here is the solution to your problem'. We can usually say, 'here is a way to understand your problem, and to develop solutions that will work in this particular context' – see the box, 'Great systems are more important than great people'.

Great systems are more important than great people

Managers have become obsessed with 'talent management', identifying and retaining the best people, the top performers, the stars, the 'top graders'. The assumption behind this fashion is that great people will produce great organizational performance. However, Jeffrey Pfeffer and Robert Sutton argue that there is no evidence to support this view of talent management. There is, however, good evidence that organizational systems are more important:

Over 15 years of research in the auto industry also provides compelling evidence for the power of systems over individual talent in a business context. Wharton Business School's John Paul MacDuffie has combined quantitative studies of every automobile plant in the world with in-depth case studies to understand why some plants are more effective than others. MacDuffie has found that lean or flexible production systems, with their emphasis on teams, training, and job rotation, and their de-emphasis of status differences between employees, build higher quality cars at a lower cost.

Toyota developed and still uses such practices, consistently achieving lower cost and higher quality than other companies – although some Honda plants give them a run for their money, and there are signs that General Motors is finally catching up. Toyota's success stems from its great system, not stunning individual talent. This starts at the top of the organization. One study showed that Toyota was the only major automobile company where a change in CEO had no effect on performance. The system is so robust that changing CEOs at Toyota is a lot like changing lightbulbs; there is little noticeable effect between the old one and the new one.

From Pfeffer and Sutton (2006, pp.97–98).

Human resource management: OB in action

Human resource management the function responsible for establishing integrated personnel policies to support organization strategy.

One of the main areas where organizational behaviour (OB) contributes to evidence-based practice is **human resource management** (HRM – or personnel management). These subjects are often taught separately, as they have their own specialized topics and methods, but there is overlap. OB is concerned with understanding micro- and macro-organizational issues, at individual, group, corporate, and contextual levels of analysis. HRM develops and implements policies which enhance the quality of working life, and encourage commitment, flexibility, and high performance from employees in the context of corporate strategy.

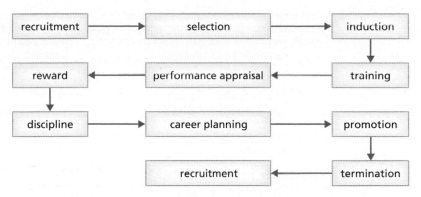

Figure 1.2: The employment cycle

In designing those policies, HRM can be seen as 'organizational behaviour in practice', and this applies to all stages of the employment cycle (Figure 1.2) – stages that you will encounter at various points in your career. At the end of this cycle, 'termination' can mean that the employee has resigned, retired, been made redundant, or been fired.

To demonstrate the relationships between HRM and OB, Table 1.5 maps the OB topics covered in this text against areas of HRM practice.

The basic model of HRM (Figure 1.3) says that, *if* you design your people policies in a particular way, *then* performance will improve. In terms of the concepts we introduced earlier, HRM policies are *independent variables* in this relationship, and the quality of working life and organizational effectiveness are *dependent variables*. However, as we will see, process theory may be more appropriate for explaining the relationship between HR policies and organizational outcomes.

Table 1.5: Human resource management and organizational behaviour

HRM functions	issues and activities	OB topics
recruitment, selection, induction	getting the right employees into the right jobs; recruiting from an increasingly diverse population; sensitivity to employment of women, ethnic minorities, the disabled, the elderly	environmental turbulence; PESTLE analysis; personality assessment; communication; person perception; learning; new organizational forms
training and development	tension between individual and organizational responsibility; development as a recruitment and retention tool; coping with new technologies	technology and job design; new organizational forms; learning; the learning organization; motivation; organizational change
performance appraisal and reward	annual appraisal; pay policy; fringe benefits; need to attract and retain staff; impact of teamwork on individual pay	motivation; expectancy theory; equity theory; group influence on individual behaviour; teamworking
managing conduct and discipline	sexual harassment, racial abuse, drug abuse, alcohol abuse, health and safety; monitoring misconduct; using surveillance; formulation and communication of policies	surveillance technology; learning; socialization; behaviour modification; organizational culture; managing conflict; management style
participation and commitment	involvement in decisions increases commitment; design of communications and participation mechanisms; managing organizational culture; tap ideas, release talent, encourage loyalty	communication; motivation; organization structure; organization culture; new forms of flexible organization; organizational change; leadership style
organization development and change	the personnel/human resource management role in facilitating development and change; flexible working practices	organization development and change; motivation and job design; organization culture and structure; leadership

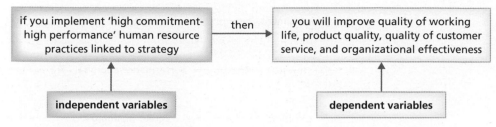

Figure 1.3: The basic model of HRM

The Bath model of HRM

This basic model needs further detail to make it work. The Bath People and Performance Model was developed by John Purcell and colleagues at the University of Bath in the UK (Purcell *et al.*, 2000, 2003; Sloman, 2002). Based on case study research in 12 organizations, this approach – summarized in Figure 1.4 – focuses on the *processes* through which HR policies influence employee behaviour and performance. Purcell and his colleagues argue that, for people to perform beyond the minimum requirements of a job, three factors, Ability, Motivation and Opportunity (AMO) are necessary:

Factor	Employees must
ability	have job skills and knowledge, including how to work well with others
motivation	feel motivated to do the work, and to do it well
opportunity	be able to use their skills, and contribute to team and organizational success

If one of these factors is weak or missing, then an individual's performance is likely to be poor. You may have the ability and the motivation, but if your supervisor prevents you from sharing ideas with colleagues and insists on 'standard procedure', then your performance is unlikely to excel. You will probably not 'go the extra mile'.

Most employees have some choice over how, and also how well, they perform their jobs. This is known as 'discretionary behaviour'. Sales assistants, for example, can decide to adopt a casual and unsympathetic tone, or they can make customers feel that their concerns have been handled in a competent and friendly way. Negative, uncaring behaviours are

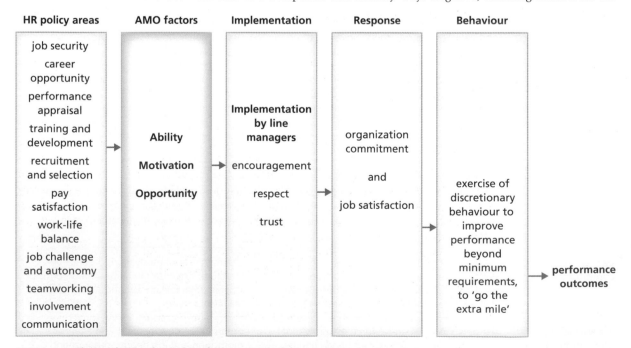

Figure 1.4: The Bath People and Performance Model

Source: Adapted from Purcell *et al.* (2003, p.7). Reprinted by permission of the Chartered Institute of Personnel and Development.

often a response to an employee's perception that the organization no longer cares about them. When one member of staff annoys a customer, and management finds out, then that employee has a problem. However, if staff collectively withdraw their positive discretionary behaviours, this can damage the performance of the organization as a whole.

What encourages employees to 'go the extra mile'? The answer lies in the model's *process theory*, which establishes a sequence of events with four linked steps.

1. Basic HR policies are required to produce the ability, motivation and opportunity central to any level of performance.
2. The line managers who 'bring these policies to life', have to communicate trust, respect and encouragement. This is achieved through the way that they give directions, and respond to suggestions.
3. The combination of HR policies with line management behaviours must lead to feelings of job satisfaction and employee commitment. Otherwise, the policies themselves will have little impact on behaviour and performance.
4. People tend to use positive discretionary behaviours when they experience pride in where they work, and want to stay there. Commitment and job satisfaction thus encourage employees to use discretionary behaviour to perform better.

In terms of our previous discussion, this is a *process theory* linking HR policies to organizational performance. While those HR policies must be in place, it is the *process* through which they are implemented that matters. The same policies, with inconsistent or half-hearted management, could lower commitment and satisfaction, leading to a withdrawal of positive discretionary behaviours. The 11 HR policies central to this model are:

1. recruitment and selection that is careful and sophisticated;
2. training and development that equips employees for their job roles;
3. career opportunities provided;
4. communication that is two-way, and information sharing;
5. involvement of employees in management decision-making;
6. teamworking;
7. performance appraisal and development for individuals;
8. pay that is regarded as equitable and motivating;
9. job security;
10. challenge and autonomy in jobs;
11. work-life balance.

This suggests that a *positive bundle* of policies which reinforce each other will produce a greater impact than the sum of individual policies. On the other hand, a 'deadly combination' of other policies can compete with and weaken each other; for example financial rewards based on individual contributions, with appraisal and promotion systems which encourage teamworking. Earlier research by Mark Huselid (1995) showed that organizations using high performance work practices had higher levels of productivity and financial performance, and lower employee turnover, and that those work practices contributed US$18,500 per employee in shareholder value and around $4,000 per employee in additional profits. Jeffrey Pfeffer (1998) similarly claims that human resource practices can raise an organization's stock market value by US$20,000 to $40,000 per employee.

Treat employees well, therefore, and your profits will rise. Comparative research by Malcolm Patterson and his colleagues (1997) at the Institute for Work Psychology at the University of Sheffield has shown that British manufacturing companies place less emphasis on empowering and capturing the ideas of employees than, for example, Australia, Japan and Switzerland, whose managers make more use of HR practices. Britain's poor comparative productivity and innovation may thus lie with work organization and management processes.

HR practices are a matter of life and death

Patients seeking the best hospital care traditionally consider the success rates of the doctors who could be treating them. Research also suggests that patients should examine hospital human resource practices, because these are linked to mortality rates.

Michael West and colleagues surveyed 61 hospitals in England, along with ten detailed case studies. Chief executives and human resource directors were asked about their hospital's characteristics, HR strategy, employee involvement, and HR practices covering all clinical, administrative, support and managerial staff groups. The survey also asked about training policies, teamworking, and staff performance appraisals.

Data were then collected on the numbers of deaths following emergency and non-emergency surgery, admission for hip fractures and heart attacks, and re-admission. Care was taken to account for variations in mortality due to region, local population, and hospital size. The ratio of doctors to patients affects mortality, as having more doctors around can mean fewer deaths. Analysis showed that mortality rates were significantly lower in hospitals with comprehensive HR practices concerning:

appraisal   extensive and sophisticated appraisal systems

training   well-developed training policies and budgets

teamwork   high numbers of staff working in teams, and trained to do so

These relationships were even stronger where the HR director was a full voting member of the hospital management board, a position of power and influence from which systematic policies could be implemented. However, it is the skills and knowledge of doctors and surgeons which affect patient care and survival, and medical staff were suspicious of these research findings. How can HR practices applied to staff who are not involved in patient diagnosis and treatment affect mortality rates? West and colleagues reply (p.35):

Our answer is simple, though it may seem strange to those who deal with individuals rather than organizations. If you have HR practices that focus on effort and skill; develop people's skills; encourage co-operation, collaboration, innovation and synergy in teams for most, if not all, employees, the whole system functions and performs better. If the receptionists, porters, ancillary staff, secretaries, nurses, managers and, yes, the doctors are working effectively, the system as a whole will function effectively.

HR practices, therefore, affect organizational processes. A hospital is a work community which depends on the interaction of all its members. Although clearly important, the skills and performance of doctors is not the only factor which affects the quality of patient care.

Based on West et al. *(2002) and*
West and Johnson (2002).

Returning to our discussion of evidence-based management, there is compelling evidence for the link between 'high performance' human resource management and organizational performance. On commercial grounds alone, surely this evidence has made an impact on organizational practice? David Guest (2000) studied 18 HR practices, surveying more than 1,000 chief executives and HR directors in 237 companies. He found that only 25 per cent of those companies used more than half of those practices, and only 1 per cent used more than 12 of them. These 'best practices' are not as common out there as they are in textbooks. Why not? David Guest and Zella King (2001) suggest five reasons:

- managers may not be aware of the research;
- managers may feel that research evidence does not apply to their organization;
- managers may believe that they already have appropriate practices;
- there may be constraints from more pressing priorities;
- implementation skills may be lacking.

While the concept of evidence-based management sounds appealing, the links between evidence and practice in organizational behaviour are complex. Management decisions are always going to be influenced by considerations other than research evidence; organization politics (preserving personal power and reputation), competitive advantage (why should we do what other companies are doing?). Management is only one stakeholder group in any organization; why should evidence not be used to promote the interests of other groups?

RECAP

1. *Explain the importance of an understanding of organizational behaviour.*

   - Organizations influence almost every aspect of our daily lives in a multitude of ways.

   - If we eventually destroy this planet, the cause will not lie with technology or weaponry. We will have destroyed it with ineffective organizations.

2. *Explain and illustrate the central dilemma of organizational design.*

   - The organizational dilemma concerns how to reconcile the inconsistency between individual needs and aspirations, and the collective purpose of the organization.

3. *Understand the need for explanations of behaviour in organizations that take account of combinations of, and relationships between factors at different levels of analysis.*

   - The study of organizational behaviour is multi-disciplinary, drawing in particular from psychology, social psychology, sociology, economics and political science.

   - Organizational behaviour involves a multi-level study of the external environment, and internal structure, functioning and performance of organizations, and the behaviour of groups and individuals.

   - Organizational effectiveness and quality of working life are explained by a combination of contextual, individual, group, structural, process and managerial factors.

   - In considering explanations of organizational behaviour, systemic thinking is required, avoiding explanations based on single causes, and considering a range of interrelated factors at different levels of analysis.

4. *Understand the difference between positivist and constructivist perspectives, and their respective implications for the study of organizational behaviour.*

   - A positivist perspective uses the same research methods and modes of explanation found in the natural sciences to study and understand organizational behaviour.

   - It is difficult to apply conventional scientific research methods to people, because of the 'reactive effects' which come into play when people know they are being studied.

   - A constructivist perspective assumes that, as we are self-defining creatures who attach meanings to our behaviour, social science is different from natural science.

   - A constructivist perspective believes that reality is not objective and 'out there', but is socially constructed.

   - A constructivist approach means abandoning scientific neutrality in the interests of stimulating social and organizational change through providing critical feedback and encouraging self-awareness.

5. *Understand the distinction between variance and process explanations of organizational behaviour.*

   - Variance theory explains organizational behaviour by identifying relationships between independent and dependent variables which can be defined and measured. Variance theories are often quantitative, and are based on a positivist perspective.

   - Process theory explains organizational behaviour using narratives which show how multiple factors produce outcomes by combining and interacting over time in a given context. Process theories can combine quantitative and qualitative dimensions, and can draw from positivist and constructivist traditions.

6. *Explain the development and limitations of evidence-based management.*

   - The concept of evidence-based management has become popular, but the links between evidence and practice are complex; evidence can help to shape the ways in which problems are understood and approached, rather than offering specific solutions.

7. *Recognize the breadth of applications of organizational behaviour theory, and in particular the contribution to human resource management practice.*

   - The Bath model of human resource management argues that discretionary behaviour to go beyond minimum requirements relies on a combination of HR policies and effective line management implementation.

   - High performance work practices increase organizational profitability by decreasing employee turnover and improving productivity, but they are not widely adopted.

Revision

1. How is organizational behaviour defined? What topics does this subject cover? What is the practical relevance of organizational behaviour?

2. Describe an example of organizational *mis*behaviour, where you as the customer were treated badly. Suggest possible explanations for your treatment.

3. What are the differences between variance and process theories, and why have variance theories been rejected as useful sources of explanations in organizational behaviour?

4. How can evidence, concepts, theories and models from organizational behaviour contribute effectively to organizational practice? Give examples.

Research assignment

Go to www.economist.com/management. This website summarizes management news, research and books. One book reviewed in 2008 argued that humour at work created competitive advantage by helping to attract and retain employees and stimulate creativity; there is a link between punchline and bottom line. Find an example of evidence-based management. Write a report in which you: (a) show whether this is a variance theory – universal law linking two or more variables, or a process theory – describing a sequence of events linking a combination of factors in a particular context; (b) assess whether or not this work would be useful to management, in terms of how easy or how costly it would be to implement, and (c) describe how you as an employee would feel if management started using this tool, technique, method, or approach on you and your colleagues.

Springboard

Bryman, A. and Bell, E., 2003, *Business Research Methods*, Oxford University Press, Oxford.

Comprehensive account of methods used in management and organizational research.

Chartered Institute of Personnel and Development, 2008, *High Performance Working*, CIPD, London.

Short briefing which explains the components of high performance working, how it can be implemented and the barriers, with examples of organizations using this approach.

Cottrell, S., 2005, *Critical Thinking Skills: Developing Effective Analysis and Argument*, Palgrave Macmillan, Basingstoke, Hants.

The nature and application of critical thinking.

Leopold, J. and Harris, L., 2009, *The Strategic Managing of Human Resources*, Financial Times Prentice Hall, Harlow, Essex (2nd edn).

Comprehensive introductory text linking human resource policies and practices to corporate strategy, with case studies.

OB in films

Antz (1998, directors Eric Darnell and Tim Johnson). This clip (7 minutes) begins immediately after the opening credits with Z (played by Woody Allen) saying 'All my life I've lived and worked in the big city'; ends with General Mandible (Gene Hackman) saying, 'Our very next stop Cutter'. This is the story of a neurotic worker ant, Z 4195, who wants to escape from his insignificant job in an authoritarian organization – the ant colony.

1. Using the field map of the organizational behaviour terrain as a guide, identify as many examples as you can of how individual, group, structural and managerial process factors influence organizational effectiveness and quality of working life in an ant colony.

2. This is animated fiction with ants. What similar examples of factors affecting organizational effectiveness and quality of working life can you identify from organizations with which you are familiar?

OB in literature

Franz Kafka, *The Castle*, Penguin Books, Harmondsworth, 1926. How does this classic novel illustrate the organizational dilemma, and how well does it describe the relationships between employees and large bureaucratic organizations?

CHAPTER EXERCISES

Best job – worst job

Objectives
1. To help you to get to know each other.
2. To introduce you to the main sections of this organizational behaviour course.

Briefing
1. Pair up with another student. Interview each other to find out names, where you both come from, and what other courses you are currently taking.

2. In turn, introduce your partner to the other members of the class.

3. Two pairs now join up, and the group of four discuss:

   What was the worst job that you had? What made it so bad?
   What was the best job that you ever had? What made it so good?

4. Appoint a scribe to record the recurring themes revealed in group members' stories about their best and worst jobs. Appoint also a group spokesperson.

5. The spokespersons then give presentations to the whole class, summarizing the recurring features of what made a job good or bad. As you listen, use this score sheet to record the frequency of occurrence of the various factors.

Factors affecting job experience

Factors	Examples	(✓) if mentioned
Individual factors	Pay: reasonable or poor Job training: comprehensive or none Personality: clashes with other people Communication: frequent or little	
Group factors	Co-workers: helping or not contributing Conflict with co-workers Pressure to conform to group norms	
Structural factors	Job tasks: boring or interesting Job responsibilities: clear or unclear Supervision: too close or little Rules: too many or insufficient guidance	
Process factors	Staff not welded into a team Changes: well or poorly implemented People management: poor or good Working atmosphere: bad or good	
Management factors	Boss: considerate or autocratic Decisions: imposed or asked for opinions Disagreements with managers: often or few	

Management versus the workers

Rate each of the following issues on this five-point scale, in terms of whether you think managers and workers have shared, partially shared, or separate interests:

1	2	3	4	5
share identical interests			have completely separate interests	

- health and safety standards
- basic pay
- introducing new technology
- levels of overtime working
- designing interesting jobs
- bonus payments
- flexible working hours
- equal opportunities
- company share price
- developing new products and/or services
- redundancy

Explain why you rated each of these issues in the way that you did.

Based on Noon and Blyton (2007, p.305).

Chapter 2 **Environment**

Key terms

environment	environmental complexity
environmental scanning	environmental dynamism
globalization	post-modern organization
consolidation	environmental determinism
PESTLE analysis	ethics
scenario planning	ethical stance
environmental uncertainty	corporate social responsibility

Learning outcomes

When you have read this chapter, you should be able to define those key terms in your own words, and you should also be able to:

1. Understand the mutual interdependence between the organization and its environment.

2. Appreciate the strengths and limitations of PESTLE analysis of organizational environments.

3. Explain contemporary organizational responses to environmental turbulence.

4. Apply utilitarianism, theory of rights and theory of justice to assess whether or not management actions are ethical, and recognize the limitations of those criteria.

5. Understand the concept of corporate social responsibility, and the practical and ethical implications of this concept for organizational behaviour.

Why study an organization's environment?

Should that have happened?

Lee and Charlie

Lee is 61 and has been director of engineering for American Semiconductor for 14 years. Intelligent and with a reputation as a good manager, he has not kept up to date with technological developments. The manufacturing process produces toxic waste, and Lee's casual approach to disposal has culminated in two court cases which could cost the company considerable sums in damages. The company's executive vice president, Charlie, has tried for

about three years to persuade Lee to prioritize the disposal problem, without success. Having decided that Lee should be removed from his position, Charlie is reluctant to fire him as that would demoralize other managers. He therefore tells colleagues, informally, that he is not satisfied with Lee's work, and exaggerates Lee's faults in these conversations. When Lee encounters a growing lack of support from colleagues, he decides to take early retirement.

Is Charlie's approach ethical?

Environment issues, trends, and events outside the boundaries of the organization, which influence internal decisions and behaviours.

An organization has to interact with the world around it, with its **environment**. The operations of any organization – local café, city hospital, multinational motor car company – can be described in terms of its 'import–transformation–export' processes. The car plant imports from its environment resources such as materials, component parts and equipment, storage facilities, staff and energy. The car plant then transforms these resources into vehicles, which are exported to a dealer network for sale to customers. The organization is involved in a constant series of exchanges with suppliers, dealers, consumers, regulatory agencies, and other stakeholders such as shareholders and trade unions.

The environment for a motor car plant in the twenty-first century is complex. There is global overcapacity in production, and the cost of oil is high and unpredictable. The industry consolidation of the late 1990s, in which smaller manufacturers (Saab, Rover, Rolls Royce, Jaguar, Volvo) were bought by larger companies (General Motors, BMW, Ford), continues (the Indian Tata Group owns the Jaguar and Land Rover brands). Competition encourages manufacturers to locate plants in low wage countries (Hungary, Brazil, Romania) generating resentment in traditional manufacturing bases (Britain, America). In Japan, *gaiatsu*, or foreign pressure, led to restructuring at Toyota, Honda and Nissan in the late 1990s.

Cost competition has also encouraged the application of 'lean manufacturing' methods, with consequences for working practices and quality of working life. There is concern over the environmental pollution generated by internal combustion engines which burn petrol and diesel oil, encouraging the development of cleaner engines to reduce carbon emissions. The volume of traffic in many cities around the world has driven governments to consider road pricing, congestion charges, and new taxation measures to encourage the use of public transport. These are just some of the factors in the external environment of a car plant. Such factors force constant adjustments to ways of thinking about the business of making cars. This means always thinking about the organization's business strategy, organization structure, use of resources, management decisions, job design and working practices.

STOP AND THINK

What other factors, trends or developments in the external environment of a car plant have not been mentioned? How will these affect the company's behaviour?

What are the main factors in the environment of your college or university? How are those factors influencing management actions – and how are these affecting you?

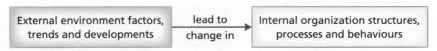

Figure 2.1: External environment–organization links

The argument of this chapter is illustrated in Figure 2.1, which argues that 'the world out there' influences 'the world in here'.

Social science texts annoy readers from other disciplines by first explaining a model, then revealing that it is wrong. As this is the strategy adopted here, an explanation is appropriate. There are three reasons for using this 'build it up, knock it down' approach.

1. We have to start somewhere, so let us begin simple and work up to complex.

2. If we construct an argument using basic assumptions, then introduce more complex and realistic assumptions, the thinking behind the model is exposed more clearly.

3. Models like Figure 2.1 are just 'one point of view', and are not beyond dispute. The search for 'the one best way' or 'the correct answer' is usually inappropriate.

An understanding of the dynamics of the environment is central to organizational effectiveness. An organization which is 'out of fit' (still making CD players now that MP3 is here) has to change, or go out of business. As the complexity and pace of environmental change seem to have increased, organizations that are able to adapt quickly to new pressures and opportunities are likely to be more successful than those which are slow to respond. (But the organization that makes a rapid jump in the wrong direction – making even better CDs to compete with MP3 – will still be in trouble.) A central concern for organizational behaviour, therefore, has been the search for 'fit' between the internal characteristics of the organization, and features of the external environment.

Analyzing the organization's environment

Identifying current and future factors 'out there' which could affect an organization usually generates a long list. The first problem, therefore, is to identify all of those factors. The next challenge is to predict their impact. The methods used to analyze the environment are known as **environmental scanning** techniques.

Environmental scanning involves collecting information from a range of sources: government statistics, newspapers and magazines, internet sites, specialist research and consulting agencies, demographic analysis, market research, focus groups. There are three major trends affecting most organizations; technology, globalization and demographics.

Environmental scanning techniques for identifying and predicting the impact of external trends and developments on the internal functioning of an organization.

Technology

Technology is probably the most tangible and visible aspect of environmental change. The pace of development appears to be unchecked. Since the last edition of this text was published three years ago, we have seen increases in the use of social networking (Facebook, MySpace, LinkedIn) and virtual worlds (Second Life), and the development of 'cloud computing' using software services on the internet rather than stored on your computer. We also have the promise of a headset – the Epoc – that will run your computer using thought control, an idea that was the basis for the movie *Firefox* (1982, director Clint Eastwood) in which Clint Eastwood steals from the then Soviet Union a jet fighter which is controlled by the pilot's thought impulses through a 'neuralink'. The implications of technology for organizational behaviour are explored in Chapter 3.

Applications of computing affect most aspects of our social and organizational lives, from entertainment to manufacturing, the provision of services, including education and how we communicate. These developments have increased the number of 'knowledge workers' (including teachers) whose value depends more on what they know than on what they can do. Software design and 'back office' support operations do not depend on location, and these kinds of knowledge work can be 'outsourced' to countries where pay is lower. A focus on computing, however, overlooks developments in other fields, such as in new materials, and in healthcare where the pace of development of new drugs, treatment regimes, and medical equipment seems to be almost as rapid as in computing, but attracts less attention.

STOP AND THINK

What new technologies, materials, medical treatments, services, processes, and so on, have affected your life and work recently? For better, or for worse?

Globalization

Business in Europe and North America was threatened in the 1970s with competition from countries on the Pacific Rim, such as Japan and Korea. These countries were able to produce cars, motor bikes and consumer electronic and entertainment products with higher quality and lower prices, using shorter production times and new operating processes. European and American businesses became more cost and quality conscious, and increased the focus on customer service. During the late 1990s, the Pacific Rim economies suffered from a combination of currency exchange rate collapses, banking system crises and cumbersome organization structures. However, their successes made a lasting impression on European and American management practice. Now, in the twenty-first century, these 'threats' continue, based on economic growth in China, and the growth of services outsourcing to remote call centres at the expense of jobs in Europe and North America. The term given to these trends and developments (Giddens, 1990, p.64) is **globalization**.

Globalization
the intensification of world-wide social and business relationships which link localities in such a way that local conditions are shaped by distant events.

Globalization involves 'the death of distance' (Cairncross, 1995, 2001), a term which means that geographical separation, of countries and individuals, is less important. Globalization means that the fate of a developing country village, dependent on export sales revenues from a single cash crop, is decided by price movements in exchanges in New York and Frankfurt. Globalization means that decisions taken in Tokyo affect employment in the English Midlands, where Toyota has an assembly plant. Globalization means that a dispute between Brussels and Washington over trade regulations can shut knitwear factories in the Borders region of Scotland. In 2008, the high-risk lending policies of banks in the United States led to the collapse of banks, other financial institutions and stock markets around the world.

BRICS and globality

Globalization used to mean 'Americanization'. Not any more. Everyone is now competing with everyone else, a new trend described as 'globality' by Harold Sirkin and colleagues (2008). Organizations in many developing economies are expanding into developed economies, buying up established businesses and brands. The famous American beer-maker Budweiser, for example, is today owned by a Brazilian–Belgian conglomerate. Chinese companies are investing heavily in Australian mining organizations. By 2008, there were over 60 companies based in 'emerging markets' on the *Fortune* 500 list of the world's biggest companies. Many of those were from the BRICs economies: Brazil, Russia, India and China. The ten largest *Fortune* Global 500 emerging market companies in 2008 were:

company	country	global rank	revenue $bn
Sinopec	China	16	159.3
Stage Grid	China	24	132.9
China National Petroleum	China	25	129.8
Pemex	Mexico	42	104.0
Gazprom	Russia	47	98.6
Petrobras	Brazil	63	87.7
Lukoil	Russia	90	67.2
Petronas	Malaysia	95	66.2
Indian Oil	India	116	57.4
Industrial and Commercial Bank of China	China	133	51.5

Other global companies from emerging economies are Haier (China, white goods), Cemex (Mexico, cement), Embraer (Brazil, aircraft), Infosys and Ranbaxy (India, software and pharmaceuticals). Lenovo is a Chinese computer manufacturer which, in 2005, bought the personal computer business of IBM for US$1.75 million, and now has annual revenues of around $17 billion. One of its products is a simple computer for farmers in rural markets, but with features (an 'express repair' key that recovers from a crash) that are used in products for sale elsewhere. The company's chairman Yang Yuanqing says, 'We are proud of our Chinese roots', but 'we no longer want to be positioned as a Chinese company. We want to be a truly global company.' Lenovo has no headquarters; management meetings rotate through the company's locations around the world; development work is done by virtual teams in different countries; the global marketing department is in Bangalore.

Virtual teams are teams which meet and collaborate using the internet and video conferencing, but rarely meet in person. Mr Yang and his family moved to North Carolina to learn about US culture and to improve their English.

Tata Group is an Indian software, tea and car and steel making conglomerate which operates in 85 countries. Tata owns Tetley, a British tea-making company, Corus, a European steel company, and Jaguar and Land Rover (bought from Ford in 2008). Like other companies mentioned here, Tata trades in markets where consumers are not as wealthy as those in developed economies, requiring 'frugal engineering' to make profitable products that those consumers can afford. Tata's new car, the Nano, will sell for around US$2,500, and may also be sold as a town car in developed economies.

Author's own work based on data in Bishop (2008).

Globalization has also been assisted by the development of free trade through national and international deregulation, which has made it easier to move goods and money around the planet, and to relocate facilities (for producing goods and services) where labour and other costs are relatively low. For some commentators, this means that the role of the single nation state in economic affairs is reduced, and we see the increasing importance of supranational bodies such as the European Union (EU), the Commonwealth of Independent States (CIS), the Council of the Baltic Sea States (CBSS), the Association of South East Asian Nations (ASEAN), the Organization for Economic Co-operation and Development (OECD) and the North American Free Trade Association (NAFTA). Access to advanced communications technology and weaponry also means that local conflicts quickly attract global attention.

Home viewing

Syriana (2006, director Stephen Gaghan) comes with the slogan, 'everything is connected', and offers insights into the nature of globalization. The film is set in the fictional Gulf state of Syriana, and is based on relations between the global oil industry and national politics, illustrating the links between power and wealth, between political, organizational and personal actions, between the decisions of corporate executives and the fate of workers. The action shifts between America, the Middle East and Europe. Friends are enemies; colleagues are crooks. One character observes, 'Corruption ain't nothing more than government intrusion into market efficiencies in the form of regulation. We have laws against it *precisely* so we can get away with it. Corruption is our protection. Corruption is what keeps us safe and warm.

Corruption is how we win.' George Clooney plays Bob Barnes, a CIA agent hunting Middle-Eastern terrorists. His role is to prevent the ageing Emir and his idealistic son from finalizing a deal with China, and not America ('I want you to take him from his hotel, drug him, put him in the front of a car, and run a truck into it at fifty miles an hour'). *Syriana* attributes the radicalization of young immigrant Muslims from Pakistan, and their suicide terrorist attack on an oil tanker, to the casual manner in which a global oil company treats its employees. George Clooney won an Oscar for his part in this movie. As you watch this movie, identify positive and negative examples of globalization in action, and assess whether the advantages outweigh the disadvantages, from the viewpoint of this film.

STOP AND THINK

How does globalization affect you personally?

In what ways could globalization influence your working life and your career?

What are the personal benefits and disadvantages?

Consider your own experience of globalization. This may involve holiday plans, working abroad, the clothes that you wear, the food and drink that you consume, and the way in which you use the internet, phones, social networking sites and different types of media technology. You probably have many direct and indirect encounters with other cultures, daily.

Disneyization

While most of us think of Disney as a company that makes animated and children's films, Alan Bryman argues that *Disneyization* is a global process infiltrating aspects of our social, cultural and economic life. In short, our surroundings are becoming more like a Disney theme park. Disneyization has four main principles:

theming — settings and objects are presented and decorated in dramatic ways that are not directly related to their purpose, such as a restaurant with a Wild West theme

hybrid consumption — the blurring of boundaries between different types of products and services that are normally distinct and separate, such as with casinos that are also hotels including numerous restaurants

merchandizing — the promotion of branded and licensed items, with copyright images and logos clearly on display, rather than just plain company products

performative labour — front line staff are hired to perform, smiling and helpful, joking and interacting with customers, to create atmosphere and mood

If your restaurant or shopping mall has been Disneyized, it will look and sound different, and give the impression of providing a novel and perhaps dramatic experience. These principles, Bryman argues, are being increasingly imitated, because they increase the appeal of goods and services and the settings in which they are provided, and encourage you to buy things that perhaps you don't really need.

Based on Bryman (2004).

Source: © Alan Bryman

The Hotel Luxor, in Las Vegas, with an 'Ancient Egpyt' theme

However, many people around the world do not have access to the goods and technologies that contribute to the experience of globalization for affluent members of developed economies. Globalization is an uneven economic and political process, and many are still excluded from the benefits. Many societies and groups reject the dislocation that globalization can bring, and object to the spread of Western culture and values, signified most clearly by brand labels. Western organizations (from fast food outlets to national embassies) have thus become terrorist targets, as well as focal points for the (often violent) demonstration of anger over perceived attempts to impose Western values on other cultures.

This seems to be an age of 'disorganized capitalism', complex and rapidly changing, in which the boundaries of large organizations in particular are blurred, and in which the nature of work itself is in a state of flux. Figure 2.2, based on the work of John Kotter (1995b), summarizes this argument. The arrows running down the figure set out a causal chain, from the technological, economic and geopolitical trends at the top, to the organizational changes at the bottom. Kotter argues that organizational changes in the direction of becoming faster, flatter and more flexible, are determined by external environmental pressures, which are driving globalization, introducing new threats and problems, and opening up market opportunities. Change seems to be inevitable; 'adapt to survive'.

Indian investment

Figures from UK Trade and Investment, which provides practical assistance to international companies establishing and expanding their businesses in the UK, show just how quickly inward investment from India is growing.

In 2000–2001 this government body supported only 21 Indian investment projects in the UK, but by 2006–2007 the number had shot up to 69, creating 5,130 new jobs and safeguarding 2,135 existing ones in that year alone. Even these figures represent just the tip of the iceberg, with the Indian High Commission in London estimating that there are now about 500 Indian companies operating in the UK.

From Arkin (2008).

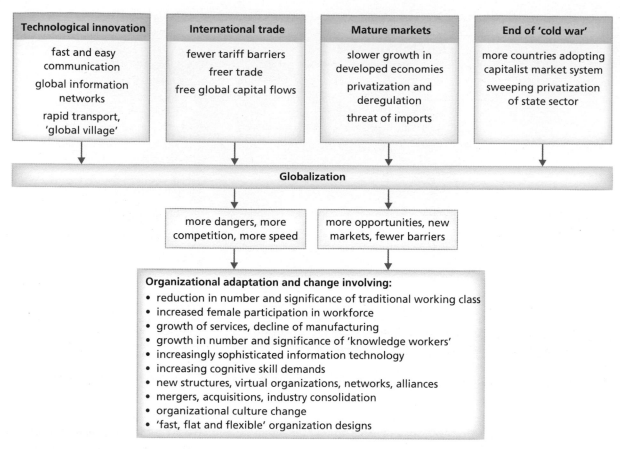

Figure 2.2: Globalization and organizational change

Consolidation the process through which company ownership in a sector becomes concentrated in a smaller number of larger and sometimes global enterprises.

Many sectors are increasingly dominated by smaller numbers of much larger companies, a process which is called **consolidation**.

In the 1970s, and for the following two decades, there were eight international accounting firms. Today, the remaining 'big four' are PricewaterhouseCoopers, Ernst & Young, Deloitte and KPMG. At the beginning of the twenty-first century, this group was known as the 'big five', but Arthur Andersen collapsed following its role in the Enron corporate scandal. It is predicted that the motor car industry will consolidate into six independent manufacturers, two each in North America, Europe and Japan. The global entertainment sector is consolidated around half a dozen international businesses. National and global consolidation has affected the hotel and catering sector, too. The next time you are in town, see how many of the restaurants (quality and fast food) are independently owned, and how many are part of national (or international) restaurant chains.

Demographics

There are several demographic trends relevant to organizational behaviour. The workforce in Western industrialized economies is ageing. In other words, the proportion of the population who have retired from employment is growing relative to the proportion of the population still in work. Organizations that discriminate against older employees (which in some cases means over 30 or 40 years of age) will find it difficult to recruit. An ageing population may have different needs as consumers, opening up new markets for organizations smart enough to identify and meet those needs, and also putting pressure on healthcare.

Several factors, including wars and improved transport and communication, have contributed to global migration. This means a higher ethnic, cultural and religious mix in a given workforce, putting a premium on the ability to manage diversity of values, needs and preferences. Another demographic trend concerns the development of the 'hourglass economy', which is split between educated and skilled knowledge workers, and poorly educated, untrained and poorly paid manual and clerical workers. Lifestyles and values are changing, affecting the formation and composition of households, patterns of living and consumption, trends in leisure and education and preferences in working patterns. Social values also change. Environmental concern, expressed in punitive fines for organizations which create toxic waste, and in public protests (over new roads and airports, for example) were uncommon before the 1980s, but are now routine, and this concern contributes to the corporate social responsibility movement, explored later in this chapter.

Working longer in Finland

Finland has the most rapidly ageing population in Europe. When people retire, knowledge and experience are lost, and it is difficult to recruit replacements. This leads to labour shortages, and younger employees, who have to work harder to compensate, suffer from burnout. Ageism is banned by the Finnish constitution, but employers discriminate against older workers, telling applicants that, 'you're menopausal', or that 'we don't take on older people to sleep in the corners and wait for retirement'. The answer is to help people to work longer, so the Finnish Institute of Occupational Health set up a Maintenance of Work Ability (MWA) programme. Between 1997 and 2004, the rate of employment for 55- to 64-year-olds rose from 36 per cent to 50 per cent. MWA ideas include:

- a network of occupational health centres
- training in 'work ability' for occupational health professionals
- fitness and therapy programmes and health check-ups for staff

- motivation and learning measures
- introduction of new working patterns
- 'tacit knowledge' programmes pairing older with younger employees
- worker-oriented job redesign and ergonomics
- tackling hazards such as noise and dust to which older workers may be sensitive
- training in new computer applications
- training for managers in leadership and age management skills

The outcomes from MWA include retention of skilled workers, and improved productivity and product quality. Finnish law allows for flexible retirement between 63 and 68; Finland is one of only a few industrialized countries where the retirement age is rising.

Based on Ball (2005).

STOP AND THINK

In what ways do your values differ from the values of your parents?

In what ways will your lifestyle differ from that of your parents?

In what ways will your experience of work differ from that of your parents?

How will your values and expectations as an employee make life easier or more difficult for the organizations that are likely to employ you?

Demographic trends make many demands on how organizations are structured and managed. The implications of these trends can be felt at different levels, from business strategy, through organization structures, to providing special facilities for particular ethnic or religious groups.

PESTLE analysis an environmental scanning tool identifying Political, Economic, Social, Technological, Legal and Ecological factors that affect an organization.

Returning to the concept of environmental scanning, one popular approach is **PESTLE analysis**, which helps to organize the complexity of dealing with trends in technology, globalization, technology and other factors providing a simple structure.

Figure 2.3 illustrates a typical range of PESTLE trends and pressures. The details under each headings are for illustration, and they are not comprehensive. The headings can overlap. For example, 'Legal' concerns regulations and laws. 'Political' concerns government policy, ideology and the actions of interest groups; but government policy can become law.

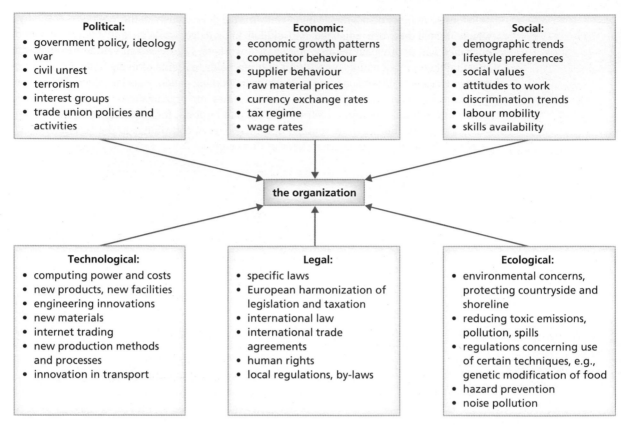

Political:
- government policy, ideology
- war
- civil unrest
- terrorism
- interest groups
- trade union policies and activities

Economic:
- economic growth patterns
- competitor behaviour
- supplier behaviour
- raw material prices
- currency exchange rates
- tax regime
- wage rates

Social:
- demographic trends
- lifestyle preferences
- social values
- attitudes to work
- discrimination trends
- labour mobility
- skills availability

the organization

Technological:
- computing power and costs
- new products, new facilities
- engineering innovations
- new materials
- internet trading
- new production methods and processes
- innovation in transport

Legal:
- specific laws
- European harmonization of legislation and taxation
- international law
- international trade agreements
- human rights
- local regulations, by-laws

Ecological:
- environmental concerns, protecting countryside and shoreline
- reducing toxic emissions, pollution, spills
- regulations concerning use of certain techniques, e.g., genetic modification of food
- hazard prevention
- noise pollution

Figure 2.3: PESTLE factors affecting the organization

The best way to approach environmental scanning is to do an analysis yourself. This will almost certainly reveal that the neat categories in the model overlap in a rather untidy way in practice. Many legislative changes are politically motivated. Ecological concerns reflect changing social values and preferences. Some technological developments (electric cars) are encouraged by economic and ecological issues (the price and pollution of petrol). However, the point of the analysis is to identify external environmental factors, their interrelationships, and their impact. It is less important to get them into the 'correct' boxes.

STOP AND THINK

Choose an organization with which you are familiar; hospital, supermarket, university or college, the place you worked last summer.

Make a list of the political, economic, social, technological, legislative and ecological factors that affect that organization.

What practical advice would you give to the management of this organization?

How would you assess the practical value of this exercise to the organization?

Diet and airline fuel costs

Why should airlines be concerned about their passengers' diets? The amount of fuel that an aircraft uses depends on the weight that it is carrying. The weight of the average American rose 10 pounds during the 1990s, resulting in an extra 350 million gallons of fuel being used by airlines in 2000, at a cost of £149 million. That extra fuel released 3.8 million tons of carbon dioxide into the environment. Airlines can reduce weight by using plastic cutlery and avoiding heavy magazines, but they cannot control passengers' weight. Southwest Airlines asks passengers who can't fit between the armrests to buy a second seat. A commuter plane crash in North Carolina in 2003, which killed 21 people, was blamed on passengers with above average weight.

To cut costs, Ryanair and FlyBe are charging passengers for each bag they check in. As an incentive to carry less luggage, passengers with cabin bags only get discounted fares, and can avoid the check-in queues. Ryanair estimates that this will reduce airport handling and fuel costs, and cut turn-around times, saving the company €30 million a year.

Based on The Daily Telegraph *(2004) and* The Economist *(2006a).*

PESTLE analysis raises a number of issues:

First, it is difficult to escape from the argument that the organization must pay attention to PESTLE trends and developments. The organization which fails to respond to those external factors will quickly run into difficulties.

Second, the long list of external factors, even under these neat headings, can be intimidating. Identifying which are most significant, and then predicting their impact, can be difficult.

Third, a full understanding of external factors can involve the analysis of a substantial amount of different kinds of data, and this takes time. How about analysing demographic trends in south-central Scotland, for example, or pan-European regulations affecting the food and drink industry, or forthcoming information technology software innovations, or collating the results of surveys concerning lifestyle changes and consumption patterns across South East Asia. The time spent on these analyses has to be balanced against the need for a rapid response.

Environmental complexity makes prediction hazardous. We can predict demographic trends with some accuracy, with respect to mortality, and gender and age profiles. We can normally predict economic trends with some confidence in the short to medium term, two to three years. Trends in social values and lifestyles, politics, technological innovation or the impact of new technology, cannot be predicted with much confidence – although that does not stop journalists and others from making the attempt. Environmental scanning can mean a lot of informed guesswork and judgement.

PESTLE analysis thus has two strengths and four weaknesses:

Strengths

1. The analysis encourages consideration of the range of external factors affecting internal organizational arrangements.

2. The analysis is a convenient framework for ordering a complex and bewildering set of factors.

Weaknesses

1. This analysis can identify many factors which may not be significant. It is difficult to strike a balance between identifying all factors, and those which are important.

2. It is difficult to anticipate 'defining events', such as wars, terrorist attacks, new discoveries, economic collapse and major political or financial upheavals which shift country boundaries or radically change government policies.

3. This analysis can involve the time consuming and expensive collection of data, some of which may be available, and some of which may have to be researched.

4. The time spent in information gathering and analysis may inhibit a rapid and effective response to the very trends being analysed.

Scenario planning in a high-risk world

Terrorism is not the only unexpected risk that might ruin a business. Outbreaks of infectious diseases such as the SARS epidemic can be equally damaging. Most companies are still well behind with contingency planning. In the past, says Bain's [a management consultancy firm] Mr Rigby, bosses were reluctant to draw up such plans in case they frightened employees and customers. Now, he says, 'it's a necessity'. The new concern with geopolitical risks has led to a revival of scenario planning. Pioneered in the 1970s by Pierre Wack at Royal Dutch/Shell (which includes three different forecasts of the global economy in its strategic planning), scenario planning has been unfashionable because the geopolitical climate appeared to be benign. Now, however, it has become popular as a way to help managers to think about and plan for future uncertainties.

At Microsoft, Brent Callinicos, the company's treasurer, keeps track of up to seven scenarios at a time. Microsoft calculates and discloses its 'value at risk' – an estimate of the greatest loss it is 95 per cent sure it will not exceed – for 20-day periods ahead. Scenarios are crucial in putting the value-at-risk calculations into context. The Economist Intelligence Unit surveyed 600 global executives in 2008 and asked them which risks were the most threatening to their business over the next decade. The top 12 were:

- increase in protectionism
- major oil price shock
- collapse in asset prices
- emergence of a disruptive business model
- international terrorism
- unexpected regulatory change
- global recession
- instability in the Middle East
- increased competition from emerging market companies
- talent shortages
- climate change
- increased industrial pollution

Only 26 per cent said that they used scenario planning regularly, 41 per cent used it on an ad hoc basis, and 29 per cent said that they would be using it in future.

Based on The Economist *(2004a) and* Cave *(2008).*

Scenario planning the imaginative development of one or more likely pictures of the dimensions and characteristics of the future for an organization.

Environmental analysis with PESTLE is used for **scenario planning**, a technique developed by the oil company Royal Dutch/Shell in the 1970s, and also known as the 'Shell method'.

Scenario planning combines environmental scanning with creative thinking, to identify the most probable future scenario as a basis for planning and action. In the field of corporate strategy, scenario planning is used to explore 'best case, worst case' possibilities, and to encourage 'out-of-the-box' and creative 'blue skies' thinking.

Environmental scanning is a useful predictive action planning tool, particularly when allied with scenario planning, and as a guide to creative decision-making. This is also a useful theoretical framework which exposes the range of external environmental influences on internal organizational behaviour, and highlights the relationships between those external factors. Environmental scanning has become a specialist field, with its own texts and tools; see Johnson *et al.*, 2008.

We can now update our model. Figure 2.4 shows the links between external environmental pressures and internal organizational responses in more detail. This model relies on a number of basic assumptions:

- It assumes that all the relevant data can be identified, collected and analyzed.
- It assumes that the analysis will lead to accurate forecasts of current and future trends, and to the construction of realistic future scenarios.
- It assumes that the analysis will be consistent, and not pull the organization in different directions at the same time.
- It assumes that the kinds of internal organizational responses indicated by the analysis can be implemented at an appropriate pace.

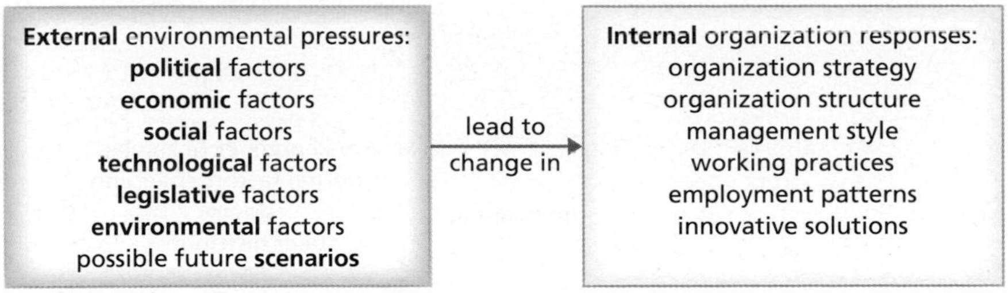

External environmental pressures:		Internal organization responses:
political factors		organization strategy
economic factors		organization structure
social factors	lead to	management style
technological factors	change in	working practices
legislative factors		employment patterns
environmental factors		innovative solutions
possible future **scenarios**		

Figure 2.4: External environment–organization link detailed

Work in 2020: colourful scenarios

The consultancy company PricewaterhouseCoopers used scenario planning to explore the future nature of work and management. They developed three possible scenarios for 2020, each with a different picture of the nature of work, and the role of management:

orange world   big companies have been replaced by networks of small specialized enterprises. People work on short-term contracts exploring job opportunities online through portals developed by craft guilds

green world   demographic change, climate and sustainability are key business drivers. Employment law, employee relations, and corporate responsibility are vital in this heavily regulated environment

blue world   huge corporations are like mini-states providing staff with housing, health, education, and other welfare benefits. Human capital metrics are sophisticated, and people management is as powerful as finance

What if none of these models turns out to be correct? Is this a waste of time? Sandy Pepper, the project leader, replies: 'You can respond more quickly to what does happen if you have trained yourself to think in a more innovative, lateral way about the future.'

Based on Arkin (2007a).

This analysis must be used carefully. Environmental scanning and scenario planning can be more useful when carried out quickly, relying on a combination of information, informed guesswork and judgement, rather than insisting on comprehensive data. The results of a painstaking analysis may be available too late to be of use.

The continuing search for 'fit'

Environmental uncertainty the degree of unpredictable turbulence and change in the political, economic, social, technological, legal and ecological context in which an organization operates.

One factor stands out in environmental scanning for most organizations: **environmental uncertainty**. Most managers feel that the speed of events is increasing, and that they lack a clear view of the way ahead, the nature of the terrain, obstacles or the final destination. How can organizations be adaptable enough to cope with continuous and unpredictable change?

Robert Duncan defined uncertainty as the lack of adequate information to reach an unambiguous decision, and argued that environmental uncertainty has two dimensions (Duncan 1972, 1973, 1974, 1979). One of these dimensions concerns degree of *simplicity* or *complexity*, and the other concerns the degree of *stability* or *dynamism*:

simple–complex   the number of different issues faced, the number of different factors to consider, the number of things to worry about

stable–dynamic   the extent to which those issues are changing or stable, and if they are subject to slow movement or to abrupt shifts

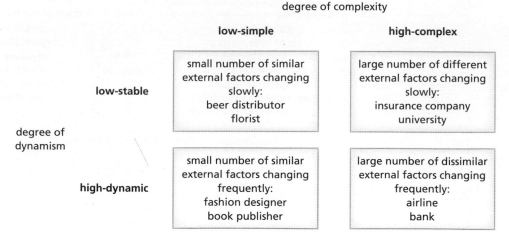

Figure 2.5: Duncan's typology of organizational environments

Environmental complexity the range of external factors relevant to the activities of the organization; the more factors, the higher the complexity.

Environmental dynamism the pace of change in relevant factors external to the organization; the greater the pace of change, the more dynamic the environment.

External factors can include customers, suppliers, regulatory agencies, competitors and partners in joint ventures. Duncan argued that the 'stable–dynamic' dimension is more important in determining environmental uncertainty. Complexity means that you just have a lot of variables to consider. Dynamism, on the other hand, is more difficult to manage because you don't know what is going to happen next most of the time. Plotting these two dimensions against each other produces the typology of organizational environments in Figure 2.5. This typology can be applied to the organization, or to business units and departments.

Duncan argues that an organization's location in this typology is dependent on *management perception*, and not on an observer's classification. In other words, if you don't perceive that your environment is turbulent, then you will probably not respond to it as such. As our perception can change, so the location of an organization on this typology is unstable.

This is different from arguing that external environments *determine* internal structures and processes. Our *perception* is selective, paying attention to some factors, while filtering out others. The same environment may be perceived differently by different managers and organizations, even in the same sector. It is management perceptions which affect decisions about organization strategy, structures and processes. In the language of Karl Weick (1979), managers *enact* rather than react to the external environment.

We have one perspective which claims that reality, the environment, is 'out there' waiting to be observed and analysed. The second perspective claims that 'the environment' is what we perceive and interpret it to be, and which therefore is enacted. This distinction between 'the truth is out there', and 'the truth is what we interpret it to be', reflects the discussion in Chapter 1 of **positivist** and **constructivist** perspectives on organizational behaviour.

STOP AND THINK

Where on Duncan's typology – Figure 2.5 – are these organizations located?

- Oxfam charity organization
- Loamshire District General Hospital
- Burger King fast food chain
- Aldi discount food retailer
- A Scotch whisky distillery in a remote Highland glen
- Hertz car rental company
- Marriott International hotels
- Oscar de la Renta perfume manufacturers

Which type of environment would you prefer to work in; stable/simple or dynamic/complex, and why? Share your choice with a colleague. You will have to consider this question every time you seek employment.

Table 2.1: Ansoff's typology of environments

	Environmental change	Organization strategy	Management attitude
1	**Repetitive** little or no change	**Stable** based on precedent	**Stability seeking** rejects change
2	**Expanding** slow incremental change	**Reactive** incremental change based on experience	**Efficiency driven** adapts to change
3	**Changing** fast incremental change	**Anticipatory** incremental change based on extrapolation	**Market driven** seeks familiar change
4	**Discontinuous** discontinuous but predictable change	**Entrepreneurial** discontinuous new strategies based on observed opportunities	**Environment driven** seeks new but related change
5	**Surprising** discontinuous and unpredictable change	**Creative** discontinuous new and creative strategies	**Environment creating** seeks novel change

Source: Ansoff (1997)

Igor Ansoff (1997) has developed this argument, generating interesting practical advice, summarized in Table 2.1. Ansoff identifies five types of environment based on the turbulence being experienced, from 'repetitive' at one extreme, to 'surprising' at the other. The first two columns of his table have to be read *vertically*, working up and down this scale from 'repetitive' at one extreme to 'surprising' at the other:

1. repetitive
2. expanding
3. changing
4. discontinuous
5. surprising

Go to level 1, the repetitive environment, and read the table *horizontally*. Ansoff argues that we can identify the most appropriate strategy and management attitude for that environment. In a stable environment, strategy should be based on precedent. What made the organization successful in the past will work in future. In a repetitive environment, the management attitude concerns stability. Change could ruin the business:

environment is repetitive, with no change → strategy should be stable and based on precedent → management should seek stability, reject change

Now go to level 5, to the surprising, discontinuous and unpredictable environment, and again read across the row. As you might expect, the recommended strategy is creative, based on new approaches, and not on what the organization has done in the past. The management attitude has to be novelty-seeking, helping to influence the environment in creative ways. Holding on to past precedents in this context will ruin the business:

surprising environment, unpredictable change → novel strategies should be based on creativity → management should embrace change, seek novelty

Now read the other three middle rows, again working *across* the table, noting the strategy and management implications for each of the other levels of change. Once that argument and the practical implications are clear, try reading the organization strategy column *vertically*. This can be read as a strategy scale, from stability (precedent driven) at one extreme to creativity (novelty driven) at the other. The final column works in the same way, with a management attitude scale, from stability (rejecting change) to creativity (embracing novelty).

Ansoff also distinguishes between *extrapolative* and *discontinuous* change, shown by the separation in Table 2.1 between levels 3 and 4. Where change is extrapolative, the future can be predicted, more or less, following (extrapolating from) current trends. When change is discontinuous, our ability to predict is limited. Ansoff (1997) claims that 80 per cent of managers say their organizations have level 4 or 5 environments.

Ansoff makes a number of cruel observations about managers who have been successful in organizations with extrapolative environments. He claims that they may lack the skills, knowledge, experience and attitudes to deal with discontinuous change. Success in a discontinuous environment requires entrepreneurial vision and creativity, anticipating change. He comments that, 'Managers incapable of developing an entrepreneurial mindset must be replaced' (1997: 76).

STOP AND THINK

Does your educational institution face extrapolative or discontinuous change?

To what extent is the institution's strategy and management attitude appropriate to that level of change?

Apply this analysis to yourself. What level of environmental change are you subject to, and how does this affect your behaviour?

Post-modern organization
a networked, information-rich, delayered, downsized, boundary-less, high commitment organization employing highly skilled, well-paid autonomous knowledge workers.

Our updated model is in Figure 2.6. This is a 'stimulus–response' model. The stimulus of external change prompts organizational responses. The scale, dynamism and complexity of environmental stimuli encourage the development of a new adaptive, environmentally responsive organizational 'paradigm', described as the **post-modern organization**.

Stewart Clegg (1990, p.181) describes the post-modern organization:

Where the modernist organization was rigid, post-modern organization is flexible. Where modernist consumption was premised on mass forms, post-modernist consumption is premised on niches. Where modernist organization and jobs were highly differentiated, demarcated and de-skilled, post-modernist organization and jobs are highly de-differentiated, de-demarcated and multiskilled.

So, bureaucracy, macho managers and boring jobs have been replaced by flexible organizations with participative, supportive managers and interesting, multiskilled, jobs.

STOP AND THINK

Have you experienced, or observed, a flexible, boundary-less, post-modern organization with skilled and autonomous employees?

Have you experienced, or observed, the opposite – a bureaucratic organization with poorly paid, boring and unskilled jobs that are controlled by autocratic managers?

Environmental determinism the argument that internal organizational responses are primarily determined by external environmental factors.

We promised that, having built a model, we would knock it down. There are four flaws in the reasoning in Figure 2.6. The first problem concerns **environmental determinism**. Duncan's argument about the role of perceptions is a powerful challenge to this perspective.

We know that internal organizational arrangements reflect the influence of a range of factors: the dynamics of the senior management team, their approach to decision-making, employee suggestions, past experience. We also know that, whatever the reality 'out there', what really matters is how the environment is understood and interpreted 'in here'. This means that the environmental 'stimulus' is just one stimulus among many, and that this stimulus is not always guaranteed either a response, or the expected response.

The second problem concerns assumptions about organizational boundaries. Can we say clearly what is 'out there' and what is 'in here'? The organization is involved in a constant process of exchange with the environment, importing staff and resources, exporting goods and

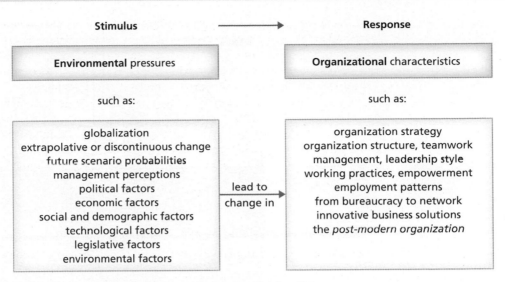

Figure 2.6: The search for environment–organization 'fit'

services. Employees are members of the wider society, whose values and preferences are thus 'inside' the organization. Many organizations operate partnerships, with suppliers and competitors, to share the costs, for example, of developing new materials, processes and products. Healthcare is delivered through networks of collaborating organizations. Some companies, such as gymnasiums and roadside motoring assistance, treat their customers as 'members'. The boundaries between organizations and their environments are often blurred.

The third problem is one of interpretation. We are considering 'environment' and 'organization' as separate domains. However, an organization chooses and influences its environment; this is a matter of strategic choice (Child, 1997). For example, a restaurant changes its environment (its customers, its suppliers, its competitors) when the owners decide to stop selling fast food and move into gourmet dining. In other words, the external environment of the organization is *enacted*: the organization creates and to some extent even becomes its own environment, rather than being 'given' or 'presented with' that environment.

The final problem concerns continuity. The model presents a picture of rapid and radical change. However, we know that is not the case. Looking back over the past century, we can identify many continuities, environmental and organizational. Many of today's well-known companies even predate the twentieth century. The German Weihenstephan Brewery was founded in 1040, the Swedish company Stora in 1288, Oxford University Press in 1478, Beretta in 1530, Lloyd's in 1688, Sumitomo in 1690, Sotheby's in 1744, Guinness in 1759.

Ethical behaviour

Organizations and managers are expected to behave ethically. The emphasis on this aspect of organizational behaviour has increased in the twenty-first century, for two reasons. The first concerns a number of high profile corporate scandals (Enron, Worldcom). The second concerns increasing media scrutiny of organization and management practices, focusing on environmental issues and the use of low cost labour. These concerns are, of course, not new, but they are seen as more important and attract more attention than they have done in the past.

Richard Daft (2008) distinguishes between the 'domain of codified law', and the 'domain of free choice'. In the domain of law, our behaviour – what we can and cannot do – is decided by legislation. Individuals are not allowed to murder or to steal, and organizations must conform with accounting, tax, health and safety and employment legislation. If we do the wrong thing, we end up in court, or in jail; organizations can be fined, and in some

**"I started to think outside the box.
Then I started to think outside the law."**

Source: www.cartoonstock.com

cases senior managers can be imprisoned. In the domain of choice, we can do what we like: smoke cigarettes, eat unhealthy food, take as little exercise as we choose. Organizations can decide which businesses to be in, where to locate their headquarters, which markets to expand.

Are we ever really 'free to choose' our behaviour? Daft (2003, p.139) points out that, even where there are no laws to guide our behaviour, there are 'standards of conduct, based on shared principles and values about moral conduct that guide an individual or company'. We have to decide whether or not to comply with those norms. The domain of ethics thus sits between the domain of law and the domain of choice. We may have to take responsibility for our actions in a courtroom (domain of codified law), in the court of our own conscience (domain of free choice), or in the court of social judgement (domain of ethics).

We need to distinguish between *individual* ethics and *business* ethics. The behavioural choices facing individuals and organizations are different, and the criteria against which we judge those actions may also be different.

Individual ethics

Managers should surely act ethically. However, there is no consensus on what constitutes 'ethical' behaviour. Different commentators use different criteria, which lead to judgements about the same behaviour. As a result, ethics is a controversial subject.

Ethics the codes of moral principles, values and rules that govern our decisions and actions with respect to what is right and wrong, good and bad.

Gerald Cavanagh, Dennis Moberg and Manuel Velasquez developed a template to distinguish ethical from unethical management actions (Cavanagh *et al.*, 1981; Velasquez *et al.*, 1983). Their perspective is based on three ethical frameworks: utilitarianism, individual rights and natural justice (Table 2.2). Instead of choosing one of these, they suggest that these criteria should be combined to reach ethical judgements.

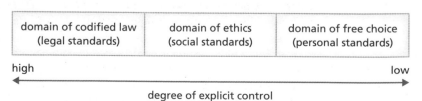

| domain of codified law (legal standards) | domain of ethics (social standards) | domain of free choice (personal standards) |

high ←   → low

degree of explicit control

Figure 2.7: Three domains of action

Table 2.2: Ethical frameworks

	strengths	**weaknesses**
utilitarianism	encourages efficiency parallels profit maximization looks beyond the individual	impossible to quantify variables can lead to unjust resource allocation individual rights may be violated
rights	protects the individual establishes standards of behaviour independent of outcomes	may encourage selfish behaviour individual rights may become obstacles to productivity and efficiency
justice	ensures fair allocation of resources ensures democratic operation, independent of status or class protects the interests of the under-represented in the organization	can encourage a sense of entitlement that discourages risk and innovation some individual rights may be violated to accommodate justice for majority

Adapted from Velasquez *et al.* (1983)

Utilitarianism

A utilitarian perspective judges behaviour in terms of outcomes; this is the classic 'ends justifies means' argument. This approach considers the 'balance sheet' of benefits and costs to those involved. Behaviour is ethical if it achieves 'the greatest good of the greatest number'. However, in even modestly complex settings, with several stakeholders, and actions with a range of consequences, calculating the costs and benefits can be challenging.

Rights

This perspective judges behaviour on the extent to which fundamental individual rights are respected. This includes the right of free consent, the right to privacy, the right to freedom of conscience, the right of free speech, the right to due process in the form of an impartial hearing. The ethical decision depends on whether or not individual rights have been violated.

Justice

This perspective judges behaviour on whether or not the benefits and costs flowing from an action are fairly, equitably and impartially distributed. Distributive justice states that rules should be applied consistently, those in similar circumstances should be treated equally, and individuals should not be held responsible for matters beyond their control. As with the utilitarian view, these issues are awkward to resolve in practice, as judgements of consistency, similarity, and responsibility are subjective and vary from one setting to another.

This produces a 'decision tree' for deciding whether an action is ethical or not (Figure 2.8). First, 'gather the facts', then ask about benefits, rights and justice. The framework also introduces three sets of circumstances which could justify unethical behaviour in some settings. 'Overwhelming factors' are issues that justify setting aside ethical criteria. Some actions may have 'dual effects', with positive and negative outcomes, and the negatives may be acceptable if they are outweighed by the positives. 'Incapacitating factors' may prevent the decision-maker from applying ethical criteria. For example, managers can be constrained by the views and actions of colleagues, and may be pressured into behaviour that they would not choose themselves. Individual managers may not have enough information on which to reach a judgement. Finally, the individual may doubt the relevance of one or more ethical criteria to a given setting. The right to free speech, for example, may not apply if this involved releasing information that would be damaging to others.

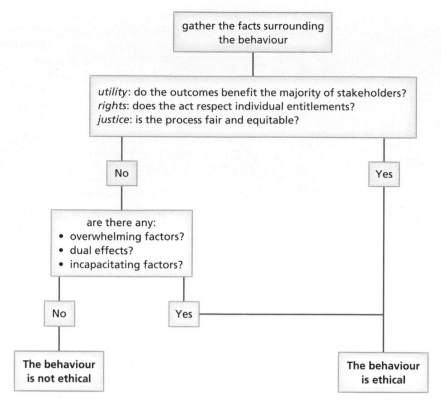

Figure 2.8: The ethical decision tree

Source: Adapted from Velasquez *et al.* (1983).

As a result, we have several escape routes which allow actions that would be prohibited by the three criteria. The urgency of the case, time pressures, resource constraints, penalties for inaction, and so on, can all be called upon as overwhelming, dual, or incapacitating factors.

Source: © Leo Cullum/Condé Nast Publications/www.cartoonbank.com

Sam and Bob: Sam and Bob are research scientists in the General Rubber product development laboratory. Sam, who is introvert, quiet, and serious, is more technically proficient; his patents have earned the company around $6 million over the past ten years. Bob does not have the same expertise, his output is 'solid though unimaginative', and he is extrovert and demonstrative. The rumour is that Bob will be moved into an administrative role. The lab offers a $300,000 fund each year for the best new product idea. Sam and Bob both submit proposals, which are assessed as having equal merit. Sam takes no further action, but Bob conducts a publicity campaign, about which he tells Sam in advance, promoting the advantages of his proposal to those who might influence the final decision. Informal pressure builds to decide in Bob's favour (Cavanagh *et al.*, 1981).

Is Bob's behaviour ethical? Does the ethical decision tree help you to reach a decision?

Cavanagh and colleagues (1981) argue that Bob's actions are unethical. From a utilitarian perspective, the outcome is acceptable, as both proposals had equal merit. From a rights perspective, Sam had the same opportunities, and he knew about Bob's informal campaign. But by introducing 'irrelevant differences' between the proposals based on personal lobbying, Bob's behaviour breached the principles of justice and was unethical.

How do you feel about this judgement? There is another view. Ideas in most organizations do not make progress on merit alone. Bob recognized that ideas benefit from good publicity. Should we praise Sam for his ethics and criticize Bob for his unfair practices? Or should we regard Sam as naive and lazy, and praise Bob for his enthusiasm and understanding of the context? Bob's actions were not secret, and he won the prize. For the company that wants to encourage innovation, Bob seems to be the better role model. This decision tree offers contradictory assessments and can lead to judgements that are controversial.

This ethical decision framework seems to offer a structured approach for resolving difficult choices. However, it can produce outcomes which are confusing, and in some cases perverse. 'Ethical' in this example describes behaviour that is careless, amateurish and naive, while contextual awareness, astuteness and professionalism are labelled unethical. This framework focuses on single incidents, but Bob and Sam have to continue working for that organization. The actions that they take, and the results they achieve, influence how they are regarded, which affects how colleagues feel about and respond to them. Whether they get results, or avoid the difficult issues, affects their career prospects and the degree of influence that they can exert in the organization in future. In other words, the way in which they handle these issues affects their reputation beyond the single incident. Maybe we should adopt a broader time horizon in reaching such decisions about ethical or unethical behaviour.

This framework can highlight the issues, but it cannot always make the decision for us. That is a matter of personal judgement. Velasquez *et al.* (1983, pp.79–80) conclude:

> The manager who is unable to use ethical criteria because of these incapacitating factors may justifiably give them a lesser weight in making decisions about what to do. However, determining whether a manager's lack of freedom, lack of information, or lack of certitude is sufficient to abrogate moral responsibility requires one to make some very difficult judgements. In the end, these are hard questions that only the individuals involved can answer for themselves.

Let's return to our opening case, 'Should that have happened?'. Was Charlie acting ethically? In the utilitarian view, his actions are acceptable. However, Cavanagh and colleagues argue that Charlie violated Lee's right to be treated honestly by damaging his reputation behind his back, and that Charlie's actions were unethical. However, Lee had not responded to Charlie's request to alter his damaging behaviour; did Lee not ignore Charlie's rights, and also ignore the rights of shareholders and the community? Charlie's actions can be seen as personally sensitive and organizationally prudent, given Lee's behaviour, his proximity to retirement, his record, and the limited options open to Charlie to solve this problem quickly. To discipline or to fire Lee would be humiliating for him, and could damage his pension entitlement. Instead, Charlie informally creates the circumstances in which Lee reaches his own decision to quit.

Business ethics and corporate social responsibility

Gerry Johnson, Kevan Scholes and Richard Whittington (2008) explore the question of business ethics using a three-level framework.

level 1: ethical stance   this concerns the extent to which the organization's minimum obligations to stakeholders and to society at large will be exceeded

level 2: corporate social responsibility   this focuses on how the organization puts its ethical stance into practice, by addressing different stakeholder interests

level 3: individual manager ethics   this concerns individual ethics, the decisions and actions of individual managers, and the ethical principles behind their behaviour

Ethical stance
the extent to which an organization exceeds its legal minimum obligations to its stakeholders and to society at large.

We explored individual ethics in the previous section. Our focus here first lies with the organization's ethical stance, deciding how far to go beyond minimum legal requirements and to contribute to the wider community.

Johnson *et al.* (2005, p.189) suggest that organizations can take progressively more intense ethical stances (Figure 2.9). Each stance incorporates an increasing range of stakeholder interests; includes a wider range of criteria; and involves a longer period over which outcomes are judged. At the start of this continuum is the minimum obligations position, focusing on the short-term financial interests of shareholders. This not really an 'ethical' position. The organization works within the law, but does not engage in additional social or environmental activities such as charitable donations. Performance is measured in financial terms.

The next step in the continuum involves a shift in language as well as focus, from shareholders to stakeholders. There are many groups with a stake in an organization: employees, suppliers, customers, local community, government, society. This stance also focuses on shareholder interests, but recognizes that these can be enhanced by the positive management of relationships with other stakeholders. A company's engagement in, for example, charitable giving, while not producing shareholder gains in the short term can enhance reputation and visibility, and contribute to long-term profits and share price. These actions can be regarded as promotional expenditure and investments in the future. Organizational performance is thus measured in financial terms over a longer period.

Moving two steps beyond minimum obligations addresses the interests and expectations of multiple stakeholders. The actions of organizations adopting this stance might include refusing to 'off-shore' jobs to countries where wages are lower, contracting with 'fair trade' suppliers, keeping uneconomic units working to preserve employment, and not selling antisocial products. While these actions increase costs, and shareholder gains may not be maximized, other stakeholders benefit. The problem is balancing the interests of all the stakeholders. Organizational performance therefore is not measured solely in financial terms.

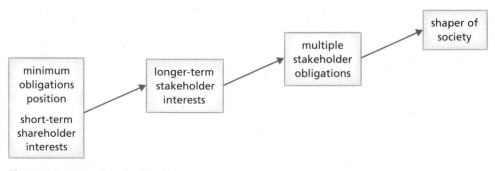

Figure 2.9: Intensity of ethical stance
Source: After Johnson *et al.* (2005)

Moving three steps beyond the minimum position, organizations can be ideologically driven, aiming to reshape society. Google appears to be one example of an organization which takes this stance (although some of their actions and aspirations are controversial). While shareholders and financial constraints can limit the actions of organizations, private companies with no shareholders find it easier to adopt this ethical stance.

Corporate social responsibility the view that organizations should act ethically, in ways that contribute to economic development, the environment, quality of working life, local communities, and the wider society.

Should organizations adopt an ethical stance that supports social and environmental issues? This can be good for business, if it attracts socially responsible customers (Donaldson and Preston, 1995). The economist Milton Friedman (1970) once argued that, 'The business of business is business.' His view is now unfashionable. The corporate social responsibility (CSR) movement expects organizations to promote social and environmental or 'green' issues. This has become a major environmental pressure, combining Political, Ecological, Social and Technological aspects of PESTLE analysis. Many organizations are addressing these issues, to strengthen their reputation as 'responsible corporate citizens'.

Is Google green?

Flying abroad on holiday uses fuel which leads to carbon dioxide emissions, which damage the environment and contribute to global warming. In contrast, sitting at your desk at home, quietly surfing the internet, is much more environmentally friendly. Or is it? To use the internet, you need power to run your computer, screen, and modem. To process your search, Google uses several large data centres – banks of servers – scattered around the world, in America, China, Europe, and Japan. These data centres need a lot of power to keep them running, and your search may pass through more than one of them. Google keeps the location of its data centres and their energy consumption secret. However, it is estimated that the global computing industry generates as much greenhouse gas as the world's airlines.

Author's own work based on Leake and Woods (2009).

The actions of large, wealthy, powerful organizations can have a major impact on local communities and national economies, world trade, the environment, employment, job security and employee health and pensions. Surely organizations must behave 'responsibly', and promote social and environmental issues? Along with management ethics, the importance of corporate responsibility has been highlighted in the twenty-first century by corporate scandals at *Enron*, *Worldcom* and the Japanese company *livedoor*, where executives were accused of fraudulent transactions which benefited them personally.

Best green companies

The newspaper *The Sunday Times* holds an annual 'best green companies' competition. This is based on a survey which explores the environmental impact of organizations, and asks staff what they think of their employers' 'green credentials'. Factors considered include energy use, recycling, carbon emissions, and what the organization is doing to meet its environmental targets. The ten best green companies in 2008 were:

rank	organization	sector	size
1	JC Atkinson and Son	manufacturing	small
2	Carillion	construction	big
3	Co-op Financial Services	financial services	big
4	Pureprint Group	printing and publishing	small
5	Skanska UK	construction	big
6	HBOS	financial services	big
7	Loughborough Students' Union	education	small
8	Saint-Gobain Glass UK	manufacturing	small
9	MCM Architecture	architects	small
10	National Magazine Company	media	mid

JC Atkinson makes coffins, and heats its factory in Tyne and Wear with a warm-air heater powered by waste wood from the manufacturing process, saving around £18,000 a year in gas or oil costs. Skylights in the factory roof reduce the electricity bill by £1,200 a year, and a biomass generator produces all the company's own electricity (and the sale of excess electricity earns them £25,000 a year).

Based on Clayton (2008).

Table 2.3 lists typical CSR policies. While this all sounds desirable, CSR has its critics. The concept is vague, and can mean different things in different settings. Managers who pay for community projects and make charitable donations are giving away money that belongs to shareholders, and which could be reinvested in the business, or used to improve pay and working conditions. Another objection is that, if you are acting legally, then by definition you are acting morally, so what's the problem? It is hard to distinguish between 'responsible' actions that reflect a concern for society, and actions designed to enhance the reputation of the company. It is also important to recognize that business laws and customs vary between countries and cultures. What constitutes fair and just ethical conduct depends on where you are in the world. Finally, CSR seems to overlook the benefits of competition, which leads to better quality products and services, and to reduced costs for consumers. Critics of CSR also argue that furthering social and environmental issues is the job of governments.

Table 2.3: CSR policies and practices

General policies include signing up to national and international ethical codes, using ethical investment criteria, and taking part in surveys of sustainability. Specific policies include:

Environment
1. Pollution control
2. Product improvement
3. Repair of environment
4. Recycling waste materials
5. Energy saving

Equal Opportunities
1. Minority employment
2. Advancement of minorities
3. Advancement of women
4. Support for minority businesses
5. Other disadvantaged groups

Personnel
1. Employee health and safety
2. Training
3. Personal counselling
4. Subcontractor code of behaviour
5. Providing medical care or insurance

Community involvement
1. Charitable donations
2. Promoting and supporting public health initiatives
3. Support for education and the arts
4. Community involvement projects

Products
1. Safety
2. Quality
3. Sustainability, percentage of materials that can be recycled

Suppliers
1. Fair terms of trade
2. Blacklisting unethical, irresponsible suppliers
3. Subcontractor code

STOP AND THINK Look at the list of CSR policies and practices in Table 2.3. What behaviours would you like to add to that list, and what benefits would you expect those behaviours to produce?

Corporate (social) responsibility

Professor David Grayson

An interview with Professor David Grayson, Director, The Doughty Centre for Corporate Responsibility, Cranfield University School of Management

Interviewer: How would you define corporate responsibility?

David: Corporate responsibility is about how business conducts its core operations. Is it behaving ethically? Does it treat its employees and its suppliers fairly? Does it market responsibly to customers? It's about maximizing positive environmental and social impacts.

Interviewer: You tied that definition to the concept of ethics.

David: I think it's hard to imagine a responsible business which is behaving unethically. Where it's complicit in bribery and corruption, or where it is misleading its consumers or its employees.

Interviewer: You don't use the term corporate *social* responsibility.

David: I think that corporate social responsibility has a much narrower meaning. If you listen to journalists and managers, when they refer to corporate social responsibility, they're talking about community programmes, staff volunteering, payroll giving, environmental projects. They're not thinking about the way the business conducts its core operations.

Interviewer: And you prefer the phrase, 'responsible business'?

David: This is about the way we do business. That's why Marks & Spencer call the senior group which oversees their corporate responsibility the 'How We Do Business' committee.

Interviewer: Why has this issue become significant?

David: Well, you could argue that this is not a new issue at all. It goes back to the nineteenth century, to the Quaker businesses like Cadbury, Rowntrees and Levers (now Unilever) which were seeking to be responsible employers, building homes for their workers, providing libraries and schools. And they were responsible in the formulation of their products.

I think the reason why many more businesses are talking about corporate responsibility is first of all because you've got a much greater role for business. If you think about what we've lived through in the last twenty years, the fall of the Berlin wall, the collapse of communism, the process of liberalization and privatization, and globalization – which means that business is centre stage in many more parts of the world. And many businesses were state-owned companies in telephony, airlines, and utilities, with public service expectations.

→

Second, look at the scale of the global challenges that we face; climate change, resource depletion, inter-faith tensions, a burgeoning population. The issues are so serious for the future of the planet, there is an expectation that business has got to help find solutions. I think you've got much higher expectations of how business should conduct itself, partly because of scandals like Bhopal in India, or Enron in the US, or recent examples with the subprime crisis – irresponsible behaviour, which is a threat if a company doesn't take these issues seriously.

Interviewer: Milton Friedman argued in the 1970s that 'the business of business is business'. What would you say to Milton today if you had the opportunity?

David: Well first, I would point to the recent McKinsey survey of 5,000 global business leaders who were asked whether they thought that 'the business of business was simply business', or whether it is to make long-term profits for the owners of the business and to address social and environmental issues. Around 84 per cent said that business needs to balance profit making with addressing environmental and social issues. And the idea that somehow this is a distraction only occurs if a business is treating it as a 'bolt on', rather than built into business strategy. I think that the best businesses are seeing that this is a way of stimulating creativity and innovation, finding new products, services, and markets.

Interviewer: What does corporate responsibility mean in practice?

David: It starts with linking to business purpose and strategy. I think we're seeing the best companies linking it explicitly to their business values. My old employer, Procter & Gamble, have recently amended their statement of global business principles to incorporate sustainability. You then need, as Procter & Gamble are doing, to translate what that means for each part of the business. You need to have leaders who are authentic in explaining why a commitment to responsible business

Innocent smoothies

Source: Innocent Ltd.

practice is an integral part of the business. It also means setting clear goals, measuring performance, and regularly communicating what you're doing, how you're doing, and engaging stakeholders along the way.

Interviewer: Could you give me another iconic example of a company that has implemented corporate responsibility?

David: One great example is Innocent Ltd which makes fruit smoothies. They started in the UK and now operate across Europe. They've got almost three quarters of the UK fruit smoothies market, selling 2 million a week. Right from the beginning, they embedded a commitment to sustainability through their business strategy, and into the business operations. They articulate the values of Innocent as a company. They recruit and train against those values. Those values are integral to decision-making, and to performance measurement, reward, and promotion for management.

Even as a small business, they recognize that they influence what's happening in their supply chain. So they teamed up with

The Rainforest Alliance, a non-governmental organization that vets conditions in plantations, where the bananas for fruit smoothies are grown.

Interviewer: How do you see the future of corporate responsibility?

David: Now there's an economic downturn, are we going to see a slowdown of commitment to responsible business? On the contrary. Economically challenging times will be a stimulus for embedding responsible business, because it will be a way of differentiating yourself from competition, identifying with your employees, and getting the best out of them. How do we use this to help us find new marketplace insights? Unilever demonstrate commitment to sustainability through their supply chain practices. They believe that if consumers see the care that they've taken, it reinforces the quality of the products and the seriousness with which the company is producing them. The global boss of Wal-Mart and about a hundred of his top business leaders are in China in a few days time, talking to their 350 Chinese suppliers about the environmental and social standards that Wal-Mart requires. We'll see more businesses putting these requirements into their own supply chains.

Interest in the social impact of business dates from the early nineteenth century, with Robert Owen, who managed New Lanark Mills, south of Glasgow, in Scotland, from 1800–1825. In contrast with other employers at the time, Owen wanted to give his employees good living and working conditions, education and healthcare. But it was not until the late 1960s that interest in corporate social responsibility and business ethics was taken more seriously. These themes are now well established in contemporary debate and organizational research.

Royal Bank of Scotland, Annual Report 2004

The first responsibility of any company in society is to be successful. Success requires us to balance the differing interests of our stakeholders. We must provide the high quality products and services that our customers want, at a price they can afford. Our shareholders demand and deserve a healthy return on the capital they entrust to us, which we achieve through growth and profit. We owe our employees stable, safe and fair employment. We must work productively with government and regulators. We attach importance to managing our environmental impact and making a genuine contribution to the communities in which we operate.

CSR has become popular for three main reasons.

CSR as self-defence

If we don't do it ourselves, we'll have it done to us. While operating within the law, organizations are still self-regulating in many spheres of their activity. However, there is always the danger that a high profile corporate scandal will create demand for new regulation. *Enron* and other similar fraud cases, for example, led to the introduction of new regulations affecting corporate governance in America (the infamous Sarbanes–Oxley Act, 2002). Expensive and cumbersome to implement, that legislation was designed to restore public confidence by improving corporate accounting controls. CSR can be seen as a strategy to demonstrate corporate concern with ethical behaviour and impact on the community.

CSR as a result of affluence

If we don't do it, they'll stop buying from us. Increased affluence encourages us to assess the behaviour of the companies from which we buy products and services. If we feel that a company is not behaving in a socially acceptable, ethical manner, then we can withdraw our custom. Patterns of customer demand can thus affect corporate actions, for example by focusing on healthy eating, the promotion of ethical investment, and concern for the environment. CSR can deflect criticism and maintain customer support.

CSR as business resource

If we explain how responsible we are, our reputation will improve profits. Each new major CSR initiative gets media attention, which is free publicity. The company that frequently makes visible and genuine contributions to society may find that their sales and market share increase. In contrast, the company that makes false claims or that exaggerates its social and environmental concerns may find its reputation tarnished. CSR can be seen as a strategy to manage the impression that the consuming public has of the organization, and as a result to get good public relations and free advertising.

Coca-Cola: thirsty for sustainability

Sensitive to accusations that it runs a wasteful, unethical, and polluting business that does not make a social contribution, Coca-Cola in Europe has responded with a series of corporate responsibility initiatives:

- restricting the marketing of its products to children
- working with the World Wildlife Fund to find ways to cut back and to replenish the 290 billion litres of water that the company uses annually
- working with Greenpeace to develop environmentally friendly beverage coolers and vending machines to reduce the emission of hydrocarbon greenhouse gasses

- monitoring the agricultural impact of the company into tea, coffee, and juice drinks which require it to purchase ingredients from around the globe

Based on Wiggins (2007).

Websites accuse the company of exaggerating the benefits of an unhealthy product, of management complicity in the deaths of union organizers in bottling plants in South America, and of reducing and polluting local water supplies in India:

www.killercoke.org
www.indiaresource.org/campaigns/coke/2004/
risingstruggles.html

Craigslist and Facebook

Craigslist is a classified ads website run by Craig Newark and Jim Buckmaster, who live in San Francisco. One of the most successful internet companies ever, their site is used by tens of millions of people daily, in more than 500 cities in over 50 countries. *Craigslist* dominates the online classified ads business. This is the eleventh most-visited website in America, and is more popular than Amazon or CNN. The '*Craigslist* community' uses the site to buy and sell just about anything, including stamps, houses, personal services, and dead moose ('a big issue in Alaska', according to Jim). Wall Street estimates the company value at US$5 billion. Craig and Jim live in rented accommodation, and drive old cars – not the stereotypes of Californian hi-tech 'dot com' entrepreneurs. Despite its global reach, this is still a 'small' company which employs 25 staff, including the two bosses (*eBay* has around 15,000 staff).

Check the simple website*, and you will find millions of personal classified advertisements, but no graphics, no animation, no pop-ups, and no corporate banners. *Craigslist* charges no fees for posting most of those listings, and does not take a percentage of successful transactions (as other websites do, including *eBay*). The company makes its revenue from employers who post job vacancies, and from property agencies who post rentals.

Craig and Jim run the business based on what they themselves describe as their 'nerd value culture'. This includes a refusal to maximize profits, and to put the needs of their users first. Their annual revenue is around US$100 million. Analysts estimate that they could earn five times that amount just by allowing banner advertising, like most other websites, and by charging for more listings. Craig explains that:

I've seen companies with too much revenue. Having too much money, too many resources, means you don't have to work smart, so you work dumb. And then you lose your market position to smaller, hungrier competitors. Also, when you have too much cash and power, you tend to attract employees who are very good at organizational politics but who are really bad at everything else. We know a lot of these really rich guys and they are no happier than anyone else. Money has become a burden to them. That reinforces the values that Jim and I share, about living simply.

However, critics complain that, by not charging for its services, *Craigslist* is undercutting classified advertising in local and national newspapers, and damaging their business.

Facebook** is the fourth most-visited website on the planet. A social network site, it was designed by Mark Zuckerberg and friends at Harvard in 2004, and now has more than 110 million users worldwide. Like *Craigslist*, this is a small company with 700 employees. In 2008, Facebook expected to make US$300 million in revenues from display advertising. But Mark is more concerned with helping people than with making money: 'The goal of the company is to help people to share more in order to make the world more open and to help promote understanding between people. If we can succeed in this mission then we will also be able to build a pretty good business and everyone can be financially rewarded'.

* http://www.craigslist.org/about/sites

** http://en-gb.facebook.com

Based on Goodwin (2008) and Harvey (2008).

STOP AND THINK

In 2008 Kenco Coffee introduced a new television advertising campaign. The old ads concentrated on the quality and taste of the product. The new ads for the Kenco Sustainable Development coffee range show the company helping coffee growers and their farming communities in developing countries with social, economic, and environmental projects.

Check their website: www.kencocoffeecompany.co.uk. Go to 'product and equipment range' – 'Kenco sustainable development'.

Do you see this as a genuine contribution to economic growth and sustainability in poorer parts of the world? Or is this a marketing tactic to persuade you to buy their coffee?

 RECAP

1. *Understand the interdependence between the organization and its environment.*

   - To survive, organizations have to adapt their internal structures, processes and behaviours to cope with complexity and the pace of external change.

   - External pressures on organizations come from the globalization of business, developments in information technology, and social and demographic trends.

2. *Appreciate the strengths and limitations of PESTLE analysis of organizational environments.*

   - PESTLE analysis provides a comprehensive framework for identifying and planning responses to external factors that can affect an organization.

   - PESTLE analysis generates vast amounts of information, creating a time-consuming analysis problem, and making predictions based on this analysis can be difficult.

3. *Explain contemporary organizational responses to environmental turbulence.*

   - Ansoff argues that organizations in turbulent environments must embrace change, be creative and seek novelty in order to survive.

   - Duncan and Weick argue that what counts is the management perception of environmental uncertainty; perception determines the management response.

4. *Apply utilitarianism, theory of rights and theory of justice to assess whether or not management actions are ethical, and recognize the limitations of those criteria.*

- The utilitarian perspective argues that behaviour is ethical if it achieves the greatest good for the greatest number.

- The theory of rights judges behaviour on the extent to which individual rights are respected, including right of free consent, right to privacy, right to freedom of conscience, right of free speech, right to due process in an impartial hearing.

- The theory of justice judges behaviour on whether or not the benefits and burdens flowing from an action are fairly, equitably and impartially distributed.

- These criteria produce different assessments of the same behaviour; and circumstances can include other factors which the application of these criteria make inappropriate.

5. *Understand the concept of corporate social responsibility, and the practical and ethical implications of this concept for organizational behaviour.*

- Businesses and their managers are expected to act in responsible and ethical ways, contributing to social and environmental outcomes as well as making profit.

- Responsible practices include, for example, the business contribution to the community, the sustainable use of resources, ethical behaviour in relationships with suppliers and customers, and the impact of the business on all stakeholders.

- Critics argue that it is government's job to deal with social and environmental issues. The role of business is to maximize profits while operating within the law. Managers who donate company funds to 'good causes' give away shareholders' money.

Revision

1. Explain the 'environment–organization fit' argument. To what trends has this argument led, in terms of organization design and working practices?

2. How can organizational environments be classified, and what are the implications of such categorization for organization structures, strategies and managers?

3. What are the dangers and the benefits of corporate social responsibility, for employees, management, organizations, society, the environment?

4. Why can it be difficult to decide whether a particular action is ethical or not?

Research assignment

Innocent Ltd started with fruit smoothies, and diversified into other drinks and soups. Look at what the company says on its website 'about us' and about 'our ethics': http://www.innocentdrinks.co.uk/. What ethical stance does this company take? In what ways do you think that this approach to running a 'sustainable business' will improve profitability? And in what ways could this approach damage profitability? Are you more or less likely to buy their products, knowing what Innocent says about its view of corporate social responsibility? In April 2009, Innocent sold a £30 million stake in the company to Coca-Cola, claiming that this would allow the company to 'do more of what Innocent is here to do'. How does this link with Coca-Cola change your assessment of Innocent's ethical stance? See Chapter 4, Culture, where the influence of founders' values on company culture, including Innocent Ltd, is explored.

Springboard

Blowfield, M. and Murray, A., 2008, *Corporate Responsibility: A Critical Introduction*. Oxford: Oxford University Press.

Text which develops a framework exploring dimensions of corporate responsibility in theory and practice, current trends, and management approaches.

Dunphy, D., Benn, S. and Griffiths, A., 2002, *Organizational Change for Corporate Sustainability*, Routledge, London.

Explores organizational 'greening', arguing that organizations must take seriously their wider environmental and ecological responsibilities.

Ritzer, G., 2008, *The McDonaldization of Society 5*. Thousand Oaks, CA: Pine Forge Press.

McDonaldization as an organizational paradigm is based on efficiency, predictability, calculability, and control. Ritzer asks (Chapter 10) if we are also seeing 'The Starbuckization of society' through 'the McDonaldization of the coffee shop business'?

Sirkin, H.L., Hemerling, J.W. and Bhattacharya, A.K., 2008, *Globality: Competing with Everyone from Everywhere for Everything*. New York and Boston: Business Plus.

Argues that we are in a 'post-globalization' world. In the past, Western organizations expanded into less affluent economies. Now companies from Brazil, Russia, India, China and Eastern Europe are capturing customers and markets in 'developed' countries.

OB in films

Thank You for Smoking (2005, director Jason Reitman) DVD track 18: 1:13:39 to 1:20:26 (7 minutes). This is the story of a tobacco company spokesperson and lobbyist for cigarettes. In this clip, Nick Naylor (played by Aaron Eckhart) testifies before a Senate hearing where issues of free choice and 'bad products' are discussed. As you watch this, identify:

1. Who are the cigarette companies' stakeholders?
2. What corporate social responsibility issues are raised here?
3. Where do you stand on the issue of freedom of choice for consumers?

OB in literature

Pattern Recognition, by William Gibson, Penguin Books, London, 2003. What does this novel reveal about the power and implications of product branding – for individuals as well as organizations – in the age of globalization and the internet?

CHAPTER EXERCISES

Ethical conduct

Objectives
1. To explore the nature of ethical and unethical work behaviours.
2. To identify what makes some behaviour ethical, and some behaviour unethical.
3. To explore individual differences in reaching ethical judgements.

Briefing
Here are examples of behaviour at work. Are these actions ethical? Tick your response in the column that best describes your opinion; is that behaviour ethical and thus acceptable in your view, or is it acceptable only in some contexts, or is it unethical in any circumstances?

Discussion
Share your answers with colleagues. Note the *differences* in your responses. Explore and explain *why* you hold different views on these issues. What makes some behaviours ethical and some behaviours unethical? Are differences between individuals linked to age, sex, experience, culture, religion, or to other factors? What are the implications of these differences for you personally and for your relationships with others? What are the implications for managing a diverse multicultural workforce?

Vermeir and Van Kenhove (2008) compared views of corporate actions and those of consumers. Using short stories or 'scenarios', they found that; the 'unethical' actions of consumers are more acceptable than corporate actions; women are more likely than men to rate a situation as unethical; and women are less likely to apply double standards.

behaviour	always ethical	ethical in some contexts	always unethical
1 claim credit for the work of others	❑	❑	❑
2 withhold information to slow others down	❑	❑	❑
3 call in sick so that you can have the day off	❑	❑	❑
4 make a false time report	❑	❑	❑
5 pad your expenses claims	❑	❑	❑
6 accept gifts for favours	❑	❑	❑
7 use friends as sources of confidential information	❑	❑	❑
8 deliberately make your boss look bad	❑	❑	❑
9 use company materials for your own purposes	❑	❑	❑
10 report colleagues who violate company rules	❑	❑	❑
11 make friends with the power brokers	❑	❑	❑
12 give others gifts or bribes in return for favours	❑	❑	❑
13 deliberately make a colleague look bad	❑	❑	❑
14 conduct personal business on company time	❑	❑	❑
15 divulge confidential information to others	❑	❑	❑
16 deliberately take your time to complete a task	❑	❑	❑
17 drink alcohol during working hours	❑	❑	❑
18 buy company products, not those of competitors	❑	❑	❑
19 vote for issues because they support this company	❑	❑	❑
20 work for more than one employer at a time	❑	❑	❑

Based on DeJong et al. (2008).

Profits versus people

Objectives 1. To explore the nature and implications of management views of ethical issues.

Briefing In the late 'noughties' (2005–2010), a lot of companies and managers found themselves accused of making a lot of money through 'suspect' business practices. Observers and commentators always say that, if they had been in charge, this would not have happened.

Individual ranking (1): Consider the following business values, and rank them in order of importance according to your own beliefs and principles:

1. career development of employees
2. concern for employees as people
3. concern for the environment
4. customer orientation
5. efficiency
6. high quality of products and services
7. integrity
8. managerial and organizational effectiveness
9. profit-making
10. social responsibility

Individual ranking (2): Now rank these items again, this time according to the values that you believe are actually given to them by practising managers.

Groupwork In groups of three:

1. Develop a consensus ranking (from top priority to bottom priority) of these business values based on the *personal sentiments and values* of your group's members.
2. Calculate the *practising managers'* rankings using the average of your group members' rankings (give 10 points to the top ranked item, 9 to the second, and so on).

Discussion How does your group's consensus ranking of personal values compare with the practising managers' ranking? Is there a difference? If so, why?

Based on Marcic (1995, pp.367–68).

Chapter 3 **Technology**

Key terms

material technology

social technology

replacement effects

compensatory effects

nonstandard work

Web 2.0 technologies

technological determinism

characteristics of mass production

job rotation

job enlargement

autonomous work group

system

open system

socio-technical system

organizational choice

lean production

Learning outcomes

When you have read this chapter, you should be able to define those key terms in your own words, and you should also be able to:

1. Explain different uses of the term technology.

2. Explain why predictions about technology and unemployment are often exaggerated.

3. Give examples of how new technology is changing the nature of work.

4. Describe the potential of Web 2.0 to transform work, and explain why that transformation is currently slow.

5. Demonstrate how the consequences of technological innovation for skill requirements depend on the organization of work, and not just on technical capabilities.

6. Define the characteristics of mass production, and describe methods to combat them.

7. Apply the socio-technical system perspective to organizational analysis and design.

8. Contrast the Scandinavian and Japanese models of team-based work organization.

Why study technology?

Technological innovation is one of the key features of our society. In this chapter we will focus on computing, telecommunications and other information technologies which affect:

how you communicate	email, mobile phone, social networking websites, video conferencing, digital cameras, voice over internet
how you buy and use goods and services	cloud computing, smart cash cards, e-commerce, internet access to news, information, films, music
how you find and apply for jobs	e-recruitment; but beware – interviewers check your profiles on Facebook and MySpace
how you spend your leisure time	MP3 player, DVD, web surfing, blogging, interactive gaming, chat rooms, social networking, e-books

Technology also affects the nature of work and organizations. While computing promises better personal and corporate performance, analyses consistently show that productivity gains are not always achieved. Technology can liberate and empower, but it can also increase workload, stress, and intensify surveillance and control. Many 'high profile' computing projects have been disasters; examples in Britain include the computerization of the London Stock Exchange, the London Ambulance Service, the Passport Office, the National Insurance system, and the Common User Data System at the Ministry of Defence. One commentator noted that, 'the bigger the project, the bigger the disaster' (Dearlove, 2000). The problems often lie not with the technology, but with organization and management issues.

Technology influences the organization of work, and the design of jobs. In the popular media, new technology is often accused of creating unemployment while deskilling the jobs that are left. However, the impact of technology is more complex than that. New technology has a mix of costs and benefits, depending on how it is used.

First, we will show that the impact of technology on employment is indeterminate. New technology creates new jobs while making 'old' jobs redundant, and has an overall skills upgrading effect while deskilling some tasks.

Second, we will consider how new technology can change the nature of work through teleworking, and through applications of Web 2.0 technologies, exploring the limitations and benefits of these developments.

Third, we will examine the argument that management motives in implementing new technology can explain the organizational consequences. Technology may have material benefits, but technology is also used to support social and political objectives, affecting the status and power of particular groups.

Finally, we consider research into technology implications, demonstrating how classic studies are perhaps more relevant and important today than they were when first developed. This particularly applies to socio-technical systems theory. We also consider the controversial argument concerning the respective merits of Swedish and Japanese approaches to work organization. While Sweden is known for the development of autonomous teamwork, Japan has a reputation for 'lean' and 'build to order' manufacturing systems. Which is better?

Active Skin

You and your computer are no longer tied to an office desk. Wireless broadband allows you to access company files and your email from home, and from most airport lounges around the planet. As a result, depending on your job, you can work anywhere, any time. The technology laboratory at BT (a British telecommunications company) first suggested that, instead of carrying that laptop computer, you could have the software that you need implanted, under your skin, in microscopic processors (sensors and memory devices). Known as 'Active Skin', these processors allow you to carry the software you need in your fingertips (literally). Other applications include identity chips that can be detected by

sensors which open security doors to restricted areas, and give you access to company databases. These processors can carry radio frequency identification devices (RFIDs). Employees at Citywatcher.com, an American surveillance equipment company based in Cincinnati, have had RFIDs each the size of a grain of rice implanted in their biceps. These devices control access to secure areas where video surveillance tapes are stored, and will in future be used to control access to the company vaults. Even the company's chief executive, Sean Darks, is reported to have an RFID implant.

Based on Govan (2006) and Jaques (2003).

Why technology predictions are often false

What is 'technology'? Langdon Winner (1977) argues that the way we use the term has changed as our concern with 'technological implications' has grown. In the eighteenth and nineteenth centuries, technology simply meant machines, tools, factories, industry, craft, engineering. Today, 'technology' refers to a range of phenomena: tools, instruments, machines, organizations, methods, techniques, supply chain and production systems.

STOP AND THINK

Which technologies shape your day-to-day experience?

How do you expect your life experiences to be different from those of your parents; and what part does technology play in creating those differences?

Rapid developments leave the language behind, and the word technology is simply a convenient umbrella term. Ambiguity in the language reflects the pace of innovation, and the concern over technology and its consequences – individual, organizational and social. Winner also observes that we tend to oversimplify and polarize; technology is either a good thing or a bad thing; you are either for it or against it.

Material technology
tools, machinery and equipment that can be seen, touched, and heard.

Alan Fox (1974) makes a useful distinction between material technology and social technology. Material technology is the stuff we can see and touch. Social technology includes job definitions, payment systems, authority relationships, communications, control systems, disciplinary codes and 'all the many other rules and decision-making procedures which seek to govern what work is done, how it is done, and the relationships that prevail between those doing it' (Fox, 1974, p.1).

Social technology
the methods which order the behaviour and relationships of people in systematic, purposive ways through structures of co-ordination, control, motivation and reward.

Research has sought to identify the effects of technology on organizations, jobs, and society at large. Technology has often been regarded as the *independent variable*, the factor whose effects are to be studied. Economic growth, employment levels, organization structures, skill requirements, and quality of working life, become the *dependent variables* that are likely to be affected by technology. This relationship is shown in Figure 3.1.

However, some definitions of 'technology' go beyond the equipment itself (the machinery *and* the work system around it) and overlap with the dependent variables. Organization structures and the design of jobs are social technology. This makes it difficult to establish cause and effect.

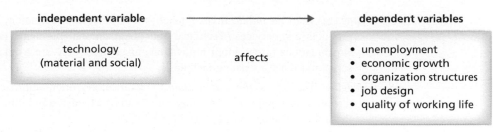

Figure 3.1: Technology as an independent variable

Advances in technology, and developments in computing and information technology in particular, often attract media predictions of doom. What does the evidence say?

STOP AND THINK

Which of the following media stories do you agree with?

- Robots are replacing people in factory jobs.
- Nobody needs to work in an office because we can work from our networked computers at home; the 'virtual organization' has arrived.
- The days of craft skill and worker autonomy are gone.

Compare your views with those of colleagues. Have the media got it wrong, or not?

Those media stories are correct. Some jobs have been eliminated and some work has been deskilled by technology. Some of us work from home at our computers. Some traditional crafts are disappearing. Should we be concerned by these stories and trends?

The myth of technological unemployment

Replacement effects processes through which intelligent machines substitute for people at work, leading to unemployment.

Compensatory effects processes that delay or deflect replacement effects, and which lead to the creation of new products and services, and new jobs.

New technology can create unemployment through what are known as **replacement effects**, which substitute equipment for people, while increasing productivity. For example, many supermarkets now use self-service checkout technology, allowing customers to scan and pay for items on their own, reducing the number of checkout operators required to staff the store.

It is natural to assume that, as machines do more, people do less. These fears date from the nineteenth century, when Luddites destroyed the mechanical looms that put them out of work. Why has technological change since then not made the problem even worse?

Technological innovation is of course consistent with economic growth. Unemployment levels are not higher today than they were in the nineteenth and twentieth centuries, and there is little evidence for a technology-led fall in job opportunities. The opposite is the case. The effects of new technology on employment also depend on **compensatory effects**.

There are six compensatory effects:

New products and services mean job creation: New products and services create demand which leads to investment in factories, offices and other infrastructure, creating jobs in manufacturing, distribution, sales, and maintenance.

Lower costs increase demand: Technical innovation improves the productivity (same output, fewer resources) of existing operations. The consequent cost reduction leads to lower prices, and hence to increased demand. This also means that consumers have more money to spend on other goods and services, increasing demand and the creation of jobs elsewhere.

Time lags delay the implications: It takes time to build new technology into existing systems, products and services. Technical and organizational problems need to be overcome. Organizations rarely adopt innovations as soon as they are available, as it is costly to scrap and replace existing facilities.

Hedging risk delays the implications: Organizations often approach experimental new technologies slowly. The 'learning curve' can be expensive and time consuming. To hedge these risks, change is introduced gradually.

What is a normal job?

We are in the midst of radical changes to the way we conduct and organize most work. In particular, more and more work is information work, and most of us generally use computers on a daily basis as an integral part of our work. Our notion of what constitutes a so-called 'normal job' is rapidly going out of fashion. Farmers shook their heads in disbelief when they saw the young men and women head for the brand new factories in the cities of the industrial revolution: 'Why are you going there? How are you going to find food to eat?' Work was then intrinsically linked to farming the land and all other jobs, apart from the priest and the schoolteacher seemed rather suspicious

occupations. Work in factories rapidly took over in defining what constituted 'normal work'. Manufacturing replaced farming as the primary occupation, then since World War II, it was replaced by the services industry. In the twenty-first century, what for most people constitutes a normal job can be quite difficult to define. In a survey of the Californian workforce in 1999, only 33 per cent of the sample fitted the description of having one, single day-shift, year round, permanent employment paid for by the firm for which the work is done and not working from home.

From Sørensen (2004, p.8).

Expectations of demand: Organizations usually implement innovations only when their market is likely to expand. In that case, the organization has to retain, if not increase, the existing workforce.

Technical limitations: New technologies do not always live up to their promise. They may, in fact, not be able to do everything that the 'old' technology could do. Existing jobs, skills and equipment are thus often found working alongside new devices. That is why, in a world of mobile phones and MP3 players, many homes still have traditional landlines, and there is a market for vinyl records.

Technology does not necessarily increase unemployment. New technology can create as many jobs as it eliminates, if not more. The impact of technology on employment is thus indeterminate, and depends on the interplay of replacement and compensatory effects.

The myth of technological deskilling

If technology does not create unemployment, then surely the remaining jobs will be deskilled? The evidence suggests that 'technological implications' are not as one-dimensional as that. Technology can deskill, but it can also increase the demands on skill and understanding.

Maarten Goos and Alan Manning argue that technology is polarizing employment, into 'lovely and lousy' jobs (Goos and Manning, 2003). Studies show that new technology can open up new opportunities for work organization and can raise demands on social and cognitive skills. Low skill, low pay manual work is more easily automated. It is much more difficult to substitute technology for people in jobs that require more complex problem-solving capabilities. Shoshana Zuboff (1988, p.76) concludes, from studies of automated process control applications, that as manual or 'action-centred' skills become automated, complex 'intellective' skills become important.

Replacement effects in action?

This article appears to suggest that technology is to blame for the lack of job opportunities in this factory. Read carefully; there is another explanation.

On the banks of the sleepy river Loire, across the valley from Amboise's historic *Château Royal*, stands a model of modern high tech French manufacturing. In a neatly landscaped business park, Pfizer, an American pharmaceutical giant, produces 80 per cent of the world's Viagra, and the entire supply for the American market. Every bottle of Viagra bought in an American drugstore will have been filled, packaged, labelled, bar-coded and shipped from this site. The Amboise factory manufactures Viagra in 227 different guises, from pill jars to blister packs. In all, the site turns out nearly 70m packs or bottle of pills of various kinds each year, labelled in 44 different languages.

Pfizer's Amboise plant shows that, for foreign investors, France remains an attractive location. This particular site offers a mix of high productivity, technical expertise (it has a big research facility, and nearby Tours is home to a pharmaceutical college) and reliability in a market troubled by fakes. Yet a visit to the gleaming, ultra-clean production line prompts another, more unsettling observation: there are hardly any workers.

No human being drives forklift trucks around the factory floors, fills pill packets or loads them into boxes. Instead, unmanned laser-guided vehicles surge down the aisles, picking up packages that have been stuffed, wrapped and labelled by machine, and delivered to the robots along conveyor belts suspended from the ceiling. All this takes place in an eerie near-silence. The factory's director, Marie-Gabrielle Laborde-Rayna, says that even visitors from the pharmaceuticals industry familiar with high-tech production are impressed by the level of automation at Amboise.

A less comforting conclusion for the French, however, is that in France firms often invest in machines rather than hire people. This is not because French workers are inefficient. On the contrary, their productivity per hour worked is marginally higher than that of their American counterparts. It is, rather, because social-security contributions are high, the working week is short, the labour code is strict and shedding jobs is slow and difficult. Taking on an employee in France is a risk, so employers avoid it as best they can.

Source: © H. Mark Weidman Photography/Alamy

Employee on the production plant line

From The Economist *(28 October 2006b).*

Studies of manufacturing show that sophisticated, flexible, expensive equipment often needs sophisticated, flexible, expensive people to operate and maintain it. Richard Walton and Gerald Susman (1987) argue that advanced technology increases:

- interdependencies between functions;
- skill requirements, and dependence on skilled people;
- capital investment per employee;
- the speed, scope and costs of mistakes;
- sensitivity of performance to changes in skill and attitudes.

Walton and Susman suggest that the response to these trends should be to develop a skilled, flexible workforce, and flat management structures. Appropriate 'people policies' are:

- job enrichment, multiskilling, teamwork, 'pay for knowledge' reward systems;
- rethinking the organizational level at which decisions are taken;
- attention to selection and training, and to management development.

The growth of nonstandard work

Nonstandard work employment that does not involve a fixed schedule at the same physical location for an extended time.

Technology encourages the development of nonstandard work, which does not involve turning up at the same place and time every day to work under management supervision with the mutual expectation that this arrangement will last for some time. Various labels are used for nonstandard work: alternative, nontraditional, market mediated, contract, telecommuting, e-lance, freelance, contingent, disposable, temporary. If you have a nonstandard job, your office or place of work is just as likely to be in your home, or in a Starbucks coffee shop. Census figures suggest that, in America, about 10 per cent of the working population have nonstandard jobs, and that these are more common for high skill–high pay knowledge workers such as independent contractors, managers and other professionals. The same trend applies in Japan, Britain, Australia, Canada, Europe and parts of Asia (Ashford *et al.*, 2007). The exercise of knowledge, creativity and problem-solving skills requires more freedom and flexibility than traditional bureaucracy allows, and technology makes this possible.

Organizations have always employed some staff on temporary and flexible contracts, so that they can expand and contract the workforce to adapt to business conditions. The employment of nonstandard workers has been encouraged by the growth in *intermediators*, such as temporary help agencies and contract companies who supply specialist staff for short periods.

STOP AND THINK

What for you are the benefits and disadvantages of nonstandard work?

If you know someone who has a nonstandard job, ask them how they feel about it. Would their experience encourage you to find nonstandard work?

However, the two main factors promoting growth in nonstandard work in the twenty-first century are *technology* and *employee preferences*. Relatively inexpensive computing and telecommunications systems mean that many kinds of work (including researching and writing this textbook) can be carried out almost anywhere. The same technology can be used to monitor employees who are not on the premises, perhaps making managers more comfortable with this style of working as they still have a degree of control.

Many of us prefer nonstandard work because it is more flexible and varied, free from direct management supervision and organization politics, is often better paid, and gives us a lifestyle in which we can more easily combine work with other personal and family interests. These preferences have been linked to the expectations of Generation Y – the Netgeneration – born since 1980 and who have grown up with today's technology. Generation Y does not have a monopoly on these preferences and lifestyles, which are also characteristic of many 'Gen Xers' and 'Baby Boomers'. One of the challenges created by these trends concerns managing a *blended workforce*, in which standard and nonstandard employees work side by side, with different working conditions and lifestyles.

Generation Y

It is widely assumed that your attitudes and traits are influenced by the culture into which you are born. As social, economic, and political circumstances change, it is likely that different generations in the same culture will develop distinctly different characteristics. The so-called Baby Boomers are those of us born between 1943 and 1960. Generation X includes those born between 1961 and 1980. Those born after 1980 are now known as Generation Y.

Research evidence suggests that, if you belong to Generation Y:

- the society in which you live is more ethnically diverse and technologically sophisticated than previous generations have experienced;

- some people think of you as a 'digital native';

- about half of you were not brought up in a traditional 'nuclear family';

- you are a multi-tasker, comfortable working in groups or collaboratively;
- you value intelligence and education and have high self-esteem and confidence;
- you have a natural ability and are comfortable with technology;
- you prefer work that is defined by task, and not by time;
- you seek creative challenges and you want to make an impact;
- you like to work asynchronously, anywhere, any time;

- telecommuting, flexitime, virtual working appeal to you, because this allows you freedom to 'have a life' and accommodate personal and family needs;
- you expect the organization to be concerned about your personal development.
- you do not expect to stay in the same job for long.

However, a recent survey showed that, although managers felt that Generation Y was distinctive in many ways, few organizations had started to develop management policies and practices to meet their needs and expectations.

From Birkinshaw and Pass (2008).

Changing the nature of work: teleworking

Another example of how technology enables us to work in different ways, but does not determine the nature of jobs, can be seen in the phenomenon of teleworking, a common form of nonstandard work. Communications with the far side of the planet, using email, mobile telephone, instant messaging, video conferencing, and old-fashioned facsimile transmission, are inexpensive and instantaneous. The world, for some, has become a virtual office.

If teleworking applies only to those who use a computer and a telecommunications link to work from home, then less than 2 per cent of the workforce in Britain and America are teleworkers. However, the terms teleworking and telecommuting cover various kinds of employment, combining technology and location in different ways. For example, you do not need to have a computer to work from home, and the distinction between home-working and teleworking is blurred. Leslie Haddon and Malcolm Brynin (2005) identify six categories:

net homeworkers	work from home using the internet
pc homeworkers	work from home using a pc
mobile users	rely on a mobile phone but are not net or pc homeworkers
day homeworkers	work at home but do not use the internet, a pc or a mobile phone
overtime workers	similar to day homeworkers but work evenings and weekends
standard workers	work at one or more workplaces excluding their home

A survey of 1,750 households in Britain, Bulgaria, Germany, Israel, Italy and Norway showed that few employees work exclusively from home. Norway and Israel had the lowest proportions of standard workers, reflecting geographical and security issues respectively. About 20 per cent of all those surveyed said that they worked from home at least once a week, and most of those did this regularly. The average weekly working hours of net homeworkers varied from 8 in Norway to 19 in Germany. In Britain, about half of all net and pc homeworkers use a pc for their work at home at least half of the time.

The survey also showed that net and pc homeworkers are mostly male, except in Israel. Mobile users were also mostly male. In contrast, homeworkers who do not use computers are more likely to be female. This may be because teleworking is more common in managerial, professional and technical jobs, and around 75 per cent of respondents were in those categories. Teleworking is clearly not a major option for those employed in more routine white collar work. However, 20 per cent of net homeworkers in Germany and 17 per cent in Britain and Italy, were employed in blue collar work, and many of those were self-employed. Net homeworkers are thus more likely to be male, professional and relatively well paid, in comparison with workplace-bound colleagues. Pc homeworkers, in contrast, are more likely to be employed in lower status jobs, with lower pay, which was shown in this survey to be less well paid than plain homeworking. In other words, teleworking and homeworking mirror traditional distinctions between jobs based on social and occupational status, and do not suggest some dramatic new shaping role for technology in the organization of work.

Home viewing

Gattaca (1997, director Andrew Niccol) is based in a future society in which employment opportunities are determined by genetic profiling. People who are engineered to possess specific characteristics are called 'valids'. Those who are not engineered, the 'love children' who lack a genetic profile, are called 'invalids'. The invalids are restricted to low skilled manual jobs. Vincent (played by Ethan Hawke) is an invalid who assumes the identity of a valid (Jude Law) so that he can get a job with the Gattaca Aerospace Corporation, in order to achieve his goal of going into space. As you watch this movie, gather evidence that would allow you to make a balanced assessment of the strengths and limitations – including the social benefits and drawbacks – of genetic engineering technology. In the end, what is your overall assessment: desirable or not? And why?

STOP AND THINK Your employer gives you a computer with a broadband internet connection and asks you to work at home. What are the advantages and disadvantages for the organization? For you? Following this analysis, will you comply or complain?

Teleworking appeared in the 1970s, and developments in computing and telecommunications have made this option more available, and potentially more attractive. Self-employed teleworkers are also sometimes called 'e-lancers'. While the popularity of teleworking is technology driven, there is no 'one best way' to do this. An IRS survey (1996) identified five main and five subsidiary reasons for introducing teleworking from a management perspective:

Five main reasons:

1. in response to requests from employees (most common);
2. to reduce costs;
3. to cope with maternity;
4. to help reduce office overcrowding;
5. following relocation of office, where some staff were unable to move.

Five subsidiary reasons:

1. to cope with illness or disability;
2. fits the kind of work that we do;
3. because staff live some distance from the office;
4. allows more undisturbed working time;
5. database connections are faster out of main working hours.

There are many personal and organizational advantages. Teleworkers do not need expensive office space. There is no office 'chit chat' and other distractions. Reduced commuting means lower travel expenses and fewer frustrations, and more effective use of employee time. Many organizations report increased efficiency, productivity, work turnaround, accuracy, speed of response, and morale. With jobs where location is not important, an organization can use people who they might not otherwise employ. For the teleworker, there is no supervisor checking, there is freedom to arrange the working day, and you become your own boss.

There are, however, a number of disadvantages:

- high set-up costs;
- staff are not able to share equipment and other facilities;
- lack of social interaction, sharing of ideas, and team spirit;
- staff lose touch with organization culture and goals;
- management cannot easily monitor and control activity;
- no access to office records and facilities;
- some customers expect to contact a 'conventional' office.

Virtual work in the virtual office

For most information workers, 'work' is mobile, and can be done just about anywhere. The concept of 'the workplace' as a permanent, static location has become redundant, as people set up their virtual office wherever they can use their laptop, wherever they can access the internet. Where managers and their staff are not co-located as they have been in conventional offices, direct supervision of employees becomes difficult, if not impractical. Interpersonal communication and performance monitoring take place through computer links.

Carsten Sørensen (2004) argues that traditional management command-and-control has to be replaced with 'coordinate and cultivate'. However, this approach depends on mutual trust. Employees have to trust management not to abuse the detailed monitoring information that can be collected concerning their movements and behaviour; intrusive surveillance damages trust. Management have to trust distant employees to do what they are being paid to do; we have to believe you when you say that you are working. He argues that:

> Failing to realize the seriousness of the challenges facing modern organizations can have monumental consequences. The primary strategic challenge is balancing the traditional hierarchical command-and-control environments with decentralized environments, that have distributed coordination of activities and cultivation of mutual trust in distributed and virtual working. Getting it wrong on either account can be a serious mistake (p.32).

As we see initial developments in the kind of systems and services supporting coordination of mobile and distributed activities, we also see the emerging need for all involved to cultivate and negotiate new perceptions of privacy and surveillance. [. . .] Mutual trust is not an added bonus of the mobile organization, it is an absolute core property. Without mutual trust it is impossible to effectively coordinate the distributed activities. Mistrust also results in the perceived need to engage in activities only serving the purpose of demonstrating ability internally and not generating business value. It has been reported that mobile phone users frequently don't divulge their exact location, instead giving out the location that will best serve their purpose (p.28).

"Richard, we need to talk. I'll E-mail you."

Source: Aaron Bacall/Condé Nast Publications/www.cartoonbank.com

Based on Sørensen (2004).

To what extent does technology *determine* the consequences for teleworkers and the organizations which employ them? Technology makes some kinds of new working arrangements possible and more attractive. However, technology simply opens up a variety of different kinds of work and organizational options, some of which may simply be computer-based versions of what people did before. The consequences depend in part on the technology, and also on how we decide to use the technology in a given setting.

Teleworking at Lloyd's

Michael Collins reports the results of an experiment in teleworking at the financial institution Lloyd's of London, looking at the impact on those involved, and at the business benefits. The experiment involved the Lloyd's Policy Signing Office (LPSO), which employed 300 full-time and 100 part-time staff providing support services to insurance syndicates, brokers, and managing agents. The work involved producing insurance policies, doing research, publishing information, providing accounting and regulatory services, and arranging cash settlements in multiple currencies. By 2001, LPSO had 52 teleworkers (47 women and 5 men), around 12.5 per cent of the department, working between 60 and 90 per cent of their time at home, using much the same technology, and performing the same tasks as colleagues in the conventional office. Detailed measurements were made of the costs involved in setting up and maintaining teleworking, and of staff performance.

The results showed that, while the quality of work was not affected, teleworkers were over 20 per cent more productive than their office-based colleagues. However, the financial benefits were almost equal to the set-up and running costs, and the experiment would not have

been justified on this basis alone. The LPSO teleworkers expressed higher levels of satisfaction with work-life balance, and also had lower levels of absence, but felt that they had fewer training and career development opportunities than their office colleagues. Cut off from the office grapevine, an 'us and them' feeling developed between teleworkers and office staff. The teleworkers also had frustrating computing problems, particularly with slow response times, made worse by the lack of readily available technical support. Nevertheless, there was a queue of office staff asking to be allowed to become teleworkers.

Collins concludes that, although the business case for teleworking in this instance was not compelling, it is important to look at the broader range of issues and to consider non-financial benefits as well. It is also important to recognize that teleworking is not without problems and unintended consequences. The issues that arise will differ from one organization to another, and these must be recognized and addressed if the approach is to be effective.

Based on Collins (2005).

Web 2.0: the impact

Web 2.0 technologies internet-based information systems that allow high levels of user interaction, such as blogs, wikis (collaborative databases), and social networking.

The internet has entered a new phase in the twenty first century. Computing has become more 'social and sociable', and these developments are known as **Web 2.0 technologies**.

Web 2.0 technologies involve a higher degree of participation and interaction between systems and users, and between users, than the old 'one-way' internet. This includes social networking, online co-ordination, blogs, podcasts, collaborative publishing and RSS (really simple syndication) feeds. Julian Birkinshaw and Sarah Pass (2008) surveyed 488 senior managers to find out how they were responding to the challenges and opportunities of Web 2.0. The managers were asked to rate their agreement with the following statements:

- Web 2.0 enables the value of a service/activity to increase with the addition of each new user (network effect);
- Web 2.0 allows systems to evolve in an emergent or organic way; users derive value not only from the services themselves but also the overall shape that a service inherits from user behaviours;

- Web 2.0 allows experiences to be tailored to individual user needs by integrating the capabilities of multiple services from different places;
- Web 2.0 allows users to participate in the creation/delivery of new policies, services or offerings;
- Web 2.0 allows users to experience services on their own terms, not those of a centralized authority such as a corporation.

Most respondents seemed not to have enough knowledge of Web 2.0, although it could radically change internal and external communication. IBM uses its corporate intranet for online 'jams' with up to 50,000 employees at a time. Comcast, AOL, and Dunkin Donuts, on the other hand, have suffered public criticism of their poor service with video clips showing on YouTube. The next question concerned how managers were actually using these new technological capabilities. The most common uses involved communication, and the recruitment and selection of staff, but the activity that received the highest level of response was, 'I have read books and articles about Web 2.0'. Using online job advertisements, application forms, and tests, are now common, but these are 'Web 1.0' methods. There was some limited evidence of wider experimentation with Web 2.0, and examples included:

- senior management communicating with staff through blogs, webcasts and podcasts;
- management podcasts which allowed staff to download company information to MP3 players, which could be used outside work;
- using blogs for knowledge-sharing, especially with regard to problem-solving;
- live online forums allowing management to interact with thousands of employees.

Two companies, Kimberly-Clark Corporation and Informa, demonstrate the possibilities:

> Kimberly-Clark Corporation has actively pushed Web 2.0 technologies for communication in response to a global employee engagement survey that highlighted the need for improvement in their communication. With the organization divided across continents and with increasing numbers of remote teams, senior executives were concerned about how to ensure employees felt engaged and able to communicate effectively within their teams. To address this problem, the organization incorporated a number of Web 2.0 technologies, including Microsoft Sharepoint Services (which they had found worked especially well with Generation Y employees), blogs and live forums. Organizational communication had been improved through the use of live forums with directors of the company, and a quarterly video message from the CEO emailed to all employees. To address communication issues around remote teams (often divided between countries), the use of frequent video-conferencing has helped to maintain effective communication.
>
> One interesting example of how Web 2.0 is being used for internal promotion and recruitment is the publishing company Informa. The company has built its own space on *Second Life*, the virtual world in which people can interact with others through their personal avatar. Informa provides access to information about job functions, competencies and opportunities. Employees go into *Second Life* and learn about particular roles, talk to ambassadors for those roles and view internal job vacancies. In some ways this is no different from the traditional ways of getting information across to employees, but the medium is sufficiently novel and fun that it increases the uptake, particularly among younger employees.
>
> *From Birkinshaw and Pass (2008, pp.13–14).*

Do you have a Second Life?

Second Life is a virtual three-dimensional online world (http://secondlife.com) in which the resident characters or 'avatars' behave and interact under the control of their real world creators. Designed for entertainment, *Second Life* is a combination of computer game and social networking site. However, some of the 'residents' are real world organizations, and there are specialist consulting firms that help companies establish their *Second Life* presence. IBM, Cisco and PA Consulting, for example, have set up their own 'islands' with virtual offices, showrooms, meeting rooms and training and conference facilities on *Second Life*. (Some of these islands are open access, and some are private.) This allows them to bring into one 'room' people from different parts of the organization, and the chief executive can speak to a shopfloor worker, and vice versa. Cisco has an island called 'Connected

Women' which allows its female employees from around the world to meet and network. IBM has around 40 different islands, one of which is used to help recruit and induct graduates.

While you can leave a chatroom without anybody noticing, others will know when your avatar stands up and leaves. Meetings in *Second Life* can be more business-like, because there is less 'small talk', and people with disabilities (a speech impediment, for example) can find the experience liberating (as discussions are conducted in text). The publishing company Informa has a careers development centre on *Second Life* illustrating different types of job, the skills required for promotion, and a 'champion' for each role whom visitors can contact.

Based on Syedain (2008a).

Graeme Martin and colleagues (2008) argue that it is more useful to think of Web 2.0 as a system which includes inputs, transfer mechanisms, and outputs (see the discussion of open systems later in this chapter). Their view of this system is shown in Figure 3.2.

Martin and colleagues note that traditional employee opinion surveys can *reduce* the sense of participation and engagement because they are designed and 'owned' by the organization, and constrain the responses that can be given. They describe how some British government departments are using Web 2.0 methods to overcome those limitations.

The Department of Communities and Local Government's Director General and Ministers Monthly Staff Webchat is chaired by a director general. Staff can ask questions directly to board executive members in an asynchronous chatroom. The online chatroom has a formal agenda, and transcripts and action points are fed back to board members. The

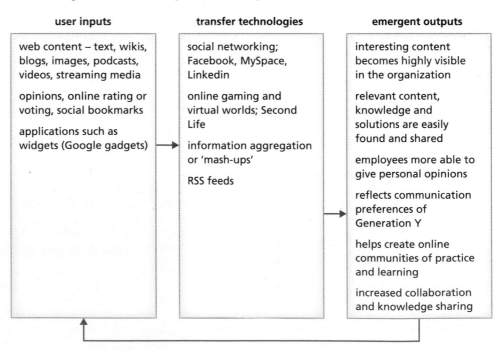

Figure 3.2: The Web 2.0 system

Source: After Martin *et al.* (2008) with the permission of the publisher, and the Chartered Institute of Personnel and Development, London (www.cipd.co.uk)

webchat is marketed internally through various channels of communication and usually attracts over 100 discussion postings a month.

Her Majesty's Revenue and Customs (HMRC) online discussion forum is an important channel for employee contributions to the corporate suggestion scheme, 'Angels and Demons'. Suggestions are being sought on how to improve work organization and processes, and on culture change, along the lines of the BBC's *Dragon's Den*. According to the website, more than 12,000 HMRC employees had registered by October 2007, 8,000 had contributed to online discussions on specific themes, and 500 innovative business ideas had been logged.

From Martin et al. *(2008, p.14).*

Birkinshaw and Pass (2008, p.15) argue that Web 2.0 could radically alter the nature of work, tapping knowledge from across the organization, encouraging informal co-ordination, and making the workplace more engaging. But most of the innovation is taking place, not in work organizations, but in web communities and social networks whose members are often not traditional salaried employees. It seems that many organizations, despite researching these new technologies and their possibilities, have done little in practice to develop and exploit the organizational and business benefits. Barriers include lack of management expertise, uncertainty over costs and benefits, and fear of loss of control over information. Many organizations seem more concerned to prevent staff exploring Web 2.0; a survey of 1,765 British employers found that 80 per cent had disciplined employees for using social networking sites at work, and many had banned their use (Martin *et al.*, 2008). Other reasons for management caution lie with perceptions of risk with regard to new technology, and with the uncertainty over how these technologies and their applications will develop. Birkinshaw and Pass conclude that, 'The future is already here; it is just unevenly distributed.'

Web 2.0 and Enterprise 2.0

Web 2.0	Enterprise 2.0
accessible from just about anywhere	companies can become more agile, modular and flexible
computers become 'virtual' machines as cloud computing resources are used only when and where they are needed	improved interpersonal collaboration and sharing – blogs, wikis, social networks, inside and outside the organization
software bought and used as an online service, when and where needed, flexible	organizational specialization; process networks of specialized firms
service-oriented architecture means using only the bit of the software relevant to you	capital expenditure becomes operational expenditure (easier and cheaper)
mash-ups; bits of software applications can be combined in creative ways	small companies can enjoy the same computing infrastructure as large competitors
wireless networks connect more devices; more products are designed with built-in radio connectivity; who needs a laptop?	cloud computing is the basis for whole new businesses (Animoto allows users to turn photos into music videos)
data centres become industrial-scale service factories*	easier to outsource business processes to networks of small specialist companies
personal and corporate data storage and protection become major concerns	collaboration and openness – on a global scale generate security risks
some organizations block employee access to social networking sites through company computers	'digital natives' are impatient with the rules of traditional corporate IT, and can now build their own tailored applications

* The telecommunications company BT has 57 data centres spread around the world, with a total of 10,000 servers. There are around 7,000 data centres in America. One of the largest, Microsoft's data centre in Northlake, Chicago, contains 2,500 servers, covers 46,000 square metres, and cost US$500 million. It is planned to hold 400,000 servers. Due to their high electricity consumption and the need for a supply of water as coolant, these data centres may not be 'environmentally friendly' (see Chapter 2).

Based on Siegele (2008).

Determinism or choice?

Different technologies make different demands on those who work with them. The technology of an organization appears to determine the nature of work. When we compare a hospital with a call centre, or a retail store with a coal mine, the technology seems to determine: the kinds of tasks that need to be done; the nature of jobs; the organization of work; the grouping of jobs; the hierarchy through which work is planned, co-ordinated and controlled; the knowledge and skills required; the values and attitudes of employees.

But does technology really determine these factors? Can we predict the shape of an organization, and the nature and content of jobs, from a knowledge of technology? As we have seen, while new technologies enable some new kinds of working arrangements, they do not uniquely determine the outcomes. The argument that technology does have predictable consequences for work and organization is known as technological determinism.

Technological determinism
the argument that technology explains the nature of jobs, work groupings, hierarchy, skills, values and attitudes in organizations.

Technological determinism assumes that work has to be organized to meet the requirements of the technology. Different technologies have different 'technological imperatives'. Arthur Turner and Paul Lawrence (1965) explained the background to their work on manufacturing jobs saying: '[T]his research started with the concept that every industrial job contained certain technologically determined task attributes which would influence the workers' response. By "task attributes" we meant such characteristics of the job as the amount of variety, autonomy, responsibility, and interaction with others built into the design.'

Technological determinism is an oversimplified perspective. Technology *suggests* and *enables*. There are three areas of choice in the new technology implementation process, concerning choice of design, of goals, and of work organization.

First, there are choices in the design of tools, machinery, equipment and systems. For example, how much control is built into the machine, and how much is left to human intervention and discretion. There are examples where automation has been removed from aircraft cockpits, ships' bridges and railway engine cabs following the discovery that pilots and drivers lose touch with the reality of their tasks when surrounded by sophisticated controls which function without their understanding or help.

Second, there are choices in the goals that technology is used to achieve. The need to reduce costs, improve quality and customer service, and improve management information can be critical. However, managers also promote innovation for personal and political reasons, to enhance power over resources and influence over decisions, to enhance status and prestige, and to exert closer surveillance and control over employees.

Third, there are choices in how work is organized. As we will see, car assembly work can be designed in several different ways, and it is not clear which of these approaches may be best.

These choices rely on the assumptions we make about human capabilities and organizational characteristics. They rely less on the capabilities of the equipment. These are called 'psychosocial assumptions', because they concern beliefs about individuals and groups. To consider the 'impact' of a technology, therefore, is to consider the wrong question. Technological innovations trigger a decision-making and negotiation process which is driven by the perceptions, goals, and assumptions of those involved. The choices that form in that process determine the 'impact'. Technology has a limited effect on work independent of the purposes of those who would use it and the responses of those who have to work with it.

Figure 3.3 summarizes this argument claiming that the consequences of technological change depend on the interaction of technical capabilities, objectives, and how work is organized.

Is this argument oversimplified? Surely technology must have *some* independent influence on the nature of work and organizations? Two commentators have challenged the 'organizational choice' argument, Ian McLoughlin and Jon Clark (1994; McLoughlin, 1999). They argue that new information technologies *do* create imperatives:

- reduction in tasks that require manual skills;
- creation of complex tasks requiring problem-solving skills;

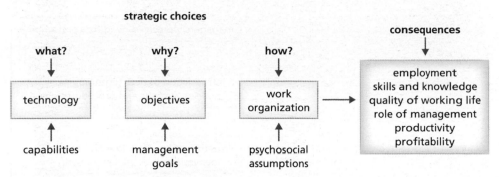

Figure 3.3: **Technological indeterminism**

- ability to combine knowledge of new with old technology;
- a relationship between technology and user that relies on informed intervention based on an understanding of system interdependencies.

In other words, 'action-centred' abilities become less important, and cognitive skills become more valued. This is not to deny the significance of organizational choice, or the role of social shaping and negotiation, in affecting the outcomes for work experience that accompany particular technological innovations. Technology appears to have 'enabling' properties; the technology of motor car production enables task fragmentation and rigid supervisory control, but it also enables multiskilled, autonomous teamwork.

The politics of technology

Commentators in the 1940s claimed that technological change increased task specialization, took skill and identity from work, and increased discipline in the workplace. This pessimistic view appeared in Harry Braverman's (1974) influential work which triggered a 'labour process debate' which still generates controversy today. Braverman's argument is that advances in technology give management progressive opportunities to reduce skill and discretion, and to tighten surveillance and control over workers. It is important to draw a distinction between what technology can achieve, and what management uses technology to achieve. Braverman's argument concerns the latter.

Humanization or intensification?

The problem as it presents itself to those managing industry, trade, and finance is very different from the problem as it appears in the academic or journalistic worlds. Management is habituated to carrying on labour processes in a setting of social antagonism and, in fact, has never known it to be otherwise. Corporate managers have neither the hope nor the expectation of altering this situation by a single stroke: rather, they are concerned to ameliorate it only when it interferes with the orderly functioning of their plants, offices, warehouses and stores.

For corporate management this is a problem in costs and controls, not in the 'humanization of work'. It compels their attention because it manifests itself in absenteeism, turnover, and productivity levels that do not conform to their calculations and expectations. The solutions they will accept are only those which provide improvements in their labour costs and in their competitive positions domestically and in the world market.

From Braverman (1974, p.36).

This argument treats technology as a political tool, which managers use to maintain their position of power, and to manipulate employees and the conditions in which they work. This is an important observation because technology is often seen as politically neutral. However,

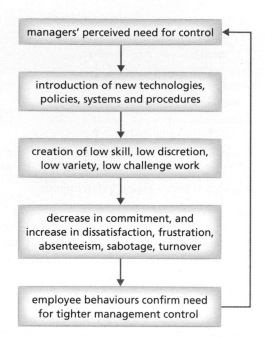

Figure 3.4: The vicious circle of control

if management can increase task specialization, and reduce the level of skill required in a job, lower wages can be offered, and the organization's dependence on those employees is reduced. If management can increase the discipline in work, improve surveillance and gain tighter control of employees, this can lead to reduced discretion and to work intensification.

Managers can manipulate employees by appealing to technological determinism: 'we have no choice but to do it this way because of the technology'. Technological determinism can be used to justify and to protect from challenge unpopular decisions; those who argue clearly don't understand the technology. Improved control can lead to lower costs and higher profits, and also maintains the status and power of management. Some 'technology implications' can be seen instead as the implications of management strategies to improve employee control. Technology's consequences are not the inescapable outcomes of the demands of machinery.

Chapter 14 explores scientific management, which is still applied today, although it was developed in the early twentieth century. Scientific management offers a rationale for task fragmentation, simplification and tighter control. The typically antagonistic human response to simple repetitive work can confirm the management view that tight control of employees is necessary, to maintain discipline, and to produce goods and services effectively. Scientific management can become self-perpetuating through the 'vicious circle of control' (Clegg and Dunkerley, 1980), illustrated in Figure 3.4.

This vicious circle can only be broken by a change in management perceptions, starting with higher trust in, and higher discretion for employees. Braverman and his followers argue that such a change is unlikely in a capitalist economy. Technological determinism is replaced in this perspective with an economic and political logic. However, other commentators argue that the effective use of technology depends on developing high levels of mutual trust between management and employees (Malone, 2004; Sørensen, 2004).

Classic studies on work and technology

One of the first studies of the relationship between technology and the nature of work was reported by Charles Walker and Robert Guest in 1952. They argued, in determinist mode, that some production technologies prevent the formation of work groups and frustrate the

Characteristics of mass production mechanical pacing of work, no choice of tools or methods, repetitiveness, minute subdivision of product, minimum skill requirements, and surface mental attention.

Job rotation a work design method in which employees are switched from task to task at regular intervals.

Job enlargement a work design method in which tasks are combined to widen the scope of a job.

social needs of employees. Their survey of 180 American automobile assembly workers identified six characteristics of mass production work, which are listed in the margin.

The assembly jobs were scored on these characteristics. Despite being content with pay and conditions, employees in jobs with a high 'mass production score' disliked their work, and had a higher rate of absenteeism than those in low-scoring jobs. In other words, scientific management had taken task specialization too far. Monotony and boredom reduced work rate, output, and morale, and led to high levels of absenteeism and complaints. The solutions to boredom and monotony were job rotation and job enlargement.

The first account of job enlargement was at the Endicott plant of the American company IBM (Walker, 1950). In 1944, machine operators' jobs were enlarged to include machine set-up and inspection of finished product. There was nothing in the technology to prevent operators doing these extra tasks. The benefits were improved product quality and a reduction in losses from scrap, less idle time for operators and machines, and a 95 per cent cut in set-up and inspection costs. Job enlargement reduced monotony and boredom and increased variety, but in a superficial way. Nevertheless, job rotation and enlargement are still in use.

Mass production characteristics also cause stress and illness. Arthur Kornhauser's (1965) study of car assembly workers in Detroit showed that factory work could lead to job dissatisfaction and poor mental health. The workers in his study had a long list of grievances:

low pay	simplicity of job operations
job insecurity	repetitiveness and boredom
poor working conditions	lack of control over the work
low status	non-use of abilities
restricted promotion opportunities	feelings of futility

the style of the supervisors

Workers in jobs with these characteristics had lower mental health, which meant that they:

were anxious and tense	were less satisfied with life
had negative self-concepts	were socially withdrawn
were hostile to others	suffered from isolation and despair

Kornhauser argued that work with mass production characteristics produces this pattern of psychological reactions. A later study showed that the most stressful jobs were those which combined high workload with low discretion (Karasek, 1979). Typical examples included assembly workers, garment stitchers, goods and materials handlers, nursing aides and orderlies and telephone operators. The main symptoms included exhaustion and depression including nervousness, anxiety and sleeping difficulties.

STOP AND THINK

What other jobs – and not necessarily in manufacturing – combine a high workload with low discretion?

Do employees in those jobs display symptoms of fatigue or depression?

What advice would you give to management to reduce workload and increase discretion in those jobs?

Swedish car makers were among the first to show that mass production characteristics can be avoided by creative work design. Saab-Scania began experimenting in 1970, when 40 workers in the chassis shop of a new truck factory were divided into production groups (Norstedt and Aguren, 1973). Group members were responsible for deciding how they would rotate between tasks, and also absorbed maintenance and quality control functions. These changes eventually affected about 600 manual workers, with the following results:

- productivity increased and product quality improved;
- unplanned stoppages of production were significantly reduced;
- costs were reduced to 5 per cent below budget;
- labour turnover was cut from 70 to 20 per cent;
- absenteeism was not affected;
- co-operation between management and workforce improved.

Saab's best known experiment was at their engine factory at Södertälje. Here an oblong conveyor loop moved engine blocks to seven assembly groups, each with three members (Thomas, 1974). Each group had its own U-shaped guide track in the floor, to the side of the main conveyor. Engine blocks were taken from the main track, assembled by the group, and then returned to the conveyor. The engines arrived with their cylinder heads, and the groups handled the fitting of carburettors, distributors, spark plugs, camshafts, and other components.

Each assembly group decided for themselves how the work was allocated. The group had half an hour to build each engine, and they decided how that time would be spent. Individual jobs on the conventional assembly track had cycle times of less than two minutes. In 1974, Saab-Scania estimated that they saved around 65,000 Swedish kroner a year on recruitment and training costs alone with this approach. This form of work organization is known as the **autonomous work group** (or self-regulating or self-managing group or team).

Autonomous work groups make their own decisions about how tasks and responsibilities will be allocated, shared and rotated. This a feature of the 'high performance work systems' discussed in Chapter 9, and was the approach used by Sweden's other car maker, Volvo. Volvo's plant at Kalmar pioneered the concept of 'dock assembly', in which teams completed whole stages of the car assembly in static bays to one side of the moving assembly track.

Autonomous work group
a team allocated to a significant segment of the workflow, with discretion over how their work will be carried out.

Technology and alienation

One classic study of the impact of technology on work was carried out by Robert Blauner, who analysed working conditions in the early 1960s in:

printing, dominated by craft work

cotton spinning, dominated by machine minding

car manufacture, dominated by mass production

chemicals manufacture, dominated by process production

Blauner identified four components of alienation, concerning feelings of:

1. *Powerlessness*: loss of control over conditions of work, work processes, pace and methods.
2. *Meaninglessness*: loss of significance of work activities.
3. *Isolation*: loss of sense of community membership.
4. *Self-estrangement*: loss of personal identity, of sense of work as a central life interest.

Printing workers set their own pace, were free from management pressure, chose their own techniques and methods, had powerful unions, practised a complex skill, had good social contacts at work, had high status, identified closely with their work and were not alienated.

Textile workers performed simple, rapid and repetitive operations over which they had little control, worked under strict supervision, and had little social contact. Alienation, however, was low. Blauner argued that this was because textile workers lived in close rural communities whose values and way of life overcame feelings of alienation arising at work.

Car assembly workers had little control over work methods, saw little meaning in the tasks they performed, were socially isolated, and developed no meaningful skills.

Chemicals processing workers operated prosperous, technically advanced plants where manual work had been automated. They controlled their own work pace, and had freedom of movement, social contact and team work. They developed an understanding of the chemical reactions which they monitored, and also developed a sense of belonging, achievement and responsibility. In addition they had close contact with educated, modern management.

Blauner concluded that advanced technology would eliminate alienation.

Based on Blauner (1964).

Socio-technical systems analysis and design

System something that functions through the interdependence of its component parts.

Open system a system that interacts, in a purposive way, with its external environment in order to survive.

Eric John Miller (1924–2002)

Albert Kenneth Rice (1908–1969)

Swedish managers did not invent the autonomous work group. The idea came from the work of British researchers at the Tavistock Institute of Human Relations in London. The Institute is still in business, although its work now focuses more on policy, change, and leadership in the public sector. According to Martyn Sloman, adviser on learning at the Chartered Institute of Personnel and Development, one reason why technology often fails to deliver productivity gains is because the lessons of the Tavistock research are overlooked (Overell, 2005, 15 March). The Tavistock group first developed the concept of the organization as a **system**.

The term system can be applied to a range of phenomena: solar system, nervous system, traffic management system, telecommunications system, waste disposal system. Any system is defined by its boundaries, which in turn depend on what one wants to study, and why. In an organizational context, we may wish to analyse a performance measurement system, a product distribution system, a supply chain management system, a production system.

The human organism and the organization share one important property. They are each dependent on their ability to conduct an exchange with their environments. We breathe air, consume food and drink, and absorb sensory information. We convert these imports into energy and actions, dispose of waste products, and expend energy in chosen behaviours. The organization, like the human body, is also an **open system**.

Open systems import resources, such as people, materials, equipment, information, and money. They transform those inputs, in organizations through producing services and goods. They then export those products back into the environment, as goods and satisfied customers. This view of organizations as living organisms is known as 'the organic analogy' (Rice, 1958, 1963; Miller and Rice, 1967).

Another property of open systems is their ability to reach a particular outcome from a variety of different starting points and through different routes. The autonomous work group at Saab, for example, could assemble an engine in many different ways, but with the same end results. A chemical reaction, on the other hand, is a closed system in which the end result depends on the concentrations and quantities of the items used to begin with. This property is known as 'equifinality', and it has an interesting consequence for organizational design. Equifinality means that it is not necessary to specify in detail the organization structure and the duties of every member. If an organization can develop its own mode of operating, and change as circumstances require, then it will only be necessary to detail the basic and most significant aspects. This approach to organizational design is called 'minimum critical specification'.

"JUST THINK OF IT AS IF YOU'RE READING A LONG TEXT-MESSAGE."

Source: www.cartoonstock.com

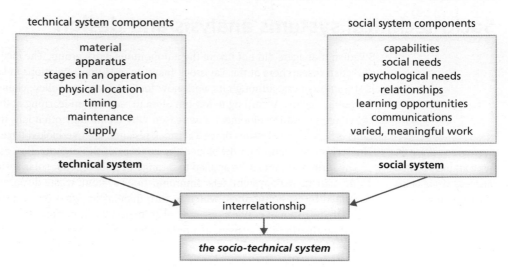

technical system components

| material |
| apparatus |
| stages in an operation |
| physical location |
| timing |
| maintenance |
| supply |

social system components

| capabilities |
| social needs |
| psychological needs |
| relationships |
| learning opportunities |
| communications |
| varied, meaningful work |

technical system

social system

interrelationship

the socio-technical system

Figure 3.5: The organization as socio-technical system

Socio-technical system system which has both a material technology (machinery, equipment) and a social organization (job specifications, management structure).

Unlike closed systems which maintain or move towards states of homogeneity, organization structures become more elaborate and adaptable in attempts to cope with their environment (Emery and Trist, 1960). This argument is consistent with demands for organizations to become more flexible and responsive in an increasingly turbulent world. One Tavistock researcher and consultant, Eric Trist, developed the concept that an organization is also a socio-technical system.

The socio-technical system concept is illustrated in Figure 3.5. The goal of socio-technical system design is to find the best fit between the social and technical dimensions. Trist argued that effective socio-technical system design could never satisfy fully the needs of both subsystems. A system designed to meet social needs, ignoring the technical system would run into problems. On the other hand, a system designed only to meet the demands of technology would raise social and organizational problems. 'Suboptimization' is a feature of socio-technical design, which aims at 'joint optimization' of social and technical needs. The resultant socio-technical system design is thus a matter of creative choice.

Several new concepts have been introduced in this section:

system	anything that functions by virtue of the interdependence of its component parts
open system	a system that has to conduct regular exchanges with its environment in order to survive
the organic analogy	the organization as an open system has properties similar to a living organism
equifinality	the same end results can be achieved with different starting points and routes
minimum critical specification	it is not necessary to specify organization and task design in detail as open systems adapt themselves as necessary
socio-technical system	the organization combines a social system (people) with a technical system (plant and machinery)
joint optimization	the social and technical systems cannot be designed in isolation; trade-offs are necessary to design for 'best fit' between the two sub-systems

Organizational choice the argument that work design is not determined by technology, that the technical system does not determine the social system.

Tavistock researchers also introduced the concept of **organizational choice**.

Eric Trist and Kenneth Bamforth developed the concept of the socio-technical system in their study of the social and psychological impact of longwall coal mining methods in the 1940s (Trist and Bamforth, 1951; Bamforth was a miner). Table 3.1 summarizes the developments in technology, work organization and job characteristics which they studied.

Table 3.1: From single place to composite longwall coal mining

technology	work organization	job characteristics
1: hand and pneumatic picks	single place	composite autonomous miner
2: mechanized coal cutters and belt conveyors	conventional cutting longwall	task fragmentation, mechanization, mass production features
3: electric coal cutters and belt conveyors	composite longwall	composite autonomous, self-regulating teams

Their research contrasted the advantages of the traditional 'composite autonomous mining' method of single place working with the problems of highly mechanized coal getting (Trist *et al.*, 1963). During their study, however, they found that some pits had developed a form of 'shortwall' working, with methods similar to those of traditional single place working.

One case, called 'The Manley Innovation' after the name of the pit, describes how miners developed a teamwork approach to shortwall mining, in response to underground conditions which made it dangerous to work long coal faces. When management tried to restore conventional longwall working, to reduce costs, the men resisted and negotiated an agreement to continue with their approach. This was based on composite, multiskilled, self-selecting groups, each with over 40 members, collectively responsible for the whole coal-getting cycle on any one shift. This contrasted sharply with conventional longwall working, in which each shift was restricted to one stage of the coal-getting cycle, and each miner was limited to one fragmented task, with limited opportunity to develop other underground skills. The Manley groups had no supervisors, but elected their own 'team captains' to liaise with management. They were paid on a common paynote, as all members made equivalent contributions.

This led to two conclusions.

1. Work in groups is more likely to be meaningful, to develop responsibility, and to satisfy human needs than work that is allocated to separately supervised individuals.

2. Work can be organized in this way regardless of the technology. Social system design is not determined by technical system characteristics and demands.

In other words, technical change is consistent with *organizational choice*, or with what John Bessant (1983) calls 'design space'.

STOP AND THINK

Coal mining is hardly 'typical' work. To what extent can the concept of organizational choice be applied to other kinds of work and organizations?

Socio-technical systems thinking remains influential, particularly in The Netherlands and Sweden. Under the influence of Ulbo de Sitter (who is Swedish) and his Dutch colleagues, (de Sitter *et al.*, 1997), a more elaborate socio-technical system design methodology has been developed (Benders *et al.*, 2000):

1. an analysis of the environment to establish the main organizational design criteria, such as market objectives, but also quality of working life and labour relations;

2. an analysis of the product flow pattern;

3. design of the production structure, first approximate and then in detail, based on semi-autonomous production units operated by 'whole task groups';

4. design of the control structure, allocating control tasks to the lowest possible level, which can be an individual workstation or an autonomous group;

5. the creation of 'operational groups' which combine support and line functions (such as maintenance and quality control) and which assist a number of whole task groups.

Contemporary examples of autonomous teamworking are explored in Chapter 13.

Team versus lean: competing paradigms of work design

Until the early 1990s, the team-based plants of the Swedish car manufacturers Saab and Volvo were 'management tourist attractions'. The team-based approach was still popular in the 1990s, one study showing that over half of American manufacturing companies had scrapped their assembly lines in favour of 'cellular manufacturing' (*The Economist*, 1994).

Volvo built a new assembly plant at Uddevalla, on Sweden's West Coast, in the late 1980s. Instead of a traditional paced assembly line, teams of eight to ten car builders handled the final assembly, on a static assembly dock. The plant had a central store from which parts and sub-assemblies were delivered to teams by automatically guided vehicles. Each team managed its own recruitment, training, maintenance, tooling and task planning. Without supervisors, teams elected spokespersons to plan and assign work, lead discussions, deal with problems, and communicate with management.

In 1990 Saab sold its motor car business to General Motors, and in 1991 closed its team-based plant at Malmo. In 1993, Volvo closed its plants at Kalmar and Uddevalla, and concentrated production at its traditional factory at Torslanda, outside Gothenburg. The Uddevalla plant was later reopened to make special vehicles. In January 1999, Volvo Car Corporation was sold to Ford Motor Company. As Swedish car makers were selling and closing their facilities, Japanese companies such as Toyota, Honda and Nissan were opening successful new plants in Europe and America based on traditional assembly line methods.

These developments helped to tarnish the image of team-based manufacturing. What went wrong? One explanation lies in the work of James Womack, Dan Jones and Daniel Roos (1990) who compared the production methods and productivity of car companies around the world. One of their measures was the number of hours of direct labour used to build, paint and finally assemble a car. The main differences in 1989, between the best and the worst companies, on the measure of labour assembly hours, were:

	Best	Worst
Japan	13.2	25.9
North America	18.6	30.7
Europe	22.8	55.7

These comparisons were damning, showing the advantages of Japanese methods, especially the approach developed by Toyota. At Uddevalla, the training time for team members was high, and the assembly time for each car was twice the European average. Womack and colleagues argued that the productivity differences were due to production methods. The Japanese advantage was based on Toyota's **lean production** methods (Oliver *et al.*, 1994).

Lean production
a manufacturing method which combines machine-pacing, work standardization, just-in-time materials flow, continuous improvement, problem-solving teams, and powerful supervision.

Lean production, also known as the Toyota Production System (TPS) combines:

- Machine-paced assembly, with task specialization, placing responsibility on workers to improve the 'one best way' for each task.

- 'Just-in-time' delivery of materials to the point of assembly, replacing the need to hold costly inventories, reducing the need for storage space, and cutting the time that elapses between receipt of order and delivery to the customer.

- Continuous improvement or *kaizen*. When the worker identifies an improvement, this is agreed with supervision and engineering, and the work procedure sheet is revised.

- Aggressive problem-solving using 'quality circles', a team approach to *kaizen*.

- A ruthless approach to reducing equipment adjustment and retooling times, and eliminating defects. In a Japanese plant, one worker can bring the plant to a halt if a problem arises. The plant is not restarted until the problem is fixed.

- Powerful first-line supervisors who monitor and encourage continuous improvement.

Teamwork in Japan, therefore, is not the same as teamwork in most Scandinavian, European or American companies (Buchanan, 2000a). The closely supervised Japanese assembler carries out a short-cycle repetitive task, and is under pressure to improve productivity. This is quite different from the experience of multiskilled autonomous team members, who decide how to allocate tasks, and who solve their own problems, at their own pace. Bram Steijn (2001) distinguishes four work systems in terms of their effects on employees:

	low autonomy	high autonomy
no teamwork	scientific management	professional work
teamwork	lean teams	autonomous teams

Source: Adapted from Steijn (2001)

Scientific management, or Taylorism, creates individual jobs with limited autonomy. However, some individual job roles, in for example the professions of accounting, law and medicine, have high autonomy. Teams in lean manufacturing have low levels of autonomy, in contrast with autonomous teams.

Is it safe to conclude that the Anglo-American-Scandinavian model of team-based manufacturing has been discredited, and that lean production is a more effective paradigm?

The evidence suggests that lean production can also be 'mean' production. The pace and intensity, the demands of *kaizen*, supervisory regulation of methods, and lack of discretion are stressful. A study of a plant run jointly by Toyota and General Motors in California – New United Motors Manufacturing Incorporated (NUMMI) – showed that this industry-standard approach to lean production was an example of 'management by stress'. Every worker motion and action was carefully timed to remove waste effort, reduce inventory, and continuously streamline production (Parker and Slaughter, 1988). Those pressures are often offset with job security and high wages, and Japanese 'transplant' factories are usually located in areas of traditionally high unemployment and low trade union membership. In addition, Japanese methods, based on traditional scientific management methods, appear to be 'natural' and 'safe' to many managers (Hammarstrom and Lansbury, 1991).

Lean services

Lean production does not just apply to manufacturing. In the financial services sector, mortgage and loan administration company HML also uses lean techniques. HML employs 2,000 people, and handles services for 35 different financial institutions, processing new loans, dealing with customer queries, chasing arrears, and recovering debts. A lot of this work is done over the telephone by staff working in call centres. Rapid growth of the business meant that traditional ways of working were no longer effective.

The company's managing director, Brian Brodie, wanted to engage staff in improving processes to improve the quality and efficiency of customer service. He first set up two 'deep dive projects' in areas of the business where improvements were most needed. The projects were run by a transformation team of 13 employees, drawn from different parts of the company, with support from external consultants. One project led to the creation of a new team responsible for producing client reports. The second redesigned the insurance processing part of the business. The lean production process involves:

- specifying what creates value for the customer;
- identifying the processes required to deliver the end product;
- providing exactly what the customer wants, in the right order;
- delivering it where and when it's wanted;
- solving the customer's problem;
- creating value flow and eliminate waste;
- continually reducing the customer's hassle in solving problems;
- seeking perfection by continually removing layers of waste.

Based on Roberts (2008).

Swedish commentators have defended their methods. Christian Berggren, at the Swedish Institute for Work Life Research in Stockholm, has been scathing of the narrow range of measures used in the American research, which focused on final assembly hours, and paid less attention to how the supply chain, from design to customer, was organized (Berggren, 1993b, 1995). Berggren also argues that Volvo's decision to close Kalmar and Uddevalla was reached despite company analyses which showed that these plants were at least as productive as the conventional, but much larger and older, plant at Torslanda. The company had excess capacity in the early 1990s, and logistics and politics made it expedient to close the smaller, experimental plants located some distance from their main facilities.

The aim of lean manufacturing is to build products only when a customer order is received instead of making items to store in warehouses until they are sold. The ability to react instantly to business changes would create the 'real time enterprise', and this is made possible with information technology. There is a growing demand in the motor manufacturing sector for vehicles tailored to individual requirements, known as 'flexible mass customization'. Manufacturers thus aim for what is known as 'build to order', or BTO. With a conventional manufacturing system, the buyer might wait months for delivery. Many companies are now attempting to reduce this to 15 days, or less, using the internet to integrate their supply chains. This improves customer service, and reduces supply chain and manufacturing costs. This approach also requires skills upgrading for assembly workers.

The Toyota Production System

The Toyota Production System (TPS) has become a global model for car manufacturing. TPS has two main principles. First, products are only made once they have been sold. Second, the manufacturing process is continuous and uninterrupted, using a 'just-in-time' flow of parts.

Traditionally, goods are made according to sales forecasts, and items are held in store until orders are placed. In TPS, manufacturing does not start until a customer has placed an order. This cuts the cost of storing goods in warehouses. Conventional production lines have separate stages, with 'buffers' where stocks of part-finished goods build up. In TPS, in-process stocks are seen as waste, or *muda*. Without buffers, a breakdown stops the whole assembly line. Breakdowns are addressed using *kaizen*, a problem-solving method in which employees continuously improve the process. While TPS is efficient, it is unpleasant for workers. The production schedule is tight, the work is repetitive, the pace is fast, the pressure is high, and the physical conditions are tough. Workers are expected to make a number of suggestions a year, linked to pay and promotion, leading to many unworkable suggestions.

In the late 1980s, Toyota had problems recruiting and retaining production staff, particularly in final assembly. The first response was to develop a more technically sophisticated production line, at the Tahara plant. However, the development and maintenance of this line were difficult, it used more space than the previous system, the reduction in staffing was marginal, there were frequent breakdowns, and workers did not like this system either. It was expensive to change the equipment each time a new model was introduced, and the investment could only be recovered with high production volumes, which market conditions did not require. Toyota abandoned this approach in the late 1990s, and developed a 'worker friendly' system with four elements:

1. segmented lines built around production modules or *kumi* (for example, the whole exhaust system) separated by small buffers of approximately five cars, giving each employee a more meaningful task and contribution to the end product;

2. ergonomically improved working conditions, such as mobile component carts or 'dollies', and *raku-raku* ('comfort') seats, based on an employee's prize-winning suggestion, which allow easier access to the car body interiors;

3. automation of selected tasks, using only simple machinery, sometimes developed by assembly workers, to reduce heavy work such as tyre assembly;

4. a modified form of *kaizen*, with a broader emphasis on self-development, and with no link to pay, although good suggestions can still improve promotion chances.

TPS is often compared to Swedish worker-friendly 'autonomous groups', which are seen as less efficient. It is striking to note that Volvo first developed group working in the 1970s at the Kalmar plant where they could not recruit workers to conventional assembly lines.

Based on Benders and Morita (2004).

Building washers and fridges to order

Bill Beer is head of the appliances division of the American manufacturing company Maytag, based in Iowa. Maytag is in the business of mass customization, making washing machines, dishwashers and refrigerators which sell at around three times the price of mainstream products. The company must be able to offer customers a range of choice, while keeping up with demand. Working towards a build to order system, Maytag has developed 'build to replenish'; production of an item only begins when one has been sold. This involves a lean manufacturing system, with close links to the retailers who sell the products:

> Walking around the floor of Maytag's washing-machine factory in Iowa is like a lesson in modern industrial archaeology. There are three levels of sophistication on show. One part of the factory makes a traditional basic model in a traditional manner, with one long assembly-line conveyor belt and lots of offline areas in which faulty machines are taken out of the loop for repair. A second line, making more sophisticated products, has a number of smaller production cells instead of a long line, and only a few offline repair areas. Instead of a conveyor belt, machines come along on little pads that stop them at each station for a while. So far, so traditional.

> But the third production area, making the most advanced Atlantis washing machines, consists of just seven cells. In these, groups of workers make whole boatloads of washers, which come off the line at the rate of one a minute. The work is less mindless than performing single repetitive tasks, and each operator can see what is going on around him. That means he can stop the line if something is wrong, or move along to help a buddy at the next station when needed. Working in such small cells means that no time is wasted by workers looking around for parts. 'Everything is brought to the worker, as if he were a surgeon', says Art Learmonth, one of Mr Beer's manufacturing lieutenants. The cell arrangement is also more flexible than one long line, in that seven different variations of a washing machine can be turned out at the same time.

> A similar reworking of the company's Jackson, Tennessee, dishwasher factory improved quality by 55%, freed up 43,000 square feet and increased capacity by 50%. Such factories can now turn out any model at any hour of the production day, in response to feedback from the department stores that sell Maytag's products.

From The Economist *(2001a, p.81).*

We are faced with a dispute between two socio-technical system paradigms, two different ways of organizing around production. The 'team versus lean' debate is far from resolution, although it appears that some lean approaches depend, at least in part, for their effectiveness on the use of small and relatively autonomous teams. While the arguments in motor car production may be unresolved, similar methods are being applied and developed in other manufacturing and service sector organizations. This debate is likely to run for some time.

The twenty-first-century factory

When work is supported by and organized within a complex hierarchical organization clearly demarcating the individual's place and time of work as well as the specific tasks to be carried out, then there is relatively little need for individual management of interaction. For example, when considering software developers we have studied who, based on relatively stable specifications, must produce parts of a technical system, then the main managerial challenge is to ensure that they are undisturbed and at the same time have sufficient access to negotiate mutual interdependencies amongst each other. This implies that the organization will place the software developers in large open-space or cubicle areas with only very few stationary telephones and a ban on the use of mobile phones. Silent interaction through instant messaging or email ensures access to colleagues without disturbing others working, and meeting rooms provide the needed context for group discussions. In this respect, the software developers' environment constitutes the factory of the twenty-first century manufacturing 'modern' machines consisting of computer code.

From Sørensen (2004, p.15).

RECAP

1. *Explain different uses of the term technology.*

   - Material technology means equipment, machines, apparatus. Social technology refers to organization structures and processes of co-ordination and control.

2. *Explain why predictions about technology and unemployment are often exaggerated.*

   - The effects of technology on employment are indeterminate, because replacement effects (job losses) are offset by compensatory effects (job creation).

3. *Give examples of how new technology is changing the nature of work.*

   - Teleworkers (telecommuters) escape direct management control and have more freedom to organize themselves, but they can become socially isolated.

4. *Describe the potential of Web 2.0 to transform work, and explain why that transformation is currently slow.*

   - Web 2.0 has the potential radically to transform communications and information-sharing in organizations.

   - Some organizations have established Web 2.0 systems to make it easier for top management and staff to communicate with each other and to exchange knowledge.

   - Many organizations are reluctant to experiment because of the uncertainty and risk attached to these new technologies.

5. *Demonstrate how the consequences of technological innovation for skill requirements depend on the organization of work, and not just on technical capabilities.*

   - The impact of technology on work and skills depends on choices concerning equipment and system design, management objectives and the organization of work.

   - New technology has reduced the need for manual labour, creating instead jobs which demand high levels of interpretative and problem-solving skills.

6. *Define the characteristics of mass production, and describe methods to combat them.*

   - Mass production characteristics include mechanical pacing, no choice of method, repetition, task fragmentation and minimum use of skills and mental attention.

   - Psychological reactions to work with mass production characteristics include anxiety and tension, hostility, isolation and despair and social withdrawal, which can be overcome to some extent by job enlargement and job rotation.

7. *Apply the socio-technical system perspective to organizational analysis and design.*

   - Socio-technical system design aims to find the best fit between social and technical subsystems, to achieve joint optimization through minimal critical specification.

8. *Contrast the Scandinavian and Japanese models of team-based work organization.*

   - Scandinavian companies use autonomous self-regulating work groups.

   - Japanese companies use 'off line' quality circles and problem-solving teams as part of a lean manufacturing approach, which has mass production characteristics.

Revision

1. Why is technology such an important aspect of organizational behaviour?

2. Japanese and Scandinavian manufacturing companies use teams as part of their organizational design. What are the differences between the Japanese and Scandinavian approaches?

3. What is nonstandard work and what part does technology play in encouraging these types of jobs and employment?

4. What are the characteristics of Web 2.0 technologies, and in what ways can these new systems affect work and organizational behaviour?

Research assignment

Material technology influences social technology. What does that statement mean? How do different authors approach these issues? Interview two people who have been working in the same organization for a significant period. Ask one of them to explain how technology has changed their personal experience of work, at the level of the job role that they do. Ask the other to explain how technology has changed the organization as a whole. Has Web 2.0 technology started to have an effect, either on individual jobs or on the organization, and how? Relate their comments to your earlier review of the technology literature.

'Job role' refers to how work is done; tasks, procedures, skills, responsibilities eliminated, new ones acquired. Impact at the organization level could concern changes to structures, teams, systems, working practices and external links with suppliers and customers. Any suitable employee will be able to answer questions about job role; a manager will be more knowledgeable about organizational changes.

Springboard

Ashford, S.J., George, E. and Blatt, R., 2007, 'Old assumptions, new work: the opportunities and challenges of research on nonstandard employment', *The Academy of Management Annals*, 1(1): 65–117.

Comprehensive review of nature, triggers, experience and challenges of nonstandard work and the new questions which these developments raise.

Boreham, P., Thompson, P. and Parker, R., 2003, *New Technology @ Work*, Routledge Business, London.

Critical examination of the effects of information and communication technology on work and organizations, arguing that technology has no independent effects but is shaped by economic and political forces.

Malone, T.W., 2004, *The Future of Work: How the New Order of Business Will Shape Your Organization, Your Management Style, and Your Life*, Harvard Business School Press, Boston MA.

Economic trends and new technology make 'command and control' management obsolete, while 'coordinate and cultivate' means organizations with 'loose hierarchies' will provide freedom, flexibility and values that traditionally feature in small organizations.

OB in films

Modern Times (1936, director Charles Chaplin). DVD track 2, 0:01:10 to 0:06:00 (5 minutes). Clip opens with flock of sheep ends when the scene cuts from the assembly line to the manager's office. Despite the date, this sequence is still one of the most powerful movie illustrations of the human being treated as a machine, of the worker caught in the cogwheels of capitalist production.

1. Are employees still subjected to such treatment in organizations today? Give examples.
2. Can you identify instances where new technology has liberated workers from this kind of treatment?
3. Chaplin's movie was set in a factory; do office workers escape from the effects of technology?

DVD track 3: 00:06:07 to 00:12:57 (6 minutes): clip begins in the manager's office as the salesmen bring in a piece of equipment; ends with the manager saying 'It's no good – it isn't practical' (caption). This is a disastrous demonstration of the Billows Feeding machine which is designed to feed employees while they work, thus improving productivity.

4. What does this scene reveal about management objectives in the use of technology?
5. What does this scene tell us about about management values in relation to employees?

 OB in literature

Lucy Kellaway, *Martin Lukes: Who Moved My BlackBerry?*, Viking Books, London, 2005. What does this comic novel reveal about the advantages and dangers of living with and constantly communicating through the fashionable BlackBerry?

CHAPTER EXERCISES

The web we weave

Objectives

1. To encourage breadth of thinking about a topic, in this case Web 2.0 technology.
2. To develop skills in producing a wide-ranging and balanced assessment.
3. To consider the extent to which technology determines or facilitates the outcomes or impacts that it produces.

Briefing

The issue for debate is: What are the individual, organizational, and social benefits and dangers of Web 2.0 technology?

Divide into groups of three. Your group's task is to think of as many relevant points as you can concerning the issue for debate. List these points on a flipchart for presentation. Time allowed: 10 to 15 minutes.

Present your points in plenary. Your points will be awarded 'quality marks' for relevance, importance, plausibility, and creativity. If your argument for a point is particularly impressive or original, you can win more quality marks. The group with the highest quality marks will be declared the winner. Time allowed depends on number of groups: up to 45 minutes.

Consider two of the main benefits and two of the main dangers that you have identified. To what extent are these inevitable consequences of Web 2.0? To what extent do these consequences depend on how individuals and organizations decide to use the technology?

CHAPTER EXERCISES

Old McDonald's Farm

Objective   To explore the integration of social and technical aspects of an organization.

Briefing   Organizations are sociotechnical systems. This means that technology – equipment, machines, processes, materials, layout – has to work alongside people – structures, roles, role relationships, job design. You can't design an organization to suit the technology while ignoring the people, because that would be ineffective. Similarly, designing an organization just to suit the people, while ignoring the requirements of the technology, would be equally disastrous. The concept of sociotechnical system design means that the social system and the technical system have to be designed so that they can work with each other.

Old McDonald's Farm

Let's consider Old McDonald's farm. On this farm, he had no pigs, cows, or chickens. He had only corn, planted in long rows that grew all year round. McDonald had a perfect environment for growing corn. The soil was rich, and the climate was perfect, twelve months every year.

McDonald's rows were so long that at one end of the row, the soil was being prepared for planting, while the next section on that row was being planted, the next section was growing, and the next was being harvested. McDonald had four of these long rows.

McDonald is a progressive and scientific farmer. He is concerned about both productivity and quality. He had an industrial engineer study the amount of effort required to complete the work in each function on each row. He found that two employees were required per section, on each row, fully employed in that function all year round. Therefore, he employed eight workers on each row.

Initially, Mr McDonald had only four rows, A, B, C and D, and a total of 32 people. But he decided to expand, adding two more rows. This added 16 more workers. Now he had 48 employees. Until this time, he had only one supervisor responsible for directing the work of all 32 employees on the initial four rows. Now he decided that there was too much work for one supervisor. He added another.

Mr McDonald now had to decide whether to reorganize the work of his managers and employees. He decided to talk to his two supervisors, Mr Jones and Mr Smith. He found that they had very different ideas.

Mr Jones insisted that the only intelligent way to organize was around the technical knowledge, the functional expertise. He argued that he should take responsibility for all employees working on the first two sections, soil preparation and planting, on all rows. Mr Smith, he acknowledged, had greater expertise in growing and harvesting, so he would take responsibility for all employees in the last two sections. They would each have an equal number of employees to supervise.

Mr Smith had a different idea. He argued that, while some specialized knowledge was needed, it was more important for the employees to take responsibility for the entire growing cycle. This way, they could move down the row, seeing the progress of the corn. He argued for organizing the employees into teams by row.

→

	soil prep	planting	growing	harvesting
row A				
row B				
row C				
row D				
row E				
row F				

Mr McDonald has hired you as a consultant to help him with his organization design. The questions that he wants you to answer are:

1. How will you organize employees on the farm, and how will you assign responsibility to Smith and Jones? You can recommend any assignment that you like, but the numbers of employees that are required will stay the same.

2. What sociotechnical principles support your recommendations? Why is your approach better than the alternatives?

If you were one of Mr McDonald's employees, which approach to organization design would you prefer, and why?

From MARCIC Organizational Behavior, 4E, © 1995 South-Western, a part of Cengage Learning, Inc. Reproduced by permission. www.cengage.com/permissions.

Chapter 4 **Culture**

Key terms

organizational culture

surface manifestations of culture

organizational values

basic assumptions

organizational socialization

pre-arrival stage of socialization

encounter stage of socialization

role modelling

metamorphosis stage of socialization

integration (or unitary) perspective on culture

differentiation perspective on culture

fragmentation (or conflict) perspective on culture

strong culture

weak culture

internal integration

external adaptation

social orientation

power orientation

uncertainty orientation

goal orientation

time orientation

Learning outcomes

When you have read this chapter, you should be able to define those key terms in your own words and you should also be able to:

1. Explain the popularity of organizational culture among managers, consultants and academics.

2. List, describe and give examples of Schein's three levels of culture.

3. Distinguish the stages of organizational socialization.

4. Contrast managerial and social science perspectives on organizational culture.

5. Assess the link between organizational culture and economic performance.

6. Distinguish different national culture dimensions.

Why study organizational culture?

Culture can be thought of as the personality of an organization. It deals with how things are done in a company on a daily basis. It affects how employees perform their work; how they relate to each other; to customers and to their managers. Organizational culture affects not only task issues – how well or badly an organization performs, but also emotional issues – how workers feel about their work and their organization. Organizational culture has been a popular topic since the early 1980s. First adopted by senior executives and management consultants as a quick-fix solution to virtually every organization problem, it was later adopted by academics as an explanatory framework with which to understand behaviour in organizations (Morgan *et al.*, 1983; Meek, 1988; Deal and Kennedy, 2000; Martin, 2001; Alvesson, 2001).

Ann Cunliffe (2008) states that organizational culture is important for four reasons. It shapes the image that the public has of an organization; it influences organizational performance; it provides direction for the company; and it helps attract and retain motivated staff. To these can be added four more. First, increasing globalization has placed organizational culture into sharp focus alongside national culture. Second, there is an enduring assumption that organizational performance depends on employee values being aligned with company strategy. Third, there is the contentious view that management can consciously manipulate culture to achieve organizational (change) objectives (Ogbonna and Harris, 2002). Finally, the increased trend to inter-organizational relationships has stimulated an interest in developing a culture of collaboration (see Chapter 17). An organization's culture can determine whether employees collaborate or compete with others.

STOP AND THINK   Think of a company whose products or services you use or which is familiar to you. How does this company differentiate itself from others in the same industry? What words would you use to describe the distinguishing features of this organization?

Rise of organizational culture

Organizational culture the shared values, beliefs and norms which influence the way employees think, feel and act towards others inside and outside the organization.

Organizational culture remains a controversial concept. Some writers argue that just as one can talk about French culture, Arab culture or Asian culture, so too it is possible to discuss the organizational culture of the British Civil Service, McDonald's, Microsoft or of Disney. Others reject this notion. In general, however, it is recognized that organizations have 'something' (a personality, philosophy, ideology or climate) which goes beyond economic rationality, and which gives each of them a unique identity. One writer referred to it as, 'The way we do things around here' (Deal and Kennedy, 1982); while another saw it as 'the collective programming of the mind' (Hofstede, 2001).

The current debates about culture are traceable to the early 1980s when four books catapulted the concept to the forefront of management attention. William Ouchi's (1981) *Theory Z*; Richard Pascale and Anthony Athos' (1982), *The Art of Japanese Management*; *In Search of Excellence*, written by Tom Peters and Robert Waterman (1982); and Terrence Deal and Allan Kennedy's (1982) *Corporate Cultures*. These publications suggested that a strong culture was a powerful lever for guiding workforce behaviour. They conceived of a company's culture as consisting of values, beliefs, heroes and symbols that possessed meaning for all employees. In addition to these books, other factors also stimulated an interest. These included Japan's industrial success during the 1970s and 1980s; the view that intangible (soft) factors such as values and beliefs impacted on financial (hard) ones: the conviction that managers could change cultures to achieve greater organizational effectiveness; and that culture might weaken union power.

Originally introduced to managers by consultants, it was not long before academics started to take an interest in it as well. Some business school professors attempted to refine the concept, seeking to operationalize it for research purposes. Edgar Schein (1984) was amongst the first of these academics. Research attention turned to the meanings and beliefs that employees assigned to organizational behaviour, and how their assigned meanings influenced the ways in which they behaved themselves in companies (Schultz, 1995).

Culture: surface manifestations, values and basic assumptions

Surface manifestation of culture culture's most accessible forms which are visible and audible behaviour patterns and objects.

Edgar Schein's (2004) model of culture is widely accepted and considers organizational culture in terms of three levels, each distinguished by its visibility to, and accessibility by individuals (Figure 4.1). Schein's first level is the surface manifestation of culture, also called 'observable culture'. It refers to the visible things that a culture produces. It includes both physical objects and also behaviour patterns that can be seen, heard or felt – they all 'send a message' to an organization's employees, suppliers and customers.

The surface level of culture is the most visible. Anyone coming into contact with it can observe it. Its constituent elements are defined below and illustrated in Table 4.1:

Edgar Henry Schein
(b.1928)

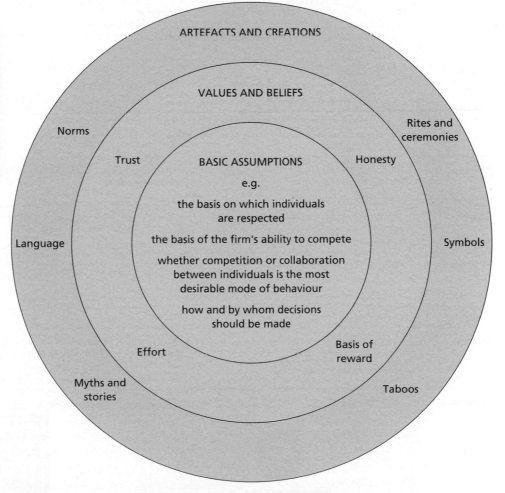

Figure 4.1: Schein's three levels of culture
Source: From Rollinson (2008, p.592).

Table 4.1: Examples of surface manifestations of culture at Motorola and Rolls Royce

Manifestation	Examples	
	Motorola	*Rolls Royce*
Artefacts	Name badges, stationery, T-shirts, promotional items, celebratory publications	Name badges. Standard workwear, issued to all staff levels in the organization. Each polo shirt is customized with the wearer's name
Ceremonials	Annual service dances, annual total customer satisfaction competition	Fun days, sporting events, commemorative shows
Courses	Basic health and safety course	Induction courses to orientate new starts to RR principles
Heroes	Paul Galvin, Joseph Galvin – founders	Henry Rolls, Charles Royce – founders
Jokes	None	'The Right Way, The Wrong Way and the Rolls-Royce Way' – humorous, self-depreciation about the evolution of certain ways of going about things, but also a reminder of the importance of individuality and identity.
Language	Employees known as 'Motorolans'. Role-naming conventions and communications remind everyone of their responsibilities as Motorolans.	Divisional/departmental naming – job roles defined within particular naming structures
Legends	The first walkie-talkies. First words communicated from the moon via Motorola technology	Commemorative window in tribute to the Rolls-Royce Spitfire's contribution to World War II
Mottoes	Total Customer Satisfaction, Six Sigma Quality, Intelligence Everywhere, Engineering Intelligence with Style	Centre of Excellence Trusted to Deliver Excellence
Norms	Ethics, Respect, Innovation	Code of Business Conduct – Quality, Excellence, Ethics, Respect
Physical layout	Semi-open plan – cubed group set up. Junior managers have separate offices beside staff; senior managers have corporate offices distanced from most employees	Open plan layouts – applies to both offices and work cells where possible
Rites	Badges – initially the identity badge, but then the service badge, given at 5 year intervals, also has a great deal of kudos	Length of Service Acknowledgement – rite of passage
Sagas	Motorola's timelined history used repeatedly to demonstrate its influence on the world and world events	The 1970s bankruptcy saga
Slogans	*Hello Moto* – modern re-invention of how the Motorola name came into being – a fusion of 'Motor' (representing a car) plus 'Hola' representing Hello in Spanish, to emphasize communications on the move.	None
Stories	About a particular vice-president who fell asleep at a very important customer meeting. A cautionary tale about what not to do!	Impact of a particular shop floor visit and how the feedback to quality managers changed thinking and processes. The tale is cautionary about how misunderstandings can generate unnecessary panics
Symbols	Motorola 'M' brand – known as the 'emsignia'	The Rolls-Royce brand – RR

Sources: Personal communication from managers who have worked for these companies. Motorola logo and Rolls Royce logo used with permission.

Artefacts are material objects created by human hands to facilitate culturally expressive activities. They include tools, furniture, appliances and clothing.

Ceremonials are formally planned, elaborate, dramatic sets of activities of cultural expression, e.g., opening events, prize-givings, graduations, religious services.

Courses and workshops are used to instruct, induct, orient and train new members, and to recognize the contributions of existing ones.

Heroes are characters, living or dead, who personify the values and beliefs; who are referred to in company stories, legends, sagas, myths and jokes; and who represent role models that current employees should emulate.

Jokes are humorous stories intended to cause amusement but whose underlying themes may carry a message for the behaviour or values expected of organizational members.

Language is the particular form or manner in which members use vocal sounds and written signs to convey meaning to each other. It includes both specialist technical vocabulary related to the business (jargon), as well as general naming choices.

Legends are handed-down narratives about wonderful events based on history, but embellished with fictional details. These fascinate employees and invite them to admire or deplore certain activities.

Mottoes are maxims adopted as rules of conduct. Unlike slogans, mottoes are rarely, if ever, changed.

Norms are expected modes of behaviour that are accepted as the company's way of doing things, thereby providing guidance for employee behaviour.

Physical layout concerns things that surround people, providing them with immediate sensory stimuli, as they carry out culturally expressive activities.

Rites are relatively elaborate, dramatic sets of activities that consolidate various forms of cultural expression into one event. They are formally planned, though not necessarily always officially sanctioned.

Sagas are historical narratives describing the unique accomplishments of a group and its leaders. They usually describe a series of events that are said to have unfolded over time and which constitute an important part of an organization's history.

Slogans are short, catchy phrases that are regularly changed. They are used for both customer advertising and also to motivate employees.

Stories are narratives describing how individuals acted and the decisions they made that affected the company's future. Stories can include a mixture of both truth and fiction.

Symbols refer to any act, event, object, quality or relation that serves as a vehicle for conveying meaning.

STOP AND THINK

Drawing upon organizations that you have had direct experience of, provide one example of *each* of the 15 surface manifestations of culture.

Organizational values the accumulated beliefs held about how work should be done and situations dealt with, that guide employee behaviour.

Schein's second level of culture concerns organizational values. These represent the accumulated beliefs held about how work should be done and situations dealt with. They are often unspoken, but guide employees' behaviours. They can be encapsulated in brief statements such as those below:

- Take risks
- Be honest
- Work hard

- Be creative
- Be cautious
- Respect authority
- Be entrepreneurial
- Maintain high standards
- Co-ordinate with others

Values are said to provide a common direction for all employees, and to guide their behaviour. 'People way down the line know what they are supposed to do in most situations because the handful of guiding values is crystal clear' (Peters and Waterman, 1982, p.76). Motorola has two 'key beliefs' – 'uncompromising integrity' and 'constant respect for people'. The Central Intelligence Agency's (CIA) core values, shown on its website, state that 'quiet patriotism is our hallmark'; 'we pride ourselves on our extraordinary responsiveness to the needs of our customers'; and their staff 'embrace personal accountability'; put 'country first and agency before self', and; they learn from their mistakes because they 'reflect on their performance'. Additionally, they 'seek and speak the truth', but they add, only 'to our colleagues and our customers'. You can go to the website of any large, private, public or voluntary organization – Microsoft, the British National Health Service, Amnesty International – and locate their values in their vision or mission statement.

Toyota values

Toyota has 580 different companies around the world; 51 factories outside Japan; and sells cars in over 170 countries. To hold its operations together, make them part of a single entity, and to encourage its employees to be both self-motivating and self-directing, the company uses its strong organization culture called 'The Toyota Way' which is based on five distinct values:

Kaizen: The process of continuous improvement, treated more as a frame of mind than a business process. Employees come to work seeking to improve on their previous day's performance.

Genchi genbutsu: Going to the source of a problem, to find the facts (rather than relying on hearsay), to build consensus upon well-supported arguments.

Challenge: Employees are encouraged to see problems as opportunities to allow them to improve their performance further.

Teamwork: Putting the company's interests above the individual's, and sharing knowledge with others within the team, a process of on-the-job training.

Respect: For other people; their skills; and their special knowledge deriving from company position. The expression of differences of opinion are encouraged, but in respectful ways.

Once these are inculcated into employees, they guide their decision-making during the working day. It obviates their need to ask their manager what to do. Everyone knows which solution to implement, thereby speeding up decision-making. Toyota's Japanese employees, who have been immersed in its culture for a long time, reach a point of 'emotional fortitude' where their behaviour is entirely consistent with the organization's culture and beliefs. Toyota employees in the West, where individual interest predominates over group interest, find it hard to reach this mental state, and this may give their Japanese colleagues an intrinsic, competitive advantage.

Based on Hindle (2006a, p.13) and Takeuchi et al. (2008).

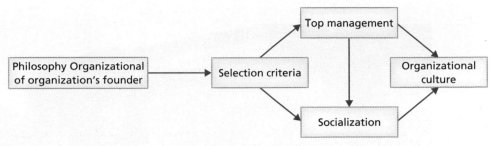

Figure 4.2: Where does organizational culture come from?

Sources of values

Values distinguish one organization from another, but where do they come from? Some authors see them as representing organizational solutions to problems experienced in the past. Another source of values are the views of the original founder, as modified by the company's current senior management (Schein, 1983). Originally, a single person (founder) has an idea for a new business, and brings in other key people to create a core group who share a common vision with the founder. This group creates an organization, brings in others, and begins to build a common history. Stephen Robbins described senior management as an organization's 'culture carriers'. Thus 'organizational' values therefore are really always the values of the current company elite (senior managers). This is similar to the way that 'organizational goals' actually represent the preferred aims of the chief executive and his management team.

Altering an organization's structure and its processes can also change its culture, by changing its values. Therefore included among the surface manifestations of culture are its current staff appraisals or performance systems; reward and incentive schemes; disciplinary procedures and promotion rules. For example, a structural change such as creating self-managing teams changes culture. Different structures give rise to different cultures. Change one and you change the other. A mechanistic structure with a tall hierarchy, centralization, standardization, little autonomy, encourages a culture which encourages caution, obeying authority, respecting tradition, predictability and stability. In contrast, an organic structure with a flat hierarchy, decentralization and reliance on mutual adjustment of staff, gives them freedom to choose and control their own activities, and creates a culture of creativity, risk taking and innovation.

Home viewing

Watch the opening 30 minutes of the film *The Firm* (1993, director Sidney Pollock) in which Harvard law graduate Mitch McDeere (played by Tom Cruise) joins a small Memphis law firm. McDeere first develops expectations about the organization during his job interview, and then experiences its reality. Which stages of the organizational socialization are being depicted here? What does he learn? Where does he learn it? How does he learn it? Have you experienced anything similar in your own work life?

These men *are* innocent

Richard Reed, Jon Wright and Adam Balon are the founders of the Innocent Drinks company. They are three Cambridge University graduates who, in 1999, resigned their day jobs, to start their own business that aimed to provide an easy way for busy people to enhance their daily vitamin intake. The business is based on values of friendship; fun, product contents, packaging and communication. The company guarantees 'that anything Innocent (produces) will always taste good and will do you good. We promise we'll never use concentrates,

→

Source: Innocent Ltd.

Innocent founders

preservatives, stabilisers or any weird stuff in our drinks.' Its packaging is either recyclable or biodegradable. In 2007, Innocent decided to trial their children's smoothies in McDonald's restaurants which proved controversial. Richard Reed stated that, 'Some people would see McDonald's at the opposite end of the spectrum. But we will never change our principles or the way we do business for anyone – McDonald's or anyone else.' In 2009, Innocent sold Coca-Cola a £30 million minority stake in itself. It is yet to be seen whether Innocent's founders' values will influence McDonald's or Coca-Cola, or whether Innocent will itself be McDonaldized and Coca-Colaized.

Based on O'Hanlon (2007); Roberts (2009); Tryhorn and Sweney (2009).

In a sense therefore, organizational values are always backward looking, despite being developed to contribute to the future development of the company. For an organizational culture to form, a fairly stable collection of people need to have shared a significant history, involving problems, which allowed a social learning process to take place. Organizations that have such histories possess cultures that permeate most of their functions (Schein, 2004). Company values come in lists. They are to be found printed in company reports, framed on company walls, and published on organizational websites.

STOP AND THINK Why do you think that companies prefer to talk about 'organizational and company values' and 'organizational or company goals' rather than senior management's or chief executive officer's values and goals?

Basic assumptions invisible, preconscious, 'taken-for-granted' understandings held by individuals within an organization concerning human behaviour, the nature of reality and its relationship to its environment.

Finally, **basic assumptions** relate to the nature of reality and the organization's relationship to its environment. They are invisible, preconscious and 'taken-for-granted'. As persons act in accordance with their values and beliefs, these become embedded as organizational basic assumptions, and direct their actions. These too can be summarized in brief statements such as:

- Quality
- Stability
- Morality
- Economy
- Excellence
- Profitability
- Predictability
- Responsibility
- Innovativeness

Deloitte's *Little Blue Book of Strategy*

In 2007, Deloitte's *Little Blue Book of Strategy* (sub-titled, *An Abridged Guide to All the Important Stuff*) was sent to thousands of its staff in the United States, and is an example of an artefact (surface cultural manifestation). It came with the instruction to be carried around and referred to often. It is only the latest in a series of corporate guides. Three years earlier, JP Morgan Chase had produced a booklet containing 123 principles for its staff to follow each day; and a year before that, Cadbury Schweppes' yellow book provided its managers with 144 rules to 'live and breathe' by. Deloitte's publication tells its staff to 'deliver loads of value, to every client, every time'. In contrast to its predecessors, it contains only four points of strategy and four corporate values. The 'important stuff' about strategy that Deloitte employees need to know about includes 'Starry starry heights' (the message is 'shoot for the moon') and clients and 'talent' matter equally. With regard to the values, staff must 'obsess over' these. One of these is diversity ('We strive to make our world comfortable for people of all stripes, thinking styles and hairdos – even when they exceed our comfort level'). There is also the an assertion that Deloitte welcomes diversity of thought. To ensure that staff are 'living the strategy', the second last page of book containing a 10 item checklist ('I reach high', 'I make things happen', 'I fuss over the grey areas'). There is a page entitled, *Our Pledge*. It says: 'The promise of our brand. To that we pledge allegiance'. Deloitte staff here are being invited to make a pledge of allegiance, not to a brand, but to a promise of a brand. Kellaway makes a comparison with Chairman Mao's *Little Red Book* distributed to 900 million Chinese in the 1960s. That became a tool for brainwashing and torture. She says that Deloitte's book is also a tool for brainwashing and torture, but adds that the brainwashing is unlikely to succeed, and it is business, logic, taste and style that is tortured. Nevertheless, this publication provides a small glimpse into this company's culture.

Based on Kellaway (2007).

Organizational socialization

Organizational socialization
the process through which an employee's pattern of behaviour, values, attitudes and motives is influenced to conform to that of the organization's.

The ultimate strength of a company's culture depends on the homogeneity of group membership, and the length and intensity of their shared experiences in a group. One learns about a company's culture through the process of **organizational socialization**. This is the process through which an employee's pattern of behaviour, values, attitudes and motives is influenced to conform to that of the organization's. It includes the careful selection of new company members, their instruction in appropriate ways of thinking and behaving; and the reinforcement of desired behaviours by senior managers.

The concept of socialization can be considered at the level of the individual and the group. Socialization is important because, as John van Maanen and Edgar Schein (1979) argue, new organization recruits have to be taught to see the organizational world as their more experienced colleagues do, if the tradition of the organization is to survive. Socialization involved newcomers absorbing the values and behaviours required to survive and prosper in an organization. It reduces variability of behaviour by imbuing employees

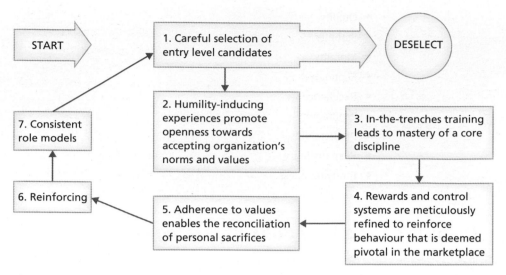

Figure 4.3: Seven steps of organizational socialization

Source: From Pascale (1985). Copyright © 1985, by The Regents of the University of California. Reprinted from the *California Management Review*, Vol. 27, No. 2. By permission of The Regents.

Pre-arrival stage of socialization the period of learning in the process that occurs before an applicant joins an organization.

with a sense of what is expected of them, and how they should do things. By providing an internal sense of how they should behave, plus a shared frame of reference, socialization standardizes employee behaviour, making it predictable for the benefit of senior management. Richard Pascale (1985) distinguished seven key steps or elements in the process of organizational socialization process that are shown in Figure 4.3:

Selection: Trained recruiters carefully select entry-level candidates seeking traits using standardized selection methods. The entrants are not 'oversold' on a particular position, because the companies rely on applicants 'deselecting', if they find that the organization does not fit in with their personal styles and values. It is also referred to as the **pre-arrival stage of socialization**.

Encounter stage of socialization the period of learning in the process during which the new recruit learns about organizational expectations.

Humility-inducing experiences: Once working, the organization encourages new entrants to question their past behaviour, beliefs and values. It does this by assigning them more work than they can possibly cope with, or giving them menial tasks to perform. The aim is to reduce their self-complacency, increase their self-examination, and prepare them to accept the organization's own norms and values. This is also the first step in the **encounter stage of socialization**.

Interviewing for Amazon.com

My first meeting with the recruiter was a revelation. She was a polite and talkative lady with thick glasses and an overbite . . . She had called me on the phone right away, she told me, because of my background.

'My background?'

'Your degree.'

'Oh, I'm sorry about that –,' I began, preparing to launch into my standard corporate apology for not having a background in human resources or political science and why I was still employable, please. Give me a chance, I won't let you down.

'I think you are exactly what we are looking for.'

That stopped me dead. No one had ever said that. I thought for a moment about what this job was: customer service. Selling books over the Internet. Unless there was a hidden element of art criticism to the job, I couldn't see how aesthetics applied.

'Oh', I said . . .

'Amazon is about broadening horizons, interfacing with technology, and taking a can-do approach to corporate solutions.'

'I like technology . . . I like horizons.' Jesus, I was giving a terrible interview. I was normally very good at interviews, better at them than at actually doing work, but I still couldn't believe that this woman actually thought I was qualified to do something . . .

Amazon is always telling us to find them freaks. 'They want the freaks, you know, people who might not fit in elsewhere. So then I saw your résumé . . . ah . . .' She lost track of her tact for a moment. 'Ah . . . I thought you would really find a home here. People need a home to work in, you know?'

'Well, I agree with that.'

She nodded vigorously, I nodded as well . . . We both sat there, nodding at each other, like a couple of windup toys, working through our hiring script. I was nodding to say: *Yes, please give me a job.* Her nodding said: *Yes, you are a freak.* We nodded all the way to signing me up for an informational meeting about the company and the job.

A. BACALL

"I *was* motivated by greed, but I blame that on the workplace culture."

Source: www.cartoonstock.com

In-the-trenches training: The training received by recruits focuses on their achieving mastery of the core disciplines of the company's business. These extensive and carefully reinforced job experiences seek to imbue them into the organization's way of doing things.

Rewards and control systems: New members' performances are carefully assessed and rewarded. The organization uses systems that are comprehensive and consistent, and which link to competitive success and its values.

Adherence to values: The employees identify with the common organizational values allowing them to reconcile the personal sacrifices that they have made in order to be a member of the organization. This creates the foundation of trust between them and their organization, and often involves linking company goals with significant higher level goals – not making profits from selling PCs but 'connecting humanity'!

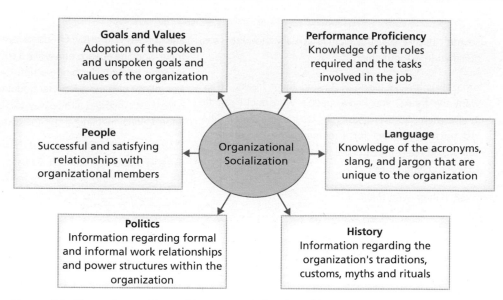

Figure 4.4: Dimensions addressed in most socialization efforts

Source: From Chao *et al*. (1994) in Colquitt *et al*. (2009, p.558). Copyright © 1994 by the American Psychological Association. Reproduced with permission. The official citation that should be used in referencing this material is Chao, G.T., O'Leary-Kelly, A.M., Wolf, S., Klein, H.J. & Gardner, P.D. (1994). Organizational socialization: Its content and consequences. *Journal of Applied Psychology*, 79, 730–743. di:10.1037/0021-9010.79.5.730

Reinforcing folklore: New entrants are exposed to the organizational stories, myths and symbols as they interact with their managers and colleagues within the workplace. These provide them with a code of conduct that clarifies, 'how we do things around here' and, by implication, how they should do it as well.

Consistent role models: Entrants also learn through **role modelling**. They are shown personnel who are judged by the company to be 'winners', that is, who possess the traits, demonstrate the behaviours and achieve the results that are recognized and valued by the firm (see Chapter 5, Learning). The learner observes established members, acquiring a mental picture of the act and its consequences (rewards and punishments), and then copies them, acting out the acquired image. This marks the **metamorphosis stage of socialization** in which the new employee adjusts to their organization's values, attitudes, motives, norms and required behaviours.

Beyond the induction period which, in some large companies may last up to a year, performance based appraisal systems and formal training programmes are also instituted by companies to visibly signal which goals new joiners should be striving for and how. Finally, senior management's behaviour, in promoting, censoring and dismissing employees, also sends information to employees about company values, expectations about norms, risk-taking, acceptability of delegation, appropriate dress, topics of discussion, and so on (see Figure 4.4).

Role modelling a form of socialization in which an individual learns by example, copying the behaviour of established organization members.

Metamorphosis stage of socialization the period in which the new employee adjusts to their organization's values, attitudes, motives, norms and required behaviours.

Inculcating Disney values into new employees

Disney begins tugging on the heartstrings of employees even before they are hired. When they walk into Disney's capacious 'casting centre', they are in Wonderland. After ascending a gentle sloping hallway whose walls are decorated with whimsical murals, they enter a vast anteroom where the centrepiece is the original model of Snow White's castle. Some 50,000 aspiring employees funnel through the Lake Buena Vista casting centre every year seeking to work in the 'Happiest Place in the World'. Disney World's 40 interviewers – all of whom started as front line workers – are most interested in personality. 'We can train for skills. We want people who are enthusiastic, who have pride in their work, who can take charge of a situation without supervision,' says the director of casting. Disney's 40 hour initial training course, *Traditions*, is attended by all new hires. It emphasizes emotions rather than policies or procedures. Guided by two unfailingly upbeat cast members, the neatly dressed neophytes sit at round tables in a small classroom discussing their earliest memories of Disney, their visions of great service, and their understanding of teamwork. Participants also learn to 'speak Disney' – staff are 'cast members'; customers are 'guests'; rides are 'attractions'; uniforms are 'costumes' and accidents are 'incidents'. The cast members receive an appearance guide which specifies, in excruciating detail, the company's requirements on grooming (length and style of hair); colour and quantity of cosmetic; hues and textures of hosiery; and the use of friendly smiles and courteous phrases. The company's top–down management style is consistent with that of its founder, who is said to have 'ruled by fear'. Supervisors hide in observation posts catching incorrectly dressed staff or those returning late from breaks. Interestingly, this close monitoring of employees by management impacts on the group cohesion of these front line workers. They come to view their supervisors as sneaks and tricksters and, in response, form cohesive units whose members look out for one another when they work (and shirk).

Based on Henkoff (1994);
Dyck and Neubert (2009, p.326).

Perspectives on culture contrasted

The debate about organizational culture takes place between two camps. The managerial writers and consultants who believe that there is a relationship between a strong culture and organizational performance. They hold that, 'A well-developed and business-specific culture in which management and staff are thoroughly socialized . . . can underpin stronger organizational commitment, higher morale, more efficient performance, and generally higher productivity' (Furnham and Gunter, 1993, p.232). Ranged against them are, mainly academic social scientists, who believe that organizational culture is a term that is overused, overinclusive, but under-defined. The description of organizational culture on the preceding pages has taken a managerial perspective. Its distinguishing feature is that it is both normative and prescriptive. The managerial–social science debate about organizational culture can be considered under four headings:

Managerial		Social science
1. Culture *has*	v.	Culture *is*
2. Integration	v.	Differentiation
		Fragmentation
3. Culture managed	v.	Culture tolerated
4. Symbolic leadership	v.	Management control

1. Culture 'has' versus culture 'is'

The *has* view holds that every organization possesses a culture, just as it has a strategy, structure, technology and employees. It is also called a *functionalist perspective*. It sees organizational culture constituting an objective reality of artefacts, values and meanings that academics can quantify and measure. The culture is a feature of the organization, 'given' to new-joiners who have not participated in its formation. From this perspective, culture is acquired by employees; is a variable, and hence represents a lever for change which senior management can use (Smircich, 1983). The writers most associated with this view are the management academic and consultants mentioned earlier in the chapter (Peters and Waterman, 1982; Schein, 2004; Deal and Kennedy, 1982; Ouchi, 1981; Pascale and Athos, 1982).

The alternative view sees organizational culture as something that the organization *is*. From this standpoint, culture constitutes a subjective reality of rites and rituals and meanings. It is also known as the *symbolic, social constructionist* or *shared cognitions perspective*. It thus rejects the notion that culture possesses any objective, independent existence that imposes itself on employees. Instead, it holds that culture cannot be easily quantified or measured, and that academics must study it the way that anthropologists study tribes. Culture is produced and reproduced continuously through the routine interactions between organization members. Hence organizational culture exists only in, and through, their social (inter) actions. This approach seeks to understand social relations within organizations, and rejects the notion that culture many be manipulated by senior management. Among researchers who take this position are Ackroyd and Cowley, 1990; Anthony, 1990; Gagliardi, 1986; Harris and Ogbonna, 1999; Knights and Willmott, 1987; Krefting and Frost, 1985; Legge, 1994; Martin, 1985, 1992; Meyerson and Martin, 1987; Ogbonna, 1993; Ray, 1986; Weick, 1979; and Willmott, 1993.

HMRC's organizational culture

In 2005, David Varney became the chairman of the British Civil Service's newly formed HMRC – Her Majesty's Revenue and Customs. It was the result of a merger of the Inland Revenue department, responsible for the collection of taxes, and the Customs and Excise department, charged with collections of duties. Within the HMRC, senior managers' responsibilities have deliberately not overlapped with the structures of the two previous departments, intentionally to enable a new organizational culture to develop. 'We didn't want an organization that was split along lines of customers, operations, policies or infrastructure. We wanted an organization where responsibility was shared.' The difficulty of bringing together two departments is exacerbated by their different traditions and cultures. Customs had greater powers of investigation and entry, some of which date back to the days of chasing brandy smugglers. Varney's aim is to have an 'HMRC way of doing things'. He hoped that both employees and customers would quickly associate themselves with the new merged entity.

Based on Financial Times *(2005, p.13)*;
The Economist *(2006d, pp.66–71)*.

2. Integration versus differentiation/fragmentation

Integration (or unitary) perspective on culture regards it as monolithic, characterized by consistency, organization-wide consensus, and clarity.

Differentiation perspective on culture regards it as consisting of subcultures, each with its own characteristics, which differ from those of its neighbours.

Joanne Martin (1992) distinguished three perspectives on culture which she labelled integration differentiation and fragmentation. These have formed the basis of research and writing on this topic. There is divergence between the integration (unitary) and differentiation perspectives. The managerial integration (or unitary) perspective on culture holds that an organization possesses a single, unified culture, consisting of shared values to which most employees subscribe. These integrating features lead to improved organization effectiveness through greater employee commitment and employee control, as measured by productivity and profitability. It includes the controversial notion of a 'strong' culture, which is defined by three characteristics: the existence of a clear set of values, norms and beliefs; the sharing of these by the majority of members; and the guidance of employees' behaviour.

In contrast, the social science emphasizes two perspectives – differentiation and fragmentation. The differentiation perspective on culture regards a single organization as consisting of many groups, each with their own subcultures. Each of these has its own characteristics, which differ from those of its neighbours. It therefore sees organizational culture as differentiated or as a plurality rather than a unified whole. Within an organization, there are diverse interest groups who have their own objectives (e.g. management v. labour; staff v. line; marketing v. production). Thus, the differentiation perspective sees 'cultural pluralism' as a fundamental aspect of all organizations; seeks to understand the complexity and the interaction between frequently conflicting subcultures; and therefore stands in direct contrast to the managerial unitary or integrationist perspective.

Table 4.2: Martin's contrasting perspectives on organizational culture

Features	Cultural perspective		
	Integration	Differentiation	Fragmentation
Orientation to consensus	Organization wide consensus	Sub-cultural consensus	No consensus – multiplicity of views
Relations between different cultural elements	Consistent	Inconsistent	Complex
Orientation to ambiguity	Exclude it	Channel it outside subculture	Focus upon it

From Martin (1992, p.13).

Joanne Martin
(b.1940)

Martin Parker (2000) is one of several writers who, on the basis of a review of popular management works, concluded that rather than having a single, strong culture, organizations possess multiple (sub)cultures. These reflect the main ways in which employees distinguish themselves within companies – by their occupation or profession; by the function they perform; by their geographical location in the firm; and by their age (e.g. senior members of the engineering department in the research building). These subcultures overlap and contradict each other. Thus the neat typologies of cultural types which are presented later in this chapter, may understate the complexities of organizational life. Thus subcultures act to obstruct management attempts to develop a unified culture which might be used to control staff.

The other social science perspective – fragmentation, sees organizations as collections of opposed groupings (e.g. management v. labour; staff v. line; production department v. marketing department) which are rarely reconciled. The fragmentation (or conflict) perspective on culture assumes the absence of consensus, the inevitability of conflict; and focuses on the variety of interests and opinions between different groups; and upon power in organizations. It is critical of managers and management consultants who underplay the differences that exist between individuals, groups and departments within a company. It sees conflict rather than consensus as the norm within organizations; and it both challenges the notion of the existence of a single organizational culture itself, and the value of the concept itself (Becker, 1982).

Fragmentation (or conflict) perspective on culture regards it as consisting of an incompletely shared set of elements that are loosely structured and constantly changing.

3. Culture managed versus culture tolerated

Since the managerialist perspective sees culture as something that an organization *has*, it further assumes that it is capable of being created and modified by corporate leaders. This has sparked three debates. First, concerning how managers can change their company's culture from 'weak' to 'strong'. Second, how culture can help a company innovate and adjust rapidly to environmental changes. Third, the part played by leaders' visions and styles of management in managing their cultures. This view assumes that senior company executives can and should exercise cultural leadership. Cultural leadership is seen as having a maintenance and an *innovation* dimension (Trice and Beyer, 1984, 1993). The contrasting, social science view holds that culture is what an organization *is*, and hence, it is incapable of being managed. Instead, it is to be tolerated and its effects on its members studied. Some 'culture managed' writers, such as Fred Luthans (1995) argue that strong cultures can be created by management's use of rewards and punishments. In contrast, the 'culture tolerated' academics argues that employees' deeply held values and beliefs cannot be modified in the short term using such external stimuli.

Creating a culture of collaboration

Taking a managerial approach which holds that culture can be manipulated, Lynda Gratton made the following recommendations as to what companies should do if they wanted to encourage a culture of collaboration among their staff:

1. Leaders model desired behaviour – employees were unlikely to behave collaboratively and to value collaboration if they saw senior executives competing with each other.

2. Careful selection – new employees should be chosen on the basis of their attitudes to sharing knowledge and collaborating with others, and inducted into the value of collaboration.

3. Reward programmes – should ensure that collaboration is rewarded. Unilever's performance management system focuses rewards on team-based activities rather than on individual achievements.

4. Increase informal collaboration – formal collaboration increased if informal collaboration occurred through shared social events, social enterprise activities and communities of practice. BT is fostering such informal networks. It provides funding and coaching to support self-selecting groups such as women's networks.

Based on Gratton (2007);
Gratton and Erikson (2007); Murray (2007).

4. Symbolic leadership versus management control

Symbolic leadership (or the management of organizational culture) is one way of encouraging employees to feel that they are working for something worthwhile, so that they will work harder and be more productive. Burman and Evans (2008) stress that it is only leaders, and not managers, who can impact culture in this way. This view treats managers as heroes, who symbolize the organization both internally to their employees, and externally to customers, governments and others (Smircich and Morgan, 1982). These leaders said Carol Ray, 'possess direct ties to the values and goals of the dominant elites in order to activate the emotion and sentiment which might lead to devotion, loyalty and commitment to the company' (Ray, 1986, p.294). The managerialist view holds that employees can be helped to internalize organizational values.

In contrast, the social science perspective argues that symbolic leadership represents an attempt to internalize managerial control. People enter organizations with different motivations, experiences and values. These natural individual differences tend to direct their behaviours in numerous, often divergent directions. To accomplish its goal and present itself as a unified entity to outsiders, organizations and their managers have to find ways of controlling and reducing the variability of employee behaviour. One such way is through culture. Carol Ray (1986) distinguished different types of management control through history (Figure 4.5).

Bureaucratic control (F.W. Taylor)
manipulation of rewards → loyalty → increased productivity

Humanistic control (Elton Mayo)
'satisfying' task or work group → loyalty → increased productivity

---

Culture (symbolic) control (Deal and Kennedy, Schein)
manipulation of culture → love firm and its goals → increased productivity including myth and ritual

---

Figure 4.5: Contrasting forms of organizational control
Source: From Carol Axel Ray (1986, p.294).

She noted the move away from *bureaucratic control* towards *humanistic control*. The former focuses on external, overt control of employees through rules, procedures, close supervision, appraisal and reward. Frederick Taylor, Henry Ford, Max Weber and Henri Fayol all recommended this rationalist approach to direct the behaviour of employees towards organizational goals. It was expensive in terms of supervisory manpower required, frequently caused resentment, and elicited grudging compliance from the workers. In contrast, humanistic control sought to satisfy employees needs' by providing a satisfying work task, or a pleasant working group life to promote internal control. Promoted by Mayo (1933, 1945), the hope was that individuals would willingly meet organization goals by meetings their individual ones (van Maanen and Barley, 1984).

Carol Ray suggested that mangers saw organizational culture as an effective control tool. It sought to affect what employees thought, believed, felt and valued. She said that 'control by corporate culture views people as emotional, symbol-loving and needing to belong to a superior entity or collectivity' (Ray, 1986, p.295). This form of control had previously only been attempted by religious organizations. A manager at a high-tech, US company summarized the approach, 'Power plays don't work. You can't make 'em do anything. They have to want to. So you have to work through the culture. The idea is to educate people without [their] knowing it. Have the religion and not know how they got it' (quoted in Kunda, 1992, p.5). Part of the reason for IBM's 72 hour, online, real time, chat ('jam') session was to revise its values because the company's senior management felt that when employees were released from central control, the strongest glue holding them together was the set of values embraced by the organization that they work for (Hindle, 2006b).

Work or play?

Peter Fleming and Andre Spicer researched what they term the social geography of self and identity. They studied a call centre company that they named Sunray, which emphasised a culture of fun, epitomized in the slogan 'Remember the 3 Fs – Focus, Fun, Fulfilment'. Their study demonstrated how the company attempted to blur the traditional boundaries that typically divide work life and private life, in an effort to extend its control over employees. It disrupted and reorganized the traditional inside / outside boundary by holding team meetings before or after work at city centre cafes or nearby parks. Its team-building meetings involved participants bringing personal items from home to the workshop. This was one example of how Sunray used the private lives of workers as a training strategy to get them to invest more of themselves in their work. It also encouraged inside-the-organization activities that normally took place outside work, e.g. wearing pyjamas, drinking alcohol; bringing home-made food to share with colleagues; decorating a work area with personal items; dressing casually – to be 'free to be themselves'. Additionally, it encouraged activities-at-home which were more appropriate inside the organization e.g. the memorizing of the company slogan; workers attending awaydays on Sundays. These actions challenged the social geography of work and non-work.

The researchers found that Sunray's cultural techniques evoked in employees feelings and identities traditionally associated outside work, but not normally found inside it. The cultural message was that all the experiences that employees normally look forward to after work, such as having fun, partying, joy, fulfilment, exhilaration and friendship could be obtained inside the company. The aim of this conscious blurring of the boundary between private life and working life was to maximize the productive demands of the company. It was the 'whole' person that the company now desired, not just the uniform corporate self, since employee creativity and innovation were now linked to staff 'being themselves'. Sunray had a conscious recruitment strategy of employing young people whom they found 'can be themselves and know how to have fun', Fleming and Spicer argue that the power of the modern corporation now extends far beyond the boundaries of work, and deep into the private lives of citizens. They cite the example of Sunray's creation of a 'culture of fun', as one attempt by major corporations around the world to absorb the lifestyles, consumption patterns and social activities of their employees by importing the positive experiences and emotions associated with non-work inside the workplace.

Fleming and Spicer demonstrated how management at this call centre used a culture management programme

→

to erode and reconstitute the spatial division between work and non-work. The programme involved activities that challenged employees' meaning of work both inside and outside the firm, so that they no longer possessed a clear physical distance between employment time and home/leisure time. The authors' analysis of space, boundaries and culture management revealed a two-way cultural process in which spatial practices that were once considered the domain of organizational life, were transferred into the homes of employees, while their 'private activities' were carried back into their company. The consideration of colour schemes, personalization of cubicles and so on, all provide examples of the surface manifestations of the culture of this call centre. The study demonstrated how cultural controls operated as political mechanisms in contemporary work places. However, the authors add that engineered corporate culture may not always be accepted or internalized by workers, who can resist and contest the boundaries between work and non-work.

Based on Fleming and Spicer (2004, 2007).

STOP AND THINK   Consider the organizational approach to culture as described in the research on Sunray. What are its strengths and weaknesses for (a) company management (b) employees, (c) customers, and (d) the wider community?

The use of organizational culture to control involves the selective application of rites, ceremonials, myths, stories, symbols, and legends by managers to direct the behaviour of employees. It is called *symbolic management*. It appeals to managers because it is cheaper, avoids resentment, and builds employee commitment to the company and its goals. This theme of 'internalized control' is at the heart of the work of Michel Foucault (1979) whose ideas will be considered in greater depth later. Writers like Willmott (1993) saw it as an attempt at 'colonizing the minds' or 'engineering of the soul' (Rose, 1990) of organization members, to encourage them to internalize desired company values and norms. External control is replaced by self-control, such as that used by professionals including doctors, teachers, lawyers and priests.

Can culture be lethal?

On 1 February 2003, the Space Shuttle *Columbia*, on its way to its landing site in Florida, blew up in the skies of East Texas. Its seven-member crew perished, and the $2 billion ship was lost. The Columbia Accident Investigation Board Report determined the causes of the disaster to be both physical and organizational. The immediate physical cause was the now infamous chunk of foam that dislodged itself from the craft's bipod ramp, and struck a heat shield tile on the left wing. The organizational cause was attributed to NASA's culture and history. Specifically, it highlighted changes from NASA's culture of excellence to a culture of bureaucracy and production.

The agency's original, and much respected, technical and management approaches, which formed its 'culture of excellence', were established at the Marshall Space Flight Centre in Huntsville, Alabama in 1958. Under the leadership of Werner von Braun, a rocket team of 120 German engineers, who had come to the United States after the war, recreated their strong German research culture. It stressed rigorous engineering precision and put safety first; set high technical standards; inculcated an awareness of risk and failure; and encouraged open communications. However, following a decision in 1972 by President Richard Nixon, to make a reusable shuttle, NASA moved to a 'culture of production'. The new managerial focus stressed efficiency over safety, and effective reproducibility over creative problem-solving. Its mantra was 'Faster, better, cheaper'. The accident board's report argued that the transition from a culture of excellence to a culture of production took 30 years. Moreover, it proved to be resistant to change; preventing staff from reading danger signals and responding adequately to events.

Based on Mason (2004).

Culture strength, performance and types

Strong and weak cultures

Strong culture
one in which an organization's core values are widely shared among employees, intensely held by them, and which guides their behaviour.

A distinction has been made between strong culture and weak culture organizations (Gordon and DiTomaso, 1992). A strong culture is defined by O'Reilly (1989) as one which possesses:

- *intensity* – organization members have a strong emotional attachment to the core values of the organization, and are willing to display approval or disapproval of fellow members who act in certain ways, and

- *sharedness* – there is widespread agreement among employees about these organization values

Weak culture
one in which there is little agreement among employees about their organization's core values, the way things are supposed to be, or what is expected of them.

In contrast, a weak culture is one in which there is little agreement among employees about their organization's core values.

Thus, the greater the number of employees who accept the organization's core values, the stronger their emotional attachment to those values is; and the more they 'walk their talk', the stronger a company's culture will be, and vice versa. A strong culture is held to unite staff, and direct their attitudes and actions (Deal and Kennedy, 1982; Peters and Waterman, 1982). Currently, Apple, Hewlett Packard, McDonald's and Disney are considered strong culture companies. Much of the managerial literature has assumed that companies with strong cultures perform better than those with weak ones.

STOP AND THINK

Is a strong organizational culture likely to improve company performance and lead it to success? What arguments can you make against this view?

Tom J. Peters
(b.1942)

Robert H. Waterman

Company success, measured in financial terms, depends on many factors other than culture (e.g. being a dominant provider like Microsoft), and is therefore likely to be found in companies that have weak cultures. A firm's financial performance may itself affect the strength of its culture. That is, company success may *cause* its culture to become strong, rather than a strong culture being the cause of success. A strong culture may only be a good predictor of performance in the short term (Gordon and DiTomaso, 1992). Many of Peters and Waterman's strong culture companies subsequently failed. Finally, a strong culture only aids success only if it is an appropriate one, that is, if is suitable for coping with the conditions faced by the organization.

Strong cultures are slow to develop and difficult to change. Strong cultures may not necessarily be 'good' cultures if they result in employees holding inappropriate attitudes and making wrong decisions. A company's strong culture may impede its success if it encourages conformist attitudes. Miller (1994) suggested that it can cause inertia (clinging to past recipes); immoderation (foolish risk taking); inattention (selective perception of signals) and insularity (failure to adapt to the environment). IBM, a corporation acknowledged for its strong culture, nearly collapsed in the 1990s when it failed to respond to Apple's challenge and initially failed to make the transition from mainframe to personal computers. Thus one can compare the advantages and disadvantages of strong cultures as shown in Table 4.3.

John Kotter and James Heskett (1992) researched the relationship between organization culture and a company's economic success. They empirically tested the cultural strength of 207 large firms from a variety of industries. They only found a moderate correlation, and discovered examples of successful weak culture companies, and unsuccessful strong culture ones. They concluded that there was evidence of a relationship, strong culture-success, but that it was insufficient as an explanation in itself.

Table 4.3: Advantages and disadvantages of a strong culture

Advantages	Disadvantages
Differentiates the organization from others	Makes merging with an organization more difficult
Allows employees to identify themselves with the organization	Attracts and retains similar kinds of employees thereby limiting the diversity of thought
Facilitates behaviour desired by management, among employees	Can be 'too much of a good thing' if it creates extreme behaviours among employees
Creates stability within the organization	Makes adapting to a changing environment more difficult

From Colquitt *et al.* (2009, p.557).

Internal integration
the process through which employees adjust to each other, work together, and perceive themselves as a collective entity.

Denison *et al.* (2004) noted that models linking organizational culture and organizational performance have to deal with the contradictions of companies attempting to achieve **internal integration** (getting all their departments and staff to work in tandem), and **external adaptation** (responding quickly and effectively to environmental changes). They write that organizations that are market-focused, and opportunistic have problems with internal integration; while those that are well-integrated and over-controlled, can have external adaptation difficulties responding to their changing environments. Similarly, organizations with a top-down vision, struggle with empowerment, to create the 'bottom-up' commitments and behaviours among employees needed to implement that vision; while those with a strong commitment to employee participation have problems deciding upon a strategic direction. The most effective companies, say these authors, are those that can resolve these contradictions without resorting to simple trade-offs.

External adaptation
the process through which employees adjust to changing environmental circumstances to attain organizational goals.

This line of argument leads us away from a 'one best culture' viewpoint, and towards a contingency approach which we will encounter with respect to organization structure, and which we shall meet again in connection with leadership. Rob Goffee and Gareth Jones (2003) take this contingency approach to culture, stating that there is no, single, 'best culture', but that the most suitable is one that is 'environmentally appropriate'. Performance is likely to be better for companies possessing cultures that are both strong *and* able to adjust sufficiently well to their environments. Thus, a firm which operates in a volatile, competitive environment will need a strong culture that not only adapts quickly but even perhaps anticipates environmental changes. In contrast, if a company has a predictable and relatively static environment, it will need a strong but less adaptable culture. A study by Jose Garmendia (2004) into companies in the health insurance industry confirmed that a strong culture had a positive impact on organizational performance (results), but only if that culture is adapted to the environment and interacts proactively with it.

Home viewing

In *Nine to Five* (1980, director Colin Higgins) three female employees (played by Jane Fonda, Lily Tomlin and Dolly Parton) work in a company called Consolidated. They capture their boss, Franklin Hart (played by Dabney Coleman) whom they see as a 'sexist, egotistical, lying, hypocritical bigot', and imprison him in his own home. They then proceed to introduce a programme of culture change which underpins their feminized approach to management. For each change that you observe, decide what you think its purpose is, suggest how it might change the culture, and suggest how it might work to improve productivity.

Table 4.4: Culture framework

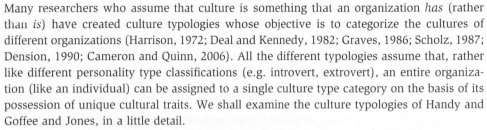

		CENTRALIZATION	
		High	Low
	High	*Role*	*Task*
FORMALIZATION	Low	*Power*	*Person*

Based on Handy (1993).

Culture typologies

Many researchers who assume that culture is something that an organization *has* (rather than *is*) have created culture typologies whose objective is to categorize the cultures of different organizations (Harrison, 1972; Deal and Kennedy, 1982; Graves, 1986; Scholz, 1987; Dension, 1990; Cameron and Quinn, 2006). All the different typologies assume that, rather like different personality type classifications (e.g. introvert, extrovert), an entire organization (like an individual) can be assigned to a single culture type category on the basis of its possession of unique cultural traits. We shall examine the culture typologies of Handy and Goffee and Jones, in a little detail.

Charles Handy's (1993) classification, developed from that of Roger Harrison (1972), is based on the degree of centralization and formalization and is shown in Table 4.4. Centralization refers to how much power and authority is centralized at the top of the organization. Formalization concerns the extent to which rules, procedures and policies govern organizational activities.

Terrence E. Deal

Allan A. Kennedy

Power cultures have a single, dominant individual who exerts their will; controlling by recruiting those of a similar viewpoint; and operating with the minimum of rules. It works on precedent, anticipating the desires of those at the centre. Decisions are based on a balance of power rather than logic, and there is little emphasis on discussion to reach consensus. For example, small companies run by their founder/owner.

Role culture organizations emphasize the importance of rules, procedures, role expectations and job descriptions. Managers within them operate 'by the book', on the basis of their position in the hierarchy and their role, and in a depersonalized way. It is based on its functional departments and specialties, and its operations are driven by logic and rationality. This culture is characteristic of bureaucracies.

Person culture organizations are focused on individuals. They exist for the benefit of their members, and may include a 'star performer'. Control is exercised only by mutual consent, and the organization is seen as subordinate to the individuals. This type of culture is rare and tends to be found in small, start-up IT firms, architects' partnerships and barristers' chambers.

Task cultures are job- or project-oriented. The task is specified at the top, but then the emphasis shifts to finding the resources, and then to getting the job done through using individuals' enthusiasm and commitment, working as a team. Influence within this culture is based on expert, rather than position or personal power. Such cultures are found where sensitivity and flexibility to an organization's environment are important, for example, in client-focused agencies such as advertising companies or management consultancies.

Rob Goffee and Gareth Jones (2003) used the dimensions of sociability and solidarity to classify cultures.

Sociability concerns emotional relationships, and describes how friendly employees are to each other. Relationships are valued for their own sakes; are sustained through face-to-face contact; and this indicates members' willingness to help each other without consideration of return favours. When sociability is high, all staff will celebrate an individual's success; will visit them if ill, and will socialize together after work.

Table 4.5: Culture contingency framework

		SOCIABILITY	
		High	Low
	High	*Communal culture*	*Mercenary culture*
SOLIDARITY	Low	*Networked culture*	*Fragmented culture*

Based on Goffee and Jones (2003).

Solidarity refers to the task-centred co-operation between dissimilar individuals and groups which is underpinned by perceived shared interests and common purpose. It is not sustained by face-to-face interaction, and does not depend on members' personal acquaintance or close friendship with one another. It is the degree to which members think and act in similar ways. It expresses the level of collectiveness as opposed to individuality within an organization. They work together smoothly, even though they may not like their colleagues.

These two dimensions combine to distinguish four types of organizational culture.

Communal culture (high sociability/high solidarity); members are friendly to each other and also think and act alike. Careful selection ensures that only those who 'fit in' are accepted. They receive an intensive induction into the core values; and regular appraisals with respect to meeting performance targets and adhering to the company's ethos. There is a high degree of cohesion and staff focus on a single goal. Members work in flexible, collaborative and mutually supportive ways.

Networked culture (high sociability/low solidarity): members are friendly to each but think and act differently. The culture stimulates creativity by encouraging teamwork, information sharing between individuals and departments, and openness to new ideas. It encourages members to go beyond their job descriptions to assist their colleagues. Performance may be impeded due to difficulty in disciplining poorly performing 'friends', and the search for consensus and compromise which does not necessarily provide the best solutions. The culture is found in companies facing highly competitive environments, and may evolve from a communal culture which is often difficult to sustain.

Mercenary culture (low sociability/high solidarity): staff may think alike but are not friendly to each other. It is found in firms operating in rapidly changing, highly competitive business environments where success and even survival depend on staff acting quickly, decisively and collectively, to beat the competition. Members 'pull their weight' and pursue efficiency. The intolerance of poor performance is not impeded by having to maintain friendly relations with everybody. Employees seek to maximize personal gains; only co-operate when they see personal benefits; are well rewarded, but are sacked if they fail to perform adequately.

Fragmented culture (low sociability/low solidarity): employees think and act differently and show little liking for their co-workers. Organization charts and job descriptions define individuals' responsibilities so everyone knows what is expected of them in their department. Small companies with this culture may only have a few employees, but these tend to be 'star' performers who compete with each other. Law firms, management consultancies or training organizations would be examples, all of which rely on key individuals doing their own job well for their client.

STOP AND THINK Why might different departments within the same organization have different cultures e.g. role culture in accounting; person culture in marketing; task culture in research and development? How fixed are these cultures over time? Would they change as personnel changed?

Source: Copyright Grantland Enterprises (www.grantland.net).

National cultures

Social orientation
relative importance of
the interests of the
individual versus the
interest of the group
– *individualism v.
collectivism.*

Power orientation
the appropriateness of
power/authority within
organizations – *respect
v. tolerance.*

**Uncertainty
orientation** the
emotional response to
uncertainty and change
– *acceptance v.
avoidance.*

National cultural stereotypes are well established: Scots are mean; Americans are brash; Germans are humourless; French are romantic; Japanese are inscrutable. However, researchers have studied how national cultures might affect organizational cultures in specific country settings. They have been interested to see how attempts to establish a common organizational culture in a multi-national firm, can be undermined by the strength of national cultures. An organization's culture, while having unique properties, is necessarily embedded within the wider norms and values of the country in which its office or factory is located, and is affected by the personal values that employees bring with them to their jobs. Fombrun (1984) saw organizational culture as being partly the outcome of societal factors, some of which were identified by Brooks (2003). Laurent (1989) argued that the national culture was more powerful and stable than organizational culture.

Awareness and understanding of cultural differences is crucial for everybody in the organization. Vanhoegaerden (1999) suggested that there were two reasons for their neglect. Many people believed that, underneath, everybody is fundamentally the same. This belief is reinforced by the impression that cultures are merging. The success of global companies such as Disney, Coca-Cola and others, can convince us that the world is becoming more alike. The convergence may exist, but at a superficial level, and cultural differences remain. Pascal, the French philosopher noted that, 'There are truths on this side of the Pyrenees, which are falsehoods on the other.' Even the archetypal global brand, McDonald's, encounters cultural obstacles as it covers the world. When it opened in Japan, it found that Ronald McDonald's clown-like white face did not go down well. In Japan, white is associated with death and was an unlikely lure to persuade people to eat Big Macs. It also found that Japanese people had difficulty in pronouncing the 'R' in Ronald, so the character was transformed to Donald McDonald.

Wal-Mart's German exit

After eight years of never making a profit, Wal-Mart said Auf Wiedersehen to Germany, announcing in 2006 that it was selling its 85 hypermarkets and pulling out of the country after incurring a £540 million pre-tax loss. It failed to understand how the American and German cultures differed. The use of 'greeters' in every American store (staff who were ordered to smile at every customer as they entered) was particularly unpopular among German customers. Neither did they like their purchases being bagged for them by store staff. At the same time, Wal-Mart's employees resisted management demands which they felt were unjust, such as a ban on dating colleagues in positions of authority; a 'no flirting' rule between workers; being forced to work beyond contracted hours; video surveillance of workers; and a telephone hotline for employees to inform on their colleagues. Legal action by its German staff forced Wal-Mart to amend its ethics manual concerning romantic attachments and to ban video monitoring.

Based on Litterick (2006); Deutsche Welle *(2006).*

At both levels of the cultural debate, the organizational and the national, one sees not only attempts to identify specific traits, but also attempts to classify organizations and countries

Goal orientation the motivation to achieve goals – *aggressive masculinity v. passive femininity.*

Time orientation the time outlook on work and life – *short-term v. long-term.*

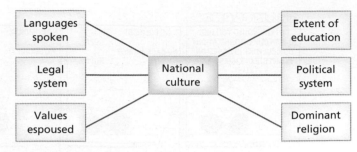

Figure 4.6: Factors affecting national culture
Source: From Brooks (2003, p.266).

Geert Hofstede
(b.1928)

into types. This creation of trait lists and typologies parallels work in personality. In the 1980s, Geert Hofstede (1986, 1991) carried out a cross-cultural study of 116,000 employees of the same multinational company located in 40 countries. Working later with Bond (Hofstede and Bond, 1988), he distinguished national cultures in terms of five orientations – social, power, uncertainty, goal and time. Each cultural orientation affects the perceptions, attitudes, values, motivation and behaviours of people who live in it. Like personality assessment, each of the orientations represents a separate continuum, so each culture can be positioned somewhere along each one as shown in Figure 4.7.

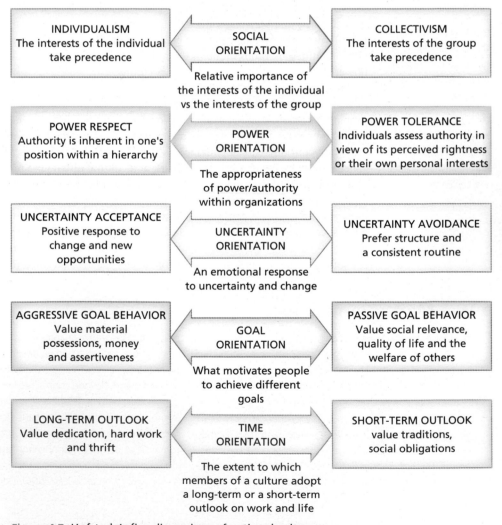

Figure 4.7: Hofstede's five dimensions of national culture
Source: From GRIFFIN, RICKY W; PUSTAY, MICHAEL W., INTERNATIONAL BUSINESS, 5th Edition, © 2007, p.102. Reprinted by permission of Pearson Education, Inc., Upper Saddle River, NJ.

Home viewing

Rising Sun (1993, director Philip Kaufman) concerns the murder of Cheryl, an American blonde, in the boardroom of the Nakamoto Corporation, a Japanese transplant in Los Angeles, during negotiations to acquire Microcon, an American defence company. John Connor (played by Sean Connery) and Web Smith (Wesley Snipes) are the detectives on the case. As you watch the film, consider first, what is says about Japanese transplants in an alien culture. How do organizational behaviour styles clash?

Second, what does it say about cross-cultural communication? Connor has to teach his partner how to do business with the Japanese. This involves explaining social norms and rituals, preserving 'face', conversation style, and interpersonal relationships. Finally, how does the film address organizational power politics, in terms of the symbolic use of architecture, the exploitation of friendships, the use of surveillance technology, and golfing relationships?

National culture and motorcar manufacture

Professor Lord Bhattacharyya, head of the Warwick Manufacturing Group claimed that it was the arrogance of the Rover managers and the lack of a learning culture in the company that prevented it from obtaining the real benefits from its partnership with the Japanese group, Honda. Later in 1992, when BMW bought the Rover business, communication with the German managers was even worse (exacerbated by political in-fighting on the German side). Failure was the inevitable, bitter result. In a similar way, the collapse of the Daimler-Chrysler link indicates poor collaboration and internal strife, which stemmed, in part, from national cultural differences and traditions between German and US managers.

Two of Hofstede's five culture dimensions help to explain the difficulties faced by Honda, BMW, Daimler and Chrysler managers. The first is *social orientation* (Table 4.6)

– the relative importance of the interests of the individual versus those of the group. Out of 100, the US scored 91, close to extreme individualism; the UK was 89; and Germany was 67 (a little above the European average). In contrast, Japan's score was 46, well towards collectivism. The other dimension is *uncertainty orientation* (Table 4.7) – the emotional response to uncertainty and change. The Japanese scored 92, close to extreme uncertainty avoidance; Germany was 65; the USA was 46; and Britain was 35. The last two are well towards the uncertainty acceptance end of the continuum. The lack of precise rules and procedures at Rover's Longbridge plant may have made the BMW team uncomfortable from the outset.

Based on Lester (2007, p.8)

Source: Bastian/© Caro/Alamy

Table 4.6: Extremes of social orientation dimension

	Collectivism	Individualism
In the family	Education towards 'we' consciousness	Education towards 'I' consciousness
	Opinions predetermined by group	Private opinion expected
	Obligations to family or in group	Obligations to self
	Harmony	• Self-interest
	Respect	• Self-actualization
	Shame	• Guilt
At school	Learning is for the young only	Continuing education
	Learn how to do	Learn how to learn
At the workplace	Value standards differ for in-groups and out-groups: particularism	Same value standards apply to allow: universalism
	Other people seen as members of their group	Other people seen as potential resources
	Relationship prevails over task	Task prevails over relationship
	Moral model of employer–employee relationship	Calculative model of employer–employee relationship

From Hofstede (1994, p.3).

Table 4.7: Extremes of uncertainty dimension

	Weak (acceptance of)	Strong (avoidance of)
In the family	What is different, is ridiculous or curious	What is different is dangerous
	Ease, indolence, low stress	Higher anxiety and stress
	Aggression and emotion not shown	Showing of aggression and emotions accepted
At school	Students comfortable with:	Students comfortable with:
	• Unstructured learning situations	• Structured learning situations
	• Vague objectives	• Precise objectives
	• Broad assignments	• Detailed assignments
	• No timetables	• Strict timetables
	Teachers may say 'I don't know'	Teachers should have all the answers
At the workplace	Dislike of rules – written or unwritten	Emotional need for rules – written or unwritten
	Less formalization and standardization	More formalization and standardization

From Hofstede (1994, p.4).

Table 4.8: Cultural dimensions of the GLOBE model

Cultural dimension	Definition: the degree to which
1. Assertiveness	Individuals are bold, forceful, dominant, confrontational or demanding in relationships with others
2. Collectivism-group	Individuals express and show pride, loyalty and cohesiveness to their organizations or families
3. Collectivism-societal	Organizational and societal, institutional practices (such as those of governments), which encourage and reward collective distribution of resources (as under socialism) and collective action.
4. Future orientation	A society encourages and rewards behaviours such as planning, investing in the future, and delaying gratification
5. Gender differentiation	A society minimizes differential treatment between men and women, such as through equal opportunity based on ability and performance.
6. Humane orientation	A society or organization encourages and rewards individuals for being fair, altruistic, generous, caring and kind to others.
7. Performance orientation	A society encourages and rewards group members for performance improvements, excellence, high standards and innovation
8. Power distance	Members of a society accept and endorse the equal (lower power distance) or unequal (higher power distance) distribution of authority, control and status privileges (such as a class structure).
9. Uncertainty avoidance	A society, organization or group relies on social norms, formal rules and formal procedures to alleviate the unpredictability of future events.

Based on House *et al.* (2004), from HELLRIEGEL/SLOCUM. *Organizational Behaviour* (with Bind-In Competency Test Web Site Printed Access Card), 12E. © 2009 South-Western, a part of Cengage Learning, Inc. Reproduced by permission. www.cengage.com/permissions.

Since 1993, Hofstede's pioneering work has been incorporated, updated and extended by the Global Leadership and Organizational Behaviour Effectiveness (GLOBE) research programme. This is a longitudinal study of leadership and organizational culture of 825 organizations located in 62 countries (Javidan and House, 2001). Whereas Hofstede's was a one-off, snapshot survey, GLOBE is a longitudinal study reporting changes over time. GLOBE contrasts national cultures on nine dimensions, which include, but also go beyond, those proposed by Hofstede.

Table 4.9 list the three highest and lowest ranking countries on each of GLOBE's nine dimensions, as well as those located in the middle.

STOP AND THINK Are interpersonal skills, motivation, group behaviour, leadership style, conflict management, structure, predominant leadership style, training and HRM practices all culturally relative?

Table 4.9: GLOBE country rankings

Dimension	Countries scoring high	Countries scoring medium	Countries scoring low
1. Assertiveness	Spain USA Greece	Egypt Ireland Philippines	Sweden New Zealand Switzerland
2. Collectivism-group	Egypt China Morocco	Japan Israel Qatar	Denmark Sweden New Zealand
3. Collectivism-societal*	Greece Hungary Germany	Hong Kong USA Egypt	Denmark Singapore Japan
4. Future orientation	Denmark Canada Netherlands	Slovenia Egypt Ireland	Russia Argentina Poland
5. Gender differentiation	South Korea Egypt Morocco	Italy Brazil Argentina	Sweden Denmark Slovenia
6. Humane orientation	Indonesia Egypt Malaysia	Hong Kong Sweden Taiwan	Germany Spain France
7. Performance orientation	USA Taiwan New Zealand	Sweden Israel Spain	Russia Argentina Greece
8. Power distance	Russia Spain Thailand	England France Brazil	Denmark Netherlands South Africa
9. Uncertainty avoidance	Austria Denmark Germany	Israel USA Mexico	Russia Hungary Bolivia

* A low score indicates collectivism.
Reprinted from *Organizational Dynamics*, 29(4), Javidan, M. and House, R.J., Cultural acumen from the global manager: lessons from the Project GLOBE, pp.289–305, copyright 2001, with permission from Elsevier.

Multicultural teamworking

Jeanne Brett, Kirstin Behfar and Mary Kern studied the day-to-day working problems encountered by members of teams that prevented them gaining the benefits of the multicultural team arrangement (knowledge of different product markets; culturally sensitive customer service; and 24-hour work rotations). The team members studied came from a variety of countries including the United States, India, Japan, Korea, Brazil, America, Mexico, UK, Poland and Greece. The authors identified four barriers to team success:

Direct–indirect communication: In Western cultures, communication is generally direct and explicit. The meaning is on the surface, and is not dependent on a listener's knowledge of the speaker or the context, for its interpretation. In cultures using indirect communication however, the meaning is embedded in the message's presentation. For example, a negotiator's preferences and priorities have to be inferred, rather than asked about directly. Uncovering and discussing real problems may have to done hypothetically – by asking

Source: Yuri Arcurs/Dreamstime.com

Teamworking picture

what would happen if some system part failed – even though the failure being discussed is real and immediate. Communication challenges reduce information sharing and create interpersonal conflict.

Trouble with accents and fluency: Despite English being the international business language, non-native speakers' accents, lack of fluency, translation and usage problems, all create misunderstandings and frustrations, and influence team members' perceptions of each others' status and competence. Non-fluency prevents the team benefiting from members' expertise; demotivates individuals, and can be another cause of interpersonal conflict.

Differing attitudes to hierarchy and authority: Teams necessarily have a flat structure, which can be uncomfortable for those members who come from cultures in which people are treated according to their organizational status. For example, deferring to higher status members is appropriate when most of

the team come from a hierarchical culture, but can be status and credibility damaging (even humiliating) if most of the team come from an egalitarian culture. A project can fail if members feel they have been treated disrespectfully.

Conflicting norms for decision-making: Cultures differ in terms of the degree of prior analysis required and speed of decision-making. US managers like to make quick decisions with little analysis compared to their Brazilian counterparts.

The most successful teams and managers used four strategies to deal with these challenges: *adaptation* – acknowledging the culture gaps openly and working around them; *structural intervention* – changing the shape of the team (size, membership); *managerial intervention* – establishing team norms early; and *exit* – removing a team member when other options have failed.

Based on Brett et al. *(2006).*

Organizational culture v. national culture

Does organizational culture erase or diminish the influence of national culture? Research by Lubatkin *et al.* (1998) suggests not. Both company managers and employees bring their cultural background and ethnicity to the workplace. In Hofstede's (2001) study, national culture explained more of the differences than did role, age, gender or race. Laurent (1983) also found more pronounced cultural differences among employees from around the world working within the same multinational company than among those working for companies in their native lands. The company's culture did not replace or eliminate national differences. Nancy Adler (2002) suggested that the pressure to conform to the culture of a foreign owned company brought out employees' resistance, causing them to cling on more strongly to their own national identities. By adulthood, she claimed, national culture may be so ingrained that a company's organizational culture cannot erase it.

RECAP

1. *Account for the popularity of organizational culture among managers, consultants and academics.*

   - For managers, the concept offers the route to economic success to match that enjoyed by Japanese organizations of the time.

   - For consultants, the concept provides an appealing, easy-to-grasp quick-fix solution to sell to managers wishing to improve their organization's performance.

   - For academics, it offers an alternative perspective with which to research and theorize about organizations and provides a new context within which to explore postmodernist ideas.

2. *List, describe and exemplify Schein's three levels of culture.*

   - Schein distinguished surface manifestations of culture at level one (e.g., artefacts, rites, ceremonials); organizational values at level two (e.g. customer obsession); and basic assumptions at level three which actually was the culture (e.g. nature of reality and truth).

3. *List the stages of organizational socialization.*

   - The stages of organizational socialization are pre-arrival, encounter and metamorphosis.

4. *Contrast managerial and social science perspectives on organizational culture.*

   - Organizational culture is something that a company either *has*, or what a company *is*.

   - Organizational culture is a single, integrated unit or a differentiated entity consisting of multiple, different subcultures, fragmented with conflicting interests.

   - An organization's culture can be managed by its leaders or it is beyond their direct control and instead has to be tolerated by them.

   - Culture signals a new era of symbolic leadership which relies on internalized forms of employee direction, or it is old style management control under a new guise.

5. *Assess the link between organizational culture and economic performance.*

   - Few research studies have been conducted which explicitly test a causal link between an organization's culture and its economic performance.

   - Those that have been conducted do not illustrate any direct causal relationship between a 'strong' culture and high economic performance suggesting, at a minimum, that other, mediating variables may be more significant.

   - There is anecdotal data as well as a logical argument, to suggest that organizations possessing a strong culture at a time of required change, may be less flexible, less able to change, and hence more less likely to perform well economically.

6. *Distinguish different national culture dimensions.*

   - Hofstede suggested that national culture could be differentiated along five dimensions: power distance; uncertainty avoidance; individualism-collectivism; masculinity-femininity (and later) short term-long term perspective.

   - The GLOBE framework for assessing national culture incorporates and extends Hofstede's dimensions and includes: assertiveness; future orientation; gender differentiation; uncertainty avoidance; power distance; collectivism – group; collectivism – societal; performance orientation; humane orientation.

Revision	1. Is organization culture capable of being managed?
	2. What guidance does the theory and research into national culture offer managers working around the world for global, multinational corporations?
	3. Consider the social orientation and uncertainty dimensions of Hofstede's model, as described in Tables 4.6 and 4.7. How are these likely to affect the behaviour of employees and managers within the workplace?
	4. To what extent, and in what ways, might a national culture affect an organization's culture?

Research assignment	First, familiarize yourself with the list of Schein's 15 surface manifestations of culture as shown on pp.102–3. Use this list to (a) interview a manager and obtain examples of as many of the surface manifestations of culture as they are able to provide you with. (b) For each manifestation, ask your manager what purpose it serves within their organization. (c) Ask them what external and internal factors have moulded the organization's culture into what it is today. (d) Select one of the two of the culture typologies (Handy or Goffee and Jones) and fit your organization into it, justifying your choice with evidence.

Springboard

Gannon, M.J. and Newman, K.L. (eds), 2001, *The Blackwell Handbook of Cross-cultural Management*, Blackwell, Oxford.

Considers the influence of national cultures on managerial and employee behaviour.

Michel, A. and Wortham, S., 2009, *Bullish on Uncertainty*, Cambridge University Press. Cambridge.

This study of two Wall Street investment banks examines how they manage their high uncertainty environments, and how their organizational cultures transform their staff.

Willmott, H., 1993, 'Strength is ignorance, slavery is freedom; managing culture in modern organizations', *Journal of Management Studies*, (30)5: 515–52.

A landmark paper in which the author proposes that culture is a particular form of control which operates, not by external regulation, but by shaping the identity (internal world) of an organization's employees.

Willmott, H.C., 2003, 'Renewing strength: corporate culture revisited', *Management*, (6)3: 73–87.

The author provides a critique of the idea that corporate culture can be managed.

OB in films

Dead Poets Society (1989, director Peter Weir): DVD track 1: 0:00:53–0:04:44 (4 minutes). To establish context, many films begin with shots of an organization to communicate its culture. The clip begins with the opening credits of the film, and ends after Mr Keating has been introduced, sits down and there is a shot of an outside scene.

1. Which surface manifestations of Welton Academy's culture are being communicated here?

2. What values can you infer about Welton Academy's organizational culture from viewing this clip?

Welton Academy culture

1. *Artefacts* are material objects created to facilitate culturally expressive activities. They include tools, furniture, appliances and clothing.

2. *Ceremonials* are formally planned, elaborate, dramatic sets of activities of cultural expression.

3. *Courses* and workshops are used to instruct, induct, orient and train new members, and to recognize the contributions of existing ones.

4. *Heroes* are characters, living or dead, who personify the values and beliefs; who are referred to in company stories.

5. *Jokes* are humorous stories intended to cause amusement but whose underlying themes may carry a message for the behaviour or values.

6. *Language* is the particular form or manner in which members use vocal sounds and written signs to convey meaning to each other.

7. *Legends* are handed-down narratives about wonderful events based on history, but embellished with fictional details.

8. *Mottoes* are maxims adopted as rules of conduct which are rarely, if ever, changed.

9. *Norms* are expected modes of behaviour that are accepted as the company's way of doing things.

10. *Physical layout* concerns things that surround people, providing them with sensory stimuli.

11. *Rites* are relatively elaborate, dramatic sets of activities that consolidate various forms of cultural expression into one event.

12. *Sagas* are historical narratives describing the unique accomplishments of a group and its leaders.

13. *Slogans* are short, catchy phrases that are regularly changed.

14. *Stories* are narratives describing how individuals acted and the decisions they made that affected the company's future.

15. *Symbols* refer to any act, event, object, quality or relation that serves as a vehicle for conveying meaning.

OB in literature

Mike Daisey, *Twenty-One Dog Years – Doing Time @ Amazon.com*, 2002, Fourth Estate. This highly amusing autobiography concerns Daisey's application to, and short period working for, Amazon in Seattle. It describes the sequences of organizational socialization and highlights many aspects of this organization's culture, and how it affects him and the other company employees.

CHAPTER EXERCISES

Surface manifestations

Exercise developed in association with Professor Phillip Beaumont, University of Glasgow.

Objectives
1. Understand how organization structure and processes affect organization culture.
2. Speculate how the organization culture might affect your views and behaviours as an employee.

Briefing Examine the five clusters of descriptions as directed by your instructor. For each one:
1. Decide what 'message' each one sends to employees about the organization's culture.
2. Speculate on the views and behaviours it might encourage or discourage among employees.

Descriptions
1. Companies value high-performing employees
   (a) Company A conducts annual staff appraisals between an employee and their manager. Those performing below standard are asked to explain their poor performance.
   (b) Company B conducts quarterly reviews between an employee and their manager. If employees exceed their annual performance target, they are given a substantial bonus in that year.
   (c) Company C conducts regular team appraisals in which team members comment on each others' strengths and weaknesses. All receive extensive, preparatory training and each person promptly gets a summarized, anonymized report of these comments about them, and this is used when promotion decisions are made.

2. Companies want their employees to have creative ideas.
   (a) Company A hires only the smartest people and then immediately after appointment, sends them on creativity workshops.
   (b) Company B has a rigorous selection procedure. Its expensive and elaborate 3-day assessment centre selection approach focuses on determining each applicant's level of creativity.
   (c) Company C has a staff restaurant with only 6-seater tables to allow different staff to meet; its rest areas have whiteboards on the walls; and there are suggestion boxes in every main corridor.

3. Companies have different approaches to employees' work spaces.
   (a) Company A encourages staff to personalize their workspaces by decorating them with photos, toys and other items brought from home. Staff are free to come to work dressed as they like.

→

(b) Company B has open space work areas for all staff. They wear business dress and address each other by their first names. Managers do not have their own offices or secretaries. The conference suite is used for department meetings to which secretarial and support staff are invited. Recycling boxes are located throughout the building.

(c) Company C believes messy desks demonstrate a lack of personal organization. It operates paperless office system and requires managers to enforce a 'clear surface' policy. Non-business-related items in workspaces are considered unprofessional and are banned. 'Dress-down Fridays' were introduced by senior management after much discussion, some time ago.

4. Companies have different approaches to employees' errors.

(a) In company A, an employee's mistake is discussed at a team meeting, recorded on the employee's file, and senior management is informed for possible disciplinary action.

(b) In Company B, the manager identifies errors made by subordinates; talks to the individuals, shows them where they went wrong, and what they should do in the future.

(c) In Company C, employees discuss their mistakes with their managers. The manager assists the subordinate to analyze their error, helps them learn from it, and agrees an action plan for future improvements.

5. Companies have different ways of rewarding their employees.

(a) In Company A, all employees receive a fixed salary negotiated by the union with their employer. The salary depends on seniority and grade.

(b) In Company B, all employees receive an inflation-based pay rise and participate in a bonus scheme based on the company's performance.

(c) In Company C, employees receive an inflation-based pay rise, and may receive in addition, a bonus based on their team's performance during the year.

(d) In Company D, each employee receives a combination of a wage and a bonus. The bonus element is uncapped and thus can be significant, and is directly related to their performance in the previous year.

Metaphors for culture

Objectives
1. To contrast students' metaphors for national culture.

2. To assess how these help to identify cultural problems and suggest solutions.

Briefing
A metaphor says that one thing is something else – 'An eye is a camera' or 'The brain is a computer'. Metaphors can be used as diagnostic tools to help understand organizational problems and offer possible solutions. This exercise shows how this can be done.

1. Students in the class, individually, complete the sentence, 'Culture is . . .'. They then make notes explaining why they chose that particular metaphor.

2. They form into small groups.

3. Within the groups, they explain their chosen metaphor to the other members. Members then consider the implications of the selected metaphor for how people learn and motivate themselves, factors affecting relationships between individuals, leadership styles, how groups work, and other aspects.

4. Once all group members have had the opportunity to explain and discuss their own metaphor, members read the following case study and, selecting each metaphor in turn, assess how it helps to identify the problem and offer a solution.

In 1993, IBM established a joint venture research team to develop a revolutionary new chip design for the next century. The other companies in the group were Siemens AG of Germany and Toshiba Corporation of Japan. Engineers from all three companies were set up in Long Island at one of IBM's research affiliates. The project was expected to last several years. People who initially were worried that the more than 100 scientists from the three countries would have difficulties working together proved to be correct. Problems began almost immediately. Individuals wanted to associate only with fellow country members, thus jeopardizing the project's success. An observer noted that the Japanese disliked the office set-up, which consisted of many small offices and few open spaces, and they had difficulty conversing in English. The Germans covered the glass walls of their offices to maintain privacy, thus offending both the Japanese and Americans. The Japanese liked to go out drinking after work, during which time they tended to develop strong group norms. The Americans, however, preferred to go home to their families. Furthermore, the Americans complained that the Germans planned too much and that the Japanese would not make decisions.

From WORKING ACROSS CULTURES by Martin J. Gannon. Copyright 2000 by Sage Publications Inc. Books. Reproduced with permission of Sage Publications Inc. Books in the format Textbook via Copyright Clearance Center.

Part 2 **Individuals in the organization**

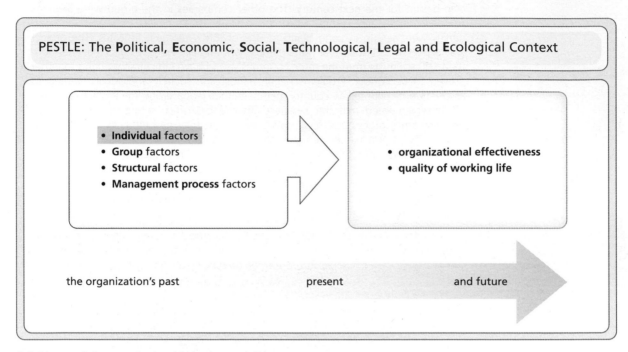

PESTLE: The **P**olitical, **E**conomic, **S**ocial, **T**echnological, **L**egal and **E**cological Context

- **Individual** factors
- **Group** factors
- **Structural** factors
- **Management process** factors

- **organizational effectiveness**
- **quality of working life**

the organization's past   present   and future

A field map of the organizational behaviour terrain

Introduction

Part 2, Individuals in the organization, explores five topics:

- *Learning*, in Chapter 5
- *Personality*, in Chapter 6
- *Communication*, in Chapter 7
- *Perception*, in Chapter 8
- *Motivation*, in Chapter 9

These aspects of psychology are closely related, although it is helpful to discuss them separately, for the purposes of explanation. Each contributes in a different way to our understanding of behaviour in general, to our understanding of behaviour in organizations in particular, and to our analysis of performance at work and quality of working life. The coverage of these topics is clearly more limited than you will find in a psychology textbook, because we are focusing on issues that help us to understand organizational behaviour, and on techniques and approaches that have shaped organization and management practice.

Invitation to see

This image is similar to one used in *The Sunday Times* (10 June, 2007) to illustrate an article titled 'addiction to work', about the phenomenon of compulsive working, or 'workaholism' (original image unobtainable). The caption said, 'stressed and harassed with too much to do, but we love it really'. The article argued that many of us enjoy high pressure 'extreme' jobs.

Source: Jay P. Morgan/Getty Images

1. **Decoding**   Look at this image closely. Note in as much detail as possible what messages you feel that it is trying to convey. Does it tell a story, present a point of view, support an argument, perpetuate a myth, reinforce a stereotype, challenge a stereotype?

2. **Challenging**   To what extent do you agree with the messages, stories, points of view, arguments, myths, or stereotypes in this image? Is this image open to challenge, to criticism, or to interpretation and decoding in other ways, revealing other messages?

3. **Sharing**   Compare with colleagues your interpretation of this image. Explore explanations for differences in your respective decodings.

What would you do? You're the employee

What advice can you give to management to help solve this problem? Base your advice on your own experience and views, as well as on the information provided.

Our company prides itself on attracting the best talent and for many years has run a successful training scheme both for graduate entrants and non-graduates. Competition for places on our schemes is always fierce and we believe that the breadth of training we provide is recognized as something of a gold standard in our industry. Newly qualified trainees invariably settle in well and make an impact in whatever area of the business they join.

However, a recent analysis of our retention rate for these trainees has made uncomfortable reading. It seems that a large number are benefiting from the training and then departing for higher salaries or prospects elsewhere. Despite being afforded every opportunity to progress within the firm, the reality is that too few of them see us as a 'job for life', or even a job for a decade – it looks like for many, we are merely the first rung on their personal career ladder.

Our schemes are a serious investment and it goes without saying that we need to retain entrants to make the expense worthwhile. Although it could be argued that we are boosting skills in the industry as a whole, we aren't in the business of altruism and are not prepared to act as a training ground for our competitors to come along and poach the best of the talent we have developed.

Of course, our employees cannot be blamed for listening to offers from our rivals, especially if they are being approached by headhunters – but our pay and benefits are more than competitive, so we do not believe that throwing money at the problem will solve anything.

What can we do to foster greater loyalty among the talent we have developed and ensure that all our good work in the recruitment field is not going to waste?

From 'Troubleshooter', People Management, *24 January 2008, p.72.*

Chapter 5 **Learning**

Key terms

learning

behaviourist psychology

cognitive psychology

feedback

positive reinforcement

negative reinforcement

punishment

extinction

Pavlovian conditioning

Skinnerian conditioning

shaping

intermittent reinforcement

schedule of reinforcement

cybernetic analogy

intrinsic feedback

extrinsic feedback

concurrent feedback

delayed feedback

behaviour modification

socialization

behavioural modelling

provisional selves

behavioural self-management

learning organization

single-loop learning

double-loop learning

tacit knowledge

explicit knowledge

knowledge management

Learning outcomes

When you have read this chapter, you should be able to define those key terms in your own words, and you should also be able to:

1. Explain the characteristics of the behaviourist and cognitive approaches to learning.

2. Explain and evaluate the technique of behaviour modification.

3. Explain the socialization process, and assess the practical relevance of this concept.

4. Explain and evaluate the technique of behavioural self-management.

5. Describe features of knowledge management and the learning organization.

Why study learning?

In an economy dominated by knowledge work and rapid, unpredictable change, the ability to learn, and to continue learning, for individuals and organizations, is crucial. The Web 2.0 technologies discussed in Chapter 3 have led to the growing use of electronic simulations or 'sims' for training and management development (Syedain, 2008b). As a general rule, the higher the level of your education, the higher your salary. In contributing to organizational effectiveness, employees have to know what to do, how to do it, and how well they are expected to perform. Learning theories thus affect management practices including:

- induction of new recruits;
- the design and delivery of job training;
- design of payment systems;
- how supervisors evaluate performance and provide feedback;
- creation of learning organizations;
- design and operation of knowledge management systems.

One of the learning mechanisms explored in this chapter is *positive reinforcement*. In practice, this means praising employees for good performance. Timothy Hinkin and Chester Schriescheim (2009) argue that, at a time of economic crisis, when financial rewards are scarce, positive reinforcement becomes a more valuable management resource.

Thinking for a living

Central to much thinking about how organizations should be restructured for the twenty-first century is the idea that innovation and growth will depend more and more on so-called knowledge workers, the sort of people who, to quote the title of a recent book by Thomas Davenport of Babson College, Massachusetts, find themselves 'Thinking for a Living'.

Lowell Bryan and Claudia Joyce at McKinsey reckon that knowledge workers 'represent a large and growing percentage of the employees of the world's biggest corporations'. In some industries, such as financial services, media and pharmaceuticals, they think the share may already be as high as 25 per cent.

Others would put it much higher. One of the secrets of Toyota's success, says Takis Athanasopoulos, the chief executive of the Japanese carmaker's European operations, is that the company encourages every worker, no matter how far down the production line, to consider himself a knowledge worker and to think creatively about improving his particular corner of the organization.

From Hindle (2006b, p.9).

Learning organization
an organizational form that enables individual learning to create valued outcomes, such as innovation, efficiency, environmental alignment, and competitive advantage.

Learning is one of the most fundamental and controversial topics in psychology. The extremes of this controversy lie in **behaviourist** and **cognitive** theories of learning. The concept of the learning organization has also been popular for some time. The learning organization is a combination of structures and policies which encourage learning, with individual and corporate benefits. Some larger companies regard learning as so important that they have established their own corporate universities. Some commentators argue that organizations, as well as individuals, are able to learn, but this is a controversial view.

Knowledge has thus become an asset more important than equipment and materials for many organizations, where understanding of processes – the 'how to' of making products and providing services – is critical. Competitive advantage means knowing *how to* make products, *how to* innovate more rapidly, *how to* bring new products and services more quickly to the marketplace, knowing *how to* meet changing customer needs. The capacity to develop new knowledge affects the organization's ability to grow and to survive, as technologies, customer requirements, government policies and economic conditions change.

What is learning all about?

1. Learning is a part of work and work involves learning; these are not separate functions but intertwined; the separation we have made of them is artificial and often does not serve us well.

2. Learning is not only or even primarily about obtaining correct information or answers from knowledgeable others; it is fundamentally about making meaning out of the experience that we and others have in the world.

3. Organizational learning results from intentional and planned efforts to learn. Although it can and does occur accidentally, organizations cannot afford to rely on learning through chance.

4. As a collective we are capable of learning our way to the answers we need to address our difficult problems. It is ourselves we must rely on for these answers rather than experts, who can, at best, only provide us with answers that have worked in the past.

From Dixon (1999, p.xiv).

The learning process

How do we learn? How do we come to know what we know, and to do what we are able to do? These questions lie at the heart of psychology, and it is not surprising that we are faced with different approaches to the topic. This variety maintains controversy, excitement and interest in the subject, and also helps to generate new thinking.

Psychology is associated with the study of rats in mazes. Rats, and other animals, have contributed much to our understanding of human behaviour, and have been widely used by psychologists concerned with the development of learning theories. Rat biochemistry is similar to ours. We have to accept that humans are animals in many respects, and that we can learn much about ourselves by studying other creatures.

The ability to learn is not unique to human beings. Animals also learn, as dog owners and circus fans can confirm. One feature that seems to distinguish us from animals is our ability to learn about, adapt to, survive in, and manipulate our environment for purposes that we ourselves define. Animals can adapt to changes in their circumstances, but their ability to manipulate their environment is limited, and they appear to have little choice over their goals. In addition, animals have developed no science, technology or engineering – or social science.

We hope that when you have finished reading this book you will be able to say that you have learned something. The test is whether or not you will be able to do things that you could not do before. You should know what the study of organizational behaviour involves, and you should be able to tell others what you know and think about it. You should be able to write essays and answer examination questions that previously you could not tackle. We can describe this process as learning, and the result as knowledge.

Learning the process of acquiring knowledge through experience which leads to a lasting change in behaviour.

It is important to note the limits on what counts as learning defined in terms of durability and experience. Behaviour can be changed temporarily by many factors, in ways which are not described as learning. Factors other than experience which alter our behaviour temporarily include maturation (in children), ageing (in adults), drugs, alcohol and fatigue.

From neurological research, we now know which areas of the brain are involved in learning and memory processes, although our understanding of these processes is incomplete. The study of learning, however, is not confined to brain surgery. We can *infer* that learning has taken place by examining changes in your behaviour. If we assume that behaviour does not alter spontaneously, for no reason, then we can look for experiences that may be causes of behaviour change. These experiences may be derived from inside the body, or they may be sensory, arising outside. The task of inferring whether or not learning has taken place may be an obvious one, but observable behaviour may not always reveal learning.

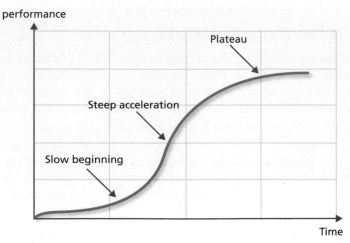

Figure 5.1: The typical manual skills learning curve

It is helpful to distinguish between two types of learning. Procedural learning, or 'knowing how', concerns your ability to carry out skilled actions, such as riding a horse or painting a picture. Declarative learning, or 'knowing that', concerns your store of factual knowledge, such as an understanding of the history of our use of the horse, or of the contribution of the European Futurist movement to contemporary art.

Changes in behaviour can be measured using a 'learning curve', one example of which is shown in Figure 5.1, concerning the development of manual skills.

The learning can be plotted for one person, for a group of trainees, or even for a whole organization. The learning curve illustrated in Figure 5.1 shows that:

1. Learning is not a smooth process, but changes in pace over time, until a stable peak performance is eventually reached.

2. The learner's ability develops slowly at first, then accelerates and develops more quickly, before finally reaching a plateau.

Learning curves for manual skills often follow this profile, but cognitive skills can develop in the same way. The shape of a learning curve depends on the characteristics of the task and of the learner. It is often possible to measure learning in this way, to compare individuals with each other, and to establish what constitutes good performance. If we understand the factors influencing the shape of the curve, we can develop ways to make learning more effective.

STOP AND THINK

Draw your own learning curve for this course.

Why is it that shape? What would your ideal learning curve look like?

How could you change the shape of this learning curve?

The experiences that lead to changes in behaviour have a number of important features.

First, the human mind is not a passive recorder of information picked up through the senses. We can often recall the plot of a novel, for example, but remember very few of the author's words. This suggests that we do not record experiences in a straightforward way.

Second, we are usually able to recall events in which we have participated as if we were another actor in the drama. We are able to reflect, to see ourselves 'from outside', as objects in our own experience. At the time when we experienced the events, those cannot have been the sense impressions that we picked up. Reflection is a valuable capability.

Behaviourist psychology
a perspective which argues that what we learn are chains of muscle movements; mental processes are not observable, and are not valid issues for study (also **stimulus–response psychology**).

Table 5.1: Behaviourist and cognitive perspectives

Behaviourist, stimulus-response	Cognitive, information processing
studies observable behaviour	studies mental processes
behaviour is determined by learned sequences of muscle movements	behaviour is determined by memory, mental processes and expectations
we learn habits	we learn cognitive structures
we solve problems by trial and error	we solve problems with insight and understanding
routine, mechanistic, open to direct research	rich, complex, studied using indirect methods

Cognitive psychology
a perspective which argues that what we learn are mental structures; mental processes can be studied by inference, although they cannot be observed directly (also **information processing psychology**).

Third, new experiences do not always lead to behaviour change. Declarative learning, for example, may not be evident until we are asked the right questions. Our experiences must be processed in some way if they are to influence our behaviour in future.

Fourth, the way in which we express our drives depends on a mix of genetics and experience. We have innate drives, which are expressed in behaviour in different ways, depending on a combination of factors. Our innate makeup biases our behaviour in certain directions, but these biases can be modified by experience.

This chapter explains two influential approaches to learning, based on behaviourist psychology and cognitive psychology. These perspectives are in many respects contradictory, but they can also be seen as complementary. Summarized in Table 5.1, these theoretical standpoints have different implications for organization and management practice.

The behaviourist approach to learning

John Broadus Watson (1878–1958)

Feedback information about the outcomes of our behaviour.

The American psychologist John Broadus Watson (1878–1958) introduced the term *behaviourism* in 1913. He was critical of the technique of introspection, a popular psychological technique at that time, in which subjects were asked to talk about their experiences and thought processes, to explore their minds, and to describe what they found there. Instead, Watson wanted objective, 'scientific' handles on human behaviour, its causes and its consequences. This took him, and many other psychologists, away from the intangible contents of the mind to study relationships between visible stimuli and visible responses. That is why behaviourist psychology is also referred to as 'stimulus–response psychology'.

Behaviourism assumes that what lies between the stimulus and the response is a mechanism that will be revealed as our knowledge of the biochemistry and neurophysiology of the brain develops. This mechanism must relate stimuli to responses in a way that governs behaviour. We can therefore continue to study how stimuli and responses are related without a detailed understanding of the nature of that mechanism. Behaviourists thus argue that nothing of *psychological* importance happens between stimulus and response. Cognitive psychology argues that something of considerable psychological importance happens here.

The oldest theory of learning states that actions that are experienced together tend to be associated with each other (touching a flame, pain). We use knowledge of the outcomes of past behaviour to do better in future (don't touch flames). You learn to get higher assignment grades by finding out how well you did last time and why. We cannot learn without feedback. Behaviourists and cognitive psychologists agree that experience affects behaviour, but disagree over how this happens.

Feedback can be rewarding or punishing. If a particular behaviour is rewarded, then it is more likely to be repeated. If it is punished or ignored, it is likely to be avoided in future. This is known as the 'law of effect', which states that we learn to repeat behaviours that have

Positive reinforcement the attempt to encourage desirable behaviours by introducing positive consequences when the desired behaviour occurs.

Negative reinforcement the attempt to encourage desirable behaviours by withdrawing negative consequences when the desired behaviour occurs.

Punishment the attempt to discourage undesirable behaviours through the application of negative consequences, or by withholding a positive consequence, following the undesirable behaviour.

Extinction the attempt to eliminate undesirable behaviours by attaching no consequences, positive or negative, such as indifference and silence.

favourable consequences, and avoid those that have neutral or undesirable outcomes. Rats can be trained to run through mazes with a combination of food pellets and electric shocks.

Behaviourism makes subtle distinctions relating to reward and punishment, illustrated in Table 5.2. With **positive reinforcement**, desired behaviours lead to positive consequences. With **negative reinforcement**, the undesirable outcomes continue until the desired behaviour occurs. As one-off **punishment** follows undesirable behaviour, this is different from negative reinforcement. Where behaviour has no positive or negative outcomes, this can lead to the **extinction** of that behaviour, as it comes to be seen as unimportant.

DESPITE YEARS OF MANAGEMENT TRAINING JOHN STILL FOUND IT DIFFICULT TO GIVE NEGATIVE FEEDBACK

Source: www.cartoonstock.com

STOP AND THINK

Some airlines, concerned about the cost of fuel, want to encourage passengers to carry less luggage (a lighter plane uses less fuel). One approach is to allow passengers with hand luggage only to skip the check-in queues. Another is to charge passengers extra for each item of luggage that they check in.

Which reinforcement regimes are being used to teach passengers to travel light?

Table 5.2: Reinforcement regimes

	behaviour	reinforcement	result	illustration
positive reinforcement	desired behaviour occurs	positive consequences are introduced	desired behaviour is repeated	confess, and stick to your story, and you will get a shorter prison sentence
negative reinforcement	desired behaviour occurs	negative consequences are withdrawn	desired behaviour is repeated	the torture will continue until you confess
punishment	undesired behaviour occurs	a single act of punishment is introduced	undesired behaviour is not repeated	fail to meet your scoring target and we kick you off the team
extinction	undesired behaviour occurs	the behaviour is ignored	undesired behaviour is not repeated	ignore an individual's practical jokes used to gain attention

Pavlovian conditioning
a technique for associating an established response or behaviour with a new stimulus (also **classical** and **respondent** conditioning).

Ivan Petrovich Pavlov (1849–1936)

The development of associations between stimuli and responses occurs in two different ways, known as **Pavlovian conditioning** and **Skinnerian conditioning**. Pavlovian conditioning, also known as **classical** and as **respondent** conditioning, was developed by the Russian physiologist Ivan Petrovich Pavlov (1849–1936).

The best-known response which Pavlov studied concerned a dog salivating at the sight of food. Pavlov demonstrated how this could be associated with a new and completely different stimulus, such as the sound of a bell. Dog owners are trained today in the use of classical conditioning methods. If you show meat to a dog, it will produce saliva. The meat is the stimulus, the saliva is the response. The meat is an *unconditioned* stimulus; the dog salivates naturally, and the saliva is an unconditioned response. Unconditioned responses are also called reflexes. Your lower leg jerks when you are struck just below the kneecap; your pupils contract when light is shone into your eyes. These are typical human reflexes. Humans also salivate, another unconditioned response, at the sight and smell of food.

Suppose we ring a bell before we show the meat to the dog. Do this often enough, and the dog will associate the bell with the meat. Soon, it will salivate at the sound of the bell, without food being present. The bell has become a *conditioned* stimulus, and the saliva is now a conditioned response. The dog has learned from experience to salivate at the sound of a bell as well as at the sight of food. It does not have to be a bell. All manner of stimuli can be conditioned in this way. Pavlov discovered this form of conditioning by accident. His research was initially concerned with salivation, but he observed that his dogs salivated at the sight and sound of his laboratory assistants, before they were given their meat. He found this more interesting, and changed the focus of his research.

STOP AND THINK   Can you recognize conditioned responses in your own behaviour? Is there a particular song, or a smell (perfume or after shave, or food cooking), that makes you think of another person, another place, another time, another experience?

Home viewing

The Truman Show

Pavlov has influenced Hollywood. In *The Truman Show* (1998, director Peter Weir), Truman Burbank (played by Jim Carrey) is adopted as a child by a television network. He believes that he is living a normal life, but he is actually a prisoner in an immense domed city-sized soundstage, simulating the town of Seahaven, where he is surrounded by actors who play members of his family, teachers, and employers. As in the *Big Brother* television series, his every action is broadcast to viewers around the world, 24 hours a day, and has created a multi-million dollar franchise for the network. If Truman were to quit, network profits would collapse. To stop him from leaving, the production team devise a plan based on Pavlovian conditioning. As you watch this movie, note how Truman's original conditioning is achieved. How does this conditioning affect Truman's daily life? How does he overcome his conditioning in his attempt to escape from Seahaven?

Suppose we now stop giving the meat to the dog after the bell. The dog will continue to salivate at the sound of the bell alone, expecting the bell to signal the arrival of food. If we continue to do this, however, the volume of saliva produced falls, and the association between the conditioned stimulus and conditioned response eventually suffers *extinction*. The conditioned response may also be invoked by stimuli similar to the original conditioned stimulus, such as a bell with a different pitch. This phenomenon is called *stimulus generalization*. A related phenomenon, *stimulus discrimination*, can be demonstrated by conditioning the dog to salivate at a bell of one pitch, but not at another.

Skinnerian conditioning
a technique for associating a response or a behaviour with its consequence (also **instrumental** and **operant** conditioning).

Burrhus Frederic Skinner (1904–1990)

Shaping the selective reinforcement of chosen behaviours in a manner that progressively establishes a desired behaviour pattern.

Skinnerian conditioning is also known as **instrumental** and as **operant** conditioning. It is the discovery of the American psychologist Burrhus Frederic Skinner (1904–1990). Instrumental conditioning demonstrates how new behaviours or responses become established through association with particular stimuli.

Where the consequence of a behaviour is desirable to the individual, then the frequency of that behaviour is likely to increase. Given a particular context, any behaviour that is rewarded or reinforced will tend to be repeated in that context. Skinner put a rat into a box (known as a 'Skinner box') with a lever which, when pressed, gave the animal food. The rat is not taught to press the lever in the box. However, wandering around the box, the rat eventually moves the lever. It may sit on it, knock it with its head, or push it with a paw. That random behaviour is reinforced with food, and so it is likely to happen again.

Classical conditioning has that name because it is the older of the two methods. Skinnerian conditioning is also called instrumental conditioning because it concerns behaviours that are instrumental in getting some material reward. Skinner's rat has to be under the influence of some drive before it can be conditioned in this way. His rats were hungry when they went into his box, and their behaviour thus led to a desired reward.

Where do the terms respondent and operant conditioning come from? Watson's stimulus–response psychology stated that there was no behaviour, or no response, without a stimulus to set it in motion. One could therefore condition a known response to a given stimulus. In other words, one could attach that response to another stimulus. Such responses are called respondents. Knee jerks, pupil contractions and salivation are well known and clearly identified responses that are amenable to conditioning.

Skinner observed that animals and humans do behave in the absence of specific stimuli, such as a rat wandering around in his Skinner box. Indeed, he argued that most human behaviour is of this kind. Behaviours that do not have identifiable stimuli are called operants. Operant conditioning thus explains how new behaviours are established, such as pressing that lever to get food. Respondent conditioning does not alter the animal's behaviour (the dog always did salivate when it thought that food was coming), only the behaviour's timing. Skinner also developed the technique of shaping, or the selective reinforcement of desired behaviours. He was able to get pigeons to play ping-pong and to walk in figures of eight – famous demonstrations of how spontaneous behaviours can be shaped by operant conditioning.

Conditioning at Amazon

Actually it *was* a bit of a sweatshop, or like something from the accounting halls of Dickens' *Bleak House* – a wasteland of cubicle dividers filled with the ceaseless murmuring of order numbers and apologies. If human misery and efficient boredom could be beautiful, there would have been a kind of beauty in the endlessly replicated, hot-desking, rack-mounted workers and their swiftly exchangeable work stations. Lit up by the dead light of our monitors, we would constantly scratch at our keyboards – it could have been sadly romantic, if it hadn't been for the sirens.

Hanging everywhere were readerboards showing the number of calls on hold and the average response time. When the numbers got too high they would turn red and a fearful, piercing whistle would go off, hooting over and over. People developed neurotic aversion to the sound, they shook and looked up like dogs when they heard it.

Msmith explained it to me. 'It's conditioning.'

'What is?'

'The sirens. they actually condition you to work faster.'

'Uh-huh.'

'No, I'm serious. Think about it: what's the most horrible sound you can think of right now?' The siren was blaring right over our head – eepEEP, eepEEP.

'I think that would be the siren.'

'Right. They make it so horrible so that you feel intense relief when the siren stops . . . Wait for it . . .' The siren stopped. 'See? Can you feel that?'

'Holy shit.' Sitting there, I could actually feel my heart rate dropping and my tension beginning to dissolve. 'It's like I'm wired to it.'

'Yeah. I heard they could have gotten a normal alarm, but the workflow analysts they hired said we'd work harder if we had something at stake.'

Source: © World Foto/Alamy

Jeff Bezos

Intermittent reinforcement
a procedure in which a reward is provided only occasionally following correct responses, and not for every correct response.

Schedule of reinforcement the pattern and frequency of rewards contingent on the display of desirable behaviour.

Skinner studied numerous variations on the operant conditioning theme. One important variation concerns the occasional reward of desired behaviour rather than delivering rewards in a continuous and regular manner. This mirrors real life more closely than the laboratory experiment. Why, for example, do gamblers keep playing when they lose much of the time? Why do anglers continue to fish when they catch nothing for hours at a time? There are many such examples of the power of intermittent reinforcement. Behaviour can be maintained without regular and consistent reinforcement every time that it occurs.

The pattern and timing of rewards for desired behaviour is known as the schedule of reinforcement. The possible variation in schedules of reinforcement is limitless, and Skinner investigated the effects of a number of these (Ferster and Skinner, 1957). However, there are two main classes of intermittent reinforcement, concerning interval schedules and ratio schedules, which are described in Table 5.3, contrasted with continuous reinforcement.

Skinner claimed to be able to explain the development of complex patterns of behaviour with the theory of operant conditioning. This shows how our behaviour is shaped by our environment, by our experiences in that environment, and by the selective rewards and punishments that we receive. Thinking, problem-solving, and the acquisition of language, he argued, are dependent on these simple conditioning processes. Skinner rejected the use of 'mentalistic' concepts and 'inner psychic forces' in explanations of human behaviour because these were not observable, were not researchable, and were therefore not necessary to the science of human psychology. Why use complicated and unobservable concepts when simple and observable phenomena seem to provide adequate explanations?

STOP AND THINK

In this cartoon, what modes of reinforcement are being discussed?

Skinner's ambitious and influential project led to the development of programmed learning, a technique of instruction designed to reinforce correct responses in the learner and to let people learn at their own pace. The **behaviour modification** techniques described later are also based on his ideas. As the behaviour of a conditioned animal is consistent and predictable, this can be used to test the effects of drugs.

Reinforcing desired behaviour is generally more effective than punishing undesirable behaviour. However, C.C. Walters and J.E. Grusek (1977), from a review of research, suggest that punishment can be effective if it meets the following conditions:

- the punishment should be quick and short;
- it should be administered immediately after the undesirable behaviour;
- it should be limited in its intensity;
- it should be specifically related to behaviour, and not to character traits;

Table 5.3: Schedules of reinforcement

schedule	description	effects on responses
continuous	reinforcement after *every correct response*	can establish high performance, but can also lead to satiation; rapid extinction when reinforcement is withheld
fixed ratio	reinforcement after a *predetermined number* of correct responses	tends to generate high rates of desired responses
variable ratio	reinforcement after a *random number* of correct responses	can produce a high response rate that is resistant to extinction
fixed interval	reinforcement of a correct response after a *predetermined period*	can produce uneven response patterns, slow following reinforcement, vigorous immediately preceding reinforcement
variable interval	reinforcement of a correct response after *random periods*	can produce a high response rate that is resistant to extinction

Based on Luthans and Kreitner (1985).

- it should be restricted to the context in which the undesirable behaviour occurs;
- it should not send 'mixed messages' about what is acceptable behaviour;
- penalties should take the form of withdrawal of rewards, not physical pain.

STOP AND THINK

To what extent should the criteria for effective punishment be used by managers when disciplining employees in an organizational context?

The cognitive approach to learning

Norbert Wiener
(1894–1964)

Cybernetic analogy
an explanation of the learning process based on the components and operation of a feedback control system.

Why should we look only at observable stimuli and responses in the study of psychology? It is possible to study the internal workings of the mind in indirect ways, by inference. Behaviourism seems to be unnecessarily restrictive, excluding those characteristics that make us interesting, different and, above all, human.

How do we select from all the stimuli that bombard our senses those to which we are going to respond? Why are some outcomes seen as rewarding and others as punishments? This may appear obvious where the reward is survival or food and the punishment is pain or death. However, with intrinsic or symbolic rewards this is not always clear. To answer these questions, we have to consider states of mind concerning perception and motivation.

The rewards and punishments that behaviourists call reinforcement work in more complex ways than conditioning theories suggest. Reinforcement is always knowledge, or **feedback**, about the success of past behaviour. Feedback is information that can be used to modify or maintain previous behaviours. This information has to be perceived, interpreted, given meaning, and used in decisions about future behaviours. The feedback has to be processed. Cognitive learning theories are thus also called information processing theories.

This approach draws concepts from the field of cybernetics which was established by the American mathematician Norbert Wiener (1954). He defined cybernetics as 'the science of communication in the animal and in the machine'. One central idea of cybernetics is the notion of the control of system performance through feedback. Information processing theories of learning are based on what is called the **cybernetic analogy**.

The elements of a cybernetic feedback control system are outlined in Figure 5.2.

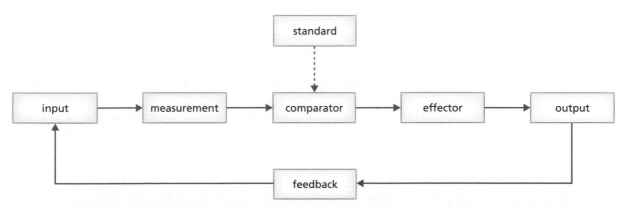

Figure 5.2: Elements of cybernetic feedback control

World of Warcraft, world of learning

If your boss tells you to stop playing that computer game and get back to work or you're fired, you now have a good answer. It's not just a game. It's a training programme, and you are learning valuable business skills that will improve your performance at work. David Edery and Ethan Mollick argue that the skills required to succeed in computer games such as *World of Warcraft* or *The Sims* are also useful organizational and managerial capabilities. These include mental, social, and creative problem-solving skills. As well as developing persistence and competition, gaming promotes community-building, as users exchange ideas and game modifications ('mods').

Games are used by companies for product placement and advertising (advergames, adverworlds), and are now also used in corporate training programmes. Medical schools use game-like simulations to train surgeons, reducing their error rate. Google uses video games to turn visitors into voluntary employees, asking them to label the millions of images on the web which Google cannot identify on its own. Games are also used to reach new customers, build brands, recruit and develop new staff, and encourage creativity and experimentation.

Games are fun and motivational. Before it releases a new operating system, Microsoft asks staff to help debug it. The Microsoftees find this boring, and project managers spend a lot of time persuading them to do it. For Windows Vista, participation in debugging quadrupled when Microsoft created a game that awarded points for bug-testing and prizes for achieving goals. Now that you have read this, is it back to work, or back to the keyboard?

Based on Edery and Mollick (2008).

Intrinsic feedback information which comes from within, from the muscles, joints, skin, and other mechanisms such as that which controls balance.

Extrinsic feedback information which comes from our environment, such as the visual and aural information needed to drive a car.

Concurrent feedback information which arrives during our behaviour and which can be used to control behaviour as it unfolds.

Delayed feedback information which is received after a task is completed, and which can be used to influence future performance.

Consider a domestic heating control system. The temperature standard is set on a thermostat, and a heater (effector) starts to warm up the room. The output of the system is heated air. Changes in temperature are measured by a thermometer. The temperature of the room is continually compared with the standard. When the room reaches the required temperature, the effector is switched off, and when the room cools, it is switched on again.

The cybernetic analogy says that this control loop is a model of what goes on inside the mind. For standard, read motive, purpose, intent, or goals. The output is behaviour. The senses are our measuring devices. Our perceptual process is the comparator which organizes and imposes meaning on the sensory data which control behaviour in pursuit of our goals. We have some kind of internal representation or 'schema' of ourselves and our environment. This internal representation is used in a purposive way to determine our behaviour, and is also known as the individual's **perceptual world** (see Chapter 8).

We formulate plans to achieve our purposes. These plans are sets of mental instructions for guiding the required behaviour. Within the master plan (get an educational qualification) there are likely to be a number of subplans (submit essays on time; pass examinations; make new friends). The organization of our behaviour is hierarchical – a concept which is also seen in computer programs where routines and subroutines are 'nested' within each other.

We can also use information on how we are doing – feedback – to update our internal representation and to refine and adapt our plans. Feedback can either be self-generated or come from an external source: it can be either intrinsic or extrinsic.

Independent of the source and nature of the feedback, timing is also important. Feedback can arrive during, or after the behaviour in which we are interested in learning: it can be either concurrent or delayed.

Intrinsic feedback is invariably concurrent. When you throw rings over pegs at the fair to win a soft toy, the intrinsic concurrent visual feedback means that you know immediately how well (or how badly) you are performing. Some extrinsic feedback is also concurrent; from a driving instructor, for example. However, for your next course assignment, feedback from your lecturer is going to be delayed. Instructors cannot provide

STOP AND THINK From your own experience, identify an example of each of the four varieties of feedback. What changes in that feedback would be required for you to be able to improve your performance (on this course, at sport, whatever)?

concurrent feedback on your essay or project, but the longer the delay, the less effective the feedback is likely to be.

Feedback, rewards and punishments, and knowledge of results, also have a *motivating* effect on behaviour, as well as a reinforcing effect. Several researchers argue that opportunities to learn new skills and knowledge, to understand more, to develop more effective ways of coping with our environment, are intrinsically motivating. The American psychologist Robert W. White (1959) suggests that we have a motive to develop 'competence' and that this gives us satisfaction. As the later section on the learning organization demonstrates, the 'urge towards discovery' and the 'will to understand' has triggered a search for novel organizational forms in which individual and organizational learning are encouraged.

Behaviourism in practice

Behaviour modification
a technique for encouraging desired behaviours and discouraging unwanted behaviours using operant conditioning.

Behaviourism led to the development of behaviour modification techniques, first used to treat mental and learning disorders, and phobias, and for psychiatric rehabilitation and accident and trauma recovery. These methods are now used in many organizational settings.

As developed by Fred Luthans (Luthans and Kreitner, 1985; Luthans *et al.*, 1998), organizational behaviour modification, or OBMod, has five steps:

1. *Identify* the critical, observable and measurable behaviours to be encouraged.
2. *Measure* the current frequency of those behaviours, to provide a baseline against which to measure improvement.
3. *Establish* the triggers or antecedents for those behaviours, and also establish the consequences – positive, neutral and negative – that follow from those behaviours.
4. *Develop* a strategy to strengthen desired behaviours and weaken dysfunctional behaviours through positive reinforcement (money, recognition) and feedback; punishment may be necessary in some cases, for example to inhibit unsafe behaviour.
5. *Evaluate* systematically the effectiveness of the approach in changing behaviour and improving performance compared with the original baseline measurement.

Fred Luthans
(b.1939)

Behaviour modification is attractive to managers who can manipulate the reinforcement of employee behaviours, and the approach focuses on behaviour rather than on internal mental states and processes. Desirable behaviours include speaking politely to customers, attending training, helping colleagues, or in a hospital, washing hands regularly to reduce infections. Undesirable behaviours include lateness, making poor quality items, and being rude to customers. OBMod uses reinforcement to eliminate undesired behaviour and to encourage desired behaviour. Suppose a manager wants more work assignments completed on time, and fewer submitted beyond deadline. The OBMod options are summarized in Table 5.4.

Table 5.4: Behaviour modification options

Procedure	Operationalization	Behavioural effect
positive reinforcement	manager praises employee each time work is completed on schedule	increases desired work behaviour
negative reinforcement	unpaid overtime continues to be mandatory until work is completed on schedule, then overtime is rewarded	increases desired work behaviour
punishment	manager asks employee to stay late when work is not handed in on time	eliminates or decreases undesired behaviour
extinction	manager ignores the employee when work is handed in late	eliminates or decreases undesired behaviour

OBMod, MRSA and ICUs

Adverse events cost the UK health service £2 billion a year, and hospital-acquired infections cost a further £1 billion. Human error seems to be the main cause, but research shows that organization culture and management systems can encourage undesirable behaviour. Could behaviour modification techniques be used to improve patient safety?

Dominic Cooper and colleagues describe a hospital OBMod programme which aimed to reduce infections, such as MRSA (methicillin-resistant *staphylococcus aureus*). The usual methods include screening, isolation, cleaning, monitoring, training, awareness-raising, and improved policies and protocols, but that wasn't enough to solve the problem. Two intensive care units (ICUs) were involved, employing 140 doctors, nurses, healthcare assistants and administrative staff. The units had many visitors, including physicians, other hospital staff, family members and friends. The programme focused on two behaviours. The first was hand-washing, to reduce the spread of infection; research shows that doctors wash their hands on less than 10 per cent of appropriate occasions. The second concerned the accuracy and completeness of nursing documents which record patients' conditions.

Staff were briefed on the aims and conduct of the programme, to engage them in problem-solving and in generating ideas (such as installing a sink at the entrance where visitors could wash before coming in). Staff were asked to identify their main concerns, and what they saw as the most common undesired behaviours. A project coordinator and eight observers were trained in behaviour modification methods; how to observe, how to give feedback, how to set improvement goals. A checklist of 36 desired behaviours was developed, so that observers could record compliance, which they did by standing at the central nursing station for 20 minutes at a randomly chosen time each day. Observation data were analysed weekly, posted on a feedback chart, and discussed in group feedback meetings.

The results showed significant changes in behaviour which along with other methods reduced MRSA infections by 70 per cent. With fewer MRSA patients, there was extra ICU capacity, reduced laboratory costs, less overtime and temporary staff costs, and reduced costs of complaints. These outcomes were attributed to motivation to provide quality care (goals), and to the weekly performance data (feedback) which let staff know that they were doing a good job. Apart from the time that staff spent training, observing, and in meetings, the programme costs came to only a few hundred pounds for clerical materials and cleaning items.

Based on Cooper et al. *(2005).*

Fred Luthans and colleagues (1998) describe how OBMod improved productivity in a Russian textile mill. For performance improvements, workers were given extrinsic rewards including American products such as adults' and children's clothing, jeans, T-shirts with popular logos, music tapes and food that was difficult to get in Russia. They were also given 'social rewards' (attention, recognition, feedback) for specific actions, such as checking looms, undertaking repairs, monitoring fabric quality, and helping others. This approach had a 'very positive impact' leading to 'highly significant increases in performance' (Luthans *et al.*, 1998, p.471). Asking the workers for ideas on how to improve performance got no response; the culture and political climate prevented them from making suggestions which would criticize methods and colleagues. Luthans concludes that OBMod 'fits' Eastern European organizational cultures where it has wide applicability.

OBMod has the following characteristics:

- It applies to clearly identifiable and observable behaviours, such as timekeeping, carrying out checks and repairs, and the use of particular work methods.
- Rewards are contingent on the performance of the desirable behaviours.
- Positive reinforcement can take a number of forms, from the praise of a superior to cash prizes, to food, to clothing.
- Behaviour change and performance improvements can be dramatic.
- The desired modification in behaviour may only be sustained if positive reinforcement is continued (although this may be intermittent).

STOP AND THINK How do you feel about being given food, T-shirts, and praise for working harder?

Do you regard this approach as practical, or as demeaning – and why?

Cognitive perspectives in practice

Socialization the process through which individual behaviours, values, attitudes and motives are influenced to conform with those seen as desirable in a given social or organizational setting.

When people join an organization, they give up some personal freedom of action. That is part of the price of membership. Employees thus accept that an organization can make demands on their time and effort, as long as these demands are perceived to be legitimate. Other members of the organization have to teach new recruits what is expected of them. The process through which recruits are 'shown the ropes' is called socialization. Cognitive psychologists regard behaviour modification as simplistic, and turn to more complex social explanations and methods for organizational behaviour change.

This perspective draws on social learning theory which is based on assumptions about human psychology different from those behind OBMod techniques. One of the most influential advocates of social learning theory has been Albert Bandura (1977, 1986), who showed that we learn new behaviours by observing and copying others, through behavioural modelling. We copy the behaviour of others without the need for rewards or punishments to encourage us to do this. However, if the behaviours that we copy are successful (in other words, rewarded or reinforced by positive results), then we are more likely to continue to act in that way. Our capabilities for reflection and self-determination are central in this perspective. We construct, through observation and experience, internal models of our environment, and plan courses of action accordingly. The ways in which we model ourselves on others is particularly apparent in children, and we continue to copy or imitate others as adults.

Albert Bandura (b.1925)

Behavioural modelling learning how to act by observing and copying the behaviour of others.

Provisional selves from observing others, the experiments that we make with the ways in which we act and interact in new organizational roles.

Bandura's argument that we learn through social experience, through observation and modelling, does not deny the importance of reinforcement. Behavioural modelling involves the four processes of attention, retention, production, and reinforcement outlined in Figure 5.3. Suppose we choose to base some of our behaviours (how to handle a job interview, how to make new friends) on a chosen model, someone who is successful in those areas. Suppose that our new approach does not lead to the desired results; didn't get the job, failed to establish relationships. Without reinforcement, we will abandon those new behaviours and look for other models. If our new methods are successful, however, we will use them again.

When we get a new job, we have to learn how to 'fit in', and this means following the norms and rules that are considered to be appropriate in the organization. From her study of financial analysts and consultants, Herminia Ibarra (1999) shows how we adapt to new roles by experimenting with provisional selves, which are based on the role models that we see around us. This process, she found, has three stages:

observing   we watch other people to see how they behave and respond

experimenting we try out some of those behaviours to see how they work for us

evaluating   we use our own assessment and feedback from others to decide which
                    behaviours to keep, and which to discard

Our observations of role models in a new organizational setting can cover a wide range of issues; physical appearance, personal style, ways of interacting, displays of skill. This does not simply mean that we copy others. We choose the behaviours that we feel are credible and consistent with how we see ourselves, and with how we want others to see us; competent, creative, enthusiastic, trustworthy – for example. We do this by experimenting, keeping those actions that we like, and discarding those that don't work, or which are inconsistent with our self-image. Comments from Ibarra's interviewees illustrate this:

There are a good half dozen to a dozen senior people I'd view as mentors. I think up until director, you're building your skills, you're trying on different styles, like different

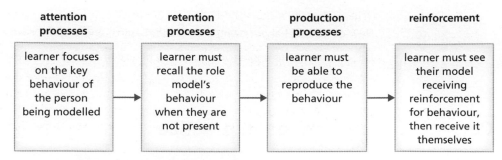

Figure 5.3: The behavioural modelling process
Source: Based on Weiss (1990).

clothes, almost. You try and figure out what styles fit your personality and fit what you're good at. And then that's how you should try to go after business (p.777).

I've been out with X and watched him in action. He's very aggressive in new business – one of the best in the firm. He has a very charismatic personality, which is something you can't teach. I don't think I could really replicate his style. I'm not as outgoing, but I think the attitude and persistence are things that I have (p.775).

I don't have an aggressive personality. I have been told I need to improve. I have adjusted to it by becoming more assertive over time. Just watching P was good. She is very vocal, asks lots of questions, always makes sure she has a point to make, is very assertive. Now I do like she does (p.780).

STOP AND THINK Think of two people who you have observed recently – one a real person, the other a character in a movie or a television programme. How have they influenced you? Which of their behaviours have you adopted? How did that work out? What behaviours have you decided not to adopt, and why? For whom are you a role model in this way?

How does social learning theory apply to organizational settings? Organizations encourage different standards concerning:

- what counts as good work performance;
- familiarity in social interactions at work;
- the amount of deference to show to superiors;
- dress and appearance;
- social activities after work;
- attitudes to work, colleagues, managers, unions, customers.

You have to learn these standards and the ways of behaving and related attitudes that they involve, to become an effective and accepted member of the organization. You do not have to believe that the organization's standards are appropriate. In order to 'fit in', what matters is that you behave *as if* you believe in those norms.

Home viewing

In the first half of *Full Metal Jacket* (1987, director Stanley Kubrick), unquestioning obedience from new recruits is demanded for membership of the US marines. In *Fight Club* (1999, director Peter Fincher), a similar level of compliance is required in order to join 'Project Mayhem'. As you watch these films, identify the different rules of membership in the two organizations. What learning processes are used to elicit conformity from members? What is the purpose of the oral intimidation to which they are exposed? How do these learning processes affect individuals' identities?

The socialization process can thus be informal. Often, newcomers learn the ropes just by watching their new colleagues. Socialization is thus achieved without planned intervention, by giving rewards such as praise, encouragement, and promotion for 'correct' behaviour. It is supported by negative reinforcements and punishments, like being ignored, ridiculed or fined for behaviour that is 'out of line'. We quickly learn what attitudes to take, what style of language to use, what 'dress code' to obey, where to take lunch and with whom, and so on. Some organizations have formal induction courses, but these are often brief, and focus on routine issues like organization structures and policies, and health and safety regulations.

STOP AND THINK
Remember when you first joined this college or university; how did you feel about the formal socialization or induction process? To what informal, unplanned socialization were you exposed? Which had the greater impact on your behaviour, the formal or the informal processes?

Note that some of the positive outcomes are material, in the form of money and desirable working conditions (bigger office and desk, subsidized meals, access to free sports and leisure facilities, a space in the car park). Some of the available rewards, on the other hand, are symbolic and social rewards such as prestige, status, recognition and public praise.

Managed socialization in action

Social learning theory argues that we learn correct behaviours through experience and through the examples or *role models* that other people provide. While this can happen naturally, some companies prefer not to leave it to chance, and to manage the process instead. For example, some companies use a 'buddy system', pairing new recruits with established employees. However, if you get a job with the American computer software company Trilogy, based in Austin, Texas, you will not be given a buddy, or a one-day induction by your new boss. Instead, you will be sent to Trilogy University (TU) for three months, to join an orientation programme modelled on Marine Corps basic training. This is a 'boot camp', intense and intimidating, designed to challenge new recruits, most of whom are university graduates with an average age of 22. Trilogy wants to familiarize them quickly with appropriate knowledge and job skills, and also with the company's 'vision and values'. Run twice a year, over 12 weeks, for between 60 and 200 recruits at a time, the boot camp has three stages.

Month one

New recruits are assigned to a section, of about 20 people, and to an instruction track. The section leader is an experienced Trilogy employee, and the tracks resemble work in the company. Along with functional training,

constantly evaluated, recruits are given a series of increasingly challenging assignments, which mirror real customer problems, but with reduced timescales. Students are stretched beyond the point of failure in order to introduce company values including humility, creativity, innovation, teamwork, customer problem-solving, and risk taking. Another goal is to develop lasting, trusting relationships with colleagues.

Month two

This is project month, and recruits are told that, 'in order for the company to survive, they have to come up with a frame-breaking great new business idea'. Teams of three to five have to generate an idea, create a business model, build the product, develop a marketing plan and present the results to the Chief Executive. These projects are real, and around 15 per cent are funded. Recruits are expected to learn about the need to set priorities, evaluate probabilities and measure results. Failure to generate a successful idea is not punished.

Month three

Most recruits move on to business-related 'graduation projects', and leave TU as they find sponsors willing to take them on. Graduation involves a meeting between the recruit, the new manager and the section leader, at which the recruit's abilities are reviewed, their personal career objectives are examined, and the manager's three- to five-year goals for the recruit (including further skill development) are agreed. Most graduates find a home in the company, but those few who cannot find a sponsor have to leave.

Since 1995, when TU was founded, projects developed by recruits have generated revenues of $25 million, and have formed the basis for $100 million in new business for the company. These innovative ideas include internet-based motor car retailing, and a website which allows shoppers to put products from several different internet retailers into a single purchase. In addition, the section leaders assigned for three months to inspire, motivate, mentor and develop the new recruits develop their leadership and change agency skills.

Based on Tichy (2001).

Behaviour modification versus socialization

Is behaviour modification a useful approach to learning at work and the development of appropriate behaviours? The evidence suggests a qualified 'yes'; there are two qualifications.

First, behaviour modification needs careful planning to identify specific behavioural goals, and procedures for reinforcing the behaviours that will achieve those goals. The method can be effective when behaviour and reinforcement are clearly identified and linked; wear your seat belt and we'll give you cash. The method is less effective when this relationship is vague; demonstrate commitment and we'll consider you for promotion.

Second, the 'rewards for good behaviour' method appears broadly consistent with American (and perhaps Eastern European) cultural values and aspirations. The transfer of this approach to other cultures is questionable. The most often cited practical examples are American.

STOP AND THINK   You are responsible for training the new shelf-stacker in your local supermarket. What combination of behaviour modification and socialization techniques will you use, and how will you apply these?

Behaviour modification is manipulative, often ignores internal needs and intrinsic rewards, and can be a threat to individual dignity and autonomy. It can be seen as a simplistic and transparent attempt to manipulate, prompting cynicism rather than behaviour change. The technique thus has limitations. However, OBMod requires the communication of goals and expectations in unambiguous terms. Many would argue that this clarity is desirable. Fred Luthans and R. Kreitner (1985) summarize the problems with behaviour modification:

1. Appropriate reinforcers may not always be available, in limited and boring work settings, for example.

2. We do not all respond the same way to the same reinforcers; what one person finds rewarding may be of little consequence to someone else.

3. Once started, a behaviour modification programme has to be sustained.

4. There may not be enough extrinsic motivators (money and luncheon vouchers, for example) available.

They also argue, however, that the technique has made significant contributions:

1. Behaviour modification techniques put the focus on observable employee behaviour and not on hypothetical internal states.

2. The method shows how performance is influenced by contingent consequences.

3. It supports the view that positive reinforcement is more effective in changing employee behaviour than punishment.

4. It is possible to show a clear causal link to performance, which is often hard to establish with other behaviour change methods, such as job enrichment.

Behavioural self-management (BSM)

Management attempts to modify the behaviour of others raises ethical questions. Self-improvement, however, is acceptable and fashionable. Fred Luthans and Tim Davis (1979) developed the technique of **behavioural self-management** for individual use.

BSM combines the behavioural focus of OBMod with the cognitive processes central to social learning theory. It is not merely a form of self-imposed behaviour modification. Social learning theory argues that we actively process stimuli and consequences, in a self-monitoring fashion, whereas behaviourism sees our behaviour shaped by rewards and punishments.

BSM involves the following steps:

1. *Identify the undesirable behaviour* that you want to change, develop or improve.

2. *Manage the situational cues* which trigger desired behaviour. Avoid situations which trigger the target behaviour, seek situations which encourage desired behaviour instead. Use 'reminders and attention focusers' such as notes stuck in prominent places, and 'self observation data' recording success and lapses. Set personal contracts, establish behavioural goals, post records of these in prominent places.

3. *Provide cognitive support* for the new behaviour. There are three ways to do this. First, through *symbolic coding*, using visual images and acronyms to support the desired behaviour (KISS, MBWA). Second, through *mental rehearsal* of the desired behaviour (a technique used by many successful sports people). Third,

through *self-talk*, which is positive and supportive of the desired behaviour change.

4. *Develop self-reinforcement*, which is within your control, and which is delivered only on condition that the desired behaviour change is achieved. This can be strengthened by arranging also for positive reinforcement from supportive friends and colleagues.

This web of situational cues, cognitive support, and self-reinforcement can be a powerful combination in helping to eliminate target behaviours and establish desired behaviours in their place. Using this technique, Rakos and Grodek (1984) report how American college students successfully modified behaviour problems concerning smoking, lack of assertiveness, poor study habits, overeating, sloppy housekeeping, lack of exercise and moodiness. Luthans and Davis (1979) describe how the technique was used to deal with management behaviour problems such as overdependence on the boss, ignoring paperwork, leaving the office without notifying anybody, and failing to fill out expense reports.

Apply behavioural self-management to yourself. Target a behaviour of current personal significance; drinking, smoking, overeating, excessive clubbing, inappropriate study habits. Establish a pattern of situational cues, cognitive support and self-reinforcement. Set a timescale, and use your experience to assess the power and relevance of this technique.

Based on Kreitner et al. (1999, pp.457–61).

Behavioural self-management a technique for changing one's own behaviour by systematically manipulating cues, cognitive processes and contingent consequences.

Socialization has the advantage of flexibility. Social learning is dependent on the cultural context, and as a process rather than a specific technique, the general approach is not restricted to one culture. American induction and socialization procedures may be quite different from Swedish, Belgian, Nigerian, Malaysian or Spanish methods.

Socialization is a process that takes place anyway, planned or not. The issue concerns appropriate socialization, with respect to existing organization culture and behavioural preferences. Because it is a 'natural' process, with no clear financial or other material benefit from investing in its operation, it may be difficult to persuade management to give socialization the attention and resource that some commentators suggest. However, as the following section demonstrates, some organizations have introduced the methods of the **learning organization**. This is an attempt to socialize an organization's members with respect to attitudes and behaviours related to the acquisition and development of new knowledge, creativity, innovation, flexibility and readiness for change.

Table 5.5 summarizes the contrasts between behaviour modification and socialization.

Table 5.5: Behaviour modification versus socialization

Behaviour modification	Socialization
feedback needed in both approaches for behaviour to change	
planned procedure	naturally occurring, even if also planned
stimulus determines responses	individual needs determine responses
externally generated reinforcements	internally generated reinforcements
focuses on observable behaviour	focuses on unobservable internal states
focus on tangible rewards and punishments (money, other material rewards)	focus on intangible rewards and punishments (social inclusion, self-esteem)
clear links between desired behaviour and consequence	intangible links between desired behaviour and consequences
compliance required by external agent	conformity encouraged by social grouping

The learning organization

Chris Argyris
(b.1923)

Donald Schön
(1930–1997)

The concept of the **learning organization** is based on the work of Chris Argyris and Donald Schön (Argyris and Schön, 1974, 1978; Argyris, 1982). Marleen Huysman (1999, p.61) offers this definition:

The learning organization concept has become significant for several reasons:

- the production of goods and services increasingly involves sophisticated knowledge;
- knowledge is, therefore, as valuable a resource as raw materials;
- many organizations have lost knowledgeable staff through retirements and delayering;
- information technologies are knowledge intensive;
- some knowledge can have a short life span, made obsolete by innovation;
- flexibility, creativity and responsiveness are now prized capabilities;
- knowledge can thus be a source of competitive advantage for an organization.

Ikujiro Nonaka and Hirotaka Takeuchi (1995) argue that the ability to create knowledge and solve problems is a 'core competence' for most organizations. For them, everyone is a knowledge worker. Anyone dealing with customers, such as the ticket clerk in a theatre run by the local council, is a source of intelligence on customer perceptions of pricing, facilities, and productions. These 'boundary workers' often have poorly paid jobs (receptionists, porters, sales staff), and their customer intelligence is overlooked as their positions are distant, in terms of physical location and organization structure, from management.

Learning is the new sex (or should be)

When Barclays Bank set up its corporate university, it wanted to develop something different. Paul Rudd, the director of Barclays University (known as 'BU') said that, 'Corporate universities are pretty ill-defined and many organizations just re-branded their training departments to make them sound sexier.' The company focus groups showed that

employees were not 'engaged' either by attending training courses, or by sitting at computer screens.

The bank set up a series of leading edge 'metro centres' in existing bank buildings, but with a radically different environment. Each metro centre cost £1 million to establish, and typical features include:

- background music
- café area
- high-tech training rooms
- Zen room in which to relax
- library
- 48-hour free ordering service for books, videos and CDs

The libraries do not have books on banking, but on subjects such as teaching children to read, t'ai chi, and anger management. The centres are open in the evenings, and also at weekends, when families are allowed to visit. Each of the bank's 65,000 staff has a £150 allowance to spend on anything that is related to learning. During the summer, the centres run courses, and there is a BU summer school for employees' children. BU's director Paul Rudd argues that:

> We're trying to develop Barclays into an employer of choice. It's something more than working in a great environment. It's something you can involve your wife, husband, partner or children in, and it's a reason for not just coming to work but to develop through your work and through the opportunities at Barclays University.

He also says that, 'learning is something we want people to see as sexy and something they want to do as opposed to being forced to do'. In other words, if learning isn't the new sex, then it should be.

Based on Persaud (2004).

Karl Weick and Frances Westley (1996, p.440) point out that the concepts of 'organization' and 'learning' are contradictory. Organization implies structure, order, stability. Learning implies change, variety, disorganization. Management is concerned with models of best practice and consulting tools. The popular book by Peter Senge *et al.* (1999) includes an 'owner registration form', to return after indicating in tick boxes your interest in speakers, seminars, further materials, or hiring the authors as consultants.

STOP AND THINK

An organization doesn't exist without its members. How can an organization 'learn'?

Peter Senge
(b.1947)

The idea of the learning organization was popularized by Peter Senge whose book, *The Fifth Discipline* (1990) was an international best-seller. Senge argues (1990, p.4) that work at all levels must become more 'learningful'. He identifies five 'learning disciplines'; Table 5.6.

Table 5.6: Five learning disciplines

Learning discipline	Explanation
1. Personal mastery	*aspiration*, concerning what you as an individual want to achieve
2. Mental models	*reflection and inquiry*, concerning the constant refinement of thinking and development of awareness
3. Shared vision	*collective commitment* to a common sense of purpose and actions to achieve that purpose
4. Team learning	*group interaction*, concerning collective thinking and action to achieve common goals
5. Systems thinking	*understanding interdependency and complexity* and the role of feedback in system development

Organizational learning in Ireland

A survey of over 260 senior human resource managers in multinational companies in Ireland showed that over half had a formal policy to facilitate organizational learning across their global operations. The most common learning methods were:

- international informal networks
- international project groups
- expatriate assignments
- international formal committees
- international secondments to external organizations.

Over 60 per cent of multinational companies used more than three of these organizational learning methods, and only 15 per cent used none. American owned multinationals, however, spent more on organizational learning than their British, European, or Irish competitors.

Based on Gunnigle et al. *(2007).*

Senge's argument is – have realistic goals, challenge your assumptions, commit to a shared vision, teamworking is good. The application of these 'disciplines', however, is problematic, and is linked to our discussion of socialization, to encouraging the 'correct' attitudes, values and beliefs among employees at all levels. The most important learning discipline is 'the fifth discipline', systems thinking, which means understanding how complex organizations function, and how they can be changed to work more effectively. The theory is:

> [T]he practice of organizational learning involves developing tangible activities: new governing ideas, innovations in infrastructure, and new management methods and tools for changing the way people conduct their work. Given the opportunity to take part in these new activities, people will develop an enduring capability for change. The process will pay back the organization with far greater levels of diversity, commitment, innovation and talent (Senge *et al.*, 1999, p.33).

In other words, the manager who wants commitment, flexibility and creativity from employees must provide them with lots of learning opportunities.

Is yours a learning organization?

A survey tool for deciding if you have a learning organization has been developed by David Garvin, Amy Edmondson and Francesca Gino. They felt that while Peter Senge and others had provided a compelling vision of the learning organization, they had not developed a practical approach to implementing the idea. The effective learning organization, they argue, has three building blocks. Here are the three blocks, their components, and a sample of the survey items used to measure how well your learning organization functions:

Block 1: Supportive learning environment

psychological safety	In this unit, it is easy to speak up about what is on your mind
appreciation of differences	Differences in opinion are welcome in this unit
openness to new ideas	In this unit, people are interested in better ways of doing things
time for reflection	Despite the workload, people in this unit find time to review how the work is going

Block 2: Concrete learning processes and practices

experimentation	This unit experiments frequently with new ways of working
information collection	This unit frequently compares its performance with that of competitors and 'best-in-class organizations'
analysis	This unit engages in productive conflict and debate during discussions
education and training	In this unit, time is made available for education and training activities
information transfer	This unit regularly shares information with networks of experts within and outside the organization

Block 3: Leadership that reinforces learning

My managers invite input from others in discussion

Managers acknowledge their limitations with respect to knowledge, information, or expertise

My managers listen attentively

These building blocks overlap with and reinforce each other, but measuring an organization's performance in each area identifies areas of excellence and opportunities for improvement.

Some commentators argue that a learning organization helps its members to learn. Others claim that the organization itself learns. How can this be? Silvia Gherardi (1997, p.542) treats the term learning organization as a metaphor which regards an organization as a biological entity, as 'a subject which learns, which processes information, which reflects on experiences, which is endowed with a stock of knowledge, skills and expertise'.

Gherardi supports the view that organizations learn with experience, the proof lying with visible changes in an organization's behaviour. For example, in the development of manufacturing processes, the staff hours required to produce a unit of output decrease with accumulated experience, even though the staff change. Another example concerns the ways in which organizations evolve and adapt to 'fit' their environment, introducing internal structural changes in response to environmental opportunities and pressures.

Carlsberg puts learning on tap

Carlsberg shut its entire Leeds brewery for one day for staff to be given additional training. The move was designed to give health and safety advice to 170 staff at the Danish lager firm, update them on new technology and hold wellness and personal development sessions. Such a large-scale initiative marks a change of thinking for Carlsberg, Natalie Steed, change manager, HR, told *People Management*.

'Stopping production for training is rare in manufacturing, if not unprecedented', said Steed. 'But feedback from staff told us it was what they wanted, and having all the trainers on site on a single day meant we could spend our training budget in the most effective way.'

Usually, training at the company is conducted in groups of eight people, which is as many as can be spared at any one time. Shutting the plant gave them time to go beyond the bare essentials, explained Steed. 'It's given us the time to carry out things we've always wanted to do – particularly around health and well-being – rather than just doing what we have to do', she said.

The day was a boost for learning at all levels. Engineers, who typically have high-level degrees, were given the chance to carry out a 'skills gap analysis' to identify areas to improve. It was also an opportunity to promote Carlsberg's new learning centre, where staff can pursue courses in numeracy, literacy and basic IT skills. The learning day idea is now set to be repeated in Carlsberg's other UK brewery, in Northampton.

From People Management
(30 October 2008, p.8).

Organizations also have available to them several different types of knowledge, not all of which are dependent on individual expertise (Gherardi, 1997, p.547). This includes learning from past experience through assessment and evaluation, and learning from the experience of other organizations. There is also knowledge 'built in' to equipment and raw materials, with formulae, ingredients, recipes, known properties and so on. Standard operating procedures can usually be found in instruction manuals, forms and job descriptions – all ways of codifying knowledge. Many organizations also possess patents and property rights.

Karl Weick and Frances Westley (1996) argue that organizational learning is best understood in terms of *organization culture*. Culture includes values, beliefs, feelings, artefacts, myths, symbols, metaphors and rituals, which taken together distinguish one organization or group from others. Organizations are thus 'repositories of knowledge' independent of their members (Schön, 1983, p.242). Organizations which accumulate stocks of codified, documented knowledge, independent of their members, can thus be said to learn.

Weick and Westley (1996) note how different organizational forms are better equipped for learning. The post-modern organization described in Chapter 2 adapts to change in its environment in an innovative, creative, responsive manner. This is an organizational form associated with creative thinking and rapid learning, and has also been described as 'adhocracy'. Bureaucracy, on the other hand, is concerned with efficiency, division of labour, rigid chain of command, and with clear distinctions and rationality.

How can 'organizational learning' be understood? Argyris and Schön (1974) developed the distinction between **single-loop learning** and **double-loop learning**.

The concept of single-loop learning comes from cybernetics, where control systems are considered in terms of norms, standards, procedures, routines and feedback; see Figure 5.2. The classic example of cybernetic control is the domestic thermostat which, by detecting temperature variations, takes action to correct deviations from a predetermined norm. In single-loop learning, the system maintains performance at that norm, and is unable to 'learn' that the norm is too high or too low. It is unable to 'learn how to learn', to challenge and rethink its values and assumptions. Limited to making small scale changes, single-loop learning is not really learning at all.

Single-loop learning the ability to use feedback to make continuous adjustments and adaptations, to maintain performance at a predetermined standard.

Double-loop learning the ability to challenge and to redefine the assumptions underlying performance standards and to improve performance.

STOP AND THINK Let us assume that you are learning during your organizational behaviour course. Is this single-loop learning, or double-loop learning? Which of these two types of learning should you be engaged in?

Learning how to learn involves double-loop learning. This means challenging assumptions, beliefs, norms, routines and decisions, rather than accepting them and working within those limitations. In single-loop learning, the question is, how can we better achieve that standard of performance? With double-loop learning, in contrast, the question becomes, is that an appropriate target in the first place? Mary Jo Hatch (1997, p.372) observes that:

> Double-loop learning, once strictly the domain of strategists and top managers, is increasingly being seen as taking place, or needing to take place, throughout organizations as they hire professionals and skilled technicians to help them adapt to the increasing rates of change they perceive as necessary to their survival. As double-loop learning diffuses, organizational stability is replaced by chaos and new organizational orders emerge from the internal dynamics of the organization rather than at the behest of top management.

Oiling the wheels of knowledge management

Shell International Exploration and Production is a knowledge intensive global oil company. A problem arising in Nigeria may have already been solved in the North Sea off the coast of Scotland. To put the people with the answers in touch with the people with problems, the company developed a knowledge management system. 'New Ways of Working' has three web-based global networks dealing with sub-surface, surface, and wells knowledge. Each business group allows members to share their knowledge with 3,000 to 4,000 other members.

- When Shell Brazil wanted help to retrieve broken tools from a borehole, engineers asked colleagues in other countries for help. This exchange of ideas saved the well, and saved the company US$7 million.

- A manager in Shell Malaysia had problems shutting down a gas turbine. Searching for ideas in the archived material on the global network, he found that teams in Australia and America had already posted solutions.
- The Shell sales company in Singapore beat bigger rivals to a contract by using the global network to gain insights into the work which they and competitors had done with that client in the past.

This idea was expanded to eleven knowledge communities covering support functions, human resources, information technology, finance and procurement. Each community has a co-ordinator responsible for controlling content and traffic flow, and encouraging people to contribute. If a particular question receives no answers, the co-ordinator attempts to find an expert in the area. Each community has developed a massive archive of knowledge which is used for personal development, problem-solving, and contacting those with specialist information and expertise. Total savings from this initiative were estimated in 2002 to be US$200 million, considering only those instances where savings could be quantified.

Based on Carrington (2002).

Tacit knowledge knowledge and understanding specific to the individual, derived from experience, and difficult to codify and to communicate to others.

Explicit knowledge knowledge and understanding which is codified, clearly articulated, and available to anyone.

Knowledge management the conversion of individual tacit knowledge into explicit knowledge so that it can be shared with others in the organization.

When we learn, we acquire knowledge – of organizational behaviour, gardening, guitar playing, accountancy, electrical engineering, and so on. Knowledge, however, is a difficult term to define clearly. For Nonaka and Takeuchi (1995), there are two types of knowledge, **tacit knowledge** and **explicit knowledge**.

Tacit knowledge includes insights, intuition, hunches and judgements, and concerns the individual's unarticulated mental models and skills. Tacit knowledge tends to be personal, specific to particular contexts, and difficult to communicate. For example, if you are able to drive a motor car with a manual gear shift, then you will know where to position your foot to 'slip the clutch' and prevent the car from rolling on a slope. You will be able to move your foot to that position, accurately and consistently, without much conscious thought. However, expect to run into difficulties when you try to explain this tacit skill to a learner driver.

Explicit knowledge on the other hand is articulated, codified, expressed, available to anyone. Nonaka and Takeuchi argue that the Japanese emphasize tacit knowledge, while Westerners emphasize explicit, formal, codified knowledge. In Western cultures, tacit knowledge is undervalued because it is intangible and difficult to measure. However, tacit and explicit knowledge are complementary. Nonaka and Takeuchi are thus concerned with 'knowledge conversion' in which tacit knowledge is made available to the organization, on the one hand, and organizational knowledge becomes the individual's tacit knowledge, on the other (Nonaka *et al.* 1999).

Organizational learning is related to, but is different from **knowledge management** (Rajan *et al.*, 1999).

Knowledge management concerns turning individual learning into organizational learning. Amin Rajan and colleagues (1999) describe how some organizations have developed 'intelligent search engines'. These are technology-based systems which facilitate access to expertise by creating a catalogue of specialists, each with their own website on the company intranet. The number of times somebody's expertise is used can be monitored and used to influence pay and promotion decisions (Rajan *et al.*, 1999, p.6).

Table 5.7 summarizes the main positive and negative aspects of the learning organization, and its related concepts of intellectual capital and knowledge management.

Knowledge management tends to be distinguished from the learning organization concept by the focus on information technology, and on the development of online databases. Company buyers and their suppliers have much better information and forecasts on which to base purchasing and delivery decisions. Zeneca Pharmaceuticals has developed a system called *Concert*, to bring together information on new drug discoveries and licences in a highly competitive sector. Managers around the company are responsible for identifying relevant knowledge, and for putting it into the system (Coles, 1998). Harry Scarbrough (1999), however, is critical of the emphasis on technological solutions, which overlook the ways in which people develop, use and communicate knowledge as part of their working activity.

Table 5.7: Learning organization positives and negatives

learning organization positives	learning organization negatives
a rich, multi-dimensional concept affecting many aspects of organizational behaviour	a complex and diffuse set of practices, difficult to implement systematically
an innovative approach to learning, to knowledge management, and to investing in intellectual capital	an attempt to use dated concepts from change management and learning theory, repackaged as a management consulting project
a new set of challenging concepts focusing attention on the acquisition and development of individual and corporate knowledge	a new vocabulary for encouraging employee compliance with management directives in the guise of 'self-development'
an innovative approach to organization, management and employee development	an innovative approach for strengthening management control
innovative use of technology to manage organizational knowledge through databases and the internet or intranets	a technology-dependent approach which ignores how people actually develop and use knowledge in organizations

The concepts of the learning organization and knowledge management are still fashionable. This popularity has been reinforced by the growth of knowledge work, by the realization that ideas generate competitive advantage, and by technological developments. However, there are barriers to the implementation of these ideals, and it will be interesting to observe whether they remain fashionable in the second decade of the twenty-first century.

 RECAP

1. *Explain the characteristics of the behaviourist and cognitive approaches to learning.*

   - Behaviourism argues that we learn chains of muscle movements. As mental processes are not observable, they are not considered valid issues for study.

   - Cognitive psychology argues that we learn mental structures. Mental processes are important, and they are amenable to study although they cannot be observed.

   - In behaviourist theory, feedback contributes to learning by providing reinforcement; in cognitive theory, feedback provides information and is motivational.

2. *Explain and evaluate the technique of behaviour modification.*

   - Respondent (or Pavlovian, classical) conditioning is a method by which an established response (good work performance) is associated with a new stimulus (supervisory encouragement).

   - Operant (or Skinnerian, instrumental) conditioning is a method by which a behaviour (good work performance) is associated with a new consequence (bonus payment).

   - Positive reinforcement, negative reinforcement, punishment and extinction condition the target by manipulating the consequences of desirable and undesirable behaviours.

   - Behaviour modification works well when rewards are linked clearly to specific behaviours, but does not work well when these links are ambiguous and vague; this manipulative approach may not be acceptable in some cultures.

3. *Explain the socialization process, and assess the practical relevance of this concept.*

   - Social learning theory argues that we learn values, beliefs and behaviour patterns through experience, through observation and modelling.

   - Socialization can be informal – this happens anyway – or it can be formally organized through induction and training programmes.

4. *Explain and evaluate the technique of behavioural self-management.*

- Behavioural self-management involves identifying the behaviour you want to change, altering the situational cues which trigger that behaviour, and establishing support and reinforcement for your new behaviour.

5. *Describe the characteristics of the learning organization.*

- A learning organization is characterized by its approach to strategy, to environmental scanning, to the use of information, to the creation of learning opportunities, and to the creation of structures that are flexible and enable employee learning, in contrast to rigid bureaucratic organizations in which learning is the employee's responsibility.

- The learning organization concept became popular as managers recognized the strategic need for more highly skilled and trained, flexible and creative workforces.

- Knowledge management is a technology-based technique for making tacit knowledge available more widely, typically through individual and corporate databases which can be accessed through the organization's intranet.

Revision

1. What are the differences between behaviourist and cognitive perspectives on learning?

2. What is the difference between Pavlovian and Skinnerian conditioning? What relevance do these and their related laboratory-based concepts have in an organizational context?

3. Describe and illustrate the technique of organizational behaviour modification, and identify the advantages and disadvantages of this technique.

4. Why are positive and negative reinforcement more effective than punishment? In what circumstances can punishment be effective in changing behaviour?

Research assignment

Review your understanding of social learning theory, behaviour modelling, and the concept of provisional selves. How do these approaches explain the ways in which new employees learn about the organization and their job? Interview a manager, a supervisor or team leader, and a front line employee in an organization of your choice. Find out how each of those three individuals learned about the organization and their work when they first joined (and/or when they moved to a new job in another part of the organization). Collect examples of behaviour modelling, and of their experiments with provisional selves. How effective were those methods in helping the new employee to 'fit in'? What other methods and sources of information did those individuals use in order to help them to 'fit in'? From this evidence, what are the strengths and limitations of behaviour modelling and provisional selves as an explanation of how new employees are socialized by organizations?

Springboard

Argyris, C., 1982, *Reasoning, Learning, and Action*, Jossey-Bass, San Francisco, CA.

Classic text on the nature of individual and organizational learning.

Davenport, T.H., 2005, *Thinking for a Living: How to get Better Performance and Results from Knowledge Workers*, Harvard Business School Press, Boston, MA.

Argues that knowledge workers have motives, attitudes, and needs for autonomy that require a new management style if their high performance is to be achieved and maintained.

Dixon, N.M., 1999, *The Organizational Learning Cycle: How We Can Learn Collectively*, Gower, Aldershot (2nd edn).

Organizational learning in practice. Cases include US Army, Bank of Montreal, Chaparral Steel, World Health Organization, Johnsonville Foods.

Edery, D. and Mollick, E., 2008, *Changing the Game: How Video Games are Transforming the Business World*. Harlow: Financial Times Prentice Hall.

Explores multiple business applications of computer games, and allows you to justify playing games at work.

 ## OB in films

A Clockwork Orange (1971 and 2000, director Stanley Kubrick) DVD track (scene) 19: 1:06:57 to 1:11.40 (6 minutes). Clip begins with doctor introducing herself: 'Good morning. My name is Dr Branom'. Clip ends with Dr Branom (played by Madge Ryan) saying, 'Dr Brodski is pleased with you. You've made a very positive response.'

This movie is based in a future totalitarian state in which the Droog (thug) Alex (played by Malcolm McDowell) is subjected to aversion therapy to cure him of his addiction to violence, rape, drugs and classical music. Fiction? Aversion therapy was used to 'treat' homosexuals in the 1960s. An extremely violent film for its time, Kubrick removed it from circulation in 1974 when it was accused of triggering copycat crimes. The film was released on the anniversary of Kubrick's death, in 2000. In this clip (which contains violence and nudity):

1. To what conditioning and reinforcement regime is Alex subjected?

2. How effective is this in changing his behaviour?

3. Does society have a moral right to interfere with individual behaviour in this way?

 ## OB in literature

Huxley, A., *Brave New World*, 1934, Penguin Books, London. Huxley describes a futuristic society which uses behaviour modification methods for social control. What modes of conditioning does this novel describe? What are the consequences of these methods? What organizational processes today work in the same manner?

CHAPTER EXERCISES

Reinforcement and behaviour

Objective   To examine the effects of positive and negative reinforcement on behaviour change.

This exercise takes about half an hour, and although it can be used with any size of group, it works particularly well with large classes.

Exercise overview   Two or three volunteers will receive reinforcement from the rest of the class while performing a simple task. The volunteers leave the room while the class is being briefed.

The instructor identifies an object which the student volunteers must find when they return to the room. This object should be unobtrusive, but it should be clearly visible to the class: a piece of paper stuck to the wall, a briefcase or bag in the corner, a mark on the wall.

The instructor specifies the reinforcement regime that will apply when each of the volunteers comes back into the room.

Negative reinforcement regime: the class will hiss, boo, make sarcastic comments, and throw harmless items at the first volunteer when they are moving away from the chosen object, and sit silently when they are moving towards it.

Positive reinforcement regime: the class will smile, cheer, applaud, and make encouraging comments with compliments when the second volunteer is moving towards the chosen object, and sit silently when they move away.

Combined reinforcement regime: the class will cheer when the third volunteer approaches the object, and boo when they move away from it.

Nominate one student to record the time that it takes each of the volunteers to find the object.

Exercise sequence   1. The first volunteer is brought back into the room, and instructed: Your task is to find and touch a particular object in the room. The class will help you, but you cannot ask questions, and they cannot speak to you. The first volunteer continues to look for the object until it is found, with the class giving negative reinforcement.

2. The second volunteer is brought back into the room, and is given the same instruction, to look for the object, with the class giving positive reinforcement.

3. The third volunteer is brought back into the room, and is instructed to find the object with the class giving a combination of negative and positive reinforcement.

Class discussion   • Ask the volunteers how they each felt during this exercise. What were their emotional responses to the different kinds of reinforcement they received?

• What effects did the different reinforcement regimes have on the behaviour of the volunteers?

• Which reinforcement regime do you think is most common in today's organizations? What are the likely effects on motivation and productivity?

This exercise is based on Marcic (1995, pp.61–63 and 122–23).

→

Branto Bakery

Branto Bakery is a large company producing a range of bakery products for the major supermarkets. Analysis by the human resources department has revealed that the sales and administration departments have the highest rates of absenteeism and latecoming. Interestingly, each of these departments also has individuals with the best absence and timekeeping records. The managing director has asked the two department heads to address these absence and timekeeping problems. Alan Anderson, head of sales, has decided to adopt a behaviour modification approach. Barbara Brown, head of administration, has chosen to develop a socialization approach with current and new staff. You have been asked to advise one of them, as an external management consultant:

1. Design either a behaviour modification programme for Anderson, or a socialization plan for Brown, that will reduce absenteeism and improve timekeeping in their departments.

2. Explain the elements of your plan, how it will address these problems, and how it will be implemented.

3. Assess the strengths and weaknesses of your plan in the short term, and in the long term.

Chapter 6 **Personality**

Key terms

personality	self-concept
psychometrics	generalized other
type	unconditional positive regard
trait	thematic apperception test
nomothetic	need for achievement
the big five	projective test
type A personality	reliability
type B personality	predictive validity
idiographic	

Learning outcomes

When you have read this chapter, you should be able to define those key terms in your own words, and you should also be able to:

1. Distinguish between type, trait and self theories of personality.

2. Identify the strengths and limitations of formal approaches to personality assessment.

3. Explain the uses and limitations of objective questionnaires and projective tests as measures of personality.

4. Explain the relationship between personality and stress, and identify appropriate individual and organizational stress management strategies.

5. Evaluate the benefits and problems of psychometric assessment as a tool to assist management decision-making, particularly in selection.

6. Assess your own personality.

Why study personality?

> ## Latin roots
>
> | | | | |
> |---|---|---|---|
> | *per sonare* | to speak through | *persona grata* | an acceptable person |
> | *persona* | an actor's mask; a character in a play | *persona non grata* | an unacceptable person |

Personality
the psychological qualities that influence an individual's characteristic behaviour patterns, in a stable and distinctive manner.

Psychometrics
the systematic testing, measurement and assessment of intelligence, aptitudes, and personality.

Who are you? How do you describe yourself? How do you differ from others? How can we define and measure those characteristics and differences? Psychology answers these questions using the concept of personality. Many managers believe that personality is related to job performance and career success, and personality assessment is a widely used selection tool. Most of us believe that we are 'a good judge of character'. Even without a formal personality assessment, you are unlikely to get that job unless 'your face fits'. What are the foundations of personality assessments, or psychometrics, and what value are they?

An internet search for 'psychometric tests' will identify numerous sites, and the use of online testing (particularly for graduates) is now widespread. In this chapter, two approaches to personality assessment are explained, called nomothetic and idiographic. Nomothetic approaches form the basis for most contemporary psychometrics. These are usually based on 'tick box' questionnaires, which are easy to administer and to score. The open-ended questions used by idiographic methods to capture the individual's unique characteristics are more difficult to interpret. Nomothetic techniques appear to be more objective and quantitative. However, idiographic techniques rely on different assumptions about human psychology. It is on the validity of these assumptions that our judgements of different methods should be based, and not simply on matters of operational convenience.

The term **psychometrics** covers a range of assessments and measurements of aptitude, intelligence, integrity and personality. An entire industry has developed, designing and supplying personality assessments which many organizations use in their selection and promotion procedures.

When measuring aspects of aptitude or intelligence, we can use the term 'test', because a high score is usually better than a low score. When measuring personality, however, it is more appropriate to use the term 'assessment'. There are no 'correct' answers in a personality assessment, and so a high score on one factor (extraversion, for example), cannot be said to be better or worse than a low score. In addition to selecting job applicants, psychometric assessment has several other applications:

- assessment of suitability for promotion;
- assessment for redeployment purposes;
- evaluation of training potential;
- team and leadership development;
- career counselling and development;
- graduate recruitment, for applicants with limited work experience;
- vocational guidance;
- redundancy counselling.

Psychometrics often complement less formal and more subjective methods, to help managers reach better-informed and objective judgements about people. However, these assessments have been criticized for being unfair and misleading, in gender and cultural terms, as well as being poor predictors of performance. Should you wish to improve your scores, or even to 'cheat' on a forthcoming assessment, you will find several 'how to' books on psychometrics and personality assessment on the popular psychology shelves in your local bookshop.

Would you pass an integrity test?

Employers want staff who are conscientious, dependable and honest. The problem is how to identify these attributes. Many companies use integrity tests to identify candidates who could pose risks, concerning dishonesty, cheating, lying, stealing, drug abuse, racism, sexism, and violent and criminal behaviour at work. After using integrity testing in 600 of its 1,900 stores, one American retailer reported a 35 per cent drop in the loss (or theft) of stock in those stores, while stock losses rose by over 10 per cent in stores that did not use integrity testing.

It can be relatively easy to fake a good score on a conventional paper-and-pencil integrity test. To make it more difficult for candidates to cheat, some organizations create special scenarios, then observe group discussions as candidates explore and resolve these. Research on integrity tests show that in the transportation, hospitality, healthcare and retail sectors around 70 per cent of candidates meet the minimum pass rate, and around 30 per cent score below standard.

Based on Arnold and Jones (2006).

Defining personality

The concept of personality underpins psychology's attempt to identify our unique characters and to measure and understand differences between individuals. Personality describes aspects of behaviour which are stable and enduring, and which distinguish the individual from others. Using the term personality in this way assumes that behaviour does have stable features, and does not change frequently, and those distinctive properties can somehow be measured.

Stability

Personality theory deals with behaviour patterns that are consistent in different contexts, and over time. We are not interested in properties that are occasional and transient. Mood swings and related behaviours caused by illness, or the consumption of drugs, are not stable and are thus not regarded as personality characteristics, unless they become permanent. However, there is a problem here. Personality appears to be flexible. The manager who is loud and autocratic in the office can be a caring and supportive parent at home. The 'stable' behaviours which we exhibit depend, in part, on social context. Some personality features (as with allergies) may only appear in specific social and physical conditions.

Distinctiveness

Personality theory is concerned with the pattern of dispositions and behaviours unique to the individual, and is not so concerned with properties that all or most other people share. You may be aggressive towards waiters, friendly with librarians, deferential to professors, and terrified of mice. You may share some of these dispositions with a friend who breeds mice.

Some psychologists argue than personality is largely inherited, determined by genetics and the biochemistry and physiology of the brain. Evidence suggests, for example, that because measures of job satisfaction are fairly stable over time and across jobs, a predisposition to be content with, or frustrated at work may have a genetic component. From this perspective, your personality is fixed at birth, if not before, and life's experiences do little to alter it.

Other psychologists argue that our characters are shaped by environmental, cultural and social factors, that our feelings and behaviour patterns are learned. Social learning theory argues that we acquire new behaviours by observing and imitating others. Motivation theory demonstrates how job satisfaction can be influenced by changes in supervisory style and the design of jobs. Every society has distinctive ways of doing things. We cannot possibly be born with this local knowledge. In this perspective, your personality is flexible, changing with experience. Psychological well-being may depend on such adaptability.

The controversy over the relative effects of heredity and environment on personality is known as the 'nature-nurture' debate. Few psychologists if any now hold the extreme positions set out here. Both genetic *and* situational factors influence behaviour. Theorists disagree over the emphases to be given to these factors, how they should be measured, and how they interact. During the 1960s and 1970s, 'nurture' was the position in vogue. Since the 1990s, biological and genetic evidence have moved thinking more in the direction of 'nature'. Steven Pinker (2002) offers a particularly scathing criticism of the view that the mind is a 'blank slate' inscribed by our environment and our experiences, arguing instead for an innate human nature based on discoveries in evolutionary biology, genetics and neurophysiology.

These debates have implications for organizational behaviour. There are many situations in which we want to be able to *explain* behaviour, and personality characteristics may give us clues. However, there are also organizational settings where it is important to be able not just to explain, but also to *predict* behaviour. Prediction is particularly important in job selection and promotion contexts. Can personality assessment help us to make more confident predictions about someone's future behaviour and job performance?

Types and traits

Type a descriptive label for a distinct pattern of personality characteristics, such as introvert, extravert, neurotic.

Descriptions of the components and structure of personality have focused on the concepts of **type** and **trait**. One of the most straightforward ways of describing and analyzing personality concerns the categorization of people into personality types.

One of the first personality theorists was Hippocrates ('The father of medicine') who lived in Greece around 400 BC. He claimed that personality type or 'temperament' was determined by bodily 'humours', generating the different behaviour patterns shown in Table 6.1.

Hippocrates
(450–370 BC)

Table 6.1: Hippocrates' type theory of personality

body humour	temperament or type	behaviours
blood	sanguine	confident, cheerful, optimistic, hopeful, active
phlegm	phlegmatic	sluggish, apathetic
black bile	melancholic	depressed, sad, brooding, prone to ill-founded fears
yellow bile	choleric	aggressive, excitable, irritable

William H. Sheldon
(1898–1970)

These temperament labels are still in use today, with the same meanings. Hippocrates' theory, however, is unsound for two reasons. First, evidence concerning the relationships between body chemistry and behaviour does not confirm the theory. Second, our personal experience suggests that there are more than four types of people in the world.

A more recent type theory was developed by William Sheldon (1898–1970), who argued that temperament was related to physique, which he called *somatotype* (Sheldon, 1942). In other words, your personality depends on your 'biological individuality', your body size and shape:

The *ectomorph*, who is thin and delicate, is restrained, inhibited, cautious, introverted, artistic and intellectual.

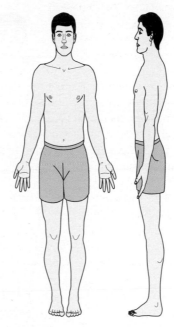

Figure 6.1: Ectomorph body shape

Source: www.kheper.net/topics.typology/somatotypes.html

The *mesomorph* is muscular, strong and rectangular, and is energetic, physical, adventurous and assertive.

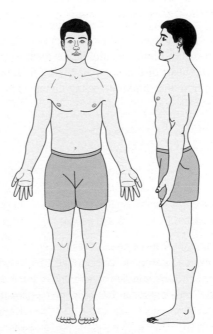

Figure 6.2: Mesomorph body shape

Source: www.kheper.net/topics.typology/somatotypes.html

The *endomorph* who is fat, soft and round, is also sociable, relaxed, easy-going and enjoys food.

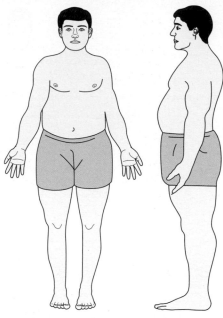

Figure 6.3: Endomorph body shape

Source: www.kheper.net/topics.typology/somatotypes.html

Carl Gustav Jung
(1875–1961)

This typology has intuitive appeal, but it may not be a good model for predicting behaviour. Can you think of an endomorph who is introverted and intellectual? Are you friendly with a mesomorph who is a relaxed gourmet – or with an ectomorph who is sociable and assertive?

Type theory owes a debt to the Swiss psychologist, Carl Gustav Jung (1875–1961) whose approach is based on *psychological preferences* for extraversion or introversion, for sensation or intuition, for thinking or feeling, and for judging or perceiving (Jung, 1953, 1971). At the heart of this complex theory lie four personality types, plotted across the sensation–intuition and thinking–feeling dimensions, illustrated in Figure 6.4.

The Ayurveda principle

The ancient Indian system of holistic medicine, Ayurveda, is founded on the principle that living matter is composed of earth, water, fire, air and ether, combining to give three basic personality types or *doshas*: *vata*, *pitta* and *kapha*:

Vata (air and ether): Slim, angular and restless. Creative and artistic, leaning towards athletics or dancing. Like to travel, can be flirtatious and emotionally insecure. Dry skin, prone to joint pains, rheumatism and depression.

Pitta (water and fire): Medium build with fair or red hair. Good leaders and executives who get things done. Articulate and impatient, can be irritable. Lunch is a very important meal. Skin is reddish. Prone to acne, rashes, ulcers and urinary infections.

Kapha (earth and water): Stocky, perhaps overweight. Loyal workers, not pushy. Patient, affectionate and forgiving. Smooth and oily skin. Prone to respiratory tract problems, asthma, bronchitis, colds and sinus problems, and to depression.

Each of us is a combination of all three *doshas*, the dominant one determining our physical and spiritual character. The key to health lies in balance, ensuring that one *doshic* personality is not too prominent. The similarities between Ayurveda and somatotyping are striking.

Based on Morris (1999).

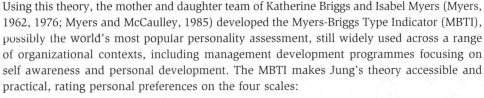

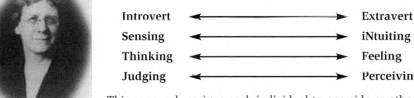

Thinking

ST: Sensation–thinking

practical, down-to earth, impersonal, wants facts, needs order and precision, dislikes ambiguity, values efficiency and clear lines of authority

NT: Intuition–Thinking

conceptual, analytical, sees future possibilities, generates creative new ideas, welcomes change, sparks enthusiasm in others

Sensation

Intuition

SF: Sensation–Feeling

gregarious, sociable, interested in other people, little or no time for personal reflection, dislikes ambiguity, enjoys getting people to care for and support each other

NF: Intuition–Feeling

creative, warm, enthusiastic, hates rules, hierarchies and procedures, persistent and committed, flexible and communicative, can be over-ambitious and idealistic

Feeling

Figure 6.4: Jung's personality type matrix

Isabel Briggs Myers (1897–1980)

Katherine Cook Briggs (1875–1968)

Trait a relatively stable quality or attribute of an individual's personality, influencing behaviour in a particular direction.

Nomothetic an approach to the study of personality emphasizing the identification of traits, and the systematic relationships between different aspects of personality.

Using this theory, the mother and daughter team of Katherine Briggs and Isabel Myers (Myers, 1962, 1976; Myers and McCaulley, 1985) developed the Myers-Briggs Type Indicator (MBTI), possibly the world's most popular personality assessment, still widely used across a range of organizational contexts, including management development programmes focusing on self awareness and personal development. The MBTI makes Jung's theory accessible and practical, rating personal preferences on the four scales:

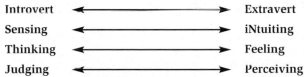

Introvert	⟷	Extravert
Sensing	⟷	iNtuiting
Thinking	⟷	Feeling
Judging	⟷	Perceiving

This approach assigns each individual to one side or other of each dimension, establishing 16 personality types, each known by its letter code; iNtuiting is known by the letter N to avoid confusion with introversion. If you are ENFP, you have been typed as Extravert, Intuitive, Feeling and Perceiving. It is useful to remember, however, that the assessments that produce individual scores reveal preferences and tendencies. The resultant profiles do not necessarily mean that individuals are trapped in those categories. While we may have a preference for impersonal analysis (T), we may when appropriate be able to use personal evaluations (F); we may prefer to focus on the immediate and concrete (S), while being able when appropriate to consider imaginative opportunities (N) (Trompenaars and Woolliams, 2002).

The MBTI has a number of applications. For example problem-solving and decision-making groups need a complementary personality mix; intuitive types need sensing types, feeling types need thinking types. This echoes the theory of effective group composition developed by Meredith Belbin (1981; 1993; see Chapter 11, Group structure).

Type approaches fit people into categories possessing common behaviour patterns. A personality **trait**, on the other hand, is any enduring behaviour that occurs in a variety of settings. While individuals belong to types, traits belong to individuals. You fit a type, you have a trait. Traits are also defined in terms of predispositions to behave in a particular way.

Examples of traits include shyness, excitability, reliability, moodiness, punctuality. The study of traits in personality research and assessment, and of how traits cluster to form personality types, is associated with the nomothetic approach in psychology.

"Well, then, when *would* be a good time to talk about your procrastination?"

Source: Copyright P.C. Vey. Originally appeared in *Harvard Business Review*

Nomothetic means 'law setting or law giving'. Psychologists who adopt this approach look for universal laws of behaviour. The nomothetic approach assumes that personality is inherited and that environmental factors have little effect; this approach sits on the nature side of the nature-nurture debate. The nomothetic approach adopts the following procedures.

First, it is necessary to identify the main dimensions on which personality can vary. Trait approaches assume that there is a common set of dimensions on which we can be compared. Traits describe aspects of temperament and character, and reflect the individual's predisposition to behave in particular ways. This approach assumes that your unique personality can be measured and compared with others on the same dimensions.

Second, the personalities of groups of people are assessed, usually through a self-report questionnaire. Popular magazines often use 'fun' versions of these questionnaires. The questions typically ask you to choose between a fixed number of answers. Responses may be confined, for example, to 'true' or 'false', to 'yes' or 'no', or to a rating scale that runs from 'strongly agree' to 'strongly disagree'. These are called 'forced choice' questions, and this procedure assumes that your answers reflect your behaviour.

Third, your personality profile is constructed across the traits measured. Your score on each dimension is compared with the average and the distribution of scores for the whole group. This enables the assessor to identify individuals around the norm, and those with pronounced characteristics that deviate from the norm. Your personal score has little meaning outside the scores of the population with which you are being compared. You cannot have a 'high' or 'low' score; you can only have scores that are high or low when compared with others.

Fourth, the group may be split into subgroups, say by age, sex or occupation. This produces other reference points, or norms, against which individual scores can be compared. Patterns of similarities and differences among and between subgroups enable general laws about personality to be formulated. One may find, for example, that successful Scottish male managers tend to be introverted, or that women under the age of 30 employed in purchasing have unusually low scores on shyness. This approach is impersonal, and it is difficult to use the results to predict individual behaviour, even with 'extreme' scores. It may be possible, however, to make probabilistic predictions about groups, in terms of behaviour tendencies.

Hans Jürgen
Eysenck
(1916–1997)

It may seem odd that one approach to individual personality assessment relies on studies of large groups. However, through this method, it is possible to find out what is normal or average (in the statistical sense) and then compare individuals with that. Individuals who 'deviate from the norm' are not social outcasts. However, assessments based on this method are often used as a guide to the profile of individuals, especially in employment selection.

One of the most influential trait theories of personality is that of Hans Jürgen Eysenck (1970, 1990), who was born in Germany in 1916, and who worked in Britain until his death in 1997. Following Jung, his research explored the key dimensions on which personality varies, including the extraversion-introversion or 'E' dimension, and the neuroticism-stability or 'N' dimension. However, unlike Jung, Eysenck sought to identify trait clusters.

Eysenck's approach is nomothetic. His sympathies lie with behaviourist psychologists who seek a scientific, experimental, mathematical psychology. Behaviourists claim, however, that behaviour is shaped by environmental influences. Eysenck's explanations of personality, on the other hand, are based on genetics and biology.

Eysenck's model offers a way of linking types, traits and behaviour. He argues that personality structure is hierarchical. Each individual possesses more or less of a number of identifiable traits – trait 1, trait 2, trait 3, and so on. Research shows how individuals who have a particular trait, say trait 1, are more likely to possess another, say trait 3, than people who do not have trait 1. In other words traits tend to 'cluster' in systematic patterns. These clusters identify a 'higher order' of personality description, which Eysenck refers to as personality types, as Figure 6.2 illustrates.

This does not mean that every individual who has trait 1 has a Type 'X' personality. It means that questionnaire analysis has shown that individuals with high scores on trait 1 are more likely to have high scores on traits 3 and 5 also, putting them into the Type 'X' category.

Eysenck presents statistical evidence from personality assessments to support the existence of personality trait clusters. However, individuals vary in a continuous distribution on trait scores. The result of an individual assessment using this approach is a personality profile across several traits rather than allocation to a single personality type.

The E dimension divides us into two broad categories of people – extraverts and introverts. American use of these terms refers to sociability and unsociability. European use emphasizes spontaneity and inhibition. Eysenck's account combines these notions. Most of us have a trait profile between these extremes on a continuum, and they are not exclusive categories. Eysenck argues that seven pairs of personality traits cluster to generate, respectively, the extravert and introvert personality types. These traits are summarized in Table 6.2.

Extraverts are tough-minded individuals who need strong and varied external stimulation. They are sociable, like parties, are good at telling stories, enjoy practical jokes, have many friends, need people to talk to, do not enjoy studying and reading on their own, crave excitement, take risks, act impulsively, prefer change, are optimistic, carefree, active, aggressive, quick tempered, display their emotions and are unreliable.

Introverts are tender-minded, experience strong emotions, and do not need intense external stimuli. They are quiet, introspective, retiring, prefer books to people, are withdrawn, reserved, plan ahead, distrust impulse, appreciate order, lead careful sober lives, have little excitement, suppress emotions, are pessimistic, worry about moral standards and are reliable.

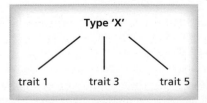

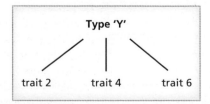

Figure 6.5: A hierarchical model of personality types and traits

Table 6.2: Trait clusters for extravert and introvert types

extravert	introvert
activity	inactivity
expressiveness	inhibition
impulsiveness	control
irresponsibility	responsibility
practicality	reflectiveness
risk taking	carefulness
sociability	unsociability

The N dimension assesses personality on a continuum from neuroticism to stability. Neurotics are emotional, unstable and anxious, can have low opinions of themselves, feel that they are unattractive failures, tend to be disappointed with life, and are pessimistic and depressed. They worry about things that may never happen and are upset when things go wrong. They are obsessive, conscientious and highly disciplined, and get annoyed by untidiness. Neurotics are not self-reliant and tend to submit to institutional power without question. They feel controlled by events, by others and by fate. They often imagine that they are ill and demand sympathy. They blame themselves and are troubled by conscience.

Home viewing

Glengarry Glen Ross (1992, director James Foley) is based in a Chicago real-estate office. To boost flagging sales, the 'downtown' manager Blake (played by Alec Baldwin) introduces a sales contest. First prize is a Cadillac Eldorado, second prize is a set of steak knives, third prize is dismissal. The sales staff include Ricky Roma (Al Pacino), Shelley Levene (Jack Lemmon), George Aaronow (Alan Arkin) and Dave Moss (Ed Harris). In the first ten minutes of the film, note how Blake in his 'motivational pep talk' conforms to the stereotype of the extravert, competitive, successful 'macho' salesman. Observe the effects of his 'pep talk' on the behaviour of the sales team. Does Blake offer a stereotype which salespeople should copy? What is Blake's own view of human nature? This part of the movie shows the construction of individual identity through a 'performance' conditioned by organizational context. This contrasts with a view of identity as genetically determined.

Why Sandhurst uses personality assessment to select British army officers

I'll never forget the words of Paul Barney, who survived the sinking of the Estonia ferry in 1994, in which 852 people died. While others froze with fear on the tilting deck, Barney made his own escape. 'I'm self-employed, single-minded, independent and not afraid to make decisions myself', he said.

His calmness under pressure – the ability to think clearly in an atmosphere of unthinkable stress – confirms a belief among psychologists that the ability to deal with extreme situations is due largely to personality type. Those scoring highly on the 'neuroticism' scale, for example, are known to crumple in anxious situations.

Those who score highly on the 'psychoticism' scale – who might be caricatured as cold risk-takers – perform very well under duress. This explains Sandhurst's rigorous approach to selection – officers must be alert but not neurotic, calm but not cold, a team player but not a conformist.

Since personality is strongly influenced by genes – indeed, biologists have even linked personality traits to particular brain chemicals that inhibit or trigger action – our response to stress is largely configured by our biology. There is further evidence for a biological input – survivors of disasters often report distorted perception, such as

Source: Adrian Gennis/AFP/Getty Images

Army officers on parade

tunnel vision or events unfolding in slow motion, which suggests that the brain shifts itself into survival mode. An estimated 15 per cent of people show this cognitive ability. Unfortunately, an estimated 10 per cent 'freeze', showing a cognitive shutdown, which has also been called 'the will to die'.

As [the reporter on whom this story was based] discovered, digesting information under extreme time pressure – and having to recall it later, while being shouted at – is also stressful. The stress triggered the release of adrenaline, leading to an increased heartbeat and raised blood pressure; these physiological pressures left [the reporter] unable to recall a fact just 30 seconds after being reminded of it.

From Ahuja (2006) © The Times, 1 March 2006.

Stable people are 'adjusted'. They are self-confident, optimistic, resist irrational fears, are easy going, realistic, solve their own problems, have few health worries and have few regrets about their past. The traits clusters for emotionally unstable and stable types are summarized in Table 6.3.

Table 6.3: Trait clusters for emotionally unstable and stable types

emotionally unstable	emotionally stable
anxiety	calm
guilt	guilt freedom
hypochondriasis	sense of health
lack of autonomy	autonomy
low self esteem	self-esteem
obsessiveness	casualness
unhappiness	happiness

Source: www.cartoonstock.com.

The questionnaire that Eysenck used to measure the E and N dimensions has 96 questions, 40 for each dimension, and 16 'lie detector' questions. The questions are mainly in the 'yes/no' format. The E and N dimensions are not correlated; if you are extraverted, you could be either stable or neurotic. If you are stable, you could be either extravert or introvert.

Is one personality type more desirable than another? The extravert may be sociable, friendly, cheerful, active and lively. However, extraverts are unreliable, fickle in friendships, and are easily bored with uninteresting or time consuming tasks. There are positive and negative sides to the extravert personality, as with the introvert. Those with extreme scores have what Eysenck calls an 'ambiguous gift'. If we are aware of such features, however, we may be able to act in ways to control and exploit them to our advantage. It is thus important to be aware of your personality, and to be aware of the characteristics that could be seen by others as strengths and weaknesses. To understand others, you must begin with an understanding of your own personality and emotions, and the effect that you have on others.

The big five

The big five trait clusters that appear consistently to capture main personality traits; Openness, Conscientiousness, Extraversion, Agreeableness and Neuroticism.

The search for trait clusters has culminated in what is known as **the big five**. The most influential advocates of this approach are Paul Costa and Robert McRae (McRae, 1992). This approach has achieved broad acceptance as a common descriptive system. Research has consistently reproduced these dimensions in different social settings and cultures, with different populations, with different forms of data collection, and in different languages. However, the labelling and interpretation of the factors and sub-traits remains controversial.

The big five (which spell OCEAN) are not personality types. These are sets of factors, 'super traits', which describe common elements among the sub-factors or traits which cluster together. Costa and McCrae identify six traits under each of the five headings, giving 30 traits in total. Table 6.4 summarizes the big five trait clusters. You can profile your own personality at the end of this chapter using this approach.

Table 6.4: The big five personality trait clusters

High ◄───► Low

explorer (O+) creative, open-minded, intellectual	**Openness** rigidity of beliefs and range of interests	*preserver* (O−) not receptive to new ideas, narrow-minded
focused (C+) organized, self-disciplined, achievement-oriented	**Conscientiousness** desire to impose order and precision	*flexible* (C−) disorganized, frivolous, irresponsible
extravert (E+) sociable, talkative, assertive	**Extroversion** level of comfort with relationships	*introvert* (E−) less sociable, quiet, introverted
adapter (A+) good-natured, compliant, sympathetic	**Agreeableness** the ability to get along with others	*challenger* (A−) quarrelsome, irritable, uncooperative
reactive (N+) anxious, depressed, self-conscious	**Neuroticism** tendency to maintain a balanced emotional state	*resilient* (N−) calm, contented, self-assured

High ◄───► Low

Paul T. Costa
(b.1943)

Robert McCrae
(b.1949)

The six traits relating to **Openness** (fantasy, aesthetics, feelings, actions, ideas, values) run on a continuum from 'explorer', at one extreme, to 'preserver' at the other. Explorer (O+) traits are useful for entrepreneurs, architects, change agents, artists and theoretical scientists. Preserver (O−) traits are useful for finance managers, stage performers, project managers and applied scientists. Those in the middle of this spectrum (O) are labelled 'moderates' who are interested in novelty when necessity commands, but not for too long.

The traits relating to **Conscientiousness** (competence, order, dutifulness, achievement striving, self discipline, deliberation) run from 'focused' to 'flexible'. Focused (C+) traits are useful for leaders, senior executives, and other high achievers. Flexible (C−) traits are useful for researchers, detectives and management consultants. Those in the middle (C) are 'balanced', and find it easy to move from being focused to being flexible, from production to research.

The traits relating to **Extraversion** (warmth, gregariousness, assertiveness, activity, excitement-seeking, positive emotions) run from 'extravert' to 'introvert' (surprise, surprise). Extravert (E+) traits are useful in sales, politics, and the arts. Introvert (E−) traits are useful for production management, and in the physical and natural sciences. Those in the middle of this spectrum (E) are 'ambiverts' who move easily from isolation to social settings.

The traits relating to **Agreeableness** (trust, straightforwardness, altruism, compliance, modesty, tender-mindedness) run from 'adapter' to 'challenger'. Adapter (A+) traits are useful in teaching, social work and psychology. Challenger (A−) traits are useful in advertising, management and military leadership. Those in the middle of this spectrum (A) are 'negotiators' who move from leadership to followership as the situation demands.

The traits relating to **Neuroticism**, or 'negative emotionality' (worry, anger, discouragement, self-consciousness, impulsiveness, vulnerability), run from 'reactive' to 'resilient'. Reactive (emotional) or 'N+' traits are useful for social scientists, academics and customer service professionals, but extreme reactivity interferes with intellectual performance. Resilient (unflappable) or 'N−' traits are useful for air traffic controllers, airline pilots, military snipers, finance managers and engineers. Those in the middle of this spectrum (N) are 'responsives', able to use levels of emotionality appropriate to the circumstances.

This analysis implies that certain traits will lead to success in particular occupations. Reviewing the research, Ivan Robertson (2001) argues that the relationship between personality and performance is not straightforward. In particular, findings suggest that:

- only two of the big five personality factors, conscientiousness and emotional stability, are consistently associated with better performance, in most occupations;
- conscientiousness is a better predictor of work performance than emotional stability;
- although openness, agreeableness and extraversion are not universally important, any of the big five personality factors could be significant in certain occupations;
- the correlations that have been found between personality factors and job performance are not strong, as performance is also affected by a range of other factors.

High conscientiousness is not always a reliable predictor of someone's suitability for a job. One study showed that employees who scored low in conscientiousness were rated by supervisors as innovative and promotable (Robertson, 2001, p.43). Organizations facing high levels of competition and change, want staff with good interpersonal skills, motivation, flexibility, and adaptability, and high conscientiousness may be less relevant.

The big five and your management career

Does success in your chosen career depend on your personality? Research has shown that *conscientiousness* is positively related to salary, promotions, and job status in most occupations. However, *neuroticism* is negatively related to performance, salary, and status. The findings for *extraversion* are inconsistent, linked to performance, salary, and job level in some studies, but not in others. These differences may depend on the type of work being studied; introverts may be better at handling routine, for example. *Openness* and *agreeableness* do not correlate consistently with job performance; these attributes could contribute to lower performance in some jobs; openness has been shown to reduce the performance of rugby referees, and agreeableness interferes with management potential.

Using The Big 5 personality assessment (you will find a short version at the end of this chapter), Joanna Moutafi, Adrian Furnham and John Crump studied 900 British managers, from ten organizations, in retailing, telecoms, manufacturing, consultancy, accounting, and legal services. They reached three main conclusions:

Conscientiousness was positively related to management level. This suggests that you are more likely to be promoted if you are capable, sensitive, effective, well-organized, thorough, dependable, reliable, ambitious and hard-working. However, it may also be the case

that high-level jobs encourage the development of those characteristics.

Neuroticism was negatively related to management level. This means that you are less likely to be promoted if you appear nervous, tense, anxious, stress-prone, unhappy, depressed, shy and unable to cope. People with those characteristics may avoid management jobs with high levels of responsibility, but the stress of those jobs may increase neuroticism.

Extraversion was positively related to management level. This implies that you are more likely to be promoted if you are dominant, socially ascendant, confident, assertive, energetic, determined, outgoing, and sociable. The researchers note that, 'Management is an extraverted activity. Managers attend meetings, give talks and socially interact all day long, which are activities more easily handled by extraverts than introverts' (p.277).

Psychometric tests of mental ability tend to be good predictors of job performance, while measures of personality traits are poorer predictors. This study suggests, however, that personality assessment could be useful in selecting people for management roles.

Based on Moutafi et al. (2007).

Personality Types A and B

Personality and health seem to be linked in a way particularly relevant to organizational behaviour. Meyer Friedman and Ray Rosenman (1974) identified two extreme 'behaviour syndromes' which explained differences in stress levels. They claim to have identified a 'stress prone' personality. Much subsequent research has focused on what they called **Type A personality** and its opposite, **Type B personality**, summarized in Table 6.5.

Type A personality
a combination of emotions and behaviours characterized by ambition, hostility, impatience and a sense of constant time-pressure.

Type B personality
a combination of emotions and behaviours characterized by relaxation, low focus on achievement, and ability to take time to enjoy leisure.

Table 6.5: Type A and Type B personality characteristics

Type A personality characteristics	Type B personality characteristics
competitive	able to take time out to enjoy leisure
high need for achievement	not preoccupied with achievement
aggressive	easygoing
works fast	works at a steady pace
impatient	seldom impatient
restless	not easily frustrated
extremely alert	relaxed
tense facial muscles	moves and speaks slowly
constant feeling of time pressure	seldom lacks enough time
more likely to suffer stress related illness	**less likely to suffer stress related illness**

Friedman and Rosenman found that Type A personalities were three times more likely to suffer heart disease than Type B personalities. The typical Type A thrives on long hours, large amounts of work and tight deadlines. These are socially and organizationally desirable characteristics, as are competitiveness and a high need for achievement. However, those who are extreme Type A may not be able to relax long enough to stand back from a complex problem to make an effective and comprehensive analysis, and may lack the patience and relaxed style required in some management positions. A further problem lies in the fact that their impatience and hostility can increase the stress levels in those who have to work with them. Like the extravert, a Type A personality can appear to have many admirable facets, but this behaviour syndrome can be dysfunctional for the individual, and for others.

STOP AND THINK

Are you a Type A or a Type B?

Do you suffer from: alcohol abuse, excessive smoking, dizziness, upset stomach, headaches, fatigue, sweating, bad breath? If 'yes', these could be stress responses to your Type A behaviour pattern. Expect your first heart attack before you are 45.

If you don't suffer stress-related symptoms, perhaps you are a Type B. However, do you think that your dozy behaviour could damage your career prospects?

Whichever your response, what are you going to do about it?

Meyer Friedman
(1910–2001)

Friedman and Rosenman argue that a Type A can change into a Type B, with awareness and training, and suggest a number of personal 're-engineering strategies':

- keep reminding yourself that life is always full of unfinished business;
- you only 'finish' when you die;
- learn how to delegate responsibility to others;
- limit your weekly working hours;
- schedule time for leisure and exercise;
- take a course in time management skills.

The problem, of course, is that the extreme Type A personality – the person most at risk – can never find enough time to implement these strategies. Another problem lies with the question of whether you can 're-engineer' your personality.

Stress management: individual and organization

The work of Friedman and Rosenman reveals a relationship between personality and health. Negative emotional states such as depression, hostility and anxiety can be linked to heart disease, respiratory disorders such as asthma, headaches and ulcers. Health risks are greater where negative states are chronic, particularly when they are part of personality. Stress is also caused by individual factors; difficulty in coping with change, lack of confidence, poor time management, poor stress management skills. Noreen Tehrani and Lisa Ayling (2008) summarize recent research findings which show that:

- stress may become the most dangerous business risk in the early twenty-first century;
- three quarters of executives say that stress adversely affects their health, home life, and performance at work;
- one in five workers (i.e., 5 million in Britain) report feeling extremely stressed at work;
- work-related stress, anxiety, or depression accounts for around 10.5 million lost working days a year in Britain.

Stress has many causes other than personality. The pace of life and constant change generate stress by increasing the range and intensity of the demands on our time. Any condition that requires an adaptive response from the individual is known as a stressor. Typical stressors that arise in organizational contexts are:

- *inadequate physical working environment*: noise, bad lighting, inadequate ventilation, lack of privacy, extremes of heat and cold, old and unreliable equipment;
- *inappropriate job design*: poor co-ordination, inadequate training, lack of information, rigid procedures, inadequate staffing, excessive workloads, no challenge, little use of skills, no responsibility or participation in decision-making, role ambiguity;
- *poor management style*: inconsistent, competitive, crisis management, autocratic management, excessive time pressures placed on employees;
- *poor relationships*: with superiors, with colleagues, with particular individuals, lack of feedback, little social contact, racial and sexual harassment;
- *uncertain future*: job insecurity, fear of unemployment or redeployment, few promotion opportunities, low-status job;
- *divided loyalties*: conflicts between personal aspirations and organizational requirements, conflict between job and family and social responsibilities.

Stress – or pressure – can also be arousing and exciting, and can enhance our sense of satisfaction and accomplishment and improve our performance. The term *eustress* describes this positive aspect of stress. The prefix 'eu' is Greek for 'good'. This contrasts with *distress*, which means the unpleasant, debilitating and unhealthy side of stress.

Stress can be episodic. When dealing with life's problems, we get anxious, cope with the problem and then relax again. Some events can be extremely stressful, such as the death of a relative, or a prison sentence. Other experiences can be stressful, such as getting a poor exam grade, being fined for speeding, or arguing with a friend, but trigger a less extreme response. Each of these episodes on its own is unlikely to cause lasting damage. However, when several of these episodes occur around the same time, the health risk is increased.

Stress can be chronic. This happens when we face constant stress, with no escape, and can lead to exhaustion and 'burnout'. This may be due to the unfortunate coincidence of several unrelated episodes. However, chronic stress also arises from the enduring features of our personal, social and organizational circumstances. If we are always under pressure, always facing multiple and unrealistic demands, always having difficulties with our work, our colleagues, and our relationships, then the health risk from stress is likely to increase.

Table 6.6: Typical stress symptoms

excessive alcohol intake	heavy cigarette smoking	dependence on tranquillizers
tiredness	low energy	dizziness
headaches	stomach upsets and ulcers	bad breath
high blood pressure	sleep problems	hyperventilation
temper tantrums	irritability	moodiness
loss of concentration	aggression	overeating
excess worrying	anxiety	inability to relax
pounding heart	feelings of inadequacy	memory loss

Stress can be a personal response to life's challenges. What you brush aside may be a problem for others. There are three factors moderating the impact of stressors on:

Condition   You are better able to cope with stress if you are in good health.

Cognitive appraisal If you believe that you are not going to cope with a particular event, this belief can become a 'self-fulfilling prophecy'.

Hardiness   Hardiness is an outlook on life characterized by a welcoming approach to change, commitment to purposeful activity, and a sense of being in control. This combination increases resilience to stress.

Stress has many symptoms which, taken on their own, do not appear significant and are not particularly threatening if they are temporary. An occasional headache is seldom cause for concern. Many of these symptoms have other causes, so they can be overlooked, and stress passes unrecognized and untreated. Table 6.6 identifies typical symptoms of stress.

Stress can have emotional consequences such as anxiety, fatigue, depression, frustration, nervousness, and low self-esteem. At the extreme, stress can contribute to mental break-down and suicide. Stress also influences behaviour in many other ways, from 'comfort tricks' involving alcohol and other drugs and excessive eating, to accident-proneness and emotional outbursts. Stress affects our ability to think, and interferes with concentration, decision-making, attention span, and reaction to criticism. There are several physiological responses, such as increased heart rate and blood pressure, sweating, and 'hot and cold flushes'.

The organizational consequences of stress can be damaging. The performance of stressed employees can be poor, and stress causes absenteeism, staff turnover, accidents, and wilful sabotage. Stress can also damage relationships (although poor relationships may cause stress in the first place), and commitment to work and to the organization are also likely to fall.

There are two broad strategies for reducing stress; *individual* emotion-focused strategies, and *organizational* problem-focused strategies.

Individual emotion-focused strategies improve resilience and coping skills and include:

- consciousness-raising to improve self-awareness;
- exercise and fitness programmes;
- self-help training, in biofeedback, meditation, relaxation, coping strategies;
- time management training;
- development of other social and job interests.

Organizational problem-focused strategies deal directly with the stressors and include:

- improved selection and training mechanisms;
- staff counselling programmes;
- improved organizational communications;
- job redesign and enrichment strategies;
- development of teamworking systems.

It is not always appropriate to 'blame' the individual for their experience of and response to stress, despite the known link to personality. Stress is also caused by organizational factors. While individual resilience can be improved, the need for problem-focused organizational solutions is inescapable.

Stress costs

In Britain, the Health and Safety Executive (HSE) estimates that, each year, 90 million working days are lost at a cost of £3.7 billion due to stress-related illness. The problem is particularly acute in the public sector, where workload and other pressures lead to exhaustion, absenteeism, staff turnover, depression, anxiety, and to mental and

Source: © Bill Varie/Corbis

physical illness. Apart from the individual suffering, another incentive for managers to consider ways to reduce stress is the increase in litigation by stressed employees. Courts have awarded substantial sums in damages. For example, Worcestershire County Council had to pay £140,000 to a former social worker who was left in charge of a residential home without any management training. The same council also had to pay £203,000 in damages to a warden for travellers' sites for the stress caused by his work.

Rather than deal openly with the issue, the danger is that managers become scared to talk about stress in case that heightens awareness of the issues and leads to legal action. A survey carried out in 2003 showed that while 75 per cent of public sector organizations provide employees with advice on stress, only 48 per cent of private organizations do this. To prevent stress at work, the management standards published by the HSE advises employers to consider *demand* (job design, training needs, flexible working), *control* (involve employees in decisions), *support* (give employees opportunities to discuss stress), *relationships* (policies for handling grievances, poor performance, bullying, other misconduct), *role* (clear and accurate job descriptions), and *change* (planned to avoid surprises, involving those affected).

Based on Braid (2003) and Empson (2004).

Figure 6.6 summarizes the argument of this section, with respect to the causes of stress, factors that moderate the experience of stress, stress symptoms and coping strategies.

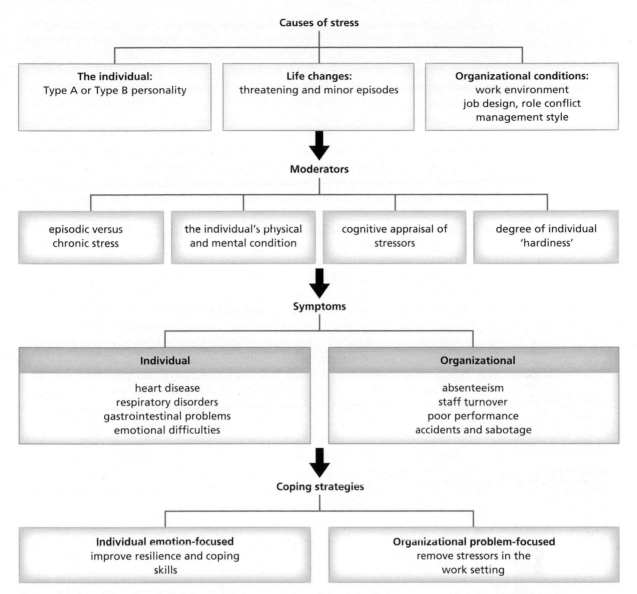

Figure 6.6: Stress causes, moderators, symptoms and coping strategies

The development of the self

Idiographic
an approach to the study of personality emphasizing the uniqueness of the individual, rejecting the assumption that we can all be measured on the same dimensions.

The nomothetic approach to the study of personality has been criticized by those who advocate an **idiographic** approach, which contrasts sharply in perspective and implications.

Idiographic means 'writing about individuals'. Psychologists who adopt this perspective begin with a detailed picture of one person, aiming to capture the uniqueness, richness and complexity of the individual. It is a valuable way of deepening our understanding, but does not readily produce universal laws of behaviour.

The idiographic approach makes the following assumptions.

First, each individual has unique traits that are not comparable with the traits of others. Your sensitivity and aggression are not necessarily comparable with my sensitivity and aggression. Idiographic research produces in-depth studies of normal and abnormal individuals, with information from interviews, letters, diaries, and biographies. The data include what people say and write about themselves, and are not restricted to scores on paper-and-pencil tests.

Second, we are not just biological machines powered by heredity. We are also socially self-conscious. Our behaviour patterns are influenced by experience, and by conscious reflection and reasoning, not just by instinct and habit.

Third, we behave in accordance with the image that we have of ourselves – our self, or self-concept. We learn about ourselves through our interactions with others. We take the attitudes and behaviours of others and use those to adjust our self-concept and behaviour.

Self-concept the set of perceptions that we have about ourselves.

Fourth, as the development of the self-concept is a social process, it follows that personality can change through social experiences. The development of personality is therefore not the inevitable result of genetic inheritance. It is through interaction with others that we learn to understand ourselves as individuals. We cannot develop self-understanding without the (tacit) help of others. In this view, there is no such thing as 'human nature'. Our character is shaped through social interactions and relationships. Remember, this contrasts starkly with the argument that human nature is largely influenced by biology and genetics (Pinker, 2002). This perspective, therefore, is on the nurture side of the nature–nurture debate.

Your self-understanding thus determines your behaviour. For example, confidence in your ability to do something is related to the successful demonstration of that ability. Ability combined with lack of confidence usually leads to failure or poor performance.

The mind's ability to reflect on its own functions is an important capability. We experience a world 'out there' and we are capable of experiencing ourselves in that world, as objects that live and behave in it. We can observe, evaluate, and criticize ourselves in the same conscious, objective, impersonal way that we observe, evaluate and criticize other people and events, and we experience shame, anxiety or pride in our own behaviour. Our capacity for reflective thought enables us to evaluate past and future actions and their consequences.

Charles Horton Cooley (1864–1929)

The American psychologist Charles Horton Cooley introduced the concept of the 'looking glass self'. Our mirror is the other people with whom we interact. If others respond warmly and favourably towards us, we develop a 'positive' self-concept. If others respond with criticism, ridicule and aggression, we develop a 'negative' self-image. The personality of the individual is thus the result of a process in which the individual learns to be the person they are. Most of us learn, accept and use most of the attitudes, values, beliefs and expectations of the society in which we are brought up.

In other words, we learn the stock of knowledge peculiar to our society. Red means stop. Cars drive on the left-hand side of the road (in Australia and Britain). An extended hand is a symbol of respect and friendship, not of hostility or aggression. These examples, on their own, are trivial. Taken together, these make up our 'recipe knowledge' of how society works. The taken-for granted 'rules' that govern our behaviour are created, recreated and reinforced through our ongoing interactions with others based on shared definitions of our reality. We interact with each other successfully because we share this understanding. How could we develop such a shared understanding on our own? What we inherit from our parents cannot possibly tell us how to behave in a specific culture. We have to learn how to become *persona grata* through social interaction.

George Herbert Mead (1863–1931)

If we all share the same ideas and behaviours, we have a recipe for a society of conformists. This is not consistent with the evidence, and the theory does not imply this. George Herbert Mead (1934) argued that the self has two components:

I   The unique, individual, conscious and impulsive aspects of the individual

Me The norms and values of society that the individual learns and accepts, or 'internalizes'.

Generalized other what we think other people expect of us, in terms of our attitudes, values, beliefs and behaviour.

Mead used the term generalized other to refer to the set of expectations one believes others have of one. 'Me' is the part of self where these generalized attitudes are organized. The 'Me' cannot be physically located. It refers rather to the mental process that enables us to reflect on our own conduct. The 'Me' is the self as an object to itself.

The 'I' is the active, impulsive component of the self. Other people encourage us to conform to current values and beliefs. Reflective individuals adjust their part in the social process. We can initiate change by introducing new social values. Patterns of socially acceptable conduct are specified in broad and general ways. There is plenty of scope for flexibility, modification, originality, creativity, individuality, variety and significant change.

STOP AND THINK

List the ten words or phrases that best describe the most important features of your individual identity. These features could concern your social roles, physical characteristics, intellectual qualities, social style, beliefs, and particular skills.

Then make a second list, putting what you regard as the most important feature at the top, and ranking all ten items with the least important at the bottom.

Starting at the bottom of your list, imagine that these items are removed from your personality one by one. Visualize how you would be different without each personality feature. What difference does its absence make to you?

This is the start of the process of establishing your **self-concept**. How much more or less valid is this approach than one based on forced choice questionnaires – and why?

Carl Ransom Rogers
(1902–1987)

Figure 6.7 illustrates what Carl Rogers (1902–1987) called the 'two-sided self'.

Our self-concept gives us a sense of meaning and consistency. But as our perceptions and motives change through new experiences and learning, our self-concept and our behaviour change. Personality in this perspective, therefore, is not stable, as the self-concept can be reorganized. We have perceptions of our qualities, abilities, attitudes, impulses and so on. If these perceptions are accurate, conscious, organized and accepted, then we can regard our self-concept as successful in that it will lead to feelings of comfort, freedom from tension, and of psychological adjustment. Well adjusted individuals thus have flexible images of themselves, that are open to change through new experiences.

Personality disorders can be caused by a failure to bring together experiences, motives and feelings into a consistent self-concept. We usually behave in ways consistent with our self-images, and when we have new experiences or feelings that are inconsistent we either:

- recognize the inconsistency and try to integrate the two sets of understanding – the healthy response; or
- deny or distort one of the experiences, perhaps by putting the blame onto someone or something else – an unhealthy defence mechanism.

Rogers argued that at the core of human personality is the desire to realize fully one's potential. To achieve this, the right social environment is required, one in which we are

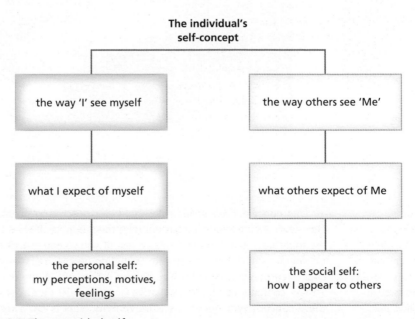

Figure 6.7: The two-sided self

Unconditional positive regard
unqualified, non-judgemental approval and respect for the traits and behaviours of the other person (a term used in counselling).

treated with **unconditional positive regard**. This means that one is accepted for whatever one is; in which one is valued, trusted and respected, even in the face of characteristics which others dislike. In this environment, the individual is likely to become trusting, spontaneous, flexible, leading a rich and meaningful life with a harmonious self-concept. However, this is far from the type of social environment in many contemporary organizations. Most of us face highly conditional regard, in which a narrow range of thoughts and behaviours is accepted.

Compared with nomothetic methods, an idiographic approach appears to be a complex, untidy view of personality and its development. It has been influential in research, but is conspicuous by its absence in contemporary psychometrics. How can the individual's self-understanding be studied? An approach based on questions worded by a researcher is not going to work; you may reject that wording as inappropriate to *your* self-concept.

Thematic apperception test
an assessment in which the individual is shown ambiguous pictures and is asked to create stories of what may be happening in them.

We need another route into the individual's mind. Well, we can ask people to write and to speak freely about themselves. These and similar techniques are in common use, including free association, interpretation of dreams, and the analysis of fantasies. Here the individual has freedom of expression and responses are not tied to predetermined categories. The researcher's job is to identify the themes that reveal the individual's preoccupations and interests, and personality. One technique is the **thematic apperception test**, or TAT.

STOP AND THINK

Write an imaginative story (100 words) about what is happening in this picture:

Need for achievement
a concern with meeting standards of excellence, the desire to be successful in competition, the motivation to excel.

This concept breaks our rule about not describing personality assessments as 'tests'. However, we have to be consistent with the literature. This is how the TAT works. First, you are told that you are about to take a test of your creative writing skills. Then you are shown photographs or drawings, typically including people, and asked to write an imaginative story suggested by what you see. The images do not imply any particular story.

The contents of your imaginative accounts are then assessed in various ways. One of these concerns your **need for achievement**. This is not a test of your imaginative writing at all.

Henry Alexander
Murray
(1893–1988)

David Clarence
McClelland
(1917–1998)

Projective test
an assessment
based on abstract or
ambiguous images,
which the subject is
asked to interpret by
projecting their feelings,
preoccupations and
motives into their
responses.

The assessment procedure first involves determining whether any of the characters in your story have an achievement goal. In other words, does somebody in your story want to perform better? This could involve doing something better than someone else, meeting or exceeding a self-imposed standard of excellence, doing something unique, or being involved in doing something well. Points are scored for the presence of these features in your story. The more achievement imagery, the higher your score.

The TAT is widely used today in psychological research, occupational choice, psychiatric evaluation, and screening candidates for high-stress jobs. The test was invented by Henry Murray and Christiana Morgan in the 1930s, and was later developed by David McClelland (1961; McClelland *et al.*, 1976) as a means of measuring the strength of need for achievement. The TAT is also used to measure the needs for power and affiliation, using similar scoring procedures, but looking for different imagery. But what can short, creative stories about ambiguous pictures tell us about your distinctive and stable personality characteristics? The thematic apperception test is a **projective test**.

The label 'projective' is used because subjects project their personalities into the stories they write. The Rorschach test is a form of projective assessment which uses random inkblots instead of pictures or photographs. McClelland argues that it is reasonable to assume that the person with a strong concern with achievement is likely to write stories with lots of achievement imagery and themes. The evidence seems to support this view. Need for achievement is important in an organizational context. People with low need for achievement are concerned more with security and status than with personal fulfilment, are preoccupied with their own ideas and feelings, worry more about their self-presentation than their performance, and prefer bright Scottish tartans. People with high need for achievement tend to have the following characteristics:

- they prefer tasks in which they have to achieve a standard of excellence rather than simply carrying out routine activities;
- they prefer jobs in which they get frequent and clear feedback on how well they are doing, to help them perform better;
- they prefer activities that involve moderate risks of failure; high risk activities lead to failure, low risk activities do not provide opportunities to demonstrate ability;
- they have a good memory for unfinished tasks and do not like to leave things incomplete;
- they can be unfriendly and unsociable when they do not want others to get in the way of their performance;
- they have a sense of urgency, appear to be in a hurry, to be working against time and have an inability to relax;
- they prefer sombre Scottish tartans with lots of blues and greens (Buchanan tartan has lots of red and yellow); unobtrusive backgrounds allow them to stand out better.

Organizations want employees with drive, ambition and self-motivation. Can the TAT be used to identify them? Unfortunately, it is not a good assessment for this purpose. Although the detailed scoring is not obvious to the untrained, the definition of achievement imagery is close to popular understanding. So, when you know what the 'test' is all about, it is easy to fake your score. We have here the same problem as with objective questionnaires. Personality assessment scores are not necessarily good predictors of job performance.

The TAT faces other problems as an organizational selection tool. The output of the assessment is hard for the untrained eye to regard as 'objective data'. The scoring procedure involves subjective interpretation. Expensive training is required in the full technical procedure to produce judges who can reach reliable assessments. With an objective questionnaire, anyone with the scoring key can calculate quickly and accurately the results.

McClelland argues that need for achievement can be increased by teaching you the scoring system, and by helping you to write high scoring stories. This increases need for achievement by encouraging you to see and to understand daily life more vividly in achievement terms. McClelland and colleagues used this approach in many different settings, for example with senior managers, entrepreneurs, police officers and social workers, and the first application outside America was with Indian businessmen in 1963. In other words, the TAT can be used both as a personality assessment, and also to change personality.

Nomothetic versus idiographic

These contrasting perspectives on personality are summarized in Table 6.7.

Table 6.7: Nomothetic versus idiographic

The nomothetic approach	The idiographic approach
positivist bias	constructivist bias
generalizing; emphasizes the discovery of laws of human behaviour	individualizing; emphasizes the richness and complexity of the unique individual
based on statistical study of large groups	based on intensive study of individuals
uses objective questionnaires	uses projective assessments (tests) and other written and spoken materials
describes personality in terms of the individual's possession of traits, and trait clusters or personality types	describes personality in terms of the individual's own understanding and interpretation of their identity
personality is composed of discrete and identifiable elements	personality has to be understood as an indivisible, intelligible whole
personality is primarily determined by heredity, biology, genetics	personality is primarily determined by social and cultural processes
personality is given and cannot be altered	personality is adaptable, open to change through experience

How can we choose between these perspectives? We can examine the logic of the arguments, consider how the evidence supports the theories, and consider the comprehensiveness of the explanations. We can resort to practical considerations and assess the methods used to treat personality disorders, and to analyze and predict behaviour. These forms of judgement miss the point, that these approaches are based on very different views of human nature. The evidence is such as to leave us debating for a considerable time without satisfactory resolution. We thus have to resort to criteria such as:

- Which theory is more aesthetically pleasing?
- Which approach 'feels' right?
- How does each approach fit with my world view?

A better approach is to regard these perspectives as complementary. They offer two broad research strategies, each of which is capable of telling us about different aspects of human psychology. What each alone reveals is interesting, but partial. Perhaps we should use both approaches and not concentrate on one alone. However, contemporary employee assessment and selection methods ignore this advice, and use predominantly nomothetic methods.

Selection methods

Choosing the right candidate for a job, or for promotion, is a critical decision. Incorrect decisions lead to frustrated employees and poor performance. Selection procedures are costly and time-consuming, and it is expensive to repeat them to recover from errors.

A selection (or a promotion) decision is a prediction about the ability of a candidate to perform well the particular job. Predictions are based on an understanding of the demands of the position to be filled, and on information about the candidates. Traditionally, candidate information has come from application forms, the testimony of referees, and interviews. The application form provides background, but is impersonal. Referees notoriously reveal only good things about candidates. Research suggests that interviews can also be unreliable, and are not suitable for all occupations (what would you think of the football team captain who selected players on the basis of how well they performed in their interview?).

Psychometrics

Psychometrics, around which a substantial commercial management consulting sector has grown, promise to improve the objectivity of selection and promotion decisions, by systematically collecting information that has predictive power. Psychometric applications developed rapidly in the last two decades of the twentieth century, and there are now over 5,000 such tests and assessments in use.

When choosing a psychometric assessment, for any purpose, two criteria are particularly important; reliability and predictive validity.

Reliability the degree to which an assessment delivers consistent results when repeated.

If the same group of people is given the same assessment on two or more occasions, and the results are the same or similar, then the assessment can be described as reliable. This is known as 'test-retest reliability'.

Predictive validity the extent to which assessment scores accurately predict behaviours such as job performance.

The validity of an assessment concerns the extent to which it actually measures what it sets out to measure. There are different types of validity; face validity (does it look right), construct validity (does it relate to other similar measures), and predictive validity. In employee selection, predictive validity is critical.

The question is, can we predict job performance from personality assessments? We can answer this question using the following method. First, assess a large applicant group. Second, hire them all regardless of their scores. Third, wait for an appropriate period (maybe five years). Finally, assess their performance, to see whether those with 'good' scores became high performers, or not. If they are, then you have a valid test.

The problem is that no one selection method can accurately predict how an individual will perform in a particular job or occupation. Most employers therefore use several methods for gathering information about candidates, although almost all organizations use interviews as part of their approach. Mick Marchington and Adrian Wilkinson (2005) report the findings of an annual survey of around 1,000 employers in Britain which showed the relative popularity of the different methods available:

selection method	% of organizations using
traditional interview	66
competency-based interview	62
tests for specific skills	60
structured interview (panel)	55
general ability tests	53
literacy and/or numeracy tests	48
personality questionnaires	46
assessment centres	43
structured interview (e.g., critical incidents)	38
telephone interview	26
online tests (selection/self selection)	6

Source: From *Human Resource Management at Work*, 3rd edn, Chartered Institute of Personnel Development (Marchington, M. and Wilkinson, A. 2005) with the permission of the publisher, the Chartered Institute of Personnel Development, London (www.cipd.co.uk)

Approaches to selection vary from country to country. Employers in Britain and America rely on interviews; graphology (handwriting analysis) is widely used in France; Britain, Germany, and The Netherlands also make extensive use of assessment centres. Blood group is a selection criterion in Japan. Marchington and Wilkinson (2005) note that the accuracy of some of these methods in predicting job performance has shown to be as follows:

method(s)	validity coefficient
perfect selection	1.0
intelligence and integrity tests	0.65
intelligence tests and structured interviews	0.63
intelligence tests and work sampling	0.60
work sampling	0.54
intelligence tests	0.51
structured interviews	0.51
integrity tests	0.41
personality assessments	0.40
assessment centres	0.37
biodata	0.35
references	0.26
years of job experience	0.18
years of education	0.10
graphology (handwriting analysis)	0.02
selection with a pin	0.0

There are two points to note from these figures. First, any method with a validity coefficient of less than 0.5 is going to be wrong more often than it is right. Second, personality assessments have relatively low predictive validity. The cost of recruitment error has been estimated to lie between £5,000 and £50,000, depending on the seniority of the appointment, and the potential for error should the wrong person be hired (Chartered Institute for Personnel and Development, 2001).

STOP AND THINK   At your next job interview, you are asked, 'Why should we employ you?'. The first part of your answer concerns your knowledge and skills. The second part of your answer concerns your personality. What are you going to say? Will this help you to get the job?

The results of personality assessments are rarely used as the sole basis of a selection decision. While these may be useful complements to other methods, personality assessments are usually poor performance predictors because:

- people are flexible and multifaceted, able to develop new skills and behaviours and to adapt to new circumstances; personality assessment captures a fragment of the whole;
- most jobs are multifaceted in their demands on skill and knowledge, and traits which enhance competence in one task may not improve overall job performance;
- job performance usually depends on many factors unrelated to personality; ability, luck, training, payment systems, physical facilities, supervisory style, organization structure, company policies and procedures;
- most jobs change over time, so predictions based on current measures are unreliable;

- nomothetic methods work with populations and large samples, against which individual profiles can be compared; these methods were not designed to make predictions about individuals, although that is how they are often used;
- in clinical and research settings, most people give honest answers about personality, but these assessments are easy to falsify when job or promotion is at stake.

Situational interviewing

Structured or situational interviewing is an approach with a relatively high predictive validity. Candidates are presented with a series of work-based problems, and asked how they would respond. Situations and questions are based on job analysis which focuses on critical knowledge, skills and abilities. Neal Schmitt and David Chan (1998, p.31) give examples of situational interview questions used for selecting emergency telephone operators:

1. Imagine that you tried to help a stranger, for example, with traffic directions, or to get up after a fall, and that person blamed you for his or misfortune or yelled at you. What would you do?

2. Suppose a friend calls you and is extremely upset. Apparently, her child has been injured. She begins to tell you, in a hysterical manner, all about her difficulty in getting her baby-sitters, what the child is wearing, what words the child can speak, and so on. What would you do?

3. How would you react if you were a sales clerk, waitress or gas station attendant and a customer talked back to you, indicating that you should have known something you did not, or telling you that you were not waiting on him or her fast enough?

Candidates' responses are rated for communication skills, emotional control and judgement, and can be compared against the actual behaviour of high level performers in this occupation.

It is difficult for candidates to cheat or to practise their responses to a situational interview, not knowing what specific behaviours and replies are being sought by assessors. Companies using these methods report a high success rate (Maurer et al., 1999).

Robert Sternberg (1988, 1999) has designed measures of *successful intelligence*, that is the ability to operate effectively in a given environment. Sternberg claims that successfully intelligent people have the three kinds of abilities shown in Table 6.8. The techniques used to assess this concept in practice are similar to those used in situational interviewing. Sternberg (1999, p.31) reports this example:

> I have developed a test in which a candidate for a sales job would make a phone call and try to sell a product to an examiner. During the call, the candidate has to reply to standardized objections to the sale. Responses to test items are compared against the responses of designated experts in each field, and scoring is done by comparative profile analysis [comparing the profile of the candidate with that of the expert].

Table 6.8: Dimensions of successful intelligence

analytical	analysing, evaluating, making judgements on abstract data removed from day-to-day practicalities
creative	finding novel, high-quality solutions, going 'beyond the given', 'making do in a rapidly changing world'
practical	the solution of real problems, application of common sense, not dependent on educational qualifications

Assessment centres

Assessment centres, which use a wide range of methods, were first used during the Second World War by British War Office Selection Boards. Groups of around 6 to 10 candidates are brought together for one to three days. They are presented, individually and as a group, with a variety of exercises, tests of ability, personality assessments, interviews, work samples, team problem-solving, and written tasks. Their activities are observed and scored. This is useful for selection and promotion, staff development, talent spotting, and for career guidance and counselling. The evidence suggests that this combination of techniques can improve the probability of selecting and promoting appropriate candidates.

Critics of assessment centres point to the investment in time and money they require to design and operate. Qualified assessors are necessary, and a lack of senior management commitment to the process can give both assessors and candidates inappropriate signals. Methods must be specifically tailored to each organization's needs. The focus on observable and measurable aspects of behaviour overlooks less apparent and less easily assessed skills.

Advocates argue that the information collected is comprehensive and comparable, and candidates have opportunities to demonstrate capabilities unlikely to appear in interviews. The self-knowledge gained can also be valuable to candidates. It is claimed that a well-designed assessment centre using a variety of methods can achieve a predictive validity of 0.8 with respect to job performance (Chartered Institute of Personnel and Development, 2001).

Does personality assessment have a future as part of the selection process? The relationships between personality constructs and job performance are modelled by Ivan Robertson (1994), shown in Figure 6.8. Robertson argues that the links between personality, performance and career success must be weak. There are too many factors to allow us to make reliable predictions. The model identifies the demands of the job, and factors in the organizational context that can influence behaviour at work independently of, or in interaction with, personality. Robertson argues, however, that it is possible to relate personality measures to specific competencies, such as judgement, resilience, sensitivity, and energy. This argument has intuitive appeal, and perhaps explains the continuing popularity of psychometric assessment in the twenty-first century. He claims that the evidence supports this view, and that this is where the future research agenda lies. He concludes that, 'When the personality constructs involved are clear and thought is given to the expected link between these constructs and work behaviour, it is likely that worthwhile information may be derived from personality measurement' (Robertson, 1994, p.85).

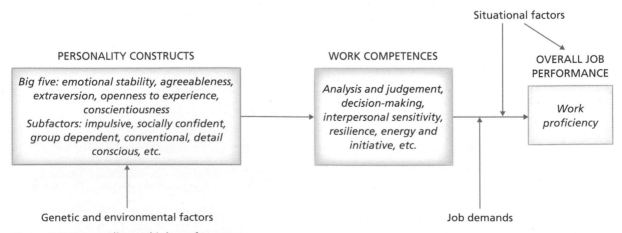

Figure 6.8: Personality and job performance

Source: From I.T. Robertson, 'Personality and personnel selection', in C.L. Cooper and D.M. Rousseau (eds), *Trends in Organizational Behaviour*, 1994, p.8. Copyright 1994 © John Wiley & Sons Limited. Reproduced with permission.

RECAP

1. *Distinguish between type, trait and self theories of personality.*

   - Type theories (Hippocrates, Sheldon, Jung) *classify* individuals using a limited number of personality categories.

   - Trait theories, based on a nomothetic perspective (Eysenck, Costa and McCrae), *profile* the individual's personality across a number of different facets.

   - Self theories, based on an idiographic perspective (Cooley, Mead), *describe* unique individual personalities.

2. *Identify the strengths and limitations of formal methods of personality assessment.*

   - Formal methods offer objective and comprehensive assessments of personality. But they are impersonal, based on group norms, and don't capture individual uniqueness.

   - Formal methods provide objective information about job candidates, but the links between personality assessment scores and job performance are often weak.

3. *Explain the uses and limitations of objective questionnaires and projective tests as measures of personality.*

   - Objective questionnaires are easy to score and offer quantitative rigour. But they can only be interpreted using group norms; individual scores are meaningless.

   - Projective tests capture the richness and uniqueness of the individual. But they have complex scoring, are subjective, and individual results cannot easily be compared.

4. *Explain the relationship between personality and stress, and identify appropriate individual and organizational stress management strategies.*

   - Type A personalities (competitive, impatient) are more stress prone than Type B personalities (easygoing, relaxed)

   - Individuals can develop physical and psychological resilience and coping skills.

   - Management has to reduce or remove work-related stressors (job design, management style, adverse working conditions, excessive workload).

5. *Evaluate the benefits and problems of psychometric assessment as a tool to assist management decision-making, particularly in selection.*

   - Psychometrics offer objective, systematic, comprehensive and quantitative information. They are also useful in career guidance, counselling and development.

   - Individual scores are meaningless outside the context of group norms.

   - It is difficult to predict job performance from a personality profile.

   - Personality assessment can identify strengths in specific areas of competence.

6. *Assess realistically the main characteristics of your own personality.*

   - Current thinking profiles personality on 'the big five' trait clusters of Openness, Conscientiousness, Extraversion, Agreeableness and Neuroticism (OCEAN). Self theories argue that the self-concept is what is important, not your test scores.

Revision

1. What is psychometrics, and what are the main applications? What are the benefits and drawbacks of psychometric assessment in organizational contexts?

2. What is 'personality' and why is this term difficult to define clearly?

3. What is the difference between 'type' and 'trait' theories of personality? Using at least one example of a trait theory, explain the benefits and problems associated with this approach to personality assessment.

4. Explain the distinction between nomothetic and idiographic views of personality. How do idiographic methods assess personality, and what are the advantages and drawbacks of these methods?

Research assignment

Interview two managers who are involved in recruiting and selecting candidates for jobs in their organizations. Choose two different types of organization for this assignment; large and small, public and private sector, manufacturing and retailing. First ask them (a) what selection methods are used by their organizations, (b) why they use those methods, and (c) what in their experience are the strengths and weaknesses of their chosen methods. Then ask them for their judgement concerning the relative importance of personality as a predictor of a candidate's future job performance. If they use psychometrics to assess personality, find out the extent to which the scores influence selection decisions. Your report will cover the following issues:

1. Describe the range of selection methods used by these organizations.

2. If the two managers reported using different methods, how can this be explained? Was this due to personal preferences, to the nature of the work for which candidates were being chosen, or to the differing nature of the organizations?

3. Summarize the strengths and weaknesses of the methods which they mentioned. Is their experience-based assessment consistent with the research evidence presented in this chapter? From what the evidence tells us about the value of different selection methods, what practical advice would you give to these two managers?

4. Prepare a brief assessment of the importance placed on personality factors by those two managers in their selection processes, compared with what the evidence says about our ability to predict job performance using personality assessment scores.

Springboard

Abbey, A. and Cranwell-Ward, J., 2005, *Organizational Stress*, Palgrave Macmillan, London.

Explores stress from organizational and individual perspectives, providing practical advice on stress management with examples and case studies.

Pinker, S., 2002, *The Blank Slate: The Modern Denial of Human Nature*, Allen Lane/The Penguin Press, London.

Explores the roots of character combining evolutionary biology and a computational theory of the mind. Presents a complex argument for 'preprogramming' with regard to a range of capabilities. For example, we are not born with a language 'hard wired' in our brains, but we do seem to have a pre-wired 'language learning module'.

Tehrani, N. and Ayling, L., 2008, *Stress at Work*, Chartered Institute of Personnel and Development, London.

Explains the significance of stress, identifies the symptoms, outlines strategies for managing stress. An excellent summary, available from the CIPD website.

Toplis, T., Dulewicz, V. and Fletcher, C., 2005, *Psychological Testing: A Manager's Guide*, Chartered Institute of Personnel and Development, London (4th edn).

Practical guide to evaluating, choosing, and using tests, including computer-administered testing.

OB in films

Who Framed Roger Rabbit (1988, director Robert Zemeckis) DVD track (scene) 7: 0:35:20 to 0:39:36 (5 minutes). Scroll into the scene to the point where Eddie enters his office; clip ends with Eddie saying to Roger, 'What's all this "we" stuff. They just want the Rabbit', when the door is shattered by gunfire and the weasels enter (from a suggestion by Champoux, 2001).

This Oscar award winning movie is a murder mystery involving a man, a woman, and a rabbit, in a world populated by cartoon characters ('toons') and ordinary people. Roger (a toon played by Charles Fleischer) has been framed for a murder, and asks detective Eddie Valiant (Bob Hoskins) to find his wife, and to clear his name. Eddie is an alcoholic who hates toons. During investigation, Eddie uncovers a plot to destroy all the toons.

1. Describe Roger's personality on 'the big five' dimensions.

2. Is Roger a Type A or a Type B personality? How do you know?

 ## OB in literature

Rupert Thomson (2006), *Divided Kingdom*, Bloomsbury Press, London. In this Huxley–Orwellian novel it is winter, and an eight-year-old boy is removed from his home and family in the middle of the night. He is the victim of an extraordinary experiment. To reform society and cut crime, the government has divided the population, and the country, into four groups, each with a different personality type; cholerics, phlegmatics, melancholics and sanguines. Borders have been established, with concrete walls, armed guards and razor wire. Our 'hero' tries to deal with his new situation, but his beliefs are challenged. What does this novel reveal about personality and how it can be altered, or not?

CHAPTER EXERCISES

The Big Five Locator

Objectives
1. To assess your personality profile on 'the big five' personality trait clusters.

2. To assess the value of this kind of personality assessment in career counselling and employment selection.

Briefing
A 'big five' personality assessment involves either a short questionnaire (the NEO-FFI with 60 questions covering the five factors) or the 'full facet' version (the NEO-PI-R with 240 questions covering all 30 traits). These assessments can also be used for management development, in leadership and interpersonal skills, and for the assessment of conflict management and decision-making styles (Howard and Howard, 1993). The Big Five Locator is an easy-to-use instrument for assessing an individual's personality profile. It is presented here for demonstration and discussion, and should be regarded as providing only an approximate measure of individual traits and individual differences.

Scoring
Calculate your **negative emotionality** score by adding the numbers you circled on the first row of each five-line grouping: row 1 + row 6 + row 11 + row 16 + row 21: score = _____

Calculate your **extraversion** score by adding the numbers you circled on the second row of each five-line grouping: row 2 + row 7 + row 12 + row 17 + row 22: score = _____

Calculate your **openness** score by adding the numbers you circled on the third row of each five-line grouping: row 3 + row 8 + row 13 + row 18 + row 23: score = _____

Calculate your **agreeableness** score by adding the numbers you circled on the fourth row of each five-line grouping: row 4 + row 9 + row 14 + row 19 + row 24: score = _____

Calculate your **conscientiousness** score by adding the numbers you circled on the last row of each five-line grouping: row 5 + row 10 + row 15 + row 20 + row 25: score = _____

Enter your five scores in this table, noting the different order (back to OCEAN).

trait	score
openness	
conscientiousness	
extraversion	
agreeableness	
negative emotionality	

On the centre scale, circle the point which most accurately describes you between each of the two terms presented. If the two terms are equally accurate in their description, then mark the middle point.

1	Eager	5	4	3	2	1	Calm
2	Prefer being with others	5	4	3	2	1	Prefer being alone
3	A dreamer	5	4	3	2	1	No-nonsense
4	Courteous	5	4	3	2	1	Abrupt
5	Neat	5	4	3	2	1	Messy
6	Cautious	5	4	3	2	1	Confident
7	Optimistic	5	4	3	2	1	Pessimistic
8	Theoretical	5	4	3	2	1	Practical
9	Generous	5	4	3	2	1	Selfish
10	Decisive	5	4	3	2	1	Open-ended
11	Discouraged	5	4	3	2	1	Upbeat
12	Exhibitionist	5	4	3	2	1	Private
13	Follow imagination	5	4	3	2	1	Follow authority
14	Warm	5	4	3	2	1	Cold
15	Stay focused	5	4	3	2	1	Easily distracted
16	Easily embarrassed	5	4	3	2	1	Don't give a damn
17	Outgoing	5	4	3	2	1	Cool
18	Seek novelty	5	4	3	2	1	Seek routine
19	Team player	5	4	3	2	1	Independent
20	A preference for order	5	4	3	2	1	Comfortable with chaos
21	Distractible	5	4	3	2	1	Unflappable
22	Conversational	5	4	3	2	1	Thoughtful
23	Comfortable with ambiguity	5	4	3	2	1	Prefer things clear-cut
24	Trusting	5	4	3	2	1	Sceptical
25	On time	5	4	3	2	1	Procrastinate

When you have calculated your five scores, transfer them to this interpretation sheet by putting a cross at the approximate point on each scale:

Big five locator score interpretation

low openness: practical, conservative, efficient, expert	preserver 10	moderator 15	explorer 20	**high openness**: curious, liberal, impractical, likes novelty
low conscientiousness: spontaneous, fun loving, experimental, unorganized	flexible 10	balanced 15	focused 20	**high conscientiousness**: dependable, organized, disciplined, cautious, stubborn
low extraversion: private, independent, works alone, reserved	introvert 10	ambivert 15	extravert 20	**high extraversion**: assertive, sociable, warm, optimistic
low agreeableness: sceptical, tough, aggressive, self-interest	challenger 10	negotiator 15	adapter 20	**high agreeableness**: trusting, humble, altruistic, team player
low negative emotionality: secure, unflappable, unresponsive, guilt free	resilient 10	responsive 15	reactive 20	**high negative emotionality**: excitable, worrying, reactive, alert

Discussion   Plenary:

- Why do you think we as individuals are interested in understanding more about our personalities?
- Why do you think organizations are interested in the personalities of job applicants?

Syndicate groups:

1. How accurate do you find your personality profile from this assessment? If it was inaccurate, why do think that was the case?

2. Compare your highest and lowest scores across the five dimensions. There is of course no 'one best score'. In what kinds of work would your highest score be most valuable, and what kinds of work would your highest score not be valuable? What types of work do you think you should avoid given your lowest score?

3. How helpful is this personality assessment to job interviewers who need to make predictions about a candidate's future job performance? What aspects of the assessment make it valuable in this respect? What aspects make it unhelpful?

4. What actions can be taken to maximize the contribution of personality assessments in selecting candidates for jobs?

Based on Howard et al. *(1996, pp.107–22).*

Biters and bleaters

It may be obvious that we all like to win and hate to lose, but it seems that some of us actually find winning stressful. To assess your own views, take the following test. Rate how you feel you would respond – strongly disagree to strongly agree – to each of these situations:

→

	strongly disagree	disagree	agree	strongly agree
I get really wound up when my sports team loses.	1	2	3	4
I really hate it when I go to a meeting to seek approval for a decision and approval is not forthcoming.	1	2	3	4
If I was in charge of a budget, and it was cut, I would willingly accept it.	4	3	2	1
You choose a fixed-rate mortgage and a month later interest rates are cut. This doesn't bother you.	4	3	2	1
You are interviewed for a job and fail to make the final shortlist. You are gutted for weeks.	1	2	3	4
You compete with a colleague for promotion. You hear on the grapevine that your competitor has got it. It doesn't bother you.	4	3	2	1
When you're in social situations and others are dominating the conversation, this frustrates you.	1	2	3	4
At the office party, your partner makes a lighthearted remark about your lack of competence at domestic chores. You are hurt.	1	2	3	4

Oliver Schultheiss at the University of Michigan suggests that we are divided between wolves, who want to win, and sheep, who are distressed by beating others. The researchers first used a projective test, asking subjects to describe what they saw in photographs of people competing. The stories were scored for 'implicit power motivation' with high scorers designated wolves, and low scorers as sheep. They were then paired and asked to compete on a task requiring speed and accuracy, but the results were fixed in advance.

Saliva samples were used to measure the level of a stress hormone. When the wolves lost, they became stressed. But when the sheep *won*, they became stressed, too. If you know the category to which you belong, you can adjust your work environment accordingly. Typical wolf occupations are: politician, teacher, stand-up comedian. Typical sheep occupations are: office worker, researcher, accountant. While some of us are competitive and find positions of power satisfying, others are less comfortable dominating others.

Which are you? To calculate your score, just add the numbers in the boxes that you ticked:

Score 8–15: Sheep. You don't hate winning, but when you lose, it doesn't baa-ther you

Score 16–24: Wolf in sheep's clothing. Winning is more important in some aspects of life (work) than in others (relationships)

Score 25–32: Wolf. You have a howl-at-the-moon obsession with winning at everything

Based on Ahuja (2006) © The Times, 31 August 2006.

Chapter 7 **Communication**

Key terms

social intelligence

communication process

coding

decoding

perceptual filters

noise

feedback

non-verbal communication

power tells

high context culture

low context culture

impression management

emotional intelligence

communication climate

Learning outcomes

When you have read this chapter, you should be able to define those key terms in your own words, and you should also be able to:

1. Describe the dimensions of social intelligence, and explain the importance of this capability.

2. Understand the main components of the interpersonal communication process.

3. Identify the main barriers to effective interpersonal communication.

4. Understand the effective use of different questioning techniques, conversation controls, and listening skills.

5. Explain the nature and significance of non-verbal communication.

6. Understand the nature and mechanisms of impression management skills and techniques.

7. Be able to explain the concept of emotional intelligence and its practical significance.

8. Understand the ways in which corporate communication can be used to manipulate understanding and encourage compliance with management directions.

Why study communication?

Communication is central to understanding organizational behaviour for several reasons:

- communication affects organizational performance and individual career prospects;
- very few people work alone, and the job of most managers involves interacting with other people, often for more than 90 per cent of their time;
- communication is seen as a problem in many organizations;
- in an increasingly diverse multi-cultural society, sensitivity to the norms and expectations of other cultures is vital to effective cross-cultural communication;
- new technology is radically changing our patterns of communication.

Organizational communication is a discipline in its own right, with its own research traditions (Jablin and Putnam, 2001). Everything significant that happens in an organization involves communication; hiring and training employees, providing feedback, purchasing supplies, solving problems, dealing with customers, deciding strategy. However, communication is often interrupted by hierarchical structures, power and status differences, the design of jobs, the nature of (part time, temporary) employment, physical layouts and rules.

Most managers spend a lot of time in meetings and in conversation, talking and listening, networking and influencing, gathering information and negotiating. Henry Mintzberg (1973) emphasized the monitoring, informational, decision-making and interpersonal aspects of the work of executives. John Kotter (1982, 1999) found that general managers spend most of their time talking to others, often on topics not related to the business, but central to maintaining networks and relationships, and to developing goals and action plans.

Social intelligence
the ability to understand the thoughts and feelings of others and to manage our relationships accordingly.

Are you able to 'feel' what others are feeling? Can you 'read' what's happening in complex social settings? Do you use that understanding to manage your relationships? If so, then you have social intelligence. Despite modern communications technology, personal interactions, one-to-one, face-to-face, 'F2F', or 'face time' are still important, perhaps even more so. Our ability to interact effectively with others was first described as social intelligence in 1920 by Edward Thorndike, but the idea was seen then as just another aspect of general intelligence. (We will explore the related concept of emotional intelligence later in this chapter.)

Daniel Goleman (2006) argues that social intelligence is a special set of capabilities, including social awareness (what we sense about others) and social facility (how we act on that awareness). Each of these dimensions has four ingredients (Table 7.1).

Social intelligence can be developed with training and experience. Goleman argues that these capabilities lead to management effectiveness. However, these capabilities are important to all of us, in social and organizational settings. Globalization and international mobility mean that we often find ourselves interacting and working with people from other countries and cultures. Different cultures have differing norms concerning how conversations should be handled, including appropriate greetings, degree of formality, the use of eye contact, suitable topics for discussion, physical distance between speakers and the interpretation of gestures. Social intelligence in a culturally diverse context becomes increasingly important.

ZITS *Jerry Scott & Jim Borgman*

Source: Reproduced with kind permission of the Zits Partnership and King Features Syndicate.

Table 7.1: Social intelligence

social awareness	primal empathy	'reading' others' emotions intuitively from small clues (such as a brief facial expression)
	attunement	understanding the other person through complete and sustained attention and careful listening
	empathic accuracy	explicit understanding, through observation and inference, of what someone feels and thinks
	social cognition	knowing how the social world works, what is expected, reading the social signals
social facility	synchrony	harmoniously orchestrating our interactions with the right gestures (smiles, nods, posture, timing)
	self-preservation	ability in interactions to trigger desired emotional responses in others, charisma
	influence	shaping the outcomes of interactions with tact and control, tuning actions to fit the circumstances
	concern	capacity for compassion, sharing others' emotions, elation or distress

Based on Goleman (2006).

Modern communications technologies have not yet overcome the need for people to meet in person. Where information is easily codified (a booking, a bank statement), and transactions are simple (pay a bill, buy a ticket), an exchange can be completed online. However, where transactions are complex and based on judgements ('what is your opinion?', 'could we do it this way?'), where emotions and feelings are as significant as facts and figures, the social and geographical context, the quality of relationships and interpersonal trust, are all crucial.

Communication between different occupational groups can be difficult. SQUAWKS, for example, are problems noted by United States Air Force pilots and left for maintenance crews to fix before their next flight. Here are some complaints logged by pilots and the replies from the maintenance crews.

pilot complaint	maintenance crew response
Test flight okay, except auto land very rough	Auto land not installed on this aircraft
DME volume unbelievably loud	Volume set to more believable level
Friction locks cause throttle levers to stick	That's what they're there for
Number three engine missing	Engine found on right wing after brief search
Target radar hums	Reprogrammed target radar with the words
Aircraft handles funny	Aircraft warned to straighten up and be serious
Dead bugs on windshield	Live bugs on order
Left inside main tyre almost needs replacement	Almost replaced left inside main tyre
Evidence of leak on right main landing gear	Evidence removed
IFF inoperative	IFF always inoperative in OFF mode
Something loose in cockpit	Something tightened in cockpit

Focus, May 1999, p.18

Interpersonal communication

> *Conversation*: a competitive sport in which the first person to draw breath is declared the listener.

In most cultures, conversation is a social imperative in which silences are discouraged (Finland is different). Normally, as soon as one person stops talking, another takes their turn. The currency of conversation is information. We ask you the time. You tell us the time. Information has been transmitted. Interpersonal communication has been achieved. However, the communication process is often more subtle and interesting.

Communication process the transmission of information, and the exchange of meaning, between at least two people.

We will first focus on interpersonal communication. A more detailed study would recognize the importance of other aspects of communication, including the use of different media, networks, and inter-organizational communication. The principles that we will explore, however, have wide application. For the moment, let us focus on 'one-on-one' or 'F2F' communication, and examine our definition of the communication process.

STOP AND THINK We all have experience of ineffective communication. Either the other person misunderstood what you had to say, or you misunderstood them. Remember the last time this happened: what went wrong? What caused that communication to fail? Share your analysis with colleagues to see whether there are common causes.

We do not receive communication passively. We have to interpret or decode the message. To the extent that we interpret communication from others in the manner they intended, and they in turn interpret our messages correctly, then communication is effective. However, communication is an error-prone process.

Interpersonal communication typically involves much more than the simple transmission of information. Pay close attention to the next person who asks you what time it is. You will often be able to tell how they are feeling, and about why they need to know, if they are in a hurry, perhaps, or if they are anxious or nervous, or bored with waiting. In other words, their question has a purpose or a meaning. Although it is not always stated directly, we can often infer that meaning from the context and from their behaviour.

Communication is an error-prone process

I rang the bell of a small bed-and-breakfast place, whereupon a lady appeared at an upstairs window. 'What do you want?', she asked. 'I want to stay here', I replied. 'Well, stay there then', she said and banged the window shut.

Chick Murray, Scottish comedian

The same considerations apply to your response. Your reply suggests, at least, a willingness to be helpful, may imply friendship, and may also indicate that you share the same concern as the person asking the question (we are going to be late; when will this film start?). However, your reply can also indicate frustration and annoyance: 'Five minutes since the last time you asked me!'. Communication thus involves the transmission of both information and meaning.

This process of exchange is illustrated in Figure 7.1 which shows the main elements of interpersonal communication. This model is based on the work of Claude Shannon and Warren Weaver (1949), who were concerned with signal processing in electronic systems, rather than with organizational communication.

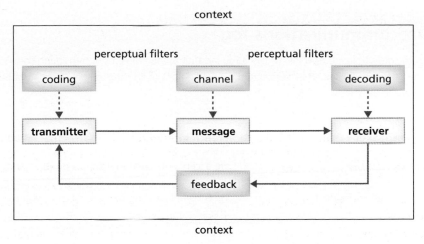

Figure 7.1: Exchanging meaning: a model of the communication process

Coding the stage in the interpersonal communication process in which the transmitter chooses how to express a message for transmission to someone else.

At the heart of this model, we have a transmitter sending a message to a receiver. We will assume that the channel is face-to-face, rather than over a telephone, or through a letter, or a video conference, or email. It is useful to think of the way in which the transmitter phrases and expresses the message as a coding process; the transmitter chooses words, and also how the message will be expressed (loud and with exasperation, quiet and in a friendly manner, for example). The success of our communication depends on the accuracy of the receiver's decoding; did they understand the language used, and appreciate the exasperation or friendship? We each have our own perceptual filters which can interfere with accurate decoding, such as predispositions to hear, or not to hear, particular types of information, and preoccupations which divert our attention elsewhere.

Decoding the stage in the interpersonal communication process in which the recipient interprets a message transmitted to them by someone else.

This model highlights the problems that arise in communication, and suggests solutions. There are many ways in which coding and decoding can go wrong; some common terms can lead to misunderstandings:

term	popular use	dictionary definition
decimate	devastate	cut by ten per cent
exotic	colourful, glamorous	from another country
aggravate	to annoy, to irritate	to make worse
clinical	cold, impersonal	caring, at the bedside of the sick
avid	enthusiastic	greedy

Perceptual filters individual characteristics, predispositions, and preoccupations that interfere with the effective transmission and receipt of messages.

The branch manager who receives from head office an instruction to 'decimate' her or his salesforce would thus be advised to check the original coding of the message before taking action. Using the dictionary definition of the word exotic implies that Daewoo, Isuzu, Kia and Skoda sell exotic motor cars in Britain. To be successful, transmitters and receivers need to share a common 'codebook'.

STOP AND THINK What other expressions create coding and decoding problems? Identify examples – which can be humorous (like the man who asked for wild duck in a restaurant. 'I don't have wild duck, sir', replied the waiter, 'But I can annoy one for you').

Eurocommunications fog

With the growth in membership of the European Union, the problems of translating communications, both written and spoken, have multiplied. This has led to the development of informal guides to what, in particular, English and French speakers actually mean:

English speaker	French interpreter	Actual meaning
I hear what you say	He accepts my point of view	I disagree and do not want to discuss it further
With the greatest respect	He is complimenting me	I think you are wrong or foolish
By the way	This is not important	The main aim of this discussion
I'll bear that in mind	I will act on that	I will do nothing about that
Correct me if I'm wrong	Correct him if he's wrong	I'm correct, please don't contradict me

French speaker	Literal English	Actual meaning
Je serai clair	I will be clear	I will be rude
Il faut la visibilité Européenne	We need European visibility	The EU must indulge in some pointless international grand-standing
Il faut trouver une solution pragmatique	We must find a pragmatic solution	I am about to propose a highly complex, theoretical, legalistic and unworkable way forward

Based on The Economist *(2004b).*

Language is also used to 'soften' or to disguise unpleasant events. Employees being made redundant, for example, may be 'given the pink slip', 'downsized', 'rightsized', 'delayered', invited to 'take gardening leave', to 'spend more time with the family', or to 'put their careers on hold'. They may also be 'counselled on', 'repositioned', urged to 'develop their careers elsewhere', or to 'explore other opportunities for their talents', but are rarely 'fired' or 'given the chop'. In some organizations, there are no 'problems and difficulties', only 'challenges and opportunities'. The fictional character Martin Lukes is advised not to compare his strengths with his weaknesses, but with his 'less strong strengths' (Kellaway, 2005).

The communication process is further complicated by the perceptual filters which affect what we say, and which in turn affect what we hear and how we hear it. When you asked what time it was, did you 'hear' the frustration or friendship in the response? Or did you simply focus on the time issue, because that was more important to you? The transmitter of a message has motives, objectives, personality traits, values, biases and prejudices, which colour the content and expression of communication. We decide the information we wish to reveal, and which to withhold or conceal from others. We do not always perform this filtering consciously. Similarly, at the receiving end, perceptual filtering can affect what is heard, what is decoded, what is not decoded, and the way in which the message is understood.

There is a further complicating factor; the physical, social and cultural context. The casual remark by a colleague across a restaurant table ('we could all be redundant by Christmas') may be dismissed. The same casual remark by a colleague across an office desk can be a source of considerable alarm. An innocent gesture in one culture causes offence in another. The style and content of our conversation depends often on our relationships with others. Status differences colour our communication. We do not reveal to the boss what we discuss with colleagues. The style and content of communication can change in a striking manner when organizational relationships are 'suspended', such as during an office party.

Noise factors outside the communication process which interfere with or distract attention from the transmission and reception of the intended meaning.

Electronics engineers use the term noise to refer to anything which interferes with a signal in the communication process.

Communication suffers from noise, a term which covers more than just the sound of machinery, telephones, and other people talking. Noise includes coding and decoding problems and errors, perceptual filters, anything that interferes with the integrity of our chosen channel, and issues arising from our relationships with others. Our motives, emotions and health can constitute noise. For example, the effectiveness of our coding and decoding is affected by anxiety, pressure, stress, and with our levels of enthusiasm and excitement.

Our past experiences also affect the way in which we see things today, and lead us to filter what we transmit and what we receive. Communication stumbles when transmitter and receiver have different frames of reference, and do not share experience and understanding, even where they share a common language. We make judgements about the honesty, integrity, trustworthiness and credibility of others, and decode their messages and act on them (or not) accordingly. People in an organizational setting may have time to reflect, or they may be under time pressure, or 'communication overload'.

There is a final aspect of our communication model which we have to consider: feedback.

Feedback processes through which the transmitter of a message detects whether and how that message has been received and decoded.

When we communicate face to face, we can usually tell if the other person likes us, if they agree with us, and if they are interested in what we have to say – or not. How do we know this? Well, they may say, 'that's interesting', or 'I disagree', or 'I have to catch my flight'. We can also tell from cues such as the tone of their replies, their facial expression, body posture, and limb gestures. We will explore the coding and decoding of non-verbal communication (also called body language) later in the chapter.

When we communicate face to face, we get instant feedback, from what others say, and how they say it. Our ability to exchange meaning effectively is assisted by this rich feedback loop. Our communication can be awkward where feedback is delayed, or absent. Feedback allows us to check constantly the accuracy of the coding and decoding processes. We ask a question, see the other person look annoyed or puzzled, realize that we have not worded our question appropriately, and we 'recode' the message. Face to face, if we are paying attention, this can work well. We can do this to some extent over the telephone, decoding the tone of the other person's voice. With more formal and distant forms of communication, feedback can be delayed or non-existent, and we need to take much more care over our coding.

STOP AND THINK   Think of the people with whom you communicate regularly. What are the main barriers to effective communication in your experience? What would you have to do to improve the effectiveness of your communication?

We can be careless coders and lazy listeners. The communication process appears to be a simple one, but it is prone to errors arising on both sides of the exchange. We cannot confidently assume that receivers will always decode our messages in a manner that leaves them with the meaning that we intended to transmit. It is obvious to argue that communication is central to organizational effectiveness, but this claim has major practical implications. We assume that organizations will function better where:

- communications are open;
- relationships are based on mutual understanding and trust;
- interactions are based on co-operation rather than competition;
- people work together in teams; and
- decisions are reached in a participative way.

These features, however, are not widespread.

Charm offensive

British soldiers in Iraq and Afghanistan were given a guide to social interaction, with advice on conversation topics, responding to hospitality, and how to read gestures:

Troops were given the following advice to avoid causing offence in the Arab world:

gestures   avoid the 'OK' sign which widely means the 'evil eye'

shaking hands   it is disrepectful for a man to offer his hand to a woman

social interaction   there is no 'personal space'; Arab culture stresses the need to 'share the breath' of a companion

conversation   men should not question other men about the women in their family

In Afghanistan, men should not have any physical contact with women in public, food is served in communal dishes and eaten with the right hand, legs should be crossed when sitting, women's legs, ankles and feet must be covered, and it is offensive to point the soles of your shoes towards someone.

The Arab world: an introduction to cultural appreciation

- Extending both open palms towards a person indicates enthusiasm or "excellent"
- A single, downward nod is the most common expression for "yes"

- Touching the outer edges of the eyes with the fingertips signifies assent or "OK"

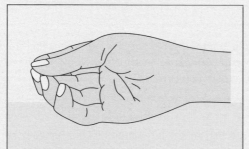

- Holding the right palm out with the palm upward, with the tips of the thumb and fingers touching and the palm moving up and down, means "calm down", "more slowly" or "be patient"

- Patting the heart repeatedly means "I've had enough" (usually used at mealtimes)

Figure 7.2: Advice on videoconferencing etiquette

Evans (2008) © The Times, 11 February 2008.

Videoconferencing skills

Television exaggerates small movements, stroking your hair, picking your nose, biting your lip. With the growth in videoconferencing, or teleworking, your performance can influence your reputation and career. Here is some advice on videoconferencing etiquette:

Choose your clothes carefully

Dress as you would for the office, and avoid 'busy' patterns. Do not wear casual shorts under the smart top, as you may have to stand up to get something.

Pay attention

Do not stare at the screen, or you will appear 'stiff'. Maintain eye contact with viewers and with those in the room. When selling an idea, lean slightly towards the camera. Do not shift your gaze frequently or appear detached. Do not frown, slouch, cup your chin in your hands, or bounce around in your chair. Do not leave the room, and do not lean back in your chair. Women appear more effective if they perch on the edge of their seat throughout the session.

Remember the camera's reach

If you roll your eyes or make some other dismissive gesture while somebody else is speaking, your viewers may see that, even if colleagues in the room do not. Do not fall asleep, and if you do, don't snore. Remember that those at the other end may be able to see and to hear you before the meeting begins formally, and will hear what you say about them in advance.

Avoid culturally insensitive gestures

For example, Asian viewers are often uncomfortable with large demonstrative hand and body movements. This is particularly important for international videoconferencing.

Calm your nerves by practising

Rehearse, role-play, sharpen your delivery, practise boldness. Make a video of yourself, and replay with the sound off to monitor your body language. Then replay without watching to monitor your vocal delivery; avoid 'squeak speak' – sounding like a mouse.

Based on Lublin (2006).

"I suppose you realize that when I tell everyone back at the office about this you wont be able to tele-commute anymore."

Source: www.cartoonstock.com

The main barriers to effective organizational communication are:

power differences research consistently shows that employees distort upward communication, and that superiors often have a limited understanding of subordinates' roles, experiences and problems

gender differences men and women use different conversational styles which can lead to misunderstanding; men tend to talk more and give information while women tend to listen and reflect more

physical surroundings room size and layout influence our ability to see others and our readiness to participate in conversations and discussions

language even within one country, variations in accent and dialect can make communication difficult

cultural diversity different cultures have different norms and expectations concerning formal and informal conversations; lack of awareness of those norms creates misunderstanding

So, how can we improve communication?

face to face when we are able to speak with someone directly, we can use the feedback constantly to check the coding and decoding processes, and to correct mistakes and misunderstandings

reality checks we should not assume that others will necessarily decode our messages in the way we intended, and we should check the way in which our messages have been interpreted

place and time the right message delivered in the wrong place or at the wrong time is more likely to be decoded incorrectly, or even ignored, so choose the time and place with sensitivity and care

empathetic listening see things from the other person's point of view, consider the thinking that may have led to their behaviour, decode the message the way they might decode it, listen attentively to feedback (Guirdham, 2002)

Verbal communication

The word 'verbal' is another term that causes decoding problems. Verbal means 'in words', which can be either spoken or written. The expressions, verbal agreement and verbal warning, can thus refer either to oral or to written communication, and both are contrasted with non-verbal communication.

Most conversations involve exchanges of information or meaning. How do we get the information we want? We achieve this through a range of questioning techniques. The main types of question are shown in Table 7.2. By using these labels, it becomes easier to analyse the questioning techniques used by others, and it is easier for us to make conscious choices about how to conduct our own side of a conversation more effectively.

The first basic distinction in questioning strategy is between closed and open questions. Closed questions invite a factual statement in reply, or a simple yes or no response. Open questions, in contrast, invite the person responding to disclose further information. Predict the differences in response to these two questions:

Will you have dinner with me this evening?

What are you doing this evening?

Table 7.2: Questioning techniques

question type	illustration	uses
closed	Did you enjoy the movie?	to get a 'yes' or 'no' answer; to obtain factual information; to establish conversation control
open	What did you think of that movie?	to introduce a subject; to encourage further discussion; to keep the other person talking
probe	Can you tell me more about that?	to follow up an open question; to get more information; to demonstrate interest
reflective	You thought the acting was poor?	to show interest and concern; to encourage further disclosure of feelings and emotions
multiple	What did you think of the movie, and wasn't the star excellent in that role, and did you think that the ending was rather sudden?	confuses the listener; gives them a choice of question to which to respond
leading	You didn't see anyone leaving the house?	to get the answer that you expect to hear (so, why ask?)
hypothetical	What would happen if . . . ?	to encourage creative thinking

It seems as though closed questions are limited while open questions are more effective. If the purpose is to get the other person to divulge lots of information, then this assessment is correct. However, closed questions are particularly useful in two settings. First, where all that is required is simple factual information: 'Are you coming to the meeting?' Open questions invite the discussion of irrelevant information, for which there may be no time. Second, interviewers often begin with a short series of closed questions in order to establish the conversation pattern. We have all had experience of conversations where the other person took control, giving us information which we did not want. Closed questioning can avoid this. Consider the following questioning sequence used at the beginning of an interview:

What is your current job title?

How long have you been in your present position?

What was your previous position?

This can help to establish the conversation pattern by signalling to the other person, 'I ask the questions, you give the answers.' Usually, by the time the third or fourth closed question has been answered, the person being interviewed will wait for the interviewer to ask their next question, and will not begin talking about some other issue.

Probes are simply another type of open question. Probes indicate that the listener is interested in what the other person is saying. In most instances, that indication of interest encourages the disclosure of further information.

The reflective statement is a powerful technique for maintaining rapport and encouraging the disclosure of information, particularly concerning feelings and emotions. All that you have to do is to mirror or reflect back to the person an emotion that they have 'given' to you. The feeling or emotion expressed can be spoken ('you didn't enjoy your holiday then') or it can reflect an unspoken, non-verbal expression ('you look happy this morning'). As with probes, reflective statements signal interest and concern and encourage the other person to continue disclosing information.

STOP AND THINK

Record a television police drama, a magazine programme, or a news broadcast. Watch somebody being interviewed; police interviewing suspect, host interviewing celebrity, news reader interviewing politician. Identify the questioning techniques used. What advice can you give the interviewer to help improve their questioning?

Replay the same interview with the sound off. Can you identify any communication barriers which made this exchange less effective than it could have been; for example, physical layout, posture, timing, non-verbal communication? What further advice would you give the interviewer to help them improve their technique?

Multiple questions and leading questions are rarely used by trained interviewers. Multiples are often heard on radio and television, particularly when politicians are being asked about their positions and views on topical subjects. Leading questions are especially ineffective when fresh information is required. Watch a police drama on television, and identify how many times witnesses and suspects are confronted with questions such as:

So you didn't see anyone else leave the house after five o'clock?

You're saying that the stolen televisions were put in your garage by somebody else?

Hypothetical questions can be useful in stimulating creative and innovative 'blue skies' thinking. Used in selection interviewing, this technique only tells us how well the candidate handles hypothetical questions, and reveals little about their future job performance.

We also control our conversations through a range of conscious and unconscious verbal and non-verbal signals which tell the parties to a conversation, for example, when one has finished an utterance and when it is somebody else's turn to speak. These signals reveal agreement, friendship, dispute and dislike – emotions which in turn shape the further response of the listener. The four main conversation control signals are explained in Table 7.3. Note that the different uses and implications of pauses in conversation depend on the context.

When conversing normally, we use these signals habitually. However, awareness of the methods being used can allow us to bring these under conscious control. Therapists and counsellors, for example, use a range of methods to shape conversations in ways that allow their clients to articulate their difficulties and to work towards identifying appropriate solutions. Managers holding selection, appraisal or promotion interviews need to understand conversation control techniques in order to handle these interactions effectively.

Table 7.3: Conversation control signals

signal	example	meaning
lubricators	'uh huh'; 'mmm, mmm' and other grunts and groans	I'm listening, keep talking, I'm interested
inhibitors	'what !'; 'really' 'oh' and similar loud interjections	I'm surprised, I don't agree, I've heard enough of this
bridges	'I'd like to leave that and move on to ask you about . . .'	I'd like to make a clean link to the next conversation topic
pauses (1)	about two seconds silence	in normal conversation: same as lubricators
pauses (2)	silence of three seconds or longer	in a threat context: I'm going to wait until I get an answer
pauses (3)	silence of three seconds or longer	in a counselling context: I'll give you time to think

Gender and communication style

**Deborah Tannen
(b.1945)**

Deborah Tannen (1990, 1995) argues that boys and girls acquire different linguistic styles, which create communication barriers and influence career prospects.

A linguistic style is a characteristic speaking pattern which includes factors such as tone of voice, speed, loudness, directness or indirectness, pacing and pausing, choice of words, and how we use jokes, stories, figures of speech, questions, and apologies. Tannen (1995, p.140) claims that, '[G]irls learn conversational rituals that focus on the rapport dimension of relationships whereas boys tend to learn rituals that focus on the status dimension.'

Boys as they grow up play in large groups, emphasize status and leadership, display their knowledge and abilities, challenge others, take 'centre stage' by telling jokes and stories, and try to acquire status in their group by giving orders to others. Girls focus on a small group of friends, sharing secrets with their best friend, emphasizing similarities, and playing down ways in which someone could be better than others. Girls tend to be more modest, appear less self-assured, and ostracize those who claim superiority.

These childhood differences affect adult behaviour in organizational settings. Men tend to think more in hierarchical terms, and are concerned with status, power, and with being 'one up'. Men strive to retain 'one up' by driving and by interrupting conversations. Men jockey for position by putting others down, appear competent by acting confidently, and appear knowledgeable by asking fewer questions. Men tend to give negative feedback quickly, and look for opportunities to criticize, rather than pay others compliments.

Women are more likely to avoid putting others down and to act in ways that are face-saving for others. Women can appear to lack self confidence by playing down their certainty and by expressing doubt more openly. Women also appear less self-assured and knowledgeable by asking more questions, tend to soften criticism by offering positive feedback first, and pay others compliments more often than men do.

These linguistic differences are particularly important when speaking of achievements. Men tend to be more direct and use 'I' more often. Women tend to speak indirectly and speak of 'we' when talking about accomplishments. In summary, men tend to adopt linguistic styles and to behave in ways that are more likely to get them recognized, and that are more likely to earn them attributions of effectiveness and competence. Women adopting a more 'masculine' linguistic style can be seen as aggressive. Tannen advises us all to be more aware of these differences in linguistic styles, and to pay attention to the dynamics of our conversations.

Based on Tannen (1990, 1995).

STOP AND THINK   To what extent does Tannen's analysis apply to linguistic styles and behavioural differences between men and women in your culture today?

Aboriginal culture and communication

Australian Aboriginal culture includes aspects of verbal and non-verbal communication which are quite different from most European and North American communication styles.

- Aborigines value brevity in verbal communication rather than detailed elaboration, and simple 'yes' and 'no' replies are common.

- There is no word for 'thank you' in Aboriginal languages. People do things for you as an obligation.

- In some Aboriginal tribes, it is unlawful to use the name of a dead person.

- The terms 'full-blood', 'half-caste', 'quarter-caste', 'native' and 'part-Aborigine' are regarded as offensive by Aborigines.

- Long silences in Aboriginal conversation are common and are not regarded as awkward.

- To some Aboriginal people, it is not acceptable to look another straight in the eye.

- Some Aboriginal groups do not allow men and women to mix freely.

- Aborigines feel that it is not necessary to look at the person who is speaking to them.

- Aborigines do not feel that it is necessary to attend meetings (an interview, for example) at specific times.

How do these norms and preferences compare with the communication style of your culture?

Based on Nelson-Jones (2000).

Non-verbal communication

Which part of the human anatomy is capable of expanding up to ten times in size when we are emotionally aroused? The answer, of course, is the pupil of your eye. When we look at something we find interesting – an image, a scene, a person – our pupils dilate. When we lose interest, our pupils contract. There is a physiological basis in non-verbal communication for the 'dark limpid pools' to which romantic novelists refer.

When we interact with others face to face, we are constantly sending and receiving messages through our signs, expressions, gestures, postures, and vocal mannerisms. In other words, **non-verbal communication** accompanies our verbal communication. We code and transmit factual information primarily through verbal communication. We also code and transmit feelings and emotions, and the strength of those feelings, through non-verbal communication.

Non-verbal communication is popularly known as *body language*. We will use the technical term for two reasons. First, non-verbal communication is rich and varied; the term body language suggests that we are only concerned with body movements and postures. Second, the term body language implies that gestures have specific meanings, that we can produce in a dictionary. That is not the case, as the meaning of non-verbal communication also depends on context. The technical term has the advantage of including a range of behaviours, and signals our concern with how these behaviours are embedded in the communication process.

Allan Pease (1985, 1997), implies in the titles of his popular books that one can 'read' somebody else's attitudes and emotions from their non-verbal communication. Is this possible? If we are careful, yes, sometimes. This 'body and mind reading' claim deserves cautious support. We can exchange meaning with non-verbal codes, as long as we evaluate the verbal and non-verbal components together, and pay close attention also to the context.

Non-verbal communication
the process of coding meaning through behaviours such as facial expressions, limb gestures and body postures.

Non-verbal hints for the job interview

When you sit down, lean forward slightly; this shows interest. Use open-handed gestures – palm upwards – to convey sincerity. Keep regular eye contact, but not for more than 60 per cent of the time, or you'll look mad. However, do it for less than 30 per cent of the time and you may seem shifty or bored.

Don't sit defensively – hands across the body, knees pressed together, hand over your mouth – it can look neurotic or unstable. Equally, don't fidget or play with your hair, or grin maniacally. Above all, don't slouch back in the chair, arms behind your head, with a challenging stare. It threatens the interviewer and makes you look arrogant and difficult.

From Burne and Aldridge (1996).

The first study of gesture was conducted by the Italian cleric Andrea de Jorio, born in 1769. To help him to decipher the Greek figures excavated by archaeologists at Herculaneum, Pozzuoli and Pompei in the early nineteenth century, he studied the facial and bodily gestures of the people of Naples, a city founded by the ancient Greeks. His book *Gesture in Naples and Gesture in Classical Antiquity* is available in translation (Kendon, 2000).

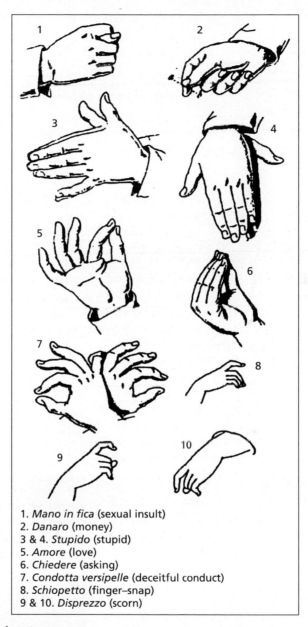

1. *Mano in fica* (sexual insult)
2. *Danaro* (money)
3 & 4. *Stupido* (stupid)
5. *Amore* (love)
6. *Chiedere* (asking)
7. *Condotta versipelle* (deceitful conduct)
8. *Schiopetto* (finger–snap)
9 & 10. *Disprezzo* (scorn)

Early Italian hand gestures

Source: Reprinted by the permission of the Syndics of Cambridge University Library.

The main dimensions of non-verbal behaviour are summarized in Table 7.4.

Maureen Guirdham (1995, p.165) lists 136 non-verbal communication behaviours, in nine categories; what we do with our mouths, eyebrows, eyelids and eyes, gaze, facial expressions, head movements, hands and arms, lower limbs and trunk movements. The sub-heading 'mouth region' lists 40 behaviours, such as tongue out, open grin, yawn, wry smile, sneer, tight lips, lower lip tremble – and so on. The subheading 'hands and arms' lists 40 behaviours; scratch, sit on hands, hand flutter, digit suck, palms up, caress, hand on neck.

Table 7.4: Dimensions of non-verbal communication

occulesics; eye behaviour
kinesics; body and limb movements
proxemics; the use of space
paralanguage; tone and pitch of voice
facial expressions
posture
chromatics; the use of colour
chronemics; the use of time
haptics; bodily contacts

Non-verbal courtship

According to Allan Pease (1997), typical male courtship gestures involving non-verbal communication include: preening (straightening tie, smoothing hair), thumbs-in-belt (pointing towards genitals), turning his body to face a female, pointing his foot towards her, holding her gaze, hands on his hips, dilated pupils, and the 'leg spread' (crotch display). Women, on the other hand, have a much richer repertoire of non-verbal courtship behaviour which includes:

- preening gestures such as touching hair, smoothing clothing;
- one or both hands on hips;
- foot and body pointing towards the male;
- extended eye contact or 'intimate gaze';
- thumbs-in-belt, but often only one, or thumb protruding from pocket or handbag;
- pupil dilation;
- flushed appearance;
- the head toss, to flick hair away from face (used even by women with short hair);
- exposing the soft smooth skin on the wrists to the male;
- exposing the palms of the hands;
- the sideways glance with drooped eyelids ('you caught me looking at you');
- wet lips, mouth slightly open;
- fondling cylindrical objects (stem of wine glass, a finger);
- the knee point, one leg tucked under the other, pointing to the male, thighs exposed;
- the shoe fondle, pushing the foot in and out of a half-on-half-off shoe;
- crossing and uncrossing the legs slowly in front of the man;
- gently stroking the thighs (indicating a desire to be touched).

How many of these non-verbal courtship gestures, male and female, are illustrated here:

Source: Colin McDougall

Courtship gestures

Another important aspect of non-verbal communication is 'paralanguage'. This concerns the rate of speech, and pitch and loudness of our voice, regardless of the words we are using. There are many different ways of saying the same sequence of words; it's not what you say, but the way that you say it. Paralanguage demonstrates some of the over-riding power of non-verbal communication. Consider the simple statement: 'That was a really great lecture'. Think of the many ways in which you can say this, the differences in gaze and posture as you say it, and particularly the differences in the tone and pitch of your voice. For some of these expressions, listeners will hear you say that you really *did* enjoy the lecture. However, there are other ways in which you can 'code' these same words, non-verbally, in such a way that listeners will be left in no doubt that you thought the lecture poor. When verbal and non-verbal messages contradict each other, it is the non-verbal message which is believed.

STOP AND THINK

Say out loud exactly the same sentence, 'This is a really interesting textbook', in two different ways, with opposite meanings.

Another aspect of non-verbal communication concerns the way in which we use distance in relationships. The study of this aspect of behaviour is known as 'proxemics'. British culture requires a 'social distance' of about half a metre or more between people in normal conversation. If you cross this invisible boundary and step into someone's 'personal space' they usually move backwards to maintain the distance; a failure to 'retreat' implies intimacy. The comfortable distance in Arab and Latin (American and European) countries is smaller, and you are likely to be regarded as arrogant and distant by trying to maintain your personal space when interacting with members of those cultures.

The power of paralanguage

Meaning 1	Why don't I take **YOU** to dinner tonight?	I was going to take someone else.
Meaning 2	Why don't **I** take you to dinner tonight?	Instead of the guy you were going with.
Meaning 3	Why **DON'T** I take you to dinner tonight?	I'm trying to find a reason why I shouldn't take you.
Meaning 4	**WHY** don't I take you to dinner tonight?	Do you have a problem with me?
Meaning 5	Why don't I **TAKE** you to dinner tonight?	Instead of going on your own.
Meaning 6	Why don't I take you to **DINNER** tonight?	Instead of lunch tomorrow.
Meaning 7	Why don't I take you to dinner **TONIGHT**?	Not tomorrow night.

From Kiely (1993).

It is possible to test the theory of personal space. At a social gathering, a party perhaps, move gradually and tactfully into someone else's space, by pretending to reach for a drink, moving aside to let someone else past, leaning forward to be heard better, and so on. You can move someone across a room in this way. The same result can be achieved while seated, if the chairs are easy to move. However, if your target does not retreat as predicted, and you are now in their intimate space, you have a decoding problem, and the textbook can't help you.

Lie detectors

Can we use non-verbal communication to detect when someone is lying? Adrian Furnham identifies several (UK) verbal and non-verbal 'lie detectors'. However, in other cultures, these cues may constitute normal interpersonal behaviour and may *not* signal deceit.

Verbal cues

Response latency	The time between the end of a question and the start of a reply. Liars take longer, hesitate more.
Linguistic distance	Not saying, 'I', but talking in the abstract: for example, 'one might believe that . . .'
Slow, uneven speech	As an individual tries to think through their lies. They might also suddenly talk quickly, attempting to make a sensitive subject appear less significant.
Too eager to fill gaps in conversation	Liars keep talking when it is unnecessary, as if a silence signifies that the other person does not believe them.
Too many pitch raises	Instead of the pitch dropping at the end of a reply, it is lifted in the same way as asking a question.

Non-verbal cues

Too much squirming	Someone shifting around in their seat is signalling their desire not to be there.
Too much eye contact, rather than too little	Liars tend to overcompensate. They need to look at you to monitor how successful they are being.
Micro-expressions	Flickers of surprise, hurt or anger that are difficult to detect. Sudden facial expressions of pain are often giveaways.
An increase in comfort gestures	These often take the form of self-touching, particularly around the nose and mouth.
An increase in stuttering and slurring	Including what are known as 'Freudian slips'.
A loss of resonance in the voice	It tends to become flatter and more monotonous.

Based on Furnham (1997, p.53).

When we are lying, we may unconsciously send non-verbal 'deceit cues', which include rapid shifts in gaze, fidgeting in our seats, long pauses and frequent speech corrections. When lying, it is important to control these cues, ensuring that verbal and non-verbal messages are consistent. Similarly, when we want to emphasize the sincerity or strength of our feelings, it is important that the non-verbal signals we send are consistent with the verbal message. Maureen Guirdham (2002, p.184) describes non-verbal communication as a 'relationship language'. This is how we communicate trust, boredom, submission, dislike and friendship without stating our feelings directly. When decoding non-verbal communication, it is important to pay attention to context, and to the pattern or cluster of behaviours on display. For example, when someone wishes to indicate liking or friendship, they are likely to turn their body towards you, look you straight in the face, establish regular eye contact and look away infrequently, and to nod and smile a lot, keeping their hands and arms by their sides or in front of them. This cluster conveys friendship, or positive non-verbal communication.

We can often identify disagreement or dislike by negative non-verbal communication. This cluster includes turning the body away, folding the arms tightly, crossing the legs such that they point away from the other person, loss of eye contact, wandering gaze, looking at someone else or at the door (suggesting a desire to leave), and a lack of nods and smiles. The cluster of behaviours producing this 'closed posture' often mean that we know that someone does not like what we are saying before they state their disagreement in words.

However, awareness of the context is critical to this decoding or 'mind reading'. People also engage in negative non-verbal communication when they are unwell, or when they are anxious about something that is perhaps unrelated to your conversation and relationship. People also 'close up' and fold their arms when they are cold and uncomfortable.

Interpreting gesture clusters

cluster signals	indicating
flexible open posture, open hands, display of palms and wrists, removing jacket, moving closer to other person, leaning forward in chair, uncrossed arms and legs, smiling, nodding, eye contact	openness
rigid, closed posture, arms and legs tightly crossed, eyes glancing sideways, minimal eye contact, frowning, no smiling, pursed lips, clenched fists, head down, flat tone of voice	defensiveness
drumming fingers, head cupped in palm of hand, foot swinging, brushing or picking lint from clothing, body pointing towards exit, repeatedly looking at watch, the exit, a book	boredom, impatience
small inward smile, erect body posture, hands open and arms extended outwards, eyes wide and alert, lively walk, expressive and well-modulated voice	enthusiasm
knitted forehead, deadpan expression, tentative nodding or smiling, one slightly raised eyebrow, strained voice, saying 'I understand' while looking away	lack of understanding
blank expression, phoney smile, tight posture, arms stiff at side, sudden eye shifts, nervous tapping, sudden mood shifts, speech toneless and soft or too loud and animated	stress

The dilation and contraction of our pupils is beyond our direct control, unlike the movements of our hands, but our eyes also send non-verbal information. Our pupils dilate in low light, and when we see something or someone interesting. Dilation conveys honesty, openness and sexual attraction. Our pupils also dilate when we are relaxed, and with the consumption of alcohol and other drugs. Context is thus critical to accurate decoding. Contracted pupils can signify low lighting conditions, or lack of interest, distrust, hatred, hostility, fatigue, stress, sorrow, or perhaps a hangover. It is only possible to decode pupil dilation or contraction with reference to other non-verbal clues, and to the context in which this behaviour appears.

Someone who is anxious usually displays 'self-manipulation'; playing with an ear lobe, stroking lips, playing with hair. Anxiety can also be signalled by shifting direction of gaze. Friendship is conveyed by an open non-verbal behaviour cluster. Other friendship signals can be amusing to use and to identify. When we meet someone to whom we are attracted, we often use 'preening gestures'; smoothing our clothes, stroking our hair, straightening our posture. Observe a group of friends together and you will often see them standing, sitting, and even holding cups or glasses in an almost identical manner. This is known as 'posture mirroring'. Sometimes you can identify the 'outsider' as the one not adopting the posture. Friendship groups also copy each others' gestures, known as 'gesture mirroring'.

We also use non-verbal communication to show how important we are with **power tells**. The power tells that dominant people display include (Collett, 2004):

Power tells
non-verbal signals that indicate to others how important and dominant someone is, or how powerful they would like us to *think* they are.

- sitting and standing with your legs far apart (men);
- appropriating the territory around you by placing your hands on your hips;
- using open postures and invasive hand gestures;
- smiling less, because a smile is an appeasement gesture;

- establishing visual dominance by looking away while speaking, implying that you do not need to be attentive;
- speaking first, and dominating the conversation thereafter;
- using a lower vocal register, and speaking more slowly;
- interrupting others, and resisting interruption by others.

The opposites of power tells, that is signals which suggest a submissive attitude, include:

- modifying your speech style to sound more like the other person;
- frequent hesitations, lots of 'ums' and 'ers';
- adopting closed postures;
- clasping your hands, touching your face and hair (self-comfort gestures).

The impact of non-verbal communication

The third and final debate, which took place at Hofstra University, New York on 15 October, was a firecracker of a show, as riveting as the two previous meetings were soporific. The candidates discussed substantive issues. They exchanged sharp blows. And, most of the time, they avoided reciting their talking points.

Source: Emmanuel Dunand/AFP/Getty Images

Mr McCain, Presidential candidate

All good stuff. But Mr McCain also made two big mistakes. Bringing up Mr Obama's association with Bill Ayers, a former terrorist, made him look petty on a day on which the Dow Jones had lost 8 per cent of its value and people have much bleaker issues on their minds. The second – and more serious – lay in his body language. Mr McCain let his contempt for the younger man shine through, harrumphing, grimacing, smirking and goggling

his eyes whenever Mr Obama got a chance to speak. The whole performance was reminiscent of Al Gore's sighing in his debate with George Bush in 2000, which many people think contributed to his defeat.

Source: Dave Weaver/Press Association Images

President Obama

Mr Obama's performance during all this was remarkable. He remained calm and unflustered. He listened respectfully to his opponent. He took every opportunity to change the subject to economics and the woes of the average American. If many of his arguments were weak, his body language was impeccable.

The instant polls all gave a big victory to Mr Obama. Mr McCain made the debate exciting, but Mr Obama got the better of the evening, surely increasing his already high chances of victory in November [Obama of course won the election].

From The Economist *(2008b).*

This is national politics. In your judgement, how important is body language or non-verbal communication in an organizational context?

Cultural differences in communication style

The use and interpretation of non-verbal communication differ from culture to culture. In Japan, smiling and nodding implies understanding, but not necessarily agreement. In Australia, raising the pitch of your voice at the end of a sentence signifies openness to challenge or question, not a lie. In some Asian cultures, it is impolite to give superiors direct and prolonged eye contact; a bowed head signifies deference and not lack of self confidence or defensiveness. People from northern European cultures prefer a lot of personal space and rarely touch each other. French, Italians and Latin Americans, in contrast, stand closer together and touch more often to indicate agreement and friendship.

Simple gestures must also be used with care. Make a circle with your thumb and forefinger, extending the other three fingers. How will this be interpreted (DuBrin, 1994)? In America, and to scuba divers, it means, 'OK'. In Japan, it means money. In France, it means zero or nothing. In some Arab countries, it signifies a curse. In Germany and Brazil, it is obscene.

High context culture
a culture whose members rely heavily on a range of social and non-verbal clues when communicating with others and interpreting their messages.

Edward Hall (1976, 1989) distinguished between high context culture and low context culture.

high context culture	low context culture
establish relationship first	get down to business first
value personal relations and goodwill	value expertise and performance
agreement based on trust	agreement based on legal contract
slow and ritualistic negotiations	fast and efficient negotiations

Low context culture
a culture whose members focus on the written and spoken word when communicating with others and interpreting their messages.

China, Korea, Japan and Vietnam are high context cultures, where people tend to take a greater interest in your position, your business card, your dress, material possessions, and other signs of status and relationships. Written and spoken communications are not ignored, but they are secondary. Agreements can be made on a handshake, on someone's word.

North America, Scandinavia, Switzerland and Germany are low context cultures, where people pay secondary attention to non-verbal messages. People in German organizations tend to be preoccupied with detailed written rules, and Americans like to have precise legal documents. Agreements are not made until the contract is in writing, signed.

These categorizations reflect tendencies and are not absolutes. Most countries have subcultures with very different norms. In addition, men tend to be more high context than women, but this observation does not apply to all men or to all women. Nevertheless, it is easy to see how misunderstanding can arise when high and low context cultures meet, unless those communicating are sensitive to their respective differences.

Impression management

**Erving Goffman
(1922–1982)**

We usually send and receive non-verbal messages unconsciously. However, it is possible to control the non-verbal signals that we send, and to be aware of and to read the cues that others are giving to us. This level of attention and control can be difficult to sustain, but it can be important in organizational settings, especially where we want to control the image or impression that others have of us. We can do this through impression management techniques, based originally on the work of Erving Goffman (1959).

Paul Rosenfeld and colleagues (2001) observe that our impression management methods are rich and varied, including:

• what we do and how we do it;
• what we say and how we say it;

Impression management
the processes through which we control the image or impression that others have of us.

- the furnishings and arrangement of our offices;
- our physical appearance including clothes and make-up;
- non-verbal communication such as facial expressions or postures.

Effective impression management means being consciously aware and in control of the cues that we send to others through verbal and non-verbal channels. This suggests that we consciously seek to manipulate the impression or perceptions that others have of us.

STOP AND THINK

Is impression management simply a form of deceit? What in your view are the ethical problems raised by the advice that we should consciously manipulate the impression that others have of us through verbal and non-verbal communication?

Do you use, or do you avoid, impression management methods when you are deciding what to wear to go to parties, clubs, job interviews?

The ethics of impression management

Richard M. Nixon

Source: Reuters/Strold

his five o'clock shadow. Kennedy got his aides to apply make-up when Nixon wasn't looking, and presented a tanned and handsome face to the nation. Nixon looked like a sweaty corpse. Radio listeners thought he did well. But on television, Kennedy won by a mile.

From The Economist *(2008a).*

In your judgement, was John F. Kennedy's behaviour ethical at that debate in 1960?

John F. Kennedy

Source: Ted Spiegel/Corbis

At first, Richard Nixon vowed he would not debate John Kennedy. He had little to gain from such an encounter, and much to lose. As vice-president, he was better known than the young senator and universally considered a heavyweight. But in the end his fear of appearing fearful overcame his caution. It was a mistake. The camera is unkind to men who look shifty.

At the first debate in 1960, Nixon was not feeling well. After hearing Kennedy turn down the offer of make-up, he turned it down too, although it might have covered

As with conversation controls, we can use impression management to manipulate the behaviour of others. We do this, for example, by 'giving off' the impression that we are friendly, submissive, apologetic, angry, defensive, confident, intimidating, and so on. The more effectively we manage our impression, the greater the control we can achieve in social interaction, and the greater our power to pursue our preferred outcomes over others.

Some people regard impression management as acting. However, we manage our impression all the time. It is hardly possible to avoid sending signals through, for example, our dress, posture, facial expressions, gestures, tone and pitch of voice, and even location in a room. We can distinguish between conscious (by implication more effective) and unconscious (by implication less effective, or misleading) impression management. Conscious impression management has many advantages. Interactions run more smoothly when we provide the correct signals to others who in turn accurately decode these signals of our attitudes and intents. Impression management is a critical skill in many organizational contexts, such as counselling, and in selection, appraisal and disciplinary interviews.

Home viewing

Catch Me If You Can (2003, directed by Steven Spielberg) is a comedy drama based on the true story of the forger and confidence trickster Frank Abagnale Jr (played by Leonardo Di Caprio) and the FBI agent Carl Hanratty (Tom Hanks) who finally apprehends him, but not before Frank has committed millions of dollars worth of fraud. Frank is a master of the art of impression management, effortlessly convincing others that he is, at various stages in his 'career'; newspaper journalist, high school teacher, airline pilot, doctor, and lawyer. He is so convincing that, when he does at one point decide to reveal the truth, his fiancée's father (Martin Sheen) does not believe him. Note examples of how Frank uses a combination of non-verbal communication, courtship techniques, avoidance of lie detection cues, paralanguage and gesture clusters, to manage the impression that he wants to convey.

Feldman and Klitch (1991) offer advice on how to manage your impression to enhance your career, suggesting six methods for creating a favourable self-image (Table 7.5).

Table 7.5: **Creating a favourable self-image**

Ingratiation	Use flattery, agree with the opinions of others, do favours to encourage people with power and influence to befriend you.
Intimidation	Convey the image of potential danger to those who could stand in the way of your advancement. Use veiled threats of exposure.
Self promotion	Win respect and admiration of superiors through embellishing your accomplishments, overstating your abilities, displaying awards.
Exemplification	Create an impression of selfless dedication and self-sacrifice, so those in positions of influence will feel guilty and offer reward or promotion.
Accounting	Distance yourself from negative events, deny personal responsibility for problems, diminish the seriousness of difficulties.
Supplication	Get those in positions of influence to be sympathetic and nurturing, for example, through requests for 'mentoring' and other support.

Will you get that job?

Summarizing research on communication in selection interviews, Fredric Jablin (2001, pp.749–50) concludes that:

- Interviewers report that applicants' communication skills are critical to selection decisions, including fluency of speech, composure, appropriate content and ability to express ideas in an organized manner.

- Interviewers rate more favourably interviewees who display appropriate levels of nonverbal immediacy, including eye contact, smiling, open posture, interpersonal distance and direct body orientation.

- Interviewers rate more highly and are more satisfied with interviewees who talk more of the time in interview, who elaborate on their answers, and whose discussion of topics closely matches the interviewer's expectations.

- Interviewers rate more favourably interviewees who display assertive impression management techniques, such as agreeing with the interviewer, emphasizing positive traits, asking positive-closed questions, claiming that they 'fit' the organization, and telling personal stories to confirm that they are competent, hardworking, goal-oriented, confident, adaptable, interpersonally skilled and effective leaders.

- Where the interviewer is seen as trustworthy, competent, composed, empathic, enthusiastic, and well-organized, the applicant is more likely to accept the job offer.

Based on Jablin (2001).

Emotional intelligence

Emotional intelligence the ability to identify, integrate, understand and reflectively manage one's own and other people's feelings.

Non-verbal communication is one way in which we display emotion. While often embarrassing, an open show of emotion can sometimes be desirable. Emotions are a key source of motivation. Inability to display and share feelings can be a handicap. Sharing feelings of frustration and anger can be as important in an organizational setting as showing positive feelings of, for example, praise, satisfaction and friendship. The ability to handle emotions can be regarded as a mental skill, which can be developed with training, but some commentators regard this skill as a personality dimension (see Chapter 6).

The concept of **emotional intelligence** was developed by Peter Salovey and John D. Mayer (1990) who argued that the concept of 'rational' intelligence ignores emotional competencies.

The concept was popularized by Daniel Goleman (1998, 2005), who argues that emotional intelligence is more important to career success than technical skills or rational intelligence. Goleman's dimensions of emotional intelligence are summarized in Table 7.6.

Goleman argues that emotional intelligence gives us an advantage, at work and in social relationships, but that it is particularly important for top management, where conventional notions of intelligence are taken for granted. At senior levels, high emotional intelligence is a mark of the 'star performer'. There are several assessments for measuring emotional intelligence (sometimes confusingly called EQ), and some commentators argue that emotional intelligence can be learned and developed through experience and training.

Woodruffe (2001) notes a paradox concerning tests which measure emotional intelligence. A typical item, to which respondents are asked to rate their agreement, is 'I can easily express emotions over the phone.' What is the 'correct' answer? Only an emotionally intelligent person, he points out, could recognize whether or not they can do this. He then asks, 'Is it emotionally intelligent to express the emotion or to be aware that you don't express it?'. Woodruffe argues that emotional intelligence is not a useful concept and that its impact on job performance is exaggerated.

Table 7.6: The five dimensions of emotional intelligence

Dimension	Definition	Hallmarks
1 Self-awareness	the ability to recognize and understand your moods, emotions and drives as well the effect you have on others	self confidence, realistic self-assessment, self-deprecating sense of humour
2 Regulating feelings	the ability to control your disruptive moods and impulses; the propensity to suspend judgement, to think before acting	trustworthiness and integrity, comfortable with ambiguity, openness to change
3 Motivation	a passion to work for reasons beyond status and money; a propensity to pursue goals with energy and persistence	high achievement need, optimism even in the face of failure, organizational commitment
4 Empathy	the ability to recognize and understand the emotional makeup of others; skill in dealing with the emotional responses of others	expertise in building and retaining talent; cross-cultural sensitivity; service to clients and customers
5 Social skills	effectiveness in managing relationships and building networks; ability to find common ground, to build rapport	effectiveness in leading change; persuasiveness; expertise in building and leading teams

Organizational communication

Communication is central to individual and organizational performance, but many managers regard communication as a problem and many employees feel that they are not fully informed about management plans. Research shows that many companies do not pay attention to communication when implementing change, resulting in absenteeism, turnover, disputes and low productivity. Employee communication has become more important. Why? One reason is the growth in the volume of other information available through the internet. A second reason is the rise in employee expectations, to be kept informed and to contribute ideas.

A recent study by the Chartered Institute of Personnel and Development (Cannell, 2007) in Britain found that only just over half of employees felt that they were being informed about what their company was doing, and only 65 per cent said that they were given enough information to enable them to do their work effectively. People who are informed and feel valued are more likely to be committed to the organization and to perform better in their work. Poor communication, therefore, is an organizational issue as well as a personal one. Clear, consistent, effective communication should be a management priority. This study found that the top four objectives that organizations try to achieve through internal communications are:

- engaging employees to achieve business goals: 85 per cent of respondents
- understanding organization goals and strategy: 81 per cent
- supporting culture change: 52 per cent
- creating an open environment for dialogue across the organization: 50 per cent

One key management problem is to persuade employees to work in the interests of the organization as a whole. However, the interests of individuals and organizations do not always coincide. How can employee behaviour be channelled in the desired directions? In their seminal contribution to organizational behaviour, James March and Herbert Simon (1958) argued that management cannot change individual behaviour directly, or by attempting to alter people's personalities. It is more effective and practical, they argued, to influence the premises on which people make their own decisions about how they will behave.

Thirteen points for an effective communication strategy

1. Convince top management of the importance of communication
2. Build alliances across the organization to support initiatives
3. Recognize that no single method will be effective
4. Use a mix of approaches and use all available channels where relevant
5. Target communication to the audience; different methods for shop floor and managers
6. Respect cultural diversity and vary approaches accordingly
7. Make sure that messages are consistent, over time and between audiences
8. Ensure clarity of message and keep things as simple as possible
9. Train managers in communication skills
10. Develop and sustain two-way communication, dialogue and feedback
11. Ensure that employees feel that they can say what they think without discomfort
12. Ensure that communication is built into the planning stages of all activities
13. Review communication initiatives to check what has worked, what hasn't, and why

Based on Cannell (2007).

How can management influence the premises – the underlying assumptions – which affect the day-to-day decisions of employees? This is simple. The basis on which pay is calculated, for example, can affect attendance, timekeeping, and work rate (through piece rates and bonuses). Company rules, how these are enforced, and the terms in which they are expressed, are also ways of 'signalling' or 'coding' desirable and undesirable behaviours. Desirable behaviours can be reinforced through the appraisal system which, in a retail store for example, can evaluate employee behaviours such as, 'expresses ideas clearly, keeps other informed, shares knowledge, provides timely communication, listens and responds to customers'.

STOP AND THINK   How does your educational institution use rewards and sanctions to influence the decisions that you make about the nature and direction of your studies? What 'signals' do teaching staff send in order to communicate to students how they expect them to behave?

These 'signalling systems' are saying, 'behave this way and you will be rewarded and/or promoted, but behave that way and you will be overlooked for promotion – or fired'. These systems are often complemented by organization vision and mission statements, and by statements of corporate values.

Better communication is often advocated by management consultants as a cure for many organizational problems such as low morale, high absenteeism and turnover, labour unrest and conflict, low productivity and resistance to change. This advice is based on the theory that, if people understand what is going on, then they will be more likely to follow management directions. A well-presented argument supported with compelling evidence should result in consensus and compliance. Is that always the case?

Organizations use a range of mechanisms for communicating with employees, such as:

- the management chain of command;
- regular meetings with senior and/or middle managers;
- in-house newspapers and magazines;
- company intranet;
- noticeboards;
- videos and in-house television;
- conferences and seminars;
- employee reports;
- team briefings;
- email, intranet, blogs, podcasts.

Those are traditionally one-way-top-down modes of communication. Two-way exchanges are more effectively achieved through methods such as:

- Web 2.0 interactive systems (see Chapter 2)
- 'speak out' programmes in which problems are taken to counsellors;
- suggestion or 'bright ideas' schemes;
- open door policies;
- the appraisal system;
- quality circles;
- attitude surveys;
- interactive email (where managers guarantee to reply).

Communication climate the prevailing atmosphere in an organization – *open* or *closed* – in which ideas and information are exchanged.

Jack Gibb (1961) developed the concept of **communication climate**.

Culture differences in organizational communication

In the 'North' [of Europe] the policy is that everyone knows. 'Southern' management discourages an open, critical attitude of younger and 'inexperienced' employees, whereas in the North such an attitude is welcomed. On the corporate information front, five years ago Unilever started 'Cascade', a system to acquaint all employees yearly with information about how the Corporation was doing financially. For this, corporate HQ prepares a big packet full of information, complete with overhead sheets and even videos. All business groups receive the same information and are expected to pass it on to their companies and eventually to all employees. Random checks among employees after the Cascade exercise have shown that in Eastern Europe all employees are very interested in corporate information and that 'coverage' is near 100 per cent; in Western Europe coverage is 'average', some 80 per cent, but in Latin countries coverage is 'difficult', at around 65 per cent, because local management seems to decide that not all information is 'necessary' or fit for their employees.

From Fourboul and Bournois (1999).

An open communication climate promotes collaborative working; people develop self-worth, feel that they can contribute freely without reprisal, know that their suggestions will be welcomed, that mistakes will be seen as learning opportunities, and they feel trusted, secure and confident in their job. In a closed communication climate, information is withheld unless it is to the advantage of the sender, and recrimination, secrecy and distrust can make working life unpleasant. This distinction is summarized in Table 7.7. These extremes are not absolutes; most organizations are likely to have a climate which lies on the continuum between open and closed, and the climate may vary between sections or departments.

Table 7.7: Open and closed communication climates

Open, supportive communication climate	Closed, defensive communication climate
Descriptive: informative rather than evaluative communication	**Judgemental**: emphasis on apportioning blame, make people feel incompetent
Solution-oriented: focus on problem-solving rather than on what is not possible	**Controlling**: conformity expected, inconsistency and change inhibited
Open and honest: no hidden messages	**Deceptive**: hidden meanings, insincerity, manipulative communication
Caring: emphasis on empathy and understanding	**Non-caring**: detached and impersonal, little concern for others
Egalitarian: everyone valued regardless of role or status	**Superior**: status and skill differences emphasized in communication
Forgiving: errors and mistakes recognized as inevitable, focus on minimizing	**Dogmatic**: little discussion, unwillingness to accept views of others or compromise
Feedback: positive, essential to maintaining performance and relationships	**Hostile**: needs of others given little importance

STOP AND THINK

How would you describe the communication climate of your educational institution? Of an organization where you have recently worked? Of your current employer?

The theory that 'people will comply if they understand' suggests that communication has an educational component. Employees who are better informed about 'economic realities' are more likely to have realistic expectations, and make reasonable demands. However, this argument equates communication with propaganda which attempts to shape attitudes and behaviours in particular directions, to generate consensus by giving the logic of managerial decision-making a greater legitimacy. With the growing use of Web 2.0-based interactive communications, alongside traditional methods such as team briefings and teamworking, management can bypass trade unions by working through team leaders instead.

Communication in an organization is not a neutral process. Organizational communication is constructed from a perspective which represents management interests. Organizational power inequalities require management to direct and dominate workforce behaviour. Information is not simply a commodity to be transmitted. Communication mechanisms are tools for manipulating employee attitudes and behaviours. The 'context' in our model of the communication process (Figure 7.1) must consider not just physical and interpersonal factors, but also the wider social and political context of organizational communication.

RECAP

1. *Describe the dimensions of social intelligence, and explain the importance of these capabilities, especially for managers.*

   - The capabilities that make up social intelligence involve a combination of awareness – what we sense about others – and facility – how we act on that awareness.

   - Managers spend lots of time interacting with others, and it becomes more important to understand the thoughts and feelings of others in a more culturally diverse population.

2. *Understand the main components of the interpersonal communication process.*

   - Communication involves an exchange of meaning, achieved through the processes of coding, transmission, decoding and feedback.

   - Face-to-face communication allows instant feedback; coding and decoding problems arise with other forms of communication where feedback is delayed or absent.

3. *Identify the main barriers to effective interpersonal communication.*

   - The main barriers to effective communication include power and gender differences, physical surroundings, language variations and cultural diversity.

   - Barriers can be overcome through face to face communication, by checking decoding, by paying attention to context, and by seeing things the way the other person does.

4. *Understand the effective use of different questioning techniques, conversation controls and listening skills.*

   - Getting appropriate information from someone else involves the effective use of different questioning methods: open, closed, probe, hypothetical and reflective.

   - Effective communication involves the use of a range of simple conversation controls: lubricators, inhibitors, bridges and pauses.

   - Active listening involves a range of verbal and non-verbal skills.

   - Communication methods differ between high context and low context cultures.

5. *Explain the nature and significance of non-verbal communication.*

   - Non-verbal communication includes facial expressions, eye behaviour, gesture and posture, distance between ourselves and others, and paralanguage.

   - If the verbal and non-verbal messages which we are sending are inconsistent, the verbal will be discounted and the non-verbal accepted.

   - Lies can be detected in non-verbal communication, but many clues are culture-specific.

6. *Understand the nature and mechanisms of impression management skills and techniques.*

   - We influence the image that others have of us through verbal and non-verbal signals.

   - We use impression management to create a favourable image through ingratiation, intimidation, self-promotion, exemplification, accounting, and supplication.

   - Impression management can be seen as natural and unconscious, or as a deliberate attempt at deceit.

7. *Be able to explain the concept of emotional intelligence and its practical significance.*

   - Emotional intelligence concerns the ability to identify, integrate, understand and reflectively manage one's own feelings, and the feelings of other people.

   - As with social intelligence, understanding your own emotions and the emotions of others is a key skill for all of us, particularly for managers, and its importance is heightened in culturally diverse organizational settings.

8. *Understand the ways in which corporate communication can be used to manipulate understanding and encourage compliance with management directions.*

   - Organizations use a range of media for communicating with employees.

   - The communication climate in an organization can be classed as open and supportive, or closed and defensive.

   - Organizational communication is not neutral, but is constructed from a management perspective in an attempt to manipulate the attitudes and behaviour of recipients.

Revision

1. What is social intelligence, and why are these capabilities now seen as ranking in importance with general intelligence, especially for managers?
2. What are the main problems affecting the communication process, and how can these problems be solved?
3. Explain, with appropriate examples, the questioning techniques which we use to obtain information from others, and the conversation control methods that we use to ensure that our interactions run smoothly, and in our favour.
4. What is non-verbal communication, and what part does it play in human interaction in general and in organizational settings in particular?

Research assignment

Choose two different television programmes which include interviews; news, political commentary, magazine programmes, chat shows. It does not matter whether the interview is about news information, or simply audience entertainment. In each case observe one interviewer or host or commentator interviewing someone, and makes notes on:

1. what questioning techniques are used, and their effectiveness;
2. what questioning techniques are not used;
3. the interviewer's use of body language;
4. does the interviewer display social intelligence, and what evidence can you cite;
5. does the interviewer display emotional intelligence, and what evidence can you cite;
6. who controls the flow of conversation – interviewer or interviewee.

Write a report comparing the similarities and differences in these two interviews. Assess the skill and effectiveness of the interviewer in each case. Where appropriate, determine from your assessment what practical advice you would give to these interviewers to help them to improve their technique. What general conclusions can you reach concerning interviewing skills in general, and television interviewing in particular?

Springboard

Crystal, D., 2005, *How Language Works*, Penguin Books, London.

Insights into the mechanics of communication, how we learn and use languages, the significance of dialects, gestures, and tone of voice, how the brain handles language, how conversations work.

Goleman, D., 2005, *Emotional Intelligence: Why It Can Matter More Than IQ*, Bantam Books, London.

This book turned emotional intelligence into a management fad. Argues that, if you are not committed to the organization, to team working, and to high performance, then you lack emotional intelligence.

Guirdham, M., 2002 and 2005, *Interactive Behaviour at Work*, Financial Times Prentice Hall, Harlow (3rd edn); and *Communicating Across Cultures at Work*, Palgrave Macmillan, London (2nd edn).

Guides to research, theory and practice in interpersonal skills, and cross-cultural and technology-mediated communication, with self-assessments and advice.

Huczynski, A., 2004, *Influencing Within Organizations*, Routledge, London.

Practical guide to the realities of influence, arguing that job skills alone are not enough to ensure career advancement. Chapters on verbal and non-verbal influencing and impression management.

OB in films

Burn After Reading (2008, directors Joel and Ethan Cohen): DVD track 6: 0:27:13 to 0:29:08 (2 minutes). Clip opens with Linda asking for 'just a tea'; clip ends with Linda saying, 'Haven't you heard of the power of positive thinking?'

Gym employee Linda Litzke (played by Frances McDormand) is talking to the gym manager, Ted Treffon (Richard Jenkins).

1. What does Linda want to achieve in this conversation?
2. What tactics does she use?
3. Why does she not achieve her goal?
4. What advice can you give to Linda about managing this conversation more effectively?
5. What does Ted want to achieve in this conversation?
6. What tactics does he use?
7. Why does he not achieve his goal?
8. What advice can you give to Ted about managing this conversation more effectively?

 ## OB in literature

Tainted Blood, by Arnaldur Indriđason (Vintage, 2005, translated from Icelandic by Bernard Scudder) is an unusual detective novel set in Reykyavík, Iceland. Detective Erlendur has problems communicating with his daughter, Eva Lind. What are the barriers to their effective communication? Describe how these barriers arise and/or are overcome in your own interpersonal relationships, with friends and colleagues as well as with family members.

CHAPTER EXERCISES

Impression management check

Objective   1. To assess aspects of the way in which you deal with other people.

Briefing   As you read each of the following 18 statements, ask yourself whether or not it applies to you, and answer (tick) 'yes' or 'no' accordingly. You will of course occasionally feel that you want to answer, 'sometimes'. But try in each case to decide where your personal preferences, strengths, and priorities really lie, and answer 'yes' or 'no' accordingly. You don't always get to sit on the fence. This is not a test with right or wrong answers. It is designed for personal reflection and group discussion.

	yes	no
1 I find it hard to imitate the behaviour of other people.		
2 At parties and gatherings, I do not attempt to do or say things that others will like.		
3 I can only argue for ideas which I already believe.		
4 I can make impromptu speeches even on topics about which I have almost no information.		

5 I guess I put on a show to impress or entertain others.		
6 I would probably make a good actor.		
7 In a group of people, I am rarely the centre of attention.		
8 In different situations and with different people, I often act like very different persons.		
9 I am not particularly good at making other people like me.		
10 I'm not always the person I appear to be.		
11 I would not change my opinions or the way I do things in order to please someone or win their favour.		
12 I have considered being an entertainer.		
13 I have never been good at games like charades, or acting.		
14 I have trouble changing my behaviour to suit different people and different situations.		
15 At a party I let others keep the jokes and stories going.		
16 I feel a bit awkward in company and do not show up quite as well as I should.		
17 I can look anyone in the eye and tell a lie with a straight face, if for an appropriate reason.		
18 I may deceive people by being friendly when I really dislike them.		

Scoring You get either one point or zero, depending on how you responded to each statement. Simply add up the number of points you got.

statement	score		your score
	yes	no	
1	0	1	
2	0	1	
3	0	1	
4	1	0	
5	1	0	
6	1	0	
7	0	1	
8	1	0	
9	0	1	
10	1	0	
11	0	1	
12	1	0	
13	0	1	
14	0	1	
15	0	1	
16	0	1	
17	1	0	
18	1	0	
		Total:	

Interpretation A score of 13 or more implies strong impression management skills:

awareness you are consciously aware of your own and other people's feelings and behaviour, and of how you affect others

flexibility you are able to adjust what you say and do to match other people's expectations, and to achieve your goals

control you are able consciously to control your behaviour, and thus to control other people; you probably enjoy this

A score of 7 or less implies weak impression management skills:

awareness   you are not always aware of your own or other people's feelings and behaviour, or of how you affect others

flexibility   you are unable to adjust what you say and do to match other people's expectations, and to achieve your goals

control   you are unable consciously to control your behaviour, and may feel uncomfortably manipulated at times

A score between 8 and 12 implies moderate impression management skills. Read over the interpretations above, and judge your strengths for yourself. Which way would you now like to go – up or down?

Analysis   Whatever your own score, consider the following key issues:

1. To what extent are impression management skills learnable and to what extent are we born with them?

2. Is it immoral or unethical to adjust one's behaviour in order to modify the feelings and behaviours of others?

3. Regardless of your own impression management score, would it benefit you to be more aware of how other people use these skills? Give specific examples.

4. In what ways would it benefit you personally to improve your own impression management skills, or to enhance your awareness of how you use them? Give specific examples.

How would you respond?

Objectives   1. To analyse the practical uses of questioning techniques and conversation controls.

2. To explore appropriate management options in dealing with employee grievances.

Briefing   1. Individual analysis: Read these sets of statements on your own, without discussing them with colleagues. In each case decide, as the supervisor:

- which of the four statements is the best, and why?
- what objective(s) you would have for this interaction – that is, what you would like to have achieved by the end?
- what are the key issues relevant to the individual, team, and organization in this context?
- what is your behavioural plan for the meeting – that is, beyond the stated comment, what else will you say and do?
- a fifth response that you think is better than those suggested.

2. Syndicate discussion: Following your instructor's advice on size of syndicate and timing, share your assessments, selections and, where appropriate, alternative responses, and attempt to reach a group consensus.

3. Plenary: Each group presents and explains its conclusions to the group as a whole.

4. Debriefing: Your instructor will lead a discussion of the implications of the different responses in each case, and of the key learning points from this exercise.

Here are three statements from employees, directed at you, their immediate supervisor.

Assistant Supervisor, age 30, computer manufacturing plant

'Yes, I do have a problem. I'd like to know more about what happened with the promotions last month. Charlie got the supervisor's job in motherboard assembly and I didn't even know he was interested. Why did you give the job to him? I would like to know more about what you think of my promotion prospects here. I've been doing this job for about three years now, and I've been with the company for almost five years. I haven't had any complaints about my work. Seems to me I've been doing a pretty good job, but I don't see any recognition for that. What do I have to do to get promoted round here?'

1. You'll make a great supervisor, Bill, but give it time. I'll do what I can to make your case. Don't be discouraged, OK? I'm sure you'll get there soon, you'll see.

2. So, you're not sure about how the company regards your work here?

3. I understand how you feel, but I have to admit it took me five years to make supervisor myself. And I guess I must have felt much the same way you do today. But we just have to be patient. Things don't always happen when we'd like them to, do they?

4. Come on, you've been here long enough to know the answer to that one. Nobody got promoted just by waiting for it to happen. Get with it, you've got to put yourself forward, make people stand up and take notice of your capabilities.

Secretary, age 45, insurance company headquarters

'Can I ask you to do something about the calendars that Mr Johnson and Mr Hargreaves insist on displaying in their offices? They are degrading to women and I find them offensive. I know that some of the other secretaries who work on their floor feel exactly the same way as I do. I have to work with these men and I can't stay out of their offices. Don't we have a company policy or something? I'm surprised you've allowed it to go on this long as it is.'

1. You and some of the other secretaries find these calendars insulting?

2. Look, you're taking this all too seriously. Boys' toys, that's all it is, executive perks. Doesn't mean anything, and there's nothing personal behind it at all. You've no cause for concern.

3. You're right, I don't like that either, but we're talking about their own offices here, and I think that they have the right, within reason, to make their own decisions about what pictures to put on the walls, same as you and I do.

4. I'll see if I can't get a chance to have a quiet word with them some time next week, maybe try to persuade them to move their calendars out of sight, OK? I'm sure they don't mean anything by it.

Personnel Officer, age 26, local authority

'I've just about had it. I can't put up with this kind of pressure for much longer. We just don't have the staff to service the level of requests that we're getting and still do a good job. And some of the people we have to deal with! If that old witch in administration calls me one more time about those files that went missing last week, she's going to get a real mouthful in return. How come you let your department get pushed around like this?'

1. You're not alone. Pressure is something that we've all had to endure at some time. I understand that, it comes with the territory. I think it's about developing the right skills and attitudes to cope.

2. You're right, this is a difficult patch, but I'm sure that it will pass. This can't go on for much longer, and I expect you'll see things start to come right at the end of the month.

3. Well, if you can't stand the heat, I suppose you just have to get out of the kitchen. And please don't refer to people who are senior to you in this organization in that manner ever again.

4. Let me check – this is not about Mrs Smith in admin is it? You're saying the strain is such that you're thinking of leaving us?

Based on Snyder, 1987, p.179.

Chapter 8 **Perception**

Key terms

perception	perceptual set
perceptual world	perceptual world
selective attention	halo effect
perceptual threshold	stereotype
habituation	self-fulfilling prophecy
perceptual filters	attribution
perceptual organization	

Learning outcomes

When you have read this chapter, you should be able to define those key terms in your own words, and you should also be able to:

1. Identify the main features of the process of perception.

2. Distinguish between the bottom-up processing of sensory information and the top-down interpretation of that information.

3. Understand the nature and implications of selective attention and perceptual organization.

4. Give examples of how behaviour is influenced by our perceptions.

5. Explain and illustrate the main processes and problems in perception, including false attributions, halo effects and stereotyping.

6. Explain some less widely appreciated sources of discrimination at work arising from characteristics of the person perception and attribution processes.

7. Suggest techniques for improving perceptual accuracy and avoiding errors.

Why study perception?

Of all the topics covered in this text, perception is perhaps the one which most clearly sets social science apart from natural science. We attach meanings, interpretations, values and aims to our actions. Our actions are influenced by how we perceive ourselves, and on how we perceive our social and physical environment. We explain our behaviour with terms like reason, motive, intention, purpose, and desire. Astronomers, chemists, engineers, and physicists do not face this complication in coming to grips with their subject matter.

Perception the dynamic psychological process responsible for attending to, organizing and interpreting sensory data.

It is our perception of reality which shapes and directs our behaviour, not some objective understanding of if. We each perceive the world around us in different ways. If one person on a hillside perceives that it is cold, they will reach for a sweater. If the person standing next to them perceives that it is warm, they will remove their sweater. These contrasting behaviours can occur simultaneously, regardless of the ambient temperature. Human behaviour is a function of the way in which we perceive the world around us, and how we perceive other people and events in that world.

STOP AND THINK

Choose a film that you have seen recently, and which you particularly enjoyed. Now find a friend or colleague who has seen the same film, and who hated it.

Share your views of that film. What factors (age, sex, background, education, interests, values and beliefs, political views, past experience) can you identify that explain the differences in perception between you and your friend or colleague?

We often find ourselves unable to understand other people's behaviour. People can say and do surprising things in settings where it is obvious to us that some other behaviour would have been more appropriate. If we are to understand why you behaved in that way in that context, we first need to discover how you perceive that context and your place in it. When we are able to 'see it the way you see it', to put ourselves in your position, what initially took us by surprise is likely to become readily understandable. To understand each others' behaviour, we need to be able to understand each others' perceptions. We need to be able to understand why we perceive things differently in the first place.

Perceptions of empowerment

How do employees perceive management attempts at empowerment? Empowerment implies flexibility and freedom to make decisions about how work is carried out. The construction industry tends to rely on collaborating teams, which work on-site at a distance from company management, and high levels of employee empowerment might be expected under these conditions. When problems are solved by those who are closest to the work, decision-making is quicker, and job satisfaction and performance can increase. Kay Greasley and colleagues interviewed sixteen workers, on four large construction projects, to find out how they perceived empowerment in practice. Four themes emerged:

The role of supervision: the style of the first line supervisor is crucial, as this is often the only manager with whom construction workers come into contact regularly. Some trusted their workers to get on with the job, but others monitored the work closely.

The employee view: employees felt more competent, trusted, and empowered when supervisory monitoring was low. However, while some workers wanted extensive decision-making powers, others were more comfortable with routine decisions.

Consequences: feeling valued, and implementing one's own ideas, prompted a positive emotional response, increasing self-esteem, job satisfaction, and pride in the work.

Barriers: supervisory style, and health and safety regulations, are barriers to empowerment in the construction industry. Senior management are too distant to encourage supervisors to adopt a more empowering approach, and the many safety regulations are stringent (although managers do not always seem to follow the same rules).

The temporary project-based nature of construction work, with distant senior managers, makes it difficult to develop a consistent approach to employee empowerment, even where this is management policy. However, if employees perceive that they are not trusted, and have little or no control over their work, they can withdraw goodwill and delay the construction process.

Based on Greasley et al. *(2005)*

Selectivity and organization

We do not passively register sense impressions picked up from the world around us. We process and interpret the incoming raw data in the light of our past experiences, in terms of our current needs and interests, in terms of our knowledge, expectations, beliefs and motives.

The main elements in the perceptual process are illustrated in Figure 8.1. From a psychological point of view, the processes of sensation, on the one hand, and perception, on the other, work together through what are respectively termed *bottom up* and *top down* processing. The bottom up phase concerns the way in which we process the raw data received by our sensory apparatus. One of the key characteristics of bottom up processing concerns the need for selectivity. We are simply not able to attend to all of the sensory information available to us at any given time. Bottom up processing screens or filters out redundant and less relevant information so that we can focus on what is important.

The top down phase, in contrast, concerns the mental processing that allows us to order, interpret, and make sense of the world around us. One of the key characteristics of top down processing concerns our need to make sense of our environment, and our search for meaning.

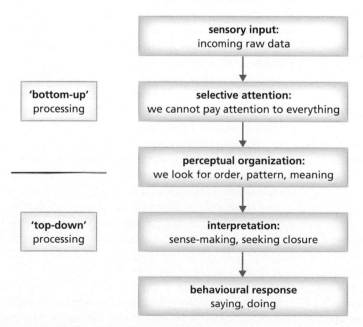

Figure 8.1: Elements in the process of perception

This distinction between sensation (bottom up) and perception (top down) can be illustrated in our ability to make sense of incomplete, or even incorrect, sensory information. The missing letter or comma, or the incorrectly spelled term does not interfere with comprehension, as you will know from text messaging:

This sent nce us incorr ct, bit yoo wull stell bi abl to udersta d it.

Our top down conceptual processing ability means that we are able to fill in the gaps and correct the mistakes, and make sense of 'imperfect' raw data.

We each have a similar nervous system and share more or less common sensory equipment. However, we have different social and physical backgrounds which give us different values, interests and expectations, and therefore different perceptions. We do not behave in, or respond to, the world 'as it really is'. This idea of the 'real world' is somewhat arbitrary. The 'real world' as a concept is not a useful starting point for developing an understanding of human behaviour in general, or organizational behaviour in particular. We behave in, and in response to, the world as we perceive it. We each live in our own **perceptual world**.

Perceptual world
the individual's personal internal image, map or picture of their social, physical and organizational environment.

Successful interpersonal relationships depend on some overlap between our perceptual worlds, or we would never be able to understand each other. Our perceptual worlds, however, are in a detailed analysis unique, which makes life interesting, but also gives us problems.

Our perceptual processing is normally carried out without much conscious deliberation or effort. In fact, we often have no effective control over the process, and fortunately, control is not always necessary. We can, however, control some aspects of the process simply by being consciously aware of what is happening. There are many settings where such control is desirable and can help us to avoid dangerous and expensive errors. Understanding the characteristics of perception can be useful in a variety of organizational settings. For example, with the design of aircraft instruments and displays for pilots, in the conduct of selection interviews for new employees, and in handling disputes and employee grievances.

Perception is a dynamic process because it involves ordering and attaching meaning to raw sensory data. Our sensory apparatus is bombarded with vast amounts of information. Some of this information comes from inside our bodies, such as sensations of hunger, lust, pain and fatigue. Some of this information comes from people, objects and events in the world around us. We do not passively record these sensory data. We are constantly sifting and ordering this stream of information, making sense of it and interpreting it.

Perception, therefore, is an information processing activity which concerns the phenomena of **selective attention** and **perceptual organization**. We will explore selective attention first.

Selective attention
the ability, often exercised unconsciously, to choose from the stream of sensory data, to concentrate on particular elements, and to ignore others.

Our senses – sight, hearing, touch, taste, smell, and the sensing of internal bodily signals or 'kinaesthesia' – each consist of specialist nerves that respond to specific forms of energy, such as light, sound, pressure, and temperature changes. There are some forms of energy that our senses cannot detect unaided, such as radio waves, sounds at very low and very high pitch, and infrared radiation. Our sensory apparatus has limitations that we cannot overcome without the aid of special equipment. We are unable to hear sound frequencies above 10,000 hertz, but many animals, including dogs and dolphins, can. We are unable to hear sounds below 30 hertz, but whales can. Owls have much better eyesight than we do.

Perceptual threshold a boundary point, either side of which our senses respectively will or will not be able to detect stimuli, such as sound, light, or touch.

The constraints imposed by our sensory apparatus can be modified in certain ways by experience. The boundary, or **perceptual threshold**, between what we can and cannot detect can be established by experiment. We can explore individual differences in thresholds across the senses, and these thresholds can sometimes be altered by training and experience.

If there happens to be a clock ticking in the room where you study, you will almost certainly not be aware of the sound, until somebody mentions it, or the clock stops. Next time you visit a library, close your eyes for few seconds and pay attention to the background noise that you do not usually hear. But surely, you must have heard it, as you must have heard the clock ticking, if your ears were working properly? Our sensory apparatus responds,

Home viewing

The Sixth Sense (1999, director M. Night Shyamalan) concerns the attempts by a disillusioned child psychologist, Malcolm Crowe (played by Bruce Willis), to cure a young boy, Cole (Haley Joel Osment), who is tormented because he sees dead people. Crowe's depression, and his eagerness to help Cole, are explained at the beginning of the film, when he is attacked at home by an ex-patient who had the same problem, but whom Crowe was unable to help. Crowe spends so much time with Cole that he ignores his wife Anna (Olivia Williams). However, this film cleverly manipulates the perceptions and assumptions of the audience. Once you have watched the film to the end, either reflect on the action, or watch it again. Notice which clues you 'saw', but either ignored or misinterpreted the first time around. Notice how your interpretation of events relied on the assumptions that you made, or rather the assumptions that you were expected to make. It is only when you know the full plot of the film that you can begin to make 'correct' assumptions and interpretations, based on exactly the same evidence you were presented with the first time around. What does this movie tell you about the ease with which your perceptions, assumptions and understanding can be manipulated?

not simply to energy, but to changes in energy levels. Having detected a stimulus, such as a clock, or the hum of air conditioning, the nerves concerned become tired of transmitting the same information indefinitely and give up, until the stimulus changes. This explains our surprise at the sudden silence which follows when machinery stops.

Once stimuli become familiar, they stop being sensed. This phenomenon, in which the perceptual threshold is raised, is known as **habituation**.

Habituation the decrease in our perceptual response to stimuli once they have become familiar.

Our sensory apparatus has design limitations which filter out some information, such as x-rays and dog whistles. Perception involves other filtering processes, as the phenomenon of habituation suggests. In particular, information that is familiar, non-threatening, and unnecessary to the task in hand is screened out of our conscious awareness.

Stand on the pavement of a busy street and pay attention to as much of the available information as you can; the noise of the traffic, the make and colour and condition of passing vehicles, the smell of rubber tyres and exhaust fumes, the pressure of the pavement on the soles of your feet, the breeze across your face, the smell of the perfume of a passing woman, the clothes of the man across the street and the type of dog he is walking, an overheard mobile telephone conversation. When you think you are taking it all in, start to cross the road. If you get across safely, you will find that your heightened awareness has lapsed, dramatically. You would be mown down fairly quickly if this were not the case. Selective attention allows us to concentrate on the important and significant, and to ignore the insignificant and trivial.

Nancy Adler (2002) offers an excellent example of habituation in our use of language. Read the following sentence, and then quickly count the number of Fs:

FINISHED FILES ARE THE RESULT OF YEARS OF SCIENTIFIC STUDY
COMBINED WITH THE EXPERIENCE OF YEARS

Most people who speak English as a second language see all six Fs. Native English speakers usually pick up only three or four, because they tend to miss out the Fs in 'of'. Native English speakers have been conditioned – habituated – to skip the 'of' because it does not contribute to the meaning of the sentence.

Perceptual filters individual characteristics, predispositions, and preoccupations that interfere with the effective transmission and receipt of messages.

Adler's explanation is that, once we stop seeing the 'ofs', we do not see them again, even as in this example when we are looking for them. There is simply too much information available at any one time for us to pay attention to all of it, so we screen out that which is apparently of little or no value. The image of the world that we carry around inside our heads can only ever be a partial representation of what is 'really out there'. This leads to the conclusion that our behavioural choices are determined not by reality, but by what we perceive that reality to be. Our perception is influenced by what are called **perceptual filters**.

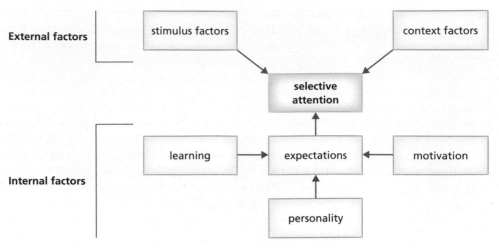

Figure 8.2: The external and internal factors influencing selective attention

The internal and external factors which affect selective attention are illustrated in Figure 8.2. The external factors affecting selective attention include stimulus factors and context factors. With respect to the stimulus factors, our attention is drawn more readily to stimuli that are:

large		small
bright		dull
loud		quiet
strong	rather than	weak
unfamiliar		familiar
stand out from surroundings		blend with surroundings
moving		stationary
repeated (but not repetitive)		one-off

Note, however, that we do not merely respond to single features, as this list might imply; we respond to the pattern of stimuli available to us.

STOP AND THINK

Identify examples of the ways in which advertisements creatively use stimulus factors to attract our attention, in newspapers, magazines, and on billboards and television.

Our attention is also influenced by context factors. The naval commander on the ship's bridge and the cook in the kitchen may both have occasion to shout 'fire', but these identical utterances mean quite different things to those within earshot, and will lead to radically different forms of behaviour (the taking and saving of lives respectively). We do not need any help to make this crucial distinction, beyond our knowledge of the context.

The internal factors affecting perception include:

- *Learning*: you've heard that argument before, so are you going to listen carefully to it again? Our past experience leads to the development of perceptual expectations or *perceptual sets*, which give us predispositions to pay attention to some stimuli, and to ignore other information.

- *Personality*: how come you (gregarious, sociable) saw the advertisement for the party, but your friend (reserved, shy) did not? Our personality traits predispose us to pay attention to some issues and events and human characteristics and not others.

- *Motivation*: do you get out of the shower to take a telephone call, perhaps expecting a party invitation or a job offer? We are more likely to perceive as important, and thus to respond to stimuli that we find motivating.

Much of perception can be described as classification or categorization. We categorize people as male or female, lazy or energetic, extrovert or shy. In fact our classification schemes are usually more sophisticated than that. We classify objects as cars, buildings, furniture, crockery, and so on, and we refine our classification schemes further under these headings. However, we are not born with a neat classification scheme 'wired in' with the brain. These categories are learned. They are social constructs. What we learn is often culture bound, or culture specific. An Indonesian visitor to one of our institutions once remarked, 'In your country, you feed the pigeons. In my country, the pigeons feed us'. The British revulsion at the thought of eating dog (classified as pet), the Hindu revulsion at the thought of eating beef (classified as sacred), and the Islamic aversion to alcohol (proscribed by the Koran), are all culturally transmitted emotions based on learned values.

Perceptual organization the process through which incoming stimuli are organized or patterned in systematic and meaningful ways.

Max Wertheimer
(1880–1943)

Problems arise when we and others act as if our culture had a monopoly on 'right thinking' on such issues. Different does not imply wrong. Different people within the same culture have different experiences and develop different expectations. The internal factors – our past experience and what we have learned, our personalities, our motivations – contribute to the development of our expectations of the world around us, what we want from it, what will happen in it, and what should happen. We tend to select information that fits our expectations, and pay less attention to information that does not.

Our categorization processes, and the search for meaning and pattern, are key characteristics of perception. This perceptual work is captured by the concept of **perceptual organization**.

The principles by which the process of perceptual organization operates were first identified by Max Wertheimer (1880–1943) in 1923. The 'proximity principle' notes that we tend to group together or to classify stimuli that are physically close to each other and which thus appear to 'belong' together. Note how you 'see' three sets of pairs rather than six blobs here:

The 'similarity principle' notes that we classify or group together stimuli that resemble each other in appearance in some respect. Note how you 'see' four pairs here, not eight objects:

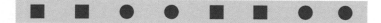

The fact that we are able to make use of incomplete and ambiguous information, by 'filling in the gaps' from our own knowledge and past experience, is known as the 'principle of closure'. These principles of perceptual organization apply to simple visual stimuli. Of more interest here, however, is the way in which these principles apply to person perception. How often do we assume that people are similar just because they live in the same neighbourhood, or work in the same section of the factory or office building (proximity principle), or just because they wear the same clothes or have similar ethnic origins (similarity principle)? How often do we take incomplete information about someone (he's Scottish) and draw inferences from this (closure principle)? This can cause the spread of false rumours in organizations through what is sometimes called 'the grapevine'.

Change blindness: just how selective can we get?

Picture the following, and prepare to be amazed. You're walking across a college campus when a stranger asks you for directions. While you're talking to him, two men pass between you carrying a wooden door. You feel a moment's irritation, but they move on and you carry on describing the route. When you're finished, the stranger informs you that you've just taken part in a psychology experiment. 'Did you notice anything change after the two men passed with the door?' he asks. 'No', you reply uneasily. He then explains that the man who initially approached you walked off behind the door, leaving him in his place. The first man now comes up to join you. Looking at them standing side by side, you notice that the two are of different height and build, and dressed differently, have different haircuts, and different voices.

It sounds impossible, but when Daniel Simons, a psychologist at Harvard University, and his colleague Daniel Levin of Kent State University in Ohio actually did this experiment, they found that fully 50 per cent of those who took part failed to notice the substitution. The subjects had succumbed to what is called change blindness. Rather than logging every detail of the visual scene, says Simons, we are actually highly selective about what we take in. Our impression of seeing everything is just that – an impression. In fact we extract a few details and rely on memory, or perhaps even our imagination, for the rest.

From Spinney (2000).

Perceptual sets and perceptual worlds

Perceptual set
an individual's predisposition to respond to people and events in a particular manner.

We have shown how the perceptual process selects incoming stimuli and organizes them into meaningful patterns. We have also argued that this processing is influenced by learning, motivation, and by personality – factors which give rise to expectations, which in turn make us more ready to respond to certain stimuli in certain ways and less ready to respond to others. This readiness to respond is called the individual's perceptual set.

Source: Artwork supplied by *The Broadbent Partnership*, London. Reproduced with permission.

Look at the drawing, made in 1915 by the cartoonist W.H. Hill. What do you see? Is she an old woman, or a young woman? The drawing is ambiguous; you should be able to 'see' two different versions of the woman. Your answer may be influenced by what you are predisposed to see, at the time you are reading this. The reactions of different individuals will not be consistent, and it does not make sense to argue over which perception is correct. We must accept that two people can observe the same thing, but perceive it in quite different ways. One other issue where perceptual variations can cause problems concerns bullying. At what point does dynamic hands-on management become harassment and bullying? There is limited agreement on the behaviours that constitute bullying, which can easily be perceived as autocratic management (Hoel *et al.*, 2001; Woodman and Cook, 2005).

Is it ethical?

Sally Power and Lorman Lundsten studied employee perceptions of ethical behaviour in the workplace. They asked 280 white collar and managerial staff to identify three ethical challenges they experienced at work. 'Ethical' was not defined, as the researchers wanted to find out how employees interpreted the term (a constructivist perspective; see Chapter 1). The 764 ethical challenges that were reported fell into six categories:

category	examples
honesty	misreporting financial figures; over-billing; hiding information; not telling the whole truth; stealing through expense reports
personal issues	stealing time from employer; lack of integrity; self-interest; acting contrary to company policy
complex business issues	concern about excess corporate profit; environmental issues; competitive practices; sexual harassment; insider trading
relationships	taking credit for others' work; favouritism; stealing ideas; inappropriate relationships; backstabbing; threat of job loss
fairness	discrimination; taking advantage of customers
other	disloyalty; bribes or rebates

"Get serious, John, we're talking business ethics not ethics."

Source: © Charles Barsotti/Condé Nast Publications/ www.cartoonbank.com

These respondents had no difficulties in identifying clearly those situations in which ethical or moral principles had been violated. Much of the academic commentary on this issue, however, is less confident about categorizing these behaviours. For example, it is often necessary to balance competing interests, and behaviour perceived as unethical in one context could be appropriate in a different setting. The two settings most often described by respondents in this study involved the treatment of employees by employers, and the treatment of customers by the company and its employees.

Based on Power and Lundsten (2005).

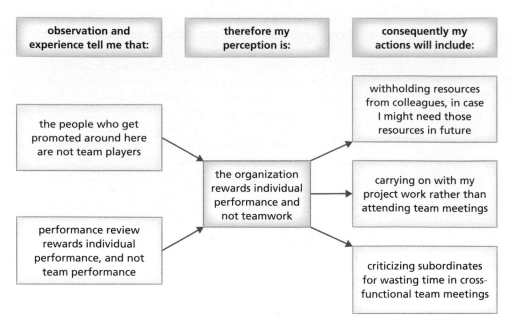

Figure 8.3: The information–perception–actions link

Failure to appreciate the importance of differences in individual perception creates many organizational problems, particularly with communication. Employees may perceive that they face chronic problems, while management perceive that such complaints are trivial and transient. It makes little sense to ask whose perceptions are correct. The starting point for resolving such issues must lie with the recognition that different people hold different, but equally legitimate, views of the same set of circumstances. Chapter 1 identified two views of human behaviour. The **positivist** perspective sets out to discover an objective world out there, as it really is. The **constructivist** perspective sets out to discover how our world is socially constructed, and how we experience and interpret that world. The argument in this chapter suggests that, 'the world out there', is not a good starting point for developing an understanding of human behaviour. We each have a unique version of what is out there and of our own place in it. We each live in our own perceptual world.

We each have a perceptual world that is selective and partial, and which concentrates on features of particular interest and importance to us. Through the processes of learning, motivation and personality development, we each have different expectations and different degrees of readiness to respond to objects, people and events in different ways. We impose meaning on received patterns of information; the meanings that we attach to objects, people and events are not intrinsic to these things, but are learned through social experience and are coloured by our current needs and objectives.

Our perceptions, that is the meanings that we attach to the information available to us, shape our actions. Behaviour in an organization context can usually be understood once we understand the way in which the individual perceives that context. Figure 8.3 (based on Dixon, 1999) illustrates the links between available information based on observation and experience, the perception based on that information, and outcomes in terms of decisions with respect to actions. This example explains why employees would ignore apparently reasonable management requests to become 'team players'.

Perceptual world
the individual's personal internal image, map or picture of their social, physical and organizational environment.

Source: R. Beau Lotto

Perception tables 1

Look carefully at this picture. The green and red tables appear to be different in size. The green table seems to be longer and thinner. But their dimensions are almost identical, as the second picture shows (note the yellow and blue lines)

Source: R. Beau Lotto

Perception tables 2

How can we get this so wrong? The designer of this illusion, Dr Beau Lotto, argues that we take into account the visual cues that we have learned in the past. We estimate size by the way in which objects appear to us in space, rather than using precise measurements. This involves the effects of light, shadow, and perspective. The 'real' world, however, is three dimensional, and we can be tricked when objects are presented in two dimensions, as in these pictures. As this chapter argues, perception always depends on context.

From Beau Lotto, TimesOnline, *2 May 2008.*
http://www.timesonline.co.uk/tol/life_and_style/health/article3861639.ece.

Cultural factors play a significant role in determining how we interpret available information and experience. You order a meal in a restaurant. Was the service fast or slow? Research into cultural differences in the perception of time suggest that your answer to this question depends to some extent on where in the world you come from. One study (Levine, 1990) compared the pace of life in six countries (Britain, Italy, Indonesia, Japan, Taiwan and the United States) by measuring:

- the accuracy of clocks in city bank branches;
- the speed at which city pedestrians walked;
- the length of time it took to buy a postage stamp.

The research revealed that Japanese cities had the most accurate clocks, the fastest pedestrians and the most efficient post office clerks. Indonesian cities, in contrast, had the least accurate clocks, and the slowest pedestrians. Italy, however, had the slowest post office clerks. The overall results of this study were as follows:

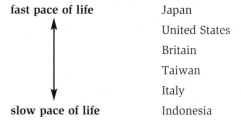

fast pace of life   Japan

United States

Britain

Taiwan

Italy

slow pace of life   Indonesia

To understand an individual's behaviour, therefore, we need to know something of the elements in their perceptual world, and the pattern of information and other cultural influences that have shaped that world. To change an individual's behaviour, therefore, we first have to consider changing their perceptions, through the information and experiences available to them. In the example in Figure 8.3, this would involve radical, visible and sustained changes in company performance review, and in promotion policies and practice.

Developing an understanding of our own perceptual world is difficult because there are many influences of which we are not aware. Information about the perceptual worlds of others

STOP AND THINK

Here is a story from the computer company, IBM. How would an understanding of the concept of perceptual world have helped Reiswig?

The IBM programmers still found things heavy-handed at times, despite Reiswig's attempts to lighten up. For instance, Reiswig at one point made fifty-hour weeks mandatory. Some of the programmers, who had been working eighty- to ninety-hour weeks, took that as an insult. They said that if IBM wanted to play those sorts of penny-ante games, then they'd work exactly fifty hours a week. Progress on OS/2 actually *slowed* after extra hours became required. An apocryphal memo began circulating among the IBM programmers about a rowing race that had supposedly taken place between IBM and Microsoft. Microsoft had one coxswain shouting orders while eight people rowed, the memo said. IBM had eight coxswains shouting orders while one rowed. Microsoft won big. So IBM launched several task forces to do some coxswain/oarsman analyses and decided after several weeks that the problem was that the oarsman wasn't rowing hard enough. When the race was rerun and Microsoft won big again, the oarsman was fired.

After a month or so, though, Reiswig figured out what was going on and removed the requirement. Hours soared, and the OS/2 project became one of the most engaging in the history of IBM.

From Carroll (1994).

is even more elusive. Although we can in principle find out how others perceive things, a lack of mutual understanding creates barriers to interpersonal communications. Unfortunately, we often forget that our own perceptual world is not the only possible or correct one.

Do we see to know or know to see?

Fortunately, we as individuals are not as isolated from each other as the argument so far suggests. We do not live in a social and organizational world of constant misunderstanding and failed communication. A high proportion of our interactions are effective, or tolerably so. Why? We are, of course, not wholly unique as individuals, and our personal perceptual worlds overlap. We share the same, or similar, sensory apparatus. We share the same basic needs. We share much of the same background social environment. Within the same society, although there are vast differences in experience, we share some of the same problems and environmental features. All this common ground makes the tasks of mutual understanding and interpersonal communication possible.

We have defined the process of perception in terms of making sense of the information available to us. We are active processors of that information, not passive recipients. However, much of that information is already processed for us. We are bombarded with sensory information, from other people, from books and newspapers and magazines, from street advertising, from radio and television, from the internet, and from various internal organizational sources – annual reports, team briefings, newsletters.

In the contemporary organizational context, employees at all levels have experienced major upheavals in recent years as organizations have introduced initiatives to improve performance. These changes, which have often led to stress, burnout, initiative fatigue and work intensification as well as to improved organizational performance (Buchanan *et al.*, 1999), have typically been communicated using arguments like this:

> In order to survive in a rapidly changing, turbulent, and highly competitive environment, we need to become more efficient, more cost conscious, more flexible and adaptable, and more customer-focused. Therefore, we need to implement the following radical changes to organization structures, procedures, and jobs.

There are two ways to read this turbulent world argument.

First, this is an unexceptional and taken-for-granted expression of contemporary organizational reality. There is nothing unusual in this argument about the need for organizational flexibility to deal with external change. People have been saying that for years. It's obvious, isn't it? This is a widely accepted view.

Second, this is an attempt to promote a particular perception of organizational reality, based on management values. After all, change is stressful and employees are likely to resist. If we can present a compelling argument that is beyond challenge, resistance can be avoided and the changes can go ahead more smoothly.

The key to this second reading lies with our use of language. One view of language is that we use it as a tool to communicate observations and understanding. An alternative view is that language, particularly the concepts that we use, constructs that understanding. You cannot 'see' 20 different types of snow until you know what they are called and can link those labels to different visual stimuli. In other words, one view of language simply says that we 'see in order to know'. The alternative view is that we need to know first, before we can 'see'. The implication of this second view of language, that 'we know to see', is that perceptions can potentially be influenced, that is can be managed, through language.

Consider the 'turbulent world so we must change' argument. What language typically accompanies this exhortation? Looking through job advertisements and other forms of organizational literature, note how many times the following kinds of statements appear:

- we need to become more *customer orientated*;
- our mission is *excellence*;

- we believe in employee *empowerment*;
- our survival depends on *efficiency* and *cost effectiveness*;
- *initiative* and *creativity* are key competencies;
- *flexibility* is the key to competitive success;
- we must strive for *continuous improvement*;
- we are a *total quality* organization.

The 'turbulent world' argument is hard to challenge. Communications of this kind have the potential to lead employees to internalize management values as their own, without question. It is difficult to argue that 'there is so little change in the business environment that we should be developing a rigid bureaucracy', or that 'customers don't matter, let's pay attention to our own staff'. However, rapid change can be personally and socially damaging; factory and office closures and relocation, loss of jobs, loss of community. An organization that ignores the well-being of its staff may find that it loses customers who feel that they have been given inadequate or discourteous service.

Language promotes a particular set of perceptions related to a specific set of values. An organization can have 'difficulties and problems' (negative), or 'challenges and opportunities' (positive). The 'turbulent world' language creates an impression of 'the way things are', of 'it makes sense doesn't it?', of 'that's obvious'. Why experience 'failure' when you can enjoy 'deferred success' instead? If you can get people to accept this kind of language and these arguments, then language becomes a tool for manipulating perceptions. If we can manipulate perceptions, we can control behaviour because, as this chapter argues, our behaviour depends not on some 'external reality' but on our perception of reality.

This 'second reading' of the 'turbulent world' argument, viewing it as an attempt to manage perception, reflects a change in our understanding of the use of language, not simply to represent the world, but also to create it. This perspective argues that 'reality out there' is not simply waiting to be discovered, but is created in social exchange through language. We don't go out and discover reality. Multiple realities are presented to us through our interactions. What matters is the version of reality in which most people come to believe. The management of perception is thus a tool for 'keeping people in their place' by inhibiting criticism. You cannot easily criticize something that appears to be, and is widely accepted as natural, obvious or inevitable without appearing deviant or eccentric.

This argument has two implications. First, it highlights the value of differences in perception, of multiple perspectives, arguing that no single perspective should be given the privilege of being correct. Second, it invites us to question the obvious, and the taken-for-granted.

Source: © Copyright 2001 United Features Syndicate, Inc.

STOP AND THINK

It seems that we are 'fed' information in language which reinforces the management definition of reality and justifies decisions in order to make employees compliant.

Find examples of managers or politicians using language in order to make what they have to say more acceptable to their audience.

Perceptual sets and assumptions

Halo effect
a judgement based on a single striking characteristic, such as an aspect of dress, speech, posture, or nationality.

Stereotype
a category, or personality type to which we allocate people on the basis of their membership of some known group.

Edward Lee Thorndike (1874–1949)

The concept of perceptual set, or perceptual expectation, applies to the ways in which we see other people, events and objects. To understand the nature of perception is to understand, at least in part, the sources and nature of many organizational problems. There are two related and prominent features of the process of people perception: the halo effect and stereotyping.

The term halo effect was first used by the psychologist Edward Thorndike in 1920. It is a natural human response, on meeting a stranger, to 'size them up', to make judgements about the kind of person they are, and whether we will like them or not. We do this to others on a first encounter; they do this to us. It seems as if first impressions really do count, after all (and we don't get a second chance to make a first impression).

However, faced with so much new information about someone – the physical and social setting, their appearance, what they say, how they say it, their posture, their non-verbal behaviour, how they respond to us – we must be selective. In terms of the model of the perceptual process shown in Figure 8.1, the halo effect is an error at the selective attention stage. Our judgements can rely on a single striking characteristic: a familiar accent, a perfume, dress or tie, hairstyle. If our judgement is favourable, we give the other person a positive halo. We may then overlook other information that could lead us to a different, more balanced, evaluation. If our judgement, on the other hand, is not favourable, we give the other person a negative halo (or horn). The halo effect can work in both directions.

The halo effect can thus act as an early screen that filters out later information which is not consistent with our earlier judgement. The problem, of course, is that what we notice first about another person is often not relevant to the judgement that we want to make. A confounding factor is that we tend to give more favourable judgements to people who have characteristics similar to ours. However, since when did somebody's voice, hairstyle, deodorant or clothes enable us to predict, say, their ability to design bridges, or manage a department in a hotel? Some people feel that they can make predictions from such limited evidence, based presumably on their own past experiences. The halo effect can apply to things as well as to people. How many examples can you think of where country of origin leads you automatically to believe that the product quality will be good or bad (Australian wine, Belgian chocolates, French perfume, German cars, Italian clothes, Scottish whisky)?

Why job applicants are not hired

A survey of 153 human resource managers in America identified the 20 most common errors made by applicants attending job interviews, listed here in order of importance:

1. Poor personal appearance.
2. Overaggressiveness.
3. Inability to express information clearly.
4. Lack of interest and enthusiasm.
5. Lack of career planning; no purpose and no goals.
6. Nervous, lack of confidence and poise.
7. Overemphasis on money.
8. Unwillingness to start at the bottom.
9. Makes excuses.
10. Lack of tact and courtesy.
11. Immaturity.
12. Condemns past employers.
13. No genuine interest in company or job.
14. Fails to look interviewer in the eye.
15. Sloppy application form.
16. Little sense of humour.
17. Arrives late at interview.
18. Fails to express appreciation for interviewer's time.
19. Fails to ask questions about the company and job.
20. Vague responses to questions.

Each of these behaviours can lead the interviewer to perceive the applicant in negative terms.

From Bedeian (1986).

Walter Lippmann
(1889–1974)

Remember the concept of perceptual organization? This phenomenon also applies to person perception. The term, stereotyping, was first used by typographers to made-up blocks of type, and was used to describe bias in person perception by Walter Lippmann in 1922. The concept refers to the way in which we group together people who seem to us to share similar characteristics. Lippmann saw stereotypes as 'pictures in the head', as simple mental images of groups and their behaviour. So, when we meet, say, an accountant, a nurse, an engineer, a poet, or a mechanical engineering student, we attribute certain personality traits to them because they are accountants, students, or whatever. Everybody knows, for example, that Scots are mean, and blondes have more fun. In terms of the model in Figure 8.1, therefore, stereotyping is an error at the perceptual organization stage in the process of perception.

No more bad hair days

During the American presidential campaign of 2007–2008, one of the key questions that was put to Hillary Clinton had nothing to do with her policies. It concerned how she was able to appear flawless, fresh and radiant at every public appearance, despite her tiring schedule.

Hilary Clinton

She was accused of using Botox and cosmetic surgery, and her campaign spending reports showed that she spent US$7,500 in one month on voice and drama coaching, along with $1,000 on a hairdo and $2,000 on a Hollywood makeup artist. As *The Times* newspaper reported, she also had the help of Kriss Soterion, a makeup artist with CNN, who softened her look and changed her lipstick to make her more appealing to women.

Appearance (style) matters more than policy (substance)? *The Times'* Washington correspondent said:

> Mrs Clinton has learnt the hard way, however, that poor grooming can distract from the message just as surely as a stunning exterior. [. . .] All of which is less to enhance her appearance than to remove her appearance as a talking point so that people will listen instead to what she has to say. Still, everyone is talking about how fabulous she looks in this most arduous of races.

Based on Philp (2008).

Source: Mike Segar/Reuters

Self-fulfilling prophecy a prediction that becomes true simply because someone expects it to happen.

Another shortcut that we make when we meet people is the self-fulfilling prophecy. For example, if you predict an avalanche in a loud voice under a large and loose overhang of snow, your prediction is likely to be self-fulfilling. In other words, we create what we expected to find in the first place. This phenomenon also applies to human behaviour. For example, if we expect people at work to be lazy, apathetic and careless, and treat them accordingly, we are likely to find that they respond to our treatment of them by displaying the behaviours that we expected. The reverse can also be true; if we treat people as though we expect them to be motivated, enthusiastic, and competent, then they are likely to respond accordingly. We will meet this phenomenon again in Chapter 9 in our discussion of motivation, and Douglas McGregor's contrast between Theory X and Theory Y.

If we know, or assume, somebody's apparent group membership in this way, our instant categorization allows us to attribute a range of qualities to them. Stereotypes are overgeneralizations, and are bound to be radically inaccurate on occasion. But they can be convenient. By adopting a stereotyped perspective, we may be able to shortcut our evaluation process, and make quicker and more reliable predictions of behaviour. We can have problems, however, with those who fall into more than one category with conflicting stereotypes: the mechanical engineer who writes poetry, for instance.

STOP AND THINK

Explore your own stereotypes by completing each of the following sentences with three terms that you think describe most or all members of the category concerned:

university lecturers are . . .

artists are . . .

mechanical engineers are . . .

trainee nurses are . . .

airline pilots are . . .

You may find it interesting to share your stereotypes with those of colleagues, particularly if some of them have friends or close relatives who are pilots, nurses, mechanical engineers . . .

Stereotyping also works at an international level. See if you can match these stereotyped (not necessarily accurate) images with the right countries:

Culture		Stereotyped image
1 **American**	A	Demonstrative, talkative, emotional, romantic, bold, artistic
2 **English**	B	Mañana attitude, macho, music lovers, touchers
3 **French**	C	Inscrutable, intelligent, xenophobic, golfers, group-oriented, polite, soft-spoken
4 **Italian**	D	Conservative, reserved, polite, proper, formal
5 **Latin American**	E	Arrogant, loud, friendly, impatient, generous, hardworking, monolingual
6 **Japanese**	F	Arrogant, rude, chauvinistic, romantics, gourmets, cultural, artistic

Clearly, while some members of each of these cultures may possess some of the attributes of their stereotype, it would be false to claim that every member of a culture shared the same attributes to the same degree. Not all Asians are keen golfers; not all English people are reserved and polite; not all Americans are arrogant and hardworking.

Sex, appearance, attractiveness and discrimination

We emphasized earlier that the perceptual process is concerned with making sense of and explaining the world around us, and the people and events in it. Our need for explanation and understanding is reflected in the way in which we search for the causes of people's actions. Our perceptions of causality are known as **attributions**.

Attribution the process by which we make sense of our environment through our perceptions of causality.

An attribution is a belief about the cause or causes of an event or an action. Attribution theory was developed in the 1950s and 1960s by Fritz Heider (1958) and Harold Kelley (1971). They argue that our understanding of our social world is based on our continual attempts at causal analysis based on how we interpret experience.

Why is that person so successful? Why did that project fail? Why are those people still arguing? If we understand the causes of success, failure and conflict, we may be able to adjust our behaviour and other factors accordingly. Attribution is simply the process of attaching causes or reasons to the actions and events we see. We tend to look for causes either in people's abilities and personalities, or in aspects of the setting or circumstances in

Fritz Heider
(1896–1988)

Harold H. Kelley
(1921–2003)

which they find themselves. This distinction is usually described in terms of internal causality and external causality. We may explain a particular individual's success, or promotion, with reference to their superior skills and knowledge (internal causality), or with reference to luck, friends in high places, and coincidence (external causality).

Research has revealed patterns in our attributions. When we are explaining our personal achievements, we point to our capabilities, but when we are explaining our lack of success, we blame our circumstances. This is known as *projection*. We project blame onto external causes that are beyond our control. However, we tend to attribute the behaviour of others to their disposition, that is, to aspects of their personality. We met **the fundamental attribution error** in Chapter 1. This refers to the tendency to exaggerate the disposition and personality of the individual rather than the context in which they find themselves.

Attribution theory can explain aspects of discrimination in organizational settings. For example, sex and appearance affect how we are paid and promoted. In Britain, Barry Harper (2000) studied over 11,000 people (belonging to the long-term National Child Development Study) aged 33 to determine the effects of looks, height and obesity on pay. This study confirmed that attractive people, men and women, earn more, that tall men earn substantially more, but that height is less important for women. Unattractive men earn 15 per cent less than colleagues with average looks, while unattractive women earn 11 per cent less. Tall men earn 10 per cent more than men of average height, but tall women earn only 5 per cent more. Obese women earn 5 per cent less than those of average weight, but obese men are not affected. While widespread, the benefits of height and the costs of being unattractive were more common in 'white collar' occupations. For women, a 15 per cent penalty for being unattractive was most common in secretarial and clerical jobs. Attractive men in customer-facing sales roles earned 13 per cent more, while tall men in 'high touch' positions earned 25 per cent more. Some commentators are critical of 'beauty bias', putting appearance before capability, as another form of unfair discrimination at work.

Short changed in China

In 2002, Jiang Tao brought a court case against the Chengdu branch of The People's Bank of China in Sichuan province for discrimination on the basis of his height. The Bank advertised a job in a local newspaper stating that male applicants should be at least 1.68 metres tall, and that female applicants should be at least 1.55 metres. Mr Jiang was three centimetres too short, and this criterion excluded around 40 per cent of the male population of Sichuan.

Height requirements are common in China. The East China University of Politics and Law in Shanghai requires male and female students to be at least 1.70 and 1.60 metres tall respectively, thereby excluding around half of the otherwise eligible students from rural areas

where average heights are lower. A teacher in Fujian province was fired because he was found to be four centimetres shorter than the required 1.60 metres.

Height in China is considered to be an important attribute for those in jobs which carry authority, in catering and leisure industries where tall is considered beautiful, and in jobs that involve contact with foreigners. This is because it is undignified to have to look up to others. Height may not be important in politics. Deng Xiaoping, who ruled China for over a decade, was only 1.50 metres tall.

Based on The Economist *(2002a).*

Why should appearance influence career progression? Our attributions are related to our stereotypes. We seem to attribute explanations of people's behaviour to aspects of their appearance. Discrimination against particular groups and individuals, on the basis of sex, sexual orientation, age or ethnic background, is now widely recognized. Legislation seeks to address sexual and racial discrimination, and social attitudes towards homosexuals and the elderly in organizational settings do appear, slowly, to be changing. However, attribution research suggests that discrimination, based on our perceptions of causal links between sex, appearance, and job performance, are more subtle, and less public.

With respect to attractiveness, sex, height, and weight, we are dealing with factors which cannot have any meaningful impact on performance for most jobs or occupations. The tall, attractive female computer programmer of average weight may be more effective in her job than the short, overweight male programmer with the unremarkable features. A moment's consideration, however, would probably lead us to reject height, weight and attractiveness as causal factors in this equation, and lead us to look for differences in education, experience and ability instead. The problem seems to be, however, that we make attribution errors by jumping quickly and unconsciously to judgements of this kind, particularly when we have little information about the other person on which to base a more careful assessment.

Hot dogs, old dogs, new tricks

Fast food outlets traditionally employ younger and less experienced staff and managers. With an ageing workforce, the supply of young employees is declining. In America, less than 8 per cent of employees and managers working in food service are over 55 years of age, and the main age group for employees is 18–24. As the sector expands, however, and proportion of the workforce in the 55- to 64-year-old range grows, the industry will have to recruit increasing numbers of older staff. But there is a problem. While younger workers are often regarded as less reliable and more accident prone than their older colleagues, research shows that stereotyped perceptions of older workers are more often negative; difficult to train, lacking in creativity, too cautious, resistant to new technology, inflexible. In the hospitality industry, some managers keep older workers out of front line positions in service areas, believing that they have a negative impact on customer perceptions of the business. Hiring more elderly staff could of course help to overcome that negative stereotype.

Robin Depietro and Merwyn Strate studied the perceptions that American managers in this sector had of older workers. They also asked these managers about the numbers of older workers they expected to employ in future. The 20 managers in this study perceived older workers to be self-motivated, disciplined, loyal and dependable, with good communication skills, lower levels of absenteeism, respect for authority and credibility with customers.

Despite these positive perceptions, only 25 per cent of the managers said that they would prefer to have older workers in their restaurants. Only 10 per cent said that they expected to employ more older workers in future, and 15 per cent said that they expected to employ fewer. Management perceptions, it seems, are not consistent with management actions in this sector. Depietro and Strate argue that fast food organizations need to rethink their human resource and organization development policies, to match management perceptions with recruitment practices, adding that there are sound business reasons for doing this:

There needs to be some thought and planning for how older workers can add some dependability and maturity into restaurants, and can possibly change part of the image of quick service restaurants. Working to actively recruit and hire older employees could add a new dimension and some new markets for quick service restaurants.

Based on Depietro and Strate (2007).

Any aspect of our appearance is a form of non-verbal communication. We cannot control our age, or height, but these factors, combined with behaviour that is under our control, send signals that others decode in the light of their experiences (age is related to reliability), expectations (tall and handsome means self confident and knowledgeable) and prejudices (short and overweight women will deter customers). This also applies to choice of clothing. This is an aspect which is, of course, within our control. Dress can indicate organizational culture, and can contribute significantly to the individual's impression management. The way in which we dress can tell others how we want to be seen (as formal, relaxed, creative, businesslike) rather than what we are really like. However, we may not always be aware how others perceive our attempts to manage our impression through our dress style.

Perceptions of personality based on voice quality

We develop perceptions about relationships between the physical characteristics of other people and their behaviour. In other words, we develop implicit personality theories. Perry Hinton (1993) notes that we base these implicit theories, in part, on voice quality, such as:

voice quality high in	male voice	female voice
breathiness	young, artistic	feminine, pretty, petite, shallow
flatness	masculine, cold: same for both sexes	
nasality	having many socially undesirable features: same for both sexes	
tenseness	old, unyielding, cantankerous	young, emotional, high-strung

There is, however, no empirical basis for these judgements. A man with a tense voice is not necessarily old and cantankerous. A woman with a breathy voice is not necessarily petite and shallow. Think of a time when you first spoke to somebody on the telephone. Later, when you met them face to face, did they appear and behave as you had expected?

Based on Hinton (1993).

Perceptual errors and how to avoid them

The main sources of errors in person perception seem to include:

1. Not collecting enough information about other people.
2. Basing our judgements on information that is irrelevant or insignificant.
3. Seeing what we expect to see and what we want to see, and not investigating further.
4. Allowing early information about someone to colour our judgement, despite later and contradictory information.
5. Allowing our own characteristics to influence our judgements of others.
6. Accepting stereotypes uncritically.
7. Attempting to decode non-verbal behaviour outwith the context in which it appears.
8. Basing attributions on flimsy and potentially irrelevant evidence.

The remedies, therefore, include:

1. Take more time and avoid instant or 'snap' judgements about others.
2. Collect and consciously use more information about other people.
3. Develop self-awareness, and an understanding of how our personal biases and preferences affect our perceptions and judgements of other people.
4. Check our attributions – the assumptions we make about the causes of behaviour, particularly the links we make between aspects of personality and appearance on the one hand and behaviour on the other.

If we are to improve our understanding of others, we must first have a well-developed knowledge of ourselves – our strengths, our preferences, our flaws and our biases. The development of self-knowledge can be an uncomfortable process. In organizational settings, we are often constrained in the expression of our feelings (positive and negative) about other people, due to social or cultural norms, and to the communication barriers erected by status and power differentials. This may in part explain the enduring appeal of training courses in social and interpersonal skills, self awareness and personal growth designed to help us overcome these problems, to 'get in touch' with other people, and to 'get in touch with ourselves'. Training in interpersonal communication skills typically emphasizes openness and honesty in relationships, active listening skills, sensitivity to non-verbal behaviour, and how to give and receive both critical and non-evaluative feedback.

Adrian Furnham's unlucky thirteen

Adrian Furnham argues that the process of making evaluations, judgements, or ratings of the performance of employees is subject to a number of systematic perception errors. This is particularly problematic in a performance appraisal context:

1. *Central tendency*: Appraising everyone at the middle of the rating scale.

2. *Contrast error*: Basing an appraisal on comparison with other employees (who may have received undeserved high or low ratings) rather than on established performance criteria.

3. *Different from me*: Giving a poor appraisal because the person has qualities or characteristics not possessed by the appraiser.

4. *Halo effect*: Appraising an employee undeservedly well on one quality (performance, for example) because they are perceived highly by the appraiser on another quality (attractiveness, perhaps).

5. *Horn effect*: The opposite of the halo effect. Giving someone a poor appraisal on one quality (attractiveness) influences poor rating on other qualities (performance).

6. *Initial impression*: Basing an appraisal on first impressions rather than on how the person has behaved throughout the period to which the appraisal relates.

7. *Latest behaviour*: Basing an appraisal on the person's recent behaviour, rather than on how they have behaved throughout the appraisal period.

8. *Lenient or generous rating*: Perhaps the most common error, being consistently generous in appraisal, mostly to avoid conflict.

9. *Performance dimension error*: Giving someone a similar appraisal on two distinct but similar qualities, because they happen to follow each other on the appraisal form.

10. *Same as me*: Giving a good appraisal because the person has qualities or characteristics possessed by the appraiser.

11. *Spillover effect*: Basing this appraisal, good or bad, on the results of the previous appraisal, rather than on how the person has behaved during the appraisal period.

12. *Status effect*: Giving those in higher level positions consistently better appraisals than those in lower level jobs.

13. *Strict rating*: Being consistently harsh in appraising performance.

Based on Furnham (2005).

The accuracy of management perception

How accurate are the perceptions of managers? Inaccurate perceptions could lead to inappropriate decisions and ineffective organizational practices. John Mezias and William Starbuck (2003) found that management perceptions of their organizations are often wrong. Management decisions are of course based on information from a range of sources: company documents, rumours overheard at the water cooler, committee meetings, articles in journals, speeches by the chief executive. Mezias and Starbuck identify ten factors that influence management perceptions of all that information, and which can lead to distortions:

subject matter	managers are more likely to notice recent incidents, larger changes, and dramatic events, but may have more accurate perceptions of older and smaller changes and routine events. People are better at perceiving sounds, symbols and objects than abstract concepts and unobservable processes
individual differences	our perceptual systems vary. Some of us are better at sight, hearing, and recall than others
experience	experience predisposes us to notice some stimuli and not others

training and job role	if you work in marketing, you learn more about customers and competitors and less about materials and production processes
memory	we find it easier to recall some experiences than others
interpersonal skills	a manager's style can either encourage colleagues to share or to conceal information
information systems	organization information systems are selective in capturing and disseminating information, usually emphasizing factors that have been relevant in the past while overlooking new and emerging trends
culture	social and organization cultures focus attention on particular phenomena and de-emphasize others, sometimes making it difficult to share experiences
seniority	managers at the top of the hierarchy see things differently from those at the bottom, often perceiving fewer and milder problems
environment	some business environments are more volatile than others, so data quickly become obsolete

Mezias and Starbuck asked managers about their companies and their business environments, including number of employees, communication practices, processes for evaluating strategies, sales growth, industry concentration, sector growth, and fluctuations in sales. These were areas where 'objective' answers could be found in documented sources, and the researchers expected that managers' perceptions would be more accurate than previous studies suggested. Instead, they found a number of perceptual errors. These particularly concerned inaccurate perceptions of sales levels (overestimates and underestimates), with some errors exceeding 1,000 per cent, with the highest being 5,000 per cent beyond the 'correct' answer. Only a third of the managers questioned had 'very accurate' perceptions, reporting errors of less than 11 per cent. Many managers also appear to underestimate the rate of change over time, reporting much smaller changes than had actually occurred.

In one of their studies, they asked senior managers questions about their company's quality improvement programme. This is what they found:

> [F]our respondents gave numerical answers having six significant digits. Obviously, these managers looked up the numbers in the quality performance reports that they were then receiving monthly. Three of these four respondents were quality specialists, and two of these specialists gave the correct numbers. The other quality specialist and a finance manager gave the same extremely precise incorrect number. They had both pulled this number from the wrong section of the quality-performance report. Thus, even having written documents in front of them and having relevant training does not assure that managers will give accurate information (Mezias and Starbuck, 2003, p.14).

These findings are not as disastrous as they appear. We don't always have to perceive problems accurately in order to solve them effectively; 'most problem-solving does not depend on accurate knowledge of current situations . . . people can act effectively without having accurate perceptions: they need only pursue general, long-term goals' (Mezias and Starbuck, 2003, p.15). John Maule and Gerard Hodgkinson (2003) agree that an incorrect judgement may not be damaging if it can be refined, with feedback, over time. That is how management perception affects most decisions, and this is not necessarily a problem. While perceptual accuracy is certainly important in some instances, perception that is 'good enough' and that can be corrected as better information is gathered is adequate for most situations.

Mezias and Starbuck suggest three strategies to improve the accuracy of management perception and reduce the cost of mistakes:

1. anticipate perceptual inaccuracy, and focus on key factors, using extra resources and backup systems where serious errors are most likely to occur;

2. arrange multi-faceted feedback about performance outcomes, so that mistakes and unpredicted outcomes can be quickly detected;

3. concentrate on incremental steps and avoid drastic changes, as small innovations are less risky.

 ## RECAP

1. *Identify the main features of the process of perception.*

   - People behave according to how they perceive the world, not in response to 'reality'.

   - The perceptual process involves the interpretation of sensory input in the light of past experience, and our store of knowledge, beliefs, expectations and motives.

2. *Distinguish between the bottom-up processing of sensory information and the top-down interpretation of that information.*

   - Sensation, or bottom up processing, determines the data to which we pay attention.

   - Perception, or top down processing, determines the way in which we organize and interpret perceived information in order to make behavioural choices.

3. *Understand the nature and implications of selective attention and perceptual organization.*

   - Selective attention is influenced by external factors relating to the stimulus and the context, and by internal factors such as learning, personality and motivation.

   - The way in which we organize and interpret sensory data in meaningful ways, even when it is incomplete or ambiguous, is known as perceptual organization.

4. *Give examples of how behaviour is influenced by our perceptions.*

   - We each have our own perceptual world, an internal mental image of our environment.

   - Different cultures lead to differences in perception and consequently in behaviour.

5. *Explain and illustrate the main processes and problems in perception, including false attributions, halo effects and stereotyping.*

   - An attribution is a belief about cause and effect. When speaking about ourselves, we tend to attribute success to personal factors and failure to external factors. When speaking about others, we tend to attribute success and failure to personality features.

   - Making a favourable judgement of someone on the basis of a single positive characteristic is known as the halo effect, and is called the horn effect if the judgement is negative.

   - Assuming that someone possesses a set of personality traits because they belong to a particular social group is known as stereotyping.

6. *Explain some less widely appreciated sources of discrimination at work arising from characteristics of the person perception and attribution processes.*

   - Aspects of behaviour are attributed to appearance, leading to discrimination. You are likely to be paid less at work if you are an overweight or underweight female, a short man, a husband with an overweight wife, and are perceived to be unattractive.

   - The fundamental attribution error leads us to emphasize individual personality and ignore social and organizational context when explaining behaviour.

7. *Suggest techniques for improving perceptual accuracy and avoiding errors.*

   - To avoid mistakes, avoid rapid judgements, take more time, collect more information, be aware of your own prejudices and biases and develop increased self-awareness.

   - To improve accuracy, expect errors to occur, use as much feedback as you can get, and take small steps rather than radical ones to reduce risks.

Revision

1. Explain the distinction between sensation and perception. What is the significance of this distinction?
2. What is the individual's perceptual world? What factors influence this construct, and how does an understanding of someone's perceptual world help us to understand their behaviour?
3. What is the difference between selective attention and perceptual organization? What factors influence the latter process?
4. What are the factors influencing selective attention? How can a knowledge of these factors be exploited in commercial settings?

Research assignment

Look carefully at the style of dress and appearance of the instructors in your educational institution, across all the subjects that you are studying. How does their appearance affect your perceptions of their:

- approachability
- subject knowledge
- professionalism
- understanding of the world beyond the academic 'ivory tower'?

Write a report that first identifies specific aspects of your instructors' dress and appearance that lead you to make judgements on those criteria. Conclude your report with advice to instructors on how they could change their dress and appearance to improve the ways in which they are perceived by students on those criteria – to make them appear more approachable, more professional, and so on.

Springboard

Goldstein, E., 2001, *Sensation and Perception*, Wadsworth, Belmont CA.

Introduction to the psychology and physiology of sensation and perception. Describes with fascinating illustrations how the senses function, exposing the complexity of perceptual processes.

Pinker, S., 1997, *How the Mind Works*, Penguin Books, London.

Pinker's explanation relies on evolutionary biology (a version of Darwinism) and the computational theory of mind. The computational theory regards the mind as a complex modular information processor. Pinker's investigation of the clues to how our information processor functions is insightful and entertaining, and his style makes complex ideas accessible.

Rosenzweig, P., 2007, *The Halo Effect: And the Eight Other Business Delusions That Deceive Managers*, Glencoe, Ill: Free Press.

Does an organization's culture determine its success, as many researchers have argued? Or does good performance lead employees to rate the company culture highly? The latter is an example of the halo effect. Rosenzweig is critical of research that argues differently because it has muddled up cause and effect.

Zalkind, S.S. and Costello, T.W., 1962, 'Perception: some recent research and implications for administration', *Administrative Science Quarterly*, (7), pp.218–35.

A much cited piece of work which is still worth reading. Explores the importance of an understanding of perception for management, which in the 1960s was called 'administration'. It is interesting to note how perceptions of 'administrators' have changed since then.

OB in films

Legally Blonde (2001, director Robert Luketic), DVD track (scene) 8; 0:21:17 to 0:22:46 (3 minutes). Clip begins with the tutor saying, 'OK, welcome to law school'; clip ends with Elle saying, 'Whoever said that orange was the new pink was seriously disturbed'.

Legally Blonde is the story of an attractive blonde sorority queen, Elle Woods (played by Reece Witherspoon), whose boyfriend leaves her to go to Harvard Law School. To get him back, she goes to Harvard, too. Every character in this movie plays a stereotyped role. In this clip, on the law school lawn, Elle and three of her classmates are asked by a tutor to introduce themselves. As you watch the clip, observe the five characters carefully and:

1. Decide on an appropriate stereotype label (e.g., 'absent-minded professor') for each character.

2. Explain why you have chosen that label, based on the evidence that each character provides (what they say, how they say it, appearance, non-verbal behaviour).

3. For each character identify two adjectives that you think would describe how they would be likely to interact socially with others.

4. Thinking of each of those characters in an organizational context, assess what you feel would be their strengths and their weaknesses.

 OB in literature

Aldous Huxley, *The Doors of Perception/Heaven and Hell*, Flamingo, 1994 (first published in 1954 by Chatto & Windus, London). This is Huxley's account of his experiment, in 1953, with the hallucinogenic drug mescalin, and with effects similar to those induced by LSD. Huxley describes how his perception of reality was altered by this experience, opening up a whole new perceptual world. In *Heaven and Hell*, the sequel, he presents his later reflections on this experience. What does this novel tell us about the distinction between the 'real' world and the world as we perceive and understand it to be?

CHAPTER EXERCISES

Person perception

Objective   To explore factors influencing our perception of other people. Research has shown, for example, that we assess others' characters from their faces. These assessments include how friendly, aggressive, trustworthy, and creditworthy another person is. The judgements that we reach based on such apparently limited information often turn out to be correct.

Briefing   1. Break into groups of three.

2. Your instructor will give you five or six photographs of people, taken from recent newspapers and magazines. You have 5 minutes to work out as much as you can about each of these people, using only what you can see in the picture. Consider characteristics such as their:

conscientiousness	approachability
intelligence	reliability
aggressiveness	other characteristics suggested by the photographs

3. Prepare a presentation based on your photographs and your assumptions. Explain clearly which items of evidence from the photographs led you to make those assessments.

You're the interviewee: what would you do?

You are about to go for a job interview, but first you will be kept waiting in the interviewer's office. During that time, you can observe clues about your interviewer and perhaps about the organization. What clues do you think are significant and revealing? What personal experiences in your own past affect how you observe and make judgements in this setting?

This exercise can be completed in class time, but is more effective if steps 1 to 3 are completed in advance. For a one hour tutorial, time will be tight without preparation.

Step 1   Read *The manager's room description* which follows, to get a feel for the setting in which you find yourself.

Step 2   Complete the analysis sheet.

In the *data* column, record those observations that you find significant and revealing about the kind of person who occupies this room.

In the *inferences* column, note the perceptions or conclusions that you reach from your data.

In the *experiences* column, record past incidents or events, recent or distant, that you think influence your inferences.

data I observe in the room	the inferences that I make	based on past experience

Step 3   Using that analysis, construct a profile of your interviewer.

Step 4   Finally, record your answers to the following questions:

1. What is the sex, marital status and ethnic background of the managing director? Identify the data in the room that lead you to your inferences.

2. How would you describe the managing director's character? What are this person's interests? What would you expect this person's management style to be like? Once again, identify the data on which you base these judgements.

3. Given your own personality, do you think that you would be happy working for this person?

4. Explain how your analysis illustrates the concepts of selective attention, perceptual organization, perceptual world, halo effect, and stereotyping.

Step 5   Present your findings, according to your Instructor's directions.

The manager's room description

You are now in the Acme Holdings company offices, top floor, for your job interview. It sounds like your ideal position. As personal assistant, you will be working for the managing director who has asked to interview you. You have arrived on time, but the managing director's secretary apologizes and tells you there will be a delay. The managing director has been called to an important meeting which will take up to fifteen minutes. The secretary tells you that you are welcome to wait in the managing director's private office, and shows you in.

You know that you will be alone here for fifteen minutes. You look around the room, curious about the person with whom you may be working. The shallow pile carpet is a warm pink, with no pattern. You choose one of six high-backed chairs, upholstered in a darker fabric that matches well with the carpet and curtains, and with polished wooden arms. In the centre of the ring of chairs is a low glass-topped coffee table. On the wall behind you is a large photograph of a vintage motor car, accompanied by its driver in leather helmet, goggles, scarf and long leather coat; you can't make out the driver's face. The window ledge holds four plants arranged equal distances apart; two look like small exotic ferns and the others are a begonia and a geranium in flower.

On the other side of the room sits a large wooden executive desk, with a black leather chair. A framed copy of the company's mission statement hangs on the wall behind the desk, and below that sits a black leather briefcase with combination locks. The plain grey waste paper basket by the wall beside the desk is full of papers. At the front of the desk sits a pen-stand with a letter opener. To the side is a 'state of the art' laptop computer and a desk lamp. In front of the lamp sits a metal photograph frame holding two pictures. One is of an attractive woman in her thirties with a young boy around eight years old. The other photograph is of a retriever dog in a field to the side of some farm buildings. In front of the framed photograph is a stack of file folders. Immediately in front of the chair, on the desk, is a small pile of papers, and a Mont Blanc pen with the Acme company logo on the barrel.

On the other side of the desk is a delicate china mug. In front of it lies what looks like a leather-covered address book or perhaps a diary, a passport and a pad of yellow paper. Beside the pad there is a pile of unopened mail with envelopes of differing sizes. On top of the mail and behind are some half-folded newspapers: *The Guardian*, *The Independent* and *The Financial Times*. You note that there is no telephone on the desk. Behind the desk is a small glass-fronted display case. There are some books lined up on top of the case: *Plugged In: The Generation Y Guide to Thriving at Work*, *The Oxford Concise Dictionary of Quotations*, *Managing Difficult Interactions* and *Shattering the Glass Ceiling*. Also on top of the case sits a small bronze statue, of a man sitting with his legs crossed in a Yoga position. There is a cheese plant on the far side of the display case. Inside the case, there are computing systems manuals and books and pamphlets on employment law, many of which deal with race and sex discrimination issues.

You decide to get up and look out the window. There is a three-seater settee under the window, covered in the same fabric as the armchairs with matching scatter cushions in the corners. From the window you can easily see people shopping and children playing in the nearby park. You turn to another table beside the settee. Several magazines sit in front of a burgundy ceramic lamp with a beige shade. There are two recent copies of *The Economist*, and a copy each of *Asia Today*, *Classic CD* and *Fortune*. As you head back to your chair, you notice that the papers on the desk in front of the chair are your application papers and curriculum vitae. Your first name, obviously indicating your sex, has been boldly circled with the Mont Blanc pen. As the managing director may return at any moment, you go back and sit in your chair to wait.

Chapter 9 **Motivation**

Key terms

extreme job

boreout

drive

motive

motivation

self-actualization

equity theory

expectancy theory

valence

instrumentality

expectancy

goal-setting theory

inner work life theory

job enrichment

motivator factors

hygiene factors

vertical loading factors

intrinsic rewards

extrinsic rewards

growth need strength

job diagnostic survey

motivating potential score

empowerment

engagement

high performance work system

Learning outcomes

When you have read this chapter, you should be able to define those key terms in your own words, and you should also be able to:

1. Understand different ways in which the term motivation is used.

2. Understand the nature of motives and motivation processes as influences on behaviour.

3. Use expectancy theory and job enrichment to diagnose organizational problems and to recommend solutions.

4. Explain the continuing contemporary interest in this field, with respect to extreme jobs, boreout and high performance work systems.

Why study motivation?

The topic of employee motivation plays a central role in the field of management – both practically and theoretically. Managers see motivation as an integral part of the performance equation at all levels, while organizational researchers see it as a fundamental building block in the development of useful theories of effective management practice. Indeed, the topic of motivation permeates many of the sub-fields that compose the study of management, including leadership, teams, performance management, management ethics, decision-making, and organizational change.

From Steers et al. *(2004).*

A motivated workforce can be a sign of a successful organization. How is that achieved? Each of us has a different reason for getting out of bed in the morning. Our motives – from the Latin *movere*, to move – are key determinants of our behaviour. If we understand your motives (desire for more leisure time), we can influence your behaviour (take a day's holiday if you finish that assignment). Evidence shows that students rate job satisfaction more highly than money; in one survey, the top two aspects of the ideal job were enjoyment, and friendly colleagues (Reade, 2003). Earning 'enough' came third, followed by passion for the industry, good location and social life. With this motivational knowledge, management can change working arrangements as well as payment levels. In other words, look for job ads which seem to suggest, 'we don't pay much, but it's fun'.

Rank and yank

Some companies, including Ford, General Electric, Cisco Systems, Intel, Conoco, Hewlett-Packard, Microsoft and Sun Microsystems, use Forced Ranking Systems (FRS) to assess employee performance. FRS asks managers to rank employees against each other, evaluating their contributions along a continuum from best to worst. Then, depending on company policy, the worst 5 or 10 per cent are likely to be fired. At General Electric, employees are divided into top 20 per cent, middle 80 per cent, and bottom 10 per cent. Managers at Kimberly-Clark must ensure that no more than 20 per cent of their employees are given one of the top two rankings, while at least 5 per cent must be allocated to the bottom two. This method can help managers to justify difficult decisions about underperforming staff.

This approach is based on the statistical observation that individual differences are normally distributed in the form of a bell curve. FRS ensures that a percentage of employees will fall into the 'worst' category. So for example, if at Ford you are graded C, the lowest grade in their system, you are not eligible for bonuses that year;

two Cs in a row are grounds for dismissal. At Sun Microsystems, FRS is used to identify the lowest-performing 10 per cent of employees who are then given 90 days 'to shape up, find another job inside Sun, or ship out'. One problem is that the criteria for ranking are increasingly qualitative and subjective, involving teamwork and communication skills, for example.

What would you predict will be the impact of this approach on employee motivation? FRS is used by some business schools in America and Europe. How would you respond if your organizational behaviour instructor used 'rank and yank' with your class examination grades? In 2001, nine employees raised a class action suit against Ford claiming that its forced ranking system discriminates against older workers. In the previous year, cases involving FRS discrimination against blacks and women were raised against Microsoft and Conoco.

Based on Arkin (2007b); Boyle (2001);
see OB Cinema *at the end of this chapter.*

Once a popular topic, research into work motivation declined in the 1990s, and there have been few major theoretical developments since. The ideas developed in the mid- to late twentieth century, however, are also 'current'. Managers still use the terms and the tools which those earlier researchers introduced. Richard Steers and colleagues (2004), however, argue that work today is more short-term in outlook, uses time as a measure of performance, emphasizes teamwork, and produces more conflicts of motives and values (company or environment, work or family). The idea of a 'job for life' has also become a novelty.

Steers and colleagues thus ask whether those twentieth century perspectives apply to today's realities. Two other trends suggest that motivation remains a core issue. One concerns the development of extreme jobs, and the other concerns the phenomenon of boreout.

Extreme jobs

Extreme job a job that involves a working week of 60 hours or more, with high earnings, combined with additional performance pressures.

Some of us are motivated by the extreme job which involves long hours, frequent travel across different time zones, and multiple other pressures.

The characteristics of extreme jobs include:

- physical presence in the office of at least 10 hours a day;
- tight deadlines and fast working pace;
- unpredictable workflow;
- inordinate scope of responsibility;
- frequent travel;
- after-hours work events;
- availability to clients 24/7;
- responsibility for profit and loss;
- responsibility for mentoring and recruiting.

Sylvia Ann Hewlett and Carolyn Buck Luce (2006) found that people in extreme jobs actually enjoy their work and feel fulfilled by it. Answers to the motives question, 'why do you do it?' included adrenaline rush, great colleagues, high pay, recognition, status and power.

There are more men than women in extreme jobs; less than 20 per cent of those in such roles in America are female. Long hours and intense pressure are also exhausting, and have implications for family life. Women in extreme jobs are concerned that their children are less disciplined, eat more junk food, and watch too much television as a result of their frequent absence. They give this example (p.49) of what an extreme job is like:

> A financial analyst we'll call Sudhir emigrated five years ago from Mumbai, India. He works at a major commercial bank in New York. Summertime, when he puts in 90 hours a week, is his 'light' season. The rest of the year, he works upwards of 120 hours a week – leaving only 48 hours for sleeping, eating, entertaining, and (he smiles) bathing. Sudhir stays late in the office even when he has nothing particularly pressing to do. His get-a-life existence is a hazard of the profession – but worth it: As a 23-year-old with a first job, he is in the top 6 per cent of earners in America.

The research of Hewlett and Luce in America also revealed that:

- 53 per cent of women in extreme jobs say that their job interferes with their sex life;
- 65 per cent of men say their extreme jobs damage relationships with their children.

Companies are dealing with 'extremists' in different ways. American Express gives high performers time to work on their own projects. Other companies encourage key managers to work from home and to take career breaks. ProLogis, a distribution company with offices in America and China, uses short-term global assignments to reduce the pressures of relocation (Millard, 2006). The motivational impact of extreme jobs thus needs to be balanced with ways to reduce the potential long-term personal and domestic costs.

Boreout boredom, demotivation and lack of energy and enthusiasm caused by uninteresting, unchallenging and monotonous work.

Boreout

According to Philippe Rothlin and Peter Werder (2008), demotivation is common, especially among office workers, and is caused by repetitive, uninteresting, unchallenging work, which leads to boreout.

They estimate that 15 per cent of office workers are affected; boreout leads to high levels of sick leave and reduces company loyalty. If you suffer boreout, you turn up for work lacking energy and enthusiasm, and spend your time surfing the internet, chatting to colleagues, and trying to look busy. The journalist Roger Boyes (2007) describes one of his tactics:

> I remember while working for the *Financial Times* in the 1970s that colleagues developed an 'Italian Jacket' system. A spare jacket, kept in the office, would be spread over the back of your chair, a half-drunk cup of coffee would be placed next to the phone – and you could disappear for a couple of hours. The editor would assume that you were briefly somewhere else in the building.

Other tactics include the fake stomach upset which creates time to read magazines in the toilet, and 'fake smokers' who use their 'addiction' as an excuse to escape from their desk. The employee who answers 'yes' to four or more of these questions may be suffering boreout:

1. Do you complete private tasks at work?
2. Do you feel under-challenged or bored?
3. Do you sometimes pretend to be busy?
4. Are you tired and apathetic after work even if you experienced no stress in the office?
5. Are you unhappy with your work?
6. Do you find your work meaningless?
7. Could you complete your work quicker than you are doing?
8. Are you afraid of changing your job because you might take a salary cut?
9. Do you send private emails to colleagues during working hours?
10. Do you have little or no interest in your work?

Today's theories about work motivation, and the techniques that influence management practice, were developed some time ago. Are they relevant to current trends involving extreme jobs and boreout? As we will see, those theories and techniques are used today in companies as diverse as Linn Products (audio equipment) and Pizza Express (fast food). We will also see how one 'new' theory of motivation is similar to a popular 'old' theory.

Drives, motives and motivation

Motivation can be explored from three distinct but related perspectives:

goals what are the main motives for our behaviour? Wealth, status and power trigger behaviours directed towards their attainment. This perspective views motivation in terms of our desired outcomes or goals. This question is addressed by *content* theories of motivation

decisions why do we choose to pursue certain goals? Why do you study hard to earn distinctions while a friend has a full social life and is happy with pass grades? This perspective views motivation in terms of the cognitive decision-making processes influencing an individual's choice of goals. This question is addressed by *process* theories of motivation

influence how can we motivate you to work harder? Managers want to motivate employees to turn up on time and be helpful to customers. This perspective views motivation as a social influence process and is addressed by *job enrichment* theories

Drive an innate, biological determinant of behaviour, activated by deprivation.

Do we inherit our goals, or are they acquired through experience? If our motives are innate, then it would be pointless to attempt to change them. If they are acquired, then they can be altered. Our behaviour is influenced by our biological equipment. We appear to have an innate need for survival. Our needs for oxygen, water, food, shelter, warmth and sex can be overpowering. These needs are triggered by deprivation and are known as **drives**.

Home viewing

American Beauty (1999, director Sam Mendes) is a story of 'the perfect family' falling apart. Lester Burnham (played by Kevin Spacey) quits his dead-end management job to work serving burgers in MrSmiley's, while his wife Carolyn (Annette Bening) has an affair with her local competitor in the real estate business. The story displays the corrosive effects of dissatisfying, demotivating work on family, personal identity, and relationships. Also of interest is the way in which the main characters define 'success' in life.

Table 9.1: Innate cognitive drives

curiosity	the need to explore, to play, to learn more
sense-making	the need to understand the nature of the world around us
order and meaning	the need for order, certainty, equity, consistency, predictability
effectance or competency	the need to exert mastery and control over the world around us
self-understanding	the need to know who and what we are

Our drives may not be restricted to basic biological needs. Some psychologists claim that we are active sensation-seekers who have the innate cognitive drives listed in Table 9.1.

The drives come with the body. We do not have to learn to be cold, thirsty or hungry. However, we can *override* these drives. Some religious orders inflict celibacy on willing members. Altruism can overcome personal safety needs in extraordinary circumstances. The idea that our behaviour is pre-programmed is too simple. Psychologists once thought that human behaviour could be explained in terms of instincts, but that turns out to be unhelpful. Animal behaviour, in contrast, is triggered by instincts. Birds and squirrels cannot override their programming, and remain locked into their niches in nature. The ways in which we, on the other hand, seek to satisfy our drives are innumerable, and vary between individuals and across cultures. Consider differences in eating habits around the world, and the range of things that individuals do to satisfy their sex drives.

Motives, in contrast, appear to be acquired through experience.

Motive a socially acquired need activated by a desire for fulfilment.

Polygamy is a crime in most Western cultures, but a sign of male achievement, wealth and status in parts of the Arab world. Our choice of goals and behaviours is shaped by the norms of our society. Those who choose not to conform are often shunned, ridiculed, and perhaps imprisoned. The distinction between drives and motives is summarized in Table 9.2.

This distinction between innate drives and acquired motives is not clear. The terms 'needs' and 'goals' are also used to refer to both drives and motives. We try to satisfy our biological drives in ways acceptable to our society. The innate drives for competency, sense-making and curiosity are socially prized in most cultures. From the constructivist perspective (Chapter 1), human behaviour is purposive. We attach reasons to our goals and behaviours. To understand your motives, and to influence your behaviour, we need to understand why you choose particular outcomes and how you decide to pursue them.

Table 9.2: Drives versus motives

drives	motives
are innate	are learned
have a physiological basis	have a social basis
are activated by deprivation	are activated by environment
are aimed at satiation	are aimed at stimulation

Motivation the cognitive decision-making process through which goal-directed behaviour is initiated, energized, directed, and maintained.

Motivation is a broad concept which includes preferences for particular outcomes, strength of effort (half-hearted or enthusiastic), and persistence (in the face of problems and barriers). These are the factors that we have to understand in order to explain your motivation and behaviour. These are the factors which a manager has to appreciate in order to motivate employees to behave in organizationally desirable ways.

Content theories

Theories of motivation based on drives and needs are known as content theories. They have this label because drives and needs are seen as part of our common 'mental luggage'. The most recent content theory of work motivation was developed by Nitin Nohria, Boris Groysberg and Linda-Eling Lee (2008). Their 'emotional needs' theory claims that we are driven by four basic and innate ('hardwired') drives:

the drive to *acquire*	obtain scarce goods, develop social status
the drive to *bond*	form connections with other individuals and groups
the drive to *comprehend*	satisfy our curiosity, master our environment
the drive to *defend*	protect against threats, promote justice

From a survey of around 700 employees of large companies, they found that an organization's ability to meet the four drives contributes to employee motivation by influencing feelings of involvement, energy and initiative, satisfaction, commitment, and intention to quit (or stay). Fulfilling employees' drive to bond has the greatest impact on commitment, while meeting the drive to comprehend is closely linked to involvement, energy and initiative. However, the best way to improve motivation is to meet all four drives; 'a poor showing on one drive substantially diminishes the impact of high scores on the other three'. How can this framework be used in practice? There is a 'primary lever' linked to each of the drives. These are the organization's reward system, its culture, the way that jobs are designed, and performance management and resource allocation processes. Organizational policies and practices in each of those areas can enhance motivation, as shown in Table 9.3.

Table 9.3: Emotional needs theory and implications for practice

drive	primary lever	management actions
acquire	reward system	differentiate good from average and poor performers tie rewards clearly to performance pay as well as your competitors
bond	culture	foster mutual reliance and friendship among coworkers value collaboration and teamwork encourage sharing of best practices
comprehend	job design	design jobs that have distinct and important roles in the organization design jobs that are meaningful and foster a sense of contribution to the organization
defend	performance management	increase the transparency of all processes emphasize their fairness build trust by being just and transparent in granting rewards, assignments, and other forms of recognition

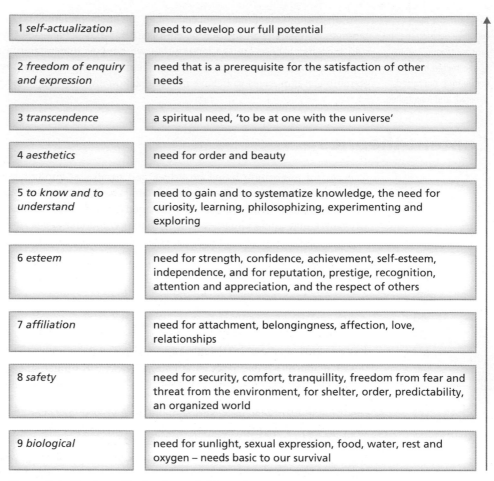

1 *self-actualization*	need to develop our full potential
2 *freedom of enquiry and expression*	need that is a prerequisite for the satisfaction of other needs
3 *transcendence*	a spiritual need, 'to be at one with the universe'
4 *aesthetics*	need for order and beauty
5 *to know and to understand*	need to gain and to systematize knowledge, the need for curiosity, learning, philosophizing, experimenting and exploring
6 *esteem*	need for strength, confidence, achievement, self-esteem, independence, and for reputation, prestige, recognition, attention and appreciation, and the respect of others
7 *affiliation*	need for attachment, belongingness, affection, love, relationships
8 *safety*	need for security, comfort, tranquillity, freedom from fear and threat from the environment, for shelter, order, predictability, an organized world
9 *biological*	need for sunlight, sexual expression, food, water, rest and oxygen – needs basic to our survival

Figure 9.1: Abraham Maslow's needs hierarchy

Abraham Harold
Maslow
(1908–1970)

Self-actualization
the desire for personal
fulfilment, to develop
one's potential, to
become everything
that one is capable of
becoming.

This emphasis on organizational factors does not mean that management behaviour is not important. On the contrary, because managers have some control over the way in which company policies are implemented, they can help to meet their employees' drives. For example, a line manager or supervisor can link performance and reward through the use of praise, recognition, favoured assignments, the allocation of bonuses, encouraging teamwork, and making jobs interesting and meaningful. Once again, employees expect their managers to address all four drives, within the constraints of the organization. Managers who are worse at fulfilling just one drive are rated poorly.

This new theory is similar to the famous framework developed several decades ago by the American psychologist Abraham Maslow (1943, 1954, 1971). Maslow also argued that we have innate needs (including drives and goals), and identified nine of these (Figure 9.1).

If our biological and safety needs are not satisfied, we die. If our needs for love and esteem are not satisfied, we can feel inferior and helpless, but if these needs are satisfied, we feel self-confident. **Self-actualization** and transcendence, Maslow argued, are our ultimate goals. While the implications of self-actualization have been widely explored, the metaphysical concept of transcendence has been largely ignored by management writers and researchers.

Maslow argued that self-actualized people are rare, and that creating the conditions for us to develop our capabilities to this extent was a challenging task. He also argued that these needs are organized in a hierarchy, with lower order biological and safety needs at the bottom, and higher order self-actualization and transcendence needs at the top, as in Figure 9.1.

STOP AND THINK Most organizational behaviour textbooks ignore needs 2 to 5 in Maslow's framework, and concentrate instead on the other five needs. One explanation is that freedom of enquiry, transcendence, aesthetics, and the need to know, are not relevant to work, organizations, or management. How valid is that explanation? How else can we explain why those needs are rarely discussed?

This hierarchy, Maslow argued, has the following properties.

1. A need is not an effective motivator until those lower in the hierarchy are more or less satisfied. You are unlikely to be concerned about the sharks (threat to safety), if you are drowning (biological deprivation).

2. A satisfied need is not a motivator. If you are well fed and safe, we would have difficulty energizing and directing your behaviour with offers of food and shelter.

3. Lack of need satisfaction can affect mental health. Consider the frustration, anxiety and depression that can arise from lack of self-esteem, loss of the respect of others, an inability to sustain relationships and an inability to develop one's capabilities.

4. We have an innate desire to work our way up the hierarchy, pursuing the satisfaction of our higher order needs once our lower order needs are more or less satisfied.

5. The experience of self-actualization stimulates desire for more. Maslow claimed that self-actualizers have 'peak experiences'. When you have had one of these, you want another. Self-actualization cannot be satisfied in the same way as the other needs.

Maslow did not intend this hierarchy to be regarded as rigid, but as a typical picture of how human motivation is likely to develop under ideal conditions.

There are two main criticisms of Maslow's theory. First, it is vague and cannot predict behaviour. Second, it is more of a social philosophy reflecting white American middle-class values in the mid-twentieth century. So, can this theory be dismissed as irrelevant in the twenty-first century? No. Maslow's thinking remains influential, particularly in

"So, does anyone else feel that their needs aren't being met?"

Source: © Tom Cheney/Condé Nast Publications/www.cartoonbank.com

Table 9.4: Nohria and Maslow compared

Nohria's needs	Maslow's needs
acquire	biological, esteem
bond	affiliation, esteem
comprehend	knowing and understanding, freedom of enquiry
defend	safety

recognizing that behaviour depends on a range of basic and higher-order needs, drives and motives. His ideas still influence management practice concerning rewards, management style and work design. Techniques such as job enrichment, total quality management, process re-design, self-managing teams, 'new leadership', and empowerment, have all been influenced by his thinking. We also find the emotional needs identified by Nohria and colleagues in Maslow's framework (Table 9.4), and the latter appears to be the more interesting and useful of the two.

China and the West: diverging or converging?

Do Western motivation theories apply to other countries, such as China? Western management thinking traditionally emphasized the role of individual tasks, performance, and rewards. Since the 1980s, however, the importance of teamwork and information sharing has been widely recognized. In contrast, Chinese attitudes to work have been influenced by the collectivist philosophy of Confucianism which stresses benevolence, right conduct, loyalty, and good manners; selfishness and materialism are shunned, and sharing is valued.

Are these cultural differences being strengthened, or eroded, by current economic trends and developments? In other words, are the work cultures of China and the West diverging or converging? Maria Rotundo and Jia Lin Xie compared Chinese and Western management attitudes to misconduct at work, to identify the differences.

While both cultures felt that stealing from the organization was wrong, Chinese managers rated more highly the importance of task completion, challenging work, and opportunity for advancement – which are all individual aspects of work. Chinese and Western managers rated co-operative working equally. Over the last 20 years, the centralized and planned economy of China has become more decentralized and market-driven. In this more competitive context, managers need to pay more attention to task completion, and Chinese workers may have become more individualistic as a result. The researchers conclude, therefore, that Western and Chinese attitudes to work behaviour and performance seem to be converging.

Based on Rotundo and Xie (2008).

The best place to work

In 2008, *The Sunday Times* newspaper, surveyed over 500 companies and 180,000 employees to identify 'the best company to work for' in the UK. The award was won by Heat, a central heating installation company based in Belfast. W.L. Gore & Associates, who won the prize in the previous four years, came eleventh. Companies were rated on eight factors:

Leadership: how employees feel about the head of the company and senior managers

Wellbeing: how staff feel about stress, pressure and the balance between work and home life

My manager: people's feelings towards their immediate boss and their day-to-day managers

My team: people's feelings about their immediate colleagues

Fair deal: how happy the workforce is with their pay and benefits

Giving something back: how much companies are thought by their staff to put back into society, and the local community

My company: feelings about the company as opposed to the people they work with

Personal growth: to what extent staff feel they are stretched and challenged by their job

Heat's managing director said that their success was based on the company's approach to communication; 'We work hard to make it simple. If you make it simple everybody understands and that makes it more likely to last'. Across the survey, the score for work-life balance saw the biggest drop on the previous year, perhaps

reflecting the impact of the economic downturn which began in 2009. The top ten companies were:

1. Heat
2. Edward Jones
3. Beaverbrooks the Jewellers
4. Hydrock
5. Pannone
6. Denplan
7. Iris
8. Office Angels
9. Sandwell Community Trust
10. Handelsbanken

None of these companies is particularly large or well-known. Heat was the top performing company for 'giving something back'. No other organization in the survey had higher scores for employees believing that their managers were excellent role models, good motivators, and excellent leaders. It also got the highest score for work not interfering with domestic responsibilities.

Source: RESO/Photolibrary.com

Based on McCall (2008).

Process theories

J. Stacy Adams

Equity theory
a process theory of motivation which argues that perception of unfairness leads to tension, which motivates the individual to resolve that unfairness.

Theories of motivation that focus on how we make choices with respect to goals are known as process theories. Unlike content theories, process theories give us a decision-making role in choosing our goals and how to pursue them. Individuals are motivated by different outcomes. Cultures encourage different patterns of motivation. We thus appear to have some choice of motives, and the means to achieve them. The theories of Nohria and colleagues, and of Maslow, are universalist – they apply to everyone, and cannot explain differences between individuals and cultures. We will explore four process theories of work motivation, equity theory, expectancy theory, goal-setting theory and inner work life theory.

Equity theory

Several theorists have argued that we look for a just or equitable return for our efforts. The calculation of what is just or equitable depends on the comparisons we make with others. Equity theory is thus based on our perceptions of fair treatment. Stacy Adams (1963, 1965) argued that we are motivated to act in situations which we perceive to be inequitable or unfair. Inequity occurs when you get either more, or less, than you think you deserve. The theory is based on perceptions of *in*equity, but is traditionally called *equity* theory.

This theory explains behaviour using perceptions of social comparisons. Equity theory argues that, the more intense the perceived inequity, the higher the tension, and the stronger the motivation to act. Adams argues that we respond differently to 'over-reward' and 'under-reward'. We tend to perceive a modest amount of over-reward as 'good luck', and do nothing, while a modest under-reward is not so readily tolerated.

Table 9.5: Strategies for reducing inequity

strategy	example
1. alter your outcomes	persuade the manager to increase my pay
2. adjust your inputs	I won't work as hard as Annika
3. alter the comparison person's outcomes	persuade the manager to cut Annika's pay
4. alter the comparison person's inputs	leave the difficult tasks to Annika
5. compare with someone else	Per gets the same as I get
6. rationalize the inequity	Annika has worked here for much longer
7. leave	get another job

How do you calculate inequity? Adams proposed that we compare our rewards (pay, recognition) and contributions (time, effort, ideas) with the outputs and inputs of others. Equity thus exists when these ratios are equal:

$$\frac{\text{my rewards (minus my costs)}}{\text{my effort and contribution}} = \frac{\text{your rewards (minus your costs)}}{\text{your effort and contribution}}$$

Rewards can include a range of tangible and intangible factors including pay, status symbols, fringe benefits, promotion prospects, satisfaction and job security. Inputs similarly relate to any factor that you believe you bring to the situation, including age, experience, skill, education, effort, loyalty and commitment. The relative priority or weighting of these various factors depends on the individual's perception.

How do you resolve inequity? Let's imagine that you are working in a restaurant in Gamla Stan (the Old Town) in Stockholm and you discover that Annika is earning 25 Swedish kroner (about US$3.0) an hour more than you, for the same work (about US$100 a week more than you). Table 9.5 lists Adams's seven strategies for reducing this inequity.

Choice of strategy is a sensitive issue, and equity theory does not predict which strategy an individual will choose. Each option has different short-term and long-term consequences. Arguing with your manager, reducing your input, or making Annika do the difficult work, may reduce inequity in the short term, but could have long-term consequences for your relationships and employment at this location.

The theory's predictions of behaviour for over- and under-reward are shown in Figure 9.2.

Evidence from laboratory research supports the theory, and confirms that people who are overpaid reduce their perceived inequity by working harder. Studies in real settings also

Figure 9.2: Equity theory – causal chains

broadly confirm equity theory predictions. Interestingly from a management perspective, perceived equity seems to lead to greater job satisfaction and organizational commitment (Sweeney *et al.*, 1990).

Equity theory has some problems. A number of quantitative and qualitative variables have to be considered when calculating an equity ratio. These variables depend on individual perception, and are difficult to measure. Different people use different timescales when calculating fairness; short term calculations may be different from long term implications. There are individual differences in tolerance levels, and not everyone will respond in the same way to a particular level of inequity. The extent to which you believe that there is a valid explanation for inequity will also moderate your response.

Equity theory also overlooks the wider organizational context in two ways. The first concerns the basis of our social comparisons, which can be extremely varied. Some of us compare our situations with immediate colleagues, while others make comparisons with people in other organizations, sectors and countries. There is no rationale for preferring one basis of comparison to another. The second way in which equity theory ignores context concerns the systemic inequities in capitalist economies. Colleagues may receive the same treatment from their employing organization (perception of equity) while being exploited by more senior individuals in positions of wealth, influence and power (perception of inequity). However, this inequity is a 'normal' feature of capitalist society, and is thus difficult to challenge.

STOP AND THINK

What actions would you take if you were earning just a little more than Annika in our example from the Stockholm restaurant?

What actions would you take if you were earning very much more than Annika?

To what extent do you think equity theory can make accurate predictions of your behaviour in inequitable situations like these?

Expectancy theory
a process theory which argues that individual motivation depends on the *valence* of outcomes, the *expectancy* that effort will lead to good performance, and the *instrumentality* of performance in producing valued outcomes.

Equity theory has implications for management practice. Employees compare pay (even in organizations that insist on pay secrecy) and perceived inequity quickly generates resentment. Comparisons are often subjective and imprecise, particularly where information is lacking and employees rely on rumour. It is important to recognize that perceptions of inequity generate tension, even where there is actually little inequity. The circulation of accurate information about rewards, and the links between effort and rewards, is thus crucial.

Expectancy theory

A motive is an outcome that has become desirable. The process through which outcomes become desirable is explained by the expectancy theory of motivation.

Cognitive theories in psychology assume that we are purposive, and that we are aware of our goals and actions. Expectancy theory is a cognitive theory, and was developed by the American psychologist Edward C. Tolman in the 1930s as a challenge to the behaviourist views of his contemporaries. Tolman argued that behaviour is directed by the expectations that we have about our behaviour leading to the achievement of desired outcomes.

For work motivation to be high, productive work has to be seen as a path to valued goals. If you need more money, and if you expect to get more money for working hard, then we can predict that you will work hard. If you still need more money, but if you expect that hard work will only result in happy smiles from the boss, then we can predict that you will decide not to work hard (unless you value happy smiles). This theory thus assumes that we behave in ways that are instrumental to the achievement of valued goals.

Edward Chace
Tolman (1886–1959)

Valence the perceived value or preference that an individual has for a particular outcome, and can be positive, negative, or neutral.

Instrumentality the perceived probability that good performance will lead to valued rewards, and is measured on a scale from 0 (no chance) to 1 (certainty).

Expectancy the perceived probability that effort will result in good performance, and is measured on a scale from 0 (no chance) to 1 (certainty).

Victor Harold Vroom (b.1932)

The American psychologist Victor H. Vroom (1964) developed the first expectancy theory of work motivation, based on three concepts: valence, instrumentality and expectancy. This is known as *valence-instrumentality-expectancy theory* – expectancy theory for short.

Instrumentality and expectancy are both *subjective probabilities*. What is important is what the individual estimates to be the likelihood of good performance leading to valued rewards, and of effort leading to good performance, respectively.

The force (F) of your motivation to work hard is the result of the product (multiplication) of these three variables and not the sum (addition). This is because, if one of the variables is zero, then, despite the value of the other two, the product, F, will be zero, and that is what we would expect. This cumbersome explanation is expressed in *the expectancy equation*:

$$F = V \times I \times E$$

What is the effect of a low 'V' value? If you do not care what grade you get for your next assignment, then you will not be motivated to work hard for it.

What is the effect of a low 'E' value? If you believe that long hard hours in the library will not get you a high assignment grade, then you will not be motivated to work hard.

What is the effect of a low 'I' value? If you believe that a good grade will not lead to a chosen qualification, or to your preferred career, then you will not be motivated to work hard.

Only when all three of the terms in the expectancy equation are positive and high will the motivating force be positive and strong. However, behaviour typically has a number of outcomes. Working hard affects our work performance, levels of fatigue, social life, today's pay and tomorrow's promotion prospects. The expectancy equation thus has to be summed for all possible outcomes. The full expectancy equation is:

$$F = \Sigma \ (V \times I \times E)$$

The sign Σ is the Greek letter sigma, which means, 'add up all the values of the calculation in the brackets'. Note that there will be only a single E value, concerning the probability that high effort will lead to high performance. However, there will be several different I values, one for each rated outcome, concerning the probability that these will be obtained.

STOP AND THINK

Measure the force of your motivation to get a high grade in organizational behaviour:

What are your V values? Identify the range of outcomes from working hard for this subject. Rate the value of each of these to you, as 1 (positive), 0 (ambivalent) or –1 (negative).

What are your I values? For each outcome, estimate the subjective probability of that occurring (you could get a high grade, you could ruin your social life).

What is your E value? Estimate the subjective probability that high effort will produce a high grade in this subject. This probability will be between 0 (little or no chance) and 1 (certainty of high grade).

Sum the calculation across all your outcomes, and compare your score with colleagues. If the theory is correct, those with higher F scores are more highly motivated to get a good grade for the organizational behaviour course.

Consider the process through which you have just worked. To what extent is this a realistic picture of the cognitive decision-making process that we undertake when deciding on aspects of our behaviour?

In summary:

- Expectancy theory states that behaviour results from a conscious decision-making process based on expectations, or subjective probabilities, that the individual has about the results of different behaviours leading to performance and to rewards.
- Expectancy theory can explain individual differences in motivation and behaviour.
- Expectancy theory measures the strength or force of the individual's motivation to behave in particular ways.
- Expectancy theory assumes that behaviour is rational, and that we are aware of our motives.

Expectancy theory has a number of management consequences:

- the link between effort and performance must be supported with adequate training, instruction and resources;
- the link between performance and rewards must be clear if rewards are to have the desired motivational effect;
- if employees are instructed to do one thing but rewarded for doing another, they will focus on the behaviours which are rewarded and ignore other instructions;
- money is only one of several extrinsic rewards, and to be motivating it must be linked clearly to performance and be seen as equitable;
- performance standards must be clear, otherwise employees will not know how best to direct their efforts;
- there is no point in offering rewards which employees do not value, or which are not valued highly enough to influence behaviour;
- if different employees value different kinds of rewards, it may help to introduce a 'cafeteria benefits' scheme, offering choices of medical insurance, health club memberships, car breakdown cover, bus passes, shopping vouchers, cinema tickets, bicycle allowances, financial planning advice, and travel insurance, for example;
- the value of different rewards may change with time and has to be monitored.

In other words, to ensure low motivation and poor performance:

1. keep performance goals vague and ambiguous;
2. provide inadequate advice and resources for goal achievement;
3. reward behaviour other than good job performance;
4. offer rewards which employees do not value;
5. concentrate on financial rewards and ignore other intrinsic and extrinsic rewards;
6. make sure performance ratings are subjective and inconsistent.

Edwin Locke
(b.1938)

Gary Philip Latham
(b.1945)

Goal-setting theory
a process theory of
motivation which
argues that work
motivation is influenced
by goal difficulty,
goal specificity, and
knowledge of results.

Goal-setting theory

Goal-setting theory is regarded as a process theory of motivation. However, the main advocate, Edwin Locke (1968; Latham and Yukl, 1975) argues that 'goal-setting is more appropriately viewed as a motivational technique rather than a formal theory' (1975, p.465). This technique relies on a series of propositions which explain and predict work behaviour, so it is entitled to be described as theory.

Goal theory has established four propositions which are well-supported by research:

Challenging goals lead to higher levels of performance than simple and unchallenging goals. Difficult goals are also called 'stretch' goals because they encourage us to try harder (unless the goal is beyond our level of ability).

Specific goals lead to higher levels of performance than vague goals such as 'try harder' or 'do your best'. It is easier to adjust our behaviour when we know precisely what is required of us, and goal specificity avoids confusion. Goals should thus be SMART: specific, measurable, attainable, realistic and time-related.

Participation in goal setting, particularly when this is expected, can improve performance by increasing commitment to those goals, but managerially assigned goals that are adequately explained and justified can also lead to high performance.

Knowledge of results of past performance – feedback – is necessary for effective goal achievement. Feedback contains information and is also motivational.

The theory has been tested mainly in situations where short term targets can be expressed in clear and quantifiable terms. It is unclear if the theory applies to longer term goals, say over a period of years, as targets are likely to be more qualitative and to change as circumstances alter. It is also uncertain whether this applies where goals are difficult to measure, such as in most types of managerial work. Another limitation is that the theory and its applications concentrate on individual goals and performance rather than on teamwork.

Goal-setting for lumberjacks

Responding to criticism that goal-setting had been tested mainly in laboratory settings, Locke (1975, pp.466–67) cited four studies in real organizational settings. In two separate studies of independent pulpwood producers, high productivity was maintained when a supervisor remained on the job with the men and set production goals for them.

In a third study of sawing crews, output per man was higher over a three-month period when specific and moderately difficult goals were assigned to the sawyers; this was not the case with other sawing crews where no specific goals were assigned.

In a fourth study, loggers were given the goal of loading trucks to 94 per cent of the legal maximum; the old average was only 60 per cent. Performance improved immediately, and loading weights remained high, averaging 90 per cent, for the next 15 months, saving a quarter of a million US dollars, as the purchase of additional trucks was avoided.

Locke points out that, in all four cases, performance improvements were quickly obtained without the offer of financial rewards for goal attainment, or penalties for failure.

The main positive feature of goal-setting theory concerns the clarity of the practical implications (Locke and Latham, 1990):

- *Goal difficulty*: set goals for performance at levels which will stretch employees, but which are not beyond their ability levels.

- *Goal specificity*: express goals in clear and precise language, if possible in quantifiable terms, and avoid setting vague and ambiguous goals.

- *Participation*: allow employees to take part in the goal-setting process to increase the acceptability of and their commitment to goals.

- *Acceptance*: if goals are set by management, ensure that they are adequately explained and justified, so that those concerned understand and accept them.

- *Feedback*: provide information on the results of past performance to allow employees to adjust their behaviour, if necessary, to improve future performance.

STOP AND THINK

Yo! Sushi, a Japanese restaurant chain, offers its staff financial bonuses of up to 20 per cent of annual salary every three months. To earn this bonus, staff have to meet restaurant targets which include the number of customers, the average bill amount, and profitability. Staff also have individual performance targets which are documented and reviewed quarterly, and which affect the bonus. One of the chain's restaurant managers, Tony Pay, claims that the scheme is effective because bonuses are frequent (not annual), and targets are agreed upon by management and staff.

What are the strengths of this scheme from the perspective of goal-setting theory?

What potential problems does this approach have, for management, for employees, and perhaps also for customers?

How would you advise management to adapt and improve this scheme?

Based on Patten (1999).

Inner work life theory

Inner work life theory a process theory of motivation which argues that our behaviour and performance at work are influenced by the interplay of our perceptions, emotions and motives.

Equity, expectancy, and goal-setting theories of motivation allow us to make choices. These perspectives, however, imply a rational, logical, reasoned approach to the decisions that shape our behaviour. They do not allow for the influence of emotions. The **inner work life theory** developed by Teresa Amabile and Steven Kramer (2007) argues that our behaviour and work performance are influenced by the way in which our perceptions, motives, and emotions interact with each other, triggered by everyday events.

Our private thoughts and feelings may not be visible to others, especially managers, but we do not leave them at home when we go to work. To find out how the dynamics of our 'inner work life' can affect performance, Amabile and Kramer asked 238 professionals from 26 project teams to complete a personal diary, in a standard format, every day for the duration of their projects. The researcher sent daily emails to each professional, asking for a description of an event that stood out in their mind that day and how that made them feel (similar to the critical incident method used by Herzberg and described earlier). This gave the researchers around 12,000 diary entries to analyse, revealing the richness and intensity of people's inner work lives, what they call 'the reality management never sees'.

Figure 9.3 summarizes the 'inner working life' model of work performance. One of the most important implications concerns the role of emotions. Neuroscience has shown that cognition (including perception) and emotion are closely linked. Events at work trigger a combination of perceptual, emotional, and motivational processes. The way in which these processes interact shapes our behaviour and our performance at work.

The researchers conclude that we perform better when our experiences at work include more positive emotions, stronger intrinsic motivation, and favourable perceptions of the work, the team, management and the organization. Positive emotions, perceptions and motivation were also linked to higher levels of creativity, and this effect can last for several days. Productivity, commitment and collegiality are also improved when we 'are in a good mood'.

The practical management implications of this research differ from that of other motivation theories, which emphasize the 'daily pat on the back' and attempts to make work fun. This research suggests that the two most important management behaviours involve 'enabling people to move forward in their work', and 'treating them decently as human beings'.

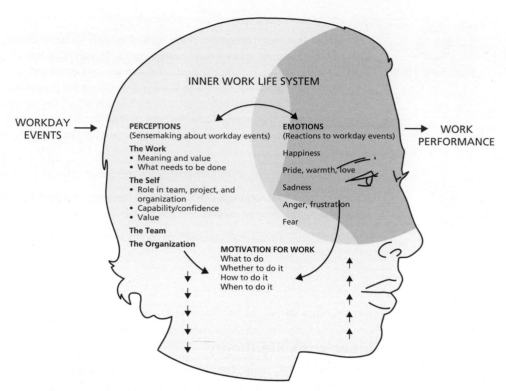

Figure 9.3: Inner working life theory

Source: Reprinted by permission of *Harvard Business Review*. Figure on p.75. From "Inner work life: understanding the subtext of business performance" by Amabile, T.M. and Kramer, S.J., 85(5). Copyright © 2007 by the Harvard Business School Publishing Corporation, all rights reserved.

1. Enable progress

The factor that made the difference between 'good days' and 'bad days' for the respondents in this study was a sense of being able to make progress. This could mean achieving a goal, accomplishing a task, solving a problem. The worst days – frustrating, sad, fearful – were characterized by setbacks, and even small delays could have this impact. Managers should:

- provide direct help and do not get in the way;
- make sure that time and other resources are adequate;
- react to successes and failures with a learning orientation;
- set clear and unambiguous goals (see earlier discussion of goal theory).

2. Manage with a human touch

Interpersonal relationships are also important, treating people fairly and with respect. These events had almost as much impact as 'enabling process' on the distinction between good and bad days. Praise in the absence of real progress had little positive impact, and can arouse cynicism. Good progress without recognition leads to anger and sadness.

The researchers conclude that:

> Managers' day-to-day (and moment-to-moment) behaviours matter not just because they directly facilitate or impede the work of the organization. They're also important because they affect people's inner work lives, creating ripple effects on organizational performance. When people are blocked from doing good, constructive work day by day, they form negative impressions of the organization, their coworkers, their managers, their work, and themselves; they feel frustrated and unhappy; and they become demotivated in their work. But when managers facilitate progress, every aspect of people's inner work lives are enhanced, which leads to even greater progress. This positive spiral benefits individual workers – and the entire organization (Amabile and Kramer, 2007, p.83).

The social process of motivating others

Motivation can also be seen as a social influence process. The advice in the previous section, about enabling progress, and 'managing with a human touch', illustrates this. The general question is, how do we motivate others to do what we want them to do? The question for management is, how do we motivate employees to perform well? Many jobs are still designed using the methods of the American engineer Frederick Winslow Taylor (1911). Taylor's *scientific management* approach to designing jobs (see Chapter 14) is as follows:

1. Decide on the optimum degree of *task fragmentation*, breaking down a complex job into a sequence of simple steps.
2. Decide the *one best way* to perform the work, through studies to discover the most effective method for doing each step, including workplace layout and design of tools.
3. *Train* employees to carry out these simple fragmented tasks in the manner specified.
4. *Reward* employees financially for meeting performance targets.

STOP AND THINK   You are employed on a job in which you repeat the same simple task every 15 seconds, perhaps wiring plugs for lamps, 9.00 am until 5.30 pm, every day (with a lunch break), five days a week. Describe your emotional response to this work.

Is it inevitable that some jobs just have to be like this, given the nature of work and technology, and the need to keep quality high and costs low?

Task fragmentation has advantages:

- employees do not need expensive and time-consuming training;
- repeating one small specialized task makes employees very proficient;
- unskilled work gets lower pay; and
- some of the problems of achieving controlled performance are simplified.

The disadvantages include:

- repetitive work is very boring;
- the individual's contribution to the organization is meaningless and insignificant;
- monotony leads to apathy, dissatisfaction, boreout, and carelessness; and
- the employee does not develop skills that might lead to promotion.

Job enrichment
a technique for broadening the experience of work to enhance employee need satisfaction and to improve motivation and performance.

Taylor's approach to job design appears logical and efficient, but it creates jobs that do not stimulate motivation or improve performance. Taylor had a simplified view of human motivation, regarding 'lower level' employees as 'coin operated' and arguing that the rewards for working as instructed should be financial. Taylor's methods are more likely to encourage absenteeism and sabotage than commitment and flexibility. Managers are thus interested in theories of motivation as sources of alternative methods for encouraging motivation and high performance. During the 1960s and 1970s, these concerns created the Quality of Working Life (QWL) movement whose language and methods are still influential. One QWL technique is **job enrichment**.

Frederick Herzberg
(1923–2000)

The concept of job enrichment was first developed by the American psychologist Frederick Herzberg (1966, 1968). While this work is about half a century old, recent research suggests that many employees still respond in ways that Herzberg's theory predicts (Bassett-Jones and Lloyd, 2005). To discover what factors affected job satisfaction and dissatisfaction, 203 Pittsburgh engineers and accountants were asked two 'critical incident' questions. They were asked to recall events which had made them feel good about their work, and events which had made them feel bad about it.

Motivator factors
aspects of work which lead to high levels of satisfaction, motivation and performance, including achievement, recognition, responsibility, advancement, growth, and the work itself.

Hygiene factors
aspects of work which remove dissatisfaction, but do not contribute to motivation and performance, including pay, company policy, supervision, status, security and working conditions.

Vertical loading factors methods for enriching work and improving motivation, by removing controls, increasing accountability, and by providing feedback, new tasks, natural work units, special assignments, and additional authority.

Intrinsic rewards valued outcomes or benefits which come from the individual, such as feelings of satisfaction, competence, self-esteem and accomplishment.

Extrinsic rewards valued outcomes or benefits provided by others, such as promotion, pay increases, a bigger office desk, praise and recognition.

Table 9.6: Motivator and hygiene factors

Motivator factors (job content)	Hygiene factors (organizational context)
achievement	pay
advancement	company policy
growth	supervisory style
recognition	status
responsibility	security
the work itself	working conditions

Analysis of these critical incident narratives showed that the factors which led to job satisfaction were different from those which led to job dissatisfaction. Herzberg called this a 'two factor theory of motivation', the two sets of factors being motivator factors and hygiene factors, summarized in Table 9.6. Motivators are also known as (job) content factors, while hygiene factors are known as (organizational) context factors.

Herzberg (1987) claimed that this pattern of motivation had been identified in Finland, Hungary, Italy, Israel, Japan and Zambia. In South Africa, however, while managers and skilled workers, black and white, produced the expected results, unskilled workers' satisfaction appeared to be dependent on hygiene. Herzberg claims that, 'the impoverished nature of the unskilled workers' jobs has not afforded these workers with motivators – thus the abnormal profile'. He also cites a study of unskilled Indian workers who were, 'operating on a dependent hygiene continuum that leads to addiction to hygiene, or strikes and revolution'.

According to this theory, the redesign of jobs to increase motivation and performance should thus focus on motivators or content factors. Improvement in the hygiene or context factors, Herzberg (1968) argued, will remove dissatisfaction, but will not increase motivation and performance. He suggested using vertical loading factors, to achieve job enrichment.

The way in which a job is designed determines the rewards available, and what the individual has to do to get those rewards. It helps to distinguish *intrinsic rewards* and *extrinsic rewards*.

Intrinsic rewards are valued outcomes within the control of the individual, such as feelings of satisfaction and accomplishment. For some of us, and for some actions, the outcome is its own (intrinsic) reward. Mountaineers, poets, athletes, authors, painters and musicians are usually familiar with the concept of intrinsic reward; few people ever get paid for climbing hills, and there are few wealthy poets on this planet. Extrinsic rewards are valued outcomes that are controlled by others, such as recognition, promotion, and pay increases.

The relationships between performance and intrinsic reward are more immediate than those between performance and extrinsic reward. Intrinsic rewards are thus more important influences on our motivation to work. 'Eat what you kill' incentive reward schemes don't work well, according to Alfie Kohn (1993). Money is not a major concern for most people, and 'bribing' people to perform can be seen as manipulative and controlling. Incentive pay schemes also discourage risk taking and creativity, and undermine interest in the job itself. Extrinsic rewards might buy compliance, but do not encourage commitment.

The Job Characteristics Model (Figure 9.4) describes the job enrichment strategy of the expectancy theorists Richard Hackman and Greg Oldham (1974; Hackman *et al.*, 1975). This model sets out the links between the features of jobs, the individual's experience, and outcomes in terms of motivation, satisfaction and performance. The model suggests that jobs can be analysed in terms of five *core dimensions*:

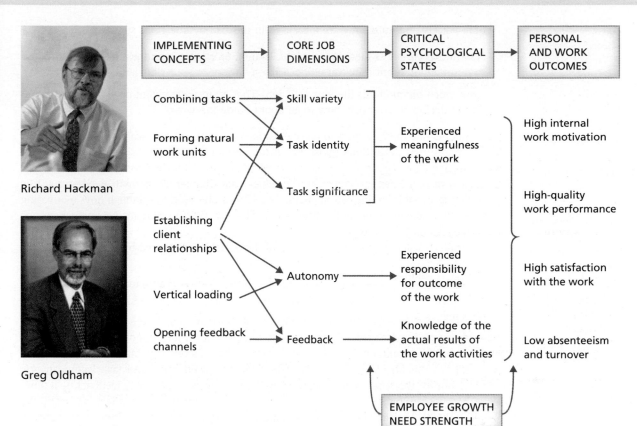

Richard Hackman

Greg Oldham

Figure 9.4: **The Job Characteristics Model**

Copyright © 1975, by The Regents of the University of California. Reprinted from the *California Management Review*, Vol. 17, No. 4. By permission of The Regents.

Growth need strength a measure of the readiness and capability of an individual to respond positively to job enrichment.

1. *Skill variety*: the extent to which a job makes use of different skills and abilities.

2. *Task identity*: the extent to which a job involves a 'whole' and meaningful piece of work.

3. *Task significance*: the extent to which a job affects the work of others.

4. *Autonomy*: the extent to which a job provides independence and discretion.

5. *Feedback*: the extent to which performance information is related back to the individual.

This model also takes into account individual differences in growth need strength, a concept based on Maslow's concept of self-actualization.

Job diagnostic survey a questionnaire which assesses the degree of skill variety, task identity, task significance, autonomy, and feedback in jobs.

Growth need strength (GNS) is an indicator of your willingness to welcome personal development through job enrichment. The causal chain, from job design, through individual experience, to performance outcomes, depends on GNS. With employees whose GNS is low, an enriched job is unlikely to improve their performance.

Jobs can be assessed on these core dimensions. Richard Hackman and Greg Oldham (1974; Hackman *et al.*, 1975) developed an opinion questionnaire called the job diagnostic survey (JDS) for this purpose.

STOP AND THINK   Your instructor offers to enrich your educational experience of studying organizational behaviour, with additional classes and tutorials, further reading, and extra feedback and revision sessions. There is no guarantee, however, that this will increase your course grades. How do you feel about this offer?

Skill variety and autonomy are measured in the JDS by questions such as:

How much *variety* is there in your job? That is, to what extent does the job require you to do many different things at work, using a variety of your skills and talents?

How much *autonomy* is there in your job? That is, to what extent does your job permit you to decide *on your own* how to go about doing the work?

Respondents rate their answers to these questions on a seven point scale. The JDS thus provides **operational definitions** (glossary) of the variables in the Job Characteristics Model. The core job dimensions are *independent variables*, and critical psychological states and performance outcomes are *dependent variables* (see Chapter 1). Growth need strength is a mediating variable in this causal chain. The JDS can be used to establish how motivating a job is, by calculating the motivating potential score (MPS), from answers across groups of employees on the same job.

The MPS is calculated using the values of the variables measured by the JDS:

Motivating potential score
an indicator of how motivating a job is likely to be for an individual, considering skill variety, task identity, task significance, autonomy and feedback.

$$\text{MPS} = \frac{(\text{skill variety} + \text{task identity} + \text{task significance})}{3} \times \text{autonomy} \times \text{feedback}$$

The first part of this equation concerns aspects of the job. The second part concerns how the work is managed. Autonomy and feedback are more important than the other dimensions. The equation reflects this by treating them as two separate components. Only the arithmetic mean of the ratings for skill variety, task identity, and task significance is used. If one of the three main components – job aspects, autonomy, feedback – is low, then the MPS will be low. A near-zero rating on either autonomy or feedback, for example, would pull the score down disproportionately (five times zero equals zero). A near-zero rating on task variety, identity or significance would not have much impact on the overall score. The five core dimensions stimulate three psychological states critical to high work motivation, job satisfaction and performance. These critical psychological states are:

1. *Experienced meaningfulness*: the extent to which the individual considers the work to be meaningful, valuable and worthwhile.

2. *Experienced responsibility*: the extent to which the individual feels accountable for the work output.

3. *Knowledge of results*: the extent to which individuals know and understand how well they are performing.

Jobs with high MPS are more likely to lead to the experience of critical psychological states than jobs with low scores. Expectancy theorists argue that all three critical states must be present if the personal and work outcomes on the right hand side of the model are to be achieved. One or two is not good enough. The MPS is only a guide to how motivating a job will be because different employees can have different perceptions of the same job. Those who put a low value on personal growth (revealed by a low GNS score) will not respond as the model suggests. No point, then, in offering them enriched jobs, unless one believes that the experience of personal development can in itself stimulate future growth need.

The model also shows how the motivating potential of jobs can be improved by applying five *implementing concepts*. These (including vertical loading, from Herzberg) are:

1. Combine tasks

Give employees more than one part of the work to do. This increases variety, and allows the individual to make a greater contribution to the product or service. For example, train call centre staff to handle a range of customer problems rather than specializing in a few areas.

2. Form natural work units

Give employees meaningful patterns of work. This increases individual contribution and task significance. For example, create teams which build the whole motor car engine, rather than assigning individual assembly workers to fragmented and repetitive tasks.

3. Establish client relationships

Give employees responsibility for personal contacts. This increases variety, gives the person freedom in performing the work, and also increases feedback. For example, staff working in a hospital pharmacy can deal directly with staff and patients on nominated wards, rather than responding on the basis of 'first come first served by whoever is free at the time'.

4. Vertical loading

Give employees responsibilities normally allocated to supervisors:

work scheduling	work methods	problem-solving
quality checks	training others	cost control
work times and breaks	deciding priorities	recruitment decisions

This gives individuals more autonomy, by removing the supervisory role, or redesigning it to involve other activities, such as training, coaching and liaising with other departments.

5 Open feedback channels

Give employees performance summaries and corporate information, as well as establishing client relationships. This improves opportunities for feedback of results. Feedback tells people how well they are doing, and provides a basis for improvement.

"But I must have a bone!
I need incentivising."

Source: www.cartoonstock.com

High performance hi-fi

Linn Products, based in Glasgow in Scotland, makes top of the range audio equipment. Despite the engineering sophistication and complexity, every product is assembled by hand, by a single employee. The company's founder and executive chairman, Ivor Tiefenbrun, explains why he abandoned the traditional assembly line in favour of 'single-stage build':

> Early on, we did use an assembly line and tried to operate like a mini General Motors. But try as I might, I couldn't get all the manufacturing processes to synchronize efficiently. So, one day, I asked one of the women on the turntable assembly line to collect all the parts of the product, assemble it, and bring it to me. She looked at me a little strangely, went and gathered the components, and assembled the turntable in 17 and a half minutes – a process that took 22 and a half minutes on the line.

> That was an 'aha' moment for me. We reorganized the factory to accommodate a single-stage build model, using computer-controlled vehicles to distribute materials to work positions, and taught everyone in the plant how to build any product we made. That way, we could do real-time manufacturing, let customer orders pull, reconfigure the factory, and shift resources as needed to produce what customers wanted that day.

> When one person builds a product from start to finish, they feel responsible for it and can see the connection between what they do and how the product performs. And since the people who build the products are often responsible for servicing them later, those employees interact with customers and see how happy – or unhappy – they are. So, they're learning a lot more than just how to assemble a product. They start to spot connections that no engineer, service technician, or assembly-line worker every would, and bring skills developed in one area to bear on what they do somewhere else. As a result, they can contribute to product quality with improvements and innovation.

Source: The Linn Klimax System

The Linn Artikulat speaker system

From Morse (2006).

Can the theory and practice of job enrichment now be abandoned? On the contrary. The language and the method have become a taken-for-granted aspect of management practice. Applications of job enrichment are no longer novel, and pass unreported. The concept of job enrichment was 're-invented' by Timothy Butler and James Waldroop (1999) with the label 'job sculpting'. This approach first identifies what interests and challenges people; applying new technology, developing theories and concepts, mentoring and counselling others, negotiating and persuading. Jobs, special assignments, and careeer paths can then be 'sculpted' to match those interests, enhance motivation and performance, and discourage people from leaving. They give the example of a bank lending officer, who was good at customer services but had an interest in theory and conceptual thinking; he was about to leave the company until it moved him to a role in competitive analysis and strategy formulation.

Topped with motivation

How can an organization motivate its top performing managers when they don't want to be promoted out of their operational roles? A successful company with an annual turnover of £255 million and profits over £42 million, Pizza Express has this problem with its 'A-list' restaurant managers, the stars who prefer the front line to a more boring senior role. If they are neglected, and leave to join the competition, they are difficult to replace.

In 2007, the company launched its *Exploration* programme, in which A-list restaurant managers are invited to pitch their innovative ideas to a senior management panel. Their human resources director, Julie MacDonald, explained:

> When we talked to the top restaurant managers about what sort of development they wanted, lots of them said they were really passionate about something. These are the people who have strong opinions and want to influence the business, but the business hasn't been engaging with them. The programme will give them the opportunity to develop a passion.

The manager presents the idea, its benefits, how it will work, and what it will cost. This could involve learning about Italian wine or developing new promotional activities, for example. The panel includes their line manager, the human resources director, the finance director, and another company director. The panel decide on the spot whether or not to fund the idea and 'just to ratchet up the tension a bit further', the meeting is filmed. A second component of the *Exploration* programme is an 'A-Club', creating a network of top restaurant managers who share ideas through regular business meetings and social events, from visiting a cookery school to reviewing the hourly pay structure for restaurant staff. The third element is a personal and professional development programme designed to strengthen key management competencies such as local marketing, sales growth, and teambuilding.

Based on Syedain (2007).

Empowerment, engagement and high performance

Practice in many organizations has gone beyond the enrichment of individual jobs, to focus on teamworking, organizational culture change, and other forms of employee empowerment. In the 1960s, an executive of American Telephone and Telegraph, concerned about low levels of staff commitment to the company, complained that, 'we have lost too many people who are still with us' (Ford, 1969). AT&T employees expected interesting, meaningful work, which was not on offer, and performance consequently suffered. Those expectations do not appear to have changed. A well-educated, media-informed, knowledge-based workforce, conscious of individual rights and social comparisons, is much less willing to tolerate bureaucratic control, and is ready to challenge management decisions and actions.

Empowerment organizational arrangements that give employees more autonomy, discretion, and decision-making responsibility.

As a result, many organizations during the 1990s reconsidered job enrichment and other approaches to improve quality of working life, through employee **empowerment**. This has more recently been linked to the related concept of employee **engagement**.

Specific techniques for improving motivation and performance through empowerment and engagement, fall into two broad categories: individual job enrichment, and self-managing or autonomous teamwork. This chapter focuses on individual motivation and jobs. Chapter 12 explores teamwork. These approaches converge in the **high performance work system**.

Engagement the extent to which people enjoy and believe in what they do, and feel valued for doing it.

The features of high performance work systems were first explored by Peter Vaill (1982, p.25). Organizations, or groups, are a high performance system if they:

1. Perform excellently against a known external standard.

2. Perform beyond what is assumed to be their potential best.

3. Perform excellently in relation to what they did before.

4. Are judged by observers to be substantially better than comparable groups.

High performance work system a form of organization that operates at levels of excellence far beyond those of comparable systems.

5. Are achieving levels of performance with fewer resources than necessary.

6. Are seen to be exemplars, as a source of ideas and inspiration.

7. Are seen to achieve the ideals of the culture.

8. Are the only organizations that have been able to do what they do at all, even though it might seem that what they do is not so difficult or mysterious.

Do we need more empowerment?

Toby Wall and Stephen Wood argue that empowerment can be an effective management tool. Their study of 80 manufacturing companies found that empowerment had a more significant impact on organizational performance than new technology, or research and development. Empowerment works best where there is uncertainty in the production process, and employees have to deal with variable demands and ambiguity. Where jobs are routine, output is unaffected by empowerment, which improves individual performance by encouraging new ideas, and by allowing employees to work more effectively. Empowerment itself is not motivating. The research also revealed international differences:

management preferences (per cent)	Britain	Japan	Australia	Switzerland
empowerment	23	21	34	47
team working	35	22	45	50
total quality management	42	61	55	54
just-in-time methods	41	40	39	61

Based on Wall and Wood (2002).

Engagement

Employers clearly want employees who are motivated and committed, who identify with their employing organization, and who are prepared to 'go the extra mile' at work. This may have become a problem, with increasing work intensity, longer working hours, and a growing concern for work-life balance. The contemporary term for this combination of attributes is *engagement*, which means more than just motivation or job satisfaction. Can engagement be measured, and what steps can management take to enhance engagement? Commitment and 'organizational citizenship' can be measured with attitude surveys, and the results can become the basis for appropriate action to strengthen engagement and employee performance.

Lucy McGee of the consultancy organization DDI argues that it is just as important to select employees who are more likely to become engaged, as it is to increase the engagement of existing staff. From cross-sectoral research involving around 4,000 employees, six characteristics are believed to predict the probability of individual applicants becoming engaged employees. The characteristics that identify 'engagement readiness' are:

adaptability	openness to new ideas, willingness to change approach
passion for work	maintaining positive view despite stress and frustration
emotional maturity	customer focus under fire, results before ego
positive disposition	eagerness to help others, outstanding teamwork
self-efficacy	confidence in one's ability
achievement orientation	the need to succeed and to excel

It is important to establish 'job fit', with work that the candidate enjoys [see our earlier discussion of job sculpting]. Ability to do a job does not necessarily mean that the person will be committed to that work for any length of time. Using a combination of 'career battery' psychometric questionnaires and situational interviews (asking candidates how they would handle typical work problems), an organization can increase the probability of employing engaged employees who are not only high performers, but who are also more likely to be good coaches, effective salespeople, and strong team players.

Based on Emmott (2006); McGee (2006).

Table 9.7: QWL versus HPWS

QWL in the 1970s	HPWS today
aimed to reduce costs of absenteeism and labour turnover and increase productivity	aims to improve organizational flexibility and product quality for competitive advantage
autonomy improves quality of work experience and job satisfaction	empowerment and engagement improve skill, decision-making, and adaptability
focused on repetitive manual and office work	focuses on challenging knowledge work
had little impact on management roles	redefinition of management roles
'quick fix' applied to problematic groups	takes time to change attitudes and behaviour
most employees broadly want the same kinds of things from work	need to cater for a wide range of individual differences in interests and expectations

Are the claims for high performance work systems justified? A recent UK report describes how organizations adopting high performance practices perform better than those which do not (CIPD, 2008). While work redesign methods have remained the same, and theories of motivation have seen little development since the 1980s, the organizational context to which these theories and techniques are applied has changed dramatically. The distinctions between the quality of working life (QWL) approach, and the high performance work systems (HPWS) approach are summarized in Table 9.7.

Empowerment has become a broad term applied to any arrangements which pass decision-making responsibilities from managers to lower-level employees. Tim Claydon and Mike Doyle (1996) argue that empowerment is more myth than reality, as changes introduced under this heading are often cosmetic, and managers are reluctant to relinquish their power. Have competitive pressures and the need to cut costs, improve quality, and enhance flexibility eroded that management reluctance? Anna Psoinos and Steve Smithson (2002) surveyed the human resource managers of the top 450 manufacturing companies in Britain. The findings suggest that empowerment is widely developed. Of the 103 companies which replied:

- 91 (88 per cent) had introduced changes that could lead to empowerment, such as delayering, downsizing, total quality management, and process re-engineering;

- of those 91 companies, 79 (87 per cent) delegated decisions to lower level staff, such as quality responsibility, problem-solving, job and shift allocations, quality control, production and maintenance scheduling, and plant modifications and improvements;

- of those 79 companies, 25 per cent said that empowerment had been unsuccessful, while 18 per cent said information was not available, or that it was too soon to tell;

- empowerment was successful in 60 per cent of companies where it had been used.

One manager said (p.139):

I think empowerment to [this company] is actually giving employees flexibility and the room to manoeuvre, to actually do their job and to do their job to a high standard. It's about providing them with the right training, providing them with the right skills and the right tools to actually look at their job and see how they're doing their job, and are they doing their job in the best way. And giving them scope to actually make decisions and have some impact on what they're doing.

However, another manager argued:

That doesn't mean to say that everybody can do what they like. You've got to have a process to say yes, this is a good idea, and you put it in, in a way that enables you to control the changes.

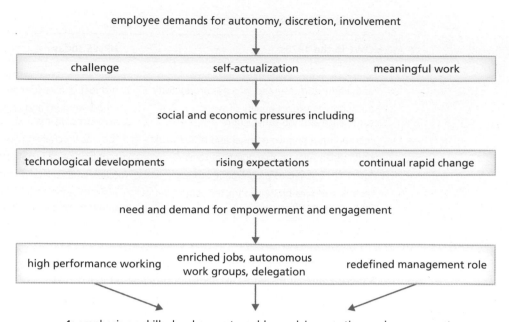

Figure 9.5: The case for high performance work systems

The main reasons for introducing empowerment concerned quality, productivity, flexibility and cost reduction, not concern for quality of working life. The main constraints on empowerment were traditional job and status demarcations, hierarchical structures, organization culture, middle management resistance, and complex production systems.

The argument of this chapter is summarized in Figure 9.5. This begins with demands for involvement and autonomy in work, and with the challenge and personal development that we desire. These needs seek fulfilment in contexts facing multiple socio-economic pressures. Addressing these needs and pressures involves job enrichment, self-managing teamwork, and other approaches to empowerment. The emphasis on personal development and continuous improvement helps to promote adaptability, product quality and customer care, thus increasing organizational effectiveness and quality of working life.

STOP AND THINK

Some commentators argue that job enrichment, high performance work systems and empowerment are a radical transformation in organization design and in management-employee relationships.

Other commentators argue that these approaches are cosmetic, having no effect on the power and reward inequalities and exploitation in contemporary organizations.

Given your own experience of work, which view do you support?

RECAP

1. *Understand different ways in which the term motivation is used.*

   - Motivation can refer to desired goals which we as individuals have or acquire.
   - Motivation can refer to the individual decision-making process through which goals are chosen and pursued.
   - Motivation can refer to social influence attempts to change the behaviour of others.

2. *Understand the nature of motives and motivation processes as influences on behaviour.*

   - Motives as desirable goals can be innate (drives) or acquired (socially learned).
   - Content theories of motivation explain behaviour in terms of innate drives and acquired motives.
   - Equity theory explains motivation in terms of perceived injustice or unfairness.
   - Expectancy theory explains motivation in terms of valued outcomes and the subjective probability of achieving those outcomes.
   - Goal-setting theory explains behaviour in terms of goal difficulty and goal specificity.
   - Inner work life theory explains behaviour in terms of the interactions between perceptions, motives, and emotions.

3. *Use expectancy theory and job enrichment to diagnose organizational problems and to recommend solutions.*

   - A job will only be motivating if it leads to rewards which the individual values.
   - Rewards motivate high performance when the link between effort and reward is clear.
   - Hygiene factors can overcome dissatisfaction but do not lead to motivation.

   - Content factors lead to job satisfaction, motivation and high performance.
   - Jobs can be enriched by applying vertical job loading factors.
   - The motivating potential of a job can be increased by improving skill variety, task identity, task significance, autonomy and feedback.
   - Job enrichment will not improve the performance of individuals with low growth need strength.

4. *Explain the continuing contemporary interest in this field, with respect to extreme jobs, boreout, and high performance work systems.*

   - Some people are motivated by extreme jobs, working long hours under pressure, for the adrenaline rush, high pay, status and power, but with personal and social problems.
   - For some office workers, their jobs are so uninteresting and lacking in challenge that they suffer boreout, becoming drained and unenthusiastic, devoting their time to the appearance of working hard, while surfing the internet and chatting to colleagues.
   - An educated, informed, knowledge-based workforce expects more participation in management decisions and opportunities for self-development.
   - In a rapidly changing competitive business environment, organizations need to motivate employees to be flexible, adaptable, committed and creative, not just to turn up on time and follow instructions.
   - High performance work systems use combinations of individual job enrichment, autonomous team-working, facilitative, coaching supervisory style, and other forms of delegation to empower lower-level employees.

Revision

1. What is an extreme job? Why would anyone want to live and work like this? What are the benefits of costs of holding an extreme job?

2. What are the causes and implications of boreout? What steps can management take to reduce or prevent boreout among office staff?

3. Explain the distinction between content and process theories of motivation. Give an example of a content theory of motivation and describe the implications for organizational practice. What are the limitations of this approach in practice?

4. How does equity theory explain motivation and behaviour, and how can equity theory be used to diagnose and improve employee motivation?

Research assignment

Linn Products is cited in this chapter as a company that uses job enrichment successfully in the manufacture of its hi-fi products. Their website is: www.LinnProducts.net. Linn also has its own record label: www.LinnRecords.com. Check out the company's websites:

- How does Linn describe the kinds of work that they provide?
- What about the working conditions?
- Their terms and conditions of employment?
- Personal development and career opportunities?

What does this tell you about the company's approach to employee motivation? What is the balance between intrinsic and extrinsic motivation? Is that what you expected to find?

Repeat this assessment with another organization of your own choice. Prepare a report describing the similarities and differences in approach to employee motivation in these two organizations, concluding with an assessment of which one you would choose on the basis of this information if both were to offer you employment.

Springboard

Bassett-Jones, N. and Lloyd, G.C., 2005, 'Does Herzberg's motivation theory have staying power?', *Journal of Management Development*, 24(10): 929–43.

Presents the results of a survey of employee attitudes, finding that money and recognition are not primary sources of motivation. Factors linked to intrinsic satisfaction were found to be more important. This is consistent with Herzberg's predictions, and the researchers conclude that his theory still has utility half a century after it was developed.

Burke, R.J. and Cooper, C.L. (eds), 2008, *The Long Work Hours Culture: Causes, Consequences and Choices*, Emerald Group Publishing, Bingley.

Some observers claim that we have developed a 'long work hours culture' which some workaholics enjoy. But working long hours creates health and domestic problems. Using recent research, this book examines what motivates people to work long hours, and explores the costs and benefits.

Chartered Institute of Personnel and Development, 2008, *High Performance Working Factsheet*, London: Chartered Institute for Personnel and Development.

Describes the components of high performance working, how to implement the approach, common barriers and how to overcome them, citing examples and further references.

Pinder, C.C., 2008, *Work Motivation in Organizational Behaviour*, Psychology Press/Taylor & Francis, Hove, East Sussex (2nd edn).

Comprehensive overview of the development of motivation theories. Emphasizes how behaviour at work is shaped by a range of factors including frustration and violence, love and sex, and power – topics which most treatments of motivation ignore. Just the text for that module assignment.

OB in films

Tough culture

Enron: The Smartest Guys in the Room (2005, director Alex Gibney): DVD track 4, 0:17:00 to 0:23:00 (6 minutes). Clip begins at the start of this track; clip ends when the trader says, 'Well I'll stomp on the guy's throat.'

The collapse of Enron is one of the largest corporate scandals in twenty-first century America. We are introduced in this clip to senior executive Jeff Skilling, hired by company president Kenneth Lay because he saw Skilling as a visionary, as 'a man with a big idea'.

1. How would you describe Jeff Skilling's management style?
2. What effect does he have on employee motivation?
3. Jeff's view of human motivation is based on competition, greed, and 'survival of the fittest'. He introduces the Performance Review Committee system which applies a 'rank and yank' approach to staff appraisals. What are the advantages and disadvantages of this system, for managers, and for employees?

 ## OB in literature

The Gum Thief, by Douglas Coupland, Random House/Vintage Canada, Toronto, 2007. This novel is set in Vancouver, Canada. What does this story tell us about (a) the intrinsic and extrinsic rewards from working in an office supplies store (*Staples*), (b) the problems created by employing older and younger workers in the same kinds of job, and (c) the issues raised where full time and part time employees work side by side?

CHAPTER EXERCISES

Chris and Pat compare salaries

Objectives
1. to identify factors affecting pay decisions.
2. to understand the complexity of pay determination.
3. to distinguish between legal and illegal bases for pay decisions.
4. to distinguish between wise and unwise pay decisions.

Briefing
- Form groups of four or five.
- Read the *Chris and Pat compare salaries* briefing.
- Individually, list all the reasons you can think of why Chris and Pat earn different salaries. You can include reasons that may be legal or illegal, wise or unwise.
- As a group, combine your reasons, where possible adding to them, so that your group list contains 20 items.

→

Chris and Pat compare salaries

Chris Clements and Pat Palmer are both computer programmers. One day, they find out that Chris earns £31,750 a year while Pat earns £40,100. Chris is surprised and says, 'I can't think of any reasons why we should be paid so differently'. Pat replies, 'I can think of at least 20 reasons'.

Based on Renard (2008).

The teaching assistant's job

I am a teaching assistant, and I work in the same primary school class every day. Although the class teacher is responsible for the whole class, after discussion with her I have identified a number of children who need extra help with spelling, reading and/or maths. While the teacher works with the rest of the class, I work with those who need the extra help, usually for short periods, individually or in small groups. I diagnose their needs, teach them, encourage them, assess them, record their results, celebrate with them when they make progress, and set them new targets. The children enjoy having more adult attention, and usually work very hard in these sessions with me. As well as this work, I support the class generally across all subjects including art, dance, geography, science, and other subjects as necessary.

For part of each day, one girl with special needs is not supported by either the class teacher or a teaching assistant. So I keep an eye on her, and if necessary take her away from the main class for some quiet time. Because I do this, the class teacher is able to concentrate on the rest of the class. This is not part of my job, and on occasions I have looked after the girl for the whole day when her own teaching assistant was absent. However, this has never been acknowledged by the class teacher or by the school's head teacher. It is very hard work as the girl's behaviour can be extremely challenging. It would be nice to have even a very small word of thanks. And I don't really know what effect my support is having on this girl.

Analysis

1. From this account, estimate the Motivating Potential Score (MPS) for the teaching assistant's job using this rating scale: 5 = high, 3 = medium, and 1 = low*:

$$MPS = \frac{(\text{skill variety} + \text{task identity} + \text{task significance})}{3} \times \text{autonomy} \times \text{feedback}$$

2. What advice can you give that would lead to an increase in the MPS for this job?

* Reminder: the core job dimensions in this model are:

1. *Skill variety*: does the job make use of different skills and abilities?

2. *Task identity*: does the job involve a 'whole' and meaningful piece of work?

3. *Task significance*: does the job affect the work of others?

4. *Autonomy*: does the job provide independence and discretion?

5. *Feedback*: is performance information related back to the individual?

Part 3 Groups and teams in the organization

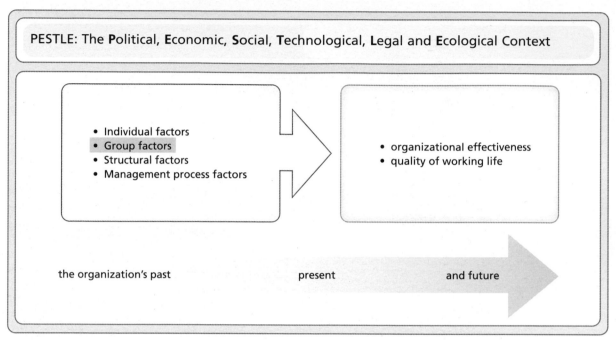

PESTLE: The **P**olitical, **E**conomic, **S**ocial, **T**echnological, **L**egal and **E**cological Context

- Individual factors
- Group factors
- Structural factors
- Management process factors

- organizational effectiveness
- quality of working life

the organization's past   present   and future

A field map of the organizational behaviour terrain

Introduction

Part 3, Groups and teams in the organization, explores the following four topics:

- *Group formation*, in Chapter 10
- *Group structure*, in Chapter 11
- *Individuals in groups*, in Chapter 12
- *Teamworking*, in Chapter 13

These topics reflect the progress of collections of people over time in organizational contexts. A number of individuals may informally develop into a group, or a team can be formally set up by management. Groups and teams often develop their own internal structures, which allow members to work together more effectively. Groups influence the attitudes and behaviours of their members, and individuals, in turn, can affect the group as a whole. Management's aim is to get individuals working together as a single, cohesive, productive unit. Groups and teams offer a distinct but related level of analysis, between the individual and the organization structure and its processes.

Invitation to see

This image from *The Times* (27 February 2009) shows a surgeon and his team in an operating theatre. This illustrated an article explaining how America and Britain could learn from the healthcare system in Switzerland. The caption read, 'the medical insurance system operating in Switzerland depends on teamwork between state and private sector'.

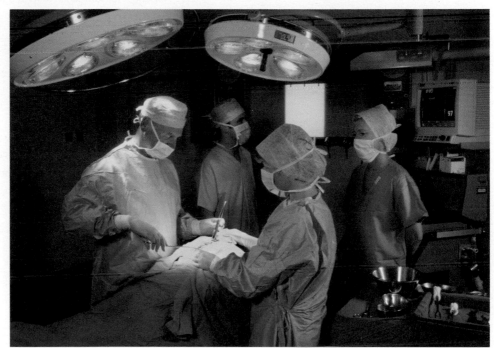

Source: Vince Bevan/Alamy

Surgical team in operating theatre

1. **Decoding**   Look at this image closely. Note in as much detail as possible what messages you feel that it is trying to convey. Does it tell a story, present a point of view, support an argument, perpetuate a myth, reinforce a stereotype, challenge a stereotype?

2. **Challenging**   To what extent do you agree with the messages, stories, points of view, arguments, myths, or stereotypes in this image? Is this image open to challenge, to criticism, or to interpretation and decoding in other ways, revealing other messages?

3. **Sharing**   Compare with colleagues your interpretation of this image. Explore explanations for differences in your respective decodings.

What would you do? You're the adviser

Obesity has become a social problem, and not only in developed economies. Here is an example of how this can affect the workplace.

I am the human resources manager for a nationwide furniture manufacturer. Recently, an employee on our delivery team gained a lot of weight. We've received reports from his colleagues that he is having difficulty carrying furniture from the van into customers' properties. He is willing to do the work and is normally very hard-working. But we're concerned that his lack of fitness is adding to the risk of injury for his colleagues. One member of staff recently spent three weeks off work with a back injury, which colleagues say was caused partly by working with this person and his inability to carry our products.

His line manager has raised the issue but he has denied any problem. The manager argues that he is not capable of performing his duties, but we are not in a position to offer him another role. Are there grounds for dismissal or a requirement for him to improve his fitness? How can we be fair to him without exposing other members of the delivery team to health and safety risks?

As an external adviser, how would you advise the manager to deal with this problem, taking into account the needs of the individual, his colleagues, and the organization as a whole?

From 'Troubleshooter', People Management, *4 September, 2008, pp.46–47.*

Chapter 10 Group formation

Key terms

group	Human Relations approach
group dynamics	formal group
aggregate	informal group
additive task	group self-organization
conjunctive task	activities
disjunctive task	interactions
the Hawthorne effect	sentiments

Learning outcomes

When you have read this chapter, you should be able to define those key terms in your own words, and you should also be able to:

1. List the key characteristics of a group.
2. Distinguish between different types of group tasks.
3. Name the four research phases of the Hawthorne studies.
4. Distinguish between a formal and an informal group.
5. Outline Homans' theory of group formation.
6. Enumerate the five stages of Tuckman and Jensen's model of group development.
7. Summarize Katzenbach and Santamaria's distinction between a team and a single-leader working group.

Why study groups?

Marion Hampton (1999, p.113) summarized both the symbolic and practical aspects of groups:

> Groups embody many important cultural values of Western society: teamwork, co-operation, a collective that is greater than the sum of its parts, informality, egalitarianism and even the indispensability of the individual member. Groups are seen as having a motivating, inspiring influence on the individual, drawing the best out of him or her, enabling him or her to perform feats that would be beyond him or herself as a detached individual. Groups can have a healing effect on individuals, bolstering their self-esteem and filling their lives with meaning.

Groups play an important role in our lives. It has been estimated that the average person belongs to five or six different groups and about 92 per cent of members are in groups of five people or less. These may include the quality control circles, new product teams, the local women's groups and sports teams. The terms 'groups' and 'teams' are often used interchangeably. People join groups because of common needs, interests or goals, physical proximity or cultural similarity, or may be assigned to them by management. Much organizational work is performed in teams, and McGrath's (1984) circumplex model classifies eight different group tasks (Figure 10.1) (Arrow and McGrath, 1995).

Group performance thus affects the success of the organization as a whole. Being able to work productively with others is so important that companies place an emphasis on their recruits being good 'team players'. To ensure this, they invest in team development activities to develop their teamworking abilities. Hayes (1997, p.1) noted that,

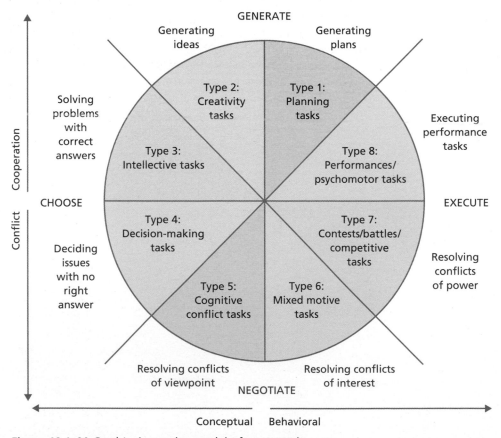

Figure 10.1: McGrath's circumplex model of group tasks

Source: From Forsyth (2006). Modified from MCGRATH, GROUPS: INTERACTION AND PERFORMANCE, 1st Edition, © 1984, p.61. Reprinted by permission of Pearson Education, Inc., Upper Saddle River, NJ.

To an ever-increasing extent, modern management has become focused on the idea of the team. Management consultants propose organizational restructuring to facilitate teamwork; directors make policy statements about the importance of the team to the organization; and senior managers exhort their junior staff to encourage team working in their departments.

Head hunters are increasingly being asked to assemble teams of top executives, and the bosses themselves are expected to be good at putting together teams (Nadler *et al.*, 2006).

Teams and knowledge production

A study that investigated 19.9 million research papers published over five decades and 2.1 million patents showed that teams increasingly outperform solo authors in the production of knowledge. Research is increasingly done in teams across nearly all fields. Teams typically produce more frequently cited research than individuals do, a trend that that has been increasing over time. Teams now also produce the exceptionally high-impact research, even where that distinction was once the domain of solo authors. These findings apply to sciences and engineering, social sciences, arts and humanities, and patents, suggesting that the process of knowledge creation has fundamentally changed.

Wuchty et al. *(2007).*

It has been argued that the modern organization is no longer a collection of individuals, but rather a network of interconnected teams (Kozlowski and Bell, 2003). Group working and teamworking has been an aspect of organizational life for a long time, yet remains controversial. The management literature promotes the benefits of group working, and stresses the commonality of interests between individual workers, organized by management into teams, and the goals of the 'organization as a whole', that is, of senior management. Critics, in contrast, contend that the extent of group-management conflict has been misinterpreted, underplayed or simply ignored.

"Individuals can and do make a difference, but it takes teamwork to really mess things up."

Source: www.cartoonstock.com

To boldly go . . . in groups

Source: EJA/NASA

Perhaps the most fictional aspect of the classic science fiction TV and film series, *Star Trek*, was how well the crew members got on with each other despite being in such close proximity in the spaceship for years. Here on Earth, Anatoly Perminov, the head of the Russian space agency, Roskosmos, revealed Russia's intention of building an inhabited space station on the moon by 2032, as a prelude to launching a manned mission to Mars. The estimated duration of a round trip to Mars, including a stay on the surface, is five hundred days. This would be as much of a psychological as a technical challenge. In preparation for this, Roskosmos and the European Space Agency (ESA) have placed three groups of six volunteers into sealed, simulation modules called *Mars-500* in Moscow's Institute of Biological Problems. Like the contestants on the TV show *Big Brother*, the subjects are ordered to complete tasks. They will be monitored for two years, to determine the effects of separation and close proximity living. During a similar experiment in IBP's *Mars Flyer* isolation chamber in 1999, two Russian cosmonauts broke into a fist fight, spluttering blood on the module walls. One of them then pressed unwelcome kisses on a Canadian crew member.

Russians psychologists claim that cosmonauts can develop 'space dementia'; become clinically depressed; and suffer from 'asthenisation', which causes irritability, low energy and leads crew members to get on badly with each other. Nick Kanas of the University of California investigated interactions between space crew and their mission controllers on the ground of *Mir* (the Soviet Union's first space station); *Skylab* (NASA's first station) and the current International Space Station (ISS). He found that the way crew coped with stress was to blame the ground staff. They converted tensions on board into feelings that the people on Earth did not care. One Skylab crew became so annoyed with mission control during its 84 days in space that they mutinied, sulked and turned off all communications. Psychologists are unsure whether a Mars mission should be crewed entirely by women (they are less likely to commit suicide or murder each when irritable); be mixed (the sexes would support each other); or consist of psychologically robust and less libidinous robots.

Based on Baker (2007); The Economist (2007b); BBC Radio 4 (2008); Wood (2001).

STOP AND THINK

Suggest reasons why group working has become so popular in organizations.

In what ways does it benefit individual employees? How does it improve organizational performance?

Definitions of groups

Group two or more people, in face-to-face interaction, each aware of their group membership and interdependence, as they strive to achieve their goals.

Interpersonal behaviour builds up into group behaviour that in turn sustains and structures future interpersonal relations. The term **group** is thus reserved for people who consider themselves to be part of an identifiable unit, who relate to each other in a meaningful fashion and who share dispositions through their shared sense of collective identity. Researchers often refer to these as *psychological groups* (Johnson and Johnson, 2008). Groups affect the behaviour of the individuals who compose them. For this reason, social psychologists study internal **group dynamics**. They ask how members of a group communicate with each other and coordinate their activities; how they influence each other; what roles they play in the group; what kind of relationships they have; which members lead, and which follow, how they balance a focus on their task with social issues; and how they resolve conflicts (see Figure 10.2).

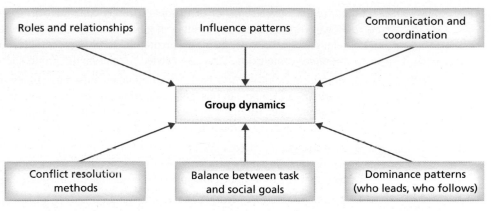

Figure 10.2: Group dynamics

STOP AND THINK

Why would only *one* of the following be considered to be a group? In what circumstances could one of the other aggregates become a group?

(a) People riding on a bus

(b) Blonde women between 20 and 30 years of age

(c) Members of a football team

(d) Audience in a theatre

(e) People sheltering in a shop doorway from the rain

Group dynamics the forces operating within groups that affect their performance and their members' satisfaction.

Aggregate a collection of unrelated people who happen to be in close physical proximity for a short period of time.

It is important to maintain a distinction between mere aggregates of individuals and what are called groups. The latter are so called because they exist not only through the (often visible) interactions of members, but also in the (not observable) perceptions of their members. In the Stop and Think example, only the football team would fulfil our criteria for a group, and we can usefully distinguish it from an **aggregate**. Aggregates are individuals who happen to be collected together at any particular time. Like the bus travellers, theatre audience or rain shelterers, they do not relate to one another in any meaningful fashion, nor consider themselves a part of any identifiable unit, despite their temporary physical proximity. By the same token, the definition allows one to exclude classes of people who may be defined by physical attributes, geographical location, economic status or age. Even though a trade union in an organization may like to believe it is a group, it will fail to meet our definition if all of its members do not interact with each other, and if they are not aware of each other. This need for all members to interact has led to the suggestion that in practice, a psychological group is unlikely to exceed twelve or so persons. Beyond that number, the opportunity for frequent interaction between members and hence group awareness, is considerably reduced.

It is possible for small aggregates of people to be transformed into a group through outside circumstances. In fact, a whole series of 'disaster movies' in the cinema have been made in which people fight for their lives on board sinking ships, hijacked aeroplanes and burning skyscraper buildings. The story typically involves aggregates of people setting out at the start of the film. The danger causes them to interact with one another, and this increases their awareness of one another and leads them to see themselves as having common problems. By the end of the film, the survivors demonstrate all the characteristics of the group as defined here. The disaster movie example helps us to understand some of the characteristics of a group. Groups differ in the degree to which they possess the five characteristics discussed below. The more of them that they possess, the more a group will be recognized as such, and the more power it will have with which to influence its members.

A *minimum membership of two people:* Groups can range from two people to over 30. However, the greater the number of group members, the higher the number of possible relationships between them, the greater the level of communication that is required, and the more complex the structure needed to operate the group successfully.

A *communication network:* Each group member must be capable of communicating with every other member. In this communication process, the aims and purposes of the group are exchanged. The mere process of interaction satisfies some of our social needs, and it is used to set and enforce standards of group behaviour.

A *shared sense of collective identity.* Each member must identify with the other members of their group, and not see themselves as an individual acting independently. They must all believe themselves to be participants in the group which itself is distinct from other groups.

Complementary goals. Members have individual objectives which can only be met through membership of and participation in the group. Their goals may differ but are sufficiently complementary that members feel able to achieve them through participation in the group. They recognize the need to work collectively and not as individuals.

Group structure. Individuals in the group will have different roles e.g. initiator/ideas person, suggestion-provider, compromiser. These roles, which tend to become fixed, indicate what members expect of each other. Norms or rules exist which indicate which behaviours are acceptable in the group and which are not (e.g. smoking, swearing, latecoming).

Size matters

Big is not always beautiful. The more people at a meeting, the harder it is to get consensus. Meetings of over 20 people, without a show of hands, last interminably. Research by Peter Klimek, a physicist from the Medical University in Vienna, used a program that simulated decision-making by different sized committees. His findings have implications for political organizations. In 1967, the Labour Prime Minster, Harold Wilson, had 21 members in his cabinet, while 40 years later, Gordon Brown had 24 in his. Klimek recommends trimming the size of the cabinet. Once a committee grows in size to over 20 members, it is difficult for it to reach consensus because too many subgroups are formed. The chairman of Marks and Spencer agreed saying that the more people there were at a meeting, the harder it was to reach consensus. Large cabinet sizes are unstable. The Sri Lankan cabinet has 54 ministers. Klimek found that 10–15 members was the best number for a cabinet, such as those in Switzerland and Hungary. However, small can also be a problem. A meeting of eight people is the worst total for decision-making. It produces neither a consensus nor a majority view, and has the highest probability of becoming deadlocked.

Based on Taher (2009).

STOP AND THINK The groups to which you belong provide you with shared goals, a sense of identity and meet your social needs. However, can they also constrain your thinking, stifle your freedom of expression, limit your behaviour, restrict your freedom of expression? What is your opinion?

As the size and complexity of modern organizations has increased, the need to integrate the work of different groups within organizations has also grown. McLaren Racing is well known in Formula 1 competition. The company is divided into four groups – those who conceive the car, those who engineer it, those who manufacture it, and those who race it (Blitz, 2007). There are many benefits of group working:

- They allow organizations to develop and deliver products and services quickly and cost-effectively while maintaining quality.

- They enable organizations to learn and retain that learning, more effectively.

Table 10.1: Issues facing any work group

Issue	Questions
1. Atmosphere and relationships	What kinds of relationships should there be among members? How close and friendly, formal or informal?
2. Member participation	How much participation should be required of members? Some more than others? All equally? Are some members more needed than others?
3. Goal understanding and acceptance	How much do members need to *understand* group goals? How much do they need to *accept* to be *committed* to the goals? Everyone equally? Some more than others?
4. Listening and information sharing	How is information to be shared? Who needs to know what? Who should listen most to whom?
5. Handling disagreements and conflict	How should disagreements or conflicts be handled? To what extent should they be resolved? Brushed aside? Handled by dictate?
6. Decision-making	How should decisions be made? Consensus? Voting? One-person rule? Secret ballot?
7. Evaluation of member performance	How is evaluation to be managed? Everyone appraises everyone else? A few take the responsibility? Is it to be avoided?
8. Expressing feelings	How should feelings be expressed? Only about the task? Openly and directly?
9. Division of labour	How are task assignments to be made? Voluntarily? By discussion? By leaders?
10. Leadership	Who should lead? How should leadership *functions* be exercised? Shared? Elected? Appointed from outside?
11. Attention to process	How should the group monitor and improve its own process? Ongoing feedback from members? Formal procedures? Avoiding direct discussion?

From Cohen et al. *(1995, p.142).*

- Cross functional groups promote improved quality management.
- Cross-functional design groups can undertake effective process reengineering.
- Production time can be reduced if tasks performed concurrently by individuals, are performed concurrently by people in groups.
- Group-based organization promotes innovation because of the cross-fertilization of ideas.
- Organizations with flat structures can be monitored, co-ordinated and directed more effectively, if the functional unit is the group rather than the individual.
- Groups can better handle the rise in organizational information processing requirements caused by increasing complexity than individuals (Mohrman *et al.*, 1995).

Types of group tasks

Borrill and West (2005) reported research estimating that 88 per cent of the variation in a group's performance could be explained with reference to the task that it was asked to perform. As McGrath's circumflex model shows, group tasks vary in terms of the number of possible solutions; intrinsic interest; need for member co-operation; unitary versus divisible; conceptual or behavioural; and level of difficulty. Ivan Steiner (1972) classified group tasks on the basis of the type of interdependence that they required between their members.

Additive task a task whose accomplishment depends on the sum of all group members' efforts

Additive task

With this type of task, all group members do basically the same job, and the final group product or outcome (group performance) is the sum of all their individual contributions. The final outcome is roughly proportional to the number of individuals contributing. There is low interdependency between these people. A group working together will normally perform better than the same number of individuals working alone, provided that all group members make their contribution. Social loafing can, however, reduce performance on an additive task. Examples of additive tasks are tug-of-war contests, pedestrians giving a stalled car a push-start (Littlepage, 1991).

Conjunctive task

Conjunctive task a task whose accomplishment depends on the performance of the group's least talented member.

In this task, one member's performance depends on another's. There is high interdependency. Thus, a group's *least* capable member determines performance. A successful group project at university depends on one member finding the information, a second writing it up, and a third presenting it. All three elements are required for success and hence co-ordination is essential in conjunctive tasks. Groups perform less well on conjunctive tasks than lone individuals. Examples of conjunctive tasks include climbing a mountain, running a relay race, and playing chamber music (Steiner and Rajaratnam, 1961).

The hand over

Yves Morieux of the Boston Consulting Group observed that relay races were often won by teams whose members did not necessarily have the fastest individual times. Members of the medal-winning French women's Olympic relay team explained that, at some point, each had to decide whether to run their guts out, and literally be unable to see straight when they passed the baton, or whether they held something back, to make a better baton change, and thus enable their team mate to run a faster time. The value of this sort of decision-making, and each individual's contribution to the team, was beyond measure.

Based on Hindle (2006c, p.13).

Disjunctive tasks

In this type of task, once again, one member's performance depends on another's. Again there is high interdependency. However, this time, the group's *most* capable member determines its performance. Groups perform better than their average member on disjunctive tasks, since even the best performer will not know all the answers, and working with others helps to improve overall group performance. Diagnostic and problem-solving activities performed by a group would come into this category. Co-ordination is important here as well, but in the sense of stopping the others impeding the top performers (Diehl and Stroebe, 1991). Examples of disjunctive task performers are quiz teams (*University Challenge*, pub quiz) and a maintenance team in a nuclear power generating plant.

Disjunctive task a task whose accomplishment depends on the performance of the group's most talented member.

Groups will tend to outperform the same number of individuals working separately when working on disjunctive tasks, than on additive or conjunctive tasks. This is provided that the most talented member can convince the others of the correctness of their answer. The attitudes, feelings and conflicts in a group setting might prevent this from happening.

Team tasks and *Extreme Programming*

Give a computer programmer complete freedom and he or she will code in their own idiosyncratic way. When other programmers need to repair it, they have to pour over the indecipherable code of colleagues. In contrast, if you teach programmers some discipline, they will code logically and clearly. This is the idea behind extreme programming (XP). It was invented in 1996 by Kent Beck, Ward Cunningham and Ron Jeffries when they were working to rescue the Chrysler Comprehensive Compensation (C3) software project from collapse. They formulated a set of directions for keeping code 'elegantly written'. Among XP's tenets, is a rule forbidding any individual from taking sole responsibility for any piece of programming. Another rule specifies that programmers must work in pairs, on a single terminal, on each bit of code. A pair, cooperating in this way, has been found to work twice as fast, and think of more than twice as many solutions, as two programmers working separately. They achieve a higher level of defect prevention and removal, leading to a higher quality product. Since software developers treat programming methodologies as rules of personal ethics, XP has provoked heated debate. XP sceptics suggest that the best coders are probably 100 times more

productive than the worst, and stories of 'Top Gun', heroic (individual) programming which kept projects on schedule abound. The same critics add that pairing such 'cowboy coders' slows each one down, and undercuts the team's overall efficiency. In their defence, XP proponents argue that the approach saves money in future programming time because code changes can be made by anybody. Many companies are keen to adopt XP's 'group approach' to programming as it helps to develop products more quickly, more cost-effectively, while maintaining quality, and enabling organizations to retain their learning internally. Extreme measures, it appears, are good for extreme times.

Based on Ziegler (2003); Williams and Kessler (2000).

The Hawthorne studies

George Elton Mayo
(1880–1949)

Fritz Jules
Roethlisberger
(1898–1974)

The famous Hawthorne studies consisted of a series of experiments conducted during the 1920s and 1930s at the Hawthorne plant of the Western Electric Company, located in Cicero, Illinois, which manufactured telephones. They resulted in creation of the human relations approach to management. At that time, factories used natural daylight or candles to illuminate the workspace of their workers. In an attempt to promote the sales of light bulbs, the company paid for a series of experiments to try to demonstrate a positive correlation between the amount of light and worker productivity. The original experiments therefore examined the effect of physical changes – originally illumination – on worker productivity (Gillespie, 1991).

The initial experiments examined productivity improvements in terms of the effect of physical factors. Later, Professor George Elton Mayo of the Harvard Business School was invited to bring an academic research team into the factory. Team members included Fritz Jules Roethlisberger (who later become the first Professor of Organizational Behaviour (holding his post in the Harvard Business School)) and William J. Dickson. It was through their 1939 book, *Management and the Worker*, that the results of the Hawthorne studies were communicated to the world (Roethlisberger and Dickson, 1939). The Hawthorne research revolutionized social science thinking.

The illumination experiments (1924–1927)

These explored the relationship between the quality of illumination and efficiency. No correlation was found between production output obtained and the lighting provided. Production even increased when the light intensity was reduced. The conclusion was that lighting was only one of several factors affecting production, and perhaps a minor one. A different study, with fewer workers, was needed to control for the effect of any single variable.

Relay Assembly Test Room experiments (1927–1933)

These focused on questions of fatigue, rest pauses, length of working day and attitudes to their work and the company. Six, self-selected female workers, drawn from the regular workforce of the Relay Assembly Department were placed in a separate room for closer observation. They had been working a 48-hour week including Saturdays with no tea breaks. A researcher was placed in the room with them, kept a note of what happened, maintained a friendly atmosphere by listening to their complaints, and told them what was going on. A total of 13 time periods were studied during which changes were made to the womens' rest pauses, hours of work and refreshment breaks.

Relay Assembly Test Room, c.1929

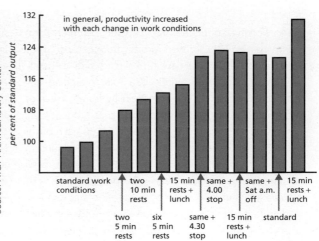

in general, productivity increased with each change in work conditions

Source: AT&T Archive&History Center
per cent of standard output

Source: Based on data from Roethlisberger and Dickson (1939). From *Behaviour in Organizations*, 6/E by Greenberg/Baron, © 1997. Reprinted by permission of Pearson Education, Inc. Upper Saddle River, NJ.

William J. Dickson (1904–1973)

The Hawthorne Effect the tendency of people being observed to behave differently than they otherwise would.

The results showed a nearly continuous increase in output over those 13 periods. This increase began when employee benefits such as rest periods, served lunches and early finishes were added, but was maintained even when these privileges were withdrawn and the women returned to their normal 48-hour week. The five reasons offered for the increases in output included:

1. the motivating effect of acquiring a special status through their selection for and involvement in the experiment;

2. the effect of participation as the women were consulted and informed by the experimenter;

3. the effect of observer friendliness which improved their morale;

4. a different and less intensive form of supervision which reduced their stress while increasing their productivity;

5. the self-selected nature of the group creating higher levels of mutual dependence and support appropriate for group working.

The increase in output due to the increased attention paid to employees in this study is now referred to as **The Hawthorne Effect**. It is defined as the tendency of people being observed, as part of a research effort, to behave differently than they otherwise would. Mayo and his colleagues became convinced that the women were not solely motivated by money or by improvements in their working conditions. Their attitudes towards and achievement of increased output seemed to be affected by the group to which they belonged. These results led management to study employee attitudes using an interviewing programme.

Interviewing programme (1928–1930)

To find out more about how employees felt about their supervisors and working conditions and how these related to morale, management instituted an interviewing programme involving over 20,000 interviews, which extended to family and social issues. These interviews also revealed the existence of many informal, gang-like groups within the formal working groups. Each had its own leaders and 'sidekicks' who controlled production output. Examining this became the focus of the next experiment.

Bank Wiring Observation Room experiments (1931–1932)

The interviews had revealed that groups exercised a great deal of control over the behaviour of their members. To find out more, a group of men were observed in another part of the company. The Bank Wiring Observation Room consisted of 14 men who were formally

Source: AT&T Archives and History Center

Men in the Bank Wiring Observation Room, c.1932

organized into three subgroups, each of which contained three wirers and one supervisor. In addition, two inspectors moved between the three groups. There were two major findings. First, the detailed observation of interactions between the men revealed the existence of two informal groups or 'cliques' within the three formal groups. The membership of these crossed the formal group boundaries.

Second, it was found that these cliques developed informal rules of behaviour or 'norms', as well as mechanisms to enforce these. The total figure for the week's production would tally with the total week's output, but the daily reports showed a steady, level output regardless of actual daily production. This group was operating below its capability and individual group members were not earning as much as they could. The norms under which the group operated were found to be the following (Roethlisberger and Dickson, 1939, p.522):

- You should not turn out too much work. If you do, you are a *rate-buster*.
- You should not turn out too little work. If you do, you are a *chisler*.
- You should not tell a supervisor anything that might get a colleague into trouble. If you do, you are a *squealer*.
- You should not attempt to maintain social distance or act officiously. If you are an inspector, for example, you should not act like one.

The researchers discovered that the Bank Wiring Observation Room men were afraid that if they significantly increased their output, the piece rate would be cut, and the daily output expected by management would increase. The men could be reprimanded and lay-offs might occur. To avoid this, the group members agreed between themselves, what was a fair day's output (neither too high nor too low). They enforced this informal output norm through a system of negative sanctions or punishments. These included:

- ridicule as when a group member was referred to as The Slave or Speed King;
- 'binging', which involved striking a norm-violator painfully on the upper arm or flicking his ear;
- total rejection or exclusion of the individual by the group as a whole.

Roethlisberger and Dickson (1939) wrote that, 'The social organization of the bankwiremen performed a twofold function (1) to protect the group from internal indiscretions and (2) to protect it from outside interference . . . nearly all the activities of this group can be looked upon as methods of controlling the behaviour of its members' (pp.523–24). These results showed that workers were more responsive to the social forces of their peer group than to the controls and incentives of management. Mayo concluded that:

- Work is a group activity and not just an individual activity.

- The social world of the adult is primarily patterned around work activities.

- At work, within their social group, people fulfil their needs for belonging and recognition, which enhances their productivity.

- A worker's complaint is a manifestation of a more basic, often psychological problem.

- Informal groups at work exercise strong social controls over the work habits and attitudes of individual workers.

- Managers need to collaborate with these informal groups to increase cohesion for the company's benefit.

Human Relations approach a school of management thought which emphasizes the importance of social processes at work.

Those conclusions led to the **Human Relations approach** to management which held that work should be a source of social relationships for individuals, a way of meeting their need for belonging, for group membership and even be a focus for their personal identity. As Rose noted (1988, p.104):

> Within work-based social relationships or groups . . . behaviour, particularly productivity or cooperativeness with management, was thought to be shaped and constrained by the worker's role and status in a group. Other informal sets of relationships might spring up within the formal organization as a whole. Modifying or overriding the official social structure of the factory which was based on purely technical criteria such as division of labour.

STOP AND THINK Reflect on the six reasons listed on p.306 to account for the increases in output among the women in the Relay Assembly Test Room. From your experience of participating or working in groups, which explanation seems (a) most and (b) least convincing to you? Why?

Group-oriented view of organizations

In his book, *The Social Problems of an Industrial Society*, Elton Mayo went on to propose a social philosophy which placed groups at the centre of our understanding of human behaviour in organizations (Mayo, 1945). He stressed the importance of informal groups, and encouraged managers to 'grow' them. He discussed *natural groups* of 3–6 workers and family *groups* of between 8–30 members. These would develop into one, large *organized group*, consisting of a plant-wide network of family groups, each with its own natural groups. Mayo's vision was of a community organization, in which all or most employees were members of well-knit, natural groups, which were linked together in common purpose. These were not the formal groups discussed earlier. Mayo invited managers to act somewhat like gardeners rather than engineers, and to use their skills, intelligence and experience, to deliberately integrate individuals within groups.

Another famous psychologist, Rensis Likert (1961) echoed the idea that organizations should be viewed and managed as a collection of groups rather than individuals. He felt that that group forces were important in both influencing the behaviour of individual work groups with regard to productivity, waste, absence and so on, and thus affected the performance of the entire organization. In his book chapter entitled, 'The principle of supportive relationships', Likert, like Mayo, attempted to derive a theory of organizational design with the group as the basic building block. He argued that:

Rensis Likert
(1903–1981)

1. work groups are important sources of individuals' need satisfaction;

2. groups in organizations that fulfil this psychological function are also more productive;

3. management's task is therefore to create effective work groups by developing 'supportive relationships';

Back to the future: Work as the new community?

Eighty years on from Mayo and the idea of the workplace taking on the functions of the community is back in vogue. For example, the workers at Google, the internet search engine company, are not offered a job but 'the chance to be part of a community of people doing meaningful work. It is not the role so much as belonging that is the key; employees are consumers of a collective experience.' Companies such as this allow staff to bring their children to work; play roller hockey; use the gym and sauna; have a massage or play the piano, all on company time and premises. Work it appears can give us friends, lovers, identity, childcare and dry cleaning. Researchers have documented a renewed appetite for community and belonging in Western democracies and 'corporate communities' and 'company families' are developing to fill the gap. Many social issues are currently being tackled through the suffix 'at work' – bullying, racism, stress, drugs. Some employers are acting as quasi-national states, offering healthcare, eye-tests and playgroups.

The work-as-community theory reflects the fact that employees spend more time at work than previous generations. For many staff, it is the most important thing in their lives. Arlie Hochschild suggests that individuals are working longer not because of employers' demands but because they find greater satisfaction at work than where they live. Work gives them order; a degree of stability; and involvement in teamwork, which replaces family relationships. In contrast, life at home is dys-functional and uncertain making work a place to which to escape. Critics respond by saying that in addition to applying to a tiny section of the professional middle class anyway, the work-as-community view merely betrays a desire to put a positive gloss on the long hours culture. It's a nice motherhood notion that makes work seem worthwhile.

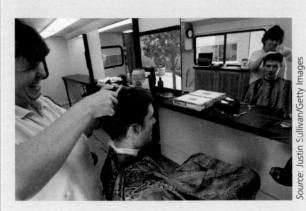

Source: Justin Sullivan/Getty Images

Based on Ignattius (2006); The Economist *(2007a); Cook (2008); Hochschild (1997).*

4. an effective organizational structure consists of democratic-participative work groups, each linked to the organization as a whole through overlapping memberships;

5. co-ordination is achieved by individuals who carry out 'linking functions'.

Likert is also remembered for proposing the concept of the overlapping group membership structure. This he termed a 'linking pin' process. The overlapping works vertically by having the leaders of related subordinate groups as members of the next higher group, with their common superior as leader and so on up the hierarchy. The organization is therefore conceived as consisting of many overlapping groups. This is shown in Figure 10.5. In his view, an organizational design based around groups rather than individuals, improves communications, increases co-operation, provides more team member commitment and produces faster decision-making.

While Likert's 'linking pin' concept focused on *vertical* co-ordination, today the stress is placed upon *horizontal* integration in the form of cross-functional teams. Nevertheless, most people in an organization are now members of several teams. This overlap of groups in organizations, due to matrix structures and cross functional team working, means that an individual can be a member of a project team and a geographical group, all at the same time. This will hinder their ability to identify with any one particular group.

Following Likert, a succession of academics and consultants have followed Mayo in promoting the cause of organizations-built-around-groups, rather than just including them. In the 1970s, Leavitt (1975) asked management to use small groups as the basic building blocks for an organization. Ouchi and Johnson (1978) echoed Mayo's thesis that people in

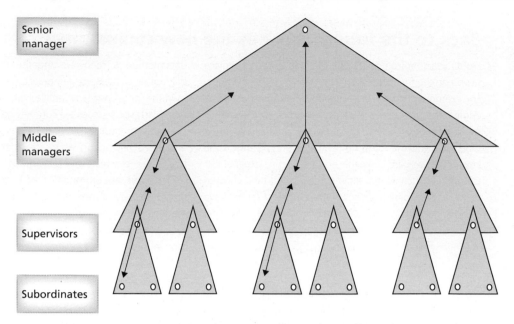

Figure 10.3: Rensis Likert's linking pin model

Source: Based on Likert (1961, p.105), copyright The McGraw Hill Companies Inc.

society lacked social support anchors which made life tolerable, and they recommended that large organizations should be organized around 'clans' (similar to Mayo's natural groups) which could provide the associational ties and cohesion for their employees. In the 1980s, Tom Peters (1987, p.296) said that, 'The modest-sized, task-oriented, semi-autonomous, mainly self-managing team should be the basic organization building block'. Finally, in the 1990s, team-based organizational models were proposed (see Chapter 17).

STOP AND THINK

You have accepted a job and your new employer tells you that you will become 'part of the team', and a 'member of one big happy family here'.

- How do you feel about the organization as your 'psychological home' in this respect?
- When managers say that they want you 'to belong' what do they *really* mean?
- Why do you think teamworking has been so consistently popular with managers interested in improving employees' performance?

Formal and informal groups

Workplace behaviour can be considered as varying along a continuum from formally to informally organized. At one extreme, formal behaviour is organized to achieve the collective purpose of an organization. This may be to make washing machines, provide a repair service, earn £200,000 profit a year or achieve a 5 per cent return on investment. To achieve such collective purposes, the organization is structured in such a way so as to use the limited resources it has at its disposal as efficiently and effectively as possible. It does this by creating what is called a formal organization. The overall collective purpose or aim is broken down into subgoals and subtasks. These are assigned to different subunits in the organization. The tasks may be grouped together and departments thus formed. Job requirements in terms of job descriptions may be written. The subdivision continues to take place until a small group of people is given one such subgoal and divides it between its members. When this occurs, there exists the basis for forming the group along functional lines. This process of identifying the purpose, dividing up tasks and so on is referred to as the creation of the formal organization. A group formed through this division of labour is called a formal group.

Formal group one that has been consciously created by management to accomplish a defined task that contributes to the organization's goal.

Managers make choices as to how technology and organization will be combined to create task orientated (formal) groups. The purpose of the groups in the production department may be to manufacture 100 cars a day, while that of the group in the design department may be to draw up a set of construction plans. Whatever type of formal group we are interested in, they all have certain common characteristics:

- they are task-oriented;
- they tend to be permanent;
- they have a formal structure;
- they are consciously organized by management to achieve organizational goals;
- their activities contribute directly to the organization's collective purpose.

Alongside these formal groups, and consisting of the same employees, albeit arranged differently, will be a number of informal groups. These emerge in an organization and are neither anticipated, nor intended, by those who create the formal organization. They emerge from the informal interaction of the members of the formal organization. These unplanned-for groups share many of the characteristics of the small social leisure groups. These function alongside the formal groups. An informal group develops during the spontaneous interaction of persons in the group as they talk, joke and associate with one another.

Informal group a collection of individuals who become a group when they develop interdependencies, influence one another's behaviour, and contribute to mutual need satisfaction.

Why do informal groups exist and what purpose do they serve? Ackroyd and Thompson (1999) introduced the concept of group self-organization to help our understanding of the nature of formal and informal groups. Group self-organization refers to the tendency of groups to:

- form interests;
- develop autonomy;
- establish identities.

Social networks of informal groups

Social networks (the 'informal organization') are generally considered to be unobservable and ungovernable by most corporations, and are consequentially treated as an 'invisible enemy'. In consequence, managers frequently try to work around or ignore them. Even where the network's existence is acknowledged and valued, managers tend to rely on intuition to nurture this social capital, but commonly misunderstand the links between their members. Cross and Prusak, who conducted a study into the social networks that existed within 50 large organizations, argue that it is possible for managers to develop informal networks systematically in order to enhance their effectiveness. The first step is for them to identify and map the many different informal networks of people within a company, which can be done using a graphical tool called *social network analysis*. The next step is for the managers to focus their attention on just a few role-players in the network whose performance is critical to the entire organization. Their research revealed four such key roles:

- *Central connectors* link most of the people within an informal network to one another. Despite not being formal leaders, they know who possesses the critical information or expertise required to get the work done.

- *Boundary spanners* connect the informal organization with other parts of the company or with similar networks in other organizations. They consult and advise individuals from many different company departments, regardless of their own functional affiliations.

- *Information brokers* keep different subgroups in an informal network together. Failure to communicate across subgroups, would lead to their splintering into smaller, less effective segments.

- *Peripheral specialists* are those members within an informal network to whom anyone can turn to for specialized expertise.

A study by Allen and his colleagues of the staff of ICI plc's research and development (R&D) department confirms

→

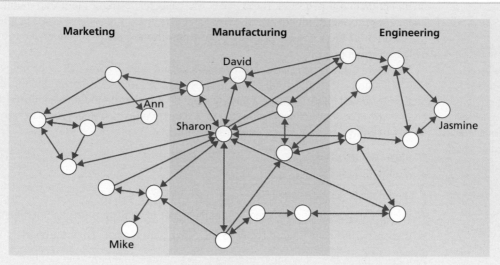

Figure 10.4: An organizational communication network
From Daft and Marcic (2009, p.568).

the earlier work. Network researchers recommend that managers transform an ineffective informal network into a productive one by focusing on these key individuals, and determining whether these people are performing their roles effectively or are being prevented from doing so – are the central connectors hoarding information? Are boundary spanners talking to the right people outside the group? Do the peripheral specialists need to be drawn more closely into the network? Additionally, managers should actively encourage social contacts by installing coffee rooms and water-coolers, where staff can meet; identify individuals who are the 'knowledge nodes' in the network and train and coach them; map the social networks to reveal any gaps; and be aware that a loss of personnel means not also a loss of formal know-how but also the collapse of their associated social network.

From DAFT/MARCIC. Management, 6E. © 2009
South-Western, a part of Cengage Learning, Inc.
Reproduced by permission. www.cengage.com/permissions.

In the Bank Wiring Room in the Hawthorne Studies, workers' interests centred around restricting their output. In so doing, they gained a degree of personal control, that is, they increased their autonomy in relation to management. The two cliques that emerged, each developed their own, separate identities. Self-interest and self-identity interact and reciprocate. These processes have implications for the behaviour of the groups concerned. This phenomenon is termed **group self-organization**.

Group self-organization the tendency of groups to form interests, develop autonomy and establish identities.

Motivation theory suggests that humans have a need for love, esteem and safety (see Chapter 9, Motivation). Love needs are concerned with belongingness and relationships; esteem needs focus on recognition, attention and appreciation; while safety needs concern security of employment. The failure to satisfy these needs may result in our inability to feel confident, capable, necessary or useful members of society. These needs concern our relationships with others. The time that we do spend at work remains considerable, and we frequently seek to satisfy these needs through our relationships with work colleagues. The difficulty is that the organizations are not primarily designed to allow individuals to meet such needs at work.

A formal organization is ostensibly designed on rational principles and is aimed at achieving the collective purpose of the organization. It thus limits employees' behaviour in order to be able to control and predict it. The individual brings their hopes, needs, desires and personal goals to their job. While the company may not be interested in these, the employee will, nevertheless, attempt to achieve their personal ambitions while at work by manipulating the situation to fulfil their unmet needs. Most other staff will generally be seeking to do the same so it will not be difficult to set up series of satisfying relationships. These relationships in turn will lead to the formation of informal groups. Because of our social nature, we have a tendency to form informal groups. The task-oriented, formal groups rarely consider the social needs of their members. Indeed these needs are frequently considered to be dispensable and counterproductive to the achievement of the formal purpose of the organization.

STOP AND THINK

Consider how your educational institution contributes to the satisfaction of your social needs while studying through your membership of social groups (class, tutorial groups, self-help and study groups, clubs and societies, sports teams). On the other hand:

- How are other aspects of your institution's structure, rules, procedures and policies blocking your satisfaction?

- How could your institution meet your social needs and those of your fellow students more effectively through different forms of group arrangement – and would these be consistent with good teaching and learning practice?

Home viewing

Office Space (1998, director Mike Judge), follows the progress of Peter Gibbons (played by Ron Livingston) an employee of the computer company, Initech. His behaviour is driven by the nature of his work and imminent loss of his job due to downsizing. Peter shows signs of alienation (see Chapter 3, Technology), particularly feelings of *powerlessness*, *meaninglessness* and *self-estrangement*. As you watch, look for the symptoms of his alienation being expressed. The fourth alienation symptom, *isolation* is not present because he is a member of an informal group which provides each with a sense of community and membership, and helps Peter cope with the futility of his work life. How does this informal group operate; what are its goals; what do its members talk about? Also, how does the film depict the idea that modern organizations deny white collar male employees their essential masculinity? How does Peter resolve this issue?

Homans's theory of group formation

George Caspar
Homans
(1910–1989)

Groups do not suddenly appear out of nowhere. Before being able and willing to contribute as part of a collective, individuals who were previously strangers have to become acquainted with each other in order to establish how best to work together to achieve the common task. George Homans addressed this question of how groups formed (Homans, 1951). His three-part model is summarized in Table 10.2, and we shall examine it in relation to management and workers in organizations.

Table 10.2: Homans' model of group formation

Environment of group	External system	Internal system	
Physical	Required activities	Emergent activities	
Technological	Required interactions	Emergent interactions	Formation of
Social	Required sentiments	Emergent sentiments	a group

Group environment

Homans proposed that every group (or *social system* in his model) exists within an environment which affects it physically, technologically and socially. This environment is created by management's decisions in three areas:

- *Physical*: these are the actual surroundings within which a group functions. It includes the spatial arrangement of physical objects and location of human activities e.g. office architecture and work furniture; placement of workers on an assembly line.

- *Technological:* this includes both material technology (the tools, machinery and equipment that can be seen, touched and heard) that group members use to do their jobs, and the social technology (the methods which order their behaviour and relationships).

- *Social*: this encompasses the norms and values of the group itself; of its managers (e.g. employees as motivated solely by money) and of the organization culture (stressing mutual support and collaboration or competition, distrust and backstabbing).

Homans argued that a group's environment was created by the organization's management through its design of the physical work place; its purchase of equipment and choices in job design; as well as its choice of strategy, structure and culture.

Homans' group environments

Physically, the context of a group in a call centre differs depending on management's choice of work furniture (see photos below). Each arrangement limits the form and nature of operators' interactions with each other, and requires them to behave in certain ways. Managers can select work furniture to isolate operators, discourage them from interacting with colleagues and thus prevent informal groups from forming. Alison Barnes's study of Australian call centres reported a manager saying 'It's not the sort of place where you can talk to the person beside you or behind you if you're not taking calls . . . it's not a job where there is a lot of interaction during the day'. Barnes noted that the lack of spaces at work where staff members could meet privately hindered their collective organization. A company policy of 'hot desking' also prevented an operator working with the same group of people.

Technologically, the context of their work consists of the material technology that requires staff to interact with customers using the telephone and computer. In addition, there are the wallboards, with their 6 inch high, LED numbers, which show the number of calls waiting

Source: Image Source/Rex Features

3 people next to each other

to be answered. This flashes faster as the length of the queue increases. Computers monitor how many calls each operator deals with, and how quickly, keeping figures on all staff. The social technology consists of the script and prompt software held in the computer that directs their conversations in certain, required ways. Socially, the norms, values and goals that make up the shared understanding within which the group will function are specific to each group and are influenced by the culture of the call centre organization in which it operates. Barnes concluded 'The design of work in the call centres – the technology such as the automatic call distribution or the focus on statistics – inhibited worker interaction. Designing an office space in order to facilitate employee communication would have been inconsistent with company objectives.'

Source: © Jagadeesh/Reuters/Corbis

Call centre – individual cells

Based on Barnes (2008).

External system

Homans' external system broadly equates to the concept of the formal organization introduced earlier. Managers have certain requirements or expectations of employees which, from the employees' perspective, are the 'givens' of their jobs. They require individuals to perform certain **activities**; to have certain **interactions** with others; and to have certain **sentiments** or feelings towards their work.

Activities in Homans's theory, the physical movements, and verbal and non-verbal behaviours engaged in by group members.

Interactions in Homans's theory, the two-way communications between group members.

Sentiments in Homans' theory, the feelings, attitudes and beliefs held by group members towards others.

For example, in a supermarket, the physical, technological, social environment is represented by the design and positioning of the checkout stations; the choice of scanning equipment; and the company's 'the customer is always right' policy. The supermarket management wants its checkout operators to scan customers' purchases (activities); greet them, offer to pack their bags, and say goodbye to them (interactions). They are also expected to have positive attitudes and feelings towards their customers and their employer (sentiments). Homans prefaced each of these elements with the term 'required' (*required activities*, *required interactions* and *required sentiments*) and referred to them collectively as the *external system*.

Each of these three elements reinforce each other. The more activities that employees share, the more frequent will be their interactions, and the stronger will be their shared activities and sentiments (how much the other persons are liked or disliked). The greater the number of interactions between persons, the more will be their shared activities and the stronger their sentiments towards each other. The stronger the sentiments people have for one another, the greater will be the number of their shared activities and interactions. Persons in a group interact with one another, not just because of spatial or geographical proximity (called propinquity), but also to accomplish goals such as co-operation and problem-solving.

Homans's required activities and interactions

Source: Monkey Business Images/www.dreamstime.com

At most supermarkets, checkout operators are expected to conform to particular patterns of non-verbal behaviour even when not serving. For example, one checkout operator, Denise (name changed) commented in an interview with the authors that, at her store, not only were the checkouts constantly monitored by closed-circuit television but supervisors regularly patrolled behind the checkouts, preventing any of the operators turning around to talk to fellow operators, by whispering the command 'FF', which meant 'Face the Front'. Denise and her colleagues were required not only to 'FF', but also to sit straight at all times; they were strictly forbidden, for example, from putting their elbows on the counter in front of them to relax their backs.

From Noon and Blyton (2007, p.189).

Internal system

Homans' internal system broadly equates to the concept of the informal organization introduced earlier. They are another, different set of group members' activities, interactions and sentiments that emerge from the physical, technological, social environment, and as a result of the required activities, required interactions and required sentiments themselves. Homans prefaced each of these elements with the term 'emergent' (*emergent activities, emergent interactions* and *emergent sentiments*) and referred to them collectively as the *internal system*. These represent the creation of informal groups within the organization.

These can occur in addition to, or in place of the latter, and are not asked for by the organization's management. For example, if the job is repetitive (technological context), operators might see how quickly they can perform it (emergent activity), so as to give their work more challenge. If employees are in close proximity to each other (physical context), they might relieve their boredom by talking to each other (emergent interaction) even though company rules forbid it. Group members may come to view customers as a nuisance and develop anti-customer feelings (emergent sentiments). For Homans, the relationship between the external and internal systems was crucial.

- *The internal and the external systems are interdependent*: a change in one system will produce a change in the other. For example, the replacement of a management-selected team leader (external system) can impact on the activities between the group members (internal system). Similarly, the sentiments of group members (internal system) can affect the way they do their work (external system).

- *The environment and the internal and external systems are interdependent*: changes in the environment produce changes in the external (formal) and internal (informal) work organization. Individuals and groups will modify what they do and how they do it, to respond to the changes they perceive.

Homans' emergent activities and interactions

The technological environment of the PowerGrid call centre includes remote, clandestine electronic surveillance of employees. If group members think they might be watched, the argument goes, they will provide the high quality of customer service expected of them (required interactions). However, the reality is that there are individual members capable of and willing to engage in forms of resistance that circumvent the surveillance possibilities.

Resistance was found which indicated that employees engaged in activities to maintain some degree of control over the labour process. Three examples of such resistance (emergence interactions) were identified. In the first, customers phoning to pay a bill, were transferred into the computer interactive system called 'cardgate'. The system does not hang up after the caller is finished, thereby giving the operator a 10-minute break to go out and have a cigarette. Second, there is the practice of 'bumping' calls that involves sending the caller, who has reached the front of the call queue, back to the end. Third, putting in an order to finalize an account that would mean the customer would have their electricity cut off. Employees are recognizing opportunities to engage in activities that impede management's ultimate goal of running a profitable venture.

Based on Townsend (2005).

Homans' model of group formation established the basis for our understanding of group behaviour. First, it highlights how the environment within which a group functions (the physical dispersion of staff; the technology that they use; and their social context), helps or hinders the process of group formation. Second, it highlights how this management-created environment imposes the required activities, required interactions and required sentiments on individuals and groups in an organization, and then how these in turn stimulate the

STOP AND THINK

Identify and explain the emergent behaviours in a workgroup of which you are a member.

- How would group members explain and assess these emergent behaviours?
- How would management respond to these emergent behaviours?

emergent activities, emergent interactions and emergent sentiments, that are not required by the external system.

Tuckman and Jensen's theory of group development

Bruce Wayne
Tuckman (b.1938)

Groups of whatever type do not come into existence fully formed. Bruce Tuckman and Mary Ann Jensen suggested that groups pass through five clearly defined stages of development which they labelled forming, storming, norming, performing and adjourning (Tuckman, 1965; Tuckman and Jensen, 1977). Of course not all groups develop through all the stages and some get stuck in the middle and remain inefficient and ineffective. Progress through the stages may be slow, but appears to be necessary and inescapable.

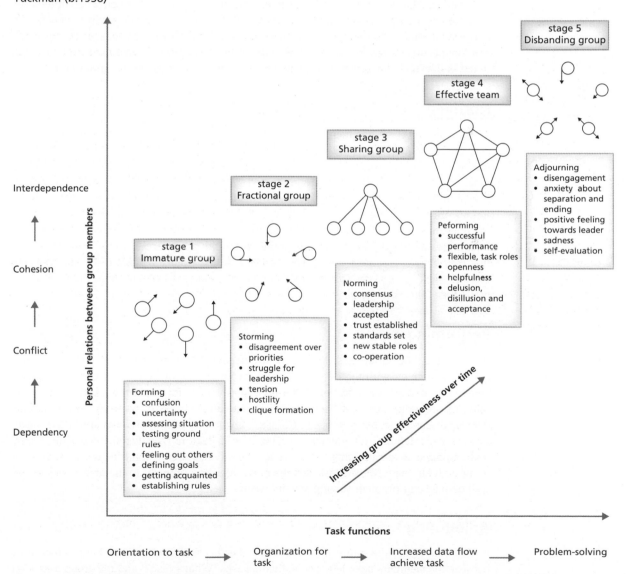

Figure 10.5: Stages of group development

Source: Based on Tuckman (1965); Tuckman and Jensen (1977); Jones (1973).

Forming

This is the orientation stage, at which the set of individuals has not yet gelled. The individual asks, 'How do I fit in?' and the group asks 'Why are we here?' Everyone is busy finding out about each other's attitudes and backgrounds, and establishing ground rules. Members are also keen to fix their personal identities in the group and make a personal impression on the others. In the personal relations area, members are *dependent* on some leader to provide them with structure in the form of ground rules and an agenda for action. Task-wise, they seek *orientation* as to what they are being asked to do, what the issues are, and whether everyone understands the task.

Storming

This is a conflict stage in the group's life and can be an uncomfortable period. The individual asks 'What's my role here?' and the group asks 'Why are we fighting over who's in charge and who does what?' Members bargain with each other as they try to sort out what each of them individually, and as a group, want out of the group process. Individuals reveal their personal goals and it is likely that interpersonal hostility is generated when differences in these goals are revealed. Members may resist the control of other group members and may show hostility. The early relationships established in the forming stage may be disrupted. The key personal relations issue in this stage is the management of *conflict*, while the task function question is *organization* – how best to organize to achieve the group objective.

Norming

In this cohesion stage, the members of the group develop ways of working to develop closer relationships and camaraderie. The individual asks, 'What do others expect me to do?' and the group asks 'Can we agree on roles and work as a team?' The questions of who will do what and how it will be done are addressed. Working rules are established in terms of norms of behaviour (do not smoke) and role allocation (Jill will be the spokesperson). A framework is therefore created in which each group member can relate to the others and the questions of agreeing expectations and dealing with a failure to meet members' expectations are addressed. The personal relations within the group stress *cohesion*. Members feel that they have overcome conflict, have 'gelled' and experience a sense of 'groupiness'. On the task side, there is an *increase in data-flow* as members become more prepared to be more open about their goals.

Performing

By this stage the group has developed an effective structure, and it is concerned with actually getting on with the job in hand and accomplishing objectives. The individual asks 'How can I best perform my role?' and the group asks 'Can we do the job properly?' The fully mature group has now been created which can get on with its work. Not all groups develop to this stage, but may become bogged down in an earlier, and less productive stage. In personal relations, interdependence becomes a feature. Members are equally happy working alone, in subgroupings or as a single unit. Collaboration and functional competition occur between them. On the task side, there is a high commitment to the objective, jobs are well defined and problem-solving activity ensues.

Adjourning

In this final stage, the group may disband, either because the task has been achieved or because the members have left. The individual asks 'What's next?' and the group asks 'Can we help members make the transition to their next task or group?' Before they do so, they may reflect on their time together, and ready themselves to go their own ways.

Tuckman and Jensen's stages need not occur in sequence. While groups do pass through these different stages, they have been found to go through more of an iterative process. They cycle back and forth between the different stages. They may pass through one stage several times, or become frozen in a certain stage for a period of time. Some groups pass through certain stages more quickly than others. Moreover, progress through to any given stage is not inevitable (Gersick, 1988, 1989).

The value of the Tuckman and Jensen framework shown in Figure 10.5 is that it can help us to explain some of the problems of group working. A group may be operating at half power because it may have failed to work through some of the issues at the earlier stages. For example, the efficiency of a project team may be impaired because it had not resolved the issue of leadership. Alternatively, people may be pulling in different directions because the purpose of the group has not been clarified, nor its objectives agreed. Members might be using the group to achieve their personal and unstated aims (so-called hidden agendas). For all these reasons, effective group functioning may be hindered.

Home viewing

The Breakfast Club (1984, director John Hughes) is set in the library of an American high school where five students have been sent to spend a whole Saturday in detention, under a teacher's less than watchful eye. Apart from the teacher and the school janitor, there are only five main characters in the film, representing different teen stereotypes: the sports 'jock', Andrew (played by Emillo Estevez); the prom queen, Claire (Molly Ringwald); the weirdo, Allison (Ally Sheedy); the nerd, Brian (Anthony Michael Hall) and the lout, Judd (John Bender). These five high school students have never met each other before, and each is being punished by this detention for a different act of organizational misbehaviour (see Ackroyd and Thompson, 1999). Shut in together in the school library for the day, they are forced to get to know each other. As the film unfolds, can you: Identify the 'break points' in the action when the students move from one group development stage to the next – from forming, to storming, to norming, and finally, to performing as a group? Establish where and why the leadership of this student group moves from one character to another? Identify any examples of organizational misbehaviour by the characters, and determine the purpose, objective or motive for that behaviour.

Source: Copyright Grantland Enterprises (www.grantland.net)

STOP AND THINK

Identify a group to which you currently belong – sports club, drama society, tutorial group, project group, etc.

- Identify which stage of development it has reached.
- What advice would you give to this group based on your analysis of its development?

Groups and teams

In the literature, the terms *group* and *team*, are used interchangeably, with the personal preference of writers and tradition guiding the choice of word, rather than conceptual distinction. For example, the 'how-to-do-it' books aimed at a management audience tend to refer to teams in organizations, while, for historical reasons, discussions about shop floor working arrangements refer to autonomous work groups. Management consultants frequently use the term team metaphorically, that is, they apply this label to a collection of employees to which it is imaginatively, but not literally, appropriate. Hayes (1997) noted that the idea of team must be one of the most widely used metaphors in organizational life. These same writers also use the term normatively, that is, to describe a collection of people as what they *should* be, or what they would *prefer* them to be, rather than as they actually are.

In their examination of the managerial practices used by the US Marine Corps to engage the hearts and minds of their front line troops, Jon Katzenbach and Jason Santamaria (1999) contrasted the characteristics of a team with that of a single-leader work group. These are summarized in Table 10.3. The authors describe the training of marines, and note that the highly cohesive groups produced by this process, learn when and how to function as a real team, and when to rely on a single leader.

Most commonly, writers focus on the transformation of a group into a team. They see the difference between the two as being in terms of a group being 'stuck' in the forming, storming or norming stage of Tuckman and Jensen's model, while a team is a group that has successfully arrived at the performing stage. From the point of view of management, a team is a group, which possesses extra, positive features. As a group comes to acquire these positive characteristics, it is seen as progressing towards the team-end of the continuum.

Table 10.3: Teams and groups: it pays to know the difference

	Team	**Single-leader work group**
Run by	The members of the team best-suited to lead the tasks at hand; the leadership role shifts among the members.	One person, usually the senior member, who is formally designated to lead.
Goals and agenda set by	The group, based on dialogue about purpose; constructive conflict and integration predominate.	The formal leader; often in consultation with a sponsoring executive, conflict with group members is avoided, and the leader integrates.
Performance evaluated by	The members of the group, as well as the leader and sponsor.	The leader and sponsor.
Work style determined by	The members.	The leader's preference.
Most appropriate business context	A complex challenge that requires people with various skill sets working together much of the time.	A challenge in which time is of the essence and the leader already knows how best to proceed; the leader is the primary integrator.
Speed and efficiency	Low until the group has learned to function as a team; afterwards however, the team is as fast as a single-leader group.	Higher than that of teams initially, as the members need no time to develop commitment or to learn to work as a team.
Primary end-products	Largely collective, requiring several team members to work together to produce results.	Largely individual and can be accomplished best by each person working on his or her own.
Accountability characterized by	'We hold one another mutually accountable for achieving the goals and performance of the team.'	'The leader holds us individually accountable for our output.'

These positive 'team traits' include co-operation, co-ordination, cohesion and so on. From this perspective, a group turns into a team once it has organized itself to fulfil a purpose. This implies a process of conscious self-management by the group's members during which they assign tasks, develop communication channels, and establish decision-making processes. Thus, the transition from a group to a team is the result of a learning process.

STOP AND THINK Management has just told you that you are not a 'real team' and that you are certainly not a 'high performance team'. How do you feel about that, and what are you doing to do about it?

Mayo's 'human relations approach' and Katzenbach and Santamaria's managerial practices to create teams, are separated by over 70 years, but have remarkable similarities. Both:

- are directed at managers who design jobs and structure organizations;
- promote the virtues of teams and groups over individuals;
- assume that teams and the individuals share common goals and interests;
- ignore or explain away areas of conflict or dissent;
- seek to use the power of the team in management's interest.

Management's practical interest grew, and they became interested not just in observing groups, but in designing and building effective teams. The general theme of making group behaviour contribute to management goals has been re-discovered at the level of the shop floor by the interest in Japanese-style team working (see Chapter 13). Writers have argued that the managerial belief that links all these contemporary writers with Elton Mayo back in the 1920s, is that the creation of a compliant and programmable workforce.

RECAP

1. *List the key characteristics of a group.*
   - The key ones are: two or more people, in face-to-face interaction, each aware of his or her membership in the group, each aware of the others who belong to the group, and each aware of their positive interdependence as they strive to achieve mutual goals.

2. *Distinguish between different types of group tasks.*
   - Groups can be assigned many different tasks, many of which can be categorized under the headings of additive, conjunctive and disjunctive.

3. *Name the four research phases of the Hawthorne studies.*
   - The Hawthorne studies consisted of four major phases – illumination experiments, Relay Assembly Test Room experiments, interviewing programme, and the Bank Wiring Observation Room experiments.

4. *Distinguish between a formal and an informal group.*
   - Formal groups can be distinguished from informal groups in terms of who creates them and the purposes that they serve.

5. *Outline Homans' theory of group formation.*
   - George Homans' theory of group formation distinguishes between background factors, and required and emergent activities, interactions, sentiments, to explain how individuals come to form groups.

6. *Enumerate the five stages of Tuckman and Jensen's model of group development.*
   - Tuckman and Jensen distinguish five stages through which groups typically proceed, which they name forming, storming, norming, performing and adjourning.

7. *Summarize Katzenbach and Santamaria's distinction between a team and a single-leader working group.*
   - They distinguish between a team and a single-leader working group.
   - They contrast a team with a single-leader working group on the dimensions of: who runs it; who sets the goals; performance evaluation; work style; business context; speed and efficiency; primary end products; and accountability.

Revision

1. You have brought together a collection of fellow students – friends, acquaintances and interested strangers – who wish to re-launch the Business and Management Society at your university. How can your knowledge of the group development model help you to achieve this objective?

2. List the principles of the Human Relations approach to management developed in the 1920s. Use your reading and work experience, to identify those that continue to be applied in organizations today, giving specific examples of how they are being implemented.

3. Give an example of a disjunctive task, a conjunctive task and an additive task that a lecturer might give in your subject, to groups of university students, as their semester team project. (a) In what ways would these project tasks differ? (b) How would each student group have to organize itself differently to complete its particular task? (c) Would the type of task assigned, affect what group members learned? Make any reasonable assumptions about numbers, time, membership, selection, etc.

4. In what ways does a formal group differ from an informal group? Suggest how one type of group may help or hinder the other in achieving its objectives.

Research assignment

Familiarize yourself with Tuckman and Jensen's model of group development through extended reading. (a) Develop a set of interview questions to determine which stage of development a group has reached. (b) Interview a few members of a group of your choice (work, social, sports or religious) to find this out. (c) Also find out how the context in which the group operates (e.g. physical conditions, technology, task) affects its stage of development. Write a brief report on how your interview data supports or contradictions the literature on group development stages.

Springboard

O'Connor, E., 1999, 'Minding the workers: The meaning of "human" and "human relations" of Elton Mayo', *Organization*, 6(2): 223–46.

A consideration of Mayo's ideas from a contemporary perspective.

Proctor, S. and Mueller, F. (eds), 2000, *Teamworking*, Houndmills, Basingstoke, Macmillan.

A collection of contemporary contributions investigating the use of teams in organizations.

Sinclair, A., 1992, 'The tyranny of team ideology', *Organization Studies*, 13(4): 611–26.

A critical review of the concept of team in managerial and organizational writings.

West, M.A. (ed.), 1998, *Handbook of Work Group Psychology*, Wiley, Chichester.

Contains writings on group and team behaviour. Provides an overview of the field and contemporary theoretical and research directions.

 ## OB in films

The Magnificent Seven (1960, director John Sturges), DVD track 6: 0:18:35 – track 12: 0:39:48 (6–11–21 minutes – sequenced). In this American western film, a group of Mexican farmers cross the border, initially with a view to buying guns in order to defend their village against bandits. Eventually, they end up hiring gunmen. The clip begins as the three villagers enter Chris's (played by Yul Brynner) hotel room. As you watch the clip of the selection process:

1. Speculate on which of Maslow's needs each of the gunmen appears to want to meet by joining the group? There may be more than one need.

Character (actor)	Needs				
	biological	safety	affiliational	esteem (self & others)	self-actualization
Chris (Yul Brynner)					
Harry (Brad Dexter)					
Vin (Steven McQueen)					
O'Reilly (Charles Bronson)					
Britt (James Coburn)					
Lee (Robert Vaughn)					
Chico (Horst Bucholz)					

OB in literature

Thomas Keneally, *Flying Hero Class*, Hodder & Stoughton, Sceptre, London, 1991. This is a story of an airline hijack. How does the plot illustrate the distinction between mere aggregates of people and groups? Under what circumstances can an aggregate of people on an airplane become a group?

CHAPTER EXERCISES

Group experiences

Objectives   1. Demonstrate how groups affect your work and social life.

Briefing   1. Individually

    (a) Make a list of all the different groups to which you belong at the present time.

    (b) Distinguish work groups from non-work groups, and formal from informal groups.

2. Form groups

    (a) Share the number of groups that you each belong to. What does this tell you about yourself and the way the world is organized?

    (b) Identify which types of groups all or most of you belong. Why is this?

    (c) Using examples, explain how being in a group affects your behaviour. Do you behave differently when in a group than when alone? Do you behave differently in different groups?

3. In your groups

    (a) Each person shares a *positive* experience that they have had while being a member of a group.

(b) Each person shares a *negative* experience that they have had while being a member of a group.

(c) Identify any common factors in your positive experiences; and in your negative experiences.

(d) What conclusions do you draw about the way that groups should be designed and managed?

Work group arrangements

Objectives

1. Analyze a group's behaviour using a theoretical framework.
2. Assess the situation from a management perspective.

Briefing

1. Form into groups.
2. Analyze the *Factory paint shop* case below using Homans' model: environment of group (physical, technological, social); external system (required activities, required interactions, required sentiments): internal system (emergent activities, emergent interactions, emergent sentiments).
3. Make the case for and against management intervention. Give your reasons and state your recommendations.

Factory paint shop case

Factory work can be boring and monotonous. Employees must work at the pace of the assembly line or machine, with output levels closely prescribed and monitored by management. It is not surprising that factory workers will try anything to break the boredom and relentless grind of the controlled activity in a factory. In a particular factory, a large paint-spraying machine was approximately 100 metres long and required a team of 24 people to keep it running. There were only 18 workstations on the machine, but the staffing plan was that six people would float between jobs, thereby allowing everyone to take a break whilst keeping the machine running. In practice, four people would be in the mess room for their entire shift running a card syndicate. Everyone else in the work team would take shorter breaks and simply drop in and out of the card game as their breaks allowed. A different team of four people would be informally 'rostered' each day so that over a period everyone had the total break time allowed by the company. The team achieved their allowed breaks in a way not intended (or approved) by management. Gambling was not allowed by the company either, but this did not bother the workers. Supervisors also turned a blind eye to the process as long as the work was completed and productivity was at acceptable levels.

From John Martin (2005, p.243).

Chapter 11 **Group structure**

Key terms

group structure

group process

power

reward power

coercive power

referent power

legitimate power

expert power

formal status

social status

sociometry

sociogram

communication network analysis

communigram

communication pattern analysis

communication pattern chart

Interaction Process Analysis

task activity

maintenance activity

social role

team role

distributed leadership

virtual team

synchronous communication

asynchronous communication

Learning outcomes

When you have read this chapter, you should be able to define those key terms in your own words, and you should also be able to:

1. List the six dimensions of group structure.

2. Identify the sources of power within the group.

3. Distinguish between two common uses of the concept of status.

4. Understand how emotional relationships within a group can be represented symbolically.

5. Distinguish between network, pattern and IPA techniques for analyzing communications between group members.

6. Distinguish between task, socio-emotional and individual classes of roles within a group.

7. Distinguish Belbin's team roles.

8. Give examples of three leadership styles identified by White and Lippitt.

9. Distinguish between a task and a socio-emotional group leader.

10. List the four key dimensions of a virtual team.

Why study group structure?

Abraham Zaleznik (1993, p.180) has argued that:

> While Americans admire the 'hero', the individual who has the 'right stuff', they worry about his (sic) recklessness, his willingness to take risks that endanger others. Frequently the 'hero' is suppressed in favour of the team player who values the performance of the group over individual recognition.

However, how the group as a whole performs, depends very much on the behaviour and contribution of its individual members. Within organizations, a great deal of work is done by individuals working with others in groups and teams. Because it is so important, management monitors how groups work, in order to pinpoint any problems and rectify them so as to raise team effectiveness. When there is a problem with a motor car, it is taken into a garage and the mechanic drives it around, listens to the engine, feels the gear changes, and attends to the smoothness of the ride. The individual parts of the car are then inspected, to ensure that all of them are performing their respective tasks, and are working together satisfactorily in combination. Individual faulty or worn out parts are replaced. Linkages between the parts, which may have become loosened, are tightened. The mechanic checks that the vehicle is performing satisfactorily and can be returned to its owner.

This analogy is a useful way of introducing the concept of group structure from a management perspective. In this view, structure is an important aspect of 'engineering the group'. When a group or team is performing poorly, a consultant may be brought in to observe its operation and to evaluate its outputs. The consultant will focus on individual team members, assessing their performance of their roles, and ensuring that everyone is working well together as a team. Individuals who are not contributing or who do not 'fit in', may be replaced by others. The consultant checks that communication between team members is timely and effective, and that leadership within the group is contributing towards the achievement of the goal. In contrast, social scientists tend to be more concerned with understanding how the structure of a group develops; how it affects the individuals who comprise the groups; and how it impacts on group functioning.

Source: www.cartoonstock.com

Team problem

There were four team members named Everybody, Somebody, Anybody and Nobody.

There was an important job to do and Everybody was asked to do it.

Everybody was sure Somebody would do it.

Anybody could have done it, but Nobody did.

Everybody was angry about that, because it was Somebody's job.

Everybody thought Anybody could do it, but Nobody realised that Everybody wouldn't.

In the end, Everybody blamed Somebody when Nobody did what Anybody could have done.

Source unknown.

Group structure

Group structure the relatively stable pattern of relationships among different group members.

A central idea in helping us to examine the nature and functioning of groups is that of structure. Group structure refers to the way in which members of a group relate to one another. The formation of group structure is one of the basic aspects of group development. When people come together and interact, differences between individuals begin to appear. Some talk while others listen; some make decisions, while others accept them; some ask for information, while others provide it. These differences between group members serve as the basis for the establishment of group structure. As differentiation occurs, relations are established between members. Group structure is the label given to this patterning of relationships.

Group structure carries with it the connotation of something fixed and unchanging. While there is an element of permanency in terms of the relationships between members, these do continue to change and modify. Group members continually interact with each other, and in consequence their relationships are tested and transformed. As we describe the structure of any group, it is useful to view it as a snapshot photograph, correct at the time the shutter was pressed but acknowledging that things were different the moment before and after the photo was taken. Differences between the members of a group begin to occur as soon as it is formed. This differentiation within a group occurs along not one, but several dimensions. The most important of these are:

- power;
- status;
- liking;
- communication;
- role;
- leadership.

There are as many structures in a group as there are dimensions along which a group can be differentiated. Although in common usage we talk about the structure of a group, in reality, a group will differentiate simultaneously along a number of dimensions. Group members will be accorded different amounts of status and hence a group will have a status hierarchy. They will be able to exert differing amounts of power and thus a power structure will emerge. In examining group functioning, social scientists have found it useful to consider the six dimensions listed above. While it is possible to examine each structural dimension of the group in turn, we need to remember that all are closely related and operate simultaneously in a group setting. Cartwright and Zander (1968) suggest that a group's structure is determined by:

1. the requirements for efficient group performance;
2. the abilities and motivations of group members; and
3. the psychological and social environment of the group.

Why does a group have structure?

Why does a patterning of relationships between individuals in a group occur and what purpose does it serve? Robert Bales (1950a) offered a psychological explanation based on the individual's desire for stability, 'need for order' and 'low tolerance of ambiguity'. He argued that meeting and dealing with other people within a group can cause an individual stress. It is the potential uncertainty and unpredictability in the actions of others that causes this. If the behaviour between group members can be made predictable, this can reduce the tension for all concerned. This, he explained, is what group structure does.

A sociological explanation would point to structure as a manifestation of power, with structure 'imposed' on groups (as a natural aspect of efficient functioning, of course) to maintain the power position of key players in the organization. All groups are overlaid with the power and cultural patterns of the organization within which they exist. Whether a group's structure results from its members' basic need for predictability, or is imposed by powerful outsiders, the effect in either case is to create differences between the individuals within the group along several dimensions at the same time (e.g. status, role, power). One person will therefore simultaneously have high status and power since each person stands at the intersection of several dimensions. The combination of all of these for each group member is referred to as their position in the group structure. A group's structure will be affected by **group process** which refers to the group activity which occurs over time, specifically to the oral and non-verbal contributions of group members. Examples of a group's process include:

Group process the patterns of interactions between the members of a group.

- Direction of communication   (Who talks to whom)
- Quantity of communication   (Number of times each group member speaks)
- Content of communication   (Type of oral utterance made)
- Decision-making style   (How decisions are made in the group)
- Problem-solving style   (How problems are approached and solved)

The structure of a group can affect its process. For example, when an individual is appointed the leader of formal group, they will tend to speak more often, and will be listened to more closely. Being group leader will therefore determine the direction, frequency and content of their communication with others in the group. Conversely, group process can determine group structure. In an informal group, the individual who speaks most often to all fellow members may come to be liked the most. Their status will rise in the eyes of the other members, and they may be given permission to take on a leadership role within the group.

When seeking to improve the performance of a group through the use of team building activities, management consultants often focus on group processes, in order to locate problems in group functioning and to suggest solutions. They look at *how* a group does things and not *what* it does. They may decide that a group is performing poorly because its members are not communicating with each other sufficiently; that there is an absence of goal clarity; that leadership within the group is poor; or that the way decisions are reached antagonizes members and fails to secure their commitment. Inevitably they will recommend that the group should become aware of its processes, and manage them better, in order to achieve improved outcomes.

Power structure

Power the capacity of individuals to overcome resistance on the part of others, to exert their will, and to produce results consistent with their interests and objectives.

Individual members of a group differ in terms of how much **power** they each possess, and hence in their ability to direct the behaviour of other members. For this reason, it becomes necessary for the group to have established control relations between members. By having a power structure, the group avoids continued power struggles that can disrupt its functioning. It can also link goal achievement activities to a system of authority which is seen as legitimate (Dahl, 1957).

Various writers have defined power in terms of influence. Power is an aspect not only in relationships between individuals within a group, but also in leadership relations and political issues. We shall therefore re-visit the work of these authors in other chapters. For now, we can draw upon the classic work of John French and Bertram Raven (1958) who saw power as a property not of the individual, but of the relationship. These authors distinguished five types of power which are defined here: reward power, coercive power, referent power, legitimate power and expert power.

Saying that power is a property of the relationship and not of the individual means that, for example, it is not having rewards to distribute or sanctions to exercise that matters, it's being *perceived* to have. So you have reward power when others believe that you have rewards up your sleeve, even when you don't.

Home viewing:

Aliens (1986, director James Cameron), is a science fiction thriller set in the distant future on the planet LV-426. The characters in this group include Lieutenant Gorman, the senior officer of the space marines; Sergeant Apone and Corporal Hicks. In addition to these military personnel, there is Burke, who represents the Weyland-Yutani Corporation that owns the facilities on the planet and employs Ripley. Watch the first part of the film from the scene where Burke and Gorman visit Ripley's quarters to persuade her to join the expedition to the point where, having escaped the creature's attack, they decide to 'nuke the planet'. Use French and Raven's five power-base classification to decide which of the characters possesses which types of power within the group. Also assess who gains and who loses which type of power. How does this happen? What does this tell us about the power structure of a group?

STOP AND THINK

- Who gains from having stable power in a group and why?
- Who loses, how and why?
- Make the argument for having an *unstable* power structure in a group.

Status structure

Status is a prestige ranking within a group that is independent of formal status or position. It is closely related to leadership, since an individual's higher status is accepted by others within the group, they can influence, control or command those around. Status ranking indicates the group's 'pecking order'. Some writers argue that status is important because it motivates people and has consequences for their behaviour. This is particularly the case when individuals perceive a disparity between their own perception of themselves and how others perceive them to be. Each position in a group has a value placed upon it. Within the organization, a value is ascribed to a position by the formal organization e.g., chief executive officer, vice-president, supervisor, and can be labelled formal status. Formal status is best thought of as being synonymous with rank as in the police or the armed forces and reflects a person's position on the 'organizational ladder'.

A second way in which value is placed on a position is the social honour or prestige that is accorded an individual in a group by the other group members. In this second sense, the word status is prefixed by the word 'social' indicating the degree of informally established value accorded to that position, as compared with other positions, as perceived by both the formal and the informal group. While one can view social status as a sort of badge of honour awarded for meritorious group conduct, it can also be viewed as a set of unwritten rules about the kind of behaviour that people in a group are expected to exhibit with regard to one another. It can indicate the degree of respect, familiarity or reserve that is appropriate in a given situation.

One of the powers possessed by an informal group is its ability to confer status on those of its members who meet the expectations of the group. These members are looked up to by their peers, not because of any formal position they may hold in the organization, but because of their position in the social group. Many people actively seek status in order to fulfil their need for self-esteem. The granting of it by the group provides them with personal satisfaction. Similarly, the withholding of status can act as a group control mechanism to bring a deviant group member into line. The status accorded by the group to a member is immediate in terms of face-to-face feedback. The recognition and esteem given to group members reinforces their identification with the group and increases their dependence upon it.

Turning to consider a formal group or team, individual members will be accorded formal status within it, based on hierarchical position and task ability. The organization is made up of a number of defined positions arranged in order of their increasing authority. The formal status hierarchy reflects the potential ability of the holder of the position to contribute to the overall goals of the organization. It differentiates the amount of respect deserved and simultaneously ranks them on a status scale. The outward symbols associated with formal status (e.g. size of office, quality of carpet) are there to inform other members in the organization of where exactly that person stands on the 'organizational ladder'. This topic leads ultimately to a consideration of organization structure, which will be considered later.

Status, authority and problem-solving in an airplane cockpit

Source: Xavier Marchant/Dreamstime.com

Commercial airplanes are piloted by groups, not individuals. The actions needed when taxying, taking off, flying, making the final approach and landing, all require the cockpit crew to work together. However, smooth group working can be impeded by status differences and group dynamics. Larger aircraft consist of a pilot, a co-pilot and a flight engineer. To indicate the relative social status and authority of each position, these roles are labelled captain, flight engineer and second officer. By law, the final authority on board rests with the captains who exert their authority and power in various ways. The US National Transportation Safety Board attributed the causes of many fatal crashes to two factors – the captain's refusal to comply with the suggestions of other crew members, and the crew's excessive obedience to the captain's authority. A near miss occurred when a captain ignored his co-pilot's warning to reduce airspeed. In the case of a DC-8 running out of fuel and crashing in Portland, Oregon, the flight recorder revealed that the captain had ignored the flight engineer's repeated reminders of their dwindling fuel. A Northwest Express Airlines co-pilot failed to correct the captain's errors on an approach, leading to a crash. Aviation authorities have now recognized the abuse of power by captains and the negative impact of excessive obedience by flight crews. Rather than attempt to change the group structure in terms of the norms of hierarchy and cockpit deference, they have sought to improve communication between all members of the flight crew. To fly safely, team members need to engage in the behaviours of *inquiring* why one member is taking certain actions; *advocating* alternative options; and *asserting* their views on matters. The accident literature is full of examples where this had not been done.

Based on Foushee (1984); Milanovich et al. (1998); National Transportation Safety Board (1994); Tarnow (2000).

What effect does the status structure have on group behaviour? Research shows that, as one would expect, higher status people in a group have more power and tend to be more influential than lower status ones (Greenberg, 1976). Knowing this, individual members may take steps to enhance their status in the eyes of their colleagues, and thereby be able to get the group to make the decisions that they want.

STOP AND THINK   Consider a group of which you are currently a member. What action could you take to change your status in this group and what impact would this have on your relationships and friendships?

Interaction with others perceived as lower in status can be threatening because of the potential identification of the person with the group or individual being associated with. Status is abstract and ascribed through the perceptions of others. One's status is therefore always tenuous. It may be withdrawn or downgraded at any time. The reference group with which one identifies and whose values and behaviour one adopts, plays an important part in establishing and maintaining one's status. To preserve that status, one cannot leave the reference group for a lower status reference group.

Status in cyberspace

The phenomenon of *status equalization* occurs when group members interact over the Internet. It refers to the tendency for one person's ideas to carry greater weight than their socio-economic status based on their organizational position. Status is much more difficult to read over the Internet since it is difficult to determine in an on-line conversation. Hence, you tend to think of the person with whom you are communicating as possessing a status, equivalent to your own. This is particularly the case if you find their ideas appealing. For this reason, there is a tendency for perceptions about members' statuses to converge. Whereas in face-to-face situations, status tends to be ascribed or linked to acquired characteristics, within the internet context, it becomes linked more closely to a person's experience or expertise.

Based on Wallace (2001).

Liking structure

Sociometry the study of interpersonal feelings and relationships within groups.

Jacob Levy Moreno
(1889–1974)

Within a group, individual members will like, dislike or be indifferent to other members, in varying degrees. Their combined feelings towards each other represent their group's liking structure. This can be studied using the technique of sociometry. The term derives from the Latin *socius* (companion) and the Greek *metron* (measure). Sociometry was devised by Jacob Moreno who coined the term in his book, *Who Shall Survive* (Moreno, 1953). Moreno and his colleagues originally used the technique in their research in the New York Training School for Girls in the 1930s. They mapped the friendship choices among girls in a reformatory.

Sociometry diagrammatically maps the emotional relationships between individual members in a group on the basis of their personal choices of selection and rejection of other group members using a few standard symbols. This network of a group's interpersonal feelings is exposed by the use of sociometric tests. These reveal the spontaneous feelings and choices that individuals in a group have and make towards each other. Moreno asked individuals to complete the test. This revealed that spontaneous feelings within a person are divided into three classes – attraction (liking), rejection (disliking) and indifference (neutral feeling). A sociometric assessment is made using a preference questionnaire through which group members are asked with whom they would prefer (or not prefer) to work, study, play

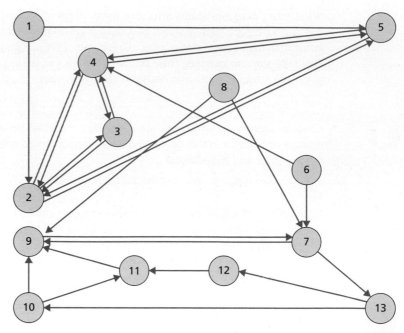

Figure 11.1: Sociogram

Sociogram a chart which shows the liking (social attraction) relationships between individual members of a group.

or live. After analysing the answers, Moreno calculated how many times an individual had been chosen as a comrade by the other members of the group for the activity in question. This feeling (the sociometric term for which is *tele*), may be one of attraction (positive *tele*) or repulsion (negative *tele*), alternatively there may merely be indifference. As shown in Figure 11.1, the members' choices are depicted on a **sociogram**, which reveals the group's liking structure by showing all the different members' positions. A sociometric assessment can reveal 'stars', 'isolates', 'neglectees', 'rejectees', 'mutual pairs' and 'mutual trios' in a group (see Table 11.1):

Table 11.1: Sociometric positions within a group

Star	Recipient of a large number of choices, sometimes described as 'over-chosen'
Isolate	Person who makes no choices at all and receives none, i.e., a relationship of mutual indifference to the remainder of the group
Neglectee	Person who, although he or she makes choices, receives none at all
Rejectee	Person who is not chosen by anyone and who is rejected by one or more persons
Mutual pair or mutual trio	Individuals who choose one another

STOP AND THINK

Look at the sociogram in Figure 11.1. Identify a 'star', an 'isolate', a 'neglectee', a 'rejectee', a 'mutual pair' and a 'mutual trio'.

Sociometry continues to be applied in organizations today under its newer label of *social network analysis* (Kilduff and Krackhardt, 2008). A company's formal organization structure is depicted on its organizational chart, but its informal organization can only be revealed through a sociometric assessment. Sociograms can be used to avoid personality clashes, raise group cohesion, and increase a group's performance (e.g. flight crews). The method can also be used to reveal the feelings of unhappy pupil isolates who may not have adjusted to their school class group, or isolate employees who have not fitted into work teams. Comparative sociograms of productive and unproductive teams can highlight areas where aspects of group structure require modification. Sociograms have also been used in the selection and training of group leaders to increase co-operation, productivity and morale amongst employees, and to anticipate turnover and conflict problems.

STOP AND THINK

Think of an organization with which you are familiar. Identify two individuals with whom you would *not* like to work in a group. List the reasons for your reluctance.

Communication structure

Communication network analysis
a technique that uses direct observation to determine the source, direction and quantity of oral communication between congregated members of a group.

Communigram a chart that indicates the source, direction and quantity of oral communication between the congregated members of a group.

Communication pattern analysis a technique that uses analysis of documents, data, and voice mail transmission, to determine the source, direction and quantity of oral and written communication between the dispersed members of a group.

Communication pattern chart indicates the source, direction and quantity of oral and written communication between the dispersed members of a group.

To understand the communication structure of a group, it is necessary to know the pattern of positions, that is, the role and status of every member, and the duration and direction of communication from position to position. Each group member depends on information provided by others. Solving a problem, making a decision or reaching agreement, all require information exchange between individuals. The members of a group may work closely together, interacting frequently, and attending regular meetings. Alternatively, they may be physically dispersed within a building or located in different buildings, and therefore only able to come together occasionally, to attend a meeting. Increasingly, different members of the same group may be located in different countries (globally dispersed groups) and interact through videoconferencing. Whatever the situation, there are different ways to determine a group's communication structure.

Communication network analysis

When group members come physically together, and participate in a meeting around a table, a **communication network analysis** of the event can be conducted. This approach was pioneered by Noel Tichy and Charles Fombrun (1979). The observer makes a note of each participant's oral utterance and to whom they direct their comment. The outcome is a **communigram** which in some ways resembles a sociogram discussed earlier, but which details not mutual liking, but answers the two questions, who spoke to whom and how often.

Communication pattern analysis

When members of a group are physically dispersed around the same building, around different buildings or are located in different countries, it is still possible to determine the source, frequency and direction of their communication with each other by using **communication pattern analysis**. Instead of observing the interactions between individuals, which is impossible, the researcher would note the initiation and direction of telephone conversations, memos, faxes and emails between the group's members. This information is documented in a **communication pattern chart**.

For example, the information flow between the members of a group, can take the form of a chain. A tells B, B tells C and so on. In his classic study, William Foote Whyte (1948) described one such chain pattern in a restaurant in which customers gave their orders to a waitress, who passed it to a runner, who passed it to a pantry worker, before it was finally delivered to the cook. This communication network could produce a distortion in the message. When information arrived through this route, the cook was unable to check it; had no opportunity to negotiate with the customer; and hence was unable to discuss any problems.

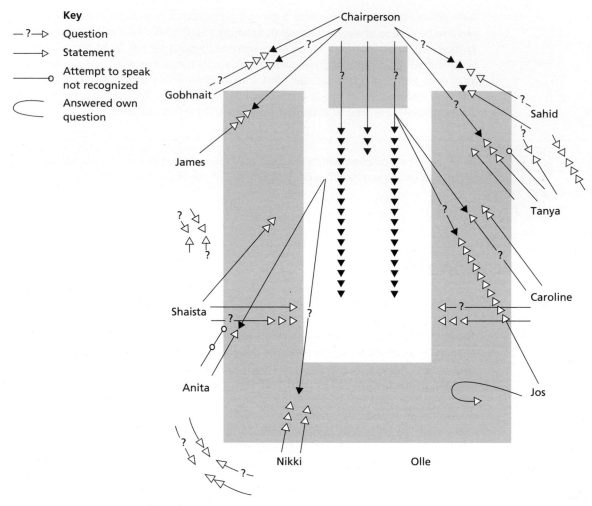

Figure 11.2: Communigram showing participation at a meeting

The aforementioned 'chain' is only one of several communication networks used by groups. To discover the full range and the effectiveness of each, Marvin Shaw (1978) conducted a laboratory experiment to test if certain group communication networks impeded or facilitated the performance of a task. While all the communication networks studied were adequate for the group to do the task, he discovered that some were superior in terms of standing up to disruption; and encouraging the emergence of leadership. Shaw studied the effects of five group communication networks on task performance and member satisfaction, and these are shown in Figure 11.3.

The way in which different communication networks affect group functioning in terms of group performance, structure and member satisfaction continues to be a subject of interest. Robert Baron and Jerald Greenberg (1990) studied the differences in performance between centralized and decentralized networks. The focus of their study was upon the type of task that a group was required to complete. The previous chapter distinguished between additive, conjunctive and disjunctive tasks. Baron and Greenberg distinguished between 'simple' and 'complex' tasks. They concluded that centralized networks are superior on simple tasks (top), and decentralized networks are superior on complex tasks (bottom). These are summarized in Figure 11.4. Managers in organizations are interested in ensuring that a group's communication network supports rather than impedes the achievement of its task. Hence, by first identifying the type of network used, and then assessing its effect, they can take steps to match the type of network with the type of group task.

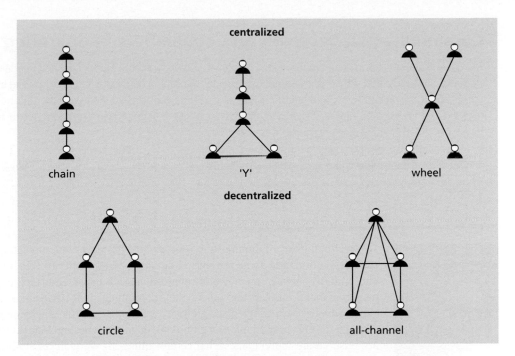

Figure 11.3: Centralized and decentralized communication patterns in groups

Source: Reprinted from *Group Processes* edited by L. Berkowitz, M.E. Shaw, Communications networks fourteen years later, pp.351–61, copyright 1978, with permission from Elsevier.

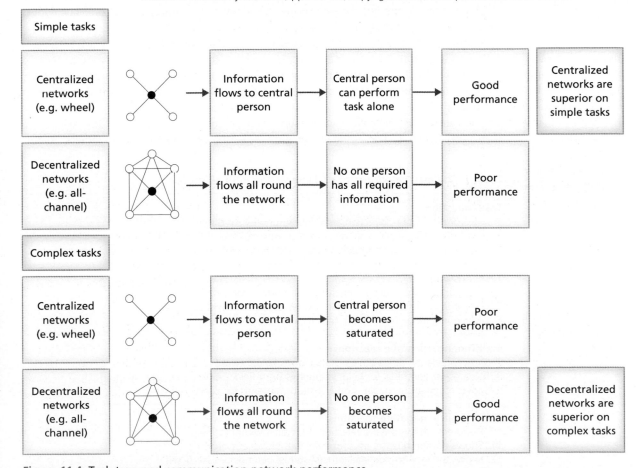

Figure 11.4: Task type and communication network performance

Source: From *Behaviour in Organizations*, 6/E, by Greenberg/Baron, © 1997 Reproduced by permission of Pearson Education, Inc., Upper Saddle River, NJ.

Communication between group members in operating theatres

Martin Makary and his colleagues from Johns Hopkins University surveyed 2,100 surgeons, anaesthesiologists and nurses about operating room communications. Surgeons received the lowest, and nurses the highest, ratings for teamwork. Another study of 60 hospitals investigated surgical mistakes (e.g. leaving a sponge inside the patient) and concluded that these could be avoided with 'better collaboration'. Nurses defined 'better collaboration' as meaning having their input respected by physicians, while the physicians defined it as nurses anticipating surgeons' needs and following surgeons' instructions.

Makary et al. *(2005, 2006).*

Interaction process analysis

Robert Freed Bales (1916–2004)

Interaction Process Analysis a technique used to categorize the content of speech.

Task activity an oral input, made by a group member, that contributes directly to the group's work task.

Maintenance activity an oral input, made by a group member that reduces conflict, maximizes cohesion and maintains relationships within a group.

The techniques of communication process analysis and communications network analysis provides information about the source, direction and quantity of verbal communication (oral and written) between members of congregated and dispersed teams respectively. However, neither of them considers the content of the communications between the individuals involved. When we observe a congregated group in action, for example, rugby players discussing their strategy for the second half, or a group of students discussing their tutorial system, what we are observe are individuals saying certain things. If we want to study the content of their oral behaviour within that group, we need a precise and reliable way of categorizing it. Robert Freed Bales (Bales 1950b) and his colleagues at Harvard University's Laboratory of Social Relations, went beyond their original research on who-talked-to-whom and how-often. He developed a technique for catgorizing the *content* of group members' oral behaviours (utterances) that he called **Interaction Process Analysis** (IPA).

Bales discovered that every group engaged in two types of oral activities which he termed **task activity** and **maintenance activity**. He found that when work groups were assigned a task, such as to solve a problem or make a recommendation, their members inevitably engaged in 12 different types of oral interactions which could be classified under four headings (Table 11.2).

One can classify or 'code' each person's oral utterance during a group discussion, into these 12 categories. For example, category 7 is 'shows solidarity, raises others' status,

Table 11.2: Bales' categories of oral interaction in small groups

Task: questions
1. Asks for orientation, direction, implying autonomy for others.
2. Asks for opinion, evaluation, analysis, expression of feeling.
3. Asks for orientation, information, repeats, clarifies, confirms.

Task: answers
4. Gives suggestion, direction, implying autonomy in others.
5. Gives opinion, evaluation, analysis, expresses feelings, wishes.
6. Gives orientation, information, repeats, clarifies, confirms.

Maintenance: positive reactions
7. Shows solidarity, raises others' status, gives help, reward.
8. Releases tension, asks for help, withdraws from field.
9. Shows antagonism, deflates others' status, defends or asserts self.

Maintenance: negative reactions
10. Disagrees, shows passive rejection, formality, withholds help.
11. Shows tension release, asks for help, withdraws out of field.
12. Shows antagonism, deflates others' status, defends or asserts self.

Based on Bales (1959).

gives help, reward'. So, if one group member said, 'That's an excellent idea from Lucy', that would be an example of a category 7 utterance. In contrast, category 12 is 'shows antagonism, deflates other's status, defends or asserts self'. If another member said, 'Jill's report was pathetic! I could do one that was twice as good in half the time', that would be an example of category 12 utterance. Bales felt that with his 12 categories, one could classify most utterances that were likely to be made by individuals in a group when they engaged in oral interaction. In his original experiments, his researchers acted as observers, and watched groups from behind a one-way mirror.

Analyzing oral interactions in a group

Below is a simplified version of Bales' Interpersonal Process Analysis (IPA) oral behaviour classification scheme. It consists of six oral behaviour categories, and each has an explanation alongside. Also provided is a chart for categorizing group members' oral contributions. There is a space for their initials along the top row. Next time you are present at a group discussion, listen to what each individual says. Every time they speak, decide in which oral category their utterance belongs, and place a tick or dot beside that category, under their name. Continue to do this, building up a record of the whole discussion.

After you have finished observing your discussion, total up your ticks or dots in the columns (horizontally) and for each group member (vertically). Your horizontal scores total gives you an indication of the behaviour of the group as a whole. For example, is this a group whose members are co-operating or competing with each other? Your vertical scores contrast the contributions of the individual group members, and can provide a clue to the roles that they are playing in the group.

proposing	any behaviour that puts forward a new suggestion, idea or course of action.
building	any behaviour that develops or extends an idea or suggestion made by someone else.
supporting	any behaviour that declares agreement or support with any individual or idea
disagreeing	any behaviour that states a criticism of another person's statement.
giving information	any behaviour that gives facts, ideas or opinions or clarifies these.
seeking information	any behaviour that asks for facts, ideas or opinions from others.

Oral interaction score sheet

Oral category	Members' names					
Proposing						
Building						
Supporting						
Disagreeing						
Giving • information • opinions • suggestions						
Seeking • information • opinions • suggestions						
TOTAL						

Bales' IPA is the most refined and exhaustive (empirically usable) method yet developed which can be used to study the content of the oral communication between individuals in groups. He provided the first rounded picture of what happens in face-to-face groups, by developing a theory of group functioning. He argued that group behaviour could be explained by showing how groups dealt with certain recurring problems such as orientation, evaluation, control, decision, tension-management and integration (Bales, 1953). His theory of group functioning thus pre-dates the Tuckman and Jensen model discussed previously.

STOP AND THINK   You have been assigned to a group and given a task to perform. You hate your job, and the management, and intend to resign shortly. What steps would you take to sabotage the work of your new group, while leaving you blameless in your boss's eyes, and confident of obtaining a good reference?

Stand back, I'm a social scientist!

To get its researchers from different fields to push new technologies through the research and development (R&D) pipeline, the Science and Technology Centre for Environmentally Responsible Solvents and Processes at Chapel Hill in North Carolina, USA, included a social scientist in each of its research teams. The idea was to analyze communication patterns between the team participants, to suggest improvements, and to make them more effective. The researchers were organized in teams according to the technical application that they were pursuing. For example, one team was developing polymers that dissolved in liquid carbon dioxide, thereby not only solving an environmental problem, but also allowing wafers to be coated with much thinner films. Getting this process to work in practice requires a range of skills and techniques. Diane Sonnenwald, a social scientist from the University of North Carolina, mapped out the pattern and level of communication between the researchers in the team. She conducted interviews to discover which colleagues within the team could most usefully collaborate.

The team leader acknowledged that Sonnenwald's input led him to appreciate the abilities of other members in the team, thereby highlighting complementary team skills. It also closed the gap between theorists and experimenters on the team. The two were stereotyped respectively as haughty high priests and pugnacious pragmatists. In fact, it was more a case of one researcher not understanding another's jargon; being afraid to ask stupid-sounding questions; or hesitating about giving up vital and hard-won information to a distant colleague. Sonnenwald was able to dismantle these types of barriers between the research team members, leading to greater co-operation between theorists and experimenters. It may be too early to judge how much this analysis of group process has accelerated development of liquid carbon-dioxide technology. However, the funding bodies are responding positively. Similar to the way in which sports teams have hired psychologists to produce a winning mind set, future technology teams may include a social scientist to help them find the shortest route from the laboratory to the marketplace.

Based on The Economist *(2001b, p.16).*

Role structure

It is a short step from identifying the main class of oral contributions that an individual makes in their group to determining their team member role. The occupants of every position in the group are expected to carry out certain functions when the members of the group interact with one another. The expected behaviours associated with a position within the group constitute the social role of the occupant of that position. **Social role** is the concept which relates the individual to the prescriptive dictates of the group. People's behaviour within the organization is structured and patterned in various ways. An understanding of role helps us to see and explain how this happens.

Social role the set of expectations that others hold of an occupant of a position.

Social role is the set of expectations that others hold of an occupant of a position in an organization structure, e.g. shop manager, bishop, head of the production department, etc.

These expectations presume attitudes, relationships and behaviours. A role is similar to a script that actors are given. The same actor changes their roles, and can act out different parts in front of different audiences. The topic of role within the context of organizational structure will be discussed later. Here, our concern is with the different roles that are played out by various members of a group or team. Totalling vertically each individual's oral contributions reveals that group members contributed in different ways to the discussion. Bales found that individuals played different roles (role differentiation) within their groups, and that this was a universal feature of face-to-face interaction in groups. As the group deals with its problems, individual members begin to 'specialize' in certain types of behaviours, thereby taking on different 'roles' within the group.

Group member roles

Kenneth Dean
Benne (1908–1992)

Within a group activity, such as a staff meeting or a tutorial discussion, some people will show a consistent preference for certain oral behaviours and not for others. The particular oral behaviour or set of behaviours that a person engages in within a group can lead them to be seen to be playing a particular role within that group. Kenneth Benne and Paul Sheats (1948) distinguished the roles that were played by the members of a group and developed three main headings. The names of their roles, under each heading, are shown in Table 11.3.

The first of these are *task roles,* which are principally directed towards achieving the group's task. The second heading, *maintenance and building roles* is concerned primarily with establishing and sustaining good relations between individual members so as to ensure the group as a whole can work together. Both of these categories of roles help the group to achieve its objective. In contrast, the third category, *individual* roles, impedes the group's efforts to achieve its aims. They have also been called 'self-interested roles' because they advance the interests of the individual member, rather than those of the group as a whole.

This distinction between behaviour that is oriented towards achieving the task, and behaviour that is focused upon individuals was originally made in the 1940s and 1950s. It has become the foundation for many subsequent teamwork theories and training, and has also laid the foundation for many theories of leadership. Following Benne and Sheats' original list of roles, many writers offered their own lists of team roles or team-player roles, which vary in number from 4 to 15 (Davis *et al.*, 1992; Margerison and McCann, 1990; Parker, 1990; Spencer and Pruss, 1992; Woodcock, 1989). All proponents of the team role concept claim to have observed the behaviours typical of that role being manifested in a variety of teams in different organizations.

Table 11.3: Benne and Sheats' roles commonly played by members of a group

Task	Building and maintenance	Individual (self-interested)
Initiator-contributor	Encourager	Aggressor
Information seeker	Harmonizer	Blocker
Opinion seeker	Compromiser	Recognition seeker
Information giver	Gatekeeper and expeditor	Self-confessor
Opinion giver	Standard setter	Playboy
Evaluator–critic	Observer and commentator	Dominator
Energizer	Follower	Help seeker
Procedural technician		Special interest pleader
Recorder		

From Benne and Sheats (1948).

Belbin's team role theory

A popular and widely used framework for understanding roles within a group or team was developed by Meredith Belbin and was based on research conducted at the Administrative Staff College, Henley (Belbin, 1981, 1993, 1996). He distinguished nine team roles. Each team role is listed and defined in Figure 11.5.

Team role an individual's tendency to behave in preferred ways which contribute to, and interrelate with, other members within a team.

Belbin argued that:

1. Within an organization people are generally appointed to a functional role on the basis of their ability or experience e.g. marketing. They are rarely selected for personal characteristics that would fit them to perform additional tasks within a team. In an ideal world, a person's functional role and their team role would coincide.

2. The personal characteristics of an individual fit them for some roles within a team, while limiting the likelihood that they will be successful in other roles. For Belbin therefore

	roles and descriptions – team role contribution	allowable weaknesses
	**Plant** Creative, imaginative, unorthodox. Solves difficult problems.	Ignores details. Too preoccupied to communicate effectively.
	**Resource investigator** Extrovert, enthusiastic, communicative. Explores opportunities. Develops contacts.	Over-optimistic. Loses interest once initial enthusiasm has passed.
	**Co-ordinator** Mature, confident, a good chairperson. Clarifies goals, promotes decision-making, delegates well.	Can be seen as manipulative. Delegates personal work.
	**Shaper** Challenging, dynamic, thrives on pressure. Has the drive and courage to overcome obstacles.	Can provoke others. Hurts people's feelings.
	**Monitor–evaluator** Sober, strategic and discerning. Sees all options. Judges accurately.	Lacks drive and ability to inspire others. Overly critical.
	**Teamworker** Co-operative, mild, perceptive and diplomatic. Listens, builds, averts friction, calms the waters.	Indecisive in crunch situations. Can be easily influenced.
	**Implementer** Disciplined, reliable, conservative and efficient. Turns ideas into practical actions.	Somewhat inflexible. Slow to respond to new possibilities.
	**Completer** Painstaking, conscientious, anxious. Searches out errors and omissions. Delivers on time.	Inclined to worry unduly. Reluctant to delegate. Can be a nit-picker.
	**Specialist** Single-minded, self-starting, dedicated. Provides knowledge and skills in rare supply.	Contributes on only a narrow front. Dwells on technicalities. Overlooks the 'big picture'.

Strength of contribution in any one of the roles is commonly associated with particular weaknesses. These are called allowable weaknesses. Executives are seldom strong in all nine team roles.

Figure 11.5: Belbin's nine team roles

Source: From Belbin (1996, p.122). Reprinted by permission of Belbin Associates.

Raymond Meredith
Belbin (b.1926)

team roles are *individual preferences* based on personality, and not the *expectations of others*, as discussed earlier in this chapter with respect to social role.

3. Individuals tend to adopt one or two team roles fairly consistently.

4. The roles that individuals are naturally inclined towards can be predicted through personality assessments, and the team role questionnaire.

5. In an ideal ('dream') team, all the necessary roles are represented, and the preferred roles of members complement each other, thereby avoiding 'gaps'. This does not mean that every team has to consist of nine people. A single member can 'double up' and play several roles, thereby enabling the overall size of the team to be reduced.

6. The assessment, selection, placement and guidance of individual employees by management is the way to improve team effectiveness. Once management knows employees' team role preferences, it can use them to compose teams in which all the required role preferences are represented.

STOP AND THINK Belbin argued that a successful team was one in which all nine of his roles were represented. What factors, inside or outside the organization, other than team role preferences, are likely to affect the success or failure of a team?

Critique of team role theory

Because of its widespread popularity, Belbin's theory has been extensively researched and continues to receive a great deal of critical assessment which has been summarized by Aitor Aritzeta *et al.* (2007). The main criticisms of the theory are summarized below. Writers variously claim that:

- There is little empirical evidence to support his theory and it is difficult to devise measures of team success that can be objectively related to team composition. It is difficult to say that a given team succeeded because it possessed all nine roles or failed because it lacked some of them.

- The questionnaire is based on respondents' self-reporting. Self-perceptions are a poor basis upon which to select team members. A more objective measure might be obtained through the use of peer ratings and an established personality assessment questionnaire.

- How individuals see their team roles is influenced as much by the roles that they habitually play, especially in teams, and what is expected of them in such roles. Thus the questionnaire scores reflect not only an individual's personality traits, but also their social learning of roles.

- The theory takes an excessively psychological perspective on role, neglecting the sociological dimension of the social position they habitually adopt, and what is expected of them in such positions by others.

- The theory does not sufficiently take into account differences in the type of task that the team is being asked to perform. Additive, conjunctive and disjunctive tasks may require different combinations of team roles to achieve success.

- Team performance is affected by a variety of different factors such as strategy and leadership, structure and management style, interpersonal skills and company resources. Focusing exclusively on team composition leads to ignoring these other critical factors.

- The concepts of team role and personality have become intertwined, being treated as interchangeable, rather than as separate but interrelated. Team roles and individual personality differences have been insufficiently related.

David Butcher and Catherine Bailey (2000) questioned the idea that a 'dream team' is one in which all members are fully committed to the team's goals; where they are all present when decisions are taken; and where all members work closely together. They felt that this was both impractical and undesirable. Managers who worked on several projects did not have time to develop close relationships, could not give full commitment to a team, and were not able to be present at all its meetings. The authors recommended instead that the task allotted to a team should indicate the required performance criteria, and members should have it explained to them how they are to work together. Butcher and Bailey concluded that organizations could benefit by understanding how teams operated in real life, rather than how they ought to work, and they rejected the idea that a team should conform to some ideal, regardless of the organizational circumstances (see also Manning *et al.*, 2006).

Leadership structure

There are many jobs to be done in a group if it is to be both productive and satisfying for its members. The emergence of a leader within any group is a function of its structure. Usually, a group makes a leader of the person who has some special capacity for coping with the group's particular problems. They may possess physical strength, shrewdness, or some other relevant attribute. The leader and the members all play roles in the group. Through them, a group atmosphere is created which enables communication, influence, and decision-making to occur. In much of the management literature, leadership is considered exclusively as a management prerogative. Authors write about 'management style' rather than 'leadership style'. This material will be dealt with in a later chapter.

Leadership styles in groups

Kurt Zadek Lewin
(1890–1947)

Ronald O. Lippitt
(1914–1986)

A classic study of leadership of groups was conducted by Kurt Lewin, Ralph White and Ronald Lippitt in the 1930s. It involved four groups of ten-year old boys, each of whom attended an after-school hobby club. Each group's members had been matched on characteristics such as age, personality, IQ, physical and socio-economic status, to be as similar as possible. The adult leaders were trained in three leadership styles:

Authoritarian leadership: The primary focus was upon achievement. The leader gave orders, praised or criticized the boys without giving reasons. He behaved in a distant and impersonal way, discouraging communication between the boys themselves.

Democratic leadership: The primary focus was on boys' choices. When the leader made comments, he explained them. He used discussions to help the boys plan their projects; allowed them to choose their own work mates; and permitted them to communicate freely with each other. He also participated in the group activities himself.

Laissez-faire leadership: The primary emphasis was minimal involvement. The leader left the boys to themselves; only gave advice and help when directly asked; and provided no praise, blame or any other comments.

As indicated above, the three leadership styles had different effects on group atmosphere and productivity and on liking for the leader. The researchers found that the autocratic leadership style led to high productivity, but only in the presence of the leader. It also created an aggressive but dependent atmosphere among the boys. The democratic leadership style led to relatively high productivity; to the boys liking their leaders most; the creation of a friendly atmosphere; and the boys proceeding with their work, irrespective of the presence or absence of the leader. The laissez-faire leadership style led to low productivity that only increased when the leader was present. It created a friendly but play-oriented atmosphere.

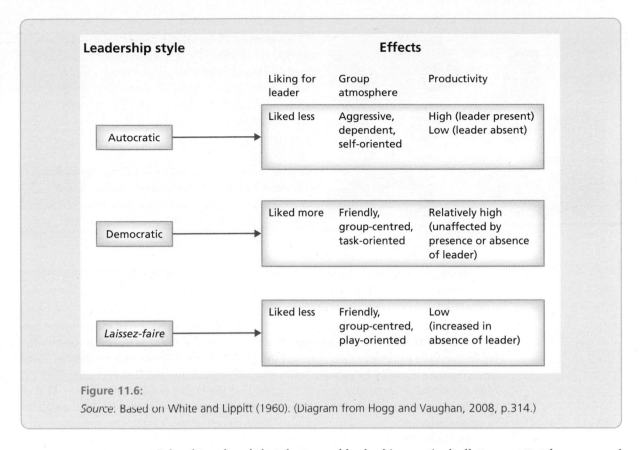

Figure 11.6:
Source: Based on White and Lippitt (1960). (Diagram from Hogg and Vaughan, 2008, p.314.)

It has been found that the type of leadership exercised affects group performance and member satisfaction. Activities are performed and actions are taken by the leader. There has been an increasing interest in **distributed leadership** within a group as opposed to individual leadership (see Chapter 19, Leadership). One can distinguish between a leader and acts of leadership. If we accept Raymond Cattell's (1951) view that the leader is any group member who is capable of modifying the properties of the group by their presence, then we can acknowledge that any member of the group can perform acts of leadership, and not just a single, designated individual. The group leadership approach considers the characteristics of small groups, seeking to understand the organizational context in which they exist, and the objectives that they seek to achieve. It seems therefore more useful to view leadership as a set of behaviours that change their nature depending on circumstances, and which switch or rotate between group members as circumstances change, rather than a static status associated with a single individual.

Distributed leadership the collective exercise of leadership behaviours, often informal and spontaneous, by staff at all levels of an organization.

Male and female ways of working

Jennifer Berdahl and Cameron Anderson (2005) argue that men and women in offices work in different ways. While women prefer to share the workload equally when working in groups, men prefer hierarchical group structures with a clearly defined leader and followers. A group containing a balance of both sexes often starts by following the male, hierarchical model, but over time, adopts the female approach. This was the finding of two studies. In one, 109 students were put into teams of about 12 – all-male, all-female and balanced teams – to work on a project for three weeks. The second involved 169 students put into teams of 4 – majority-male, majority-female, and balanced teams – for a 10-week project. Both studies showed that female-dominated groups developed less centralized patterns of leadership than male-dominated ones. Women's preferences for equality became integrated within mixed-sex groups over time, and centralization decreased in balanced groups. Asked about their preferences, women, more than men, described their companies as those which had egalitarian cultures.

Source: Pressmaster/Dreamstime.com

The second study considered the performance of groups, and found that quality suffered when leadership was highly centralized, and when a majority of group members did not perform leadership tasks, or contribute to the group's efforts. Previous research has shown that generally, centralized leadership reduced performance in tasks such as brainstorming, judgement and decision-making. However, situations that require planning and co-ordinating, such as large groups doing complex tasks, may benefit from the more hierarchical male model. Further research is needed as centralized leadership is also associated with high levels of tardiness, absenteeism and turnover, and low levels of cohesion and satisfaction in the workplace.

Based on Berdahl and Anderson (2005).

The relationship between the group's leader, at a given point in time, and the followers may be thought of as one of social exchange. The leader provides rewards for the group by helping its members to achieve their own and the group's goals. They in turn reward the leader by giving the individual heightened status and increased influence. However, members can rescind that influence at any time if they feel that the leader is no longer worthy of their respect. Viewed as a social exchange process, the leader has power in terms of their ability to influence the behaviour of those around them. Nevertheless, it is the group members who give the leader the power to influence them.

Original research by Robert Bales and Philip Slater (1956) into newly constituted groups found that two leaders regularly emerged. One was the *task leader* who specialized in making suggestions, giving information, expressing opinions and generally contributing to helping the group achieve its objective. The other was the *socio-emotional leader* who helped maintain relationships between group members, allowing them to express their ideas and positive feelings. This person made jokes, and released tensions in the group, and helped to maintain the group as a functioning entity. Although there was some rivalry, the two group leaders, *task* and *socio-emotional*, typically co-operated and worked together well. Lynda Gratton and her colleagues (Gratton *et al.*, 2007) confirmed this distinction 50 years later when investigating teams which demonstrated high levels of collaboration. They found that the flexible behaviour of their team leaders, both task and relationship-oriented, was crucial. Successful group leaders changed their style. Initially, they emphasized task leadership – clarifying goals, committing members and defining individual responsibilities. Later, they switched to a relationship orientation, once the tensions around sharing knowledge emerged. Ambidextrous team leaders, possessing both task and relationship skills, appeared to be essential.

Virtual teams

Virtual team one that relies on technology-mediated communication, while crossing boundaries of geography, time, culture and organization, to accomplish an interdependent task.

Increasing competition and globalization is forcing organizations to speed up their development and production of new products and services. Simultaneously, advancing communications hardware is allowing individuals to interact with others anywhere in the world, on the move, via laptop or mobile phone. Additionally, project-management software ('groupware') links the members of a team electronically, allowing them instantly to share and analyze project information. This combination of market-push and technology-pull has led companies to explore new types of working arrangements and organizational forms. One such development is the virtual team.

Virtual teams give companies access to the most qualified individuals to do a particular job irrespective of their geographical location; allow them to respond faster to competition; and give individuals greater flexibility in working from home. The virtual team has disrupted many aspects of traditional group structures – power, status, liking, communication, role and leadership. Much current social science research is devoted to describing and explaining the changes involved. According to Yuhyung Shin, virtual teams can be distinguished on four dimensions that are listed below (Shin, 2005):

Synchronous communication occurs when people are online at the same time, engaging in a real time conversation with others, somewhat similar to normal face-to-face discussions.

spatial dispersion the extent to which team members work in different geographical locations

cultural dispersion the extent to which a team consists of employees from different countries or cultures

temporal dispersion the extent to which team members work at different times

organizational dispersion the degree to which team members work across organizational boundaries

Asynchronous communication occurs when participants start a discussion topic (or thread), post replies to each other and, after delays, individuals read to catch up with the discussion. It is similar to a dialogue conducted by post.

Virtual teams can choose from a range of communication technologies to supplement or replace face-to-face interaction (Bell and Kozlowski, 2002; Griffith *et al.*, 2003). Their choice is affected by spatial dispersion, i.e. the spread of team members at different geographical locations or different workplaces at the same geographic location; and by temporal dispersion, i.e. the timing of members' communications (synchronicity) with each other, as they seek to accomplish their team's task. These can take the form of either synchronous or asynchronous communications. **Synchronous communication** is when you get an immediate answer to your question (e.g. telephone). **Asynchronous communication** is when you send a message and wait for an answer (e.g. email). If a virtual team member is dealing with a colleague in another country who speaks a different first language, asynchronous communication gives them more time to think and react. It is a disadvantage to them if they have to think in real time.

Home viewing

In *The Bourne Ultimatum* (2007, director Paul Greengrass), the CIA are in pursuit of one of their agents, an amnesiac, Jason Bourne (played by Matt Damon). The CIA team demonstrate the characteristics of a virtual team. Members are located in Langley, London, Madrid and Tangiers. Their 'assets' (mainly assassins) come from their different home countries. The CIA members in both the USA and Europe appear to be all working at the same time. They constantly interact to give, receive and carry out orders. Although the story involves action at various CIA sub-stations around the world, they are all part of the same security organization. By texting instructions, 'assets' can either act immediately on receiving their orders, or else catch up with them later. As you watch the film, note the examples of virtual team characteristics of spatial, cultural, temporal and organizational dispersion and asynchronous communication, each time they appear.

Cultural dispersion refers to the fact that a virtual team is composed of individuals from diverse cultural backgrounds, while organizational dispersion relates to the fact that the members of a virtual team may be members of more than one company, and could include suppliers, retailers and even consumers. It is therefore not uncommon for differences to exist in members' assumptions, motivations, knowledge bases and working styles (Shapiro *et al.*, 2002). The differences in time and place associated with different forms of information exchange possibilities were summarized by James Bowditch and Anthony Buono (2001) and are shown in Figure 11.7. According to this table, the members of a team may be present in the same place (co-located) or in different places (distributed), when receiving or giving information. Similarly, their communication may be synchronous or asynchronous. Successful collaboration within virtual teams requires participants to establish contact with each other,

		PLACE			
		Same		**Different**	
TIME	**Same**	**Co-located/Synchronous** • Face-to-face meetings • Technography • Decision-support rooms I	II	**Distributed/Synchronous** • Audio (telephone) • Videoconferencing • Distance whiteboarding	
	Different	III	IV		
		Co-located/Asynchronous • Resource centre • Team rooms • 'War' room		**Distributed/Asynchronous** • Voice mail, e-mail • Computer conferencing • Groupware & intranets	

Figure 11.7: Time and place dimensions of team information exchange

Source: From Bowditch and Buono (2001, p.170).

agree lines of communication and build trust. This is done more easily face to face. Psychologists recommend that virtual team members who typically interact through email, telephone and videoconference, should occasionally meet physically to become aware of each other's personal and cultural contexts (Newing, 2007).

IBM and Linux: virtual team problem-solving

Following Hurricane Katrina, IBM resolved a technical problem by using its Blue Pages Plus expertise locator, on its corporate internet. It found the staff members it wanted within two hours, and established a *wiki* (a web page that can be edited by anyone with access), and used it as a virtual meeting room. A team of IBMers from the US, Germany and the UK joined together to offer a solution to the problem in the space of just a few days. Teamworking within Linux, the open source software community, managed to create a barrier to protect the system against a virus that had breached a vulnerable spot. 'Despite the need for the highest security, a group of some 20 people, scarcely any of whom had ever met, employed by a dozen different companies, living in as many time zones, and straying far from their job descriptions, accomplished in about 29 hours what might have taken colleagues in adjacent cubicles weeks or months.'

Based on Hindle, 2006d, pp.15–18, 2006e, p.16; Evans and Wolf (2005).

Current thinking about virtual teams is moving away from viewing them as a special type of team that exists in contrast to 'traditional' face-to-face teams, but focuses instead on the concept of *virtualness*, as a potential characteristic of all teams. The phrase, virtual team, immediately conjures up images of desktop videoconferencing. However, the members of every team, when communicating with each other, are likely to use other ('lower') technology such as telephones, email, real-time calendar/scheduling systems, electronic bulletin boards, websites and so on. That is why Shin (2005) argues that the more any team possesses the four characteristics of spatial, temporal, cultural and organizational dispersion, the more virtual it becomes. In consequence, discussion conceives of a continuum, with face-to-face teams at one end, and virtual teams on the other, and real teams being placed somewhere along that continuum, depending on their characteristics (Griffith and Neale, 2001).

Organizations are increasingly taking advantage of electronic media to support group work activity through a variety of software tools that allow group members to engage in voting, sorting, prioritizing, collaborative document editing, online chatting, interactive video

Technology and trust in virtual teams

Technology plays a central role in collaborative efforts, especially when the players are virtual. Lynda Gratton found that while most of the teams that she studied used asynchronous technology in the form of voicemails and emails, many fewer used videoconferencing. In a virtual world, visual identification can be enormously useful. As visitors to *Second Life* know, working together remotely goes against our natural human instincts. Ceri Roderick, an occupational psychologist, said that 'We are optimally evolved to talk at the range of about 5 feet in groups of no more than 90 people . . . We respond to a rich stream of information and judge nuances such as pronunciation or slight facial expressions.' This enables us to assess people's motives, reliability and trustworthiness. As organizations become more global and their staffs more dispersed, the limits of normal human interaction are stretched. Roderick states that the objective of technology is to replicate the rich stream of information when the communication between dispersed members of a team is particularly important, for example, when building relationships, developing trust, solving problems or reviewing their progress. Doing this without travelling requires video-conferencing. The purpose of many videoconferences is not to get things done, but merely to make contacts and build trust between participants – people want to know who they are dealing with. The growth of videoconferencing has been limited due to poor video and sound quality, no eye contact, no gaze awareness, no body language, small people images and no depth of field. Most of these problems can now be fixed.

Conceived by Kenneth Crangle at Hewlett-Packard, a major computer and printer corporation, *telepresence* is a videoconferencing system that has been so upgraded that participants at a meeting forget or stop caring, that those at the other end of the room are on different continents. The use of improved live video and audio feeds and enlarged screens (see photo above), creates the illusion that the parties are talking across a table. Studies of

Source: B. Busco/Getty Images

videoconferencing by Andrew Davis and Ira Weinstein of Wainhouse Research found that its deficiencies – fiddling-with-controls delays; watching tiny faces on TV screens; conversations as a series of time-delayed interruptions and missed social signals – all meant that users felt alienated, and even keener to meet each other face-to-face.

To overcome these problems, people in *telepresence* meetings must appear life-sized; the tables and rooms at the two ends must blend seamlessly; participants must feel that they are making eye contact; and sound must be perceived to be coming from the mouth of the person speaking. Sight and sound delays must be negligible (i.e. below 250 milliseconds, the threshold at which the human brain starts to notice), so as to allow members to interrupt each other naturally. The aim is to make the participants not only task-involved but also emotionally involved. Achieving this involves enormous computing power, multiple cameras, and rooms around the world having the same furniture and wallpaper. At about $300,000 per room, *telepresence* is not cheap. However, it reduces travel bills, is environmentally friendly and saves time.

Based on Gratton (2007); Newing (2007);
The Economist (2007c, pp.63–4).

Source: Copyright Grantland Enterprises; www.grantland.net

and collective decision-making. The effectiveness of virtual workgroups is a significant issue, and we need to know how the quality of the working life of their members, as well as their dynamics and productivity, are affected by members not being in face-to-face contact with each other. Why are organizations experimenting with virtual teams? Antony Townend *et al.* (1998) offer a number of reasons:

- the trans-nationalization of trade and business activity;
- heightened worker expectations about participation and involvement;
- the increasing prevalence of flat or horizontal organization structures;
- environmental pressures that require inter-organizational co-operation;
- the on-going shift from production to service/knowledge based environments.

Information and communication technologies can potentially increase the effectiveness of teamworking by removing barriers of place, and enabling individual team members to work together across organizational and geographical boundaries. However, it is more difficult for a virtual team to be successful since there is a greater potential for misunderstandings to arise and for more things to go wrong. Bowditch and Buono (2001) explain that while team leaders are skilled in dealing with Quadrant I interactions (same time/same place), they lack the experience and expertise to guide and facilitate interactions in the other three quadrants. These authors believe that the only way to build trust and resolve conflicts between individuals, especially in the early stages of projects, is to give them the full sensory information that only person-to-person interactions provide. Bowditch and Buono report that some companies are experimenting with 'hybrid meetings' where one part is physical and the other is virtual. Some members are physically present in the room, while the others are 'attending' from their offices via desktop videoconferencing and instant messaging technologies. They conclude that moving virtual teams beyond being just vehicles for information sharing mechanisms, and towards having them complete organizational tasks and resolve project-related issues, raises unique challenges for managers and their organizations.

Software development and group communication

Source: Studio/Dreamstime.com

Some observers believe that computer science is really social science. Alberto Espinosa and his colleagues showed the importance of technical, temporal and process coordination which resulted in cost savings, reduced development cycles and better integrated products. Jonathan Pincus, an expert on software reliability and a past employee of Microsoft

Research observed that the key issues in programming related not to technical matters but to people – how they organized themselves and communicated with each other. Grady Booch of IBM Rational tracked 50 software developers for 24 hours and discovered that only 30 per cent of their time was spent on coding. The remainder was devoted to talking to their fellow team members. Programmers generally work together using a software platform called an 'integrated development environment'. This keeps track of the different pieces of code developed by different individuals and, when required, assembles these codes into a single, complete programme or 'build', for testing. However, few companies have their developers and testers either in the same office or even in the same country any longer. Hence, software programming tools now require additional features to allow coders to communicate with each other, request design changes and to report problems.

Based on The Economist *(2008c, pp.22 and 24);*
Espinosa et al. *(2007).*

 **RECAP**

1. *List the six dimensions of group structure.*
   - The six main dimensions along which the members of a group differ are – power, status, liking, communication, role and leadership. A person may be placed high on one dimension and simultaneously low on another.
   - The group's structure acts to increase the predictability of behaviour between the group's members.

2. *Identify the sources of power within the group.*
   - There are six bases or types of power – reward, coercive, referent, legitimate, expert and informational.

3. *Distinguish between two common uses of the concept of status.*
   - The status structure of a group is determined by how much status an individual member possesses. There is formal status and social status.

4. *Understand how emotional relationships within a group can be represented symbolically.*
   - The liking (emotional) structure of a group is revealed through the use of sociometry, a technique developed by Jacob Moreno.

5. *Distinguish between communication network analysis, a communication pattern analysis, and IPA analysis.*
   - Communication network analyses of a group maps the direction and quantity of oral communication in a group. It is depicted on a communigram.
   - Communication pattern analysis analyses documents, data, and voicemail transmission, to determine the source, direction and quantity of both oral and written communication between the dispersed members of a group. It is depicted as a 'chain', 'Y', 'wheel', 'circle' or 'all channel'.

   - Interpersonal Process Analysis (IPA) classifies the content of oral communications between group members. It was developed by Robert Bales.

6. *Distinguish between task, socio-emotional and individual classes of roles within a group.*
   - The role structure of a group can differentiate those members who perform task-focused roles, relations-oriented roles, and self-oriented roles. This distinction was made by Benne and Sheats.

7. *Distinguish Belbin's team roles.*
   - Meredith Belbin's team role theory distinguishes the roles played by the members of a team. They are plant, resource investigator, co-ordinator, shaper, monitor evaluator, teamworker, implementer, completer and specialist.

8. *Give examples of three leadership styles identified by White and Lippitt.*
   - White and Lippitt distinguished three leadership styles which they labelled authoritarian, democratic and laissez-faire.

9. *Distinguish between a task and socio-emotional group leader.*
   - Bales and Slater suggested that a group often had both a task leader and a socio-emotional leader. The first drove the group towards task achievement, while the second maintained the group as a co-operative working unit.

10. *List the four key dimensions of a virtual team.*
    - Spatial dispersion – the extent to which team members work in different geographical locations: cultural dispersion – the extent to which a team consists of employees from different countries or cultures; temporal dispersion – the extent to which team members work at different times; and organizational dispersion – the degree to which team members work across organizational boundaries.

Revision

1. Select any two groups with which you are familiar. Contrast them in terms of any group structure dimensions that are relevant – power, status, communication, liking, roles and leadership. Suggest possible reasons for the similarities and differences that you have highlighted.

2. Describe situations in which a (i) team role analysis and (ii) a sociogram would be relevant to improve a group's functioning. How would you apply these two techniques? How would you use the results?

3. What are the strengths and weaknesses of Belbin's team role theory as a guide for the manager wishing to construct a team that will be effective?

4. What are some of the problems that a new leader of a group faces? How can they be overcome?

5. Identify some of the problems of virtual teamworking for (a) the companies which establish them, and (b) the individuals who work in them. How might these problems be overcome?

Research assignment

Studies suggest that people spend 5–6 hours a week in meetings (Daft and Marcic, 2009, p.615). Get invited to a real meeting that takes place in an organization which is likely to last at least 30 minutes. Consult the box 'Analysing oral interactions in a group' on page 337, making several copies of the oral interaction score sheet that you will find there. Read and follow the instructions detailed in the box. After 30 minutes of silently observing and scoring, excuse yourself and leave the meeting quietly. After you have added up your scores, write a brief report which comments on (a) the way this group as a whole was working, (b) the roles played by its individual members, and (c) the adequacy of your scoring sheet and its underlying assumptions. Make recommendations as to how your group's members' interactions could be improved.

Springboard

Kilduff, M. and Krackhardt, D., 2008, *Interpersonal Networks in Organizations*, Cambridge University Press, Cambridge.

The authors apply a social network perspective to a range of organizational behaviour issues including leadership and decision-making.

Montoya, M.M., Massey, A.P., Hung, Y.C. and Crisp, C.B., 2009, 'Can you hear me now?: Communication in virtual product development teams', *Journal of Product Innovation Management*, 26(2): 139–55.

These researchers investigated the problems experienced by members of virtual teams when using information and communication technologies during new product development projects.

Nunamaker, J.F., Reinig, B.A. and Briggs, R.O., 2009, 'Principles for effective virtual teamwork', *Communications of the ACM*, 52(4): 113–17.

The authors compare managing virtual teams and face-to-face teams; discuss the challenges of establishing cohesive relationships necessary for achieving objectives; and consider the practical problems of assimilating new technologies into daily work routines.

Wheelan, S.A., 1999, *Creating Effective Work Teams*, Sage, London.

Using a version of the Tuckman and Jensen framework, the author offers a range of strategies for building and supporting well-managed, high performing teams. The book is more of a practical guide than a theoretical discourse.

OB in films

Network (1976, director Sidney Lumet), DVD track 16: 1:48:00–1:53:00 (5 minutes). This film is set in the US television industry. Because of his falling ratings, the Union Broadcasting System (UBS) fires its leading news anchorman Howard Beale (played by Peter Finch). Beale's on-air behaviour then becomes increasingly bizarre, after he promises to kill himself on television. Initially, his ratings sky-rocket as he becomes the 'Mad Prophet of the Airways', but they then decline, affecting UBS's other programmes and its revenue. The clip begins as network executives assemble for a meeting, and ends with Diana saying 'let's kill the son-of-a-bitch'. Hackett (played by Robert Duvall) sits at the desk and begins the meeting by describing the problem.

Listen to the discussion between the six individuals in the room. Each time one of them speaks, decide into which of the six oral categories it fits, and indicate this by putting a tick or dot under their name. Continue until the clip has finished.

B	C	D	E	F
Joe	Man in chair	Man in armchair	Herb (standing)	Diana

A
Hackett

Oral interaction score sheet							
Oral category	Meeting participants						
	A Hackett	B Joe	C Main in chair	D Man in armchair	E Herb (standing)	F Diana	TOTAL
Proposing							
Building							
Supporting							
Disagreeing							
Giving • information • opinions • suggestions							
Seeking • information • opinions • suggestions							
TOTAL							

OB in literature

William Golding, *Lord of the Flies*, Faber & Faber, London, 1954. In this novel (also a film), a party of schoolboys are marooned following an airplane crash. They form a society-in-microcosm. What group norms and sanctions develop? What aspects of group structure, group power and conflict are illustrated?

CHAPTER EXERCISES

Tasks and groups

Objectives   1. To distinguish between the different types of tasks that a group may perform.

2. To examine group processes including member roles, decision-making and leadership.

Briefing   (a) Form groups.

(b) Nominate a group observer to sit silently near the group and make a note of how the group went about its task; which people played which roles; how decisions were made; and how leadership was exercised.

(c) You have 15–20 minutes to complete four tasks which vary in their nature.

(d) The tasks are:

Task 1 – Rhyming words

Task 2 – Word equations

Task 3 – Whose job?

Task 4 – Motoring advice

(e) Group observers provide feedback to their groups.

(f) Instructor explains the difference between different tasks and supplies solutions.

(g) Groups compare their answers and are provided with the correct answers.

(h) All the groups then,

- identify the unique characteristics of each type of task they performed
- provide other examples of each type of task in social or work life
- consider the effect of task type on group aspects such as choice of members, ways of working, methods of decision-making

Group tasks   **Task 1 – Rhyming words**. Generate words that rhyme with the 15 words listed below.

feast	beard	battle	flowers	hissed
hurried	profit	world	orange	load
sorrow	song	accounting	great	smiles

Task 2 – Word equations. Solve each of the word equations below by substituting the appropriate words for the letters e.g. 3F = 1Y (3 feet = 1 yard)

1. '1B in the H = 2 in the B'	7. 23Y – 3Y = 2D
2. 8D – 24H = 1W	8. 3P = 6
3. E – 8 = Z	9. C + 6D = NYE
4. HH & MH at 12 = N or M	10. A & E were in the G of E
5. 4J + 4Q + 4K = CC	11. 29 – D. in F. in a L.Y.
6. S&M&T&W&T&F&S are D of W	12. 'NN = GN'

Task 3 – Whose job? Discover which person has which job.

Betty, Tom, Edward, Sid and Dave comprise the employees of the firm and fill the jobs of clerk, administrator, manager, accountant and surveyor, but not in that order. Read the information below to determine which person holds which job. Use the grid overleaf as a bingo card, eliminating individuals, as you go.

The administrator bandaged the surveyor's finger when he cut it.

While the manager and the surveyor were away from the office, the accountant docked their subordinates – Dave and Sid – a half day's pay each, for taking the afternoon off.

The accountant is a fine bridge player, and Tom admires his ability.

Dave invited the administrator for lunch but his invitation was not accepted.

→

Betty	clerk	administrator	manager	accountant	surveyor
Tom	clerk	administrator	manager	accountant	surveyor
Edward	clerk	administrator	manager	accountant	surveyor
Sid	clerk	administrator	manager	accountant	surveyor
Dave	clerk	administrator	manager	accountant	surveyor

Task 4 – Motoring advice. Suggest the best route between your educational establishment and the nearest coastal town or city.

Exercise idea and Task 1 from Dodd-McCue, D., Journal of Management Education *15(3), pp. 335–9, copyright © 1991, OBTS Teaching Society for Management Educators. Reprinted by Permission of SAGE Publications.*

Team role questionnaire

Objectives
1. To introduce team role theory.
2. To identify your preferred team roles.

Instructions

Listed below are statements that describe behaviours that members use when they are participating in a team. As a student, you may demonstrate these behaviours at work, in team projects, student organizations and societies, or in interactions with your flatmates.

Use a 1–5 scale below to indicate how frequently you engage in these behaviours when part of a team. Place a number from 1 to 5 in the space to the left of each statement.

1	2	3	4	5
Very infrequently				Very frequently

_____ 1. I organize and use other people's abilities and talents productively.

_____ 2. I react strongly when meetings look like losing track of the objective.

_____ 3. I start to look around for possible ideas and openings.

_____ 4. I often produce a new approach to a long-continuing problem.

_____ 5. I analyse other people's ideas objectively for their merits and flaws.

_____ 6. I can be relied on to see that the work we need to do is organized.

_____ 7. I am always ready to support good suggestions that help us resolve a problem.

_____ 8. I notice omissions and have an eye for getting the details right.

_____ 9. I like to employ my experience, training and qualifications.

_____ 10. I often draw out contributions from other team members.

_____ 11. I am ready to make my personal views known in a forceful way if necessary.

_____ 12. A broad range of personal contacts is important to my style of working.

_____ 13. I like to use my imagination to suggest completely new approaches.

_____ 14. I like to weigh up several alternatives thoroughly before choosing, which may take time.

_____ 15. I am interested more in practicalities than in new ideas.

_____ 16. I am concerned to help others with their problems.

_____ 17. I keep a watchful eye on areas where difficulties may arise.

_____ 18. I usually only contribute when I really know what I'm talking about.

_____ 19. I am happy to take the lead when action is needed.

_____ 20. It is worth incurring some temporary unpopularity to get my views across.

_____ 21. I like to discover the latest ideas and developments as I get easily bored.

_____ 22. I can quickly see how ideas and techniques can be used in new relationships.

_____ 23. I approach the topic in a carefully analytical way.

_____ 24. Given an objective, I can sort out the concrete steps to achieve it.

_____ 25. I get on well with others and work hard for the team.

_____ 26. I like to finish my current work before I start something new.

_____ 27. My technical knowledge and experience are usually my major contributions.

Transfer the points from each of the 27 statements into the table below, placing them next to the statement number. Then add up the points in each of the nine columns. Enter these in the 'Total' row. This indicates the roles that you most frequently play in a team. The higher the score, the more you see yourself taking that role.

Co-ordinator	Shaper	Resource investigator	Plant	Monitor evaluator	Implementer	Team worker	Completer finisher	Specialist
1.	2.	3.	4.	5.	6.	7.	8.	9.
10.	11.	12.	13.	14.	15.	16.	17.	18.
19.	20.	21.	22.	23.	24.	25.	26.	27.
TOTAL								

Briefing

1. Divide into groups.

2. Remind yourself of each of the nine team roles.

3. In your groups:

   (a) Compare your top two team role scores with those of the other members of your group. Give an example of behaviours that demonstrate your performance of that role.

   (b) Identify which roles are preferred among students in this group (high scoring roles). Identify which roles avoided, rejected or are missing (low scoring roles).

   (c) If this was a real management or project team, what could be done to cover the missing roles?

   (d) Decide whether certain roles are more important in certain phases of a team's operation. For example, which two-team roles are likely to be crucial in the getting-started phase of a team's work; the generating-ideas phase; the developing-the-ideas phase; and the implementing-the-decision phase?

   (e) Decide to what extent your preferred team roles are a reflection of your personality.

   This questionnaire was adapted from one developed by Nancy Foy, building on the work of Meredith Belbin. It appeared in Boddy and Buchanan (1987), pp.32–35, Crown Copyright.

Chapter 12 **Individuals in groups**

Key terms

social identity

self-concept

self-esteem

social representations

shared frame of reference

social influence

social facilitation

synergy

social loafing

free rider

group norm

pivotal norm

peripheral norm

group sanction

conformity

obedience

group cohesion

group socialization

organizational socialization

deindividuation

compliance

conversion

Learning outcomes

When you have read this chapter, you should be able to define those key terms in your own words, and you should also be able to:

1. Explain the basic tenets of social identity theory and social representation theory.

2. Distinguish between social facilitation and social loafing.

3. Understand how groups use norms to regulate the behaviour of their members.

4. Understand the process of group socialization of individuals.

5. Explain why individuals conform to the dictates of their group.

6. Distinguish between conformity and obedience, and between compliance and conversion.

Why study individuals in groups?

Marion Hampton (1999, p.113) warns:

> Yet groups are also endowed with a darker side, one which is highlighted in mobs and crowds. They are seen as taking over the individual's mind, depressing intelligence, eliminating morale responsibility and forcing conformity. They can cause their members a great deal of suffering and despair and can perpetuate acts of great cruelty. If groups are capable of great deeds, they are also capable of great follies.

There is now extensive research evidence which demonstrates the power of groups to affect the behaviour of their individual members. This was originally revealed in the research conducted by Elton Mayo at the Hawthorne plant in the 1920s. Since that time, managements have harnessed this power by creating groups and teams which police and discipline their own members, keeping their behaviour in line with organizational (management) objectives. The most developed form of such management-initiated group control is to be found within Japanese team-working which will be described in the next chapter. However, this chapter introduces the basic concepts of group norms, socialization and sanctions.

The power of the group to affect the perceptions, performance and attitudes of its individual members is well established. However, since the 1980s, there has also been a growing body of research that shows how a lone individual can have an influence on a majority. The two concepts of compliance and conversion have generated a great deal of interest in this field.

STOP AND THINK

Think of three things that you do alone that you would not do if someone else was with you at work.

- Why would you not do these things in the presence of others?
- What would be the consequences in each case if you did?

Is such self-control beneficial to yourself, your employer or both? Explain how.

The individual and the group

Henri Tajfel and John Turner (1986) argued that as long as individuals see themselves as more important than their group, then the latter cannot function effectively. Participants have to stop seeing themselves as individuals, and instead identify themselves as group members, treating the group's values as their own. Such an attitudinal 'switch' and commitment, facilitates the long-term existence and success of their group. This question of how much an individual should be part of the group (for their own well being, for that of their group, and for the organization) and how much separate from it (to remain creative, critical and for their own mental health), is a continuing debate in the literature.

Social identity that part of the self-concept which comes from our membership of groups and which contributes to our self-esteem.

Let us first consider some theories which seek to explain the relationship between the individual and their group. **Social identity** theory was developed by Henri Tajfel and John Turner (1986). It holds that a person's self-concept is based not only on their individual characteristics or personal identity (*I am reserved, I am interested in music, I have blond hair*), but also on their group membership (*I am French, I work for ABC corporation, I am a member of the accounting profession*). They then compare themselves to other individuals and groups. Group formation can be seen as an adaptive process as one moves from feeling and thinking as an individual (personal identity), to feeling and thinking as a representative of a group (social identity). It holds that group membership affects people's sense of who they are. The groups or social categories to which we belong (e.g. student course member; management team member, parent or sports club secretary) are an integral part of

Self-concept the set
of perceptions that we
have about who we are.

our self-concept. Our own self-concept is the way in which we see ourselves, the set of perceptions that we have about ourselves. It affects both how we feel about ourselves and how we act within a group. This is because joining a group lowers our self-awareness and raises our group awareness. The roles that we play within different groups, especially those that are important to us, influence and shape our attitudes and behaviours.

The part of an individual's self-concept that comes from their membership of a group is called social identity and fulfils two functions. First, it defines and evaluates a person (e.g. 'she's a member of the design team'). Such definition and evaluation is done both by others and by the person themselves. Second, it prescribes appropriate behaviour for them. They think and behave in characteristically 'design team' ways. How this happens is through social comparison. According to Tajfel, in order to evaluate their own opinions and abilities, individuals not only compare themselves with other individuals with whom they interact, but they also compare their own group with similar, but distinct, out-groups. The dimensions that are used to make these comparisons are called social categorizations. Categorization leads to assumptions of similarity among those who are categorized together. It minimizes the perceived differences between members of the in-group, and maximizes the differences between the in-group and out-groups. When this happens, the individuals who are part of the in-group, will have assumed a social identity, and will view other people from this standpoint.

We all see ourselves as members of various social groupings, which are distinguishable and hence different from other social groupings. The consequence is that by identifying with certain groupings but not others, we come to see the world in terms of 'us-and-them'. There are two benefits for us from this. First, our understanding of the world is enhanced by classifying everybody this way. Second, our self-esteem can be maintained or even enhanced. Membership of a high status group gives us prestige, which in turn raises our self-esteem. We are highly motivated to feel proud to belong to the group of which we are members. If we cannot achieve this feeling of pride, we will either try to change the group's perceived status, or to detach ourselves from it. Although such social identification can potentially lead to conflict between different groups within an organization, it can also be effectively managed in a way that improves the performance of both groups.

Self-esteem that
part of the self which
is concerned with how
we evaluate ourselves.

Categorizing people into groups and identifying with some of these groups, appears to be a fundamental human characteristic which derives from the fact that human beings are social animals. Because of these two basic needs for differentiating themselves from others and for belonging, individuals expose themselves to the control of others. Within the organizational context, we offer control to fellow group members who wish to direct our attitudes, thoughts and ideas in line with what the group considers appropriate; and also to managers who seek both to motivate and control us, through instituting various team working arrangements.

STOP AND THINK Which group memberships do you cite when you introduce yourself to others? From the 'us-and-them' perspective, who are 'us', and who are 'them', for you? Has this helped your own group improve its performance? Has it raised your own self-esteem? Has the management in your organization used this distinction to motivate or control your group? How?

Group influences on individuals' perceptions

How does a group affect the perceptions of its individual members? One explanation was offered at the start of the book with the *social construction of reality* perspective. This argued that our social and organizational surroundings possess no ultimate truth or reality, but are determined instead by the way in which we experience and understand those worlds which we construct and reconstruct for ourselves, in interaction with others. In short, we don't see things as they are – we see things as *we* are. Among these important 'others' with whom we interact and with whom we experience and understand the world, are the members of our psychological group.

Another explanation is provided by social representations theory which was formulated by Serge Moscovici (1984). This refers to the finding that when individuals join a new group, its members will construct and transmit complex and unfamiliar ideas to them, in straightforward and familiar ways. This process creates what are termed, social representations which come to be accepted, in a modified form, by the new members of a group, and these help the new recruits to make sense of what is going on around them within the group and the organization. The explanation of some occurrence is simplified, distorted and ritualized by the group, and becomes a 'common sense explanation' which is accepted as orthodoxy among its members, and is then communicated to new members. Social representations are theories about how the world works and are used to justify actions. The prefix, 'social' in both phrases, reminds us about the collective way in which reality is jointly manufactured, accepted and shared. How does a group affect the perceptions of its individual members?

As a new company recruit, you discuss your role in the group with existing members. During these interactions, representations are presented, developed, adapted and negotiated before being incorporated into your own, existing, belief framework. This happens during the period of socialization, shortly after you join the group. It is not a matter of you, as a new recruit, being given and accepting a bundle of existing group assumptions, ideas, beliefs and opinions to absorb. Moscovici's theory emphasizes the interactive nature of the process between you as an individual, and the other group members. Once incorporated, the group representations are revealed in all members' speech and actions.

Through these social representations, group members gain a shared frame of reference. Over time, new-joiners learn about the different assumptions, ideas, beliefs and opinions held by their fellow group members about their common work situation. Some agreement on perception and meaning is essential among the members of a group if they are to interact, communicate, agree on goals and generally act in concert on a common task. Such a shared view is essential for a group if it is to continue and develop. Moreover, as we work in groups we find that our views coalesce with those of other members of the group. A shared frame of reference and social representations suggest a group-level equivalent of the concept of organizational culture. Together, these determine the meaning that group members attach to events and other people's behaviour.

Social representations the beliefs, ideas and values, objects, people and events that are constructed by current group members, and which are transmitted to its new members.

Shared frame of reference assumptions that are held in common by group members, which shape their thinking, decisions, actions and interactions, while being constantly defined and reinforced through those interactions.

Global teams and cross-cultural working

Organizations that operate in a global business environment create teams whose members are culturally diverse and who can have difficulty understanding, communicating, and working with each other. For example, the International Air Transport Association (IATA) represents 230 airlines, employs 1,600 staff from 140 nationalities, operates in 74 countries, and has its headquarters in Geneva (Switzerland) and Montreal (Canada). Companies have traditionally used either the 'colonial' approach, using skilled expatriates from the base country, or a 'cultural translators' approach, using staff who have working experience in more than one cultural setting. Western companies operating in mainland China, for example, often fill management roles with Chinese staff from Taiwan, Singapore and Hong Kong. However, cultural differences can limit the effectiveness of expatriates, and cultural translators are in high demand which makes them expensive. Chinese, Indian and many Asian cultures are 'collectivist' and are acutely aware of status differences, known as 'high power-distance' (see Chapter 4). In contrast, Western European and North American cultures are more individualist with 'low power-distance'. Junior team members from lower power-distance cultures share their ideas and challenge others, including more senior members of the team. In contrast, Chinese staff are cautious about making such interventions and defer to senior team members.

IATA developed a special training programme for 20 of their change agents, 10 from East Asia and 10 from European and American cultures. This programme was launched in Beijing by IATA's chief executive Giovanni Bisignani and his top team. This group was then paired to co-lead ten teams whose members were high-potential junior employees in different locations. This meant that each member of the co-management pair had to learn about and adjust their approaches to each other, as well as to their team members. The teams worked on defined projects, in addition to their routine jobs, for a couple of months. The change agents also had to provide skills training to another ten-person team, such as teamwork, project management, and cross-cultural awareness. This programme had powerful learning effects. For example, one participant said, 'Being Chinese, it was surprising how much I learnt about Chinese culture from the programme – but it was from the perspective of my western colleagues, so my insight now has a stereo effect.' The experience led to this plan for integrating different cultures:

- identify two cultures that need to collaborate
- nominate leaders from each culture
- allocate appropriate pairs of co-leaders
- use real projects as the basis for teamworking
- establish a realistic time-frame
- share practices, both good and bad
- adapt for the next cross-cultural challenge

The IATA chief executive concluded that this programme was 'helping me and my senior management team to accelerate the process of building a leadership pool within our Asian employee ranks. And it has exposed our current high-potential leaders to other cultures and sensitized them to doing business with Asian cultures'.

Based on Jonsen and Bryant (2008).

STOP AND THINK Has the effect of ethnic or national background in explaining the behaviour of individuals within multi-cultural groups been exaggerated (see Chapter 4)? Are members' personal characteristics and life experiences (see Chapter 6) more important in explaining the challenges faced by multi-cultural teams?

Group influences on individuals' performance

Social influence
the process where attitudes and behaviour are changed by the real or implied presence of others.

Social facilitation
the strengthening of the dominant (prevalent or likely) response due to the presence of others.

The presence of another person or a group of people changes our attitudes and behaviour. **Social influence** refers to the process where attitudes and behaviour are influenced in some way, by the real or implied presence of others. What type of student behaviour does the presence of a university invigilator in an examination hall seek to influence? The presence of others can either improve or reduce an individual's performance. Elliott Aronson and his colleagues (Aronson *et al.*, 1994, 2010) suggested two alternative reactions by an individual to having one or more people present when performing a task – **social facilitation** and social loafing. Their model stresses the importance of evaluation, arousal and task complexity (Figure 12.1). Psychologists distinguish between group process gains and losses. The former refers to the benefits gained by people working together as a group, rather than individually. The latter refers to the opposite, as when individuals expend less effort because their input within the group is less visible.

Social facilitation

Early research investigated individuals performing various physical tasks. Norman Triplett (1898) studied children winding fishing reels and cyclists racing. The children were found to turn the reels faster when other children were present, and the cyclists performed 20 per cent faster when accompanied by a pacemaker than when alone, even in a non-racing situation. He found that they performed better in the presence of another person (a co-actor). Later studies focused on non-physical tasks. Floyd Allport (1920) discovered that students completed mathematical calculations faster in the company of other students than when alone, and coined the term, social facilitation, to indicate that task was made easier, or was 'facilitated' by the presence of others.

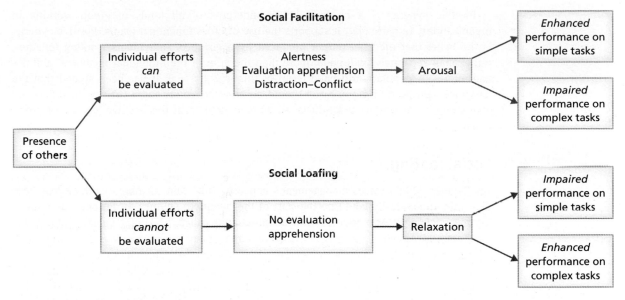

Figure 12.1: Social facilitation and social loafing
Source: From Aronson *et al*. (1994, 2010).

Check this out

Economists Alexandre Mas and Enrico Moretti, were interested in 'peer effects' – what happens when an unusually hardworking (or lazy) worker joins a team? Their results were based on scarily detailed data! They persuaded a supermarket to provide them with every single checkout ('beep') transaction, for 370 workers in six stores, timed by the second, for two years. Each worker's productivity can be measured by the second, and changes identified, depending on who else is working at the same time. The prediction is not obvious, as customers join fast moving queues; quick workers lighten the load on their colleagues. This might encourage them to either work harder or slacken off. Mas and Moretti found that the positive effect dominated. A cashier sitting near someone who was 10 per cent faster than average raised their own performance by 1.7 per cent. Is the effect illusionary? The researchers think not. They could distinguish busy from quiet times; knew that checkout staff (and not their managers) chose their own hours; and measured productivity changes every 10 minutes and not over an entire shift. They offer two explanations. Either workers are spurred on to greater efforts when contemplating the greater speed of their colleague (psychologically plausible but economically irrational); or (more cynically), workers dislike faster colleagues looking at them, because they fear being accused of slacking off. At the checkout, each worker is looking towards one colleague, with his back to a second colleague who is looking at him. The findings show that facing the back of a fast worker makes no difference, but having a fast worker *face you*, does encourage you to speed up your scanning rate.

Based on Harford (2006, p.12).

Synergy the positive or negative result of the interaction of two or more components, producing an outcome that is different from the sum of the individual components.

Social facilitation appears to be the result of two fundamental psychological processes. First, when in the presence of others, individuals experience increased emotional arousal, feeling more tense and excited. Second, when aroused, people perform their most dominant response, that is, their most likely behaviour in that setting, which is also likely to be a correct one. In contrast, if the behaviour in question is newly learned and hence not established, the dominant response is likely to be incorrect. Also relevant here is the concept of synergy which refers to the positive or negative result of the interaction of two or more individuals which produces an outcome (which can be positive or negative) that is different from the sum of the individuals operating separately.

Positive synergy is a concept which underpins of all kinds of group working in organizations. In particular, it supports the use of cross-functional teams. Positive synergy is the belief that the final output produced by a group of individuals working together, rather than separately, will equal more than the sum of the individual members' abilities and efforts. A popular short-hand term for this is 2 + 2 = 5. It has been argued that the designated purpose of group tasks should necessarily *require* more than its members are able to offer working as individuals, so as to benefit from the positive aspects of group dynamics.

Social loafing

Jos Benders (2005) traces management's concern with team members working less hard than they theoretically could, to the start of the twentieth century. In Europe, the famous German sociologist, Max Weber, wrote about what he called 'braking' (Weber, 1924). At the same time in America, Frederick Taylor the management consultant, was concerned with 'systematic soldiering' among the workers (see Chapter 14). This shirking, 'social loafing' or withholding of effort can explain why teamworking can reduce productivity. Max Ringelmann, a French professor of agricultural engineering, conducted the original studies in the late 1920s on subjects pulling ropes (Kravitz and Martin, 1986). People in the first position in the apparatus pulled less hard when they thought that people behind them were also pulling.

Research suggests that when individuals perform additive tasks (i.e. where members perform similar tasks and their output is pooled), individual effort tends to decrease as the size of the group increases. Ringelmann found that three people pulling together, only achieved two and a half times the average individual rate, while eight 'pullers' achieved less than four times the individual rate. Ingham *et al.* (1974) later repeated these experiments and reported an 18 per cent variation in effort. The 'Ringelmann effect' was renamed **social loafing** in the 1970s by Bibb Latane following investigations at Ohio University to confirm Ringlemann's original work (Latane *et al.*, 1979).

Social loafing the tendency for individuals to exert less effort when working as part of a group on an additive task, than when working alone.

Social loafing is an example of negative synergy. Teamwork of all kinds is fraught with tensions, conflicts, obstacles and problems. If these are not managed effectively, rather than surpassing the best member's capabilities, the total group output may actually equal *less* than the weakest members' efforts. This is caused by various, so-called 'processes losses' which can hinder effective group functioning (Steiner, 1972). The mathematical equivalent would be 2 + 2 = 3. This challenges the idea that 'unity is strength'. If the aforementioned group process losses exceed group process gains, then one will have a situation of negative synergy. One example of this is the tendency for individuals to exert less effort when working as part of a group than when working alone. Suggestions have been offered at both the individual and the social levels to account for social loafing (George, 1992; Karau and Williams, 1993; Comer, 1995; Liden *et al.*, 2004). The process losses in a group have been ascribed to various causes:

- Equity of effort ('others are not contributing, why should I?')
- Dispersion of responsibility ('I'm hidden in the crowd, no one will notice me')
- Negative effect of group reward ('everyone will get the same, why should I work harder?')
- Problems of co-ordination ('people are getting in each others' way')

Two theories have been put forward to explain social loafing. *Social impact theory* explains it in terms of a force acting upon a group, such as the task needing to be completed. Such a force becomes divided equally among the available members. The greater the size of the group, the lower will be the impact of that force upon any one member, and vice versa. As group size increases, responsibility for task completion becomes diffused more widely among all members and the pressure on each individual declines. Each person will thus feel less responsibility for acting responsibly (Latane and Nida, 1980).

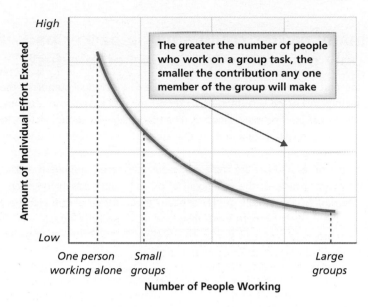

Figure 12:2: The social loafing effect
Source: From Greenberg (1999, p.158).

Collective effort theory is an expectancy theory of social loafing. It holds that it is the result of participants' realization that the relationship between their own individual effort to group performance and rewards cannot be evaluated on an individual basis, and so leads them to withhold their full effort when contributing to additive group tasks (Karau and Williams, 1993). Laboratory studies have revealed key situational factors. Social loafing was found to occur most often when the:

- task was perceived as unimportant, simple or boring;
- group members thought their individual output was not identifiable;
- the nature of each person's contribution was similar to that of the others;
- group members expected their colleagues to loaf.

The solutions offered to managers to overcome social loafing assume that it is our natural state, and that something has to be added to a situation to avoid it. Suggestions include (Greenberg and Baron, 1997; Baron and Byrne, 2000):

make the work more involving	keep people interested, thereby increasing their commitment to successful task performance, and hence encourage them perform at a high level
upgrade task	increase the perceived importance of the task in the group members' eyes
identify workers	point out each member's individual contribution prevents their getting away with a 'free ride'
reward contributions to the group	reward members for helping others achieve the common goal, and not just for their individual contributions
threaten punishment	fear of punishment prevents loafing and gets members to 'pull their weight' in the group
strengthen group cohesion	make the group size small, membership attractive and stable, common goals, facilitate member interaction

How many pickles could a pickle packer pack if pickle packers were only paid for properly packed pickles?

What are the problems facing production line workers in a pickle factory? A key job is stuffing dill pickle halves into jars. Only dill halves of a certain length can be used. Those that are too long will not fit and those that are too short will float and dance inside and look cheap and crummy. The dill halves and jars are carried on separate high-speed conveyor belts past the contingent of pickle stuffers. If the stuffers don't stuff quickly enough, the jars pile up at the workers' stations while they look for pickles of the appropriate length, so stuffers have a great temptation to stuff whichever pickles come to hand. The individual outputs of the stuffers are unidentifiable, since all jars go into a common hopper before they reach the quality control section. Responsibility for the output cannot be focused on one worker. This combination of factors leads to poor performance and improper packing. This research suggests making individual production identifiable and raises the question, 'How many pickles could a pickle packer pack if pickle packers were only paid for properly packed pickles?'

Based on Williams et al. *(1981).*

Free rider a member who obtains benefits from team membership without bearing a proportional share of the costs for generating that benefit.

Social loafing is related to the free riding (Frohlich and Oppenheimer, 1970; Kerr, 1983). A free rider obtains benefits from team membership without bearing a proportional share of the costs for generating the benefit. Hogg and Vaughan (2008) give the example of a tax evader who uses the health care service, the education system and the roads. The main difference between social loafing and free riding is that although loafers reduce effort on team tasks, they still contribute something to the group goal. The loss involved is one of *motivation*. In contrast, free riders exploit the group product, as in the case of a team project where a student gets the same grade as all the others, without having contributed anything whatsoever to the team's final report.

Free riding dooms a team to ineffectiveness and is abhorrent to team members for three reasons. It violates an equity standard – members baulk at others receiving the same benefits for less input of effort. It violates a social responsibility standard – everyone should contribute their fair share. Finally, it violates a reciprocity standard – members exchange their contributions with each other. The basic strategy for management to counteract free-riding is to broaden the individual's concept of self-interest and arrange matters so that an individual's personal goals are attained by the achievement of the group's collective goal (Albanese and van Fleet, 1985).

Source: www.phdcomics.com.

STOP AND THINK

Are you a social loafer or free rider in your educational or work context? How is social loafing/free riding reducing or improving your studies or work performance? What advice would you give to your instructor or manager to improve your performance and that of your colleagues, either through social facilitation or by discouraging social loafing in relation to particular tasks or activities?

Interestingly, Earley's study (1993) found that social loafing was not a worldwide phenomenon. In collectivist cultures such as Israel and China, there was little social loafing, and people performed better as members of a group than they did alone as they did not want to let their fellow group members down. In contrast, in individualistic cultures like the United States, social loafing occurred, and individuals performed better alone than in groups.

Group influences on individuals' behaviour

Group norm expected mode of behaviour or belief that is established either formally or informally by a group.

Elton Mayo originally noted the existence of group norms, and their enforcement through sanctions, during the Bank Wiring Observation Room studies at the Hawthorne works. The men there restricted their output to conform to a group-agreed norm or standard. In another study which has now become a classic in experimental social psychology, Muzafer Sherif (1936) showed how group norms emerged.

Sherif's work showed that in a situation where doubt and uncertainty exist and where first hand information is lacking, a person's viewpoint will shift to come into line with those of other group members. In essence this situation leads to the creation of a group norm. This occurs quickly amongst group members who have had little previous experience of the group's work, but it also occurs amongst those who have had experience, although somewhat more slowly. Few of the subjects who took part in Sherif's experiments felt conscious that others had influenced their judgements. Sherif's work suggested that in order to organize and manage itself, every group developed a system of norms. Norms are behavioural expectations and they serve to define the nature of the group. They express the

Sherif's study of the emergence of group norms

Muzafer Sherif (1906–1988)

Muzafer Sherif placed a group of three subjects in a darkened room and presented them with a small spot of light. He then asked them to track the apparent movement of the spot, and to say, aloud, each in turn, the direction in which they thought that the light was moving. The apparent movement is an optical illusion known as the 'autokinetic effect'. The light does not move. Sherif's subjects made three series of 100 estimates on successive days. Initially, there were quite wide individual differences in the response to this situation. Some subjects saw little movement while others saw a lot. However, Sherif discovered that they started to agree on the amount of apparent movement quite quickly. Having exchanged information on their judgements, their behaviour changed. They began seeing the light moving in the same direction as those who had spoken earlier.

Gradually, all the members came to see the light as moving in the same direction at the same time. There was of course no 'real' movement of the light. Each individual began to see the light in the same way as the group saw it. The results Sherif obtained with two-person and three-person groups are shown in the diagram overleaf. When a group norm emerged it was found that it became the basis for subsequent judgement when subjects were re-tested independently. The group norm therefore became a relatively permanent frame of reference for individual behaviour.

Based on Sherif (1936).

→

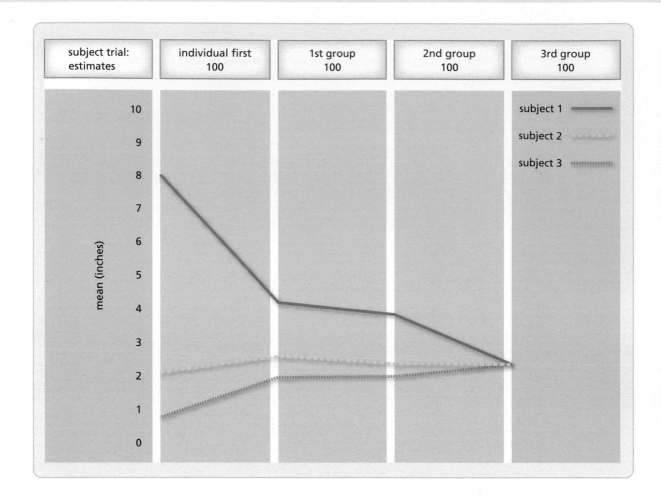

| subject trial: estimates | individual first 100 | 1st group 100 | 2nd group 100 | 3rd group 100 |

Pivotal norms socially defined standards relating to behaviour and beliefs that are central to a group's objective and survival.

Peripheral norms socially defined standards relating to behaviour and beliefs that are important but not crucial to a group's objective and survival.

values of the members of the group and provide guidelines to help the group achieve its goals. A group may develop them consciously or unconsciously.

Norms guide behaviour and facilitate interaction by specifying the kinds of reactions expected or acceptable in a particular situation. Not all group norms have equal importance. **Pivotal norms** guide behaviour which is central to the group. For example, the level of output or the amount of work preparation done. In contrast, **peripheral norms** guide behaviour that is important but not essential, for example, the choice of clothing or break time activities. Group members who violate pivotal norms can impede group objectives or endanger its survival. Therefore the consequences for such transgressing individuals are severe. In contrast, violation of peripheral norms, although frowned upon, has fewer negative consequences for the offender.

Bloody beefers and hanging beef tongues

Over a nine-week period, William Thompson used the observational data collection method to study the day-to-day activities of assembly line workers in a beef processing plant in the American Midwest. He reported that, 'working in the beef plant is "dirty" work, not in the literal sense of being drenched with perspiration and beef blood, but also in the figurative sense of performing a low status, routine and demeaning job'. Thompson and his fellow workers had to hang, brand and bag between 1,350 and 1,500 beef tongues during an eight-hour shift. The work was both monotonous and routine.

Thompson described the camaraderie that existed among the 'beefers' as they called themselves. Because of the noise, the need for earplugs, and the isolation of

Source: Marriens Bezvidenhout/Dreamstime.com

eliminated it, the workers' desire for social interaction won out and interaction flourished'.

To reduce the feeling of alienation and retain a sense of humanity, the beefers developed certain coping mechanisms. They replaced the formal, managerially imposed norms of the workplace with their own informal ones. At certain times, instead of working at a steady speed which matched the line speed, they would work at a frantic pace, and get ahead of the line. While such behaviour added only a few precious minutes to their scheduled break time, its importance was primarily symbolic, in that it challenged the company's dictates concerning the speed of the line, and it gave the men a small measure of control over the work process.

The informal group norms also encouraged certain types of rule breaking. Indeed, Thompson noted that the, 'workers practically made a game out of doing forbidden things simply to see if they could get away with it'. For example, at Thompson's workstation, despite strict rules to the contrary, workers covered in beef blood washed their hands, arms and knives in a tub of water which was reserved for cleaning tongues. In addition, workers often cut out pieces of meat, and threw them at other employees. If not noticed by the supervisor or inspector, the thrown meat chunks might be picked up off the floor, and put back on the line – a blatant violation of hygiene rules. Thompson concluded that such, 'artful sabotage served as symbolic way in which workers could express a sense of individuality, and hence self-worth'.

certain work areas, it was virtually impossible for the men on the assembly line to speak to each other. Instead, they communicated using an elaborate system of communication symbols. These included exaggerated gestures, shrill whistles, 'thumbs up' and 'thumbs down', and the clanging of knives against stainless steel tables and tubs. Thompson observed that, 'in a setting which apparently

Based on Thompson (1983).

STOP AND THINK   It is important to feel that you fit in with your peers (others in your group, school or neighbourhood). However, sometimes you may find yourself doing something because others are doing it, and that makes you feel uncomfortable or unsafe. Sometimes it is hard to say no to your friends. Can you think of an occasion when you experienced such a situation? How did you feel?

Why do norms develop within a group? David Feldman (1984) argued that their purpose was to:

- *Facilitate group task achievement or group survival:* groups develop norms which increase their chances of being successful and protect themselves from outsiders.

- *Increase the predictability of group members' behaviours:* predictability means that internally, members can anticipate and prepare for the actions of colleagues, thereby smoothing social interaction. Externally, it allows them to relate appropriately to outsiders.

- *Reduce embarrassing interpersonal problems for group members*: knowing what to do and say in a group (and what not to) increases an individual member's comfort.

- *Express the group's core values and define its distinctiveness*: norms allow members to gain a sense of the essence of the group.

Discovering the norm

In a now classic study, Donald Roy, a researcher who acted as a participant observer in a factory, described the pressures that were placed on an individual to adhere to the group norm. Roy's earnings, and those of others, were based on a piece rate system. The more he produced the more he earned. 'From my first to my last day at the plant I was subject to warnings and predictions concerning price cuts. Pressure was the heaviest from Joe Mucha, who shared my job repertoire and kept a close eye on my production. On November 14, the day after my first attained quota, Joe Mucha advised: "Don't let it go over $1.25 an hour, or the time-study man will be right down here! And they don't waste time, either! They watch the records like a hawk!" I got ahead, so I took it easy for a couple of hours. Joe told me that I had made $10.01 yesterday and warned me not to go over $1.25 an hour . . . Jack Starkey spoke to me after Joe left. "What's the matter? Are you trying to upset the applecart?" Jack explained in a friendly manner that $10.50 was too much to turn in, even on an old job. "The turret-lathe men can turn in $1.35", said Jack, "but their rate is 90 cents and ours is 85 cents." Jack warned me that the Methods Department could lower their prices on any job, old or new, by changing the fixture slightly or changing the size of the drill. According to Jack, a couple of operators . . . got to competing with each other to see how much they could turn in. They got up to $1.65 an hour, and the price was cut in half. And from then on they had to run that job themselves, as none of the other operators would accept that job. According to Jack, it would be all right for us to turn in $1.28 or $1.29 an hour, when it figured out that way, but it was not all right to turn in $1.30 an hour. Well now I know where the maximum is – $1.29 an hour.'

From Roy (1960).

Feldman (1984) also noted that group norms developed in four ways:

- *Explicit statement by a supervisor or co-worker*: this person may explicitly state certain expectations. The project leader may tell the newcomer that the group meetings starts promptly on the hour, when all members are expected to be present.

- *Critical events in the group's history*: a shop floor employee makes a suggestion for an improvement to his supervisor who criticizes and ridicules him. Group members ensure that in the future, none of them offer any more suggestions.

- *Initial pattern of behaviour*: the first behaviour pattern that emerges in a group can establish group expectations. For example, if the first speaker shares his feelings and anxieties with the other group members, the discussion of emotions in a group can become a norm.

- *Transfer behaviours from past situations*: when individuals carry over behaviours from past situations, they can increase the predictability of group members' behaviours in new settings. For example, instructors and students transfer constant expectations from class to class.

It appears that once established, group norms are difficult to change. Since the group members originally created the norms, it is they who ultimately change them. Members will tend to resist any attempts by managers or any other outsiders, to modify their group's norms. Once a group has established a set of norms, it will enforce them in order to:

- ensure its survival;
- help it achieve its task;
- clarify or simplify how members are to behave;
- avoid embarrassing situations between members;
- clarify its central values or unique identity.

Group sanction a punishment or a reward given by members to others in the group in the process of enforcing group norms.

Some examples of norms and the reasons for their enforcement are shown in Table 12.1. To enforce its norms, a group develops a set of sanctions with which to police them. The term, **group sanction** refers to the punishments and rewards that are given by a group to its members, in the process of enforcing group norms. Punishment is a negative sanction and a reward is a positive sanction.

Table 12.1: Norms and sanctions

Norm	Enforcement reason	Examples of sanctions to enforce the norm
Members attend all group meetings regularly and arrive on time.	Group survival	Absentees or latecomers are first teased or ridiculed, and then criticized.
All members are required to prepare written work before the group meetings to avoid delay at meeting.	Group task achievement	Group members compliment individuals whose preparation has been particularly thorough.
Members listen to each other's ideas without interrupting allowing them to fully present their thoughts and opinions.	Clarification of behavioural expectations	A member who interrupts is taken aside after the meeting, and asked, in future, to let the person finish speaking.
Members do not discuss their private lives with colleagues at work.	Avoidance of embarrassment	Members who insist on discussing such matters are ostracized until they stop doing so.

The earliest examples of negative sanctions exercized in groups were revealed by the Bank Wiring Observation Room phase of the Hawthorne studies. The researchers discovered that persons who broke the group norm, for example, producing either over or under the group norm were 'binged'. This involved a group member flicking the ear of the norm-transgressor or tapping him painfully on the upper part of their arm. Both actions were intended to indicate physically to the man, that his behaviour was unacceptable to the other group members. Other negative sanctions can also be used by the group, and can be placed in ascending order of severity as shown in Figure 12.3. If negative sanctions represent the 'stick' to enforce group norm compliance, then the positive sanctions represent the 'carrot'. Such carrots for the conforming individual include accolades from other members, emotional support, increase in social status, and acceptance of their ideas by others (Doms and van Avermaet, 1981).

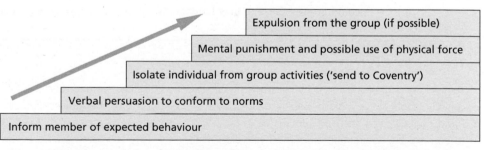

Figure 12.3: Escalating group pressure to secure individual conformity to group norms

Sent to Coventry

Being 'sent to Coventry' means becoming a social outcast. Individuals in a group can be punished in this way by their colleagues, who ignore them, refuse to speak to them, and isolate them from group activities. During the English Civil War (1642–1651) fought between the Royalists and the Parliamentarians, the city of Coventry was a strong outpost of parliamentary support. Royalist prisoners who were captured in the Midlands were frequently sent to the city of Coventry, where the local population would have nothing to do with them.

Conformity a change in an individual's belief or behaviour in response to real or imagined group pressure.

Conformity with norms tends to increase under certain conditions. An increase in norm conformity is associated with a decrease in the size of the group; and also with an increase in the group's homogeneity, visibility and a stable experience. Members who perceive themselves to have low status within the group will tend to conform more, and feel that they have to 'earn' the right to be deviant. High conformers are also those who feel that they are not fully accepted by the others. Diagnosing a team's norms and its members' conformity to them, can help to explain group behaviour (Rothwell, 1992). Conformity can be contrasted with **obedience**, a situation in which an individual changes their behaviour in response to direction from others.

Obedience a situation in which an individual changes their behaviour in response to direct command from another.

If you want to deviate from a group norm you have several options. You can attempt to persuade others to your viewpoint, and thus alter the group norm. Of course, the other members may respond by persuading you to conform to the existing norm. The higher your status, the more power you will have in the group and the more you will be able to change the behaviours and beliefs of the other members (and the less likely they will be to change your own). What other options are there? If the group is of little importance to you, and if you are free to leave the group, you will do so. Conversely, if you are of little importance to the group, you may be forced to either conform to its norms or else be rejected by its members. If, however, your presence is important to your group (e.g. because you possess high status, power, popularity or special skills), then the group may tolerate your deviant behaviour and beliefs in order to avoid the threat of losing you as a valued member. Hence, the power that a group has to influence its members towards conformity to its norms depends on three main factors:

- the positive and negative sanctions (rewards and punishments) that the group has at its disposal;
- the member's desire to avoid negative sanctions such as social and physical punishments or expulsion from the group; and
- the degree of attraction that the group has for an individual member and the attraction that group members have for each another.

Group cohesion the number and strength of mutual positive attitudes towards other group members.

This last factor in the list above above is called **group cohesion**. It refers to the number and strength of mutual positive attitudes towards group members. As Table 12.2 shows, how cohesive a group is can have a major impact on how it functions and what it achieves (Pearce *et al.*, 2002).

Having established a set of norms and the sanctions to enforce them, a group has to communicate these to new individuals who join the group. The new group member 'learns

---

Home viewing

The film *Big* (1988, director Penny Marshall) is a fantasy-comedy about a boy, Josh Baskin (played first by David Moscow, and then by Tom Hanks) whose wish to become 'big' is granted, and his 13-year-old's mind comes to occupy the body of a 35-year-old man. Josh joins the Macmillan Toy Company, and is promoted to product testing because of his unique childlike insights into the business. During his time at the company, he is a member of several groups. As you watch the film, consider how his behaviour affects the other members of his group, and also how they affect what he does.

STOP AND THINK

Consider a group of which you are a member, and its norms and sanctions. Reflect on a situation in which a member (perhaps yourself) broke a norm and received a sanction.

Assess the positive and negative outcomes of this occurrence for the individual group member concerned and the group as a whole.

Table 12.2: Group cohesion – contributors and consequences

Contributors to group cohesion	Consequences of group cohesion
Small size	
External threat	
Stable membership	Group success
Past success of group	Member satisfaction
Difficulty of entry to the group	Productivity high or low
Members sharing common goals	Greater conformity by members
Opportunity to interact with others	Member's evaluations become distorted
Attractiveness of group to individuals	Increased interaction between members
Fairness of rewards between members	Increased group influence over members
Members' agreement about their statuses	Co-operative behaviour between individuals

the ropes', and is shown how to get things done, how to interact with others and how to achieve a high social status within the group. An important aspect of achieving such status is to adhere to the group's rules or norms. Initial transgressions will be gently pointed out. However, the continued violation of norms by a group member puts at risk the cohesion of the group. When there is disagreement on a matter of importance to the group, the preservation of group effectiveness, harmony and cohesion requires a resolution of the conflict. Hence pressure is exerted on the deviating individual through persuasive communication to conform. The name given to this 'educational' process which the new member undergoes is **group socialization** and it occurs within most groups in all types of organizations (Figure 12.4).

Group socialization
the process whereby members learn the values, symbols and expected behaviours of the group to which they belong

If new recruits are thoroughly socialized, they are less likely to transgress group norms and require sanctions to be administered. However, while such pressure to go along with the majority of other members may be beneficial in many respects for the group, it also carries costs. If conformity is allowed to dominate, and individuals are given little opportunity to present alternative and different views, there is the danger of the group collectively making errors of judgement, leading them to take unwise actions. Chapter 20 will consider the

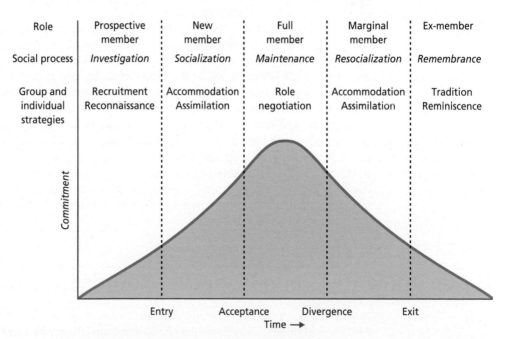

Figure 12.4: A model of the process of group socialization
Source: Moreland and Levine (1982).

Table 12.3: Comparison of stages of group development to stages of socialization

	Group development	**Organizational socialization**
Stage 1: Orientation	1. Forming • Establish interpersonal relationships • Conform to organizational traditions and standards • Boundary testing in relationships and task behaviours	1. Getting in (anticipatory socialization) • Setting of realistic expectations • Determining match with the newcomer
Stage 2: Redefinition	2. Storming • Conflict arising because of interpersonal behaviours • Resistance to group influence and task requirements	2. Breaking in • Initiation to the job • Establishing interpersonal relationships • Congruence between self and organizational performance appraisal
Stage 3: Co-ordination	3. Norming • Single leader emerges • Group cohesion established • New group standards and roles formed for members	3. Settling in (role management) The degree of fit between one's life interests outside work and the demands of the organization Resolution of conflicts at the workplace itself
Stage 4: Formalization	4. Performing • Members perform tasks together • Establishing role clarity • Teamwork is the norm	

From Gordon (1993, p.184).

concept of groupthink which, through internal conformity and external group pressure, leads individual members collectively to make poor decisions. It is important to remember that while a work group will be attempting to get its new member to adopt its own values, symbols and expected behaviours, the organization which recruited the person, will be endeavouring to do the same (see Table 12.3).

Some companies, such as Disney, are famous for, and put much time, money and effort into getting their new joiners to adopt the 'company way' of doing things. This equivalent process is called **organizational socialization** (see Chapter 4, Culture). At Disney this includes realistic job previews, a 'Traditions' class for new hires (about history, language, organization goals and values); training courses, and job assignments (debasement experiences) to 'unfreeze the newcomer's preconceptions about his or her role in the organization, and to maximize the newcomer's willingness to accept the organization's authority' (Chao, 1988, p.38). If the picture of organizational life that the newcomer is presented with by the organization is congruent with the picture held by the workforce, they will accept it. If not, the newcomer is more likely to adopt the picture held by their own work group, as this is 'where emotional control is probably the most effective, for it is stage managed by those with whom members must spend most of their time' (van Maanen cited in Novak and Fine, 1996, p.15).

Organizational socialization the process through which an employee's pattern of behaviour, values, attitudes and motives is influenced to conform to that of the organization.

Group influences on individuals' attitudes

Why do members conform to group pressure? Group norms increase the predictability of the behaviour of others, and reduce the chances of individuals embarrassing each other when interacting, for example, when speaking or dressing at social events. Complying with group norms may be of such personal benefit to us that we are willing to abide by them and in so doing, suppress our own personal desires and reduce our individual freedoms. Moreover, we also punish those who violate the group's norms and reward those who do not. Additionally, individuals have a desire for order and meaning in our lives. They view uncertainty as disturbing and as something that should be reduced to the absolute minimum. Norms, and the adherence to norms, help us 'make sense' of seemingly unconnected facts and events, provides us with explanations of 'what's going on', and allows us to feel in control of the situations in which we find ourselves. The earliest experimental studies into conformity to group norms were carried out by Solomon Asch.

Solomon Asch (1907–1996)

In the early 1950s, Solomon E. Asch constructed a laboratory experiment into individual conformity in groups.

The subject

Only number 6 was a real subject (second from the right). The remainder were Asch's paid accomplices.

The problem

In experiment conditions, the accomplices had been instructed to lie about which line was correct. Under pressure, the subject (no. 6) shows signs of conflict, of whether to conform to the group judgement or give the response he judges to be correct.

The situation

Seven men sat around a table supposedly to participate in a study on visual perception.

The task

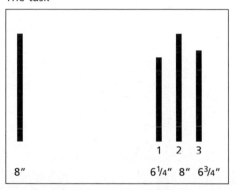

8"   1 2 3   6¼" 8" 6¾"

The task was an easy one: to judge which of three lines was equal in length to one they had seen earlier.

The results

Members making at least one error	76%
Times average member conformed	37%
Members who never conformed	24%
Members who conformed over 10 times	11%
Members who made at least one error when tested alone	5%

Solomon Asch (1951, 1952, 1956) found that those subjects who yielded to group pressure did so for different reasons. He distinguished three types of yielding:

Distortion of perception. These subjects seem to have convinced themselves that they actually did see the lines the way the other group members stated their judgements. Yielding at the perceptual level was rare, and occurred primarily among those who displayed a lack of trust in themselves. They were unaware that their estimates had been displaced or distorted by the majority.

Distortion of judgement. These subjects yielded either because they were unsure that they understood the task set for them, or because they did not want to 'spoil the experiment'. They suffered from primary doubt and lack of confidence. The factor of greatest importance was their decision that their perceptions were inaccurate, and that those of the majority were correct (akin to independence without confidence). Distortion of judgement occurred frequently.

Distortion of action. The subjects did not suffer a modification of perception, nor did they conclude that they were wrong. They yielded because they feared being excluded, ostracized or considered eccentric. These subjects suppressed their observations, and voiced the majority position with a full awareness of what they were doing.

Asch's experiment was replicated more than 30 years later, this time with five individuals using PCs who were told that they had been linked together. Whereas Asch had found that the number who refused to conform to the group trial was just 25 per cent, in the repeat study, 69 per cent of the subjects made no errors. Maybe a computer-mediated communication environment reduces our tendency to conform to a unanimous group position (Doms and Averinaet, 1981).

STOP AND THINK   Think of an occasion when you have given an opinion or supported a decision contrary to your own feelings and judgement, but consistent with those around you at the time.

How can you live with yourself for acting in such a socially compliant and submissive manner? What is your pathetic excuse for having done so?

Milgram's 'electric shock' experiments

Stanley Milgram, experimenter (1933–1984)

Volunteer subject, accomplice 'learner' and accomplice experimenter

probably reply with little hesitation. In a series of now famous and highly controversial experiments, Stanley Milgram examined people's level of obedience to authority. The research involved ordinary people of different ages, sexes, races and occupations. Groups of psychiatrists, postgraduate students and social science lecturers were asked by Milgram to predict how many of the research subjects would actually obey the experimenter's order. There was a high agreement that virtually all subjects would refuse to obey. Only one in a hundred would do it, said the psychiatrists, and that person would be a psychopath.

A study by Stanley Milgram showed that a group can aid the individual to defy authority. Would you torture another person simply because you were told to do so by someone in authority? Of course not, you would

Milgram's experiment involved volunteer subjects participating in a learning experiment. They were to act as teachers of people who were trying to learn a series of simple word pairs. As teachers they were told to punish the student when he failed to learn by giving him an electric shock. At the start the shocks were small in intensity but every time the learner made a mistake, the teacher was told to increase the size of the shock. In carrying out the experiments Milgram found that two out of every three subjects tested administered the electric shocks up to a level which was clearly marked 'fatal' simply because an authority figure told them to do so. In fact, no electric shocks were ever actually given although the volunteer 'teachers' believed that the learners were really receiving the shocks they administered. An earlier experiment by Asch had shown that it only needed one other person to agree with a deviant for the conformity effect to be counteracted. In one variation of his experiment, Milgram placed two of his accomplices alongside the subject, so that the testing of the wired-up learner would be done by a group and not by a single subject. This experimental situation is thus similar to Asch's.

The experiment began with one of the accomplices administering the shocks. He then refused to continue, argued with the experimenter and withdrew sitting in the corner of the room. The second accomplice then took over, continued for a bit, and then refused just as the previous one had done. The real subject now remained to administer the shocks himself. Milgram repeated this procedure 40 times, each with a different subject. In 30 of these 40 cases, he found that once the subjects had seen their group colleagues defy the experimenter, they also defied him. When group pressure (or support) for such defiance was lacking, only 14 subjects defied the authority figure. Milgram concluded that peer rebellion is a very powerful force in undercutting the experimenter's authority. Milgram offered seven explanations of why the group was effective in helping the individual to do this. The reasons are the same as those that explain the power the group has over the individual:

1. Peers instil in the subject the idea of defying the experimenter.
2. The lone subject has no way of knowing if defiance is a bizarre or common occurrence. Two examples confirm that it is a natural reaction.
3. The act of defiance by the accomplice defines the act of shocking as improper. It provides social confirmation for the subject's suspicion that it is wrong to punish a subject against his will, even in a psychological experiment.
4. By remaining in the room, the accomplices' presence carries with it a measure of social disapproval for the subject.
5. As long as the accomplices participated in the experiment, there was dispersion of responsibility among group members for the shocking. As they withdrew, the responsibility focused on the subject.
6. The subject witnessed two instances of disobedience and observed that the consequences of defying the experimenter were minimal.
7. Failing to keep the accomplices performing as required diminishes the experimenter's power.

A recent replication of Milgram's experiment by Jerry Burger revealed that things have not changed greatly in the intervening 45 years. A total of 70 per cent of his participants (compared to Milgram's 82.5 per cent) were prepared to continue delivering shocks after the learner had cried out in pain at 150 volts. Contrary to expectations, participants who saw a confederate refuse the experimenter's instructions, obeyed as often as those who did not see such behaviour modelled in front of them. Men and women did not differ in their rates of obedience.

Based on Milgram (1973) and Burger (2009).

Deindividuation

Deindividuation
an increased state of anonymity that loosens normal constraints on individuals' behaviour, reducing their sense of responsibility, and leading to an increase in impulsive and antisocial acts.

Social facilitation explains how groups can arouse individuals, while social loafing shows that groups can diffuse and hence diminish individual responsibility. Together, arousal and diffused responsibility combine to decrease normal, social inhibitions, and create deindividuation. **Deindividuation** refers to a person's loss of self-awareness and self-monitoring. It involves some loss of personal identity and greater identification with the group.

The writings of Gustave LeBon led to the theory of deindividuation which was first proposed by Leon Festinger, Albert Pepitone and Theodore Newcombe (1952). However, it is Marion Hampton (1999, p.112) who neatly captures the experience of deindividuation when she writes:

There are moments when we can observe ourselves behaving irrationally as members of crowds or audiences, yet we are swept by the emotion, unable to check it. In smaller groups too, like committees or teams, we may experience powerful feelings of loyalty, anxiety or anger. The moods and emotions of those around us seem to have an exaggerated effect on our own moods and emotions.

The influence of the crowd in history

Source: Luchschen/Dreamstime.com

Gustave LeBon stated that the crowd is, 'always intellectually inferior to the isolated individual . . . mob man is fickle, credulous, and intolerant showing the violence and ferocity of primitive beings'. He added, 'by the mere fact that he forms part of an organized crowd, a man

descends several rungs in the ladder of civilization. Isolated he may be a cultivated individual, in a crowd he is a barbarian – that is a creature acting by instinct' (LeBon, 1908, p.12). In his book, *The Crowd*, originally published in 1895, he hypothesized that humans had a two-part personality. The upper half was conscious, unique to each individual and contained dignity and virtue. The lower half, in contrast, was unconscious, was shared with everyone else, and contained bad desires and instincts. LeBon attributed this primitive behaviour to three things:

Anonymity	Individuals cannot be easily identified in a crowd.
Contagion	Ideas and emotions spread rapidly and unpredictably.
Suggestability	The savagery that is just below the surface is released by suggestion.

Based on LeBon (1908).

Edward Diener (1980) considered self-awareness (i.e. awareness of oneself as an object of attention) to be the crucial element in the deindividuation process. The environmental conditions which reduce self-awareness and thereby trigger deindividuation, as well the consequences of deindividuation are summarized in Figure 12.5.

Anonymity within a crowd or large group lessens inhibitions. Warriors in a tribe paint their faces and wear masks. In his novel, *Lord of the Flies*, William Golding (1954) describes how a group of boys marooned on a desert island, through their shouting, clapping and face painting, 'hype themselves up' and reduce their self-consciousness, turning themselves into a single organism, within which the individual members lose their identity. The unrestrained behaviours are provoked by the power of the group. When attention is drawn away from the individual in crowd and group situations, their anonymity is increased, and they are more likely to abandon their normal restraints and to lose their sense of individual responsibility.

This can lead to antisocial behaviour, such as attacking a police officer during protest demonstrations. In military organizations, members have always worn uniforms; but increasingly companies are requiring their staff to dress in corporate clothing. While this may get them to identify more closely with their organizations, it can also increase their anonymity.

Studies of deindividuation on the internet suggest that when dispersed members communicate using computers, there is a higher frequency of insults, swearing and name-calling between them. When working in computer-mediated mode, there tends to be more hostility than when individuals are in face-to-face interaction. Much internet communication occurs under conditions in which participants, rightly or wrongly, believe that they cannot be personally identified. However, once names are attached to members' messages, the number of inhibited remarks tends to fall significantly.

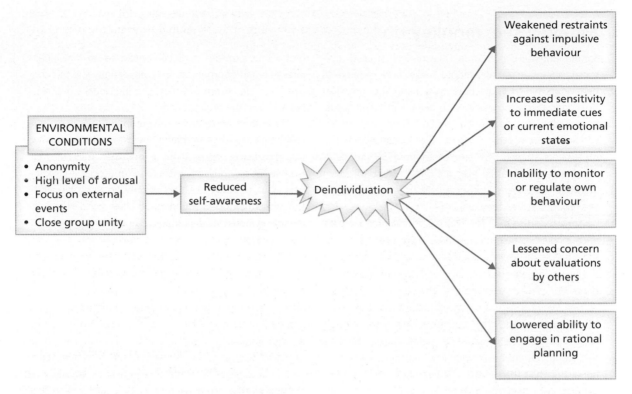

Figure 12.5: Self awareness and deindividuation
Source: From Hogg and Vaughan (2008, p.424).

STOP AND THINK   What deindividuating tendencies can you identify in the organizations with which you are familiar? Are these being created consciously or unconsciously? What effect are they having on organizational employees and clients?

A great number of different factors influence conformity to norms. The personality characteristics of individuals play a part in predisposing them to conform to group norms. The kind of stimuli eliciting conformity behaviour is also important. That people conform to norms when they are uncertain about a situation was demonstrated by the Sherif experiments. He also discovered that a person with a high degree of self-confidence could affect the opinions and estimates of other group members. Asch found that if even only one confederate in his experiment broke the unanimity with his dissenting voice, the dramatic effects of conformity were erased, and the experimental subject felt free to give the correct answer that seemed obvious all along. Upbringing (including formal education) also plays an important part. Bond and Smith's (1996) analysis showed a steady decline in conformity since the original Asch studies. Collectivist countries showed higher levels of conformity than individualist countries (see Chapter 4, Culture)

STOP AND THINK   Think of a time when you conformed to some aspect of your workgroup's behaviour. Why did you do this? How did you feel about it?

Monkey see, monkey do

Sandra Robinson and Anne O'Leary-Kelly studied anti-social actions in organizations. These were defined as behaviours which could potentially harm the individual or organizational property. Such actions included sexual harassment, stealing, insubordination, sabotage, rumour spreading, withholding effort and absenteeism. The researchers studied 187 employees from 35 groups in 20 organizations. They examined the extent to which individual employees' antisocial actions were shaped by the group in which they worked.

They found that as the richness of the group experience increased, members became more likely to match their individual level of antisocial behaviour to that of the group in general. The stronger the group's antisocial behaviour climate, the more it affected an individual's actions. Where individuals in the group relied on each other to complete a task, their behaviour was more strongly related to the level of antisocial behaviour exhibited by the group. Where an individual exhibited less antisocial behaviour than the group in general, he or she was less satisfied with their co-workers. Groups can display high levels of either antisocial or prosocial behaviour, and can encourage similar behaviour from their members. The group thus provides a social context to an individual's interpretation of organization-level systems, and this context has a significant effect on the individual's antisocial behaviour in the organization.

The authors also point to the group-induced, *contagion effect* that explains the spread or clustering of aggressive acts in particular organizations or industries. They conclude that antisocial groups encourage antisocial individual behaviour, and that isolating or ignoring them is unlikely to change them. They found that the likelihood of punishment was more effective than closeness of supervision in weakening the group-individual behaviour link.

Antisocial behaviour was thus not solely an individual-level phenomenon. Although individual characteristics such as personality, prior learning of aggressive behaviour, family background and upbringing, all played part, they argued that the social context of the work group exerted a major influence on whether individuals behaved in an antisocial way at work. Managers had both the ability and the responsibility to influence antisocial behaviour by shaping work group dynamics.

Based on Robinson and O'Leary-Kelly (1998).

Individual influences on group attitudes and behaviour

Compliance a majority's influence over a minority.

Conversion a minority's influence over a majority.

So far, the focus has been on the group influencing its members. Does this mean that an individual can never influence their group? Clearly not, since history recounts numerous instances of individuals – revolutionaries, rebels, radical thinkers, religious zealots – who created minority groupings, and as minorities successfully persuaded majorities. Indeed, leadership can be considered an example of minority influence. The theoretical underpinning to the process of a minority's influence on a majority is provided by Serge Moscovici's (1980) social influence theory. He used the term, **compliance**, to describe what happens when a majority influences a minority, through its possession of various kinds of power and its ability to implement positive and negative sanctions. He applied the term, **conversion**, to describe a minority's persuasion of a majority. The concept of conversion is illustrated every time an employee persuades their company to adopt a new product or create a new division.

In their review of 143 studies of minority influence, Wood *et al.* (1994) found that minorities had the ability to change the opinions of those who listened to them, especially if the listeners were not required to publicly acknowledge such a change. Moscovici (1980) stressed the importance of consistency in the conversion process. The individual persuading the group had to stick unswervingly to his or her point of view. Moscovici's original work on conversion has stimulated much research, and we now possess a growing body of research, and an understanding of how a minority can influence a majority (Nemeth, 1986). These different writings have been summarized by Huczynski (2004) who listed what the minority influencer of a majority has to do:

Become viable:	take a position that others are aware of; make yourself heard; get yourself noticed, and generally overcome the illusion of unanimity.
Create tension:	motivate those in the majority to try to deal with your ideas.
Be consistent:	stick unswervingly to the same position. Do not take a variety of positions that disagree with the majority.
Be persistent:	restate your consistent position in the face of others' opposition to you.
Be unyielding:	being firm and unyielding involves digging your heels in and not compromising.
Be self-confident:	this is conveyed by one's consistency and persistence. It raises self-doubts among the majority leading it to reconsider its position.
Seek defectors:	defections from the majority increases the self-doubt of the remaining majority and frees its doubters who may have self-censored themselves to speak out, perhaps encouraging more converts.

Before the 1980s, the idea that a minority could influence a majority was not a widely held view among social psychologists. However, through their research and publications, Moscovici and his colleagues presented an alternative view that possessed all the above characteristics. Minority influencing has now become an accepted and recognized phenomenon which regularly features in social psychology texts.

Home viewing

In the film, *Twelve Angry Men* (1957, director Sidney Lumet) a jury retires to deliberate and to decide on the guilt or innocence of a youth from a slum background. At the outset, 11 of the 12 jurors are convinced of the boy's guilt and are keen to find him guilty without further discussion. Only one member of the jury, played by Henry Fonda, has reservations and persuades the other members to take the time to review the evidence.

Fonda manages to change the guilty votes of the other 11 jurors, and persuades them to acquit the young defendant. The film illustrates the concept of *conversion*. Watch Fonda's behaviour carefully. At first sight it appears that it is random. But then, you'll see a pattern. What behaviours do you see him repeating? What influencing tactics does he use? Which types of power is possessed by which characters in the film?

The eyes have it

In an online work group, how are minority opinions expressed and received by the majority? Will a dissenter feel freer to express their opinion than in a face-to-face situation? A study by Poppy McLeod and her colleagues gave partial information about three different companies to group members who discussed it either face-to-face, or in a synchronous chat. Their task was to share the information to make the best investment decision. The data were organized in such a way that if all the information was made available to all the members, company A would be recognized as the best choice. However, the most revealing piece of information was provided to only one of the group's members, ensuring they would be the minority opinion holder. These individuals were found to

be particularly vocal when their contributions were online and anonymous, but also, they were ineffective at changing the majority's opinion. In consequence the online workgroups made poor decisions and bad investments. The researchers highlight the role of 'pain-gain'. In a face-to-face setting, a minority opinion holder has to stick their neck out and risk censure when voicing their opinions, and this alone may make the others pay attention to them. In contrast, online, the dissenter's pain is considerably reduced, particularly if their contributions are anonymous, so the gain will be lower as well.

Based on McLeod et al. (1997).

RECAP

1. *Explain the basic tenets of social identity theory and social representation theory.*

   - Social identity theory holds that aspects of our identity derive from the membership of a group.

   - Groups construct social representations consisting of beliefs, ideas and values which they transmit to their new members.

   - Such representations, together with group social-ization lead to all members sharing a common frame of reference.

2. *Distinguish between social facilitation and social loafing.*

   - Individual behaviour is variously modified by the presence of others or by being a part of a group.

   - The concepts of social influence, social facilitation, synergy and social loafing distinguish the direction and nature of such modifications.

3. *Understand how groups use norms to regulate the behaviour of their members.*

   - Social norms guide the behaviour of individuals in a group. They can be pivotal or peripheral.

   - Social norms are established in four ways – explicit statement, critical events, initial behaviour and transfer behaviour.

   - Sanctions are administered by members to those individuals who transgress or uphold the group's norms. Sanctions can therefore be negative (verbal abuse) or positive (praise). Groups possess an esca-lating hierarchy of ever-stronger negative sanctions.

4. *Understand the process of group socialization of individuals.*

   - Groups teach new members about their norms and incorporate them into their shared frame of reference through the process of group socialization.

5. *Explain why individuals conform to the dictates of their group.*

   - As individuals, we tend to conform to group norms because of benefits for us individually if others abide by the agreed rules; our desire for order and meaning in our lives; and a need to receive a satisfying response from others.

   - The 'cost' to the person who is a member of a group is the deindividualization that member-ship entails. Group membership brings with it anonymity and becoming 'lost in the crowd'. This can reduce our sense of individual responsibility, lower our social constraints, and lead us to engage in impulsive, antisocial acts.

6. *Distinguish between compliance and conversion.*

   - Group orientation differs in depending on the culture in which an individual lives.

   - Research shows both that a majority influences an individual (called *compliance*), and that a minority can influence a majority (called *conversion*).

Revision

1. Your instructor is proposing to set a student group assignment as part of the con-tinuous assessment for this course. However, you are concerned about the effect that social loafing and free riding might have on your group's overall performance. How would your respond to your instructor's proposal?

2. Is conformity by the individual within organizations a bad thing, which should be eliminated or a good thing that should be encouraged?

3. Critically evaluate the empirical research on individual conformity to group pressure.

4. Suggest how an individual might go about persuading a majority.

Research assignment	Choose an organization with which you are familiar, and interview some employees who work there. Ask each interviewee how their co-workers would react, if they:

1. Were seen being rude or indifferent to a customer.

2. Criticized a co-worker who was not performing satisfactorily.

3. Performed their work at a level noticeably higher than that of their co-workers.

4. Approached management offering a solution to a problem they had identified.

5. Expressed concern to management about the well being of their fellow workers.

6. Expressed concern about the poor quality of the organization's product or service.

7. Actively developed their skill and knowledge about the organization's operations and products.

Finally, ask if there are things that any employee should do or not do, if they wanted to get on well with their co-workers in the organization. Use the information obtained from your interviewees to determine (a) on which topics there appear to be group norms (b) which norms are pivotal and which are peripheral (c) what effects these norms have on the behaviour of the individuals, the operation of the group and the performance of the department.

Springboard

Burger, J.M., 2009, 'Replicating Milgram: Would people still obey today?', *American Psychologist*, 64(1): 1–11.

A modern replication of Milgram's classic obedience experiment.

Doms, M. and Avermaet, E. van, 1981, 'The conformity effect; A timeless phenomenon?', *Bulletin of the British Psychological Society*, 36: 180–88.

These authors replicated Solomon's Asch's classic studies on individual conformity in groups and obtained similar results.

Latane, B., Williams, K. and Harkins, S., 1979, 'Many hands make light the work: The causes and consequences of social loafing', *Journal of Personality and Social Psychology*, 37(6): 822–32.

This is a full account of the recreation of the Ringelmann experiment that first revealed the existence of the phenomenon of social loafing.

Nicholson, N., 2003, 'How to motivate your problem people', *Harvard Business Review*, 81(1): 57–65.

Provides useful advice if you are in a student project team where one member is not pulling their weight.

 ## OB in films

The Secret of My Success (1987, director Herbert Ross) DVD track 4: 0:17:00–0:20:00 (3 minutes). In this film, Brantley Foster (played by Michael J. Fox) leaves his home in Kansas to make his career as an executive in New York City. However, the only job he can get is in the mailroom of the Penrose Corporation. The clip begins with the mailroom manager saying 'You can't come in here bozo, take your crap to the mail slot', and ends with Melrose saying, 'you put these things away'. On his first day, Brantley learns a great deal about the organization.

1. What are the sources of his information?

2. What does he learn from each?

3. In your current or last job, what did you learn? How?

Source of information	Information gained

 ## OB in literature

Aleksandr Solzhenitsyn, 1963, *One Day in the Life of Ivan Denisovich*, Penguin Books, Harmondsworth. The novel vividly conveys the barbarity of Stalin's labour camps. It follows Ivan Denisovich Shukhov through a single day in his life in the camp in a freezing winter. Life there is unfathomably hard. Shukhov describes the activities of his work team as they perform their tasks. As you read the book consider what pressures are exerted by the group on its members; what motivates each of them, and what is the group's goal.

CHAPTER EXERCISES

Group controls work

Objectives

1. Analyze a group's behaviour using a theoretical framework.

2. Assess the situation from a management perspective.

Briefing

1. Individually, read the case, *Factory paint shop* on p.324, and answer the questions below:

   (a) As an existing employee, imagine that you had been transferred to a job on the machine described. Would you be happy to go along with the break system described? What would you do if you were not a card player?

   (b) What would you do if you were a new employee to the company who had been allocated to work on that machine?

   (c) If you were an existing group member, and a new member had been transferred into your unit, and was reluctant to participate in the group's informal work arrangements described in the case, how might your group persuade them?

   (d) Should management ignore such adjustments to official policy and intentions? What are the advantages and disadvantages of doing so?

   (e) Have you ever been in a job when something similar has occurred?

3. Form into groups of 3–5 members and nominate a spokesperson.

4. Discuss your individual answers to the questions and prepare a group response.

5. Your spokesperson will report back to the class as a whole, as directed by your instructor.

From Organizational Behaviour and Management, *3rd edn, Martin, J., Copyright 2005 Thomson. Reproduced by permission of Cengage Learning.*

Team member from hell

Objective

1. To evaluate a student group's attempt to change the behaviour of one of its members.

Briefing

1. Form groups.

2. Each group considers the questions specified by their instructor.

Discussion questions

1. What motivates John?

2. What mistakes did the group make in trying to motivate John?

3. How did the team contribute to John's motivational problem?

4. Given what you know about effective group performance, how well did the group handle its problem with John?

5. What suggestions would you make to help the group both achieve its goal and to motivate John?

Let me tell you about my team member from hell. Someone with no desire to succeed is the worst kind of person to have as a member in your student project group, because it is nearly impossible to induce him to do the work and perform it well. It was apparent from the beginning that John had no motivation. After our group had already been created by the course lecturer, a latecomer came to class, and the lecturer assigned him to our group. His name was John. Already I was a little wary. Students who turn up to a class a couple of days after it has started are the slackers; they have either skipped the first few days of class or haven't got their schedule of courses organized.

At our first meeting my expectations were confirmed. I found out that John was a member of the university drinking club, and he did nothing but talk about his social life. I must say though, John was entertaining. He could make us laugh, mainly because he didn't seem to know what he was talking about. Unfortunately, John could also be loud and obnoxious and often his jokes simply were not funny: He just didn't understand the difference between social time and work life. Although John planned to work in his family's business when he graduated, he was working 20–30 hours a week to earn money to pay for his tuition fees and cover his living expenses. I don't think he wanted to be at university really, and he might have dropped out if it wasn't for all his friends. John seemed like someone you would always have to push a little harder in order to get anything done. He made no attempt to discuss anything about our team project or about the courses he was taking. All he ever talked about was partying.

In our team, we began by discussing what we would prepare for our next meeting. John did not volunteer his services for any of the tasks and when we assigned him one, he seemed very annoyed and dissatisfied. At the next meeting, John showed up late and was unprepared. I was disappointed, but not surprised. It wasn't the end of the world, but I couldn't help but look ahead at the complex project we had to complete. If this was the attitude and work ethic that John brought to only our second meeting, how were we ever going to get a reasonable project finished? I intend to make something of myself when I graduate, so I am concerned with my grades and don't want to be dragged down by someone who doesn't care. I would almost rather do things on my own.

→

We decided to distribute the workload evenly among all the members of the group. Each person chose a certain task, and we all began working to complete it. Things seemed to be going quite well until another group member and I realized that John was not completing his part of the work. He had a bad attitude about university that was not very positive, and was not doing well in classes. We tried to motivate him by explaining that if we completed the project successfully, he would complete the course and get a good grade. This seemed to work initially, but we soon learned he was still not completing the work. We discussed the situation and offered to help him if he was having difficulties. Again this worked temporarily but he fell back into his same old pattern.

It wasn't as though the group didn't make an effort to get him involved. Two of us kept reminding him to do his part of the project. However, John would just smile; give a little chuckle, and reply, 'I don't really care about this stupid course. I don't know why we have to do this anyway.' We also sent him numerous e-mails, practically begging him to attend our meetings, so that we could have his input as well as to save his grade. He never responded to any of the messages. At the meetings that he did show up to, we confronted him, and asked him to make more of an effort to attend regularly. He was really laid back and would always just tell us that he was busy, and that he would do what he could.

Eventually one of the members exploded with anger at him. She told him that he was being extremely disrespectful, and that if he didn't want to do any work, he shouldn't show up at the meetings at all! After that, the only thing that changed was that he began coming to our meetings, but he didn't contribute and still did almost no work. He just walked in, sat there while we did the work, and then took credit for work that he had not done.

As time went on, we noticed that John was trying to make small attempts to slowly work his way back into the group. I think he began to notice what a good time we were having working together to complete the project. Although he became more vocal and offered some opinions, we really didn't want to listen to what he had to say. We were well advanced with the project and didn't need his input by this time. Also, we no longer trusted him and did not feel that we could rely on him. I didn't take anything that John said seriously any more, and when he offered to do something, I didn't expect him to do it. He continued to derail our meetings with stories of his weekend parties. He began to complain and make sarcastic comments such as 'Oh, I guess nobody hears me.'

As the project deadline approached, the group agreed to meet at the start and end of the week and then again, over the weekend, for one final time. However, after thinking about the plans just made, John realized that his club's formal dance was scheduled for the same weekend, and he claimed there was no time to work on the project. His statement really annoyed me. Did he expect the rest of us to finish the project for him? Did he really have the nerve to change our plans, just so that he could get drunk all weekend? What were his priorities – university or partying? Suddenly, after this occurred to me, I felt a tremendous pressure. Not only did I and my other team members have to organize everything to finish the project, but we were also the only ones who cared about the quality of the work we produced. We could have talked to John again about his performance, but we never did. We just wanted to get the work done and go home as soon as we could. We decided to speak to the course lecturer to see if we could get John removed from our group. We told John of our intentions and he realized that he would not be able to successfully complete the project on his own, which he would have had to do if he was removed from our group. John agreed to fulfil his duties and, although we had done a large part of the required work that had been assigned to him, he did successfully complete the rest himself.

Chapter 13 **Teamworking**

Key terms

team

group

team autonomy

advice team

quality circles

action team

project team

cross-functional team

production team

high performance work system

autonomous work group

empowerment

Japanese teamworking

total quality management

just-in-time system

kaizen

external work team
   differentiation

internal work team
   differentiation

external work team integration

team performance

team viability

Learning outcomes

When you have read this chapter, you should be able to define those
key terms in your own words, and you should also be able to:

1. Understand why 'team' is a contested concept in the
    organizational literature.

2. List the nine dimensions of team autonomy.

3. Differentiate between four major types of teams and give an
    example of each.

4. Discuss the types of obstacles to effectiveness experienced by each
    type of team.

5. Contrast Western with Japanese concepts of teamworking.

6. List the three main elements of the ecological framework for
    analyzing work team effectiveness.

7. Understand the continuing importance of teamworking.

Why study teamworking?

As organizations grow in size and become structurally more complex, groups of people are needed who work together in co-ordinated ways to achieve objectives and contribute to the overall aims, effectiveness and competitiveness of the organization. Teamworking provides the flexibility needed to respond effectively, appropriately and more quickly than competitors to the constantly changing demands in the organization's environment, and provides a mechanism for bringing together a range of expertise and skills required to complete complex work tasks. Teams have become the building blocks of organizations.

This view was expressed by Borrill and West (2005), discussed the great contribution that teamworking has made to organizational effectiveness. The potential of teamworking to contribute to organizational (management) goals has been re-discovered at the level of the shop floor by the interest in Japanese teamworking, seen by many critics as a means of creating a compliant and programmable workforce. The teamwork literature reveals a continuing, worldwide, organizational trend towards the introduction of teamworking. Teams are popular in organizations and are positively perceived by their members, managers and society at large. Companies appear to believe that teams are an effective way of:

- improving performance;
- reducing production costs;
- speeding up innovations;
- improving product quality;
- increasing work flexibility;
- introducing new technologies;
- increasing employee participation;
- achieving better industrial relations;
- meeting the challenge of global competition;
- identifying and solving work-related problems.

Indeed, some critics claim that teamworking is seen as simple solution to virtually all organizational problems. Allen and Hecht (2004) discuss this 'romance of teams' which they define as a faith in the effectiveness and even superiority of team-based work, that is not supported by convincing empirical research. The reason that teams are increasingly used, they claim, is not because they are more effective, but because their fulfil certain psychological, social and political needs. Teams make people more satisfied and bolster their confidence; they promote the idea that everyone is unique and has something different to contribute to a task; that individuals should pull together; and teams fit in with currently attractive ideas of empowerment, participation and democracy. Thus, despite being inappropriate or ineffective in certain circumstances, teams continue to be used uncritically within organizations (Naquin and Tynan, 2003; Sinclair, 1992). Thus, a reason for studying teamworking is to determine whether or not teams are superior to individuals working alone, and in which circumstances.

The T-word and team job design

Team a group whose members share a common goal that they pursue collaboratively; and who can only succeed or fail collectively.

The word, team, derives from the old English, Fresian and Norse word for a bridle and thence to a set of draught animals harnessed together and, by analogy, to a number of persons involved in joint action (Annett and Stanton, 2000). It refers to a group whose members share a common goal that they pursue collaboratively; and who can only succeed or fail collectively. Nicky Hayes saw teams as a sporting metaphor used frequently by managers and consultants. Sainsbury's, a large British supermarket chain, uses the employee job title of 'checkout *captain*'. The metaphor stresses both inclusiveness and similarity – members sharing common values and co-operating to achieve common goals; while also emphasizing differences, as various individuals play distinct, albeit equally valuable roles, and have different responsibilities. She wrote that,

> The idea of 'team' at work must be one of the most widely used metaphors in organizational life. A group of workers or managers is generally described as a 'team', in much the same way that a company or department is so often described as 'one big family'. But often, the new employee receiving these assertions quickly discovers that what was described as a '"team" is actually anything but'. The mental image of cohesion, co-ordination and common goals which was conjured up by the metaphor of the team, was entirely different from the everyday reality of working life (Hayes 1997, p.27).

Robert Jackall (1988) concluded that the language of team playing derived from American football and was used to discipline individuals into conforming. From his research, he argued that advancement in large organizations relied on being seen as a 'team player', and by not standing out from the team by displaying strong convictions or distinctive characteristics. Jos Benders and Geert van Hootegem (1999a, 1999b) felt that after decades of experimentation, teams had finally achieved the status of 'good management practice' in Western organizations. The terms 'group' and 'team' are words which are frequently used interchangeably in the management literature. Katzenbach and Smith (1993) suggest that the key distinction between a work group and a team relates to performance results. They wrote:

> A working group's performance is a function of what its members do as individuals. A team's performance includes both individual results and what we call 'collective work products'. A collective work product is what two or more members work on together . . . [it] reflects the joint, real contribution of team members (1993, p.112).

Paulus and van der Zee (2004) explained how, historically, research into groups and that into teams had followed distinct and separate paths, with the groups literature appearing in psychology textbooks, and the teams literature being found mainly in management and organizational behaviour texts. The also wrote that 'team is a word for managers' – an appealing word used as a rhetorical strategy through which managers hope to achieve their goals. It conveys the view that we are all now part of a classless society and the interests of workers and big business are the same. Other critics have argued that management's promotion of the team concept was a union-busting device – a way of threatening the existence of unions as independent institutions promoting workers' interests and increasing

Group two or more people, in face-to-face interaction, each aware of their group membership and interdependence, as they strive to achieve their goals.

employees' personal insecurity. They imply that, in contrast, **group** is a word that is used by those academics who study human behaviour in organizations.

Discussing the problem of defining the word 'team', Benders noted the taken-for-granted assumption that it was inherently associated with high levels of autonomy. The adjectives that frequently precede the word 'team' in the organizational literature are *autonomous*, *semi-autonomous*, *self-managing*, *self-regulating* or *self-directing*. Yet, as Benders takes pains to explain, the aforementioned adjectives, and the word 'team' are mutually contradictory.

> team members sell their labour capacity to the employing organization in exchange for wages. In other words, employees agree to work under the authority of managers who are appointed by their employing organizations. Thus the organization sets the boundaries within which any employee, thus also a team member, may act. Within these boundaries, employees may expect to be given directives. Full autonomy, is the sense of complete freedom to act is thus an illusion for any employee (2005, p.56).

He goes on to explain that team members are assigned specific goals by their managers, that they are expected to achieve which are in the interests of the profit-seeking organizations that employ them. In his view, the autonomy available to the members of one team is limited firstly by the autonomy exercised by other teams, and second, by the fact that all team members are subject to organizational control. Many types of teams, for example, those in the archetypal Japanese system of lean production, are not necessarily participative, let alone self-managing (Procter and Currie, 2004).

Football teams

The golden years of the Ajax Amsterdam football team were the 1970s, and included the legendary Johan Cruyff and Piet Keizer. The players enjoyed unparalleled freedom at the highest level of the modern game. There has been nothing since to compare with the giddy, unintended experiment in football democracy. It was probably as close as anyone has ever come to running a major football club like a workers' co-operative: not only did the team practically pick itself, but the players also determined most of their own tactics and decided which friendly matches they would play. It was the custom every year for the Ajax team captain to be chosen by the players without the presence of the coach. Teamwork in Dutch football was based on the fact that the team had to be the star, not its players.

Confirming this view, John Kay argued that in the 2006 World Cup, while the conquering Italian team was more than the sum of its individual parts, the Brazilian team (the final losers) was not. What distinguishes a great team from a group of great players? Kay highlights two factors. Firstly, the quality of a club's 'organizational learning', particularly its post-match debriefings, and its pre-match communication with players about other players, other clubs and pitches. His second factor has to do with personal benefit. Kay says, 'A player can choose to kick for goal or pass to a better situated player. His choice of behaviour will depend on the degree to which his incentives relate to the performance of the team rather than his performance as an individual and on his expectations about whether the next player will shoot or pass in turn. Because an individual's behaviour depends on the expectations of the behaviour of others, teams will become locked into particular states'. Italy's success was testimony to the fact that outstanding teams can defeat groups of outstanding individual players. – 'A team of champions can be beaten by a champion team'.

Based on Winner (2001) and Kay (2006).

Home viewing

The film, *Any Given Sunday* (1999, director Oliver Stone) has, as one of its themes, the contrast between individual performance within a team, and team performance. A team with a star can be neutralized if that individual is absent or incapacitated. Similarly, a 'dream team' of exceptional individual performers who are not working cohesively may be beaten by a lesser collection of individuals, working more cohesively together – a team of champions may be beaten by a champion team. Look for examples of these differences as presented in this movie.

Collaboration conundrums

Major corporations rely on large, diverse teams of highly educated specialists to implement major changes or launch initiatives. For example, the BBC covering the World Cup or the Olympics; or the Marriott Hotels developing an enhanced IT system. Research by Lynda Gratton and Tamara Erickson into team behaviour in 15 multinational companies discovered the paradox that the four qualities required for team success were the same ones that undermined that success. These were large size, diversity, virtual participation and high educational levels.

- *Size*: past teams of 20 now typically consist of 100 or more members. The increase is due to new technologies; wider stakeholder involvement; co-ordination of diverse activities; and harnessing of multiple skills. Negatively, they found that beyond 20 members, the natural level of co-operation between members decreases.

- *Diversity*: tasks require the rapid assembly of people from different backgrounds and perspectives, few of whom have ever previously met. Dissimilar views and knowledge can trigger innovation. Negatively, the greater the diversity and the number of strangers in a team, the less likely they are to share their knowledge.

- *Virtual participation*: complex tasks require insights and knowledge from people from many locations, so virtual teamworking is common. Negatively, as teams become more virtual, collaboration declines.

- *Higher education levels*: teams draw on members who possess highly specialized skills and knowledge. Negatively, the greater the proportion of highly educated specialists on a team, the more likely it is to disintegrate into unproductive conflicts.

The authors went on to recommend eight management practices that helped teams overcome these difficulties, and led them to success:

- relationship practices that bonded staff;
- executives role modelling collaboration;
- establishing a 'gift culture' in which managers support employees by mentoring them;
- training in relationship skills, such as communication and conflict resolution;
- a sense of community, fostered by group activities;
- leadership that is both task-oriented and relationship-oriented;
- using heritage relationships by having teams whose members know and trust each other;
- role clarity and task ambiguity by defining individual roles in detail but giving teams latitude to decide on approaches.

Based on Gratton and Erickson (2007)
and Gratton (2007).

Types of teams

Eric Sundstrom, Kenneth de Meuse and David Futrell (1990) distinguished four types of teams – advice, action, project and production (see Table 13.1). Advice teams provide information to management to be used in its own decision-making, e.g. quality circles. Action teams execute brief performances that are repeated under new conditions, e.g., football teams. Project teams bring together employees from different departments to accomplish a specific task, e.g. new product development. Production teams consist of individuals who share a production goal. Their labels indicate their output, which is also their distinguishing feature. Each team type is further differentiated along five dimensions:

Degree of differentiation from other units: how similar (low differentiation) or different (high differentiation) is this team from others within the department or organization?

Degree of co-ordination: is its work closely related to and intertwined with that of other work units within the organization (high co-ordination); or does it operate relatively independently (low co-ordination)?

Degree of technical specialization: are members required to apply special, technical skills acquired through higher education or extensive training (high differentiation); or do they draw upon their members' general experience and problem-solving ability (low differentiation)?

Work cycles: how much time does the team need to achieve its aims? Does it perform short, repetitive work cycles, or a single, long one?

Typical outputs: what does the team produce as its output?

Sundstrom *et al.*'s team typology allows you to categorize existing teams in organizations for research and performance improvement purposes. It allows you to compare and contrast different teams and their processes, analyze their outputs, and suggest ways of making improvements.

Team autonomy the extent to which a team experiences freedom, independence and discretion in decisions relating to the performance of its tasks.

Teams differ in terms of how much autonomy management grants them. **Team autonomy** refers to the extent to which a team experiences freedom, independence and discretion in decisions related to the performance of its tasks. When encountering an example of a supposed 'autonomous team' within a company, it is necessary to ask: who decides about what, and to what extent?

Table 13.1: Types of teams and their outputs

Types and examples	Degree of differentiation from other work units	Degree of co-ordination with other work units	Degree of technical specialization	Work cycles/time frame	Typical outputs
ADVICE Committees Review panels and boards Quality control circles Employee involvement groups Advisory councils	Low	Low	Low	Work cycles can be brief or long; one cycle can be a team life span	Decisions Selections Suggestions Proposals Recommendations
ACTION Sports teams Entertainment groups Expeditions Negotiating teams Surgery teams Cockpit crews Military platoons and squads	High	High	High	Work cycles brief, repeated under new conditions	Competitive events Expeditions Contracts Lawsuits Concerts Surgical operations Flights Combat missions
PROJECT Research groups Planning teams Architect teams Engineering teams Development teams Task forces	High	Low (for traditional units) or High (for cross-functional teams)	High	Work cycles typically differ for each new project; one cycle can be a team's life span	Plans Designs Investigations Presentations Prototypes Reports Findings
PRODUCTION Assembly line teams Manufacturing cells Mining teams Hospital receptions Data processing groups Maintenance crews	Low	High	High	Work cycles typically repeated or continuous process; cycles often briefer than team life span	Food Chemicals Components Assemblies Retail sales Customer service Equipment repairs

From Sundstrom et al. *(1990, p.125).*

Jan Gulowsen (1979), a Norwegian researcher, provided a framework which enabled more specific assessments to be made about team autonomy for comparative purposes (Table 13.2). He distinguished nine 'task areas' or dimensions in a team's working which offered the potential for autonomy. Within each area, he specified four possible levels of team input. This allows different teams to be distinguished in terms of the level of autonomy that they possess, and allows them to be compared and contrasted.

Researchers use four, specific criteria to distinguish autonomous from semi-autonomous teams:

1. members work together as a team

2. team members are responsible for specific products or services

3. team members jointly decide how work is done

4. team appoints its own leader

To be classed as 'semi-autonomous', a team must fulfil the first three criteria, while a fully autonomous team meets all four requirements (Proctor and Burridge, 2008). Table 13.3 lists in order the types of tasks that self-managing teams are most likely to perform for themselves. (*Training*, 1996):

Table 13.2: Team task areas, levels of team input and team autonomy levels

Team task area / dimensions

1. Selection of the team leader
2. Acceptance of a new member into the team
3. Distribution of work
4. Time flexibility
5. Acceptance of additional work
6. Representation outside the team
7. Production methods (choice of)
8. Production goals (output determination)
9. Production goals (quality determination)

Team input levels

1. *None* – No team participation and total management control. Managers make all the decisions and teams implement them. Team members have no input into the decision-making process; there is no element of participation, not even in the form of suggestions or requests.
2. *Some* – Teams have some input into decisions concerned with their immediate working environment. They can make suggestions, requests and have discussions with management who may adopt their ideas.
3. *Joint* – A situation of co-decision-making, in which teams share decision-making power with management, having an equal role in the taking and implementing of decisions.
4. *Autonomy* – Teams are fully trusted by management, the teams are truly autonomous, reaching their decisions with no input from management whatsoever. Management accepts them as full and equal partners.

Team autonomy level

low autonomy teams	moderate autonomy teams	high autonomy teams
assembly line workers	quality circles	autonomous work groups
supermarket checkouts	semi-autonomous groups	high performance teams
		self-directed team

Based on Gulowsen (1979).

Table 13.3: Tasks performed by self-managing teams themselves

A survey conducted for the *Training* magazine of 1,456 organizations in the United States with over 100 employees, found the following:

Task	%
Set own work schedules	67
Deal directly with external customers	67
Conduct own member training	59
Setting own production quotas/performance targets	56
Deal with suppliers/vendors	44
Purchase equipment/services	43
Develop budgets	39
Do their own performance reviews on members	36
Hire co-workers	33
Fire co-workers	14

From Training (1996, p.69).

STOP AND THINK   If you are a member of a team (work, sports, musical, religious, social), what level of decision input do you and your fellow team members have on which tasks, in relation to your supervisor, coach, choirmaster, priest, club president?

Make a list of tasks relevant to your team and then identify those which your team performs itself.

The reality of autonomous team working

Armelle Gorgeu and Rene Mathieu described the operation of autonomous teams in car seat upholstery factories in France in the mid 1990s. These teams consisted of 2–4 people, depending on the vehicle. The members organized themselves as they wanted, but were given a time limit for assembling all the seats for each car. They received team bonuses, especially for quality. Competition existed within the team's members as they received different wages, and the supervisor distinguished slow workers from those who took the role of leader. The teams allowed individuals to work at fixed positions, because the seat was removed from the assembly line, assembled, and then put back onto the conveyor belt. This job was easier than working on the conveyor belt where the manual operator had to follow along the line while working. However, it was still difficult because of the weight of the material; the physical effort involved; the manual stapling of the seat covers; and the stress caused by the speed of the physical movements required.

Each worker assembled a complete seat and had to know how to assemble the two front seats and the back seat. With the multiplication of the different models, there was a succession of different assembly kits that did not necessarily resemble each another. When the company worked on two vehicles from the same range, the personnel went from one to the other. Working fast and well, in harmony with the other workers in the unit involved a team based on affinity. In theory, the workers within a given team needed to alternate frequently between the different job positions. In practice, however, at full production rate, assembly was allocated according to the efficiency of each member – some assembled the front seats, others the back ones. 'After a difficult apprenticeship, a production worker who has mastered the operations at a particular position does not usually want to repeat the learning experience for another position', said one of the interviewees. Each group managed its own quality and productivity, and their results were displayed in the factory. This enabled team members to make comparisons with other teams.

Based on Gorgeu and Mathieu (2005).

Advice teams

Advice team a team created primarily to provide a flow of information to management to be used in its own decision-making.

Quality circle shop floor employees from the same department, who meet for a few hours each week to discuss ways of improving their work environment.

An **advice team** is created primarily to provide a flow of information to management for use in its own decision-making. Advice teams require little in the way of co-ordination with other work units in the company. Following a major accident or disaster, governments often set up committees of experts and eminent people to advise it on future action. The committee reviews the events that occurred and makes recommendations about improvements.

In organizations, the **quality circle** (also known as a *kaizen* team) has been the best known and most publicized advice team of recent times. The original concept was of a team of 6 to 12 employees from the shop floor of the same manufacturing department, meeting regularly to discuss quality problems, investigating their causes and recommending solutions to management. In practice, a wide range of different arrangements was established under this label. Circles varied in terms of the number of members; were applied in service as well as manufacturing contexts; included supervisory staff; discussed non-quality issues; and some had authority to implement their suggestions. All these matters depended on the basis upon which the circle was established by management in the particular organization.

Quality circles are a Japanese export, and have been used world-wide. They were introduced into the West during the 1980s in an effort to emulate Japanese successes. The first quality circle in the United States is claimed to have been at the Lockheed Missile and Space Company at Sunnyvale in California in 1974. The first one in Britain appeared at Rolls Royce in Derby in 1978. Although originally used in manufacturing, quality circles have been applied extensively in the service industries, government agencies, voluntary sector, the British National Health Service, and many other types of organizations. Despite their differences, which were mentioned earlier, quality circles do possess some common features:

● Membership is voluntary, and members are drawn from a particular department.

● No financial rewards are given for team suggestions.

● Members receive training in problem-solving, statistical quality control and team processes.

● Their problem-solving domain is defined by management (often, but not always quality, productivity and cost reduction).

● Meetings are held weekly, usually in company time, often with trained facilitators helping members with training issues and helping them to manage the meetings.

● The decision to install quality circles is made at the top of the organization, and the circles are created at the bottom.

Management's objectives for introducing quality circles varied greatly – quality improvement, quality enhancement and employee involvement. Although an organization may claim to have introduced quality circles, even at the height of their popularity, only a small proportion of the employees ever took part (Marchington, 1992). Quality circles represent one of the largest experiments in the use of advice teams to improve organizational performance during the 1980s. During the 1990s, quality circles begun to be superseded by the 'total quality movement' (Hill, 1991).

Action teams

Action team a team that executes brief performances that are repeated under new conditions. Its members are technically specialized, and it needs to co-ordinate its output with those of other work units.

The members of an action team are specialized in terms of their knowledge, skill and contribution to the team's objective. The 'performance' of an action team is brief, and is repeated under new conditions each time. Additionally, both the specialized inputs of the various team members and the need for individuals to co-ordinate with other team members is high.

If a football player sustains a serious injury on the field, an action team consisting of the club physiotherapist and his assistants work on him. If the injury is serious, he may be taken to hospital where another action team – a surgeon and her co-workers operate on him. Finally, when recuperating in his private room, he may watch TV and see a film created by more action teams. In all these situations, action team members have to exhibit peak performance on demand.

One example of an action team is a *crew*. This term is frequently used to refer to employees who work on aircraft, boats, spacecraft and film sets. A distinguishing feature of a crew is that it is equipment- or technology-driven. If the technology is changed, then so too is the nature of the crew. A crew depends on its technology which transforms difficult, cognitive tasks into easy ones. The crew's 'tools' affect the division of labour among its members; and crewmembers use various techniques to co-ordinate their activities (Hare, 1992; Hutchins, 1990).

Ginnett (1993) reported how, on a Boeing 727 aircraft, the crew members' roles were determined by the location of their seats in the cockpit. The captain sat in the left seat from which he tested all the emergency warning devices. He was the only one who could taxi the aircraft, since the nose wheel gear steering was located on that side of the cockpit. The first officer, who started the engines and who communicated with the tower, occupied the right hand seat. The flight engineer sat sideways, facing a panel that allowed him to monitor and control the various sub-systems in the aircraft. He was the only one able to reach the auxiliary power unit. In other transportation craft, the relationship of roles to equipment would be different. Airplane personnel consists of those in the cockpit – flight crew (pilot, co-pilot, flight engineers) and those outside it – the cabin crew (flight attendants). Between 1959–1989, 70 per cent of all severe aircraft accidents were at least partly attributable to flight crew behaviour (Weiner *et al.*, 1993). Thus, it is a more common cause than either pilot error or mechanical failure.

STOP AND THINK

Nearly all commercial airlines now rotate members of their flight crews. Pilots, co-pilots and flight attendants bid for schedules on specific planes (e.g. Airbus 380, Boeing 737) and receive a monthly schedule. Thus, a given flight crew is rarely together for more than a few days at a time. Senior pilots on large planes often fly with a different co-pilot on every trip during a month. What are the advantages and disadvantages of this arrangement?

Mending a broken heart

During cardiac surgery, a patient is rendered functionally dead – the heart stops beating, the lungs stop pumping air – while a surgical team repairs or replaces damaged arteries or valves. A week later, the patient walks out of the hospital. The team that performs this task is as important as the technology that allows them to do it. It consists of different specialists – a surgeon, an anaesthesiologist, a perfusionist and a scrub nurse working closely and co-operatively together. It exemplifies an *action team* where a single error, miscommunication or slow response by any member can result in failure. Individuals are in *reciprocal interdependence* with each other, *mutually adjusting* their actions to match those of fellow members.

Edmondson and her colleagues found that since this type of team performed hundreds of cardiac operations annually, it established a sequence of individual tasks that became very well-defined and routine. Indeed, team members often needed only to look at, rather than speak to, one another, to signal the initiation of the next stage of the procedure. The change from traditional, open-heart surgery procedures to minimally invasive ones involved several changes. The new procedure not only required individual team members to learn new, unfamiliar tasks, but also necessitated that a number of familiar tasks were performed in a different order. Thus, team members had to unlearn old routines before learning new ones. Additionally, the new technology required a greater degree

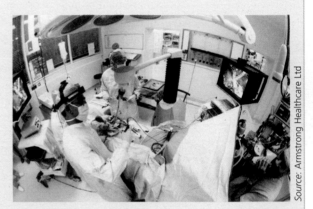

Operating theatre

Source: Armstrong Healthcare Ltd

of interdependence and communication between team members. For example, the surgeon relied more on team members for essential information than before. This not only disrupted the team's routine but also changed the surgeon's role as order-giver in the operating room's tightly structured hierarchy.

By trying out things that might not work, making mistakes and pointing out problems, learning was accelerated. Such a climate was fostered by the words and actions of surgeons acting as team leaders.

Based on Edmondson et al. *(2001).*

Project teams

A **project team** consists of individuals who have been brought together for a limited period of time, from different parts of the organization, to contribute towards a management-specified task. The task may be developing a product, refining a service or commissioning

Project team a collection of employees from different work areas in an organization brought together to accomplish a specific task within a finite time.

a new plant (Cohen and Bailey, 1997). Once this has been completed, the team is either disbanded or else its members are given new assignments. Project teams are created when:

- creative problem-solving is required involving the application of different types of specialized knowledge;
- there is a need to closely co-ordinate the work on a specific project e.g. design and development, production and testing of a new product.

Every university has hundreds of project teams who are conducting research. Most of their members are on 2–3-year contracts which span the period of the research project. Team members are recruited on the basis of their specialist knowledge, and their output consists of a research report, book and journal articles.

Cross-functional team employees from different functional departments who meet as a team to complete a particular task.

Within the organizational context, one of the best known and most common types of project team is the cross-functional team. Jack Gordon (1992) reported the spread of work teams in the United States, reporting that in organizations with more than 100 employees, 82 per cent had staff working in teams, of which 18 per cent were in cross-functional teams. Another survey, this time by the Hay Group, revealed that approximately 25 per cent of US companies had implemented cross-functional teams (Leshner and Brown, 1993, p.39). Emmerson, an electronics company based in St Louis, Missouri, established cross-functional teams in the 1990s to deal with large customers who bought from several of its divisions. The teams cut across the company's long-standing boundaries and allowed customers to see Emmerson as a single, integrated supplier rather than a collection of independent divisions (Hindle, 2006f; Knight, 2005).

Traditionally, organizations have been divided into tall, functional 'boxes' or 'chimneys'. It has been argued that by forming teams consisting of people from these different boxes, organizations could break down the boundaries between their functions (e.g. accounting, marketing, research, product design, human resources), improve co-ordination and integration; release the creative thought of their employees; and increase the speed and flexibility of their responses to customers. They are established with the objective of combining a wide range of expertise in order to reach a more informed and rounded outcome than would otherwise be possible.

Cross-functional teams comprise employees who traditionally work in different departments or work areas. Sometimes, they may also include customers, suppliers and external consultants. They are supported by their organization's structures, systems and skills which enable the teams to operate successfully as a more independent unit (less bound by functional ties) towards goals which transcend the combined abilities of individual members.

Proponents of cross-functional teams claim that they are beneficial to their customers, employees, and to the organization as a whole. Customers obtain more attractive and customized products, and have their needs met more rapidly. Team members benefit through having more challenging and rewarding jobs with broader responsibilities; greater opportunities for gaining visibility in front of senior management; increased understanding of entire processes across the organization; a 'fun' working environment and closer relationships with colleagues. The organization gains through:

- increased productivity;
- improved co-ordination and integration;
- significantly reduced processing times;
- improving market and customer focus;
- reducing the time needed to develop new products;
- improving communications by having boundaries between functions spanned.

Cross-functional teams differ from other types of teams in three important respects:

- *representative*: they are representative in that their individual members usually retain their position back in their 'home' functional department;

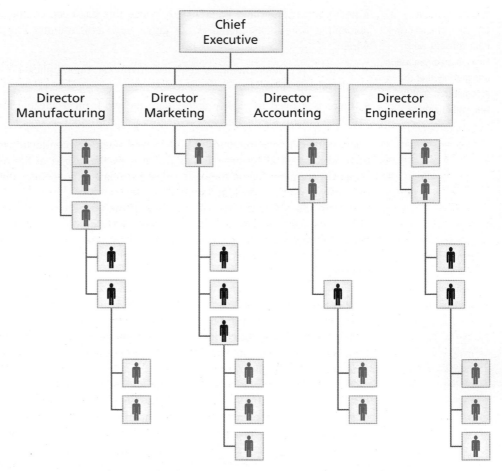

Figure 13.1: Cross-functional team

- *temporary*: they have a finite life, even if their end is years in the future;
- *innovation*: they are established to solve non-conventional problems and meet challenging performance standards.

The most common application of cross-functional teams has been in new product development, innovation, or in research and development (R&D). However, they have also been used whenever an organization requires an input of diverse, specialist skills and knowledge. For example, in manufacturing and production (e.g. Motorola); in IT development, automation and support simultaneously developing the 'soft' (interpersonal, motivational, leadership) skills of technically-oriented IT staff (e.g. Procter & Gamble); to implement quality, cost, speed improvements and process re-engineering initiatives (e.g. USAir, Hallmark Cards, Inc.); to implement customer service improvements (e.g. Unisys Client Server Systems Groups); to streamline purchasing and procurement; streamlining and optimization; for market research; for creativity and business improvement (e.g. Konica Imaging); or for benchmarking.

Cross-functional team members, since they are departmental representatives, owe their true allegiance to their home, functional (chimney) department. They are therefore likely to experience a higher degree of pressure and divided loyalties, than in other teams. Their temporary nature also places strains on members who have quickly to develop stable and effective working group processes. Cross-functional teams place great demands on the organizational support system and can have a negative effect on the individual team member. Organizations and managers need to clearly define cross-functional team assignments in order to maintain order and accountability.

Management cross-functional teams at Nissan

Following the strategic alliance between Renault and Nissan in 1999, Carlos Ghosn went to Tokyo to lead Nissan back to profitability. He wanted to introduce changes that went both against the company's long-standing operating practices, and some of the behavioural norms of Japanese society. Rather than imposing these changes from the top, he established nine cross-functional teams (CFTs) comprising Nissan's middle management, and made these the centrepiece of his turnaround plan. While executives preferred working in teams consisting of similarly oriented colleagues, Ghosn wanted them to look beyond the functional or regional boundaries that defined their direct responsibilities, and to ask difficult questions. Cross-functional teamworking would, in his view, encourage his managers to think in new ways and to challenge existing practices. In this organizational context, the teams would also provide a means for explaining the need for change, and for communicating difficult messages across the whole company. Ghosn quickly established nine CFTs, each with its own area of responsibility: business development; purchasing; manufacturing and logistics; research and development; sales and marketing; general and administrative; finance and cost; phase out of products and parts complexity management; and organization.

Together, the CFTs addressed all the key drivers which determined Nissan's performance. Each team consisted of about 10 middle managers, and created its own sub-teams to investigate some issues in greater depth. To give each CFT authority within the company, two 'leaders' (to prevent a single function's perspective predominating) from the executive committee were appointed to it. They served as that team's sponsors, helping to smooth its path, and removing institutional obstacles to its work. To avoid charges of top-down, imposed change, these leaders took a back seat, and rarely attended team meetings, leaving the real work to the team's 'pilot' who progressed the work and led the discussions.

All the CFTs were given three months, and asked to review the company's operations, and recommend ways of returning Nissan to profitability and uncovering opportunities for future growth. None of them had any decision-making responsibility. The outcome was a detailed blueprint for the Nissan Revival Plan developed by Nissan's own executives. They proposed major changes to some Nissan business practices (e.g. in engineering specifications and reducing some quality standards); and 'harsh medicine' in the form of plant closures and headcount reductions (which challenged Japanese business traditions).

Based on Ghosn (2002).

STOP AND THINK You are a middle manager at Nissan who has been a member of one of the nine cross-functional teams (see case study above). Do you feel pleased to have been given the responsibility to participate in setting the company's future direction, or resentful that the senior management seems to have manipulated you and your colleagues, through the means of cross-functional teams, into proposing unpalatable solutions that they lacked the courage to make themselves?

Production teams

Production team a stable number of individuals who share production goals, and who perform specific roles which are supported by a set of incentives and sanctions.

Typically, a **production team** consists of individuals who are responsible for performing day-to-day, core operations. These may be product-oriented teams such as those assembling a computer on a factory floor; construction workers placing a bridge in position across a motorway; or teams assembling sound and light systems for a rock concert. The degree of technical specialization required of the team members varies from medium to low, depending on the nature of the duties performed. However, the degree of required co-ordination, both between the members of each team, and between the team and other work units, is high. It is these other units that are either responsible for providing support activities such as quality control and maintenance, or who provide the inputs to, or receive the outputs of that team.

The modern concept of teamworking goes back to Eric Trist and Kenneth Bamforth (1951) who analyzed the psychological and emotional responses to underground working by miners. The socio-technical paradigm was developed during the 1960s, but became more widely known through applications, in the late 1960s and 1970s.

Suitable autonomous work team settings

There are different of teams, work tasks and work settings. Some are suitable for autonomous teamworking, while others are not. Louis Davis and George Wacker cited situational factors which they believed facilitated autonomous group working.

1. When the work is not entirely unskilled.

2. When the work group can be identified as a meaningful unit of the organization: when inputs and outputs are definable and clearly identifiable; and when different groups can be separated by stable buffer areas.

3. When turnover in the group can be kept to a minimum.

4. When there are definite criteria for performance evaluation of the group and group members.

5. When timely feedback is possible.

6. When the group has resources for measuring and controlling its own critical variances in workflow.

7. When the tasks are highly interdependent, so that group members must work together.

8. When cross training is desired by management.

9. When jobs can be structured to balance group and individual tasks.

From Davis and Wacker (1987).

The focus of 1970s' experiments into employee participation and industrial democracy sought to raise productivity by providing employees with more interesting and varied work. In contrast, team-based working innovations of the 1990s represent a greater concern with efficiency and effectiveness. They were stimulated by the need for companies to remain competitive in a fiercely aggressive global environment. The rationale is that in the race to improve service quality or reduce new product cycle times, technology only gives an organization a short-term advantage, and one which can be copied anyway. It is the way that human resources are organized and developed that is more critical.

Skylab strike

Source: NASA Images

Friday, 27 December 1973 was a red-letter day in the history of industrial relations. The Apollo astronauts in Skylab 4 (the American precursor to the International Space Station) conducted the first ever, day-long, sit-down strike in outer space. Why did this occur? A breakdown in trust occurred at the start when ground control at Houston reprimanded the astronauts for not reporting a bout of space sickness. Tensions mounted when, in an effort to maximize the amount of information gained, Houston had minutely scheduled the astronauts' activities. The crew soon found themselves tired and behind schedule. By removing all their discretion, they made them into robots. Houston shortened their meal breaks, reduced the set up times for experiments, and told them they were not working long or hard enough. Every day, it sent up six feet of information to the astronauts' teleprinter, containing 42 different sets of instructions. These included directions as to where to point the telescope, which scientific instruments to use and so on, arranging their entire day for them. Astronauts normally follow such instructions to the letter.

However, the astronauts wanted Houston to provide them with only a general schedule and a 'shopping list' of things to do, so that they could decide how best to do them. Houston's view was that many jobs interfered with one another (one crew member riding a bicycle ergometer and shaking the space station while another tries to film a solar flare), and could not be performed simultaneously. Other, more interesting tasks could distract the astronauts and prevent them from performing more mundane, albeit, vital ones. In the Taylorist style, ground control had defined itself as the planners (management) and had defined the astronauts as the implementers (workers). Eventually, the relationship between mission control and the astronauts broke down completely. The crew mutinied against mission control, turned off the communication and refused to work for a 24-hour period, spending the time relaxing and enjoying the panoramic views. Eventually, their workload was reduced but NASA ensured that none of them ever flew again.

Based on Weick (1977).

Management's interest in production teams has always been in finding ways of improving employee motivation and performance. Employee participation in decision-making can take the form of increasing their autonomy. Bram Steijn distinguished between *individual* autonomy for the employee who was not part of a team, for example, in the form of job enrichment (see Chapter 9), and team autonomy which was 'the *(collective)* autonomy for the workers *as a team* to do a task' (Steijn, 2001, p.193). It is the latter that is considered in this chapter. The individual and the teamworking approaches have converged in practice in what has been become known as the **high performance work system**. The contrast between traditional hierarchical management and team management is summarized in Table 13.4.

High performance work system a form of organization that operates at levels of excellence far beyond those of comparable systems.

Alan Jenkins (1994) argued that management had become preoccupied with autonomous (or self-managed) teamworking, and that such teams had come to be seen as the basis for effective organizational designs. Other authors have noted some of the social and historic

Table 13.4: Hierarchical and team management compared

Hierarchical management: hierarchically ordered supervision	Team management: shift to self-management
The supervisor has precise supervisory responsibilities.	The supervisor is replaced by a team of 10 to 15 people, who take over the responsibilities of their former supervisor.
The supervisor gives instructions.	Self-managing employees gather and synthesize information, act on it, and take collective responsibility for their actions.
Management relies on formal rules and authority expressed in terms of disciplines that seek to reinforce this authority.	Management provides a value-based corporate vision that guides day-to-day actions by being a reference point from which employees infer appropriate action.
The supervisor checks that instructions have been followed.	The self-managing team guides its own work and co-ordinates with other areas of the company.
The supervisor ensures that each employee fulfils his or her job description.	The self-managing team is responsible for completing a specific, well-defined job-function for which all members are cross-trained. All members of the team have the authority and responsibility to make essential decisions, set work schedules, order materials, and co-ordinate with other teams.

Reprinted by permission of SAGE Publications, London, Los Angeles, New Delhi and Singapore from Clegg, S.R., Kornberger, M. and Pitsis, T., *Managing and Organizations*, Copyright (© Sage Publications 2008).

Autonomous work group a team allocated to a significant segment of the workflow, with discretion over how their work will be carried out.

processes that have led to the emergence of the autonomous work group. This is a team (confusingly labelled 'group' in the research literature) that is allocated to a significant segment of the workflow, given discretion over how their work will be carried out. It is argued that such teams reduce costs by eliminating the need for having supervisors, and their members produce more, because they are more motivated and committed to their jobs (Langfried, 2000; Kirkman *et al.*, 2001; Chansler *et al.*, 2003).

There has been confusion about the use of the concept of teamworking in different countries and in different companies. Western teamworking emphasizes enhanced employee control and job satisfaction through participation, and represents an example of worker empowerment. This refers to organizational arrangements that give employees more autonomy, discretion and decision-making responsibility. Japanese teamworking, in contrast, operates at the other end of the autonomous teamwork continuum. It uses the scientific management principles of 'minimum manning, multi-tasking, multi-machine operation, pre-defined work operations, repetitive short cycle work, powerful first line supervisors, and a conventional managerial hierarchy' (Buchanan, 1994, p.219). Japanese work teams tend to be advice teams mistaken for production teams. They meet and function as teams 'off line' (outside the production context) in contrast to autonomous work groups which function as teams 'on line' (inside the production context).

Empowerment organizational arrangements that give employees more autonomy, discretion, and decision-making responsibility.

With respect to shop floor production teams, Marchington and Wilkinson (2005, pp.78–79) suggest that there may be limits to the possibility of introducing self-managed forms of teamworking. They point to situations in which:

> workers are unable to enlarge their jobs to embrace higher level skills or where there are legal or technical reasons that prevent workers from making certain types of decision. Moreover, the prospect of teamworking is limited where the rotation of a large range of low-level jobs means that one boring job is merely swapped for another boring job on a regular basis. In situations such as these, teamworking may only serve to make work more stressful and intrusive, and adds nothing to the skills or initiative that workers are able to deploy.

A self-managing orchestra

Orpheus Chamber Orchestra

Source: Larry Fink/studio 55

In the dictatorial world of orchestras, it is the conductors who choose the repertoire, organize rehearsals and tell musicians how to play. In contrast, the Orpheus Chamber Orchestra in New York shares and rotates leadership roles on a weekly basis. The orchestra chooses a concertmaster and the principal players for each section. These represent the core group who decide on the initial interpretation of the piece, and work with the whole ensemble, shaping the rehearsal process. Initially, this chaotic democracy led to inefficient rehearsals and bruised egos, but has improved despite remaining a long process, requiring twice as many rehearsals than with a conductor. Musicians rely on being able to see and hear each other and so limit their number to 40 players. Playing without a conductor is risky, but triggers spontaneity. If a great conductor makes all the important decisions, musicians start to play in a more passive way. One clarinettist said, 'Sometimes, I'm tired and don't feel like thinking and just want someone to guide me. On the other hand, conductors aren't inspiring and just get in the way.'

Based on The Economist; *Levine and Levine (1996).*

Additionally, van den Broek *et al.* (2002) distinguished between 'teams' and 'teamworking'. A number of organizations use team structures, yet design work to be done individually. Call centre companies offer a good example of this. Individuals, who work within these so-called 'teams', are unable to influence the activities of their fellow workers or control the nature of their work, yet still can 'look after their mates'. Asking why management would want to introduce a team structure that did not empower the employees, Townsend (2005) concluded that it was a way of exercising control over employees through group norms and company culture. To recap therefore, in companies, teamworking is not necessarily synonymous with employee empowerment.

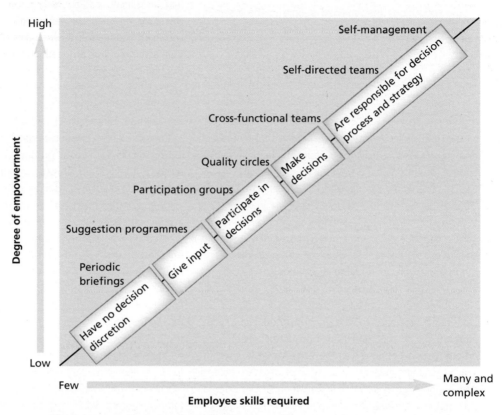

Figure 13.2: A continuum of empowerment
Source: From Daft and Noe (2001, p.218).

Source: Copyright Grantland Enterprises; www.grantland.net.

The end of the Swedish model?

During the 1970s, Volvo's Kalmar plant in Sweden constructed cars using autonomous work groups instead of assembly lines (see photos). The aim had been to make the work meaningful and significant for employees. Pehr Gyllenhammar, Volvo Car's chief executive at the time wrote,

> Acting in the belief that we couldn't really organize the work to suit the people unless we also changed the technology that chained people to the assembly line, we took some steps that seemed risky at the time – especially because they were irreversible. In a new factory we broke up the inexorable line to which the workers were subservient, and replaced it with individual carriers that moved under control of the workers.

By 1990, fuller empowerment meant that employees had greater responsibility for production planning, quality control, organizational development and personal issues, and the 'economy of the plant' improved dramatically. During the late 1980s, Volvo's Uddevalla plant, also in Sweden, introduced radical changes in workers' learning and knowledge development by making them responsible for significant aspects of car building and autonomous group working leading to a merging of employee and supervisor roles. Both flexibility and individual and group capability increased. Why then did the company revert back to assembly-line production in the early 1990s on the shop floor and greater hierarchical differentiation? Ann Westenholz argues that neither the Volvo managers nor unions at these plants were able to gain support for these work arrangements from external stakeholders. Despite the ideology in Swedish organizational and political life at the time that employees should design their own workplaces, when it came to actual practice, Volvo's senior management felt that auto-nomous work group arrangement provided them with insufficient control to achieve its production goals. Senior union staff at Volvo feared the process could lead to the exploitation of the workforce.

Terry Wallace described the changes that took place at Volvo's truck cab plant in Umeå, Northern Sweden. He reported how, in 2002, the company replaced its cell-based, teamworking form of work organization which it had introduced earlier, with assembly line production. His study revealed the factors affecting management's choice of production technologies. Management found that assembly line production was less complex, more programmable and more visible than the teamworking system, making it easier to control; it found that not all operators had the skill or motivation to learn how to perform all the tasks required; and a failure by management to impose rigid production targets on each of the teams led to a failure to meet production targets. Thus, the reversion to assembly line working was due less to technology or productivity and more to employment relationships and management's attempts to regain control over production cycles. Moreover, the 'typical Swedish model' was itself changing. Wallace noted political changes reflected in the Swedish Social Democratic Party's shift to the right; Volvo's reduced interest in involving trade unions at local level beyond what was required by law; and the company's increasing globalization reflected in the decline in Volvo's Swedish employees from 74 per cent to 33 per cent between 1985–2005 and a decline in the number of trucks assembled in Sweden from 50 per cent to 10 per cent in the 1970–2005 period. Volvo, he claimed, has been at the forefront of dismantling the 'good work' (human-centred work organization) strategies.

Based on Westenholz (2003); Wallace (2008);
Gyllenhammar (1977).

Japanese teamworking use of scientific management principles of minimum manning, multi-tasking, multi-machine operation, pre-defined work operations, repetitive short cycle work, powerful first-line supervisors and a conventional managerial hierarchy.

Total quality management a philosophy of management that is driven by customer needs and expectations, and which is committed to continuous improvement.

Just-in-time system managing inventory (stock) in which items are delivered when they are needed in the production process, instead of being stored by the manufacturer.

Kaizen Japanese term for 'improvement', refers to an element within total quality management in which employees are given responsibility, within limits, to suggest incremental changes to their work practices.

Japanese teamworking (also known as *Toyotaism*) refers to a particular form of work organization that possesses four distinguishing characteristics as described by Masaya Morita (2001):

1. Multiskilled workers.
2. Workers' continuous skill development.
3. Assignment of tasks to work units rather than individual workers.
4. Supervisors' roles as models for workers and a buffer between labour and management.

It is called lean production because, compared with other mass production plants, it has higher labour flexibility by using multi-skilled employees who operate different machines; fewer workers not directly involved in product manufacture; a minimum of unfinished products (work in progress/process); and requires very little rectification of work already carried out. In a Toyota production system, work operations are highly standardized. After three days, new workers are able to perform any particular job specified on a standard operation sheet. These highly standardized jobs are combined with similarly standardized ones, so as to extract the maximum amount of effort from employees with minimum labour input. Japanese teamworking also incorporates total quality management (TQM) and just-in-time system (JIT).

Japanese teamworking is not the same as the teamworking that came to prominence in most Scandinavian and American companies during the 1960s and 1970s (MacDuffie, 1988). The differences are summarized in Table 13.5.

Benders (2005) notes that within total quality management, continuous improvement (or *kaizen*) is achieved by using standardized operating procedures. He quotes Taiichi Ohno, the engineer responsible for the Toyota Production System, who devised detailed descriptions which specify how tasks are to be performed:

The first thing I did was standardization of jobs. The shop floor of those days was controlled by foremen – craftsmen. Division managers and section managers could not control the shop floor, and they were always making excuses for production delays. So we first made manuals of standard operating procedures, and posted them above the work station so that supervisors could see if the workers were following the standard operations at a glance. Also, I told the shop floor operators to revise the standard operating procedures continuously (Fujimoto, 1999, p.64).

Ohno's account echoes the approach adopted by Frederick Taylor who developed his scientific management approach to work design at the start of the twentieth century (see Chapter 14). Yet the last sentence introduces the *kaizen* principle. Conti and Warner (1993, p.39) noted this contradiction in labour process with 'employees working four hours a month in a very non-Taylorian manner to make their work for the rest of the month even more Taylor-like'. The participation of employees in teams, in this non-routine task of suggesting improvements, takes up a small percentage of their total working time, but has the effect of making the remaining bulk of their work time even more routine.

Another key aspect of the Toyota production system has been not only to minimize inventory (stockholding) to that required, but also to eliminate wasted effort and employees. Martin Parker and Jane Slaughter (1988) were critical of Japanese teamworking describing it as part of an overall management package which they labelled 'management-by-stress'. In their view, what appears to be participation is in fact a new form of exploitation. Innovations like the 'team concept' increase the pace and pressure of work, despite the rhetoric of worker empowerment. The innovation expands management's control by getting workers to 'participate' in the intensification of their own exploitation. The outcome is a low

Table 13.5: A comparison of Japanese and Swedish approaches to the organization of production and work

Variables	Japan: Toyota	Sweden: Volvo
Production flow design	Trimmed lines. JIT techniques.	Socio-technical design. Job enrichment.
Relations between groups	High degree of sequential dependence. Elimination of buffers.	Group control of boundaries. Independence through buffers.
Supervision	High density production. Emphasis on the authority and role of the supervisor.	Low density production. Emphasis on planning and co-ordination by supervisors.
Administrative control	Leading hands appointed by management. Suggestions are encouraged but decisions are hierarchically determined to ensure standardization.	Leading hands appointed by the group. Job rotation.
Work load and performance	Intensive peer and supervisory pressure for maximum job performance and low absenteeism.	Regulated by union management agreements.
Role of unions	Management exclusively decides about work organization and wage systems. Weak union influence.	Job content and wage system regulated by agreement. Union involvement in production design and development.

From Hammarstrom and Lansbury (1991, p.89).

skill, repetitive ('lean and mean'), mass production system. Japanese teamworking contains the following elements (Garrahan and Stewart, 1992, p.88):

1. Interchangability, meaning the workers are required or induced (through pay-for-knowledge) to be capable of doing several jobs.

2. Drastic reduction of classifications, giving management increased control to assign workers as it sees fit.

3. Detailed definition of every job step increasing management control over the way jobs are done.

4. Workers' participation in increasing their own workload.

5. More worker responsibility, without more authority, for jobs previously performed by supervisors.

6. A management attempt to make workers aware of the inter-relatedness of the plant's departments and the place of the individual in the whole.

7. An ideological atmosphere that stresses competition between plants and workers' responsibility for winning work away from other plants.

Benders (2005) noted that some companies had allowed their employees to participate in the design of their work. He suggested several reasons for this. The daily immersion of workers in the detail of their work, made these shop floor/front-line employees experts in what they were doing. Using the workers' own knowledge was likely to increase their willingness to use the system that they had themselves developed, and they were more likely to accept the working conditions that they had helped to create. Karen Legge (2005) asked why there was not more overt opposition from these production line workers, who appeared to be colluding in their own subjugation? She offers first three explanations, to which Ruth Milkman (1998) adds a fourth.

1. *Careful selection of employees*: on green field sites, new staff are chosen on the basis of their behavioural traits (rather than relevant skills), and for having the 'right attitude' towards teamworking and flexibility.

2. *Team leaders role*: the role of the trade (labour) union representative on the shop floor has been marginalized through developing the role of the team leader. This individual is responsible both for achieving production targets and for the social organization of the group.

3. *Innate appeal*: the appealing aspects of this teamworking approach – mutual support, limited participation, collective endeavour, emphasis on consensus – coupled with the company's 'family orientation', the potential to enhance job satisfaction and to save jobs, all make it appealing to recruits.

4. *Contrast with past*: workers who have experienced both the traditional, authoritarian management system and the new, participatory initiatives, prefer the latter despite some criticism of it.

STOP AND THINK

- What is your reaction to teamworking?
- Under what circumstances would you welcome it? Resent it?
- To both management and workers, teamworking appears a reasonable way of working. Make a case *against* it.

Ecological framework for analyzing work team effectiveness

Eric Sundstrom, Kenneth de Meuse and David Futrell's (1990) ecological framework for analysing work teamwork effectiveness, provides a perspective which looks at teams as embedded within their organization (Figure 13.3). The framework emphasizes the interactions between a team and the different aspects of its environment. It also provides a reminder that the organizations can facilitate or impede a team achieving effectiveness. It therefore offers a way to consider factors contributing to effectiveness. The framework holds that the effectiveness of any work team is best understood in terms of both its external surroundings and its internal processes – external to the team, but internal to the organization. The framework is intentionally vague about causation and timing, seeing team effectiveness as more of an on-going process than a fixed end-state. The framework also makes extensive use the concept of boundary. Boundaries act to:

- distinguish (differentiate) one work unit from another;
- present real or symbolic barriers to the access to, or transfer of information, goods or people;
- serve as points of external exchange with other teams, customers, peers, competitors or other entities;
- define what constitutes effectiveness for the team within its particular organization context.

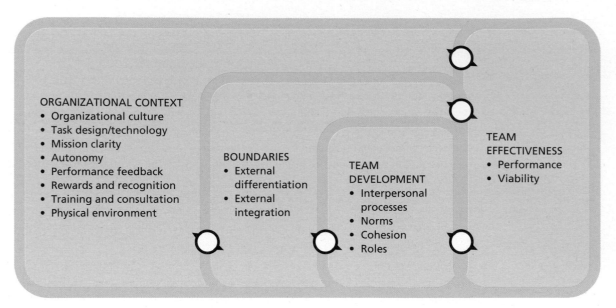

Figure 13.3: Ecological framework for analyzing work team effectiveness
Source: From Sundstrom *et al.* (1990, p.122).

The framework suggests that, at any time, a team's effectiveness is the outcome of team development and the organizational context, mediated by the team's boundaries. Each of these four sets of variables will be described in turn.

Organizational context

The first major variable in Sundstrom *et al.*'s framework is the organizational context of the work team. This refers to those features of an organization which are external to the work team, but which are relevant to the way it operates. The framework lists a total of eight such features.

1. Organizational culture

Every team operates within an organization that has its own culture and in a wider, national cultural context. How do these values and beliefs impact on team effectiveness? Certain companies have a multi-stakeholder culture (e.g. Germany) where teamworking is more likely to succeed than in a shareholder culture (e.g. USA, Britain).

2. Task design and technology

Every team works to complete its given task in a particular way. What impact do different types of tasks have on team effectiveness? Social technology refers to the way of working that is permitted or required (see Chapter 3) and may dictate the social organization of individual team roles.

3. Mission clarity

If a team has a clearly defined mission or purpose within the organization, it can assist those work units who are closely related to, or synchronized with, the team's work. How clear is the team's mission and how clearly has it been communicated to others?

4. Autonomy

Externally, management will determine a team's autonomy. Internally, it will depend on the role of the leader and how they delegate their authority within the team. Every effective team has to co-ordinate and integrate the contributions of its individual members. Which type of team leadership best achieves this?

5. Performance feedback

Does the team receive accurate, timely feedback on its performance from dependable measurement systems?

6. Rewards and recognition

These can range from financial rewards to oral praise. Are rewards sufficiently connected to performance in a way that contributes to team effectiveness?

7. Training and consultation

Training and consultation in technical skills and interpersonal processes are seen as key elements in achieving team effectiveness. Cross-training in technical skills is very often a prerequisite for job rotation which itself can be an aspect of autonomous group working.

8. Physical environment

The proximity of team members to one another affects both their ability to communicate and their level of team cohesion. Whether communicating across a table during a meeting, or between workstations on a factory shop floor, territories can reinforce team boundaries and encourage or inhibit exchanges. Physical environments are therefore central to group boundaries (Sundstrom and Altman, 1989).

Tenerife air disaster

Source: PA PHOTOS/Press Association Images

At 5.01 p.m. on 27 March 1977 at Tenerife airport in the Canary Islands, two 747–100 jets began taxiing along the runways, their captains in communication with the airport's traffic controllers. Four minutes later, Pan Am 1736 and KLM 4805 collided on the tarmac when the Dutch aircraft took off without permission. It led to the death of 583 people, to this day, the biggest air fatality in history. A number of contextual factors came together, interrupting the routines of the cockpit and air-traffic control crews, and generating stress. These included Dutch law, difficult manoeuvres and unpredictable weather. In this stressful setting, KLM cockpit crew interaction broke down. More stress improves team performance but reduces individual performance by lowering task complexity. Hence the importance of cockpit crew members coalescing into a team with a distinctive identity, rather than falling apart and acting more like individuals.

Karl Weick stated that it was unclear whether the KLM crew experienced negative synergy, defined as a form of interaction between team members which caused a failure of co-ordination within the team so severe that nobody knew what they were supposed to be doing. It might have been that the three individuals in the cockpit acted independently and in parallel, falling back on their most familiar and well-rehearsed response routines, rather than behaving as a team. The interruption of their normal operating procedures induced a high level of arousal in the crew members which reduced their cognitive information processing abilities, and led them to ignore important cues. As a result, the flight and air-traffic control crews made the wrong responses, resulting in the deadly crash. This was an example of the context influencing individuals and teams, who responded in a way that changed the context as the events unfolded. A well-functioning, high-integrated cockpit crew might have responded to the increased stress with increased performance.

Based on Weick (1990).

Work team boundaries

The second major variable in Sundstrom *et al.*'s framework is the set of work team boundaries. The boundary for a team is like the fence around a piece of property. It allows its members to know who is a member and who is not. It defines both physically and psychologically on whom group members can rely, and thereby indicates when it may be necessary for them to go beyond their own team for assistance and resources. For example, the boundary for an aircraft cockpit crew is physically defined by the design of the aircraft. A Boeing 727 has seats for three cockpit members and hence there is an expected boundary of three for the crew of that airplane.

While working to complete an assigned task (e.g. improving a procedure; designing a new product; winning a match), a team has to meet the needs of the larger organization within which it is embedded (external integration). At the same time, it has to secure enough independence to allow it to get on with its own work (external differentiation). These two features define every team's boundary, and boundary management refers to the process by which teams manage their interactions with other parts of their organization. How successfully a team manages its boundaries will affect its performance.

External work team differentiation refers to the team as a whole in relation to the rest of the organization (team-organization focus). For example, a temporary team may be assembled by management and given resources to deal with a crisis. This team thus stands out, and hence *differs* from, other work units within the company by virtue of containing an identifiable collection of people (membership), working in a specific place (territory), over a set period of time (temporal scope), on a unique task.

These four features define the team's boundary, distinguishing it from other work units within the organization:

External work team differentiation the degree to which a work team stands out from its organizational context, in terms of its membership, temporal scope and territory.

team membership	the identity of the individuals treated as members by both the team and the organization is crucial. Who decides the composition and size of a work team?
team territory	a work team has to have its 'own turf' to establish its identity and manage its external relations, especially in teams whose missions demand both external integration and differentiation
temporal scope	the longer a work team exists and the more time its members spend co-operating, the greater will be its temporal scope and differentiation as a work-unit

Differentiation within the peloton

The Tour de France cycle race was first run in 1903 and now involves about 150 top cyclists. The racers cover over 2,700 miles during their 23-day journey, and the winner receives the €400,000 prize. The competitors ride together in the *peloton* – the picturesque mob of competing teams that fly like birds in formation, across the French countryside every summer. Despite the focus on individual riders, the Tour is a sport structured around the teams sponsored by different organizations. In the past, there has been Lance Armstrong's Team Discovery and Jan Ulrich's T-Mobile team. There are 20 different teams in the race. During each 125 mile-, 5-hour stage, team members fight to put their leader in a position to win. What appears to be a random mass of bicycles is really an orderly, complex web of shifting alliances, crossed with brutal competition, designed to keep or acquire the market's most valuable currency – energy. A cycling team consist of nine riders, each of whom is a specialist. The *rouleurs* are fast riders who create drafts for their team's leader over flat terrain. Riding close behind a *rouleur* can reduce drag by 40 per cent. *Grimpeurs* are hill specialists who create a slipstream (a field of low wind resistance) for their leader as he goes up mountains; and *domestiques* are riders who carry supplies. Towards the end of the race, team members will bunch together ahead of their sprinter, shielding him from the wind for as long as possible, while leaving a space to let him break out near the finish line.

Based on Hochman (2006).

Internal work team differentiation the degree to which a team's members possess different skills and knowledge that contributes towards the achievement of the team's objective.

External work team integration the degree to which a work team is linked with the larger organization of which it is a part.

team task

the task given to the team may be *additive* (accomplishment depends on the sum of all members' efforts); *conjunctive* (depends on the performance of the least talented member); or *disjunctive* (performance of the most talented member)

Internal work team differentiation refers to the degree to which a team's members possess different skills and knowledge that contribute towards the achievement of the team's objective. A team may have high differentiation with its members having special, perhaps unique, skills, such as the cockpit crew in an aircraft; or it may have low differentiation, when the knowledge and contributions of members tend to be similar, as in a quality circle team.

External work team integration refers to the degree to which a work team is linked with the larger organization of which it is a part. It is measured in terms of how its goals and activities are co-ordinated and synchronized with those of other managers, peers, customers and suppliers inside and outside the company. The degree to which a team's goals and activities need to be co-ordinated and synchronized with those of other work units, will depend on the type of team and its task.

"Every detail of the proposal must be perfect!
Get Davidson to write the vowels, Mulroy to write the
consonants, Schwartz to write the punctuation and
Lewis to put the spaces between the words."

Source: Copyright 2003 by Randy Glasbergen, www.glasbergen.com

Team boundary management

Deborah Ancona and D. Caldwell studied the boundary management activities of 45 new product teams in five high-technology companies. They found that team members engaged in four types of intergroup activities:

- *Ambassador*: representing the team to others. For example, protecting it from interference; 'talking it up' to obtain outside resources; reporting its progress to higher management; checking threats or opposition.

- *Co-ordinating*: communicating laterally to co-ordinate team's effort on its task with other work units. For example, discussing problems; negotiating; obtaining feedback on team progress; and securing information on the progress of other teams.

- *Scouting*: scanning the teams' immediate environment. For example, gaining information on what was going on elsewhere in the organization.

- *Guarding*: keeping information and resources within the group. For example, preventing another team or individual from acquiring its resources.

The researchers also found that the teams' boundary management activities differed over the period of the product development cycle. In the first, creation phase, members were exploring issues, and hence ambassador, co-ordinating and scouting activities were high. In the second, development phase, members were exploiting the information and resources that they had acquired.

→

Task co-ordinating remained high, while ambassador and scouting activities were reduced. In the third, diffusion phase, members were exporting the work that they had completed and persuading others to make their product a priority. External interaction levels were highest in this phase. The researchers also found that high-performing new product teams carried out more external activity than low-performing teams, even when controlling for the project cycle phase. They not only responded to, but also initiated, communications with other work units. While internal group operations to integrate information gained from outside are important, it is the organization and management of interactions with other groups that appears to be critical.

Based on Ancona and Caldwell (1990).

Team development

The third major variable in Sundstrom *et al.*'s framework concerns the internal development of the team. Four factors are relevant here – interpersonal processes, roles, norms and cohesion.

1. Interpersonal processes

A group of individuals passes through a series of stages before achieving effective performance at the performing stage. Tuckman's and Jensen's model describes the characteristics of each preceding stage – forming, storming and norming (see Chapter 10, group formation).

2. Roles

Roles in general are a defining feature of a team, and the role of a leader is much studied. Are the required member roles being performed given the group's tasks, and are the task and interpersonal aspects of the leadership role being fulfilled?

3. Norms

Are the norms and rules of behaviour which are agreed on by the team members supportive or in conflict with effective performance? Can organizational culture be used to modify team norms?

4. Cohesion

Team cohesion can engender mutual co-operation, generosity and helping behaviour, motivating team members to contribute fully. However, it can also stifle creative thinking, as individuals seek to 'fit in' and not 'rock the boat'. Small group size, similar attitudes and physical proximity of workspaces, have all been found to encourage cohesion. Does the level of cohesion aid or impede the team's effectiveness?

Team performance
external measure focused on meeting the needs and expectations of management, customers or shareholders.

Team viability
internal measure focused on meeting the needs and expectations of team members.

Team effectiveness

Team effectiveness is the dependent variable in Sundstrom *et al.*'s framework, and is measured using two criteria – performance and viability. Team performance is externally focused and concerns meeting the needs and expectations of outsiders such as customers, company colleagues or fans. It is assessed using measures such as quantity, quality and time. Meanwhile, team viability is the social dimension, which is internally focused and concerns the enhancement of the group's capability to perform effectively in the future. Team viability indicators include degree of group cohesion, shared purpose, and the level of member commitment. The two are closely related since there is a possibility that a team may get a job done but self-destructs in the process. Based on his study of 27 different types of teams, Richard Hackman (1990) identified three hurdles that every team had to surmount to achieve effectiveness. The team's members had to:

- expend sufficient effort to achieve the task that they had been given (motivation);
- bring sufficient knowledge and skill to their group task (composition);
- use group processes appropriate for the task and its setting (processes).

Authors have sought to explain the continuing popularity of teamworking. Buchanan (2000a) and Marchington and Wilkinson (2005) have pointed to the fact that in Western societies, the word, 'teamworking' conveys the notion of collaboration, mutual support and commitment. It carries with it connotations of shared skills, problem-solving and making decisions together. These are all things that companies and their managers would like to be associated with, in the eyes of their employees and customers. Employers have come to see teamworking as a fundamental component of organizational success. Teams are used as a vehicle for pooling employees' ideas to improve work processes; as a way of making better decisions; and a means of finding more creative solutions. Employees who work in teams report higher levels of job satisfaction than those working in more traditional arrangements. Thus, teamworking has become a required competency that employers look for when selecting new employees.

The flexibility of the teamworking concept makes it both very popular and meaningless, at the same time. Companies can claim to have teams consisting of between 3 and 33 employees (and even more) working together, thereby appealing to the social and individual values of their stakeholders. However, as Wilson (2004) reminds us, the meaning of the term varies over time and between settings. The distinction between Japanese, 'off-line' teams, such as quality circles – whose normal work arrangements are tightly prescribed and whose work is closely monitored; and 'on-line' teams, whose members are involved in daily decisions about work organization, are so great, that it seems foolish to refer to both using the same word. It allows management to give the impression of devolving power and influence downwards without actually doing so. Companies may therefore benefit from blurring the distinction between different types of teams. Wilson states that it is important continually to ask how teams are being used in particular organizations, and whose interests this choice of work arrangement serves.

 RECAP

1. *Understand why 'team' is a contested concept in the organizational literature.*

   - Teamworking is being increasingly adopted as a favoured form of work organization in different companies and industries around the world.

   - The different purposes and ways in which managers have introduced this innovation, has meant that the term 'team', is used to describe a wide range of radically different working arrangements.

2. *List the nine dimensions of team autonomy.*

   - Gulowsen's nine dimensions of team autonomy are selection of the team leader; acceptance of a new member into the team; distribution of work; time flexibility; acceptance of additional work; representation outside the team; production methods (choice of); production goals (output determination); production goals (quality determination).

3. *Differentiate between four major types of teams and give an example of each.*

   - Teams in organizations can be classified as advice (quality circles); action (e.g. surgery team); project (cross-functional team) or production (autonomous work team).

4. *Discuss the types of obstacles to effectiveness experienced by each type of team.*

   - Advice teams frequently lack authority to implement their recommendations. Action teams can fail to integrate their members' contributions sufficiently closely. Project team members can suffer 'divided loyalties' between their team and their home department. Production teams may lack autonomy for job satisfaction.

5. *Contrast Western with Japanese concepts of teamworking.*

• The Western concept is based upon principles of empowerment and on-line teamworking, while the Japanese concept is based upon management principles of individual working on-line, and teams advising off-line.

6. *List the three main variables in the ecological framework for analyzing work team effectiveness.*

   • Team development; work team boundaries; and organizational context affect team effectiveness.

7. *Understand the continuing importance of team working.*

   • Japanese forms of teamworking (Toyotaism) have influenced the production processes used in both manufacturing and service industries all around the world.

   • As a concept, teamworking has an appeal in a management philosophy that stresses egalitarianism, non-hierarchy and inclusiveness within organizations.

Revision

1. Self-managing or autonomous work teams are heavily promoted in the literature. What are the costs and benefits of these to (a) managers who may have to train and be responsible for them, and (b) individuals who are members of such teams?

2. What impact can technology have on the behaviour and performance of teams. Discuss positive and negative effects, illustrating your answer with examples.

3. 'Autonomous team is a relative term'. Discuss the concept of team autonomy explaining why similarly labelled teams may, in practice, operate very differently, and consider why management might have difficulty in increasing the autonomy that it gives to a team.

4. Highlight briefly the main differences between West European and Japanese-style teamworking. Then, using references to the literature, consider its positive and negative aspects of both systems for **either** shop floor workers **or** management.

Research assignment

Consult the research and management literature on effective teamworking and devise a list of best practice 'do's' and 'don'ts', and use it to develop a list of questions. Select two organizations and in each of them, interview a team member, a team leader or a manager responsible for a team, and begin by determining the team's purpose, method of working, performance and the challenges that it faces. Write a brief report comparing these two teams, and assessing them against your best practice list items.

Springboard

Beirne, M., 2006, *Empowerment and Innovation: Managers, Principles and Reflective Practice*, Edward Elgar Publishers, Northampton.

Reviews the research on employee empowerment at the individual, team and organizational levels, summarizing past and present research, and raising questions about managerial and organizational practices.

Benders, J., 2005, 'Team working: a tale of partial participation', in Harley, B., Hyman, J. and Thompson, P. (eds), *Participation and Democracy at Work: Essays in Honour of Harvie Ramsey*, Palgrave Macmillan, London, pp.55–74.

This chapter examines issues of employee involvement from the teamworking perspective.

Jenkins, A., 1994, 'Teams: from "ideology" to analysis', *Organization Studies*, 15(6): 849–60.

An article defending management's interest in teams.

Sinclair, A., 1992, 'The tyranny of a team ideology', *Organization Studies*, 13(4): 611–26.

An article attacking management's obsession with teams.

OB in films

The Dish (2000, director Rob Sitch): DVD track 8: 0:35:55–0:53:07 (18 minutes sequenced). It is July 1969, and Apollo 11 is heading towards the moon. On earth, the Parkes Radio Telescope in New South Wales, Australia, the largest in the southern hemisphere, has been designated by NASA as the primary receiving station for the moonwalk, which it will broadcast to the world. Then, due to a power cut, it 'loses' Apollo 11! Parkes' director, Cliff Buxton (played by Sam Neill) and his team of scientists Mitch (Kevin Harrington); Glenn (Tom Long); and Al (Patrick Warburton) – all have to work hard (and quickly), to solve the problem. The clip begins with the lights going out during the dance, and ends with Al saying, 'Just enough time to check the generator.'

Identify examples of each of the elements of Sundstrom *et al.*'s ecological framework for analyzing work team effectiveness as the team members deal with the crisis.

Sundstrom framework element	Example
Organizational context	
1. Organizational culture	
2. Task design/technology	
3. Mission clarity	
4. Autonomy	
5. Performance feedback	
6. Rewards and recognition	
7. Physical environment	
8. Training and consultation	
Work team boundaries	
9. External differentiation	
10. External integration	
Team development	
11. Interpersonal processes	
12. Norms	
13. Cohesion	
14. Roles	

 OB in literature

Tracy Kidder, *The Soul of a New Machine,* Random House, New York, 1997. This is a true story which has been 'fictionalized'. It is based on how teams worked together to design and build a new computer. What aspects of effective teamworking and work team management does the story illustrate?

CHAPTER EXERCISES

Factors affecting team performance

Objectives   1. Identify the various factors that influence a team's success or failure.

2. Practise using the Sundstrom *et al.*'s model as an explanatory framework.

Briefing   1. Individually

   (a)   Remind yourself of Sundstrom *et al.*'s ecological framework for analyzing team effectiveness (pp.405–11).

   (b)   Reflect on a situation from your experience, where a team of which you were a member (work team, sports team, church team, other) failed to achieve its goal and also, one where a team of which you were a member, *succeeded* in achieving its goal.

   (c)   Identify which of Sundstrom's 14 factors (or any others), in your view, contributed to your team's failure or success.

2. Form groups and nominate a spokesperson.

   (a)   Go round each member in turn and ask them to describe their own experiences of team failure, and to identify what they consider might have been the contributing factors.

   (b)   After all team members' failures have been shared, ask the group to identify any recurring factors in the different accounts.

   (c)   Ask the group to highlight any 'missing' (i.e. non-Sundstrom) factors.

   (d)   Ask each group then to discuss what could have been done to avoid the failure in their first examples.

   (e)   Go round each member in turn and ask them to describe their own experiences of *team success* and to identify what they consider to have been the contributing factors.

   (f)   After all team members' successes have been shared, ask the group to identify any recurring factors in the different accounts.

   (g)   Ask the group to highlight any 'missing' (non-Sundstrom) factors.

   (h)   Then ask each group in turn to discuss how such future success can be ensured in similar teams in the future.

3. The class reforms. The spokespersons for each group report back,

   - identifying the most common factors leading to team failure and suggesting how these could have been avoided

   - identifying the most common factors leading to team success and suggesting how these can be ensured in the future

Patchwork Traditional Food Company

Objectives   1. To assess the degree of autonomous teamworking within an organization.

2. To identify conditions favouring and impeding the introduction of empowerment.

Briefing   1. Individually, read the case study and, using the checklist at the end of it, estimate the degree of team autonomy possessed by Patchwork's self-managed team. Score them on each of the ten tasks on a four-point scale – 1: no autonomy; 2: some; 3: jointly with management; 4: full autonomy.

2. Divide into groups, nominate a spokesperson, and:

   (a) consider each of the nine dimensions (see grid below); discuss your members' estimates (represented by their individual scores) and agree a group score.

   (b) discuss:

   (i) what features of the company's present situation are conducive to implementing the empowerment of employees

   (ii) what company changes in the future, either inside or outside the company, might make the current working arrangements difficult to sustain?

   (c) consider the views and reactions of Margaret Carter and her employees. What issues do they raise about the introduction and operation of empowerment within the workplace?

3. Group spokespersons should be ready to report their group's scores on each dimension and justify the rating.

Team: Patchwork Traditional Food Company

	Level of team participation				
Team tasks	**None**	**Some**	**Joint**	**Autonomy**	**Total**
1. Selecting their own team leader					
2. Accepting a new member into the team					
3. Distributing work to members					
4. Scheduling work assignments (timing)					
5. Accepting additional work					
6. Representing the team to outsiders					
7. Choosing own production methods					
8. Setting own production goals (quantity)					
9. Setting own production goals (quality)					
TOTAL TEAM SCORE					

Patchwork Traditional Food Company

Patchwork is a small company consisting of ten employees based in the Clwyd region of North Wales. It produces a range of pies, chutneys, jams and pâtés and other foods made with fresh ingredients to traditional recipes targeted at a niche market. Its owner, Margaret Carter, saw a gap in the market for handmade, low-volume, high-quality foods, which could be sold at a premium price. By personally ensuring the highest standards, she hopes to retain and increase her company's market share. As the business developed, Margaret needed to be out on the road a lot more, promoting her products to potential customers. She is responsible for taking the orders. These have varied considerably from month to month, but she has personally ensured that all products are delivered to customers in good time. This is one reason why she transformed her group of employees into a self-managing team. She explained that, 'Everybody is empowered to make their own decisions, and be in control of their day, in their working environment.' Margaret Carter realized that it was unnecessary for her employees to seek permission from her office to do what needed to be done in the production area. As a team, she felt, they already knew that, better than anyone else. However, after being given the power by her to make their own decisions, her employees' first reaction was one of uncertainty and fear. The workers were anxious that now, they had nobody to blame but themselves if something went wrong. Obviously, this was an issue, which had to be discussed and resolved between all concerned.

After the team had overcome their initial doubts, they went about making the new arrangements work. While they each knew their individual jobs, they were less familiar with the day-to-day running of the factory. They felt that they needed someone who could take an overview of the whole situation. Their past experience had taught them that everybody in the factory tended to do the jobs that they liked, while leaving the less pleasant tasks to others. Also, receiving advice from one person rather than two, would eliminate differing priorities and would avoid conflict. To meet this need, the self-managing team turned to Chris, one of their co-workers. Although Chris felt that her colleagues saw her as a supervisor, she sees herself as a team leader. She explains, 'I'm here for anybody to come to me if they need advice or help with their job, and I'm here to train up new members who come to work with us. I'm there if they need me, like a mother'.

Since what is produced is determined by how it is produced, Margaret had very clear ideas as to how her pâtés, soups and other products should be made. Her views were based on her own experience of cooking. As production volumes have increased, team members have commented that the prescribed cooking methods are difficult to operate. Following a series of meetings, she and her staff have now agreed modifications to the original practices which, while addressing the need for higher production volumes, also maintain her quality standards. The team runs the factory without the involvement of any management. Staff are responsible for ordering stock; recruiting staff; and they decide their own working hours and holidays. Every morning, they get together to talk about what they've got to do that day.

What is the reaction of employees and the management to this empowering of a self-managing team? Company workers seem generally positive about the change: 'It works very well because we all have a sense of what needs to be done, and when it needs doing'. 'It's more enjoyable because you get more job satisfaction out of being involved in everything yourself.' 'Everybody knows what everybody else is doing, what you have got to do, and it's much nicer.' However, they are aware of differences in response. One employee stated, 'Some of us enjoy taking on responsibilities, but there are a few who have not got into that yet. These are early days, but we shall get there eventually. I think that some people are just slightly frightened. They are doing it gradually, and they are all picking it up a bit at a time, and I think taking on the new responsibilities will come to them quite easily after a length of time'.

Speaking as the owner–manager of the company, Margaret Carter noted that the change had given her time to find new markets for her products, thereby providing job security for the team; and has also enabled her to spend more time developing new recipes with one of the other team members, Penny. She commented that, 'I would not have implemented a self-directed team if I did not fully trust my people which, in my view, is one of the most important factors. The main upside of the new work arrangement is that it has become a really happy team. I believe that this team happiness goes right through to our suppliers, to our product and to our customers. Her view about empowerment is that it needs to be total, 'You have to genuinely and completely let go, not half-heartedly and not pretending that you are letting go, because it will not work!'

Based on 20 Steps to Better Management*, 'Letting Go', BBC Enterprises Ltd, 1996.*

Part 4 **Organization structures**

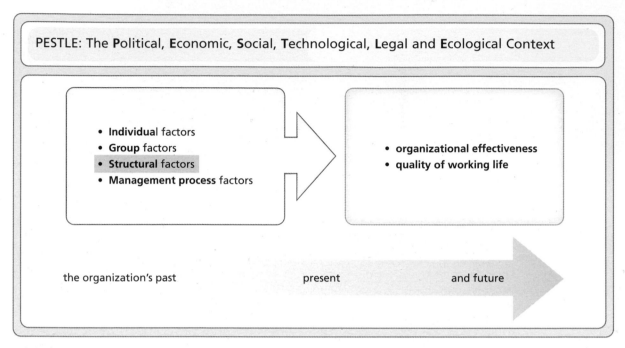

PESTLE: The **P**olitical, **E**conomic, **S**ocial, **T**echnological, **L**egal and **E**cological Context

- **Individual** factors
- **Group** factors
- **Structural** factors
- **Management process** factors

- **organizational effectiveness**
- **quality of working life**

the organization's past   present   and future

A field map of the organizational behaviour terrain

Introduction

Part 4, Organization structures, explores four related topics:

- *Traditional work design*, in Chapter 14
- *Elements of structure*, in Chapter 15
- *Early organization design*, in Chapter 16
- *Organizational architecture*, in Chapter 17

These topics consider how the way in which work is defined and designed affects employee behaviour. Chapter 14 on Traditional work design provides a historical foundation for the earlier Chapter 3 on Technology. It links technology to structure by highlighting how choices about the former have an impact on design decisions concerning the latter. Chapter 15 on Elements of structure provides an introduction to the key concepts, theories, models and authors in this field. This 'vocabulary' is then used to understand early organization design, particularly in the work of Max Weber, Henri Fayol, Tom Burns and George Stalker, and Henry Mintzberg. The final chapter in Part 4 explains how contemporary thinking about structures in the field of organization behaviour has merged with debates about corporate strategy and strategic management. It also brings the consideration of structural forms up to date by exploring hollow, modular, virtual and collaborative structures. The structural perspective offers a separate but related level of analysis after individuals and groups.

Invitation to see

This image was used by *The Sunday Times* (2 November 2008) to illustrate an article describing how Amazon, the online retailer, was expecting record-breaking sales over Christmas despite the economic recession. The photo shows Amazon's largest UK distribution centre in Swansea. The photo had no caption, but the article was titled, 'Online sales defy slump'.

Source: Jacky Parker/Alamy

1. **Decoding**   Look at this image closely. Note in as much detail as possible what messages you feel that it is trying to convey. Does it tell a story, present a point of view, support an argument, perpetuate a myth, reinforce a stereotype, challenge a stereotype?

2. **Challenging** To what extent do you agree with the messages, stories, points of view, arguments, myths, or stereotypes in this image? Is this image open to challenge, to criticism, or to interpretation and decoding in other ways, revealing other messages?

3. **Sharing**   Compare with colleagues your interpretation of this image. Explore explanations for differences in your respective decodings.

What would you do? You're the team leader

You are the research team leader in this situation. Focus on the objective. Using your knowledge of the concepts, theories, authors, models and frameworks acquired so far from course lectures and reading, as well as your personal experience, evaluate the advantages and limitations of each of the four options, which are the only options available to you at this time. Decide which one you would choose, and why.

Your problem

Lynette joined your research team six months ago, making five members, including yourself. Her knowledge of the topic (organizational change) is limited, but she has superb references and an excellent theoretical and practical grounding in social research. There is no problem in transferring her expertise to this project. She starts work with enthusiasm. You and colleagues brief her on the project aims and provide background reading. Two months into her appointment, she has produced none of the outputs that you have been expecting: review of wider literature; details of research methods; appropriate first contacts; and so on. In an informal meeting, it emerges that her understanding of the research aims and scope are still unclear, so you go over these issues again. You are reassured by this discussion. Four months into the project, she has still to produce any useful output. In another informal meeting, she indicates that the support she expected from colleagues is lacking. You promise to speak to the team, and remind her of the research aims and timescale. Six months into the project, Lynette has still not produced any material that will help to make progress towards the research aims. Before meeting with her again, a reliable senior colleague tells you in confidence that he has been told by a trustworthy friend that Lynette has been setting up a management

development and consulting business, specializing in organization development and change; you check this for yourself, and you have now seen her website. Academic research projects have deadlines, and you are not going to meet this one unless you can resolve this problem. Failure to meet the project aims on time jeopardizes future research funding, and threatens the jobs of other members of the research team.

Your objective

Your overarching objective is to meet the research project deadline, now 18 months away, while dealing with Lynette's failure to contribute to the work.

Your options

1. Hold another meeting with Lynette, to establish why her contribution has been so limited, to clarify misunderstandings, and to agree new performance objectives.

2. Confront Lynette with the knowledge that she has not been contributing to this project because she has been setting up her own business. If she does not have a convincing response to this allegation, terminate her employment immediately.

3. The lack of subject knowledge is more of a problem than you first thought. Pair Lynette with an experienced researcher, who will mentor her closely for the next six months, with regard to both the research topic and the proposed methods.

4. The UK Standing Conference on Organizational Change at University of Loamshire runs a highly-regarded research methods training programme which runs for four days in May. Send Lynette on this course, all expenses paid, to familiarize her in depth with the research topic and appropriate methods.

Chapter 14 **Traditional work design**

Key terms

rationalism

scientific management

systematic soldiering

functional foremanship

initiative and incentive system

time-and-motion studies

Fordism

systems concept

control concept

mass production

McDonaldization

intrinsic rewards

extrinsic rewards

instrumental orientation

introjection

identification

concertive control

chimerial control

Learning outcomes

When you have read this chapter, you should be able to define those key terms in your own words, and you should also be able to:

1. Understand how scientific management met the needs of its historical context.

2. Describe the main objectives and principles of the scientific management approach.

3. Critically assess Taylorism.

4. Enumerate the contributions of the Gilbreths and Gantt to scientific management.

5. Understand how Fordism developed out of Taylorism.

6. Understand the deskilling debate, and the contribution of Braverman and Ritzer.

7. Critically assess the evidence for and against the deskilling thesis.

8. Provide examples of scientific management in contemporary society.

Why study traditional work design?

Only a handful of theories can claim to be truly revolutionary, and to have had an enduring and worldwide impact on organizational thought and management practice. Frederick Winslow Taylor's scientific management and Henry Ford's assembly line are two of them. Many textbooks only mention these briefly, locating their place in history, before implying that these ideas are no longer relevant to our modern, hi-tech, organizational lives. This chapter will argue the complete opposite. Specifically, it contends that both are having a wider and more pervasive impact on society today than they did a hundred years ago. One needs only to visit a fast food restaurant; buy a mobile phone; or attend a university course, to see how the provision of goods and services have been affected by these ideas.

Developments in information technology have increased rather than reduced their relevance. Look at the interest in Total Quality Management, ISO 9000, and similar management techniques for bringing greater discipline into manufacturing, clerical and professional work (including education). For example, one current academic debate focuses on whether the virtual organization is a new organizational arrangement or a refinement of scientific management thinking. Taylorism and Fordism are alive and well and thriving at the start of the twenty-first century (Jones, 1997; Wilson, 2004). They affect us all as students, employees, consumers and citizens. It is just that most of us do not realize this. By pointing out examples of them in contemporary life, we hope to raise your awareness.

The birth of scientific management

Between 1880 and 1910, the United States underwent major and rapid industrialization, including the creation of the first, large corporations. Complex forms of organization were emerging, with new technologies of production and large workforces. Many of today's well known organizations such the Standard Oil Trust (Esso), United States Steel, General Motors and Ford, were created at that time. The workers in these new factories came from agricultural regions of America, or were immigrants from Europe. Directing the efforts of workers with little knowledge of the English language, few job skills, and no experience of the disciplined work of a factory, was a major organizational problem. Scientific management offered a solution, and represented one of the first organizational practices capable of being applied to different companies.

Before the 1880s, work organization on the factory shop floor was based upon the authority of subcontractors and supervisors. Owners employed workers indirectly, and it was labour masters and gang bosses who recruited, paid and disciplined them. However, these informal, personal methods of control created inefficiencies. During this period of economic growth, scientific management ended such internal contracting, enabling owners to employ workers directly, and thereby introduced a formal system of industrial discipline. In this period, most products were hand-made by skilled operators who handcrafted items using general-purpose machine tools such as lathes. It took these craftsmen years of training to acquire the necessary skills and experience. They could read a blueprint, visualize the final product, and possessed a level of hand–eye co-ordination and gentleness of touch that allowed them to manufacture the required item (Littler, 1982). However, there were insufficient numbers of them to permit mass production.

Rationalism the theory that reason is the foundation of certainty in knowledge.

It was against this background that Frederick Taylor and Henry Ford developed and implemented their ideas. They and their supporters all shared a belief in rationalism, which is the theory that reason is the foundation of certainty in knowledge. They believed that if one understands something, one should be able both to state it explicitly, and to write a law or a rule for it. They held that the human mind could discover innate laws that governed the workings of the universe. The consequence of developing and applying rules, laws and procedures is to replace uncertainty with predictability, both in the human and non-human spheres.

All manufacturing (e.g. turning a piece of wood into a chair leg), involves three separate activities: (1) the transformation of work pieces (2) the transfer of work pieces between workers and operations and (3) the co-ordination and control of these two processes, ensuring sufficient raw material was available to operators to work on, and that finished pieces flow smoothly through assembly. Originally, each of these three processes was performed manually, and the history of work transformation has involved the mechanization of each one. The first major approach to work rationalization, that of scientific management or Taylorism, focused on the first of these three stages – the transformation of the work piece (Gill, 1985). Taylor's approach is known by two names. Scientific management is the collective term for his ideas coined by his supporters. *Taylorism* is an eponym which, although applied by his supporters, was used mainly by his opponents who regarded the other term as specious. In this chapter, the two terms are used interchangeably.

Scientific management a form of job design which stresses short, repetitive work cycles; detailed, prescribed task sequences; a separation of task conception from task execution; and motivation based on economic rewards.

Taylorism

Frederick Winslow Taylor (1856–1915)

Systematic soldiering the conscious and deliberate restriction of output by operators.

Taylor was born into a wealthy Quaker Philadelphia family in 1856. The city was the industrial heart of 1800s America. It contained many manufacturers who had ready access to the Pennsylvanian coal and iron mines. Taylor became an apprentice machinist in a firm of engineers before joining the Midvale Steel Company in 1878 where he developed his ideas. The company manufactured locomotive wheels and axles, and it was here that he rose to the position of shop superintendent by 1887. In this role, he observed that workers used different and mostly inefficient work methods. He also noticed that few machinists ever worked at the speed of which they were capable. He contrasted natural soldiering (i.e. the inclination to take it easy), with what he labelled systematic soldiering. Taylor attributed systematic soldiering to a number of factors:

- The view among the workers that an increase in output would result in redundancies.
- Poor management controls which enabled them to work slowly, in order to protect their own best interests.
- The choice of methods of work which were left entirely to the discretion of the workers who wasted a large part of their efforts using inefficient and untested rules-of-thumb.

Appalled by what he regarded as the inefficiency of industrial practices, Taylor took steps to increase production by reducing the variety of work methods used by the workers. He set out to show how management and workforce could both benefit from adopting his more efficient work arrangements. His objectives were to achieve:

- *Efficiency* by increasing the output per worker and reducing deliberate 'underworking' by employees.
- *Predictability* of job performance by standardizing tasks by dividing up tasks into small, standardized, closely specified subtasks.
- *Control* by establishing discipline through hierarchical authority and introducing a system whereby all management's policy decisions could be implemented.

Table 14.1: Frederick Taylor's five principles of scientific management

1. A clear division of tasks and responsibilities between management and workers.
2. Use of scientific methods to determine the best way of doing a job.
3. Scientific selection of the person to do the newly designed job.
4. The training of the selected worker to perform the job in the way specified.
5. Surveillance of workers through the use of hierarchies of authority and close supervision.

"It has come to my attention gentlemen, that you've been doing the work of two men."

Source: www.cartoonstock.com.

Soldiering

Robert Kanigel explained that the word 'soldiering' had nautical roots. It related to soldiers who, when transported by ship, acted as privileged passengers. They were exempt from the work on board that the seamen had to perform. To the sailors, such work avoidance came to be known as 'soldiering'. Frederick Taylor distinguished, on the one hand, the tendency of workers to take it easy. This he labelled 'natural soldiering'. He considered it unfortunate, but almost excusable. On the other hand, and more insidious in his view, was 'systematic soldiering' which was the organized, collective behaviour of workers in the whole workshop, who restricted their production, prevented their employers knowing how fast they could work, and thus allowed them to pursue their own narrow self-interest.

Based on Kanigel (1997).

Taylor's approach involved studying each work task. He chose routine, repetitive tasks performed by numerous operatives where study could save time and increase production. Many variables was measured including size of tools, location of tools, height of workers and type of material worked. His studies tried to answer the question, 'How long should it take to do any particular job in the machine shop? He wanted to replace rules-of-thumb with scientifically designed working methods. Taylor experimented with different combinations of movement and method to discover the 'one-best-way' of performing any task. Table 14.2 shows a 'one-best-way' guide to operating a shop till given to us by one of our students who works part-time in a shop.

It was not only shop floor workers who had their jobs fragmented. Taylor felt that every employee in an organization should be confined to a single function. He proposed a system called **functional foremanship**, which never became popular. The job of the general foreman was to be divided and distributed among eight separate individuals. Each of these would oversee a separate function of the work and would be called:

Functional foremanship dividing the job of a general foreman into its constituent parts and assigning a different foreman to each part, who would oversee and be responsible for that aspect of all workers' jobs.

1. Inspector
2. Order of work and route clerk
3. Time and cost clerk
4. Shop disciplinarian
5. Gang boss
6. Speed boss
7. Repair boss
8. Instruction card clerk

Table 14.2: One-best-way of operating a shop till

1. Acknowledge each individual customer by giving him or her welcoming smile.
2. Enter the department numbers and the cost of the items.
3. Subtotal the sale and tell the customer the subtotal figure.
4. Accept the customer's form of payment, and in the case of cash, state how much the customer has actually given you.
5. Give the customer their change, telling them how much you are giving them.
6. Bag the goods and put the receipt in the bag.
7. Give the customer the bag and smile once again, thanking them.

STOP AND THINK You are a product line manager in a large factory in the English Midlands making chocolate biscuits. This guy, Frederick Taylor, a management consultant, has told you that what you need in your factory to improve efficiency is functional foremanship. In replying, 'I don't think so, Mr Taylor', give four reasons for rejecting his professional advice.

Source: Bethlehem Steel Corporation

Machine Shop No. 2 at Bethlehem Steel Works in Bethlehem, Pennsylvania, USA

In 1898, Taylor was hired by the Bethlehem Iron Company (later part of the Bethlehem Steel Corporation), to improve work methods. For many years, the product of the company's blast furnaces had been handled by 75 pig iron handlers who loaded an average of twelve-and-a-half tons [tonnes] per man per day. Taylor estimated that a first-class pig iron handler ought to handle between 47 and 48 long tons [tonnes] per day. Taylor introduced his experimental changes; raised productivity by a factor of four; and increased workers' wages by 60 per cent. The savings achieved with his improved work plan were between $75,000 and $80,000 per annum at 1911 prices. The cost of handling pig iron dropped substantially, and the employed men did the work previously done by many more. Taylor specified what tools workers were to use and how to do their jobs. His 'deal' with his workers was as follows:

Source: Bethlehem Steel Corporation

Pig iron handlers at the Bethlehem Steel Works.

You do it my way, by my standards, at the speed I mandate, and in so doing achieve a level of output I ordain, and I'll pay you handsomely for it, beyond anything you might have imagined. All you do is take orders, give up your way of doing the job for mine (Kanigel, 1997, p.214).

It was among the first attempts to align the goals of the workers with those of management.

Lean and mean?

The 'Lean Programme' is a £7 million initiative directed by logistics consultants, Unipart, on civil servants working in the National Insurance department (part of HM Revenue and Customs) at Longbenton, Northumberland in England. It aims to increase efficiency by reducing desktop clutter. Black tape on staff desks indicates where their pens, pencils, computer keyboards and phones should be correctly located. The union criticized the efficiency drive as 'demeaning and demoralizing', while a spokesperson for the HMRC said, 'Lean is all about how we can work more efficiently to deliver an even better service to our customers'. About 44 offices in Britain are part of this programme with trials taking place in the Lothians (Scotland), as well as in Portsmouth and Cardiff.

Based on Horsnell (2007, p.5); Fletcher (2007).

Initiative and incentive system
a form of job design in which management gives workers a task to perform; provides them with the financial incentive to complete it, but then leaves them to use their own initiative as to how they will perform it.

Taylor's scientific management was a powerful and largely successful attempt to wrest the organization of production from the workers and place it under the control of management. Before Taylor, the use of the initiative and incentive system within the company involved management specifying production requirements; providing workers with incentives in the form of a piece-rate bonus; and leaving them to use their own initiative in deciding how best to organize their work. In Taylor's view, not only did this result in wasted effort but also, and more importantly, workers kept their craft secrets to themselves, and worked at a collectively agreed rate that was below their ability. Taylor argued that managers should exercise full responsibility for the planning, co-ordinating and controlling of work, including selecting the tools to be used (management work), thereby leaving workers free to execute the specified tasks (shop floor work).

Management–workers relations, in Taylor's eyes, should be co-operative rather than adversarial. He saw the two pulling together to produce as much product as possible for their mutual benefit. His techniques were meant to improve the efficiency and social harmony of industrial life, and they required, in his phrase, a 'Mental Revolution' by both parties. By this he meant the application of the principles of science to determine the best way to perform any given task and the acceptance of the results obtained thereby, by both workers and management. He also believed that his 'scientific' approach would end arbitrary management decisions. Management would plan and organize the work and labour would execute it, all in accordance with the dictates of science. Once his methods had been introduced within a company, trade unions and collective bargaining would, in his view, become redundant. Scientific assessment would eliminate all ambiguity and argument. This, and all his other ideas were detailed in his book, *The Principles of Scientific Management* (Taylor, 1911).

Taylorized call centres

In their case study of customer service call centres run by two British companies, Martin Beirne, Kathleen Riach and Fiona Wilson found strong continuities with Taylorism, both in terms of their design and operation. They found the work to be pressurized and highly paced, stoked by management's preoccupation with cost minimization and productivity. Most of the jobs they studied, both front-line and supervisory, were narrowly defined and closely monitored. The time duration of each call taken; the content of the conversation with each customer; and the advice to be given, were all closely prescribed. There was a high level of task fragmentation, scripting and call streaming. The majority of operators on both sites were trained to deal with just one aspect of incoming enquiries, and were force-fed a diet of *supposedly* standardized calls by automatic systems that could *ostensibly* discriminate between all possible variants, allocating them, as necessary, to the 'appropriate skill set'.

As a corollary, cost minimization was a key theme in training, keeping budgets within tight limits, and against high levels of staff turnover, by packaging knowledge for rapid assimilation and to plug people into the system in the shortest possible time. There was also abundant evidence of bureaucratic support systems operating to police adherence and 'safeguard' customer service. Company B used scripting in all parts of the call. Agents were given their opening paragraphs, appropriate greetings, the order to list any benefits, three prompts to include in every conversation, and instruction on how to close [*the sale*]. One manager offered the justification that 'this helps the operator to structure the call into a coherent and professional interaction'. The monitored workers were disciplined for abandoning scripts, regardless of their success in converting calls into business. Teams within call centres resemble manufacturing industry lean production teams.

From Beirne et al. *(2004).*

Workers were concerned that scientific management just meant 'work speed-up' – that is, more work for less pay. Taylor was adamant that after the implementation of his methods, workers would be rewarded by large pay increases and managers would secure higher productivity and profits. Sometimes workers complained about the inequality of pay increases as when a 300 per cent productivity increase resulted in a 30 per cent pay increase.

Symphonic engineering

Here is the way in which a literal-minded industrial engineer reported on a symphony concert: 'For considerable periods the four oboe players had nothing to do. The number should be reduced and the work spread more evenly over the whole concert, thus eliminating peaks and valleys of activity. All the twelve violins were playing identical notes, this seems unnecessary duplication. The staff of this section should be drastically cut. If a larger volume of sound is required, it could be obtained by means of electronic apparatus. Much effort was absorbed in the playing of demi-semi-quavers; this seems to be an unnecessary refinement. It is recommended that all notes be rounded up to the nearest semi-quaver. If this were done, it would be possible to use trainees and lower grade operatives more extensively.

There seems to be too much repetition of some musical passages. Scores should be drastically pruned. No useful purpose is served by repeating on the horns something which has already been handled by the strings. It is estimated that if all redundant passages were eliminated

→

the whole concert time of 2 hours could be reduced to 20 minutes and there would be no need for an intermission. In many cases the operators were using one hand for holding the instrument, whereas the introduction of a fixture would have tendered the idle hand available for other work. Also, it was noted that excessive effort was being used occasionally by the players of wind instruments, whereas one compressor could supply adequate air for all instruments under more accurately controlled conditions.

Finally, obsolescence of equipment is another matter into which it is suggested further investigation could be made, as it was reported in the programme that the leading violinist's instrument was already several hundred years old. If normal depreciation schedules had been applied, the value of this instrument would have been reduced to zero and purchase of more modern equipment could then have been considered.'

From Fulmer and Herbert (1974, p.27).

Taylor argued that his approach enabled people to do more work, in less time, using less effort because of the more efficient physical movements. Since they were expending less effort, this had to be taken into account when calculating their wage increases. The efficiency savings also led to the requirement for fewer workers. Would existing workers be re-deployed or made redundant? In later years the unions became reconciled with work-study and accepted it, especially if financial benefits followed.

Criticisms of Taylorism

The following criticisms are commonly found in textbooks and historical accounts of Taylorism. It:

1. Assumed that the motivation of the employee was to secure the maximum earnings for the effort expended; and neglected the importance of other rewards from work (achievement, job satisfaction, recognition), which later research has found to be important.

2. Neglected the subjective side of work – the personal and interactional aspects of performance, the meanings that employees give to work and the significance to them of their social relationships at work.

3. Failed to appreciate the meanings that workers would put on new procedures and their reactions to being timed and closely supervised.

4. Had an inadequate understanding of the relation of the individual incentive to interaction with, and dependence on, the immediate work group. Taylor did attribute 'underworking' to group pressures, but misunderstood the way in which these worked. He failed to see that these might just as easily keep production and morale up.

5. Ignored the psychological needs and capabilities of workers. The one-best-way of doing a job was chosen with the mechanistic criteria of speed and output. The imposition of a uniform manner of work can both destroy individuality and cause other psychological disturbances.

6. Had too simple an approach to the question of productivity and morale. It sought to keep both of these up exclusively by economic rewards and punishments. However, the fatigue studies undertaken by the Gilbreths during the 1920s did signal the beginnings of a wider appreciation of the relevant factors than had initially been recognized by Taylor. Incentive approaches under the scientific approach tended to focus on the worker as an individual and ignored their social context.

7. Functional foremanship was deemed to be too complex and an unwieldy mode of supervision.

STOP AND THINK

You have travelled back through time and are able to meet Taylor. What three things would you congratulate him for, and what three things would you criticize him for?

Development of Taylorism

Lillian Moller
Gilbreth
(1878–1972)
Frank Bunker
Gilbreth
(1868–1924)

Frank Bunker Gilbreth's background resembled Taylor's in that both were practising engineers and managers. Gilbreth's experience was in the construction industry, and his most famous experiments involved bricklayers. His main contribution was to refine the techniques for measuring work. His wife Lillian was a trained psychologist and her contribution was in the area of the human aspects of work.

Motion study: This refers to the investigation and classification of the basic motions of the body. Gilbreth developed motion study. Taylor had looked mainly at time, and had not focused as closely on motions. Gilbreth rectified this omission and published his ideas in his book, *Motion Study*, in 1911.

Research techniques: To study and improve workers' body movements, Gilbreth used *stroboscopic pictures*. Small electric lamps were attached to workers' fingers, hands and arms, and the camera lens left open to track their changing positions. The resulting *chronocyclegraphic* photograph showed the workplace with motion paths superimposed. From these he made wire models, which allowed the work task to be analyzed in detail, and re-designed to be performed more efficiently. He used also used *motion picture cameras* to record a worker's movements, including a clock, calibrated in hundreds of a minute, within the film frame, enabling the worker's motions, the time taken and the conditions surrounding the job, to be all recorded simultaneously.

Therbligs: In motion and time study, the elementary movement was visualized as the building block of every work activity. Gilbreth developed a system for noting such elementary movements, each with its own symbol and colour. These he called 'therbligs' – his name spelt backwards. Like dance, all the movements of the worker's body performing a particular task were noted down using the therbligs notation. In addition, Gilbreth developed a standard time for each job element, thereby combining time study with motion study. **Time-and-motion studies** are conducted to this day, and are used for designing wage payment systems whose universal application Gilbreth advocated.

Time-and-motion studies measurement and recording techniques used to make work operations more efficient.

Time-and-motion study, Hoover factory, Perivale, West London, 1948

Source: NMPT/Walter Nurnberg/Science&society Picture Library

Henry Laurence Gantt (1861–1924)

Lillian Gilbreth's contribution came from psychology. Her book, *The Psychology of Management*, highlighted the importance of human factors in organizations and was published in 1916 (Gilbreth and Gilbreth, 1916). Her work complemented her husband's. She studied motions to eliminate unnecessary and wasteful actions, so as to reduce the fatigue experienced by workers. Since all work produced fatigue for which the remedy was rest, the aim was to find the best mixture of work and rest to maximize productivity. To do this, they focused on the total working environment, and not just on selecting first-class workers as Taylor had done. They shortened the working day; introduced rest periods and chairs; and instituted holidays with pay. They studied jobs to eliminate fatigue-producing elements. Changes were also made to heating, lighting and ventilation. The final ingredient was termed the 'betterment of work'. It included introducing rest rooms, canteens, entertainment and music into the factory. In the work of the Gilbreths we see the first realization that workers may have a variety of different needs. They thought that individual work performance depended as much on attitudes, needs and the physical environment as on correct work methods, suitable equipment and financial incentives. In 1916, the Gilbreths published their book, *Fatigue Study*, which linked Frank's development of Taylor's scientific management ideas, with Lillian's work in industrial psychology.

Gantt's contributions

In 1887, Henry Laurence Gantt joined the Midvale Steel Company and became an assistant to the company's chief engineer – F.W. Taylor. Gantt supported Taylor's approach, but humanized scientific management to make it more acceptable (Gantt, 1919). He tempered Taylor's work with greater insight into human psychology, and stressed method over measurement. He believed that Taylor's use of incentives was too punitive and lacked sensitivity to the psychological needs of the workers. He believed in consideration for, and fair dealings with, employees and felt that scientific management was being used as an oppressive instrument by the unscrupulous. He made three major contributions:

Best-known-way-at-present: Gantt's system was based on detailed instruction cards in the best scientific management tradition. However, he replaced Taylor's 'one-best-way', with his own 'best-known-way-at-present', which involved a much less detailed analysis of jobs than Taylor had suggested.

Task-and-bonus payment scheme: He replaced Taylor's differential piece-rate wage system with his own task-and-bonus scheme. Each worker was set a task, received a set day rate and an additional 20–50 per cent bonus.

'Gantt Chart': He developed a bar chart used for scheduling (i.e. planning) and co-ordinating the work of different departments or plants. His chart depicted quantities ordered, work progress and quantities issued from store. Although he never patented it, it is still in use today, and bears his name (Figure 14.1).

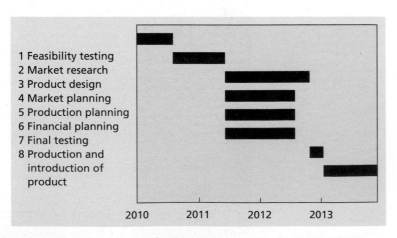

1 Feasibility testing
2 Market research
3 Product design
4 Market planning
5 Production planning
6 Financial planning
7 Final testing
8 Production and introduction of product

2010   2011   2012   2013

Figure 14.1: Gantt chart for new product development plan beginning 2010

Fordism

Henry Ford
(1863–1947)

Fordism a form of
work design that
applies scientific
management principles
to workers' jobs; the
installation of single
purpose machine tools
to manufacture
standardized parts;
and the introduction
of the mechanized
assembly line.

By 1920, the name of Henry Ford had become synonymous not only with his Model T motor car, but also with his revolutionary techniques of mass producing it. In terms of the three separate manufacturing activities distinguished by Gill (1985) earlier, Ford developed the last two – the transfer of work pieces between workers and operations; and the co-ordination and control of these processes, ensuring that sufficient raw material was available to operators and that finished pieces flowed smoothly through assembly. Thus he moved on from the mechanization and rationalization of work on the individual work piece or object pioneered by Taylor, to mechanizing the flow of objects between operatives. The process by which this was done is known as Fordism. In this sense, Fordism is distinguishable from Taylorism in that it represents a form of work organization designed for efficient mass production.

Ford established his company in 1903. In the 1890s, it was skilled craftsmen who built motor cars. Ford claimed that there were not enough of them to meet the level of car production that he wanted, and that was why, in his view, the deskilling of work was necessary. Others argue that deskilling made labour easier to control and replace. Ford's goal was 'continuous improvement' rather than the 'one best way'. His objective was to increase his control by reducing or eliminating uncertainty (Ford and Crowther, 1924). Among his major innovations were:

- analysis of jobs using time-and-motion techniques;
- installation of single purpose machine tools to manufacture standardized parts;
- introduction of the mechanized assembly line.

Analyzing jobs

Ford applied the principles of scientific management to remove waste and inefficiency. Ford established a Motion Picture Department that filmed work methods in different industries, so as to learn from them. He applied the principles of work rationalization, employees were allocated simple tasks, all of which had been carefully designed to ensure maximum efficiency. Ford's approach was entirely experimental, very pragmatic and always open to improvements – try it, modify it, try it again, keep on until it's right. The Ford mechanic, originally a skilled craftsman, became an assembler who tended his machine, only performing low-grade tasks. For example, the wheelwright's job was divided into almost a hundred operations, each performed by a different man using specialized equipment.

Installation of single purpose machine tools to produce standardized parts

Ford used rigid and heavy machine tools, carbon alloy tool steels and universal grinding machines. This ensured that each part was exactly like the next, and hence interchangeable, thus facilitating the division of labour and increasing certainty. The single purpose machines that he designed for his factory were called 'farmer machines' because farm boys, coming off the land, could be quickly trained to use them. Their operators did not have to be skilled, just quick. The skill was now incorporated within the machine, which eliminated the need for skilled workers, as anybody could now assemble an automobile.

Creation of the mechanized assembly line

Despite the aforementioned innovations, employees could still work at their own speed. In 1913, it still took 90 minutes to assemble a car. To overcome this problem, instead of moving the men past the car, the car was moved past the men. The mechanized assembly line imposed upon employees the working speed that Ford wanted. By 1914, the plant had installed a continuous automatic conveyor that met Ford's technical and philosophical objectives. The engineers arranged work in a logical order. The materials and semi-completed parts passed through the plant to where they were needed. The conveyor belt took radiator parts to assemblers, and then carried their work away to solderers, who finished off the product (Gartman, 1979).

Assembly line aircraft and paintings

Boeing manufactures its 737s at its Renton factory in Seattle. The plant used to be full of planes parked at angles, with mechanics swarming over them. The aircraft were pre-positioned at the end of each shift, in an adjacent bay, ready for the next day's work to be done on them. Now, the factory uses lean manufacturing techniques and resembles a Toyota car plant. In at one end come the aircraft fuselages that are hooked onto a moving assembly line. Nose-to-tail, they move along at a rate of two inches a minute through the final assembly process. Out at the other end roll off complete aircraft with wings, tails, cockpits, toilets, galleys and seats. There are other features of the Toyota system – the visual displays of work in progress; and alarms to stop production if a quality problem emerges. Since November 2006, Boeing has been building its 777 jetliners in a similar way. Elizabeth Lund, director of manufacturing for the 777 programme stated that, 'A moving line is the most powerful tool available to identify and eliminate waste in a production system . . . [it] drives efficiency throughout the system because it makes problems visible and creates a sense of urgency to fix the root causes of those problems.'

There are about 300 officially licensed artists working in the Place du Tertre in the Paris quarter of Montmartre, selling their works to French and foreign visitors. It is big business, over 10 millions tourists pass through annually, and many buy paintings of Parisian landmarks to take home as souvenirs. Although perhaps not great artists, their creators are skilled painters. However, their livelihoods are being threatened because local souvenir shops are selling cheap, mass-produced paintings from China and Eastern Europe. Costing a fraction of those sold by the Montmartre artists, these oil paintings are produced on mass assembly lines, where one person paints the sky; a different person does a tree; another inserts figures and so on. One of the street artists comments, 'It isn't art, it's decoration.'

Based on The Economist *(2005a); BBC News Channel (2006a); Boeing website; Chazon (2009).*

Source: Larry MacDougal/Press Association Images

Boeing factory

Systems concept a management perspective which emphasizes the interdependence between the various parts of an organization and also between the organization and its environment.

Control concept the process of imposing a pattern on previously haphazard activities, such as the operation of machinery, the interaction of machinery with people or the interactions between individuals.

After integrating various production processes, Ford's engineers produced a continuously moving line fed using overhead conveyors. Each worker was feeding, and being fed by, the assembly line. In 1908, when the Model T was introduced, production ran at 27 cars per day. By 1923, when the River Rouge plant had been completed, daily production had reached 2,000 cars. The credit for the original concept of the assembly line concept is disputed. Some stories tell of Henry Ford getting the idea at an abattoir where beef carcasses, suspended from moving hooks, were being disassembled. Other accounts have him visiting a watch plant, and seeing the staged assembly process of timepieces (Collier and Horowitz, 1987).

Taylor's ambition had always been to wrest control of the production process from the workers and place it into the hands of management. Under Fordism, this was broadly achieved. Ford's objective was to allow unsophisticated workers to make a sophisticated product in volume. He sought to make his workforce as uniform and interchangeable as the parts that they handled. He created an authoritarian work regime with closely monitored, machine-paced, short-cycle, unremitting tasks.

Ford's legacy continues to dominate twenty-first century organizations. He showed his successors how the world could be organized to solve problems using the closely related concepts of system and control. What Ford built was not just a factory, but an entire production system. This system included the factory, but went beyond its walls. What made his system so effective was the nature and the degree of control that he exerted upon it. It has been said that Ford sought complete control of all aspects of the manufacture and sale of his car. That he nearly succeeded testifies to his genius (Zaleznik and Kets de Vries, 1975).

First moving assembly line

The photograph below shows men working on the first moving assembly line at Ford's Highland Park factory in 1913.

Collection of Henry Ford Museum and Greenfield Village.

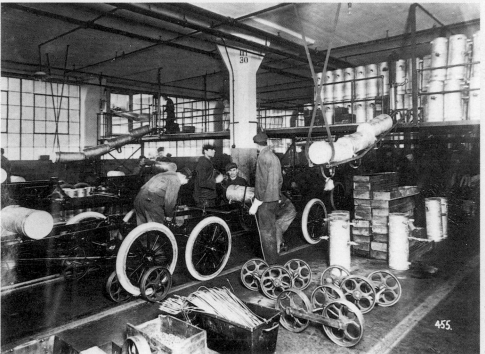

First moving assembly line

Source: Ford Motor Company

His control over the manufacturing process was achieved through the logical organization of his plants. The output of one group of workers became the input to anothers'. His factory production system was like one giant river, fed by the tributaries that constantly flowed into it.

Control over the worker was exerted through task specialization and assembly-line working. Such control was both invisible and non-confrontational. It was the system, not the supervisor, that told the employee to work faster. It de-personalized the authority relationship to such a degree that workers were no longer aware that they were being directed. Control over the environment was achieved through purchase of vital raw materials. Ford experienced production hold-ups when his suppliers had strikes. To avoid this he sought to control all aspects of the production process. In the Brazilian rain forest, he carved out rubber plantations the size of Connecticut which was called 'Fordlandia'. He bought coalmines in Kentucky; iron mines in Michigan; as well as glassworks, shipping lines and railways. He was determined to control every element of the manufacturing process, both inside and outside his company. By 1920, one Ford car rolled off the line every minute, and by 1925, the figure was one every ten seconds. In 1935, Ford's River Rouge plant in Dearborn, on the outskirts of Detroit, spread over 1096 acres; had 7.25 million square feet of floor space; possessed 235 acres of glass windows; 90 miles of railway track; employed 100,000 men; and built 2 million cars each year. Little wonder that it was called the *Cathedral of Industry*.

Ford's legacy was twofold. First, he created what came to be defined as the characteristics of **mass production** work:

1. mechanical pacing of work

2. no choice of tools or methods

3. repetitiveness

4. minute subdivision of product

5. minimum skill requirements

6. surface mental attention.

Second, he raised peoples' standard of living. Having shown that something as complicated as a motor car could be built using the techniques of mass production, it was recognized that the manufacture of other, simpler products was also possible – radios, washing machines, refrigerators, vacuum cleaners, personal computers, mobile phones. Mass production led to mass consumption, giving more people more access to more goods than ever in human history. In the 50 years to 1970, the standard of living of Americans sky-rocketed. Other countries that adopted Ford's system of manufacturing production also benefited. While Taylorism and Fordism had many similarities, they also had some differences as Table 14.3 shows.

Mass production
a form of work design that includes mechanical pacing of work, no choice of tools or methods, repetitiveness, minute subdivision of product, minimum skill requirements, and surface mental attention.

Table 14.3: Differences between Taylorism and Fordism

	Taylorism	Fordism
Approach to machinery	Organized labour around existing machinery	Eliminated labour with new machinery
Technology and the work design	Took production process as given and sought to re-organize work and labour processes	Used technology to mechanize the work process. Workers fed and tended machines
Pace of work	Set by his workers or the supervisor	Set by machinery – the speed of the assembly line

Cathedral of Industry

In the 1930s, the Mexican artist, Diego Rivera (1886–1957), was commissioned by the Detroit Institute of Art to paint frescos devoted to the city's motor car industry. His panels feature Ford's River Rouge plant. Rivera was an independent artist with a Marxist perspective. He painted the factory workers and the machines that they used. The ethnic mix of the workforce is depicted. The panels show various stages in the production of the automobile. The men in the murals are depicted as sullen and angry, working amid the clamour and din of the machinery around them. The strength shown in their faces was perceived as intimidating by some observers who accused Rivera of producing left-wing propaganda.

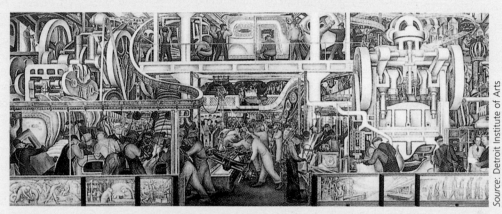

Source: Detroit Institute of Arts

Detroit Industry (South Wall) Diego Rivera, 1932–1933

Critics have argued that Ford destroyed craftsmanship and de-skilled jobs. He did indeed change the work process by introducing greater amounts of rigidity and regulation, thereby affecting the skill content of jobs. Others argue that since there were insufficient numbers of skilled workers available to do the original jobs, Ford had to redesign the tasks so that the existing, pre-industrial labour force could cope with them. In their view, it was less a question of forcing a highly-skilled, high-priced employee to accept a cheapened, dead-end job, and more an issue of identifying tasks appropriate for unskilled people to do who would otherwise have performed even less enjoyable, back-breaking work. The same critics also assert that short cycle repetitive jobs have caused worker alienation and stress, and have subjugated human beings to the machine. The assembly line is vilified for exerting an invidious, invisible control over the workers. The debate over the balance of costs and benefits of Fordism and its precursor, Taylorism, continue to this day as the next section illustrates.

Fordism in the orchestra

What do assembly line workers in car plants and musicians in professional orchestras have in common? Both have limited autonomy in their jobs. Research has found that these musicians had high internal motivation; they also had lower levels of job satisfaction than their counterparts playing in string quartets and small chamber ensembles. The reason was that the members of prestigious orchestras, with their sought-after positions, had little freedom to perform their jobs as they personally wanted. Historically, orchestra musicians have been under the strict direction of the often dictatorial maestros with their batons on the podium. The conductor is in charge, and makes all the decisions, down to exactly how a particular note is to be played. At the other end of the musical continuum are the players in jazz bands who are not only allowed, but encouraged to improvise. In between are the smaller musical groups whose members have autonomy to interpret their pieces and use more of their talents which increases their involvement in the performance.

Based on Levine and Levine (1996);
Allmendinger et al. (1994).

Today, Henry Ford's legacy in motor manufacturing is discussed in terms of the development and application of the Toyota Production System (TPS). As Tommaso Pardi (2007) noted, that critics' claims that TPS's aim of constant improvement, reduction in costs through the systematic elimination of waste using the assembly line system, represents a continuity with the classic Fordist approach, and uses the 'management by stress' approach (Durand and Hatzfeld, 2003; Parker and Slaughter, 1988b). He observed:

> The work tasks in the TPS are completely standardized, to the point that each standard worksheet does not only state the whole sequence of the operations, but also the exact positions and movements that the worker must perform. The capability of executing the standard task according to the standard task sheet is evaluated every month by the team leader (Pardi, 2007, pp.9–10).

In contrast, other writers see TPS as different from the Fordist approach in that the Taylorist principle separates the design of work from its execution (jobs designed upstairs by industrial engineers in the shop office and are performed downstairs by the workers on the assembly line). By involving industrial workers in the process of constant improvement through teamwork organization, the system increases their participation in, and satisfaction from, work (Womack *et al.*, 1990).

Home viewing

In *Clockwatchers* (1997, director Jill Sprecher), four women – Iris (played by Toni Collett), Margaret (Parker Posey), Paula (Lisa Kudrow) and Jane (Alana Ubach) – separately join the Global Credit Corporartion, as temporary secretarial staff. One theme of the film is the nature of their work. What degree of intrinsic motivation does it possess? What feelings do these women have about their jobs? How satisfied are they likely to be with their employment? A second theme concerns the work group. Being separated from the permanent staff, these 'temps' work together. As you watch the film, identify what this informal group's goals are, and how they attempt to achieve them. What techniques do they develop for dealing with their jobs? How do these secretaries introduce meaning into their work? On what is that meaning based? What causes the changes in their work environment, and what effect do these changes have on this informal group of women?

After Ford: the deskilling debate

The idea of fragmenting work tasks and simplifying jobs was begun by Taylor and developed by Ford. Since that time, has this process of deskilling work continued and been extended to other occupations and types of workers? Or, on the contrary, has work become more complicated, employees better trained and educated, and the jobs that they do more skilled? Taylor and Ford placed the issue of job skill at the centre of all subsequent discussions about work transformation and work organization. The deskilling debate provides a useful perspective from which to consider the plethora of theoretical, empirical and prescriptive writings produced by academics, managers and consultants during the twentieth century on the topic of work design.

Mike Noon and Paul Blyton (2007) provide a clear exposition of the deskilling debate, and this section draws heavily upon their explanatory structure. It stresses their contention that deskilling theory has failed to provide a satisfactory explanation of the diverse empirical evidence obtained by researchers. Instead, these authors offer an exploratory framework. We shall see how Noon and Blyton reached their conclusion. Before proceeding however, we need to go back briefly in time.

The last half of the twentieth century witnessed two, seemingly contradictory trends in work design. From the 1950s, both in the United States and Europe, there was a reaction against Taylorism, and a steady and consistent interest in more 'people-oriented' approaches.

Labels like human relations, socio-technical systems, quality of working life, organization development and human-centred manufacturing reflected this inclination. Then, during the 1970s, Japanization, and in particular, the success of Japanese 'lean production' manufacturing techniques and Japanese teamworking, became prominent. The contradiction was very apparent. On the one hand, lean production involved many features of Taylorist and Fordist work designs; while on the other, it appeared to incorporate numerous people-oriented features like teamworking. This paradox generated much research and debate.

At the same time, the gathering pace of the information technology signalled the increasing importance of knowledge-based jobs, and of the need for so-called 'knowledge workers' to fill them. The necessity of having a well-educated and trained workforce to perform these more technically complex jobs was widely discussed. The question asked by many commentators was whether a fundamental change was taking place in the nature of work, and if so whether it was resulting in people being deskilled, and their work degraded, or upskilled (or enskilled), and their work and working lives enriched. This then is the 'deskilling debate'. Although the deskilling and upskilling positions stand in opposition to one another, the deskilling one has, to date, generated the greatest amount of research and literature.

The deskilling position

Harry Braverman
(1920–1976)

Crudely summarized, the deskilling of work thesis holds that the principles and practices of Taylorism and Fordism continue to be ever more widely applied within modern organizations. The thesis first appeared in 1974 in the book, *Labor and Monopoly Capital: The Degradation of Work in the Twentieth Century*. The book was written by Harry Braverman (1920–76), an American theorist, who had originally been trained as a craftsman copper smith, and who had worked in naval shipyards, railway repair shops and steel plants, before becoming a journalist and sociologist. Braverman died shortly after his book was published, and he was not around to enjoy the reputation that his book brought, or to contribute to the debate – the labour process debate – that his work triggered (Littler and Salaman, 1982).

The Braverman deskilling thesis

There is a long-run tendency through fragmentation, rationalization and mechanization for workers and their jobs to become deskilled, both in an absolute sense (they lose craft and traditional abilities) and in a relative one (scientific knowledge progressively accumulates in the production process). Even when the individual worker retains certain traditional skills, the degraded job that he or she performs does not demand the exercise of these abilities. Thus, a worker, regardless of his or her personal talents, may be more easily and cheaply substituted in the production process.

From Zimbalist (1979, p.xv).

The 'Braverman thesis', as it came to be known, has stimulated a wide-ranging debate among labour process theorists. It was based on Marxist economic theory and the crisis of capitalism in industrial societies. Braverman saw scientific management as a method of direct employee control. Managers removed the surplus value of their employees' labour (the difference between the sales price and production cost) and realized that value when the good was sold. He called this process *valorization*. To increase their own control, managers reduced the autonomy and discretion exercised by workers in how they performed their jobs, thereby deskilling their work. Braverman contrasted two types. The first type, *organizational deskilling*, involved Taylor's separation of task conception from task execution. Workers no longer planned their work or solved their problems since these were now dealt with by managerial or technical staff. The second type, *technological deskilling*, involved using technology, in the form of software development and equipment replacement, to do the same thing. This trend, he felt, was growing in all forms of capitalist enterprises, and was being extended to clerical, administrative and other occupational (non-shop floor) groups (Braverman, 1974).

Deskilling at the Rural Payments Agency

In 2005, various farming subsidies were to be replaced by a single European Union payment. The change required the UK government's Department of Environment, Farming and Rural Affairs' (DEFRA) Rural Payments Agency (RPA) to distribute £1.5 billion to 116,000 English farmers. However, many farmers experienced long delays before receiving their payments. Some had to take out loans, while others went bankrupt. The parliamentary select committee which investigated the problem reported that part of it was due to the replacement of the old claims-based system with a new 'task-based' approach adopted. Instead of having one application form being dealt with by one official who worked through all aspects of the farmer's support claim, the ministry divided up all the tasks to be performed on each application form into separate, electronically identifiable pieces of work, which were performed by different people. Each official was doing their own bit of a process-driven workflow, for which no one had an overall responsibility. The jobs at the RPA were deskilled. As a result, no one could report what progress was being made in processing farmers' applications. DEFRA's attempt at Taylorization went badly wrong.

Based on BBC Radio 4, Farming Today, *17 January 2007.*

McDonaldization a form of work design aimed at achieving efficiency, calculability, predictability and control through non-human technology, to enhance organizational objectives by limiting employee discretion and creativity.

George Ritzer
(b.1940)

Braverman sought to counter the popular view in social science and business literature that Taylorism has been superseded by human relations and other, more sophisticated approaches, and that it no longer determined work design or management methods. On the contrary, he argued, far from being superseded, Taylorism was institutionalized, and formed the basis of production control within organizations. Following this impetus, researchers rushed to study organizations to test the thesis. They conducted case studies to determine the existence and nature of deskilling in a wide range of different organizations in both production and service industries. The Braverman deskilling thesis was proposed in 1974, but by the 1990s was being discussed as the McDonaldization thesis. This followed the publication in 1993 of a book by George Ritzer, *The McDonaldization of Society* (Ritzer, 1993/2007).

In his book, Ritzer argued that the process of **McDonaldization** was affecting many areas of our social and organizational lives. He used the term to refer to the process by which the principles of fast food restaurants were coming to dominate more and more sectors of American society as well as the rest of the world (Ritzer, 2004). He has no particular complaint against McDonald's restaurants; he merely used this fast food chain as an illustration of the wider process which was the real focus of his attention. For Ritzer, the new model of rationality, with its routinization and standardization of product and service, and represented by McDonald's, had replaced the bureaucratic structures of the past, as described by Max Weber (Ritzer, 2006). He saw the McDonald's approach as possessing four key elements:

Efficiency: Every aspect of the organization is geared towards the minimization of time. The optimal production method is the fastest production method. For McDonald's customers, it is the fastest way to get from hungry to full.

Calculability: An emphasis on things being measurable. The company quantifies its sales, while its customers calculate how much they are getting for their money. McDonaldization promotes the notion that quantity is equivalent to quality, e.g. that a large amount of product delivered quickly represents a quality product.

Predictability: Provision of standardized, uniform products and services, irrespective of time or location. It is the promise that irrespective of whichever McDonald's you are visiting in the world, you will receive the same product in the same manner.

Control: Standardized and uniform employees perform a limited range of tasks in a precise, detailed manner complemented by non-human technology which is used to replace them whenever possible.

Ritzer's argument is that the process of McDonaldization is spreading and that, while it yields a number of benefits, the associated costs and risks are, in his view considerable. His own view is that this trend is undesirable. He looks at the issue primarily from the point of view of what the consumer, client or citizen is receiving – a uniform, standardized product or service. However, he recognizes that to achieve this, the jobs of producers have to be deskilled. In addition to the simplified jobs that McDonald's employees perform, their work is also limited by the sophisticated technology of fast food preparation, which gives them little or no discretion in how they prepare and deliver food to customers. Given our definition of action teams, it is perhaps appropriate that McDonald's restaurant employees are referred to by the company as 'crew members'. Crews are a form of team which are equipment- or technology-driven, and if that technology changes, then so too does the nature of the crew.

Hamburger grilling instructions are precise and detailed, covering the exact positioning of burgers on the grill, cooking times and the sequence in which burgers are to be turned. Drinks dispensers, french-fry machines, programmed cash registers – all limit the time required to carry out a task and leave little or no room for discretion, creativity or innovation on the part of the employee. Such discretion and creativity would, of course, subvert the aims of efficiency, calculability, predictability and control.

The McJob debate

Melinda Mattos wrote that the word, *McJob* first emerged in the USA during the 1980s, referring to an article in the 1987 *Washington Post* entitled 'McJobs are bad for kids' which brought the expression into the public eye. The term was popularized by Douglas Coupland, a Canadian novelist, in his 1991 novel, *Generation X*, who used it to describe a 'low-prestige, low-dignity, low-benefit, no-future job in the service sector'. Its increased usage in everyday conversation led to it being included in the online version of the Oxford English Dictionary in 2001 and in the 2003 Merriam-Webster dictionary. The varying dictionary definitions of McJob include references to 'unstimulating', 'low-wage with few benefits', 'requires little skill', 'often temporary', 'offers minimal opportunity for promotion'.

In the United Kingdom, the McDonald's Corporation fought back, complaining that, 'The current definition is extremely insulting to the 67,000 people who work for us in the UK. It is also insulting for everyone else who works in the wider restaurant and tourism sectors.' It challenged the definition by citing its regular appearance on 'good employer' and 'best place to work' surveys. It stated that 80 per cent of its UK branch managers and 50 per cent of the company's executive team had joined the company as hourly paid crew members; and highlighted its commitment to investing in its workforce through development and training. Its campaign to change the definition included commissioning research by a university professor into how its employment helped young people (published as *Brighter Futures*); and it ran a series of 18 different advertisements at each of its locations and on giant screens in London's Piccadilly Circus, which highlighted the perks of working in the company, with the tagline, 'Not bad for a McJob'. In 2007, it launched a petition to get the definition changed, and this was supported by a letter to the *Financial Times*, signed by 14 eminent business people, academics and two MPs. Since dictionaries only reflect contemporary usage, whatever it may be, their publishers declined to change their McJob entries. By 2008, it appeared that McDonald's had admitted defeat in its battle to secure a definition change. Instead, it launched a recruitment drive under the title *My McJob* (which included the strap line 'Not bad for a McJob'), which attempted to change peoples' perceptions of the company's employment practices.

Based on BBC News Channel (2003, 2007a, 2007b);
Stern and Wiggins (2007, p.1); The Times 100 website
(4 June 2007); wheretowork website
(www.wheretowork.com); Mattos (2007, p.1);
Personnel Today (2008, p.4).

STOP AND THINK Robin Leidner's (1993) research revealed that McDonald's workers do not say that they are dissatisfied with their jobs. Do you find this disturbing or expected? Suggest an explanation for this finding.

The significance of this development is that much of current literature about the nature of work and workplace organization is discussed in terms of Ritzer and his McDonaldization thesis, rather than in terms of Braverman and his deskilling and work degradation thesis. The key point however, is that both writers address broadly the same issues. Warhurst and Thompson (1998) reported that Ritzer acknowledged the links between his own work and that of Braverman, and between Max Weber's theory of rationalization and Karl Marx's theory of exploitation. There have been many criticisms of Braverman and his deskilling thesis. These include the following (Noon and Blyton, 2007 (pp.157–59); Fincham and Rhodes, 2005):

Ignores alternative management strategies

It ignores management's ability to choose between using Taylorism to deskill a job or empowering workers to create responsible autonomy. Leaving employees with some discretion can be to management's advantage. Thus, employee empowerment facilitates greater worker interchangeability, thereby allowing better assembly line balancing. These employees are not deskilled, but management nevertheless continues to control the labour process. This suggests that deskilling is neither inevitable nor necessarily always desirable.

Overstates management's objective of controlling labour

The thesis underestimates the diversity and complexity of management objectives and plurality of interests, many of which may be competing (Buchanan and Boddy, 1983; Child, 1985). Marketing, technological, financial and political considerations may have as much, if not more impact, on work organization. The cost of direct labour is, in many cases, only a small proportion of the total cost of a product, and its control today may not be as significant a factor as it was in the past.

Treats workers as passive

The thesis treats workers as passive and compliant, yet there is evidence of collective, union and individual resistance to deskilling. The manifestations of such resistance have been extensively documented, although not widely discussed (Ackroyd and Thompson, 1999; Wilson, 2004). Historically, management's shift from direct Taylorist forms of control to technological, bureaucratic and now to a cultural type of control, is a testimony to the existence and effect of such resistance (Ray, 1986).

Underestimates the employee consent and accommodation by employees

There is contrary evidence of workers welcoming rather than resisting the opportunity to Taylorize their own jobs. This phenomenon was originally proposed by Burawoy (1979), and has been observed by managers. 'They [workers] understood the technique because it had been done *to* them for years, and they liked the idea because now they had the chance to do it for themselves' (quoted both in Adler, 1993a, p.106 and in Boje and Winsor, 1993, p.62).

Ignores gender

Braverman's concept of skill ignores gender dimensions. Acting as a social group, men have, in the past, socially constructed their notion of skill to benefit them and to disadvantage women. Research by Suchman (1996) in a law firm employing lawyers (mainly men) and support staff (female) illustrated this. The use of image-processing technology called 'litigation support' required skilled coding and retrieval of documents by the women. The males described this work as 'mindless labour' which could be automated, thereby rendering this form of knowledge work invisible by their gendered definition of skill.

Overlooks skill transfer possibilities

Deskilling in one area may be balanced by upskilling in another. The 'area' may be different national economies, different jobs within the same plant, or perhaps even different aspects of one person's job. Observers of Japanese just-in-time (JIT) production systems note that one facet of a production worker's job can be upskilled (e.g. when they participate as a group in a job's design), while another aspect of it can be deskilled (e.g. when they have to perform the job that they themselves have 'Taylorized') (Conti and Warner, 1993).

STOP AND THINK The obvious way to resolve the deskilling debate is to ask individual employees whether they think that their job now possesses a higher or lower level of skill requirement and responsibility compared to five years ago. Or, if they have a new job, whether that requires more skill to perform it than their previous job. Why is this approach unlikely to provide a reliable answer?

Source: Copyright Grantland Enterprises; www.grantland.net.

The upskilling position

Noon and Blyton (2007) traced the genesis of the upskilling position back to the 1960s with the economics of human capital theory (Becker, 1964; Fuchs, 1968). The theory held that 'human capital' (i.e. employees) were more important than physical assets such as machinery or buildings in accumulating profits. Companies, it was claimed, would invest in their workforce through the provision of education and training, to help them cope with the greater complexity of work tasks. The upskilling position holds that the general tendency to greater technical sophistication of work requires higher levels of skill among employees, with flexible specialization being one such trend.

This original view has now been developed and expanded by both popular business and academic writers. It has been incorporated into what Warhurst and Thompson (1998, p.3) describe as, 'claims of an emerging knowledge economy . . . third waves, information societies and computopia'. Upskilling is now most commonly discussed in terms of whether or not there is a growth in 'knowledge workers'. Proponents of the upskilling thesis draw upon the features of the post-industrialist economy (Bell, 1999) to support their claim that:

- success depends more on 'brains than brawn' (Barley, 1996);
- the information age has replaced the machine age (Hamel and Prahalad, 1996);
- locating vital information and using it to help understand what is happening in a turbulent environment has become a major determinant of organizational success (Quah, 1997);

- providing services is more important than making tangible products;
- a small group of core workers with steady jobs and fixed salaries will be outnumbered by a growing number of 'portfolio workers' offering their skills to clients (Handy, 1984);
- the work of symbolic analysts who trade and manipulate symbols is too complex, domain-specific and esoteric to be subject to managerial control (Reich, 1993).

Writers like Baruch Lev have highlighted the steep rise in recent years of intangible but talent-intensive assets (Wooldridge, 2006). These include everything from a skilled workforce to patents to know-how. It is claimed that these now account for half the market capitalization of America's public companies. Accenture, a management consultancy, has estimated that among leading companies, the value of their intangible assets has risen from 20 per cent to 70 per cent in the 1980–2007 period. McKinsey, another management consultancy, divided American jobs into three classes:

transformational jobs: extracting raw materials or converting them into finished products;

transactional jobs: interactions that can be easily scripted or automated;

tacit jobs: complex interactions requiring a high level of judgement.

In the 2000–2006 period, it estimated, tacit knowledge jobs had grown two-and-a-half times as fast as employment in general, and constituted 40 per cent of the American labour market in 2006, accounting for 70 per cent of all jobs created there since 1998. It is expected that this trend will affect other countries too.

Noon and Blyton (2007, pp.164–67) listed five criticisms of the upskilling thesis, saying that it:

1. falsely assumes that the growth of the service sector will create skilled jobs
2. overstates the extent to which advanced technology requires higher-level skills from employees
3. overstates the extent of change
4. oversimplifies the skill-enhancing impact of new working methods
5. needs to be put into a global perspective.

What is needed is a conceptual framework to analyze and then map the actual cases of job design. Noon and Blyton (2007, pp.172–73) offer just such a conceptual framework that is capable of being developed into an analytical tool. These authors conceptualize the work performed by employees as varying along two dimensions – *range of work* and *discretion in work*. These are shown in Figure 14.2.

Range of work

The vertical range of work dimension distinguishes at one extreme those workers who repeatedly perform a single task. For example, factory workers attaching a wheel on a car on an assembly line. Their work range would be narrow. At the other end of this dimension, there might be a shop assistant serving staff, re-stocking shelves, stocktaking and changing window displays. Since she performed many different tasks, her range of work would be wide.

Discretion over work

The horizontal control over work dimension distinguishes at one extreme those workers who, because of the specificity with which their work is defined, have little or no discretion as to how to perform it. For example, our assembly line operator who attaches a wheel on a car will follow a detailed, written specification of how they should perform their job. Their work discretion over would be labelled low. At the other end of this dimension, would be a person who had wide discretion as to how to perform their work, for example, a potter, a plumber or a doctor. Their control over their work would be high. Noon and Blyton's framework distinguishes four classes or types of jobs that they label as follows:

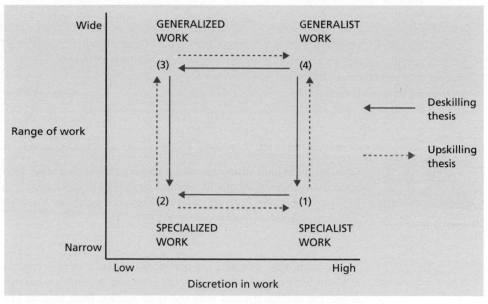

Figure 14.2 Work categorization framework and trends in skill change
Source: From Noon and Blyton, 2007, p.173.

specialist work	high discretion over a narrow range of work
specialized work	a narrow range of prescribed tasks
generalized work	a wide range of prescribed tasks
generalist work	high discretion over a wide range of tasks

Specialist work – playing three-dimensional chess!

German Air Traffic Control's (Deutsche Flugsicherung GmbH) four centres direct over 3 million flights each year within Germany's airspace. One of these is at Langen, south of Frankfurt. The staff there work in a large, windowless room, a 1,700 square-metre space, with over 100 workstations. Its walls are covered in soundproof panels at a temperature of 22.2°C. They are seated in large chairs with headsets, in front of long consoles equipped with computer monitors, display screens, switches, buttons and microphones. Their eyes are fixed on small, yellow squares, set against a black background; each has its own letter and number. These indicate the position of each aircraft, its call number, height, sink and climb rates, and velocity. The data constantly changes as the coordinates change. The job is complicated. Although there are airways and predefined routes in the sky, in order to manage the air space according to traffic volume, the controllers have to improvise. At peak times, up to 600 aircraft are in German air space. Each needs to be guided safely, precisely and as fast

Source: Action Press/Rex Features

as possible, to its destination. It is like playing chess in three dimensions. Each staff member has to think several steps ahead. The work is exceptionally strenuous, requiring extreme concentration and precision; and errors are not acceptable. Ulrike Münzer, a long-serving controller, says that you have to keep calm in stressful situations,

➞

react quickly, and be able to process all kinds of information simultaneously. Such skills tend to deteriorate with the ticking of the biological clock. Each controller is only allowed to work two consecutive hours, after which they are required to take a prescribed half-hour break. The job is so hard on the nerves that controllers are sent on compulsory regeneration courses every four years. None of the controllers is over 55.

Based on Bielefeld (2009, pp.30–33).

STOP AND THINK Consider an organization with which you are familiar – a school, university, church, current employer. Give one of example of *specialist, specialized, generalized* and *generalist* work. What effect did it have on your satisfaction and motivation?

The framework can be used both to trace trends in skill changes, and also to compare different work organization initiatives described in empirical case studies. Noon and Blyton depict the deskilling trend with the solid arrows, from high to low on the range of work dimension, and from high to low control on the discretion over work dimension. Its most extreme position labelled is (1) Specialist work. The upskilling trend is shown with dotted arrows in the opposite direction with its extreme position labelled as (4) Generalist work. Instead of looking for any general trends, Noon and Blyton's 'map' allows for the possibility of a single group, workplace, industry or industrial sector, to be represented.

Back to the future?

Intrinsic rewards valued outcomes or benefits which come from within the individual, such as feelings of satisfaction, competence, self-esteem and accomplishment.

Just how alienating and demotivating is Taylorism? Paul Adler (1999) offers an interesting counter-argument to this established view, claiming that Taylorism actually represents a fundamental emancipatory philosophy of job design. He reports that at the New United Motors Manufacturing Inc. (NUMMI) auto plant in Freemont, California, which uses a classical Taylorist approach, workers show relatively high levels of motivation and job commitment (Adler, 1993a, 1993b). How can this be? Adler's argument is that his research findings reveal two fundamental flaws in the standard view that is based on two psychological assumptions. These are first, that work is only truly motivating to the extent that it resembles free play; and second, that workers need to have autonomy.

Extrinsic rewards valued outcomes or benefits provided by others, such as promotion, pay increases, a bigger office desk, praise and recognition.

Adler states that the standard critique of Taylorism just presents motivation through extrinsic and intrinsic rewards as polar opposites; and holds that since Taylorized work lacks intrinsic rewards potential, it only leaves employees the possibility of obtaining extrinsic rewards. In so doing, it develops in them an instrumental orientation to work.

Adler draws upon the work of Richard Ryan and James Connell (1989) to argue that between the extrinsic and intrinsic polarities, there are two other intermediate positions – introjection and identification. These are presented in Table 14.4.

Instrumental orientation an attitude that sees work as an instrument to the fulfilment of other life goals.

Adler argues that job design at NUMMI taps into the identification motivation base. This focuses upon the internalization of company values, goals, and the means by which these are absorbed and adopted. Instead of motivating through 'free play', NUMMI employees are motivated through:

- The desire for excellence, the instinct of craftsmanship, and a job well done.
- Their 'psychological maturity' which recognizes the reality of the competitive situation, encouraging them to compete on quality and productivity with other autoworkers around the workplace.
- Respect and trust shown to them by management that elicits reciprocal commitment.

Introjection a formerly external regulation or value that has been 'taken in' and is now enforced through internal pressures such as guilt, anxiety or related self-esteem dynamics.

Identification the incorporation of another's thoughts, feelings and actions into one's self-esteem, thereby transforming oneself.

Table 14.4: **Four bases of motivation**

Extrinsic rewards	Introjection	Identification	Intrinsic rewards
• Following rules • Avoidance of punishment	• Self- and other-approval • Avoidance of disapproval	• Self-valued goal • Personal importance	• Enjoyment • Fun
• Because I'll get into trouble if I don't • Because that's what I'm supposed to do • So the teacher won't yell at me • Because that's the rule	• Because I want the teacher to think I'm a good student • Because I'll feel bad about myself if I don't • Because I'll feel ashamed of myself if I don't • Because I want other students to think I'm smart • Because it bothers me when I don't • Because I want people to like me	• Because I want to understand the subject • Because I want to learn new things • To find out if I'm right or wrong • Because I think it's important to • Because I wouldn't want to do that (negative behaviour)	• Because it's fun • Because I enjoy it

From Adler (1999, p.9).

Adler then considers the autonomy issue at the individual and team levels. Critics of Taylorism hold that the choice over work methods and pace of work is crucial for sustaining high levels of motivation and involvement. Adler argues that his research suggests it is not as important as claimed. NUMMI's use of the Japanese form of teamworking offered little in the way of team autonomy. The teams were organized by engineers, managers and workers; they were tightly coupled with other teams, both upstream and downstream, through just-in-time kanban systems; and with teams on other shifts. Yet workers endorsed such interdependence (low autonomy) as an effective way of managing. Adler (1999, p.12) quotes one worker:

> The work teams at NUMMI aren't like the autonomous teams, you read about in other plants. Here we're not autonomous, because we're all tied together really tightly. But it's not like we're getting squeezed to work harder, because it's us, the workers, that are making the whole thing work – we're the ones that make the standardized work and the *kaizen* suggestions. We run the plant – and if it's not running right, we stop it.

Adler argues that when workers establish a feeling of organization-wide responsibility for the effectiveness of their work, and they come to perceive their Taylorized jobs as an effective way of accomplishing the necessary interdependent tasks, then low individual and team autonomy can co-exist with high morale.

Thompson and McHugh (2002) argued that companies had been persuaded of the financial advantages of teamwork, less as a way of enhancing employees' quality of working life, and more as a way of facilitating greater flexibility, problem-solving and continuous improvement. Unlike Taylor or Ford, who were wary of the effect of group dynamics, modern management has found that it can be directed towards organizational goals and outcomes. Promoters see teams facilitating cohesion, co-operation and productivity; while critics highlight self-surveillance, peer pressure and socialization of members into the organization's culture.

One would expect that, in contrast to traditional, hierarchical-oriented, Taylorist or Fordist supervision, employees working as an autonomous or self-managing team, would be less strictly supervised. James Barker (1993) found that often, this was not the case. He

Concertive control
control exercised by the workers themselves who collaborate to develop the means of their own control by negotiating a consensus which shapes their own behaviour according to a set of core values such as those of the corporate vision statement.

and Tompkins and Cheney (1985) discuss the concept of concertive control, which is exerted not by management, but by the workers themselves. Through the discipline exerted by their team, members collaborate, and develop a way to control themselves. Barker labels this 'soft domination' because of the subtlety of the techniques involved. In this way, external values of the company become internalized, and managerial control becomes social control through the group. The team achieves first accommodation, then assimilation, then identification, and finally, internalization. The process is described by Barker:

1. Group members have discussions, and develop a consensus over values, based on their company's 'vision statement' e.g. 'We are a principled organization that values teamwork' (Barker, 1999, p.183).

2. This value consensus is then translated into group rules or norms of behaviour based on the agreed vision statement. Team members agree that being principled involves each one arriving at work on time and ensuring that all the others do so as well. Authority over the individual thus transfers from the company hierarchy and its formal rules, down to the team, with its socially created, informal rules.

3. Guidelines on how members are to behave are then specified (to provide a sense of stability and predictability for members).

Chimerial control a combination of management pressure exercised vertically on the individual through bureaucracy, technology, surveillance and the manipulation of culture; and team pressure exercised horizontally through the group norms and sanctions.

4. These devised norms, rules and guidelines are easily understood by new group members, who subject themselves to them.

What is most interesting, is that, as Barker (1993, p.433) notes, 'The teams were said to be their own masters and their own slaves.' The teams ended up doing management's work for them by dealing with their uncommitted workers by making them 'feel unworthy as a team mate' (1993, p.436). When members are simultaneously exposed to the vertical pressure of management through its bureaucracy, technology, surveillance and manipulation of culture; together with horizontal pressure through the team structure, they are said to experience chimerial control – named after the beast of Greek mythology. From his research, Benders (2005) noted that 'employees tend to experience teamwork as a mixed blessing, on the one hand welcoming the increased latitude that it provides them while, on the other, expressing concerns about work intensification (Townsend, 2005; Sewell, 1998).

STOP AND THINK

Is concertive control a totally new form of control over employees, or does it represent a modification and updating of traditional Taylorist and Fordist ideas?

RECAP

1. *Understand how scientific management met the needs of its historical context.*

   - At the start of the twentieth century, European emigration to the United States and internal migration from rural to urban areas, produced a large workforce with poor English language skills and lacking in work discipline.

   - The same period saw the establishment of large corporations and the development of technology that permitted, for the first time, the mass manufacture of products. These factories required a large workforce.

2. *Describe the main objectives and principles of the scientific management approach.*

   - The objectives are efficiency, by increasing the output per worker and reducing deliberate 'underworking'; predictability of job performance – standarizing tasks by dividing them up into small and closely specified subtasks; and control by establishing discipline through hierarchical authority and introducing a system whereby all management's policy decisions can be implemented.

   - The principles are: a clear division of tasks and responsibilities between management and workers;

use of scientific methods to determine the best way of doing a job; scientific selection of employees; the training of the selected worker to perform the job in the way specified; and the surveillance of workers through the use of hierarchies of authority and close supervision.

3. *Critically assess Taylorism.*

- It has been criticized for its assumptions about human motivation: neglecting the subjective side of work; ignoring the impact of the work group; disregarding the psychological needs and capabilities of workers; and taking a too simplistic approach to the question of productivity and morale.

4. *Enumerate the contributions of the Gilbreths and Gantt to scientific management.*

- Frank Gilbreth's contributions were micromotion study, the chronocyclograph and the 'therbligs' notation system. Lillian Gilbreth contributed fatigue study based on physiological and psychological principles.
- Laurence Gantt supplied the 'best-known-way-at-present' approach to job design; the task-and-bonus payment scheme; and the 'Gantt Chart'.

5. *Understand how Fordism developed out of Taylorism.*

- Ford developed the analysis of jobs; installed single-purpose machine tools to produce standardized parts; and established the mechanically paced assembly line.
- The twin concepts of system and control underpinned his approach.

6. *Understand the deskilling debate and the contribution of Braverman and Ritzer.*

- The 'Braverman thesis' holds that there is a long-run tendency for workers and their jobs to become deskilled through fragmentation, rationalization and mechanization.
- Some argue for the deskilling thesis, while others reject it claiming that technological developments have upskilled both workers and jobs and created new, high-skill industries.
- The deskilling debate is often discussed in the context of Ritzer's McDonaldization process, which refers to an approach to work design based on efficiency, calculability, predictability and control.

7. *Provide examples of scientific management in contemporary society.*

- Apart from fast food restaurants, the process of credit-granting through credit card; semesterization and modularization of university courses; TV programmes; food packaging.

Revision

1. Taylorism has been much criticized. Which criticisms do you feel are valid and which are not? Give reasons for your assessment.

2. Have quality and flexibility requirements in modern organizations rendered Fordism redundant?

3. To what extent are performance-based pay, just-in-time (stock) inventory and business process reengineering, just modern-day applications of Frederick Taylor's scientific management?

4. Identify non-food examples of the McDonaldization process. Analyze them in terms of Ritzer's four key elements.

Research assignment

Visit your local McDonald's or a comparable fast food restaurant that uses a similar form of work organization. Observe and make notes on the behaviour of its employees ('crew members'), both those at the counter and those in the kitchen. Arrange to interview one or two crew members – perhaps you already know someone who currently works or has worked in this type of organization in the past. Ask them about the best and worst aspects of that job. Relate their answers to Ritzer's thesis, as well as to what you have read about Taylor, Ford, Braverman and Noon and Blyton. Are the criticisms of McDonald's and similar organizations unfair?

Springboard

Allan, C., Bamber, G.J. and Timo, N., 2006, 'Fast-food work: are McJobs satisfying?', *Employee Relations*, 28(5): 402–20.

McJobs in the fast food industry are a major source of youth employment. This paper explores young people's perceptions of this industry.

Barker, J.R., 2005, 'Tightening the iron cage: concertive control in self-managing teams', in Grey, C. and Willmott, H. (eds), *Critical Management Studies: A Reader*, Oxford University Press, Oxford, pp.209–43.

This chapter describes a change from Taylorist-type to group-type control of workers' behaviour.

Bryman, A., 2004, *The Disneyization of Society*, Sage, London.

Considers how the principles of Disney – theming, hybrid consumption, merchandizing and performance – impact on society. Interesting to explore the links with McDonaldization (see Chapter 2).

Edwards, P. and Wajcman, J., 2005, 'What is happening to jobs?', *The Politics of Working Life*, Oxford University Press, Oxford, pp.19–43.

This chapter, which focuses on bad jobs and good jobs, updates the classic debates of job design introduced in this chapter, and raises contemporary concerns.

 OB in films

The Rebel (1961, director Robert Day): DVD track 2: 0:05:00 – 0:11:30 (7 minutes). In this film, the comedian Tony Hancock plays himself, as a London office worker who finds the routine of his job oppressive. The clip begins with a shot of the office, and ends with the manager saying to Tony, 'Off you go'. As you watch this clip:

1. Identify the design principles underlying the office jobs that Tony and his (all male) colleagues are performing at United International.

2. Complete this matrix, indicating the advantages and disadvantages to management and to employees of designing jobs in this way:

	advantages	disadvantages
for management		
for employees		

3. Tony's manager diagnoses his problem and suggests some solutions. How appropriate do you think his suggestions are?

4. Is this movie out of date, because management practice and office technology have changed since the 1960s? Or can you identify jobs that you have personally had, or which you have recently observed, that are designed in the same way. What would be – or what has been – your reaction to work like this?

OB in literature

Aldous Huxley, *Brave New World*, Penguin Books, Harmondsworth, 1932. Where in the plot are the techniques of Frederick Taylor and Henry Ford effectively deployed in the society which Huxley describes? This story also illustrates Pavlovian conditioning in action. Which aspects of Huxley's fictional account are found in some form in contemporary society?

CHAPTER EXERCISES

The call centre experience

Objectives
1. To distinguish different forms of control within an organizational context.
2. To explain the reasons for the popularity of call centre companies.
3. To identify the problems experienced by call centre employees and how they might be addressed.

Briefing
1. Individually consider
   (a) What is meant by the term *control* within an organizational context?
   (b) In what different ways does the company that you work for control your behaviour on the job?
2. Form into groups and discuss the following questions:
   (a) What benefits do companies gain from running their call centres?
   (b) What problems does the way that work is organized in a call centre create for its employees?
   (c) How would you improve the quality of working life of call centre employees?

Redesigning the workplace

Objectives
1. Identify aspects of Taylorist and Fordist work organization.
2. Redesign work arrangements to improve productivity and increase employee job satisfaction.

Briefing
1. Form groups.
2. Which principles and practices of Taylorist and Fordist forms of work organization are being followed and which are not?
3. Management consultants have reported that these arrangements are not very efficient. It has proved impossible to balance the line effectively so that staff at each workstation are fully occupied and each machine is fully utilized. How might this process and the jobs associated with it be more effectively designed to (a) maximize output, and (b) benefit the employees?

Bacon processing line

Imagine a factory in which sides of bacon (weighing about 20kg) are cut into slices and vacuum packed into pack sizes ranging from 500 grams to 3kg. The small sizes are sold

$\rightarrow$

to supermarkets for domestic purchases and the larger packs sold directly to hotel and catering outlets for commercial use. The bacon curing process leaves the meat wet and slippery and it has to be kept at low temperature in order to preserve it. In practice, before a side of bacon is sliced by the machine it has to be frozen in order to make it cut easily and retain its shape during the packing process. This makes the working conditions cold, damp and unpleasant. The overall process involves the slicing and packaging of bacon, and includes the following jobs and activities:

- a frozen side of bacon needs to be fed into a machine which then cuts it into slices;

- the slices need to be separated and stacked into the pack quantity on a moving conveyor belt;

- the individual stacks of bacon need to be placed into a packing machine;

- the packing machine needs to be set up for the type of pack to be produced and needs to be monitored during the packing process;

- the packed bacon needs to be weighed, priced and labelled;

- the packs need to be checked for presentation, label accuracy and quality;

- individual packs of bacon need to be put into cardboard boxes ready for cold storage and despatch to customers;

- the cardboard boxes need to be labelled with the contents and customer details;

- the cardboard boxes need to be stacked onto wooden pallets and moved to the cold store for despatch to customers.

The layout diagram below represents the machine layout and people workstations identified using a work study-based job simplification exercise. The simplified tasks in this job involved:

slicing   one person is responsible for obtaining the bacon, setting and cleaning the slicing machine and pacing the slicing processes to keep the other workstations fully utilized. This operator could wear gloves to keep their hands warm when picking up the frozen sides of bacon and feeding them into the machine.

stacking   four people working on either side of a conveyor belt splitting the cut bacon into stacks of the right quantity as it passes them by. The conveyor belt speed and rate of slicing sets the pace the work for these operators. This operation is rather like separating out a specific number of pages from a sheaf of papers; it requires dexterity and the ability to use the fingers and fingernails to separate out the correct number of frozen slices

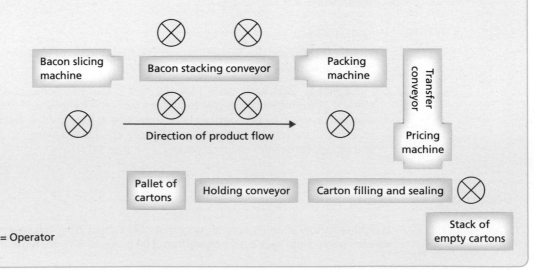

	of bacon. It is difficult to do this wearing gloves, making the work very cold and not the most pleasant of tasks.
packing	one person is responsible for setting the machine, placing individual stacks of bacon into it, and generally ensuring a smooth operation. They would also monitor the quality of the packed product.
pricing and boxing	one person is responsible for setting the automatic weighing and pricing machine, boxing the packs of bacon, sealing and labelling the boxes and stacking the cartons on a pallet ready for transport to the cold store. This person would also monitor pack quality, rejecting faulty packs and stopping the line to reset the machine if necessary.
transport	someone else would remove loaded pallets and bring empty ones as part of a similar job for other packing stations.

In addition to these direct production activities there would be a need to keep records of output and quality. Also the group would need to ensure that the whole process worked smoothly with individuals working as a team. Using work measurement techniques, the number of operators (and tasks) needed at each workstation illustrated in the diagram would be determined in order to produce the highest possible levels of output. In this case it is suggested in the diagram that a balanced line contains eight people (including one shared with other lines). However, it could be that the slicer operator is only working for 50 per cent of the time. Under these circumstances it would be common to recalculate the line speeds or redesign the jobs to keep worker utilization as high as possible.

From Organizational Behaviour and Management, *3rd edn, Martin, J.,*
Copyright 2005 Thomson. Reproduced by permission of Cengage Learning.

Chapter 15 **Elements of structure**

Key terms

organization structure	staff employees
delegation	functional relationship
work specialization	formal organization
job definition	informal organization
job description	sexuality
organization chart	sex
hierarchy	gender
span-of-control	role
authority	role conflict
responsibility	rules
accountability	formalization
line employees	centralization
chain of command	decentralization

Learning outcomes

Once you have read this chapter, you should be able to define those key terms in your own words, and you should be able to:

1. Explain how organization structure affects human behaviour in organizations.

2. List the main elements of organization structure.

3. Relate the concept of span-of-control to the height of the organization hierarchy.

4. Identify line, staff and functional relationships on an organization chart.

5. Distinguish between the formal and the informal organization of a company.

6. Understand the nature and impact of sexuality on organizational behaviour.

Why study elements of structure?

People's attitudes and behaviour can be shaped as much by the structure of the company within which they work, as by the personalities that they possess and the groups and teams of which they are a part. The constraints and demands of the job, imposed through the roles that they play, can dictate their behaviour, and even change their personalities. For this reason, it is impossible to explain the behaviour of people in organizations solely in terms of individual or group characteristics. Jay Lorsch described organization structure as management's formal and explicit attempts to indicate to organizational members what is expected of them. This involved the definition of individual jobs and their expected relationship to each other as indicated in organizational charts and in job descriptions. In his words, 'this was management's attempt to draw a map of whom they want to do what' (Lorsch, 1977, p.3).

Alan Fox argued that explanations of human behaviour in organizations must consider structural factors (Fox, 1966). He was critical of those who insisted on explaining human behaviour in organizations exclusively in terms of personalities, personal relationships, and leadership. Such explanations were highly appealing to common sense. This was because such variables were clearly visible, while the effects of structure were generally hidden. The structural approach stands in contrast to the psychologistic approach, which holds that it is the internal (individual) factors that are the main determinants of human behaviour in organizations. As a business magazine noted:

> Structure matters. Much of the large increase in the ratio of firms' stock market value to their book value since the early 1990s is due to the market's growing awareness of the role of human and organizational capital in the creation of value. For companies such as Wal-Mart and Dell, their structure is the main source of their competitive advantage. For companies currently in difficulty, such as General Motors and the big American airlines, structural re-organization will be a necessary part of any recovery (Hindle, 2006c, p.3).

STOP AND THINK Consider the behaviour of the instructor teaching this course. Identify aspects of their behaviour that you like and do not like. Decide if these positive and negative behaviours are influenced by that person's personality or by the organization structure within which they work.

Organization structuring

Organization structure the formal system of task and reporting relationships that control, co-ordinate and motivate employees to work together to achieve organizational goals.

At the start of the book, organizations were defined as social arrangements for achieving controlled performance in pursuit of collective goals. One aspect of this 'arrangement' is the creation of a structure. The purpose of organization structure is first, to divide up organizational activities and allocate them to sub-units; and second, to co-ordinate and control these activities so that they achieve the aims of the organization.

Because organization structure is an abstract concept, it is useful to begin by listing the seven things that it is concerned with – the elements of structure; these are shown in Table 15.1. Senior management's decisions regarding each element will have a major impact (either positive or negative) on the employees' work satisfaction and organizational performance. A recurring theme running through these decisions is delegation which refers to managers granting decision-making authority to employees at lower hierarchical levels.

Delegation managers granting decision-making authority to employees at lower hierarchical levels.

work specialization: to what degree should work tasks in an organization be subdivided into separate jobs? Should there be high specialization or should workers do several, different jobs (low specialization)? What are the implications for time, cost of training and employee motivation?

Table 15.1: Elements of organization structure

Element	Concerns
Work specialization	Division of work tasks
Hierarchy	Levels in the organization
Span-of-control	Supervision of workers
Chain of command	Reporting relationships
Departmentalization	Grouping of jobs
Formalization	Extent of rules
Centralization	Location of decision-making

hierarchy: should there be many layers or levels of management (tall hierarchy) or few (flat hierarchy). What are the implications in terms of communication, employee motivation and staff costs?

span-of-control: how many subordinates should a single manager or supervisor be responsible for – many (wide span-of-control) or few (narrow span-of-control)?

chain of command: to whom should a given individual or group report to with respect to their work?

departmentalization: should jobs be grouped within departments whose staff share a common expertise (functional); or according to the product or service they offer; the geographical area they operate in; the type of customer they serve or some other basis?

formalization: should written rules, records and procedures be used to co-ordinate and control the activities of different individuals and groups (high formalization) or should these be kept to the minimum (low formalization)?

centralization: should decisions be made at the top of the company by senior managers (centralized) or should decision-making be delegated down to more junior staff lower in the organizational hierarchy (decentralized)?

Why drug dealers live with their moms

Sudhir Venkateosh and Steven Levitt investigated the working of a Chicago-based, crack cocaine dealing organization called the Black Gangster Disciple Nation. They found that it was structured similarly to the fast food chain, McDonald's – 'if you were to hold a McDonald's organizational chart and a Black Disciple org chart side by side, you could hardly tell the difference' (Levitt and Dubner, 2005, p.87). The operation was divided into about a hundred branches (or franchises). J.T., the leader of one such franchise (gang), reported to about 20 men called (without irony), the board of directors, to whom he paid nearly 20 per cent of his revenues for the right to sell crack in a designated 12-square-block area. The remainder of the money, he distributed as he saw fit. Three officers reported directly to J.T. – an enforcer (who ensured the gang's safety); a treasurer (who watched over the gang's liquid assets); and a runner (who transported large quantities of drugs and money to and from the supplier). Below these officers were 25–75 street-level salesmen known as foot soldiers who aspired to become officers themselves one day. At the very bottom of the hierarchy were 200 members known as the rank-and-file. These were not actually gang employees, but they did pay dues to the gang, for either protection from rival gangs, or for the chance to secure a job as a foot soldier. A drug dealing organization works like a standard capitalist enterprise. You have to be near the summit to make a lot of money. The 120 men at the top of the Black Disciples organizational pyramid were paid very well (2.2 per cent of gang members took home more than half of all the money), with the top 20 bosses netting $500,000 each. J.T. the gang-leader (franchise holder) earned $66 dollars an hour; his three officers each received $7 dollars an hour; and the foot soldiers made $3.30 an hour – less than the US minimum wage. The authors concluded that, except for the top cats, drug dealers don't make much money, and that's why they live with their mothers.

Based on Levitt and Dubner (2005); Venkatesh and Levitt (2000, 2001); Levitt and Venkatesh (2000).

A popular way of depicting the structure of any large organization is that of a pyramid or triangle as in Figure 15.1. This is only one of many possible shapes for an organization's structure, several others will be presented later in the chapter. For the time being, we can note that the pyramidal form shows that an organization has both a vertical and a horizontal dimension. Its broad base indicates that the vast majority of employees are located at the bottom, and are responsible for either manufacturing the product or providing the service (e.g. making refrigerators, selling insurance). Proponents of the formal system claim that the reporting relationships co-ordinate, motivate and control employees, so that they work together to achieve organizational goals.

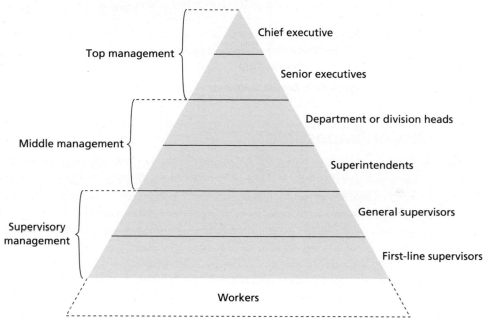

Figure 15.1: Organization structure

In Figure 15.1, each of the six successive levels above the workers represents a layer of management. On the left-hand side of the diagram, the managerial ranks are divided into three groupings: supervisory or first-line management; middle management; and senior or top management. The diagram's right-hand side lists the commonly used job titles of managers who are members of each grouping. The layers also represent differences in status. While most people will recognize an organization structure, they are less clear about its purpose. Robert Duncan (1979, p.59) said that,

> Organization structure is more than boxes on a chart; it is a pattern of interactions and co-ordination that links the technology, tasks and human components of the organization to ensure that the organization accomplishes its purpose.

For him, the purpose of a structure was two-fold. First, it facilitated the flow of information within a company in order to reduce the uncertainty in decision-making that was caused by information deficiency. Second, a structure achieved effective co-ordination and integration of the diverse activities occurring within different departments within a firm.

Harold Leavitt has suggested that organizations can be viewed as complex systems which consist of four mutually interacting independent classes of variables: organizational objectives, company structure, technology used and people employed. All of these were affected by the firm's environment such as the economic, political or social situation. The differences in organization structure can be partly accounted for by the interactions of these elements (Figure 15.2).

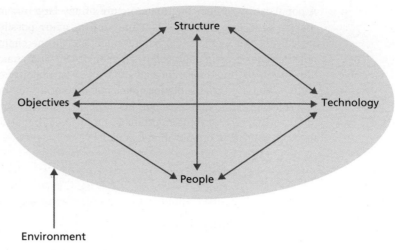

Figure 15.2: Leavitt diamond

FBI: Mission impossible?

Established in 1908, the Federal Bureau of Investigation (FBI) now has a budget of $6 billion, employs 31,000 staff, and has 56 US field offices and 50 foreign outposts. Historically, its agents have caught bank robbers, drug barons, organized crime leaders, corrupt politicians and serial killers. The FBI was organized to solve crimes efficiently *after* they had been committed – it was reactive. After 9/11 it was required to stop crimes *before* they were committed – it had to become proactive. The new environment has meant that the FBI must change nearly everything about itself. First, its objectives have been changed. It has been mandated to take the lead in counter-terrorism and counter-intelligence, and charged with protecting Americans from terrorist attacks on US soil. To achieve this, it needs to replace its past 'shoot-from-the-hip', small-picture, strategic planning approach, with a big-picture strategy involving good resource management, co-ordination and teamwork. Second, its structure needs to be changed. In the past, it had a highly compartmentalized and decentralized structure which relied on individual field officers' talents and intuition to sniff out corruption and wrongdoing. Fighting terrorism required a much more centralized approach.

Third, the FBI needs to change its people. It has doubled the number of both its linguists and intelligence analysts, and upgraded the pay of the latter. However, the bureau's cumbersome hiring and training systems are being overwhelmed processing new hires. The integration of new analysts is increasingly a challenge. Finally, on the technology side, FBI agents have only recently all acquired the basic tools of a computer, email access and an investigation database that was developed in 2004. Upgrading to a new $425 million system called Sentinel is proving problematic. In the future, its staff will have to become familiar with hostile intent systems which are currently being developed. These use 'pre-crime' technology of the type featured in Philip K. Dick's short story, *Minority Report* and the film based on it. The jury is still out on whether the bureau can achieve the necessary organizational changes being implemented by its director, Robert Mueller, so that it operates in a completely different way. A past member of the US Government Accountability Office described the challenge thus: 'You're trying to accomplish this transformation in an environment that's moving constantly. It's as if you're changing tyres on a moving car *and* you need to upgrade the vehicle you're travelling in *and* the terrain you're on is dicey and unstable.'

Based on Brazil (2007); The Economist *(2008d).*

Types of jobs

An important series of decisions on organization design relate to what types of jobs should be created. How narrow and specialized should these be? How should the work be divided and what should be the appropriate content of each person's job? The detailed answer will of course depend on the type of job considered. Is it the job of a nurse, engineer, car assembly worker, teacher or politician that is being designed? How well defined ought work tasks be? This is the question about work specialization. Some argue that newly appointed staff should know exactly what their duties are in detail. They suggest that this high degree of job definition helps to motivate employees by letting them know exactly what is expected of them. Such detail can also assist in the appraising of their past performance.

Specialization is a feature of knowledge, clerical and manual jobs. After their general medical training, some doctors become paediatricians, other chose obstetrics. On the assembly line, some workers fit car tyres, while others fix on the doors. The choice concerning the extent and type of specialization depend on the criteria being used by the organization designer. These will be affected by their values, beliefs and preferences. It may be a case of trading off efficiency of production against job satisfaction. A value position might be to seek to maximize both elements. Too rigid specialization can lead to demarcation disputes. Once the elements of the job have been decided, it is possible to advertise the post.

Other commentators believe that, far from being motivating, a high level of job definition acts to control people's behaviour and sets minimum performance standards. What is needed, they argue, is for the employee to create their own job. In practice, a detailed job definition is provided to those doing low level manual and clerical jobs, while at more senior levels there is a greater degree of own job-making. The physical manifestation of the choice about how much to define the job is the piece of paper on which is written the job description. A job description will usually contain the following information:

- job title and the department in which it is located;
- job holder's position in the hierarchy;
- to whom the job holder is responsible;
- the objectives of the job;

Work specialization the degree to which work tasks in an organization are subdivided into separate jobs.

Job definition determining the task requirements of each job in an organization. It is the first decision in the process of organizing.

Job description a summary statement of what an individual should do on the job.

HANDS ON CHIEF EXECUTIVE

**To bring bags of presence and enormous energy
to a unique global distribution operation**

A package with bells on + sleigh   **Far North**

This intensely private operation, which has a brand that is recognised throughout the world, has carved a unique position in a highly seasonal business. Its President and owner, who has always maintained a close personal involvement in every aspect of the operation, has decided that it's time to hand over the reins. The opportunities and challenges presented by technological change, and the potential threat of imitators, are issues which call for fresh ideas, new perspectives and, candidly, younger eyes. Ideal candidates, probably entering their second century and quite possibly retired recruitment consultants, will have the maturity which goes with white hair, the vision to penetrate the darkest night, a lightness of touch, and the leadership to direct a diminutive yet dedicated team. Skills in more than one language and sensitivity to a wide range of cultures will be essential, and experience of working with quadrupeds, especially reindeer, will help. Above all, we will be looking for the humour to overcome the intense seasonal pressures and the ability to appear to be in several places simultaneously. Please post full career details, quoting reference WE2512, up the nearest chimney, and share the joy, mystery, and magic of this special time with those you value most—with best wishes to our readers, candidates and clients, Ward Executive Limited, 4–6 George Street, Richmond-upon-Thames, Surrey TW9 1JY.

WARD EXECUTIVE
LIMITED
Executive Search & Selection

Source: From *Daily Telegraph*, Appointments, 31 December 1998.

- duties required of the job holder (regular, periodical and optional);
- liaison with other workers, staff, supervisors, and managers;
- authority to carry out the task – the degree of freedom permitted to exercise own judgement in carrying out the job.

The name game

Canterbury Cathedral is the headquarters of the Anglican Communion and the seat of the Archbishop of Canterbury. The cathedral employs 220 paid, full-time and part-time people, and has 400 volunteers. Paid staff include stone-masons, choristers and chefs, while volunteers include 'holy dusters' (cleaners), bell ringers and guides. Security staff are not permitted to enter the cathedral unless invited in by the *vesturer* or member of chapter. The *receiver general* is the cathedral's operations director and line manager for most of the senior managers, and has an overall responsibility for its finance and fabric (stained glass windows, flying buttresses). The receiver general is a member of the cathedral's chapter which is equivalent to a board of directors. The chapter consists of the dean, two archdeacons, three canons and three laymen and women. These clergy, along with the *precentor* (who is responsible for the organization of services) make up the full time clergy in the cathedral. The dean and chapter were constituted by Royal Charter in 1541, although there have been clergy at Canterbury Cathedral since AD 597 when St Augustine arrived from Rome to convert the Anglo-Saxons.

Based on Beagrie (2006).

Organization chart
a pictorial record that shows the formal relations that the company intends should prevail within it.

The specialization of work activities and the consequent division of labour is a feature of all large complex organizations. Once tasks have been broken down (or 'differentiated') into subtasks, these are allocated to individuals in the form of jobs. Persons carrying out the jobs occupy positions on the organization's hierarchy. Particular levels of responsibility and authority are allocated to these positions. The division of labour and the relationship of one position to another is shown on the organization chart which can act as a guide to explaining how the work of different people in the organization is co-ordinated and integrated (Chandler, 1988).

Job Description

Job title: Logistics Manager

Department: Production Department

Responsible to: Production Director

Relationships: Head of a five-member logistics team

Main objectives:

(a) To co-operate with the sales department to ensure that orders are executed without delays.

(b) To control the inventory in order to minimize the costs and inform the production lines.

(c) To deal with all our sales representatives in order to reduce further delivery times.

(d) To work with IT department to design and produce the new software for receiving orders.

Specific duties:

Duty 40% co-operation with sales department

1. Meets every day with sales manager for the orders of the day.

2. Meets weekly with the marketing director to deal with the orders.

3. Gathers daily the numbers of orders and classifies them.

4. Checks any delays and personally takes immediate action.

Duties 30% inventory control

1. Works with production line manager and checks the rate of production. In weekly meetings, they decide the priorities in production of each product.

2. Personally checks the capacity of the storehouse and fills in the reports for the production line.

3. Meets with employees in storehouse and resolves any problems they face.

Duty 15% sales representatives

1. Communicates with the main distributors on a weekly basis.

2. Meets once a month with the area representatives to discuss past performance.

3. Travels once a month to visit the representatives in their areas.

Duty 15% development of software

1. Meets weekly with the head of the IT department to discusses the evolution of the company's order receiving software.

2. Provides the numbers of orders to IT departments.

Let us consider the organization charts in Figures 15.3a and 15.3b, since an examination of them can help to clarify some of the basic aspects of an organization's structure that are introduced in this chapter. These include chain of command; formal communication channels; division of labour; departmentalization; span of control and levels of hierarchy. **Hierarchy** refers to the number of levels of authority to be found in an organization. In a company that has a flat organization structure, such as that shown in Figure 15.3a, only one level of hierarchy separates the managing director at the top from the employees at the bottom. In contrast, the organization structure depicted in Figure 15.3b, has four levels in between the top and the employees at the bottom.

Hierarchy the number of levels of authority to be found in an organization.

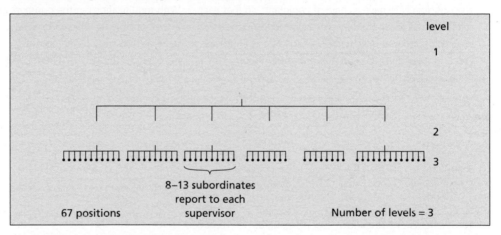

Figure 15.3a: Flat organization structure

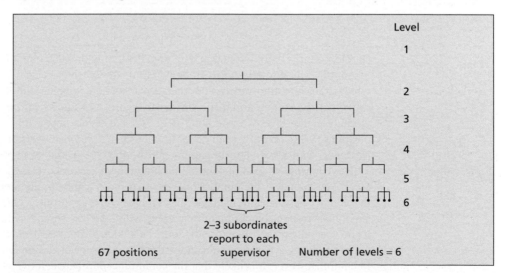

Figure 15.3b: Tall organization structure

It is useful to distinguish between organizations which have many levels in their hierarchy, such as the armed forces, the police and the civil service (referred to as having a 'tall' hierarchy), and organizations which manage to operate with relatively few levels of hierarchy such as small businesses and universities (referred to as possessing a 'flat' hierarchy). The Roman Catholic Church with its 800 million members, which has been in existence for over 1,500 years, operates with five hierarchical layers – parish priest, bishop, archbishop, cardinal and Pope.

Span-of-control the number of subordinates who report directly to a single manager or supervisor.

Span-of-control refers to the number of subordinates who report to a single supervisor or manager and for whose work that person is responsible. Comparing the two organization charts in Figure 15.3, it can be seen that in the one with a flat hierarchy, there are many employees reporting to each supervisor. Hence, that person has a wide span of control. In a tall organization structure, fewer employees report to each manager and hence the span of control of each of the managers is narrow. The larger the number of subordinates reporting to one manager, the more difficult it is for her to supervise and co-ordinate them effectively. General Sir Iain Hamilton once said that, 'No one brain can effectively control more than six or seven other brains.'

The army's span-of-control

The principle is to have a chain of command, so that each soldier knows to whom they are responsible and there can be units of different managerial sizes for different purposes. For example, according to Xenophon counting on the fingers of two hands, the divisions of Cyrus's army were:

	Form	Under	
5 men	1 squad	corporal	5
2 squads	1 sergeant's squad	sergeant	10
5 sergeant's squads	1 platoon	lieutenant	50
2 platoons	1 company	captain	100
10 companies	1 regiment	colonel	1,000
10 regiments	1 brigade	general	10,000

With modifications in the numbers in different units, this is the principle on which armies have been organized. The general does not have to control 10,000 men directly; he controls the ten regimental colonels, and so on. In modern armies this would be considered an excessive span of control and two or three armies would form an army group, but the principle remains. Split the task up into manageable proportions and do not have an excessive span of control so that real control is lost.

Jervis (1974, p.87).

Harold Koontz (1966) wrote that if an organization with 4,000 employees widened its span-of-control from 4-to-1 to 8-to-1, it could eliminate two hierarchical layers of management, which translates into nearly 800 managers. Stephen Robbins and Timothy Judge (2007) explained the simple arithmetic involved. Figure 15.4 shows an organization with 4,096 workers at the level 7 – the shop floor. All the levels above this, represent managerial positions. With a narrow span-of-control of 4-to-1, 1,365 managers are needed (levels 1–6). However, with a wide 8-to-1 span-of-control, only 585 would be required (levels 1–4).

The concepts of span-of-control and hierarchy are closely related. The wider a span-of-control is, the fewer the number of levels that there will be in the hierarchy. At each level, the contact between the manager and each of those reporting to him will be reduced. A supervisor responsible for eight operatives will have less contact with each operative than if she was only responsible for only four. This wide span-of-control, with few levels of hierarchy produces a flatter organization structure with fewer promotion steps for employees to climb. However, it is likely that the communication between the levels will be improved as there are fewer of them for any message to pass through.

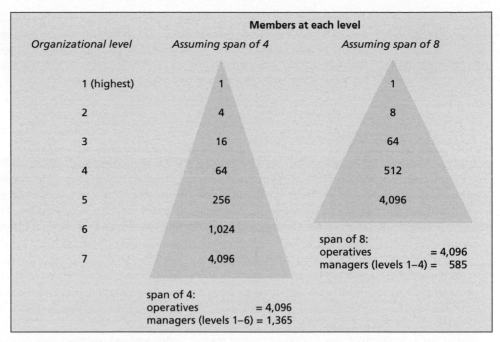

Figure 15.4: Contrasting spans-of-control
Source: Robbins (1990, p.88).

With a narrow span-of-control of one supervisor to four workers, the daily contact between the boss and her staff will be closer. This narrower span creates vertical differentiation and a taller hierarchy. Although it provides more steps in a career ladder for employees to rise through, communication tends to deteriorate as the message has to go through an ever-increasing number of layers both upwards and downwards. Because resources are always limited, they restrict the decision-making process. Many factors affect the choice of a span-of-control, and the main ones are listed in Table 15.2.

Table 15.2: Factors determining the choice of span-of-control

1. *Similarities of tasks* – The more similar the tasks carried out by subordinates are, the wider the span-of-control (and vice versa)
2. *Geographic proximity* – The more physically dispersed subordinates are, the narrower the span-of-control
3. *Subordinate characteristics* – The more subordinates are competent, responsible and able, the wider the span-of-control
4. *Interaction requirements* – The lower the interaction required with subordinates, the wider the span-of-control
5. *Standardized procedures* – The more standardized procedures there are, the wider the span-of-control
6. *New problems* – The higher the frequency of new problems experienced by subordinates, the narrower the span-of-control
7. *Knowledge gap* – The greater the gap between the manager's and subordinates' expertise, the narrower the span-of-control
8. *Task complexity* – If the work activities to be performed by employees are complex, the narrower the span-of-control
9. *Manager's job* – The greater the non-supervisory element in a manager's job, the narrower the span-of-control
10. *Planning and co-ordination* – The less planning and less coordination that is required of subordinates' work, the wider the span of control

STOP AND THINK Can a lecturer's span-of-control (class size) ever be too narrow or too wide? What factors determine the number of students that a single instructor can deal with in terms of teaching, assessment and course administration? What are the effects of high and low class sizes on (a) lecturers and (b) students?

Structure at Amazon.com

Our lives were structured around the 'quad', a term of unknown origin that signified a manageable clump, the size of a squad or platoon. CS [customer service] management broke us up into these groups to manage workflow and make certain that everyone had someone with an eye on them, but mostly it just helped create job positions above email gerbil to which people could aspire. Each quad had a 'quad leader' and the quad leader had two lieutenants known as 'leads' who were there to provide guidance and to be leaders-in-training with ill-defined job descriptions. In addition, quads had six Tier 1s (greenhorns) and six Tier 2s (veterans). It was much like a combat team, sans guns, combat and machismo. The weirdest thing about the entire structure was how totally unnecessary it was. We never spoke to anyone on our team with regard to our work. You were surrounded by co-workers, but you never needed to have a meeting or 'interface' with anybody. The only people you spoke with were four to six hundred customers a shift, on the phone and via email. Every couple of days you might have a question, but you just asked whoever was next to you, and they'd tell you what to do . . . We named our quads after pop-culture detritus: Graceland, Route 66, Area 51, *Barbarella* – the list was endless. I lived in Dagobah, Yoda's camp.

Adapted and reprinted with the permission of The Free Press, a division of Simon & Schuster, Inc., from 21 DOG YEARS @ Amazon.com by Mike Daisey. Copyright 2002 by Mike Daisey. All rights reserved.

Although flat hierarchies imply a wider span-of-control and fewer promotion opportunities, they also force managers to delegate their work effectively if they are not to be faced with an intolerable workload. Evidence suggests that individuals with high self-actualization needs prefer flat hierarchies, while those who emphasize security needs tend to gravitate towards organizations with tall hierarchies. Hierarchy is a co-ordinating and integrating device intended to bring together the activities of individuals, groups and departments that were previously separated by the division of labour and function.

At one time it was believed that the narrower the span-of-control was, the greater would be the level of employee productivity (Meier and Bohte, 2000). However, research by Theobald and Nicholson-Crotty (2005) suggests that due to negative consequences of a narrow span, it is a moderate span of control that maximizes productivity, as show in Figure 15.5. To

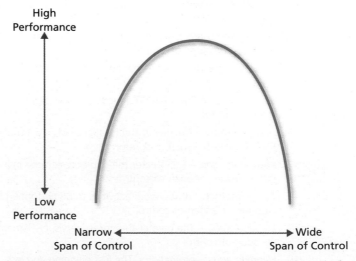

Figure 15.5: Relationship between organizational performance and span-of-control
Source: Based on Theobald and Nicholson-Crotty (2005).

recap, an organization structure performs three functions. First, it designates the formal reporting relationships, specifying both managers' spans of control and the number of hierarchical levels. Second, it groups together individuals into departments. Finally, it specifies systems within the firm, to ensure that the communication, co-ordination and integration between different departments is effective.

The graph in Figure 15.5 shows that organizational performance and span-of-control both increase to the point at which the supervisor or manager is unable any longer to co-ordinate or monitor the large number of subordinates who report to her. Companies differ, and each seeks to find the span best for it. In recent years, however, spans-of-control have generally tended to widen considerably.

Pyramid working

In modern discussions, an organizational structure is often both referred to, and shown as, a pyramid. The ancient Egyptians, who built the original pyramids, relied neither on complex machines nor animals for any of their labour. To build such monumental structures, they needed a highly organized workforce. From tomb inscriptions and labourers' instructions, researchers can draw a modern organizational chart of these ancient workers. As Ann Roth, an Egyptologist who has studied groups of workers in detail explains:

> Every project, like a pyramid, had a crew of workers, and each group was responsible for one part of the pyramid complex. There was one group for building the interior granite roofs, and separate groups for raising the chamber walls. Each crew of workers was divided into four or five smaller units which Egyptologists call *phyles* (after the Greek for 'tribe'). Each phyle carried a name such as 'Great One' or 'Green One'. The phyles too were broken up into forces of 10 or 20 men, and these had names like 'Endurance' and 'Perfection'.

They had to be very organized to build these things as they did. To construct a pyramid in a time period of 20 years, the workers had to set a stone in place every two minutes, a phenomenal pace! To keep that kind of workforce functioning at top speed, a highly developed support system was also needed to feed and house the workers. Tombs have been found bearing the titles of middle and senior level managers, which demonstrates the tight organization of the ancient Egyptian workforce. These administrators had to co-ordinate the arrival of rotating teams of labourers and shipments of supplies from all over Egypt. What really blossomed in the Fourth Dynasty was not the realization of how to work large blocks of stone; but rather the discovery of how to organize a large labour force. Raising the pyramids was as much a feat of organization as of engineering.

Based on Morell (2001, pp.78–99).

Pyramid working

Line, staff and functional relationships

Within any organization structure, individuals will have different relationships with one another. These can be *line*, *staff* and *functional*. The line relationship is a feature of every organization, irrespective of its size or simplicity. The staff and functional types are modifications of this basic line relationship which have become necessary because of the increased complexity of an organization's operations. The staff and the functional relationship usually exist in combination with the line relationship.

To explain the differences between these types of relationships, it is first necessary to introduce and define the concepts of authority, responsibility and accountability. You cannot be held accountable for an action, unless you are first given the authority to do it. In a situation where your manager delegates authority to you, they remain responsible for your actions to senior management.

Authority is vested in organizational positions, not in the individuals who occupy them. Military personnel salute the rank, not the person holding it. Authority is accepted by subordinates who comply because they believe the position holder has a legitimate right to exercise the authority. Authority flows down the vertical hierarchy of the organization, along the formal chain of command.

The line relationships in an organization are depicted vertically, and connect the positions at each level with those above and below it. It is this set of manager–subordinate relationships that are collectively referred to as the organization's chain-of-command. Using the analogy of a river, the line relationships are the designated channels through which authority flows from its source at the top of the organizational pyramid, through the middle management ranks, down via the supervisors, to employees at the desk or on the factory floor. Thus the most junior employee has some linkage to the most senior manager. All non-managerial employees have some authority within their jobs, which may be based on custom-and-practice or formally defined in their job descriptions.

Every organization possesses line employees if it has formally appointed leaders who have subordinates who report to them. All individuals in an organization report to a 'manager' from whom they receive instructions, help and approval. Managers have the authority to direct the activities of those in positions below them on the same line. Thus in the organization chart shown in Figure 15.6 the Operations Manager (Completions) has the authority to direct the activities of the four area managers. The Operations Manager (Completions) in turn, can be directed by the Director of Production. All the aforementioned individuals are in the same line relationship. The line relationships in a company are found within departments and functions. Line managers are responsible for everything that happens within their particular department.

Given the pyramidal nature of companies, managers located towards the top of an organization have more authority to control more resources than those below them. For this reason, lower level managers are forced to integrate their actions with those above them, by having to ask their bosses to approve some of their actions. In this way, managerial control is exercised down through the organization by the chain (or line) of command. Figure 15.7 shows 18 'links' in the chain-of-command in the British Royal Navy.

The line structure is the oldest and most basic framework for an organization, and all other forms are modifications of it. It is indispensable if the efforts of employees are to be co-ordinated. It provides channels for upward and downward communication, and links different parts of the company together with the ultimate source of authority. As long as an organization is small and simple, and its managers can exercise effective direction and control, then an organization based exclusively on line relationships will be adequate. However, once a company becomes large and more complex, requiring perhaps an expertise in human resources (HR), information technology (IT) or legal matters, then some modifications to its existing structure will be required. These new activities support, but do not directly progress, the company's core task. In the way that an old man may lean on his walking stick or staff pole for support, so line managers can lean on their specialist staff employees for advice and guidance on the above technical matters.

Authority the right to guide or direct the actions of others and extract from them responses that are appropriate to the attainment of an organization's goals.

Responsibility the obligation placed on a person who occupies a certain position in the organization structure to perform a task, function or assignment.

Accountability the obligation of a subordinate to report back on their discharge of the duties for which they are responsible.

Line employees workers who are directly responsible for manufacturing goods or providing a service.

Chain of command the unbroken line of authority that extends from the top of the organization to the bottom and clarifies who reports to whom.

Staff employees workers who occupy advisory positions and who use their specialized expertise to support the efforts of line employees.

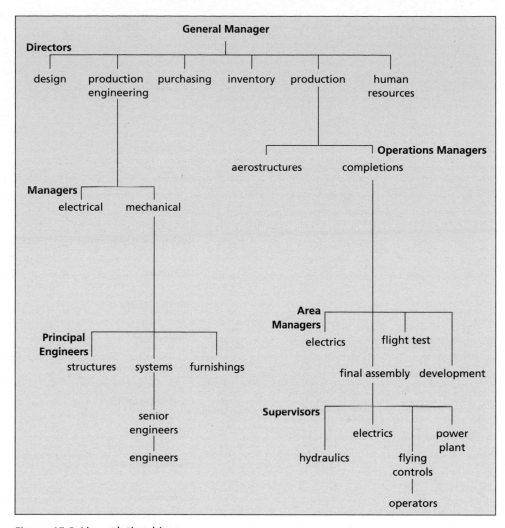

Figure 15.6: Line relationships
Source: Boddy (2005, p.308).

One way to provide line managers with advice and support is to appoint an 'assistant to' an existing line manager. The line manager can delegate tasks and projects to their assistant. The assistant has no authority of their own, but acts in the name of their line manager and with their authority. Because the assistant is not in a line relationship, they do not constitute a level in the hierarchy. Another way of providing advisory support is to establish a separate department headed by staff specialists. This is a modification of the basic line structure, and is referred to as a *line-and-staff structure*. These staff departments (HR, IT or legal) aid the line managers in achieving their departmental objectives. As with the 'assistant-to' example, the staff department performs its tasks through the line structure, and not independently of it.

Staff departments can only plan for, recommend, advise or assist other departments and their managers, since they lack the authority to insist that their advice is taken. Thus the human resources department cannot direct shop floor workers, even when dealing with a personnel problem. It has to work with the line manager of the shop floor workers concerned. Staff authority is usually subordinate to line authority, and its purpose is to facilitate the activities being directed and controlled by the line managers. Each staff department (HR, IT or legal) will of course have its own line relationships within it.

A **functional relationship** may exist in an organization between those employees who occupy specialist (staff) positions and the managers who occupy line positions. Staff

Functional relationship one in which staff department specialists have the authority to insist that line managers implement their instructions concerning a particular issue.

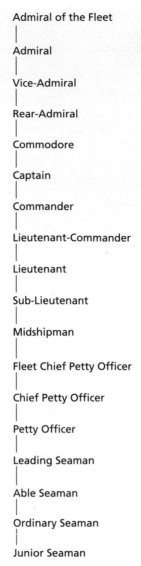

Figure 15.7: British Royal Navy: Chain-of-command

Source: From Royal Navy Museum website. http://www.royalnavalmuseum.org/info_sheets_nav_rankings.htm

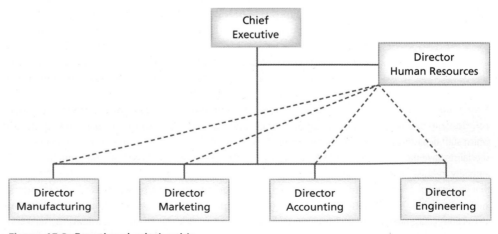

Figure 15.8: Functional relationship

specialists in departments offer their advice to line managers in all company departments, e.g. manufacturing, marketing, accounting and engineering, as shown in Figure 15.8. However, the former usually have no authority to compel the managers from the latter departments to follow their advice. This can be a problem as specialists typically have more, up-to-date knowledge than line managers, in their area of expertise. If the chief executive of the company decides that line managers must follow the advice given by staff specialists, he or she will delegate their own authority to these staff specialists on specific matters (e.g. diversity practices, computer purchase or contracts drafting), and insist that all line managers follow the advice they receive from the staff specialists. Under such circumstances a functional relationship is said to exist between the two aforementioned departments.

The functional specialists remain accountable to their own functional departmental manager – human resources, information technology or legal services – in whose name they issue instructions to line managers. Although they may have a functional relationship with other managers in other departments, within their own department, these specialists have a line relationship with their own seniors and subordinates. Traditionally, the different relationships between the various positions on an organizational chart – line, staff and functional – are depicted using various types of lines. Both these points are illustrated in Figure 15.9.

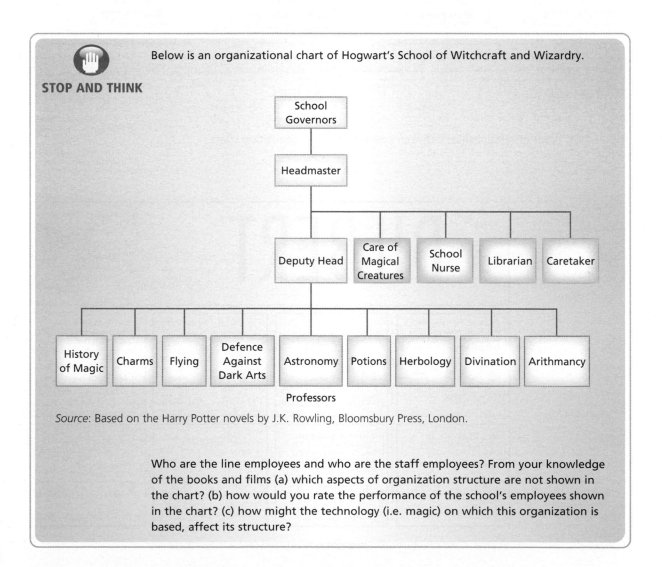

STOP AND THINK

Below is an organizational chart of Hogwart's School of Witchcraft and Wizardry.

Source: Based on the Harry Potter novels by J.K. Rowling, Bloomsbury Press, London.

Who are the line employees and who are the staff employees? From your knowledge of the books and films (a) which aspects of organization structure are not shown in the chart? (b) how would you rate the performance of the school's employees shown in the chart? (c) how might the technology (i.e. magic) on which this organization is based, affect its structure?

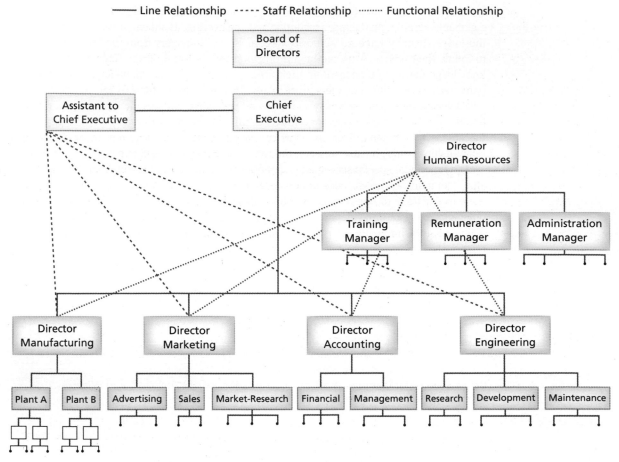

Figure 15.9: Types of relationships between positions on an organization chart

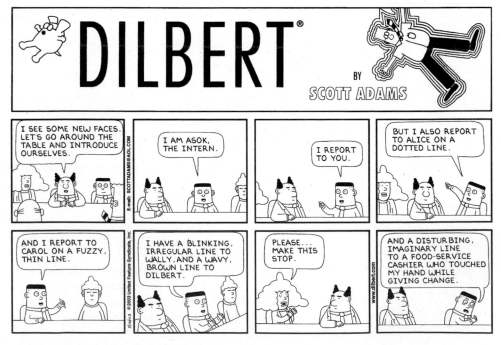

Terrorism and organization structure

The US Department of Homeland Security was created in 2002, and was one of the biggest mergers ever. It consolidated 22 units from 12 different departments. It has 180,000 employees, and an annual turnover of $37 billion. It is there to protect the US from terrorism and natural disasters. When the DHS was first established, many asked if it had the appropriate organizational structure. It brought together the main functions of domestic security under one roof. Huge agencies were seized from other departments – the Immigration and Naturalization Service (39,500 employees) from Justice; the Coast Guard (43,600) from Transportation; the Customs Service (21,700) from the Treasury. Other independent entities – like the Federal Emergency Management Agency (5,100) – were gobbled up whole.

To co-ordinate the various functions, it was argued that having a single department with budgetary control was necessary. The powers of the various units are vested in the DHS's head (Homeland Security Secretary), in order to eliminate duplication and to enforce the adoption of common standards. He delegates authority back to the bits as he sees fit. To have folded everything into a traditional, giant department would have been logical but impractical, as the job requires specialization and expertise. To have left agencies scattered around would have been no good either. For example, if there was an attack on a nuclear power plant, one agency would distribute anti-radiation treatment if you lived within 10 miles; a different one, if you lived outside that circle; a third would control the drug stockpile; and a fourth would take over if the attack also happened to be within 10 miles of a nuclear-weapons facility. The president saw the benefits of rationalization. In 2005, the head of the DHS announced a restructuring. Critics complained that it was 'weighed down with bureaucratic layers'; 'rife with turf warfare'; and lacked 'a structure for strategic thinking'. The new head commented that 'our enemy constantly changes and adapts, so we as a department must be nimble and decisive'. The new organizational structure is shown in the organization chart below (1 February 2008). To get the last, comparable US governmental reorganization right – the establishment of the Department of Defence – took 40 years and several congressional interventions.

Based on The Economist *(2005b):* The Economist, *(2002b); US Department of Homeland Security website, 1 February 2008.*

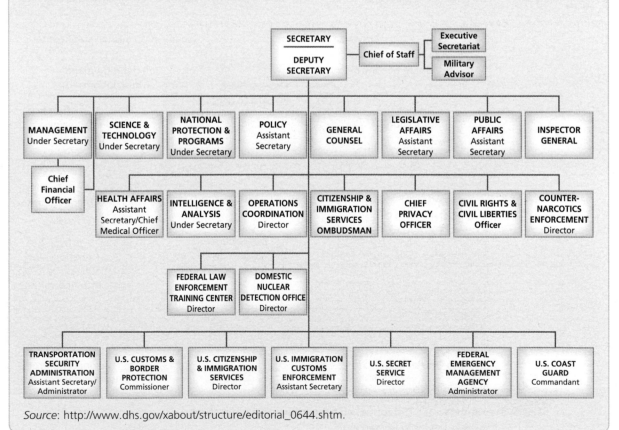

Source: http://www.dhs.gov/xabout/structure/editorial_0644.shtm.

Formal organization the documented, planned relationships, established by management to co-ordinate the activities of different employees towards the achievement of the organizational goal.

Informal organization the undocumented relationships that arise spontaneously between employees as individuals interact with one another to meet their own psychological and physical needs.

Decisions about job descriptions, organization charts, types of authority and so on, all relate to designing the formal organization. This refers to the documented, planned relationships, established by management to co-ordinate the activities of different employees towards the achievement of a common goal, using the division of labour and the creation of a hierarchy of authority. These relationships between employees are all written down, and can be checked and modified, as required. However, to understand and explain the behaviour of people in organizations, it is also necessary to become familiar with the informal organization.

The informal organization refers to the undocumented relationships that arise spontaneously between individuals in the workplace as they interact with one another, not only to do their jobs, but also to meet their psychological and physical needs. These interactions lead to the creation of relationships between individual employees (see below) and to the development of informal groups, each with their own values and norms of behaviour, which allow people to meet their social needs (see Chapter 10). These groups are separate from those specified by the formal organization. Compared to the formal organization, the informal has a more transient membership, making it looser and more flexible, with interactions between individuals being more spontaneous and more emotional, resulting in their relationships being less clearly defined, and their involvement being more variable. The relationship between the formal and the informal organizations is shown in Figure 15.10. However, the informal organization created by employees can be in conflict with the formal organization established by management. Together, the two affect the human behaviours that occur within an organization. Some of the differences between the two are shown in Table 15.3.

The informal organization arises spontaneously as individuals interact with one another, not only to do their jobs, but also to meet their psychological needs. These interactions also lead to the development of informal groups, each with their own values and norms of behaviour, which allow people to meet their social needs. The informal organization created by employees can be in conflict with the formal organization established by management.

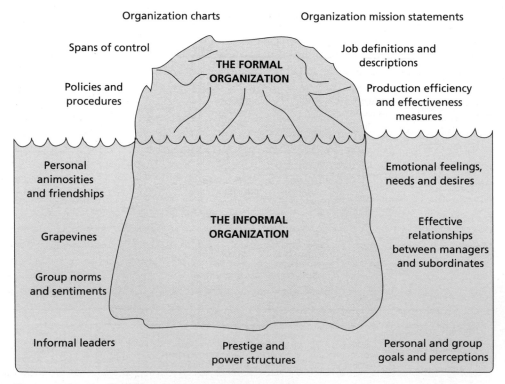

Figure 15.10: The formal and the informal organization
Source: From Lysons (1997).

Table 15.3: The formal and the informal organization compared

	Formal organization	Informal organization
A structure		
(a) origin	planned	spontaneous
(b) rationale	rational	emotional
(c) characteristics	stable	dynamic
B position terminology	job	role
C goals	profitability or service to society	member satisfaction
D influence		
(a) base	position	personality
(b) type	authority	power
(c) flow	top down	bottom up
E control mechanism	threat of firing or demotion	physical or social sanction (norms)
F communication		
(a) channels	formal channels	grapevine
(b) networks	well defined, follow formal lines	poorly defined, cut across regular channels
G charting	organizational chart	sociogram
H miscellaneous		
(a) individuals included	• all individuals in work group	• only those 'acceptable'
(b) interpersonal relations	• prescribed by job description	• arise spontaneously
(c) leadership role	• assigned by organization	• result of membership
(d) basis for interaction	• functional duties or position	• personal characteristics status
(e) basis for attachment	• loyalty	• cohesiveness

Based on Gray and Starke (1984, p.412).

Sexuality and the informal organization

Sexuality the expression of our social relations to physical, bodily desires, real or imagined, by or for others, or for oneself, together with related bodily states and experience.

Sex the basic physiological differences between men and women.

Gender culturally specific patterns of behaviour which may be attached to either of the sexes.

In contrast to the formal organization just described, the informal organization includes personal animosities and friendships, prestige and power structures, relationships between managers and subordinates, as well as emotional feelings, needs and desires. **Sexuality** is an important feature of the informal organization. It has been defined as the expression of our social relations to physical, bodily desires, real or imagined, by or for others, or for oneself, together with related bodily states and experience (Hearn et al., 1989). It is useful to contrast this concept with **sex**, which refers to the basic physiological differences between men and women, and with **gender**, which refers to culturally specific patterns of behaviour which may be attached to either of the sexes (Oakley, 1972). Many of the themes of this chapter – such as jobs, hierarchy, authority and roles – are significantly influenced by sexuality, an issue that is frequently overlooked or ignored.

Sexuality rarely features in mainstream organizational or management textbooks. One reason for this could be because organizations treat sexuality as something that should not occur within them. A distinction is made between the public and private spheres, and sexuality is seen as belonging to the latter. The sociologist, Max Weber argued that bureaucracies were based on impersonality, and strict rules, with a clear division between the public sphere, which was rational and efficient, and the private sphere, which consisted of a person's emotional and personal life. The suppression of sexuality was one of bureaucracy's first tasks, as sexuality was considered irrational and emotional, caused distractions, and thus interfered with the goal of efficiency (Bilimoria and Piderit, 2006).

However, sexuality is an integral part of every employee's personality and identity, and affects their interactions with other workers (Riach and Wilson, 2007). It refers to the entire way that a person goes about expressing themselves as a sexual being. Sexuality surrounds people in every way and in many forms. Rosemary Pringle says that it is 'alluded to in dress and self-presentation, in jokes and gossip, looks and flirtations, secret affairs and dalliances, in fantasy' (1989, p.90). Various other commentators have also written that organizations are a complex of work and play; that when you enter most organizations, you are entering a world of sexuality; and that since human beings are sexual, so too will be the places where they work (Hearn, 1993; Williams *et al.*, 1999). Moreover, sexuality is closely related to power – the first reinforces the second. Both shape, control and maintain human interaction between employees, and therefore their behaviours. Power can be expressed through sexuality, and sexuality can be used to subordinate others to a lower status. Rosabeth Moss Kanter (1977) suggested that what may look like sex differences may in reality be power differences. Sexuality affects employees' work experiences and job performance, as well as the organizational balance of power (Fleming, 2007).

Fiona Wilson (2004) observes that within the context of the workplace, sexuality refers to sex roles, sexual preference, sexual attractiveness and notions of masculinity and femininity. According to Michel Foucault (1979), notions of masculinity and femininity are based on social meanings that have been socially and culturally constructed. These meanings therefore are not fixed, but are subject to a process of ongoing revision, through which sex is used to shape and control human relationships. Within organizations, sexuality manifests itself in issues of sexual attractiveness; gender stereotyping; sex typing of jobs; the glass ceiling; the gender pay gap; work-life balance; office romances; sexual harassment and emotional labour (Table 15.4).

Since the 1960s, women have joined men in organizations. In Western societies, most people will spend more than a third of their adult life in the workplace, working in close proximity to one another. This, plus the social trends for later marriage and the long-hours culture, means that the boundaries between work and home have become blurred. Much courtship and mate selection now occurs within the sphere of the workplace. It is not surprising that about 30 per cent of co-workers will date at some point in their careers (Nardi, 2008). Many relationships begin (and end) in the workplace, even though some companies have policies banning office romances.

Table 15.4: **Issues of sexuality in organizations**

Issue	Description
Sexual attractiveness	Men and women using their physical appearance to influence outcomes, e.g. decisions on appointments, promotions, pay.
Gender stereotyping	Assumption that men and women possess different personality traits, e.g. men as strong, rational and firm; women are caring, emotional, passionate.
Sex-typing of jobs	Stereotyped attitudes towards men's and women's abilities, so that jobs are sex-typed e.g. 'male jobs' (engineering) or 'female jobs' (nursing).
Glass ceiling	Limitation of the seniority level to which women can rise – percentage of women occupying chief executive officer positions; on boards of directors; in top leadership positions.
Office romances	Emotional, physical or sexual involvement with another employee affecting organizational behaviour: includes daydreaming; flirting; handholding; sexual intercourse in the office.
Sexual harassment	Unwanted sexual attention that is perceived as threatening or offending; can be physical, verbal or non-verbal.
Emotional labour	The management of feelings to create publicly observable facial and bodily displays.

Sexuality and organizational image

Sexuality is also present in the way that a company may wish to be perceived by others. Virgin Atlantic Airlines' 2009 campaign for their 25th year anniversary had the slogan 'Still Red Hot'. Their television commercial featured a male pilot as well as female cabin crew wearing glamorous and sexy red suits while walking through an airport. As they do so, mostly men ogle the group of gorgeous hostesses, and one inadvertently squirts hamburger filling over himself. The 90 second commercial caused an uproar (which perhaps it was designed to do), and complaints were sent to the Advertising Standards Authority. It was claimed that the advertisement was insulting to all women, especially those working in the aviation industry, as the all-female crew members were being promoted as the main reason for choosing the airline. The ASA responded by saying that even although some viewers might have found the representation of the women and men in the advertisement distasteful, it was unlikely to be seen as sexist towards men or women, or to reinforce those stereotypes.

Based on Sweney (2009a, 2009b).

Source: The Advertising Archives

Virgin cabin crew

STOP AND THINK　Why might companies and business academics be reluctant to admit to the existence of sexuality within the workplace? What negative consequences might it have for them?

Managers, secretaries and their informal relationships

Using interviews, Rosemary Pringle investigated how managers exercised power over their secretaries, which the latter either accommodated or resisted. In her book, *Secretaries Talk*, Pringle revealed the variety of relationships that existed or were sought between bosses and their secretaries. The first pair studied consisted of Paul, a divisional manager in his late forties, married with children; and Suzanne, who was in her mid-twenties, and who had recently remarried and had no children. Paul has made it very clear that he wanted the stereotypical 'sexy' secretary who would always be there, at his 'beck and call'. Her presence was not as an object of desire, but to help him establish a masculine appearance. Here, sexuality was used as a tool for the manager to look successful and attractive. However, Suzanne resisted Paul's way of making her into an object of sex appeal by wearing presentable clothes that she herself had chosen. She also limited her work time to protect her private life. Pringle stated that Paul was seeking a *master–slave relationship*, even though Suzanne resisted this.

Tom was in his early fifties and a bachelor, while Carol was twenty-one and also single. Tom's and Carol's relationship was informal. Carol often did out-of-office errands for Tom, and even drove to his home to pick things up for him. She felt very relaxed with her manager and the two often had a laugh together. Tom liked Carol to look attractive in the workplace. He often commented on her clothing and appearance and liked her to wear feminine outfits like a skirt and blouse or a dress. He also controlled Carol's breaks and even her private life. Pringle classified this as a *father–daughter relationship*. The third pair was Mr Howard who was a divisional chief in his late forties, married with children. His secretary Jane was in her 30s and single. She did not use his first name. He made no requests for personal services and gave her no access to his diary. Jane felt undervalued and resented that he did not delegate more to her. Mr Howard wanted to desexualize the office atmosphere. He claimed that sexual attraction would weaken his authority and he believed that women tried to gain advantages by using sexuality. Pringle labelled this a formal, *professional relationship*. She then identified two other boss–secretary relationships. One was the *mother/nanny–son relationship* in which the secretary was the subject and the boss was positioned as the 'naughty boy'. The other was the *team relationship* which stressed equality and modernity, where the secretary worked with, rather than for, her boss. Pringle concluded that bosses exerted power over their secretaries by seeking to break down the barriers between their work and home lives by either getting them to perform non-work tasks; or by intruding into their non-work lives. Bosses controlled their secretaries by means of a detailed knowledge of their private lives.

Based on Pringle (1989).

Source: Copyright Grantland Enterprises; www.grantland.net.

Sexuality through informal relationships between employees in organizations can have both negative and positive aspects. The negative consequences for individuals and their fellow employees include creating jealousies; distractions from work; decreased productivity; increased errors; reduced professionalism; and exposure to sexual harassment. For the organization, the dangers include having to fire an employee; losing valuable talent; staff replacement costs; law suits; as well as bad publicity. There are positive consequences as a good work atmosphere can develop when informal relationships are encouraged. Rather than being a limitation on bureaucracy, sexuality can actually contribute to efficient operation. It can make work more fun and exciting for employees, thereby reducing their absenteeism and latecoming, increasing their motivation and job satisfaction, and thus raising overall company performance. Some commentators have treated sexual behaviour as inappropriate, and as having nothing to do with work itself. However, they do acknowledge that sexuality is present within the workplace. Others say that informal relations are as important as formal relationships in order to motivate employees and make the organization function. An awareness of the effects of sexuality in the workplace provides a new perspective on organizational behaviour, and increases our ability to understand and manage it.

Home viewing

Erin Brockovich (2000, director Steven Soderbergh) is an unemployed single mother (played by Julia Roberts) with three children. After losing a car accident personal injury claim in court, she joins her attorney's law firm as a filing clerk. She discovers a systematic cover-up of the poisoning of a town's water supply by the Pacific Gas and Electric Company. The film demonstrates the sexualization of work. Brockovich makes her sexuality explicit in the way that she dresses and behaves. She wears her long blonde hair loosely, and dresses in tight, low-cut tops, short skirts, see-through blouses, and high heels. Her sexuality and lack of self-control is shown as disrupting and threatening order in the office. Observe how she uses her sexual skills on a young male worker to obtain official documents. How does she persuade the working-class families of the town to agree to become plaintiffs in the law suit?

For further information about sexuality, feminine relational skills, gender stereotypes and power themes in this movie, see Bell (2008).

Roles in organizations

Role the pattern of behaviour expected by others from a person occupying a certain position in an organization hierarchy.

Roles are a central feature of every organization structure, and are specified in the organization hierarchy. All organization structuring occurs through the specification of the roles that employees are expected to play. It follows that if individuals occupying different positions in the hierarchy have mutual and complementary expectations, then the patterning and predictability of their behaviour is increased. The formal positions identified on an organization chart of a company imply the expectation of certain behaviours from any person occupying that office. This becomes the person's role. Roles are thus associated with positions in the organization and are involved in interactions. A single person plays many different and sometimes conflicting roles in life, both sequentially and simultaneously (e.g., mother, team leader, union official).

Subordinate swapping

The roles we play in organizations affect our behaviour. One company used role theory to resolve employee performance problems. Department managers met regularly to consider the possibility of exchanging their 'worst' performing subordinates. These discussions were based on the assumption that poor performance was the result of the role that a person was being asked to perform in the company. That is, that there were role expectations that the person could not meet. The company philosophy was that there were no 'bad' people (individuals with poor attitude, inadequate motivation or the wrong personality), but only individuals who were occupying roles that were unsuitable for them. The trading was a way of finding the poorly performing employee a different and more suitable role in the organization.

Based on Gray and Starke (1984, p.124).

People's roles in organizations are ranked by status. Individuals occupying the role of managers are generally accorded more status that those occupying that of cleaner. In other companies, the ranking of roles is less obvious. John van Maanen (1991) described the rank ordering of occupations at Disneyland:

1. Disneyland Ambassadors and Tour Guides. These were the upper class, prestigious, bilingual women in charge of ushering tourists through the park.

2. Ride operators who either performed skilled work such as live narration, or who drove costly vehicles such as antique trains, horse drawn carriages or the Monorail.

3. All the other ride operators.

4. Sweepers who kept the concrete grounds clean were designated as *proles*.

5. There was a still lower, fifth category of *sub-prole* or peasant status.

6. The 'lowest of the low' included food and concession workers, pancake ladies, peanut pushers, coke blokes, suds drivers and soda jerks.

Organizations are, to a degree, co-operative arrangements that are characterized by give-and-take, mutual adjustment and negotiation. Their members get on with one another, often without explicit guidance, instruction or direction. The concept of role aids our understanding of this aspect of organizational life by stressing that employees monitor and direct their own work behaviour in the light of what they know is expected of them.

STOP AND THINK It is common for people to refer to an organizational title or position (e.g. supervisor, scientist, manager) as the supervisor's role, scientist's role and manager's role, as though it were merely an established way of referring to these positions. What assumptions and problems does this use of the concept fail to appreciate?

Philip Zimbardo
(b.1933)

Many of the tasks involved in any job have been learned and assimilated so well by the employee that they become accepted as being part of the person. It raises the question of whether, in behaving in a certain way, we are ourselves or just conforming to what the organization (and society) expects of us. Role relationships therefore are the field within which behaviour occurs. People's behaviour at any given moment, is the result of:

- their personalities;
- their perception and understanding of each other;
- their attitudes to the behavioural constraints imposed by the role relationship;
- the degree of their socialization with respect to constraints;
- their ability to inhibit and control their behaviours.

Prison experiment

Do our attitudes, values and self-image affect how we play roles in organizations (e.g. of a student, lecturer, doctor or doorman) or is it those organizational roles that determine our attitudes, values and self-image? In a classic experiment, Philip Zimbardo created his own prison at Stanford University to answer this question. He selected 21 young men who had responded to a newspaper advertisement, interviewing them to ensure they were mature, emotionally stable, normal, intelligent North American male students from middle class homes with no criminal record. Each volunteer was paid $15 a day to participate in a two week study of prison life. A toss of a coin arbitrarily designated these recruits as either prisoners or guards. Hence, at the start of the study, there were no measurable differences between the two groups assigned to play the two roles (10 prisoners and 11 guards).

Those taking the role of guards had their individuality reduced by being required to wear uniforms, including silver reflector glasses which prevented eye-contact. They were to be referred to as Mr Correction Officer by the prisoners, and were given symbols of their power which included clubs, whistles, hand-cuffs and keys. They were given minimal instructions by Zimbardo, being required only to 'maintain law and order'. While physical violence was forbidden, they were told to make up and improvise their own formal rules to achieve the stated objective during their 8-hour, 3-man shifts.

Those assigned the role of prisoners were unexpectedly picked up at their homes by a city policeman in a squad car. Each was searched, hand-cuffed, finger-printed, booked in at the Palo Alto police station, blindfolded and then transferred to Zimbardo's 'Stanford County Prison' in the basement of the university's psychology building. Each prisoner's sense of uniqueness and prior identity was minimized. They were given smocks to wear and had nylon stocking caps on their heads to simulate baldness. Their personal effects were removed; they had to use their ID numbers; and were housed in stark cells. All this made them appear similar to each other and indistinguishable to observers. Six days into the planned 14-day study, the researchers had to abandon the experiment. Why?

In a matter of days, even hours, a strange relationship began to develop between the prisoners and their guards. Some of the boy guards began to treat the boy prisoners as if they were despicable animals, and began to take pleasure in psychological cruelty. The prisoners in turn became servile, dehumanized robots who thought only of their individual survival, escape and mounting hatred of the guards. About a third of the guards became tyrannical in their arbitrary use of power, and became quite inventive in developing techniques to break the spirit of the prisoners, and to make them feel worthless. Having crushed a prison rebellion, the guards escalated their aggression, and this increased the prisoners' sense of dependence, depression and helplessness. Within 36 hours, the first 'prisoner' had to be released because of uncontrolled crying, fits of rage, disorganized thinking and severe depression. Others begged to be paroled and nearly all were willing to forfeit their money if the guards agreed to release them.

Zimbardo attributed these changes to a number of causes. First, the creation of a new environment within which both groups were separated from the outside world. New attitudes were developed about this new 'mini-world', as well as what constituted appropriate behaviour within it. Second, that within this new 'mini-world' of the prison, the participants were unable to differentiate clearly between the role that they were asked to play (prisoner or guard) and their real self. A week's experience of imprisonment (temporary) appeared to undo a lifetime of learning. Human values and self-concepts were challenged, and the pathological side of human nature was allowed to surface. The prisoners became so programmed to think of themselves as prisoners, that when their requests for parole were

(a)   (b)

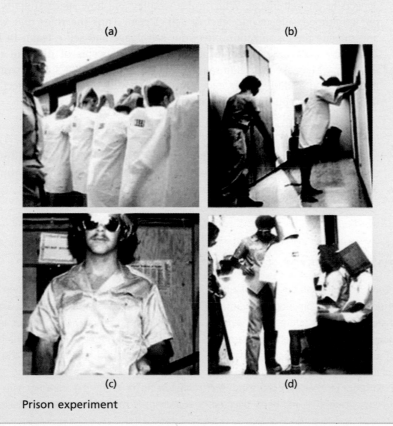

(c)   (d)

Prison experiment

→

refused, they returned docilely to their cells, instead of feeling capable of just withdrawing from an unpleasant psychological research experiment.

Zimbardo concluded that individual behaviour is largely under the control of social and environmental forces, rather than being the result of personality traits, character or willpower. In an organizational context such as a prison, merely assigning labels to people and putting them in situations where such labels acquire validity and meaning, appears sufficient to elicit a certain type of behaviour. The power of the prison environment was stronger than each individual's will to resist falling into his role. Zimbardo considered the relevance of the findings of his research, conducted in the 1970s, with the behaviour of US soldiers in Abu Ghraib prison in Baghdad in 2004.

Based on Zimbardo (2007); Photos from http://thesituationist.wordpress.com/2008/04/28/ lessons-learned-from-the-abughraib-horrors/. Archive for April 2008, 'Lessons from the Abu Ghraib Horrors', posted by Philip Zimbardo, 28 April 2008.

Home viewing

Das Experiment (2001, director Oliver Hirschbiegel) is a German film (with local language subtitles), based on Philip Zimbardo's Stanford experiment. The first half of the film shows the research but then, to achieve dramatic effect, it moves into fiction. As you watch the first part of the film, focus on how the research subjects, who had never been in a prison before, fall into their defined organizational roles. Ask yourself, how did they know how to behave in these new circumstances? Consider how you would have behaved in similar circumstances.

Role conflict the simultaneous existence of two or more sets of role expectations on a focal person in such a way that compliance with one makes it difficult to comply with the others.

The roles that we play are part of our self-concept, and personality theory tells us that we come to know ourselves through our interactions with others. We play different roles throughout our lives, and these require us to use different abilities, thereby adding more aspects to our self-image. Which roles we play and how successfully we play them during our adulthood, affects our level of self-esteem. Thus the roles that we play both inside and outside the organization affect our self-image and self-esteem. In his research, Philip Zimbardo showed that people possess mental concepts of different roles, and conform to them when asked or required to do so (Zimbardo, 2007). The woman who is both a manager and a mother may experience **role conflict** when the expectations in these two important roles pull her in opposite directions.

STOP AND THINK Identify any two roles that you currently occupy simultaneously in different social contexts, e.g. work, home, leisure. Identify a role conflict that you regularly experience as a result of such multiple role occupancy.

Changing roles: master and servant?

Sharon Bolton and Carol Boyd studied the work of airline cabin crew. In an effort to gain a competitive advantage through superior customer service, international airlines have introduced highly selective recruitment programmes for cabin crew staff that identify those applicants who possess the particular qualities required for the job. However, contrary to popular belief, possessing the 'right' personality, is not enough. Having been selected, successful candidates undergo intensive training and culture management programmes. The airline goes to great lengths to inculcate its values into its new hires. Interestingly, customer service training takes the same amount of training time as safety and emergency training; while training in areas relating to the health and well-being of crew (e.g. dealing with violence, manual handling) is minimal or may not take place at all. The resounding message received by cabin crews is that what is most important is how they present themselves to passengers. As one respondent noted, 'Over the years the airline industry has taught its cabin crews to be very subservient.' Flight attendants, like organizational actors, are asked to assume a particular identity that helps them to perform their work role more efficiently. In their case, they are asked to assume the status of servant in relation to the customer who is the master.

One respondent stated that crew encountered verbal abuse on a daily basis; and that many people had no respect for them, seeing them as servants who were expected to carry their bags and place them in the over-

head lockers. Another flight attendant with 21 years of experience who had had to suffer passenger rudeness, said that the 'passenger is always right' and they are fully aware of this; and take advantage of the situation. They know that they can say anything they like to cabin staff, usually do, and get away with it. The airline requires the work routines to be predictable and to correspond continually to predetermined standards. Temporal and spatial constraints mean that there is little room for any variation in routine: the airline needs to be able to rely on employees to give a homogeneous role performance on every occasion.

Based on Bolton and Boyd (2003).

Source: Peter Jordan/Alamy

Formalization

Rules procedure or obligations explicitly stated and written down in organization manuals.

Defining characteristics of every bureaucratic structure are its rules. From the 1930s, senior managements in large organizations increasingly adopted systems of bureaucratic (rule-governed) control. Formalization became widespread. This complemented the control exercised through machinery, and replaced that exercised through supervisory commands. Rules serve to regulate and control what individuals do and, to the extent that employees comply with company rules, they can ensure the predictability of human behaviour within organizations. Both parties benefit. For employees, rational and fair rules avoid managers' personal biases. This is true despite the fact that the rules are devised and policed by management, who could relax or ignore them at their discretion. Unions use rules to restrict the arbitrary power of employers, and demarcation rules protect jobs. Although rules can cause frustration to employees, they also reduce role ambiguity, and offer them high organizational identification and low self-estrangement.

Formalization the degree to which an organization has written rules, operating procedures, job descriptions, organizational charts and uses formal, written communication.

Management also benefits from rules. It uses formal rules and procedures to co-ordinate the activities of different employees, and establish conformity. Bureaucratic structures create job hierarchies with numerous job titles, each with its own pay rate. Elaborate formal rules (based on apparently 'objective' criteria) provide a basis for evaluating employee performance and determining rewards. This allows results to be traced back to the individual employee. This is all part of management's attempt to 'routinize' tasks which, together with the use of forecasting, planning, creating buffer stocks, and so on, seeks to remove the uncertainties involved in dealing with the environment. Provided that that environment is stable and unchanging, it is likely to be an effective strategy.

All over in a flash

'The first thing the three technicians pouring the uranium oxide solution into a precipitation tank at Tokaimura on September 30, 1999 noticed was a blue flash. Then they began to experience waves of nausea and some difficulty in breathing. What they did not realize was that they had accidentally dumped in more than six times as much fissile uranium as they had meant to, and had therefore triggered a runaway chain reaction . . . In one sense, they were lucky. They poured in 16kg of the solution. Had they poured in 40kg, they could have built themselves an amateur nuclear bomb.'

Popular management and media writers consistently condemn the effects of bureaucracy, calling instead for employees to use their own initiative; not be bound by rules, to look at the 'bigger picture'; avoid rigid, programmed behaviour, etc. However, the moment that an accident occurs, being it rail, road, aircraft, space or, as in this case, nuclear, the search is on for those who failed to adhere strictly to the rules and procedures that had been set down. A consideration of the main features of bureaucracy illustrates that it was precisely such occurrences, that this form of organization structure sought to anticipate and avoid. In the case of the uranium-processing plant in Tokaimura, initial reports identified four causes of the accident:

1. The company had illegally compiled a manual which encouraged workers to cut corners in order to reduce costs. Instead of dissolving the uranium-nitrate acid in a cylindrical tower through which nitrogen gas is bubbled for three hours to agitate the mixture, as officially specified, the workers were instructed to mix it by hand in 10-litre, stainless steel buckets, and to tip their contents into the precipitation tank.

2. The workers making the fuel lacked the knowledge and experience to do it correctly and safely.

3. Because the workers were allowed to bypass the time-consuming mixing process in the tower, with its automatic control controls for preventing such things happening, they were free to dump their material into a vessel that was not designed to take it. This further aggravated the problem.

4. The company procedure did not anticipate the possibility of such an accident occurring, and hence lacked any containment facility.

Two of the three workers inside the plant received more than the lethal dose of seven sieverts (a sievert is the unit that measures the intensity of radiation's impact on the body). Two workers died; a further 46 employees were exposed to radiation as they sought to contain the problem; and hundreds of local villagers were irradiated. The International Atomic Energy Agency classified the accident in Tokaimura, Japan as level 4 on a seven-point scale, making it the world's most serious since the level-7 disaster at Chernobyl in the Ukraine in 1986. Since then, falsification of inspection and repair reports in 2002 forced the temporary closure of 17 Japanese nuclear power plants; and a broken steam pipe that had not been inspected for two decades killed five workers in Western Japan. While bureaucratic rules and procedures may be in place, to ensure safety, they have to be actively enforced.

Based on The Economist *(1999b, 2000, 2006f).*

STOP AND THINK   Think of some of the rules that you have encountered in organizations to which you currently belong, or used to belong. How effective are they in directing the behaviour of individuals? What problems do they cause, and what advantages did they offer, and for whom?

Strengths and weaknesses of hierarchy of authority

John Child referred to the 'paradox in hierarchical organization'. He argued that the hierarchy of authority was responsible for most of the problems found within companies possessing bureaucratic organization structures. He explained that, 'Hierarchy is a means of getting work done through allocating tasks and responsibilities, as well as co-ordinating and controlling that work. At the same time, hierarchy is also the basis for distributing rewards, privileges, and powers differently, as well as creating different social identities. Fundamentally, this means that any organization based on hierarchy divides people at the same time as it endeavours to unite them. On the one hand, hierarchy provides a vertical division of labour for allocating different decisions and tasks to be undertaken within a collective effort. On the other hand, it takes on the attributes of a status ladder, distinguishing 'superiors' from 'inferiors' (Child, 2005, p.394).

The writers who are critical of bureaucracy have argued that the challenge for management is to create work environments in which employees have the opportunity to grow and to mature as individuals. In their view, this means moving away from bureaucratic organization forms and towards some other type of organization design. They say that in the twenty-first century, the bureaucratic organization will be too expensive to maintain; will be incapable of responding sufficiently quickly to change; and will not be using the innovative resources of its members. Failure to achieve profit targets will result in company collapse and large-scale redundancies. Their argument is that now that the slimming down has been completed in many companies, the new-look, leaner organizations are experimenting with radically different forms of structures which overcome the dysfunctions of bureaucracy (see Chapter 17).

Centralization v. decentralization

A fundamental question faced by every chief executive is what kinds of decisions are to be made and by whom. The answer determines both the distribution of power within an organization (see Chapter 22) and the allocation of company resources. Some senior executives prefer to retain decision-making power in their hands, and thus run highly centralized organizations. Centralization refers to the concentration of authority and responsibility for decision-making power in the hands of managers at the top of an organization's hierarchy. Others choose to delegate their power, giving junior managers individual autonomy; self-directed teams greater freedom; and introducing job enrichment for shop floor workers. Thus, their organizations are much more de-centralized in their structure. Decentralization refers to the downward dispersion of authority and responsibility for decision-making to operating units, branches and lower level managers. New technology has facilitated this by making information easily available to all levels of employees, right down to the shop floor. The question of whether and how much to centralize or decentralize, has been one of the major topics discussed in organization structuring. Each approach has its own advantages:

Centralization the concentration of authority and responsibility for decision-making power in the hands of managers at the top of an organization's hierarchy.

Decentralization the downward dispersion of authority and responsibility for decision-making to operating units, branches and lower level managers.

Centralization advantages

- A greater uniformity in decisions possible.
- Senior managers are more aware of an organization's future plans and are more likely to make decisions in its best interests.
- Fewer skilled (and highly paid) mangers are required.
- Greater control and cost effectiveness in company resources.
- Less extensive planning and reporting procedures are required.

Decentralization advantages

- Lower-level decisions can be made faster.
- Lower-level management problems can be dealt with quickly by junior staff.
- Lower-level managers have an opportunity to develop their decision-making skills.
- Increases creativity, innovation and flexibility.
- Increased motivation of lower-level employees entrusted to make decisions rather than always following orders issued at higher level.
- An organization's workload is spread so as to allow top-level managers more time for strategic planning.

 **STOP AND THINK** As a shop floor employee, would you prefer your company to be centralized or decentralized? Why?

A single organization can have a combination of both centralization and decentralization. Parts of Motorola are centralized, while other parts are not, and these change over time. Motorola's 'skunk works' are decentralized to encourage innovation, while its accountants are centralized – 'We don't want highly innovative financial accounting', said one of the company's senior managers. Centralization and decentralization also affect an organization's culture (see Chapter 4). A decentralized company which empowers its employees, and encourages and rewards creativity, creates a culture of innovation and risk taking. However, in certain organizations such as oil exploration platforms and nuclear power stations, it is important that employees do not make decisions on their own. Here, centralization can be used to create cultural values that reinforce rule-following, obedience to authority and sharing of information with managers.

Motorola and Microsoft

Twenty years ago, Motorola, the co-inventor of the mobile phone, was a tightly centralized business. Three men in its headquarters at Schaumburg, Illinois (including Bob Galvin, the founder's son), were in control of almost everything that went on. As the company grew, they decided to decentralize. But by the mid-1990s the company's mobile phone business was growing so fast that the decentralization made it impossible to control. 'While the numbers are getting bigger, an organization can be falling apart', says Pat Canavan, Motorola's chief governance officer. In 1998, the company laid off 25,000 people and repatriated control back to Schaumburg headquarters.

In 2005, Microsoft had a decentralized structure consisting of seven business units. The company's senior management decided that infighting, miscommunication and a lack of synergy between these units were causing slow product innovation. Their solution was centralization by merging the activities of these seven groups into three divisions – Business; Platform Products and Services; and Entertainment and Devices. The effect has been to concentrate decision-making in the hands of the three division directors, and to add an additional layer of hierarchy.

Based on Hindle (2006f).

Arthur Bedeian and Raymond Zammuto (1991) argued that the balance between centralization and decentralization changes on an on-going basis. It does so, in their view, in response to changes in company size, market opportunities, developments in new technology, and not least, the quality of existing decision-making. Somewhat more cynically, Anthony Jay (1970) felt that whichever of the two is currently the fashionable, it will be superseded by the other in due course. This may occur for no other reason than the incoming chief executive wishes to make a highly visible impact on their managers, employees, shareholders and financial analysts.

RECAP

1. *Explain how organization structure affects human behaviour in organizations.*

   - The procedures employees are required to follow, and the rules by which they are required to abide, all control and direct their behaviour in specified directions.

   - The roles that people play, and the expectations that others have of role holders, all direct the behaviour of employees. Indeed, in the long term, these may even lead to a change in personality of the employee.

2. *List the main elements of organization structure.*

   - The main elements include: chain-of-command; hierarchical levels; line employees; rules; staff employees; role expectations; span-of-control; departmentalization; authority; and job description.

3. *Relate the concept of span-of-control to the height of the organization hierarchy.*

   - The narrower the span-of-control, the taller the organization hierarchy (and vice versa); and the greater the consequences for employees of having one or the other.

4. *Identify line and staff relationships on an organization chart.*

   - Line relationships are depicted vertically on a organization chart, indicating that those above possess the authority to direct the behaviours of those below.

   - The seniors have responsibility for the work of the juniors, while the juniors are accountable for their work to their seniors.

   - Staff relationships are depicted horizontally on a organization chart, indicating that those who possess specific expertise e.g. in personnel, computing matters, advise those in line positions.

5. *Distinguish between the formal and the informal organization of a company.*

   - The formal organization refers to the collection of work groups that have been consciously designed by senior management to maximize efficiency and achieve organizational goals, while the informal organization refers to the network of relationships that spontaneously establish themselves between members of the organization on the basis of their common interests and friendships.

   - The two forms consist of the same people, albeit arranged in different ways.

6. *Understand the nature and impact of sexuality on organizational behaviour.*

   - Sexuality refers to sex roles, sexual preferences, sexual attractiveness and notions of masculinity and femininity in organizations.

   - Sexuality manifests itself in issues of sexual attractiveness; gender stereotyping; sex typing of jobs; the glass ceiling; the gender pay gap; work-life balance; office romances; sexual harassment and emotional labour.

Revision

1. Is hierarchical control an inevitable part of organization design or a just a management convenience? Discuss.

2. Suggest how an understanding of sexuality can help you to understand and manage the relationships within the informal organization.

3. What is meant by role? Suggest how a manager's role in an organization might be affected by (a) his or her level in the hierarchy; (b) the size of the organization and (c) its culture.

4. Consider the different types of rules to be found in organizations, and where they are to be found, giving examples from your personal experience. To what extent do rules control and make the behaviour of employees predictable, and to what extent are they ignored?

Research assignment Using the internet or personal contacts, find an organization which allows you to answer the following questions. What does its organizational chart look like? On what basis is it departmentalized? How many levels of hierarchy are there? What is the range of managers' span-of-control? Is decision-making centralized or decentralized? What staff functions are provided, and how do these relate to line personnel within the departments? How does the structure affect employees and managers? What are its advantages and disadvantages? If possible, interview employees or managers who work in the organization. Assess the effectiveness of this company's structure by relating it to the relevant theories, models and frameworks in the textbook and other reading.

Springboard

Duncan, R., 1979, 'What's the right organization structure?: Decision tree analysis provides the answer', *Organizational Dynamics*, 7(3): 59–80.

Provides a structured framework with which managers can determine which type of organization structure is most suitable for their particular company.

Fleming, P., 2007, 'Sexuality, power and resistance in the workplace', *Organization Studies*, 28(2): 239–56.

The author considers whether the expression of sexuality in organizations represents an opportunity for employee resistance or increased management control.

Galbraith, J.R., 1974, 'What's the point of organization structure?', *Interfaces*, 4(3): 28–36.

Discusses the function of organization structures as a basis for assessing the appropriateness of different types of structures for different companies.

Hinings, B. and Munro, R., 2003, '"Organization" and "disorganization"', in Westwood, R. and Clegg, S. (eds), *Debating Organization*, Blackwell Publishing, Oxford, pp.273–97.

Chapter 9 contains a debate between these two authors about the nature of organization structure.

 OB in films

Aliens (1986, directed by James Cameron): DVD track 15: 1:15:41–1:23:13 (8 minutes). The second film in this science fiction series is set in the distant future on planet LV-426. The characters include Lieutenant Gorman, the senior officer of space marines, Sergeant Apone, Corporal Hicks, Private Hudson and others. In addition to these military personnel, there is Burke, who represents the Weyland-Yutani Corporation, which owns the facilities on the planet, and Ripley (played by Sigourney Weaver), who is employed by it. The clip begins with Ripley shouting at Gorman 'Get them out of there, do it now', and ends at the point at which Corporal Hicks says 'It's the only way to be sure. Let's do it!' Which concepts of organizational structure are illustrated in this clip?

OB in literature

Kazuo Ishiguro, *The Remains of the Day*, Faber & Faber, 1989. Stevens has spent the best part of his life as head butler to Lord Darlington. He narrates the story, set before, during and just after the Second World War. He discusses his career and his relationships with his master, with the housekeeper and then with his new (American) master. The main characters are 'trapped' in their respective hierarchical roles in the social and organization structure of their time. This is a story of how one's place in an organization structure and definition of role expectations shapes role relationships and individual attitudes and behaviour in quite stark and poignant ways. What type of relationship does Stevens have (a) with the housekeeper and (b) with his own father? How are these relationships affected by the respective positions of these characters in the organization structure of the household?

CHAPTER EXERCISES

Reorganizing the American Paint Company

Objectives   1. To identify problems of inappropriate organization structure and to suggest solutions.

Briefing   Study the organizational chart of the American Paint Company. The company has grown over recent years without much attention being paid to its organization structure. There are now at least 15 problems. Focus on structural issues such as job titles, hierarchical levels, span-of-control and so on, identify what these problems are, and suggest how they might be solved.

Human button

Objectives   1. To list the elements of organization structure.

2. To identify examples of organization structure elements.

3. To assess how structure elements contribute to achieving organizational goals.

Briefing   1. What are the main organization structure elements/key terms? Can you define them?

2. Read the case study *Human Button* below, and look for examples of these.

3. What are this organization's goals? How does this organization structure operate to achieve them?

Human button

In 2010, the responsibility for the British nuclear deterrent rests with the Royal Navy. Its fleet of four ballistic submarines – the SSBNs (Ship Submersible Ballistic Nuclear) is based at Faslane in Scotland. One of the submarines – HMS *Vanguard*, *Victorious*, *Vigilant* or *Vengeance* – is always on patrol, undetectable, in the North Atlantic. They patrol for 90 days at a time; do not surface except in an emergency; and are not allowed any communication out of the boat. Every day, the captain is required to write a patrol report and a narration, explaining why certain things were done. Each SSBN is organized into departments, each headed by a senior officer who reports to the captain: Logistics

→

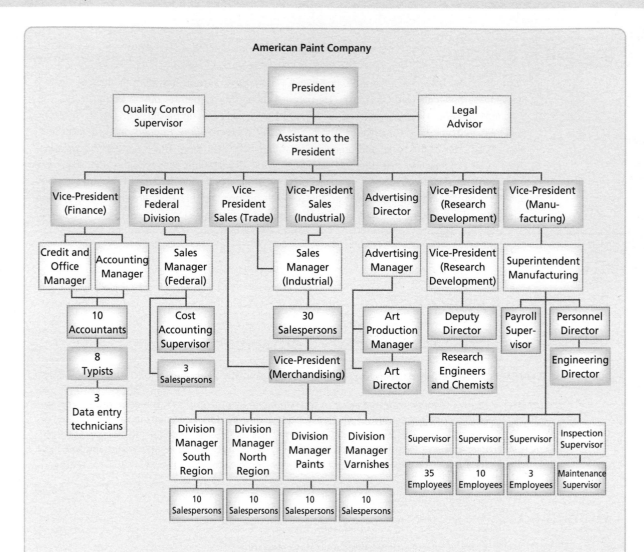

(divided into Catering Services; Supply Chain; and Personnel); Marine Engineering; Medical; Warfare; and Weapons Engineering. Only a few of the most senior officers are allowed to know its location. Each is armed with up to 16 Trident II, D5 submarine-launched, ballistic missiles whose destructive power is equivalent to all the explosives used in the Second World War. Even if the country has been utterly destroyed in a surprise attack, that one, lone submarine will always be ready and able to strike back with overwhelming force. That is the theory of nuclear deterrence.

There is a human button communication system that triggers the retaliation procedure and has many built-in, redundancy factors to anticipate problems. At one end of the communication chain is the British Prime Minister who makes the final decision. The PM's directive, detailing the target and release time, is sent from the government emergency room, somewhere below Whitehall. It is conveyed through his Chief of Defence Staff to the bunker facility at Northwood, under the Chiltern Hills in the South of England, known as 'The Hole'. Located there is Task Force 345's operations room from where the command and control of Britain's nuclear deterrent is exercised. At Northwood, the prime ministerial directive is authenticated, first by one A-list and then, one-B-list officer. The National Firing Message, as it is known, is then put onto the system and goes onto the broadcast, which is continuously transmitted to the SSBN at sea. On board the submarine, the firing order is scrutinized by two officers, and checked against codes in the submarine's safe. Three keys are engaged, and the captain gives the order to fire.

What happens if the Prime Minister is killed or The Hole is destroyed in a pre-emptive nuclear attack? In anticipation of this, the PM nominates an *alternate* – that is, a decision-maker from the Cabinet, who will make a decision in their place, if required. In addition, early in each new Prime Minister's tenure, the Cabinet Secretary briefs the PM on the choices to be made from beyond the grave. Since the 1960s, each Prime Minister has written what is known as a *Letter of Last Resort*. It details what the PM's wishes are in the event of a nuclear attack on the United Kingdom. There are believed to be four options: retaliate; do not retaliate; put yourself under the command of the United States or Australian Navy; or 'submarine captain to use his own judgement'. The Prime Minister makes his choice, writes the letter in long hand, signs it personally, and a copy of it is placed in the safe of each of the four nuclear submarines. Britain is the only nuclear power that uses this letter system. When the Prime Minister demits from office, his letter of last resort is destroyed unread.

In a deteriorating geo-political situation, if the submarine captain loses contact with Northwood, he first assures himself that Britain is an irradiated ruin and much of its population is dead. His orders are then to go, with his Executive Officer, to the safe in the submarine floor, remove the PM's letter of last resort, and act on its contents. However, it is not the captain who pulls the trigger. The submarine is brought up to hover position, still submerged, before firing, and the launch order is communicated by the captain to his Weapons Engineering Officer (known as 'The Weo'), who has the rank of Lieutenant Commander. It is he who pulls the trigger on the Colt 45 pistol handle whose wire runs from its butt. This allows the Weo to check other data on his control panels while holding the nuclear trigger in his hand. The trigger can only be activated if the captain turns a key on a panel in the control room. Below is the verbatim transcript of the final section of the launch procedure, as used in the practice drill. It represents the end of the firing chain which began with the Prime Minister's order. Below is the oral exchange between the commanding officer (A), and his various subordinates (B) who respond by confirming orders, and asking for permission. After the sound of a click, the Weo says 'One away'. The first missile will have gone, and the end of the world will have arrived:

A: *Hover command, commence hovering.*
B: *Commence hovering.*
A: *Stop engine.*
B: *Stop engine.*
A: *Ship control in condition 1SQ.*
B: *Condition 1SQ, Roger.*
A: *Weo in the missile control centre – clocks.*
B: *Check.*
A: *Come IRT.*
B: *Check.*
A: *Slow ready handover.*
B: *Semi-package has been shifted, we're on the active target package, in access to the safe, missile spinning up.*
A: *I have the system . . .*

A: *We are fire control. Fire control in condition 1SQ for strategic launch.*
B: *Fire control in condition 1SQ for strategic launch, Roger.*
A: *Command Weo, weapons system in condition 1SQ for strategic launch.*
B: *Weo requires permission to fire.*
A: *Supervisor Weo, initiate fire 1.*

(click)

Weo: One away

Case based on 'The human button', BBC Radio 4 programme, 2 December 2008: Richard Knight, 'Whose hand is on the button?', 2 December 2008, BBC website, http://news.bbc.co.uk/1/hi/uk/7758314.stm; Royal Navy website: http://royalnavy.mod.uk.

Chapter 16 Early organization design

Key terms

traditional authority

charismatic authority

legitimate authority

bureaucracy

managerial activities

managerial roles

contingency approach to organization structure

technological determinism

technical complexity

technological interdependence

mediating technology

long-linked technology

intensive technology

task variety

task analyzability

environmental determinism

mechanistic structure

organic structure

differentiation

integration

strategic choice

enacted environment

managerial enactment

resource dependence theory

vertical integration

Learning outcomes

When you have read this chapter, you should be able to define those key terms in your own words, and be able to:

1. Distinguish between charismatic, traditional and legitimate forms of authority.

2. State the main characteristics of a bureaucratic organization structure as specified by Max Weber.

3. Distinguish Fayol's six managerial activities and the main ideas of the classical management school.

4. Distinguish Mintzberg's ten managerial roles.

5. Identify the writers who comprize the early contingency approach and state their main individual contributions.

6. Discuss the strengths and weaknesses of early ideas on the design of organization structure and the practice of management.

7. Identify the influence of early organization design ideas on contemporary organizations.

Why study early organization design?

Organization design refers to the process by which managers select and manage various dimensions and components of organization structure so that it achieves their goals. Organization design affects what they and others do, and how they spend their time. Many textbooks mention early twentieth-century writings on organization design only briefly, before turning to explore team-based, network, virtual and similar contemporary developments in organization structure. This chapter will demonstrate that these early ideas, far from being either out-of-date or superseded, continue to exert a pervading influence on organizational life. In addition, their source and form, exercise a similar, enduring influence on modern management and organizational thinking.

Max Weber's ideas on bureaucracy were developed at the start of the twentieth century, and implemented from that time onwards. Today, the vast majority of employees in industrial societies around the world continue to work in bureaucratic organizations whose structures Weber would easily recognize. Moreover, they will continue to work under these structural arrangements for the foreseeable future. It is most likely that your own university is structured in this way. In contrast, at present, your chances of joining a so-called network or virtual organization are relatively slim. A significant feature of early management thought was its source and form. Little of it was based on systematic, empirical research. Max Weber was himself a historian and philosopher, while his contemporary, Henri Fayol, was a colliery manager. Fayol and his successors developed an approach to management knowledge which was based wholly on the experiences of, mainly successful, managers. Moreover, the form it took was of principles, based on that experience. Organization structure designs conceived in the past, which may have been updated, continue to have a significant impact upon the present. This raises a number of questions:

- What are the benefits and costs of a bureaucratic organization structure?

- Why have the early structure arrangements remained so influential?

- In what ways has bureaucracy become modified?

- What does this imply for the nature of jobs?

Max Weber and bureaucracy

Max Weber
(1864–1920)

Max Weber, a German sociologist and philosopher writing at the turn of the twentieth century, was the first to address the topic of organization structure in his theory of bureaucracy. If Frederick Taylor was interested in the 'one-best-way' to perform a task, Weber was interested in the one-best-way to structure an organization. Literally, bureaucracy means 'rule by office or by officials'. His work stemmed from his interest in power and authority. In this textbook, the term power is used to refer to the capacity of individuals to overcome resistance on the part of others, to exert their will, and to produce results consistent with their interests and objectives. Weber studied societies in history and distinguished three different types of authority – traditional, charismatic and legitimate authority.

It is legitimate authority that concerns us here, and it carries with it, position power. Because of the process of rationalism in modern society (the belief that the human mind can discover innate laws which govern the workings of the universe), legitimate authority has predominated. Bureaucracy is the form of organization structure associated with legitimate authority.

Within a bureaucracy, we do what managers, civil servants and university lecturers tell us, not because we think that they have a natural right to do so, or because they possess some divine power, but because we acknowledge that their exercise of power is legitimated and hence supported by two factors:

Legitimate authority based on formal, written rules which have the force of law, e.g. the authority of presidents, managers, lecturers.

- The demonstrable logical relevance of their requests, directions and instructions to us. Their commands must seem rational by being justified through their relevance to the tasks of the bureaucracy and ultimately, to its objectives.

- A shared belief in the norms and rules of the bureaucracy that have been arrived at rationally (not based on tradition or personal whim) and which possess a law-like character.

Traditional authority the belief that the ruler had a natural right to rule. This right was either God-given or by descent, e.g. the authority of kings and queens.

Weber believed that an organization based on legitimate authority would be more efficient than one based on either traditional or charismatic authority. This was because its continuity was related to formal structure and positions within it, rather than to a particular person who might leave or die. Not every formal organization will possess all the characteristics that Weber identified. However, the more of them that it has, the more closely it approximates to the 'ideal type' that he had in mind. Weber's description of bureaucracy is known as an 'ideal type'. It is not meant to describe any particular existing organization, but rather, it represents a model or a checklist, against which to compare and assess real organizations.

Characteristics of Weberian bureaucracy

1. *Work specialization*: The work is broken down into simple, routine and well-defined job tasks that are assigned to individuals to perform.

2. *Authority hierarchy*: Positions are in a hierarchy of authority, with each position under the authority of a higher one. A clear chain-of-command and workers clearly know to whom they are responsible.

3. *Employment and career*: All personnel are selected and promoted on the basis of their technical qualifications and offered a full time career.

4. *Recording*: Administrative acts and decisions are recorded in writing. Record keeping provides an organizational memory and continuity over time.

5. *Rules and procedures*: All employees are subject to rules and procedures that ensure reliable, predictable behaviour.

6. *Impersonality and impartiality*: Procedures and rules are impersonal, applying to managerial and non-managerial employees alike; and are applied in an unbiased way.

Based on Weber (1947, pp.328–37).

Charismatic authority the belief that the ruler had some special, unique virtue, either religious or heroic, e.g. the authority of religious prophets, charismatic politicians and film stars.

Bureaucracy legal–rational type of authority underpinning a form of organization structure that is characterized by a specialization of labour, a specific authority hierarchy, a formal set of rules, and a rigid promotion and selection criteria.

Weber used the term bureaucracy to describe a particular type of organization structure, that is, concerned how work was divided, co-ordinated and controlled. It was a structure that was both impersonal and rational. Whereas in the past, authority had been based on nepotism, whim or fancy, in bureaucratic organizations, it was based on rational principles. For this reason, it offered the possibility of being the most efficient ever, in comparison with what had preceded it. Bureaucracy for him was a form of organization that emphasized speed, precision, regulation, clarity, reliability and efficiency. This was achieved through creating a fixed division of tasks, imposing detailed rules, regulations and procedures and monitoring through hierarchical supervision.

Many aspects of Weber's model reflected the organizational circumstances at the time in which he was writing. In the early twentieth century, establishing employment relationships on the basis of professional selection, and creating continuity of employment and career structures, was important when the methods commonly used at the time were amateur, personal and haphazard. Because they were adopted so widely, so long ago, it is difficult to believe that there was a time when organizations did not keep detailed written records.

The strength of bureaucracy lay in its standardization. Employee behaviour was controlled and made predictable. In Weber's conception, this was achieved not through time-and-motion study, but through the application of rules, regulations and procedures. This ensures that different people in the same organization carry out their work in the same way. Bureaucratic organizations have a reasonably consistent set of goals and preferences. They devote few resources to time-consuming information searches or the analysis of current activities to check if these are meeting stated goals. Instead, they rely on rules, tradition, precedent and standard operating procedures. Little time is spent on decision-making since decisions follow from the established routines, and few action alternatives are considered. The ideological emphasis is on stability, fairness and predictability (Pfeffer, 1981).

Weber was struck by how the bureaucratic structure of a company routinized the processes of its administration, in a way similar to how a machine routinized production. Weber's ideas developed independently, but neatly complement those of Frederick Taylor's. While Taylor focused on the worker on the shop floor, Weber's interest lay in a body of knowledge, administrative rules and organization hierarchy, progressing from the top of the organization downwards. Nevertheless, Weber would have approved of the disciplining, rational conditioning and training of workers proposed by Taylor. Different organizations can be compared in terms of the degree of their bureaucratization using the previously defined dimensions of job specialization, hierarchy, span-of-control, chain of command, departmentalization, formalization and centralization.

Bureaucrats look to Kafka

France has created a 'Kafka index' that measures the complexity of a project or law against its usefulness to cut red tape. The index's name refers to Franz Kafka's novel *The Trial*, which describes one man's fight against a nightmarish bureaucracy. It uses a scale of one to 100, measuring how many hurdles, forms, letters or phone calls are needed to win state permits or aid for a project.

'It is an indicator to measure objectively the most complex procedures so that we can simplify them', said a government spokesman. The index will be regularly updated on a website, raising the prospect of a hit parade of France's most Kafkaesque ministries.

From Samuel (2006, p.17).

In modern usage, the term bureaucracy has acquired a pejorative meaning amongst the public and the media. For example, when people come up against obstructiveness in any aspect of organizational life, they complain about there being 'too much red tape'. In response, governments and companies promise to remove or reduce it. Weber's view was in direct opposition to this. For him, bureaucracy was the most efficient form of social organization precisely because it was coldly logical and did not allow personal relations or feelings to get in the way of achieving goals. Rules and bureaucratic procedures provide a standard way of dealing with employees that avoids favouritism and personal bias. Everyone knows what the rules are and receives equal treatment. However, there is often frustration at having to follow what appear to be seemingly illogical rules, and thereby experience delays. This change in meaning has occurred because the principles of bureaucracy, originally designed to maximize efficiency, also resulted in inefficiencies. These negative aspects, costs or 'dysfunctions' of bureaucracy were the focus of debates in organizational behaviour during the 1950s and 1960s (Merton, 1940; Gouldner, 1954; Blau, 1966).

In contrast, there are other writers who are supportive of bureaucratic organization structures, in part or in whole. They note that most large organizations possess many of the features of Weber's model; and that their longevity and continued existence, confirms that they can achieve an acceptable level of efficiency. In contrast, they cite examples of companies which have not adopted bureaucratic features and have failed. There is a prevailing view that organizations should be structured on the basis of rationality. This means that organization designers should accept that a hierarchical structure is more likely to produce rational decisions and better control within the organization than any other structure of authority (for example, one based on teams).

Table 16.1: Positive and negative consequences of a bureaucracy

Characteristic	Positive consequence	Negative consequences	
		For the individual	**For the organization**
1. Work/job specialization	Produces efficient, repetitive working	Over specialization of employees' skills and knowledge prevents them recognizing or caring about problems not in their domain	Inhibits rotation and hence flexible use of personnel, and thus can reduce overall productivity
2. Authority hierarchy	Clarifies who is in command	Prevents employees contributing to decisions	Allows errors to be hidden
3. Employment and career	Most appropriate person appointed to a position	Can restrict the psychological growth of the individual in their job	Individuals throughout the company are promoted to their level of incompetence
4. Recording	Creates an organization history that is not dependent on individual memory	Employees come to see record-keeping as an end in itself rather than means to an end	Recorded precedents stifle attempts at company innovation; inhibits flexibility, adaptability and responsiveness
5. Rules and procedures	Employees know what is expected of them	Introduces delays; stifles initiative and creativity	Leads to individual and sub-unit goals replacing organization objectives; rules define *minimum* levels of acceptable performance
6. Impersonality	Fosters efficiency, reduces bias	Dehumanizes those it purports to serve – officials prevented from responding to unique features of clients who are treated as standard cases	Creates a climate of alienation through the firm as employees come to see themselves as small cogs in a wheel

Insufficient bureaucracy?

Two of the most important requirements for the operation of an efficient bureaucracy are rule-following and recording. Rules and procedures within organizations are designed to make the behaviour of different employees and departments consistent and predictable. It is only when they are broken or not followed, that outsiders get to hear about them. In 2007, Her Majesty's Revenue and Customs (HMRC), a government department, lost two CDs containing the (password-protected but not unencrypted) personal and financial details of 25 million British households relating to child benefit payments. The data were sent by TNT courier service from the HMRC offices in Washington, Tyne-and-Wear to the National Audit Office in London. The two institutions should have transmitted the information using the secure government intranet which had been established at the cost of tens of million of pounds. The Prime Minister commented on the problem of 'enforcing procedures'. The Poynter Report that investigated the disk loss said it was 'entirely avoidable'.

In 2008, Her Majesty's Crown Court Prosecution Service Inspectorate, an independent body, assessing the operation of the Crown Court Prosecution Service (CPS) in England and Wales concluded that, 'the majority of CPS files are not maintained in a satisfactory way'. It concluded a third of all prosecution files had not been properly maintained. Omissions concerned the listing of defendants' bail status; requests for follow-up work; and the recording of the outcome of hearings. The inspectorate stated that court cases were being dropped because prosecutors were not keeping up to date with the paperwork. The CPS denied that these problems regularly led to cases being abandoned. Both events illustrate the failure to conform to Weber's bureaucratic organization principles. In the first case, principle 5 – rules and procedures were broken; while in the second, principle 4 – recording – was breached.

Based on The Economist *(2008e);*
BBC News Channel *(2007c); Allen, N. (2008).*

© Copyright 2007 Scott Adams, Inc.

Henri Fayol and classical management theory

Henri Fayol
(1841–1925)

Classical management theory resembles bureaucracy even though it originated in France in the early twentieth century with the work of Henri Fayol. Fayol qualified as a mining engineer in 1860 after which he joined the Commentary-Fourchambault combine, a company in which he was to spend his entire working life. In 1866, he became manager of the Commentary collieries and, in 1888 at the age of 47, he was appointed to the general manager position at a time when the financial position of the company was critical. By the time he retired in 1918, he had established financial stability in the organization. Fayol's list of managerial activities provides a definition of management. Indeed, he is credited with 'inventing' management, that is, distinguishing it as a separate activity, and defining its constituent elements. Interestingly, the word *management* is not translatable into all languages, nor does the concept exist in all cultures. Managing of course occurs, but is not always treated as anything special or separate.

It was in 1916, the year after Frederick Taylor died, that Fayol's book, *General and Industrial Administration* was published. In it, Fayol put down in a systematic form, the experience that he had gained while managing a large organization. He stressed methods rather than personalities, seeking to present the former in a coherent and relevant scheme. This formed his theory of organization. While Taylor focused on the worker on the shop floor – a bottom-up approach, Fayol began from the top of the hierarchy and moved downwards. However, like Taylor, he too believed that a manager's work could be reviewed objectively, analyzed and treated as a technical process which was subject to certain definite principles which could be taught. Fayol identified six managerial activities that supported the operation of every organization and needed to be performed to ensure its success. Although his list of management activities was originally developed over 80 years ago, it continues to be used to this day. It is shown in Table 16.2.

The six management activities are interrelated. For example, a company management team begins by *forecasting* the demand for its product, for example, steel wire. It requires a sales forecast and will use market research to develop one. Once it is clear that there is a market for the product, the next activity, *planning*, will take place. For Fayol, planning

Managerial activities activities performed by managers that support the operation of every organization and need to be performed to ensure its success.

Table 16.2: Fayol's six managerial activities

Forecasting	Predicting what will happen in the future
Planning	Devising a course of action to meet that expected demand.
Organizing	Mobilizing materials and resources by allocating separate tasks to different departments, units and individuals.
Commanding	Providing direction to employees, now more commonly referred to as *directing* or *motivating*.
Co-ordinating	Making sure that activities and resources are working well together towards the common goal.
Controlling	Monitoring progress to ensure that plans are being carried out properly.

involved, 'making a programme of action to achieve an objective'. He collectively referred to the two activities, forecasting and planning, as *purveyance*. Because they are so closely related, some authors and books treat them as a single management activity.

Having made the plan, the third activity to be performed is *organizing*. This involves bringing together the money, materials and people needed to achieve the objective. It also involves breaking down the main task into smaller pieces, and distributing them to different people. In a company structured along functional lines (accounting, production, marketing), the organizing of people may involve creating a special, temporary project team, consisting of members from the different functions. This is the matrix structure to be discussed in a later chapter.

Fayol used the word, *commanding*, to describe his fourth management activity. It has been defined as, 'influencing others towards the accomplishment of organizational goals'. We would now refer to it as either *directing* or *motivating*. Whichever term is chosen, performing this activity involves the manager ensuring that employees give of their best. To do this, managers must possess a knowledge of both the tasks to be done and of the people who are to do them. This management activity is mainly, although not exclusively, performed in a face-to-face situation. Earlier, organizing involved distributing task elements to various individuals. Now those separate elements have to be brought together. This represents the *co-ordinating* activity. Co-ordination can be achieved through memos, meetings and personal contacts between the people carrying out their unique activities.

The sixth and final activity of managers is *controlling*. This involves monitoring how the objectives set out in the plan are being achieved, with respect to the limitations of time and budget that were imposed. Any deviations are identified, and action taken to rectify them. It may be that the original plan will have to be amended. Although the six managerial activities have been presented as a sequence, in reality they occur simultaneously in a company. However, forecasting and planning tend to be primary. There are also loops when original plans have to be changed because certain resources are found to be unavailable (when organizing) or when cost overruns are discovered (through controlling).

Fayol's ideas are referred to as *classical management theory* (also dubbed, *scientific administration*). Many felt that these mirrored, at the macro-organizational level, what scientific management offered at the micro-organization level. Classical management considered that there is one, best organization structure which would suit all organizations, irrespective of their size, technology, environment or employees. This structure was based on the application of certain key principles which reflected the 'logic of efficiency' which stressed:

- functional division of work;
- hierarchical relationships;
- bureaucratic forms of control;
- narrow supervisory span;
- closely prescribed roles.

Airbus 380: a failure of coordination

The Airbus 380 passenger jet was unveiled in January 2005 in a grand ceremony in France. Six months later, a series of delivery delays began to be announced. Heads rolled, both at Airbus and its parent company, EADS. The immediate cause of the problem was a breakdown in the snap-together, final assembly process in Toulouse. The A380s rear fuselages are made in Hamburg, and are supposed to arrive in Toulouse with all their wiring ready to plug into the forward parts coming in from factories in north and west France.

Each A380 contains 500km of wiring, weighing 580 tonnes with 100,000 electrical connections, and this is woven through its walls and floor (see diagram below). When the two halves of the airplane arrived, they did not match up. The wires were too short to connect up with each other. Hamburg's failure to use the latest three-dimensional modelling software meant that nobody anticipated the effect of using lightweight aluminium wiring rather than copper. The aluminium makes the bends in the wiring looms bulkier. Worse still, engineers who scrambled to fix the problem did so in different ways. So the early aircraft all have their own, one-of-a-kind wiring systems. The greater complexity of the super-jumbo has shown up the weaknesses of Airbus's production system, and highlighted the need for a higher level of co-ordination.

Based on The Economist *(2006g);* Fortune *(2007).*

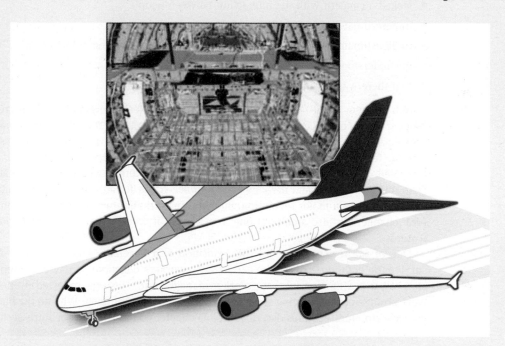

Source: www.popularmechanics.com

 **STOP AND THINK**   What are the advantages and disadvantages of having management principles based on the experience of successful managers?

Criticism of classical management

When considering classical management theory, it is important to locate it in its historical context. The managers of the period were dealing with larger, more complex organizations than had existed hitherto. At the beginning of the twentieth century many new companies developed. They employed vast numbers of people, had numerous plants and employed new technologies. All of this needed co-ordinating. With no model or experience to fall back on, those who managed these organizations had no choice but to develop their own principles and theories as to what to do to run them well. Inevitably these principles were grounded in their day-to-day experience of managing, and owed much to the models offered by military, religious and governmental organizations. Over the years, various writers have criticized Fayol's principles (Thomas, 2003; Child, 1969, March and Simon, 1958; Peters and Waterman, 1982). Their criticisms include:

- misleadingly proposed a single, standardized organizational model as the optimum one;
- promoted a militaristic, mechanistic organization, which stressed discipline, command, order, subordinates and *esprit de corps*;
- overlooked the negative consequences of tight control and narrow task specialization which can demotivate employees and hinder efficiency;
- over-emphasized an organization's formal structure, while neglecting processes such as conflict management, decision-making and communication;
- underestimated the complexity of organizations;
- were based on unreliable personal knowledge, rather than systematic research evidence;
- lacked a concern with the interaction between people;
- underestimated the effects of conflict;
- underestimated the capacity of individual workers to process information;
- misunderstood how people thought;
- that there was no one-best-way of organizing a company.

Gareth Morgan (1989) presents a continuum of different organization structural forms ranging from a bureaucratic one possessing classical features at one extreme, to an flexible, organic structure at the other (see Figure 16.1). The latter possesses little task specialization, few rules, a high degree of individual responsibility and authority, and much delegated decision-making authority. He stated that a bureaucracy could probably evolve from numbers 1 to 3, and perhaps even number 4. But for an organization to move to 5 or 6 would require a major revolution. Such a transformation would require not only a structural change, but also a cultural one. If achieved, it would mean a loss of its bureaucratic features.

One of the few examples of this transition is a Brazilian company called Semco. To survive the liquidity crisis of the early 1990s, workers negotiated a pay cut, coupled with a shift towards a more democratic worker management. This was reflected in more flexible work arrangements involving self-managed teams and outsourcing. Why do the bureaucratic-classical structural features described in this chapter continue to be a feature of the majority

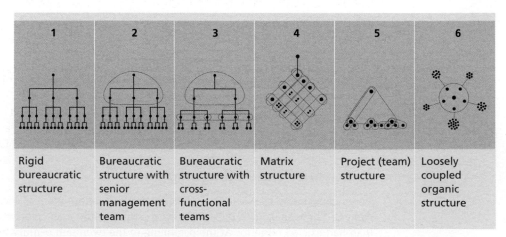

Figure 16.1: Types of organization structure
Source: From Morgan (1989, p.66).

of large companies to the present day? Stephen Robbins and Timothy Judge (Robbins, 1990; Robbins and Judge, 2007) suggested seven reasons to account for their continued existence:

1. *Success*: for the most part, over the last 100 years, irrespective of technology, environment and people, and irrespective of whether it has been a manufacturing, medical, educational, commercial or military organization, it has worked.

2. *Large size*: successful organizations survive and grow large, and the bureaucratic form is most efficient with large size.

3. *Natural selection favours bureaucracy*: bureaucracy's natural features, the six identified at the start of this chapter, are inherently more efficient than any others, and thus allow the organization to compete more effectively.

4. *Static social values*: the argument is that Western values favour order and regimentation and bureaucracy is consistent with such values. People are goal-oriented and comfortable with authoritarian structures. For example, workers prefer clearly defined job responsibilities.

5. *Environmental turbulence is exaggerated*: the changes currently being experienced may be no more dynamic than those at other times in history. Management strategies can also reduce uncertainty in the environment.

6. *Emergence of professional bureaucracy*: bureaucracy has shown its ability to adjust to the knowledge revolution, by modifying itself. The goal of standardization has been achieved in a different way among professional employees.

7. *Bureaucracy maintains control*: bureaucracy provides a high level of standardization, coupled with centralized power, which is desired by those in command. For this reason senior managers who control large organizations favour this organization design.

Harold Leavitt (2005) too believed that the bureaucratic hierarchy in modern organizations was increasing rather than declining, and it was being helped by advances in technology. The authoritarian structures remain intact today, but are cloaked by a veil of humanism. According to Leavitt, organizational hierarchies are particularly resilient, managing to change, while retaining their basic nature. They can favour one management style over others (participate, analytical or 'hot groups'), and make that the basis of their organizational culture. They can also isolate some of their characteristics in separated subunits (e.g. Xerox's Palo Alto Research Centre) whose creation involved separating a 'hot group' from the rest of the company. They can break into smaller units; form into matrix structures; and even use technology to get rid of people. Despite these transmutations, the basic core of the hierarchical management model remains unharmed.

In modern organizations, power and authority continue to lie with those at the top of the hierarchy. This hierarchy, argues Child (2005, p.394), panders to some of the weaknesses in human nature. It

> offers some people better rewards than others, often on the basis of seniority rather than performance; it indulges people's need to feel more important than others; gives people a sense of personal progression through promotion up the ladder and legitimizes the exercises of power by some people over others.

Both of the last reasons of Robbins and Child can explain the appeal of bureaucratic structures to senior management. It centralizes power in their hands, and allows them to control those at the bottom of the hierarchy. In the end, the decision to replace bureaucracy may be a political one.

Rigid bureaucratic structure

This is Weber's classic bureaucratic structure. The organization operates in a very stable environment. Its structure is pyramid-shaped, and under the control of a single chief executive. Since all important principles have been codified, and since every contingency is understood and has been anticipated, it is unnecessary for the executive to hold meetings.

Bureaucratic structure with senior management team

The environment is generating novel problems which cannot be anticipated, and for which responses cannot be codified. The chief executive creates a management team of departmental heads who meet regularly to deal with non-routine problems. Department heads have authority over their area of responsibility.

Bureaucratic structure with cross-functional teams

For problems requiring an interdepartmental view, a team is assembled consisting of lower level staff from different departments. Members attend discussions as departmental representatives. They giving the 'departmental view'; report back on developments to their department head; convey problems and information up to that person; and receive decisions down. They operate as a less rigid bureaucracy.

Matrix structure

This is the matrix structure described in the next chapter. It attaches as much importance to projects or customer groups as to functional departments such as marketing and production. It also possesses the benefits discussed above.

Project team structure

In this design, the majority of the organization's core activities are tackled through project teams. If functional departments do exist, they play a background role. The task consists of completing a series of projects, and the vehicle for task achievement is the team. These teams are given the freedom to manage themselves within the strategic parameters defined by senior management. The organization possesses more of the features of a network of interaction than of a bureaucratic structure.

Loosely coupled organic structure

A small core of staff represent the organization and set its strategic direction. They form its 'inside' centre and sustain a network which is coupled to others, located 'outside'. They use contracting to get key operational activities performed. This network of firms is held together by its current product or service. The firm is really an open-ended system of firms, ideas and activities. It lacks a clear organization structure and a definable boundary, making it difficult to determine what or who is inside or outside.

Henry Mintzberg
(b.1939)

Henry Mintzberg's managerial roles

While Henri Fayol focused on managerial activities, Henry Mintzberg, a Canadian management academic, studied the different roles performed by managers. He researched how managers spent their time. His work led to a re-assessment of the nature of managerial work within organizations, and a re-definition of the roles of the manager within organizational structures. Mintzberg (1973, 1975) studied chief executives in large and medium sized companies, categorizing the different behaviours associated with each of their positions, and distinguished ten managerial roles which he classified under the three headings of *interpersonal*, *informational* and *decisional* as shown in Table 16.3. Through their interpersonal roles managers acquired information; through their informational roles they determined the priority of information; and through their decisional roles they put it to use.

Managerial roles behaviours or tasks that a manager is expected to perform because of the position that they hold within a group or organization.

It revealed a difference between what managers actually did, and what they said they did. He showed that a manager's job was characterized by pace, interruptions, brevity and fragmentation of tasks. In addition, managers preferred to communicate verbally and spent a great deal of time in meetings or in making contacts with others outside meetings. Mintzberg argued that the ten roles that he identified could describe the nature of managerial work

Table 16.3: Mintzberg's ten managerial roles

Role	Description	Examples
Interpersonal roles arise directly from a manager's formal authority and concern relations with others.		
Figurehead	Performs symbolic, representative obligatory ceremonial, legal and social duties.	Greets visitors, presents retirement gifts, signs contracts, takes clients to lunch, opens premises, attends annual dinners
Leader	Creates the necessary culture and structure to motivate employees to achieve organizational goals.	Increases productivity through hiring, staffing, developing, coaching, training and directing employees. Provides challenging assignments.
Liaison	Maintains network of contacts with those inside and outside own unit or organization who provide information and favours.	Attends staff and professional meetings, lunches with customers, meets departmental managers. Also uses email and phone.
Informational roles concern how information is used in the manager's job, where it comes from and to whom it is communicated.		
Monitor	Scans environment for information to understand the working of own organization and its environment.	Questions subordinates and contacts, receives information from network contacts, reads business magazines, talks to customers and attends conferences.
Disseminator	Transmits information received from outsiders to the members of own organization (*internal* direction)	Makes phone calls; sends memos and emails; writes reports; holds meetings with bosses; peers and subordinates.
Spokesperson	Transmits information to outsiders on organization's views, policies, actions and results (*external* direction).	Gives press conferences, media interviews, speeches to external groups, prepares weekly status reports, conducts internal team briefings
Decisional roles: their requirements are determined by the manager's role, seniority and availability of information.		
Entrepreneur	Searches the organization and its environment for new opportunities, and initiates planned, *voluntary* changes.	Develops new products, processes and procedures, reorganizes departments, and implements innovative employee payment systems.
Disturbance handler	Takes corrective action when organization has to react to important, *involuntary*, unexpected changes.	Intervenes to avoid a strike, deals with customer complaints, resolves personal conflicts between staff.
Resource allocator	Allocates resources to different departments by making approval decisions.	Budgets, schedules programmes, assigns personnel, plans strategically, determines manpower load, sets targets.
Negotiator	Participates in sales or labour negotiations. Resolves inter-departmental arguments.	Negotiates merger details, supplier contracts, wage settlements, and in internal disputes

Based on Mintzberg (1973, 1975).

more accurately that other frameworks. The concept of role was introduced earlier in this chapter. One aspect of it is that any role-holder can choose how to carry it out. In the case of a manager, he or she can decide how they wish to blend the ten listed roles, taking into account organizational constraints and opportunities. A consequence of this is that management becomes more of an art, rather than a teachable science, that can be reduced to a set of prescriptions that can be easily taught.

Source: www.cartoonstock.com.

Mintzberg stated that all managerial work encompassed these roles, but that the prominence of each role depends on the managerial level in the company hierarchy and the type of business. His study has provided the modern focus for all the subsequent research into and debates about, the nature of managerial work. It is most frequently contrasted with the work of Henri Fayol. While Fayol identified *which* managerial activities needed to be performed, Mintzberg described *how* managers performed them.

Home viewing

Watership Down (1978, director Martin Rosen) is based on the book by Richard Adams. The amorphous group of ten rabbits are united by having to flee their home warren. They encounter several difficult and dangerous situations before finally establishing a permanent warren on Watership Down. A major theme of the story is how a shrewd, buoyant, young rabbit, Hazel, becomes transformed into the great leader, Hazel-rah. As you watch the film, make a note of which of Mintzberg's roles Hazel plays, and when in the story. Decide which roles he does not play himself and which he delegates to other rabbits. Which of his behaviours shows leadership?

Contingency approach to organization structure

The contingency approach in organizational behaviour asserts that the appropriate solution in any specific, organizational situation depends (is *contingent* upon) the circumstances prevailing at the time. The approach has been influential in topics such as work design, leadership and not least, in organization structuring. The contingency approach to organization structure argues that to be effective, an organization must adjust its structure in a manner that takes into account the type of technology it uses; the environment within which it operates; its size; and other contextual factors.

The contingency approach holds that managers need to analyze their own organization and its environment; decide and implement the most appropriate structure for the time; continually monitor the situation as it changes; and revise the structure as and when necessary.

Contingency approach to organization structure a perspective which argues that to be effective, an organization must adjust its structure to take into account its technology; its environment; its size; or other contextual factors.

Thus, organizational design is an on-going management task. Thus, Weber's bureaucratic organization structure, described earlier in this chapter, is said to be appropriate for (matches) a stable environment, while a turbulent environment requires a more flexible, or organic structure. The contingency approach as a reaction to management thinking in the first half of the twentieth century which was dominated by the search for the 'one-best-way'. Taylor, Weber and Fayol all recommended single, universal solutions to management problems, often in the form of laws or principles. Subsequent contributions to the contingency school came from many different researchers who studied wage payment systems, leadership styles, and job design. They sought to identify the kinds of situations in which particular organizational arrangements and management practices appeared to be most effective.

Determinism versus strategic choice

The main debate within the contingency approach to organization structuring is between two of its sub-schools – the determinists and the strategic choice thinkers. The determinists assert that 'contextual' factors, like an organization's size, ownership, technology or environment, impose certain constraints on the choices that their managers can make about the type of structure to adopt. If the structure was not adapted to context, then opportunities would be lost, cost would rise and the organization's existence threatened. They view the aforementioned variables as *determining* organizational characteristics. Meanwhile, strategic writers contend that a company's structure is always the outcome of a *choice* made by those in positions of power within organizations. Linked to the question of the shape of the organization's structure, is that of its performance and efficiency. Both sub-schools are interested in discovering if certain structural arrangements are more conducive to organizational success than others.

Contingency and technological determinism

Technological determinism the argument that technology can explain the nature of jobs, work groupings, hierarchy skills, values and attitudes in organizations.

Joan Woodward, James Thompson and Charles Perrow are the leading figures in the school of technological determinism. They all agree that technology requires that certain tasks be performed, and that this in turn determines jobs, organization structures and attitudes and behaviours. However, they differ in both the way in which they classify technologies, and in how they conceive of the relationship been technology and organization structure.

Joan Woodward and technological complexity

Joan Woodward was a British academic whose work from the 1950s continues to have an impact today for at least three reasons. First, she created a typology for categorizing and describing different technologies, which gives us a 'language' with which to discuss them. Second, by discovering that no single organization structure was appropriate for all circumstances, she ended the supremacy of classical management theory, and ushered in the modern, contingency approach to the design of organization structures. Third, by recognizing the impact of technology on organization design, she began a research tradition that has enhanced our understanding of the relation of new technologies to organizational forms.

Woodward studied 100 firms in south-east England. Having established their levels of performance, she correlated them with various aspects of organization structure which had been proposed by Weber, Fayol and other classic writers. These included the number of hierarchical levels, the span-of-control, the level of written communication, and so on. She had expected her analysis to reveal the relationship between some of these aspects of organization structure and the level of company performance, but it failed to do so. In her search for an alternative explanation, she noted that her firms used different technologies. She classified their technologies producing a ten-step categorization based on three main types

Joan Woodward
(1916–1971)

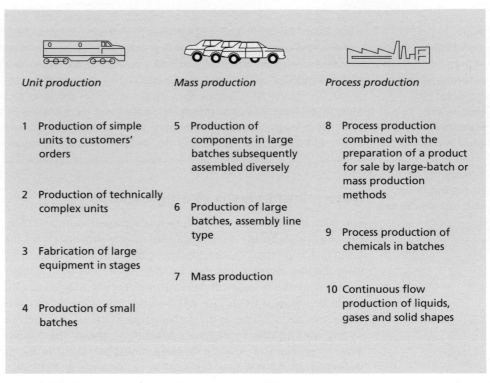

Figure 16.2: Woodward's classification of 100 British manufacturing firms according to their systems of production

Source: From Woodward (1958, p.11).

Technical complexity the degree of predictability about, and control over the final product permitted by the technology used.

(unit, mass and process) which was based on increasing **technical complexity** (1 = least complex; 10 = most complex) as shown in Figure 16.2. In unit production, one person works on a product from beginning to end, for example, a cabinet maker producing a piece of hand built furniture. In mass production, the technology requires each worker to make an individual contribution to a larger whole, for example, fitting a windscreen on a car assembly line. In process production, workers do not touch the product, but monitor machinery and the automated production processes, for example, chemical plants and oil refineries. Technical complexity is usually related to the level of mechanization used in the production process.

STOP AND THINK Woodward's classification of technologies is based on the manufacture of products. How well does it fit the provision of services? Consider services such as having your windows cleaned, buying a lottery ticket, insuring your car, having a dental check-up, etc. What alternative classification system would you need for these?

Woodward discovered that a firm's organization structure was indeed related to its performance, but through an important, additional variable – technology. Thus, the 'best' or most appropriate organization structure, that is, the one associated with highest performance, depended (or was *contingent* upon), the type of technology employed by that firm. Thus, it was Woodward (1965) who first introduced the notion of the technological imperative – the view that technology determines an organization's structure. Specifically, she held that it was the complexity of the technology used that determined the structure.

Woodward identified differences in the technical complexity of the process of production, and examined the companies' organization structures. She found that as the technology became more complex (going from type 1 through to type 10), two main things occurred.

James David Thompson (1920–1973)

First, the length of the chain-of-command increased, with the number of management levels rising from an average of 3 to 6. The proportion of managers to the total employed workforce rose, as did the proportion of indirect to direct labour. Her second major finding was that the increasing complexity of technology meant that the chief executives' span-of-control increased, and that of supervisors. The span-of-control of first line supervisors was highest in mass production and lowest in process production. Span-of-control refers to the number of subordinates supervised by one manager, and represents one of the ways of co-ordinating the activities of different employees.

Woodward argued that a relationship existed between a company's economic performance and its technology. Her conclusion was that, 'there was a particular form of organization most appropriate to each technical situation' (Woodward, 1965, p.72). The reasoning underlying this conclusion is that the technology used to manufacture the product, or make available the service, places specific requirements on those who operate it. Such demands, for example, in the need for controlling work or motivating staff, are likely to be reflected in the organization structure. The technology-structure link is complemented by the notion of effective performance which held that each type of production system called for its own characteristic organization structure.

James Thompson, technology and interdependence

The second contributor to technological determinist perspective school was a sociologist, James Thompson (1967). He was not interested in the complexity of technologies (as with Woodward), but on the characteristic types of technological interdependence that each technology created. His argument was that different types of technology create different types of interdependence between individuals, teams, departments and firms. These specified the appropriate type of co-ordination required which, in turn, determined the structure needed (see Figure 16.3).

Mediating technology creating pooled interdependence

Mediating technology allows individuals, teams and departments to operate independently of each other. Pooled task interdependence results when each department or group member

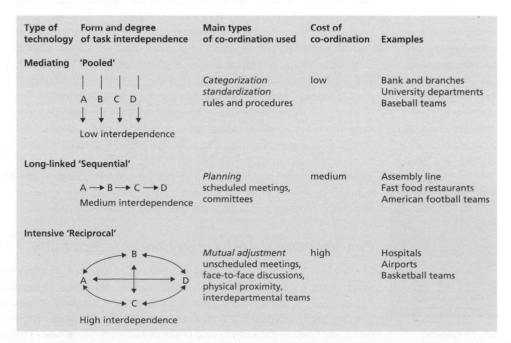

Figure 16.3: Thompson's typology of technology, interdependence and co-ordination

makes a separate and independent contribution to the company or team performance. The individual outputs are pooled; lecturers running their own courses, secretaries in a firm, sales representatives on the road, insurance claims units, and supermarket checkout operators. In each case, the individual contributor's performance can be easily identified and evaluated; and hence the potential for conflict between departments or individuals is low.

Thus, pre-determined rules, common forms, and written procedures, all act to co-ordinate the independent contributions of different units and separate employees, while clearly defined task and role relationships integrate the functions. This produces a bureaucratic organization form in which the costs of co-ordination are relatively low.

Long-linked technology: created sequential task interdependence

Long-linked technology technology that is applied to a series of programmed tasks performed in a predetermined order.

Long-linked technology requires specific work tasks to be performed in a pre-determined order. Sequential task interdependence results when one department or individual group member must perform their task before the next can complete theirs. For example, in an organizational behaviour course taught by three lecturers, sequential task interdependence means that the first one has to complete their sessions on individual psychology, before the second can teach group psychology, who is then followed by the third, who presents the material on organization structure. In a car factory, a car has to be assembled before it can be painted. Sequential task interdependence means that a department's or group member's performance cannot be easily identified or evaluated, as several individuals, groups or departments, make a contribution to a single product or service.

At the company level, co-ordination is achieved through planning and scheduling which integrates the work of different departments. At the group level, co-ordination is achieved by close supervision of workers, forming work teams consisting of employees of similar levels of skills; and motivating by rewarding group rather than individual performance. The relative cost of co-ordination with this type of technology is medium.

Intensive technology created reciprocal task interdependence

Intensive technology technology that is applied to tasks that are performed in no predetermined order.

Task variety the number of new and different demands that a task places on an individual or a function.

Intensive technology creates reciprocal interdependence, where all the activities of all the different company departments or all of the team members are fully dependent on one another. The work output of each, serves as the input for another. For example, in an organizational behaviour course which uses the group project method, a group of students can call upon different lecturers to provide them with knowledge or skill inputs to enable them to solve the project problems. Each lecturer would notice what the other had done, and would contribute accordingly. For this reason, with reciprocal task interdependence, the sequence of required operations cannot be predetermined.

Thus, the mechanisms of co-ordination include unscheduled meetings, face-to-face contacts, project groups, task forces and cross-departmental teams. This in turns necessitates a close physical grouping of reciprocally interdependent units, so that mutual adjustment can be accomplished quickly. Where this is impossible, then mechanisms like daily meetings, email, teleconferencing are needed to facilitate communication. The degree of co-ordination required through mutual adjustment goes far beyond what is necessary for the other technologies discussed, and is thus the most expensive of the three.

Charles Perrow, technology and predictability

Charles Bryce Perrow (b.1925)

Charles Perrow (1970) is the third contributor to the technological determinist school. He saw technology's effect on organization structure as working through its impact on the predictability of providing the service or manufacturing a product. He considered two dimensions. The first he labelled **task variety**. This referred to the frequency with which unexpected events occurred in the transformation (inputs to outputs) process. Task variety would be high if many unexpected events occurred during a technological process. The second, he termed,

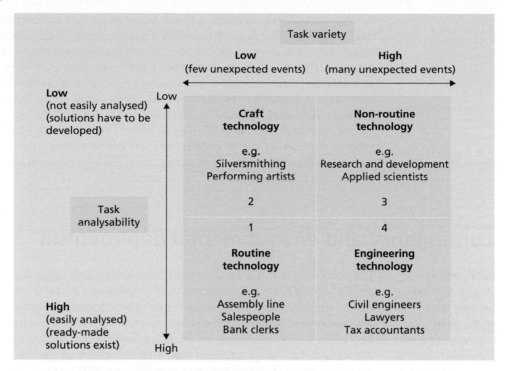

Figure 16.4: Perrow's model of technology

Source: From Perrow, Charles. *Organizational Analysis*. 1E. © 1970 Wadsworth, a part of Cengage Learning, Inc. Reproduced by permission www.cengage.com/permissions.

Task analyzability
the degree to which standardized solutions are available to solve the problems that arise.

task analyzability. This term referred to the degree to which the unexpected problems could be solved using readily available, off-the-shelf solutions. Task analyzability would be low if individuals or departments had to search around for a solution, and rely on experience, judgement, intuition and problem-solving skills (see Figure 16.4).

Types of technology

On the basis of these two dimensions, Perrow categorized technologies into four types, and discussed the effects of each one upon an organization's structure. He was particularly interested in co-ordination mechanisms, discretion, the relative power of supervisors and the middle managers who supervised them.

1. *Routine technology*: in cell 1 are tasks which are simple and where variety is low (repetitive task). Task analyzability is high (there are standard solutions available). Examples include supermarket checkout operations, and fast food hamburger restaurants.

2. *Craft technology*: in cell 2 is craft technology, characterized by low task variety and low task analyzability. The number of new problems encountered is small, but each requires some effort to find a solution. A plumber fitting a bath or shower; an accountant preparing a tax return.

3. *Non-routine technology*: in cell 3 are complex and non-routine tasks, where task variability is high (with many new or different problems encountered); and task analyzability is low (need to find a solution to the problem is difficult). The tasks performed by research chemists, advertising agencies, high tech product designers, and top management teams are all examples of non-routine technology.

4. *Engineering technology*: in cell 4 is engineering technology, characterized by high task variety and low task analyzability. Many new problems crop up, but each is relatively simple to solve. Civil engineering companies which build roads and bridges exemplify this type of technology, as well as motor manufacturers producing customized cars.

When an organization's tasks and technology are routine, its structure is likely to resemble that proposed by Weber and Fayol. With a tall hierarchy, channels of authority and formal, standardized operating procedures are used to integrate the activities of individuals, groups, units and departments. In contrast, when a firm's tasks and technology become non routine and complex, an organization will tend to use a flatter hierarchy, more cross-functional teamworking, greater face-to-face contact to allow individuals, groups units and departments to observe, and mutually adjust to each other, and to engage in decision-making and problem-solving. The differences between the two structures will be manifested in the number and types of formal rules and procedures used; the degree to which decision-making is centralized; the skill levels of workers employed; the width of supervisors' span-of-control; and the means used for communication and co-ordination.

Contingency and environmental determinism

Environmental determinism the argument that internal organizational responses are primarily determined by external environmental factors.

Environmental complexity the range of external factors relevant to the activities of the organization; the more factors, the higher the complexity.

Environmental dynamism the pace of change in relevant factors external to the organization; the greater the pace of change, the more dynamic the environment.

The second strand of determinism in organization structuring has been environmental. Several writers have had an interest in the relationship between a company's environment and its structure. Some of them argue that company success depends on securing a proper 'fit' or alignment between itself and its environment. For them, environmental determinism means that the environment determines organization structure. One prominent environmental determinist, Paul Lawrence, even said, 'Tell me what your environment is and I shall tell your what your organization ought to be' (Argyris, 1972, p.88).

The environmental determinists see the organization as being in constant interaction with the environment within which it exists (see Figure 16.5). That environment consists of 'actors' or 'networks' (e.g. competitors, investors, customers). It includes the general economic situation, the market, the competitive scene and so on. Each organization has its own unique environment. The more actors or networks that are relevant to a given company, the more complex its environment is said to be. Organizations vary in the relative degree of their environmental complexity (Duncan, 1972, 1973, 1974, 1979).

Those same actors and networks in an organization's environment can also change a great deal or remain the same. They thus differ in their degree of environmental dynamism.

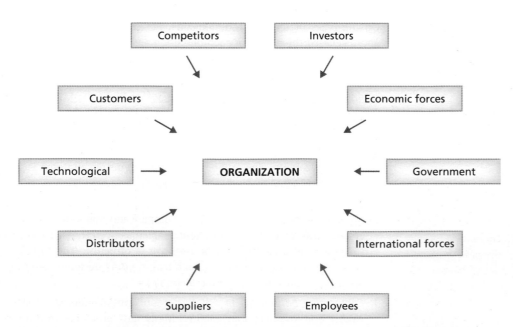

Figure 16.5: An organization depicted in its environment consisting of different actors, stakeholders and networks

Different industries vary widely in their degree of dynamism. At one extreme of stability is the mainframe computer industry where new players must confront the barriers of an entrenched set of standards and the costs of switching are high. Here, the concepts of market segmentation, economies of scale, and pre-emptive investment are all still important. Mainframe computers are not immune to change as the mini-computer and PC revolutions showed, but there are periods of considerable stability. In the middle of the range, one finds businesses like branded consumer goods. Substitution ranges from medium to high, and new entrants can replace established ones but not overnight. Survival and success depend upon capabilities and network relationships. Most industries are located in this middle ground. At the extreme of turbulence, is a situation where customers can constantly and easily substitute. It consists of networks of players whose positions and prospects change suddenly and unpredictably. Many internet businesses are located at this end of the spectrum.

Environmental determinists argue that because a company is dependent on its environment for its sales, labour, raw materials and so on, that environment constrains the kind of choices a organization can make about how it structures itself. As the environmental situation changes, the organization-environment relationship also changes. Hence, to be effective, a company has to structure and re-structure constantly to maintain alignment. The environmental determinists use the key concepts of environmental uncertainty and complexity in their explanations.

Tom Burns, George M. Stalker, mechanistic and organic organization structures

George McDonald Stalker (b.1925)

Mechanistic structure an organization structure that possesses a high degree of task specialization, many rules, tight specification of individual responsibility and authority, and centralized decision-making.

Organic structure an organization structure that possesses little task specialization, few rules, a high degree of individual responsibility and authority, and one in which decision-making is delegated.

In the late 1950s in Britain, Tom Burns (1914–2002) and George McDonald Stalker studied the behaviour of people working in a rayon mill. Rayon is a yarn or fibre produced by forcing and drawing cellulose through minute holes. They found that this contented, economically successful company, was run with a management style which, according to contemporary wisdom about 'best' management practice, should have led to worker discontent and inefficiency. Some time later, the same authors studied an electronics company. Again it was highly successful, but used a management style completely different from that of the rayon mill studied earlier. This contradiction gave the authors the impetus to begin a large scale investigation to examine the relationship between the management systems and the organizational tasks. They were particularly interested in the way management systems changed in response to changes in the commercial and technical tasks of the firm (Burns and Stalker, 1961).

The rayon mill had a highly stable, highly structured character, which would have fitted well into Weber's bureaucratic organizational model. In contrast, the electronics firm violated many of the principles of classical management. It discouraged written communications, defined jobs as little as possible, and the interaction between employees was on a face-to-face basis. Indeed, staff even complained about this uncertainty. Burns and Stalker gave the label mechanistic structure to the former and organic structure to the latter. These represented organization structures at opposite ends of a continuum. Most firms would be located somewhere in between.

Burns and Stalker argued that neither form of organization structure was intrinsically efficient or inefficient, but that rather that it all depended on the nature of the environment in which a firm operated. In their view, the key variables to be considered were the product market and the technology of the manufacturing process. These needed to be studied when the structure of a firm's management system was being designed. Thus, a *mechanistic structure* may be appropriate for an organization which uses an unchanging technology and operates in relatively stable markets. An *organic structure* can be more suitable for a firm that has to cope with unpredictable new tasks. Later, Rosabeth Moss Kanter (1983) relabelled these two constructs *integrative* and *segmentalist*, arguing that segmentalist systems stifled creativity, while integrative ones were more innovative (see Chapter 18).

Table 16.4: Characteristics of mechanistic and organic organization structures

Characteristic	Rayon mill (Mechanistic)	Electronics (Organic)
Specialization	High – sharp differentiation	Low – no hard boundaries, relatively few different jobs
Standardization	High – methods spelled out	Low – individuals decide own methods
Orientation of members	Means	Goals
Conflict resolution	By superior	Interaction
Pattern of authority, control and communication	Hierarchical – based on implied contractual relation	Wide net based upon common commitment
Locus of superior competence	At top of organization	Wherever there is skill and competence
Interaction	Vertical	Lateral
Communication content	Directions, orders	Advice, information
Loyalty	To the organization	To project and group
Prestige	From the position	From personal contribution

Based on Litterer (1973, p.339).

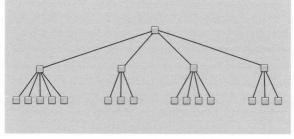 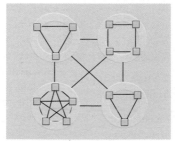

mechanistic	organic
• High specialization • Rigid departmentalization • Clear chain of command • Narrow spans of control • Centralization • High formalization	• Cross-functional teams • Cross-hierarchical teams • Free flow of information • Wide spans of control • Decentralization • Low formalization

Figure 16.6: Mechanistic versus organic structures compared

Source: From ROBBINS, STEPHEN P.; JUDGE, TIMOTHY A., ORGANIZATIONAL BEHAVIOR, 12th Edition, © 2007. Reprinted by permission of Pearson Education, Inc., Upper Saddle River, NJ.

Oticon: to organic and back again

Oticon is a Danish manufacturer of hearing aids that, in 1988, was being seriously challenged by larger competitors such as Siemens and Philips. Incoming CEO Lars Kolind radically restructured ('disorganized') it, to create what he termed the 'spaghetti organization'. The company had been very bureaucratic. Vertically, it had a tall hierarchy with six levels of management, Horizontally, it was separated into divisions, and the two main ones – Electronics (product development) and International (sales) – communicated poorly with each other. Within each division, employees' work was organized around specific departments and tasks.

Kolind re-organized the work around projects instead of divisions. Project leaders (basically, anyone with a compelling idea), were appointed by a 10-person management team (the last vestige of the company's previous mechanistic structure). Project leaders competed to attract resources and recruit people to deliver results. Employees decided whether or not to join, and could only do so with the agreement of their current project leaders. The company had a hundred or so projects at any one time, so most people worked on several at once. Additionally, they needed to be multi-skilled, so a software engineer had also to develop skills in marketing and aspects of production. Project owners (management team members) provided advice and support, but made few actual decisions. As a consequence, Oticon's organization structure became a fluid affair with no departments or divisions which could encourage local interests, impede communications, or make adjustments in workloads. Instead, project teams formed and reformed as they were needed. The potential problems of this 'managed chaos' were kept at bay by the company having a clear purpose and a set of common values, which all employees knew about and subscribed to.

This allowed Oticon to dispense with the traditional features of a mechanistic structure. There were no job titles, and employees did whatever they felt was appropriate at the time. The company did not abandon physical space completely, and continued to use its headquarters building near Copenhagen, where about 150 staff were based. However, within the building there were few formal offices, only work stations with networked computers. These were often deserted as staff frequently moved around the building. Each employee had a small personal trolley for their personal belongings which they wheeled to wherever they were working on that day. The building also had a conference room for teams to meet for problem-solving and brainstorming.

Oticon's culture continued to value face-to-face contact, but did not dictate either its form or location. Staff members used mobile phones and e-mail to participate in the activities of their teams, while away from the office. The environment stressed motion and activity, rather than sitting at desks waiting for something to happen.

Oticon's organization structure reflected its own needs and own culture, and mixed virtual and tangible elements which allowed the maximum use of knowledge and human capital, while, at the same time, increasing efficiency. Over the first four years of its new, organic structure, Oticon doubled its size, and its operating profits increased by almost 1000 per cent. It had 1200 staff in Denmark. Koland noted that, 'Hardware companies have organizations that look like machines: a company that produces knowledge needs an organization that looks like a brain, i.e. which looks chaotic and unhierarchical'. However, in 1996, Oticon incurred a number of unanticipated costs, and reversed its radical restructuring. These included problems associated with co-ordination; employee time allocation; and the demotivating effect of managers having to intervene after projects had been approved. Additionally, management sought to align new project initiatives more closely with the company's strategic goals. The company partially abandoned its spaghetti organization, and gradually adopted a more traditional, matrix structure. The company is still characterized by considerable decentralization and delegation, but many of the key elements of the spaghetti organization have now been abandoned.

Based on Bjorn-Andersen and Turner (1994);
Rivard et al. (2004); Foss (2003).

Paul Lawrence, Jay Lorsch, organization design and environmental needs

Paul Roger Lawrence (b.1922)

Differentiation the degree to which the tasks and the work of individuals, groups and units are divided up within an organization.

During the 1960s, Paul Lawrence and Jay Lorsch (1967) built on the work of Burns and Stalker, using the concepts of *differentiation* and *integration*. Differentiation refers to the process of a firm breaking itself up into sub-units, each of which concentrates on a particular part of the firm's environment. A university differentiates itself in terms of different faculties and departments. Such differentiation inevitably leads to the sub-units developing their own goals, values, norms, structures, time frames and inter-personal relations that reflect the job that they have to do, and the uncertainties with which they have to cope.

First, consider differentiation, which takes two forms. *Horizontal differentiation* is concerned with how work is divided up between the various company departments and who is responsible for which tasks. *Vertical differentiation* is concerned with who is given authority at the different levels of the company's hierarchy. High horizontal differentiation created many different departments, producing a flat structure as shown on an organization chart. High vertical differentiation resulted in many hierarchical levels, creating a tall structure. Lawrence and Lorsch found that effective organizations increased their level of differentiation as their environment became more uncertain. These adjustments allowed staff to respond more effectively to their specific sub-environment for which they were

Jay William Lorsch (b.1932)

Integration the required level to which units in an organization are linked together, and their respective degree of independence.

responsible. On the other hand however, the more differentiated the sub-units became, the more their goals would diverge, the more they would perceive the some things differently, and hence the more conflict there would be between them.

Turning next to integration, this refers to co-ordinating the work performed in the previously divided (differentiated) departments, so as to ensure that it all contributes to accomplishing the organizational goal. Thus, having divided the university into faculties, departments and research units, there is the need to ensure that they all contribute to the goals of high quality research, excellent teaching and income generation. Lawrence and Lorsch found that as environmental uncertainty increased, and thus the degree of differentiation increased, so organizations had to increase the level of their integration (co-ordination) between different departments and their staffs, if they were to work together effectively towards the common goal. Co-ordination is achieved through the use of rules, policies and procedures; goal clarification and communication; temporary task forces; permanent project teams; liaison roles; and integrator roles.

When environmental uncertainty is low, differentiation too is correspondingly low. Because the units share common goals and ways of achieving them, the hierarchy of authority in a company and standard procedures are sufficient to integrate the activities of different units and individuals. However, as uncertainty increases, so does the need for integration, and so too do the number of integrative devices used. While integration is expensive, using up the resources of time, money and effort, so too can a failure to integrate, leading to conflict between departments which has to be resolved. Lawrence and Lorsch argued that the level of uncertainty in the environment that a firm has to cope with, will determine the organization structure that is most appropriate for it.

STOP AND THINK How well are the activities performed by your educational institution differentiated and integrated? Identify the problems and recommend solutions that would improve organizational performance from the student perspective.

Strategic choice

John Child (b.1940)

Strategic choice the view that an organization's environment, market and technology is the result of senior management decisions.

The debate about contemporary organization design involves a consideration of the decisions that managers make about their organizations within their environments. Thus, strategic choice and environment are central concepts. Both Tom Burns and George Stalker (1961) and Paul Lawrence and Jay Lorsch (1967) stressed the importance of an organization's environment. Their original contributions were concerned primarily with the market conditions, and took a deterministic perspective. Their critics however, pointed to the neglect of *choice* in decisions about organization structure. John Child (1972) rectified this omission, arguing that there was no one best organization structure, and that companies could have different structures. However, he disagreed with the contention that those structures were *determined* by 'external, operational contingencies'. Instead, he stressed the part played by powerful leaders and groups, who exerted their influence to create organizational forms which suited their particular values and preferences.

Strategic choice holds that decisions about the number of levels of hierarchical levels, the span-of-control, etc. are ultimately based on the personal beliefs and political manoeuvrings of those who make them. Strategic choice researchers continue to focus on companies' environments, but they became interested in how senior managers make the choices that link their firms' strategies to their organization structures. These commentators have criticized the deterministic writers on a number of issues:

1. *The idea that an organization should 'fit' its environment*: that is, while there are choices about organization structure design, these will be relatively limited. Thus, for two similar

companies operating in a stable environment to succeed, each would make similar choices about the shape of their organization structures. However, there are examples of companies making very different structural choices in the same circumstances and both succeeding.

2. *The idea that cause and effect are linked in a simple (linear) manner*: this ignores the fact that organizations are part of a larger, complex environmental system consisting of other organizations with which they interact. Managers can create their own environments, and the idea that organizations merely adapt to their environment is too simple a view.

3. *The assumption that the choice of organization structure is an automatic reaction to the facts presented*: studies show that decisions are made by managers on the basis of the interpretations that they have made about the nature of their environment. The same environment can be perceived in different ways, by various managers who might implement different structures, which can be equally successful.

4. *The view that choices of organization structure are not political*: linked to the previous point, political factors will impinge on choices about structure as much as issues of perception and interpretation.

Child suggested that organization structuring was a political process in which power and influence were used to decide on the types of jobs, levels of hierarchy, spans-of-control, etc. that were to be adopted and, by implication, which markets to enter and with which companies to link up. His work stimulated discussion in three main areas (Child, 1997):

- The human agents (individuals or groups) who exercise choice in the design of organizations.
- The nature of the environment within which an organization exists.
- The relationships between organizational agents (e.g. managers) and that environment.

The first of the two major strategic choice perspectives was presented by Karl Weick (1979) who introduced the concept of enacted environment. This is the notion that organization and environment are created together (enacted) through the social interaction processes of key organizational participants – usually managers (Smircich and Stubbart, 1985; Westwood and Clegg, 2003). The environment within which managers work and make decisions, does not consist of a simple set of objective conditions which are just 'given'. Here we use Tony Watson's definition of managerial enactment.

The environment of an organization exists for its members by virtue of the interpretations that they make of what is occurring 'outside' the organization, and the way in which their own actions influence or shape those occurrences. He illustrates it with the example of a market and a product (Watson, 2002, p.203). A business organization does not go out and 'find' a market which it then satisfies in order to stay in business. Instead, its managers first strategically identify the *possibility* of a market relationship with certain would-be customers outside the organization. They then work at their product in the light of the possibilities and potentials that they envisage. Next they present the product to the would-be customers, in a way that will *persuade* them to trade with the organization, again in the light of their *interpretations* of the inclinations of these potential customers. Active sense-making is central to all this.

Ian Brooks offered another example of enactment, this time from the football industry. He noted that a number of football teams are relegated annually from the higher divisions, and commented that, according to press reports, many had given up the struggle well before the end of the season. He noted that they stopped spending money on new players and prepared themselves for leaner times in lower divisions. By doing this, they increased their chances of being relegated since, without new players or the motivation to stay up, their performance remained poor, or even declined, and they were indeed, relegated. When this happened, the clubs looked back and said that since they knew that they were going down, they did the sensible thing, and saved their money and energy for the following season. He asked whether these football clubs could have stayed up had they adopted a

Enacted environment the environment of an organization that exists for members by virtue of the interpretations they make of what is occurring 'outside' the organization, and the way their own actions influence or shape those occurrences.

Managerial enactment the active modification of a perceived and selected part of an organization's environment by its managers.

different strategy, or did they enact their environment (Brooks, 2003)? In Weick's view, managers *enact*, rather than *react* to their environments. That is, they *create* their organization's environment, making it easier for them to understand and modify it. The managerial enactment view differs from that of the environmental determinist school discussed in the chapter.

Resource dependence theory states that although organizations depend on their environments to survive, they seek to assert control over the resources they require, in order to minimize their dependence.

The second major strategic choice perspective – resource dependence theory – answers the question of how managers make choices. It was developed by Jeffrey Pfeffer and Gerald Salancik (1978). Their theory sees every organization as being at the mercy of its environment, needing resources from it in the form of employees, equipment, raw materials, knowledge, capital and outlets for its products and services. The environment gives a firm its power, but also controls access to these resources. It thus makes the firm dependent on its environment – hence the name of the theory. The environment (in the form of customers, suppliers, competitors, government and other stakeholders) uses its power to make demands upon the organization to provide, not only desirable products and services at competitive prices, but also efficient organization structures and processes.

Pfeffer and Salancik argue that although organizations are dependent on their environments, their managers have still to achieve their chosen objectives. To do this, they need to identify the critical resources needed – defined as those without which the company cannot function. They then trace these back to their sources in their environment and identify the nature of their dependence. For practical reasons, only the most critical and scarce resources are focused on. While it is possible to distinguish and discuss a single dependency relation between an organization, in practice, a firm will be experiencing a complex set of dependencies between itself and the various elements in its environment. When costs or risks are high, companies will team up to reduce their dependencies and risks of bankruptcy.

For example, for McDonald's fast food restaurants, having beef, buns and cheese is critical, having plastic customer seating is not. Scarcity refers to how widely available that resource is in the organization's environment. Control of resources that are most critical and scarce gives environmental elements the greatest power over a company. Pfeffer and Salancik state that the first step in applying the approach is to understand the organizational environment with respect to criticality and scarcity of resources. The second step is for managers to find ways of reducing that dependency, eliminating it altogether, or making the others dependent on their organization. Companies use their power differences to avoid excessive dependence on their environment, in order to maintain control over required resources, and thereby reduce uncertainty and increase their autonomy.

Vertical integration a situation where one company buys another in order to make the latter's output its own input, thereby securing that source of supply through ownership.

There are a number of dependence-reduction strategies. If you are a manufacturer, you could develop long-term contracts with suppliers; have several suppliers for your crucial components; purchase part-ownership of your suppliers; establish a joint venture; or simply buy up all the resources that are critical to your company. In the case of a motor manufacturer, these would mean steel for car bodies, rubber for tyres, coal to fire factory furnaces, and ships and railways to transport this material. In order to secure access to the critical resources that he needed, we know that Henry Ford bought iron mines, coal mines, rubber plantations, shipping lines and railways. This corporate strategy, which involves acquiring related businesses assimilated into the purchaser, is called vertical integration. Although a popular strategy, mergers and acquisitions are only one of many kinds of relationship that one company can have with another, as it seeks to reduce its dependency on its environment.

STOP AND THINK   Select an organization that you have read about or have first hand experience of. What is its strategy? How effective is it? What advice or recommendations would you make to its chief executive and the company board?

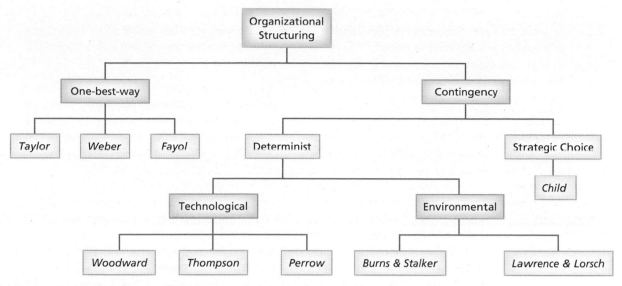

Figure 16.7: Contrasting theoretical approaches to organization structuring

 RECAP

1. *Distinguish between charismatic, traditional and legitimate forms of authority.*

   - Traditional authority is based on the belief that the ruler had a natural right to rule.

   - Charismatic authority is based on the belief that the ruler had some special, unique virtue, either religious or heroic.

   - Legitimate authority is based on formal written rules which had the force of law.

2. *State the main characteristics of a bureaucratic organization structure as specified by Max Weber.*

   - Job specialization; authority hierarchy; employment and career; recording and keeping of all administrative acts and decisions; rules and procedures to which all employees are subject; and impersonality of those procedures and rules meaning that they apply to all equally.

3. *Distinguish Fayol's six managerial activities and the main ideas of the classical management school.*

   - Fayol distinguished six managerial activities: forecasting, planning, organizing; commanding; co-ordinating; and controlling.

   - The classical management school was based on the experience of managers and consultants rather than researchers.

4. *Distinguish Mintzberg's ten managerial roles.*

   - His ten managerial roles are figurehead, leader, liaison, monitor, disseminator, spokesperson, entrepreneur, disturbance handler, resource allocator and negotiator.

5. *Identify the writers who comprise the contingency approach and state their main individual contributions.*

   - Contingency writers challenged Max Weber and Henri Fayol's view that there was one best way to structure an organization.

   - They held that there was an optimum organization structure that would maximize company performance and profits, and that this structure would differ between firms.

   - Technological contingency theorists Joan Woodward, Charles Perrow and James Thompson, saw technology determining appropriate organization structure.

   - Environmental contingency theorists, Tom Burns and G.M. Stalker, Paul Lawrence and Jay Lorsch, saw the environment determining appropriate organization structure.

6. *Discuss the strengths and weaknesses of early ideas on the design of organization structure and the practice of management.*

   - Provides a rationally designed, organizational model that allows complex tasks to be performed efficiently. Persons who are best qualified to do it, carry out the work. It provides safeguards against personal bias and individual favouritism.

- It creates dysfunctional consequences of members only interested in their own jobs; following rules obsessively; and slow to respond to changes. Bureaucracies perpetuate themselves.

7. *Identify the influence of early organization design ideas on contemporary organizations*.

- Modern organizations continue to possess the features first described by Weber and Fayol over a century ago.

- Early design principles have been successful; have helped large organizations to survive; reflect the static social values of many nations and cultures; are capable of withstanding environmental turbulence; and allow senior management to retain power.

Revision

1. Commentators argue that both too much and too little bureaucracy in an organization de-motivates employees and causes them stress. How can this be?

2. How does uncertainty affect the successful operation of rationally designed organization structures such as those proposed by Weber and Fayol?

3. Define and distinguish differentiation from integration. Using an example from your experience or reading, illustrate these two processes in operation, and highlight some of the problems that can be encountered.

4. Explain how technology and environment might influence the structure of an organization. Consider their effect on co-ordinating activities.

Research assignment

Which factors have the greatest influence on the choice of an organization's structure – changes in size, strategy, company performance, technology, environment, globalization, diversification or something else? Search the literature (newspapers, business magazines, academic research studies) to discover past and recent examples of companies restructuring themselves. In each case, identify which factors triggered the decision to restructure or which type of structure was adopted. Relate your findings to the theories discussed in this chapter.

Springboard

Leavitt, H.J., 2005, *Top Down: Why hierarchies are here to stay and how to manage them more effectively*, Harvard Business School Press, Boston, MA.

The subtitle exactly describes the book's content.

Olsen, J.P., 2006, 'Maybe it is time to rediscover bureaucracy', *Journal of Public Administration Research and Theory*, 16(1): 1–24.

This article questions the view that bureaucracy is obsolete and undesirable, and argues that it complements market and network based forms of organization.

Smircich, L. and Stubbart, C., 1985, 'Strategic management in an enacted world', *Academy of Management Review*, 10(4): 724–35.

Contrasts three models for knowing the organizational environment – objective, perceived and enacted.

Willmott, H. 2005, 'Studying managerial work: a critique and a proposal', in Grey, C. and Willmott, H. (eds), *Critical Management Studies: A Reader*, Oxford University Press, Oxford, pp.324–47.

Beginning with Mintzberg's study of managerial roles, this chapter critically considers other research into what managers do.

OB in films

Crimson Tide (1995, director Tony Scott), DVD track 4: 0:26:49–0:33:30 (7 minutes). This is the story of how a global emergency provokes a power play onboard a nuclear submarine, between the battle-hardened Captain Frank Ramsay (played by Gene Hackman) who 'goes by the book', and his Executive Officer, Lieutenant Commander Ron Hunter (Denzil Washington). The captain regularly runs a weapons systems readiness test in preparation for launching nuclear missiles. The clip begins with a loudspeaker announcement saying, 'Attention all hands, the fire has been contained', and ends with Ramsey saying to Hunter, 'We're here to defend democracy, not to practise it'.

As you watch this clip of the weapons test, identify an example of each of Weber's six principles of bureaucracy.

Bureaucratic principle	Examples
1. Work specialization	
2. Authority hierarchy	
3. Employment and career	
4. Recording	
5. Rules and regulations	
6. Impersonality and impartiality	

 OB in literature

Nice Work, 1988, David Lodge, Penguin Books, London. The worlds of Vic Wilcox, the managing director of a foundry, and Dr Robyn Penrose, a female lecturer in post-structural analysis in the English Department of a university, collide when they participate in an industry–university shadowing scheme. The novel explores the nature of work and the processes of management in two contrasting types of organization. Beyond identifying examples of managerial activities and roles performed by the characters in the book, consider what this novel tells you about managerial work and organizational life that Fayol's prescriptions and Mintzberg's research do not.

CHAPTER EXERCISES

Deborah's diary

Objectives
1. To contrast management roles with management activities.

2. To identify examples of each.

Briefing
1. Remind yourself of Mintzberg's ten management roles and Fayol's six managerial activities.

2. Form groups and nominate a spokesperson.

3. Read the case *Deborah's Day* and then:

   (a) Identify one example of each of Mintzberg's ten roles played by Deborah.

   (b) Do any of her tasks involve playing more than one role?

   (c) Consider the six staff members she met (Angela, Brian and the others). In which managerial activity was each engaged?

Deborah's Diary

Deborah is the chief executive of a large private hospital in London. In an effort to manage her time better, she keeps a diary of the tasks that she has performed at work.

Task	Mintzberg	Fayol
1. Submitted architectural plans for the new hospital extension to the hospital's board of directors for approval.		
2. Had a meeting with our Director of Finance and representatives of the bank which was financing our extension.		
3. Noted that Angela was organizing the annual hospital review and was briefing the various departmental heads about the inputs that she would be requiring from them.		
4. The city planning authority had approved our extension plans so our Director of Buildings and I had a meeting with our architect and building contractor to discuss the plans.		
5. Noted that Brain was reviewing the food purchase data to ensure that all foodstuffs had been obtained in accordance with procedures laid down by the hospital, and that the quantities of food supplied by vendors had been specified.		
6. Showed our local Member of Parliament around the hospital and answered questions alongside him at the press conference.		
7. The Director of Human Resources and I discussed plans for a senior management development programme, and a continuing professional development course for doctors and nurses.		
8. Noted that Claire was busy assessing the training needs of our nursing staff.		
9. Spent two hours surfing the web to discover how our hospital compares in terms of numbers of patients and staff as well as facilities, with our competitors here and abroad.		
10. Had a meeting with the doctor in charge of the X-Ray department to resolve a dispute between him and his technicians.		
11. Noted that David was holding a meeting with the Directors of Medicine, Nursing, Buildings and Hospitality to ensure that the superbug eradication policy was being consistently implemented.		
12. Went to the local radio station to be interviewed about the work of our hospital and to answer listeners' calls.		
13. Noted that Eva was preparing a timetable of staff performance reviews to ensure that all categories of staff received an appraisal by the end of the year.		
14. Had an opportunity to buy a CAT scanner at a huge discount price, if we acted immediately. I called each of the board members to get them to agree to the investment. Some were unsure, but I managed to persuade them.		
15. Noted that Frank was devising a new 'pay-for-performance' system through which staff who exceeded their targets received additional bonuses.		
16. Circulated the latest findings on the causes of, and procedures for, dealing with hospital 'superbugs' – MRSA and C.difficile.		

I detest bureaucracy

Objectives

1. Understand how an organization stripped of most of Weber's bureaucratic features would operate.

2. Assess whether or not you would feel comfortable working in such an organization.

Briefing

1. Form groups

2. Discuss:

   (a) How would you describe the organization structure of this company?

   (b) Why does it work at TechTarget?

   (c) Could this structure be applied in other organizations?

   (d) Strakosch claims that he 'detests bureaucracy' and seems to think that he has eradicated it with his 'open leave' policy. Identify Weber's six characteristics of bureaucracy (p.490) that are likely to be applied in TechTarget.

   (e) Would you like to work at TechTarget?

TechTarget

TechTarget Inc. is an online information technology interactive media company based in Needham, Massachusetts that employs 210 staff. Founded in 1999, it became a public $100 million company in 2007, and now provides products to over 1,000 advertisers including Cisco, Dell, EMC, HP, IBM, Intel, Microsoft and SAP. Its co-founder and Chief Executive Officer is Greg Strakosch. What is distinctive about this organization is that it has an 'open leave' policy. There are no set policies or rules concerning staff working hours or specifying sick, personal or on holidays. If you want to work between midnight and 6.00am, that's OK. If you want to take a day off, to take your family to the seaside, that's OK too. However, the company is not a holiday camp. TechTarget is an entirely results-oriented business. Managers set quarterly goals and timetables, and employees are measured by their contribution to the company and the results that they achieve. They are given a great deal of freedom to accomplish these but, in exchange for this flexibility, employees are expected to remain in close contact with their managers via e-mail, cell phone, instant-messaging and laptops. The company says that it enthusiastically rewards performance with greater opportunity, compensation and recognition. While the hours are flexible, employees can put in 50 hours in some weeks. However, at other times, staff use their time to study or to travel. The company employs 25 mothers with kids under 10, who find the working arrangements ideal. The management team set high performance expectations, and have little tolerance for failure. Despite a painstaking hiring process that weeds out all but the most autonomous applicants, 7 per cent of the workforce was dismissed in the last twelve months. 'We don't carry people who underachieve' said Strakosch. Other employees have been fired for abusing the policy. The company's success is based on hiring a team of smart, self-motivated, enthusiastic, ambitious, hard-working people and giving them autonomy and flexibility while holding them accountable for their results. It is a fast-paced, stimulating work environment that fosters teamwork. Its entrepreneurial culture encourages innovation and rewards individual achievement. The company seeks to provide its employees with satisfying careers and an environment that enables them to achieve a work/life balance. Strakosch is quoted as saying, 'I detest bureaucracy and silly policies'. In the middle of 2008 TechTarget was recognized as one of the best places to work by a local business journal, but at the end of the year it was planning to made 76 of its staff redundant.

Based on Saucer (2003); Boston Business Journal *(2008a);*
Boston Business Journal *(2008b);* www.techtarget.com.

Chapter 17 Organizational architecture

Key terms

organizational architecture

organizational design

departmentalization

functional structure

divisional structure

matrix structure

team-based structure

cross-functional team

production team

boundaryless organization

collaborative relationship structure

outsourcing

offshoring

hollow organization structure

modular organization structure

virtual organization structure

co-opetition

strategic alliance

joint venture

user contribution system

crowdsourcing

restructuring

Learning outcomes

When you have read this chapter, you should be able to define those key terms in your own words, and you should also be able to:

1. Appreciate the reason for chief executives' need to design and redesign their organization's structure.

2. Distinguish three eras of organizational design and what factors stimulated each.

3. Distinguish between functional, divisional, matrix and team-based organization structures.

4. Distinguish between an outsourcing relationship and hollow, modular and virtual organization structures.

5. Understand the trend towards companies' collaborative relationships with competitors and customers, and their involvement in virtual communities.

6. Identify the factors influencing a chief executive's choice of organization structure.

Why study organizational architecture?

Organizational architecture the framework of linked internal and external elements that an organization creates and uses to achieve the goals specified in its vision statement.

Organizational architecture refers to the framework that an organization creates and uses to achieve the goals specified in its vision statement. It thus not only includes the internal arrangements that a firm makes to deploy its various business processes, but also considers how these may be linked with those of outsiders (other individuals, groups and organizations), who come together to form a temporary system, for their mutual benefit. The first part of the chapter will focus on internal structural arrangements, while the second part will consider external linkages.

Senior management decides on job duties, lines of authority, bases of departmentalization and so on. They are under pressure to design structures that balance the current internal pressures and external demands in order to make their companies effective, efficient and profitable. While a particular organization structure will not in itself ensure the achievement of a company's goals, an inappropriate structure could impede it.

Organizational design senior management's process of choosing and implementing a structural configuration through which their organization seeks to accomplish their goals.

Organizational design refers to senior management's process of choosing and implementing a structural configuration through which their organizations seeks to accomplish their goals. Chief executives actively make this choice. Whittington, Mayer and Smith (2002) highlight the twin pressures of increasing scale of business (the US retailer, Wal-Mart, has 1.2 million employees worldwide) and the intensity with which knowledge flows through it (Unilever, a consumer goods group, processes one million emails daily). They note that business is too big and too complex to allow an inappropriate organization structure to interfere with creating shareholder value and ensuring long-term company survival.

Organizational structures had been a way of institutionalizing and managing stability, but now, they have had to become flexible and adaptive to accommodate uncertainty in the form of discontinuous change. In the past, it was thought that an organizational arrangement whereby the company performed all its tasks internally was the best way to gain competitive advantage. Indeed, at the start of the twentieth century, Henry Ford owned railway lines, steam ship companies, iron mines and rubber plantations. A century later however, increased competition, globalization and technological developments, have all meant that working with others has come to be seen as the best way to reduce costs and increase efficiency and productivity. Consequently, answers to the question of 'who does what' now extend beyond the organization's own boundary to encompass its partners, competitors, customers and other communities of interest.

Historically, the initial problem for management was building and maintaining large-scale production processes and the organizations that operated them. Then attention focused on co-ordinating and controlling these large, complex organizations and facilitating their orderly growth. Most recently, the focus has shifted onto inter-organizational relationships. Building on the work of Robert Duncan (1979) (see Chapter 2), Narasimhan Anand and Richard Daft (2007) traced changes in the design of organization structures. They distinguish three eras of organizational design shown in Table 17.1, illustrating how management thinking about organization structure changed from vertical organization to horizontal organizing, and now to open boundaries via outsourcing and partnering. We shall draw heavily on these authors' explanatory structure and use their framework to compare and contrast the changes that have occurred in the design of organizations.

Table 17.1: Eras of organizational design

Era 1	Era 2	Era 3			
Mid 1800s–late 1970s	1980s–mid-1990s	Mid-1990s to date			
Self-contained organization structures	Horizontal organization structures	Boundaryless organization structure			
		Hollow	Modular	Virtual	Collaborative

Based on Anand and Daft (2007).

Think of an example of a change to the structure of an organization with which you are familiar. Has this restructuring changed the way that you or others do your work?

Era of self-contained organization structures

The first era identified by Anand and Daft (2007) lasted over a century from the mid-1800s to the late 1970s. During that time, the ideal organization was held to possess the following characteristics: being self-contained; having clear boundaries between itself and its suppliers, customers and competitors; transforming the inputs from suppliers into completed products or services; and meeting its transformation process requirements internally. Its design emphasized the need to adapt to environmental conditions, and to maximize control through reporting relationships and a vertical chain of command (Galbraith, 1973). Anand and Daft (2007, p.335) list the underlying design principles of a self-contained organization structure as:

Departmentalization
the process of grouping together activities and employees who share a common supervisor and resources, who are jointly responsible for performance, and who tend to identify and collaborate with each other.

- group people into functions or departments;
- establish reporting relationships between people and departments;
- provide systems to co-ordinate and integrate activities both horizontally and vertically.

A department designates a distinct area or branch of an organization over which a manager has authority for the performance of specified activities. Thus job grouping or the departmentalization of jobs constitutes an important aspect of organizational design. During this era, the functional, divisional and matrix became the favoured organization structures. All three rely on vertical hierarchy and the chain of command.

Functional structure
an organizational design that groups activities and people according to the similarities in their work, profession, expertise, goals or resources used.

Functional structure

A functional structure groups activities and people, from the bottom to the top, according to the similarities in their work, profession, expertise, goals or resources used, e.g. production, marketing, sales, and finance (Figure 17.1). Each functional activity is grouped into a specific department. In a hospital, functional grouping will be physiotherapy, nursing, medical physics. A university business school may group its staff into the main subject fields (finance; human behaviour; strategy and marketing; and operations management).

Divisional structure
an organizational design that groups departments together based on the product sold, the geographical area served, or type of customer.

Divisional structure

A divisional structure split an organization up into self-contained entities based on their organizational outputs – products or services provided; the geographical region operated in; or the customer groups served. Each division is likely to have its own functional structure

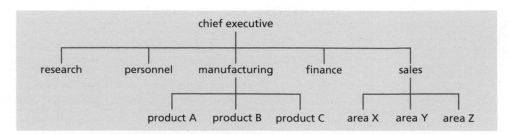

Figure 17.1: Function-based organization structure

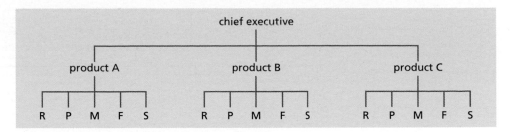

Figure 17.2: Product-based organization structure

replicated within it or receive functional support (e.g. marketing, human resources) from its headquarters. Each division operates as a stand-alone company, doing its own research, production, marketing, etc. (Chandler, 1962).

Product- or service-based

A single motor company can organize around its different automotive brands. For example, Daimler's divisions include Mercedes-Benz and Smart, while BMW's include BMW and Mini. Most university business schools offer undergraduate, postgraduate and non-graduating courses. A product- or service-based organization structure is shown in Figure 17.2.

In recent years, the Sony Corporation has failed to take advantage of changing market conditions. Its structure is based on product divisions, e.g. televisions, computer entertainment. These separate 'chimneys' or 'silos' which divide the company, have become disconnected entities that fail to communicate with each other effectively, and which no longer focus on Sony's corporate goals. Sir Howard Stringer, the CEO of Sony, will be seeking to restructure the company so as to realign the organization's structure with its corporate strategy (Colquitt *et al.*, 2009).

Geography-based

Grouping on this basis is used where the product or service is provided within a limited distance. It meets customers' needs effectively and economically, and lets senior management check and control how these are provided. Hotels and supermarkets are organized in this way. A university business school may have a main campus, a city centre location and an out-of-town, residential (hotel) facility. A geography- (or region- or location-) based organization structure is shown in Figure 17.3.

Customer-based

The company can be structured around its main customers or market segments. A large bank's departments may be personal, private, business and corporate. A university business school's clients include students, companies and research-funders. BT is divided into BT Retail (business and residential customers) and BT Wholesale (corporate customers). A customer-based organization structure is shown in Figure 17.4.

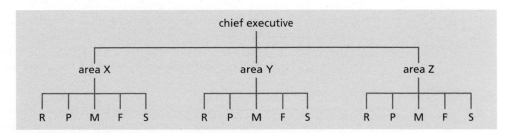

Figure 17.3: Geography-based organization structure

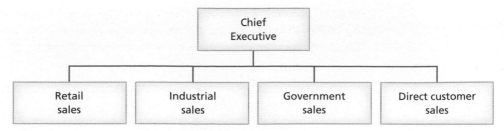

Figure 17.4: Customer-based organization structure

Matrix structure

Matrix structure an organizational design that combines two different types of structure resulting in an employee having two reporting relationships simultaneously.

A **matrix structure** combines a vertical structure with a strong horizontal overlay. The former provides downward control over the functional departments, and the latter allows inter-departmental co-ordination. This structure comprises employees working in temporary teams composed of employees from different functions (e.g. marketing, human resources, production) contributing to specific projects. This structure has two lines of authority. Each team member reports to two bosses – his project team manager and his functional manager (e.g. the head of production). There is thus a dual, rather than a single, chain of command (Bartlett and Ghoshal, 1990; Lawrence and Davis, 1979; Davis and Lawrence, 1978).

The most likely place that you would encounter a matrix structure is on your course or module, if it is taught by lecturers from a number of different university departments. These contributing lecturers report to two different bosses. One of these is responsible for

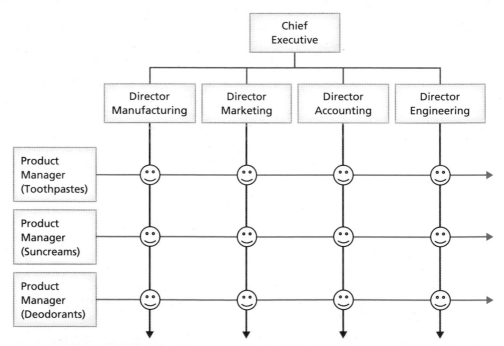

— The director of each functional department exercises line authority through the vertical chain-of-command.

— The product manager exercises authority through the horizontal chain of command, over those staff from the functional departments who have been assigned to work on the product.

☺ Employees at the intersections have two bosses. They report simultaneously to the director of their functional department (manufacturing, marketing, accounting or engineering) as well as to their product manager (toothpastes, suncreams or deodorants)

Figure 17.5: Matrix organization structure

the function, in this case the university academic department (e.g. Accounting, Economics, Law or Management). Their other 'boss' is the programme or module co-ordinator responsible for the teaching, tutoring and assessments for the module.

Philips the matrix master

Philips, a Dutch electrical giant was one of the earliest champions of the matrix structure. After the Second World War it established both national organizations and product divisions. The head of its washing machine division in Italy would have two bosses – the head of Philips in Italy and the washing machine supremo in the Netherlands. Co-ordinating committees were used to hold the two lines of command that had been created together, and to resolve the conflicts between the two lines of command that had been created. By 1991, Philips was in deep financial trouble and was reviewing its structural arrangements. It had experienced problems of accountability (was the country boss or product head responsible for the profit-and-loss account?), and power plays between country heads and business bosses (consumer electronics, medical products). Bartlett and Ghoshal concluded that matrix structures led to conflict and confusion; that the proliferation of channels created informational log jams; that multiple committees and reports bogged down the organization; and that overlapping responsibilities produced turf battles and a loss of

accountability. Academic commentators have described the matrix structure as one of the least successful organizational forms.

Since 2003, Philips has been drawing back from its matrix structure without actually re-organizing it, to counter criticisms of an over-focus on technology and under-focus on customers. Gerard Ruizendaal, head of corporate strategy said that whenever it creates a new organization, it creates a new problem. Under its 'One Philips' slogan, the company has been encouraging its employees to work across different business units, and has made awards for business initiatives that have created value for the company by involving staff collaborating with others, outside their immediate units. Philips staff are expected to move between different geographical regions and work in different product areas. Last year, Philips ran workshops for its top 1,000 managers who had been brought together in order to talk about issues that cut across organizational boundaries.

Based on Hindle (2006g); Bartlett and Ghoshal (1990).

Home viewing

The film *Other Peoples' Money* (1991, director Norman Jewison) shows a how a firm's failure to react to an external threat leaves it vulnerable to a hostile take-over. New England Wire and Cable (NEWC) is an old-fashioned manufacturing company, paternalistically led for 26 years by Andrew Jorgenson (played by Gregory Peck) who values stability and predictability. However, he is unaware of the developing problems in one of his company's divisions which requires urgent re-engineering and

diversification. Meanwhile, Garfield Investment Corporation (GIC), headed by Lawrence Garfield (played by Danny DeVito) looks for firms that are ripe to be taken over, and expects to make a substantial profit by liquidating NEWC. As you watch the film, consider some of the reasons that corporate re-structuring takes place. How does Jorgenson's leadership and decision-making style leave his company vulnerable to a take-over?

Era of horizontal organization structures

The second era identified by Anand and Daft (2007) lasted under two decades between the 1980s and the mid-1990s and promoted horizontal organization structures with a team- and process-based emphasis. It developed in response to the limitations of the earlier organization structures. These included difficulties of inter-departmental co-ordination; the ineffectiveness of vertical authority-based reporting systems; and the opportunities offered by computers and networks to increase organizational information processing capacity.

During this time, emphasis was placed on re-shaping (eliminating) organizations' internal boundaries to improving horizontal coordination and communication. Anand and Daft (2007, p.332) list the underlying design principles of a horizontal organization structure as:

- organize around complete workflow processes rather than tasks;
- flatten hierarchy and use teams to manage everything;
- appoint team leaders to manage internal team processes and co-ordinate work;
- permit team members to interact with suppliers and customers facilitating quick adaptation;
- provide required expertise from outside the team as required.

Team-based structure

Team-based structure an organizational design that consists entirely of project-type teams that co-ordinate their activities, and work directly with partners and customers to achieve their goals.

The above principles were predominantly implemented by means of a team-based structure which treats teams as organizing units of work. Here, individual employees are assembled into teams in a way similar to being assigned to traditional, functional departments. In one version, the organization consists *entirely* of different teams, each of which co-ordinate their own activities, and work with their partners and customers, to achieve their goals. Each team member possesses a different expertise (e.g. marketing, manufacturing, finance, human resources), which contributes to the team's completion of its task or project. In order for the different members to co-ordinate their contributions successfully, they must share information effectively with each other (Cherns, 1976).

These teams are characterized by horizontal communication; shared or rotated leadership; and delegated decision-making that gives authority to junior staff to make decisions on their own. Once, the goal has been achieved, the team moves onto a new project, perhaps reforming its membership before embarking on its next task. A true team-based structure is rare, and tends to be found in smaller organizations. A team structure, where it exists, is very flat, as shown in Figure 17.6. A university department may use a team structure. Academic staff may be members of a multidisciplinary research team contributing to a research council funded project; of a teaching team responsible for delivering lectures and tutorials; and of an administrative team, ensuring rooms are booked, student grades awarded and legal requirements complied with.

There are few organizations with this type of team-based structure. Square D, a large US manufacturer of electrical equipment based in Lexington, Kentucky, introduced a team-based structure in 1998. Its 800 employees were divided into 20–30 self-managed teams which are wholly responsible for their own products from start to finish. Whole Food Markets Inc, also in the United States, a retailer of natural foods, is another rare example. Each of its shops is an autonomous profit centre consisting of about ten teams. Each small, decentralized team (e.g. grocery, vegetables, bakery, prepared food), has its own team leader. It also has complete control over who joins. Using team-based hiring, after 90 days,

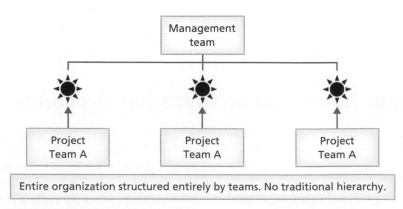

Figure 17.6: Team-based organization structure

potential hires need two-thirds of the team's support to join the staff permanently (Erickson and Gratton, 2007). The team leaders in each shop are a team; the shop leaders in each region are a team; and the company's six regional presidents are also a team (Fishman, 2007a).

Imagination in teams

Established in 1978 and based in London, Imagination Ltd is Europe's largest, independent design and communications agency, and has won a number of awards for its innovative, theatrical programmes. It is unusual because it has a team-based structure. Its work includes graphic design, website construction, product launches, visitor centres and lighting buildings. The company's website states that while the company is driven by the contribution of the talented individual, it delivers through the team. When a client consults the company, it quickly assembles a cross-functional team drawn from the company's in-house community, with the occasional outside specialist. Depending on the project, participants may include an eclectic mix of designers, architects, lighting experts, writers, theatre specialists, film directors, artists, IT experts and the occasional choreographer. New team members are selected for each new project. 'Imagination brings people together and provides the environment that encourages them to work to the best of their abilities'.

Once Imagination and the client agree on the scope of a project, team members develop a goal statement which guides their work. Being a non-hierarchical organization, only four people have formal job titles, and most projects rarely have a leader. Instead every member accepts responsibility for the project's success and makes contributions that move the whole team nearer to achieving its goal. The underpinning ethos is that the team is greater than the talent of its individual members, and that everybody can learn from each other. Teams meet weekly with intensive participation from all those present. The company ensures that people gain an understanding of, and respect for, the contribution of others, so as to keep their input in perspective.

Based on Fishman (2007b) and Imagination Ltd website (consulted 2009).

Cross-functional team employees from different functional departments who meet as a team to complete a particular task.

It is far more common for a traditionally structured company, to adjust work arrangements so that only staff members at the lower and middle levels of the hierarchy, who are responsible for manufacturing the product, providing the service or managing the delivery of either, operate as teams rather than as individuals. When this type of work arrangement is used on a regular basis, the organization may claim to be using a team-based structure. In reality however, all that has happened, is that it has grafted a teamworking format onto the lower hierarchical levels of an existing functional or divisional structure. Its organizational chart will look like this (Figure 17.7):

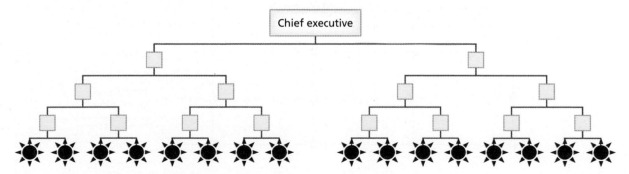

Figure 17.7: Traditional organization structure with teams at lowest level

This 'teams-at-the bottom' structure may use a **cross-functional team** approach in which a number teams consisting of employees from various functional departments, at about the same hierarchical level, are formed to complete particular tasks (see Chapter 13). As before,

Production team
a stable number of individuals who share production goals, and who perform specific roles which are supported by a set of incentives and sanctions.

the benefits of this arrangement include access to the different expertise of members, improved horizontal communication and better inter-departmental coordination. Typical issues addressed by cross-functional teams are solving a problem; developing or launching a new product or initiating a change programme. The development of the Ford Motor Company's Escape gas-electric hybrid sports utility vehicle involved cross-functional teamworking.

Another version of the 'teams-at-the-bottom' structure, is to arrange for the work to be done or service to be delivered by employees working together as **production team**, rather than making individual, sequential contributions to the final task (see Chapter 13). Since the height of the functional or divisional hierarchical structure above these production teams remains unaltered, claiming that the company is operating a team-based structure is somewhat disingenuous.

Boeing's production teams

The 787 Dreamliner is a medium-sized, wide-bodied, twin-engine, jet capable of carrying 210 to 330 passengers. To produce it, the company created an organization structure consisting of Life Cycle Product Teams (LCPTs) that have responsibility for the life-cycle cost of their product. Each LCPT has a team leader – an engineering leader, a manufacturing leader, finance and business leader and a global partner leader. Each is like a small company with responsibility for the design, production and delivery of their product on schedule and on cost to the 787 programme. The LCPTs are like little companies within the bigger programme. They are of two types – vertical and horizontal.

Vertical LCPTs are responsible for the plane's structural components such as fuselage, interior, wings, propulsion, vertical tail, and the landing gear. Their task is to deliver their product into final assembly where it all gets integrated with the others and built into the airplane. Horizontal LCPTs address matters relevant to all the different structural component teams. They are labelled systems, services, and production operations. The Systems LCPT is responsible for the architecture, testing and the systems that go into the airplane. It ensures the systems architecture for hydraulics, electrical and other systems on the airplane are all integrated. The Services LCPT is responsible for obtaining the input for the structural repair manual, which comes from managers in the horizontal teams. Production Operations LCPT is responsible for putting this airplane together and their work begins once the final assembly of the airplane is initiated.

Based on John Dodge (2007a, 2007b).

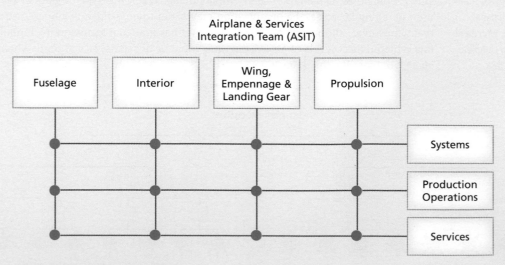

Life Cycle Product Teams (LCPTs)

Source: Boeing 787 Dreamliner Engineering Chief Describes Partners Organization, *Design News* (15 May 2007), http://www.designnews.com/article2659-Boeing_787_Dreamliner_Engineering_Chief_Describes_Partners_Organization.php. Used with permission of Design News copyright © 2009. All rights reserved.

Source: Hanusa/AP/Press Association Images

Final assembly of 787 aeroplane

There are many different forms that the structures of Era 1 and Era 2 organizations can take. To help our understanding, Christopher Mabey and his colleagues offered a conceptual framework based on the juxtaposition of various dimensions that are critical when making a decision about the internal structure of a firm (Mabey *et al.*, 1998, p.235). Their framework considers re-structuring within conventional organizational boundaries. We have modified these authors' examples, but have retained their three cross-cutting dimensions. These are shown in Figure 17.8. The top horizontal axis considers decision-making. It runs from centralized (decisions made at the top) through to decentralized (power

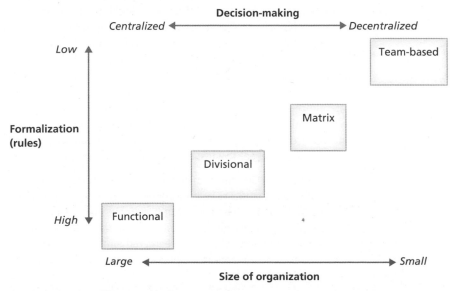

Figure 17.8: Era 1 and 2 organization structures
Source: Adapted from Mabey *et al.* (1998, p.235).

delegated for people to make decisions lower in the hierarchy). The vertical dimension on the left, distinguishes the degree of formalization (written rules, operating procedures, job descriptions, organizational charts and uses formal, written communication). It runs from low down to high. The bottom horizontal axis relates to the size of the organization.

Moving from bottom left, we begin with a structure based on the main organization functions, where people sharing the same expertise are placed together. This reflects Weber's bureaucracy. Then we have various divisional structures (product/service, geography, customer), selected to be most suited to a company's activities. Next comes the matrix stricture, creating cross-functional teams consisting of individuals from different departments of the company. Finally, arriving at top right, we have a structure based on teams which are given limited autonomy to complete an entire production process.

Era of boundaryless organizations

Boundaryless organization one possessing permeable internal and external boundaries which give it flexibility and thus the ability to respond to change rapidly.

Collaborative relationship structure a structure that involves a relationship with another, sharing with them ideas, knowledge, staff and technology for mutual benefit.

The third era identified by Anand and Daft (2007) began in the mid-1990s and continues to this day. It is characterized by the development of an architecture called the **boundaryless organization**. This concept views firms as possessing permeable boundaries, both internally and externally. It behaves like an organism encouraging better integration among its functional departments and closer partnerships with outsiders, so as to facilitate the free exchange of ideas and information, in order to maximize its flexibility and be able to respond rapidly to change (BNET Business Dictionary, 2009). The concept of the boundaryless organization was developed at General Electric and was originally described by Ron Ashkenas and his colleagues in 1995 (Ashkenas *et al.*, 2002). The term was coined by the former chief executive of General Electric (GE) Jack Welch, who wanted to eliminate barriers inside his company (horizontally, between GE's different departments and vertically, between different levels of GE's management hierarchy); and also to break down external barriers between his company and its customers, suppliers and other stakeholders.

Many organizations are adopting this approach in order to become more effective. Companies now rarely innovate on their own, and the number of potential partners with whom they can collaborate has expanded enormously. Adopting this type of organizational design involves establishing collaborative relationships with suppliers, competitors, customers, third parties, and participants in online communities. Increasingly, we are seeing examples of loosely interconnected assemblages of companies operating different types of **collaborative relationship structures** (Schilling and Steensma, 2001).

This approach has been facilitated by the opportunities created by improved communication technology (internet, mobile phones) and the rise of emerging economies (China, India), as well as by management's acceptance that an organization cannot efficiently perform alone, all the tasks required to make a product or offer a service. Organizational structuring involves translating company policy into practices, duties and functions that are allocated as specific tasks to individuals and groups. However, increasingly these individuals and groups can be located outside the company. In the last 20 years, the accent has moved from hierarchy to heterarchy; from bureaucracy to adhocracy; from structures to processes; from real to virtual; and from closed to open. John Child wrote:

> During the 1990s the transition from an economy based on the processing of materials to one based on flows of information became ever more apparent, especially in the developed economies. The transition unfettered many aspects of organizations from their former physical constraints, permitting, for example, activities in dispersed locations to be effectively integrated as those gathered on the same site. Increased information intensity is today the fundamental development to which organizational designs must respond (Child, 2005, p.27).

Outsourcing contracting with external providers to supply the organization with the processes and products that were previously supplied internally.

Underpinning all the structural developments of this era has been **outsourcing**. This describes a situation in which an organization contracts with another firm to provide it with

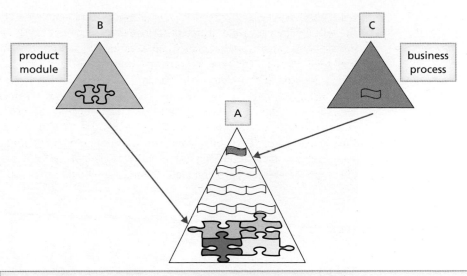

Firm B supplies organization A with one of its product modules; firm C provides it with one of its business processes.

Figure 17.9: Outsourcing relationship

either a business process, e.g. paying its staff wages (payroll); running its courses (training); delivering its goods to customers (logistics); or supply it with a component of its final product, e.g. a computer hard drive, a steering wheel, the packaging box. The company itself will have previously provided or made these itself (Figure 17.9).

Outsourcing ranges along a continuum. At one end, there is minimal outsourcing, as when an organization only hires a property maintenance company to clean its offices for it, or a drinks manufacturer arranges with a paper firm to provide it with specialist packaging for its bottles, doing everything else itself. At the other end of the continuum, there are the companies that have outsourced the majority of what they previously did and made. In the private sector, the Nike factory in Vietnam is an example; in the public sector, in Iraq, the United States military has outsourced many tasks to private security contractors such as Blackwater Worldwide and two other security firms (Scahill, 2007). When a business process or a product is supplied to an organization by a firm located in a different country, it is referred to as offshoring (*The Economist*, 2007d, 2008f). Many companies have changed their business models to reduce costs, through outsourcing and working closely with risk-sharing partners.

Offshoring contracting with external providers in a different country to supply the organization with the processes and products that were previously supplied internally.

Outsourcing has become one of the most contentious inter-organizational arrangements. In 2008, Boeing experienced a strike related to its 787 airliner, 80 per cent of whose parts are outsourced to Asian and European firms before being assembled in its Seattle plant. The union concern was that previous agreements allowed outsourcers to deliver parts straight onto the factory floor. It feared that external contractors would start fitting those parts onto the planes themselves, on the production line, displacing Boeing staff (*The Economist*, 2008g). The seven-week strike by 27,000 Boeing employees cost the company $5 billion in revenues. The management conceded to the union's demands. It agreed that outside vendors would be allowed to deliver parts to its factories, but only union members would be permitted to take them to the aircraft (Weitzman, 2008).

However, an OECD study reported that offshoring was not a big cause of job losses and had an overall positive effect on economies (Görg *et al.*, 2008; *The Economist*, 2008a). It investigated outsourcing between 1996–2005 by large British multinationals with foreign subsidiaries and found that offshoring increased by 35 per cent in manufacturing and 45 per cent in services, but still accounted for only 5 per cent of GDP in 2004. Only 4–8 per cent of the multinationals had Indian and Chinese subsidiaries, most international outsourcing was done in other developed countries, especially within the European Union. In 2005, offshoring

Source: Richard Vogel/AP/Press Association Images

Source: Marwan Naamani AFP/Getty Images

accounted for 3–5 per cent of job losses, but the resultant increased production had improved their competitiveness, resulting in compensatory job gains. In the period, offshoring is estimated to have created 100,000 UK jobs. The authors concluded that on balance, offshoring has been good for the UK economy, making domestic firms more productive, and generating jobs both at home and abroad. Anand and Daft identify three types of organization structure adopted in this boundaryless organization, all based on the outsourcing principle – hollow, modular and virtual. To these we can add a fourth – collaborative.

Outsourcing manufacturing

Valmet Automotive Inc. in Finland is one of the world's niche car makers. It was established in 1969 as a joint venture with Saab to build the classic Saab 96. Now, it is a brand-independent, European contract manufacturer of exclusive, high quality, specialty cars, and a part of Finland's Metso Corp., the world's leader in paper processing and automation. It currently employs 1100 workers and in 2005, it built 21,233 vehicles. The company currently produces the second generation Boxster and Cayman S cars for Porsche AG at its headquarters and 900,000-square-foot plant complex in Uusikaupunki (pronounced oo-see-cow-punky), about 140 miles north of Helsinki. Its website offers a virtual factory tour. Valmet provides complete vehicle projects from developing the car as a

product through to manufacturing the model in a way that meets the expectations of its major automotive customers such as Posrche and Saab. As subcontractors, their core competencies are in assembly, projects and convertible technologies. They offer the large automobile manufacturers the possibility of bringing, high-quality, specialty car models onto the market quickly and cost-effectively. Since 1969, it has produced almost the whole range of Saab models from the 95 to the 9000 Cabriolet, and more recently, the AWD Opel Calibra coupe and the Talbot Horizon.

Based on Valmet Automotive Newsletter *(2005);*
Brooke (2001); www.valmet-automotive.com.

Source: Valmet Automotive, Inc.

Hollow organization structure

Hollow organization structure an organizational design based on outsourcing an organization's non-core *processes* which are then supplied to it by specialist, external providers.

Outsourcing the majority of a company's non-core *processes* such as human relations, payroll, purchasing, logistics and security creates a hollow organization structure. Specialist suppliers then provide these for the company. Some automobile manufacturers have even outsourced the assembly of their entire vehicles (*The Economist*, 2002c). This leaves the company free to concentrate on those things which represent the core of their activity; those that it does best; and those which lead to more value creation e.g. research, design, market-ing. John Child (2005, p.180) explained that the removal of previously internally-provided

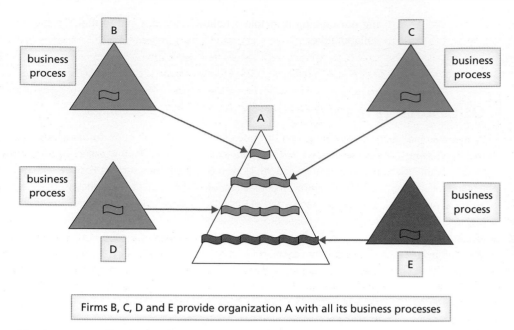

Firms B, C, D and E provide organization A with all its business processes

Figure 17.10: Hollow organization structure

processes or services 'hollows out' the organization, reducing its size and workforce, hence the name. Its remaining small number of core staff concentrate on strategic matters, including the integration of the contributions of the multiple external providers that it has created.

Anand and Daft (2007, p.335) list the underlying design principles of a hollow organization structure as:

- determine the non-core processes that are not critical to business performance; do not create current or potential business advantage; are unlikely to drive growth or rejuvenation;
- harness market forces to get non-core processes done efficiently;
- create an effective and flexible interface;
- align incentives between the organization and its outsourcing provider.

Nike, the sports goods company, considers its core competencies to be in marketing and distribution, rather than in manufacturing. In consequence, the company relies on contract manufacturers located in low cost labour areas of the world which produce merchandise bearing Nike's well-known swoosh logo.

Cycling into the hollow

Narasimhan Anand and Richard Daft give the example of Strida, a British company that sells lightweight, foldable bicycles, which changed its traditional, era 1 functional organization structure, to become an era 3 hollow organization. The Strida 1 was designed by Mark Sanders as a solution to traffic congestion. The authors explain how in 2001, the company received a large order from a customer willing only to buy at a price that was below the cost of production. The chief executive decided to close the company's vertically integrated production plant in the UK and to find a Far East partner, which could make the bicycles more efficiently at lower cost. The production facilities were moved in 2001 to Ming Cycle Industrial Co. Ltd. in Taiwan, one of the world's largest bike production manufacturers. In addition, specialist contractors were engaged by Strida to develop new models, to design owners' manuals and to manage the company website. The company uses internet communications to ensure effective communication between designers and manufacturers, as well as to manage accounts, materials and documents. The company owned back-end operations of warehouse management, order fulfilment, inventory control, customer service, inbound container management and accounts generation were all transferred to a long-established vendor. The effect of the transformation for the company was reduced overheads and the ability to alter production in response to market fluctuations. The focus of the company's chief executive officer's job became managing the various relationships that now constituted the business.

Based on Anand and Daft (2007) and
Strida company website: www.strida.com.

Modular organization structure

Modular organization structure an organizational design that involves assembling product chunks (modules) provided by internal divisions and external providers.

A modular organization structure is also based on outsourcing. However, unlike the hollow structure discussed earlier, in which outsources *processes* such as logistics, payroll or warehousing are supplied by outsiders, a modular structure outsources the production of *parts* of the total product. Internal and external contractors supply component parts that the company then assembles itself. A company can break down its product's design into chunks that are then supplied by both its internal divisions and external contractors. NASA's Space Shuttle, and computer hardware and software companies, aircraft manufacturers and household appliances firms, all organize themselves in this way. The analogy most often used is that of a Lego structure in which the different bricks are manufactured by a variety of different, external companies (Schilling and Steensma, 2001).

Anand and Daft (2007, p.337) list the underlying design principles of a modular organization structure as:

- break products into self-contained modules or chunks, capable of stand-alone manufacture;
- design interfaces to ensure different chunks work together;
- outsource product chunks to external contractors who can make them more efficiently;
- ensure that the company can assemble the chunks that are produced internally and those supplied by external providers.

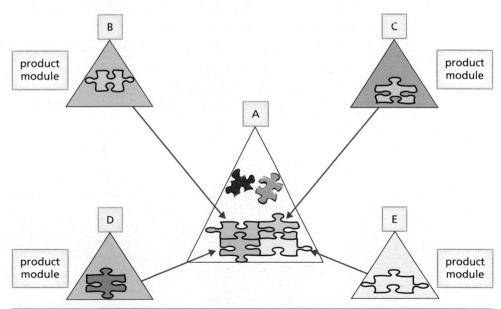

Firms B, C, D and E provide different product modules to organization A which produces its own as well, and assembles all of them

Figure 17.11: Modular organization structure

This involves a single large hub-company, located at the network's centre that outsources chunks of its production functions to external providers except those it deems to be strategically vital and close to its core competence. The distinguishing feature of a dominated network is most of the communication is in the form of a series of one-to-one, hub-node interactions between the hub company and its providers, and only a limited amount between the smaller node-companies.

Modular partners

In 2006, Boeing Commercial Airplanes dramatically altered the process for developing and manufacturing its 787 Dreamliner model, in effect, creating a dominated, network organization. This organizational design involves a single large hub-company, located at the network's centre, outsourcing chunks of its production functions to external providers while retaining those deemed to be strategically vital and close to its core competence. The distinguishing feature of a dominated network is most of the communication is in the form of a series of one-to-one interactions between the hub company and its providers, and only a limited amount *between* the smaller node-companies. For the first time, Boeing shared with others, the engineering design work, that it had previously done itself. It realized that it had to compete with an increasingly successful Airbus; and that having multiple suppliers impeded that goal. Instead of suppliers, it looked around the world for 'risk-sharing partners' (RSPS). Whereas traditional suppliers only provide what a company asks for, partners share the responsibility for a project. Boeing reduced its suppliers from 700 to under a 100 from around the world. Collectively, these were responsible for 70 per cent of the airplane. These partners spent time at Boeing's headquarters in Seattle, working together on the configuration of the plane, using a single design system. On returning home, they built their own production faculties, to make the bits of the aircraft for which they were responsible.

This form of organizational structure did not work for Boeing. Mike Blair, the executive responsible for the 787 programme reported that the company had experienced mounting production delays, and he attacked some of the companies recruited to build the plane. In future, he said, Boeing would not entrust design work to partners who 'proved incapable of doing it' and would make suppliers build their factories close to Boeing's main assembly operation, rather than flying semi-finished sections of the aircraft round the world on huge, modified 747 transporters with a grotesquely swollen bodies (dubbed Dreamlifters). Boeing has taken back some work in-house that had previously been outsourced. Has the company renounced this form of collaboration in the face of 'seven-late-seven' jibe made by its critics? Initially, it expects to produce fewer Dreamliners than planned.

Based on Hindle (2006h); The Economist *(2007e, 2007f, 2008g);* Financial Times *(2007);* BusinessWeek *(2008).*

Virtual organization structure

Virtual organization structure an organizational design that uses technology to transcend the constraints of legal structures, physical conditions, place and time, and allows a network of separate participants to present themselves to customers as a single entity.

The virtual organization structure consists of a temporary network of nodes (entire organizations, parts of organizations, teams, specific individuals) linked by information technologies which flexibly co-ordinate their activities, combine their skills and resources in order to achieve common goals, without requiring traditional hierarchies of central direction or supervision. In this structure, the outsourcing company becomes primarily a 'network co-ordinator', and when supported by sophisticated technology – a virtual organization. Virtual organizations, and indeed all new forms of working, have been brought about by a variety of changes in the environment in which businesses operate. These include communications technology and the globalization of production and sales (Hindle, 2006e). A virtual organization is viewed as a single entity from outside by its customers despite consisting of a network of separate companies.

Anand and Daft (2007, p.339) list the underlying design principles of a virtual organization structure as:

- create boundaries around a temporary organization with external partners;
- use technology to link people, assets and ideas;

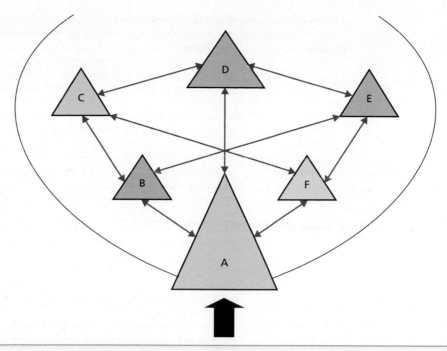

An organizational design that uses technology to allow a network of separate companies to present themselves as a single entity to customers

Figure 17.12: Virtual organization structure

- each partner contributes their domain of excellence;
- disband or absorb after opportunity ends.

Many see virtual organizations as a panacea for many of the current organizational problems. A virtual organization has the capacity to form and reform to deal with problems, and (potentially) provide a flexibility of response to organizational needs and changing circumstances. The concept has generated considerable discussion and debate among managers, management consultants and business commentators, although they disagree about its nature. In the light of this, Warner and Witzel (2004) list the six features that nearly all virtual organizations have in common (Table 17.7).

Warner and Witzel (2004) argue that organizations should not be classified into virtual or non-virtual categories. All firms can possess some degree of virtuality, and that virtuality can take different forms. They say that every organization is a mixture of virtual and tangible elements and identify six dimensions along which companies can choose to organize their activities on a virtual or a tangible basis:

- nature of product;
- nature of working;
- relationship with suppliers;
- relationship with customers;
- relationship between firm's elements;
- relationship between managers and employees.

A supermarket's internal operations are traditionally physical and tangible, but their links with their suppliers are virtual, using an automated product reordering system. Thus the question to ask of an organization is not whether it is virtual or non-virtual, but to what degree, and in what ways, does it possess virtuality. Additionally, whatever an organization's virtual–tangible 'asset mix' may be, it can be managed in a virtual or in tangible way.

Table 17.2: Features of virtual organizations

Feature	Description
1. Lack of physical structure	Less physical presence than conventional organizations. Fewer tangible assets such as offices or warehouses, and those possessed are physically dispersed.
2. Reliance on communication technologies	Technology is used dynamically to link people, assets and ideas. Communication networks replace the physical structure of a conventional organization, to define it and give a shape to its activities.
3. Mobile work	Communication networks reduce the importance of where work is physically located, meaning that individuals and team members no longer have to be physically co-located, to work together on a common task.
4. Hybrid forms	Short or long term collaboration between agencies can take various forms, called hybrids, including networks, consortia, and webs, to achieve a mutual goal.
5. Boundaryless and inclusive	Not confined to legal entities, they but can encompass suppliers and distributors, working with producers, and even involving customers in the production process.
6. Flexible and responsive	Can be rapidly assembled from a variety of disparate elements, to achieve a certain business goal, and then, as required, dismantled or reconfigured.

Based on Warner and Witzel (2004), pp.3–5.

Source: © Christopher Weyant/Condé Nast Publications/www.cartoonbank.com.

David Nadler of Mercer Delta Consulting, an organizational structure ('architecture') consultancy company, sees companies increasingly consisting of a number of strategically aligned businesses, 'linked closely where there are opportunities to create value by leveraging shared capabilities, but only loosely where the greater value lies in the undifferentiated focus' (Hindle, 2006h). This implies that close and loose relationships will co-exist within

Table 17.3: Example of collaborative relationships

	Non-contractual arrangements	Contractual arrangements	Equity-based arrangements
Multilateral arrangements	• **Lobbying coalition** (e.g. European Roundtable of industrialists) • **Joint standard setting** (e.g. Linux coalition) • **Learning communities** (e.g. Strategic Management Society)	• **Research consortium** (e.g. Symbian in PDAs) • **International marketing alliance** (e.g. Star Alliance in airlines) • **Export partnership** (e.g. Netherlands Export Combination)	• **Shared payment system** (e.g. Visa) • **Construction consortium** (e.g. Eurotunnel) • **Joint reservation system** (e.g. Galileo)
Bilateral arrangements	• **Cross-selling deal** (e.g. between pharmaceutical firms) • **R&D staff exchange** (e.g. between IT firms) • **Market information sharing agreement** (e.g. between hardware and software makers)	• **Licensing agreement** (e.g. Disney and Coca-Cola) • **Co-development contract** (e.g. Disney and Pixar in movies) • **Co-branding alliance** (e.g. Coca-Cola and McDonald's)	• **New product joint venture** (e.g. Sony and Ericsson in cell phones) • **Cross-border joint venture** (e.g. DaimlerChrysler and Beijing Automotive) • **Local joint venture** (e.g. CNN Turk in Turkey)

From Strategy Synthesis: Text and Readings, de Wit, B. and Meyer, R., Copyright 2005 International Thomson Business Press, Reproduced by permission of Cengage Learning.

and between organizations. Bob de Wit and Ron Meyer (2005) provide taxonomy of inter-organizational, collaborative relationships (Table 17.3). In the traditional organization structures, units were either within an organization – 'densely connected' or outside the organization, and not attached at all. In both situations, relations with external suppliers are at arm's length. Nadler argues that many of today's companies cohabit – using joint ventures and strategic alliances. He says that what is inside and outside the company, previously clear, is now becoming blurred. However, when different businesses become connected to varying degrees, it causes them problems of dependency and uncertainty, which in turn create risk. What happens when a partner in a joint venture goes bankrupt? How do banks ensure that employees of companies to whom they have outsourced services, do not steal their customers' PIN numbers?

Commentators even suggest that companies now need an 'extended organizational form' – one shape for their external operations, and another for their in-house activities (Hindle, 2006f).

Collaborative organization structure

Collaborative structures take the form of different relationships that organizations have with their suppliers, competitors and third parties.

Collaboration with suppliers

McLaren and partnerships

However successful this year's McLaren Formula 1 racing car is, it will bear little relation to next year's. Such is the pace of change in F1 engineering that 95 per cent of it will be different. The planning and design take place in McLaren's Technology Centre in Woking, Surrey, but the ideas generated are implemented in far-flung corners of the globe. A McLaren F1 racing car contains 15,000–16,000 separate parts that are manufactured by 750 companies. Jonathan Neale is McLaren Racing's managing director. His job is to co-ordinate all this activity. 'I can just pick up the phone and say, "I can't solve this problem. I need some help. I can tell you what the problem is but I don't know how to solve it",' he says. Partnerships are the lifeblood of McLaren and its rival teams.

→

A lot of this is about management process and organization. I run a high speed organization, but it's a small-to-medium enterprise of 500 people. I can't possibly expect to have the world's leading know-how in fuel lubrication, boding and adhesive material, yet I need that to compete. So how do we get that? We plug into our partners. I have access to global research and developments in fuel lubrication.

McLaren illustrates that technological developments, speed of change and globalization mean that a single organization, however successful, can no longer 'do it all themselves'. Even the largest companies have had to develop collaborative relationships with outsiders.

Based on Blitz (2007, pp.22–23).

Morgan Witzel (2007, p.4) noted that, 'Whereas collaboration used to be a matter of integrating organizations, now it is increasingly seen as a matter of integrating activities. In other words, tasks are carried out by the person or organization that is most suited to the specific issue.' Hence, discussions of organization structure and the alternatives to bureaucracy now focus increasingly on collaborative, inter-organizational relationships. Lynda Gratton argued that the emergence of collaboration was the result of four, intersecting environmental, social and technological trends (Gratton, 2007, Gratton *et al.*, 2007):

Rise of partnership strategies: a change in perception away from seeing companies as competing for a piece of a finite cake (*value appropriation*), and towards their making the cake bigger (*value creation*). To create new markets, competitors and customers have to work together in a process of co-creation. The pharmaceutical industry has, in the past, created and marketed its products through strategic alliances and joint ventures. The participating firms draw upon a greater pool of experience and talent; are forced to build their collaborative capabilities and their partnership skills; and treat their suppliers more like peers. In several industrial sectors (e.g. telecommunications and IT), it is no longer possible to operate individually.

Knowledge economy: the move towards the knowledge economy and the focus on the innovation of products and services. Historically, innovation has occurred through collective experience and interactions between different groups. Mutual respect and trust is a perquisite for working and sharing knowledge with others. Innovation requires a collaborative culture.

Working styles of Generation Y: the post-war, baby-boomer generation of current CEOs and senior managers were brought up in a world of competition and individual endeavour to secure a higher education, a job and career advancement, and honed their competitive skills and practices as they progressed up the hierarchy. In contrast, Generation Y (up to 27 years) is a community-based cohort that is particularly adept at, and places value upon, collaborating with others. Thus, those who have a positive attitude towards, and a competency in, collaboration, as well as experience of using social media technologies that underpin it, are progressively replacing today's senior management.

Advances in collaborative technology: many companies' collaborative experiences occur in complex forms, supported by advanced technology. Collaboration requires synchronous (videoconferencing) and asynchronous communication (email and voicemail). It involves sharing information that requires a common repository of knowledge. While the business world is currently struggling to work out how to use Web 2.0 technologies (social networks, wikis and blogs), when the current, wired-up generation of *Facebook* and *Second Life* users join the commercial world, they are likely to prefer different ways of communicating, which will affect collaboration within and between businesses (Newing, 2007).

Co-opetition
a form of cooperation between competing organizations which is limited to specified areas where both believe they can gain mutual benefit.

Collaboration with competitors

Collaboration with competitors can take the form of 'cooperative competition' which is called **co-opetition**. This occurs when two or more organizations decide that they do not

Signs of the social networking times.

Source: www.joyoftech.com.

possess an individual competitive advantage in a field, want to share common costs, or wish to innovative quickly but lack the necessary resources, knowledge or skill to do so (Brandenburger and Nalebuff, 1997). For instance, the cooperation between Peugeot and Toyota on shared components for a new city car for Europe in 2005. In this case, companies will save money on shared costs, while remaining fiercely competitive in other areas. For co-opetition to work, companies need to very clearly define where they are working together, and where they are competing. Co-opetition can take the legal–structural form of a strategic alliance or joint venture.

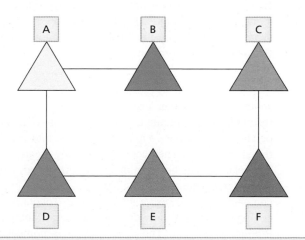

Organizations A, B, C, D, E and F co-operate, providing resources, to achieve specific objectives while remaining independent entities

Figure 17.13: Strategic alliance

Strategic alliance an arrangement in which two or more firms agree to co-operate to achieve specific objectives while remaining independent organizations.

Strategic alliance A strategic alliance is a tight, formalized, contractual relationship with a legal element, in which firms co-operate over the medium to long term, to achieve certain commercial objectives for mutual advantage, while remaining independent entities. Each alliance partner provides their own resources, products, equipment, expertise, production facilities or funding. In a strategic alliance, companies merge a limited part of their domain with each other, and attempt to achieve the competitive advantage that might have individually eluded them. Alliances tend to be established over a single, specific initiative, although they may be later extended to cover other activities between the participating companies (Figure 17.13).

Skyteam Alliance

The Skyteam Alliance is one of three mega-alliances in the international airline industry, the other two being The Star Alliance and the One World Alliance. Skyteam consists of 10 airlines, including Air France-KLM and North West Airlines, and three associate airlines. Collectively, its members provide over 15,000 daily flights to 791 destinations in 162 countries. Members can offer their own customers destinations anywhere in the world without having to fly there themselves. Together, Skyteam, Star and One World account for 69 per cent of the world's air revenue passenger miles. Each individual airline seeks to build on its own strengths, and compensates for the others' weaknesses. Next time you are on an airplane, read the in-flight magazine and listen to the announcements to determine the alliance to which your particular carrier belongs.

Based on Holland Herald (2008, p.68) and websites of www.staralliance.com; www.oneworld.com; www.alliance.com.

One reason that strategic alliances are created by companies is to bring about organizational learning. Rather than the partners being involved in skill substitution (one produces, while the other sells), they are interested in learning from each other, thereby strengthening the areas in which each is weakest. The primary reason for alliance creation is to secure specific competencies and resources to survive and succeed in globalizing markets, particularly those in which technologies are rapidly changing. However, research shows that often they end in disappointment for the organizations involved (Koza and Lewin, 1999).

STOP AND THINK

Back in 1997, arch-rivals Microsoft and Apple entered into a five-year, strategic alliance to develop Macintosh-compatible versions of Microsoft® Office 98, Internet Explorer 4 and Java technologies. The latest edition of *Office for Mac* was recently released. What benefits do you think each of these long time competitors saw for themselves in this alliance collaboration?

Joint venture an arrangement in which two or more companies remain independent, but establish a new organization that they jointly own and manage.

Joint venture Another form of co-opetition is the joint venture. Competitors may wish to pool resources or collaborate to challenge other competitors. Here, two companies remain independent, but establish a new organization into which they both contribute equity and which they jointly own. They control the newly-created firm, sharing its expenses and revenues. The relationships between them are formalized, either through shareholding arrangements or by agreements specifying asset-holding and profit distribution. Airbus is a well known company which is also a joint venture. Toyota has a number of joint venture plants with companies around the world (e.g. General Motors, Peugeot), all of which use the Toyota Production System. The joint venture is popular with Western companies operating in China, providing companies with low cost entry into new markets. Sony Ericsson was established as a joint venture in 2001 to produce mobile phones. It combines Sony's consumer electronics expertise with Ericsson's know how in technological communication. Both companies stopped making their own mobile phones (Figure 17.4).

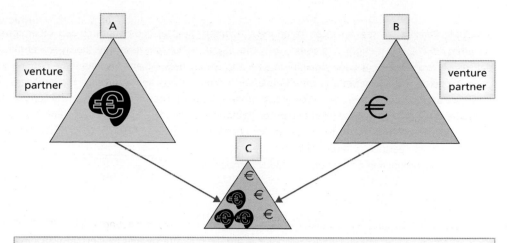

Organization A and organization B invest equity in a newly created, jointly-owned, firm C.

Figure 17.14: Joint venture

The odd couple

If you are on a short haul flight, the chances are that your aircraft's engines were made by CFM International. CFM is an unusual yet durable joint venture between US-based General Electric (GE), the world's most successful conglomerate and standard bearer of raw Anglo-Saxon capitalism, and Snecma which until recently, was a French, state-owned enterprise (and now is owned by SANFRAN). CFM's engines power 71 per cent of the world's fleet of single-aisle aircraft. They can be found in Boeing 737s, DC8s, Airbus A320s and the AWACS. It supplied 400 commercial and military customers world-wide. These are the workhouses of aviation, and constitute the largest market for engines, much bigger than

that for wide-bodied jumbos. The joint venture began in 1974 when both companies wanted to expand beyond their mostly military customers into the growing civilian business. This was dominated at the time by Pratt & Whitney, which had the best-selling engine for single aisle planes. As the technological leader, it saw no need to collaborate with anyone. Snecma decided against linking up with Rolls Royce, after a failed collaboration on Concorde engines. That left GE, which was anxious to get close to Airbus which was founded in 1970, and was then Europe's nascent aircraft consortium.

The European home of this odd pairing is an old military airfield on the edge of the forest of Fontainebleau,

Source: Ferenc Szelepcsenyi/Alamy

→

outside Paris, while the American component is based within GE's aero-engine division in Cincinnati, Pennsylvania. Despite a huge disparity in size, the two firms operate their joint venture on a simple and equitable basis. In both factories, the core module of the CFM engine (a GE design originally developed for fighter aircraft) is married to a French front fan and low-pressure turbine. Each partner is responsible for the research, design and production of its modules. Many companies set up joint ventures and other forms of collaboration, but few have one that is so central to their entire business. GE and Snecma share nothing but engine parts and sales, and they split the proceeds roughly 50–50. Jet engines may be awesomely complicated machines worth millions of dollars each. But the secret to making them successfully seems to be keep it simple.

From The Economist *(2007g).*

Collaboration with third parties

In late 2008, T-Mobile, a mobile operator owned by Germany's Deutsche Telecom, presented its new phone, the G1, which is made by HTC, a Taiwanese manufacturer. The device is the first to be based on software called Android, made by Google, the largest internet company (*The Economist*, 2008i). Android is a fully 'open' operating system and Google hopes to encourage third parties such as other telephone operators and handset makers like South Korea's Samsung and LG to adopt Android for their smartphones rather than going to the expense of developing their own software. Being 'open' also means that software companies and individual developers can, free of charge, devise mobile internet services that run on the phone (Taylor and Parker, 2008; Beaumont, 2008). It promises users the ability to customize their devices, as they have done with Linux adding features and downloading new and probably free applications. Google is hoping to make Android the dominant platform ('the Microsoft Windows') of the phone. In contrast, Apple's iPhone uses proprietary technology which enables it to keep a tight grip over what software applications are loaded onto its device and how it is used by consumers. However, Apple needs third-party developers to ensure the ongoing success of the iPhone. In mid-2008, it released its software development kit (SDK) for its iPhone and iPod Touch. The SDK tools allow these people to develop software applications that make the most of these two devices' innovative features. Apple allows developers to set their own prices for their programs, and retain 70 per cent of the sales revenue. However, Apple will be in total control of the applications programs produced. It will decide which ones to approve, and these will be distributed only through its iTunes music store. Apple has to ensure that the constraints that it places on third party developers do not drive them to competitors, and that it fosters their creativity rather than stifles it.

Collaborating with users At first glance, Amazon, eBay, Google, wikipedia, YouTube, the Mozilla Foundation, Facebook, and MySpace appear to have little in common. Some charge users, others are free. Some are profit-making organizations, others are not. However, they all use what are called user contribution systems, and these are responsible for much of their success. The idea is not new. Firms have always used customer satisfaction surveys and focus groups to provide them with feedback to improve their products. When Maxwell House wanted to develop a new brand of instant coffee, it avoided the usual market testing approach. Instead, it approached its customers directly, obtained data from them, created a model for the 'ideal' coffee, and used this as the basis for developing the new product (Witzel, 2007). However, Scott Cook (2008) argues what is new is that commercial companies are now developing ways in which unlimited numbers of people outside them can volunteer their time, energy and expertise, to improve things for their customers, and increase their profits. They do this by creating user contribution systems which are methods for aggregating and leveraging people's contributions or behaviours in ways that are useful to other people. User contribution systems are underpinned by a range of new, consumer-based technologies, collectively referred to as Web 2.0 (see Chapter 3, Technology).

User contribution system a method for aggregating and leveraging people's contributions or behaviours in ways that are useful to other people.

User contribution systems can involve customers, sales prospects as well as people with no previous connection with the company. The contribution of users can be active, as when they donate their work, expertise or information, or it can be passive (and even unknowing), as in the case of behavioural data gathered from them automatically when they participate in a transaction. Wikipedia, a non-profit organization, offers a free encyclopaedia written and frequently updated by unpaid amateurs. eBay makes a profit without any inventory because its customers fill its shelves. Less obviously, Google's search engine relies on the algorithmic aggregation of links created by others on websites, while its advertisement placement system depends on data from people's click behaviour.

Firefox

Firefox is the web browser whose code was created from the ashes of Netscape which AOL had acquired in 1998, when it become clear that it had lost the 'browser war' to Microsoft's *Internet Explorer*. Today, the Mozilla Foundation manages the code that claims a market share of 14 per cent in America, and 20 per cent in Europe. The organization structure of the open source method consists of a number of concentric circles. At the centre is a core group of a dozen full time programmers employed by the foundation. Beyond them, there are about 400 contributors trusted to offer code into the source tree, following a two-stage review. Further out, thousands of people submit software patches to be sized up. Beyond them, is a ring of tens of thousands of people who weekly download the full source code, and scrutinize bits of it. Finally, over half a million people use the test versions of the forthcoming releases, 20 per cent of them reporting problems in bug reports. The organization of open source projects is critical to their quality. These projects are not anarchic activities, driven by magical, creativity from cyberspace, as sometimes implied. Instead, they possess formal, hierarchical governance, real structure, checks and balances, and leadership. Mozilla is an example of one of the largest, contemporary collaborations between producers and users, and represents a growing organizational trend.

Based on The Economist *(2006h).*

Most user contribution systems offer no financial incentives, so what motivates individuals to contribute? Scott Cook (2008) suggests six reasons:

- *By-product*: involuntary involvement when they provide data as a by-product of a transaction e.g. every Amazon shopper adds to its recommendation engine.
- *Practical solutions*: to obtain short term, practical benefits, e.g. using the delicious.com website, users can organize their own website bookmarks which when aggregated, produce an index to the web useful to others.
- *Social rewards*: to gain interaction with others, to become a member of a community of common interests e.g. Facebook.
- *Reputation*: to gain recognition (e.g. receiving Amazon's badge for being a 'Top 1,000 reviewer') or the admiration of peers.
- *Self-expression*: to have the opportunity to air their thoughts, opinions or creative expression, or to gain feedback from others (e.g. 6 million videos on YouTube).
- *Altruism*: to help others or to let the truth be known.

Why are companies developing user contribution systems? The systems create value for businesses as a consequence of the value that they deliver to its users. User benefits include: personalized purchase recommendations; obtaining hard-to-find items; reduced prices; establishing new personal and business relationships; as well as membership of a community. Company benefits include: improved products; better served customers; more business; reduced costs and improvements in employee performance. Cook (2008) provides a user contribution taxonomy which is shown in Figure 17.15.

Crowdsourcing the act of taking a task traditionally performed by a designated agent (employee or contractor), and outsourcing it to an undefined, generally large group of people, in the form of an open call for assistance.

Crowdsourcing Crowdsourcing is a term coined by Jeff Howe in *Wired* magazine (Howe, 2006). It refers to the act of taking a task traditionally performed by an employee or a contractor and outsourcing it to an undefined, generally large group of people, in the form of an open call for assistance (Howe, 2009). BBC Radio's Traffic Unit regularly asks motorists stuck in traffic jams to call in on their mobile phones and report holdups which are then broadcast over the air.

User contribution systems aggregate and leverage various types of user input in ways that are valuable to others.

User Contribution Systems

Active		Passive	
Aggregates content	Aggregates stuff for sale	Aggregates behavioral data	Aggregates resources
Opinion & ratings: Zagat guides	Goods: eBay online marketplace	Buying behaviors: Amazon's product recommendations	Computing capacity: Skype internet-based phone system
Expertise: Wikipedia encyclopedia	Advertising: Google's AdWords advertising placement system	Web-linking behavior: Google's search engine algorithm	Computer sensing capabilities: Honda's InterNavi traffic information service
Software code: Firefox web browser	Services (and goods): Craigslist online marketplace	Company behavior: Westlaw's PeerMonitor law firm database	
Creative expression: YouTube video-sharing site			
Social connections & personal information: Facebook social networking site			

Figure 17.15: User contribution taxonomy

Source: Reprinted by permission of *Harvard Business Review*. From "The contribution revolution: Letting volunteers build your business" by Cook, S., 86(10). Copyright © 2008 by the Harvard Business School Publishing Corporation, all rights reserved.

User contribution systems

Scott Cook cites several examples of the applications of user contribution systems. In the field of marketing, Unilever has a user forum called *In the Motherhood*, where mothers share their experiences and submit and vote on plots in an online TV comedy series. The users benefit by exchanging information, participating in a community and being entertained. Unilever gains by increasing its brand awareness and customer loyalty to some of its products. In the area of design and development, a T-shirt manufacturer called *Threadless* has 600,000 collaborators who submit about 600 designs weekly. Participants vote on these and the company manufactures T-shirts based on the winning designs. The contributing designers gain exposure and recognition for their designs, while the voters obtain a sense of ownership of selected designs. The company's R&D and stock holding costs fall as fewer professional designers are needed, and its inventory turnover rate rises as user-selected designs sell out. In the field of television, *Pop Idol* and its copies (e.g. *American Idol*) are examples of contribution-defined TV shows. Millions of viewers vote to select a star from a group of amateur singers. The viewer–voters obtain entertainment and a feeling of ownership of the results. The TV company benefits from low-cost talent, reduced production costs and high advertising revenue.

Based on S. Cook (2008) and Pisano and Verganti (2008).

Operationally, it involves organizations asking crowds of internet users for creative ideas; to analyze data; supply information; help develop a new technology; carry out a design task (also known as community-based design or distributed participatory design), an algorithm or help capture, systematize or analyze large amounts of data. The Library of Congress has asked the users of *Flickr*, a popular photo-sharing site, to identify unknown people in its old photo collections. Clearly, this description indicates an overlap with the activities of organizations such as *Wikipedia, Linux,* an open source software development project, and *Firefox*, the open source web browser. However, Scott argues that crowdsourcing is not a user contribution system because the company stands between the input and the output. It sifts through people's ideas, selects those it wants, and then invests the resources needed to develop them. A second distinguishing feature is that, while companies may receive free contributions, they are also willing to pay for them. Additionally, some contributors make a living from their contributions. Other commentators consider crowdsourcing to be just another variant of a user contribution system.

Commercial companies are also creating or participating in collaborative communities using crowdsourcing. Google is sending its positioning devices to India, and asking volunteers to chart its country's roads on Google Maps. Pharmaceutical company Eli Lilley set up a network of over 90,000 of scientists (called 'solvers') on the InnoCreative website. Launched in 2001, the company aims to draw upon the brainpower of outsiders to help develop its drugs and speed them to market. Other companies (called 'seekers') including Boeing, Du Pont and Procter & Gamble pay to use the InnoCreative website, and post their most intractable problems on it. Anyone on the network can take a shot at cracking them. Solvers come from diverse backgrounds and many of them are hobbyists. Often, successful solvers contributed to fields in which they had no formal expertise, thus confirming Mark Granovetter's central tenet of network theory, that of 'the strength of weak ties' – that the most efficient networks are those that link to the broadest range of information, knowledge and experience (Howe, 2006).

However, there are problems in using ideas or information supplied by community members. The firm has to check that these have not been sent to rivals; infringe copyright; or been stolen. Second, volunteers become reluctant to contribute if they feel that someone is profiting from their hard work, hence the success of non-profit collaborations. Successful solvers in the InnoCreative network are paid between $10,000 and $100,000. A survey of marketing bosses found that 62 per cent had used crowdsourcing in some way. Obviously, getting unpaid or cheaper members of the public to do your work for you is less expensive than hiring your own staff or paying consultants (*The Economist*, 2008j). Structurally, in the case of both non-profit and commercial organizations, the organizational boundary becomes perforated, as contributions to the organizational goals come from both internal, company staff and from volunteer outsiders.

STOP AND THINK Have commercial companies confirmed P.T. Barnum's contention that 'There's a sucker born every minute' by persuading online users to contribute their time, creativity and effort for free, in return for a spurious sense of participation in some sort of 'community' or a sense of 'ownership' of something?

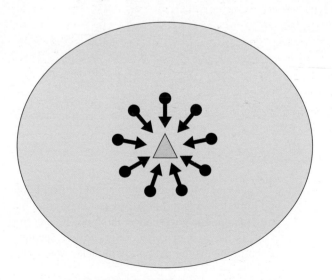

Organization uses the contributions of countless, individual volunteers to help it achieve its goals

Figure 17.16: User contribution system

Second Life as a collaboration tool

While virtual worlds are used by many to escape reality, increasing numbers of companies use them to replicate reality. They use them to help employees, business partners and customers to collaborate and learn from each other. Silicon Image, a semiconductor manufacturer, conducts part of its staff training there, and BP has simulated a pipeline location to help its engineers identify safety and construction problems. However, IBM is probably the best-known corporate user. In 2006, IBM joined the *Second Life* online community and is running a number of ongoing experiments using personal avatars.

Explaining what the company might learn from the brave new world of virtual gaming, Irving Wladowasky Berger, IBM's Vice-President of Technical Strategy and Innovation, stated that his colleagues were designing a set of conference centres to use for business with their customers; public policy issues; and internal collaborations.

They are creating meeting spaces for ex-IBMers and current employees to meet, catch up, and even collaborate, as part of a new alumni programme called The Greater IBM Connection. It has already held a virtual IBM alumni reunion. IBM has embraced *Second Life* more than any other major company at the present time. It has over 230 employees spending time in-world, and owns half a dozen islands. Most are private, with restricted access to the public. Within these environments, through a trick of the brain, people feel that they are actually present with others. More than videoconferencing, virtual worlds allow participants who meet to share a space, pass a virtual object between them, or have a chance encounter. They are becoming an important collaborative tool, but how long will they last?

Based on Shankland (2006); Gratton (2007); Hemp (2008).

Source: AFP/Getty Images

What mode of collaboration should a firm adopt when linking with others? Gary Pisano and Roberto Verganti (2008) suggest that senior managements should decide about network participation and governance. First, given its corporate strategy, how open or closed does it want its network of collaborators to be? Second, who should have the power to decide which problems the network will tackle and which solutions will be adopted?

Participation: open or closed?

Collaborative networks differ in terms of participation. Totally open collaboration means that anyone can join the network (suppliers, customers, hobbyists, institutions – even competitors).

The sponsor announces a problem, and requests contributions from an unlimited number of problem-solvers. It is like a throwing an open house party – you set the date and location and hope that the right people will come. Open source software projects like Linux, Apache and Mozilla, all exemplify open collaboration networks, as does threadless.com, the T-shirt retailer. In contrast, in a closed network, a firm will tackle its problem with one or two parties, which it chooses on the basis of their possession of the required capabilities. This is like a private club which you are invited to join. Alessi, an Italian company famous for the post-modern design of its home products invited 200 collaborators to submit designs.

Governance: hierarchical or flat?

Collaborative networks also differ in terms of governance. This relates to who gets to define the problem and choose the solution. In a hierarchical network, the 'kingpin' firm alone decides on the importance of problems, how they will be addressed, what represents an acceptable solution and which solutions will be implemented. This allows it to control and secure a larger part of the innovation's value. In contrast, in a flat network, the different parties are equal partners and share the power to decide key issues. Such decentralized decision-making, say Pisano and Verganti, allows collaborators to share costs, risk and the technical challenges of innovating.

Using the dimensions of participation and governance, Pisano and Verganti propose four basic modes of collaboration (Figure 17.17). They label these – *elite circle* (closed and hierarchical network); *innovation mall* (open and hierarchical); *innovation community* (open and flat) and *consortium* (closed and flat). These authors state that each has its own particular advantages and challenges; offers a company access to different capabilities assets; and is suited to specific types of problems, as discussed here.

		PARTICIPATION	
Innovation Mall A place where a company can post a problem, anyone can propose solutions, and the company chooses the solutions it likes best. **Example:** *InnoCentive.com website where companies can post scientific problems*	**Innovation Community** A network where anybody can propose problems, offer solutions and decide which solutions to use. **Example:** *Linux open-source software*		**Open**
Elite Circle A select group of participants chosen by a company that also defines the problem and picks the solutions **Example:** *Alessi's handpicked group of 200-plus design experts who develop new concepts for home products*	**Consortium** A private group of participants that jointly select problems, decide how to conduct work, and choose solutions. **Example:** *IBM's partnerships with select companies to jointly develop semiconductor technology*		**Closed**
GOVERNANCE			
Hierarchical	**Flat**		

Figure 17.17: Four ways to collaborate

Source: Reprinted by kind permission of *Harvard Business Review*. From "Which kind of collaboration is right for you?" by Pisano, G. and Verganti, R. 86(12). Copyright © 2008 by the Harvard Business School Publishing Corporation, all rights reserved.

With respect to participation, by choosing an open network, a firm gains access to an extremely large number of problem-solvers, and thus to the possibility of obtaining a vast quantity of ideas. Moreover, it does not need to specify its contributors beforehand. The disadvantages are that it does not attract the best contributors, and that its chance of it finding the best solutions from among the mountain of submissions is low. Pisano and Verganti state that open networks are most effective when participating in them is easy with the problem being divided into small, well-defined chunks that contributors can work on independently; when there is one or just a few solutions that can be clearly defined; when the proposed solutions can be evaluated at low cost; when the difference between an ideal solution and an average solution is not large; and when the chance of missing out on a greatly superior solution proposed by an elite participant is small.

With a closed network, a firm receives solutions from the best contributors in a selected knowledge domain (e.g. software); the best partners prefer to participate in closed networks; the chance of receiving a few suitable ideas from a small number of collaborators is high. Closed networks are most effective when a firm knows the knowledge domain from which the best solution is likely to emerge; when it can pick the best experts itself; when the problem is large and cannot be broken up into parts; and when everyone's expertise is required. With respect to governance, hierarchical form is best when a firm possesses the capabilities and knowledge to define a problem and evaluate the submitted solutions; when it can choose the direction to take; understands users' needs; and can first divide and then integrate outsiders' contributions. Flat forms work best when no single company possesses total capability on its own, and when all collaborators have a vested interest in how a problem is solved; and want a role in decision-making.

Changing an organization's structure

At the start of the book, an organization was defined as a social arrangement for achieving controlled performance in pursuit of collective goals. Thus, an organization is a tool to get things done through collective action. In the same way that different jobs require the use of different tools, so too with organizations. Contingency theory tells us that as circumstances change, an organization's structure must adapt to remain relevant and appropriate because it provides the foundation for everything that goes on within the company. A firm's current structure, whether functional, divisional, matrix, or incorporating one or more inter-organizational collaborative relationships, is not permanent, but subject to regular revision. For example, General Motors has restructured six times during the last two decades (Taylor, 2004). Amongst the factors the chief executive and the senior management team will take into account when restructuring are:

size   larger companies have more complex and formal structures

strategy   goals established by senior management

technology   type of production process used by the organization

environment   degree of change existing in the company's environment

globalization   number of countries organization operates in

diversification   number of different businesses which a company has

An organization can acquire a particular structure almost unconsciously. When a group of computer programmers hire an administrator and a secretary to 'deal with the paperwork' while they are doing their technical jobs, they are in fact designing structure. When a newly appointed chief executive of a multinational corporation creates new departments or increases the number of levels of management, he is consciously restructuring the company. Between these two extremes, incremental, ad hoc changes can be made. The point is that the structure of organizations evolves as often as it gets 'designed', and both can be messy processes.

This is to ensure that the structure remains relevant to the company's goals, as defined by its corporate strategy. It is held that 'structure follows strategy', that is, as a company changes

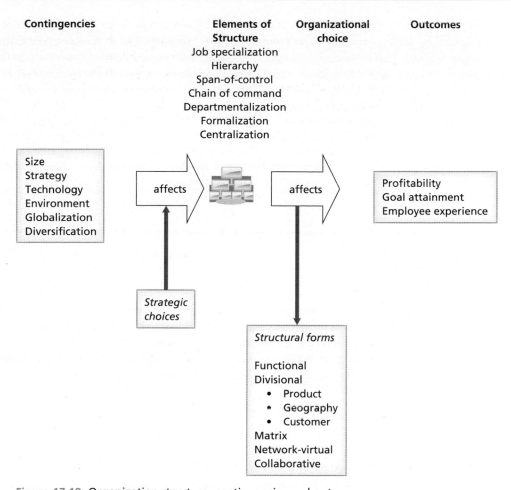

Figure 17.18: Organization structure: contingencies and outcomes
Source: Based on Colquitt *et al.* (2009, p.535) and Knights and Willmott (2007, p.222).

Restructuring
the act of partially or wholly modifying an organization's structure.

its goals or changes how it seeks to pursue those goals, it will also change its structural arrangements to match. This name given to this process is restructuring or organizational redesign. Previously separate departments may be merged, or those that have grown excessively large by the ad hoc acquisition of new responsibilities, may be divided up. Business magazines and newspapers regularly report how organizations are being restructured – both in the private and public sectors. The choice about organization structure in private firms is made by senior management, while politicians make the structural choices in government.

London and Beijing: additions and subtractions

In 2005, Her Majesty's Revenue and Customs (HMRC) was formed by an integration of two, large and previously separate central government departments – the Inland Revenue, responsible for the collection of taxes, and the Customs and Excise, charged with collections of duties. The new, unified department has 106,000 employees working in 800 offices, operating 250 computer systems, who annually had 276 million interactions, and made 50 million telephone calls. It represents one fifth of the entire Civil Service. In 2007, the Home Office, a central

government department with a budget of £14 billion and 75,000 directly employed staff, was split, with a newly established Ministry of Justice, taking over some of its previous responsibilities. Reorganizations among government departments are common. During the 1990s, the education and employment departments, and then the environment, transport and regions departments were merged. These mergers were subsequently reversed.

On the other side of the world in 2008, China's National People's Congress re-ordered the central government's

→

structure by folding separate departments into five 'superministries'. Human Resources merged with Social Security; Housing with Construction; Health expanded by taking responsibility for food and drug safety; the Environmental Protection Agency was upgraded to ministry status; and a new National Energy Commission was established. Similarly ambitious restructurings to streamline China's sprawling bureaucracy have been taken six times during the last twenty years, but have failed due to inertia and internal politics. It will be interesting to see if this attempt is any more successful.

Based on Financial Times *(2005, 28 July), p.13;*
The Economist *(2008k); and Timmins (2007, p.15).*

As one method of implementing organizational change (see Chapter 18), restructuring can have a negative effect on work performance, at least in the short term. It causes confusion among employees as to how they should do their jobs, reduces their trust in their employer and increase their level of stress. The consequence is reduced emotional attachment by staff to their organization. Repeated re-structuring organizations can have longer term negative impact. Critics often quote the Roman consul Petronius writing in AD66, who said,

> We trained hard . . . but it seemed that every time we were beginning to form up into teams we would be reorganized. I was to learn later in life that we tend to meet any new situation by reorganizing; and a wonderful method it can be for creating the illusion of progress while producing confusion, inefficiency, and demoralization.

More recently, Sir Roy Griffiths, a past managing director of the supermarket chain, J. Sainsbury, stated 'Reorganization is the thing you should do when everything else has failed' (Timmins, 2007).

STOP AND THINK   Think of the structure of an organization that you are familiar with or the university at which you are studying. What are its main goals? How is the organization divided up in order to achieve these goals? From your experience as a student, does this division of organizational parts help or hinder you? Should it be restructured? How?

Getting organizational design correct for the moment may be critical for senior management, but 'keeping it correct' can be problematic. Good design can lift a company's stock price (12 per cent in the case of DuPont's division into five business units in early 2002, raising its worth by $7 billion) or lower expectations (as in the case of Procter & Gamble's failure to implement a fully integrated structure by the summer of 2000). Speed of change, in the form of acquisitions, mergers, customer realignments, rationalizations, all involve, to a greater or lesser degree, the modification of a company's structure. Thus, one might speak more accurately of 'organizational *structuring*', as an on-going process dedicated to keeping structure aligned with strategy. Microsoft has reorganized four times in the last five years. An Oxford University study of 50 top UK companies between 1991 and 2000 revealed that, at the start of that decade, 20 per cent underwent major reorganizations to their structures annually, a figure that rose to 30 per cent by the end of the decade. It concluded that, at present, the average business could expect a major reorganization every three years (Whittington *et al.*, 2002; Whittington and Mayer, 2002).

Whittington *et al.* (2002), conducted a survey, in association with the Chartered Institute of Personnel and Development in the UK, of 300 chief executives and 500 human resource professionals. It revealed 800 reorganization initiatives ranging from corporate transformations at one extreme through to mergers of departments at the other. In half the cases, the reorganization occurred immediately after the installation of a new chief executive; half were linked to major changes in top management membership, and leadership culture and style changes; and in 90 per cent of cases, either chief executives or unit heads, were represented on reorganization steering committees. The authors draw several conclusions. First, re-organizations have only about a 40 per cent chance of being on time and a 50 per cent chance of success. Only 60 per cent meet external objectives such as improving market share or customer responsiveness. Under half meet internal effectiveness targets such as increased flexibility, or morale and retention of key employees (33 per cent). Second, the chief executive's personal credibility is put on the line during reorganizations, leaving them exposed and vulnerable. Third, reorganizations are now tightly managed. Those undertaken with clear objectives, timescales, milestones, project champions, regular reviews and detailed budgeting, are more likely to be completed on time, to budget, meet their objectives and raise efficiency.

McKinsey consultants Lowell Bryan and Claudia Joyce argued that despite the dramatic changes that have taken place in recent years in the way that people work (mobile phones, BlackBerrys, telecommuting, etc.), the organizations in which they carry out their work have changed much less. They say that, 'today's big companies do very little to enhance the productivity of their professionals. In fact, the vertically oriented organizational structures, retrofitted with ad hoc and matrix overlays, nearly always make professional work more complex and inefficient' (Hindle, 2006a). Essentially, twenty-first-century organizations are not fit for twenty-first-century workers. Inappropriate organization structures obstruct employees seeking to achieve their aims, lower their morale and thus reduce a company's productivity and competitiveness. In contrast, Cunliffe (2008, p.5) argues for the importance of creating appropriate structures which will allow employees to:

- deal with contingencies such as changing technology, markets and competition;
- gain a competitive advantage by developing the core competences and strategies to enable them to outperform other companies;
- work in an effective, supportive and responsive environment;
- increase efficiency and innovation.

While corporate strategy specifies the *goals* that a company pursues, organization structure directs the *means* by which these will be achieved. John Child (2005, pp.17–21) noted that inappropriate structure could obstruct the achievement of organizational goals by causing at least five problems:

1. *Motivation and morale*: can fall if inappropriate delegation and spans-of-control lead to too little or too much responsibility being given to employees, resulting in feelings of either under-achievement or stress. Ill-defined roles, as well as unclear priorities, work schedules and performance standards, all lead to staff not knowing what is expected of them.

2. *Decision-making*: may be experienced by staff as arbitrary and inconsistent if there is a lack of rules. Decisions are often of poor quality and made slowly if the company has too many hierarchical levels; if the separate decision-makers are isolated from each other in their own departments and their activities not co-ordinated, and where decision-making is over-centralized.

3. *Conflict and lack of co-ordination*: occurs if the structure does not emphasize a single set of company-wide objectives. Departmental priorities can then take precedence over product, project or company goals. Conflict also ensues if there is failure to co-ordinate the activities of individuals, teams and departments, whose work is interdependent.

4. *Changing circumstances*: may not be responded to imaginatively if the structure lacks people performing forecasting and planning roles; if it does not give priority to innovation and change planning top management support and adequate resources; and if team-working is not used to bring together individuals' expertise and views to respond to new challenges.

5. *Rising costs*: costs can rise due to many expensive bosses in tall hierarchies with narrow spans of control; where new staff are hired to administer excessive rules, procedures, paperwork and targets.

Restructuring the British National Health Service

Since the Health Service (NHS) began in Britain 60 years ago, there has always been a division of labour been general practitioner doctors (GPs) and hospital-based doctors (consultants). GPs are usually patients' first point of contact when they are ill. They provide primary care in their local practices. A typical practice has 4–5 GPs, but some GPs continue to work on their own. Secondary care is provided in hospitals, whose consultants provide specialist treatments. Currently, the government is considering a controversial restructuring. The proposed new work arrangement is called a *polyclinic*, a halfway house between district hospitals and local GP practices. It would blur the division between primary and secondary care; and it would represent a new way of running the NHS. Each polyclinic would house not one but three GP practices, providing 12 family doctors for over 20,000 patients. Additionally, it would offer some medical services previously only available from hospitals, such as treatments for leg ulcers. While the current proposed crossover between primary and secondary care is extremely modest, if the German model was to be followed in Britain, many more hospital-like services, including day surgery would be offered in polyclinics. The strategy underpinning this organizational restructuring is that, in future, polyclinics will be the place where most routine healthcare needs of patients will be met and where all GPs will eventually work. The BMA, the doctors' union, is campaigning against the restructuring.

Based on The Economist *(2008l, 2008m); Devlin (2008, p.1).*

RECAP

1. *Appreciate the reason for chief executives' need to design and redesign their organization's structure.*

   - Organization structure is one of the ways of achieving organizational goals.

   - An organization's structure will be changed as a result of changes in its size, strategy, technology, environment, globalization and diversification.

2. *Distinguish three eras of organizational design and what factors stimulated each.*

   - Era 1: mid-1800s–late 1970s – self-contained organization structures.

   - Era 2: 1980s–mid-1990s – horizontal organization structures.

   - Era 3: mid-1990s to date – boundaryless organization structure (hollow, modular, virtual, and collaborative).

3. *Distinguish between functional, divisional, matrix and team-based organization structures.*

   - A functional structure groups activities and people according to the similarities in their work, profession, expertise, goals or resources used.

   - A divisional structure splits an organization up into self-contained entities based on their organizational outputs; geographical region operated in; or the customer groups served.

   - A matrix structure combines two different types of structure e.g. function and product.

   - A team-based structure consists entirely of project-type teams that co-ordinate their activities, and work directly with partners and customers to achieve their goals.

4. *Distinguish between an outsourcing relationship and hollow, modular and virtual organization structures.*

   - An outsourcing relationship involves contracting with external providers to supply the organization with the processes and products that were previously supplied internally.

   - A hollow organization structure is based on outsourcing an organization's non-core *processes* which are then supplied to it by specialist, external providers.

   - A modular organization structure involves assembling product chunks (modules) provided by internal divisions and external providers.

   - A virtual organization structure uses technology to transcend the constraints of legal structures, physical conditions, place and time, and allows a network of separate participants to present themselves to customers as a single entity.

5. *Understand the trend towards companies' collaborative relationships with competitors and customers, and their involvement in virtual communities*.

- Collaboration has become a matter of integrating activities rather than integrating organizations.
- Factors contributing to increased collaboration include the rise of partnership strategies, the knowledge economy, the working style of generation Y and advances in collaborative technology.

- The increasing speed of change means that individual organizations lack the necessary resources, knowledge or skill to respond individually so have to collaborate with others.

6. *Identify the factors influencing a chief executive's choice of organization structure*.

- An organization's structure will be redesigned as a result of changes in its size, strategy, technology and environment, as well as the result of globalization and diversification.

Revision

1. Why might Max Weber and Henri Fayol be surprised by developments in contemporary organizational design arrangements?

2. Suggest how changes in organization structuring over the last 50 years have affected what workers and managers do, and how they do it.

3. In the literature, developments in all forms of inter-organizational collaboration, are presented as the way forward for the future. Consider the potential negative consequences of these arrangements for companies involved, and their employees and managers.

4. Why are network and virtual structures preferred by managers seeking to encourage entrepreneurship and innovation?

Research assignment

This chapter reported Warner and Witzel's (2004) view that every organization possessed a mixture of virtual and tangible elements (p.535). They identified six dimensions along which organizations can chose to organize their activities on a virtual or tangible basis:

- nature of product
- nature of working
- relationship with suppliers
- relationship with customers
- relationship between teams
- relationship between managers and employees

Review the discussion on virtuality and organizations in this chapter. Through personal contact, gain access to two different organizations. Using the six dimensions above as a basis for discussion, interview a manager from each organization to determine its virtual-tangible elements balance.

1. Write a report on the strengths and weaknesses of the balance based on your interview findings.

2. What effects does the balance have on employees' working patterns?

3. Identify where your findings are consistent with, and where they contradict the textbook account of strengths and weaknesses of virtual forms of organization.

Springboard

Anand, N. and Daft, R.L., 2007, 'What is the right organization design?', *Organizational Dynamics*, 36(4): 329–44.

Sets developments in choices about organization structure within a historical context.

Child, J., 1997, 'Strategic choice in the analysis of action, structure, organizations and environment: Retrospective and prospective', *Organization Studies*, 18(1): 43–76.

The author provides an overview of the strategic choice debate. A challenging read for those wishing to understand current thinking about organization structuring.

Cook, S., 2008, 'The contribution revolution', *Harvard Business Review*, 86(10): 60–69; Pisano, G. and Verganti, R., 2008, 'Which kind of collaboration is right for you?, *Harvard Business Review*, 86(12): 78–86.

Two contributions to the debate about collaborative relationships.

Hansen, M.T., 2009, 'When internal collaboration is bad for your company', *Harvard Business Review*, 87(4): 82–88.

The author considers some of the negative consequences of inter-departmental collaboration that is so frequently promoted by management academics and consultants.

 ## OB in films

In Good Company (2004, director Paul Weitz): DVD track 6: 0:19:54–0:28:43 (9 minutes). In the film, Globecom International, a multinational conglomerate buys Waterman Publishing, the parent company which owns the flagship magazine, Sports America. Globecom appoints its own 26-year-old, business school prodigy and corporate ladder climber, Carter Duryea (played by Topher Grace) to be boss. In this clip, he meets his staff for the first time. It begins with Duryea (drinking down a coffee) says 'Yeah, just keep them coming', and ends with two seated employees talking, one of whom says, 'My money's on Dan, he's prehistoric.' As you watch the clip decide:

1. What is Duryea's objective in holding this meeting with company employees?

2. How successful is he in communicating with his staff?

3. What are Sports America employees' concerns likely to be at this time?

 ## OB in literature

Mulholland, A., Thomas, C.S. and Kurchina, P., 2007, *Mashup Corporations: The End of Business as Usual*, Evolved Technologist publisher, New York; Mulholland, A. and Earle, N. 2008, *Mesh Collaborations*, Evolved Technologist, New York. These are novels embedded in management guides. The first tells the story of Jane Moneymaker, the CEO of Vorpal Inc., a fictional appliance manufacturer, as she uses mashups, Web 2.0 and service-oriented architecture to overturn established business and IT structures and achieve culture change. In the second novel, fictional companies and characters are used to chart the transformation of two companies from traditional, vertically integrated businesses to being providers of services and using Web 2.0 tools to collaborate with customers who start to look more like partners.

CHAPTER EXERCISES

University of Grantchester Business School

Objectives
1. To design alternative organization structures for a business school based on different criteria of departmentalization.
2. To assess their benefits to different stakeholders.

Briefing
1. Form groups.
2. Read the information about the University of Grantchester Business School (UGBS) below.
3. Draw alternative organizational charts for the UGBS depicting organizational structures based on the five criteria shown below. Duplicate the provision of products/services as required.

   (a) Academic subjects taught by academic staff

   (b) Products/services delivered by academic staff

   (c) Functions performed by academic staff

   (d) Geography, where the product/service is delivered

   (e) Clients who consume the product/service provided

4. Which organization structure would you prefer and why, if you were

   (a) a full time undergraduate or postgraduate student

   (b) an academic staff member?

Information about the University of Grantchester Business School

(a) Academic subjects taught: The 100 UGBS's academics are equally divided between the four main subject areas (equivalent to company functions): human behaviour (HB); financial management (FM); strategy and marketing (SM); and operations management (OM).

(b) Products offered: The UGBS offers the following products:

   U- Undergraduate teaching – BA full time students who fund themselves, taught on the main campus

   P1- Postgraduate teaching – MBA full time students who fund themselves, taught on the main campus

   P2- Postgraduate teaching – MBA part time – working managers, funded by their companies, taught in the city centre campus

   T- Together, these three constitute teaching (T=U+P1+P2);

   R- Research conducted by academics funding by the research councils

   D- Doctoral – supervision of conducted by doctoral (postgraduate) students who fund themselves, on the main campus

   C- Consultancy – consultancy provided by academics for companies, bought by them, and provided on the companies' premises

   S- Short courses – short (non-graduating) courses, taught by academics for working managers, paid for by their companies, and run on company premises

→

(c) Services: The school performs three major functions: teaching, research and consultancy.

(d) Geography: Academics can work in four locations; main campus; city centre; seaside residential facility; on the company's own premises.

(e) Customers: The school has three classes of customers: students; research council-funders; and companies.

Team-based organizational structuring

Objectives
1. To design alternative organization structures based on different criteria of departmentalization.
2. To assess their advantages and disadvantages to different stakeholders.

Briefing
1. Why did the functional structure not suit the company's strategy?
2. How did the team-based structure help?
3. What problems could the team-based approach create?

Saab Training Systems

In the 1990s Saab Training Systems was a high-tech company working in the defence industry. It was a fully owned subsidiary of the Swedish company Saab. In 1997 the company had 260 employees and a turnover of about £52m. It sold computer-aided equipment for military training – for example, laser-based simulators. The market was characterized by long, complicated and politicized negotiations with clients, fierce global competition and overcapacity as defence budgets reduced as a result of the 'peace dividend'. This high degree of uncertainty and need for flexibility had forced the company to react. It shunned external alliances, which were common in the industry, and focused on exploiting its core competence in laser-based simulation. But it also needed to drastically speed up throughput times in both development and production to get new product to commercialization faster and then to shorten delivery times.

The company decided to abandon its traditional functional structure in favour of a more flexible team-based structure and a more business process oriented way of doing business. Before these changes the company was organized into functions (production, development, marketing and purchasing). Each function had its own internal hierarchy. This structure created problems with cross-functional coordination and communication. In the new structure 40 teams were created that reported directly to the senior management team. Team sizes were between six and eight. If they got bigger they were split. The teams were built around the business processes. There were five *business teams* who negotiated contracts with customers and monitored contracts. Each team was responsible for one or more products and particular geographical markets. When a contract was signed it became a 'Project' to which other teams were assigned: a *delivery team* (who planned production and tested products prior to shipping); a *purchasing team* (responsible for sourcing materials and components); and an *applications team* (who adapted the company's 'standard' products to the need of particular customers). Finally, production was assigned to one of 14 *product teams* (who were also responsible for product development). In addition to these 'front-line' teams there were central functions such as personnel and finance.

Coordination of the various teams involved in a customer's order was very important since the particular mix of teams assigned to that order was temporary. It was dissolved as soon as the order was delivered to the customer. Also, product teams were working on more than one project at any time. The responsibility for coordination of any project was shared between the business team (commercial responsibility) and delivery teams (production planning).

Reproduced by permission of SAGE Publications, London, Los Angeles, New Delhi and Singapore, from Mullern, T., 'Integrating team-based structure in the business process', in Pettigrew, A.M. and Fenton, E.M. (eds) The Innovating Organisation, Copyright (© Sage Publications 2000).

Part 5 **Management processes**

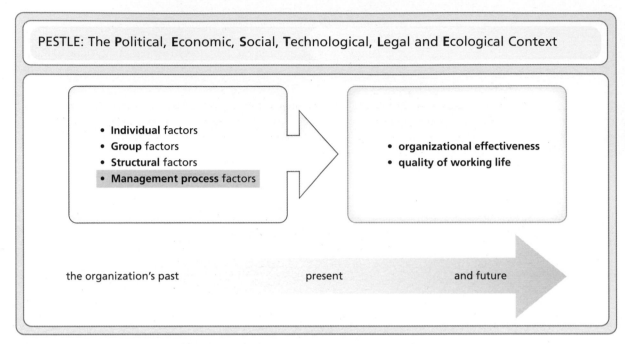

PESTLE: The **P**olitical, **E**conomic, **S**ocial, **T**echnological, **L**egal and **E**cological Context

- **Individual** factors
- **Group** factors
- **Structural** factors
- **Management process** factors

- **organizational effectiveness**
- **quality of working life**

the organization's past   present   and future

A field map of the organizational behaviour terrain

Introduction

Part 5, Management processes, explores the following five topics:

- *Organizational change*, in Chapter 18
- *Leadership*, in Chapter 19
- *Decision-making*, in Chapter 20
- *Conflict*, in Chapter 21
- *Power and politics*, in Chapter 22

Each of these topics has an enormous impact on how employees are managed; how they experience their work environment; and how successful their organization is in achieving its goals. Each topic concerns the process of managing, which involves both managers and non-managers. Thus, the most junior of employees may be called upon to exercise their leadership skills; become involved in group decision-making; attempt to resolve a conflict between colleagues – while engaging in political behaviour in order to increase their power.

Chapter 21 on Leadership begins with a historical introduction to the topic which identifies common themes in different leadership theories, and highlights contemporary debates about the nature of leadership. Chapter 22 on Decision-making considers different models of decision-making; different types of decisions; different decision-makers; and different problems in decision-making. It challenges the notion that most decisions are made logically for the benefit of the organization by managers who possess the necessary information and authority. Chapter 23 on Conflict considers the topic from the point of view of contrasting perspectives on conflict, and stresses how the way you perceive a situation influences what actions you take. It examines how the way a company is organized, itself engenders conflicts which, in turn have to be managed through the incorporation of conflict resolution devices. Finally, Chapter 24 addresses the highly abstract, but possibly the most crucial of all the concepts used to explain the behaviour of people in organizations – that of power and politics. The political perspective provides an alternative to the rational standpoint predominantly found in managerially oriented textbooks. It challenges readers to go back over earlier chapter topics, to re-assess their contents from this alternative viewpoint.

Invitation to see

This image from *The Times* (30 November 2009) is titled, 'In line for a job'. The caption read: 'Applicants for China's annual Civil Service exam wait patiently outside Huazhong University of Science and Technology at Wuhan, in the central province of Hubei. More than one million people were expected to take the annual entrance exam yesterday, competing for 15,000 places'.

Source: China Daily/Reuters

1. **Decoding**   Look at this image closely. Note in as much detail as possible what messages you feel that it is trying to convey. Does it tell a story, present a point of view, support an argument, perpetuate a myth, reinforce a stereotype, challenge a stereotype?

2. **Challenging** To what extent do you agree with the messages, stories, points of view, arguments, myths, or stereotypes in this image? Is this image open to challenge, to criticism, or to interpretation and decoding in other ways, revealing other messages?

3. **Sharing**   Compare with colleagues your interpretation of this image. Explore explanations for differences in your respective decodings.

What would you do? You're the consultant

This manager has asked for your advice as an external management consultant, concerning problems that are going to arise with regard to a forthcoming merger:

> Our company is set to merge with a competitor in the next year and over the next few months we will be carrying out a review of our internal resources. The two companies are headquartered in different towns, with some duplication in head office functions, and in the reorganization there will undoubtedly be restructuring and redundancies. Our staff know this and are already feeling insecure: office gossip suggests that many are already looking to move on. With so many challenges ahead, the last thing we need is a talent drain, but we are unsure what messages to send out to reassure people. On the one hand we want to retain our brightest people to forge the best future for the new organization, but on the other we cannot promise a future for everybody. To add to this, we have a trade union that is clamouring for information and consultation. What actions can we take to maintain morale and treat people fairly?

From 'Troubleshooter', People Management, *13 November 2008, p.62.*

Chapter 18 **Change**

Key terms

triggers of change

initiative decay

initiative fatigue

strategic change

adhocracy

the coping cycle

the Yerkes-Dodson law

readiness for change

resistance to change

stakeholder

organization development

processual/contextual theory

change agent

innovation

sustaining innovations

disruptive innovations

operational innovation

Learning outcomes

When you have read this chapter, you should be able to define those
key terms in your own words, and you should also be able to:

1. Outline the contemporary debate concerning repeat change and
   painless change.
2. Identify the main external and internal triggers of organizational
   change.
3. Understand the typical characteristics of human responses to
   change.
4. Understand the nature of resistance to change and approaches to
   overcoming it.
5. Explain the advantages and limitations of participative methods of
   change management.
6. Explain the strengths and weaknesses of the processual/contextual
   perspective on change.
7. Understand the significance of innovation, and the distinction
   between sustaining, disruptive, and operational innovations.
8. Outline the skill requirements for an effective change agent.

Why study change?

'Built-to-change' organizations

Edward E. Lawler and Christopher Worley argue that

To survive in a world that is changing increasingly quickly, businesses need to be able to anticipate change and to keep reconfiguring themselves. To do this, they need a built-in capacity to change continuously. Organizations that wait for an overwhelming mandate to engage in change efforts are very likely to be left behind and may struggle to survive. We believe that the only way for organizations to change rapidly enough is to design themselves so that they can adjust their strategic intents, structures and human capital deployments as a matter of routine. That means starting with a new set of core principles about what an organization should look like:

- don't assume that the future will be like the present;
- ensure no employee is more than two steps from the external environment;
- share business information with staff;
- use frequent goal-setting reviews, rather than job descriptions, to manage talent;
- stress that individuals' employment depends on their willingness to accept change and learn new skills;
- encourage managers at all levels to take advantage of leadership opportunities.

From Lawler and Worley (2009)

Richard Whittington and Michael Mayer (2002) argue that 'adaptive reorganization', the ability to redesign structures frequently, is now critical to organizational performance. Their research followed the top 50 companies in Britain from 1992 to 2000 and found that they reorganized every five years. By 2000, major changes were taking place on average every three years, with regular minor changes in between. In April 2002, Microsoft announced its fourth major 'reorg' in five years. This pattern of 'repeat change' is driven by:

1. intensified competition and stockmarket turbulence in the private sector, consumerism and government pressures in the public sector;
2. the pace of technological innovation;
3. increased knowledge-intensity.

They found that the results of changes were often disappointing. Improvements in flexibility and responsiveness were accompanied by poor financial returns and lower morale. With major change, expensive new information systems and complex new structures attract attention, while people are forgotten. When asked about the aims of reorganizations, managers emphasized customers, market share and efficiency, and ranked improving employee morale and retention lowest. Despite commitment to communication, there was little employee participation in the design and implementation of change.

People policies affect change processes and outcomes in a number of ways. Can we recruit staff with the right capabilities? Can we train and reward employees so that they will be motivated to perform well and to stay? Are change agents trained in implementation, and can they handle sensitive emotional responses? Will senior management succession plans produce a new top team which has the same goals and methods? Is the organization culture receptive to change? Change may be unsuccessful if human resource policies and practices concerning recruitment, training, reward, retention, management development, succession planning, and career management policies are not supportive.

However, only one in five of the organizations studied involved human resource managers in a lead role in change. Whittington and Mayer (2002) argue that, for change to be successful, the 'soft' human issues need to be integrated with 'hard' structures and systems. This requires skilled change agents, an organization culture which welcomes change and appropriate management styles. In this chapter, we will:

- explore the 'soft' issues, including emotional responses to change and causes of resistance;
- consider different perspectives on change, including implementation methods and processes, and the nature of innovation;
- identify the expertise required of the change agent.

Why reorganize?

This quote is taken from a 'joke' research article in a medical journal, illustrating the cynicism that many people feel about constant organizational change.

We identified several over-lapping reasons for reorganizations, including money, revenge, money, elections, money, newly appointed leaders, money, unemployment, money, power-hunger, money, simple greed, money, boredom, and no apparent reason at all.

The internal justifications for reorganizing identified in our mega-analysis include:

- you need to hide the fact that an organization has no reason to continue to exist;
- it has been 3 years since your last reorganization;
- a video conferencing system has just been purchased out of your employees' retirement fund;

- your CEO's brother is an organizational consultant;
- the auditor general's report on your organization is about to be released.

The external justifications for pushing for a reorganization of someone else's organization include:

- you are threatened by their organization;
- you discover that their organization is functioning effectively;
- you would like to direct attention away from your own organization's activities.

These justifications must never be made public. The fundamental rule is: 'Never let on why – really – you are reorganizing.'

From Oxman et al. (2005).

The paradoxical nature of change

STOP AND THINK

How would you respond to these 'true or false' questions?

People have a natural resistance to change.	true or false?
People get bored with routine and seek out new experiences.	true or false?
Older people are more resistant to change.	true or false?

Did you answer 'true' to all three statements? A moment's thought should suggest that these positive responses are inconsistent with each other, and contradict the evidence. For example, many people when they retire from work take up radically new activities and hobbies: painting, acting, community involvement, learning a musical instrument. We cannot have natural resistance to change and seek new experiences at the same time.

Change is a recurring theme throughout this text. In Part 1, we noted how environmental and technological trends encourage organizational changes. In Part 2, we explored changing human learning, personality, communication skills, perceptions and motivation. In Part 3, we examined how individual behaviour changes in group settings, and how group functioning can be changed to improve performance. In Part 4, we explored trends in organization design. In Part 5, we explore organizational processes, including change, and also consider how leaders can change employee behaviour, and whether leaders themselves can change their styles.

The need for organizational change can be prompted by many different **triggers of change**.

Triggers of change
disorganizing pressures indicating that current systems, procedures, rules, organization structures and processes are no longer effective.

External triggers for organizational change include:

- changing economic and trading conditions, domestic and global;
- new technology and materials;
- changes in customers' requirements and tastes;
- activities and innovations of competitors, mergers and acquisitions
- legislation and government policies;
- shifts in local, national and international politics;
- changes in social and cultural values.

Internal triggers for organizational change can include:

- new product and service design innovations;
- low performance and morale, high stress and staff turnover;
- appointment of a new senior manager or top management team;
- inadequate skills and knowledge base, triggering training programmes;
- office and factory relocation, closer to suppliers and markets;
- recognition of problems triggering reallocation of responsibilities;
- innovations in the manufacturing process;
- new ideas about how to deliver services to customers.

These lists of triggers makes organizational change sound like a reactive process. Clearly this is not always the case. In many instances, organizations anticipate events and trends, and are proactive in implementing appropriate changes.

One of the best known metaphors for change was developed by Kurt Lewin (1951) who argued for the need to *unfreeze* the current state of affairs, to *move* to a desired new state, then to *refreeze* and stabilize those changes. However, refreezing no longer seems to be an option. 'Repeat change' is the norm; 'permanent thaw' is a better metaphor. Many organizations face a 'high velocity' environment (Buchanan, 2000b) in which turbulent external conditions translate into a complex stream of initiatives affecting work and organization design, resource allocation, and systems and procedures in a continuous attempt to improve performance.

The environment for most organizations seems likely to remain turbulent, and change problems will be on the management agenda for some time. The study of change, however, is paradoxical, for several reasons:

- as the triggers and consequences of organizational change are many and complex, establishing cause and effect is problematic;
- organizational change has to be studied at different levels of analysis – individual, group, organizational, social – which are interrelated in complex ways;
- change that affects a number of different stakeholders is difficult to evaluate as there may be no agreed criteria on which to base judgements;
- change is a process, a series of events unfolding over time, and not a static or time-bounded event, raising questions concerning the appropriate time frame for analysis;
- change can only be understood in relation to continuity, with respect to what has not changed.

When thinking of change, we must also be aware of what is *not* changing. It is not difficult to list features of technology, jobs, organizations and society in the first decade of the twenty-first century that have not changed since the beginning of the twentieth. Personal transport still relies on internal combustion engines fuelled by petrol. Finding employment remains a social norm and is central to most people's definition of personal identity. If you commit a serious crime in Britain, you will still be tried in front of a jury of your peers in a sombre courtroom with a judge in a strange wig, as you would have been over 100 years ago.

Change has never been so fast (since when?)

That this is an age of change is an expression heard frequently today. Never before in the history of mankind have so many and so frequent changes occurred. These changes that we see taking place all about us are in that great cultural accumulation which is man's social heritage. It has already been shown that these cultural changes were in earlier times rather infrequent, but that in modern times they have been occurring faster and faster until today mankind is almost bewildered in his effort to keep adjusted to these ever increasing social changes. This rapidity of social change may be due to the increase in inventions which in turn is made possible by the accumulative nature of material culture [i.e., technology].

From Ogburn (1922).

Initiative decay
an organizational phenomenon where the benefits from a change initiative 'evaporate', when attention shifts to focus on other issues and priorities.

Initiative fatigue
the personal exhaustion and apathy resulting from the experience of too much organizational change.

Another paradox, related to continuity, has recently emerged in this field. The literature on change in the twentieth century was concerned with making things happen, and happen faster. An opposite concern in the twenty-first century is that we need to slow things down, and perhaps keep some things the same. One problem concerns **initiative decay**, also called 'improvement evaporation', where the benefits of a change are lost as the organization moves on to deal with new priorities. With the need for change, there is concern with how to *sustain* changes and improvements that are already in place (Buchanan *et al.*, 2006).

Another problem is **initiative fatigue**, as people become tired of constant demands to do things differently, work better, work smarter, work harder. Research suggests that initiative fatigue is widespread, affecting all organizational levels, including management (Buchanan *et al.*, 1999). Initiative fatigue lowers enthusiasm for more change.

To address these problems, Eric Abrahamson (2000) argues for 'painless change'. This means small and continuing changes such as the redesign of existing practices and business models rather creating new ones. Organizations should stop changing all the time, as this causes cynicism and burnout. Abrahamson argues that change needs to be more carefully paced, with major initiatives interrupted by periods of 'tinkering' (small incremental changes) and 'kludging' (larger-scale tinkering).

Some commentators thus argue for repeat rapid organizational changes, while others advocate more stability and continuity. Those who argue for more stability do not deny the need for major changes, but are concerned with the number and timing of these initiatives, and their relationship to other changes that may be taking place at the same time.

Strategic change: the contemporary imperative

Strategic change
organizational transformation that is radical, frame-breaking, mould-breaking, or paradigmatic in its nature and implications.

What kind of change are we discussing? Some changes are major, long term, expensive and risky, while others are more straightforward. One way to distinguish types of change is to consider how deeply they penetrate the organization. This approach (Roger Collins, personal communication), is shown in Table 18.1. In most organizations, many change initiatives are likely to be under way at the same time, at different levels. This classification does not lead to an argument that 'all change must be deep change'. Deep change is appropriate when dealing with 'deep problems', while fine tuning is an appropriate response to minor concerns.

Many commentators argue that organizational change is a strategic imperative. This means that radical shifts, or **strategic change** in organizational design and functioning is necessary in order to cope with unpredictable changes happening in the wider social, economic, political and technological environment. If you are studying strategic management or corporate strategy as part of your course, you will be familiar with this argument.

Table 18.1: Depth of organizational intervention

surface	**Fine tuning**: focus on efficiency
↓	**Restructure**: centralize, decentralize
shallow	**Reallocate resources**: grow some departments, cut others
↓	**Improve business planning**: symbolize a shift in thinking
penetrating	**Change the leadership**: new CEO with major change remit
↓	**Change the organization's definition of success**: create new goals, objectives, targets to change behaviour
deep	**Change the mission, vision, values and philosophy**: symbolize a radical shift in thinking and behaviour
↓	
transformational	**Paradigm shift**: change how we think, how we solve problems, how boundaries are defined, the way we do business: frame-breaking, mould-breaking, fundamental, strategic change

STOP AND THINK   If you want a high-flying, fast track career, you are unlikely to get far if you focus your energies on shallow changes. Shallow changes do not contribute much to organizational performance, and will not improve your visibility or reputation. You would be advised to work on deep changes, as long as they are successful.

What happens if all ambitious managers try to drive major changes in the interests of progressing their careers?

Alvin Toffler (b.1928)

Adhocracy an organization design which is temporary, adaptive and creative, in contrast with bureaucracy which tends to be permanent, rule driven and inflexible.

Strategic suggests scale, magnitude, depth. Whether change is strategic or not depends on circumstances. What is strategic in one context may be routine in another (new furniture may be strategic for a hotel, insignificant for an oil company). This strategic imperative is usually expressed in terms of the need for organizations to become more flexible, more adaptable, more 'fluid', and more responsive. It is often argued that bureaucratic organizations cannot handle complexity and unpredictability. Bureaucratic structures work better with impersonal, autocratic management, and with stability and routine. Tom Burns and George Stalker (1961) famously distinguished between rigid, *mechanistic* management systems, and fluid, *organic* systems. Alvin Toffler (1970) used the term adhocracy. (The idea of the flexible post-modern organization – see Chapter 2 – was fashionable in the 1990s; Clegg, 1990.)

Management theorists consistently suggest flexible approaches to coping with uncertainty. We seem to want organizations that are flexible enough to adapt to change, but that are also stable enough to sustain those changes. In theory, the ad hoc organization may be appropriate for handling unpredictability. However, these kinds of structures can be insecure and uncomfortable places in which to work, and may not deliver in terms of performance. Doug Stace and Dexter Dunphy (2001) identify organizations which they describe as 'prudent mechanistics', which retain traditional structures, avoid the 'organizational fashion show', and perform well. Harold Leavitt (2003) argues that, while rigid bureaucratic structures encourage 'authoritarianism, distrust, dishonesty, territoriality, toadying, and fear', they also provide ways of handling complexity, give us structure and predictability, and offer 'psychological rewards' by fulfilling needs for order and security. The benefits of flexibility must be set alongside the need for stability and sustainability.

Change and the individual

One influential approach to understanding the individual psychological consequences of rapid change comes from studies of how we cope with traumatic personal loss, such as the death of a close relative. Elizabeth Kübler-Ross (1969) argued that we deal with loss by moving through a series of stages, each characterized by a particular emotional response. **The coping cycle** has been used to understand responses to radical organizational change.

The five stages in the Kübler-Ross coping cycle are defined in Table 18.2. This is the 'ideal' model. We may not all experience the same five sets of responses. We may omit particular stages, revisit some stages, or pass through some of them more or less quickly than others. From an organizational perspective, this can be a useful explanatory and diagnostic tool. If we can work out where in the response cycle a person may be, we could provide useful support.

Just how much pressure can we take from organizational change? Psychology has long argued that the relationship between arousal, or sensory stimulation, on the one hand, and human performance, on the other, varies systematically, in the form of an 'inverted U' function. This is known as **the Yerkes-Dodson law**, shown in Figure 18.1, after the originators Robert M. Yerkes and John D. Dodson (1908).

The Yerkes-Dodson law argues that task performance increases with arousal, stimulation, and pressure. This explains why, for example, the time you spend revising for an examination

The coping cycle the emotional response to trauma and loss, in which we experience first denial, then anger, bargaining, depression, and finally acceptance.

The Yerkes-Dodson law a psychology hypothesis which states that performance increases with arousal, until we become overwhelmed, after which performance falls.

Table 18.2: The coping cycle

stage:	response:
denial	unwillingness to confront the reality; 'this is not happening'; 'there is still hope that this will all go away'
anger	turn accusations on those apparently responsible; 'why is this happening to me?'; 'why are you doing this to me?'
bargaining	attempts to negotiate, to mitigate loss; 'what if I do it this way?'
depression	the reality of loss or transition is appreciated; 'it's hopeless, there's nothing I can do now'; 'I don't know which way to turn'
acceptance	coming to terms with and accepting the situation and its full implications; 'what are we going to do about this?'; 'how am I going to move forward?'

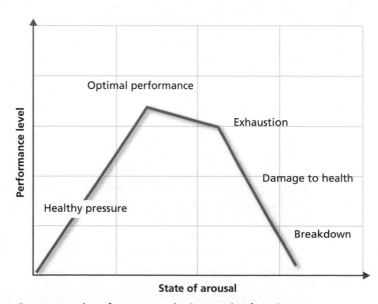

Figure 18.1: Pressure and performance – the inverted-U function

"Your proposal is innovative. Unfortunately, we won't be able to use it because we've never tried something like this before."

Source: www.cartoonstock.com.

seems to become more productive as the examination date draws closer. Here is the basis for the claim, 'I work better under pressure'. However, this hypothesis also says that, if the pressure continues to grow, the individual will eventually become stressed and exhausted, and performance will start to fall. This explains why, for example, when you delayed all of your revision until the night before, you did badly the following day.

This suggests that performance will be low if arousal is low, perhaps because the job is repetitive and boring. Performance can sometimes be improved in such settings with background music, conversation, and job rotation. Now suppose that the job is enriched and becomes more interesting, responsible and demanding, making more use of the individual's skills and knowledge. As the level of pressure increases, performance is likely to increase. However, a point will eventually be reached where the pressure becomes so great that it is overwhelming rather than stimulating. At this point fatigue and stress set in, and eventually ill-health and breakdown can occur if the pressure continues to escalate.

Can organizational change induce such pressure? From their survey of the management experience of change, Les Worral and Cary Cooper (2006) conclude that pressures to cut costs, intensify work, and improve performance, were damaging loyalty, morale, job security and sense of well-being. Factors that particularly affected well-being included:

- unmanageable workloads;
- having little control over aspects of the job;
- work interfering with home and personal life;
- not having enough time to do the job as well as they would like;
- working longer hours than they wanted to;
- having little or no influence over performance targets;
- unrealistic objectives;
- not being involved in decisions affecting their work;
- ideas and suggestions not being taken into account.

The Yerkes-Dodson law applied to work settings is summarized in Table 18.3, which plots changes in response, experience, and performance for escalating pressure levels.

Table 18.3: The pressure–performance relationship explained

Pressure level	Response	Experience	Performance
very low	boredom	low levels of interest, challenge and motivation	low, acceptable
low to moderate	comfort	interest aroused, abilities used, satisfaction, motivation	moderate to high
moderate to high	stretch	challenge, learning, development, pushing the limits	high, above expectations
high to unrealistic	stress	overload, failure, poor health, dysfunctional coping behaviour	moderate to low
extreme	panic	confusion, threat, loss of self-confidence, withdrawal	low, unacceptable

Managers' emotional responses to change

Mike Broussine and Russ Vince asked 86 senior and middle managers in six public sector organizations (local government and health care) to 'draw a picture which expresses your feelings about change at work in your organization'. This use of visual imagery is novel in organizational research, and potentially allows respondents to reveal ideas and emotions that would be more difficult to express in language. The organizations from which these managers came had experienced considerable upheaval in the few years before this study. Analysis of the managers' drawings displayed a range of emotions about change:

Emotional responses	Typical drawings
anxiety, fear, dread	organizational ship swamped by tidal wave, hospital being demolished
fear of personal catastrophe	gravestones, menacing clouds, unhappy faces, football team with three dead members
anger, violence, revenge	organization as decapitated maiden, castle blown apart by cannon
opportunity for personal development	ugly duckling becoming a swan, smiling face on strong body, flourishing tree
denial and rationalization	holiday scenes, oasis, idyllic surroundings
paradox, optimism and pessimism	angry politician pushing boulder uphill along with a ship sailing towards sunset and a gold cup for a prize, double edged sword, kamikaze and astronaut
powerlessness and debility	piles of paperwork, long queues of people, computer spewing out information, very small tree in an empty landscape with a single acorn
destabilization, alienation	manager on a treadmill with sign reading 'business as usual during alterations'
a journey to endure	castles in the air, beach scenes, horse and cart in an ominous valley, vaulting barriers, boats tossed on shark-infested ocean close to tropical island

The researchers conclude that this approach reveals, 'the paradoxical, sometimes contradictory and generally messy emotional reality that managers experience in a period of tremendous change'. The category with the smallest number of illustrative drawings was the one concerned with opportunity for personal development.

Based on Broussine and Vince (1996).

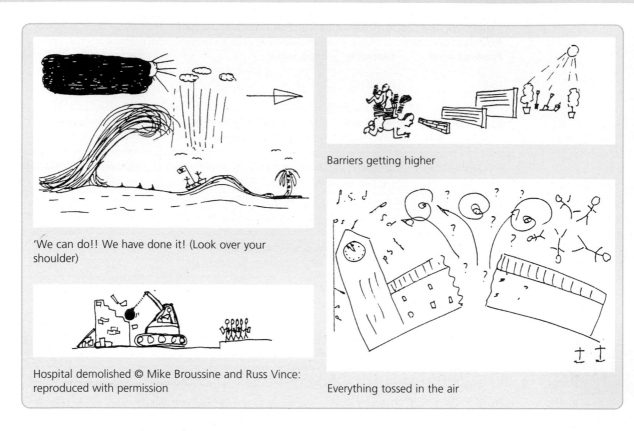

'We can do!! We have done it! (Look over your shoulder)

Barriers getting higher

Hospital demolished © Mike Broussine and Russ Vince: reproduced with permission

Everything tossed in the air

Deciding the optimal level of pressure is awkward, because this depends on the individual. Also, appropriate levels of stimulation depend on the difficulty of the task. If the task is easy, more stimulation can be applied. This explains why music destroys our concentration during a chess game, but is enjoyable while backing up computer files.

How can we tell what levels of pressure people are experiencing, or when people are getting 'too close to the edge'? We can ask them, but that may not always be appropriate. Fortunately, there are many proxy measures that show when people are suffering excess pressure: high staff turnover, sickness rates, unexplained absences, and increases in accidents and mistakes, customer complaints, and employee grievances. Physical appearance changes as people become stressed, and interpersonal relationships become strained.

Readiness and resistance

From a practical change implementation perspective, it is usually useful to ask the question: are the conditions right, or do we have to do some preliminary work before we go ahead? One approach to preparing the ground is based on the concept of readiness for change.

Readiness for change is a predisposition to welcome and embrace change.

Where readiness is high, change may be straightforward. When readiness is low, some 'groundwork' may be required. Tony Eccles (1994) identifies eight preconditions for successful change:

1. Is there *pressure* for this change?
2. Is there a clear and shared *vision* of the goal and the direction?
3. Do we have effective *liaison and trust* between those concerned?
4. Is there the *will and power* to act?
5. Do we have enough *capable people* with sufficient resources?
6. Do we have suitable *rewards* and defined *accountability* for actions?
7. Have we identified actionable *first steps*?
8. Does the organization have a *capacity to learn* and to adapt?

Where the answers to these questions are 'yes', the organization's readiness for change is high, and resistance is likely to be localized and insignificant. Where the answers are 'no', readiness is low, and implementing change will be more difficult. The concept of readiness draws attention to two other issues. One is timing. Some readiness factors may improve by waiting. The second concerns action, to heighten the impatience for change, or to strengthen a welcoming predisposition. In other words, these readiness factors can be managed.

Using this kind of diagnosis, it is often possible to anticipate both positive and negative responses to change, and to use that understanding to develop support, and also to address resistance to change.

Change has positive and negative aspects. On the one hand, change implies experiment and the creation of something new. On the other hand, it means discontinuity and the destruction of familiar arrangements and relationships. Despite the positive attributes, change can be resisted because it involves confrontation with the unknown, and loss of the familiar. It is widely assumed that resistance to change is natural. Many people find change both painful and frustrating. Arthur Bedeian (1980) cites four common causes of resistance to change.

Resistance to change an unwillingness, or an inability to accept or to discuss changes that are perceived to be damaging or threatening to the individual.

Parochial self-interest

We want to protect a status quo with which we are content and regard as advantageous. Change may threaten to push us out of our 'comfort zone', away from what we prefer and enjoy. We develop vested interests in organization structures and technologies. Change can mean loss of power, prestige, respect, approval, status and security. Change can also be personally inconvenient. It may disturb relationships and other arrangements that have taken time and effort to establish. It may force an unwelcome move in location, and alter social opportunities. Perceived as well as actual threats to interests and values are thus likely to generate resistance. We may identify ourselves more closely with our specific functions and roles than with the organization as a whole. We then have a personal stake in our specialized knowledge and skills, and may not be willing readily to see these made redundant or obsolete.

Misunderstanding and lack of trust

We are more likely to resist change when we do not understand the reasons behind it, or its nature and consequences. Resistance can thus be reduced by improved understanding. If managers have little trust in their employees, information about change may be withheld, or distorted. If employees distrust managers, management information about changes may not be believed. Incomplete and incorrect information creates uncertainty and rumour. This has the unfortunate result of increasing perceptions of threat, and increasing defensiveness. The way in which change is introduced can thus be resisted, rather than the change itself.

Contradictory assessments

We each differ in how we see and evaluate the costs and benefits of change. A major threat for me can be a stimulating challenge for you. Our personal values decide which changes are welcomed and succeed, and which are resisted and fail. Contradictory assessments are more likely to arise when communication is poor. Bedeian points out that contradictory analyses of change can lead to constructive criticism and improved proposals. Resistance to change is not necessarily dysfunctional, but can sometimes lead to more effective outcomes.

Low tolerance for change

We differ in our abilities to cope with change and uncertainty. Change that requires us to think and behave in different ways can challenge our self-concept. We each have ideas about our abilities and our strengths. One response to change may thus be self-doubt: 'can I handle this?'. Some people have a low tolerance for ambiguity and uncertainty. The anxiety and apprehension that they suffer may lead them to oppose even potentially beneficial changes.

Table 18.4: Methods for dealing with resistance to change

method	advantages	disadvantages	use when resistance is caused by
education and communication	increases commitment, reconciles opposing views	takes time	misunderstanding and lack of information
participation and involvement	reduces fear, uses individual skills	takes time	fear of the unknown
facilitation and support	increases awareness and understanding	takes time and can be expensive	anxiety over personal impact
negotiation and agreement	helps to reduce strong resistance	can be expensive and encourage others to strike deals	powerful stakeholders whose interests are threatened
manipulation and cooptation	quick and inexpensive	future problems from those who feel they were manipulated	powerful stakeholders who are difficult to manage
explicit and implicit coercion	quick and overpowers resistance	change agent must have power; risky if people are angered	deep disagreements and little chance of consensus

Source: Based on Kotter and Schlesinger (2008)

Stakeholder anyone who is concerned with how an organization operates, and who will be affected by a change or a programme of changes.

How can resistance be managed? Different individuals and groups are likely to be affected in different ways, and are therefore likely to react differently. To anticipate and manage these reactions, it helps to understand each stakeholder, or stakeholder group affected by a particular change.

Stakeholder analysis is a useful first step in planning change:

1. draw up a list of stakeholders affected by the proposed changes;
2. establish what each will gain or lose if the change goes ahead;
3. use the potential benefits to strengthen support;
4. find ways to address the concerns of those who feel they will lose out, by altering the nature of the changes, or reducing the losses in other ways.

Different stakeholders must be managed differently. Partners and allies need to be 'kept on side', while opponents need to be converted, or perhaps discredited and marginalized. John Kotter and Leo Schlesinger (2008) identify six methods for managing resistance. The advantages and disadvantages of each of these methods are summarized in Table 18.4. These methods can of course be used in combination. While education, participation and support are most likely to be the norm, there will be situations where negotiation, manipulation and coercion become necessary.

1. Education and commitment

Resistance can be based on misunderstanding and inaccurate information. Management needs to explain why changes are necessary through training, counselling, group meetings, memos and reports. Getting the facts straight can help to reconcile opposing views.

2. Participation and involvement

Resistance can arise from fear of the unknown. To reduce opposition and encourage commitment, those who will be affected should be involved in planning and implementation. This also makes use of individuals' skills and knowledge.

3. Facilitation and support

Anxiety about the personal impact of change can create resistance. It may be necessary to develop individual awareness of the need for change, as well as the self-awareness of feelings towards change and how these can be altered.

4. Negotiation and agreement

Powerful individuals and groups may resist changes that damage their interests. It may be necessary for management to compromise and negotiate, adjusting the changes to meet the concerns of powerful resistors. This can create a precedent for future changes, which may also have to be negotiated, although the circumstances may be different.

5. Manipulation and co-optation

This involves covert attempts to sidestep potential resistance. Management puts forward proposals that appeal to the specific interests of key stakeholders. The information is selective, emphasizing benefits and playing down disadvantages. Co-optation involves giving key resistors direct access to the decision-making process, perhaps giving them well-paid, high-status management positions.

6. Implicit and explicit coercion

Where there is profound disagreement between those concerned with the change, and where there is little chance of anyone shifting their ground, it may be appropriate for management to abandon attempts to achieve consensus, and resort to force and threat (not violence). It may be sufficient to offer to fire, transfer or demote individuals, or to block their career prospects.

STOP AND THINK

Faced with resistance to a desirable change, would you use manipulation and threat, or would you regard these methods as unprofessional or unethical?

Participation and dictatorship

Remploy is a British manufacturing company that provides employment for people with disabilities and health conditions. In 2007, the company decided that it had to cut costs by closing half of its 83 factories, while quadrupling the number of jobs that it found annually for its staff in mainstream employment. A support plan was developed, to prepare employees and to help them through the change, with leadership meetings, roadshows, face-to-face and written briefings, helplines, group sessions, and a specialist career transition company to support individual employees. Remploy funded training for trade union representatives, to help them interpret the company's business information. Union consultations led to 15 fewer closures than planned, to a voluntary redundancy scheme at the remaining factories, and to increased sales to the public sector (Jessop, 2008). This participative approach to major organizational change has now become conventional practice.

This approach dates from the work of Lester Coch and John French (1948) at the Harwood Manufacturing Corporation in Marion, Virginia. The company made pyjamas, and employees were complaining about frequent changes in work methods and pay rates. Absenteeism was high, efficiency was low, output was restricted deliberately, and employees were aggressive towards supervisors. Most of the grievances concerned the fact that, as soon as they had learned a new job, and started to earn bonuses, they were moved to another task. This meant that they had to start learning all over again, during which time they lost the bonus.

Coch and French designed an experiment with three production groups, each with a different level of participation in changes. One group of 18 hand pressers had to accept changes imposed by the production department. A second group of 13 pyjama folders sent three representatives to discuss and approve new methods. In a third group of 15 pyjama examiners, everyone took part. The performance of the non-participating group did not improve, and hostility to management remained high. In contrast, the performance of the 'total participation' group rose to a level higher than before the experiment. Some months later, the initial non-participation group were brought together again for a new pressing job. This time, they participated fully in the changes, which resulted in a rapid increase in efficiency. This experiment confirmed that it was not the people involved but the way in which they were treated that affected resistance to or acceptance of change.

Since that study, employee participation has been standard advice for managers seeking to encourage a welcoming and creative approach to change and avoid resistance. Richard Pascale, Mark Millemann and Linda Gioja (1997) urge managers to involve 'every last employee'. However, participative methods have been challenged by the work of two Australian researchers, Doug Stace and Dexter Dunphy (Stace and Dunphy, 2001). They first define the scale of change using four categories:

fine tuning   refining methods, policies and procedures, typically at the level of the division or department

incremental adjustment distinct modifications to strategies, structures and management processes, but not radical enough to be described as strategic

modular transformation restructuring departments and divisions, potentially radical, but at the level of parts of the organization and not the whole

corporate transformation strategic change throughout the organization, to structures, systems, procedures, mission, values and power distribution

They then identify four categories of change leadership style:

collaborative widespread employee participation in key decisions affecting their and the organization's future

consultative limited involvement in setting goals relevant to employees' areas of responsibility

directive the use of managerial authority in reaching decisions about change and the future and about how change will proceed

coercive senior management impose change on the organization

Plotting scale of change against change leadership style produces the matrix in Figure 18.2. This matrix identifies four strategies: Participative evolution, Charismatic transformation, Forced evolution, and Dictatorial transformation. Four types of change leader are identified. *Coaches* are people-centred, inspirational communicators who lead participative evolutions.

Style of change leadership	Scale of change			
	Fine tuning	Incremental adjustment	Modular transformation	Corporate transformation
Collaborative	**Type 1**		**Type 2**	
Consultative	Participative evolution		Charismatic transformation	
Directive	**Type 3**		**Type 4**	
Coercive	Forced evolution		Dictatorial transformation	

Figure 18.2: Scale of change and leadership style

	Incremental change strategies	Transformative change strategies
	Participative evolution	*Charismatic transformation*
Collaborative–consultative modes	Use when the organization needs minor adjustment to meet environmental conditions, where time is available, and where key interest groups favour change	Use when the organization needs major adjustments to meet environmental conditions, where there is little time for participation, and where there is support for radical change
	Forced evolution	*Dictatorial transformation*
Directive–coercive modes	Use when minor adjustments are required, where time is available, but where key interest groups oppose change	Use when major adjustments are necessary, where there is no time for participation, where there is no internal support for strategic change, but where this is necessary for survival

Figure 18.3: The Dunphy–Stace contingency approach to change implementation

Captains are systematic, task-oriented, authority figures who lead forced evolutions. *Charismatics* are 'heroic' figures committed to their own dramatic and challenging vision who lead (you guessed) charismatic transformations. *Commanders* are purposeful, decisive, tough-minded and forceful, able and willing to neutralize or remove resistance, to implement dictatorial transformations.

Dunphy and Stace argue that participative strategies are time-consuming as they can expose conflicting views that are difficult to reconcile. Where organizational survival depends on rapid and strategic change, dictatorial transformation is appropriate:

> Perhaps the toughest organizational change program in Australia in recent years has been the restructure of the New South Wales Police Force. The person leading that restructure and playing a classic Commander role is Police Commissioner Peter Ryan. Ryan was appointed from the United Kingdom to stamp out corruption in the force and modernize it. In his own words, he initially adopted a management style that was 'firm, hard and autocratic, and it had to be that because that is what the organization understood' (Stace and Dunphy, 2001, p.185).

The approach to change implementation which Dunphy and Stace advocate is summarized in Figure 18.3. This is a contingency model which recommends using an approach which fits the context. For example, where circumstances suggest that it is appropriate for senior managers to adopt a dictatorial approach, middle managers implementing changes may find a more collaborative style useful.

 **STOP AND THINK**   Dictatorial transformation? Coercion? Surely this kind of approach is more likely to generate hostility and resistance, reducing organizational performance? In what circumstances – if any – do you think it is appropriate to exclude others from participating in change that affects them?

The argument of Stace and Dunphy challenges the model of participative change. The argument has intuitive appeal, as any form of consultation takes time, and time may not always be available in a rapidly changing environment. However, Stace and Dunphy have empirical evidence from Australian organizations to support their case.

N-step recipes for change

The six phases of a project

1. enthusiasm   4. search for the guilty

2. disillusionment   5. punishment of the innocent

3. panic   6. praise and rewards for the non-participants

Although change is a familiar feature of the organizational landscape, it does not appear to have become any easier to implement. However, much is known about the factors which contribute to effective change, and also about the barriers. That knowledge has been codified by numerous authors advising on 'best practice'. John Kotter (1995a) outlines 'eight steps to transforming your organization':

1. Establish a sense of urgency.

2. Form a guiding coalition.

3. Create a vision.

4. Communicate the vision.

5. Empower people to act on the vision.

6. Create 'short-term wins'.

7. Consolidate improvements to produce further change.

8. Institutionalize new approaches.

There are many models like Kotter's in the management literature, and they all say much the same things about vision, leadership, communication, and involvement. David Collins (1998) refers to these as 'n-step guides', or simple 'recipes'. These models of change have one striking feature in common; they assume that planned change unfolds in a logical sequence. Solutions are not identified until the problem has been clearly defined. The best solution is not chosen until the options have been evaluated. Implementation does not begin until there is agreement on the solution. The key actors in the process have clearly defined roles and responsibilities. Implementation is monitored and deviations from plan are corrected. The process is bounded in terms of resources and time, and has a clear completion date.

The underlying assumptions of rationality and linearity in these accounts of the change process have attracted much criticism. Organizations rarely operate in such a tidy and predictable manner, particularly with respect to strategic (major, messy, radical) change. Bernard Burnes (2004) argues that there can be no 'one best way', and develops an approach based on the range of choices in change implementation. Collins (1998) also argues that n-step guides fail on three counts. First, they offer simple universal advice that does not take into account the unique circumstances of the organization. Second, they do not capture the complex, untidy, and iterative nature of the change process. Third, they do not encourage a critical perspective with regard to what is being changed, and the ways in which change can maintain and reinforce power differences. In other words, these accounts are contextually, processually, and politically naive. Collins advises managers to take a more theoretically sophisticated approach, and urges academics to take a more critical stance.

These 'recipe-based' approaches to change implementation have two advantages:

1. They codify what research and experience suggest are the main factors contributing to effective change, even if many of the factors (clear goals, good communications) seem to be common sense.

2. They offer a framework, a checklist for action, for those involved in planning change, even more useful when accompanied by stakeholder analysis and readiness analysis.

Home viewing

In 2002, the celebrity chef Jamie Oliver tried to change the food being served in British schools, to create 'a better, cooler, cleverer, healthier nation'. A real-time documentary programme was produced, *Jamie's School Dinners* (Fresh One Productions/Fremantle Home Entertainment, 2005). The four episodes follow Jamie through the following stages:

1. he pilots a new menu in two schools, in Greenwich and Durham, the latter having the reputation of being in the unhealthiest region in the country

2. the new menus are 'rolled out' across other schools in Greenwich, which involves negotiating new contracts with suppliers

3. Jamie lobbies the British government in an attempt to change the level of funding for meals provided by state schools

The documentary is inspirational and salutary, presenting a dramatic and emotional picture of the complexity of the change process. As change agent, Jamie moves from the rational aim to produce healthy menus, to the realization that he is 'brainwashing and retraining the bad habits of kids'.

As you watch the programme, consider the following questions:

- **Stakeholders**: who are the stakeholders in this change, and what will each stand to gain or lose?

- **Tactics**: what works and what doesn't work for Jamie, and why?

- **Personal attributes**: what personal attributes contribute to Jamie's effectiveness as a change agent, and what personal attributes interfere with his effectiveness?

- **Work-life balance**: how does Jamie's role as a change leader affect his family life?

- **Advice**: based on your observations, what practical advice can you give to Jamie?

However, these approaches have two limitations:

1. They are theoretically weak, and rely heavily on retrospective accounts of 'what went well' and 'what went wrong'. There is nothing intrinsically wrong with this research method. However, such an analysis does not contribute to the development of our theoretical understanding of change processes and of how these processes may themselves be changing.

2. While research and experience confirm that change is untidy, politicized, iterative and apparently irrational in terms of the way events unfold, these approaches assume that change either is, or should be, a rational linear process. There is a presumption that, if change is messy, then it must be because managers have 'failed to follow the textbook'. That may not be the case at all if change is intrinsically untidy.

Organization development

Organization development
the systematic use of applied behavioural science principles and practices to increase individual and organizational effectiveness.

Organization development (OD) approaches change with the assumption that problems in organizations are due to conflict caused by poor communication and lack of understanding. OD has a toolkit, based on core values concerning how organizations should treat their employees. OD was created in the 1960s, but it is still influential and is widely used. OD aims to improve both organizational effectiveness and individual capabilities, through the systematic application of social and behavioural science knowledge and techniques.

Stephen Robbins and Timothy Judge (2008, p.654) outline the OD values:

- **Respect**. Individuals should be treated with dignity and respect.

- **Trust**. The healthy organization is characterized by trust, authenticity and openness.

- **Power equalization**. Effective organizations do not emphasize hierarchical control.

- **Confrontation**. Problems shouldn't be hidden; they should be openly confronted.

- **Participation**. If those who are affected by change are involved in the decisions, they will be more committed to its success.

Table 18.5: Bureaucratic diseases and OD cures

bureaucratic disease	symptoms	OD cures
rigid functional boundaries	conflict between sections, poor communications	team building, job rotation, change the structure
fixed hierarchies	frustration, boredom, narrow specialist thinking	training, job enrichment, career development
information only flows down	lack of innovation, minor problems escalate	process consultation, management development
routine jobs, tight control	boredom, absenteeism, conflict for supervisors	job enrichment, job rotation, supervisory training

OD argues that 'bureaucracy is bad' and that the caring, sharing, empowering organization is a better place to work, and is financially and materially more effective. The 'bureaucracy-busting' agenda relies on the diagnosis of problems and solutions summarized in Table 18.5.

One of the founders of OD, Kurt Lewin, argued that the process of change must pass through the three stages of unfreezing, transition, and refreezing. People need to understand the need for change (unfreezing), before they will move (transition), and changes have to be embedded (refreezing) to prevent people from reverting back to old routines. OD interventions are thus designed to help with these stages. Table 18.6 shows some common OD interventions.

There are three criticisms of OD. First, it ignores the realities of organizational power inequality, claiming that conflict is due to poor communication, and not to the fundamental clash of interests between management and employees. Second, it focuses on 'soft' attitudes and values, rather than on the 'hard' operational and financial results that matter. Third, OD interventions take time. Improved effectiveness, difficult to measure, based on intangible values, in the long run, after an expensive programme – this is not a compelling promise in a fast-moving, competitive world. However, the benefits of OD include (Warrick, 1984):

1. improved productivity, morale, commitment to success;
2. better understanding of organizational strengths and weaknesses;
3. improved communications, problem-solving and conflict resolution;
4. creativity, openness, opportunities for personal development;
5. decrease in politicking, playing games;
6. better management and teamwork, and increased adaptability;
7. better able to attract and retain quality people.

STOP AND THINK

Do current economic conditions encourage or discourage the use of OD, and why?

Table 18.6: Common OD interventions

intervention	explanation	application
action research	results from a study are used to design improvements which are the subject of further study	to solve known problems which have unclear solutions
sensitivity training	technique for improving self- and others' awareness through unstructured group discussions	to develop interpersonal skills and emotional intelligence
structure change	job rotation, job enlargement and enrichment, autonomous teams, organization restructuring	various uses – empowerment, improve information flow, signal priorities, new directions
force-field analysis	method for assessing the driving and restraining forces with respect to change	to plan actions to manage the force-field in order to facilitate the change process
process consultation	external consultant facilitates problem-solving by helping clients to develop own insights	to solve problems while developing the organization's own diagnostic capabilities
survey feedback	employee opinion survey findings are fed back to help identify actions to improve performance	to generate evidence which can help to solve leadership, culture, communications, morale and other problems
team building	various methods to identify team roles, and to rate factors influencing team effectiveness	to help team members understand their roles and improve collaboration
intergroup development	clarify the mutual expectations of groups that must work together to be effective	to improve understanding and resolve conflict between sections or functions
role negotiation	clarify the mutual expectations of individuals who must work together to be effective	to reconcile differences between two individuals and to improve collaboration and interaction

The process and context of change

**Processual/
contextual theory**
a perspective arguing
that it is necessary
to understand how
the substance, context,
and process of
organizational change
interact to create the
outcomes.

The theoretical sophistication advocated by Collins (1998) and others, can be found in **processual/contextual theory**.

We discussed process theory in Chapter 1 (p.22), as one major approach to understanding organizational behaviour. This perspective has been particularly influential in helping to understand organizational change. Andrew Pettigrew (1985, 1987) cautions against looking for single causes and simple explanations for change. He points instead to the many related factors, individual, group, organizational, social, and political, which influence the nature and outcomes of change. Pettigrew argues that change is a complex and 'untidy cocktail' of rational decisions, mixed with competing individual perceptions, stimulated by visionary leadership, spiced with 'power plays' and attempts to recruit support and build coalitions behind particular ideas. Pettigrew argues that the unit of analysis should be 'the process of change in context', highlighting two related issues. First, this means paying attention to the flow of events, and not thinking of change as static or time-bounded. Second, this means paying attention to the wider context in which change takes place, and not thinking in terms of a particular location in time or geographical space (this new machine in this factory bay).

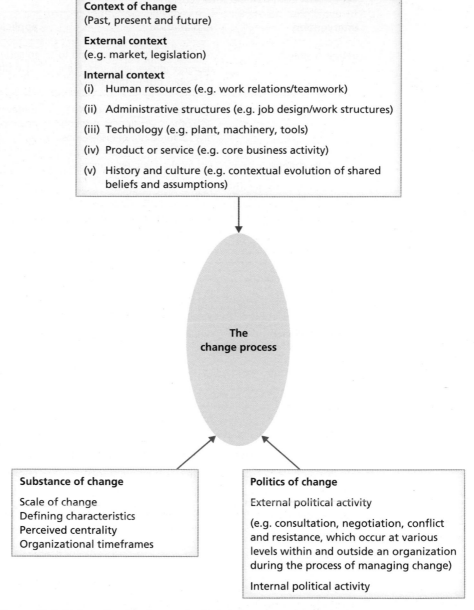

Figure 18.4: Determinants of organizational change
Source: From Dawson (2003a).

The processual/contextual perspective has been developed by Patrick Dawson (2003a and 2003b) who argues that, to understand the organizational change process, we need to consider:

1. The past, present and future *context* in which the organization functions, including external and internal factors.
2. The *substance* of the change itself, which could be new technology, process redesign, a new payment system, or changes to organization structure and culture.
3. The transition *process*, tasks, activities, decisions, timing, sequencing.
4. *Political* activity, both within and external to the organization.
5. The *interactions* between these factors.

This argument is summarized in Figure 18.4. The organization's history is critical, and relates to our earlier discussion of change and continuity in two ways. First, it is easy to forget how previous events have shaped current perceptions and responses. Second, it is also easy to forget the continuities, to ignore those aspects of the past which have not changed and which are still with us, and which again condition our current thinking.

Pettigrew and Dawson argue that the change agent must be willing to intervene in the political system of the organization. The key management task is to legitimize change proposals in the face of competing ideas. The management of change can thus be described as 'the management of meaning', which involves symbolic attempts to establish the credibility of particular definitions of problems and solutions, and to gain consent and compliance from other organization members. Part of the management task, therefore, is to do with 'the way you tell it', or more accurately with 'the way you *sell* it' to others.

Dawson identifies five aspects of the internal context: human resources, administrative structures, technology, product or service, and the organization's history and culture. He also identifies four key features of the substance of change: the scale, its 'defining characteristics', its perceived centrality, and the timeframe of change initiatives. The substance of change influences the scale of disruption to existing structures and jobs. The transition process may be slow and incremental, or rapid. In addition, managers can draw upon evidence from the context and substance of change to marshal support and to legitimate their own proposals through political action. It is the *interaction* between context, substance and political forces which shape the process of organizational change.

Combing his findings from case studies of change processes, Dawson (2003a, pp.173–75) identifies ten 'general lessons':

1. There are no simple universal prescriptions for how best to manage change.
2. Change strategies must be sensitive to people and context.
3. Major change takes time.
4. Different people experience change in different ways.
5. We can learn from all change experiences, not just the successful ones.
6. Employees need to be trained in new methods and procedures, often overlooked.
7. Communication must be ongoing and consistent.
8. Change strategies must be tailored to fit the substance and context.
9. Change is a political process.
10. Change involves the complex interaction of often contradictory processes.

A processual/contextual perspective on change has three strengths.

1. Recognizes the complexity of change, drawing attention to the many factors at different levels, and the interaction between these factors, shaping the nature, direction and consequences of change.
2. Recognizes change as a process with a past, a present and a future, rather than as a static or time-bounded event or discrete series of events.
3. Establishes clear recommendations for researchers studying organizational change, advocating longitudinal research across individual, group, organizational and social levels of analysis.

A processual/contextual perspective has three limitations:

1. Change in this perspective is in danger of being presented as over-complex and overwhelmingly confusing, and as unmanageable.
2. The people involved in the change process are sometimes portrayed as minor characters in a broad sequence of events, relegated to the role of pawns controlled by social and organizational forces rather than as proactive 'movers and shakers'.

3. This perspective does not lend itself readily to the identification of practical recommendations for the more effective management of change, beyond generalized advice such as 'recognize complexity' and 'think processually'.

The expertise of the change agent

The new agents of change: athletes not cowboys

Our new heroic model should be the athlete who can manage the amazing feat of doing more with less, who can juggle the need to both conserve resources and pursue growth opportunities. This new kind of business hero avoids the excesses of both the corpocrat and the cowboy. Where the former rigidly conserves and protects, the latter relentlessly speculates and promotes. But the business athlete has the strength to balance somewhere in the middle, taking the best of the corpocrat's discipline and the cowboy's entrepreneurial zeal. Business athletes need to be intense, lean and limber, able to stretch, good at teamwork, and in shape all the time.

From Kanter (1989).

Change agent
any member of an organization seeking to promote, further, support, sponsor, initiate, implement or help to deliver change.

Rosabeth Moss Kanter (b.1943)

What does it take to be an effective change agent? Two trends make this question urgent. First, most managers now combine change roles with their regular duties. Despite the use of project managers and external consultants, many functional managers are also key change agents. The second trend concerns the increased involvement of all levels of organizational membership on change teams. This distribution of change agency means that more people need to have the skills and knowledge required (Gronn, 2002; Bennett *et al.*, 2003).

Change agents are not necessarily senior managers, and do not need formal job titles. Change agents who are formally appointed are often selected for their expertise in the substance of the change. IT specialists, for example, are typically chosen to manage IT projects. However, rather than technical expertise, change agents require interpersonal and managerial skills, in communication, presentation, negotiation, influencing and selling, organization politics, and in managing the change process. This is consistent with the way in which change is portrayed by processual/contextual theory: untidy, many factors, many players, politicized.

Rosabeth Moss Kanter (1989) identifies seven essential change agency skills:

1. Ability to work independently, without management power, sanction and support.

2. An effective collaborator, able to compete in ways that enhance co-operation.

3. The ability to develop high trust relationships, based on high ethical standards.

4. Self-confidence, tempered with humility.

5. Respect for the process of change, as well as the content.

6. Able to work across business functions and units, 'multifaceted and ambidextrous'.

7. The willingness to stake reward on results and gain satisfaction from success.

Kanter's 'person specification' for the change agent seems to be consistent with what is known about flexible, organic organization structures, about participative management, and about the practice and implications of process re-engineering. Kanter speaks of this 'superhuman' change agent, with wide-ranging expertise, as a 'business athlete'.

STOP AND THINK

Are you an athlete or a cowboy? Do you have the personal qualities required to make you an effective change agent? Match your expertise against Kanter's list.

What further skills development do you need to be effective in a change role?

The effective change agent seems to be someone with a broad and well-developed range of skills and qualities. In a large organization, this can be a lonely and vulnerable role. However, the personal and career rewards can be significant. The high-flying, fast-track career is more readily built on contributions to strategic organizational change. Very few management careers are made by introducing minor, slow, incremental changes.

Why change, when you can innovate?

Is 'change' an appropriate response to a fast-paced unpredictable world? To keep ahead of the competition, organizations must encourage creativity and be innovative. In the public sector, innovation is necessary in order to meet rising public and political expectations with regard to service cost and quality.

Innovation involves the adoption of any device, system, process, programme, product, or service new to that organization.

Innovation is not limited to new products. Most organizations also want to create new ways to organize, to develop new and better working practices, and to provide customers, clients or patients with innovative services. As a result, the term **innovation** is usually defined in broad terms, to mean the adoption of any device, system, process, programme, product, or service *new to that organization*. This definition means that an idea may have already been developed and applied elsewhere, but if it is 'new in this setting', then it can be regarded as an innovation *here*.

Innovation and creativity are often seen as attributes of the *individual*, and inventors are sometimes seen as mavericks. However, innovation and creativity also have *organizational* dimensions. Despite commercial pressures, some organizational norms, systems, and practices are receptive to innovation, while others encourage risk avoidance.

Calvin and Hobbes

Source: CALVIN AND HOBBS © 1989 Watterson. Dist. By UNIVERSAL UCLICK.
Reprinted with permission. All rights reserved.

Sustaining innovations
innovations which make improvements to existing processes, procedures, services and products.

Disruptive innovations
innovations which involve the development of wholly new processes, procedures, services and products.

The innovation process also has a *cultural* dimension. Manufacturing in Britain has been criticized for its lack of innovation (Porter and Ketels, 2003), which results in a prosperity and productivity gap between Britain and other competitor economies, such as the United States, Germany and France. These differences are difficult to explain. Porter and Ketels argue that managers in Britain are slow to adopt new techniques. They attribute this to a combination of low investment in new technology, and weak employee training policies. The individual, organizational, and national cultural influences on innovation are summarized in Figure 18.5.

Clayton Christensen, Richard Bohmer and J. Kenagy (2000) distinguish between **sustaining innovations** and **disruptive innovations**. Sustaining innovations improve existing products and processes; a more efficient motor car, a mobile phone with video capability. Disruptive innovations introduce wholly new processes and services, such as the motor car and the mobile phone when they were first invented. Despite the term, disruptive innovations do not necessarily imply chaos and upheaval, as what is disrupted is often traditional ways of thinking and acting. However, truly disruptive innovations may be harder to manage, because they are riskier, and because there are no established routines for handling them.

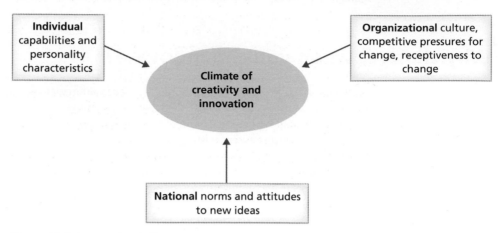

Figure 18.5: Innovation influences

STOP AND THINK

Identify three to five sustaining innovations that have affected you over the past year.

Identify three to five disruptive innovations that have affected you. Did you welcome these innovations because they were beneficial, or did you have cause to complain?

?What if!: Creating an innovative culture

?What If! is a London-based company (with offices in Manchester, York and Shanghai) that helps other companies to innovate, with an annual turnover of £30 million. Their reception area is described as looking more like an art-school cafeteria. Instead of 'new product development', they have a 'Death or Glory' team, known as Dogs. The company's advice for encouraging creativity and innovation is:

1. Find the key to an innovative culture by creating a virtuous circle of structure, attitude, behaviours and skills.

2. Identify the behaviours you want and encourage leaders to model them. Innovation is about people and how they behave together.

3. Communicate, communicate, communicate. Openness and trust provide a basis for an innovative culture.

4. Take creativity out of the hands of 'creative people' and put it back where it belongs – with everyone.

5. Hire for attitude and teach skills – successful teams are created, not inherited.

6. Practise followership rather than leadership. If you walk the floor and reward for risk, people will come with you.

From Chynoweth (2008).

Operational innovation inventing entirely new ways of doing work.

Commercial companies have always focused on innovations with new technology, products and services. Michael Hammer (2004) also advocates a focus on operational innovation finding new ways to lead, organize, work, motivate and manage (Hamel, 2006).

Hammer describes a motor vehicle insurance company which introduced 'immediate response claims handling', operating 24 hours a day. This involved scheduling visits to claimants by claims adjusters who worked from mobile vans, and who would turn up within nine hours. Previously, when the adjusters were office-based, it could take over a week to inspect a damaged vehicle. Handling 10,000 claims a day, adjusters were empowered to estimate damage and write a cheque on the spot. These operational innovations led to huge cost savings, with fewer staff involved in claims handling, lower vehicle storage costs, better fraud detection, and reduction in payout costs. Customer satisfaction and loyalty were improved.

The lean production system developed by the car manufacturing company Toyota (see Chapter 3) is another example of an operational innovation which improves product quality and reduces costs by redesigning the manufacturing process, but without directly affecting the design of the product. Wal-Mart has introduced innovations in purchasing and distribution, such as the use of 'cross-docking', where goods are switched from one truck to the next at distribution centres without going into storage. The computer company Dell and its 'build to order' business model is another example of successful operational innovation.

The best practices puzzle

Why do 'best practices' not spread more quickly? One problem with innovation is that new ideas and methods that are developed and work well in one context are often not adopted elsewhere. Known as 'the best practices puzzle', this is a long-running concern. Don Berwick (2003) observes that the treatment for scurvy, first identified in 1601, did not become standard practice in the British navy until 1865, over 260 years later.

The stethoscope will never be popular

That it [the stethoscope] will ever come into general use, not withstanding its value, I am extremely doubtful; because its beneficial application requires much time, and it gives a good deal of trouble both to the patient and practitioner, and because its whole hue and character is foreign, and opposed to all our habits and associations. It must be confessed that there is something ludicrous in the picture of a grave physician formally listening through a long tube applied to a patient's thorax, as if the disease within were a living being that could communicate its condition to the sense without.

(John Forbes, in the preface to his translation of De L'Auscultation Mediate ou Traite du Diagnostic des Maladies des Poumons et du Coeur [A Treatise on Diseases of the Chest and on Mediate Auscultation], by R.T.H. Laennec, T & G Underwood, London, 1821.)

Everett Rogers (1995) argues that the probability of an innovation being adopted is increased when it is seen to have the following six properties:

1. advantageous when compared with existing practice;
2. compatible with existing practices;
3. easy to understand;
4. observable in demonstration sites;
5. testable;
6. adaptable to fit local needs.

For innovations to diffuse effectively, Rogers argues that the perceptions of adopters, and properties of the organizational context, are as important as the innovation itself. Unless you believe that an innovation will help you to improve on current methods, you are unlikely to be persuaded. New ideas have to be adapted (sometimes significantly) to fit local conditions.

Table 18.7: From innovators to laggards

innovators	usually the first in their social grouping to adopt new approaches and behaviours, a small category of individuals who enjoy the excitement and risks of experimentation
early adopters	opinion leaders who evaluate ideas carefully, and are more sceptical and take more convincing, but take risks, help to adapt new ideas to local settings, and have effective networking skills
early majority	those who take longer to reach a decision to change, but who are still ahead of the average
late majority	even more sceptical and risk averse, wait for most of their colleagues to adopt new ideas first
laggards	viewed negatively by others, the last to adopt new ideas, even for reasons that they believe to be rational

Rogers also argues that the adoption of innovations follows a pattern. Initially, small numbers adopt, followed by 'take-off', then achieving a critical mass of adopters. Finally, the pace slackens as saturation is reached, typically short of 100 per cent (you can never convince everyone). This is usually shown as an S-shaped diffusion curve. Recognizing that the shape of the curve depends on local circumstances, Rogers argues that this pattern is influenced by the five broad groups summarized in Table 18.7.

Diffusion of a new product or idea relies initially on innovators and early adopters, and subsequently on the pace at which the early and late majority are swayed. These are not fixed categories. An individual may be an early adopter of one idea, but a late adopter of another, depending on circumstances. To be an innovator or a laggard depends as much on the social or organizational context as on the individual. This perspective suggests two conclusions, however. First, diffusion behaviour is rarely a sudden event, but a protracted process, triggered and developed by contextual factors as well as individual perceptions and interpersonal communications. Second, there is no 'one best way' to influence people to change; interventions must consider individual needs and perceptions.

Star envy: how politics stop good ideas from spreading

Richard Walton predicted 'relatively little diffusion of potentially significant restructuring in the workplace'. He followed successful work redesign experiments from the 1960s in eight organizations, including two American, two Canadian, one British, two Norwegian, and one Swedish. There was little or no diffusion in seven companies, and only at Volvo (a pioneer in work redesign) was the diffusion 'truly impressive'. What went wrong?:

- projects decayed through internal design inconsistencies, loss of top management support, union opposition, and premature turnover of key staff such as project leaders;

- crises encouraged a return to authoritarian management;

- experiments and their leaders became isolated from the rest of the organization;

- some pilots were seen as poor models for change elsewhere;

- resources, such as training, were often inadequate;

- vested interest in stability, and threat to those whose skills were no longer required;

- 'star envy' caused resentment when pilot sites attracted publicity, visitors, and management attention.

Walton identified two 'political' issues. First, while innovators got credit, those who later adapted their ideas got less praise, even though they too were successful (and had they failed, they probably would have lost more standing than the pioneers would have lost had they failed). Second, the leaders in innovative units were involved in arguments with superiors and staff groups, where they had to defend their positions aggressively, thus damaging their careers. Colleagues wanted to avoid a similar fate; 'The more successful the pioneer, the less favourable are the payoffs and the greater the risks for those who follow' (p.21). Those barriers and deterrents explain why, although lack of diffusion undermines a demonstrator project, a successful pilot does not necessarily diffuse. Walton offers the following advice:

- introduce several projects at the same time;
- avoid over-exposure and 'glorification' of those projects;

- ensure that the programme is identified with top management from the start.

Based on Walton (1975).

Killer cultures

Max McKeown defines a 'killer culture' as one which constantly replaces its products and services by developing better options. Creativity doesn't come from hiring the right people, but from creating the right conditions. Features that block innovation are rules and mission statements (too rigid), efficiency drives (no slack resources), and leaders who stifle ideas before their value can be demonstrated. McKeown's 'five truths about innovation' are:

1. **Even useless can be useful**. *Chindôgu* – the Japanese art of the unusual – describes inventions that solve a problem but cause so many new problems that they are, in effect, useless. But we could all benefit from the *Chindôgu* philosophy because it allows us the freedom to develop new ideas.
2. **Quick fixes reveal real needs**. *Jugaad* – the Hindi word for working around – describes a quick fix necessary because of limitations of resources, including wooden cars build by carpenters and powered by water pump engines. Such quick and dirty solutions reveal real needs including, for example, that for the world's cheapest car; the new £1,200 Tata Nano developed by Indian engineers.
3. **Small differences make a big difference**. If you're like many people, you'll be looking for something BIG. After all, how can you change the world with a small idea? Well, you can because often the biggest advances come from focusing on the smallest things.
4. **New ideas are made of old ideas**. Mankind has mixed and remixed ideas to arrive at our current global society. And it is to new combinations of old ideas that we must look for innovation.
5. **Power is originality's best friend**. Powerful people need ideas. And most ideas need powerful people to facilitate, legitimize, popularize and even legislate for their adoption.

McKeown cites the following examples:

The Motorola Razr was discovered as a discarded prototype on a chance visit by a newly appointed chief executive and went on to sell over 100 million units. The first iPod prototype came from ideas developed by Tony Fadell, an engineer who had failed to find funding for the project until he arrived at Apple. The three ideas that transformed Disney were all generated by existing members of the company in the first three months of Michael Eisener's tenure as CEO. He adopted a style that was playful and bold, holding informal staff lunches to liberate creativity. He led by example, proposed off-the-wall ideas, and encouraged his team to give him the ideas that might embarrass them, that went too far. When told that a concept for standalone Disney retail stores was a small business with low margins, he answered: 'Can't a company our size try something every once in a while just because it feels right? What if it does fail? It's still not going to cost as much as one expensive movie script.'

From McKeown (2008); the article was developed from McKeown, M. (2008), The Truth About Innovation, *London: Prentice Hall.*

Building a creative climate

Rosabeth Moss Kanter (1983, 1989) contrasts what she calls *segmentalist* organization cultures from *integrative* cultures. A segmentalist culture is preoccupied with hierarchy, compartmentalizes its decision-making, and emphasizes rules and efficiency. An integrative culture is based on teams and collaboration, adopts a holistic approach to problem-solving, has no time for history or precedent, and emphasizes results. It is not surprising to find Kanter arguing that bureaucratic, mechanistic segmentalist cultures tend to be 'innovation smothering', and that adaptable, organic, integrative cultures are innovation stimulating. Kanter (2002) is also well known for her 'rules for stifling innovation'.

In with the integrative, out with the segmentalist

I found that the entrepreneurial spirit producing innovation is associated with a particular way of approaching problems that I call 'integrative': the willingness to move beyond received wisdom, to combine ideas from unconnected sources, to embrace change as an opportunity to test limits. To see problems integratively is to see them as wholes, related to larger wholes, and thus challenging established practices – rather than walling off a piece of experience and preventing it from being touched or affected by any new experiences . . .

Such organizations reduce rancorous conflict and isolation between organizational units; create mechanisms for exchange of information and new ideas across organizational boundaries; ensure that multiple perspectives will be taken into account in decisions; and provide coherence and direction to the organization. In these team-oriented co-operative environments, innovation flourishes . . .

The contrasting style of thought is anti-change-oriented and prevents innovation. I call it 'segmentalism' because it is concerned with compartmentalizing actions, events, and problems and keeping each piece isolated from the others [. . .]. Companies where segmentalist approaches dominate find it difficult to innovate or to handle change.

From Kanter (1983, pp.27–28).

Table 18.8: Dimensions of the creative organization climate

Dimension	Promoting innovation	Inhibiting innovation
Challenge	people experience challenge, joy and meaning in work and invest high energy	people are alienated, indifferent, unchallenged, and are apathetic
Freedom	people make contacts, give and receive information freely, discuss problems, make decisions, take initiative	people are passive, rule-bound, anxious to remain within their well-established boundaries
Idea support	people listen to each other, ideas and suggestions are received in a supportive way by bosses and colleagues	suggestions are quickly rejected with counter arguments, usual response is to find faults and obstacles
Trust and openness	high trust climate, ideas can be expressed without fear of reprisal or ridicule, communications are open	low trust climate, people are suspicious of each other, afraid to make mistakes, fear having their ideas stolen
Dynamism and liveliness	new things happening all the time, new ways of thinking and solving problems, 'full speed'	slow jog with no surprises, no new projects or plans, everything as usual
Playfulness and humour	relaxed atmosphere with jokes and laughter, spontaneity	gravity and seriousness, stiff and gloomy, jokes improper
Debates	many voices are heard, expressing different ideas and viewpoints	people follow an authoritarian pattern without questioning
Conflicts	conflict of ideas not personal, impulses under control, people behave in a mature manner, based on psychological insight	personal and emotional tensions, plots and traps, gossip and slander, climate of 'warfare'
Risk taking	decisions and actions prompt and rapid, concrete experimentation is preferred to detailed analysis	cautious, hesitant mentality, work 'on the safe side', 'sleep on the matter', set up committees before deciding
Idea time	opportunities to discuss and test fresh ideas that are not part of planned work activity, and these chances are exploited	every minute booked and specified, pressures mean that thinking outside planned routines is difficult

Exploring how organizations smother and stimulate innovation, Göran Ekvall (1996; Ekvall and Ryhammer, 1999) developed the concept of *creative organization climate*. Climate is a combination of attitudes, feelings, and behaviours, which exists independently of the perceptions and understandings of individual members. The ten dimensions of the creative climate are summarized in Table 18.8.

STOP AND THINK

Think of an organization with which you are familiar, perhaps one where you are currently employed, or one where you have worked recently.

Assess that organization's climate on Ekvall's ten dimensions, in terms of how it promotes or inhibits innovation.

Where the organization inhibits innovation, what practical steps could management take to strengthen the creative climate, to promote innovation?

Much commentary on this topic has a 'pro-innovation bias', assuming that 'new' must be better. But some innovations can be damaging. A good idea may not work as well as better ideas that have been sidelined. What works in one context may not work well in another. Research and experience have shown that 'best practice' is contingent, that there is no 'one best way'. In addition, groups who are advised to implement 'best practice' may be insulted by the implication that they are currently using 'worst practice'. Nevertheless, innovation is and will remain an organizational and managerial preoccupation for the foreseeable future.

Rules for stifling innovation

1. Regard a new idea from below with suspicion, because it's new, and because it's from below.

2. Insist that people who need your approval to act first go through several other levels of management to get their signatures.

3. Ask departments or individuals to challenge and criticize each others' proposals. That saves you the job of deciding; you just pick the survivor.

4. Express criticism freely, and withhold praise. That keeps people on their toes. Let them know that they can be fired at any time.

5. Treat identification of problems as signs of failure, to discourage people from letting you know when something in their area isn't working.

6. Control everything carefully. Make sure people count anything that can be counted, frequently.

7. Make decisions to reorganize or change policies in secret, and spring them on people unexpectedly. That keeps people on their toes.

8. Make sure that requests for information are fully justified, and make sure that it is not given out to managers freely. You don't want data to fall into the wrong hands.

9. Assign to lower level managers, in the name of delegation and participation, responsibility for figuring out how to cut back, lay off, move people around, or otherwise implement threatening decisions you have made. And get them to do it quickly.

10. And above all, never forget that you, the higher-ups, already know everything important about this business.

From Kanter (2002).

Change is now a central management issue. While participation is socially and ethically appropriate, there is a willingness to accept directive methods, accompanied by recognition of the role of organization politics (Butcher and Clarke, 2008). There is also recognition of the need for rapid and continual adjustment to events and trends. Change is no longer something which periodically disturbs the stable fabric, but is an ever present feature.

However, some commentators argue that repeat change is damaging, and that the initiative stream should be carefully timed and paced. The significance of context factors, in shaping

Table 18.9: Trends in organizational change

change in the twentieth century	change in the twenty-first century
one theme among many	an organizational preoccupation
importance of participation and involvement	significance of political motives and actions
rational-linear model of project management	messy, untidy cocktail of reason and motive
small number of senior change agents	large number of distributed change agents
content skills are critical	process skills are critical
implementation method is critical	implementation must be tailored to context
changes must be frequent and fast	need to consider timing and pacing with care
focus on improvement	focus on innovation
aimed at organizational effectiveness	aimed at competitive advantage and survival

the opportunities for and directions of change, is now better understood and appreciated. Finally, while change may still be relevant to improving effectiveness, the organizational capability to change rapidly and often is viewed by many as a factor contributing to competitive advantage and survival. These trends are summarized in Table 18.9.

 RECAP

1. *Outline the contemporary debate concerning repeat change and painless change.*

   - Some commentators argue that constant adaptive reorganization is necessary to compete and survive in a rapidly changing and unpredictable environment.

   - Some commentators argue that constant change causes initiative decay and fatigue which damage organizational performance.

   - While rapid and continuing 'repeat change' may appear necessary, 'painless change' where initiatives are timed and paced more carefully may be more effective.

2. *Identify the main external and internal triggers of organizational change.*

   - Change can be triggered by factors internal and external to the organization, and can also be proactive by anticipating trends and events.

   - Organizational changes vary in depth, from shallow, fine tuning, to deep, paradigmatic or strategic change.

   - The broad direction of change in most organizations is towards becoming less mechanistic and bureaucratic, and more adaptive, responsive and organic.

3. *Understand the typical characteristics of human responses to change.*

   - Emotional responses to traumatic changes differ, but the typical coping cycle passes through the stages of denial, anger, bargaining, depression and acceptance.

   - The Yerkes-Dodson Law states that the initial response to pressure is improved performance, and that increasing pressure leads to fatigue, and ultimately breakdown.

   - The evidence suggests that continuous organizational changes lead to work intensification, burnout and initiative fatigue.

4. *Understand the nature of resistance to change and approaches to overcoming it.*

   - Resistance to change has many sources, including self-interest, lack of trust and understanding, competing assessments of the outcomes, and low tolerance of change.

   - One technique for addressing possible resistance to change, as well as identifying and strengthening support for change, is stakeholder analysis.

   - The main prescribed approach for avoiding or dealing with resistance is participative management, in which those affected are involved in implementation.

- The use of manipulation and coercion to implement change are advocated by some commentators, but the 'political' role of management in change is controversial.

5. *Explain the advantages and limitations of participative methods of change management.*

   - Participative methods can generate creative thinking and increase employee commitment to change, but this process is time-consuming.

   - Some commentators argue that rapid and major corporate transformations are more successful when implemented using a dictatorial or coercive style.

6. *Explain the strengths and weaknesses of the processual/contextual perspective on change.*

   - Processual/contextual theory emphasizes the interaction of the substance, process, politics and context of change, at individual, group, organizational and social levels of analysis, and considers how past events shape current and future thinking and actions.

   - Processual/contextual theory is analytically strong, but is weak in practical terms.

7. *Understand the significance of innovation, and the distinction between sustaining, disruptive, and operational innovations.*

   - Innovation has become a strategic imperative in order to compete and to survive.

   - Sustaining innovations are those which improve existing services and products.

   - Disruptive innovations introduce completely new services and products.

   - Operational innovations concern new ways of organizing, managing and working.

   - The organization's creative climate affects both how innovative people are, and how receptive the organization is to their new ideas.

8. *Outline the skill requirements for an effective change agent.*

   - The change agent has to be more skilled in managing the change process, than knowledgeable about the substance of the change. This involves 'soft' management skills of communication, presentation, selling, negotiating, influencing, and providing feedback and support.

Revision

1. What value do practical 'n-step guides' have for managers attempting to implement organizational change, and what are the limitations of this kind of advice?

2. What are the main sources of resistance to organizational change, and how can resistance be overcome?

3. While some commentators argue that 'repeat change' is a strategic imperative, others claim that this is damaging. Why, and what is the alternative?

4. What are the main types of innovation, and how can an organization develop a climate of creativity and innovation?

Research assignment

Choose an organization that has experienced major change, or changes. Arrange to interview two of the managers who were involved in implementing these changes. Using John Kotter's eight-step guide to corporate transformation, find out how the changes were managed. For each step, what was involved, how was it done, how well did that work:

1. Establish a sense of urgency.

2. Form a guiding coalition.

3. Create a vision.

4. Communicate the vision.

5. Empower people to act on the vision.

6. Create 'short-term wins'.

7. Consolidate improvements to produce further change.

8. Institutionalize new approaches.

Finally, ask your managers for their assessment of these changes. Once you have discovered how the changes were managed, rate the organization on a 1 to 10 scale for each heading (1 = very poor; 10 = very good). A score of 8 suggests disaster; a score of 80 implies success. To what extent is your assessment consistent with that of the managers who you interviewed?

Now develop an action plan that answers the following questions:

- based on your analysis, what should management have done differently in implementing these changes?

- what, if anything, should management do now in order to repair any damage that may have been done during the implementation of these changes?

- what should management do differently the next time when implementing organizational change?

One final question: how useful was Kotter's model as a basis for assessing this organization's changes? How would you improve this model?

Springboard

Buchanan, D.A., Fitzgerald, L. and Ketley, D. (eds), 2006, *The Sustainability and Spread of Organizational Change: Modernizing Healthcare*, Routledge, London.

Explores the 'improvement evaporation effect' and 'the best practices puzzle'. Why do successful changes decay, and why are good new ideas and better working practices not adopted more rapidly?

Cummings, T.G. and Worley, C.G., 2005, *Organization Development and Change*, South-Western College Publishing/Thomson Learning, Mason OH (8th edn).

Classic text exploring the history, underpinning, interventions, and applications of OD.

Kotter, J.P., 2008, *A Sense of Urgency*, Harvard Business Press, Boston.

Follows his earlier work, explaining how to create and sustain 'real urgency' to trigger continuous change.

Palmer, I., Dunford, R. and Akin, G., 2009, *Managing Organizational Change: A Multiple Perspectives Approach*. Boston, MA: McGraw Hill International (2nd edn).

Comprehensive discussion of the nature and reasons for change, theoretical perspectives, practical tools, roles of change agents, sustaining change, illustrated with case studies.

 OB in films

Charlie's Angels (2000, director Joseph McGinty Nichols – 'McG' – 2000): DVD track 14: 0:35:57 to 0:38:10 (3 minutes). Clip begins outside the company headquarters; clip ends when Alex says, 'Better yet, can anyone show me?' Alex (played by Lucy Liu) masquerading as an 'efficiency expert' leads the Angels into the Red Star corporation headquarters, in an attempt to penetrate their security systems. As you watch this three minute clip, consider the following questions:

1. Is this an organization that stimulates or smothers creativity and innovation?

2. How do you know? What are the clues, visual and spoken, that support your assessment of the organization culture?

OB in literature

Jeff Torrington, *The Devil's Carousel*, Martin, Secker & Warburg/Minerva, London, 1996. Set in the Main Assembly Division (MAD) of the Chimeford plant of the Centaur Car Company. The crimson-collared overalls of the senior foremen earn them the nickname Rednecks, while Greybacks are junior foremen wearing all-grey overalls to distinguish their lower rank. Senior managers are called Martians by the shop floor employees. Identify the symptoms and causes of resistance to change in Centaur cars. What factors explain the plant closure? What strategic changes could management have implemented to save the plant? In implementing those changes, would it have been more appropriate to use dictatorial transformation or participative evolution, and why?

CHAPTER EXERCISES

Implementation planning

Objectives
1. To apply change implementation theory to a practical setting.

2. To assess the value of 'best practice' textbook advice on how to implement change effectively.

Briefing
Due to a combination of space constraints and financial issues, your department or school has been told by senior management to relocate to another building seven kilometres from your existing site within the next three months. Your management have in turn been asked to draw up a plan for managing the move, which will affect all staff (academic, technical, secretarial, administrative), all students (undergraduate, postgraduate), and all equipment (classroom aids, computing). The new building will provide more space and student facilities, but offices for academic staff are smaller, the building is on a different bus route, and car parking facilities are limited. Senior management have reassured staff that email will allow regular contact to be maintained with colleagues in other departments and schools which are not being moved.

You have been asked to help management with their planning. Your brief is as follows:

1. Conduct a stakeholder analysis, identifying how each stakeholder or stakeholder group should be approached to ensure that this move goes ahead smoothly.

2. Conduct a readiness for change analysis, identifying any 'groundwork' that may have to be done to ensure the move goes ahead smoothly.

3. Determine a change implementation strategy. Is a participative approach appropriate, or is dictatorial transformation required? Justify your recommendation by pointing to the advantages and limitations of the various options you have explored.

4. Using one or more of the n-step guides described in this chapter, draw up a creative and practical action plan for implementing this change effectively.

Prepare a presentation of your results to colleagues.

In discussion, identify what this analysis reveals about the benefits and problems of turning organizational change theory and 'best practice' advice into practical management action.

→

Force-field analysis

Objective   1. To demonstrate the technique of force-field analysis in planning change.

Briefing   Force-field analysis is a method for assessing the issues supporting and blocking movement towards a given set of desirable outcomes, called the 'target situation'. The forces can be scored, say from 1 (weak) to 10 (strong), to calculate (approximately) the balance of forces.

If the driving forces are overwhelming, then the change can go ahead without significant problems. If the resisting forces are overwhelming, then the change may have to be abandoned, or delayed until conditions have improved.

If the driving and resisting forces are more or less in balance, then the force field analysis can be used to plan appropriate action. The extent to which the force field is balanced is a matter of judgement. Used in a group setting, this method provides a valuable way to structure what can often be an untidy discussion covering a wide range of factors and differing perceptions.

For this analysis, your target situation is 'to double the time that I spend studying organizational behaviour'. In groups of 3, complete the analysis using the following table as a guide. First identify as many driving and restraining forces as you can. Then, reach a group consensus on a score for each of those forces, from 1 (weak) to 10 (strong). Finally for this stage of the analysis, calculate the totals for each side of the force-field.

target situation: to double the time that I spend studying organizational behaviour

scores	driving forces >>>>>	<<<<< restraining forces	scores
	= total driving forces score	total restraining forces score =	

When you have completed this analysis, and added the scores, estimate the probability (high, medium, or low) of reaching your target situation *if the force-field stays the same*.

Now draw up a practical action plan for managing the field of forces that you have identified in order to increase the probability of reaching the target situation. In devising your action plan, remember that:

1. Increasing the driving forces can often result in an increase in the resisting forces. This means that the current equilibrium does not change, but is maintained with increased tension.

2. Reducing the resisting forces is preferable as this allows movement towards the desired outcomes or target situation without increasing tension.

3. Group norms are an important force in shaping and resisting change.

Chapter 19 **Leadership**

Key terms

leadership	initiating structure
great man theory	contingency theory of leadership
power	least-preferred coworker score
reward power	structured task
coercive power	unstructured task
referent power	situational leadership
legitimate power	new leader
expert power	superleader
information power	transactional leader
affiliation power	transformational leader
group power	distributed leadership
consideration	

Learning outcomes

When you have read this chapter, you should be able to define those key terms in your own words, and you should also be able to:

1. Explain the apparent difference between the concepts of leadership and management.

2. Understand why there is little relationship between personality traits and effective leadership.

3. Understand the bases of a leader's power and the role of followers in creating and supporting leaders.

4. Understand why effective leaders either adapt their style to fit the organizational and cultural context in which they operate, or find contexts which fit their personal style.

5. Explain contemporary trends in this field concerning new leadership, distributed leadership, and the argument that leaders are unnecessary.

Why study leadership?

Capital shifts are only one of the mega-trends producing economic uncertainty. Add to that global demographics, migration, massive infrastructural spend, rapid consumption of natural resources including fuels, environmental risk and international terrorism, and you have a pretty volatile mix. And what typically happens? Businesses panic and shoot themselves in the foot. Once again recruitment freezes, major cut-backs in development budgets, and lay-offs in the city are already evident. Let me state my position clearly: I believe that leadership is going to be crucial if organizations are going to survive the downturn and even thrive. Maintaining your investment in developing the leaders of the future will produce significant pay-back and enable you to gain competitive advantage through turbulent times.

From Holbeche (2008).

Leadership appears to be a critical determinant of organizational effectiveness, whether we are discussing an army, an orchestra, a hockey team, a street gang, a political party, a group of rock climbers or a multinational corporation. It is not surprising to find, therefore, that leadership continues to be the focus of research and controversy. This focus is a relatively recent phenomenon. Frank Heller (1997) notes that in 1896, the United States Library of Congress had not one book on leadership. The global literature on the subject is now vast.

Why is leadership so controversial? This is a subject with many paradoxes. We hear the complaint that 'we need more leadership'. However, the organizational hierarchy and formal authority that underpin leadership positions are often challenged. We equate leadership with positions of power, influence and status. However, leadership can be seen at all levels of the organization. Leaders have job titles and working conditions which symbolize their status. But flat structures, team-based working, the growth of knowledge work, and virtual and networked organizational forms, all weaken traditional leadership positions based on hierarchy and symbolism. Ralph Stogdill (1950), an influential early commentator on the topic, defined leadership as an influencing process aimed at goal achievement.

Leadership the process of influencing the activities of an organized group in its efforts toward goal setting and goal achievement.

Stogdill's definition has three components. First, it defines leadership as an interpersonal process in which one individual seeks to influence the behaviour of others. Second, it sets leadership in a social context, in which the other members of the group to be influenced are subordinates or followers. Third, it identifies a criterion for effective leadership – goal achievement – which is one practical objective of leadership theory and research. Most definitions of leadership share these processual, contextual and evaluative components.

STOP AND THINK

Consider those who you would call leaders, in business and politics. What characteristics, skills, abilities, and personality traits do they have in common?

Which of those leaders had a positive impact, and which had a negative impact? Do those whose impact was negative deserve the label of 'leader'?

Your list of leaders might include:

Megawati Sukarnoputri	Usama Bin Laden	Richard Branson
Gordon Brown	Benazir Bhutto	Barack Obama
Mother Teresa	Robert Mugabe	Vladimir Putin
Nelson Mandela	AnSan su Kyi	Bill Gates

How can the term 'leader' be applied to such a diverse group of individuals, whose actions have had a range of different consequences? This chapter explores six perspectives which adopt quite different views on the nature of leadership:

Trait-spotting   identifies the personality traits and related attributes of the effective leader, in order to facilitate the selection of leaders

Style-counselling   characterizes different leadership behaviour patterns to identify effective and ineffective leadership styles, in order to improve the training and development of leaders

Context-fitting   contingency theories argue that the leadership effectiveness depends on the organizational and cultural setting

New leadership   'new leaders', 'superleaders' and 'transformational leaders' (terms which overlap) are heroic, inspirational visionaries who give purpose and direction to others, emphasizing top executives and politicians whose motivational role appears to be central to organization strategy and effectiveness

Distributed leadership leadership behaviour is not confined to those with formal senior roles, but can be observed across the organization

Who needs leaders?   transformational leaders can destabilize an organization by driving too much change too quickly, causing burnout and initiative fatigue; middle managers with change implementation skills are more effective

Ken Parry and Alan Bryman (2006) note that these perspectives developed chronologically. Trait-spotting was popular until the 1940s when inconsistent research findings led to disillusionment. Style-counselling was then popular until the late 1960s, but appeared oversimplified in the face of the contingency theories which dominated thinking until the early 1980s. At that point, the 'new leadership' movement emerged. Towards the close of the twentieth century, the distributed nature of leadership attracted more attention. Moving into the twenty-first century, several commentators challenged the value of leadership, observing that 'celebrity bosses' were responsible for the rapid and radical changes that caused initiative fatigue, and organizational destabilization. Each shift in emphasis has not replaced earlier accounts, and all of those perspectives can be seen in today's research, commentary and practice.

Leaders are men with special qualities

Discussion of leadership is so often overloaded with vague but emotive ideas that one is hard put to it to nail the concept down. To cut through the panoply of such quasi-moral and unexceptionable associations as 'patriotism', 'play up and play the game', the 'never-asking-your-men-to-do-something-you-wouldn't-do-yourself' formula, 'not giving in (or up)', the 'square-jaw-frank-eyes-steadfast-gaze' formula, and the 'if . . . you'll be a man' recipe, one comes to the simple truth that *leadership is no more than exercising such an influence upon others that they tend to act in concert towards achieving a goal which they might not have achieved so readily had they been left to their own devices*.

The ingredients which bring about this agreeable state of affairs are many and varied. At the most superficial level they are believed to include such factors as voice, stature and appearance, an impression of omniscience, trustworthiness, sincerity and bravery. At a deeper and rather more important level, leadership depends upon a proper understanding of the needs and opinions of those one hopes to lead, and the context in which the leadership occurs. It also depends on good timing. Hitler, who was neither omniscient, trustworthy nor sincere, whose stature was unremarkable and whose appearance verged on the repellent, understood these rules and exploited them to full advantage. The same may be said of many good comedians.

From Dixon (1994, pp.214–15;
emphasis added).

Leadership versus management

What is the difference between leadership and management? Some commentators argue that leadership is simply one facet of the management role. Others argue that leaders and managers make different contributions; leaders have followers, managers have subordinates.

Leaders are often seen as visionaries who drive new initiatives; in contrast, managers seek to achieve stability. Warren Bennis and Burt Nanus (1985, p.21) observe that managers do things right, while leaders do the right thing. The leader is prophet, catalyst, mover-shaker, strategist. The manager is technician and problem-solver. John Kotter's (1990) contrast between leaders and managers is shown in Table 19.1. The leader influences others to sign up to their vision, inspires them to overcome obstacles, and generates positive change. The manager establishes plans and budgets, designs and staffs the organization structure, monitors and controls performance, and delivers order and predictability.

Joseph Rost (1991) argues that this is a 'good guys, bad guys' caricature. Kotter's perspective elevates leadership and denigrates management. If you really want to find out just how much people value the consistent, predictable manager, Rost suggests:

deliver payroll cheques late;

cut off the supplies and services which people need to do their jobs;

run the buses, trains and planes late and switch off traffic lights;

deliver unworkable products to customers;

base promotions and salary increases on arbitrary criteria.

Rost concludes that, 'Down with management and up with leadership is a bad idea'. Many commentators ignore this advice. What is the value of order, predictability and consistency in today's turbulent, hostile organizational context in which innovation is at a premium? Setting visions and strategies is much more fun than planning and budgeting.

If they are not leaders, what do managers do? From observing how managers spend their time, Henry Mintzberg (1977) identified ten roles under three main headings (see Chapter 16):

interpersonal roles   leader, figurehead, liaison

informational roles   monitor, disseminator, spokesperson

decisional roles   entrepreneur, disturbance handler, resource allocator, negotiator

Table 19.1: Leadership versus management

	leadership functions	management functions
creating an agenda	*Establishes direction* vision of the future, develops strategies for change to achieve goals	*Plans and budgets* decides actions and timetables, allocates resources
developing people	*Aligning people* communicates vision and strategy, influences creation of teams which accept validity of goals	*Organizing and staffing* decide structure and allocate staff, develop policies, procedures and monitoring
execution	*Motivating and inspiring* energize people to overcome obstacles, satisfy human needs	*Controlling, problem-solving* monitor results against plan and take corrective action
outcomes	*Produces positive and sometimes dramatic change*	*Produces order, consistency and predictability*

Based on Kotter (1990).

Mintzberg's research suggested that, in practice, the distinction between leadership and management is blurred. The roles overlap. Leadership is one dimension of a multifaceted management role. The effective manager requires at least some leadership qualities. The neat conceptual distinction between leader and manager does not translate neatly into practice.

Trait-spotting

For the first half of the twentieth century, researchers assumed that they could identify the personality traits and other attributes of leaders. It would then be possible to select individuals who possessed those markers, and to promote them to leadership positions.

The qualities of successful leaders

General intelligence, although not necessarily being very much brighter than the people they are leading.

Technical or professional knowledge and competence in their particular fields – how otherwise would leaders be respected?

Personality: leaders should be energetic and committed, maintain contact with their people, and understand their strengths and weaknesses.

The ability to inspire, although this quality may be rarer than some of the others and is perhaps the most difficult to develop.

Listening, sharing and delegating skills (and not interfering unnecessarily), because in groups of more than five people it becomes impossible to know all the necessary detail.

Self-knowledge, to understand their strengths and weaknesses, which in turn will enable them to turn to others in their group to compensate for their own biases or deficiencies.

From Cannell (2008).

Great man theory
a historical perspective which argues that the fate of societies, and organizations, is in the hands of powerful, idiosyncratic (male) individuals.

This search for the qualities of good leaders was influenced by **great man theory**.

Great man theory focused on political figures, arguing that leaders reach positions of influence from which they dominate and direct the lives of others by force of personality. It is interesting to note that there is no equivalent 'great woman theory'. Great men are born leaders, and emerge to take power, regardless of the social, organizational or historical context. Research thus focused on identifying the traits of these special people. Ralph Stogdill reviewed hundreds of trait studies (1948, 1974) and compiled this typical list:

- strong drive for responsibility
- focus on completing the task
- vigour and persistence in pursuit of goals
- venturesomeness and originality in problem-solving
- drive to exercise initiative in social settings
- self-confidence
- sense of personal identity
- willingness to accept consequences of decisions and actions
- readiness to absorb interpersonal stress
- willingness to tolerate frustration and delay
- ability to influence the behaviour of others
- capacity to structure social systems to the purpose in hand

Ralph M. Stogdill
(1904–1978)

*"Some men are born great, some achieve greatness,
and some are allowed to work for great men like me."*

It is difficult to challenge these qualities. Can we say that leaders should lack drive, persistence, creativity, and the ability to influence others? These are desirable qualities in many positions, and do not appear to be unique to leaders.

Research did not find a consistent set of leadership traits, and as studies covered a wider range of settings, more qualities were identified. Almost 80 characteristics were reported from a review of 20 studies of leadership traits (Bird, 1940). More than half of these traits had been identified in only one study, very few appeared in four or more investigations, and only 'intelligence' was reported in at least half of the studies reviewed. A further problem is that many of these traits are vague. Willingness to tolerate delay? Capacity to structure social systems? Readiness to absorb stress? It is difficult to see how trait-spotting can be used in a leadership selection context, as originally intended.

It was clear by 1950 that there was limited value in trying to identify leadership traits, although some weak generalizations did emerge (Shaw, 1976; Fraser, 1978). Leaders tend to score higher on average on measures of:

ability   intelligence, relevant knowledge, verbal facility

sociability   participation, co-operativeness, popularity

motivation   initiative and persistence

The trait-spotting approach was abandoned at that time as researchers switched attention, first to leadership behaviour patterns, and then to characteristics of context. However, the belief has persisted that leadership traits can be isolated, and the search for personality markers has since resumed. Paradoxically, trait-spotting has become a contemporary perspective, and can be seen in many attempts to develop leadership 'competency models'.

Power: what is it, and how can I get more?

Leadership is about influencing the behaviour of others. One cannot be a leader without followers, and followers must be willing to obey. To understand why people are influenced by some individuals and not others, we need to understand the nature of compliance.

Power the capacity of individuals to overcome resistance on the part of others, to exert their will, and to produce results consistent with their interests and objectives.

Reward power the ability of a leader to exert influence based on the belief of followers that the leader has access to valued rewards which will be dispensed in return for compliance.

Coercive power the ability of a leader to exert influence based on the belief of followers that the leader can administer unwelcome penalties or sanctions.

Referent power (also called charisma) the ability of a leader to exert influence based on the belief of followers that the leader has desirable abilities and personality traits that can and should be copied.

Legitimate power (also called position power) the ability of a leader to exert influence based on the belief of followers that the leader has authority to issue orders which they in turn have an obligation to accept.

Expert power the ability of a leader to exert influence based on the belief of followers that the leader has superior knowledge relevant to the situation and the task.

Information power the ability of a leader to exert influence based on the belief of followers that the leader has access to information that is not public knowledge.

Affiliation power the ability of a leader to exert influence based on the belief of followers that the leader has a close association with other powerful figures on whose authority they are able to act.

Group power the ability of a leader to exert influence based on the belief of followers that the leader has collective support from a team or group.

Power is a useful concept with which to explain interpersonal influence. Power is a critical dimension of leadership, and we can define power as the ability of an individual to control or to influence others, to get someone to do something that they would perhaps not otherwise do (Astley and Sachdeva, 1984; Pettigrew and McNulty, 1995).

John French and Bertram Raven (1958) identified five bases of power. If someone promises you promotion or money to act as they require, then they are using reward power. If they threaten you with demotion or redundancy, they are using coercive power. Where they rely on their charming personality, they are using referent power. If they rely on their formal organizational position to get you to comply, they are using legitimate power. Where they can claim better knowledge and understanding of the situation, they are using expert power.

Referent power is also known as charisma (in German, *Ausstrahlung*, force of personality). Legitimate power is also called position power, as it relies on the person's formal organizational role and title. Table 19.2 summarizes the more recent work of Robert Benfari, Harry Wilkinson and Charles Orth (1986) who identify eight power bases, adding information power (access to confidential information), affiliation power (access to other powerful individuals), and group power (the team are on my side).

Benfari and colleagues suggest that developing referent power in particular is valuable and straightforward, and doesn't cost anything:

- get to know the motives, preferences, values and interests of your colleagues;
- respect differences in interests and don't attack another person's style;
- give 'positive strokes', use reward power, confirm others' competence;
- invite reciprocal influence, show that you respect their opinions;
- share information, give your expertise, particularly where you stand to benefit;
- minimize concerns with status, put signs of office aside;
- develop communication skills, use clear and consistent messages;
- understand how people react to stress and crisis;
- get to know the informal political structure of your organization.

Several points follow from these definitions of power bases.

First, as shown in the right hand column of Table 19.2, the exercise of power is not always seen as negative (P−). Rewards are usually welcomed (P+). The exercise of 'strong leadership' in a crisis is rarely criticized. Referent power is by definition positively perceived. When expertise is given freely to help those in difficulty, it is perceived positively, but can trigger a negative response when used in a condescending or intrusive manner. The exercise of affiliation and group power can also be either positive or negative depending on how the leader uses them.

Second, these power bases depend on the beliefs of followers. A leader may be able to control rewards and penalties, and have superior knowledge. However, if followers do not believe that the leader has these attributes, then they may not be compliant. Similarly, leaders may be able to persuade followers that they possess power which they do not have. Power is thus a property of the *relationship* between leader and followers, not a property of the leader.

Third, these power bases are linked. The exercise of one may affect a leader's ability to use another. The leader who uses coercion may lose referent power. The leader may be able to use legitimate power to enhance both referent and expert power.

STOP AND THINK   Which combination of power bases would you expect to be most effective for an organization leader? What are the power bases of your organizational behaviour instructor(s)? What countervailing power bases do students possess?

Table 19.2: The effective use of power

Power base	Explanation	Perceived as
Reward	positive strokes, remuneration, awards, compliments, other symbolic gestures of praise	*P* +
Coercion	physical or psychological injury, verbal and non-verbal put-downs, slights, symbolic gestures of disdain, physical attack, demotion, unwanted transfer, withholding resources	*P* −
Authority	management right to control, obligation of others to obey, playing 'the boss' and abusing authority	*P* −
	leadership based on authority in times of crisis or need	*P* +
Referent	identification based on personal characteristics, sometimes on perception of charisma; or	*P* +
	reciprocal identification based on friendship, association, sharing personal information, providing something of value to the other, and on common interests, values, viewpoints and preferences; creation of reciprocal 'IOUs'	
Expert	possession of specialized knowledge valued by others, used to help others, given freely when solicited	*P* +
	unsolicited expertise, seen as unwarranted intrusion; continual use can create barriers; expertise offered in a condescending manner can be seen as coercive; withholding expertise in times of need	*P* −
Information	access to information that is not public knowledge, because of position or connections; can exist at all levels in the organization; those at the top may know less about what is going on; secretaries and personal assistants to senior executives often have information power, and can control information flows to and from superiors	*P* −
Affiliation	'borrowed' from an authority with whom one is associated – executive secretaries and staff assistants act as surrogates for their superiors; acting on the wishes of the superior	*P* +
	acting on self-interest; using negative affiliation power by applying accounting and personnel policies rigidly	*P* −
Group	collective problem-solving, conflict resolution, creative brainstorming; group resolution greater than the individual contribution	*P* +
	a few individuals dominating the proceedings, 'groupthink'	*P* −

Based on Benfari, Wilkinson and Orth (1986).

Finally, leaders can use a combination of different bases, in different contexts and at different times. Few leaders may be able to rely on a single power base.

Prestige job titles no longer give legitimacy to bosses' orders. Employees have their own sources of power which they can use to undermine a leader's position. The most effective leadership style seems to be one in which power is shared with followers. Some managers feel that more power for subordinates means less power for them. However, power sharing can increase subordinate satisfaction, and confidence in the leader. Granting discretion and access to information are also symbolic rewards. Leaders who appear to 'give power away' can thus strengthen, and not weaken, their influence over their followers.

Are you an alpha male or alpha female?

According to Kate Ludeman and Eddie Erlandson, around 75 per cent of the world's testosterone-driven, high-achieving executives are 'alpha males'. They take charge, dominate, conquer and make things happen. Clever and effective, they can also cause damage to themselves and to the companies they lead. Persistence can become stubbornness. Self-confidence leads to an unwillingness to listen to others. Those strengths, in other words, can be fatal weaknesses. There are fewer alpha women, and they do less damage because they empathize rather than confront, and are less angry and impatient. There are four types of alpha leader, each with good and bad characteristics:

commanders	intense, magnetic, push others hard, but ignore rules and create fear
visionaries	creative, inspiring, but ignore reality, and are closed to input
strategists	quick, analytical, but opinionated, not team players, and don't admit mistakes
executors	problem solvers, eye for detail, get things done, overcritical micromanagers

Organizations run by dysfunctional alphas have higher rates of illness, staff turnover, absenteeism, burnout, and early retirement. To find out if you have what it takes to be an alpha, score each of these items from 'strongly disagree' (zero) to 'strongly agree' (10)?

- No matter what, I don't give up until I reach my goal.
- When I play a game, I like to keep score.
- I sometimes rant and rave when I don't get my way.
- My opinions and ideas are usually the best ones.
- When others don't agree, I lose my temper.
- I am accustomed to being the centre of attention.
- People have described me as a 'natural born leader'.
- I believe the end usually justifies the means.
- I only collaborate with peers when I have to.
- There are a lot of people who are just plain stupid.

Scoring

0–25	Absolute wimp; keep tissues on your desk.
26–50	Bit of a pushover.
51–75	Ambitious but afraid to wield the knife.
76–100	Congratulations, you're an alpha.

Based on Ludeman and Erlandson (2006); Rushe (2006).

Jobs for the boys?

For most of the twentieth century, it was assumed that leaders had to be *men*. Most of the research was done by men whose subjects were men. Women are still poorly represented in management roles, and were largely ignored in leadership research until the 1990s. However, Fiona Wilson (2002) argues that we are now seeing a 'feminization of management' as flatter structures need skills in communication, collaboration, consensus decision-making, teamwork, networking, and developing others – qualities associated with women.

In America, all of the Fortune 100 (largest) companies have female board members. In Britain in 2008, only five of the top 100 companies had female chief executives; 39 of those companies had two or more women on their boards, compared with 13 companies in 1999 (Singh and Vinnicombe, 2008). Of the 149 appointments to the boards of the top 100 companies in Britain in 2008, only 16 were women, and 22 of those companies still had all-male boards of directors. Less than 9 per cent of senior judges in Britain are women, and less than 20 per cent of Britain's members of parliament are women, compared with around 25 per cent in Iraq and 30 per cent in Afghanistan (Driscoll, 2008). Spain is the first country in Europe to elect a government which has more female than male parliamentarians, but Spanish women make up just over 4 per cent of company boards (the European average is 11 per cent). Since January 2008, Norwegian companies must by law ensure that at least 40 per cent of their board of directors are women (traditionally 7 per cent).

A more diverse board can be more effective. Alison Konrad and Vicki Kramer (2006) found that women directors make three contributions that men are less likely to make. First, they broaden the discussion to take into account a wider range of stakeholders; employees, customers, the wider community. Second, they are more persistent in getting answers to awkward questions; men don't like to admit that they don't understand everything. Third, they are more collaborative, which improves communications. However, having one or two women on the board makes little difference. When there are three or more women, they are treated like other directors, and are less likely to be isolated or ignored.

Career and family

Does career success for women mean sacrificing family life? Sylvia Ann Hewlett surveyed over 1,100 successful women in America in two age groups, 28–40, and 41–55. She defined high achievers as those earning between US$55,000 and US$65,000, and ultra-achievers as those earning more than US$100,000. For comparison, 470 men were also included in the research. Her findings showed that:

percentage childless between ages 41 and 55

high-achieving women	33
corporate women	42
high-achieving men	25
ultra-achieving men	19
ultra-achieving women	49

High- and ultra-achieving women were also less likely to be married than their male colleagues. Hewlett quotes a young professional woman:

I know a few hard-driving women who are climbing the ladder at consulting firms, but they are single or divorced and seem pretty isolated. And I know a handful of working mothers who are trying to do the half-time thing or the two-thirds-time thing. They work reduced hours so they can see their kids, but they don't get the good projects, they don't get the bonuses, and they also get whispered about behind their backs. You know, comments like, 'If she's not prepared to work the client's hours, she has no business being in the profession' (p.73).

Around a third of high- and ultra-achieving women worked more than 55 hours a week (13 hours a day including commuting), and some were occasionally working 70 hours. Hewlett argues that, for many women, 'the brutal demands of ambitious careers, the asymmetries of male-female relationships, and the difficulties of bearing children late in life conspire to crowd out the possibility of having children'.

Based on Hewlett (2002).

Deborah Tannen (1995) argues that women and men acquire different linguistic styles in childhood (see Chapter 7). Girls learn to focus on rapport, while boys focus on status. Men think in hierarchical terms, and of being 'one up', are more likely to jockey for position by putting others down, and appear confident and knowledgeable. Women can appear to lack self-confidence by playing down their certainty and expressing doubt, and women who adopt a 'masculine' linguistic style are regarded as aggressive. Reinforcing these conclusions Deborah Rees (2004) identifies three categories of women in management:

corporate high-flyers motivated by influence and power, have pursued management careers and achieved senior roles

soloists and pioneers motivated by freedom and self-control, work on their own, or set up their own businesses

submarines as work is neither rewarding nor flexible enough, do not pursue traditional careers and put energies elsewhere

Rees discovered many women who felt that the financial rewards of senior positions did not compensate for the lack of flexibility. Submarines were frustrated by the way in which their organizations discouraged them from balancing work and non-work commitments. Soloists, pioneers and submarines also said that they disliked the 'overtly political and clubby' atmosphere at the top of male-dominated organizations, with the focus on empire building, and the absence of teamwork. For male managers, it seemed, 'winning and beating others is good', and being 'nice' to others is not seen as a valuable attribute. Despite working longer hours, soloists and pioneers expressed higher levels of satisfaction and self-fulfilment. From her research, Susan Pinker (2008) also found many women who had given up a corporate career, not because of discrimination, but because they wanted something different from life.

Home viewing

In *Harry Potter and the Goblet of Fire* (2005, director Mike Newell), Harry (played by Daniel Radcliffe) is unexpectedly chosen to take part in the challenging and dangerous Triwizard Tournament. This is a competition between three schools of wizardry – Harry's own school Hogwarts, Beauxbatons Academy, and the Durmstrang Institute. The film illustrates several aspects of leadership and the exercise of power. As the action unfolds, identify instances where characters influence the decisions and actions of others through the exercise of reward power, coercive power, legitimate power,

referent power, and expert (or information) power. The headmaster of Hogwarts is Albus Dumbledore (Michael Gambon). Dumbledore is a transformational leader. Identify where in the movie Dumbledore displays 'the four Is' of transformational leadership to influence and develop others: intellectual stimulation, idealized influence, individualized consideration, and inspirational motivation.

For further information about the power and leadership themes in this movie, see Rosser (2007).

Debate concerning the problems facing women who aspire to leadership roles has focused on 'the glass ceiling', the invisible barrier erected by male-dominated company boards. Men's careers are helped by a 'glass escalator'. Research by Michelle Ryan and Alexander Haslam (2005) suggests that women who are promoted to senior roles face another set of problems.

Research shows that companies are more likely to change the composition of their boards of directors when performance drops, than when it is improving. Ryan and Haslam suggest that poor company performance can trigger the appointment of women to the board, on the basis that diversity leads to higher performance. They also note that this means promoting women into positions that carry a high risk of failure. As women are a minority among senior managers, they are more visible in these roles, and their performance tends to be scrutinized more closely. The researchers conclude that women were being 'set up to fail'. They were being placed on a 'glass cliff', by being appointed in difficult organizational circumstances. As a consequence, their position in the company was particularly precarious. In such cases, women may find that they are held responsible for poor performance created by conditions that were in place before they were promoted. Thus, while women may be under-represented in senior management ranks, they may be over-represented in vulnerable senior positions.

Alice Eagly and Linda Carli (2007) argue that the 'glass ceiling' argument is misleading. They suggest that the image of the 'labyrinth' is more useful, as women face many obstacles and challenges to their careers at different stages. The difficulties do not just lie with senior roles. Male prejudice and family responsibilities are not the only problems. Women tend to have less time for socializing, and have weaker professional networks. Suggesting that women need persistence and self-awareness to negotiate this labyrinth, other remedies include changing the long-hours culture, and developing women at an early stage in their careers with challenging management assignments.

 **STOP AND THINK** What power bases can women exploit in order to strengthen their organizational positions and achieve promotion to more senior managerial positions?

Women don't ask

A survey carried out by a large retail chain store company over Christmas 2005 revealed that, on average, parents in England spend about £100 more on presents for their sons than for their daughters. When asked to explain, parents said that boys asked for more items, and what they asked for was more expensive. Boys also complained more loudly if they were disappointed. The most expensive toy in the top five best-sellers for girls was the Amazing Amanda doll (£69.99), compared with the boys' Playstation Portable (£179.99).

The unwritten rule that says, 'if you don't ask, you don't get', also seems to apply to adults. Research in America (Babcock and Laschever, 2003) suggests that after graduating from university, women are more likely to accept the starting salary that they are offered, while men are more likely to ask for, and get, more. This may explain why women in Britain who work full time are paid 18 per cent less than men, and why part-timers are paid 40 per cent less. Can this inequality be explained by the observation that women tend to leave employment to look after children? Not entirely, because the difference in salary between equally well-educated men and women is 15 per cent, five years after graduation, long before those women begin to start families (according to Equal Opportunities Commission figures).

Why should women be less demanding? One explanation is that men do not need to feel that they are liked by their colleagues, and are less embarrassed about complaining and asking for more money. Women, in contrast, tend to be more concerned with maintaining relationships, and assume that if they were worth a higher salary, then their boss would pay them more.

Based on Webb (2006).

Style-counselling

Disillusionment with the traits approach meant that leadership, management and supervisory style became a major focus for research. Attention switched from selecting leaders on the basis of personality traits, to training and developing leaders in appropriate behaviour patterns. This research tradition argues that a considerate, participative, democratic and involving leadership style is more effective than an impersonal, autocratic and directive style.

Two projects, the Michigan and Ohio studies, underpinned the investigation of management style. Based mainly on a study of foremen at the International Harvester Company, the work of the Survey Research Center in Michigan in the 1940s and early 1950s (Katz *et al.*, 1950), identified two dimensions of leadership behaviour:

1. **employee-centred behaviour**: focusing on relationships and employee needs;
2. **job-centred behaviour**: focusing on getting the job done.

Consideration
a pattern of leadership behaviour that demonstrates sensitivity to relationships and to the social needs of employees.

Initiating structure
a pattern of leadership behaviour that emphasizes performance of the work in hand and the achievement of product and service goals.

This work ran concurrently with the influential studies of Edwin Fleishman and Ralph Stogdill, at the Bureau of Business Research at Ohio State University (Fleishman, 1953a, 1953b; Fleishman and Harris, 1962; Stogdill, 1948 and 1950; Stogdill and Coons, 1951). The Ohio results also identified two categories of leadership behaviour which they termed consideration and initiating structure. The considerate leader is relationships and needs oriented. The leader who structures work for subordinates is task or job-centred.

The considerate leader is interested in and listens to subordinates, allows participation in decision-making, is friendly and approachable, and supports subordinates with personal problems. The leader's behaviour indicates trust, respect, warmth and rapport. This enhances subordinates' feelings of self-esteem and encourages the development of communications and relationships in a work group. The researchers first called this dimension 'social sensitivity'.

The leader who initiates structure decides how things are going to get done, structures tasks and assigns work, makes expectations clear, emphasizes deadlines and expects subordinates to follow instructions. The leader's behaviour stresses production and the achievement of organizational goals. This is the kind of emphasis that the scientific management school (see Chapter 14) encouraged, but task orientation in this perspective has a positive, motivating aspect. The researchers first called this leadership dimension 'production emphasis'.

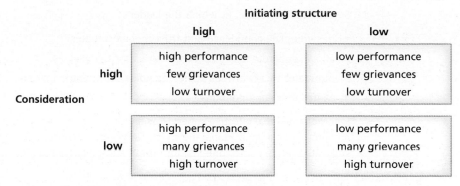

Figure 19.1: The Ohio State leadership theory predictions

The Michigan and Ohio studies developed the dichotomy between democratic and autocratic leadership, dimensions that have been confirmed in numerous other studies. Consideration and structure are independent behaviour patterns, and do not represent the extremes of a continuum. A leader can emphasize one or both. Job satisfaction is likely to be higher, and grievances and labour turnover lower, when the leader emphasizes consideration. Task performance, on the other hand, is likely to be higher when the leader emphasizes the initiation of structure. Inconsiderate leaders typically have subordinates who complain and who are more likely to leave the organization, but can have comparatively productive work groups if they are high on initiating structure. This theory is summarized in Figure 19.1.

The influential work of another Michigan researcher, Rensis Likert (1961), reinforced the benefits of considerate, performance-oriented leadership. From interviews with 24 supervisors and 419 clerks in an American insurance company, he found that supervisors in highly productive sections were more likely to:

- receive general as opposed to close supervision from their superiors;
- give general as opposed to close supervision to their subordinates;
- enjoy their responsibility and authority, and spend more time on supervision;
- be employee rather than production-oriented.

Rensis Likert
(1903–1981)

Likert and his team identified four systems of leadership:

System 1: *Exploitative autocratic*, in which the leader

- has no confidence and trust in subordinates;
- imposes decisions; never delegates;
- motivates by threat;
- has little communication and teamwork.

System 2: *Benevolent authoritative*, in which the leader

- has superficial, condescending trust in subordinates;
- imposes decisions; never delegates;
- motivates by reward;
- sometimes involves subordinates in solving problems.

System 3: *Participative*, in which the leader

- has some incomplete confidence and trust in subordinates;
- listens to subordinates but controls decision-making;
- motivates by reward and some involvement;
- uses ideas and opinions of subordinates constructively.

System 4: *Democratic*, in which the leader

- has complete confidence and trust in subordinates;
- allows subordinates to make decisions for themselves;
- motivates by reward for achieving goals set by participation;
- shares ideas and opinions.

Likert claimed that effective supervisors adopted either system 3 or system 4, which he called an 'alternative organizational life style'. However, recent research by Roderick Kramer (2006) suggests that, in some contexts, an intimidating leadership style can be effective, too.

The great intimidators

Roderick Kramer challenges the view that managers must be nice and not tough, and should be humble and self-effacing rather than intimidating. Kramer argues that intimidation is an appropriate style when an organization has become rigid or unruly, stagnant or drifting, faces resistance or inertia. Abrasive leadership gets people moving. Intimidators are not bullies, but can use bullying tactics when time is short, and the stakes are high: 'They are not averse to causing a ruckus, nor are they above using a few public whippings and ceremonial hangings to get attention. They're rough, loud, and in your face' (p.90).

"In his mysterious way, God has given each of us different talents, Ridgeway. It just so happens that mine is intimidating people."

Source: Copyright © Joseph Mirachi.

Intimidators have 'political intelligence'. The socially intelligent manager focuses on leveraging the strengths of others, with empathy and soft power. The politically intelligent manager focuses on weaknesses and insecurities, using coercion, fear, and anxiety. Working for an intimidating leader can be a positive experience. Their sense of purpose can be inspirational, their forcefulness is a role model, and intimidators challenge others to think clearly about their objectives. Kramer quotes a journalist who said, 'Don't have a reputation for being a nice guy – that won't do you any good' (p.92). Intimidation tactics include:

Get up close and personal. Intimidators work through direct confrontation, invading your personal space, using taunts and slurs to provoke and throw you off balance.

Get angry. Called 'porcupine power', this involves the 'calculated loss of temper' (use it, don't lose it), using rage and anger to help the intimidator prevail.

Keep them guessing. Intimidators preserve an air of mystery by maintaining deliberate distance. Transparency and trust are fashionable, but intimidators keep others guessing, which makes it easier to change direction without loss of credibility.

Know it all. 'Informational intimidators' can be very intimidating. It doesn't matter whether 'the facts' are correct, as long as they are presented with total confidence at the right time.

Based on Kramer (2006).

Beverly Alimo-Metcalfe and Margaret Bradley (2008) also argue that a participative, engaging style improves performance. They studied 46 mental health teams involved in implementing organizational change, and found that engaging leadership increases employee motivation, job satisfaction, and commitment while reducing stress. Each team had a designated leader, but as teams were on call around the clock, different members took the leadership role at different times. Engaging leadership had the following dimensions:

Table 19.3: Which leadership dimensions have most impact

	leadership dimension		
	engaging with others	visionary leadership	leadership capabilities
high job satisfaction	☑		☑
high motivation to achieve	☑	☑	☑
strong sense of job commitment	☑		
strong organizational commitment	☑		
high sense of fulfilment	☑	☑	
high self-esteem	☑	☑	
high self-confidence	☑		☑
low job-related stress	☑	☑	
low emotional exhaustion	☑	☑	
strong sense of team spirit	☑		
strong sense of team effectiveness	☑	☑	☑

Source: Alimo-Metcalf and Bradley (2008, table on p.41).

- *involving stakeholders early*: this helps to establish lasting relationships;
- *building a collective vision*: this means that the team 'owns' the work and the goals;
- *no team hierarchy*: leadership devolves as appropriate, even with an appointed leader;
- *supportive culture*: informal support from colleagues, formal support from supervision, so people can share problems, seek advice, and take risks;
- *successful change management*: team members are consulted about change and their views are taken into account.

Engaging with others was one of three dimensions of leadership identified in this study. *Visionary leadership* involves having clear goals, being sensitive to stakeholder needs and interests, and inspiring them with passion and determination. *Leadership capabilities* involves competencies such as understanding strategy, ensuring goal clarity, setting success criteria, commitment to high standards, and designing supportive systems and procedures. Of these three dimensions, engaging with others had the greatest impact on attitudes and performance, while leadership capabilities had only limited effects, as Table 19.3 shows.

This study suggests that efforts to develop leadership competencies would be better spent on developing a culture of engagement, at all levels of the organization.

Context-fitting

The Michigan and Ohio perspectives offer leaders 'one best way' to handle followers, by adopting the 'high consideration, high structure' ideal. This advice is supported by the fact that most people *like* their leaders to be considerate, even when they are performance oriented as well. The main criticism of this perspective lies with the observation that one leadership style may not be effective in all circumstances. Several commentators have developed frameworks showing how the effectiveness of leadership style depends on context.

Robert Tannenbaum and Warren Schmidt

Departing from 'one-best-way', Robert Tannenbaum and Warren Schmidt (1958) presented the autocratic-democratic choice as a continuum, from 'boss-centred leadership' at one extreme to 'subordinate-centred leadership' at the other. This is illustrated in Figure 19.2.

Robert Tannenbaum (1913–2003)

Warren H. Schmidt

Boss-centred leadership ⟶   ⟵ Subordinate-centred leadership

Use of authority by the manager

Area of freedom for subordinates

| Manager makes decision and announces it | Manager 'sells' decision | Manager presents ideas and invites questions | Manager presents tentative decision subject to change | Manager presents problem, gets suggestions, makes decision | Manager defines limits, asks group to make decision | Manager permits subordinates to function within limits defined by superior |

Figure 19.2: The Tannenbaum–Schmidt continuum of leadership behaviour

Source: Reprinted by permission of *Harvard Business Review*. From "How to choose a leadership pattern" by Tannenbaum, R. and Schmidt, W.H., Vol. 37, March–April reprinted in May–June, 1973, Copyright © 1958 by the Harvard Business School Publishing Corporation, all rights reserved.

The steps in this continuum are presented as alternatives for the leader; their article was subtitled, 'should a manager be democratic or autocratic – or something in between?'. Tannenbaum and Schmidt argue that the answer depends on three sets of forces:

forces in the manager   personality, values, preferences, beliefs about employee participation, confidence in subordinates

forces in the subordinates   need for independence, tolerance of ambiguity, knowledge of the problem, expectations of involvement

forces in the situation   organizational norms, size and location of work groups, effectiveness of teamworking, nature of the problem

> **Contingency theory of leadership**
> a perspective which argues that leaders must adjust their style in a manner consistent with aspects of the context.

Having concentrated on 'forces in the manager', and challenged the notion of 'one-best-way' to lead, research turned to consider aspects of the context in which the leader was operating. These included the people being led, the nature of the work they were doing, and the wider organizational setting. This perspective suggests that leaders must be able to 'diagnose' the context, and then decide what behaviour will 'fit'. As the best style is contingent on the situation, this approach is known as the **contingency theory of leadership**.

STOP AND THINK

Leadership research and theory seems to be consistent in arguing that a considerate, employee-centred, participative and democratic style is more effective.

In what context would an inconsiderate, goal-centred, impersonal and autocratic leadership style be effective? (See OB in films, this chapter, for a possible answer.)

Fred Fiedler

> **Least preferred coworker score** an assessment of the kind of person with whom a leader feels they could not work effectively.

The contingency theory of Fred Fiedler (1967; Fiedler and Chemers, 1974, 1984) provides a systematic approach to diagnosing contextual factors. Fiedler worked with groups whose leaders were clearly identified and whose performance was easy to measure, such as basketball teams and bomber crews. Fiedler first developed a new measure of a leader's approach to managing people – the **least preferred coworker score** (or LPC score).

Table 19.4: High and low LPC leaders

The low LPC leader	The high LPC leader
self-esteem based on task completion	self-esteem based on interpersonal relations
puts the task first	puts people first
is hard on those who fail	likes to please others
considers competence a key attribute	considers loyalty a key attribute
likes detail	is bored with detail

Frederick Edward Fiedler (b.1922)

Structured task
a task with clear goals, few correct or satisfactory solutions and outcomes, few ways of performing it, and clear criteria of success.

Unstructured task
a task with ambiguous goals, many good solutions, many ways of achieving acceptable outcomes, and vague criteria of success.

The leader is asked to think of the most difficult person they have ever had to work with, and to rate that individual on dimensions such as 'tense–relaxed', 'nasty–nice', and 'quarrelsome–harmonious'. Leaders with a high LPC score tend to see their least preferred coworkers more positively, and tend to be accepting, considerate, and permissive. Leaders with a low LPC score tend to be controlling and directive. The differences between high (relationships-oriented) and low (task-oriented) LPC leaders are summarized in Table 19.4.

Fiedler seems to have found another way to uncover a manager's predispositions towards consideration and initiating structure. It should not be surprising, therefore, to find that his attempts to correlate the LPC scores of leaders with the performance of their groups was not successful. This led Fiedler to argue that effectiveness is influenced not just by leadership orientation but also by three other sets of factors:

1. The extent to which the task in hand is structured.

2. The leader's position power.

3. The nature of the relationships between the leader and followers.

This argument distinguishes between a structured task and an unstructured task.

STOP AND THINK   Would you describe the task of writing an essay for your organizational behaviour instructor as structured or unstructured?

As a student, would you prefer this task to be more or less structured, and how would you advise you instructor to achieve this?

Fiedler identifies three typical sets of conditions under which a leader may have to work.

Condition 1

- The task is highly structured.
- The leader's position power is high.
- Subordinates feel that their relationships with the boss are good.

Task-oriented (low LPC score) leaders get good results in these conditions. They detect that events are under their control, set targets, monitor progress and achieve good performance. Relationships-oriented (high LPC score) leaders get poor results, because they try to build and maintain good relationships with and between their subordinates. However, when relationships are already good, and the other conditions are favourable, the leader may take subordinates for granted and start to pursue other personal objectives.

Condition 2

- The task is unstructured.
- The leader's position power is low.
- Subordinates feel that their relationships with the boss are moderately good.

Relationship-oriented (high LPC) leaders get better results in these moderately favourable circumstances where the maintenance of good relationships is important to the leader's ability to exert influence over subordinates and to getting the work done. In contrast, the task-oriented (low LPC) leader ignores deteriorating relationships and, as the task lacks structure and the leader lacks position power, the results are likely to be poor.

Condition 3

- The task is unstructured.
- The leader's position power is low.
- Subordinates feel that their relationships with the boss are poor.

Task-oriented (low LPC) leaders get better results in these very unfavourable conditions. In contrast, the relationships oriented (high LPC) leader is unwilling to exert pressure on subordinates, avoids confrontations that might upset or anger them, gets involved in attempts to repair damaged relationships and ignores the task. Meanwhile, the task-oriented leader gets impatient, tries to structure the situation, ignores resistance from subordinates, reduces the ambiguity surrounding the work and achieves good performance.

The evidence to support Fiedler's theory is positive but weak. There are four problems:

1. The key variables, task structure, power and relationships, are difficult to assess. The leader who wants to rely on this framework to determine the most effective style for a given situation has to rely more on intuition than on systematic analysis.
2. The concept of the 'least preferred coworker' is unusual, negatively worded and confusing. It is another indicator of employee-centred versus task-centred behaviour.
3. The framework does not take into account the needs of subordinates.
4. The need for a leader to have relevant technical competence is ignored.

This theory has two strengths. First, it confirms the importance of contextual factors in determining leader behaviour and effectiveness. It reinforces the view that there is no one ideal set of traits or best behavioural pattern. Second, it provides a systematic framework for developing the self-awareness of managers concerned about their leadership style.

Most contingency theories argue that leaders should change their style to fit the context. However, Fiedler felt that most managers and supervisors have problems in changing their styles. To be effective, he argued, *leaders have to change their context*, choosing conditions in which their preferred style was most likely to be effective. This could mean changing work group or department, or even moving to another organization.

Paul Hersey and Ken Blanchard

Another influential contingency theory of leadership was developed by Paul Hersey and Ken Blanchard (1988). Like Fiedler, they argue that the effective leader 'must be a good diagnostician' and adapt style to meet the demands of the situation in which they operate. Unlike Fiedler, they believe that leaders can alter their style to fit the context. Hersey and Blanchard call their approach SITUATIONAL LEADERSHIP®.

SITUATIONAL LEADERSHIP®
an approach to determining the most effective style of influencing, considering the direction and support a leader gives, and the readiness of followers to perform a particular task.

Their theory of SITUATIONAL LEADERSHIP® is summarized in Figure 19.3, which describes leadership behaviour on two dimensions.

The first dimension (horizontal axis) concerns 'task behaviour', or the amount of direction a leader gives to subordinates. This can vary from specific instructions, at one extreme, to delegation, at the other. Hersey and Blanchard identify two intermediate positions, where leaders either facilitate subordinates' decisions, or take care to explain their own.

The second dimension (vertical axis) concerns 'supportive behaviour', or the social backup a leader gives to subordinates. This can vary from limited communication, to considerable listening, facilitating and supporting. The model thus described four basic leadership styles:

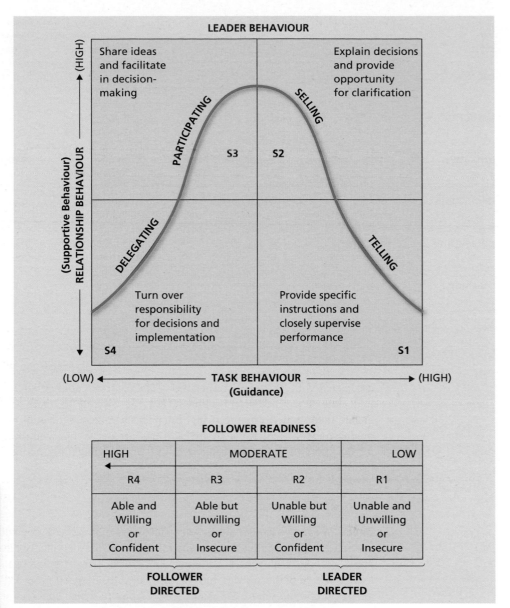

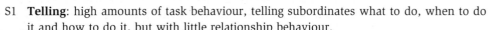

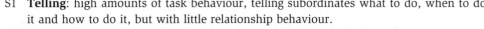

Figure 19.3: SITUATIONAL LEADERSHIP® theory

Source: © Copyright 2006 Reprinted with the permission of the Center for Leadership Studies, Escondido, CA 92025. www.situational.com. All Rights Reserved.

Paul Hersey

Kenneth H.
Blanchard (b.1939)

S1 **Telling**: high amounts of task behaviour, telling subordinates what to do, when to do it and how to do it, but with little relationship behaviour.

S2 **Selling**: high amounts of both task behaviour and relationship behaviour.

S3 **Participating**: lots of relationship behaviour and support, but little direction or task behaviour.

S4 **Delegating**: not much task behaviour or relationship behaviour.

Hersey and Blanchard argue that the willingness of followers to perform a task is also a key factor, as shown in the 'readiness continuum' in the lower part of Figure 19.3. At one extreme, we have insecure subordinates, reluctant to act. At the other, we have confident and able followers. Superimpose the readiness continuum on the top half of the model and you have a basis for selecting an effective leadership style. The view that insecure subordinates need telling, while willing groups can be left to do the job, is consistent with other theories.

Table 19.5: Goleman's six leadership styles

style	in practice	in a phrase	competencies	when to use
coercive	demands compliance	'Do what I tell you'	drive to achieve, self-control	in a crisis, with problem people
authoritative	mobilizes people	'Come with me'	self-confidence, change catalyst	when new vision and direction is needed
affiliative	creates harmony	'People come first'	empathy, communication	to heal wounds, to motivate people under stress
democratic	forges consensus	'What do you think?'	collaboration, teambuilding	to build consensus, to get contributions
pacesetting	sets high standards	'Do as I do, now'	initiative, drive to achieve	to get fast results from a motivated team
coaching	develops people	'Try this'	empathy, self-awareness	to improve performance, to develop strengths

Based on Goleman (2000).

Alan Bryman (1986, p.149) argues that there is no clear reason why S2 and S3 should be associated with R2 and R3 respectively. The S3 style could be appropriate for groups in a high state of 'psychological readiness' (R2), but without the depth of experience that would enable them to perform effectively. Bryman also notes the lack of evidence to support the model. As with Fiedler, the strengths of this perspective lie with the emphasis on the need for flexibility in leadership behaviour, and with highlighting the importance of contextual factors.

Daniel Goleman

Daniel Goleman (2000) reports research by the management consulting firm Hay McBer involving 4,000 executives from around the world. This identified six leadership styles which affect 'working atmosphere' and financial performance. The findings suggest that effective leaders use all of these styles, like an 'array of clubs in a golf pro's bag'. Each style relies on an aspect of emotional intelligence (see Chapter 6) which concerns skill in managing your emotions, and the emotions of others. Goleman's six styles are summarized in Table 19.5.

While coercion and pacesetting have their uses, the research showed that these styles can damage 'working atmosphere', reducing flexibility and employee commitment. The other four styles have a consistently positive impact on climate and performance. The most effective leaders, Goleman concludes, are those who have mastered four or more styles, particularly the positive styles, and who are able to switch styles as the situation commands. This is not a 'mechanical' matching of behaviour to context, as other contingency theories imply, but a flexible, fluid, sensitive and seamless adjustment.

David Snowden and Mary Boone

David Snowden and Mary Boone (2007) also argue that leaders have to adjust their style to suit the context. Contexts vary in terms of how simple or complex they are. The *Cynefin* framework (pronounced ku-*nev*-in) identifies four different types of context; simple, complicated, complex and chaotic. Leaders can use this approach to determine how best to operate. *Cynefin* is a Welsh term that refers to the many factors in our environment. Simple and complicated contexts are ordered and predictable, and correct choices can be based on evidence. Complex and chaotic contexts are untidy and unpredictable, and decisions

Table 19.6: Context and leadership

context	characteristics	the leader's job
simple	repeating patterns, consistent events clear causal relationships; right answers known knowns fact-based management	sense, categorize, respond ensure processes are in place delegate; use best practices clear, direct communications; intensive interaction unnecessary
complicated	expert diagnosis required causal relationships discoverable, more than one right answer known unknowns fact-based management	sense, analyze, respond create panels of experts listen to conflicting advice
complex	flux and unpredictability no right answers; emergent patterns unknown unknowns many competing ideas; need for creativity and innovation pattern-based leadership	probe, sense, respond experiment, allow patterns to emerge increase interaction and communication use methods to generate ideas encourage dissent and diversity
chaotic	high turbulence no clear causal relationships, no point looking for right answers unknowables many decisions, no time to think high tension pattern-based leadership	act first, sense, respond look for what works, not for right answers immediate action to re-establish order (command and control) clear, direct communication

have to be based on emerging patterns. Effective leaders can change their styles to match the changing environment. This approach is summarized in Table 19.6.

Being effective in one or two of these contexts is not good enough. Depending on the issues, a leader may be faced with all four contexts at the same time, relating to different aspects of the task in hand. Snowden and Boone conclude that, 'Good leadership requires openness to change on an individual level. Truly adept leaders will know not only how to identify the context they're working in at any given time but also how to change their behaviour and their decisions to match that context' (p.75).

Contingency theories argue that the most effective leadership style depends on the context. Organization structures, management skills, employee characteristics, and the nature of their tasks, are unique. No one style of leadership is universally best. There is, however, a good deal of research which indicates that a considerate, participative or democratic style of leadership is generally more effective. There are two main reasons for this.

First, participative management is part of a wider social and political trend which has raised expectations about personal freedom and quality of working life. These social and political values encourage resistance to manipulation by impersonal bureaucracies, and challenge the legitimacy of management decisions. Participation thus reflects democratic social and political values. Many commentators would note, however, that individual freedom, quality of working life, and genuine participation are still lacking in many organizations.

Second, participative management has been encouraged by research which has shown that this style is generally more effective, although an autocratic style can be effective in some circumstances. A participative style can improve organizational effectiveness by tapping the ideas of people with knowledge and experience, and by involving them in a decision-making process to which they then become committed. This is reinforced by the growth in numbers of knowledge workers who expect to be involved in decisions affecting their work, and whose knowledge makes them potentially valuable contributors in this respect.

People who are involved in setting standards or establishing methods are thus more likely to experience 'ownership' of such decisions, and are more likely to:

- accept the legitimacy of decisions reached with their help;
- accept change based on those decisions;
- trust managers who ultimately ratify and implement decisions;
- volunteer new and creative ideas and solutions.

Autocratic management stifles creativity, ignores available expertise and smothers motivation and commitment. However, autocratic management can be more effective:

- when time is short;
- when the leader is the most knowledgeable person;
- where those who could participate will never all agree on a decision.

The contingency theories discussed so far have attracted some criticisms.

One criticism concerns the questionable ability of leaders to diagnose the context in which they are operating, given the relatively vague nature of the situational variables identified by different theories. In addition, contingency theories often overlook other key dimensions of context, such as the organization culture, degree of change and levels of stress, working conditions, external economic factors, organizational design and technology. All of these factors potentially influence the leadership process in ways not addressed by any of these theoretical accounts (Hughes *et al.*, 1996).

A second criticism concerns whether leaders can adapt their styles to fit the context in the ways the theories suggest. Personality may not be flexible enough. Some theorists argue that personality is inherited, inhibiting managers from being participative in some circumstances and dictatorial in others. The manager who is motivated by affiliation and who values the friendship of others may find it hard to treat employees in an impersonal and autocratic way.

"You've demonstrated some fine leadership skills, but have you forgotten we hired you to be a follower?"

Source: Copyright P.C. Vey. Originally appeared in *Harvard Business Review*.

A third criticism is that the expectations of other managers can influence what is 'acceptable'. There are advantages in honesty and consistency. People may not accept the fickle behaviour of the participative manager who adopts an autocratic style on some occasions. The leader who changes style from one situation to another may not inspire confidence or trust. However, leaders should be able to change style to suit the circumstances:

1. It is now broadly accepted that leaders and managers can learn from experience to adjust their behaviour according to the circumstances.

2. Organizations are not rigid arrangements with fixed tasks and structures. With the growth in demand for flexibility, adaptability, improved quality of working life and worker participation, leaders and managers who fail to respond will face problems.

3. The leader or manager who adapts in a flexible way to changes in circumstances may be seen as more competent than one who sticks rigidly to traditional routines.

New leadership

New leader an inspirational visionary, concerned with building a shared sense of purpose and mission, creating a culture in which everyone is aligned with the organization's goals and is skilled and empowered to achieve them.

In the search for new ideas in the late twentieth century, the key role of heroic, powerful, visionary, charismatic leaders was recognized. Several new terms were invented to describe this role. We had the **new leader**, an inspirational figure motivating followers to higher levels of achievement. However, we also had the **superleader** who is able to 'lead others to lead themselves' (Sims and Lorenzi, 1992, p.295). These terms clearly overlap, and are closely related to the popular and influential concept of transformational leadership.

Transformational leadership

The new leadership movement began with the work of James McGregor Burns (1978), whose study of political leaders distinguished between the **transactional leader** and the **transformational leader**. Transactional leaders see their relationships with followers in terms of trade, swaps or bargains. Transformational leaders are charismatic individuals who inspire and motivate others to perform 'beyond contract'.

Transformational chefs

Katharina Balazs argues that the *chefs de cuisine* who run the best restaurants in France are transformational leaders. Following a chance conversation with one top chef, she decided to interview others. The top rating of three stars in the *Guide Rouge Michelin* applies to only 30 restaurants in the world, and 22 of those are in France. Balazs interviewed these chefs and their staff, observed the preparation of meals in their kitchens, and spoke to customers, to find out how these chefs made their restaurants outstanding. The findings showed that the leadership role of chefs combines two dimensions, *charismatic* and *architectural*.

Charismatic
visioning — providing a luxurious and extraordinary 'total dining experience' that delights customers

empowering — giving staff a voice, showing confidence and trust, allowing staff to influence what they do, expecting high standards

energizing — communicating vision, making staff feel part of something special, aiming for perfection, excitement, joy, passion in the work

Architectural
designing structure — small, organic structure with chef as 'superstar', team culture based on mutual support and collaboration

controls — managing relationships with suppliers ('only the best is good enough'), controlling quality of the product

rewards	offering recognition, personal growth and 'employability' in a context where pay is low, hours are long, and the work is intense	individual's creation, implementation demands rigorous attention to detail, and a large team of support staff is required. Those other sectors include film and theatre production, opera, fashion and architecture.

Balazs claims that this transformational leadership style applies in other sectors where the starting point is an

Based on Balazs (2001, 2002).

Superleader a leader who is able to develop leadership capacity in others, empowering them, reducing their dependence on formal leaders, stimulating their motivation, commitment and creativity.

Noel Tichy and Mary Anne Devanna (1986) argue that transformational leaders have three main roles; recognizing the need for revitalization, creating a new vision, institutionalizing change. Bernard Bass and Bruce Avolio (Bass, 1985a, 1985b; Bass and Avolio, 1990, 1994) similarly claim that transformational leadership involves 'the Four Is':

- *Intellectual stimulation*: encourage others to see what they are doing from new perspectives.
- *Idealized influence*: articulate the mission or vision of the organization.
- *Individualized consideration*: develop others to higher levels of ability.
- *Inspirational motivation*: motivate others to put organizational interests before self interest.

Transactional leader a leader who treats relationships with followers in terms of an exchange, giving followers what they want in return for what the leader desires, following prescribed tasks to pursue established goals.

The Transformational Leadership Questionnaire developed by Beverly Alimo-Metcalfe and John Alban-Metcalfe (Metcalfe and Metcalfe, 2002, 2003) identifies 14 behaviours in three categories:

Leading and developing others
- showing genuine concern;
- empowering;
- being accessible;
- encouraging change.

Personal qualities
- being transparent;
- acting with integrity;
- being decisive;
- inspiring others;
- resolving complex problems.

Transformational leader a leader who treats relationships with followers in terms of motivation and commitment, influencing and inspiring followers to give more than mere compliance to improve organizational performance.

Leading the organization
- networking and achieving;
- focusing team effort;
- building shared vision;
- supporting a developmental culture;
- facilitating change sensitively.

Research with public sector managers and employees suggests that these behaviours can increase job satisfaction and motivation, and reduce stress. Metcalfe and Metcalfe also found that women were seen as more transformational than men on most of these behaviours, and were rated as better than men on being decisive, focusing effort, mentoring, managing change, inspiring others and openness to ideas. Are these new labels a fresh development in leadership theory and practice? George Hollenbeck and colleagues (2006) argue that identifying the characteristics or competencies of transformational leaders takes us back to the 'great person' view of leadership and trait-spotting, overlooking what we know about the influence of context on leadership effectiveness.

STOP AND THINK Considering business and political leaders with whom you are familiar, directly or through the media, which come closest to these definitions of new leader, superleader and transformational leader?

The new, super, transformational leader looks like a 'one-best-way' approach. Does this vindicate trait-spotting and discredit contingency perspectives?

Distributed leadership

Distributed leadership the collective exercise of leadership behaviours, often informal and spontaneous, by staff at all levels of an organization.

Do we need visionary superheroes? Recent studies show how changes can be implemented by people at all levels of an organization. This is known as distributed leadership.

Leadership theory traditionally assumes that others will not act, and change will not happen, without 'strong and effective' leadership. We need leaders to generate the ideas and to provide the directions, the 'orders from above', which inspire followers, don't we? Peter Gronn (2002) contrasts the traditional idea of focused leadership, emphasizing the individual, with distributed leadership. Distributed leadership involves many people acting in concert, in formal and informal, spontaneous and intuitive roles (Bryman, 1996; Caldwell, 2005). These roles may not be permanent. Leadership functions can be shared. The leadership role can move from one person or group to another, as circumstances change. Leadership can thus involve role-sharing and turn-taking, rather than belonging to one person.

Distributed leadership is encouraged by flatter organization structures, teamwork, knowledge work, and 'network' organization forms. In current turbulent economic conditions, many organizations are unstable and are evolving in novel ways. This often means creating new types of inter-organizational collaborations. The scale and complexity of these changes means that many more people are involved, compared with change that only affects one part of a single organization. These trends combine with the fashion for employee empowerment and engagement (see Chapter 9). Debra Meyerson (2001a and 2001b) highlights the importance of behind-the-scenes, 'below the radar' change leadership of middle managers. Joseph Badaracco (2002) describes a 'quiet approach to change leadership', emphasizing 'small things, careful moves, controlled and measured efforts'. In short, in appropriate conditions, staff with the motivation and capabilities can lead and implement change covertly, quietly, by stealth, just as effectively as 'celebrity bosses', but without destabilizing the organization and burning out colleagues in the process.

One of the problems with distributed leadership is that the capabilities and contributions that are involved may not be recognized. Sylvia Ann Hewlett and colleagues (2005) observe that members of ethnic minority groups, while holding junior posts in their organizations, often have major community leadership roles, with capabilities and talent that are neither recognized nor used by their main employer. These are the 'unsung heroes' who take personal responsibility, and risk, for driving change without always waiting patiently for others, or simply following directions.

David Buchanan and colleagues describe how complex changes to improve cancer services in a British hospital were implemented by a large number of people acting together to meet the same goals and targets, without formal change management plans, structures, and roles. Although four key people were involved at different stages, they were not senior managers, and the change process also involved 19 other individuals, and 26 managerial, administrative and clinical groups, patients' representatives, and other organizations. Their contributions were informal and fluid, and complemented each other. The researchers note how responsibility for these changes 'migrated' around various groups and individuals. They conclude that implementing change with 'nobody in charge' can be just as effective as traditional change methods (Buchanan *et al.*, 2007). This approach is not dependent on individuals or small teams, and survives the departure of the lone change agent.

In the distinction between leadership and management, orientation to change is a distinctive 'mark of the leader' (Zaleznick, 1977). These examples suggest that leadership is a widely distributed phenomenon. Leadership functions are best carried out by those who have the interest, knowledge, skills and motivation to perform them effectively. This observation is reinforced by the development of self-managing teams which often have no formal leaders, or which have 'coach-facilitators' whose role is to develop team members' skills.

Leadership qualities: acting the part

It is not enough to be an innovative, visionary, strategic thinker to qualify as a leader. You also need visible qualities such as confidence and the ability to communicate clearly.

1. **Get out and about**. Introduce yourself to other departments. Network until you drop. Speak up at meetings. Sit in the front row at presentations. Volunteer for high-profile tasks, such as chairing events, meeting clients and giving presentations.

2. **Allow yourself to shine**. Deliver clear, positive, and inspirational messages with enthusiasm. Delete the whingeing, moaning and waffling.

3. **Make a great entrance**. You have three seconds in which to make a first impression. Do not walk into the room with the stress of the journey on your face. Take a moment to compose yourself. Breathe, straighten up, relax your face. Carry your case in your left hand to leave your right hand free for greetings.

4. **Walk with confidence and energy**. Never loiter or lurk. Wear a focused expression. Always greet colleagues in passing, even if they don't respond.

5. **Listen**. Appear to have time for other people. Active listening makes you appear charming and in touch. Face the speaker with eye contact. Pace your nods to match the energy of their words. Do not speed up or it will look like you are interrupting.

6. **Mingle**. Choose your group or individual and approach them with energy. Use body language to mirror the group mood while waiting your turn to speak. Introduce issues relevant to the conversation, or ask a question. Do not sound aggressive or opinionated. If necessary, follow your comment with a quick, audible introduction.

7. **Offer a good handshake**. Avoid the 'dead fish' and the 'bone cruncher'. Firm, dry palm, look the other person in the eye, smile with your eyes as well as your mouth.

8. **Never fiddle**. Do not play with jewellery, pens, spectacles or paper clips. This is called 'leakage', and signals anxiety which distracts the listener and can suggest incompetence.

9. **Use open gestures**. Folded arms makes you look uncomfortable and negative. Use gestures that emphasize key messages.

10. **Dress the part**. Whatever the corporate culture, always appear well groomed. Use only one or two colours at a time. Choose high contrasts for a high status appearance. Look like a leader.

Based on James (2003).

Recognition of distributed leadership does not imply a complete shift of focus away from formal, senior figures. Senior figures with prestige titles continue to exercise leadership roles and functions as well. We need a 'twin track' approach in which visionary individual leaders, and a widely dispersed leadership decoupled from high office, work together. The new leader is not a dictator, or a charismatic figure. The emphasis of the 'new leader' lies more with the 'soft' skills of enthusing and inspiring, of coaching and facilitating.

Many commentators argue that a hostile, rapidly changing competitive climate, and pressured conditions of work, require participative, visionary and inspirational styles of leadership. An autocratic, task-oriented style encourages little more than compliance with directions. The new, transformational superleader, in contrast, encourages commitment, initiative, flexibility and high performance. The behaviour of new leaders also seems appropriate to the motivation of knowledge workers and the development of learning organizations. The new leadership concept thus draws together the main strands of twentieth-century thinking:

the theory	the new transformational superleader
trait-spotting	must have the right personality, appearance, attributes, voice
style-counselling	must be caring, inspirational and visionary, ethical, risk taker
context-fitting	style is consistent with a hostile and rapidly changing environment, with the need to develop flexible organizational forms, with the need to motivate knowledge workers and develop a learning organization

Who needs leaders?

Throughout the twentieth century, it was unquestioningly accepted that leadership was indispensable. A novel perspective emerged in the opening years of the twenty-first century, challenging the enthusiasm for charismatic, visionary, transactional superleaders. Here is a perspective which argues that some leaders are *dangerous*.

Nick Morgan (2001, p.3) is critical of 'larger-than-life leaders and their grand strategies', arguing for 'a quieter, more evolutionary approach to change, one that relies on employee motivation instead of directives from on high'. He argues that organizations should reduce the amount of change, focus instead on incremental improvements, and 'above all lose the notion that you need heroic leaders in order to have meaningful, sustained change' (p.2). This is consistent with views explored in Chapter 18 on organizational change, particularly Eric Abrahamson's (2000) approach to 'painless change' which is carefully staged and paced.

Quy Huy (2001) also dismisses the role of visionary leadership, arguing that it is middle managers who achieve the balance between change and continuity, and that radical change imposed from the top makes this difficult. Jim Collins (2001) argues that 'larger than life' leaders are not always effective, and that the most powerful senior executives display what he calls 'level 5 leadership', combining humility with persistence. Debra Meyerson (2001a and 2001b) praises the less visibly heroic, behind the scenes, 'below the radar' efforts of middle managers and 'tempered radicals', who are not top managers, but who are nevertheless instrumental in initiating and driving change. Joseph Badaracco (2001, p.126 and 2002) describes a 'quiet approach to leadership', emphasizing 'small things, careful moves, controlled and measured efforts', describing leadership as 'unglamorous, not heroic'.

Rakesh Khurana (2002, p.62) is scathing in his assessment of transformational leaders. The popular stereotype concerns the charismatic individual who wins the confidence of investors and the business press, inspires and motivates employees, defeats overwhelming competition, and turns around dying companies. This is the white knight, the lone ranger, the heroic figure, and these images are exhilarating. Khurana offers four criticisms of such figures:

1. They 'reject limits to their scope and authority [and] rebel against all checks on their power and dismiss the norms and rules that apply to others'. In other words, they can be beyond the influence and control of other senior colleagues.

2. They rely on 'the widespread quasi-religious belief in the powers of charismatic leaders'. This belief allows them to 'exploit the irrational desires of their followers'.

3. They encourage the attribution error of understanding success in terms of the actions of prominent leaders, while overlooking 'the interplay of social, economic, and other impersonal forces that shape and constrain even the most heroic individual efforts'.

4. New chief executives often deliberately destabilize their organizations, to foster revitalization. However, this can be harmful, if not disastrous, as a number of corporate scandals in the early twenty-first century illustrated.

Vicious circles of redisorganization

This quote is taken from a 'joke' research article in a medical journal, illustrating the cynicism that many people feel about the impact of 'new leaders'.

New leaders typically take up their posts intoxicated with the prospect of transformation and radical revision. This triggers an avalanche of constant and hectic activity. Repeated redisorganizations result in exhausted managers who rush from one meeting to another with no time to step back and reflect. By the time the organization decides to saddle somebody with the blame for the resulting chaos, the leader has left to foul up some other organization. The end result is a perpetual cycle of redisorganization.

While all new leaders feel compelled to redisorganize, it is nonetheless possible to distinguish among several breeds of leaders based on their canine redisorganization behaviour:

Mutts	the most common type of leader: self-focused, with a need to piss all over everything to mark territory
Bulldogs	well meaning, but incompetent, and dangerous when aroused
German shepherds	bureaucratic, commonly suffer from anal retentiveness, which makes them irritable
Poodles	ideological, focused on a specific peculiar aim derived from a specific peculiar way of looking at the world, to the exclusion of empirical evidence, practical experience and common sense

These four breeds display, to varying degrees, the eight 'secrets of success': meet a lot, sniff a lot (yes, they can smell fear), talk a lot, listen infrequently, change a lot, delegate (particularly responsibility without authority), disappear and move on.

From Oxman et al. (2005).

Seven failures of really useless leaders

what really useless leaders do	how they do it	how to avoid the same trap
1 kill enthusiasm	micromanagement, coercion and disrespect	try better delegation and informal feedback, plus better, easier appraisal
2 kill emotion	aggression, lack of emotional intelligence, lack of empathy, no work-life balance	publish a personal work-life balance manifesto; develop greater empathy; encourage assertiveness
3 kill explanation	partial, inconsistent communication	make communication consistent, clear, two-way
4 kill engagement	individual objectives dictated by managers; limited team goals	allow teams to set their own goals; encourage participation in decision-making
5 kill reward	rewarding the wrong things and offering the wrong sort of reward (eg, money for someone not motivated by money)	give the right rewards to the right people at the right time; establish team rewards; give managers flexibility in rewarding staff
6 kill culture	ignoring the differences in cultures during mergers and acquisitions; punishing risk-taking while trying to introduce a culture of innovation	offer training for managers on influencing culture; allow managers to evolve their own personal mistakes policy
7 kill trust	unfair recruitment or reward decisions	offer training for managers in procedural justice and fairness; help managers to develop trust in others

From Sonsino (2007).

Khurana thus regards the transformational leader as a 'dangerous curse'. This backlash against 'new leaders' has two interesting dimensions.

- The combined views of Morgan, Huy, Collins, Myerson, Badaracco and Khurana take the debate back to the distinction between leadership and management. We saw that, crudely, there is a perspective which argues, 'leadership is good – management is bad'. Now this argument is reversed, with the argument that leaders can be dangerously destabilizing while managers drive effective change.

- In this approach, effective change depends on competent managers with change agency skills, and not on heroic visionaries with charismatic personalities.

 RECAP

1. *Explain the apparent difference between the concepts of leadership and management.*
   - Leaders are typically portrayed as inspiring, change-oriented visionaries.
   - Managers are typically portrayed as planners, organizers and controllers.
   - In practice, the roles overlap and can be difficult to distinguish.

2. *Understand why there is little relationship between personality traits and effective leadership.*
   - Many factors, besides personality traits, influence leadership effectiveness.
   - It has proved difficult to establish a consensus on specific traits.
   - The characteristics of the leader's role also influence behaviour and effectiveness.
   - Power and influence contribute to leader effectiveness, as well as personality.

3. *Understand the bases of a leader's power in organizations and the role of followers in creating and supporting leaders.*
   - A leader's power bases include reward, coercive, referent, legitimate, expert, information, affiliation and group power.
   - Leaders only have power if followers perceive them to possess it.
   - Women are traditionally powerless by discrimination and exclusion by male behaviour.
   - Women have social and interpersonal leadership qualities, improve performance by widening management discussions, and are now more likely to be promoted on merit.

4. *Understand why effective leaders either adapt their style to fit the organizational and cultural context in which they operate, or find contexts which fit their personal style.*
   - Considerate behaviour reduces labour turnover and improves job satisfaction.
   - Initiating structure improves performance but reduces job satisfaction.
   - Effective leaders combine consideration with initiating structure.
   - Contingency theory argues that leaders are more or less effective depending on how structured the task is, how powerful the leader is, and how good relationships are.
   - Situational leadership advises the manager to use telling, selling, participating and delegating styles depending on the task, relationships, and employee readiness.
   - Some commentators argue that leaders cannot change their behaviour and that they have to move jobs when less effective to a context more favourable to their style.
   - Most commentators argue that leaders can and should adapt their behaviour to fit the context and the culture in which they are operating.

5. *Explain contemporary trends in this field concerning new leadership, the dispersal of leadership, and the argument that leaders are unnecessary.*
   - One trend emphasized charismatic, visionary, inspirational new leaders.
   - New leadership, superleader and transformational leadership are close synonyms.
   - Distributed leadership can be observed at all organizational levels.
   - The new visionary leader helps to develop leadership capability in others.
   - The new leader has the right traits, and the right style, for the contemporary context, thus combining notions of trait-spotting, style-counselling and context-fitting.
   - A more recent trend views charismatic, visionary leaders as dangerous because they can destabilize an organization; change management capabilities are more important.

Revision

1. What is the difference between leadership and management, and why is it difficult to separate these concepts in practice?
2. Why is trait-spotting such a popular theme in leadership research, what has trait-spotting told us about the personality markers of successful leaders, and what are the problems with this perspective?
3. Leaders are, traditionally, men with special qualities. Why are women now more likely to be considered as effective leaders?
4. What is power, and how can the exercise of power be regarded in positive terms as well as negative? What has the leader's power got to do with his or her followers?

Research assignment

Choose one of the massively multiplayer online role-playing games (MMORPGs). Examples include *World of Warcraft*, *Eve Online*, *EverQuest*, *Lineage* and *Star Wars Galaxies*. What leadership skills are developed by players of these games, and how are those skills relevant to the way that organizations operate and are managed today? Option one: reflect on and note your answers to these questions as you play one of these games yourself. Option two: observe in action and question someone that you know who plays one of these games. Prepare a report that describes how MMORPGs can be used in a leadership development programme. (This assignment is based on research by Reeves, Malone and O'Driscoll, 2008.)

Springboard

Gill, R., 2006, *Theory and Practice of Leadership*, Sage Publications, London.

A review of the vast literature on leadership, comparing theoretical and practical perspectives. Uses examples from Europe, America and Britain.

Jackson, B. and Parry, K., 2007, *A Very Short, Fairly Interesting and Reasonably Cheap Book about Studying Leadership*, Sage Publications, London.

Short, entertaining, critical and challenging, contrasting a wide range of perspectives on leadership.

Kellerman, B., 2004, *Bad Leadership: What It Is, How It Happens, Why It Matters*, Harvard Business School Press, Boston, MA.

Barbara Kellerman develops a typology of bad leadership types; incompetent, rigid, intemperate, callous, corrupt, insular and evil.

Western, S., 2007, *Leadership: A Critical Text*, Sage Publications, London.

Challenges the notion of leader as hero and visionary, and develops the concept of distributed leadership.

OB in films

The Devil Wears Prada (2006, director David Frankel): DVD track 2: 0:03:20 to 0:09:47 (7 minutes). Track 2 begins with Andy coming out of the lift and heading for the office reception desk; clip ends when she is called back into the office as she is walking away.

Based on the novel by Lauren Weisberger, this movie tells the story of a naive, young aspiring journalist, Andrea (Andy) Sachs (played by Anne Hathaway) who gets a job as assistant to the famous editor-in-chief of the fashion magazine *Runway*. The magazine's powerful and ruthless editor, Miranda Priestly (Meryl Streep) is a legend. In this clip, we see Andy arriving for her job interview as 'second assistant' with Miranda's 'first assistant' Emily Charlton (Emily Blunt). Miranda, however, decides to conduct the interview herself.

1. How would you describe Miranda Priestley's leadership style?
   Identify specific behaviours to support your conclusions.

2. What impact does Miranda's leadership style have on those around her?
   Identify specific employee behaviours to support your conclusions.

3. Good boss or bad boss: what is your assessment of this leadership style?
   Cite specific evidence of her impact on individual performance and organizational effectiveness to support your judgement.

4. To what extent does this leadership style apply in the real world, beyond Hollywood?
   Consider aspects of individual personality, organizational context, and industry sector in making this judgement.

5. Why do you think Miranda Priestly gave Andy the job?

 ## OB in literature

Norman Augustine and Kenneth Adelman, *Shakespeare in Charge: The Bard's Guide to Leading and Succeeding on the Business Stage*, Hyperion Books, 1999; Paul Corrigan, *Shakespeare on Management: Leadership Lessons for Today's Managers*, Kogan Page, London, 1999. *Henry V* faces numerous leadership challenges. Is his position legitimate? How should he deal with those plotting against him? How should he influence his troops to follow him into battle against overwhelming odds at Agincourt? *Julius Caesar* explores the nature and ethics of organization politics. *The Merchant of Venice* exposes male-female differences in perceptions of justice and mercy. *Hamlet* is a study of leadership in an uncertain world. *Macbeth* is a leader who is obsessed with power.

CHAPTER EXERCISES

Management and leadership

Objectives 1. To explore differences in the definition of the terms management and leadership.

2. To consider whether and how our understanding and use of these terms is changing.

Briefing Are leadership and management different roles, or do they overlap? Look at this list of activities. Are these leadership activities, or management activities, or could they fall into both categories? Use the activities matrix to locate each of those activities depending on whether you feel they are management-oriented, leadership-oriented, or both.

→

Activities list

1 delegate tasks	11 act as interface between team and others	21 use analytical data to support recommendations
2 plan and prioritize steps to achieve task goals	12 motivate staff	22 explain goals, plans and roles
3 ensure predictability	13 inspire people	23 appeal to people's emotions
4 coordinate effort	14 coordinate resources	24 share a vision
5 provide focus	15 give orders and instructions	25 guide progress
6 monitor feelings and morale	16 check task completion	26 create a positive team feeling
7 follow systems and procedures	17 ensure effective induction	27 monitor budgets and tasks
8 provide development opportunities	18 unleash potential	28 use analytical data to forecast trends
9 monitor progress	19 look 'over the horizon'	29 take risks
10 appeal to rational thinking	20 be a good role model	30 build teams

Based on Gillen (2004).

Activities matrix

very high on management	managerially oriented	elements of management and leadership	leadership oriented	very high on leadership

Class discussion

Consider why you placed each of those activities in those categories:

1. What makes an activity a management activity?

2. What is distinctive about leadership activities?

3. If you put some activities in the middle, why did you do that?

4. In what ways, if at all, is society's view of leadership changing, and why?

5. Are there any current trends and developments which encourage managers to monitor and control rather than to exercise leadership?

Leadership style preferences

Objectives

1. To assess your preferred leadership style.

2. To explore the diversity of style preferences across your group.

Briefing

This assessment is designed to help you assess your preferred leadership style. Complete this questionnaire honestly, in relation to your behaviour and preferences, with respect either to your leadership behaviour, or in relation to how you think you would like to behave in a leadership role. Put a tick in the appropriate response column on the right depending on how accurate you feel each statement describes your behavioural preferences, using this scale:

A = Always   **B** = Often   **C** = Sometimes   **D** = Seldom   **E** = Never

Employee-centred or consideration score

You get one point if you ticked either A or a B in response to these questions

2 _____   10 _____   22 _____

4 _____   12 _____   24 _____

6 _____   18 _____   28 _____

8 _____   20 _____

And you get one point if you ticked either D or E in response to these questions:

14 _____   16 _____   26 _____   30 _____

Total employee-centred score is:_____

Job-centred or initiating structure score

You get one point if you ticked either A or B in response to these questions:

1 _____   13 _____   25 _____   34 _____

3 _____   15 _____   27 _____   35 _____

5 _____   17 _____   29 _____

7 _____   19 _____   31 _____

9 _____   21 _____   32 _____

11 _____   23 _____   33 _____

Total job-centred score is:_____

Leader behaviours	A	B	C	D	E
1 I would always act as the spokesperson for my group	❑	❑	❑	❑	❑
2 I would allow subordinates complete freedom in their work	❑	❑	❑	❑	❑
3 I would encourage overtime working	❑	❑	❑	❑	❑
4 I would let subordinates use their judgement to solve problems	❑	❑	❑	❑	❑
5 I would encourage the use of standard procedures	❑	❑	❑	❑	❑
6 I would needle members for greater effort	❑	❑	❑	❑	❑
7 I would stress being ahead of competing groups	❑	❑	❑	❑	❑
8 I would let subordinates work the way they thought best	❑	❑	❑	❑	❑
9 I would speak as representative for subordinates	❑	❑	❑	❑	❑
10 I would be able to tolerate postponement and uncertainty	❑	❑	❑	❑	❑
11 I would try out my ideas on subordinates	❑	❑	❑	❑	❑
12 I would turn subordinates loose on a job and let them go at it	❑	❑	❑	❑	❑
13 I would work hard for promotion	❑	❑	❑	❑	❑
14 I would get swamped by details	❑	❑	❑	❑	❑
15 I would speak for subordinates when visitors were around	❑	❑	❑	❑	❑
16 I would be reluctant to let subordinates have freedom of action	❑	❑	❑	❑	❑
17 I would keep the work pace moving rapidly	❑	❑	❑	❑	❑
18 I would give some subordinates authority that I should keep	❑	❑	❑	❑	❑
19 I would settle conflicts which occur among subordinates	❑	❑	❑	❑	❑
20 I would let subordinates have a high degree of initiative	❑	❑	❑	❑	❑
21 I would represent subordinates at external meetings	❑	❑	❑	❑	❑
22 I would be willing to make changes	❑	❑	❑	❑	❑
23 I would decide what will be done and how it will be done	❑	❑	❑	❑	❑
24 I would trust subordinates to exercise good judgement	❑	❑	❑	❑	❑
25 I would push for increased production	❑	❑	❑	❑	❑
26 I would refuse to explain my actions to subordinates	❑	❑	❑	❑	❑
27 Things usually turn out as I predict	❑	❑	❑	❑	❑
28 I would let subordinates set their own work pace	❑	❑	❑	❑	❑
29 I would assign subordinates to specific tasks	❑	❑	❑	❑	❑
30 I would be able to act without consulting subordinates	❑	❑	❑	❑	❑
31 I would ask subordinates to work harder	❑	❑	❑	❑	❑
32 I would schedule the work that had to be done	❑	❑	❑	❑	❑
33 I would persuade others that my ideas were to their advantage	❑	❑	❑	❑	❑
34 I would urge subordinates to beat their previous records	❑	❑	❑	❑	❑
35 I would expect subordinates to follow set rules and regulations	❑	❑	❑	❑	❑

Your two scores can be interpreted together as follows:

employee-centred score	job-centred score	your leadership style
0–7	0–10	you are not involved enough with either the work or with your employees
0–7	10–20	you are autocratic, a bit of a slave-driver, you get the job done but at an emotional cost
8–15	0–10	people are happy in their work but sometimes at the expense of productivity
8–15	10–20	people enjoy working for you and are productive, naturally expending energy because they get positive reinforcement for good work

From Marcic. Organizational Behavior, 3E. © 1992 South-Western, a part of Cengage Learning, Inc. Reproduced by permission. www.cengage.com/permissions.

Chapter 20 **Decision-making**

Key terms

decision-making

classical decision theory

rational economic model

rationality

rational decisions

descriptive models of decision-making

behavioural theory of decision-making

bounded rationality

maximizing

satisficing

prescriptive model of decision-making

explanatory model of decision-making

heuristic

bias

certainty

risk

uncertainty

routine decisions

adaptive decisions

innovative decisions

group polarization

risky shift phenomenon

caution shift phenomenon

groupthink

brainstorming

escalation of commitment

Learning outcomes

When you have read this chapter, you should be able to define those key terms in your own words, and you should also be able to:

1. Distinguish between prescriptive, descriptive and explanatory models of decision-making and provide an example of each.
2. Distinguish different decision conditions on the basis of risk and programmability.
3. Consider the advantages and disadvantages of group decision-making.
4. Identify the factors used to decide whether to adopt individual or group decision-making.
5. Match organizational conditions with the decision-making processes that favour them.

Why study decision-making?

Decision-making
the process of making choices from among several options.

Decision-making is fundamentally the process of making a choice from a number of alternatives. Why are senior company executives paid such high salaries? One reason is that they are there to make crucial decisions. The consequences of their decisions can lead to an increase in company profits, raised market share, raised stock price or the chance to take over a competitor. Alternatively, those decisions might have the opposite consequences and the company itself might being taken over, and their employees made redundant. Can you think of managers whose decisions have led their companies to success or failure? However, decisions are made at all levels of the organization, not just at the top. Both managers and non-managers make them. Given the central role that decision-making plays in the life of all organizations, and the effect that decision outcomes have on the lives of all organization members, it is not surprising that it has attracted the attention of practising managers and consultants, management academics and social science researchers.

Herbert Simon (1957) felt that management theory should be based around the question of choice and decision-making as the core of management. He argued that it was the art of getting things done. The questions that followed were: what was to be done – how, why, when and by whom? Henry Mintzberg (1989) felt that, 'decision-making is one of the most important, if not the most important – of all managerial activities, and represents one of the most common and crucial work tasks of managers'. Decision-making has been studied in order to both understand how decisions are actually made in practice, and to advise managers how to make better decisions. It can be analyzed at a number of different as Table 20.1 shows. Each level focuses on its own key issues and possesses its own theoretical perspectives. The levels however, are interrelated with one influencing and being affected by the others.

Table 20.1: Levels of decision-making

Level of analysis	Key issues	Theoretical perspectives
individual	Limits to information processing Personal biases	Information processing theory Cognitive psychology
group	Effects of group dynamics on individuals' perceptions, attitudes and behaviours	Groupthink. group polarization and group cohesiveness
organizational	Effects of conflicts, power and politics	Theories of organization conflict, power, politics and decision-making

Models of decision-making

The traditional approach to understanding individual decision-making is based upon classical decision theory and the rational economic model. These were originally developed in economics, and they make certain assumptions about people and how they make decisions.

The rational economic model of decision-making is described in Figure 20.1. It is still popular among economics scholars in suggesting how decisions should be made. However, to understand its weaknesses, it is necessary to list its assumptions and demonstrate how they fail to match up to reality; these are shown in Table 20.2.

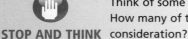

STOP AND THINK Think of some personal or organizational decisions that you have recently made. How many of the steps and assumptions from the classical model featured in your consideration?

Classical decision theory assumes that decision-makers are objective, have complete information and consider all possible alternatives and their consequences before selecting the optimal solution.

Rational economic model assumes that decision-making is and should be a rational process consisting of a sequence of steps that enhance the probability of attaining a desired outcome.

Rationality the use of scientific reasoning, empiricism and positivism, as well as the decision criteria of evidence, logical argument and reasoning.

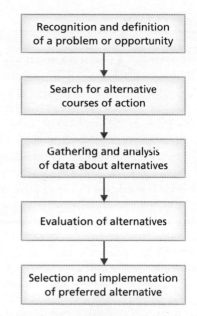

Figure 20.1: Rational economic model of decision-making

Table 20.2: Rational economic model assumptions and reality

Assumption	Reality
All alternatives will be considered	• Rarely possible to consider all alternatives since there are too many • Some alternatives will not have occurred to the decision-maker
The consequences of each alternative will be considered	• Impractical to consider all consequences • Impractical to estimate many of the consequences considered • Estimation process involves time and effort
Accurate information about alternatives is available at no cost	• Information available is rarely accurate, often dated, and usually only partially relevant to the problem • It costs money to be generated or purchased • Decisions have to be made on incomplete, insufficient and only partly accurate information
Decision-makers are rational beings	• Individuals lack the mental capacity to store and process all the information relevant to a decision • Frequently they lack the mental ability to perform the mental calculations required

Rational decisions choices based on rationality, that is, on a rational mode of thinking.

The classical view of decision-making employs the concepts of **rationality** and **rational decisions**, in its discussions and prescriptions. Rationality is equated with scientific reasoning, empiricism and positivism; and with the use of decision criteria of evidence, logical argument and reasoning. Rational decisions are decisions which are based on rationality, that is, on a rational mode of thinking (Simon, 1986: Langley, 1989).

The classical view has now been accepted as not providing an accurate account of how people typically make decisions. Moreover, its prescriptions for making better decisions have often been incorrect. Instead, contemporary cognitive research by psychologists has revealed the ways in which decisions are made based on heuristic models, judgements and tacit knowledge.

Descriptive models of decision-making investigate how individuals actually make decisions.

Behavioural theory of decision-making recognizes that bounded rationality limits the making of optimal decisions.

Bounded rationality individuals making decisions by constructing simplified models that extract the essential features from problems without capturing all their complexity.

Source: www.joyoftech.com.

Richard Michael Cyert (1921–2001)

James Gardiner March (b.1928)

Herbert Alexander Simon (1916–2001)

Descriptive models of decision-making focus on how individuals actually make decisions. Each decision made by an individual or group is affected by a number of factors. Some of these include:

- individual personality;
- group relationships;
- organizational power relationships and political behaviour;
- external environmental pressures;
- organization strategic considerations;
- information availability (or lack of).

The aim of these models is to examine which of these factors are the most important, and how they interrelate prior to a decision being made.

One of the earliest, and still among the most influential descriptive models, is the **behavioural theory of decision-making**. It was developed by Richard Cyert, James March and Herbert Simon (Simon, 1960; Cyert and March, 1963; March, 1988). It is called 'behavioural' because it treats decision-making as another aspect of individual behaviour. For example, if a research study interviewed brokers who bought and sold shares in the stock market to determine what factors influenced their decisions, it would be an example of a descriptive approach to decision-making. It is also sometimes referred to as 'administrative model' and it acknowledges that, in the real world, those who make decisions are restricted in their decision processes, and therefore have to settle for a less than an ideal solution. Behavioural theory holds that individuals make decisions while they are operating within the limits of **bounded rationality**. Bounded rationality recognizes that:

Table 20.3: Rational decision-making and bounded rationality contrasted

Rational decisions-makers . . .	Bounded rationality decision-makers . . .
Recognize and define a problem or opportunity thoroughly	Reduce the problem to something that is easily understood
Search for a extensive set of alternative courses of action, gathering data on each	Develop a few, uncomplicated and recognizable solutions, comparable to those currently being used
Evaluate all the alternatives at the same time	Evaluate each alternative as it is thought of.
Select and implement the alternative with the most value (*maximize*)	Choose the first, acceptable alternative (*satisfice*)

Based on Simon (1979); Kahneman (2003).

Maximizing a decision-making approach where all alternatives are compared and evaluated in order to find the best solution to a problem.

Satisficing a decision-making approach where the first solution that is judged to be 'good enough' (i.e. satisfactory and sufficient) is selected, and the search is then ended.

Prescriptive model of decision-making an approach that recommends how individuals should behave in order to achieve a desired outcome.

- The definition of a situation is likely to be incomplete
- It is impossible to generate all alternatives
- Impossible to predict all the consequences of each alternative
- Final decisions are often influenced by personal and political factors

The effect of personal and situational limitations is that individuals make decisions that are 'good enough' rather than 'ideal'. That is, they 'satisfice', rather than 'maximize'. When maximizing, decision-makers review the range of alternatives available, all at the same time, and attempt to select the very best one. However, when satisficing, they evaluate one option at a time in sequence, until they alight on the first one that is acceptable. That chosen option will meet all the minimum requirements for the solution, but may not be the very best (optimal) choice in the situation. Once an option is found, decision-makers will look no further. The contrast between the rational decision-making described previously, and the bounded rationality discussed here, is shown in Table 20.3.

 **STOP AND THINK**   When you chose your current partner – girlfriend, boyfriend, wife or husband, did you maximize or satisfice? Is this distinction a useful way of explaining the decision-making process?

Victor Harold Vroom (b.1932)

Phillip W. Yetton (b.1943)

Prescriptive models of decision-making recommend how individuals *should* behave in order to achieve a desired outcome. This makes the classical model, described earlier, also a prescriptive one. Such models often also contain specific techniques, procedures and processes which their supporters claim will lead to more accurate and efficient decision-making. They are often based on observations of poor decision-making processes, where key steps might have been omitted or inadequately considered. They are developed and marketed by management consultants as a way of improving organization performance through improved decision-making.

One of the best known prescriptive models of decision-making was developed by Victor Vroom and Philip Yetton (1973), later expanded by Vroom and Arthur Jago (Vroom and Jago, 1988). The focus is on decision-making *situations*, and on seven factors to identify the decision-making *style* that is likely to be most effective in any given situation. It focuses on *decision style*, concerning *how* a leader decides in a given decision situation, rather than *what* a leader decides. It also concentrates on *subordinate participation* – the appropriate amount of involvement of the leader's subordinates in making a decision. The model consists of three main elements:

1. Decision participation styles.

2. Diagnostic questions with which to analyze decision situations.

3. Decision rules to determine the appropriate decision participation style.

The model is underpinned by two key concepts – quality and acceptability. The quality of the decision relates to it achieving the aim; the cost of its implementation; and the time taken to implement it. The acceptability of the decision relates to subordinates and anyone else either affected by the decision or who has to implement it. Leaders and managers generally select the highest quality decision that is acceptable.

1. Decision participation styles

Five decision participation styles were identified – decide, consult individually, consult group, facilitate and delegate. These are shown ranging along a continuum (Table 20.4). They reflect different amounts of subordinate participation in the leader's decision. Moving from left to right on the continuum:

- The leader discusses the problem or situation more with others.
- Others' input changes from merely providing information to recommending solutions.
- Ownership and commitment to the decision increases.
- The time needed to arrive at a decision increases.

Table 20.4: Participation in decision-making processes

	Leader-centred				Group-centred
Description	**(D)** **Decide**	**(CI)** **Consult Individually**	**(CG)** **Consult Group**	**(F)** **Facilitate**	**(D)** **Delegate**
	As leader, you feel your have the information and expertise to make the decision alone and then you either announce or 'sell' it to the group.	As leader, you lack the required information or expertise. You therefore obtain this from your group members individually, either telling them the problem or not. You then make the decision alone.	As leader, you explain the situation and provide information to your group. Together, solutions are generated and discussed. You then review these recommendations and then make the decision alone.	As leader, you explain the situation and provide information to your group. Acting as facilitator, you reconcile differences and negotiate a solution acceptable to everyone. The final decision is made by you and your group together.	As leader, you explain the situation, provide information, and set the boundaries for the decision to be made. You then delegate responsibility and authority for the final decision to the group who make it themselves. You accept and implement it.
Participants	Leader	Leader and others	Leader and others	Leader and others	Leader and others
Role of participants	Leader generates and evaluates solution alone	Individuals provide leader with skill or information	Group generates solutions or recommendations	Group negotiates a solution with leader	Group generates, evaluates and makes the decision
Who makes the decision?	Leader	Leader	Leader (perhaps reflecting group inputs)	Leader and group together	Group

Based on Vroom (2000, p.84).

2. Diagnostic questions with which to analyze situations

It was found that leaders used different decision participation making styles in different situations; and all of these various styles could be equally effective, depending on the situation. The question that is raised is how do you determine which style is most suitable in a given situation. To answer this, Vroom asks seven diagnostic questions of any situation to identify which decision participation style is most effective in that situation. The answers to these seven questions, in the form of 'high' (H) or 'low' (L), should determine the appropriate level of subordinate participation in the decision-making process.

Decision significance	How significant is this decision to the success of the project or organization? If significance is high, then the leader needs to be closely involved.
Importance of commitment	How important is subordinate commitment in implementing the decision? If importance is high, then leaders should involve subordinates.
Leader expertise	What is the level of the leader's information, knowledge or expertise in relation to the problem? If it is low, the leader should involve subordinates to obtain it.
Likelihood of commitment	If the leader were to make the decision alone, would subordinates' commitment to it be high or low? If the answer is high, then subordinate involvement is less important.
Group support for goals	What is the level of subordinate support for the team's or organization's goals with respect to this situation? If it is low, the leader should not allow the group to make the decision alone.
Group expertise	What is the level of skill and commitment that group members have in working together as a team to solve the problem? If it is high, then more responsibility for the decision can be given to them.
Team competence	What is the level of subordinates' skills and commitment in working together as a team to solve the problem? If their skill and desire to work together co-operatively is high, then more responsibility for the decision can be given to them.

3. Decision rules

The Vroom–Yetton–Jago model provides a set of decision rules in the form of a decision tree to allow the selection of the most appropriate style.

Vroom and Yetton at the battle of Gettysburg

Jack Duncan, Kelvin La France and Peter Ginter applied the Vroom and Yetton model of decision-making to the battlefield behaviour of ten commanding generals in six major battles in the American Civil War (1861–1865) – Gettysburg, Shiloh, Antietam, Chancellorville, Chickamauga and Nashville. They used official war records, biographies, autobiographies and scholarly works, to reconstruct the thinking of the decision-makers. The authors did not argue that appropriate decision-making was the determining factor in the outcome of the battle. However, they felt there was an identifiable relationship between the actions that people took and the results obtained. They found that when the commanding generals on the battlefield acted consistently with the prescriptions of the Vroom and Yetton model, they were more often successful in accomplishing the goals of their campaign. Also, even though commanders favoured the autocratic (decide) decision style, the lack of information sharing and

→

	1 — Decision significance	2 — Importance of commitment	3 — Leader expertise	4 — Likelihood of commitment	5 — Group support for goals	6 — Group expertise	7 — Team competence	
Question	How significant is this decision to the success of the project or organization?	How important is subordinate commitment in implementing the decision?	What is the level of the leader's information, knowledge or expertise in relation to the problem?	If the leader were to make the decision alone, would subordinates' commitment to it be high or low?	What is the level of subordinate support for the team's or organization's goals with respect to this situation?	What is the level of skill and commitment that group members have in working together as a team to solve the problem?	What is the level of subordinates' skills and commitment in working together as a team to solve the problem?	
P R O B L E M S T A T E M E N T	H	H	H	H	–	–	–	Decide
	H	H	H	L	H	H	H	Delegate
	H	H	H	L	H	H	L	Consult group
	H	H	H	L	H	L	–	Consult group
	H	H	H	L	L	–	–	Consult group
	H	H	L	–	H	H	H	Facilitate
	H	H	L	–	H	H	L	Consult individually
	H	H	L	–	H	L	–	Consult individually
	H	H	L	–	L	H	–	Facilitate
	H	H	L	–	L	L	–	Consult group
	H	L	H	H	–	–	–	Decide
	H	L	L	–	H	–	–	Facilitate
	H	L	L	–	L	–	–	Consult individually
	L	H	–	H	–	–	–	Decide
	L	H	–	L	–	H	–	Delegate
	L	H	–	L	–	L	–	Facilitate
	L	L	–	–	–	–	–	Decide

Figure 20.2: Time-driven model of leadership

Source: Adapted from Vroom (2000).

consensus building resulted in serious disadvantages. Duncan, La France and Ginter draw three conclusions. First, in most cases, the choice of a decision-making style did matter. Second, that there is a need to revise the ideal of great military leadership to be the decisive and autocratic commander ('there is nothing so much as god on earth as the general on the battlefield'). The commander needs to use the knowledge, expertise and experience of the officers below him, including his second-in-command.

Third, management is needed on the battlefield as much as leadership. Commanders had ample time to plan the battle and, in the battle itself, the time available for decision-making appeared not to be a factor. The authors question the appropriateness of the universal application of autocratic (decide) decision style in military situations where information is lacking or troop support is not certain.

Based on Duncan et al. *(2003).*

Explanatory model of decision-making an approach that accounts for how individuals, groups and organizations make decisions.

Heuristic a simple and approximate rule, guiding procedure, shortcut or strategy that is used to solve a problem.

Bias a prejudice predisposition or a systematic distortion caused by the application of a heuristic.

Daniel Kahneman
(b.1934)

Amos Tversky
(1937–1996)

Home viewing

Thirteen Days (2001, director Roger Donaldson) is based on the true story of the Cuban Missile Crisis of October 1962, a diplomatic conflict between the United States and (the then) Soviet Union which nearly triggered a nuclear war. It stars Kevin Costner who plays an aide to President John F. Kennedy. As you watch the film, apply the Vroom–Yetton–Jago decision tree model to Kennedy's problem. The quality of the decision is crucial – the wrong one could lead to war. Does Kennedy's decision style match that recommended by the model? Also notice how strategic decisions are shaped by interacting processional, contextual, social, emotional, temporal and behavioural factors, as well as by the rational consideration of evidence.

An **explanatory model of decision-making** looks at what decisions were made and aims to provide an explanation of how they occurred. For example, there are studies of military fiascos which examine why generals took or failed to take, certain actions. Often these explanations draw upon personality and leadership concepts and theories. The poor decisions made by teams have also been studied using concepts from the group level of analysis such as groupthink and group polarization. These will be examined later in this chapter. Finally, decisions such as whether to acquire or merge with another company have drawn upon the theories of conflict, power and politics, and have been explained at the organizational level.

The judgement **heuristics** and **biases** model represents the current thinking in decision-making (*The Economist*, 1999c). The studies have highlighted the limits to rationality and introduced the concept of bounded rationality. What else might affect the individual who makes a decision? Decision-making involves choice, and choice requires both careful thought and much information. Excessive information can both overload and delay us. Many managers believe that making the right decision late is the same as making the wrong decision. Hence we speed up the process by relying on judgement shortcuts called heuristics.

Decision-making using heuristics can be considered a separate model, and one that represents a further step away from the classical model. The meaning of the word heuristic goes back to the Greek word 'eurisco' meaning 'I discover'. The leading authors in this field have been Daniel Kahneman and Amos Tversky. Their work is contained in a series of articles (Kahneman and Tversky, 1984, 2000). Their work, and that of Robert Cialdini, have highlighted certain decision biases. It revealed that heuristic-based decision-making, although faster and simpler, exposes its users to biases which are inherent in human intuition. Biases operate at the subconscious level, are virtually undetectable, and have a powerful and immediate impact on individuals' judgement.

Robert Cialdini (2009) identified the decision-making biases and heuristics that could be used by individuals to influence the decisions made by others. He called them 'weapons of influences'.

Contrast

This bias of human perception affects the way that we see the difference between things that are presented one after another. If the second item is fairly different from the first, we will tend to see it as more different than it actually is. If you lift a light object first, and then a heavy object, the latter will appear heavier than it actually is.

Reciprocation

A basic norm in society is reciprocation, that is, one person must try to repay in kind in the future, what another has provided them with in the past. We are socialized from childhood to abide by the reciprocation rule or suffer social disapproval and a feeling of personal guilt. Such reciprocation leads to concession-making, and allows different individuals' initial, incompatible demands to become compromised, so that they finally work together towards common goals.

Commitment and consistency

Commitment is a state of being in which individuals become bound to their actions, and through these, to their beliefs. Commitment sustains action in the face of difficulties. In these circumstances it is behaviour which is being committed. It represents a visible indicator of what we are and what we intend doing. After taking an initial decision, people will adjust their attitude to make it consistent with their action, and become committed to it.

Social proof

People decide what to believe or how to act in a situation, by looking at what others believe and do. In situations of uncertainty and ambiguity, they observe and follow others, especially those they perceive to be similar to themselves. Such similarity is defined in terms of status, social background, dress, manner or language. Market research suggests that 95 per cent of people are imitators and only 5 per cent are initiators.

Liking

We enjoy doing things for people we like. That liking encourages us to comply with their requests. The liking bias is so powerful, that the person concerned does not even have to be present for it to be activated. Often, just the mention of a friend's or mutual acquaintance's name will be sufficient.

Authority

Each of us has a deep-seated duty to authority, and will tend to comply when requested by an authority figure. Since the opposite is anarchy, we are all trained from birth to believe that obedience to authority is right. The strength of this bias to obey legitimate authority figures comes from systematic socialization practices designed to instil in people the perception that such obedience constitutes correct conduct. Different societies vary its terms of this dimension.

Scarcity

Things and opportunities that are difficult to obtain are more valued. We use information about an item's availability as a shortcut to decide quickly on its quality. As things become less available, we lose freedoms, and since we hate this, we react against it, and want these things more than before.

As individual decision-makers, we all use judgement heuristics to reduce the information demands placed upon us. Considerable mental activity is saved by summarizing past experiences into the form of heuristics, and using them to evaluate the present problems. In a similar way, managers in organizations substitute such simplifying strategies to save having to collect complex information and analyze it. While helpful in many situations, heuristics can lead to errors and systematically biased judgements. Although the three main biases have been discussed, many other errors, fallacies and biases exist. People have ideas about order, randomness, chance and so on. Studies have shown how peoples' judgements become biased, and hence less rational.

Decision conditions: risk and programmability

Risks of decisions

Certainty a condition in which managers possess full knowledge of alternatives; a high probability of having these available; being able to calculate the costs and benefits of each alternative; and having high predictability of outcomes.

Table 20.5 distinguishes different types of environmental conditions faced by organizations and labels these 'stable equilibrium', 'bounded instability' (or chaos), and 'explosive instability'. The conditions under which a decision is made affects both how it is made and its outcome. Decisions differ in terms of their degree of risk involved and their programmability. Every decision is made under conditions of certainty, risk or uncertainty. We shall consider each in turn.

In a situation of certainty, no element of chance comes between the alternative and its outcome, and all the outcomes are known in advance with 100 per cent certainty. In such circumstances, all that the individual has to do is to select the outcomes with the largest benefit. A situation of total certainty is so rare as to be virtually non-existent. Some writers, struggling to find an example, cite the example of government bonds which guarantee a fixed rate of interest over a period of time which will be paid barring the fall of the government. However, as the Russian government default in the late 1990s demonstrated, even government bonds carry an element of risk.

Perhaps the main reason for discussing a generally non-existent state is that it suggests one of the reasons that most senior executives and managers of the world's leading companies are paid so much. As the trading conditions become more volatile, and technological changes such as the internet dramatically change established practices, the future becomes ever more difficult to predict. Those few individuals who have shown themselves capable of making what have turned out to be the correct decisions enter a seller's market for their skills. Or, to look at it another way, if decisions were made in conditions of certainty, managers would not be needed, and junior, cheaper operatives, supplied with a rulebook could replace them. Indeed, in conditions of certainty, a computer could quickly and accurately identify the consequences of the available options and select the outcomes with the greatest benefits. Managers are paid to make those tricky 'judgement calls' in uncertain conditions.

Risk a condition in which managers have a high knowledge of alternatives; know the probability of these being available; can calculate the costs and know the benefits of each alternative; and have a medium predictability of outcomes.

Probably the most common real life decisions are made under conditions of risk. When managers can assess the likelihood of various outcomes occurring on the basis of their past experience, research or other information, decision-making can be said to take place under conditions of risk.

Decisions made under uncertainty are the most difficult since the manager even lacks the information with which to estimate the likelihood of various outcomes and their associated probabilities and payoffs (March and Simon, 1958, p.137). Conditions of uncertainty prevail in new markets, or those offering new technologies, or those aimed at new target customers. In all these cases there is no historical data from which to infer probabilities. In each case, the situation is so novel and complex that it is impossible to make comparative judgements.

Uncertainty a condition in which managers possess low knowledge of alternatives; a low probability of having these available; can to some degree calculate the costs and benefits of each alternative; but have no predictability of outcomes.

Without uncertainty as to what course of action to take, there would be no decision to be make. Hence, a decision-making manager would not be required. It is for this reason that so many writers over the years have emphasized the centrality of decision-making in management. Having considered the various conditions under which decisions are made, let us investigate the greater complexity of each of the activities associated with the decision-making model presented earlier.

Table 20.5: Environmental and decision-making conditions

Environmental condition	Decision-making condition	Characteristics	Illustration
Stable equilibrium is a state in which the elements are always in, or quickly return to, a state of balance	Certainty	Alternatives and outcomes known and fully predictable	Fixed interest rate savings accounts
Bounded instability (or chaos) is a state in which there is a mixture of order and disorder, many unpredictable events and changes, and in which an organization's behaviour has an irregular pattern	Risk	Known alternatives with only probable outcomes predictable	Tomorrow's weather
Explosive instability is a state in which there is no order or pattern	Uncertainty	Alternatives and outcomes poorly understood	Developing a new product

STOP AND THINK

Identify three separate events in your university career or work life involving certainty, risk and uncertainty. Consider each situation and think how it could change, or did actually change, from one condition to one of the other two.

Certainty
- From certainty to risk
- From certainty to uncertainty

Risk
- From risk to certainty
- From risk to uncertainty

Uncertainty
- From uncertainty to risk
- From uncertainty to certainty

From Samaras (1989, p.51).

Programmability of decisions

Routine decisions
decisions made according to established procedures and rules.

Organization members make many different decisions every day. Some decisions are routine while others are not. **Routine decisions** are those which involve the use of pre-established organizational procedures or rules. Routine decision-makers are given considerable guidance as to what to do and how to do it through a well-established process, clearly defined goals, and the provision of information sources and decision rules. Examples of routine decisions include the re-ordering of stock items which have fallen to a certain level; the efficient routing of delivery vans; and the scheduling of equipment use. All these decisions tend to be repetitive and programmed, and are made by low level employees on their own who rely on pre-determined courses of action.

Adaptive decisions
decisions that require human judgement based on clarified criteria and are made using basic quantitative decision tools.

Adaptive decisions typically require human judgement to be used. It is a form of judgement that no computer program, however complex, could produce. Once certain judgements are clarified, adaptive decisions can be made, using relatively basic quantitative decision tools such as break-even analysis, a pay-off matrix or a decision tree.

Table 20.6: Routine, adaptive and innovative decisions

Decision type	Routine	← Adaptive →	Innovative
Goals	Clear, specific		Vague
Level	Lower level employees		Upper management
Problem	Well structured		Poorly structured
Process	Computational		Heuristic
Information	Readily available		Unavailable
Level of risk	Low		High
Involvement	Single decision maker		Group decision
Consequences	Minor		Major
Solution basis	Decision rule and procedures		Judgement, creativity
Decision speed	Fast		Slow
Time for solution	Short		Relatively long

Innovative decisions
decisions which address
novel problems, lack
pre-specified courses of
action, and are made by
senior managers.

Finally, innovative decisions are made when a unique situation is confronted that has no precedent; when there are no off-the-shelf solutions; and when a novel answer has to be found. Innovative decisions are an outcome of problem-solving; they frequently deal with areas of the unknown; and company professionals or top managers typically make them. Within the organizational context, such decisions tend to be rare. For example, the decision whether to acquire another company; to invest in a new technology; or to adopt a new marketing approach. Many innovative decisions concern some aspect of company strategy, and hence are more likely to be made by groups than by an individual.

STOP AND THINK   Think of three very different decisions that you have recently made. How well did they fit into this routine, adaptive, innovative decision framework presented? What additional decision-type categories would you add?

Individual and group decision-making

One of the main reasons why organizational activities are arranged around groups and teams is management's assumption that group decisions are better than individual decisions. The common sense belief is that with many members contributing their diverse skills, knowledge and experiences, they will make better decisions than individuals (Hill, 1982). However, experimental research data show that while the average quality of a decision made by a group is higher than the average quality of a decision made by an individual, the quality of work group decisions is consistently below that made by their most capable individual members (Rogelberg *et al.*, 1992).

STOP AND THINK   Suggest reasons why, despite the evidence of ineffectiveness, organizations continue to promote group-based decision-making.

Table 20.7: Advantages and disadvantages of group decision-making

Advantages	Disadvantages
Greater pool of knowledge: A group can bring much more information and experience to bear on a decision or problem than can an individual alone	*Personality factors*: Traits such as shyness can prevent some members offering their opinions and knowledge to the group
Different perspectives: Individuals with varied experience and interests help the group see decision situations and problems from different angles	*Social conformity*: Unwillingness to 'rock the boat' and pressure to conform may combine to stifle the creativity of individual contributors
Greater comprehension: Those who personally experience the give-and-take of group discussion about alternative courses of action tend to understand the rationale behind the final decision	*Diffusion of responsibility*: Members feel able to avoid responsibility for their actions, believing it can be shouldered by the others present
Increased acceptance: Those who play an active role in group decision-making and problem-solving tend to view the outcomes as 'ours' rather than 'theirs'	*Minority domination*: Sometimes the quality of group action is reduced when the group gives in to those who talk the loudest and longest
Training ground: Less experienced participants in group action learn how to cope with group dynamics by actually being involved	*Logrolling*: Political wheeling and dealing can displace sound thinking when an individual's pet project or vested interest is at stake
	Goal displacement: Sometimes secondary considerations such as winning an argument making a point, or getting back at a rival, displace the primary task of making a sound decision or solving a problem
	Group brainstorming: Reduces rather than increases the quantity and quality of ideas compared to individual performance
	'Groupthink': Sometimes cohesive 'in-groups' let the desire for unanimity override the sound judgement when generating and evaluating alternative courses of action
	Satisficing: Making decisions which are immediately acceptable to the group rather than the best ones

Based on West et al. *(1998, pp.1–48); Kreitner (1989, p.238).*

On the positive side, multiple individuals in a group can supply a greater range of knowledge and information to deal with the more complex questions. They can generate more alternatives; can have a better comprehension of the problem using multiple perspectives; and permit the specialization of labour, with individuals doing those tasks for which they are best suited. The effect of this is to improve the quality of group effort, and facilitate wider decision acceptance since more members will understand the decision better and have a feeling of ownership of it through participation. On the negative side, there are concerns that groups work more slowly; that the disagreements within them can create group conflict; and that group members may be intimidated by their group leader, creating only pseudo-involvement in decision-making.

Research has revealed that two main factors determine whether groups should be preferred to individuals. These are first, how structured the task is, and second, who are the

Table 20.8: Individual and group performance compared

Factor	Individuals when	Group when
Type of problem task	Creativity or efficiency is desired	Diverse skills and knowledge are required
Acceptance of decision	Acceptance is not important	Acceptance by group members is valued
Quality of the solution	'Best member' can be identified	Several group members can improve the solution
Characteristics of the individuals	Individuals cannot collaborate	Members have experience of working together
Decision-making climate	Climate is competitive	Climate is supportive of group problem-solving
Time available	Relatively little time is available	Relatively more time is available

From Gordon (1993, p.253).

individuals. If the task to be performed is structured (has a clear, correct solution), then groups are better, although they take longer (Weber, 1984). In the case of unstructured tasks (no single correct answer, and creativity required), individuals are better. Hence the counter-intuitive finding that performance of brainstorming groups is inferior to that of individuals.

Problems with group decision-making

Group polarization a situation in which individuals in a group begin by taking a moderate stance on an issue related to a common value and, after having discussed it, end up taking a more extreme decision than the average of members' decisions. The extremes could be more risky or more cautious.

Risky shift phenomenon the tendency of a group to make decisions that are riskier than those that the members of the group would have recommended individually.

Caution shift phenomenon the tendency of a group to make decisions that are more risk averse than those that the members of the group would have recommended individually.

It is the very strengths of a group that are also its weaknesses. The cost of bringing individuals together in one place counters the benefits of getting contributions from supposedly independent minds. Four problems will be examined here: group polarization, groupthink, brainstorming and escalation of commitment.

Group polarization refers to the phenomenon that occurs when a position that is held on an issue by the majority of group members is intensified (in a given direction) as a result of discussion (Lamm, 1988). This tendency can lead to irrational and hence to ineffective group performance. Social psychologists have documented the situation in which individuals in a group begin by taking a moderate stance on an issue related to a common value and then, after having discussed it, end up taking a more extreme stance. James Stoner conducted one of the earliest of these studies in the 1950s. He found that groups of management students were willing to make decisions involving greater risks than their individual preferences (Stoner, 1961). This phenomenon was referred to as the **risky shift**. However, the opposite can also occur, and is called the **caution shift**. Here a group can become more risk averse than the initial, average risk averse tendencies of its individual members (Lamm and Myers, 1978; Isenberg, 1986).

Patricia Wallace (2001) believed that group polarization may be partly responsible for the extremism often found on the internet, and the apparent absence of a moderate voice. An individual might hold a relatively moderate view about an issue initially, but after talking with others about it over the internet, they is likely to move away from the middle view towards one of the fringes. Factors that contribute to group polarization are present on the Internet in abundance. First people talk and talk endlessly. Second, members are selective about what they share with others. As talk progresses, members become increasingly reluctant to bring up items that might contradict the merging group consensus. This creates a biased discussion where alternatives are not considered during discussion.

Online bias

Ross Hightower and Lutfus Sayeed studied online groups that used groupware that allowed synchronous chat and had online voting capabilities to collaborate in making a personnel decision. Group members were given the resumes (job application forms) of candidates applying for the position of a marketing manager. The researchers rigged the applicants' positive and negative attributes so that only one applicant was best suited for the job because he most closely matched the criteria in the job description. They distributed information packets containing a subset of information from the resumes, so that each group member knew only part of the story. Some three-person groups met face-to-face, while others discussed the job from separate locations using groupware.

Almost none of the group – face-to-face or online – chose the best candidate. Neither type shared information in a way that would allow them to make an objective decision based on the whole picture. However, the degree of bias was most skewed when discussion was held online. Bias was determined by which titbits of information members chose to share. In the most biased discussion, they shared positive information (but not negative) about the winning candidates, and negative information (but not positive) about losing candidates. Each item contributed would thus reinforce the march towards group consensus, rather than add complications to fuel the debate. This trend was found to be twice as prevalent in online groups than in the face-to-face ones.

Based on Highwater and Sayeed (1995).

Groupthink a mode of thinking in a cohesive in-group, in which members' strivings for unanimity override their motivation to appraise realistically the alternative courses of action.

Irving Lester Janis (1918–1990)

Groupthink is a mode of thinking that occurs when the members' strivings for unanimity override their motivation to appraise realistically the alternative courses of action. One of the reasons groups perform badly on complex, unstructured tasks is due to the dynamics of group interaction. Groups and teams can develop a high level of cohesiveness. This is generally a positive thing, but it also has negative consequences. Specifically, the desire not to disrupt the consensus can lead to a reluctance to challenge the group's thinking which in turn, results in bad decisions. Irving Janis studied a number of American foreign policy 'disasters' such as the failure to anticipate the Japanese attack on Pearl Harbour in 1941; the Bay of Pigs fiasco in 1961 when the President John F. Kennedy administration sought to overthrow the government of Fidel Castro; or the prosecution of the Vietnam War between 1964 and 1967 by President Lyndon Johnson. Janis concluded that it was the cohesive nature of these important committees which made these decisions, and which prevented contradictory views being expressed. He named this process, groupthink. He listed the symptoms of groupthink as well as how these could be prevented. These are outlined in Table 20.9.

Groupthink led to a failure by the group to make the best decision. The group discussed a minimum number of alternatives; the courses of action favoured by the majority of the group were not re-examined from the view of hidden risks and other alternatives. The group failed to use the expert opinion that it had, and when expert opinion was evaluated, it was done with a selective bias which ignored the facts and opinions which did not support the group view.

In the groups studied by Janis, while individual doubt may have been suppressed and the illusion of group unanimity and cohesiveness maintained, the group paid a high price in terms of its effectiveness. The factors affecting group cohesiveness are listed in Table 20.10. Thus, while group cohesion can make a positive contribution to group effectiveness, it may also have negative consequences on the process of group decision-making. Group loyalty, instilled through cohesion, acts to stifle the raising and questioning of controversial issues which in turn leads to the making of poor decisions. At the heart of groupthink is the tendency for groups to seek concurrence and the illusion of unanimity. To prevent groupthink occurring, individuals who disagree with the group's evolving consensus, must be willing to make their voices heard.

Victoria Medvec of the Kellogg business school argues that when people sit around a table together, they tend to seek confirmation of what everyone already knows. She suggests two ways of avoiding this. First, before anyone makes a verbal contribution to the

Table 20.9: Groupthink: symptoms and prevention steps

When groups become very cohesive, there is a danger that they will become victims of their own closeness.

Symptoms	Prevention steps
1. *Illusion of invulnerability*: members display excessive optimism that past successes will continue and will shield them, and hence they tend to take extreme risks	(A) Leader encourages open expression of doubt by members
2. *Collective rationalization*: members collectively rationalize away data that disconfirm the assumptions and beliefs upon which they base their decisions	(B) Leader accepts criticism of his/her opinions
3. *Illusion of morality*: members believe that they, as moral individuals, are unlikely to make bad decisions	(C) Higher status members offer opinions last
4. *Shared stereotypes*: members dismiss disconfirming evidence by discrediting its source (e.g. stereotyping other groups and its leaders as evil or weak)	(D) Get recommendations from a duplicate group
5. *Direct pressure*: imposition of verbal, non-verbal or other sanctions on individuals who explore deviant positions (e.g. those who express doubts or question the validity of group beliefs). Perhaps use of assertive language to force compliance	(E) Periodically divide into subgroups
6. *Self-censorship*: members keep silent about misgivings about the apparent group consensus and try to minimize their doubts	(F) Members get reactions of trusted outsiders
7. *Illusion of unanimity*: members conclude that the group has reached a consensus because its most vocal members are in agreement	(G) Invite trusted outsiders to join the discussion periodically
8. *Mind guards*: members who take it upon themselves to screen out adverse, disconfirming information supplied by 'outsiders' which might endanger the group's complacency	(H) Assign someone to the role of devil's advocate (I) Develop scenarios of rivals' possible actions

Based on Janis (1982).

discussion, they should write down what they think about the different items on the agenda. Second, they should rate the strength of their views on a one to ten scale. This will enable them to remember their original views on a topic before they were influenced by other group members (Hindle, 2006d).

Although less than two dozen experimental, laboratory studies have been conducted on groupthink (Turner and Pratkanis, 1998), an overview of these supports a link between the level of cohesion in the group, and the occurrence of groupthink (Mullen *et al.*, 1994). However, the strongest evidence supports the effective of directive leadership. Directive leadership is linked to less information being considered by the group; the discouragement of dissent; fewer solutions being found; and more self-censorship by members (Flowers, 1977; Leana, 1985; McCauley, 1989; Moorhead and Montanari, 1986). It appears that if the group leader is strong; states their position at the start; and appears to have a strong preference for a particular outcome, the group is less likely to consider alternative information or solutions.

Table 20.10: Factors affecting group cohesiveness

Size	Smaller groups are more cohesive than larger ones, partly because their members interact more frequently
Duration	The longer members are together, the more opportunity they have to find out about one another
Threats	An external threat can often (although not always) serve to harden against 'the enemy'
Isolation	Leads a group to feel distinct and hence special
Rewards	Group rewards can encourage co-operation to achieve the group goal
Restricted entry	Difficulty of membership increases identification with the group
Similarities	Where individuals share common goals and attitudes, they enjoy being in one another's company

The Space Shuttle *Challenger* Disaster – a case of groupthink?

On 28 January 1986, 73 seconds after its launch from Cape Canaveral, Florida, the space shuttle *Challenger* exploded, killing all seven members of its crew, including a civilian schoolteacher, Christa MacAuliffe. The evidence suggested that the physical cause of the explosion was an O-ring rubber seal that failed to do its job, due to the freezing overnight temperatures at the launch pad. A presidential commission established to investigate the causes of the accident cited flawed decision-making as one of the causes of the disaster. The subsequent analysis of documents and testimony by researchers has led some of them to argue that the negative symptoms of groupthink increased in the 24 hours prior to the launch in the group that consisted of Morton Thiokol, the builders of the rocket boosters, and NASA management personnel. Thiokol engineers argued for the cancellation of the launch because the O-rings would not withstand the pressure at the launch time temperatures. The engineers were pressured by their bosses to stifle their dissent, and their opinions were devalued. The past record of success led to overconfidence, and various pieces of information were withheld from key individuals. In consequence, the group failed to consider fully the alternatives; failed to evaluate the risks associated with their preferred course of action; used information that was biased when making their decision; and failed to work out a contingency plan. Although the physical cause of the disaster was an O-ring seal, many researchers claim that the actual cause was the flawed decision-making process that had been infected by groupthink.

Based on Esser and Lindoerfer (1989) and Moorhead et al. *(1991).*

Source: NASA Images

Brainstorming a technique in which all group members are encouraged to propose ideas spontaneously, without critiquing or censoring others' ideas. The alternative ideas so generated are not evaluated until all have been listed.

Brainstorming is usually presented as a technique that seeks to improve group decision-making. However, it can be argued that it represents a problem in group decision-making. Brainstorming asserts the superiority of a group's performance over that of an individual's. Alexander F. Osborn, a principal of the New York advertising agency Batten, Barton, Durstine and Osborn invented brainstorming in 1939. He coined the term to mean using the *brain* to *storm* a problem creatively. It is based on the belief that under given conditions, a group of people working together will solve a problem more creatively than if the same people worked separately as individuals. The presence of a group is said to permit members to 'bounce ideas off each other', or gives individuals the chance to throw out half-baked ideas which other group members might turn into more practical suggestions.

The purpose of the technique is to produce creative, new ideas. Members of brainstorming groups are required to follow four main rules of procedure:

1. Avoid criticizing others' ideas.
2. Share even fanciful or bizarre suggestions.
3. Offer as many comments as possible.
4. Build on others' ideas to create your own.

The proponents of brainstorming argue that the flow of ideas in a group will trigger off further ideas whereas the usual evaluative framework will tend to stifle the imagination. A brainstorming group may, on occasions, perform better than an individual who applies these rules to his own thought processes. However, if one has four individuals working alone, they can generally greatly outperform a group of four in terms of the number of ideas generated. Research has consistently shown that group brainstorming actually *inhibits* creative thinking. Taylor *et al.* (1958) carried out one of the earliest studies and compared the performance of brainstorming groups with 'pseudo-groups' (constructed by the experimenter from individual members' scores). They discovered that pseudo-groups were superior to the brainstorming groups on criteria of idea quantity, quality and uniqueness. Over the intervening years, these original conclusions have been investigated by researchers (Yetton and Bottger, 1982; Diehl and Stroebe, 1987, 1991; Mullen *et al.*, 1991; Brown and Paulus, 1996, Furnham, 2000; Paulus *et al.*, 2002; Litchfield, 2008). It may be that brainstorming is most effective with established or specially trained groups.

Electronic brainstorming

While face-to-face brainstorming has been proved of little value, electronic brainstorming may prove to be superior. A support tool had participants sitting at their PCs, entering their ideas in one window, after which it appeared in a second window, with the ideas of the other participants. It was found that in large groups, this electronic support, improved performance. The reason given was that it by-passed the production-blocking problem, allowing individuals to glance at colleagues' contributions at any time, but not have their train of thought interrupted. The environment may have triggered disinhibition, making members feel freer to express their wildest notions without concern for negative reactions.

From Connelly (1997); Cooper et al. (1998);
Dennis and Valacich (1993); Paulus et al. (2001).

 **STOP AND THINK**   Despite the research evidence, members of brainstorming groups firmly believe that group brainstorming is more productive that individual brainstorming, both in terms of the number and quality of the ideas generated. Why might this be?

Advocacy versus inquiry: The Bay of Pigs and the Cuban Missile Crisis

Garvin and Roberto distinguish between the *advocacy* approach to decision-making, which sees it as an event made by a manager at a discrete point in time, and the *inquiry* approach, which treats it as a process to be explicitly designed and managed.

	Advocacy	Inquiry
Concept of decision-making	A contest	Collaborative problem-solving
Purpose of discussion	Persuasion and lobbying	Testing and evaluation
Participants' role	Spokespeople	Critical thinkers
Patterns of behaviour	Strive to persuade others Defend your position Downplay weaknesses	Present balanced arguments Remain open to alternatives Accept constructive criticism
Minority views	Discouraged or dismissed	Cultivated and valued
Outcome	Winners and losers	Collective ownership

Source: Reprinted by permission of *Harvard Business Review*. Exhibit on p.110. From "What you don't know about making decisions" by Garvin, D.A. and Roberto, M.A., 79(8). Copyright © 2001 by the Harvard Business School Publishing Corporation, all rights reserved.

The contrast can be illustrated by two critical foreign policy decisions faced by President John F. Kennedy and his administration. During his first two years in office, Kennedy dealt with the Bay of Pigs invasion and the Cuban Missile Crisis. Both problems were assigned to cabinet-level task forces, and involved many of the same individuals, the same political interests and extremely high stakes. However, the outcomes were completely different, largely because the two groups operated in different ways.

The first group, which had to decide whether to support an invasion of Cuba by a small army of US-trained Cuban exiles, worked in an advocacy mode. The outcome of its deliberations was widely considered to be an example of flawed decision-making. Shortly after taking office, President Kennedy learned of the planned attack on Cuba developed by the CIA during Eisenhower's administration. Backed by the Joint Chief of Staff, the CIA argued forcefully for the invasion. It understated the risks, and filtered the information that it presented to the president to reinforce its own position. Knowledgeable individuals from the Latin America desk were excluded from deliberations because of their likely opposition. Some members of Kennedy's own staff opposed the plan, but kept silent for fear of appearing weak in the face of the strong advocacy by the CIA. As a result, there was little debate, and the group failed to test some critical underlying assumptions. For example, whether the landing would ignite a domestic uprising against Castro; and whether the exiles could hide in the mountains if they met with strong resistance. The resulting invasion is generally considered to be one of the low points of the Cold War. About 100 lives were lost, and the remaining exiles were taken hostage. The incident was a major embarrassment to the Kennedy administration and dealt a blow to America's global standing.

After the botched invasion, Kennedy conducted a review of the foreign policy decision-making process and introduced five major changes, essentially transforming the process to one of inquiry. First, people were urged to participate in discussions as 'sceptical generalists' – that is, as disinterested critical thinkers rather than as representatives of particular departments. Second, Robert Kennedy and Theodore Sorensen were assigned the role of intellectual watchdog, and expected to pursue every possible point of contention, uncovering weaknesses and untested assumptions. Third, task forces were urged to abandon the rules of protocol, eliminating formal agendas and deference to rank. Fourth, participants were expected to split occasionally into subgroups to develop a broad range of options. Finally, President Kennedy decided to absent himself from some of the early task force meetings to avoid influencing other participants and thereby slanting the debate.

This inquiry mode of decision-making was used to great effect in October 1962, when President Kennedy learned that the Soviet Union had placed nuclear missiles on Cuban soil, despite repeated assurances from the Soviet ambassador that this would not occur. Kennedy immediately convened a high level task force, which contained many of the same men responsible for the Bay of Pigs invasion, and asked them to frame a response. The group met around the clock for two weeks, often inviting additional members to join in their deliberations to broaden their perspective. Occasionally, to encourage the free flow of ideas, they met without the president. Robert Kennedy played his new role thoughtfully, critiquing options frequently, and encouraging the group to develop additional alternatives. In particular, he urged the group to move beyond a simple go or no-go decision on a military air strike.

Ultimately, subgroups developed two positions, one favouring a blockade and the other, an air strike. These groups gathered information from a broad range of sources, viewed and interpreted the same intelligence photos, and took great care to identify and test underlying assumptions, such as whether the Tactical Air Command was indeed capable of eliminating all Soviet missiles in a surgical air strike. The subgroups exchanged position papers, critiqued each other's proposals, and came together to debate the alternatives. They presented Kennedy with both options, leaving him to make the final choice. The result was a carefully framed response, leading to a successful blockade and a peaceful resolution of the crisis.

Based on Garvin and Roberto (2001).

Escalation of commitment an increased commitment to a previously made decision, despite negative information suggesting one should do otherwise.

Escalation of commitment is the final problem in group decision-making to be considered. Have you ever waited for a lift (elevator) that did not arrive, and the longer that you waited, the less inclined you were to use the stairs instead? The concept refers to the tendency of individuals to increase their commitment to a course of action in the future, despite the evidence of negative outcomes from the past. In addition to waiting situations, this tendency has been noticed in interpersonal relations, gambling, economic investment and policy-making.

Barry Staw (1976, 1981) first demonstrated escalation of commitment as an individual phenomenon, leading to much subsequent work on the topic (Whyte, 1986; Brockner, 1992). However, later research on group polarization and on groupthink supports Whyte's (1993) contention that groups escalate more than individuals. Risky-shift findings shows us that groups make riskier decisions than individuals, and the decision to escalate in the light of past failure, can be viewed as risk-seeking. From a groupthink perspective, since a majority view is sufficient to induce dissenters to conform to a decision to escalate, reliance on a group rather than on an individual to resolve an escalation dilemma, is likely to increase the frequency with which escalation occurs. Figure 20.3 shows the factors that Ross and Staw (1993) identified as contributing to a commitment escalation by a group or an individual. Note that although individual (psychological) variables play a part, a range of other determinants are equally, if not more important.

Task factors

The characteristics of the task itself – shooting a film, constructing a building, implementing a military tactic – are a major influence. A project like a movie or even a relationship can have had such a large amount of assets (money or emotions) previously invested in it, that it reaches the point where its abandonment would involve unacceptable financial or personal costs. The task may lack clearly defined goals, performance standards to measure those goals or unambiguous feedback that can allow a regular check on progress. Since the benefits of a task are often delayed, decision-makers are tempted to remain with it until the end. When doing so, they tend to attribute setbacks to temporary causes that they believe can be rectified with additional expenditure.

Psychological factors

Most psychological factors stem from the ego-involvement of the decision-makers for whom failure of the activity will threaten their self-esteem. Reinforcement traps mean that a person is reluctant to withdraw from a previously rewarding activity believing that, from past

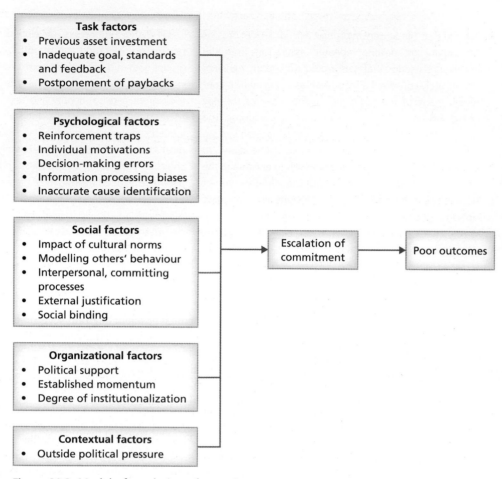

Figure 20.3: Model of escalation of commitment
Source: Based on Ross and Staw (1993).

history, it can be made to succeed. Individual motivation also plays a part, especially the need for self-justification. All sorts of decision-making errors are committed as people take risks to recover previously invested resources. They begin to process information in a biased way, becoming overconfident and slanting facts to suit pre-existing beliefs. Often they fail to determine the true cause of the problem by attributing negative outcomes to external rather than internal factors.

Social factors

In many countries, cultural norms favour consistent (no 'U-turns') leadership which 'triumphs in the end'. Members are likely to be under pressure from a hostile audience to justify their actions, as well as from friendly colleagues who want to 'save face'. This need to rationalize their actions to other parties, when challenged, results in producing renewed justifications leading, in turn, to greater commitment. Seeking direction, decision-makers are likely to make a social comparison with others, modelling their behaviour on what someone else has done in a similar situation.

Organizational factors

The idea of projects continuing because of the political support of key organizational players is well understood. Also important is the momentum towards the continuation of the task or project, that is generated by the company having already recruited expert staff, invested in specialized equipment, and entered or withdrawn from certain lines of business activity.

A final important variable here is how closely the project is tied to the company's values and objectives. Its degree of organizational institutionalization may be high or low.

Contextual factors

A decision taken within an organization involves forces outside its boundaries. Political, economic, societal, technological, legal and ethical variables can all play a part. External forces that are unconnected with, but which have an interest in, the rescue or continuance of a 'permanently failing organization' can contribute to an escalation of commitment.

Organizational decision-making

The making of decisions has been examined at the level of the individual and of the group. It now remains to consider it at the organizational context. The administration of any organization has two main tasks. First, to co-ordinate the work activities within the organization (e.g. ensure that jobs are divided among departments and performed). Second, to adjust to circumstances outside the organization (e.g. regulate contracts with suppliers; adhere to government regulations; respond to customers). Individuals in the organization (mainly but not exclusively managers) have to deal with the fact that rules, procedures and precedents seldom determine what should be done in every particular case. Decisions which are 'unprogrammed', have to be made. This means that discretion has to be used, judgements have to be made, and decisions promulgated. This ambiguity and uncertainty provides the political context within which decision-making occurs within organizations.

Sociologists have studied how power and politics impact on the decision-making process and prevent the operation of the classical decision-making process described at the start of this chapter. Decisions in organizations involve power and conflict between individuals and groups in organizations. The more sources of uncertainty there are, the more possibility there is for individuals and groups to take up political positions. From this perspective, a particular decision is less an expression of the organization's goals, and more a reflection of the ability of a particular individual or group to impose their view or 'definition of the situation' and solution, onto other groups.

As noted earlier, Herbert Simon criticized the classical model of decision-making, saying that it ignored the internal politics of the organization system. He and his colleagues, Richard Cyert and James March, were influential in introducing politics into the consideration of decision-making in organizations. They linked the cognitive limits to rationality with political limits. The classical model had assumed that:

- decision-makers possessed a consistent order of preferences;
- there was agreement among the stakeholders about the goals of the organization;
- decision rules were known and accepted by everyone.

In contrast to it, the bounded rationality view stressed that decision-makers could not make the types of decisions that the classical model recommended for two reasons. First, there was ambiguity over which direction to take on an issue. That is, people disagreed about which goals to pursue or which problems to solve. Second, there was the issue of uncertainty. This concerned the degree to which people felt certain that a given action would produce a given outcome (cause-and-effect).

The condition of uncertainty was examined earlier, and it was noted that extra information could reduce it. However, that same, new information could also increase ambiguity since it provided extra points over which different decision-makers could disagree. James Thompson and Arthur Tuden used the dimensions of agreement or disagreement over goals and beliefs about cause-and-effect relations, as a way of distinguishing four different situations faced by decision-makers (Thompson and Tuden, 1959; Thompson, 1967). These are described in Figure 20.4.

		\multicolumn{2}{c}{**Consensus on goals or problem definition?**}
		agree	*disagree*
Beliefs about cause and effect relationships	*certainty*	I Computational strategy Rational model	III Compromise strategy Political model
	uncertainty	II Judgmental strategy Incremental model	IV Inspirational strategy Garbage can model

Figure 20.4: Conditions favouring different decision-making processes
Source: Based on Thompson and Tuden (1959); Thompson (1967).

Any given choice situation can be mapped on these two continua: the degree of agreement that exists between parties on the goals to be pursued; and the level of certainty that a specified outcome can be achieved through the use of a given action. Each such situation can thus be defined as falling into one of the four quadrants above. The most likely form of decision-making model for each quadrant was specified.

I. Computational strategy – rational model

In this case, those concerned are clear and agreed on what outcome they desire (no ambiguity) and certain about the consequences of their actions (high certainty). For example, as demand for ice cream increases in the summer, the company introduces an extra shift. The rational model has already been considered, and may be capable of being applied in this situation since the management know about the capabilities of their machines, costs of extra manning, and the income from extra sales. The company can therefore calculate the costs and returns using a *computational strategy*.

II. Judgmental strategy – incremental model

In this case, those concerned are clear and agreed on what outcome they desire (no ambiguity), but are uncertain about the consequences of their actions (low certainty) because information is inadequate. In the case of the ice cream makers, new equipment may need to be purchased whose performance is unknown. Charles Lindblom (1959) built on Simon's notion of bounded rationality, saying that the limited search for and evaluation of alternatives meant that those which were offered differed only slightly (i.e. incrementally) from what already existed. Hence, current judgement choices were made on the basis of past decisions. Decision-making in his view was thus remedial, concerned with 'fixing the past' by moving away from it, rather than oriented to achieving goals in the future. Decisions therefore were continually adjusted as they unfolded, and problems were continually attacked. For Lindblom, policy formulation was thus not a single event, but the outcome of countless small, separate, often disjointed decisions, made individually, by different individuals and groups, over a period of years. He referred to the process that he described as *incrementalism* or *disjointed incrementalism*, although it is more popularly referred to as the 'science of muddling through'.

III. Compromise strategy – political model

In this case, those concerned are unclear or divided as to what outcomes they desire (high ambiguity). Increasing production to manufacture a large number of extra low profit products or a smaller volume of higher mark-up items might be equally appealing. The use of the technology provides certainty that either option can be achieved (high certainty). In this case, a compromise strategy is used.

These sorts of unprogrammed decisions are bound to be resolved, ultimately, by reasoning, judgement, influence and politics. When faced with a question such as how should we reformulate strategy for 2015, reasonable people will always disagree. Political behaviour is therefore an inevitable consequence of the prevalence of unprogrammed management decisions.

Many writers view an organization as a coalition of interests. Each department has its own goals, is interdependent with others, and competes for scarce resources. The task of senior management is to balance these demands and resolve any ensuing conflicts. It does so by engaging in politics, in an effort to manage or manipulate the decision-making process, to 'cut a deal'. In such circumstances, a decision is not the result of the classical decision-making process, but something that is the outcome of horse-trading, and which is acceptable to all those involved. From this perspective, individuals and groups unite their interests, propose alternatives, assess their power, join with others, negotiate and form coalitions. In conditions of high ambiguity, decision-makers look for alternatives that can accommodate the interests of the parties involved. They are not greatly concerned with searching for information.

IV. Inspirational strategy – garbage can model

In this case, those concerned are unclear or are divided as to what outcomes they desire (high ambiguity). They are also uncertain about the consequences that their actions are likely to have (high uncertainty). When there is neither agreement on goals, nor certainty about cause and effect relationships, ambiguity and uncertainty prevail, and decision-making becomes random. If there is no preference between high volume/low profit ices and low volume/high profit ices, or certainty about what will happen if they do launch them, then the *inspirational strategy* is an inspired leap into the dark!

In such circumstances, Cyert and March's decision-making processes become 'uncoupled' from the decisions actually made. That is, a link ceases to exist between the problems identified and the solutions proposed or implemented. The garbage can model was developed by James March and Johan Olsen and turned the classical model on its head. Whereas both the classical and the bounded rationality models treated decisions as the outcomes of a reasoned approach of information-gathering and evaluation, the garbage can model contended that the elements that came to constitute decision problems were independent phenomena that came together in random ways (Cohen *et al.*, 1972; March and Olsen, 1976; Einsiedel, 1983).

In their view, the various logical models of decision-making had failed to recognize the amount of confusion that surrounded decision-making situations. Instead, they labelled these situations *organized anarchies*. Within these, a decision 'occurred' rather than was consciously taken. Thus, decision-making involved streams of activities which served to cope with uncertainty over time. It occurred when four separate but interdependent streams fortuitously met. The four streams were:

Choice opportunities	Every organization has a stream of 'occasions' at which there is an expectation of a decision e.g. weekly staff meetings, product review meetings, government cabinet meetings
Participants	A stream of people who have an opportunity to make a choice
Problems	A stream of problems which represent matters of concern for individuals both inside and outside the organization e.g. declining sales; need to recruit staff; increasing hospital waiting lists
Solutions	The existence of a stream of solutions or answers, all seeking problems and questions, and all available from internal staff advisors or external consultants.

From this perspective, the choice opportunities act as the container (garbage can) for the mixture of problems, solutions and participants that are there at the time. Because of the disorder that characterizes managerial work, preferences are rarely well ordered, they often change, and the criteria for judging the relevance of information are vague. Thus the classical rational model, with its logic and order does not describe what happens. For example, choices are made before problems are understood; solutions sometimes discover problems; and only rarely are problems resolved after choices are made. The actual decisions made are often irrelevant to the people concerned. For them, the priority may have been to blame others, pay off debts, store up favours, punish others or position themselves in a power struggle. March and Olsen (1976, p.52) felt that:

> choice situations are not simply occasions for making substantive decisions. They are also arenas in which important symbolic meanings are developed. People gain status and exhibit virtue. Problems are accorded significance. Novices are educated into the values of the society and organization. Participation rights are certification of social legitimacy; participation performances are critical presentations of self.

"My team has created a very innovative solution, but we're still looking for a problem to go with it."

Source: Copyright Randy Glasbergen. www.glasbergen.com.

 RECAP

1. *Distinguish prescriptive, descriptive and explanatory models of decision-making and provide an example of each.*

   - Prescriptive models of decision-making recommend how individuals should behave in order to achieve a desired outcome. The original prescriptive model is the rational economic model, while a recent one was devised by Victor Vroom and Philip Yetton.

   - Descriptive models of decision-making reveal how individuals actually make decisions. The behavioural theory of decision-making is the earliest and most influential descriptive models and was developed by Herbert Simon, John March and Richard Cyert.

   - Explanatory models of decision-making look at what decisions were made and aim to provide an explanation of how they occurred. The heuristics and biases model developed by Daniel Kahneman and Amos Tversky, and Irving Janis' groupthink concept illustrate such explanations.

2. *Distinguish different decision conditions on the basis of risk and programmability.*

   - Decision conditions can be classified as those involving: certainty, risk and uncertainty.

   - Decisions can be classified as routine, adaptive and innovative.

3. *Consider the advantages and disadvantages of group decision-making*.

- Groups offer the advantages of a greater pool of knowledge; different perspectives; greater problem comprehension; and increased acceptance of decisions.

- Disadvantages of groups can be considered under the headings of personality factors; social conformity; diffusion of responsibility; minority domination; logrolling; goal displacement; group brainstorming, groupthink and satisficing.

4. *Identify the factors used to decide whether to adopt individual or group decision-making*.

- Individual or group decision-making has been made on the basis of the following factors: type of problem task; acceptance of decision; quality of the solution; characteristics of the individuals; and decision-making climate.

5. *Match organizational conditions with the decision-making processes that favour them*.

- When there is certainty about cause-and-effects and there is consensus on goals or problem definition then a computational strategy involving the rational decision-making model is favoured.

- When there is uncertainty about cause-and-effects, but there is consensus on goals or problem definition, then a judgmental strategy involving an incremental decision-making model is favoured.

- When there is certainty about cause-and-effects, but disagreement about goals or problem definition then a compromise strategy involving a political decision-making model is favoured.

- When there is neither certainty about cause-and-effects, nor agreement about goals or problem definition, then an inspirational strategy involving the garbage can model of decision-making is favoured.

Revision

1. What are the strengths and weakness of the Vroom–Jago time-driven, decision-making model?

2. How does a 'satisficing' decision differ from a 'maximising' one? Provide examples of each from your own experience. In what circumstances would one be preferable to the other?

3. 'No decision that is ever made by a manager is truly rational.' Do you agree or disagree with this statement? Support your view with arguments and examples.

4. Should decision-making by groups be avoided or encouraged by organizations?

5. Suggest how political factors impact on the making of decisions by individuals and groups within the organization.

Research assignment

Familiarize yourself with Cialdini's seven weapons of influence through extended reading. (a) Develop a set of interview questions to determine the nature of their use. (b) Interview a few managers, co-workers or friends. Explain each of the weapons, and ask them for examples of weapons being used on them, or when using them on others. (c) Use the data collected to write a report discussing the popularity of the different weapons of influencing, giving examples of their use.

Springboard

Bazerman, M.H., 2005, *Judgement in Managerial Decision Making*, 6th edn, Wiley, New York.

A comprehensive, entertaining and interactive description of the judgement heuristics identified by the research of Daniel Kahneman and Amos Tversky.

Buchanan, D. and Badham, R., 2008, *Power, Politics and Organizational Change*, 2nd edn, Sage, London.

The book focuses on theories and research dealing with power and politics in decision-making within a context of organizational change. It has a practical approach which includes consideration of ethical issues.

Cialdini, R.B., 2009, *Influence: Science and Practice*, 5th edn, Pearson Education, New York.

Interesting and entertaining account of the biases that we experience in everyday life with suggestions on how to avoid them.

Hardman, D., 2009, *Judgement and Decision Making*, Wiley-Blackwell, Bognor Regis.

Considers the ways in which individuals and groups make decisions under conditions of risk and uncertainty in business, medicine, sports, economics and law.

 OB in films

Network (1976, director Sidney Lumet): DVD track 16: 1:48:00–1:53:00 (5 minutes). This film is set in the US television industry. Because of his falling ratings, the Union Broadcasting System (UBS) fires its leading news anchorman Howard Beale (played by Peter Finch). Beale's on-air behaviour then becomes increasingly bizarre, after he promises to kill himself on television. Initially, his ratings skyrocket, but then decline, affecting UBS's other programmes and its revenue. In this clip, network executives have a meeting in Frank Hackett's office. Hackett (Robert Duvall) sits at his desk and describes the problem. The clip begins as network executives assemble for a meeting, and ends with Diana saying 'let's kill the son of a bitch'. The members have to make a decision:

1. What decision options do the executives have?
2. Which decision-making model is being used to make their final decision?
3. How is the decision actually made in the group in the room?
4. How might the individuals justify this decision to themselves?

 OB in literature

Michael Crichton, *Airframe*, Arrow Books, London 1997. A mid-air disaster aboard a commercial airliner leaves three people dead and 56 injured. The pilot lands the plane, and a frantic investigation begins by the aircraft's manufacturers to determine what occurred. The plot involves company managers seeking to determine the cause of the accident. Consider their approach to arriving at a decision. What factors affect both the decision-making process and its outcome?

CHAPTER EXERCISES

Decision types

Objectives
1. To allow you to distinguish between different types of decisions.
2. To make you aware of the requirements of each type of decision.

Briefing
The chapter defined and distinguished between routine, adaptive and innovative types of decisions. This exercise gives you the opportunity to identify and deal with each of the three types.

1. Class divides into groups. Each group represents the executive committee of a small manufacturing company which meets regularly to review and decide upon a list of problems. The list consists of items submitted by employees for decision. This week's list of issues is shown below.

2. Each group is to sort the items on the list into three decision categories – routine, adaptive and innovative.

3. Once all the items have been sorted into three piles, each group is to select one item from the routine pile and one item from the innovative pile, and develop an action plan for each. They should also select one adaptive decision issue, and indicate what approach might be appropriate for working on that decision.

4. After 20–30 minutes, the executive committees/small groups reassemble in a class plenary session. Each group presents *one* of the decisions that it has worked on, and describes its conclusions.

5. Class discusses:

   • Was a routine or innovative decision harder to deal with? Why?

   • Did group members and groups categorize the decision items in the same way?

   • Over which items did group members disagree?

   • How were disagreements over categorization dealt with by the group?

List of decision items

1. An assembly worker wants the committee to decide on a more equitable method for allocating scarce parking spaces.

2. A departmental manager wants a decision as to whether one of his programmers can be given a special bonus for developing a popular software item.

3. The facilities manager wants to know if part time employees are eligible to join the company health club.

4. A division manager wants a decision on whether to open a new office in Paris, Berlin or Moscow.

5. The cafeteria manager has asked for a decision on how to choose among suppliers of foodstuffs.

6. The marketing manager wants a decision on a new product that will not compete with other manufacturers' products, but will be popular because it fills an unmet need.

7. A supervisor has asked whether overtime should be given to those who ask first or to those who have the most seniority.

8. A decision has to be made whether to emphasize desktop or laptop computers during the next quarter.

9. The research department has developed an innovative and cheap memory chip which is capable of being incorporated in many devices. It has asked what direction your committee wants to take in developing applications for this chip.

10. The board of directors has told your committee to consider whether it would be better to open company-owned retail outlets in five major cities or to franchise the outlets.

From SASHKIN, MARSHALL; MORRIS, WILLIAM C.; HELLRIEGE, DONALD,
EXPERIMENTAL EXERCISES MANAGEMENT BOOK, © *1987 pp.73–74, Reprinted by permission of Pearson Education, Inc., Upper Saddle River, NJ 07458*

→

Choosing decision styles

Objectives
1. To introduce students to different types of decision-making styles.
2. To apply the Vroom–Yetton–Jago model of decision-making.
3. To evaluate the strengths and weaknesses of this decision-making model.

Briefing
1. Form into groups.
2. Read the scenarios as directed by your instructor.
3. Apply the Vroom–Yetton–Jago model (p.634) using the decision-making sheet below.
4. Agree the most appropriate decision-making style in each scenario.
5. Based on your experience of this approach, what problems would a manager encounter in trying to apply this model?

	Question	1 NM	2 SSR	3 RB
1. Decision significance	How significant is this decision to the success of the project or organization? If significance is high, then the leader needs to be closely involved			
2. Importance of commitment	How important is subordinate commitment in implementing the decision? If importance is high, then leaders should involve subordinates			
3. Leader expertise	What is the level of the leader's information, knowledge or expertise in relation to the problem? If it is low, the leader should involve subordinates to obtain it			
4. Likelihood of commitment	If the leader were to make the decision alone, would subordinates' commitment to it be high or low? If the answer is high, then subordinate involvement is less important			
5. Group support for goals	What is the level of subordinate support for the team's or organization's goals with respect to this situation? If it is low, the leader should not allow the group to make the decision alone			
6. Group expertise	What is the level of group members' knowledge and expertise in relation to the problem? If it is high, then more responsibility for the decision can be given to them			
7. Team competence	What is the level of subordinates' skills and commitment in working together as a team to solve the problem? If their skill and desire to work together co-operatively is high, then more responsibility for the decision can be given to them			
Decision style				

Decision-making scenarios

1. New machines

You are a manufacturing manager in a large electronics plant. The company's management has recently installed new machines and put in a new, simplified work system. To everyone's surprise, the expected rise in productivity has not occurred. In fact, production has begun to drop off, quality has fallen, and the amount of staff turnover has increased. You do not believe that there is anything wrong with the machines. Other companies using them confirm this opinion, and representatives from the firm that built the machines report that they are operating at peak efficiency. You suspect that some parts of the new work system may be responsible for the change, but this view is not widely shared among your five immediate subordinates – four first-line supervisors, each in charge of a section, and your supply manager. They are all as concerned as you are, since it affects company profitability and thus their jobs. Each one has their own explanation based on their specialist knowledge. The drop in production has been variously attributed to poor training of the operators, lack of an adequate system of financial incentives, and poor morale. Clearly, this is an issue about which there is considerable depth of feeling among individuals and a source of potential disagreement among your subordinates. This morning you received a phone call from your divisional manager. He had just received your production figures for the last six months and was calling to express his concern. He indicated that the problem was yours to solve in any way you thought best. However, he wanted to know within a week what steps you planned to take. You share your divisional manager's concern with the situation.

2. Sugar Substitute Research

You are the head of research and development (R&D) unit for a major beer company, overseeing the work of a team of scientists. They work together well, successfully contributing to different projects. One of the scientists in your unit seems to have tentatively identified a new chemical compound that has few calories but tastes more like sugar than current sugar substitutes. The company has no foreseeable need for this product, but it could be patented and licensed to manufacturers in the food industry, and be a money-earner. Since the sugar substitute discovery would require considerable time and resources to make it commercially viable, these would need to be taken away from other projects in the lab. The sugar substitute project is beyond your technical expertise, but some of the lab researchers are familiar with that field of chemistry. The amount of research needed to perfect the substitute is difficult to determine, and you do not know how much demand there would be for it. There are no rules about funding projects that would be licensed but not used by the organization. The company's R&D budget is limited, and the scientists in your work group have recently complained that they require more resources and financial support to complete their current projects. Some of these have a potential for increasing future beer sales. You believe that most researchers in the R&D unit are committed to ensuring that the company's goals are achieved.

3. Repertory theatre

You are the director of a repertory theatre responsible for both its artistic and financial direction. While recognizing the importance of both sets of responsibilities, your own interests and talent have led you to focus on securing the highest level of quality for the theatre's productions. Four departmental heads responsible for administration, production, marketing and development report to you. Over the years, they have worked together effectively to mount numerous successful productions. Last week you received a report from an accounting firm commissioned to assess the financial health of your theatre. You were surprised to discover that the theatre's expenses were greatly exceeding its income, and shocked by the report's conclusion that unless expenses were reduced, the theatre might have to close in a year's time. You have circulated the report to your staff, and have been surprised at the variety of their reactions to it. Some dispute the report's conclusions, challenging its assumptions and methods of calculation. Others accept the findings but, shaken by its implications, are divided about what steps should be taken and when. However, what everybody is agreed on, is that the theatre should not be closed.

Scenario 1 (Kreitner and Kinicki, 2001, p.375);
Scenario 2 (Colquitt et al., 2009, p.482);
Scenario 3 (Vroom, 2000, p.90).

Chapter 21 Conflict

Key terms

conflict

frame of reference

unitarist frame of reference on conflict

pluralist frame of reference on conflict

interactionist frame of reference on conflict

functional conflict

dysfunctional conflict

conflict resolution

distributive bargaining

integrative bargaining

arbitration

mediation

conflict stimulation

radical frame of reference

organizational misbehaviour

resistance

alienation

labour process

emotional labour

emotions

felt emotions

displayed emotions

emotional dissonance

surface acting

deep acting

display rules

feeling rules

expression rules

emotional harmony

Learning outcomes

When you have read this chapter, you should be able to define those key terms in your own words, and you should also be able to:

1. Distinguish between the four major frames of reference on conflict.
2. Distinguish between functional and dysfunctional conflict.
3. Explain the relationship between organizing, co-ordinating and conflict.
4. List the causes of conflict in organizations.
5. Distinguish different organizational co-ordination devices.
6. Explain the conditions in which conflict is resolved and stimulated.
7. List Thomas' five conflict resolution approaches.
8. Distinguish between distributive and integrative bargaining.

Why study conflict?

Conflict is a fundamental force governing all aspects of life. Conflict specialists see the phenomenon as occurring both in various contexts (e.g. political, economic, social, psychological); and at a number of social levels (e.g. personal, domestic, organizational, communal, national and international). Within an organization, conflicts can occur between individuals, groups and departments; they can arise from the exercise of power and politics; emanate from particular leadership styles and decision-making processes; or arise from structural and cultural changes.

Conflict a process that begins when one party perceives that another party has negatively affected, or is about to negatively affect, something the first part cares about.

Conflict is a state of mind. It has to be perceived by the parties involved. If two or more parties are not aware of a conflict, then no conflict exists. This broad definition encompasses conflicts at different levels within an organization. Typically conflicts are based upon differences in interests and values. They occur when the interests of one party come up against the different interests of another. Parties may include shareholders, managers, departments, professional and groups; while conflict issues can include dividends, manager bonuses and employee wage levels.

There has been a longstanding debate concerning whether or not conflict within organizations is harmful. Dean Tjosvold (2008) argued that conflict was an inevitable aspect of all organizations; that properly conducted, it led to a better understanding between individuals, as well as to better ways of working. Since conflict was essential to successful teamwork and organizational effectiveness, it should be welcomed and managed appropriately. In contrast, Carsten De Dreu (2008) stated that conflict was always detrimental, and that the research support for the beneficial aspects of workplace conflict was weak. He said that conflict was beneficial in only a very few, specific situations; and that even in these, it had negative consequences which outweighed the positive ones. He felt that organizations had to make efforts to manage conflict, not because it had positive effects but so as to minimize its negative ones.

STOP AND THINK

Can you provide examples from your work own experience where conflict led to positive and negative outcomes?

Contrasting frames of reference: unitarist, pluralist, interactionist

Frame of reference a person's perceptions and interpretations of events, and involve assumptions about reality, attitudes towards what is possible, and conventions regarding correct behaviour.

A frame of reference, explained Roger Bennett (1991, p.131), refers to

> the influences which structure a person's perceptions and interpretations of events. These involve assumptions about reality, attitudes towards what is possible, and conventions regarding what is correct behaviour for those involved in a dispute. The adoption of differing frames of references by opposing sides can impair the effective resolution of conflicts.

Bennett gives the example of a labour dispute, where the unions and management look at the industrial relations bargaining situation from completely different points of view. Management assumes that the natural state of affairs is one in which there is no inherent conflict of interest between the different individuals, groups or collectivities that constitute the industry. It assumes that they possess shared goals, and that a united and disciplined workforce expends their collective efforts to achieving these. From this frame of reference, co-operation is the norm, and all dissent is seen as unreasonable. Senior management cannot conceive how or why their authority might be challenged or why employees might engage in disruptive behaviour. In contrast, labour assumes differing and conflicting demands. It sees profits as something to be fought over with senior management and company shareholders. From labour's frame of reference, each party seeks legitimately to maximize its own rewards. Industrial action aims to maximize the revenues going to labour, and is explainable in these terms.

The literature distinguishes four different frames of reference on conflict, based on the distinctions made by Alan Fox. They are labelled *unitarist, pluralist, interactionist* and *radical* (Fox, 1966, 1973). In this section, the first three will be introduced and contrasted, while the fourth, the radical, will be subjected to a more detailed analysis in its own section later. These frames are neither 'right' nor 'wrong', only different.

- *unitarist*: sees organizations as essentially harmonious and any conflict as bad;
- *pluralist*: sees organizations as a collection of groups, each with their own interests;
- *interactionist*: sees conflict as a positive, necessary force for effective performance;
- *radical*: sees conflict as an inevitable outcome of capitalism.

Moreover, academics will also adopt one of these frames when they teach the topic to their students or research it. Neither organization employees nor academics will necessarily make their chosen frame explicit, and hence students need to ask or deduce which conflict frame of reference the person holds.

Pronoun test

Robert Reich, described the 'pronoun test' that he used to evaluate the nature of the employment relationship in the companies that he visited as US Secretary of Labour during the first Clinton Administration, in the following way:

'I'd say, "Tell me about the company". If the person said "we" or "us", I knew people were strongly attached to the organization. If they said "they" or "them", I knew there was less of a sense of linkage.'

Cited in Rousseau (1999).

Most of us are capable of bringing different frames of reference to bear on the situations that we face. It we analyze it this way, we reach these conclusions, but if we analyze it from another perspective, we reach different conclusions. Some people (students, academics, managers) *may* be wedded to a particular perspective. This becomes obvious in their conversations, actions or writings. Their chosen frame of reference on conflict will determine:

- what they will notice in their environment;
- how they will interpret those noticed events;
- how they expect others to behave;
- how they will behave themselves.

However, there is value in being able to view conflicts from a number of different standpoints, to 'switch between frames', in part, so that we can understand the viewpoints of others.

Unitarist frame of reference on conflict
a perspective that regards management and employee interests as coinciding and which thus regards (organizational) conflict as harmful and to be avoided.

The **unitarist frame of reference on conflict** views organizations as fundamentally harmonious, co-operative structures, consisting of committed, loyal, worker–management teams that promote harmony of purpose.

Stephen Ackroyd and Paul Thompson (1999) and Johnston (2000) identified the key features of the unitarist or unitary frame of reference:

1. Assumes a commonality of interests between an organization's workers and managers and, by implication, the company's owners (shareholders).
2. Accepts unquestioningly the political, economic and social framework within which management is performed, and adopts the language, assumptions and goals of management itself, which it supposedly seeks to study and understand.

3. De-politizes the relationships between individuals, groups and classes within the workplace; treating conflicts and contradictions as peripheral.

4. Explains actual, observed instances of workplace conflict in terms of either a failure of co-ordination problems, or psychological terms (the personal malfunction or abnormal behaviour of deviant individuals).

5. Applies a liberal-humanistic, individually focused approach to conflict resolution, which is rooted in the human relations movement and its developments.

6. Holds that managers are capable of permanently changing the behaviour of employees in a conflict situation in organization through the application of conflict resolution techniques.

7. Claims that economic, technological and political developments had, by the 1990s, meant that management had virtually eliminated non-sanctioned employee behaviour within the organization.

8. Moves rapidly over the consideration of causes of conflict within the workplace, in order to focus on conflict resolution techniques.

9. Uses communication failures between management and employees (and the interference of 'third party agitators', normally unions) to explain workplace conflict.

Pluralist frame of reference on conflict
a perspective that views organizations as consisting of different, natural interest groups, each with their own potentially constructive, legitimate interests, which makes conflict between them inevitable.

The **pluralist frame of reference on conflict** views organizations as a collection of many separate groups, each of which has their own legitimate interests, thereby making conflict between them inevitable as each attempts to pursue its own objectives. This frame of reference therefore rejects the view that individual employees have the same interests as the management, or that an organization is one big happy family.

The pluralist frame takes a political orientation in that it sees that some of the time, the interests of the different groups will coincide, while at other times, they will clash and so cause conflict between them. The outbreak of conflict provides a 'relationship regulation' mechanism between the different groups. That is, it provides a clear sign to both parties as to which issues they disagree fundamentally about, and thus provides a sort of 'early warning system' of possible impending breakdown which would be to the disadvantage of all concerned. The most common clashes may be between unions and management, but will also include differences between management functions (production versus marketing); levels of management (senior management v. middle management); and between individual managers.

These differences do not prevent an organization from functioning since all groups recognize that compromise and negotiation are essential if they are to achieve their goals even partially. Hence, from this perspective, the job of management becomes that of keeping the balance between potentially conflicting goals, and managing the differences between these different interest groups. This involves seeking a compromise between the different constituents such as the employees, managers, shareholders, and others, so that all these stakeholders, to varying degrees, can continue to pursue their aspirations. Underlying the pluralist view is the belief that conflict can be resolved through compromise to the benefit of all. However, it requires all parties to limit their claims to a level which is at least tolerable to the others, and which allows further collaboration to continue. A mutual survival strategy is agreed.

Acceptance of the pluralist frame implies that conflict is inevitable, indeed endemic. However, it does not see conflict as harmful and to be eliminated, but believes that it must be evaluated in terms of its functions and dysfunctions. For while it may reinforce the status quo, it can also assist evolutionary rather than revolutionary change, acting as a safety valve, and keep the organization responsive to internal and external changes while retaining intact its essential elements such as the organizational hierarchy and the power distribution. The inevitable conflict which results has to be managed so that organizational goals are reconciled with group interests for the benefit of mutual survival and prosperity. This on-going internal struggle is seen as generally acting to maintain the vitality, responsiveness and efficiency of the organization.

Interactionist frame of reference on conflict a perspective that views conflict as a positive and necessary force within organizations that is essential for their effective performance.

Functional conflict a form of conflict which supports organization goals and improves performance.

Dysfunctional conflict a form of conflict which does not support organization goals and hinders organizational performance.

The **interactionist frame of reference on conflict** views it as a positive force within organizations that is necessary for effective performance. It can be considered as part of the pluralist tradition. It accepts the inevitability of conflict and argues that, to be dealt with constructively, conflict has to be institutionalized within the organization through systems of collective bargaining. The interactionist frame not only accepts the inevitability of conflict, but also contains the notion that there is an optimum level of it (not too little or too much), and that the way to achieve that level is through the intervention of the manager.

The interactionist frame believes that conflict should be encouraged whenever it emerges, and stimulated if it is absent. It sees a group or a department that is too peaceful, harmonious and co-operative as potentially apathetic and unresponsive to changing needs. It fears that extreme group cohesion can lead to groupthink, as identified by Irving Janis (1982) and Cosier and Schwenk (1990). This frame therefore encourages managers to maintain a minimum level of conflict within their organizations so to as to encourage self-criticism, change and innovation and thereby counter apathy. However, that conflict has to be of the appropriate type. Thus, **functional conflict** supports organization goals and improves performance, but **dysfunctional conflict** hinders organizational performance.

The relationship between the two is depicted on a bell-shaped curve shown in Figure 21.1. Insufficient conflict, and the unit or group does not perform at its best; too much conflict and its performance deteriorates. Performance improvements occur through conflict exposing weaknesses in organizational decision-making and design which prompts changes in the company.

Condition	1	2	3
Conflict level	Too little	Optimal	Too great
Organizational performance (High ↑ / Low ↓)	Low ←	Level of conflict	→ High
Organizational performance level	Low	High	Low
Organization's internal characteristics	• Apathy • Stagnation • Poor focus • Unmotivated • Few changes • Slow to adapt • Not integrated • Few new ideas	• Cohesive • Productive • Co-operation • Organizational goal focused • Innovative and changing • Solution searching • Creatively adapting to environment	• Chaotic • Disruptive • Distracted • Politicized • Uncooperative • Hostile to other groups
Probable impact on organization	Dysfunctional	Functional	Dysfunctional
Managerial action required	Stimulate conflict	Leave alone	Reduce conflict

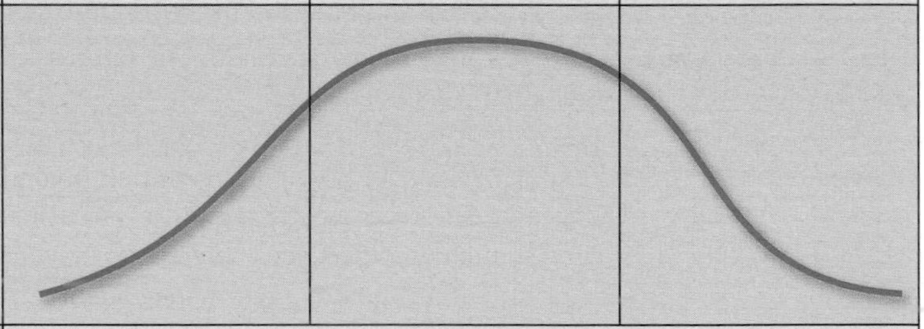

Figure 21.1: Types of conflict, internal organizational characteristics and required management actions

Source: Based on Hatch (1997, p.305); Robbins (1998, p.464).

Figure 21.1 is also sometimes referred to as the contingency model of conflict because it recommends that managers should increase or decrease the amount of conflict in their organizations depending on the situation (Hatch, 1997, p.304: Hatch with Cunliffe, 2006). Thus for example, in condition one there is too little conflict, and so they need to stimulate more. In contrast, in condition three, there is too much conflict and they need to reduce it. In both cases they seek to achieve an optimum level of conflict depicted in column two. Taffinder (1998) felt that at optimal intensity (condition two in Figure 21.1), conflict produced organizational benefits which managers rarely exploited and even suppressed by applying conflict resolution approaches too rapidly. Amongst the benefits of functional conflict that he listed were:

- Motivating energy to deal with underlying problems.
- Making underlying issues explicit.
- Sharpening people's understanding of real goals and interests.
- Enhancing mutual understanding between different groups of employees.
- Stimulating a sense of urgency.
- Discouraging engagement in avoidance behaviour.
- Preventing premature and often dangerous resolution problems.

Co-ordination failure and conflict

The process of organizing by senior managers acts to differentiate activities, and an outbreak of conflict can thus be seen as a symptom of management's failure to adequately co-ordinate these same activities later on. The co-ordination–conflict four-stage model organizes the diverse theoretical discussions and research findings into a framework that explains how conflict in organizations arises and how it might be managed (Figure 21.2). Such management may involve either the use of conflict resolution approaches (to reduce or eradicate conflict) or conflict stimulation approaches (to encourage and increase conflict).

Organizing

The first stage of the model consists of organizing, defined as the process of breaking up of a single task, and dividing it among different departments, groups or individuals. For example, a car company allocates the work involved in building a new vehicle to its different subdivisions (departments, groups and individuals) – personnel, accounting, production, sales and research. Such functional specialization is one of many bases on which to divide the total work involved. Specialization is rational because it concentrates specialists in proper departments, avoids duplication, allows performance goals to be established and specifies practices.

All forms of horizontal specialization result in each subunit becoming concerned with its own particular part of the total objective and work process. The degree of such separation of tasks can vary, but it creates the conditions in which conflict can potentially arise. It does so because, by definition, each department, group or individual receives a different part of the whole task to perform. This makes it distinct from the other departments on six different areas:

1. Goals orientation and evaluation
2. Self-image and stereotypes
3. Task interdependencies
4. Time perspective
5. Overlapping authority
6. Scarce resources

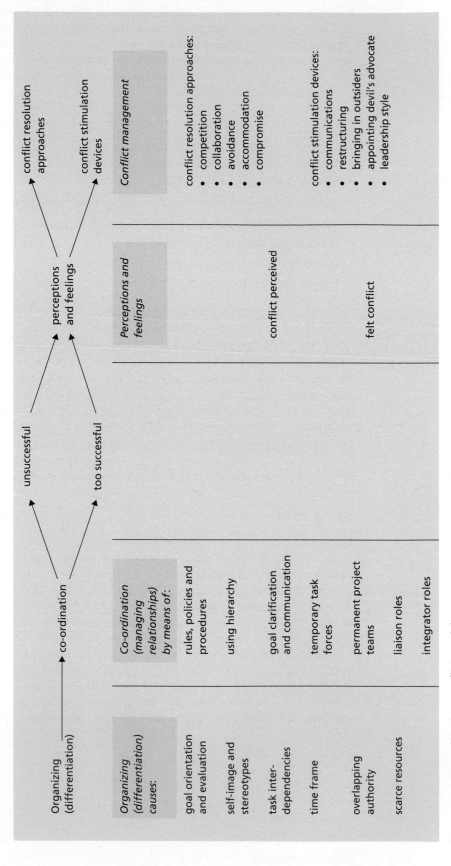

Figure 21.2: Co-ordination–conflict model

1. Goals orientation and evaluation

Each department is given its own goal, and its members are evaluated on the extent to which they achieve it. Ideally, the goals of different departments, groups and individuals, although different should be complementary, but in practice this may not be so. Moreover, the measurement process can reinforce differences. Each department's unique goals and evaluation methods lead it to have its own view about company priorities, and how these are best achieved.

2. Self-image and stereotypes

Employees in each department become socialized into a particular perception of themselves and seeing the other departments in the company. A group may come to see itself as more vital to a company's operations than others, and comes to believe that it has higher status or prestige. Such an evaluation can engender an 'us-and-them' attitude. The higher status groups may cease to adapt their behaviours to accommodate the goals of other groups, and indeed, may try to achieve their objectives at the cost of others, thus creating conflict. Whenever differences between groups and departments are emphasized, stereotypes are reinforced, relations deteriorate, and conflict develops. Departments will often blame each other for problems and shortcomings (see Table 21.1).

3. Task interdependencies

The process of organizing results in differentiation, makes individuals, groups and departments, dependent on each other to perform satisfactorily their own jobs and achieve their objectives. The degree of such interdependence varies. An earlier chapter considered James Thompson's (1967) three types of interdependence – *pooled*, *sequential* and *reciprocal*. Groups in sequential interdependence, and even more, in reciprocal interdependence, required a high degree of co-ordination between their activities. If this was achieved, then each group would perform effectively and its members would experience satisfaction. When such co-ordination was absent, the result would be conflict between them. From this viewpoint, conflict results from a failure in co-ordination.

Table 21.1: Areas of potential goal conflict between marketing and manufacturing departments

Goal conflict	*Marketing* operating goal is customer satisfaction	versus	*Manufacturing* operating goal is production efficiency
conflict area	*typical comment*		*typical comment*
1 Breadth of product line	'Our customers demand variety'		'The product line is too broad – all we get are short, uneconomical runs'
2 New product introduction	'New products are our lifeblood'		'Unnecessary design changes are prohibitively expensive'
3 Production scheduling	'We need faster response. Our lead times are too long'		'We need realistic customer commitments that don't change like a wind direction'
4 Physical distribution	'Why don't we ever have the right merchandise in inventory?'		'We can't afford to keep huge inventories'
5 Quality	'Why can't we have reasonable quality at low cost?'		'Why must we always offer options that are too expensive and offer little customer utility?'

Source: Reprinted by permission of *Harvard Business Review*. Adapted exhibit on p.115 From "Can marketing and manufacturing coexist?" by Shapiro, B.S. 55 (September–October). Copyright © 1977 by the Harvard Business School Publishing Corporation, all rights reserved.

4. Time perspective

Paul Lawrence and Jay Lorsch's (1967) study found that people's perceptions of the importance accorded to different items, depended on the time frame that governed their work and their goal orientations. Groups with different perceptions would find it difficult to co-ordinate their activities, and this would result in greater inter-group conflict. This is partly because their time frames differ. These different goals are often incompatible, hindering communication, impeding co-ordination and encouraging conflict.

5. Overlapping authority

Demarcation disputes have always caused difficulties, and ambiguity over responsibility or authority is one example of this. Individuals or groups may be uncertain as to who is responsible for performing which tasks or duties; and who has to authority to direct whom. Each party may claim or reject responsibility, and the result can be conflict. Groups may fight for the control of a resource, while individual managers may attempt to seize one another's authority.

6. Scarce resources

Once a task is allocated to an individual, group or department, it is also allocated resources to achieve it. Since resources are finite, conflict can arise with respect to how personnel, money, space or equipment are shared out. From a win-lose perspective, one party's gain is another's loss. For this reason, conflicts often arise at times of budget cuts, reduced promotion opportunities, and no increase in salaries or wages.

Conflict in virtual teams

Virtual teams consist of geographically dispersed individuals who are assembled using a combination of telecommunication and information technologies for the purpose of accomplishing an organizational task. This definition forms the basis of Yuhyung Shin's study into what causes interpersonal conflict in them and how it can be resolved.

The four dimensions that distinguish these teams also constitute the sources of the conflict within them. First, the members of these teams have *spatial dispersion* and *temporal dispersion*. Being in different places and working at different times, members operate without face-to-face interaction or direct supervision. This makes it difficult for them to receive guidance, instruction or clarification of their tasks and roles from their supervisors or peers, compared to face-to-face members. The effect is that virtual team members experience task, role and responsibility ambiguity, all of which increase the chances of conflict. Second, *cultural dispersion*, the fact that virtual teams are more likely to consist of individuals from many different cultures with diverse backgrounds who have not met before, means that variations in values, personalities, work and communication styles, can all ignite conflict. For example, members from individualistic cultures will emphasize the needs, values and goals of the individual rather than of the group, while for those from collective cultures, the group will take precedence over the individual. The absence of face-to-face interaction makes it difficult to resolve the inevitable misunderstandings which lead to conflict. Third, there is the problem caused by *organizational dispersion*, the fact that a virtual team can consist of individuals working for different organizations. As their team forms and then disbands, there is little opportunity for group cohesiveness to develop. Individuals can find that their membership and

relationships within virtual teams can be temporary and tenuous with the result that they experience conflicts associated with identity issues.

The spatial, temporal, cultural and organizational dispersion of team members collectively acts to reduce the trust between them in a number of ways. The lack of traditional control through supervision, and little opportunity to see each other, means that individuals are reluctant to share information and ideas or to collaborate. This limited interaction and their diverse backgrounds, also means that individuals do not possess knowledge of each others' competences or past performances. All of these factors can trigger conflict. Workplace conflicts are usually resolved using negotiation, mediation, facilitation, arbitration or litigation. Shin goes on to recommend and describe how a virtual negotiation system and a virtual mediation system might work. Since more interpersonal conflict can be expected within virtual than face-to-face teams, she suggests that this should be anticipated, and that team members should be taught conflict resolution skills.

Based on Shin (2005); Kankanhalli et al. *(2007).*

STOP AND THINK   How complete is this list of conflict causes – goals orientation, self-image, interdependencies, time frame, overlapping authority and scare resources? Think of two conflict situations with which you have been involved in an organization. Do these causes satisfactorily account for your conflicts or would you wish to add other causes?

Co-ordinating

If organizing involved breaking up the task into bits, then co-ordinating is bringing the bits together again. Co-ordination involves ensuring that the previously divided tasks that were allocated between different departments, groups and individuals, are brought together in the right way and at the right time. Co-ordination entails synchronizing the different aspects of the work process. The three general classes of co-ordination devices are listed in Table 21.2.

Provided that the relationships between the differentiated departments, units, groups or individuals are successfully co-ordinated, then conflict will not occur. By effectively using inter-party co-ordination devices, a company can prevent conflict breaking out in the first place. The devices are designed to manage the relationships between the different individuals, groups, units and departments so that the reasons for conflict to arise are eliminated. It is only if and when these co-ordination devices fail, and conflict occurs, that conflict resolution techniques will be required. Organizations use seven devices to co-ordinate:

1. Rules, policies and procedures
2. Using hierarchy
3. Goal clarification and communication

Table 21.2: Devices for co-ordinating relationships in organizations classified by class

Class of co-ordination	Description	Device
Formal direction	Written guidelines and adjudication by senior staff	• Rules, policies and procedures • Using hierarchy
Mutual adjustment	Members carrying out the work adjust to each other	• Goal clarification and communication • Temporary task force • Permanent project team
Special liaison	Specially employed co-ordinators use consultation and communication	• Liaison roles • Integrator roles

Source: Adapted from *Managing Through Organization*, Hales, C., copyright 1993 Routledge, Reproduced by permission of Cengage Learning.

4. Temporary task forces

5. Permanent project teams

6. Liaison roles

7. Integrator roles

1. Rules, policies and procedures

All of these specify how one party is to interact with another. For example, a standardized operating procedure will specify when additional staff can be recruited to a department. Rules and procedures reduce the need for both interaction and information flow between parties. They are most useful when inter-party activities are known in advance; when they occur frequently enough to merit establishing rules and procedures to handle them; and when there is sufficient stability to make them relevant.

2. Using hierarchy

Co-ordination of different parties' activities is achieved efficiently, by referring any problems to a superior located higher in the organizational hierarchy. The supervisor uses their legitimate authority, based on their position in the hierarchy, to resolve a conflict. Team members unable to agree take the problem to their mutual boss (Grant, 2002). Resorting to hierarchy is only effective in the short term to provide solutions to specific, urgent problems.

3. Goal clarification and communication

By specifying and communicating its goals to the others in advance, each party knows what the other is attempting to do. At the individual level this may mean clear job descriptions, while at the departmental level, it could be a statements of objectives. Parties can meet to ensure that they do not compete or interfere with the goals of others. Such discussions reduce the chances of each party misperceiving the others' intentions.

4. Temporary task force

This involves representatives from several different departments coming together on a temporary basis, to form a task force. Once the specific problem they were created for is solved, the task force disbands, and members return to their usual duties and departments. During their membership, individuals come to understand the goals, values, attitudes and problems of their fellow members. This helps to resolve their differences effectively, especially if more than two parties are involved.

5. Permanent project team

For complex tasks, a project team may be established consisting of cross-functional members (e.g. from engineering, marketing, finance). This creates a matrix structure, since each individual retains a responsibility to the permanent team leader and to their functional department. This solution allows co-ordination to occur at the team level, thus improving communication and decision-making.

6. Liaison roles

If differences remain unresolved by senior management, then a liaison role may be created. It would be used most by departments between whom the potential for conflict was highest. The occupant of this role has to be well informed about the needs and technology of the units involved, be seen to be unbiased, and be interpersonally skilled. By holding meetings, supplying units with information, liaison personnel keep the employees in different sections in touch with each other.

7. Integrator roles

An individual or department may be dedicated to integrating the activities of several, highly conflicting departments, e.g. production, sales and research (Figure 21.3) A scientist with financial and sales experience may be recruited to occupy an integrating role. By having a 'foot in each camp', this person can assist the departments to co-ordinate their activities. The integrator checks that the departments' objectives complement each other, and that the output of one becomes the timely input to the other.

Perceptions and emotions

The conditions described in the previous stage can exist without igniting a conflict. Perception plays an important part. It is only if one party, individual, group or department, becomes aware of, or is adversely affected by them, and cares about the situation, that latent conflict turns into perceived conflict. It occurs only when one party realizes that another is thwarting its goals. It is at this stage that the conflict issue becomes defined, and 'what it is all about'

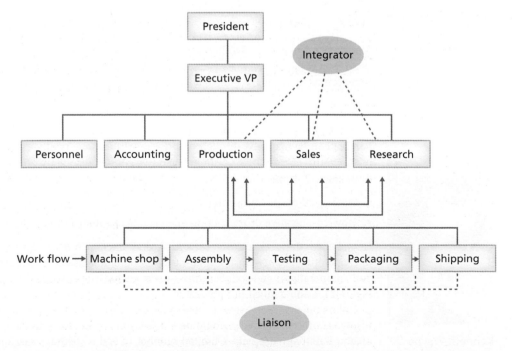

Figure 21.3: Co-ordinating using liaison and integrator roles

Home viewing

In the film, *Twelve Angry Men* (1957, director Sidney Lumet) a jury retires to decide on the guilt or innocence of a youth from a slum background. At the outset, 11 of the 12 jurors are convinced of the boy's guilt and are keen to find him guilty without further discussion. Only one member of the jury, played by Henry Fonda has reservations and persuades the other members to take the time to review the evidence. The film can be broken down into a series of 'conflict episodes', each of which ends with a vote (conflict reduction) or a juror's change of mind. The film illustrates many aspects of conflict. In each episode, ask yourself how do perceived and felt conflict manifest themselves in the characters' behaviour? How does each vote become the latent conflict for the next episode? Watch Fonda's behaviour carefully. At first sight it appears that it is random. But then you'll see a pattern. What is that pattern? Consider what types of power are possessed by the characters in the film? Finally, notice how the group's decisions are influenced by processional, contextual, social, emotional, temporal and behavioural factors.

gets decided. Specifically, each party considers the origins of the conflict, why it emerged, and how the problem is being experienced with the other party. The way that the conflict is defined at this stage will determine the type of outcomes that the parties are willing to settle for in the later stages. In American society, the issue of racism did not attain conflict status, until black people realized how severely it affected them.

Not only must a party perceive a conflict, but it must also feel it. That is, it must become emotionally involved in experiencing feelings of anxiety, tenseness, frustration and hostility towards the other party. The emotional dimension of conflict shapes perceptions. For example, negative emotions result in an oversimplification of issues, reductions in trust and negative interpretations of other parties' behaviour. Positive emotions, in contrast, increase the chances of the parties taking a broader view; seeing the issue as a problem to be solved; and developing more creative solutions.

Conflict resolution methods: negotiation, arbitration and mediation

Conflict resolution a process which has as its objective the ending of the conflict between the disagreeing parties.

Managers may judge the existing co-ordination devices to be inadequate, thereby causing conflict. They will therefore manage the situation by implementing conflict resolution approaches to reduce or eliminate the immediate conflict, before adjusting the co-ordination mechanism to prevent it occurring in the first place. Alternatively, they may consider that the co-ordination devices are working too well, thereby causing complacency and apathy. In this case, they may introduce conflict stimulation approaches to increase conflict. Thus, within organizations conflict can be managed through **conflict resolution** and conflict stimulation approaches.

Kenneth Thomas (1976) distinguished five conflict resolution approaches based upon the two dimensions of:

- How assertive or unassertive each party is in pursuing its own concerns.
- How co-operative or unco-operative each is in satisfying the concerns of the other.

Kenneth Wayne Thomas (b.1943)

He labelled these *competing* (assertive and uncooperative); *avoiding* (unassertive and uncooperative); *compromising* (mid-range on both dimensions); *accommodating* (unassertive and co-operative); and *collaborating* (assertive and co-operative). They are summarized in Figure 21.4 and defined in Table 21.3.

Unless the managers were flexible and capable of switching between styles, their ability to resolve conflicts effectively would be limited. In practice, all individuals, whether managers or not, habitually use only a limited number of styles (perhaps just one) to resolve all the conflicts in which they are involved. It is not surprising that their success is limited.

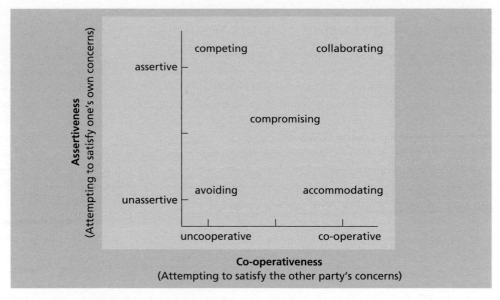

Figure 21.4: Conflict resolution approaches
Source: From Ruble and Thomas (1976, p.145).

Table 21.3: Conflict resolution approaches compared

approach	objective	your posture	supporting rationale	likely outcome
1. Competing	Get your way	'I know what's right. Don't question my judgement or authority'	It is better to risk causing a few hard feelings than to abandon the issue	You feel vindicated, but the other party feels defeated and possibly humiliated
2. Avoiding	Avoid having to deal with conflict	'I'm neutral on that issue. Let me think about it. That's someone else's problem'	Disagreements are inherently bad because they create tension	Interpersonal problems don't get resolved, causing long-term frustration manifested in a variety of ways
3. Compromising	Reach an agreement quickly	'Let's search for a solution we can both live with so we can get on with our work'	Prolonged conflicts distract people from their work and cause bitter feelings	Participants go for the expedient rather than effective solutions
4. Accommodating	Don't upset the other person	'How can I help you feel good about this? My position isn't so important that it is worth risking bad feelings between us'	Maintaining harmonious relationships should be our top priority	The other person is likely to take advantage
5. Collaborating	Solve the problem together	'This is my position, what's yours? I'm committed to finding the best possible solution. What do the facts suggest?'	Each position is important though not necessarily equally valid. Emphasis should be placed on the quality of the outcome and the fairness of the decision-making process	The problem is most likely to be resolved. Also both parties are committed to the solution and satisfied that they have been treated fairly

From Whetton et al. (2000, p.345).

Choosing and using conflict resolution styles

Neil Brewer and his colleagues examined the relationship between biological sex, gender role, organizational status and conflict resolution style of 118 males and females in three organizations. Males were highest on the competing (or dominating) conflict management styles; females were highest on the avoiding style; and androgynous individuals were highest on the collaborative (or integrating) style. Individuals from the upper (more senior) levels in the organization were higher on collaborative styles, and lower status individuals reported greater use of avoiding and accommodating styles. Friedman *et al.* argued that a person's chosen style can shape their work environment, affecting the level of on-going conflict and the stress that they experience. Their study of a clinical hospital department found that those using a collaborative (or integrative) style experienced lower levels of task conflict, reduced their relationship conflict and thereby their stress. Those who used a more competing or avoiding style experienced higher levels of task conflict, thereby increasing relationship conflict and their stress. They concluded that employees' work environments were, in part, of their own making.

Based on Brewer et al. *(2002) and*
Friedman et al. *(2000).*

STOP AND THINK   Some individuals resolve conflict in one fixed way in different situations. Others change their approach to suit the circumstances. Think about a specific domestic, friendship or organizational context that involved conflict. How did you deal with it? Did you compete, avoid, compromise, accommodate or collaborate?

Distributive bargaining a negotiation strategy in which a fixed sum of resources is divided up. It leads to a win–lose situation between the parties.

Richard Walton and Robert McKersie's (1965) research into negotiation behaviour distinguished distributive bargaining strategies from integrative bargaining strategies.

Distributive bargaining operates under zero sum conditions. It seeks to divide up a fixed amount of resources – a win–lose situation. Purchasing a new car exemplifies this. The more the buyer pays, the more profit the seller makes and vice versa. Here the pie is fixed, and the parties bargain about the share each receives. Within an organization, distributive bargaining takes place between the trade (labour) unions and management. Issues involving wages, benefits, working conditions and related matters are seen as a conflict over limited resources. Integrative bargaining is the type of bargaining that seeks one or more settlements that can create a win–win solution. A union–management agreement which increases productivity and profits, and wages in line with both, would be an example of integrated bargaining because the size of the total pie is increased. Integrative bargaining is preferable to distributive bargaining because the latter makes one party a loser. It can create animosities and deepens divisions between people who have to work together on an ongoing basis.

Integrative bargaining a negotiation strategy that seeks to increase the total amount of resources. It creates a win-win situation between the parties.

Studies have revealed similarities between conflict resolution strategies and negotiation strategies (Savage *et al.*, 1989; Smith, 1987). Of the five conflict resolution strategies described earlier, four of them (competing, avoiding, compromising and accommodating) involve one or more of the parties sacrificing something, and would therefore be classified as distributive. David Whetton and colleagues (1996) suggested that these distributive strategies matched the natural inclination of those individuals who approached conflicts with a 'macho man', 'easy touch' or 'split the difference' style, and they thereby engendered competition, exploitation or irresponsibility. Over the last two decades, the major developers of the integrative bargaining concept have been Roger Fisher and William Ury (1981) from the Harvard Negotiating Project. Their scheme of 'principled negotiation' sets out guiding principles to apply when preparing and engaging in face to face negotiations. More recent work in this project has dealt with how negotiators should proceed if the other side does not 'play the game' (Ury, 1991; Ury and Patton, 1997).

Arbitration a process in which a third party to a conflict has the authority to impose an agreement that is binding on the parties in conflict.

If two parties, such as a union and an employer or two companies cannot agree a matter, and do not wish to take the matter to court to be resolved by litigation, they can choose to go to arbitration. This may occur if negotiations between unions and management have

Table 21.4: Bargaining strategies

Integrative bargaining Win–win strategy	Distributive bargaining Win–lose strategy
1. Define the conflict as a mutual problem	1. Define the conflict as a win–lose situation
2. Pursue joint outcomes	2. Pursue own group's outcomes
3. Find creative agreements that satisfy both groups	3. Force the other group into submission
4. Use open, honest and accurate communication of group's needs, goals and proposals	4. Use deceitful, inaccurate and misleading communication of group's needs, goals and proposals
5. Avoid threats (to reduce the other's defensiveness)	5. Use threats (to force submission)
6. Communicate flexibility of position	6. Communicate high commitment (rigidity) regarding one's position

After Johnson and Johnson, JOINING TOGETHER, pp.182–183, © 1975. Reproduced by permission of Pearson Education, Inc.

reached an impasse; if a grievance is presented and the arbiter listens to both sides. In this process, the dispute is referred to a third party who is given the power to formulate a settlement that is binding on both parties. This is similar to a judge in a courtroom. Arbitration may be voluntary or compulsory; the former occurs when both parties involved have the choice of whether or not to have a decision imposed on them. Compulsory arbitration, perhaps due to government regulations, denies them that choice.

Mediation a process in which a neutral third party to the conflict assists in the achievement of a negotiated solution by using reason, persuasion and the presentation of alternatives.

Alternatively, the two parties can choose **mediation**. This involves bringing in a third party in order to help the two sides resolve the dispute. In a negotiation situation, the behaviour and feelings of the parties can become sharply polarized, and each becomes isolated from the other. When this happens, a mediator can maintain contact and communication between the parties in dispute. In hostage-taking situations and local wars, independent third parties are often brought in to act as mediators. They do not control the agreement, but influence the conflict resolution process, helping the two sides to come to an agreement. They guide the two parties to discover the solution to their problem. With increasing numbers of cases log-jammed in the courts, the frequency and importance of mediation is increasing (*Harvard Business Review*, 2000).

Mediation: knocking heads together

Organizations seeking to resolve disputes through the courts often find the process both time-consuming and expensive. The Bank of Credit and Commerce International's lawsuit against the Bank of England lasted 13 years and cost £100m in legal fees. Hence, instead of litigation, many companies initially turn to arbitration, especially in commercial cross-border disputes. However, arbitration has not necessarily proved to be cheaper, fairer or quicker. In the US, the time between filing a complaint and getting a decision was an average of 16.7 months. For these reasons, out-of-court, alternative dispute resolution (ADR) procedures, such as mediation, have become increasingly popular. Had the BCCI and Bank of England agreed to mediation, it would have probably taken a day to resolve the matter and cost a few thousand pounds. The London-based Centre for Effective Dispute Resolution (CEDR) is one of European's largest mediation bodies. Of the 3,000 commercial disputes that are subject to its mediation process annually, 70–80 per cent are resolved in one or two days, while 10–15 per cent are settled within weeks.

Whereas arbitration mimics a courtroom setting with lawyers on both sides and a neutral decision-maker; mediation is more akin to counselling or bargaining, with

→

the parties encouraged to talk to each other and strike a deal. Here the mediator's task is not to judge the outcome but to prompt the discussion. There has been a global interest in mediation among countries with diverse legal traditions such as France, Russia, Cameroon, Saudi Arabia, Japan, Bangladesh and China. As a way of solving disputes, mediation has been found to be swifter, cheaper and more flexible; it causes less damage to long-term relationships; and is safer in countries where judicial corruption is common.

Based on The Economist *(2007h).*

Mediation techniques include asking each party to state the problem; to state the other's view of the problem; and to ask it to confirm the accuracy of the other's repetition. Once the initial positions have been presented and understood, alternative solutions are generated using brainstorming. The use of recesses in the mediating process is valuable. These can help calm the parties after an emotional encounter; be used to conduct private enquiries about interests; and can help to de-escalate conflict.

Interactionists argue that there are conditions in organizations when what is needed is more and not less conflict, i.e. **conflict stimulation** (Sternberg and Soriano, 1984; Robbins, 1974). John Kotter (1996) discussed the dangers of complacency, and the need to drive employees out of their comfort zones. Amongst the complacency-smashing and potentially conflict-stimulating techniques used by senior management were the following:

Conflict stimulation the process of engendering conflict between parties where none existed before, or escalating the current conflict level if it is too low.

- Create a crisis by allowing a financial loss to occur or an error to blow up.
- Eliminate obvious examples of excess like corporate jet fleets and gourmet dining rooms.
- Set targets like income, productivity and cycle times so high that they can't be reached by doing business as usual.
- Share more information about customer satisfaction and financial performance with employees.
- Insist that people speak regularly to dissatisfied customers, unhappy suppliers and disgruntled shareholders.
- Put more honest discussions of the firm's problems in company newspapers and management speeches. Stop senior management's 'happy talk'.

Various techniques can be used to stimulate conflict, where none existed before, in order to encourage different opinions, and engender new thinking and problem-solving.

1. *Communications*

Managers can withhold information 'to keep them guessing' or send large amounts of inconsistent information ('we're expanding, we're going bust) to get people arguing. They might send ambiguous or threatening messages.

2. *Re-structuring a company*

Re-aligning working groups and altering rules and regulations, so as to increase or create interdependence between previously independent units. This can easily stimulate conflict, particularly if the goals of the newly interdependent departments are made incompatible, e.g. one department's objective being to minimize costs, the other's to maximize market share.

3. *Bringing in outsiders*

Adding individuals to a group whose backgrounds, values, attitudes or management styles differ from those of existing members. For example, recruiting senior executives with a career experience in automobile manufacture to manage health care organizations.

4. Devil's advocate method

Within an organization, a person is assigned the role of critic, to stimulate critical thinking and reality testing. For example, in deciding to embark on an e-commerce strategy, one team member might be assigned the devil's advocate role to focus on its pitfalls and dangers.

5. Dialectic method

This method explores opposite positions called 'thesis' and' antithesis'. The outcome of the debate between the two is the 'synthesis' which in turn, becomes the new thesis to be opened up for debate. Before deciding on a take-over, a company may establish two or more teams, give them access to the same information, and give them the task to argue for and against the acquisition decision. The conflict of ideas throws up alternatives, which can be synthesized into a superior, final decision.

6. Leadership style

Organizations can appoint managers who encourage non-traditional viewpoints, rather than authoritarian ones who might be inclined to suppress opposing viewpoints. Leadership style has been found to be a key element in organization change programmes, and in particular those involving changes in organization culture.

The radical frame of reference

Radical frame of reference on conflict a perspective that views organizational conflict as an inevitable consequence of exploitative employment relations in a capitalist economy.

Newspapers and human resource management magazines regularly carry accounts of company problems such as sexual harassment, racial harassment, theft and pilferage, bullying, organizational romance, sabotage and strikes. These are all examples of human behaviour in organizations, yet the previous unitarist, pluralist and interactionist frames of reference on conflict have difficulty in explaining such actions. Indeed, it is only the radical frame of reference on conflict that draws attention to such behaviour in organizations. The other conflict perspectives may recognize but then ignore them. In contrast, the radical frame sees the workplace as an arena of conflict between managers (in their role as agents of the owners) who are the controllers of the means of production, and who exploit the employees. It holds that the logic of profit maximization involves managers relentlessly driving down the costs of production and controlling the manufacturing process. As conflict is an endemic property of capitalist employment relations, it cannot be resolved by any 'techniques'.

Bossnapping in France

The global recession has resulted in factory closures and job losses. In France, after two decades, the 'sequestration' or temporary kidnapping of executives has come back into fashion with charges of 'hostage-taking' and 'industrial terrorism' being levelled at workers. Francois-Henri Pinault, the boss of Christie's, Printemps and FNAC, was ambushed in a taxi in the 15 arrondissement in Paris, and held for an hour while negotiating with 50 angry employees who had blocked the street. He was finally freed by police. Nicholas Polutnik, director of the Caterpillar's bulldozer plant in Grenoble and three of his management team, were forced to spend the night in their offices. The firm planned to cut 700 jobs in France. Additionally, Serge Foucher, head of Sony France was held for a short time, while at 3M's pharmaceutical factory in Pithiviers, south of Paris, the head of its French operations, Luc Rousselet was shut in his office by 20 workers. All these events, triggered by the recession, have brought into sharp focus the different circumstances and interests of different groups. Reports of job losses for workers have been juxtaposed in the media with constant news of bonuses and 'golden parachutes' for failed bosses and the government's introduction of tax concessions for the wealthy. The banners of the protestors who trapped M. Pinault in his taxi read 'Shareholders get Euros 420m, FNAC employee lose 400 jobs'.

Based on Lichfield (2009).

Table 21.5: Employee survival strategies

Survival Strategy	Definition	Objectives	Examples	Interpreted as a form of consent	Interpreted as a form of resistance
Making out	Elaborate system of informal employee behaviour that regulates work processes and ensures targets are met, yet allows workers to reassert some control of their working day	Economic gain Fatigue reduction Time passing Boredom relief Social and psychological rewards Avoiding social stigma	Refuse collection staff 'totting' – searching through rubbish bins for valuables to keep or sell. Shop floor workers manipulating their piece-rate payment schemes	Acts of 'game playing' within the organization's rules which result in mutual benefit for employees and managers	Acts that undermine management control by bending the rules to satisfy the self-interest of employees
Fiddling	Illegitimately acquiring company products, services or time for personal use	Economic gain Proving interest and excitement Expressing frustration or resentment	Stealing office supplies, inflating expense claims, personal phone calls from work, 'cyber-loafing'; Supermarket staff 'grazing' – consuming crisps, sweets	'Deserved' perks that help subsidize wages and confer status on employees	Theft that affects profitability and undermines the integrity of everyone in the organization
Joking	A permitted or required interaction in which one party makes fun of the other, who in turn, is required to take no offence	Maintaining social order Releasing frustration and tension Challenging authority Forging group identities Alleviating work monotony	Joke telling Banter Playful insults Teasing (permitted disrespect) Practical jokes, initiation rituals	Forms of group regulation that preserve the status quo and provide a way of letting off steam	Challenges to management authority that undermine the status and policies of managers and make them appear foolish
Sabotage	An intentional, malicious attempt to disrupt or destroy a work process or a product	Way of expressing temporary frustration with work process, rules, managers or any other aspect of the organization Way of asserting control over the work process	Spreading computer viruses Reporting company malpractices to the press Being intentionally rude to customers Disabling a photocopier	(a) Expressions of frustration or irresponsible behaviour (letting off steam) (b) Well-meaning actions that have unintended negative consequences	(a) Malicious acts against property and people, intended to 'get even' with the organization (b) Well-meaning actions intended to 'expose' the organization (whistleblowing)
Escaping	Removing oneself temporarily or permanently from one's work tasks	Coping with boredom	Physical withdrawal through late-coming, absenteeism or resignation; mental withdrawal through dreaming, 'going robotic', cynical distancing from company values	Acts of withdrawal that result in employees accepting the status quo, even though they disagree with management policy or objectives	Acts that result in withdrawal of goodwill or mental and physical effort, thereby reducing organizational performance and undermining management objectives

Based on Noon and Blyton (2007, p.272).

Organizational misbehaviour anything that workers do in the workplace which management considers they should not do.

Stephen Ackroyd and Paul Thompson (1999) explained that management establishes a boundary that distinguishes employee behaviour that is and is not acceptable. Employee actions are then defined as falling on one or other side of that boundary. The authors use the term, organizational misbehaviour, to refer to anything that workers do in the workplace which management considers they should not do.

Although much of the literature refers to 'conflict' in organizations, in reality, overt conflict is actually very rare. Thus, for Richard Edwards (1979) the struggle between capital and labour is the main dynamic which shapes the employment relationship. He refers to *structural antagonisms* rather than to conflict, and sees these as arising from the clash over the distribution of the surplus. Carter Goodrich (1975) wrote about the 'frontiers of control' and the notion of *resistance*. Management's attempt to exert control is met by employee resistance, and that produces clashes over interests. The notion of resistance carries with it the connotation of something: intermittent (occurring regularly but not continually), changing (frontier being pushed forward and back), and occurring below the surface. This is in contrast to conflict, with its connotations of a single, visible, explosion (Jermier *et al.*, 1994; Sagie *et al.*, 2004).

Resistance more or less covert behaviour that counteracts and restricts management attempts to exercise power and control in the workplace.

Alienation feelings of powerlessness, meaninglessness, isolation and self-estrangement engendered within employees by the design of the jobs that they perform.

The concept of resistance has an application at all levels of the organizational hierarchy, from shop floor employees developing ways of combating alienation through informal processes and actions; through professionals like engineers, academics or hospital doctors resisting management directions; right up to senior management resisting the control exercised by the board of directors. It also allows a consideration of how that resistance moves to different areas within the organization; and how the parties acquire and relinquish different types of power, and gain and lose ascendancy over each other.

Noon and Blyton (2007) list five survival strategies that workers use to counter alienation (Table 21.5). They explain that each can be interpreted either as a form of employee consent or employee resistance by an outside observer; and that these strategies may be condoned and tolerated by management or judged to be unacceptable and punished. The authors also highlight the problem of interpreting the meaning of those engaging in these behaviours and their motivations. All this affects the nature and degree of conflict that may ensue between the workers and management.

Gripe sites and work bloggers – dissent on the internet

An increasing number of employees, and customers are choosing to express their anger and frustration with organizations by posting uncensored comments on the web. This can take several forms. First, there are the collective gripe or complaint sites such as VaultReports.com, where employees of many different companies – JP Morgan, Microsoft, Goldman Sachs – can make their views known. Second, there are the company-specific gripe sites such as the one for Shell, royaldutchshellplc.com, and others which can be accessed by entering the company name into a search engine, followed by the word 'sucks'. Third, there are the social network sites. Virgin Atlantic fired 13 of its employees who posted derogatory comments on a Facebook forum about the airline's safety standards (planes infested with cockroaches) and its customers (described as 'chavs' – people with flashy bad taste). A posting by BA staff on Facebook, which described their customers as 'smelly and annoying', was being investigated by the company. Typically, most comments are com-

plaints and cover issues relating to company practices, recruitment, pay and staff morale. The comments, which are made anonymously, are unsupported, and the company has no right of reply.

Managements are concerned about this form of dissent because the sites can be easily accessed by the public; may attract media attention; can tarnish company image; and undermine employee morale. On the other hand, they provide management with feedback on matters that it needs to focus on. Customers have also used the internet, for example to force HSBC bank into a U-turn over graduate overdrafts after the National Union of Students campaign used Facebook to generate a massive protest. When many consumers complain and somebody hits a chord, a blog swarm occurs. Finally, there are the work bloggers. Joe Gordon, one time employee of the Waterstone's bookshop chain, was sacked for gross misconduct and bringing the company into disrepute after referring in his personal blog to his employer as

'Bastardstones', and to his manager as 'Evil Boss'. Empirical research by James Richards based on an analysis of 744 work blogs and a survey of 207 work bloggers showed blogging to be a new way for employees to express workplace conflict, resist the labour process and express dissent. While employers see these as a threat, Richards found that 'the vast majority of work blogs represent nothing more than employees posting honest accounts of the jobs they do and the places where they work on the internet' (p.100). He found that workblogs' contents consisted mainly of employees sharing experiences of their jobs over time; educating and influencing others about their profession; and expressing their enthusiasm for or venting their frustrations about work. Only two of Richards' 207 bloggers claimed to blog as an act of outright defiance. The study suggests that work blogging is a creative way of coping with, rather than resisting work, and that cyberspace has become the latest meeting point for powerless and rudderless labour.

Based Brimelow (2005); Donkin (2008); Garside (2007); Richards (2008); The Economist (2008)

STOP AND THINK   Which of Noon and Blyton's employee survival strategies – making out, fiddling, joking, sabotage, escaping – have you personally engaged in at work? Have you observed other employees engaging in any of these behaviours?

Edwards (1979) noted that the perpetual struggle for control in organizations is not always constant, obvious or visible. Because employees' tactics of resistance are often covert some knowledge of a particular organizational context is required for researchers (and indeed for managers) to become fully aware of what is going on. Resistance, as opposed to conflict, in the workplace is reflected in 'soldiering' (output restriction); pilferage; absenteeism; sabotage; vandalism; practical joking; and sexual misconduct. Reviewing the managerial and academic literature on the presence and absence of such misbehaviour at work, Ackroyd and Thompson (1999) concluded that typically it:

- Provided sanitized accounts of employee behaviour that depicted employees as invariably constructive, conforming and dutiful.

- Saw employees' behaviour as being orderly, purposeful and directed towards the attainment of organizational (managerial) goals.

- Defined 'normal' employee behaviour as that which was programmed by management ('pro-social) and which complied with managerial norms and values; and treated employees' deviations from those (management-) expected standards of behaviour, as *mis*behaviour.

- Assumed that when there was a lack of correspondence between management direction and the employees' response to it (i.e. occurrence of misbehaviour), what needed to change was the latter.

Four perspectives within the radical frame of reference

David Collinson and Stephen Ackroyd (2005) distinguish four contemporary perspectives on organizational misbehaviour and resistance which explain employee behaviours such as those listed above, which have 'an oppositional or subversive intent or effect within the workplace' (p.305). This section draws heavily on their framework.

- Managerialist organizational behaviour perspective
- Labour process theory perspective
- Post-structuralism perspective
- Feminist studies perspective

Managerialist/organizational behaviour perspective

This perspective is held by American OB academics who share the values of managers and identify with their organizations and problems. The objective is to secure employee obedience and compliance. Originally it was assumed that if workers were treated reasonably, they would act responsibly. However, incidents of workplace aggression and violence led those within this tradition to see employee misbehaviour as unprincipled and even dangerous. To explain employees' actions, these writers use concepts such as resistance, revenge, workplace deviance, and antisocial, dysfunctional and counterproductive behaviour. They see such employee actions as harmful for organizations. They seek to help managers identify acceptable behaviour and aid them in imposing appropriate sanctions (Ackroyd and Thompson, 1999; Hollway, 1991).

Labour process theory perspective

Labour process the work that employees perform, the conditions in which they do it, and the social relations that they engage in while doing it.

The labour process refers to the social relations that employees engage in at work, the work that they perform, and the conditions in which they do it. The labour process theory offers a Marxist analysis that is discussed in terms of Harry Braverman's 'degradation of work' thesis. It stresses conflict and contradiction. The main features of the labour process theory are that:

1. It rejects the notion of a correspondence of interests between managers (as agents of the owners), and workers (labour) within capitalist organizations. It sees conflict rather than consensus as the fundamental and central dynamic in organizational life.

2. It sees the workplace as a 'contested terrain' (Edwards, 1979) where employees, individually and collectively, seek to protect and extend their own interests in production process, and resist management's attempts to change working conditions to extract profit from labour.

3. It highlights the contradictions of management behaviour: treating the workforce as the company's 'most important asset' and seeking its commitment while, simultaneously, treating it as dispensable through redundancy, delayering and plant closure. Encouraging staff involvement and creativity on the one hand, while rejecting increased employee discretion in decision-making (empowerment); and seeking to manufacture consent, while exercising coercion.

4. It holds that the degree to which managers can alter employee behaviour has been exaggerated. Ackroyd and Thompson (1999) distinguish between *tractability*, which refers to management's capacity to induce, through its actions, marginal, temporary changes in employee behaviour; and *corrigibility*, the permanent 'correction' of behaviour to conform with management expectations. They say that employee behaviour may be tractable, but that it is rarely corrigible.

5. It challenges taken-for granted assumptions by asking questions such as: why do managers have to:

   * motivate employees (why are employees not already motivated)?
   * overcome employees' resistance to change (what do employees fear)?
   * create a 'strong' organization culture to gain employees' commitment (why are employees not already committed to their companies)?
   * manage conflict with employees (what are employees resisting)?

6. Given that management control can never be complete, it examines the opportunities for different forms of worker resistance.

7. It explains actual, observed instances of workplace conflict in terms of differences of interests, power, politics, domination, control, etc.; and also in economic terms, focusing on capital maximization and profit distribution.

Post-structuralism perspective

This perspective on organizational misbehaviour and resistance focuses on how employees' behaviour is controlled by management's monitoring of them. It stresses surveillance and draws upon Michel Foucault's (1979) ideas on discipline (see Chapter 22). Popular, contemporary techniques of surveillance include monitoring employees' use of computers; recording their telephone conversations; videotaping work areas; issuing them with smart cards to enter and exit work areas; and implanting chips under their skins to locate them geographically (Gurchiek, 2006). More traditional surveillance techniques include setting performance targets which are linked appraisal and reward systems. According to Foucault, the use of such management power produces resistance as employees defy management's attempts to control their behaviour. Post-structuralists recommend that employee resistance be examined in terms of its causes – what gave rise to it; its process – what are the motives, meanings and practices of these involved); and its consequences – what is the effect on those involved and the organization (Collinson, 2003; Jermier *et al.*, 1994).

Feminist studies perspective

Studies within this perspective focus on gender and sexuality (see Chapter 15). Fleming and Spicer (2007) observe that organizations are considered formally desexualized spheres in which management have historically attempted to expunge erotic and romantic relations. They wrote that the issue of sexuality and its relationship to conflict has received little attention in the studies of work. They consider how sexuality has important implications for relations of power and resistance between employees and managers and between employees themselves; and they discuss the claim that sex is promoted in some workplaces as a method of management control. Traditional workplaces are now recognized as having an important sexual component, and sexuality widely imbues organizational life. Mainstream organizational behaviour research has typically ignored sex and work. However, as Rosemary Pringle (1989, p.162) noted:

> Far from being marginal to the workplace, sexuality is everywhere. It is alluded to in dress and presentation, in jokes and gossip, looks and flirtations, secret affairs and dalliances, in fantasy, and in the range of coercive behaviours that we now call sexual harassment.

However, since Gibson Burrell's (1984) analysis, research on the topic, where it exists, has been discussed in terms of power, control and resistance. Wal-Mart's attempt to ban work romances in Germany illustrates this (see Chapter 4, Culture). One manifestation of resistance in the workplace that has received a great deal of attention relates to the varying reaction of employees to what is called emotional labour. It is to this topic that we turn in the next section.

STOP AND THINK   Empirical research from within the radical perspective, utilizing one of the four perspectives described above, is now rare. Most studies discussed are ten and more years old. Why may there be reluctance by social scientists to investigate this type of human behaviour in organizations?

Conflict in cyberspace

The internet allows expressions of discontent to be aggregated, thereby giving workers the opportunity to stage protests without actually going on strike. A dramatic example occurred on 27 September 2007 at IBM Italy. Employees of the computer giant staged a virtual protest against a new pay settlement at IBM's corporate campus in *Second Life*, an online virtual world. They logged on from home to avoid legal problems. The RSU, the official trade union representing IBM's workers asked for as many avatars as possible to man the picket lines.

Staff aimed to hit the company's virtual islands, as well as putting real life protesters on picket line duty outside its Italian facilities. These virtual islands are being heavily promoted by IBM as a new communication and service link with customers, as well as a vehicle for work activities. Disrupting some of them could have an impact. The union also hoped that this protest would prove attractive to its younger, computer-savvy members. There are no industrial relation laws in *Second Life*, so no chance of being arrested for secondary picketing. More than 1,850 people across 30 countries logged onto their computers to take part in the virtual industrial dispute. Within *Second Life*, they moved their avatars (virtual reality characters) to seven IBM locations to protest against the computer giant's real world activities. The British TUC (Trades Unions Congress) sent some avatars of its own to show solidarity. A month later, the head of IBM Italy and the RSU union agreed on a new pay deal with the company.

Based on The Economist *(2008o);* Personnel Today *(2007, 2 October, p.3).*

Emotional labour

As a student, have you worked in a bar, operated a checkout in a supermarket, or waited on tables in a restaurant, dealing with people face-to-face? What emotions did you experience when dealing with your customers – anger, fear, joy, love, sadness, surprise? Did you express those feelings to them at the time; or did you bite your tongue and say nothing; or did you suppress your emotions and act in the opposite way to which you felt? If you did either of the last two, then you performed emotional labour, which is the act of expressing organizationally required emotions during interactions with others at work. It involves expending psychological effort to keep in check both one's internal emotions and external behaviours.

Emotional labour the act of expressing organizationally required emotions during interactions with others at work.

Emotions intense, short-lived reactions that are linked to a specific cause and which interrupt thought processes and behaviours.

Emotions are intense, short-lived reactions that are linked to a specific cause and which interrupt thought processes and behaviours. Since an emotion cannot be directly seen, it is communicated verbally and non-verbally. Thus one's 'performance' of an emotion consists of 'a complex combination of facial expression, body language, spoken words and tone of voice' (Rafaeli and Sutton, 1987, p.33). Most work tasks involve two elements – physical labour and mental labour. The physical refers to walking, carrying, lifting, talking, and similar behaviours. The mental involves knowing, understanding, analysing, applying and evaluating people, things and situations. However, there are many jobs that now require a third kind of labour – emotional. Arlie Hochschild first coined the term, emotional labour, in her book, *The Managed Heart: Commercialization of Human Feeling*. In it, she discussed employees' management of their feelings to create publicly observable facial and bodily displays (Hochschild, 1983).

Arlie Russell Hochschild (b.1940)

As a result of the increasing similarity of the offerings provided to customers by different companies in the airline, fast food, financial services, tourism, hotel and call centre industries, some organizations have attempted to differentiate themselves from their competitors by the way that their employees deal with customers. Hochschild drew attention to the importance of social interaction in service provision. The emotional style of offering a service has not only become part of the service itself (Hochschild, 2003), but increasingly is now often more important than the service itself. The interactions between service providers and their customers have become the determining element in the latter's evaluation of satisfaction. In this way, the psychological aspects of service provision now take priority over the physical ones (Noon and Blyton, 2007). While Hochschild (2003) was concerned that emotion was being commodified through the 'commercialization of intimate life', other writers considered the harnessing of employees' emotional energy to improve customer service as a good thing (Kinnie *et al.*, 2000).

Historically, staff members have always been encouraged, in a general way, to provide 'service with a smile' or to 'put on a good show'. However, in recent years, emotional labour has become a specific part of the employment contract and the employee's discretion concerning which feelings to show and how to show them is reduced or completely eliminated. Emotional labour occurs when employees, as part of the wage-effort bargain, are required by their bosses to display emotions which cause customers to feel and respond in particular ways. The employer thus buys not only an employee's physical and mental labour, but also their emotional labour, in return for a wage. As Bolton (2000, p.163) states, 'employees' private emotional systems have been appropriated by management as a renewable resource' (Bolton, 2005). To ensure that employees perform as required, companies use a combination of three elements:

1. **Careful applicant selection.** Choosing the appropriate employee is the first step. Disney World interviews 50,000 aspiring employees annually, and is most interested in their personality, wanting people who are enthusiastic, and who exhibit a clean and honest appearance (Henkoff, 1994, van Maanen and Kunda, 1989). The McDonald's Corporation rejects applicants who are too poker-faced or who fail to demonstrate pleasure when describing a pleasant experience to interviewers (Slocum and Hellriegel, 2009).

2. **Employee training.** Companies run training courses for new starts whose jobs involve face-to-face or voice-to-voice interaction with customers, to develop their abilities to display appropriate emotions. Disney has overhauled its new hires orientation courses, putting less emphasis on policies and procedures, and more on emotion (Henkoff, 1994).

3. **Employee monitoring.** Organizations monitor staff interactions with customers to ensure that they display the required emotions. Ghost travellers on airlines and mystery shoppers in stores act as customers, to check staff performance. In a telesales and call centres, supervisors randomly record conversations for review purposes (Taylor, 1998). Companies also use customer questionnaires to assess whether staff are eliciting the desired responses.

Emotional labour consists of five key elements. First, employees consciously manage their emotions (either inducing or suppressing them) as part of their paid work requirement. Second, they do this when interacting with others (customers, clients, as well as other staff) within the workplace. Third, they do so with the objective of creating in the recipient, a particular state of mind ('I am being well treated'); a particular feeling (satisfied customer) or a particular response ('I'll use their service again'). Fourth, emotional labour should boost the self-esteem of its receiver. Finally, it is done to serve the interests of the employer (achieving organizational goals) who prescribes, supervises and monitors the performance of that emotional labour (Taylor, 1998).

Felt emotions
emotions that employees actually feel in a work situation.

Displayed emotions
emotions that employees are required by management to show as part of their jobs.

In every work situation, there are the emotions that employees actually feel – felt emotions – and those emotions that they are required to show by management as part of their jobs – displayed emotions. Richard Layard (2005) provides an example of the difference during an Olympic medal awards ceremony. He says that all three medallists on the rostrum display feelings of happiness and joy in front of the cameras and the crowd. In this particular 'work situation', the expressed feelings of the gold medallist and the bronze medallist, are probably also their felt emotions – the former because they won, and the latter, because they expected no medal at all. In contrast, the silver medallist's felt emotion may actually be disappointment due to a failure to win the gold (Medvec et al., 1995).

Compare the emotional displays of the gold and bronze medal winners (centre and left respectively) with that of the silver medallist (right) in the photo.

In our Olympic example, the silver medallist is experiencing a disjunction between her felt emotions and her expressed emotions. You may experience a similar situation when

Source: Mike Powell/Getty Images

internally you have feelings of anger and loathing towards your customers or co-workers, but externally, you display feelings of calm and interest through your facial expression, tone of voice, and content of speech. This gap between the emotions that you feel and those that you actually display is called emotional dissonance. This refers to the disparity between an individual's felt and displayed emotions. It can ignite conflict in organizations when employees are unable to sustain their emotional dissonance. Their suppressed real emotions can lead to exhaustion, burnout and aggression (Medvec *et al.*, 1995).

Emotional dissonance the disparity between an individual's felt and displayed emotions.

In addition to performing physical and mental labour, employees in organizations are also expected to expend the emotional labour that is appropriate for their job or profession. Individuals are appointed to positions in organizations, and are given job titles and job descriptions. In playing the role of a production manager, team leader or salesperson, they may display certain emotions and suppress others. Thus, for those around the person, 'what you see is not necessarily how they feel'. Thus individuals at all levels of the organizations, disguise their true feelings and manufacture false ones, either because it helps them to do their jobs, or because a failure to do so would be punished by management.

Employee	Should display emotions of
Undertaker	Solemnity, sadness
Debt collector	Disapproval
Police interrogator	Hostility
Supermarket checkout assistant	Friendliness
Nightclub bouncer	Anger
Flight attendant	Happiness, reassurance
Security officer	Irritation

Emotional labour involves employees manipulating and 'acting out' their emotions in a way that an actor might do in the theatre. Employees come to give 'performances' during their work in front of an audience of customers. Hochschild (1983) distinguished two types of

Surface acting hiding one's felt emotions and forgoing emotional expressions in response to display rules.

acting. **Surface acting**, which involves either not displaying the emotions that you do feel (emotion suppression), or displaying emotions that you do not feel (emotion simulation). In the first instance, you hide your felt emotions; in the second, you display emotions that you are not experiencing. For example, a waitress who is angry with a rude customer continues to smile, despite his rude behaviour towards her. Here, the employee complies with display rules but without internalizing emotions which they only fake. In contrast, **deep acting** is the process of attempting to modify one's felt emotions based on display rules, so that they really experience them. By developing these inner feelings about their organizational role and the customers they serve, the employee's outward behaviour becomes automatic.

Deep acting attempting to modify one's felt emotions based on display rules.

Surface acting has been found to be more stressful to employees and the source of greater conflict, because it involves feigning one's true feelings (Grandey, 2003; Grandey *et al.*, 2004). Stress tends to occur when emotional displays are prolonged; when employees are asked to take them to a level considered 'unacceptable; when they consider it to be inappropriate for the job; or when they are asked to maintain their emotional display while customers are being rude or offensive.

Fly and smile

Source: Paul Doyle/Alamy

In the photograph above, an experienced flight attendant demonstrates the facial expression that she uses at work. Is she performing genuine warmth, or is it concealed irritation?

Flight attendants are under strong pressure from the airlines to show only 'positive' expressions of emotion. This is sometimes a challenge, since not all passengers are pleasant and cooperative. She and the other attendants have learned that you can say anything to a passenger as long as you smile. In the photograph, she performs the smile that she uses while dealing with unruly or inebriated

passengers. The verbal content of what she says is quite negative, but as long as the attendant smiles while saying it, the passenger accepts the information without complaint. Were you correct?

The earliest studies into emotional labour were conducted on flight attendants and this occupational group continues to receive much research attention. On a flight, cabin crew will always display reassurance, even if they are afraid: 'Even though I'm an honest person, I have learned not to allow my face to mirror my alarm or my fright.' Airline management sees the nature of the interaction between flight attendants and passengers as central to the latter's perceptions of service quality. Competitive pressures have stimulated managerial initiatives to manage the 'natural' delivery of quality customer service during customer-attendant interactions. Taylor and Tyler found that three particular uses of body language were fundamental in establishing rapport – walking softly, making eye contact and always smiling. Emotional labour was required when, dealing with sick and nervous passengers and applying 'tender loving care' (TLC) and confronting emergency situations. Being friendly, cheerful and helpful involves an emotional display. In organizations with a 'customer is always right' philosophy, service workers are taught to diffuse customer hostility, and in consequence, end up absorbing a raft of verbal abuse during the course of a normal working day. They come to accept such verbalized customer dissatisfaction, no matter how upsetting, as 'just part of the job'. The growing incidence of both verbal and physical customer violence in Britain is likely to increase both the volume and intensity of emotional labour in service industries. The drive for competitive advantage through enhanced customer service

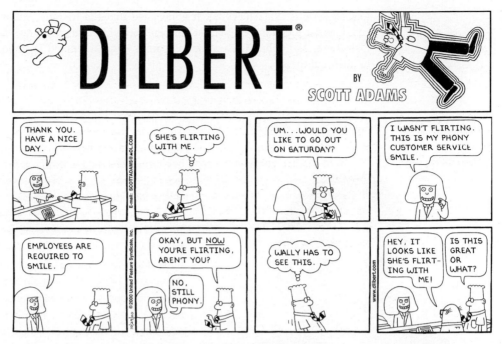

Source: © Copyright 2000 United Feature Syndicate. Inc.

means that an integral part of every service worker's job is to transform customer dissatisfaction to satisfaction. When management failed to invest in violence reduction strategies, exposing service workers to increasing levels of customer violence, it increasingly exploited the emotional labour of their staff. Thus there was the paradoxical situation in which cabin crew had to deploy their emotional labour (calming customers, etc.) to compensate for management's failure to remove the causes of customer abuse. However, the more successful that they were in doing this, the less management felt pressured to address the sources of customer violence.

Based on Hochschild (1983); Taylor and Tyler (2000).

Display rules organizational scripts concerning which feelings are appropriate in a given setting and how they should be displayed.

Feeling rules dictate which feelings should be displayed in particular settings.

Expression rules dictate how displayed feelings should be expressed in particular settings.

Emotional labour in an organization is governed by **display rules** (Ashforth and Humfrey, 1993; Hopfl, 2002). These are determined by management and take the form of an emotional script which specifies two types of rules. **Feeling rules** dictate which feelings should be displayed in particular settings. Your lecturer is supposed to feel enthusiastic and not bored when teaching you; a funeral director is expected to be solemn and not cheerful when assisting you to despatch a deceased relative; and managers are expected to be annoyed when disciplining poor performers. **Expression rules** dictate how these feelings should be expressed in particular settings. Enthusiasm by a lecturer in front of students is appropriately conveyed by tone of voice, speed of delivery and body language. Dressing up in strange clothing and singing the lecture is inappropriate. Enthusiasm by a new employee at a client meeting is appropriately shown by paying attention to the person speaking, asking questions and making comments. Inappropriate expression is applauding the speaker's contribution. Expression rules are frequently specified in a verbal repertoire or script that a call centre or a restaurant employee learns during their training. Meika Loe (2002) described how waitresses at 'Bazoom' restaurant had to behave as actresses, following the rules established by management and be cheerful, polite, smiling, attentive to customers and sexy, while avoiding showing bad feelings such as sadness or anger.

While display rules are organization-specific, they can differ between cultures, creating problems for companies. The smiling rule, a key component of customer care training in the United States and Britain, is inappropriate in Muslim countries and in Japan. In Israel, smiling supermarket cashiers are perceived as inexperienced, and are therefore encouraged to look serious (Rafaeli, 1989). It is believed that the friendly, smiling greeter welcoming customers in German Wal-Mart stores contributed to that company's failure in that country. Elsewhere, as the box illustrates, companies have attempted to impose their display rules in alien cultures.

Emotions training in Japan

Source: Pathathai Chungyam/Dreamstime.com

Hiroshi Leyoshi and other gas station attendants are gathered for a three-hour training session on learning how to smile. 'It's easy to say you should smile at customers' says Leyoshi, a 39-year-old gas attendant, after the seminar. 'But to be honest, it all depends on I how I feel at the moment'. Leyoshi isn't the only person who has trouble

smiling at customers. In the Japanese culture, hiding one's emotions is considered a virtue because the lack of expression minimizes conflict and avoids drawing attention to the individual. Tomoko Yoshi is a customer relations training expert who works at the Sheraton Hotels in Japan. He teaches hotel employees never to show emotions while talking with a guest. In particular, even if the employee is upset, they are instructed never to point with their finger. Pointing is considered rude. Using one's whole hand shows more effort and is considered more polite and businesslike. Similarly, if a customer is sitting in a restaurant and the waiter raises their voice, it signals to the customer that the waiter wants the guest to leave and isn't welcome any longer. Yoshida also instructs bellmen not to use their feet to close a door or move a customer's bags or toys even if the bellman is upset. Why? In Japan, people believe that the ground is where they walk in shoes. When they go home, they take their shoes off because they don't want to mix the outside ground with the inside ground. Yoshikihiko Kadokawa, author of *The Power of Laughing Face,* found that even in Japan's culture, the friendliest clerks in some of Japan's biggest retail stores consistently rang up the highest sales. His research found that smiling salesclerks reported 20 per cent more sales than non-smiling salesclerks.

From Slocum and Hellriegel (2009, p.61).

How much of a problem is emotional labour for employees? Hochschild (1983) was concerned with the detrimental effects on employees of unacceptable levels of emotional display. Information about its effects of is both limited and contradictory. It is the negative consequences that have been emphasized in the literature. For those employees who do experience emotional dissonance, creating and maintaining a separation between these two sets of feelings, at a high level, and over an extended period of time, can entail severe socio-emotional costs. These include low self-esteem, depression and cynicism. In extreme circumstances, it may even affect their social relationships and their mental health.

Noon and Blyton (2007) remind us that emotional labour is a variation of what already occurs in many work contexts. For those employees who perform mundane, service jobs, smiling at customers and interacting with them in a friendly way, provides meaning and pleasure, increasing their job satisfaction. There are therefore employees who engage in emotional labour, who neither act (surface or deep) nor experience emotional dissonance or stress (Ashforth and Humfrey, 1993; Ashforth and Tomiuk, 2000; Lewig and Dollard, 2003). Their felt emotions and expressed emotions match, so that they experience **emotional harmony** (Mann, 1999).

Emotional harmony a match between an employee's felt emotions and their expressed emotions within the workplace.

The distinction between felt and displayed emotions may not be as fixed as some writers claim, partly because they are already used to performing various types of emotional scripts inside and outside work. Some research studies, such as those into the jobs of adventure guides (Sharpe, 2005) report high degrees of emotional harmony, while other research among flight attendants (Williams, 2003) revealed that the emotional labour they performed was a source of both stress *and* satisfaction for them. These types of people enjoy serving customers and obtaining a positive response from them. Many identify closely with their work roles, and thus the emotional display rules that others consider to be so onerous and stressful are, for them, wholly consistent with their personal values and identity. For these people, task performance, complete with emotional displays, is likely to enhance rather than to reduce their psychological well being.

From his empirical study of banking and health employees, Wharton (1993) found no simple relationships. Whether a person who engaged in emotional labour would find their job satisfying or emotionally exhausting, depended on a number of variables. These included the 'fit' between an individual's personal characteristics and the requirements of their job; the level, range and duration of the emotional labour required in the role (intense, extensive and prolonged or low, narrow and brief, or some other combination); their ability to disengage ('switch off') from their job after leaving the workplace; and finally, their degree of autonomy in performing their job, with greater autonomy being associated with lower emotional exhaustion.

STOP AND THINK   Has the importance of emotional labour been overstated? Is it even a valid concept to study? We all engage in impression management all the time (Chapter 7, Communication). We can 'put on a smile' without necessarily being happy. At what point does normal impression management become emotional labour?

 RECAP

1. *Distinguish between the four major frames of reference on conflict.*

   - The unitarist frame sees organizations as essentially harmonious and any conflict as bad.

   - The pluralist frame sees organizations as a collection of groups, each with their own interests.

   - The interactionist sees conflict as a positive, necessary force for effective performance.

   - The radical frame sees conflict as an inevitable outcome of capitalism.

2. *Distinguish between functional and dysfunctional conflict.*

   - *Functional conflict* is considered by management to support organizational goals, and it improves organizational performance.

   - *Dysfunctional conflict* is considered to impede the achievement of organizational goals and reduces company performance.

3. *Explain the relationship between organizing, co-ordinating and conflict.*

   - Organizing concerns dividing up a large task (e.g. designing, building and marketing of a car), into sub-tasks, and assigning them to groups (e.g. design department, production department, etc.). Co-ordination brings those previously divided subtasks together to ensure that all activities are directed towards organizational goals. In the process of subdivision, departments acquire their own subordinate goals and interests, which differ from organizational ones. Conflict ensues when these divergent interests and goals clash.

4. *List the causes of conflict in organizations.*

   - Individual, groups, units and departments may be in conflict with each other due to the differences in their goal orientation and evaluations; self-image and stereotypes; task interdependencies; time perspectives; as well as overlapping authority and scarce resources.

5. *Distinguish the different organizational co-ordination devices.*

   - Co-ordination devices include rules, policies and procedures; using hierarchy; goal clarification and communication; temporary task force; permanent project teams; liaison roles and integrator roles.

6. *Explain the conditions under which conflict is resolved and stimulated in organizations.*

   - Some writers contend that conflict which is dysfunctional, that is, does not achieve organizational goals, wastes time, de-motivates staff, wastes resources and generally lowers individual and hence organizational performance. In such cases it needs to be eliminated.

   - Commentators argue that conflict stimulation is necessary if employees enter 'comfort zones'; are reluctant to think in new ways; and find it easier to maintain the status quo. In rapidly changing organizational environment such behaviour not only reduces organizational success, but may endanger its very existence.

7. *List Thomas' five conflict resolution approaches.*

   - Thomas' five conflict resolution approaches are avoidance; accommodation; compromise; collaboration; and competition.

8. *Distinguish between distributive and integrative bargaining.*

   - Distributive bargaining refers to a negotiation situation in which a fixed sum of resources is divided up. It leads to a win–lose situation between the parties.

   - Integrative bargaining, seeks to increase the total amount of resources, and create a win–win situation between the parties.

Revision

1. 'The unitarist frame of reference on conflict is the most dominant in the literature and practice'. Do you agree? Give reasons for your view and illustrate with examples.

2. 'Since every unit and department in an organization has its own goals and interests, conflict will always be a feature of organizational life'. Consider the costs and benefits of this for organization stakeholders. Giving your reasons and illustrate with examples.

3. Kenneth Thomas distinguished five conflict resolution approaches. Suggest the difficulties for an individual seeking to switch between them.

4. Is emotional labour as great a problem as some of the literature suggests? What defensive mechanisms can employees use to cope with the emotional labour demands of their jobs?

Research assignment

Type 'gripe sites' or 'complaint sites' into a search engine; or type in the name of a company and add 'sucks' after it. Read the posted comments. Analyze and categorize the content of messages posted about the organization. What topics are the complaints about? How valid or representative are these comments? In what ways do they contradict the image projected by the company (visit and analyze its own website)? What purpose do these websites serve? Write a report using one or more of the conflict perspectives discussed in this chapter to explain what you have found.

Springboard

Ackroyd, S. and Thompson, P., 1999, *Organizational Misbehaviour*, Sage, London.

Adopting a radical frame of reference on conflict, the authors review the empirical and theoretical work on organizational misbehaviour, setting it within the context of employee resistance, conflict and social identity.

Collins, D., 1998, *Organizational Change: Sociological Perspectives*, Routledge, London.

Chapters 7 and 8 provide extended descriptions and examples of each of the four frameworks of reference on conflict.

Kolb, D.M., 1983, 'Strategy and tactics of mediation', *Human Relations*, 36(3): pp.247–68.
In this classic article, the author considers the conflict resolution strategy of mediation.

Weiss, J. and Hughes, J. 2005, 'Want Collaboration?', *Harvard Business Review*, 83(3): 93–101.
Adopting an interactionist frame of reference on conflict, the authors argue that effective collaboration is only achieved by seeing conflict as natural and necessary, and managing it effectively.

 ## OB in films

There Will be Blood (2007, director Paul Thomas Anderson) DVD track 5: 01.27:00–01.31:00 (5 minutes). This film is set in 1898 and tells the story of a silver miner turned oil man, Daniel Plainview (played by Daniel Day-Lewis), who is engaged in a ruthless quest for wealth during Southern California's oil boom. His son, HW is badly injured in a gusher accident which leaves him profoundly deaf, and Plainview is very sensitive about this. The clip begins with Plainview and his brother Henry (Kevin J. O'Connor) going into a meeting, shaking hands and sitting down at a table. They are going to negotiate with two investors who want to buy his oil wells. The investors appear to be offering him lots of money. If Plainview accepts the deal, he will be a very rich man. The clip ends with Henry and his brother walking out of the meeting.

1. Why does this negotiation session collapse into irreconcilable conflict? (Pay attention to the physical setting of the meeting, the way it is run, the nature of the conversation, the personalities involved, and the power bases of the participants.)

2. How could things have been handled better, by whom?

 ## OB in literature

Lodge, D., *Nice Work*, Penguin Books, Harmondsworth, 1989. The novel concerns Vic Wilcox, a middle-aged, male, managing director of a foundry, Midland Amalgamated, and Robyn Penrose, a committed feminist intellectual and member of a university English department on a short term contract. She hopes that agreeing to participate in a 'manager shadowing' scheme will help her to renew her contract. Which frame of reference on conflict do Vic and Robyn hold respectively? How might they have come to adopt that frame? How does it affect their perception of events in the company?

CHAPTER EXERCISES

Organizational misbehaviour

Objectives
1. To find examples of organizational misbehaviour.

2. To suggest reasons for its occurrence in the workplace.

3. To propose management action to address it.

Briefing
1. Make a list of employee misbehaviours that you have engaged in yourself while at work, observed others engaging in, or which you have read about.

2. Form into groups and discuss:

   (a) What are the causes of such organizational misbehaviour?

   (b) What options do employees have who engage in organizational misbehaviour themselves or see others doing it?

   (c) What actions can senior management take to do to eliminate or reduce organizational misbehaviour?

Resolving group conflict

Objectives   1. To demonstrate conflict and ways of resolving it.

2. To contrast individual and group decision-making.

3. To explore the impact assumptions and perceptions.

Briefing   1. Individually, read the story and complete the worksheet below by circling 'T' (true), 'F' (false) or '?' (unknown) in response to each of the 11 statements about it.

Statements about the story

A businessman had just turned off the lights in the store when a man appeared and demanded money. The owner opened a cash register. The contents of the cash register were scooped up, and the man sped away. A member of the police was notified promptly.			
1. A man appeared after the owner had turned off his store lights.	T	F	?
2. The robber was a man.	T	F	?
3. A man did not demand money.	T	F	?
4. The man who opened the cash register was the owner.	T	F	?
5. The store owner scooped up the contents of cash register, he ran away.	T	F	?
6. Someone opened a cash register.	T	F	?
7. After the man who demanded the money scooped up the contents of the cash register, he ran away.	T	F	?
8. While the cash register contained money, the story does *not* state *how much*.	T	F	?
9. The robber demanded money of the owner.	T	F	?
10. The story concerns a series of events in which only three persons are referred to: the owner of the store; a man who demanded money; and a member of the police force.	T	F	?
11. The following events in the story are true: someone demanded money; a cash register was opened; its contents were scooped up, and a man dashed out of the store.	T	F	?

2. Divide into groups and reach a group consensus on the 11 statements. Each group appoints an observer who notes how decisions are made and how differences between group members are resolved.

3. Class re-assembles, observers report back, and there is a discussion on different forms of decision-making and conflict resolution in groups.

From Haney (1973).

Chapter 22 **Power and politics**

Key terms

power	rational model of organization
strategic contingencies	political model of organization
influencing	organizational politics
acceptance	need for power
compliance	Machiavellianism
resistance	locus of control
rationalism	risk-seeking propensity
rationality	

Learning outcomes

When you have read this chapter, you should be able to define those
key terms in your own words, and you should also be able to:

1. Appreciate the importance of power and politics in organizational
   life.
2. Compare and contrast different perspectives on power.
3. Distinguish different bases of power.
4. Identify organizational factors which enhance the power of
   departments.
5. Differentiate between power tactics and influencing tactics.
6. Distinguish between the rational and political models of
   organization.
7. Identify the characteristics of individuals most likely to engage in
   political behaviour.
8. Explain how women use and are affected by organizational
   politics.

Why study power and politics?

Organizations have a political dimension as well as a social, technological, economic and a cultural one. David Buchanan and Richard Badham (2008) observe that as organizational structures become flatter and subject to regular change, and as hierarchical power becomes less significant, the scope for political manoeuvring increases. In other words, current organizational trends and developments place a premium on political skills. Power and politics are inextricably entwined, affecting behaviour in organizations. Power is the ability to get other people to do what you want them to do, while politics is the use of techniques and tactics to do this. Some writers believe that much management failure can be attributed to political incompetence, political naiveté, and the inability or unwillingness to perform effectively the required political tasks in an organization (Kotter, 1985; Yates, 1985).

Politics is about overcoming the problem of resolving situations where different organization members bring different values to their work, and consequently do not share common goals or views, but yet have to continue to work with one another (Kakabadse, 1983). Even when they do share aims about company objectives, they may disagree about the means to those ends, and will fight (figuratively) for what they believe is the appropriate line of action. Ian Mangham (1979) felt that most significant organizational decisions were the outcome of social and political forces, and only partly influenced by evidence and rational argument – shaped by 'the pulling and hauling that is politics' (p.17). Henry Kissinger, an American diplomat, confirmed this view when he wrote:

> Before I served as a consultant to [President] Kennedy, I had believed, like most academics, that the process of decision-making was largely intellectual and all one had to do was to walk into the President's office and convince him of the correctness of one's view. This perspective, I soon realized is as dangerously immature as it is widely held (cited in Pfeffer, 1992a, p.31).

Lee Bolman and Terrence Deal (1991) summarized this political view of organization, seeing goals and decisions as emerging from bargaining, negotiation and jockeying for position by individuals and coalitions. These coalitions were composed of varied individuals and interest groups which possessed enduring differences of values, preferences, beliefs, information and perceptions of reality. Many observers feel that political behaviour plays a more significant role in organizational life than is commonly realized or admitted; and that the academic management literature does not adequately explore the shaping of political behaviour in organizational change.

Power in organizations

Michel Foucault wrote that 'power is everywhere, not because it embraces everything, but because it comes from everywhere' (Foucault, 1979, p.93). Power is a contested concept around which a number of contrasting perspectives have developed. There is, therefore, value in being able to view this complex and slippery notion from different angles, and to be aware of, and be able, to draw on the strengths and limitations of different perspectives. For these reasons, power is difficult to define and measure with precision. Power has been defined as the capacity of individuals to overcome resistance on the part of others, to exert their will and to produce results consistent with their interests and objectives.

Power the capacity of individuals to overcome resistance on the part of others, to exert their will, and to produce results consistent with their interests and objectives.

Being abstract, power is also a difficult topic to conceptualize. For this reason, a number of different viewpoints are offered. They share similarities and differences. The first, 'power-as-a-property' viewpoint, sees power as an attribute or characteristic, and distinguishes three different perspectives. It is associated with writers such as Pfeffer, and French and Raven. The second, 'face of power' viewpoint, considers it in terms of its visibility to outsiders. It is most closely associated with Steven Lukes. The third viewpoint focuses on disciplinary power and is associated with the work of Michel Foucault.

Power-as-a-property viewpoint

This viewpoint distinguishes three different perspectives, 'frames of reference' or ways of looking at power. These perspectives are similar to conflict perspectives considered in the previous chapter. Each provides a different lens through which we can see power being formed and activated. Each is distinguished by the attribute or characteristic of power that is considered to be crucial. The three perspectives are:

- Power as a property of individuals.
- Power as a property of relationships.
- Power as an embedded property of structures.

Power as a property of individuals

This perspective sees power as something that you possess, a set of resources that you ac-cumulate. It asks questions such as how much power does an individual have; where did it come from; and how can the person acquire more power? Jeffrey Pfeffer (1992b) listed the sources of managers' power. Notice how some of these come from the position that the manager occupies within the organization hierarchy (structural sources) while others relate to their personal attributes like personality, communication and motivation (individual sources).

Table 22.1: Power as an individual property: sources

Structural sources of individual power include:

- Formal position and authority in the organization structure
- Ability to cultivate allies and supporters
- Access to and control over information and other resources
- Physical and social position in the organization's communication network
- The centrality of your own unit or section to the business
- Role in resolving critical problems, in reducing uncertainty
- Degree of unity of your section, lack of internal dissent
- Being irreplaceable
- The pervasiveness of your activities in the organization

Personal sources of individual power include:

- Energy, endurance and physical stamina
- Ability to focus energy and avoid wasteful effort
- Sensitivity and ability to read and understand others
- Flexibility in selecting varied means to achieve goals
- Personal toughness; willingness to engage in conflict and confrontation
- Able to 'play the subordinate' and 'team member' to enlist the support of others

---

Based on Pfeffer (1981).

Waiter power

A prominent US politician and ex-basketball superstar, Bill Bradley, was invited to make a speech at a large political banquet. During the meal, the waiter came round and served Bradley with a pat of butter. Bradley reacted to this by asking if he could have two pats of butter.

'Sorry,' the waiter replied. 'Just one pat of butter each.'

'I don't think you know who I am,' Bradley responded, 'I'm Bill Bradley, Rhodes Scholar, professional basketball player, world champion, United States senator.'

'Well,' the waiter said, 'maybe you don't know who I am.'

'As a matter of fact I don't,' Bradley replied, 'Who are you?'

'I'm the guy,' said the waiter, 'who's in charge of the butter.'

From Kettle (1999) in Jackson and Carter (2000, p.250).

From this perspective, since power is something you accumulate, individuals act to strengthen, as much as possible, both their structural and individual sources of power.

 **STOP AND THINK**   How would the structural sources of power in this perspective explain why typically, accountants tend to be more powerful and influential in most organizations than, for example, human resource managers?

Bertram Herbert
Raven (b.1926)

Power as a property of relationships

The second perspective on power sees it as a *relationship* between individuals and groups which develops over time (Crozier, 1973). Power is generated, maintained and lost, in the context of relationships with others. It derives from the work of John French and Bertram Raven who distinguished five power bases – reward, coercion, referent, legitimate and expert (Table 22.2). From this perspective, these power bases depend on the *perceptions* of others. Perception shapes our behaviour as much as reality. An individual may have access to rewards or possess expertise, but if his followers believe that he does not, they may be unwilling to comply. Similarly, a person may lack reward capacity or expertise, but will gain compliance from others because she persuades them that she possesses these. An individual can manipulate followers' perceptions to gain compliance. It is because two parties and their perceptions are involved, that this view sees power as a *relational* construct, and not solely the personal property of the individual who accumulates it.

Table 22.2: Bases of power

Reward power	is based on the belief of followers that the leader has access to valued rewards which will be dispensed in return for compliance with instructions
Coercive power	is based on the belief of followers that the leader can administer penalties or sanctions that are considered to be unwelcome
Referent power	is based on the belief of followers that the leader has desirable abilities and personality traits that can and should be copied
Legitimate power	is based on the belief of followers that the leader has authority to give directions, within the boundaries of their position or rank
Expert power	is based on the belief of followers that the leader has superior knowledge relevant to the situation and the task in hand

After French and Raven (1958).

 **STOP AND THINK**   The five power bases are interrelated and using one will increase or decrease a person's ability to use another. What are the effects of your manager exercising coercive power over you? Your team leader using expert power? How is their use of other types of power affected?

Additionally, power is dynamic, changing in form and amount as the situation around the individual and followers changes. For example, a person's initial recommendation, based on their expertise, may initially be discounted by others. However, when that person is proved to be correct by circumstances, others' assessment of that person change, and their expert power may be enhanced. David Knights and Hugh Willmott (1999) remind us that power can only be successful, 'if those over whom power is exercised are tempted by the material rewards offered' (p.166). Reward power is only effective if what is offered is seen as desirable. Allan Cohen and David Bradford (1989, 1991) identified eight types of

Table 22.3: Organizational currencies

Currencies	Examples
• Resources	Lending or giving money, personnel or space.
• Information	Sharing specific technical or company knowledge.
• Advancement	Providing a task that can assist in another's promotion.
• Recognition	Acknowledging another's effort or achievement.
• Network/contacts	Providing opportunities for linking with others.
• Personal support	Giving personal and emotional support.
• Assistance	Helping others with their projects.
• Co-operation	Responding quickly to requests, approving a project.

Based on Cohen and Bradford (1989, 1991).

rewards which they call *organizational currencies* (Table 22.3). They show how these can be used to persuade others to comply with your requests.

Third, individuals can operate from several bases of power, and use different power bases in different combinations in different contexts at different times. The American gangster Al Capone is reputed to have said that you could get more done with a kind word *and* a gun, than with a kind word alone (McCarty, 2004). The relationship issue here manifests itself in terms of the existence of different groups of followers, and different issues being dealt with. In one relationship, certain power bases may be effective, whereas in a different one, others may be more appropriate. Similarly, situations change over time. In the past, leadership was based first on coercion, then on legitimate power, now on expert power and increasingly on referent power. French and Raven listed five bases of power, since one's power base will depend on whatever resources are available and appropriate in the circumstances. Hence, the list of potential power bases is potentially infinite (Clegg and Hardy, 1996; Hardy, 1995).

Expert power on the rostrum

Toscanini

The story is told of the great conductor; Arturo Toscanini who, shortly before a concert was about to begin, was approached by a distraught member of the orchestra who reported that one of the keys on his instrument was broken. He did not know how he would be able to play in the concert. Toscanini thought for a moment, and replied, 'All is well. That note is never played in tonight's performance.'

Based on Greenberg and Baron (2007, p.473).

Source: © Interphoto/Alamy

Power as an embedded property of structures

The third perspective on power focuses on how power is used to control the behaviour of individuals through less obvious means. It pays attention to the way in which power is woven into an organization's fabric – into what we take for granted, the order of things, the social and organizational structures that we find ourselves and the rule systems that appear to constitute the 'natural' running of day-to-day procedures. Being embedded in this way makes power less visible and less detectable by those who are not sufficiently observant. Even if detected, it is difficult to challenge 'the ways things are'. It is in the interest of those who can manipulate and exploit this unequal distribution of power, that it is accepted and not challenged. While this embedded or hidden power may be less easily detected, analyzed and challenged, it is no less potent.

The embedded perspective sees power as so expertly woven into the fabric of the organization, that we accept it, in a 'taken-for-granted' way, in the same way that we accept that offices have desks. We accept the social and organization structure of the company – our job description, the operating rules and policies, the targets we are set, the equipment which we are given to use, and how we will be rewarded. All of these we consider a perfectly 'natural' way of running an organization on a day-to-day basis. When power becomes so embedded, it becomes virtually invisible. Even when detected, it becomes difficult, if not impossible to challenge.

Embedded power controls

The six control strategies described by Don Hellriegel and John Slocum exercise power over individuals in a way that is not immediately obvious.

Control through organization structure: large organizations give their employees job descriptions that set out their tasks and responsibilities. These can be narrow, detailed and specific, or general, broad and vague. They also specify communication flows and the location of decision-making responsibility.

Control through policies and rules: written policies and rules guide employees' actions, structure their relationships, and aim to establish consistency of behaviour. Rules lay down standards, define acceptable behaviour and establish levels of required performance.

Control through recruitment and training: companies wish to avoid having people who behave in unstable, variable, spontaneous, idiosyncratic and random ways. To achieve predictability, they select stable, reliable individuals, while consistency and reliability is achieved through training them.

Control through rewards and punishments: employees receive extrinsic rewards in the form of material, monetary incentives and associated fringe benefits like company cars and free meals. Intrinsic rewards include satisfying work, personal responsibility and autonomy. Offering to provide or withdraw these rewards gains employees' compliance.

Control through budgets: individuals and sections in organizations are given financial and resource targets to guide their performance. These may relate to expenditure, level of cost incurred, or sales volume to be achieved in a month. Production budgets include labour hours used and machine downtime.

Control through technology: includes both material technology (machinery, tools, equipment) as well as social technology (work processes that order the behaviour and relationships of employees). Developments in IT have increased the possibilities of electronic surveillance of staff.

Based on Hellriegel and Slocum (1978).

Strategic contingencies events and activities, both inside and outside an organization, that are essential for it to attain its goals.

Strategic contingencies are events and activities which must occur, either inside or outside an organization, for it to attain its goals. This concept can explain the differences in the relative power of different departments (Hickson *et al.*, 1971; Salancik and Pfeffer, 1974, 1977). In the short term, a firm must manufacture a product and sell it to a customer at a profit to survive. Developing the next product or counting the money it has received is less important. In this short-term example, the sales department and production department

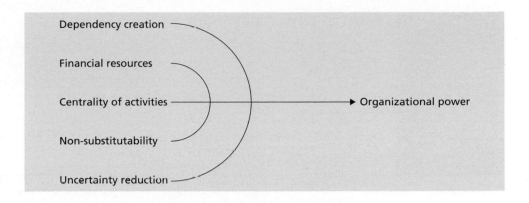

provide greater strategic value to the company than do the R&D or the finance departments. Hence, individuals, groups or departments which are responsible with dealing with the key issues and dependencies in the company environment, which solve its pressing problems or which deal with a current crisis, will be more powerful than those that do not (Astley and Sachdeva, 1984; Mintzberg, 1983).

The power sources that indicate a department's ability to respond to strategic contingencies include dependency-creation, financial resources, centrality of activities, non-substitutability and ability to decrease uncertainty. These five sources overlap, and the more of them a department possesses, the greater the power that it will exert within its organization.

1. *Dependency-creation*: A department is powerful if other units and departments depend on its products or services. These may include materials, information, resources and services which flow between departments. The receiving department is always in an inferior power position. The number and strength of the dependencies is also important.

2. *Financial resources*: A department's ability to control financial resources gives it power. Money can be converted into many different resources that are required and valued by others. Because of the power-enhancing value of financial resources, departments in all organizations compete with others to grasp new projects or tasks which have new financial budgets attached to them.

3. *Centrality*: Centrality refers to the degree to which a department's activities are critical to achieving the organization's goal. The more central it is, the more powerful it is, compared to other departments. Low centrality departments like training, payroll management, computer management, human resources and advertising, can be closed down and their work subcontracted out.

4. *Non-substitutability*: If what a department does cannot easily be done by another department, either inside or outside the organization, then it has great power. The more specialized its work, the greater the skill and knowledge required to do it, and hence the more power that accrues to it.

5. *Uncertainty reduction*: Those who have the ability to reduce uncertainty can gain significant reputations and positions of influence, by offering clear definitions of problems and by specifying solutions, thereby restoring an otherwise confused situation.

STOP AND THINK

Do you think that the pursuit of power interferes with or contributes to, improved organizational performance?

Steven Lukes
(b.1941)

Faces of power viewpoint

A second viewpoint on power was provided by Steven Lukes (2005). For him, it ranged from power as clearly visible (overt) and self-evident to an observer, through to power being subtle, less visible (covert) and then on to institutionalized, that is, embedded in the structure of the organization in which individuals work. He conceptualized it as having three dimensions or 'faces':

Dimension 1   Power that is exercised to secure a decision in situations where there is some observable conflict or disagreement.

Dimension 2   Power that is exercised to keep issues on or off the decision-making agenda, so that potential conflicts or disagreements are precluded and therefore unobservable.

Dimension 3   Institutionalized power is used to define reality for its members. If norms and meanings become internalized by employees, they will accept and act in accordance with those defined for them by senior management, even if it goes against their 'real' interests.

The first dimension is the most obvious, and concerns a clash of interests between those making a decision. It focuses on the *observable behaviour* of individuals or groups that determine or influence the form or content of a decision. For example, in the army, a sergeant threatens to put a private on a charge unless he completes his assigned task before midnight. The sergeant's words (verbal and paraverbal behaviour) and manner (non-verbal) can both be observed by an on-looker who notices their effect on what the soldier decides to do (works more quickly).

The second dimension of power concerns the manipulation of issues and non-issues. This acts to constrain the scope for decision-making. The interests of certain groups are excluded from a particular bargaining or decision-making arena. The focus here is on the *non-observable behaviour* that is involved in keeping issues on or off an agenda. In your dissertation, you initially include research by a writer whom your supervisor has a low opinion of. On reflection, you decide this might reduce your grade, so you remove it from your report. There has been no direct pressure placed upon you, but implicitly, issues which are important or irrelevant, have been shaped. Bachrach and Baratz (1962) noted that this can be manifested as much through *non-decisions* (not doing something) as through direct decisions (Wolfinger, 1971; Pettigrew, 1973). The powerful can use this form of power to avoid completely any overt conflict or resistance to their intentions.

This form of power can keep controversial issues from ever reaching the public domain either to be discussed or decided upon. Unlike in the first case where individuals or groups, though they may be overruled are nevertheless involved in the decision-making process, here, in the second, they are not admitted into the arena in the first place. Power is most commonly associated with someone doing something, such as making a decision or acting in a particular way (Bachrach and Baratz, 1962).

The third dimension of power involves shaping people's perceptions, cognitions and preferences, so that they accept their existing situation because they cannot see an alternative. They see it as natural and unchangeable; or as divinely ordained and beneficial to them. Fleming and Spicer (2007) referred to it as 'power as domination' which leads us to act against our own objective interests. This power dimension is characterized by harmony, as overt conflict is avoided. Those subject to its consequences are not aware of it. It involves the 'powerful' defining reality for the 'powerless' within the organization. For example, they may promote the single criterion of maximizing profit or reducing costs, and this then becomes a fundamental reality. They secure the support of those whom they disadvantage by the exercise of their power. The true interests and potential grievances of the 'powerless' are obscured or distorted, and they are distracted from them, becoming instead pre-occupied by events that are more immediate and understandable to them. The public exposure of power is avoided.

The distinguishing feature of institutionalized power, is that it is difficult to associate it with the actions of any specific individual who may be influencing a decision (first dimension); or with backstage manoeuvring conducted by individuals and groups, who are seeking to prevent contentious issues being discussed (second dimension). Power-holders, by defining reality for employees and getting them to internalize selected norms and meanings, in a way 'cast a spell' over them, whereby the powerless become unable to formulate consciously their real interests or imagine alternatives. Institutional power helps to sustain the dominance of senior management by reducing the ability of subordinates to dissent.

Disciplinary power viewpoint

Michel Foucault (1926–1984)

Michel Foucault, a French philosopher and historian, has provided a third viewpoint on power. His work can be related to Lukes's third dimension of power, the institutional, which focuses on the way that management sustains its dominance by reducing subordinates' ability to dissent by creating their reality and managing meanings for them. Two concepts – bio-power and disciplinary power are central to an understanding of his ideas.

Bio-power

Bio-power operates by establishing and defining what is normal or abnormal, socially deviant or acceptable in thought and behaviour. Bio-power is targeted at society as a whole, and is achieved through a variety of *discursive practices*: talk, writing, debate, argument, representation. The media play a major role in sustaining and altering what we conceive of as socially normal. Bio-power exercises its control over us through 'constituting the normal' and operates through our individual cognition and understanding. If you accept without challenge 'the way things are', the way a situation is currently represented ('the constitution of the normal' as Foucault puts it) then bio-power takes on a self-disciplining role with regard to your thinking and behaving.

> As you walk onto the street, you realize just how late it is. You can't believe that you have been at work for so long. You should be used to this by now. Most days you spend twelve hours in the office, with only a fading tourist photograph of an Indian village to remind you of what it was like to be free. There isn't anyone holding a gun to your head, is there? But long hours have their drawbacks . . . Even though you might want a family, you know that is impossible. Anyway, you have made your decision. You're out to achieve big things, and this requires a few small sacrifices (Fleming and Spicer 2007, p.19).

There is no manager or supervisor telling you what to do or how to behave. Sets of procedures, instructions and controls are applied by individuals to themselves in pursuit of goals that they have been persuaded are their own, but which are, to a substantial degree, those of the self-interested organizations and the elites that control them. These 'technologies of the self' as Rose (1989) termed them mean that, rather than having individuals' behaviour regulated through external systems of monitoring and control (e.g. supervisors, technology, appraisal systems), these more intrusive controls get inside the 'hearts and minds' of organization members, to establish their self-regulation. As one writer noted 'the whips are inside men' (Mills, 1951, p.234).

STOP AND THINK How is bio-power affecting you? At university, which goals have you been persuaded are your own? In your work, current or past, which procedures, instructions and controls have you uncritically accepted and conformed to? How might you have challenged these?

Disciplinary power

For Foucault, disciplinary power operates through the construction of social and organizational routine, and is targeted at individuals and groups. He thus regards power as a set of techniques whose effects are achieved through *disciplinary practices*. These practices are the tools of surveillance and assessment that are used to control and regiment individuals, rendering them docile and compliant. The techniques or mechanisms that achieve compliance include (Hiley, 1987, p.351):

- the allocation of physical space in offices or factories which establishes homogeneity and uniformity, individual and collective identity, ranks people according to status and fixes their position in the network of social relations;

- the standardization of individual behaviour through timetables, regimentation, work standardization and repetitive activities;

- the 'composition of forces' where individuals became parts of larger units such as cross-functional teams or assembly-lines;

- the use of job ladders and career systems which, through their future promises, encourage consent to organizational demands.

We would not normally consider office layouts, timetables, career ladders and work allocations to be manifestations of power. However, they do shape and discipline our daily activities and interactions, controlling and regimenting us, guaranteeing our compliance with the social and organizational norms and expectations. It is exactly because they are 'micro techniques' – so small and so embedded in the organization's structure, that they are hardly noticed by employees. Foucault's concept of power is very different from the traditional concept, as contrasted in Table 22.4. It can be of value to organization managers who wish to secure workers' willing compliance with managerial instructions.

Table 22.4: Foucault versus traditional concepts of power

Traditional concepts of power	Foucault's concepts of power
Power is possessed, is accumulated, is vested in the individual	Power is pervasive, is a totality, is reflected in concrete practices
Power is in the hands of social and organizational elites; resistance is futile	Power is to be found in the micro-physics of social life; power depends on resistance
We are subject to the domination of those who are more powerful than we are	We construct our own web of power in accepting current definitions of normality
Power is destructive, denies, represses, prevents, corrupts	Power is productive, contributes to social order, which is flexible and shifting
Power is episodic, visible, is observable in action, is deployed intermittently, is absent except when exercised	Power is present in its absence, discreet, operating through taken-for-granted daily routines and modes of living
Knowledge of power sources and relationships is emancipatory, can help us overcome domination	Knowledge maintains and extends the web of power, creating further opportunities for domination

Source: Reproduced by permission of SAGE Publications, London, Los Angeles, New Delhi and Singapore, from Buchanan, D.A. and Badham, R.J., *Power and Organizational Change: Winning the Turf Game*, Copyright (© Sage Publications 2008).

STOP AND THINK How are disciplinary practices affecting you? Give examples of those that you have been subjected to at university or at work, and which have shaped and directed your daily activities and interactions.

Foucault talks of people being trapped within a 'field of force relations', a sort of web of power which they help to create, and which is constantly being re-created by them in an on-going way. Individuals are both and simultaneously, creators of that web and prisoners within it. Within that web at the organizational level, specific disciplinary practices condition employees' thought processes, leading them to treat techniques like performance-based pay as being perfectly 'natural', and not to question it (Hardy and Clegg, 1996). That 'field of force relations' is neither stable nor inevitable. Instead, it changes as points of resistance are encountered; fissures open up, old coalitions break up and new ones are formed. It is a shifting network of alliances, not only in organizations, but in society in general (Clegg, 1989). If employees do recognize them, the practices are difficult to argue against. Resistance by employees to them, said Foucault, merely demonstrates and reinforces the necessity for such discipline. Over the last decade, the British government has established targets in all the public services – police, health, education, transport, housing. Foucault encourages us to take a critical, questioning stance towards what we might consider to be 'normal', or 'routine' within organizations. While such company practices may appear neutral, their political role in controlling and regimenting individuals is often obscured or hidden.

Foucault uses the metaphor of the *panopticon* for his paradigm of disciplinary technology. The panopticon is a prison whose design allows all the inmates to be observed in their cells by one observer who remains unseen by them. The prisoners know that they cannot hide or escape from this surveillance, and that it is constant and regular, but they do not know exactly when they are being observed. The consequence is that they behave as *if they* are being watched. They 'self-survey' and become obedient and compliant, by self-disciplining themselves. As McAuley *et al.* (2007, p.263) state: 'We are not necessarily compelled to act as we do by some external agency. Instead, through society's disciplines of schools, hospitals, prisons and military, we have internalised it [*power*] to become self-governed or "normalized".'

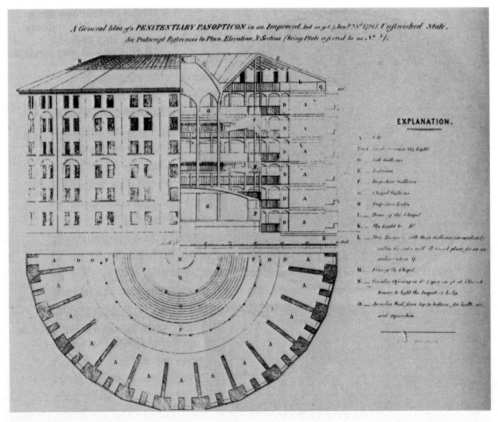

Bentham's Panopticon

- Over the last few years in Britain, many lorries and trucks have had a panel attached to their rear doors with lettering large enough to be read by following drivers. The panel reads, 'Well driven? Call 0800-22-55-33'
- Office stationery from a British bank carries the following statement at the bottom of the page, 'To help us to improve our service we may record or monitor phone calls'

Research by Sewell and Wilkinson (1992) into its application in the manufacturing sector, suggested that it had become a modern version of the 'panoptical gaze' (Foucault, 1979). Like Buchanan and Badham's 'embedded power' and Lukes's institutionalized power, Foucault's bio-power and panoptical structure provide an on-going, pervasive exercise of power, in which people's behaviour is constantly being controlled, but is done so by the individuals themselves, through their own self-monitoring. Employees are watched and they watch themselves. Put another way, Foucault argues that individuals are party to their own situation. Rules are not only devised and imposed by others, but also accepted by them. To become subject to rules implies an acceptance of them. For him, organizations are prisons, with their processes of decision-making, information technology and human resource management only refining the process of 'capture'.

Power and influencing tactics

How do individuals use their power and get others to do what they want? One definition of power is the ability 'to produce intended effects' in line with one's perceived interests (Pettigrew and McNulty, 1995). These effects can be produced in a way that those upon whom the power is being exercised, are both aware of it and may also be often resentful. Alternatively, those effects can be obtained in such a way that those being affected are unaware, only occasionally resentful, but more often actually grateful. We can thus distinguish two approaches – the 'power push' and the 'influencing pull'. Both see power as a property of the individual which is exercised in a relationship with other people, albeit in different ways.

Power-push

Buchanan and Badham (2008) provide a typology of power tactics (Table 22.5). Their examples come from interviews and discussions with managers attending executive development programmes in Australia, Britain, Sweden and Finland. They were confident that these represent the taken-for-granted 'recipe knowledge' of many experienced managers around the world.

Influencing pull

Influencing the ability to affect another's attitudes, beliefs or behaviours, seen only in its effect, without using coercion or formal position, and in a way that influencees believe that they are acting in their own best interests.

This perspective also considers power as a property of the individual, which forms the basis for their influencing. Individuals in organizations are seen as possessing varying amounts of different types of power, as discussed earlier. The more of each power type a person has, the greater the number of influencing strategies that they can use, and the greater the likelihood of achieving a desired outcome. Moreover, the amount of power possessed is not fixed. Organizational members both gain and lose power depending on what they do or fail to do, as well as what those around them do.

Following his review of the influencing literature, Andrzej Huczynski (2004) defined influencing as one person's ability to affect another's attitudes, beliefs or behaviours. Its distinguishing feature is that generally it is seen only in its effect, and is done without the use of either coercion or the use of formal position. If performed successfully, the person being influenced – the *influencee* – will believe that they are acting in their own best interests. Robert Cialdini (2009; Cialdini and Sagarin, 2005) identified six principles of influence by observing 'compliance professionals' who persuade for a living; salespeople, fund-raisers, advertisers, political lobbyists, cult recruiters and con artists. He argues that we have learned

Table 22.5: Power tactics

Image building	We all know people who did not get the job because they didn't look the part – appearance is a credibility issue. Appropriate dress, support for the 'right' causes; adherence to group norms; air of self-confidence.
Information games	Withhold information to make others look foolish, bending the truth, white lies, massaging information, overwhelming others with complex technical information, timed data release
Scapegoating	Ensure someone else is blamed, avoid personal blame yourself, take credit for your and others' success
Alliances	Do a deal with influential others to form a critical mass, a coalition, to win support for your proposals
Networking	Make friends in influential positions. 'Wine-and-dine' them to get your initiatives onto the senior management agenda and improve visibility
Compromise	Give in on unimportant issues to create allies for subsequent, more important issues
Rule games	Refuse requests on the grounds of not following correct procedures or being 'against company policy', but grant identical requests from allies on the grounds of 'special circumstances'
Positioning	Switch to, and choose roles that make you look successful and visible; avoid or withdraw from failing projects; locate yourself appropriately in the building; position yourself in your office
Issue selling	Package, present and promote your ideas and plans in ways that make them more appealing to your target audience
Dirty tricks	Keep dirt files for blackmail, spy on others, discredit and undermine competitors, spread false rumours, corridor talk

Based on Buchanan and Badham (2008, p.16); Buchanan (2008). Reproduced by permission of SAGE Publications, London, Los Angeles, New Delhi and Singapore, from Buchanan, D.A. and Badham, R.J., *Power, Politics and Organizational Change: Winning the Turf Game*, Copyright (© Sage Publications 2008).

a number of automatic responses to familiar social cues, and that compliance professionals and others can exploit those socialized responses.

Reciprocity   we are more likely to comply with a request from someone who has given us a gift, favour, or concession

We have a socially trained sense of obligation, to give 'something in return', even when the gift is unsolicited. Survey researchers include small payments to increase questionnaire response rates; restaurant staff increase tips by giving customers sweets with their bills.

The door-in-the-face technique: The influencer begins with an extreme request (join a long-term blood donor programme), that is usually rejected, then makes the request which they intended (make a one-off donation). The influencer has made a concession, and expects a concession from the target. This is also known as the 'reciprocal concessions' tactic.

Social validation   we are more likely to comply with a request, or to adopt a behaviour, which is consistent with what similar others are thinking or doing

If other people think it is correct, then we tend to agree. If others are doing it (driving fast on a stretch of road), then we feel justified in doing the same. Bartenders 'salt' their jar of tips to indicate that tipping is 'appropriate' behaviour. Church ushers use the same method, and evangelical preachers use 'ringers' who are briefed to 'spontaneously' come forward at predetermined moments during the service.

The list technique: the influencer makes a request after the target has seen a list of others who have already complied (donated, purchased). Research shows that, the longer the list, the greater the effect.

Commitment/ we are more likely to comply with a request which leads to actions that
consistency are consistent with our previous actions and commitments

Consistency is linked to intellect, rationality, honesty, and integrity, and tends to be valued; we like to appear to be consistent. If we can get you to commit to something, then it will be easier to persuade you to behave in ways that are consistent with that prior commitment.

The four walls technique: doorstep salespeople use this to gain permission to enter. The technique involves asking a series of questions to which the target's answer is likely to be yes. To be consistent with their earlier answers, the target then has to agree to the final – crucial – question. The encyclopedia salesperson asks you:

(1) Do you feel that education is important for your children?

(2) Do you think that homework contributes to the quality of education?

(3) Don't you agree that a good set of reference books helps with homework?

(4) Well, you'll be interested in these encyclopedias that we're now offering at a very good price. Can I come in and show you?

The foot-in-the-door technique: the influencer first asks for a small favour that is almost certain to be granted (wear a small pin to promote a charity), followed by a bigger related request (donate cash). Those who agree to the small request are more likely to agree to the larger one.

The bait-and-switch procedure: this is illustrated by retailers who advertise goods (e.g., furniture) at an especially low price, but when the customers show up, the products are either poor quality, or they are sold out. Customers have made a commitment to purchasing at that store, and are more likely to consider alternative products without going elsewhere.

The low-ball technique: the salesperson 'throws a low ball', by persuading the customer to buy (e.g., a car) at a low price, or by offering an inflated trade-in for their old vehicle. But then a calculation error is discovered, or an assessor disallows the trade-in valuation. Having already committed to the purchase, most customers will go ahead even at the higher price.

Friendship/liking we are more likely to comply with requests from friends, or others whom we like

Tupperware parties use friends and neighbours, rather than company sales staff, to persuade participants to purchase. Charities recruit volunteers to collect donations in their local area. Compliance professionals as strangers, however, have to find ways to get us to like them.

Physical attractiveness: attractive individuals are generally more persuasive. Those whom we believe to be attractive are also attributed with traits such as talent, kindness, honesty and intelligence.

Similarity: we tend to like, and to be persuaded more readily, by those who are similar to us, in opinions, background, lifestyle, personality, dress. In one study, a survey response rate was doubled by giving the person sending the questionnaire a name similar to that of the respondent;

Compliments: praise encourages liking, unless it is obvious that the flatterer's intent is manipulative.

Co-operation: co-operation enhances compliance. Salespeople often appear to 'do battle' on the customer's behalf with a remote 'villain' of a sales manager. This co-operation in a shared outcome leads to liking, which promotes sales.

Scarcity we are more likely to comply with requests that will lead to the acquisition of opportunities that are scarce

Opportunities tend to be more highly valued when they are less available, and items that are difficult to possess are 'better' than items that can be easily acquired, including information.

The limited number tactic: customers are told that products, services, membership opportunities are in short supply and will not last long. 'Hurry, buy now.'

The deadline technique: an official time limit is placed on the opportunity to purchase or acquire: 'offer available for one week only'. This may be accompanied by a statement indicating that the item will either be unavailable, or become more expensive, once the deadline has expired.

Authority   we are more likely to comply with requests from those in positions of legitimate authority

Position power can be extremely persuasive. The title 'doctor' often commands blind obedience to dangerous instructions, such as administering an unsafe level of a drug. People are more likely to comply with instructions from a security guard in uniform, and the expensive business suit can have a similar effect.

The bank examiner scheme: a man in a business suit comes to your house claiming to be a bank official investigating irregularities in transactions by a local teller. Will you help? All you have to do is withdraw your savings from that teller's window, so that they can be caught in the act. Then, pass your money to the uniformed security guard, who will return it to your account (allegedly).

Gary Yukl reviewed the research into influencing managers, co-workers and subordinates. He identified 12 influencing tactics and judged their effectiveness (Table 22.6). Both Cialdini's and Yukl's work on influencing is based on the pioneering contribution of Kahneman and Tversky who investigated how individuals made decisions (see Chapter 20, Decision making).

Whether using power-push or influencing-pull, individuals will respond in one of three ways – acceptance, compliance or resistance. Acceptance refers to their agreeing to the request and carrying it out enthusiastically with commitment, and hence with a high probability that it will be fulfilled. In this situation, there is a change in both their attitude and behaviour. Alternatively, their response may be compliance, reluctantly doing what the influencer asks. They will be apathetic, unenthusiastic, will make a minimal effort, and will need to be prodded to meet minimum requirements. They change their behaviour, but not their attitude. Finally, their response might be resistance. They reject the influencer's request, and take steps to avoid having to do it by means of either excuses or a direct refusal. Here there is no change in either their attitude or their behaviour.

Acceptance agreeing with and becoming committed to an influencing request both attitudinally and behaviourally.

Compliance superficial, public and transitory change in behaviour in response to an influencing request reluctantly, which is not accompanied by attitudinal change.

Resistance rejecting an influencing request by means of a direct refusal, making excuses, stalling, or making an argument against, indicating neither behavioural nor attitudinal change.

STOP AND THINK

How would you go about increasing your own power bases (e.g. reward, coercive, referent, etc.) within your organization?

What steps would you take to reduce the power bases of those around you?

Source: Copyright Grantland Enterprises: www.grantland.net.

Table 22.6: Influencing tactics

	Most effective	
Tactic	**Description**	**Examples**
Rational persuasion	Relying on the presentation of factual evidence and logical argument to support a request	'As you can see from this cost comparison, the second tender is 20 per cent lower'
Consultation	Allowing the influencee to participate in deciding *how* to carry out or implement your request	'I need you to work 20 hours of overtime over the next month, but you decide how to put in those hours'
Inspirational appeal	Appealing to the influencee's values, ideals or aspirations to elicit an emotional or attitudinal reaction	'It not about you staying an extra hour after work without overtime pay, it's about improving the health of the nation!'
Collaboration	Making it easy for the influencee to agree to your request by providing resources or removing impediments to agreement	'If you agree to lead the team, I'll give you administrative support, and re-allocate your existing work to others'
	Moderately effective	
Ingratiation	Using favours, compliments and friendly behaviour ('sucking up' or 'brown-nosing') – 'I don't understand this spreadsheet at all'	'You're so clever. I wonder if you could re-analyze these figures for me'
Exchange	Negotiating and exchanging benefits based upon the social norms of obligation and reciprocity	'If you cover my evening shift, I'll do your weekend one for you'
Personal appeal	Influencing request based on personal friendship or loyalty	'Emma – we've worked together now for over four years. I wonder if you could take your annual leave later than normal this year'
Apprising	Explaining to influencee how complying with your request benefits them personally. The benefit is not received directly, as in an exchange, but results from their action	'If you agree to join the team, you'll be presenting your ideas to senior management, and you'll have the opportunity to impress them and perhaps get a promotion'
	Least effective	
Pressure	Making strident verbal statements and regularly reminding the influencee of your request	'As I said yesterday, it's vital that your presentation tomorrow is of the highest standard'
Coalitions	Mobilizing other people in the organization to support you, and thereby strengthening your request	'Claire and Peter are also affected, and that's why we would all like you to change'
Upward appeals	Seeking the assistance of someone senior to your influencee, either through the use of their authority or as mediator	'Since I can't persuade you, let's have a meeting with our boss, and see what she thinks'
Legitimating	Basing a request on your own authority, organizational rules, policies or expressed/implied support of superiors	'As the project leader, I'm asking you to postpone your holiday until the task is completed which is normal company policy'

Based on Yukl (2000, 2005); Yukl and Falbe (1990).

Organizations: rational or political?

Rationalism the
theory that reason
is the foundation of
certainty in knowledge.

Rationality the use
of scientific reasoning,
empiricism and
positivism, as well
as the decision criteria
of evidence, logical
argument and
reasoning.

**Rational model
of organization**
a perspective that holds
that organizational goals
are clear; objectives are
defined, alternatives are
identified; and choices
are made on the basis
of reason in a logical
way.

The question of whether organizations are *rational* or *political* continues to be debated. The form and nature of the assessment of the role of power and politics within organizations depends on whether or not one considers organizations to be political entities. The rational model is summarized on the left-hand side of Table 22.7, while the political is described in the right-hand side column. These two models have different implications for how people are understood to operate within organizations, and which interests they are held to give priority to.

The rational model of organization is based on rationalism and rationality.

Rational actions are undertaken on the basis of reason; a person adopts the same actions in the same circumstances; and choices are made objectively, on valid knowledge rather than on intuition. In the organizational context, the beliefs of the rational model of organization are summarized in the left-hand column of Table 22.7. They are contrasted with those held by the political model, against its eight organizational characteristics. At the very heart of this perspective is the view that an employee possesses goals that conform to, and are compatible with the goals of the other organization members. Individuals are considered to share a collective purpose that can even be called the 'organizational goal'. All the remaining features of the model assume the existence of this goal.

The rational model of organization thus holds that peoples' behaviour in companies is not to be random or accidental, but instead directed towards the achievement of the aforementioned organizational goal. Rationalists argue that when making a choice, the decision-maker is guided by the norm of optimization, that is, seeking the most favourable outcome for a particular end. In this process, the various available alternatives are uncovered, their likely consequences assessed, and the risks of each considered. Finally, the course of action is selected which best meets the organizational goal which, as mentioned earlier, is held to exist and be shared by all.

Table 22.7: Rational versus political models of organization

Organizational characteristic	Rational model	Political model
Goals, preference	Consistent across participants	Inconsistent, pluralistic within the organization
Power and control	Centralized	Decentralized, shifting coalitions and interest groups
Decision process	Orderly, logical, rational	Disorderly, characterized by push and pull of interests
Rules and norms	Norm of optimization	Free play of market forces; conflict is legitimate and expected
Information	Extensive, systematic, accurate	Ambiguous, information used and withheld strategically
Beliefs about cause–effect relationships	Known, at least to a probability estimate	Disagreements about causes and effects
Decisions	Based on outcome-maximizing choice	Result of bargaining and interplay among interests
Ideology	Efficiency and effectiveness	Struggle, conflict, winners, losers

Based on Pfeffer (1981, p.31).

Rationalists hold that this is the best way to make choices on issues such as the introduction of new technology, work organization, distribution of rewards, organization structure, and so on. However, rational writers are not only *prescriptive*, saying how, in their view, things should be done, but also claim to be *descriptive*, that is, they claim to be describing how decisions are actually made in real organizations.

STOP AND THINK Suggest reasons that might account for the popularity of the rationalist view of organizations among managers, management consultants and management academics.

Political model of organization a perspective that holds that organizations are made up of groups that have separate interests, goals and values, and in which power and influence are needed in order to reach decisions.

In contrast, there is the **political model of organization**. Rationalism has not gone unchallenged. James March (1962) was amongst the earliest writers to highlight that the rationalist model failed to take into account the differences of interests and objectives that existed between individuals within organizations. Indeed, March described business firms as *political coalitions*.

The political model of organizations holds that normally there is no overarching organizational goal to which all members subscribe; that the behaviour of individuals and cliques within organizations can be explained with reference to their attempts to achieve their own unique goals; and that those who possess the greatest amounts of power will be the most successful in furthering their interests and achieving their goals. In contrast, the rational model, asserts that individual and departmental goals typically fit into the main organizational objective.

Other researchers investigated how decisions were actually made in organizations. They discovered an absence of the use of reason, consistency, empirical data or means-end sequencing that was supposed to characterize rational organizational decision-making. In the place of consensus they found conflict, and discovered decisions being made on the basis of bargaining and compromise (Allison, 1971). In the place of an organization-wide consensus on the organizational goal, they found individuals, groups, units and departments which had their own objectives; which were in conflict with each other to attain their own parochial ends; and which resolved issues through negotiation and the use of power.

These studies have led another group of writers to promote the political model of organization (Baldridge, 1971). The key characteristics of organizations, as they see them, are summarized in the right-hand column of Table 22.7. Their point of departure is the view that this is no overarching organizational goal to which all members subscribe, and even where there is a written, company 'mission statement', decisions are rarely made which further its achievement. This is because people's goals are considered to be different, and not the same. For example, the differences between management and workers' goals were examined with the concept of the *organizational dilemma* in Chapter 1.

Which is political and which is an example of effective management? The constructivist view of politics holds that a person's perception determines their judgement. Krell *et al.* (1987) illustrated how the same behaviour might be labelled differently depending on a person's standpoint (Table 22.8).

STOP AND THINK Suggest reasons that might account for the relative unpopularity of the political view of organizations among managers, management consultants and management academics.

From your experience of organizations (school, club, church, company) does the rationalist or the political model best explain the behaviour of people within it?

Table 22.8: Politics is in the eye of the beholder

'Political' label	'Effective management' label
Blaming others	Fixing responsibility
'Kissing up'	Developing working relationships
Apple polishing	Demonstrating loyalty
Passing the buck	Delegating authority
Covering your rear	Documenting decisions
Creating conflict	Encouraging change and innovation
Forming coalitions	Facilitating teamwork
Whistle-blowing	Improving efficiency
Scheming	Planning ahead
Overachieving	Competent and capable
Ambitious	Career-minded
Opportunistic	Astute
Cunning	Practical minded
Arrogant	Confident
Perfectionist	Attentive to detail

Based on Krell et al. (1987) in Robbins and Judge (2007), p.483.

The rational and the political models of organization take a different view of the nature of organizations, and also of how the behaviour of people within them can be best explained. Rather like the *nature–nurture* debate on personality, the 'rationalists' and the 'politicals', each have their own supporters, each can provide theoretical and empirical evidence in their defence, and each is necessarily partial, not giving the full picture of what is happening. One view is neither better, nor more realistic than the other. Perhaps it is best to treat the rational and political models as 'different ways of seeing' what goes on in organizations.

Organizational politics

Organizational politics the techniques and tactics used to acquire, develop, retain and use power to obtain preferred outcomes in a situation in which there is uncertainty or an absence of consensus about choices.

The study of **organizational politics** is the study of who gets what, when and how. Engaging in political behaviour or performing political acts, involves individuals engaging in activities to acquire, develop, retain and use power, in order to obtain their preferred outcomes. When decisions are unstructured and complex; cannot be made by following rules; where there is uncertainty; and where employees are in competition with each other, they are made using political processes. Political behaviour concerns the actions that individuals take to influence the distribution of advantages and disadvantages within their organizations (Allen *et al.*, 1979; Farrell and Petersen, 1982). Why does political behaviour occur within organizations? Chanlat (1997) distinguishes four sets of factors – personal, decisional, structural and organizational change – which account for such behaviour.

STOP AND THINK

The main problem with political behaviour in organizations is that most people lack the skills necessary to engage in it effectively. Do you agree or disagree?

Personal factors

Organizations hire individuals who possess ambition, drive, creativity, and ideas of their own. Thus organizational recruitment, appraisal and training and promotion policies directly encourage political behaviour. For example, staff selection methods seek to identify candidates who possess the personality traits that have been related to a willingness to use power and engage in political behaviour. These are the *need for power*, *Machiavellianism*, *locus of control* and *risk-seeking propensity* (House, 1988).

Need for power

Need for power (*nPow*) the desire to make an impact on others, change people or events, and make a difference in life.

In the 1940s, David McClelland (1961) proposed the theory that people culturally acquired, that is learned, three types of needs. These were the need for power (*nPower*), for achievement (*nAch*), and for affiliation (*nAff*). In any single individual the strength of these three needs varied. Some individuals had a strong desire or motive to influence and lead others, and thus were more likely to engage in political behaviour within organizations. Since a desire to control others and events, and thus to have an impact on what is going on, is often associated with effective management, it is not surprising that selectors look for this trait in candidates for managerial jobs (McClelland and Boyatzis, 1982).

US presidents' needs for power, achievement and affiliation

US President	Needs		
	Power (*nPow*)	**Achievement** (*nAch*)	**Affiliation** (*nAff*)
Clinton, Bill	Moderate	High	High
Bush, George (senior)	Moderate	Moderate	Low
Reagan, Ronald	High	Moderate	Low
Kennedy, John F.	High	Low	High
Roosevelt, Frank D.	High	Moderate	Low
Lincoln, Abraham	Moderate	Low	Moderate
Washington, George	Low	Low	Moderate

Based on House *et al.* (1991, p.395).

Machiavellianism

Machiavellianism a personality trait or style of behaviour towards others characterized by (1) the use of guile and deceit in interpersonal relations; (2) a cynical view of the nature of other people; and (3) a lack of concern with conventional morality.

A second trait possessed by those who tend to engage in the use of power and politics in companies is termed Machiavellianism. Niccolo Machiavelli was a sixteenth-century Florentine philosopher and statesman who wrote a set of guidelines for rulers to use in order to secure and hold governmental power. These were published in a book called, *The Prince*, and suggested that the primary method for achieving power was the manipulation of others (Machiavelli, 1961). Since that time, Machiavelli's name has come to be associated with the use of opportunism and deceit in interpersonal relations. Thus we speak about a peoples' Machiavellian behaviour, or describe them as being Machiavellians. Christie and Geis (1970) discussed Machiavellian personality characteristics.

'High-Machs', those who score highly on a pencil-and-paper tests to measure their level of Machevellianism, would agree to statements such as:

Niccolo Machiavelli (1469–1527)

- The best way to deal with people is to tell them what they want to hear
- It is simply asking for trouble to completely trust someone else
- Never tell anyone the real reason you did something unless it is useful to do so

In behaving in accordance with Machiavellian principles, they prefer to being feared than being liked; effectively manipulate others using their persuasive skills, especially in face-to-face contacts; initiate and control interactions; use deceit in relationships; engage in ethically questionable behaviour; and believe that any means justify the desired ends. One might add here that a desire for revenge and retribution, especially if one has been on the receiving end of others' politicking, may be considered both acceptable and satisfying.

Locus of control

Locus of control an individual's generalized belief about internal (self-control) versus external control (control by the situation or by others).

The third personality trait affecting the likelihood of an individual engaging in political behaviour is the locus of control. Some people believe that what happens to them in life is under their own control. These are said to have an internal locus of control. Others hold that their life situation is under the control of fate or other people. This group is classed as having an external locus of control (Rotter, 1966). It is 'internals', those who believe that they control what happens to them, who tend to be more political in their behaviour than 'externals'. Internals are more likely to expect that their political tactics will be effective, and are also less likely to be influenced by others.

Risk-seeking propensity

Risk-seeking propensity the willingness of an individual to choose options that entail risks.

The final personality trait that is likely to determine whether a person engages in political behaviour is their risk-seeking propensity. Engaging in political behaviour in companies is not risk-free, and there are negative as well as positive outcomes for those who do it. They could be demoted, passed over for promotion, or given low performance assessments. Some people are natural risk-avoiders while others are risk-seekers (Sitkin and Pablo, 1992; Madison et al., 1980). Generally speaking, risk-seekers are more willing to engage in political behaviour, than risk-avoiders. For the latter, the negative consequences of a failed influencing attempt outweigh the possible benefits of a successful outcome.

Possession of these personality traits is associated with a high desire for career advancement. Every organization will contain a proportion of ambitious people who compete with each other by arguing and lobbying for their personal ideas; innovations, projects and goals. However, traditional organizational structures are pyramidal or triangular in shape. That is, at each successive, higher level, there are fewer positions available. Hence, these ambitious people are in constant competition with each other to secure a scarce, desirable, more senior post within the company.

Decisional factors

The extent to which politicking enters the decision-making process depends on the type of decisions that are being made and the context of the decision-making process. Decisions vary depending on whether they are structured or unstructured. Structured decisions are programmable, that is, they can be resolved using decision rules. Routine, day-to-day decisions, such as how much stock to order, are of this type. In a standard situation, if a decision is structured or programmed, or if there is no opposition to what a manager wants to do, then it is unnecessary to use politics.

In general however, the number of management decisions that can be reached unambiguously, using information, analysis and logical reasoning, tends to be small. Unstructured decisions are more common. These are unprogrammable and cannot be made in the way previously described, using the bureaucratic rules and procedures that Max Weber would have liked. Moreover, they have implications for inter-unit relationships which is an aspect of organizational integration, and is the most difficult to subject to routinization and techno-economic logic so beloved of rationalists (Beeman and Sharkey, 1987). In these circumstances, the competition between individuals and groups is strong; managerial discretion is high; and decisions have widespread consequences for success or failure at work. Most of the significant decisions in organizations, and virtually all at senior management levels, tend to be unstructured. They cannot be based on reason and logic alone, but involve, in some way, the values and preferences of key organizational members. Examples of unstructured, senior management decisions include:

- Should we seek to maximize profitability now, or seek to extend our market share?
- Should the role of the human resource management function be developed?
- Should we develop our expertise in this sector or take-over a company that already possesses it?

Home viewing

The film *Contact* (1997, director Robert Zemeckis) is about Dr Eleanor (Ellie) Arroway (played by Jodie Foster). It recounts humankind's first contact with alien life. The whole endeavour of searching for extra-terrestrial life is fraught with personal, scientific, economic, political and ethical uncertainties. While she may be an excellent scientist, Ellie is not a particularly good organizational politician. As you watch the film, answer the following questions. What organizational political mistakes does Ellie make? What organizational political skills does Dr David Drumlin display? What mistakes does Ellie make in the President's advisory committee meeting? What tactics does Drumlin use to maintain his controlling position? What advice would you give Ellie if she wanted to become a more effective organizational politician?

Jeffrey Pfeffer
(b.1946)

In such circumstances, one can expect different managers with their own unique past experiences, personal opinions, differing values, and current preferences, to disagree. That debate is normal and valuable. Put another way, 'When two people always agree, one of them is unnecessary' (Pfeffer and Sutton, 2006, p.31). Since information, analysis and logical reasoning cannot resolve an unstructured decision, what strategy is left? In such circumstances difficult choices will be made using political means (Drory, 1993; Schilt, 1986). The managers concerned will use various tactics to gain the support of the people around the table, while deflecting the resistance of others, in order to win the debate, and have their preferred course of action endorsed by the decision-making meeting. To win the competition of ideas, players will do whatever they can, within the constraints imposed by the social norms, to ensure that their ideas prevail over others. The success or failure of rivals will have an impact on their individual position, reputation and career progression, and the status of their department, section or occupational group within the organization.

Thus, political behaviour is a direct consequence of the numerical superiority of unstructured over structured decisions, which explains its predominance in the higher levels of organizations, where such decisions tend to be made most frequently. It also emanates from the tendency of informed and interested parties to disagree with each other, partly on the interpretation of information and analyses, and partly because they hold differing, beliefs, values and preferences. Pfeffer (1992b, p.37) observed that:

> Power is more important in major decisions, such as those made at higher organizational levels, and those that involve crucial issues like reorganization and budget allocations; for domains in which performance is more difficult to assess such as staff rather than line production operations; and in instances in which there is likely to be uncertainty and disagreement.

Structural factors

Organization structuring creates roles and departments which compete with each other. Jeffrey Pfeffer (1981) described how such structuring produced the conditions within organizations where power came to exercised and politicking engaged in (Figure 22.1). Our starting point is the observation that in large organizations, tasks are divided up among a number of departments. *Differentiation* (1) is the term used to refer to this specialization of both departments and employees' jobs in an organization by task. This division of labour enables an organization to achieve certain economies. However, it also has a number of

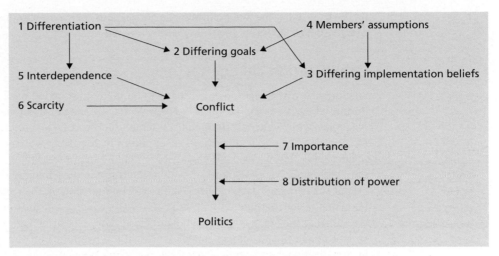

Figure 22.1: Structural conditions producing the use of power and politics in organizational decision-making

Source: Reuse of figure, p.69 'Structural conditions producing the power . . .' from POWER IN ORGANIZATIONS by JEFFREY PFEFFER. Copyright © 1981 by Jeffrey Pfeffer, Reprinted by permission of HarperCollins Publishers.

divisive consequences. First, it creates differences in *goals* (2) and understandings about what the company does, or should do, because each department is assigned its unique goal as part of the differentiation process. Marketing's task may be to maximize sales, while Production's may be to minimize costs. Such objectives are frequently in conflict. Second, different departments receive different sets of information. Marketing receives data on sales, while Production receives data on costs. This causes parochialism, with each employee seeing the world through their own department's perspective.

Differentiation also causes the creation of differences in *beliefs* about how something should be done (3). Individuals can agree on a goal, yet disagree on decisions and their outcomes. They can have different views as to what are the appropriate means to achieve the stated, and perhaps agreed, ends. Individuals are physically recruited into a department, not a company. For example, research and development department (R&D) recruits scientists, while the human resources department hires personnel specialists. The differing personalities and backgrounds of the staff who compose the different company departments, socialization, background, training and way of addressing business problems, affects not only how they see their department's goals, but also their *assumptions* as to how these should be achieved (4).

Differentiation also creates *interdependence* between people and departments, where the actions of one affect the other (5). It thus ties groups and individuals together, making each concerned with what the other does and gets in terms of resources. Scarce resources are the most valuable. Labelling a resource as *scarce* produces a vigorous action to obtain it, and greater dissatisfaction with its apparent unavailability (6). Gandz and Murray (1980) saw scarcity as existing in the following organizational areas: promotions and transfers; hiring; pay; budget allocation; facilities and equipment allocation; delegation of authority; interdepartmental co-ordination; personnel policies; disciplinary penalties; work appraisals; and grievances and complaints.

The combined existence of these factors can certainly lead to conflict between departments, groups and individuals, as was shown in the previous chapter. However, will these conditions inevitably result in the use of power and politicking? Pfeffer argues that they will if two further conditions are met. It depends partly on how important it is to those involved, and *importance* is relative (7). The exercise of power and engagement in political behaviour requires time and effort, so will tend to be reserved for the more important issues. Finally, it depends on how widely *power is distributed* within an organization (8). Politicking, bargaining and coalition formation only occur when power is dispersed, widely, and not when it is centralized at the top. Political behaviour is thus an inevitable consequence of structural differentiation (Johnson and Gill, 1993).

Organization change factors

Such unstructured decisions often have to be made in a period of change and uncertainty during which an organization is unlikely to have a single, unambiguous, clearly defined objective, with which all its members agree. Such a context provides the greatest scope for political behaviour. It creates an opportunity for those who possess the appropriate political skill, knowledge and expertise, to deploy them most effectively because the usual rational arguments and empirical evidence surrounding each argument may be lacking, or because reason and 'facts' are not sufficiently compelling on their own. Who knows what the demand for the product will be in two years time? What the costs of not entering the e-commerce market now are unknown. These four sets of factors – personal, decisional, structural and organizational change – present a powerful combination. Political behaviour in organizational settings is a naturally occurring phenomenon, resistant to management attempts to stifle or eradicate it.

Women and organizational politics

Carly Fiorina (2006, p.70), the ousted chief executive officer of Hewlett Packard, noted in her autobiography that, 'Life isn't always fair, and is different for men than for women.' Sex role stereotyping associates management with masculinity: 'think manager – think male' (Ryan and Haslam, 2005, 2007); systematic underestimation of their abilities; and the consequent hostility, all continue to be the common experience of senior female managers in large corporations. Women are as likely to experience and use organizational politics as their male colleagues. However, research suggests that there are differences between the sexes. These are subtle but real, and have different consequences for those involved. We need to begin by providing a description of some of the gender differences, and then offering explanations for them.

Descriptions of differences

Table 22.9 summarizes the research evidence which contrasts female and male stereotypes concerning attitudes towards organization politics, and appears to confirm the cliché that 'men are bad *but* bold and women are wonderful *but* weak'. However, these are predispositions, broad patterns or general tendencies, and as such must be treated with caution. Differences between the sexes should not be confused with individual differences, and the reinforcement of inaccurate or over-generalized stereotypes should be avoided.

Women in organizations appear not to use power or influencing tactics to the same degree or in the same way as their male counterparts. The consequence of this is their well-documented failure to rise up to occupy senior management roles (Singh and Vinnicombe, 2005). Women are less successful in acquiring organizational power (Mann, 1995). Perrewé and Nelson (2004) argue that women are more likely to suffer 'political skill deficiency'. Since political competence is most important at senior organizational levels, women either struggle in the competition to secure those top jobs for themselves, or else they struggle once they have been appointed to those senior posts. Arroba and James (1988) say that women tend to lack confidence and (perceived) competence in organizational politics. Summarizing the broad findings of the available evidence on influence tactics, Ferris *et al.* (2002, p.103) noted that:

- women tend to use fewer influence tactics than men;
- the tactics most used by women tend to be consistent with female stereotypes;

Table 22.9: Gender stereotypes in approach to organizational politics

wonderful but weak female stereotype	bad but bold male stereotype
socialized to be passive and accommodating	socialized to be proactive and competitive
politically innocent, naive	politically aware, skilled
emphasize rapport; 'we'	emphasize status; 'me'
strive for equity	seek to win
want to be liked	want to be one up
are less prepared to hurt others	are more prepared to hurt others
organizational power is difficult to acquire	organizational power is readily acquired
freely express doubt and uncertainty	freely express confidence and certainty
use passive or 'soft' influence tactics such as coalition forming	use aggressive or 'hard' influence tactics such as threats and assertiveness
use fewer influence tactics	use a wide range of influence tactics
use fewer impression management tactics	use many impression management tactics
use formal systems to get information	use informal systems to get information
narrow network of friends and colleagues	wide network of friends and colleagues
political behaviour is unnecessary	political behaviour is necessary
political behaviour is distasteful	political behaviour is routine
career depends on doing a good job	career depends on self-promotion
uncomfortable with self-promoting behaviour	self-promotion taken for granted
politics interferes with the job	politics necessary to get the job done

Reproduced by permission of SAGE Publications, London, Los Angeles, New Delhi and Singapore, from Buchanan, D.A. and Badham, R.J., *Power, Politics and Organizational Change: Winning the Turf Game*, Copyright (© Sage Publications 2008).

- organizational norms reward those who use traditional 'masculine' influence tactics;
- women who use 'male' tactics may attract organizational rewards (promotion, pay rises) but may receive less social support from colleagues.

Singh *et al.*'s (2002) studies of managers' use of impression management tactics (see Chapter 7, Communication) revealed that networking, ingratiation and self-promotion were reportedly used more by men than women. The differences between male and female managers were greatest at junior levels, and those female managers who used impression management reported that they began doing so after they had noticed that men with equivalent experience and qualifications were being preferred for promotion.

Explanations of differences

What are the reasons for these differences? Explanations by various authors have been offered under a number of headings, individual, social and structural.

He was luckier... the desk allowed him to work
in his underwear.

Source: www.joyoftech.com.

Individual

Personality differences: While variations in individuals' attitudes and behaviours may be attributable to sex, they may also be the result of innate personality traits and predispositions. Some psychologists argue that these are genetically acquired, while others believe that socialization, in the form of upbringing and cultural norms, have a major impact on personality (see Chapter 6, Personality). Women are socialized to be more passive and accommodating than men. Deborah Tannen (1990, 1995) argued that boys and girls acquired different linguistic styles in childhood, which had knock-on effects on their working styles and career prospects later in their lives.

Ignorance: This argument states that women are ignorant of, or deny, the importance of organizational politics. Mann (1995) labelled this 'political naiveté'. As a consequence, they adopt 'innocent' behaviours in the workplace and place their faith in rationality and the formal organization. They believe that they can mobilize the resources that they need through formal channels, and secure promotion by working hard without the need to influence others. In their view, politics only interferes with the process of getting the job done. They are therefore less likely to use informal relationships, loyalties' ties or use favours (granted to and owed by others) to achieve their goals.

Personal preferences: Singh *et al.*'s (2002) study found that, despite apparent gender differences, women understood as well as men, the need to 'read' the organization and 'play the game' in order to be recognized and increase their promotion chances. However, women reported they were uncomfortable having to behave in a self-promoting manner and that networking was not a natural female behaviour. Thus, women in this study understood the rules of the game, but some deliberately chose not to play.

Inauthentic: Women who seek or acquire senior management positions have the option of employing the 'take charge', dominant male stereotype of male leadership. Alice Eagly (2005) noted that women who moderated their display of femininity, and who modelled the confident, authoritative masculine behaviours, were more likely to feel that they were inauthentic, unnatural and play-acting.

Personal motivation: General Electric's study of its 135,000 professional workers found that voluntary turnover among female staff was 8 per cent compared to 6.5 per cent among men. The research firm, Catalyst reported that 26 per cent of professional women who were not yet in the most senior posts said that they did not want those jobs. Of the 108 women who had appeared in the Fortune 500 lists of the most powerful women over the last five years, at least 20 had left their prestigious positions, most of them of their own volition. Apparently, it is not that women cannot get high-level jobs, rather they're choosing not to. The study found that senior, organizational women did not greet promotions eagerly. Some did not actively seek promotions; some declined them outright; while others replied to the invitation, out of modesty, with the question, 'Are you sure?'. Hillary Clinton suggested that many women pushed less strongly for promotion than men, not because they were reining in their ambition, but because they did not hang their egos on the next rung of the corporate ladder. Some women reject the offer of greater power because they are unwilling to make personal sacrifices; while others demand a lot more satisfaction in their lives than men do (Sellers, 2003).

Social

Others' perceptions of appropriate behaviour: Eagly (2005) reported that women had the option of employing the dominant male stereotype of male leadership (aggressive, assertive, competitive, clear, intense). However, those who did so, reported feeling inauthentic, and prompted others to ask whether it was appropriate for a woman to behave like this. It appears that certain behaviours are perceived as being reserved for men, and hence tough female managers are often labelled with epithets such as *battle axe*, *dragon lady*, *bitch* and *bully broad*. Unbridled ambition is still less acceptable in women than in men. (Eagly, 2005, p.464) noted a double bind:

> If a leadership role requires a highly authoritative or competitive behaviour that is perceived as masculine, the mere fact that a woman occupies the role can yield disapproval . . . the more confidently a woman conveys those values, the less effective she may become because of her challenge to traditional gender norms and her overturning of the expected gender hierarchy.

Other writers concur, saying that women are more likely to meet with disapproval from others for failing to conform to expectations concerning appropriate female behaviour, and can be seen as unacceptably pushy (Ryan and Haslam, 2007).

Structural

Work experience: Both Kanter (1979) and Oakley (2000) have argued that women are rendered 'structurally powerless' by being limited to routine, low-profile jobs; having restricted access to line management roles early in their careers; and facing male discrimination in promotion decisions due to secretive promotion and reward systems, unequal power distribution and 'old boy networks' (Oakley, 2000).

Working practices: Hillary Clinton asked, 'Are women willing to pay the price of corporate life?' They have to play by the same rules as the men, and right now, there are really brutal rules for women who want to have families. Bunting (2004, p.124) quotes Harvey, a manager at Microsoft UK, who says, 'Women look at how big those jobs are, and take a choice'. That explains the 80–20 per cent split of men to women at senior levels, but he insists that the senior ladies are getting through. The average age of employees at Microsoft UK is 34, and most of those Bunting met had no children. The male-dominated culture of organizations increasingly encourages long working hours. This discourages women who have family responsibilities, preventing them from participating in formal working breakfast meetings or socially in late evening drinks. It also excludes them from informal male gatherings in inaccessible locations such as the golf club or the men's locker room in the gym.

This neat categorization separates and presents a set of individual explanations for the underrepresentation of women in senior management roles. Mann (1995) however, offers a more integrated 'spiral of female powerless', linking several of them, when she suggests that the existing male-dominated culture, with its power bias towards men, means that women are less successful in acquiring organizational power than men. Because they have less access to power, they are therefore less likely to engage in and make use of organizational politics, and rely instead on formal means (achieving stated targets) to advance up the executive ladder. Such political career incompetence leads to their stunted career progression within the organizational hierarchy.

 RECAP

1. *Appreciate the importance of power and politics in organizational life.*
   - Whether real or perceived, greater turbulence in the context of organizations, has created increased fluidity, uncertainty, ambiguity and discontinuity, providing the ideal conditions in which power and politics can be exercised.

2. *Compare and contrast different perspectives on power.*
   - Power can be considered from the 'power-as-property'; the 'faces of power'; and the 'disciplinary power' viewpoints.
   - The 'power-as-property' viewpoint offers three perspectives seeing power as a property of individuals; of relationships and as an embedded property of structures.
   - The 'faces of power' viewpoint offers three dimensions: seeing power as overt and observable; as covert and unobservable; and as internalized by employees.
   - Disciplinary power reduces subordinates' ability to dissent by creating and managing meanings for them.

3. *Distinguish different bases of power.*
   - The five bases of power are reward, coercion, referent, legitimate and expert.

4. *Identify organizational factors which enhance the power of departments.*
   - Factors enhancing the power of departments are dependency-creation; financial resources; centrality; non-substitutability and uncertainty reduction.

5. *Differentiate between power tactics, influencing tactics and influencing responses.*
   - Power tactics can be classified under the headings of image building; selective information; scapegoating;

formal alliances; networking' compromise; rule manipulation; as well as covert 'dirty tricks' methods.
   - Influencing tactics include rational persuasion; consultation; inspirational appeal; collaboration; ingratiation; exchange; personal appeal; apprising; pressure; and coalitions.
   - Influencing responses are acceptance, compliance and resistance.

6. *Distinguish between the rational and political models of organization.*
   - The rational model of organizations sees behaviour in organizations as guided by clear goals and choices made on the basis of reason, the *political model of organization* sees no such logical behaviour, but sees organizations made up of groups possessing their own interests, goals and values, and in which power and influence are needed in order to reach decisions.

7. *Identify the characteristics of individuals most likely to engage in political behaviour.*
   - Persons most likely to engage in political behaviour have a high need for power (nPow); a high Mach score; an internal locus of control; and a risk-seeking propensity.

8. *Explain how women use and are affected by organizational politics.*
   - Sex role stereotyping associates management with masculinity leading to a systematic underestimation of women's abilities.
   - Women appear to use power, influencing and impression management tactics differently to men.
   - Differences between men and women in organizations can be considered under the three headings of individual, social and structural.

Revision

1. How can someone low in the organizational hierarchy obtain power?

2. Discuss the costs and benefits to an organization of its employees engaging in political behaviour.

3. 'Power is most potent when it appears to be absent'. What does this statement mean? Do you agree with it? Give reasons and examples to support your view.

4. Why are some departments, units or groups in organizations more powerful than others?

Research assignment

Read the literature on the difference between rational and political decision-making beginning at p.709 in this book. Interview three managers from the same or different organizations, ideally at junior, middle and senior manager levels. (a) Ask each one to give you a specific example of 'workplace politics in action' (b) Make three copies of the scoresheet from p.724. Ask each manager to rank each type of decision according to the extent that they believe politics plays a part in it in their organization (1 = most political; 11 = least political). They should enter their ranking in column three (c) Ask them what makes a decision 'political' in their organization.

Springboard

Buchanan, D. and Badham, R., 2008, *Power, Politics and Organizational Change*, 2nd edn, Sage, London.

Revised and updated edition considers the use of power and politics with respect to a change agent.

Mintzberg, H., 1983, *Power In and Around Organizations*, Prentice Hall, Englewood Cliffs, NJ.

A major contribution from a North American perspective.

Pfeffer, J., 1992, *Managing With Power: Politics and Influence in Organizations*, 2nd edn, Harvard Business School Press, Boston MA.

A discussion of power and politics for a management audience by a leading academic researcher and author.

Yukl, G., 2000, 'Using power effectively' in Locke, E.A. (ed.), *The Blackwell Handbook of Principles of Organizational Behaviour*, Blackwell Business, Oxford, pp.241–56.

Introduction to different types of power and influencing tactics.

OB in films

Dirty Rotten Scoundrels (1988, director Frank Oz). DVD track 2: 0:07:42–0:10:55 (4 minutes). In the film, Freddy Benson (played by Steve Martin) is a conman working the French Riviera. The clip begins with a shot of Zurich railway station platform and ends with Martin saying 'Thank you.' Martin persuades a woman on a train, a complete stranger, to buy him a meal. How does he achieve this?

1. What impression management techniques does he use?

2. What influencing tactics does he employ?

OB in literature

Paul Palmer, *Balance of Power*, Coronet Books/Hodder & Stoughton, London, 2000. The premature death of the American President Tyler Forrester, and the discovery of evidence suggesting that he may have been corruptly accepting bribes, prompts his wife Elizabeth to investigate. The story revolves around the power bases and power plays of senior political and administrative figures and the less influential figures who they cynically manipulate. Many political tactics are illustrated, including the use and exploitation of relationships and networks, spreading carefully timed rumours to discredit people, image manipulation, using blackmail to get 'inside' information, and removing opposition by sideways 'promotion'. Although perhaps overstated in this fictional account, these tactics are broadly typical examples of political behaviour in large complex organizations.

CHAPTER EXERCISES

Power in a changing environment

Objectives

1. Introduce students to different types of power.

2. Introduce students to the PESTLE change drivers in the environment which impact on the power of employees.

3. To understand how power in organizations is gained and lost as a result of these environment changes.

Briefing

1. Form groups and nominate a spokesperson.

2. Read each of the five scenarios in order. For each one, decide:

   (a) Which environment change driver is affecting the organization in this scenario?

   (b) What types of activities are likely to increase/become more important in the company, as a result?

   (c) Which five company employees' power will *increase* most in the light of this changed environmental condition?

   (d) Why did you select these persons?

   Each scenario is separate from the others. Make any reasonable assumptions as you discuss the matter.

3. Each group's spokesperson presents and justifies their conclusions to the entire class.

Situation

Your medium-sized company manufactures portable, petrol-driven, electric power generators that are sold to domestic and office customers, often for use in emergencies.

Advertising expert (m)	Chartered accountant (m)
Chief financial offer (f)	General manager (m)
Operations manager (f)	Marketing manager (f)
Industrial engineer (m)	Computer programmer (f)
Product designer (m)	Industrial chemist (m)
Public relations expert (m)	In-house legal advisor (m)
Company trainer (m)	Human resource manager (f)

Employees (m) = male; (f) = female

Environmental change scenarios

1. The existing small batch production of engines will be replaced by a state-of-the-art, automated assembly line.

2. New laws about engine and factory emissions are being passed by the European Parliament.

3. Sales are greatly reduced, and the industrial sector seems to be shrinking.

4. The company is planning to go international in the next year or two.

5. The Equality Commission is pressing companies to establish better male–female balance in senior posts and is threatening to 'name-and-shame' companies.

Exercise adapted from Barbuto, J.E., Power and the changing environment in Journal of Management Education, 24(2), pp.288–96, Copyright © 2000, OBTS Teaching Society for Management Educators, reprinted by permission of SAGE Publications.

Politics in decision-making

Objectives
1. To contrast perceptions about the use of politics in decision-making.
2. To predict when and where politics will be used in organizations.
3. To contrast political with rational decision-making processes.

Briefing
1. Individually, using the worksheet, rank each of the 11 organizational decisions in terms of the extent to which you think politics plays a part. Rank the most political decision as '1' and the least political as '11'. Enter your ranking in the first column on your worksheet – 'Individual ranking'.

2. Form groups of 4–7. Rank the 11 items again, this time as a group. Use consensus to reach agreement, that is, listen to each person's ideas and rationale before deciding. Do not vote, bargain, average or toss a coin. Base your decision on the logical arguments made by group members rather than your personal preference. Enter your rankings in the second column on the scoresheet – 'Team ranking'.

3. After all teams have finished, your instructor will read out the rankings produced by a survey of managers which indicates the frequency with which they believe that politics plays a part in each type of decision. As these are read out, enter them in column 3 on the scoresheet – 'Manager ranking'.

4. In your existing groups:

   (a) Compare the individual rankings (column 1) of group members. On which decisions did group members' perceptions differ significantly? Why might that be?

   (b) Compare your group ranking (column 2) with the manager ranking (column 3). On which decisions did group and managers' perceptions differ significantly? Why might that be?

→

Scoresheet

'To what extent do you believe politics plays a part in the decision?'

1 = most political   11 = least political

Decision	1 Individual ranking	2 Team ranking	3 Manager ranking
1. Management promotions and transfers			
2. Entry level hiring			
3. Amount of pay			
4. Annual budgets			
5. Allocation of facilities, equipment, offices			
6. Delegation of authority among managers			
7. Interdepartmental co-ordination			
8. Specification of personnel policies			
9. Penalties for disciplinary infractions			
10. Performance appraisals			
11. Grievances and complaints			

5. Re-form as a total group and answer the questions as directed by your instructor:

(a) What distinguishes the most political decisions items (ranked 1–4 in column 3) from the least political (ranked 8–11)?

(b) In what circumstances might a rationale decision process be used in making a decision, and when would a political process be used?

(c) Research suggests that political behaviour occurs more frequently at higher rather than lower levels. Why should this be so?

(d) How would you

  • apply rationality to those decisions currently possessing a large political element?

  • politicize decisions currently made using rational processes?

(e) How would you advise a manager who felt that politics was bad for the organization and should be avoided at all costs?

Based on Daft and Sharfman (1990, pp.339–41);
Baker and Paulson (1995, pp.18–22).

Glossary

Acceptance agreeing with and becoming committed to an influencing request both attitudinally and behaviourally.

Accountability the obligation of a subordinate to report back on their discharge of the duties for which they are responsible.

Activities in Homans's theory, the physical movements, and verbal and non-verbal behaviours engaged in by group members.

Action team a team that executes brief performances that are repeated under new conditions. Its members are technically specialized, and it needs to co-ordinate its output with those of other work units.

Adaptive decisions decisions that require human judgement based on clarified criteria and are made using basic quantitative decision tools.

Additive task a task whose accomplishment depends on the sum of all group members' efforts.

Adhocracy an organization design which is temporary, adaptive and creative, in contrast with bureaucracy which tends to be permanent, rule driven and inflexible.

Advice team a team created primarily to provide a flow of information to management to be used in its own decision-making.

Affiliation power the ability of a leader to exert influence based on the belief of followers that the leader has a close association with other powerful figures on whose authority they are able to act.

Aggregate a collection of unrelated people who happen to be in close physical proximity for a short period of time.

Alienation feelings of powerlessness, meaninglessness, isolation and self-estrangement engendered within employees by the design of the jobs that they perform.

Arbitration a process in which a third party to a conflict has the authority to impose an agreement that is binding on the parties in conflict.

Asynchronous communication occurs when participants start a discussion topic (or thread), post replies to each other and, after delays, individuals read to catch up with the discussion. It is similar to a dialogue conducted by post.

Attribution the process by which we make sense of our environment through our perceptions of causality.

Authority the right to guide or direct the actions of others and extract from them responses that are appropriate to the attainment of an organization's goals.

Autonomous work group a team allocated to a significant segment of the workflow, with discretion over how their work will be carried out.

Balanced scorecard an approach to defining organizational effectiveness using a combination of quantitative and qualitative measures to assess performance.

Basic assumptions invisible, preconscious, 'taken-for-granted' understandings held by individuals within an organization concerning human behaviour, the nature of reality and its relationship to its environment.

Behaviour modification is a technique for encouraging desired behaviours and discouraging unwanted behaviours using operant conditioning.

Behavioural modelling learning how to act by observing and copying the behaviour of others.

Behavioural self-management a technique for changing one's own behaviour by systematically manipulating cues, cognitive processes and contingent consequences.

Behavioural theory of decision-making recognizes that bounded rationality limits the making of optimal decisions.

Behaviourist psychology a perspective which argues that what we learn are chains of muscle movements; mental processes are not observable, and are not valid issues for study (also **stimulus-response psychology**).

Bias a prejudice, predisposition or a systematic distortion caused by the application of a heuristic.

the big five trait clusters that appear consistently to capture main personality traits; Openness, Conscientiousness, Extraversion, Agreeableness and Neuroticism.

Boreout boredom, demotivation, and lack of energy and enthusiasm caused by uninteresting, unchallenging and monotonous work.

Boundaryless organization one possessing permeable internal and external boundaries which give it flexibility and thus the ability to respond to change rapidly.

Bounded rationality individuals making decisions by constructing simplified models that extract the essential features from problems without capturing all their complexity.

Brainstorming a technique in which all group members are encouraged to propose ideas spontaneously, without critiquing or censoring others' ideas. The alternative ideas so generated are not evaluated until all have been listed.

Bureaucracy legal-rational type of authority underpinning a form of organization structure that is characterized by a specialization of labour, a specific authority hierarchy, a formal set of rules, and a rigid promotion and selection criteria.

Caution shift phenomenon the tendency of a group to make decisions that are more risk averse than those that the members of the group would have recommended individually.

Centralization the concentration of authority and responsibility for decision-making power in the hands of managers at the top of an organization's hierarchy.

Certainty a condition in which managers possess full knowledge of alternatives; a high probability of having these available; being able to calculate the costs and benefits of each alternative; and having high predictability of outcomes.

Chain of command the unbroken line of authority that extends from the top of the organization to the bottom and clarifies who reports to whom.

Change agent any member of an organization seeking to promote, further, support, sponsor, initiate, implement or help to deliver change.

Characteristics of mass production mechanical pacing of work, no choice of tools or methods, repetitiveness, minute subdivision of product, minimum skill requirements, and surface mental attention.

Charismatic authority the belief that the ruler had some special, unique virtue, either religious or heroic, e.g. the authority of religious prophets, charismatic politicians and film stars.

Chimerial control a combination of management pressure exercised vertically on the individual through bureaucracy, technology, surveillance and the manipulation of culture; and team pressure exercised horizontally through the group norms and sanctions.

Classical decision theory assumes that decision-makers are objective, have complete information and consider all possible alternatives and their consequences before selecting the optimal solution.

Coding the stage in the interpersonal communication process in which the transmitter chooses how to express a message for transmission to someone else.

Coercive power the ability of a leader to exert influence based on the belief of followers that the leader can administer unwelcome penalties or sanctions.

Cognitive psychology a perspective which argues that what we learn are mental structures; mental processes can be studied by inference, although they cannot be observed directly (also **information processing psychology**).

Collaborative relationship structure a structure that involves a relationship with another, sharing with them ideas, knowledge, staff and technology for mutual benefit.

Communication climate the prevailing atmosphere in an organization – *open* or *closed* – in which ideas and information are exchanged.

Communication network analysis a technique that uses direct observation to determine the source, direction and quantity of oral communication between congregated members of a group.

Communication pattern analysis a technique that uses analysis of documents, data, and voicemail transmission, to determine the source, direction and quantity of oral and written communication between the dispersed members of a group.

Communication pattern chart indicates the source, direction and quantity of oral and written communication between the dispersed members of a group.

Communication process the transmission of information, and the exchange of meaning, between at least two people.

Communigram a chart that indicates the source, direction and quantity of oral communication between the congregated members of a group.

Compensatory effects processes that delay or deflect replacement effects, and which lead to the creation of new products and services, and new jobs.

Compliance (in the context of a group) a majority's influence over a minority (Chapter 12).

Compliance superficial, public and transitory change in behaviour in response to an influencing request reluctantly, which is not accompanied by attitudinal change (Chapter 22).

Concertive control control exercised by the workers themselves who collaborate to develop the means of their own control by negotiating a consensus which shapes their own behaviour according to a set of core values such as those of the corporate vision statement.

Concurrent feedback information which arrives during our behaviour and which can be used to control behaviour as it unfolds.

Conflict a process that begins when one party perceives that another party has negatively affected, or is about to negatively affect, something the first part cares about.

Conflict resolution a process, which has as its objective the ending of the conflict between the disagreeing parties.

Conflict stimulation the process of engendering conflict between parties where none existed before, or escalating the current conflict level if it is too low.

Conformity a change in an individual's belief or behaviour in response to real or imagined group pressure.

Conjunctive task a task whose accomplishment depends on the performance of the group's least talented member.

Consideration a pattern of leadership behaviour that demonstrates sensitivity to relationships and to the social needs of employees.

Consolidation the process through which company ownership in a sector becomes concentrated in a smaller number of larger and sometimes global enterprises.

Constructivism a perspective which argues that our social and organizational worlds have no ultimate objective truth or reality, but are instead determined by our shared experiences, meanings, and interpretations.

Contingency approach to organization structure a perspective which argues that to be effective, an organization must adjust its structure to take into account its technology; its environment; its size; or other contextual factors.

Contingency theory of leadership a perspective which argues that leaders must adjust their style in a manner consistent with aspects of the context.

Control concept the process of imposing a pattern on previously haphazard activities, such as the operation of machinery, the interaction of machinery with people, or the interactions between individuals.

Controlled performance setting standards, measuring performance, comparing actual with standard, and taking corrective action if necessary.

Conversion a minority's influence over a majority.

Co-opetition a form of cooperation between competing organizations which is limited to specified areas where both believe they can gain mutual benefit.

Coping cycle the emotional response to trauma and loss, in which we experience first denial, then anger, bargaining, depression, and finally acceptance.

Corporate social responsibility the view that organizations should act ethically, in ways that contribute to economic development, the environment, quality of working life, local communities, and the wider society.

Cross-functional team employees from different functional departments who meet as a team to complete a particular task.

Crowdsourcing the act of taking a task traditionally performed by a designated agent (employee or contractor), and outsourcing it to an undefined, generally large group of people, in the form of an open call for assistance.

Cybernetic analogy an explanation of the learning process based on the components and operation of a feedback control system.

Decentralization the downward dispersion of authority and responsibility for decision-making to operating units, branches and lower level managers.

Decision-making the process of making choices from among several options.

Decoding the stage in the interpersonal communication process in which the recipient interprets a message transmitted to them by someone else.

Deep acting attempting to modify one's felt emotions based on display rules.

Deindividuation an increased state of anonymity that loosens normal constraints on individuals' behaviour, reducing their sense of responsibility, and leading to an increase in impulsive and antisocial acts.

Delayed feedback information which is received after a task is completed, and which can be used to influence future performance.

Delegation managers granting decision-making authority to employees at lower hierarchical levels.

Departmentalization the process of grouping together activities and employees who share a common supervisor and resources, who are jointly responsible for performance, and who tend to identify and collaborate with each other.

Descriptive models of decision-making investigate how individuals actually make decisions.

Differentiation the degree to which the tasks and the work of individuals, groups and units are divided up within an organization.

Differentiation perspective on culture regards it as consisting of subcultures, each with its own characteristics, which differ from those of its neighbours.

Disjunctive task a task whose accomplishment depends on the performance of the group's most talented member.

Display rules organizational scripts concerning which feelings are appropriate in a given setting and how they should be displayed.

Displayed emotions emotions that employees are required by management to show as part of their jobs.

Disruptive innovations innovations which involve the development of wholly new processes, procedures, services and products.

Distributive bargaining a negotiation strategy in which a fixed sum of resources is divided up. It leads to a win–lose situation between the parties.

Distributed leadership the collective exercise of leadership behaviours, often informal and spontaneous, by staff at all levels of an organization.

Divisional structure an organizational design that groups departments together based on the product sold, the geographical area served, or type of customer.

Double-loop learning the ability to challenge and to redefine the assumptions underlying performance standards and to improve performance.

Drive an innate, biological determinant of behaviour, activated by deprivation.

Dysfunctional conflict a form of conflict which does not support organization goals and hinders organizational performance.

Emotions intense, short-lived reactions that are linked to a specific cause and which interrupt thought processes and behaviours.

Emotional dissonance the disparity between an individual's felt and displayed emotions.

Emotional harmony a match between an employee's felt emotions and their expressed emotions within the workplace.

Emotional intelligence the ability to identify, integrate, understand and reflectively manage one's own and other people's feelings.

Emotional labour the act of expressing organizationally required emotions during interactions with others at work.

Employment cycle the sequence of stages through which all employees pass in each working position they hold, from recruitment and selection, to termination.

Empowerment organizational arrangements that give employees more autonomy, discretion, and decision-making responsibility.

Enacted environment the environment of an organization that exists for members by virtue of the interpretations they make of what is occurring 'outside' the organization, and the way their own actions influence or shape those occurrences.

Encounter stage of socialization the period of learning in the process during which the new recruit learns about organizational expectations.

Engagement the extent to which people enjoy and believe in what they do, and feel valued for doing it.

Environment issues, trends, and events outside the boundaries of the organization, which influence internal decisions and behaviours.

Environmental complexity the range of external factors relevant to the activities of the organization; the more factors, the higher the complexity.

Environmental determinism the argument that internal organizational responses are primarily determined by external environmental factors.

Environmental dynamism the pace of change in relevant factors external to the organization; the greater the pace of change, the more dynamic the environment.

Environmental scanning techniques for identifying and predicting the impact of external trends and developments on the internal functioning of an organization.

Environmental uncertainty the degree of unpredictable turbulence and change in the political, economic, social, technological, legal and ecological context in which an organization operates.

Equity theory a process theory of motivation which argues that perception of unfairness leads to tension, which motivates the individual to resolve that unfairness.

Escalation of commitment an increased commitment to a previously made decision, despite negative information suggesting one should do otherwise.

Ethical stance the extent to which an organization exceeds its legal minimum obligations to its stakeholders and to society at large.

Ethics the codes of moral principles, values and rules that govern our decisions and actions with respect to what is right and wrong, good and bad.

Evidence-based management systematically using the best available research evidence to inform decisions about how to manage people and organizations.

Expectancy the perceived probability that effort will result in good performance, and is measured on a scale from 0 (no chance) to 1 (certainty).

Expectancy theory a process theory which argues that individual motivation depends on the *valence* of outcomes, the *expectancy* that effort will lead to good performance, and the *instrumentality* of performance in producing valued outcomes.

Expert power the ability of a leader to exert influence based on the belief of followers that the leader has superior knowledge relevant to the situation and the task.

Explanatory model of decision-making an approach that accounts for how individuals, groups and organizations make decisions.

Explicit knowledge knowledge and understanding which is codified, clearly articulated, and available to anyone.

Expression rules dictate how displayed feelings should be expressed in particular settings.

External adaptation the process through which employees adjust to changing environmental circumstances to attain organizational goals.

External work team differentiation the degree to which a work team stands out from its organizational context, in terms of its membership, temporal scope and territory.

External work team integration the degree to which a work team is linked with the larger organization of which it is a part.

Extinction the attempt to eliminate undesirable behaviours by attaching no consequences, positive or negative, such as indifference and silence.

Extreme job a job that involves a working week of 60 hours or more, with high earnings, combined with additional performance pressures.

Extrinsic feedback information which comes from our environment, such as the visual and aural information needed to drive a car.

Extrinsic rewards valued outcomes or benefits provided by others, such as promotion, pay increases, a bigger office desk, praise and recognition.

Feedback information about the outcomes of our behaviour.

Feedback (in the process of interpersonal communication) processes through which the transmitter of a message detects whether and how that message has been received and decoded.

Feeling rules dictate which feelings should be displayed in particular settings.

Felt emotions emotions that employees actually feel in a work situation.

Fordism a form of work design that applies scientific management principles to workers' jobs; the installation of single purpose machine tools to manufacture standardized parts; and the introduction of the mechanized assembly line.

Formal group one that has been consciously created by management to accomplish a defined task that contributes to the organization's goal.

Formal organization the documented, planned relationships, established by management to co-ordinate the activities of different employees towards the achievement of the organizational goal.

Formal status the collection of rights and obligations associated with a position, as distinct from the person who may occupy that position.

Formalization the degree to which an organization has written rules, operating procedures, job descriptions, organizational charts and uses formal, written communication.

Fragmentation (or conflict) perspective on culture regards it as consisting of an incompletely shared set of elements that are loosely structured and constantly changing.

Frame of reference a person's perceptions and interpretations of events that involve assumptions about reality, attitudes towards what is possible, and conventions regarding correct behaviour.

Free rider a member who obtains benefits from team membership without bearing a proportional share of the costs for generating that benefit.

Functional conflict a form of conflict which supports organization goals and improves performance.

Functional foremanship dividing the job of a general foreman into its constituent parts and assigning a different foreman to each part, who would oversee and be responsible for that aspect of all workers' jobs.

Functional relationship one in which staff department specialists have the authority to insist that line managers implement their instructions concerning a particular issue.

Functional structure an organizational design that groups activities and people according to the similarities in their work, profession, expertise, goals or resources used.

Fundamental attribution error the tendency to emphasize explanations of the behaviour of others based on their personality or disposition, and to overlook the influence of wider social and contextual influences.

Gender culturally specific patterns of behaviour which may be attached to either of the sexes.

Generalized other what we think other people expect of us, in terms of our attitudes, values, beliefs and behaviour.

Globalization the intensification of world-wide social and business relationships which link localities in such a way that local conditions are shaped by distant events.

Goal orientation the motivation to achieve goals – *aggressive masculinity* v. *passive femininity*.

Goal-setting theory a process theory of motivation which argues that work motivation is influenced by goal difficulty, goal specificity, and knowledge of results.

Great man theory a historical perspective which argues that the fate of societies, and organizations, is in the hands of powerful, idiosyncratic (male) individuals.

Group two or more people, in face-to-face interaction, each aware of their group membership and interdependence, as they strive to achieve their goals.

Group cohesion the number and strength of mutual positive attitudes towards other group members.

Group dynamics the forces operating within groups that affect their performance and their members' satisfaction.

Group norm expected mode of behaviour or belief that is established either formally or informally by a group.

Group polarization a situation in which individuals in a group begin by taking a moderate stance on an issue related to a common value and, after having discussed it, end up taking a more extreme decision than the average of members' decisions. The extremes could be more risky or more cautious.

Group power the ability of a leader to exert influence based on the belief of followers that the leader has collective support from a team or group.

Group process the patterns of interactions between the members of a group.

Group sanction a punishment or a reward given by members to others in the group in the process of enforcing group norms.

Group self-organization the tendency of groups to form interests, develop autonomy and establish identities.

Group socialization the process whereby members learn the values, symbols and expected behaviours of the group to which they belong.

Group structure the relatively stable pattern of relationships among different group members.

Groupthink a mode of thinking in a cohesive in-group, in which members' strivings for unanimity override their motivation to appraise realistically the alternative courses of action.

Growth need strength a measure of the readiness and capability of an individual to respond positively to job enrichment.

Habituation the decrease in our perceptual response to stimuli once they have become familiar.

Halo effect a judgement based on a single striking characteristic, such as an aspect of dress, speech, posture, or nationality.

Hawthorne Effect the tendency of people being observed to behave differently than they otherwise would.

Heuristic a simple and approximate rule, guiding procedure, shortcut or strategy that is used to solve a problem.

Hierarchy the number of levels of authority to be found in an organization.

High context culture a culture whose members rely heavily on a range of social and non-verbal cues when communicating with others and interpreting their messages.

High performance work system a form of organization that operates at levels of excellence far beyond those of comparable systems.

Hollow organization structure an organizational design based on outsourcing an organization's non-core *processes* which are then supplied to it by specialist, external providers.

Human Relations approach a school of management thought which emphasizes the importance of social processes at work.

Human resource management the function responsible for establishing integrated personnel policies to support organization strategy.

Hygiene factors aspects of work which remove dissatisfaction, but do not contribute to motivation and performance, including pay, company policy, supervision, status, security and working conditions.

Identification the incorporation of another's thoughts, feelings and actions into one's self-esteem, thereby transforming oneself.

Idiographic an approach to the study of personality emphasizing the uniqueness of the individual, rejecting the assumption that we can all be measured on the same dimensions.

Impression management the processes through which we control the image or impression that others have of us.

Influencing the ability to affect another's attitudes, beliefs or behaviours, seen only in its effect, without using coercion or formal position, and in a way that influencees believe that they are acting in their own best interests.

Informal group a collection of individuals who become a group when they develop interdependencies, influence one another's behaviour, and contribute to mutual need satisfaction.

Informal organization the undocumented relationships that arise spontaneously between employees as individuals interact with one another to meet their own psychological and physical needs.

Information power the ability of a leader to exert influence based on the belief of followers that the leader has access to information that is not public knowledge.

Initiating structure a pattern of leadership behaviour that emphasizes performance of the work in hand and the achievement of product and service goals.

Initiative and incentive system a form of job design in which management gives workers a task to perform; provides them with the financial incentive to complete it, but then leaves them to use their own initiative as to how they will perform it.

Initiative decay an organizational phenomenon where the benefits from a change initiative 'evaporate', when attention shifts to focus on other issues and priorities.

Initiative fatigue the personal exhaustion and apathy resulting from the experience of too much organizational change.

Inner work life theory a process theory of motivation which argues that our behaviour and performance at work are influenced by the interplay of our perceptions, emotions, and motives.

Innovation involves the adoption of any device, system, process, programme, product, or service new to that organization.

Innovative decisions decisions which address novel problems, lack pre-specified courses of action, and are made by senior managers.

Instrumental orientation an attitude that sees work as an instrument to the fulfilment of other life goals.

Instrumentality the perceived probability that good performance will lead to valued rewards, and is measured on a scale from 0 (no chance) to 1 (certainty).

Integration the required level to which units in an organization are linked together, and their respective degree of independence.

Integrative bargaining a negotiation strategy that seeks to increase the total amount of resources. It creates a win–win situation between the parties.

Integration (or unitary) perspective on culture regards it as monolithic, characterized by consistency, organization-wide consensus, and clarity.

Intensive technology technology that is applied to tasks that are performed in no predetermined order.

Interaction process analysis a technique used to categorize the content of speech.

Interactionist frame of reference on conflict a perspective that views conflict as a positive and necessary force within organizations that is essential for their effective performance.

Interactions in Homans' theory, the two-way communications between group members.

Intermittent reinforcement a procedure in which a reward is provided only occasionally following correct responses, and not for every correct response.

Internal integration the process through which employees adjust to each other, work together, and perceive themselves as a collective entity.

Internal work team differentiation the degree to which a team's members possess different skills and knowledge that contributes towards the achievement of the team's objective.

Intrinsic feedback information which comes from within, from the muscles, joints, skin, and other mechanisms such as that which controls balance.

Intrinsic rewards valued outcomes or benefits which come from the individual, such as feelings of satisfaction, competence, self-esteem and accomplishment.

Introjection a formerly external regulation or value that has been 'taken in' and is now enforced through internal pressures such as guilt, anxiety or related self-esteem dynamics.

Japanese teamworking use of scientific management principles of minimum manning, multi-tasking, multi-machine operation, pre-defined work operations, repetitive short cycle work, powerful first line supervisors, and a conventional managerial hierarchy.

Job definition determining the task requirements of each job in an organization. It is the first decision in the process of organizing.

Job description a summary statement of what an individual should do in the job.

Job diagnostic survey a questionnaire which assesses the degree of skill variety, task identity, task significance, autonomy, and feedback in jobs.

Job enlargement a work design method in which tasks are combined to widen the scope of a job.

Job enrichment a technique for broadening the experience of work to enhance employee need satisfaction and to improve motivation and performance.

Job rotation a work design method in which employees are switched from task to task at regular intervals.

Joint venture an arrangement in which two or more companies remain independent, but establish a new organization that they jointly own and manage.

Just-in-time system managing inventory (stock) in which items are delivered when they are needed in the production process, instead of being stored by the manufacturer.

Kaizen Japanese term for 'improvement', refers to an element within total quality management in which employees are given responsibility, within limits, to suggest incremental changes to their work practices.

Knowledge management the conversion of individual tacit knowledge into explicit knowledge so that it can be shared with others in the organization.

Labour process the work that employees perform, the conditions in which they do it, and the social relations that they engage in while doing it.

Leadership the process of influencing the activities of an organized group in its efforts toward goal setting and goal achievement.

Lean production a manufacturing method which combines machine-pacing, work standardization, just-in-time materials flow, continuous improvement, problem-solving teams, and powerful supervision.

Learning the process of acquiring knowledge through experience which leads to a lasting change in behaviour.

Learning organization an organizational form that enables individual learning to create valued outcomes, such as innovation, efficiency, environmental alignment, and competitive advantage.

Least preferred co-worker score an assessment of the kind of person with whom a leader feels they could not work effectively.

Legitimate authority based on formal, written rules which have the force of law, e.g. the authority of presidents, managers, lecturers.

Legitimate power (also called position power) the ability of a leader to exert influence based on the belief of followers that the leader has authority to issue orders which they in turn have an obligation to accept.

Line employees workers who are directly responsible for manufacturing goods or providing a service.

Locus of control an individual's generalized belief about internal (self-control) versus external control (control by the situation or by others).

Long-linked technology technology that is applied to a series of programmed tasks performed in a predetermined order.

Low context culture a culture whose members focus on the written and spoken word when communicating with others and interpreting their messages.

McDonaldization a form of work design aimed at achieving efficiency, calculability, predictability and control through non-human technology, to enhance organizational objectives by limiting employee discretion and creativity.

Machiavellianism a personality trait or style of behaviour towards others characterized by (1) the use of guile and deceit in interpersonal relations, (2) a cynical view of the nature of other people; and (3) a lack of concern with conventional morality.

Maintenance activity an oral input, made by a group member that reduces conflict, maximizes cohesion and maintains relationships within a group.

Managerial activities activities performed by managers that support the operation of every organization and need to be performed to ensure its success.

Managerial enactment the active modification of a perceived and selected part of an organization's environment by its managers.

Managerial roles behaviours or tasks that a manager is expected to perform because of the position that they hold within a group or organization.

Mass production a form of work design that includes mechanical pacing of work, no choice of tools or methods, repetitiveness, minute subdivision of product, minimum skill requirements, and surface mental attention.

Material technology tools, machinery and equipment that can be seen, touched and heard.

Matrix structure an organizational design that combines two different types of structure resulting in an employee having two reporting relationships simultaneously.

Maximizing a decision-making approach where all alternatives are compared and evaluated in order to find the best solution to a problem.

Mechanistic structure an organization structure that possesses a high degree of task specialization, many rules, tight specification of individual responsibility and authority, and centralized decision-making.

Mediating technology technology that links independent but standardized tasks.

Mediation a process in which a neutral third party to the conflict assists in the achievement of a negotiated solution by using reason, persuasion and the presentation of alternatives.

Metamorphosis stage of socialization the period in which the new employee adjusts to their organization's values, attitudes, motives, norms and required behaviours.

Modular organization structure an organizational design that involves assembling product chunks (modules) provided by internal divisions and external providers.

Motivating potential score an indicator of how motivating a job is likely to be for an individual, considering skill variety, task identity, task significance, autonomy and feedback.

Motivation the cognitive decision-making process through which goal-directed behaviour is initiated, energized, directed, and maintained.

Motive a socially acquired need activated by a desire for fulfilment.

Motivator factors aspects of work which lead to high levels of satisfaction, motivation and performance, including achievement, recognition, responsibility, advancement, growth, and the work itself.

Need for achievement a concern with meeting standards of excellence, the desire to be successful in competition, the motivation to excel.

Need for power (*n*Pow) the desire to make an impact on others, change people or events, and make a difference in life.

Negative reinforcement the attempt to encourage desirable behaviours by withdrawing negative consequences when the desired behaviour occurs.

New leader an inspirational visionary, concerned with building a shared sense of purpose and mission, creating a culture in which everyone is aligned with the organization's goals and is skilled and empowered to achieve them.

Noise factors outside the communication process which interfere with or distract attention from the transmission and reception of the intended meaning.

Nomothetic an approach to the study of personality emphasizing the identification of traits, and the systematic relationships between different aspects of personality.

Nonstandard work employment that does not involve a fixed schedule at the same physical location for an extended time.

Non-verbal communication the process of coding meaning through behaviours such as facial expressions, limb gestures and body postures.

Obedience a situation in which an individual changes their behaviour in response to direct command from another.

Offshoring contracting with external providers in a different country to supply the organization with the processes and products that were previously supplied internally.

Open system a system that interacts, in a purposive way, with its external environment in order to survive.

Operational definition the method used to measure the incidence of a variable in practice.

Operational innovation inventing entirely new ways of doing work.

Organic structure an organization structure that possesses little task specialization, few rules, a high degree of individual responsibility and authority, and one in which decision-making is delegated.

Organization a social arrangement for achieving controlled performance in pursuit of collective goals.

Organizational architecture the framework of linked internal and external elements that an organization creates and uses to achieve the goals specified in its vision statement.

Organizational behaviour an interdisciplinary body of knowledge and field of research, concerned with how formal organizations, behaviour of people within organizations, and salient features of their context and environment, evolve and take shape, why all these things happen the way they do, and what purposes they serve.

Organization chart a pictorial record that shows the formal relations that the company intends should prevail within it.

Organization structure the formal system of task and reporting relationships that control, co-ordinate and motivate employees to work together to achieve organizational goals.

Organizational choice the argument that work design is not determined by technology, that the technical system does not determine the social system.

Organizational culture the shared values, beliefs and norms which influence the way employees think, feel and act towards others inside and outside the organization.

Organizational design senior management's process of choosing and implementing a structural configuration through which their organization seeks to accomplish their goals.

Organizational development the systematic use of applied behavioural science principles and practices to increase individual and organizational effectiveness.

Organizational dilemma how to reconcile inconsistency between individual needs and aspirations on the one hand, and the collective purpose of the organization on the other.

Organizational effectiveness a multi-dimensional concept defined differently by different stakeholders, including a range of quantitative and qualitative measures.

Organization misbehaviour anything that workers do in the workplace which management considers they should not do.

Organizational politics the techniques and tactics used to acquire, develop, retain and use power to obtain preferred outcomes in a situation in which there is uncertainty or an absence of consensus about choices.

Organizational socialization the process through which an employee's pattern of behaviour, values, attitudes and motives is influenced to conform to that of the organization.

Organizational values the accumulated beliefs held about how work should be done and situations dealt with, that guide employee behaviour.

Outsourcing contracting with external providers to supply the organization with the processes and products that were previously supplied internally.

Pavlovian conditioning a technique for associating an established response or behaviour with a new stimulus (also **classical** and **respondent** conditioning).

Perception the dynamic psychological process responsible for attending to, organizing and interpreting sensory data.

Perceptual filters individual characteristics, predispositions, and preoccupations that interfere with the effective transmission and receipt of messages.

Perceptual organization the process through which incoming stimuli are organized or patterned in systematic and meaningful ways.

Perceptual set an individual's predisposition to respond to people and events in a particular manner.

Perceptual threshold a boundary point, either side of which our senses respectively will or will not be able to detect stimuli, such as sound, light, or touch.

Perceptual world the individual's personal internal image, map or picture of their social, physical and organizational environment.

Peripheral norms socially defined standards relating to behaviour and beliefs that are important but not crucial to a group's objective and survival.

Personality the psychological qualities that influence an individual's characteristic behaviour patterns, in a stable and distinctive manner.

PESTLE analysis an environmental scanning tool identifying Political, Economic, Social, Technological, Legal and Ecological factors that affect an organization.

Pivotal norms socially defined standards relating to behaviour and beliefs that are central to a group's objective and survival.

Pluralist frame of reference on conflict a perspective that views organizations as consisting of different, natural interest groups, each with their own potentially constructive, legitimate interests, which makes conflict between them inevitable.

Political model of organization a perspective that holds that organizations are made up of groups that have separate interests, goals and values, and in which power and influence are needed in order to reach decisions.

Positive reinforcement the attempt to encourage desirable behaviours by introducing positive consequences when the desired behaviour occurs.

Positivism a perspective which assumes that the world can be understood in terms of causal relationships between observable and measurable variables, and that these relationships can be studied objectively using controlled experiments.

Post-modern organization A networked, information-rich, delayered, downsized, boundary-less, high commitment organization employing highly skilled, well-paid autonomous knowledge workers.

Power the capacity of individuals to overcome resistance on the part of others, to exert their will, and to produce results consistent with their interests and objectives.

Power orientation the appropriateness of power/ authority within organizations – *respect* v. *tolerance*.

Power tells non-verbal signals that indicate to others how important and dominant someone is, or how powerful they would like us to *think* they are.

Pre-arrival stage of socialization the period of learning in the process that occurs before an applicant joins an organization.

Predictive validity the extent to which assessment scores accurately predict behaviours such as job performance.

Prescriptive model of decision-making an approach that recommends how individuals should behave in order to achieve a desired outcome.

Process theory an approach to explaining organizational behaviour based on narratives which show how many factors, combining and interacting over time in a particular context, are likely to produce the outcomes of interest.

Processual/contextual theory a perspective arguing that it is necessary to understand how the substance, context, and process of organizational change interact to create the outcomes.

Production team a stable number of individuals who share production goals, and who perform specific roles which are supported by a set of incentives and sanctions.

Project team a collection of employees from different work areas in an organization brought together to accomplish a specific task within a finite time.

Projective test an assessment based on abstract or ambiguous images, which the subject is asked to interpret by projecting their feelings, preoccupations and motives into their responses.

Provisional selves from observing others, the experiments that we make with the ways in which we act and interact in new organizational roles.

Psychometrics the systematic testing, measurement and assessment of intelligence, aptitudes, and personality.

Punishment the attempt to discourage undesirable behaviours through the application of negative consequences, or by withholding a positive consequence, following the undesirable behaviour.

Quality circle shop floor employees from the same department, who meet for a few hours each week to discuss ways of improving their work environment.

Quality of working life an individual's overall assessment of satisfaction with their job, working conditions, pay, colleagues, management style, organization culture, work-life balance, and training, development, and career opportunities.

Radical frame of reference on conflict a perspective that views organizational conflict as an inevitable consequence of exploitative employment relations in a capitalist economy.

Rationalism the theory that reason is the foundation of certainty in knowledge.

Rationality the use of scientific reasoning, empiricism and positivism, as well as the decision criteria of evidence, logical argument and reasoning.

Rational economic model assumes that decision-making is and should be a rational process consisting of a sequence of steps that enhance the probability of attaining a desired outcome.

Rational model of organization a perspective that holds that organizational goals are clear; objectives are defined, alternatives are identified; and choices are made on the basis of reason in a logical way.

Rational decisions choices based on rationality, that is, on a rational mode of thinking.

Readiness for change is a predisposition to welcome and embrace change.

Referent power (also called charisma) the ability of a leader to exert influence based on the belief of followers that the leader has desirable abilities and personality traits that can and should be copied.

Reliability the degree to which an assessment delivers consistent results when repeated.

Replacement effects processes through which intelligent machines substitute for people at work, leading to unemployment.

Responsibility the obligation placed on a person who occupies a certain position in the organization structure to perform a task, function or assignment.

Resistance (in conflict) more or less covert behaviour that counteracts and restricts management attempts to exercise power and control in the workplace.

Resistance (in influencing) rejecting an influencing request by means of a direct refusal, making excuses, stalling, or making an argument against, indicating neither behavioural nor attitudinal change.

Resistance to change an unwillingness, or an inability to accept or to discuss changes that are perceived to be damaging or threatening to the individual.

Resource dependence theory states that although organizations depend on their environments to survive, they seek to assert control over the resources they require, in order to minimize their dependence.

Restructuring the act of partially or wholly modifying an organization's structure.

Reward power the ability of a leader to exert influence based on the belief of followers that the leader has access to valued rewards which will be dispensed in return for compliance.

Risk a condition in which managers have a high knowledge of alternatives; know the probability of

these being available; can calculate the costs and know the benefits of each alternative; and have a medium predictability of outcomes.

Risk-seeking propensity the willingness of an individual to choose options that entail risks.

Risky shift phenomenon the tendency of a group to make decisions that are riskier than those that the members of the group would have recommended individually.

Role the pattern of behaviour expected by others from a person occupying a certain position in an organization hierarchy.

Role conflict the simultaneous existence of two or more sets of role expectations on a focal person in such a way that compliance with one makes it difficult to comply with the others.

Role modelling a form of socialization in which an individual learns by example, copying the behaviour of established organization members.

Routine decisions decisions made according to established procedures and rules.

Rules procedure or obligations explicitly stated and written down in organization manuals.

Satisficing a decision-making approach where the first solution that is judged to be 'good enough' (i.e. satisfactory and sufficient) is selected, and the search is then ended.

Scenario planning the imaginative development of one or more likely pictures of the dimensions and characteristics of the future for an organization.

Schedule of reinforcement the pattern and frequency of rewards contingent on the display of desirable behaviour.

Scientific management a form of job design which stresses short, repetitive work cycles; detailed, prescribed task sequences; a separation of task conception from task execution; and motivation based on economic rewards.

Selective attention the ability, often exercised unconsciously, to choose from the stream of sensory data, to concentrate on particular elements, and to ignore others.

Self-actualization the desire for personal fulfilment, to develop one's potential, to become everything that one is capable of becoming.

Self-concept the set of perceptions that we have about ourselves.

Self-esteem that part of the self which is concerned with how we evaluate ourselves.

Self-fulfilling prophecy a prediction that becomes true simply because someone expects it to happen.

Sentiments in Homans' theory, the feelings, attitudes and beliefs held by group members towards others.

Sex the basic physiological differences between men and women.

Sexuality the expression of our social relations to physical, bodily desires, real or imagined, by or for others, or for oneself, together with related bodily states and experience.

Shaping the selective reinforcement of chosen behaviours in a manner that progressively establishes a desired behaviour pattern.

Shared frame of reference assumptions that are held in common by group members, which shape their thinking, decisions, actions and interactions, while being constantly defined and reinforced through those interactions.

Single-loop learning the ability to use feedback to make continuous adjustments and adaptations, to maintain performance at a predetermined standard.

SITUATIONAL LEADERSHIP® Ran approach to determining the most effective style of influencing, considering the direction and support a leader gives, and the readiness of followers to perform a particular task.

Skinnerian conditioning a technique for associating a response or a behaviour with its consequence (also **instrumental** and **operant** conditioning).

Social facilitation the strengthening of the dominant (prevalent or likely) response due to the presence of others.

Social identity that part of the self-concept which comes from our membership of groups and which contributes to our self-esteem.

Social influence the process where attitudes and behaviour are changed by the real or implied presence of others.

Social intelligence the ability to understand the thoughts and feelings of others and to manage our relationships accordingly.

Social loafing the tendency for individuals to exert less effort when working as part of a group on an additive task, than when working alone.

Social orientation relative importance of the interests of the individual versus the interest of the group – *individualism* v. *collectivism*.

Social representations the beliefs, ideas and values, objects, people and events that are constructed by current group members, and which are transmitted to its new members.

Social role the set of expectations that others hold of an occupant of a position.

Social status the relative ranking that a person holds and the value of that person as measured by a group.

Social technology the methods which order the behaviour and relationships of people in systematic, purposive ways through structures of co-ordination, control, motivation and reward.

Socialization the process through which individual behaviours, values, attitudes and motives are influenced to conform with those seen as desirable in a given social or organizational setting.

Sociogram a chart which shows the liking (social attraction) relationships between individual members of a group.

Socio-technical system system which has both a material technology (machinery, equipment) and a social organization (job specifications, management structure).

Sociometry the study of interpersonal feelings and relationships within groups.

Span-of-control the number of subordinates who report directly to a single manager or supervisor.

Staff employees workers who occupy advisory positions and who use their specialized expertise to support the efforts of line employees.

Stakeholder anyone who is concerned with how an organization operates, and who will be affected by a change or a programme of changes.

Stereotype a category, or personality type to which we allocate people on the basis of their membership of some known group.

Strategic alliance an arrangement in which two or more firms agree to co-operate to achieve specific objectives while remaining independent organizations.

Strategic change organizational transformation that is radical, frame-breaking, mould-breaking, or paradigmatic in its nature and implications.

Strategic choice the view that an organization's environment, market and technology is the result of senior management decisions.

Strategic contingencies events and activities, both inside and outside an organization, that are essential for it to attain its goals.

Strong culture one in which an organization's core values are widely shared among employees, intensely held by them, and which guides their behaviour.

Structured task a task with clear goals, few correct or satisfactory solutions and outcomes, few ways of performing it, and clear criteria of success.

Superleader a leader who is able to develop leadership capacity in others, empowering them, reducing their dependence on formal leaders, stimulating their motivation, commitment and creativity.

Surface acting hiding one's felt emotions and forgoing emotional expressions in response to display rules.

Surface manifestations of culture culture's most accessible forms which are visible and audible behaviour patterns and objects.

Sustaining innovations innovations which make improvements to existing processes, procedures, services and products.

Synchronous communication occurs when people are online at the same time, engaging in a real time conversation with others, somewhat similar to normal face-to-face discussions.

Synergy the positive or negative result of the interaction of two or more components, producing an outcome that is different from the sum of the individual components.

System something that functions through the interdependence of its component parts.

Systems concept a management perspective which emphasizes the interdependence between the various parts of an organization, and also between the organization and its environment.

Systematic soldiering the conscious and deliberate restriction of output by operators.

Tacit knowledge knowledge and understanding specific to the individual, derived from experience, and difficult to codify and to communicate to others.

Task activity an oral input, made by a group member, that contributes directly to the group's work task.

Task analyzability the degree to which standardized solutions are available to solve the problems that arise.

Task variety the number of new and different demands that a task places on an individual or a function.

Team a group whose members share a common goal that they pursue collaboratively; and who can only succeed or fail collectively.

Team autonomy the extent to which a team experiences freedom, independence and discretion in decisions relating to the performance of its tasks.

Team performance external measure focused on meeting the needs and expectations of management, customers or shareholders.

Team role an individual's tendency to behave in preferred ways which contribute to, and interrelate with, other members within a team.

Team viability internal measure focused on meeting the needs and expectations of team members.

Team-based structure an organizational design that consists entirely of project-type teams that co-ordinate their activities, and work directly with partners and customers to achieve their goals.

Technical complexity the degree of predictability about and control over the final product permitted by the technology used.

Technological determinism the argument that technology can explain the nature of jobs, work groupings, hierarchy skills, values and attitudes in organizations.

Technological interdependence the extent to which the work tasks performed in an organization by one department or team member, affect the task performance of other departments or team members. It can be high or low.

Thematic apperception test an assessment in which the individual is shown ambiguous pictures and is asked to create stories of what may be happening in them.

Time-and-motion studies measurement and recording techniques used to make work operations more efficient.

Time orientation the time outlook on work and life – *short term* v. *long term*.

Total quality management a philosophy of management that is driven by customer needs and expectations, and which is committed to continuous improvement.

Traditional authority the belief that the ruler had a natural right to rule. This right was either God-given or by descent, e.g. the authority of kings and queens.

Trait a relatively stable quality or attribute of an individual's personality, influencing behaviour in a particular direction.

Transactional leader a leader who treats relationships with followers in terms of an exchange, giving followers what they want in return for what the leader desires, following prescribed tasks to pursue established goals.

Transformational leader a leader who treats relationships with followers in terms of motivation and commitment, influencing and inspiring followers to give more than mere compliance to improve organizational performance.

Triggers of change disorganizing pressures indicating that current systems, procedures, rules, organization structures and processes are no longer effective.

Type a descriptive label for a distinct pattern of personality characteristics, such as introvert, extravert, neurotic.

Type A personality a combination of emotions and behaviours characterized by ambition, hostility, impatience and a sense of constant time-pressure.

Type B personality a combination of emotions and behaviours characterized by relaxation, low focus on achievement, and ability to take time to enjoy leisure.

Uncertainty a condition in which managers possess low knowledge of alternatives; a low probability of having these available; can to some degree calculate the costs and benefits of each alternative; but have no predictability of outcomes.

Uncertainty orientation the emotional response to uncertainty and change – *acceptance* v. *avoidance*.

Unconditional positive regard unqualified, non-judgemental approval and respect for the traits and behaviours of the other person (a term used in counselling).

Unitarist frame of reference on conflict a perspective that regards management and employee interests as coinciding and which thus regards (organizational) conflict as harmful and to be avoided.

Unstructured task a task with ambiguous goals, many good solutions, many ways of achieving acceptable outcomes, and vague criteria of success.

User contribution system a method for aggregating and leveraging people's contributions or behaviours in ways that are useful to other people.

Valence the perceived value or preference that an individual has for a particular outcome, and can be positive, negative, or neutral.

Variance theory an approach to explaining organizational behaviour based on universal relationships between independent and dependent variables which can be defined and measured precisely.

Vertical loading factors methods for enriching work and improving motivation, by removing controls, increasing accountability, and by providing feedback, new tasks, natural work units, special assignments, and additional authority.

Vertical integration a situation where one company buys another in order to make the latter's output its own input, thereby securing that source of supply through ownership.

Virtual organization structure an organizational design that uses technology to transcend the constraints of legal structures, physical conditions, place and time, and allows a network of separate participants to present themselves to customers as a single entity.

Virtual team one that relies on technology-mediated communication, while crossing boundaries of geography, time, culture and organization, to accomplish an interdependent task.

Weak culture one in which there is little agreement among employees about their organization's core values, the way things are supposed to be, or what is expected of them.

Web 2.0 technologies internet-based information systems that allow high levels of user interaction, such as blogs, wikis (collaborative databases), and social networking.

Work specialization the degree to which work tasks in an organization are subdivided into separate jobs.

the Yerkes-Dodson law a psychology hypothesis which states that performance increases with arousal, until we become overwhelmed, after which performance falls.

References

Abbey, A. and Cranwell-Ward, J. (2005) *Organizational Stress*. London: Palgrave Macmillan.

Abrahamson, E. (2000) 'Change without pain', *Harvard Business Review*, 78(4): 75–79.

Ackroyd, S. and Cowley, P. (1990) 'Can culture change be managed?: working with "raw" material: the case of the English slaughterman', *Personnel Review*, 19(5): 3–13.

Ackroyd, S. and Thompson, P. (1999) *Organizational Misbehaviour*. London: Sage Publications.

Adams, J.S. (1963) 'Toward an understanding of inequity', *Journal of Abnormal and Social Psychology*, 67(4): 422–36.

Adams, J.S. (1965) 'Inequity in social exchange', in L. Berkowitz (ed.), *Advances in Experimental Social Psychology*. New York: Academic Press, pp.267–99.

Adams, R. (1973) *Watership Down*. London: Puffin Books.

Adcroft, A. and Willis, R. (2000) 'Innovation or optimization: facing up to the challenge of the global economy', in Jim Barry, John Chandler, Heather Clark, Roger Johnston and David Needle (eds), *Organization and Management: A Critical Text*. London: Thomson Learning, pp.171–91.

Adler, N.J. (2002) *International Dimensions of Organizational Behaviour*. London: International Thomson, (4th edn).

Adler, P.S. (1993a) 'Time-and-motion regained', *Harvard Business Review*, 71(1): 97–108.

Adler, P.S. (1993b) 'The learning bureaucracy: New United Motors Manufacturing, Inc', in B.M. Staw and L.L. Cummings (eds), *Research in Organizational Behaviour*. Greenwich, CT: JAI Press, pp.111–94.

Adler, P.S. (1999) 'The emancipatory significance of Taylorism', in M.P.E. Cunha and C.A. Marques (eds), *Readings in Organization Science – Organizational Change in a Changing Context*. Lisbon: Instituto Superior de Psicologia Aplicada, pp.7–14.

Adler, P.S. (2005) 'Market, hierarchy and trust: the knowledge economy and the future of capitalism', in G.C. and H. Willmott (eds), *Critical Management Studies: A Reader*. Oxford: Oxford University Press, pp.171–208.

Ahuja, A. (2006) 'Sink or swim: which personality type are you?' *The Times*, Times 2 Supplement, 1 March, p.5.

Ahuja, A. (2006) 'Born to lose?' *The Times*, Times 2 Supplement, 31 August, pp.4–5.

Aiello, J.R. and Svec, C.M. (1993) 'Computer monitoring of work performance: extending the social facilitation framework to electronic presence', *Journal of Applied Social Psychology*, 23(7): 537–48.

Albanese, R. and van Fleet, D.D. (1985) 'Rational behaviour in groups: the free rider tendency', *American Academy of Management Review*, 10(2): 244–55.

ALCS News (2006) 'Google update', January, p.5.

Alderfer, C. (1972) *Human Needs in Organizational Settings*. New York: The Free Press.

Alimo-Metcalfe, B. and Bradley, M. (2008) 'Cast in a new light', *People Management*, 14(2): 38–41.

Allen, J., James, A.D. and Gamlen, P. (2007) 'Formal versus informal knowledge networks in R&D: a case study using social network analysis', *R&D Management*, 37(3): 179–96.

Allen, N. (2008) 'Court cases hampered by poor paperwork', *The Daily Telegraph*, 22 May.

Allen, N.J. and Hecht, T. (2004) 'The romance of teams: towards an understanding of its psychological underpinnings and implications', *Journal of Occupational and Organizational Psychology*, 77(4): 439–61.

Allen, R.W., Madison, D.L., Porter, L.W., Renwick, P.A. and Mayes, B.T. (1979) 'Organizational politics: tactics and characteristics of actors', *California Management Review*, 22(1): 77–83.

Allison, G.T. (1971) *Essence of Decision*. Boston, MA: Little, Brown and Co.

Allmendinger, J., Hackman, R. and Lehman, E.V. (1994) *Life and Work in Symphony Orchestras: An Interim Report of Research Findings, Report No.7, Cross-national Study of Symphony Orchestras*. Cambridge MA: Harvard University Press.

Allport, F.H. (1920) 'The influences of the group upon association and thought', *Journal of Experimental Psychology*, 3: 159–82.

Alvesson, M. (2001) *Understanding Organizational Culture*. London: Sage Publications.

Alvesson, M. and Ashcraft, K.L. (2009) 'Critical methodology in management and management and organization research', in David A. Buchanan and Alan Bryman (eds), *The Sage Handbook of Organizational Research Methods*. London: Sage Publications.

Amabile, T.M. and Kramer, S.J. (2007) 'Inner work life: understanding the subtext of business performance', *Harvard Business Review*, 85(5): 72–83.

Anand, J. (1999) 'How many matches are made in heaven?' *Financial Times, Mastering Strategy Supplement*, 25 October, pp.6–7.

Anand, N. and Daft, R.L. (2007) 'What is the right organization design?' *Organizational Dynamics*, 36(4): 329–44.

Ancona, D. and Caldwell, D. (1990) 'Improving the performance of new product teams', *Research Technology Management*, 33(2): 25–29.

Anderson, N. and Shackleton, V. (1993) *Successful Selection Interviewing*. Oxford: Blackwell.

Anderson, D. and Mullen, P. (eds) (1998) *Faking It: The Sentimentalization of Modern Society*, London: Penguin Books.

Annett, J. and Stanton, N.A. (2000) 'Team work: a problem for ergonomics?' *Ergonomics*, 43(8): 1045–51.

Ansoff, I. (1997) 'Measuring and managing for environmental turbulence: the Ansoff Associates approach', in Alexander Watson Hiam (ed.), *The Portable Conference on Change Management*: HRD Press Inc., pp.67–83.

Anthony, P.D. (1990) 'The paradox of the management of culture or "he who leads is lost"', *Personnel Review*, 19(4): 3–8.

Argyris, C. (1972) *The Applicability of Organizational Sociology*. London: Cambridge University Press.

Argyris, C. (1982) *Reasoning, Learning, and Action*. San Francisco, CA: Jossey-Bass.

Argyris, C. and Schön, D. (1974) *Theory in Practice*. San Francisco, CA: Jossey-Bass.

Argyris, C. and Schön, D. (eds) (1978) *Organizational Learning*, Cambridge, MA: Addison-Wesley.

Aritzeta, A., Swailes, S. and Senior, B. (2007) 'Belbin's team role model: development, validity and applications for teambuilding', *Journal of Management Studies*, 44(1): 96–118.

Arkin, A. (2007a) 'The generation game', *People Management*, 13(24): 24–27.

Arkin, A. (2007b) 'From soft to strong', *People Management*, 13(8): 30–33.

Arkin, A. (2008) 'The empire strikes back', *People Management*, 14(7): 24–29.

Arnold, D.W. and Jones, J.W. (2006) 'Who the devil's applying now?' from www.crimcheck.com/employment_testing.htm.

Aronson, E., Wilson, T.D. and Akert, R.M. (eds) (1994) *Social Psychology*, New York: HarperCollins.

Aronson, E., Wilson, T.D. and Akert, R.M. (2010) Social Psychology@ The Heart and Mind, 7E, New Jersey: Pearson Education Inc.

Arroba, T. and James, K. (1988) 'Are politics palatable to women managers?: how women can make wise moves at work', *Women in Management Review*, 3(3): 123–30.

Arrow, H. and McGrath, J.E. (1995) 'Membership dynamics in groups at work: a theoretical framework', *Research in Organizational Behaviour*, 17: 373–411.

Asch, S.E. (1951) 'Effects of group pressure upon the modification and distortion of judgements', in H. Guetzkow (ed.), *Groups, Leadership and Men*. Pittsburgh, PA: Carnegie Press, pp.177–90.

Asch, S.E. (1952) *Social Psychology*. Englewood Cliffs, NJ: Prentice Hall.

Asch, S.E. (1956) 'Studies of independence and submission to group pressure: a minority of one against a unanimous majority', *Psychological Monograph: General and Applied*, 9(416): 1–70.

Ashford, S.J., George, E. and Blatt, R. (2007) 'Old assumptions, new work: the opportunities and challenges of research on nonstandard employment', *The Academy of Management Annals*, 1(1): 65–117.

Ashforth, B.E. and Humfrey, R. (1993) 'Emotion in the work place: a reappraisal', *Human Relations*, 48(2): 97–125.

Ashforth, B.E. and Tomiuk, M. (2000) 'Emotional labour and authenticity: views from service agents', in S. Fineman (ed.), *Emotion in Organizations*. London: Sage Publications, (2nd edn) pp.184–203.

Ashkanasy, N.M. (2003) 'The case for culture', in R. Westwood and S. Clegg (eds), *Debating Organization*. Oxford: Blackwell, pp.300–11.

Ashkenas, R., Ulrich, D., Jick, T. and Kerr, S. (2002) *The Boundaryless Organization: Breaking the Chains of Organization Structure*. San Francisco, CA: Jossey-Bass, (2nd edn).

Astley, W.G. and Sachdeva, P.S. (1984) 'Structural sources of intra-organizational power: a theoretical synthesis', *Academy of Management Review*, 9(1): 104–13.

Atkinson, J. (1985) 'The changing corporation', in David Clutterbuck (ed.), *New Patterns of Work*. Aldershot: Gower, pp.13–24.

Augustine, N. and Adelman, K. (1999) *Shakespeare in Charge. The Bard's Guide to Leading and Succeeding on the Business Stage*. Hyperion Books.

Babcock, L. and Laschever, S. (2003) *Women Don't Ask: Negotiation and the Gender Divide*. Princeton, NJ: Princeton University Press.

Bachrach, P. and Baratz, M.S. (1962) 'The two faces of power', *American Political Science Review*, 56(4): 947–52.

Bachrach, P. and Baratz, M.S. (1963) 'Decisions and nondecisions: an analytical framework', *American Political Science Review*, 57(3): 641–51.

Badaracco, J.L. (2001) 'We don't need another hero', *Harvard Business Review*, 79(8): 121–26.

Badaracco, J.L. (2002) *Leading Quietly: An Unorthodox Guide to Doing the Right Thing*. Boston, MA: Harvard Business School Press.

Baker, G. (2007) 'Russia enters "space race" to build moon base', from http://www.telegraph.co.uk/news/worldnews/1561846/Russia-enters-space-race-to-build-moon-base.html, accessed January 2009.

Baker, H.E. and Paulson, S.K. (1995) *Experiential Exercises in Organization Theory*. Englewood Cliffs, NJ: Prentice Hall.

Balazs, K. (2001) 'Some like it haute: leadership lessons from France's great chefs', *Organizational Dynamics*, 30(2): 134–48.

Balazs, K. (2002) 'Take one entrepreneur: the recipe for success of France's great chefs', *European Management Journal*, 20(3): 247–59.

Baldridge, J.V. (1971) *Power and Conflict in the University*. New York: John Wiley.

Bales, R.F. (1950a) *Interaction Process Analysis*. Reading, MA: Addison-Wesley.

Bales, R.F. (1950b) 'A set of categories for the analysis of small group interaction', *American Sociological Review*, 15(2): 257–63.

Bales, R.F. (1953) 'The equilibrium problem in small groups', in T. Parsons, R.F. Bales and E.A. Shils (eds), *Working Papers in the Theory of Action*. New York: The Free Press, pp.111–61.

Bales, R.F. (1959) 'Task roles and social roles in problem-solving groups', in E.E. Maccoby, M. Newcomb and E.L. Hartley (eds), *Readings in Social Psychology*. New York: Holt, Rinehart and Winston, pp.437–59.

Bales, R.F. and Slater, P.E. (1956) 'Role differentiation in small decision-making groups', in T. Parsons and R.F. Bales (eds), *Family, Socialization and Interaction*. London: Routledge, pp.259–306.

Ball, C. (2005) 'The Finnish line', *People Management*, 11(11): 40–42.

Bandura, A. (1977) *Social Learning Theory*. Englewood Cliffs, NJ: Prentice Hall.

Bandura, A. (1986) *Social Foundations of Thought and Action: A Social Cognitive Theory*. Englewood Cliffs, NJ: Prentice Hall.

Banks, I. (1999) *The Business*. London: Little, Brown and Company.

Barbour, M. (1999) 'British fat cats take the cream', *The Times*, 29 March, p.48.

Barbuto, J.E. (2000) 'Power and the changing environment', *Journal of Management Education*, 24(2): 288–96.

Barker, J.R. (1993) 'Tightening the iron cage: concertive control in self-managing teams', *Administrative Science Quarterly*, 38(3): 408–37.

Barker, J.R. (1999) *The Discipline of Teamwork*. London: Sage Publications.

Barker, J.R. (2005) 'Tightening the iron cage: concertive control in self-managing teams', in C. Grey and H. Willmott (eds), *Critical Management Studies: A Reader*. Oxford: Oxford University Press, pp.209–43.

Barley, S. (1996) *The New World of Work*. London: British-North American Committee.

Barnes, A. (2008) 'The construction of control: the physical environment and the development of resistance and accommodation within call centres', *New Technology, Work and Employment*, 22(3): 246–59.

Baron, R.S. (1986) 'Distraction–conflict theory: progress and problems', in L. Berkowitz (ed.), *Advances in Experimental Social Psychology, Vol.20*. New York: Academic Press, pp.1–40.

Baron, R. and Byrne, D. (2000) *Social Psychology*. London: Allyn & Bacon, (9th edn).

Baron, R.A. and Greenberg, J. (1990) *Behaviour in Organizations*. Upper Saddle River, NJ: Allyn & Bacon, (3rd edn).

Baron, R.S. and Kerr, N.L. (2003) *Group Process, Group Decision, Group Action*. Milton Keynes: Open University Press, (2nd edn).

Bartlett, C. and Ghoshal, S. (1990) 'Matrix management: not a structure, a frame of mind', *Harvard Business Review*, 68(4): 138–45.

Bass, B.M. (1985a) *Bass and Stogdill's Handbook of Leadership: Theory, Research and Managerial Applications*. New York: The Free Press, (3rd edn).

Bass, B.M. (1985b) *Leadership and Performance Beyond Expectations*. New York: The Free Press.

Bass, B.M. and Avolio, B.J. (1990) 'The implications of transactional and transformational leadership for individual, team and organizational development', *Research and Organizational Change and Development*, 4: 321–72.

Bass, B.M. and Avolio, B.J. (1994) *Improving Organizational Effectiveness through Transformational Leadership*. Thousand Oaks, CA: Sage Publications.

Bassett-Jones, N. and Lloyd, G.C. (2005) 'Does Herzberg's motivation theory have staying power?' *Journal of Management Development*, 24(10): 929–43.

Bateson, G. and Mead, M. (1942) *Balinese Character: A Photographic Analysis*. New York: New York Academy of Sciences, Special Publications 2.

Bavelas, A. (1967) 'Communication patterns in task-orientated groups', in D. Cartwright and A. Zander (eds), *Group Dynamics: Research and Theory*. London: Tavistock, (3rd edn).

Bavelas, A. and Barrett, D. (1951) 'An experimental approach to organizational communication', *Personnel Review*, 27: 367–71.

Bazerman, M.H. (2005) *Judgement in Managerial Decision-making*. New York: Wiley, (6th edn).

Bazerman, M.H. and Gillespie, J.J. (1999) 'Betting on the future: the virtues of contingent contracts', *Harvard Business Review*, 77(5): 155–60.

Bazerman, M.H. and Chugh, D. (2006) 'Decisions without blinders', *Harvard Business Review*, 84(1): 88–97.

BBC News Channel (2003) 'McDonald's anger over McJob entry', 9 November.

BBC News Channel (2006a) 'Boeing begins use of moving assembly line for 777 jetliners', 8 November.

BBC News Channel (2006b) 'Paperwork hampers court cases', 22 May.

BBC News Channel (2007a) 'McDonald's begins McJob petition', 23 May.

BBC News Channel (2007b) 'The flipside of a McJob', 8 June.

BBC News Channel (2007c) 'Brown orders data security checks', 21 November.

BBC News Channel (2008) 'Discs loss "entirely avoidable"', 25 June.

BBC Radio 4 (2008) 'Mission to Mars, Frontiers programme', 5 May.

Beagrie, S. (2006) 'Order in the cathedral', *Personnel Today*, 31 January, pp.24–25.

Beardwell, I. and Holden, L. (2001) *Human Resource Management: A Contemporary Perspective*. Harlow, Essex: Financial Times Prentice Hall, (3rd edn).

Beaumont, C. (2008) 'Has Apple really unlocked the toolbox?' *The Daily Telegraph*, Review section, 15 March, p.21.

Becker, G. (1964) *Human Capital*. New York: National Bureau of Economic Research.

Becker, H. (1982) 'Culture: a sociological view', *Yale Review*, 71: 513–27.

Bedeian, A.G. (1980) *Organization Theory and Analysis*. Homewood, IL: The Dryden Press.

Bedeian, A.G. (1986) *Management*. New York: CBS International.

Bedeian, A.G. and Zammuto, R.F. (1991) *Organizations: Theory and Design*. London: The Dryden Press.

Beeman, D.R. and Sharkey, T.W. (1987) 'The use and abuse of corporate politics', *Business Horizons*, 30(2): 26–31.

Beer, M. and Spector, B. (1985) 'Corporate wide transformations in human resource management', in R.E. Walton and E.R. Lawrence (eds), *Human Resource Management Trends and Challenges*. Boston, MA: Harvard Business School Press.

Behar, R. (1989) 'Joe's bad trip', *Time*, 24 July, pp.54–59.

Beirne, M. (2006) *Empowerment and Innovation: Managers, Principles and Reflective Practice*. Northampton: Edward Elgar Publishers.

Beirne, M., Riach, K. and Wilson, F. (2004) 'Controlling business?: agency and constraint in call centre working', *New Technology, Work and Employment*, 19(2): 96–109.

Belanger, J. (2006) 'Technology and work', in M. Korczynski, R. Hodson and P. Edwards (eds), *Social Theory at Work*. Oxford: Oxford University Press, pp.325–55.

Belbin, R.M. (1981) *Management Teams: Why They Succeed or Fail*. London: Butterworth Heinemann.

Belbin, R.M. (1993) *Team Roles at Work*. Oxford: Butterworth Heinemann.

Belbin, R.M. (1996) *The Coming Shape of Organizations*. London: Butterworth Heinemann.

Bell, D. (1999) *The Coming of Post Industrial Society*. New York: Basic Books (reprint of 1976 edn).

Bell, E. (2008) *Reading Management and Organization in Film*. London: Palgrave Macmillan.

Bell, B.S. and Kozlowski, S.W.J. (2002) 'A typology of virtual teams: implications for effective leadership', *Group and Organizational Management*, 27(1): 14–49.

Benders, J. (2005) 'Team working: a tale of partial participation', in B. Harley, J. Hyman and P. Thompson (eds), *Participation and Democracy at Work: Essays in Honour of Harvie Ramsey*. London: Palgrave Macmillan, pp.55–74.

Benders, J. and van Hootegem, G. (1999a) 'How the Japanese got teams', in S. Proctor and F. Mueller (eds), *Teamworking*. London: Macmillan, pp.43–59.

Benders, J. and Van Hootegem, G. (1999b) 'Teams and their context: moving the team discussion beyond existing dichotomies', *Journal of Management Studies*, 36(5): 609–28.

Benders, J. and Morita, M. (2004) 'Changes in Toyota Motors' operations management', *International Journal of Production Research*, 42(3): 433–44.

Benders, J., Doorewaard, H. and Poutsma, E. (2000) 'Modern sociotechnology', in M. Beyerlin (ed.), *Work Teams: Past, Present and Future*. New York: Kluwer Academic Publishers.

Benfari, R.C., Wilkinson, H.E. and Orth, C.D. (1986) 'The effective use of power', *Business Horizons*, 29(3): 12–16.

Benne, K.D. and Sheats, P. (1948) 'Functional roles of group members', *Journal of Social Issues*, 4(2): 41–49.

Bennett, N., Wise, C. and Woods, P. (2003) *Distributed Leadership*. Nottingham: National College for School Leadership.

Bennett, R. (1991) *Organizational Behaviour*. London: M & E Handbook Series.

Bennis, W.G. and Nanus, B. (1985) *Leaders: The Strategies for Taking Charge*. New York: Harper & Row.

Berdahl, J. and Anderson, C. (2005) 'Do groups need an alpha animal?' *Group Dynamics: Theory, Research and Practice*, 9(1): 45–57.

Berger, P. and Luckmann, T. (1966) *The Social Construction of Reality*. Harmondsworth: Penguin Books.

Berggren, C. (1993a) *Alternatives to Lean Production*. Basingstoke: Macmillan.

Berggren, C. (1993b) 'The Volvo Uddevalla plant: why the decision to close it is mistaken', *Journal of Industry Studies*, 1(1): 75–87.

Berggren, C. (1995) 'The fate of the branch plants – performance versus power', in Ake Sandberg (ed.), *Enriching Production: Perspectives on Volvo's Uddevalla Plant as an Alternative to Lean production*. Aldershot: Avebury, pp.105–26.

Bernick, C.L. (2001) 'When your culture needs a makeover', *Harvard Business Review*, 79(6): 53–61.

Berwick, D.M. (2003) 'Disseminating innovations in health care', *Journal of the American Medical Association*, 289(15): 1969–75.

Bessant, J. (1983) 'Management and manufacturing innovation: the case of information technology', in Graham Winch (ed.), *Information Technology in Manufacturing Processes*. London: Rossendale, pp.14–30.

Beynon, H. (1975) *Working for Ford*. Harmondsworth: Penguin Books.

Bielefeld, M. (2009) 'Regissure der Lüfte', *Lufthansa Magazin*, April, pp.30–33.

Bilimoria, D. and Piderit, S.K. (2006) *Handbook on Women and Business in Management*. Northampton: Edward Elgar Publishing.

Bird, C. (1940) *Social Psychology*. New York: Appleton-Century.

Birkinshaw, J. and Pass, S. (2008) *Innovation in the Workplace: How are Organizations Responding to Generation Y and Web 2.0 Technologies?* London: Chartered Institute for Personnel and Development.

Bishop, M. (2008) 'A bigger world: a special report on globalization', *The Economist (supplement)*, 20 September.

Bjorn-Andersen, N. and Turner, J. (1994) 'Creating the twenty-first century organization: the metamorphosis of Oticon', in R. Baskerville (ed.), *Transforming Organizations with Information Technology*. North Holland, Amsterdam: Elsevier Science, pp.379–94.

Blass, T. (2007) *The Man Who Shocked the World: The Life and Legacy of Stanley Milgram*. New York: Basic Books.

Blau, P.M. (1966) *The Dynamics of Bureaucracy*. Chicago, IL: University of Chicago Press, (2nd edn).

Blauner, R. (1964) *Alienation and Freedom: The Factory Worker and his Industry*. Chicago, IL: University of Chicago Press.

Blitz, R. (2007) 'Winning formula', *Financial Times Magazine*, 11 August, pp.22–23.

Blowfield, M. and Murray, A. (2008) *Corporate Responsibility: A Critical Introduction*. Oxford: Oxford University Press.

BNET Business Dictionary (2009), from http://dictionary.bnet.com/, accessed January 2009.

Boddy, D. (2002) *Managing Projects: Building and Leading the Team*. Harlow: Financial Times Prentice Hall, (2nd edn).

Boddy, D. (2007) *Management: An Introduction*. Harlow: Financial Times Prentice Hall, (4th edn).

Boddy, D. and Buchanan, D.A. (1987) *Management of Technology. The Technical Change Audit: Action for Results, 5: The Process Module*. Moorfoot, Sheffield: Manpower Services Commission.

Boje, D.M. and Winsor, R.D. (1993) 'The resurrection of Taylorism: total quality management's hidden agenda', *Journal of Organizational Change Management*, 6(4): 57–70.

Bolman, L. and Deal, T. (1991) *Re-framing Organizations*. San Francisco, CA: Jossey-Bass.

Bolton, S. (2000) 'Emotion here, emotion there, emotional organizations everywhere', *Critical Perspectives on Accounting*, 11(2): 155–71.

Bolton, S. (2005) *Emotion Management in the Workplace*. Basingstoke: Palgrave Macmillan.

Bolton, S.C. and Boyd, C. (2003) 'Trolley dolly or skilled emotion manager: moving on from Hochschild's managed heart', *Work, Employment and Society*, 17(2): 289–308.

Bond, R. and Smith, P.B. (1996) 'Culture and conformity: a meta-analysis of studies using Asch's (1952b, 1956) line judgment task', *Psychological Bulletin*, 119(1): 111–37.

Boozer, J. (2002) *Career Movies: American Business and the Success Mystique*. Austin, TX: University of Texas Press.

Boreham, P., Thompson, P., Parker, R. and Hall, R. (2007) *New Technology @ Work*. Abingdon, Oxon: Routledge.

Borrill, C. and West, M. (2005) 'The psychology of effective teamworking', in N. Gold (ed.), *Teamwork*. London: Palgrave Macmillan, pp.136–60.

Borum, F. (1995) *Organization, Power and Change*. Copenhagen: Handelshøjskolens Forlag.

Boston Business Journal (2008a) 'TechTarget recognized as one of area's "Best Places to Work"', 10 June.

Boston Business Journal (2008b) 'TechTarget to cut 76 positions', 12 December.

Bowditch, J.L. and Buono, A.F. (2001) *A Primer on Organizational Behaviour*. New York: John Wiley.

Boyd, C. (2002) 'Customer violence and employee health and safety', *Work, Employment and Society*, 16(1): 151–69.

Boyes, R. (2007) 'Forget burnout, now it's boreout', *The Times*, 15 September, p.3.

Boyle, M. (2001) 'Performance reviews: perilous curves ahead', *Fortune*, 28 May, pp.103–04.

Bracewell, M. (2002) *Perfect Tense*. London: Vintage, The Random House Group.

Braid, M. (2003) 'Public sector counts the cost of stress', *The Sunday Times*, 23 November, p.9.

Brandenburger, A.M. and Nalebuff, B.J. (1997) *Co-opetition*. London: Profile Business Books, (2nd edn).

Braverman, H. (1974) *Labor and Monopoly Capital: The Degradation of Work in the Twentieth Century*. New York: Monthly Review Press.

Bray, P. (1999) 'Falling under the psychologist's spell', *The Sunday Times: The Restless Customer Supplement*, 13 June, p.9.

Brazil, J.J. (2007) 'Mission impossible?' from http://www.fastcompany.com/magazine/114/features-mission-impossible.html?page=0%2C0, accessed 19 December 2007.

Bredin, A. (1996) *The Virtual Office Survival Handbook: What Telecommuters and Entrepreneurs Need to Succeed in Today's Nontraditional Workplace*. New York: John Wiley.

Brett, J., Behfar, K. and Kern, M.C. (2006) 'Managing multicultural teams', *Harvard Business Review*, 84(11): 84–91.

Brewer, N., Mitchell, P. and Weber, N. (2002) 'Gender role, organizational status and conflict management styles', *International Journal of Conflict Management*, 13(1): 78–94.

Brimelow, R. (2005) '"Blog" dismissal should prompt policy on usage', *Personnel Today*, 1 February, p.5.

Brockner, J. (1992) 'The escalation of commitment to a failing course of action: toward theoretical progress', *Academy of Management Review*, 17(1): 39–61.

Brooke, L. (2001) 'Strong to the Finnish – Valmet Automotive', from www.allbusiness.com/periodicals/article/796663-1.html.

Brooks, I. (2003) *Organizational Behaviour: Individuals, Groups and Organization*. Harlow: Financial Times Prentice Hall, (2nd edn).

Broussine, M. and Vince, R. (1996) 'Working with metaphor towards organizational change', in Cliff Oswick and David Grant (eds), *Organization Development: Metaphorical Explorations*. London: Pitman, pp.57–72.

Brown, M. (1998) *Richard Branson*. London: Michael Joseph.

Brown, R. (2000) *Group Processes*. Oxford: Blackwell.

Brown, V. and Paulus, P.B. (1996) 'A simple dynamic model of social factors in brainstorming', *Small Group Research*, 27: 91–114.

Bryman, A. (1986) *Leadership and Organizations*. London: Routledge & Kegan Paul.

Bryman, A. (1988) *Doing Research in Organizations*. London: Routledge.

Bryman, A. (1989) *Research Methods and Organization Studies*. London: Routledge.

Bryman, A. (1996) 'Leadership in organizations', in Stewart R. Clegg, Cynthia Hardy and Walter R. Nord (eds), *Handbook of Organization Studies*. London: Sage Publications, pp.276–92.

Bryman, A. (2001) *Social Research Methods*. Oxford: Oxford University Press.

Bryman, A. (2004) *The Disneyization of Society*. London: Sage Publications.

Bryman, A. and Bell, E. (2003) *Business Research Methods*. Oxford: Oxford University Press.

Buchanan, D.A. (1994) 'Cellular manufacture and the role of teams', in J. Storey (ed.), *New Wave Manufacturing Strategies: Organizational and Human Resource Management Dimensions*. London: Paul Chapman Publishing, pp.204–25.

Buchanan, D.A. (1996) 'The limitations and opportunities of business process re-engineering in a politicized organizational climate', *Human Relations*, 50(1): 51–72.

Buchanan, D.A. (2000a) 'An eager and enduring embrace: the ongoing rediscovery of teamworking as a management idea', in Stephen Procter and Frank Mueller (eds), *Teamworking*. Houndmills and London: Macmillan Business, pp.25–42.

Buchanan, D.A. (2000b) 'The lived experience of high velocity change: a hospital case study', paper presented at the American Academy of Management Conference, Symposium on Strategy as Dynamic and Pluralistic, Toronto, August.

Buchanan, D.A. (2001) 'The role of photography in organizational research: a re-engineering case illustration', *Journal of Management Inquiry*, 10(2): 151–64.

Buchanan, D.A. (2003) 'Demands, instabilities, manipulations, careers: the lived experience of driving change', *Human Relations*, 56(6): 663–84.

Buchanan, D.A. (2004) 'Creativity and innovation in healthcare: barriers and possibilities', paper presented at the Australia and New Zealand Academy of Management Conference, University of Otago, Dunedin, New Zealand, December.

Buchanan, D.A. (2008) 'You stab my back, I'll stab yours: Management experience and perceptions of organization political behaviour', *British Journal of Management*, 19(1): 49–64.

Buchanan, D.A. and Boddy, D. (1983) *Organizations in the Computer Age: Technological Imperatives and Strategic Change*. Aldershot: Gower.

Buchanan, D.A. and Preston, D. (1992) 'Life in the cell: supervision and teamwork in a "manufacturing systems engineering" environment', *Human Resource Management Journal*, 2(4): 55–76.

Buchanan, D.A. and Wilson, B. (1996a) 'Next patient please: the operating theatres problem at Leicester General Hospital NHS Trust', in John Storey (ed.), *Cases in Human Resource and Change Management*. Oxford: Blackwell Business, pp.190–205.

Buchanan, D.A. and Wilson, B. (1996b) 'Re-engineering operating theatres: the perspective assessed', *Journal of Management in Medicine*, 10(4): 57–74.

Buchanan, D. and Huczynski, A. (2004) 'Images of influence: Twelve Angry Men and Thirteen Days', *Journal of Management Inquiry*, 13(4): 312–23.

Buchanan, D.A. and Badham, R.J. (2008) *Power, Politics, and Organizational Change: Winning the Turf Game*. London: Sage Publications, (2nd edn).

Buchanan, D.A., Claydon, T. and Doyle, M. (1999) 'Organization development and change: The legacy of the nineties', *Human Resource Management Journal*, 9(2): 20–37.

Buchanan, D.A., Fitzgerald, L. and Ketley, D. (eds) (2006) *The Sustainability and Spread of Organizational Change: Modernizing Healthcare*, London: Routledge.

Buchanan, D.A., Addicott, R., Fitzgerald, L., Ferlie, E. and Baeza, J. (2007) 'Nobody in charge: distributed change agency in healthcare', *Human Relations*, 60(7): 1065–90.

Bunting, M. (2004) *Willing Slaves: How the Overwork Culture is Ruling Our Lives*. New York: HarperCollins.

Buono, A.F., Bowditch, J.L. and Lewis, J.W. (1985) 'When cultures collide: the anatomy of a merger', *Human Relations*, 38(5): 477–500.

Burawoy, M. (1979) *Manufacturing Consent*. Chicago, IL: University of Chicago Press.

Burger, J.M. (2009) 'Replicating Milgram: would people still obey today?' *American Psychologist*, 64(1): 1–11.

Burgoyne, J. (1999) 'Design of the times', *People Management*, 5(11): 38–44.

Burke, R.J. and Cooper, C.L. (eds) (2008) *The Long Work Hours Culture: Causes, Consequences and Choices*, Bingley: Emerald Group Publishing.

Burman, R. and Evans, A. (2008) 'Target zero: a culture of safety', in R. Oddy (ed.), *Defence Aviation Safety Centre Journal*. RAF Bentley Priory, Stanmore: MoD Aviation Regulatory and Safety Group, pp.22–27.

Burne, J. and Aldridge, S. (1996) 'Who do you think you are?' *Focus Extra*: 1–8.

Burnes, B. (2004) *Managing Change: A Strategic Approach to Organizational Dynamics*. Harlow: Financial Times Prentice Hall, (4th edn).

Burns, J.M. (1978) *Leadership*. New York: Harper & Row.

Burns, T. and Stalker, G.M. (1961 and 1994) *The Management of Innovation*. London: Tavistock Publications and Oxford University Press.

Burns, P. and Jewhurst, J. (eds) (1996) *Small Business and Entrepreneurship*, Houndmills, Basingstoke: Macmillan Business.

Burrell, G. (1984) 'Sex and organizational analysis', *Organization Studies*, 5(2): 97–118.

Burrell, G. (1998) *Pandemonium: Towards a Retro-Theory of Organization*. London: Sage Publications.

Burrell, G. and Morgan, G. (1979) *Sociological Paradigms and Organizational Analysis*. London: Heinemann.

Burt, T. and Larsen, P.T. (2003) 'DirecTV is about changing the whole model of News Corp's output in the US', *Financial Times*, Wednesday 12 February, p.15.

BusinessWeek (2008) 'Globalization bites Boeing', 24 March, p.32.

Butcher, D. and Bailey, C. (2000) 'Crewed awakenings', *People Management*, 6(16): 35–37.

Butcher, D. and Clarke, M. (2008) *Smart Management: Using Politics in Organizations*. Houndmills, Basingstoke: Palgrave, (2nd edn).

Butcher, D. and Harvey, P. (1999) 'Be upstanding', *People Management*, 5(13): 37–42.

Butler, T. and Waldroop, J. (1999) 'Job sculpting: the art of retaining your best people', *Harvard Business Review*, 77(5): 144–52.

Cairncross, F. (1995) 'The death of distance: a survey of telecommunications', *The Economist*, special supplement, 30 September.

Cairncross, F. (2001) *The Death of Distance 2.0: How the Communications Revolution will Change our Lives*. Boston, MA: Harvard Business School Press.

Caldwell, R. (2005) *Agency and Change: Rethinking Change Agency in Organizations*. Abingdon: Routledge.

Callahan, C.V. and Pasternack, B.A. (1999) 'Corporate strategy in the digital age', *Strategy and Business*, 15: 10–14.

Cameron, K.S. and Quinn, R.E. (2006) *Diagnosing and Changing Organizational Culture: Based on the Competing Values Framework*. San Francisco, CA: Jossey Bass, (2nd edn).

Cannell, M. (2007) 'Employee Communication', London: Chartered Institute of Personnel and Development.

Cannell, M. (2008) *Leadership: An Overview*. London: Chartered Institute of Personnel and Development.

Carlowe, J. (2003) 'The EI test', *Focus Extra*, 130: 78–83.

Carr, N.G. (1999) 'Being virtual: character and the new economy', *Harvard Business Review*, 77(3): 181–90.

Carrington, L. (2002) 'Oiling the wheels', *People Management*, 8(13): 31–34.

Carroll, P. (1994) *Big Blues: The Unmaking of IBM*. London: Orion Books.

Carroll, M., Cooke, F.L., Grugulis, I., Rubery, J. and Earnshaw, J. (2002) 'Analysing diversity in the management of human resources in call centres', paper presented at the Human Resource Management Journal Conference on Call Centres, King's College, London.

Cartwright, D. and Zander, A. (eds) (1968) *Group Dynamics: Research and Theory*, London: Tavistock Publications, (3rd edn).

Cattell, R. (1951) 'New concepts for measuring leadership in terms of group syntality', *Human Relations*, 4(2): 161–68.

Cave, A. (2008) 'Build up your resilience to risk', *The Daily Telegraph*, 5 April, p.30.

Cavanagh, G.F., Moberg, D.J. and Velasquez, M. (1981) 'The ethics of organizational politics', *Academy of Management Review*, 6(3): 363–74.

Champoux, J.E. (2001) *Organizational Behaviour: Using Film to Visualize Principles and Practices*. Cincinnati, OH: South-Western College Publishing.

Champoux, J.E. (2005) *Our Feature Presentation: Organizational Behaviour*. Mason, OH: Thomson South-Western.

Champoux, J.E. (2006) 'At the cinema: aspiring to a higher ethical standard', *Academy of management Learning and Education*, 5(3): 386–90.

Champoux, J.E. (2007) *Our Feature Presentation: Human Resource Management*. Mason, OH: Thomson South-Western.

Chandler, A.D. (1962) *Strategy and Structure: Chapters in the History of American Industrial Enterprise*. Cambridge, MA: MIT Press.

Chandler, A.D. (1988) 'Origins of the organization chart', *Harvard Business Review*, 66(2): 156–57.

Chandler, A.D. (1990) *Scale and Scope: The Dynamics of Industrial Capitalism*. Cambridge, MA: Harvard University Press.

Chandler, A.D., Hagstrom, P. and Sölvell, Ö. (eds) (1998) *The Dynamic Firm: The Role of Technology, Strategy, Organization, and Regions*, Oxford: Oxford University Press.

Chanlat, J.-F. (1997) 'Conflict and politics', in A. Sorge and M. Warner (eds), *Handbook of Organization Behaviour*. London: International Thompson Business Press, pp.472–80.

Chansler, P.A., Swamidass, P.M. and Cammann, C. (2003) 'Self-managing work teams: an empirical study of group cohesiveness in "natural work groups" at a Harley-Davidson Motor Company Plant', *Small Group Research*, 34(1): 101–21.

Chao, G.T. (1988) 'The socialization process: building newcomer commitment', in M. London and E.D. Mone (eds), *Career Growth and Human Resource Strategies: The Role of the Human Resource Professional in Employee Development*. New York and London: Quorum Books, pp.31–47.

Chao, G.T., O'Leary-Kelly, A.M., Wolf, S., Klein, H.J. and Gardner, P.D. (1994) 'Organizational socialization: its content and consequences', *Journal of Applied Psychology*, 79(5): 730–43.

Chartered Institute of Personnel and Development (1998) 'Key Facts: Stress at Work', London: Chartered Institute of Personnel and Development.

Chartered Institute of Personnel and Development (2001) 'Quick Facts: Assessment Centres for Recruitment and Selection', London: Chartered Institute of Personnel and Development.

Chartered Institute of Personnel and Development (2008) 'High Performance Working Factsheet', London: Chartered Institute of Personnel and Development.

Chazon, D. (2009) 'Paris artists vie with false imports', *BBC News Channel*, 22 January.

Cherns, A.B. (1976) 'The principles of socio-technical design', *Human Relations*, 29(8): 783–92.

Child, J. (1969) *British Management Thought*. London: George Allen and Unwin.

Child, J. (1972) 'Organizational structure, environment and performance: the role of strategic choice', *Sociology*, 6(1): 1–22.

Child, J. (1985) 'Managerial strategies, new technology and the labour process', in D. Knights, H. Willmott and D. Collinson (eds), *Job Redesign*. Aldershot: Gower, pp.107–41.

Child, J. (1997) 'Strategic choice in the analysis of action, structure, organizations and environments: retrospect and prospect', *Organization Studies*, 18(1): 43–76.

Child, J. (2005) *Organization: Contemporary Principles and Practice*. Oxford: Blackwell.

Christensen, C.M., Bohmer, R. and Kenagy, J. (2000) 'Will disruptive innovations cure health care?' *Harvard Business Review*, 78(5): 102–12.

Christie, R. and Geis, F.L. (1970) *Studies in Machiavellianism*. New York: Academic Press.

Chynoweth, C. (2008) 'Ideas on the bottom line', *People Management*, 14(9): 28–32.

Cialdini, R.B. (2009) *Influence: Science and Practice*. London: Allyn and Bacon, (5th edn).

Cialdini, R.B. and Sagarin, B.J. (2005) 'Principles of interpersonal influence', in T.C. Brock and M.C. Green (eds), *Persuasion: Psychological Insights and Perspectives*. Newbury Park, CA: Sage Publications, (2nd edn.) pp.143–69.

Clarke, A. (1999) 'Employees under surveillance', *The Times*, 6 April, p.35.

Clarry, T. (1999) 'Premium Bonding', *People Management*, 5(17): 34–39.

Claydon, T. and Doyle, M. (1996) 'Trusting me, trusting you: the ethics of employee empowerment', *Personnel Review*, 25(6): 13–25.

Clayton, M. (2008) 'Make rival companies turn green with envy', *The Sunday Times*, Appointments, 12 October, p.4.

Clegg, S.R. (1989) *Frameworks of Power*. London: Sage Publications.

Clegg, S.R. (1990) *Modern Organizations: Organization Studies in the Postmodern World*. London: Sage Publications.

Clegg, S.R. and Dunkerley, D. (1980) *Organization, Class and Control*. London: Routledge & Kegan Paul.

Clegg, S.R. and Hardy, C. (1996) 'Organizations, organization and organizing', in Stewart R. Clegg, Cynthia Hardy and Walter R. Nord (eds), *Handbook of Organization Studies*. London: Sage Publications, pp.1–28.

Clegg, S.R. and Hardy, C. (1996) 'Conclusion: representations', in Stewart R. Clegg, Cynthia Hardy and Walter R. Nord (eds), *Handbook of Organization Studies*. London: Sage Publications, pp.676–708.

Clegg, S.R., Kornberger, M. and Pitsis, T. (2008) *Managing and Organizations*. London: Sage Publications, (2nd edn).

Clegg, S.R., Hardy, C., Lawrence, T. and Nord, W.R. (eds) (2006) *The Sage Handbook of Organization Studies*, London: Sage Publications, (2nd edn).

Coch, L. and French, J.R.P. (1948) 'Overcoming resistance to change', *Human Relations*, 1(4): 512–32.

Cohen, A.R. and Bradford, D.L. (1989) 'Influence without authority: the use of alliances, reciprocity and exchange to accomplish work', *Organizational Dynamics*, 17(1): 5–18.

Cohen, A.R. and Bradford, D.L. (1991) *Influence Without Authority*. New York: Wiley.

Cohen, A.R., Fink, S.L., Gadon, H. and Willits, R.D. (1995) *Effective Behaviour in Organizations*. Homewood, IL: Irwin, (6th edn).

Cohen, S.G. and Bailey, D.E. (1997) 'What makes teams work: group effectiveness research from the shopfloor to the executive suite', *Journal of Management*, 23(3): 239–90.

Cohen, M.D., March, J.G. and Olsen, J.P. (1972) 'Garbage can model of organizational choice', *Administrative Science Quarterly*, 17(1): 1–25.

Colebatch, H. and Lamour, P. (1993) *Market, Bureaucracy and Community*. London: Pluto Press.

Coles, M. (1998) 'Unlock the power of knowledge', *The Sunday Times*, 20 September, p.7.28.

Collett, P. (2004) 'Show and tell', *People Management*, 10(8): 34–35.

Collier, J. and Collier, M. (1986) *Visual Anthropology: Photography as a Research Method*. Albuquerque: University of New Mexico Press.

Collier, P. and Horowitz, D. (1987) *The Fords: An American Epic*. London: Futura Collins.

Colling, T. (1995) 'Experiencing turbulence: competition, strategic choice and the management of human resources in British Airways', *Human Resource Management Journal*, 5(5): 18–33.

Collins, D. (1998) *Organizational Change: Sociological Perspectives*. London: Routledge.

Collins, J. (2001) 'Level 5 leadership: the triumph of humility and fierce resolve', *Harvard Business Review*, 79(1): 67–76.

Collins, M. (2005) 'The (not so simple) case for teleworking: a study at Lloyd's of London', *New Technology, Work and Employment*, 20(2): 115–32.

Collinson, D.L. (2003) 'Identities and insecurities: selves at work', *Organization*, 10(3): 527–47.

Collinson, D. and Ackroyd, S. (2005) 'Resistance, misbehaviour and dissent', in S. Ackroyd, R. Batt, P. Thompson and P.A. Tolbert (eds), *The Oxford Handbook of Work and Organization*. Oxford: Oxford University Press, pp.305–26.

Colquitt, J.A., LePine, J.A. and Wesson, M.J. (2009) *Organizational Behaviour: Improving Performance and Commitment in the Workplace*. London: McGraw Hill.

Comer, D.R. (1995) 'A model of social loafing in real work groups', *Human Relations*, 48(6): 647–67.

Connelly, T. (1997) 'Electronic brainstorming: science meets technology in the group meeting room', in S. Kiesler (ed.), *Culture of the Internet*. Mahwah, NJ: Lawrence Erlbaum Associates, pp.263–76.

Conti, R.E. and Warner, M. (1993) 'Taylorism, new technology and just-in-time systems in Japanese manufacturing', *New Technology, Work and Employment*, 8(1): 31–42.

Cook, J. (2008) 'Perks make Google office hardly feel like work', from http://www.seattlepi.com/business/347434_google16.html, accessed 18 January.

Cook, S. (2008) 'The contribution revolution: Letting volunteers build your business', *Harvard Business Review*, 86(10): 60–69.

Cooper, C. (ed.) (2000) *Theories of Organizational Stress*, Oxford: Oxford University Press.

Cooper, W.H., Gallupe, R.G., Pollard, S. and Cadsby, J. (1998) 'Some liberating effects of anonymous electronic brainstorming', *Small Group Research*, 29(2): 147–78.

Coopey, J. (1995) 'Managerial culture and the and the stillbirth of organizational commitment', *Human Resource Management Journal*, 5(3): 56–76.

Cosier, R.A. and Schwenk, C.R. (1990) 'Agreement and thinking alike: ingredients for poor decisions', *Academy of Management Executive*, 4(1): 69–74.

Costa, P. and McCrae, R.R. (1992) *NEO PI-R: Professional Manual*. Odessa, Florida: Psychological Assessment Resources.

Cottrell, S. (2005) *Critical Thinking Skills: Developing Effective Analysis and Argument*. Basingstoke, Hants: Palgrave Macmillan.

Cottrell, N.B., Wack, K.L., Sekerak, G.J. and Rittle, R. (1968) 'Social facilitation in dominant responses by presence of an audience and the mere presence of others', *Journal of Personality and Social Psychology*, 9(3): 245–50.

Cross, R. and Prusak, L. (2002) 'The people who make organizations go – or stop', *Harvard Business Review*, 80(6): 104–12.

Cross, R. and Parker, A. (2004) *The Hidden Power of Social Networks*. Cambridge, MA: Harvard Business School Press.

Crozier, M. (1973) 'The problem of power', *Social Research*, 40(2): 211–18.

Crystal, D. (2005) *How Language Works*. London: Penguin Books.

Cummings, T.G. and Worley, C.G. (2005) *Organization Development and Change*. Mason, OH: South-Western College Publishing/Thomson Learning, (8th edn).

Cunliffe, A., L. (2008) *Organization Theory*. London: Sage Publications.

Cyert, R.M. and March, J.G. (1963) *A Behavioural Theory of the Firm*. Englewood Cliffs, NJ: Prentice Hall (2nd edn 1962, Oxford: Blackwell Business).

Czarniawska, B. (1998) *A Narrative Approach to Organization Studies*. Thousand Oaks, CA: Sage Publications.

Czarniawska, B. (1999) *Writing Management: Organization Theory as a Literary Genre*. Oxford: Oxford University Press.

Czarniawska, B. and Sevón, G. (eds) (2003) *The Northern Lights: Organization Theory in Scandinavia*, Copenhagen: Copenhagen Business School Press.

Czarniawska-Joerges, B. and de Monthoux, P.G. (eds) (1994) *Good Novels, Better Management: Reading Organizational Realities in Fiction*, Reading UK: Harwood Academic Publishers.

Daft, R. (2003) *Management*. Mason, OH: Thomson-South Western.

Daft, R. (2008) *Management*. Mason, OH: Thomson South-Western, (6th edn).

Daft, R. and Marcic, D. (2009) *Management: The New Workplace*. London: South-Western Cengage Learning, (6th edn).

Daft, R.L. and Noe, R.A. (2001) *Organizational Behaviour*. Mason, OH: South-Western College Publishing/Thomson Learning.

Daft, R.L. and Sharfman, M.P. (1990) *Organization Theory: Cases and Applications*. Eagan, MN: West Publishing.

Dahl, R.A. (1957) 'The concept of power', *Behavioural Science*, 2(3): 201–15.

Daisey, M. (2002) *21 Dog Years: Doing Time @ Amazon.Com*. London: Fourth Estate.

Daniels, K., Lamond, D.A. and Standen, P. (eds) (2000) *Managing Telework*, London: Business Press, Thomson Learning.

Davenport, T.H. (1993) *Process Innovation: Re-engineering Work Through Information Technology*. Boston, MA: Harvard Business School Press.

Davenport, T.H. (2005) *Thinking for a Living: How to get Better Performance and Results from Knowledge Workers*. Boston, MA: Harvard Business School Press.

Davidow, W. and Malone, M. (1992) *The Virtual Corporation*. New York: HarperCollins.

Davidson, M.J. and Cooper, C.L. (1992) *Shattering the Glass Ceiling: The Woman Manager*. London: Paul Chapman Publishing.

Davis, L.E. and Taylor, J.C. (1975) 'Technology effects on job, work, and organizational structure: a contingency view', in L.E. Davis and A.B. Cherns (eds), *The Quality of Working Life: Problems, Prospects and the State of the Art*. New York: The Free Press, pp.220–41.

Davis, L.E. and Taylor, J.C. (1976) 'Technology, organization and job structure', in R. Dubin (ed.), *Handbook of Work, Organization and Society*. Chicago, IL: Rand McNally, pp.379–419.

Davis, S.M. and Lawrence, P.R. (1978) 'Problems of matrix organizations', *Harvard Business Review*, 56(3): 131–42.

Davis, L.E. and Wacker, G.J. (1987) 'Job design', in G. Salvendy (ed.), *Handbook of Human Factors*. New York: Wiley, pp.431–52.

Davis, D., Millburn, P., Murphy, T. and Woodhouse, M. (1992) *Successful Team Building: How To Create Teams That Really Work*. London: Kogan Page.

Dawson, P. (1994) *Organizational Change: A Processual Approach*. London: Paul Chapman Publishing.

Dawson, P. (1996) *Technology and Quality: Change in the Workplace*. London: International Thomson Business Press.

Dawson, P. (2003a) *Reshaping Change: A Processual Approach*. London: Routledge.

Dawson, P. (2003b) *Understanding Organizational Change: The Contemporary Experience of People at Work*. London: Sage Publications.

de Bruxelles, S. (2001) 'Pupils sum up maths teachers as fat nerds', *The Times*, Wednesday 3 January, p.11.

De Dreu, C.K.W. (2008) 'The virtue and vice of workplace conflict: food for (pessimistic) thought', *Journal of Organizational Behaviour*, 29(1): 5–18.

de Jorio, A. (2001) *Gesture in Naples and Gesture in Classical Antiquity*. (Adam Kenton, Trans.) Indiana: Indiana University Press.

de Sitter, L.U., den Hertog, J.F. and Dankbaar, B. (1997) 'From complex organizations with simple jobs to simple organizations with complex jobs', *Human Relations*, 50(5): 497–534.

de Wit, B. and Meyer, R. (2005) *Strategy Synthesis: Text and Readings*. London: International Thomson Business Press.

Deal, T.E. and Kennedy, A.A. (1982) *Organization Cultures: The Rites and Rituals of Organization Life*. Reading, MA: Addison Wesley.

Deal, T.E. and Kennedy, A.A. (2000) *The New Corporate Cultures*. New York and London: Texere Publishing.

Dearlove, D. (2000) 'Productivity myth knocks the shine off IT', *The Times*, 28 September, p.5.

Deetz, S. (2000) 'Describing differences in approaches to organization science: rethinking Burrell and Morgan and their legacy', in P.J. Frost, A.Y. Lewin and R.L. Daft (eds), *Talking About Organization Science: Debates and Dialogue from Crossroads*. Thousand Oaks, CA: Sage Publications.

DeJong, P., Lancaster, J., Pelaez, P. and Munoz, J.S. (2008) 'Examination of correlates of ethical propensity and ethical intentions in the United States, Australia, and the Philippines: a managerial perspective', *International Journal of Management*, 25(2): 270–78.

Denison, D.R. (1990) *Corporate Culture and Organizational Effectiveness*. New York: Wiley.

Denison, D.R., Haaland, S. and Goelzner, P. (2004) 'Corporate culture and organizational effectiveness: is Asia different from the rest of the world?' *Organizational Dynamics*, 33(1): 98–109.

Denning, S. (2004) 'Telling tales', *Harvard Business Review*, 82(5): 122–29.

Denning, S. (2005) *The Leader's Guide to Storytelling: Mastering the Art and Discipline of Business Narratives*. San Francisco, CA: Jossey-Bass.

Dennis, A.R. and Valacich, J.S. (1993) 'Computer brainstorms: more heads are better than one', *Journal of Applied Psychology*, 78(4): 531–37.

Denzin, N.K. and Lincoln, Y.S. (eds) (2000) *Handbook of Qualitative Research*, Thousand Oaks, CA: Sage Publications, (2nd edn).

Department of Health (2002) *NHS Leadership Qualities Framework*. London: Modernization Agency Leadership Centre.

Depietro, R.B. and Strate, M.L. (2007) 'Management perceptions of older employees in the US quick service restaurant industry', *Journal of Foodservice Business Research*, 9(2): 169–85.

Deutsche Welle (2006) 'World's biggest retailer Wal-Mart closes up shop in Germany', from http://www.dw-world.de/dw/article/0,,2112746,00.html.

Devlin, K. (2008) 'Patients recruited in fight to save surgeries', *The Daily Telegraph*, 17 May, p.1.

Diehl, M. and Stroebe, W. (1987) 'Productivity loss in brainstorming groups: towards the solution of a riddle', *Journal of Personality and Social Psychology*, 53(3): 447–509.

Diehl, M. and Stroebe, W. (1991) 'Productivity loss in idea generating groups: tracking down the blocking effect', *Journal of Personality and Social Psychology*, 61(3): 392–403.

Diener, E. (1980) 'Deindividuation: the absence of self-awareness and self-regulation in group members', in H.B. Paulus (ed.), *The Psychology of Group Influence*. Hillsdale, NJ: Lawrence Erlbaum Associates, pp.209–42.

Dixon, N.F. (1994) *On The Psychology of Military Incompetence*. London: Pimlico.

Dixon, N.M. (1999) *The Organizational Learning Cycle: How We Can Learn Collectively*. Aldershot: Gower, (2nd edn).

Dixon, N.M. (2000) *Common Knowledge: How Companies Thrive by Sharing What They Know*. Boston, MA: Harvard Business School Press.

Dodd-McCue, D. (1991) 'Led like sheep: An exercise for linking group decision-making to different types of tasks', *Journal of Management Education*, 15(3): 335–39.

Dodge, J. (2007a) 'Designing around the clock, and the world', from http://www.accessmylibrary.com/coms2/summary_0286–30960578_ITM, accessed 4 June.

Dodge, J. (2007b) 'Boeing 787 Dreamliner engineering chief describes partners organization', from http://www.designnews.com/article/CA6441528.html, accessed 15 May.

Doherty, N. and Tyson, S. (1998) *Mental Well Being in the Workplace: A Resource Pack for Management Training and Development*. London: Health and Safety Executive.

Doms, M. and van Avermaet, E. (1981) 'The conformity effect: a timeless phenomenon?' *Bulletin of the British Psychological Society*, 36(1): 180–88.

Donaldson, T. and Preston, L. (1995) 'The stakeholder theory of the corporation: concepts, evidence, and implications', *Academy of Management Review*, 20(1): 65–91.

Donkin, R. (2008) 'It's a matter of opinion, but workers' views count', *Financial Times*, 8 February, p.9.

Dreu, C. and Van de Vliert, E. (1997) *Using Conflict in Organizations*. London: Sage Publications.

Driscoll, M. (2008) 'Why these women and top jobs aren't mixing', *The Sunday Times*, 7 September, p.17.

Drory, A. (1993) 'Perceived political climate and job attitudes', *Organization Studies*, 14(2): 59–71.

Drory, A. and Romm, T. (1990) 'The definition of organizational politics: a review', *Human Relations*, 43(11): 1134–54.

Drucker, P.F. (1988) 'The coming of the new organization', *Harvard Business Review*, 66(1): 45–53.

Drummond, G. (1994) 'Irresistible science of the super-sellers', *Focus Extra*, November, p.24 and 26.

Druskat, V.U. and Wolff, S.B. (2001) 'Building the emotional intelligence of groups', *Harvard Business Review*, 79(3): 81–90.

Du Gay, P. (2000) *In Praise of Bureaucracy*. London: Routledge.

DuBrin, A.J. (1994) *Applying Psychology: Individual and Organizational Effectiveness*. Englewood Cliffs, NJ: Prentice Hall.

Duncan, R.B. (1972) 'Characteristics of organizational environments and perceived environmental uncertainty', *Administrative Science Quarterly*, 17(3): 313–27.

Duncan, R.B. (1973) 'Multiple decision making structures in adapting to environmental uncertainty: the impact on organizational effectiveness', *Human Relations*, 26(3): 273–91.

Duncan, R.B. (1974) 'Modifications in decision making structures in adapting to the environment: some implications for organizational learning', *Decision Sciences*, 5(4): 705–25.

Duncan, R.B. (1979) 'What is the right organization structure?: decision tree analysis provides the answer', *Organizational Dynamics*, 7(3): 59–80.

Duncan, W.J., La France, K.G. and Ginter, P.M. (2003) 'Leadership and decision making: A retrospective application and assessment', *Journal of Leadership and Organizational Studies*, 9(4): 1–20.

Dunphy, D., Benn, S. and Griffiths, A. (2002) *Organizational Change for Corporate Sustainability*. London: Routledge.

Durand, J.-P. and Hatzfeld, N. (2003) *Living Labour: Life on the Line at Peugeot France*. London: Palgrave.

Dyck, B. and Neubert, M.J. (2009) *Principles of Management*. London: South-Western Cengage Learning.

Eagly, A.H. (2005) 'Achieving relational authenticity in leadership: does gender matter?' *Leadership Quarterly*, 16(3): 459–74.

Eagly, A.H. and Carli, L.L. (2007) 'Women and the labyrinth of leadership', *Harvard Business Review*, 85(9): 62–71.

Earley, P.C. (1993) 'East meets West meets Mideast: further explorations of collectivist and individualistic work groups', *Academy of Management Journal*, 36(2): 319–48.

Easterby-Smith, M. and Araujo, L. (1999) 'Organizational learning: current debates and opportunities', in Mark Easterby-Smith, Luis Araujo and John Burgoyne (eds), *Organizational Learning and the Learning Organization*. London: Sage Publications, pp.1–21.

Easterby-Smith, M., Burgoyne, J. and Araujo, L. (eds) (1999) *Organizational Learning and the Learning Organization: Developments in Theory and Practice*, London: Sage Publications.

Eccles, T. (1994) *Succeeding With Change: Implementing Action-Driven Strategies*. London: McGraw-Hill.

Eckles, C.H. (1956) *Dairy Cattle and Milk Production*. New York: Macmillan.

Edery, D. and Mollick, E. (2008) *Changing the Game: How Video Games are Transforming the Business World*. Harlow: Financial Times Prentice Hall.

Edmondson, A., Bohmer, R. and Pisano, G. (2001) 'Speeding up team learning', *Harvard Business Review*, 79(9): 125–32.

Edwards, R.C. (1979) *Contested Terrain: The Transformation of Industry in the Twentieth Century*. London: Heinemann.

Edwards, P. and Wajcman, J. (2005) *The Politics of Working Life*. Oxford: Oxford University Press.

Einsiedel, A.A. (1983) 'Decision making and problem solving skills: the rational versus the garbage can model of decision-making', *Project Management Quarterly*, 14(4): 52–57.

Ekvall, G. (1996) 'Organizational climate for creativity and innovation', *European Journal of Work and Organizational Psychology*, 5(1): 105–23.

Ekvall, G. and Ryhammar, L. (1999) 'The creative climate: its determinants and effects at a Swedish university', *Creativity Research Journal*, 12(4): 303–10.

Elsworth, C. (2005) 'Jackson jurors face testing time as world tunes into courtroom', *The Daily Telegraph*, 29 January, p.15.

Emery, R.E. and Trist, E.L. (1960) 'Socio-technical systems', in C.W. Churchman and M. Verhulst (eds), *Management Science, Models and Techniques, Volume 2*. London: Pergamon Press, pp.83–97.

Emmison, M. and Smith, P. (2000) *Researching the Visual: Images, Objects, Contexts and Interactions in Social and Cultural Inquiry*. London: Sage Publications.

Emmott, M. (2004) 'Britain's real working lives', *People Management*, 10(13): 14–15.

Emmott, M. (2006) 'What drives employee engagement?' *Impact: Quarterly Update on CIPD Policy and Research*, 16(August): 4–5.

Empson, S. (2004) 'Anxiety attack', *People Management*, 10(25): 18–19.

Engardio, P., Bernstein, A. and Kripalani, M. (2003) 'The new global job shift', *Business Week*, 3 February, pp.36–48.

Erickson, T.J. and Gratton, L. (2007) 'What it means to work here', *Harvard Business Review*, 85(3): 104–12.

Espinosa, J.A., Slaughter, S.A., Kraut, R.E. and Herbsleb, J.D. (2007) 'Team Knowledge and Coordination in geographically distributed software development', *Journal of Management Information Systems*, 24(1): 136–69.

Esser, J.K. and Lindoerfer, J.S. (1989) 'Groupthink and the space shuttle Challenger accident', *Journal of Behavioural Decision Making*, 2(3): 167–77.

Evans, M. (2008) 'Charming the locals: a soldier's guide', *The Times*, 11 February, p.14.

Evans, P. and Wolf, B. (2005) 'Collaboration rules', *Harvard Business Review*, 83(7–8): 96–104.

Eysenck, H.J. (1970) *The Structure of Human Personality*. London: Methuen, (3rd edn).

Eysenck, H.J. (1990) 'Biological dimensions of personality', in L.A. Pervin (ed.), *Handbook of Personality, Theory and Research*. New York: Guilford Press, pp.244–76.

Farrell, D. and Petersen, J.C. (1982) 'Patterns of political behaviour in organizations', *Academy of Management Review*, 7(3): 403–12.

Feldman, D.C. (1984) 'The development and enforcement of group norms', *Academy of Management Review*, 9(1): 47–53.

Feldman, M. (1991) 'The meanings of ambiguity: learning from stories and metaphors', in P. Frost, L. Moore, M. Louis, C. Lundberg and J. Martin (eds), *Reframing Organization Culture*. Newbury Park, CA: Sage Publications, pp.145–56.

Feldman, D. and Klitch, N. (1991) 'Impression management and career strategies', in K. Giacalone and P. Rosenfeld (eds), *Applied Impression Management: How Image Making Affects Managerial Decisions*. London: Sage Publications, pp.67–80.

Ferris, G.R., Hochwater, W.A., Douglas, C., Blass, F.R., Kolodinsky, R.W.and Treadway, D.C. (2002), 'Social influence processes in organizations and human resource systems', *Research in Personnel and Human Resource Management*, (21): 65–127.

Ferris, G.R., Treadway, D.C., Kolodinsky, R.W., Hochwarter, W.A., Kacmar, C.J., Douglas, C. and Frink, D.D. (2005) 'Development and Validation of the Political Skill Inventory', *Journal of Management*, 31(1): 126–52.

Ferster, C.S. and Skinner, B.F. (1957) *Schedules of Reinforcement*. New York: Appleton-Century-Crofts.

Festinger, L., Pepitone, A. and Newcomb, T. (1952) 'Some consequences of deindividuation in a group', *Journal of Abnormal and Social Psychology*, 47(2): 382–89.

Fiedler, F.E. (1967) *A Theory of Leadership Effectiveness*. New York: McGraw-Hill.

Fiedler, F.E. and Chemers, M.M. (1974) *Leadership and Effective Management*. Glenview IL: Scott, Foresman.

Fiedler, F.E. and Chemers, M.M. (1984) *Improving Leadership Effectiveness: The Leaders Match Concept*. New York: Wiley, (2nd edn).

Financial Times (2005) 'More than a just a change of customs', 28 July, p.13.

Financial Times (2007) 'Manufacturing enters a new era', 18 June, p.6.

Fincham, R. and Rhodes, P.S. (2005) *The Individual, Work and Organization*. Oxford: Oxford University Press, (4th edn).

Fiorina, C. (2006) *Tough Choices: A Memoir*. London and Boston: Nicholas Brealey Publishing.

Fisher, R. and Ury, W. (1981) *Getting to Yes: Negotiating Agreement Without Giving In*. London: Hutchinson.

Fishman, C. (2007a) 'Whole foods is all teams', from http://www.fastcompany.com/magazine/02/team1.html, accessed 18 December.

Fishman, C. (2007b) 'Total teamwork: Imagination Ltd', from http://www.fastcompany.com/magazine/33/imagination.html, accessed 19 December.

Fleishman, E.A. (1953a) 'The description of supervisory behaviour', *Journal of Applied Psychology*, 37(1): 1–6.

Fleishman, E.A. (1953b) 'The measurement of leadership attitudes in industry', *Journal of Applied Psychology*, 37(3): 153–58.

Fleishman, E.A. and Harris, E.F. (1962) 'Patterns of leadership behaviour related to employee grievances and turnover', *Personnel Psychology*, 15(1): 43–56.

Fleming, P. (2007) 'Sexuality, power and resistance in the workplace', *Organization Studies*, 28(2): 239–56.

Fleming, P. and Spicer, A. (2004) 'You can checkout anytime, but you can never leave: Spatial boundaries in a high commitment organization', *Human Relations*, 57(1): 75–94.

Fleming, P. and Spicer, A. (2007) *Contesting the Corporation: Struggle, Power and Resistance in Organizations*. Cambridge: Cambridge University Press.

Fletcher, S. (2007) 'Messy desk? Have £7 million', from http://www.hrzone.co.uk/item/163568, accessed 9 January.

Flowers, M.L. (1977) 'A laboratory test of some implications of Janis's groupthink hypothesis', *Journal of Personality and Social Psychology*, 35(12): 888–96.

Fombrun, C.J. (1984) 'Organization culture and competitive strategy', in C.J. Fombrun, N.M. Tichy and M.A. Devanna (eds), *Strategic Human Resource Management*. New York: Wiley.

Ford, R.N. (1969) *Motivation Through the Work Itself*. New York: American Management Association.

Ford, H. and Crowther, S. (1924) *My Life and Work*. London: William Heinemann.

Ford, R.C. and Fottler, M.D. (1995) 'Empowerment a matter of degree', *Academy of Management Executive*, 9(3): 21–29.

Foreman, J. and Thatchenkery, T.J. (1996) 'Filmic representations for organizational analysis: the characterization of a transplant organization in the film *Rising Sun*', *Journal of Organizational Change Management*, 9(3): 44–61.

Forsyth, D.R. (2006) *Group Dynamics*. London: Thomson Wadsworth, (4th edn).

Fortune (2007) 'The big picture', 5 March, pp.57–64.

Foss, N.J. (2003) 'Selective intervention and internal hybrids: interpreting and learning from the rise and decline of the Oticon spaghetti organization', *Organization Science*, 14(3): 331–49.

Foucault, M. (1979) *Discipline and Punish*. Harmondsworth: Penguin Books.

Fourboul, C.V. and Bournois, F. (1999) 'Strategic communication with employees in large European companies: a typology', *European Management Journal*, 17(2): 204–17.

Foushee, H.C. (1984) 'Dyads and triads at 35,000 feet: factors affecting group process and air crew performance', *American Psychologist*, 39(8): 885–93.

Fox, A. (1966) *Industrial Sociology and Industrial Relations, Research Paper 3*. London: Royal Commission on Trade Unions and Employers' Associations.

Fox, A. (1973) 'Industrial relations: a social critique of pluralist ideology', in John Child (ed.), *Man and Organization*. London: Allen & Unwin, pp.185–233.

Fox, A. (1974) *Man Mismanagement*. London: Hutchinson.

Fraser, C. (1978) 'Small groups: structure and leadership', in Henri Tajfel and Colin Fraser (eds), *Introducing Social Psychology*. Harmondsworth: Penguin Books, pp.176–200.

French, J.R.P. and Raven, B.H. (1958) 'The bases of social power', in D. Cartwright (ed.), *Studies in Social Power*. Ann Arbor, Michigan: Institute for Social Research, University of Michigan Press, pp.150–67.

Friedman, M. (1970) 'The social responsibility of business is to increase its profits', *New York Times Magazine*(13 September).

Friedman, M. and Rosenman, R.F. (1974) *Type A Behaviour and Your Heart*. New York: Knopf.

Friedman, R.A., Tidd, S.T., Currall, S.C. and Tsai, J.C. (2000) 'What goes around comes around: the impact of personal conflict style on work conflict and stress', *International Journal of Conflict Management*, 11(1): 32–55.

Frohlich, N. and Oppenheimer, J. (1970) 'I get by with a little help from my friends', *World Politics*, 23: 104–20.

Fuchs, V. (1968) *The Service Economy*. New York: Basic Books.

Fujimoto, T. (1999) *The Evolution of the Toyota Production System*. New York: Oxford University Press.

Fulmer, R.M. and Herbert, T.T. (1974) *Exploring the New Management*. New York: Macmillan.

Furnham, A. (1997) *The Psychology of Behaviour at Work*. Hove, Sussex: Psychology Press/Taylor & Francis.

Furnham, A. (1999) 'Anti-hierarchy gurus fall flat on their faces', *The Daily Telegraph, Appointments Section*, appointments, p.A3.

Furnham, A. (2000) 'The brainstorming myth', *Business Strategy Review*, 11(4): 21–28.

Furnham, A. (2005) *The Psychology of Behaviour at Work*. Hove, Sussex: Psychology Press/Taylor & Francis, (2nd edn).

Furnham, A. and Gunter, B. (1993) 'Corporate culture: definition, diagnosis and change', in Cary L. Cooper and Ivan T. Robertson (eds), *International Review of Industrial and Organizational Psychology, vol.8*. Chichester: John Wiley, pp.233–61.

Gabriel, Y. (2004) *Myths, Stories, and Organizations: Premodern Narratives for our Times*. Oxford: Oxford University Press.

Gagliardi, P. (1986) 'The creation and change of organizational cultures: a conceptual framework', *Organization Studies*, 7(2): 117–34.

Galbraith, J. (1973) *Designing Complex Organizations*. Reading, MA: Addison Wesley.

Galbraith, J.R. (1974) 'Sexuality, power and resistance in the workplace', *Interfaces*, 4(3): 28–36.

Gallie, D., White, M., Cheng, Y. and Tomlinson, M. (1998) *Restructuring the Employment Relationship*. Oxford: Clarendon Press.

Gallupe, R.B., Bastianutti, L.M. and Cooper, W.H. (1991) 'Unblocking brainstorms', *Journal of Applied Psychology*, 76(1): 137–42.

Gandz, J. and Murray, V.V. (1980) 'The experience of workplace politics', *Academy of Management Journal*, 23(2): 237–51.

Gannon, M.J. and Newman, K.L. (eds) (2001) *The Blackwell Handbook of Cross-cultural Management*, Oxford: Blackwell.

Gantt, H. (1919) *Organizing for Work*. New York: Harcourt, Brace and Hove.

Garmendia, J.A. (2004) 'The impact of company culture on company performance', *Current Sociology*, 52(6): 1021–38.

Garrahan, P. and Stewart, P. (1992) *The Nissan Enigma: Flexibility at Work in a Local Economy*. London: Mansell Publishing.

Garside, J. (2007) 'Online revolutionaries', from www.telegraph.co.uk/finance/migrationtemp/2815430/Online-revolutionaries.html, accessed 18 June 2009.

Garten, J. (2002) *The Politics of Fortune: A New Agenda for Business Leaders*. Boston, MA: Harvard University Press.

Gartman, D. (1979) 'Origins of the assembly line and capitalist control of work at Ford', in A.S. Zimbalist (ed.), *Case Studies on the Labour Process*. London: Monthly Review Press, pp.193–205.

Garvin, D.A. and Roberto, M.A. (2001) 'What you don't know about making decisions', *Harvard Business Review*, 79(8): 108–16.

Garvin, D.A., Edmondson, A. and Gino, F. (2008) 'Is yours a learning organization?' *Harvard Business Review*, 86(3): 109–16.

George, J.M. (1992) 'Extrinsic and intrinsic origins of perceived social loafing in organizations', *Academy of Management Journal*, 35(1): 191–202.

Gersick, C.J. (1988) 'Time and transition in work teams', *Academy of Management Journal*, 31(1): 9–41.

Gersick, C.J. (1989) 'Marking time: predictable transitions in task group', *Academy of Management Journal*, 32(2): 274–309.

Gherardi, S. (1997) 'Organizational learning', in Arndt Sorge and Malcolm Warner (eds), *The Handbook of Organizational Behaviour*. London: International Thomson Business Press, pp.542–41.

Ghosn, C. (2002) 'Saving the business without losing the company', *Harvard Business Review*, 80(1): 37–45.

Gibb, J.R. (1961) 'Defensive communication', *Journal of Communication*, 11(3): 141–48.

Gibson, W. (2003) *Pattern Recognition*. London: Penguin Books.

Giddens, A. (1990) *The Consequences of Modernity*. Cambridge and Oxford: Polity Press and Blackwell.

Gilbreth, F.B. (1911) *Motion Study: A Method for Increasing the Efficiency of the Workman*. New York: Van Nostrand.

Gilbreth, L. (1914) *Psychology of Management*. First published in serial form: *Industrial Engineering and Engineering Digest–11* (May–June 1912; July–Dec 1912; Jan–May 1913) New York: Sturgis & Walton.

Gilbreth, F.B. and Gilbreth, L. (1916) *Fatigue Study*. New York: Sturgis & Walton.

Gill, C. (1985) *Work, Unemployment and the New Technology*. Cambridge: Polity Press.

Gill, R. (2006) *Theory and Practice of Leadership*. London: Sage Publications.

Gillen, T. (2004) *Leadership or Management: The Differences*. London: Chartered Institute of Personnel and Development.

Gillespie, R. (1991) *Manufacturing Knowledge: A History of the Hawthorne Experiments*. Cambridge: Cambridge University Press.

Ginnett, R.C. (1993) 'Crews as groups: their formation and leadership', in E.L. Wiener, B.G. Kanki and R.L. Helmreich (eds), *Cockpit Resource Management*. San Diego, CA: Academic Press, pp.71–98.

Gluck, F.W. (2005) 'God's line manager', *FT Magazine*, 17 May, pp.16–20.

Goffee, R. and Jones, G. (2003) *The Character of a Corporation: How Your Company's Culture Can Make or Break Your Business*. London: Profile Business.

Goffman, E. (1959) *The Presentation of Self in Everyday Life*. New York: Doubleday Anchor.

Gog, S.K. (2007) 'At Google, hours are long, but the company is free', from http://www.washingtonpost.com/wp-dyn/content/article/2007/01/23/AR2007012300334.html, accessed 24 January.

Golding, W. (1954) *Lord of the Flies*. London: Faber & Faber.

Goldratt, E. and Cox, J. (1993) *The Goal*. Aldershot: Gower Publishing, (2nd edn).

Goldstein, E. (2001) *Sensation and Perception*. Belmont, CA: Wadsworth.

Goldthorpe, J.H., Lockwood, D., Bechhofer, F. and Platt, J. (1968) *The Affluent Worker: Industrial Attitudes and Behaviour*. Cambridge: Cambridge University Press.

Goleman, D. (1998) *Working with Emotional Intelligence*. London: Bloomsbury Publishing.

Goleman, D. (2000) 'Leadership that gets results', *Harvard Business Review*, 78(2): 78–90.

Goleman, D. (2005) *Emotional Intelligence: Why It Can Matter More Than IQ*. London: Bloomsbury Publishing (first published 1995).

Goleman, D. (2006) *Social Intelligence: The New Science of Human Relationships*. London: Hutchinson.

Golzen, G. (1989) 'Maestro, learn the company score', *The Sunday Times*, appointments section, 25 June, p.8.

Goodrich, C.L. (1975) *The Frontier of Control*. London: Pluto Press.

Goodwin, C. (2008) 'Shucks, we just can't help making billions', *The Sunday Times*, Ingear Supplement, 7 September, pp.6–9.

Goos, M. and Manning, A. (2003) 'Lousy and lovely jobs: The rising polarization of work in Britain', *London School of Economics, Discussion Paper Series* No. 614.

Gordon, J. (1992) 'Work teams – how far have they come?' *Training*, 29(10): 59–65.

Gordon, J. (1993) *A Diagnostic Approach to Organizational Behaviour*. Boston, MA: Allyn & Bacon.

Gordon, G.G. and DiTomaso, N. (1992) 'Predicting corporate performance from organizational culture', *Journal of Management Studies*, 29(6): 783–98.

Görg, H., Greenaway, D. and Kneller, R. (2008) *The Economic Impact of Offshoring*. Nottingham: Globalization and Economic Policy Centre, University of Nottingham.

Gorgeu, A. and Mathieu, R. (2005) 'Teamwork in factories within the French automobile industry', *New Technology, Work and Employment*, 20(2): 88–101.

Gouldner, A.W. (1954) *Patterns of Industrial Bureaucracy*. New York: The Free Press.

Gouldner, A.W. (1957) 'Cosmopolitans and locals: towards an analysis of latent roles', *Administrative Science Quarterly*, 2(3): 281–306.

Govan, F. (2006) 'I've got the office under my skin', *The Daily Telegraph*, 14 February, p.11.

Grandey, A.A. (2003) 'When "the show must go on": surface acting and deep acting as determinants of emotional exhaustion and peer-related service delivery', *Academy of Management Journal*, 46(1): 86–96.

Grandey, A.A., Dickter, D.N. and Sin, H. (2004) 'The customer is not always right: customer aggression and emotion regulation of service employees', *Journal of Organizational Behaviour*, 25(3): 397–418.

Grant, R.M. (2002) *Contemporary Strategy Analysis: Concepts, Techniques and Applications*. Oxford: Blackwell, (4th edn).

Gratton, L. (2007) 'Building bridges for success', *Financial Times*, Understanding the Culture of Collaboration supplement, 29 June, pp.2–3.

Gratton, L. and Erickson, T.J. (2007) 'Ways to build collaborative teams', *Harvard Business Review*, 85(11): 101–09.

Gratton, L., Voight, A. and Erickson, T. (2007) 'Bridging fault lines in diverse teams', *Sloan Management Review*, 48(4): 22–29.

Graves, D. (1986) *Corporate Culture: Diagnosis and Change*. New York: St Martin's Press.

Gray, J.L. and Starke, F.A. (1984) *Organizational Behaviour: Concepts and Applications.* Columbus, OH: Merrill Publishing, (3rd edn).

Greasley, K., Bryman, A., Dainty, A., Price, A., Soetanto, R. and King, N. (2005) 'Employee perceptions of empowerment', *Employee Relations*, 27(4): 354–68.

Greenberg, J. (1976) 'The role of seating position in group interaction: a review with applications for group trainers', *Group and Organizational Studies*, 1(3): 310–27.

Greenberg, J. (1999) *Managing Behaviour in Organizations.* Upper Saddle River, NJ: Prentice Hall, (2nd edn).

Greenberg, J. and Baron, R.A. (1997) *Behaviour in Organizations.* Englewood Cliffs, NJ: Pearson/Prentice Hall, (6th edn).

Greenberg, J. and Baron, R.A. (2007) *Behaviour in Organizations.* Englewood Cliffs, NJ: Pearson/Prentice Hall, (9th edn).

Greenhalgh, L. (2001) 'Managers face up to the new era', *Financial Times (Mastering People Management supplement)*, 11 October.

Greiner, L.E. (1998) 'Evolution and revolution as organizations grow', *Harvard Business Review*, 76(3): 55–68.

Grey, C. (2005) *A Very Short, Fairly Interesting and Reasonably Cheap Book About Studying Organizations.* London: Sage Publications.

Griffin, R. and Putsay, M.W. (2007) *International Business: A Managerial Perspective.* Upper Saddle River, NJ: Pearson/Prentice Hall.

Griffith, T.L. and Neale, M.A. (2001) 'Information processing in traditional, hybrid and virtual teams; from nascent knowledge to transactive memory', *Research in Organizational Behaviour*, 23: 379–421.

Griffith, T.L., Sawyer, J.E. and Neale, M.A. (2003) 'Vitualness and knowledge in teams: Managing the love triangle of organizations, individuals and information technology', *MIS Quarterly*, 27(2): 265–87.

Griffiths, J. (2005) 'A marriage of two mindsets', *Financial Times*, 16 March, p.15.

Gronn, P. (2002) 'Distributed leadership as a unit of analysis', *Leadership Quarterly*, 13(4): 423–51.

Groth, L. (1999) *Future Organizational Design.* Chichester: Wiley.

Guest, D. (2000) 'Piece by piece', *People Management*, 6(15): 26–31.

Guest, D. and King, Z. (2001) 'Personnel's paradox', *People Management*, 7(19): 24–29.

Guest, D. and King, Z. (2004) 'Power, innovation and problem-solving: the personnel managers' three steps to heaven?' *Journal of Management Studies*, 41(3): 401–23.

Guirdham, M. (1995) *Interpersonal Skills at Work.* Hemel Hempstead: Prentice Hall, (2nd edn).

Guirdham, M. (2002) *Interactive Behaviour at Work.* Harlow: Financial Times Prentice Hall, (3rd edn).

Guirdham, M. (2005) *Communicating Across Cultures at Work.* London: Palgrave Macmillan, (2nd edn).

Gulowsen, J. (1979) 'A measure of work-group autonomy', in L.E. Davis and J.C. Taylor (eds), *Design of Jobs.* Santa Monica: Goodyear, (2nd edn.) pp.206–18.

Gunnigle, P., Lavelle, J. and McDonnell, A. (2007) *Human Resource Practices in Multinational Companies in Ireland: A Large-Scale Survey.* Limerick: University of Limerick Employment Relations Research Unit.

Gurchiek, K. (2006) 'Security gets under employees' skin: workers have chip implanted to access restricted areas', from *HRMagazine* http://goliath.ecnext.com/coms2/summary_0199-5465346_ITM, accessed 1 April.

Gyllenhammar, P.G. (1977) *People at Work.* Reading, MA: Addison-Wesley.

Hackman, J.R. (1990) *Groups That Work (and Those That Don't).* San Francisco, CA: Jossey-Bass.

Hackman, J.R. and Oldham, G.R. (1974) *The job diagnostic survey: an instrument for the diagnosis of jobs and the evaluation of job redesign projects, Technical Report no.4.* Department of Administrative Sciences, Yale University.

Hackman, J.R., Oldham, G., Janson, R. and Purdy, K. (1975) 'A new strategy for job enrichment', *California Management Review*, 17(4): 57–71.

Haddon, L. and Brynin, M. (2005) 'The character of telework and the characteristics of teleworkers', *New Technology, Work and Employment*, 20(1): 34–46.

Hales, C. (1993) *Managing Through Organization*. London: Routledge.

Hall, E.T. (1976) *Beyond Culture*. New York: Doubleday/Currency.

Hall, E.T. (1989) *Understanding Cultural Differences*. Yarmouth, ME: Intercultural Press.

Hamel, G. (2006) 'The why, what, and how of management innovation', *Harvard Business Review*, 84(2): 72–84.

Hamel, G. and Prahalad, C.K. (1996) 'Competing in the new economy: managing out of bounds', *Strategic Management Journal*, 17(3): 237–42.

Hammarstrom, O. and Lansbury, R.D. (1991) 'The art of building a car: the Swedish experience re-examined', *New Technology, Work and Employment*, 6(2): 85–90.

Hammer, M. (1990) 'Reengineering work: can't automate, obliterate', *Harvard Business Review*, 68(4): 104–12.

Hammer, M. (2004) 'Deep change: how operational innovation can transform your company', *Harvard Business Review*, 82(4): 84–93.

Hammer, M. and Champy, J. (1993) *Reengineering the Corporation: A Manifesto for Business Revolution*. London: Nicholas Brealey Publishing.

Hammer, M. and Stanton, S.A. (1995) *The Reengineering Revolution – A Handbook*. New York: HarperCollins.

Hampton, M.M. (1999) 'Work groups', in Yiannis Gabriel (ed.), *Organizations in Depth*. London: Sage Publications, pp.112–38.

Handy, C. (1984) *The Future of Work*. Oxford: Blackwell.

Handy, C. (1993) *Understanding Organizations*. Harmondsworth: Penguin Books, (4th edn).

Handy, C. (1995) 'Trust and the virtual organization', *Harvard Business Review*, 73(3): 4–50.

Haney, W.V. (1973) *Communication and Organizational Behaviour*. Homewood, IL, Richard D. Irwin.

Hansen, M.T. (2009) 'When internal collaboration is bad for your company', *Harvard Business Review*, 87(4): 82–84.

Hardman, D. (2009) *Judgement and Decision Making*. Bognor Regis: Wiley-Blackwell.

Hardy, C. (ed.) (1995) *Power and Politics in Organizations*, Aldershot: Dartmouth Publishing.

Hardy, C. and Clegg, S.R. (1996) 'Some dare call it power', in Stewart R. Clegg, Cynthia Hardy and Walter R. Nord (eds), *Handbook of Organization Studies*. London: Sage Publications, pp.622–41.

Hardy, C. and Palmer, I. (1999) 'Pedagogical practice and postmodern idea', *Journal of Management Education*, 23(4): 377–95.

Hare, A.P. (1992) *Groups, Teams and Social Interactions*. New York: Praeger.

Harford, T. (2006) 'Check this out', *FT Magazine*, 16 December, p.12.

Harley, B. (2005) 'Hope or hype: high performance work systems', in B. Harley, J. Hyman and P. Thompson (eds), *Participation and Democracy at Work: Essays in Honour of Harvie Ramsay*. Basingstoke, Hants: Palgrave Macmillan, pp.38–54.

Harper, B. (2000) 'Beauty, stature and the labour market: a British cohort study', *Oxford Bulletin of Economics and Statistics*, 62(S1): 771–800.

Harper, C.R., Kidera, G.J. and Cullen, J.F. (1971) 'Study of simulated airline pilot incapacitation, phase II: subtle or partial loss of function', *Aerospace Medicine*, 42(9): 946–48.

Harris, M. (1998) 'Re-thinking the virtual organization', in P.J. Jackson and J.M. van der Wielen (eds), *Telework: International Perspectives*. London: Routledge.

Harris, L.C. and Ogbonna, E. (1999) 'Developing a market oriented culture: a critical evaluation', *Journal of Management Studies*, 36(2): 177–98.

Harrison, R. (1972) 'Understanding your organization's character', *Harvard Business Review*, 50(3): 119–28.

Harrison, M.I. (1994) *Diagnosing Organizations: Methods, Models and Processes*. Thousand Oaks, CA: Sage Publications.

Harrison, A. (1999) 'Getting the message: resistance to corporate communication in three British organizations', paper presented at the Working Class Academics Conference, University of Arkansas, Little Rock.

Harvard Business Review (2000) *Harvard Business Review on Negotiation and Conflict Resolution*. Boston, MA: Harvard Business School Press.

Harvard Business Review (2008) 'Archive: a field is born', 86(7–8): 164.

Harvey, M. (2008) 'With friends like these – 110 million of them – making a profit should be easy, shouldn't it?' *The Times*, 20 October, pp.44–45.

Haspeslagh, P. (1999) 'Managing the mating dance in equal mergers', *Financial Times; Mastering Strategy Supplement*, 25 October, pp.6–7.

Hassard, J.S. and Buchanan, D.A. (2009) 'From *Modern Times* to *Syriana*: feature films as research data', in David A. Buchanan and Alan Bryman (eds), *The Sage Handbook of Organizational Research Methods*. London: Sage Publications.

Hassard, J. and Holliday, R. (eds) (1998) *Organization-Representation: Work and Organizations in Popular Culture*, London: Sage Publications.

Hatch, M.J. (1997) *Organization Theory: Modern, Symbolic and Postmodern Perspectives*. Oxford: Oxford University Press.

Hatch, M.J. and Schultz, M. (eds) (2005) *Organizational Identity: A Reader*, Oxford: Oxford University Press.

Hatch, M.J. and Cunliffe, A.L. (2006) *Organization Theory*. Oxford: Oxford University Press, (2nd edn).

Hatchett, A. (2000) 'Ringing true', *People Management*, 6(2): 40–41.

Hayes, N. (1997) *Successful Team Management*. London: International Thomson Business Press.

Hearn, J. (1993) 'Emotive subjects: organizational men, organizational masculinities and the (de)construction of emotions', in S. Fineman (ed.), *Emotion in Organizations*. London: Sage Publications, pp.142–66.

Hearn, J.R., Sheppard, D.L., Tancred, P. and Burrell, G. (eds) (1989) *The Sexuality of Organization*, London: Sage Publications.

Heath, C. and Sitkin, S.B. (2001) 'Big-B versus Big-O: what is *organizational* about organizational behavior?', *Journal of Organizational Behavior*, 22(1): 43–58.

Heider, F. (1958) *The Psychology of Interpersonal Relationships*. New York: John Wiley.

Heil, G., Bennis, W. and Stephens, D.C. (2000) *Douglas McGregor Revisited*. New York: John Wiley.

Helft, M. (2007) 'Google: master of online traffic helps its workers beat the rush', *New York Times*, 10 March, pp.1–3.

Heller, F. (1997) 'Leadership', in Arndt Sorge and Malcolm Warner (eds), *The Handbook of Organizational Behaviour*. London: International Thomson, pp.340–49.

Hellriegel, D. and Slocum, J.W. (1978) *Management: Contingency Approaches*. Reading, MA: Addison-Wesley.

Hemp, P. (2008) 'Getting real about virtual worlds', *Harvard Business Review*, 86(10): 27–28.

Henkoff, R. (1994) 'Finding and keeping the best service workers', *Fortune*, 3 October, pp.52–58.

Henry, J. and Hartzler, M. (1998) *Tools for Virtual Teams: A Team Fitness Companion*. Milwaukee, Wisconsin: ASQ Quality Press.

Hersey, P. and Blanchard, K.H. (1988) *Management of Organizational Behavior: Utilizing Human Resources*. Englewood Cliffs, NJ: Prentice-Hall International.

Herzberg, F. (1966) *Work and the Nature of Man*. New York: Staples Press.

Herzberg, F. (1968) 'One more time: how do you motivate employees?' *Harvard Business Review*, 46(1): 53–62.

Herzberg, F. (1987) 'Workers' needs the same around the world', *Industry Week*, 21 September, pp.29–32.

Hewlett, S.A. (2002) 'Executive women and the myth of having it all', *Harvard Business Review*, 80(4): 66–73.

Hewlett, S.A. (2002) *Baby Hunger: The New Battle for Babyhood*. London: Atlantic Books.

Hewlett, S.A. and Luce, C.B. (2006) 'Extreme jobs: the dangerous allure of the 70-hour workweek', *Harvard Business Review*, 84(12): 49–59.

Hewlett, S.A., Luce, C.B. and West, C. (2005) 'Leadership in your midst: tapping the hidden strengths of minority executives', *Harvard Business Review*, 83(11): 74–82.

Hickson, D. and Pugh, D.S. (2002) *Management Worldwide: The Impact of Societal Culture on Organizations Around the Globe*. Harmondsworth: Penguin Books, (2nd edn).

Hickson, D.J., Hinings, C.R., Lee, C.A., Schneck, R.E. and Pennings, J.M. (1971) 'A strategic contingencies theory of intra-organizational power', *Administrative Science Quarterly*, 16(2): 216–19.

Higgs, M. (2003) 'Good call', *People Management*, 9(2): 48–49.

Highwater, R. and Sayeed, L. (1995) 'The impact of computer-mediated communication systems on biased group discussion', *Computers in Human Behaviour*, 11(1): 33–44.

Hiley, D.R. (1987) 'Power and values in corporate life', *Journal of Business Ethics*, 6(5): 343–53.

Hill, G.W. (1982) 'Group versus individual performance: are N + 1 heads better than one?' *Psychological Bulletin*, 91(3): 517–39.

Hill, S. (1991) 'Why quality circles failed but total quality management might succeed', *British Journal of Industrial Relations*, 29(4): 541–68.

Hindle, T. (2006a) 'Inculcating culture: the Toyota way', *The Economist, The New Organization: A Survey of the Company*, 21 January, p.13.

Hindle, T. (2006b) 'Thinking for a living', *The Economist, The New Organization: A Survey of the Company*, 21 January, pp.9 and 12–14.

Hindle, T. (2006c) 'Take a deep breath', *The Economist, The New Organization: A Survey of the Company*, 21 January, pp.5, 6 and 8.

Hindle, T. (2006d) 'Teaming with bright ideas', *The Economist, The New Organization: A Survey of the Company*, 21 January, pp.15–18.

Hindle, T. (2006e) 'Big and no longer blue: A totally new, improved IBM', *The Economist, The New Organization: A Survey of the Company*, 21 January, p.16.

Hindle, T. (2006f) 'The new organization', *The Economist, The New Organization: A Survey of the Company*, 21 January, pp.3–5.

Hindle, T. (2006g) 'The matrix master: a survey of the company', *The Economist*, 21 January, p.6.

Hindle, T. (2006h) 'Partners in wealth', *The Economist, The New Organization: A Survey of the Company*, 21 January, pp.18–19.

Hinings, B. and Munro, R. (2003) '"Organization" and "disorganization"', in R. Westwood and S. Clegg (eds), *Debating Organization*. Oxford: Blackwell, pp.273–97.

Hinkin, T.R. and Schriesheim, C.A. (2009) 'Performance incentives for tough times', *Harvard Business Review*, 87(3): 26.

Hinton, P.R. (1993) *The Psychology of Interpersonal Perception*. London: Routledge.

Hochman, P. (2006) 'Pack mentality', from http://money.cnn.com/2006/05/26/magazines/ fortune/peloton_greatteams_fortune_0612/index.htm, accessed 1 June.

Hochschild, A. (1983) *The Managed Heart*. Berkeley, CA: University of California Press.

Hochschild, A.R. (1997) *The Time Bind: When Home Becomes Work and Work Becomes Home*. New York: Owl Books.

Hochschild, A. (2003) *The Commercialization of Intimate Life*. Berkeley, CA: University of California Press.

Hochschild, A. (2003) *The 2nd Shift*, New York: Penguin.

Hoel, H., Cooper, C.L. and Faragher, B. (2001) 'The experience of bullying in Great Britain: the impact of organizational status', *European Journal of Work and Organizational Psychology*, 10(4): 443–65.

Hofstede, G. (1986) 'Editorial: the usefulness of the concept of organization culture', *Journal of Management Studies*, 23(3): 253–57.

Hofstede, G. (1991) *Cultures and Organizations*. London: McGraw-Hill.

Hofstede, G. (1994) 'The business of international business is culture', *International Business Review*, 3(1): 1–14.

Hofstede, G. (2001) *Culture's Consequences: International Differences in Work-related Values*. London: Sage Publications, (2nd edn).

Hofstede, G. and Bond, M. (1988) 'The Confucian connection: from cultural roots to economic growth', *Organizational Dynamics*, 16(4): 4–21.

Hogg, M.A. and Vaughan, G.M. (2008) *Social Psychology*. Harlow: Pearson Education Ltd, (5th edn).

Holbeche, L. (2008) 'The leadership paradox', *Futures*, 1(1): 2–4.

Holland Herald KLM Magazine (2008) 'Our worldwide alliance', March, p.68.

Hollenbeck, G.P., McCall Jnr, M.W. and Silzer, R.F. (2006) 'Leadership competency models', *Leadership Quarterly*, 17(4): 398–413.

Hollway, W. (1991) *Work Psychology and Organizational Behaviour*. London: Sage Publications.

Holman, D. and Thorpe, R. (eds) (2003) *Management and Language: The Manager as a Practical Author*, London: Sage Publications.

Holpp, L. (1994) 'Applied empowerment', *Training*, 31(2): 39–44.

Homans, G.C. (1951) *The Human Group*. London: Routledge and Kegan Paul.

Hope, V. and Hendry, J. (1995) 'Corporate culture – is it relevant for the organization of the 1990s?' *Human Resource Management Journal*, 5(4): 61–73.

Hopfl, H. (2002) 'Playing the part: reflections on aspects of mere performance in the customer-client relationship', *Journal of Management Studies*, 39(2): 255–67.

Horsnell, M. (2007) 'The £7 million guide to a tidy desk', *The Times*, 5 January, p.5.

House, R.J. (1988) 'Power and personality in complex organizations', in B.M. Staw and L.L. Cummings (eds), *Research in Organizational Behaviour: Volume 10*. Greenwich, CT: JAI Press, pp.305–57.

House, R.J., Spangler, W.D. and Woycke, J. (1991) 'Personality and charisma in the US presidency: a psychological theory of leader effectiveness', *Administrative Science Quarterly*, 36(3): 364–96.

House, R.J., Hanges, P.J., Javidan, M., Dorfman, M. and Gupta, V. (eds) (2004) *Culture, Leadership and Organizations: The GLOBE Study of 62 Societies*, Thousand Oaks, CA: Sage Publications.

Howard, P.J. and Howard, J.M. (1993) *The Big Five Workbook: A Roadmap for Individual and Team Interpretation of Scores on the Five-Factor Model of Personality*. Charlotte, NC: Center for Applied Cognitive Studies.

Howard, P.J., Medina, P.L. and Howard, J.K. (1996) 'The big five locator: a quick assessment tool for consultants and trainers', in, *The 1996 Annual: Volume 1 Training*. San Diego, CA: Pfeiffer & Company, pp.107–22.

Howe, J. (2006) 'The rise of crowdsourcing', from http://www.wired.com/wired/archive/14.06/crowds.html, accessed 14 June.

Howe, J. (2009) *Crowdsourcing: Why the Power of the Crowd is Driving the Future of Business*. London: Crown Business.

Huczynski, A.A. (2004) *Influencing Within Organizations*. London: Routledge, (2nd edn).

Huczynski, A. and Buchanan, D. (2004) 'Theory from fiction: a narrative process perspective on the pedagogical use of feature film', *Journal of Management Education*, 28(6): 707–26.

Huczynski, A. and Buchanan, D. (2005) 'Feature films in management education: beyond illustration and entertainment', *Journal of Organizational Behaviour Education*, 1(1): 73–94.

Hughes, R.L., Ginnett, R.C. and Curphy, G.J. (1996) *Leadership: Enhancing the Lessons of Experience*. Chicago, IL: Irwin.

Huselid, M.A. (1995) 'The impact of human resource management practices on turnover, productivity, and corporate financial performance', *Academy of Management Journal*, 38(3): 635–72.

Hutchins, E. (1990) 'The technology of team navigation', in J. Galegher, R.E. Kraut and C. Egido (eds), *Intellectual Teamwork; Social and Technological Foundations of Co-operative Work*. Hillsdale, NJ: Lawrence Erlbaum Associates, pp.191–220.

Huxley, A. (1932) *Brave New World*. Harmondsworth: Chatto and Windus/Penguin Books.

Huxley, A. (1954) *The Doors of Perception/Heaven and Hell*. London: Chatto and Windus/ Flamingo.

Huy, Q.N. (2001) 'In praise of middle managers', *Harvard Business Review*, 79(8): 72–79.

Huysman, M. (1999) 'Balancing biases: a critical review of the literature on organizational learning', in Mark Easterby-Smith, Luis Araujo and John Burgoyne (eds), *Organizational Learning and the Learning Organization*. London: Sage Publications, pp.59–74.

Ibarra, H. (1999) 'Provisional selves: experimenting with image and identity in professional adaptation', *Administrative Science Quarterly*, 44(4): 764–91.

Ignattius, A. (2006) 'In search of the real Google', *Time*, 20 February, pp.32–42.

Ilgen, D.R. and Knowlton, W.A. (1980) 'Performance attributional effects on feedback from superiors', *Organizational Behaviour and Human Performance*, 25(3): 441–56.

Incomes Data Services (1999) *Pay and Conditions in Call Centres 1999*. London: Incomes Data Services.

Ingham, A.G., Levinger, G., Graves, J. and Peckham, V. (1974) 'The Ringelmann effect: studies of group size and group performance', *Journal of Experimental Social Psychology*, 10(4): 371–84.

IRS Employment Review (1996) 'Turn on, tune in, churn out: a survey of teleworking', *IRS Employment Review*, 609(June): 6–15.

Isenberg, D.J. (1986) 'Group polarization: a critical review and meta-analysis', *Journal of Personality and Social Psychology*, 50(6): 1141–51.

Jablin, F.M. (2001) 'Organizational entry, assimilation, and disengagement/exit', in Fredric M. Jablin and Linda L. Putnam (eds), *The New Handbook of Organizational Communication: Advances in Theory, Research, and Methods*. Thousand Oaks, CA: Sage Publications, pp.732–818.

Jablin, F.M. and Putnam, L.L. (eds) (2001) *The New Handbook of Organizational Communication: Advances in Theory, Research, and Methods*, Thousand Oaks, CA: Sage Publications.

Jackall, R. (1988) *Moral Mazes: The World of Corporate Managers*. London: Sage Publications.

Jackson, N. and Carter, P. (2000) *Rethinking Organisational Behaviour*. Harlow, Essex: Financial Times Prentice Hall.

Jackson, B. and Parry, K. (2007) *A Very Short, Fairly Interesting and Reasonably Cheap Book about Studying Leadership*. London: Sage Publications.

Jacobs, J.H. (1945) 'The application of sociometry to industry', *Sociometry*, 8: 81–98.

James, J. (2003) 'You've got the look', *People Management*, 9(7): 46–47.

Janis, I.L. (1982) *Victims of Groupthink*. Boston, MA: Houghton Mifflin, (2nd edn).

Jaques, R. (2003) 'The chip under your skin', *The Times*, 2 October, p.4.

Javidan, M. and House, R.J. (2001) 'Cultural acumen for the global manager: Lessons from the Project GLOBE', *Organizational Dynamics*, 29(4): 289–305.

Jay, A. (1970) *Management and Machiavelli*. Harmondsworth: Penguin Books.

Jenkins, A. (1994) 'Teams: from ideology to analysis', *Organization Studies*, 15(6): 849–60.

Jermier, J.M., Knights, D. and Nord, W.R. (eds) (1994) *Resistance and Power in Organizations*, London: Routledge.

Jervis, F.R. (1974) *Bosses in British Business*. London: Routledge and Kegan Paul.

Jessop, A. (2008) 'How I made a difference at work', *People Management*, 14(12): 44.

Johnson, D.W. and Johnson, F.P. (1975) *Joining Together: Group Theory and Group Skills*. Englewood Cliffs, NJ: Prentice Hall.

Johnson, D.W. and Johnson, F.P. (2008) *Joining Together: Group Theory and Group Skills*. Englewood Cliffs, NJ: Pearson, (10th edn).

Johnson, P. and Gill, J. (1993) *Management Control and Organizational Behaviour*. London: Paul Chapman/Sage Publications.

Johnson, G., Scholes, K. and Whittington, R. (2005) *Exploring Corporate Strategy: Text and Cases*. Harlow: Financial Times Prentice Hall, (7th edn).

Johnson, G., Scholes, K. and Whittington, R. (2008) *Exploring Corporate Strategy: Text and Cases*. Harlow: Financial Times Prentice Hall, (8th edn).

Johnston, R. (2000) 'Hidden capital', in J. Barry, J. Chandler, H. Clark, R. Johnston and D. Needle (eds), *Organization and Management: A Critical Text*. London: International Thomson Business Press, pp.16–35.

Jones, J.E. (1973) 'Model of group development', in, *The 1973 Annual Handbook for Group Facilitators*. San Francisco, CA: Pfeiffer/Jossey-Bass, pp.127–29.

Jones, O. (1997) 'Changing the balance?: Taylorism, TQM and work organization', *New Technology, Work and Organization*, 12(1): 13–24.

Jonsen, K. and Bryant, B. (2008) 'Stretch target', *People Management*, 14(17): 28–31.

Joseph, M. (1989) *Sociology for Business*. Oxford: Blackwell.

Jung, C.G. (1953) *Collected Works*. New York: Bollingen Series/Pantheon.

Jung, C.G. (1971) *Psychological Types, (The Collected Works of C.G. Jung, Volume 6)*. Princeton, NJ: Princeton University Press (first published 1923).

Kafka, F. (1926) *The Castle (Das Schloss)*. (Willa Muir and Edwin Muir, Trans.) Munich/Harmondsworth: Wolff/Penguin Books (1957).

Kahneman, D. (2003) 'Maps of bounded rationality: Psychology for behavioural economists', *American Economic Review*, 93(5): 1449–75.

Kahneman, D. and Tversky, A. (1984) 'Choices, values and frames', *American Psychologist*, 39(4): 341–50.

Kahneman, D. and Tversky, A. (eds) (2000) *Choices, Values and Frames*, Cambridge: Cambridge University Press.

Kahneman, D., Slovic, P. and Tversky, A. (eds) (1982) *Judgement Under uncertainty: Heuristics and Biases*, Cambridge: Cambridge University Press.

Kakabadse, A. (1983) *The Politics of Management*. Aldershot: Gower.

Kanigel, R. (1997) *The One Best Way: Frederick Winslow Taylor and the Enigma of Efficiency*. London: Little Brown.

Kankanhalli, A., Tan, B.C.Y. and Wei, K.-K. (2007) 'Conflict and performance in global virtual teams', *Journal of Management Information Systems*, 23(3): 237–74.

Kanter, R.M. (1977) *Men and Women of the Corporation*. New York: Basic Books.

Kanter, R.M. (1979) 'Power failure in management circuits', *Harvard Business Review*, 57(4): 65–75.

Kanter, R.M. (1983) *The Change Masters: Corporate Entrepreneurs at Work*. London: George Allen & Unwin.

Kanter, R.M. (1989) *When Giants Learn to Dance: Mastering the Challenge of Strategy, Management and Careers in the 1990s*. London: Simon & Schuster.

Kanter, R.M. (2002) 'Creating the culture for innovation', in Frances Hesselbein, Marshall Goldsmith and Iain Somerville (eds), *Leading For Innovation And Organizing For Results*. San Francisco: Jossey-Bass, pp.73–85.

Karasek, R.A. (1979) 'Job demands, job decision latitudes, and mental strain: implications for job redesign', *Administrative Science Quarterly*, 24(2): 285–308.

Karau, S.J. and Williams, K.D. (1993) 'Social loafing: meta-analytic review and theoretical integration', *Journal of Personality and Social Psychology*, 65(4): 681–706.

Katz, D., Maccoby, N. and Morse, N.C. (1950) *Productivity, Supervision, and Morale in an Office Situation*. Ann Arbor, MI: University of Michigan Institute for Social Research.

Katzenbach, J.R. (1998) *Teams at the Top*. Cambridge, MA: Harvard Business School Press.

Katzenbach, J.R. and Smith, D.K. (1993) *The Wisdom of Teams: Creating the High Performance Organization*. Boston, MA: Harvard Business School Press.

Katzenbach, J.R. and Santamaria, J.A. (1999) 'Firing up the front line', *Harvard Business Review*, 77(3): 107–17.

Katzenbach, J.R., Beckett, F., Dichter, S., Feigen, M., Gagnon, C., Hope, Q. and Ling, T. (1997) *Real Change Leaders: How Do You Create Growth and High Performance at Your Company*. London: Nicholas Brealey Publishing.

Kay, J. (2006) 'Football's example can help companies score', from http://www.ft.com/cms/s/0/6667847e-1079–11db-8eec-0000779e2340.html?nclick_check=1, accessed 10 July.

Keenoy, T. (1990) 'Human resource management: rhetoric, reality and contradiction', *International Journal of Human Resource Management*, 1(3): 363–84.

Keenoy, T. (1999) 'HRM as hologram: a polemic', *Journal of Management Studies*, 36(1): 1–23.

Kellaway, L. (2005) *Martin Lukes: Who Moved My BlackBerry?* London: Viking Books.

Kellaway, L. (2007) 'A motivational missive that amounts to torture', *Financial Times*, Business Life, 2 July, p.16.

Kellerman, B. (2004) *Bad Leadership: What It Is, How It Happens, Why It Matters*. Boston, MA: Harvard Business School Press.

Kelley, H.H. (1971) *Attribution: Perceiving the Causes of Behaviour*. New York: General Learning Press.

Kemske, F. (1996) *Human Resources: A Business Novel*. London: Nicholas Brealey.

Kenton, A. (2000) *Gesture in Naples and Gesture in Classical Antiquity*, A Translation. Bloomington, IL: Indiana University Press.

Kerr, N.L. (1983) 'Motivation losses in small groups: a social dilemma analysis', *Journal of Personality and Social Psychology*, 45(4): 819–28.

Kettle, M. (1999) 'Ten Steps to the White House', *The Guardian*, 1 March, p.7.

Khurana, R. (2002) 'The curse of the superstar CEO', *Harvard Business Review*, 80(9): 60–66.

Kiely, M. (1993) 'When "no" means "yes"', *Marketing*, October, pp.7–9.

Kilduff, M. and Krackhardt, D. (2008) *Interpersonal Networks in Organizations*. Cambridge: Cambridge University Press.

Kinnie, N., Hutchinson, S. and Purcell, J. (2000) 'Fun and surveillance: the paradox of high commitment management in call centres', *International Journal of Human Resource Management*, 11(5): 967–85.

Kirkman, B.L., Gibson, C.B. and Shapiro, B.L. (2001) 'Exporting teams: enhancing the implementation and effectiveness of work teams in global affiliates', *Organizational Dynamics*, 30(1): 12–29.

Knight, C. (2005) *Performance Without Compromise*. Cambridge, MA: Harvard Business School Press.

Knights, D. and Willmott, H. (1987) 'Organizational culture as management strategy: a critique and illustration from the financial services industry', *International Studies of Management and Organization*, 17(3): 40–63.

Knights, D. and Willmott, H. (1999) *Management Lives: Power and Identity in Work Organizations*. London: Sage Publications.

Knights, D. and Willmott, H. (eds) (2000) *The Reengineering Revolution: Critical Studies of Corporate Change*, London: Sage Publications.

Knights, D. and Willmott, H. (2007) *Introducing Organizational Behaviour and Management*. London: Thomson Learning.

Kohn, A. (1993) 'Why incentive plans cannot work', *Harvard Business Review*, 71(5): 54–63.

Kolb, D.M. (1983) 'Strategy and tactics of mediation', *Human Relations* 36(3): 247–68.

Konrad, A.M. and Kramer, V.W. (2006) 'How many women do boards need?' *Harvard Business Review*, 84(12): 22.

Koontz, H. (1966) 'Making theory operational: the span of management', *Journal of Management Studies*, 3(3): 229–43.

Kornhauser, A. (1965) *Mental Health of the Industrial Worker*. New York: John Wiley.

Kotter, J.P. (1982) *The General Managers*. New York: The Free Press.

Kotter, J.P. (1985) *Power and influence*. New York: The Free Press.

Kotter, J.P. (1990) *A Force for Change: How Leadership Differs from Management*. New York: The Free Press.

Kotter, J.P. (1995a) 'Leading change: why transformation efforts fail', *Harvard Business Review*, 73(2): 59–67.

Kotter, J.P. (1995b) *The New Rules: How to Succeed in Today's Post-Corporate World*. IL: The Free Press.

Kotter, J.P. (1996) 'Kill complacency', *Fortune*, 5 August, pp.122–24.

Kotter, J.P. (1999) 'What effective general managers really do', *Harvard Business Review*, 77(2): 145–59.

Kotter, J.P. (2008) *A Sense of Urgency*. Boston, MA: Harvard Business Press.

Kotter, J.P. and Heskett, J.L. (1992) *Corporate Culture and Performance*. New York: The Free Press.

Kotter, J.P. and Schlesinger, L.A. (2008; first published 1979) 'Choosing strategies for change', *Harvard Business Review*, 57(2): 106–14.

Koza, M.P. and Lewin, A.Y. (1999) 'Putting the S-word back in alliances', *Financial Times Mastering Strategy Supplement*, 1 November, pp.12–13.

Kozlowski, S.W.J. and Bell, B. (2003) 'Work groups and teams in organizations', in W.C. Boreman, D.R. Ilgen and I.B. Weiner (eds), *Handbook of Industrial and Organizational Psychology, Vol.12*. New York: Wiley, pp.333–76.

Krackhardt, D. and Hanson, J.R. (1993) 'Informal networks: the company behind the chart', *Harvard Business Review*, 71(4): 104–11.

Kramer, R.M. (2006) 'The great intimidators', *Harvard Business Review*, 84(2): 88–96.

Kravitz, D.A. and Martin, B. (1986) 'Ringelmann re-discovered: the original article', *Journal of Personality and Social Psychology*, 50(5): 936–41.

Krefting, L.A. and Frost, P.J. (1985) 'Untangling webs, surfacing waves, and wildcating: a multiple metaphor perspective on managing culture', in P.J. Frost, L.F. Moore and M.R. Louis (eds), *Organizational Culture*. Beverley Hills, CA: Sage Publications.

Kreitner, R. (1989) *Management*. Boston, MA: Houghton Mifflin, (4th edn).

Kreitner, R., Kinicki, A. and Buelens, M. (1999) *Organizational Behaviour*. London: McGraw-Hill.

Kreitner, R. and Kinicki, A. (2001) *Organizational Behaviour*. New York: Irwin McGraw-Hill, (5th edn).

Krell, T.C., Mendenhall, M.E. and Sendry, J. (1987) 'Doing research in the conceptual morass of organizational politics', paper presented at the Western Academy of Management Conference, Hollywood.

Kübler-Ross, E. (1969) *On Death and Dying*. Toronto: Macmillan.

Kunda, G. (1992) *Engineering Culture: Control and Commitment in a High Tech Corporation.* Philadelphia, PA: Temple University Press.

Kwiatkowski, R. and Lawrence, S. (1996) 'Orchestral metaphors and organizational reality: or "Taylor rides again"?' paper presented at the British Psychological Society, Occupational Psychology Conference, Eastbourne, January.

Lamb, J. (1999) 'Face value gains credence in "unwritten" HR policies', *People Management*, 5(23): 14–15.

Lamm, H. (1988) 'A review of our research on group polarization: eleven experiments on the effects of group discussion on risk acceptance, probability estimation and negotiation positions', *Psychological Reports*, 62: 807–13.

Lamm, H. and Myers, D.G. (1978) 'Group induced polarization of attitudes and behaviour', in L. Berkowitz (ed.), *Advances in Experimental Social Psychology Vol.11*. New York: Academic Press, pp.145–95.

Langfried, C.W. (2000) 'Work group design and autonomy', *Small Group Research*, 31(1): 54–70.

Langley, A. (1989) 'In search of rationality: the purposes behind the use of formal analysis in organizations', *Administrative Science Quarterly*, 34(4): 598–631.

Langley, A. (2009) 'Studying processes in and around organizations', in David A. Buchanan and Alan Bryman (eds), *Handbook of Organizational Research Methods*. London: Sage Publications, pp.409–29.

Lashinsky, A. (2007) 'Search and Joy', *Fortune*, 22 January, pp.70–82.

Latane, B. and Nida, S. (1980) 'Social impact theory and group influence: a social engineering perspective', in P.B. Paulus (ed.), *Psychology of Group Influence*. Hillsdale, NJ: Lawrence Erlbaum Associates, pp.3–34.

Latane, B., Williams, K. and Harkins, S. (1979) 'Many hands make light work: the causes and consequences of social loafing', *Journal of Personality and Social Psychology*, 37(6): 822–32.

Latham, G.P. and Yukl, G.A. (1975) 'A review of research on the application of goal setting in organizations', *Academy of Management Journal*, 18(4): 824–45.

Laurent, A. (1983) 'The cultural diversity of Western conceptions of management', *International Studies of Management and Organization*, 13(1–2 whole issue).

Laurent, A. (1989) 'A cultural view of organizational change', in P. Evans, Y. Doz and A. Laurent (eds), *Human Resource Management in International Firms*. London: Macmillan, pp.83–94.

Lawler, E.E. (1996) *From the Ground Up: Six Principles for Building the New Logic Corporation*. San Francisco, CA: Jossey-Bass.

Lawler, E.E. and Worley, C. (2009) 'The rebirth of change', *People Management,* 14(23): 28–30.

Lawler, E.E., Mohrman, S.A. and Ledford, G.E. (1998) *Strategies for High Performance Organizations*. San Francisco, CA: Jossey-Bass.

Lawrence, P.R. and Lorsch, J.W. (1967) *Organization and Environment*. Boston, MA: Addison Wesley.

Lawrence, S. and Davis, P. (1979) *Matrix*. Reading, MA: Addison Wesley.

Layard, R. (2005) *Happiness: Lessons from a New Science*. London: Penguin Books.

Leake, J. and Woods, R. (2009) 'Google and you'll damage the planet', *The Sunday Times*, 11 January, p.6.

Leana, C.R. (1985) 'A partial test of Janis's groupthink model: Effects of group cohesiveness and leader behaviour on defective decision making', *Journal of Management*, 11(1): 5–17.

Leavitt, H.J. (1975) 'Suppose we took groups seriously', in E.L Cass and F.G. Zimmer (ed.), *Man and Work in Society*. London: Van Nostrand Reinhold, pp.67–77.

Leavitt, H.J. (2003) 'Why hierarchies thrive', *Harvard Business Review*, 81(3): 96–1022.

Leavitt, H.J. (2005) *Top Down: Why Hierarchies Are Here To Stay and How To Manage Them More Effectively*. Boston, MA: Harvard Business School Press.

LeBon, G. (1908; first published 1895 by Ernest Benn) *The Crowd: A Study of the Popular Mind*. London: Unwin.

Legge, K. (1994) 'Managing culture: fact or fiction', in Keith Sisson (ed.), *Personnel Management: A Comprehensive Guide to Theory and Practice in Britain*. Oxford: Blackwell, pp.397–433.

Legge, K. (2005) *Human Resource Management: Rhetorics and Realities*. Houndmills, Basingstoke: Macmillan Business, (2nd anniversary edn).

Leidner, R. (1993) *Fast Food, Fast Talk: Service Work and the Routinization of Everyday Life*. Berkeley, CA: University of California Press.

Leopold, J. and Harris, L. (2009) *The Strategic Managing of Human Resources*. Harlow, Essex: Financial Times Prentice Hall, (2nd edn).

Leshner, M. and Brown, A. (1993) 'Increasing efficiency through cross-training', *Bet's Review*, 95(8): 39–40.

Lester, T. (2007) 'Masters of collaboration', *Financial Times*, Understanding the Culture of Collaboration supplement, 29 June, p.8.

Levine, R.V. (1990) 'The pace of life', *American Scientist*, 78(5): 43–53.

Levine, S. and Levine, R. (1996) 'Why they're not smiling: Stress and discontent in the orchestra workplace', *Harmony*, April, pp.15–25.

Levitt, S.D. and Dubner, S.J. (2005) *Freakonomics*. London: Penguin Books.

Levitt, S.D. and Venkatesh, S.A. (2000) 'An economic analysis of a drug-selling gang's finances', *Quarterly Journal of Economics*, 115(3): 755–89.

Lewig, K.A. and Dollard, M.F. (2003) 'Emotional dissonance: emotional exhaustion and job satisfaction in call centre workers', *European Journal of Work and Organization Psychology*, 12(4): 366–92.

Lewin, A.Y. and Stephens, C.U. (1994) 'CEO attributes as determinants of organization design: an integrated model', *Organization Studies*, 14(2): 183–212.

Lewin, K. (ed.) (1951) *Field Theory in Social Science*, New York: Harper & Row.

Lichfield, J. (2009) 'Bossnapped! (It's French for industrial action)', *The International Independent*, 2 April, p.27.

Liden, R.C., Wayne, S.J., Jaworkski, R.A. and Bennett, N. (2004) 'Social loafing: a field investigation', *Journal of Management*, 30(2): 285–304.

Likert, R. (1961) *New Patterns of Management*. New York: McGraw-Hill.

Lindblom, C. (1959) 'The science of muddling through', *Public Administration Review*, 34(4): 79–88.

Litchfield, R.C. (2008) 'Brainstorming reconsidered: a goal-based approach', *Academy of Management Review*, 33(3): 649–68.

Litterer, J.A. (1973) *The Analysis of Organizations*. Chichester: John Wiley.

Litterick, D. (2006) 'Wal-Mart quits Germany but insists Asda is safe', *The Daily Telegraph*, 29 July, p.31.

Littlepage, G.E. (1991) 'Effects of group size and task characteristics on group performance: a test of Steiner's model', *Personality and Social Psychology Bulletin*, 17(4): 449–56.

Littler, C.R. (1982) *The Development of the Labour Process in Capitalist Societies*. London: Heinemann.

Littler, C. and Salaman, G. (1982) 'Bravermania and beyond: recent theories and labour process', *Sociology*, 16(2): 251–69.

Locke, E.A. (1968) 'Towards a theory of task performance and incentives', *Organizational Behaviour and Human Performance*, 3(2): 157–89.

Locke, E.A. (1975) 'Personnel attitudes and motivation', *Annual Review of Psychology*, 26: 457–80.

Locke, E.A. and Latham, G.P. (1990) *A Theory of Goal Setting and Task Performance.* Englewood Cliffs, NJ: Prentice Hall.

Locock, L. (2001) *Maps and Journeys: Redesign in the NHS.* Birmingham: The University of Birmingham, Health Services Management Centre.

Loe, M. (2002) 'Working for men: At the intersection of power, gender and sexuality', in C.L. Williams and A. Stein (eds), *Sexuality and Gender.* Oxford: Blackwell, pp.221–38.

Lorsch, J.W. (1977) 'Organizational design: a situational perspective', *Organizational Dynamics*, 6(2): 2–14.

Lubatkin, M., Calori, R., Very, P. and Veiga, J. (1998) 'Managing mergers across borders: a two nation explanation of a nationally bound administrative heritage', *Organizational Science*, 9(6): 670–84.

Lublin, J.S. (2006) 'Some do's and don'ts to help you hone videoconference skills', *The Wall Street Journal (Marketplace Supplement)*, 7 February, p.B1.

Ludeman, K. and Erlandson, E. (2006) *Alpha Male Syndrome: Curb the Belligerence, Channel the Brilliance.* Boston, MA: Harvard Business School Press.

Lukes, S. (2005) *Power: A Radical View.* London: Macmillan, (2nd edn).

Luthans, F. (1995) *Organizational Behaviour.* New York: McGraw-Hill, (7th edn).

Luthans, F. and Davis, T.R.V. (1979) 'Behavioural self-management: the missing link in managerial effectiveness', *Organizational Dynamics*, 8(1): 42–60.

Luthans, F. and Kreitner, R. (1985) *Organizational Behaviour Modification and Beyond.* Glenview IL: Scott, Foresman, (2nd edn).

Luthans, F., Stajkovic, A., Luthans, B.C. and Luthans, K.W. (1998) 'Applying behavioural management in Eastern Europe', *European Management Journal*, 16(4): 466–74.

Lysons, K. (1997) 'Organizational analysis', *British Journal of Administrative Management*, special supplement(18).

Mabey, C., Salaman, G. and Storey, J. (1998) *Human Resource Management: A Strategic Introduction.* Oxford: Blackwell, (2nd edn).

MacDonald, S. (1999) 'Femininity rules, OK', *The Times, First Executive Supplement*, 30 September, p.2.

MacDuffie, J.P. (1988) 'The Japanese auto transplants: challenges to conventional wisdom', *ILR Report*, 26(1): 12–18.

Machiavelli, N. (1961) *The Prince.* (George Bull, Trans.) Harmondsworth: Penguin Books.

Madison, D.L., Allen, R.W., Porter, L.W. and Mayes, B.T. (1980) 'Organizational politics: an exploration of managers' perceptions', *Human Relations*, 33(2): 79–100.

Makary, M.A., Sexton, J.B., Freischlag, J.A., Holzmueller, C.G., Millman, E.A., Rowen, L. and Pronovost, P.J. (2005) 'Operating room teamwork among physicians and nurses: teamwork in the eye of the beholder', *Journal of the American College of Surgeons*, 202(5): 746–52.

Makary, M.A., Sexton, J.B., Freischlag, J.A., Millman, E.A., Pryor, D., Holzmueller, C. and Pronovost, P.J. (2006) 'Patient safety in surgery', *Annals of Surgery*, 243(5): 628–35.

Malone, T.W. (2004) *The Future of Work: How the New Order of Business Will Shape Your Organization, Your Management Style, and Your Life.* Boston, MA: Harvard Business School Press.

Mangham, I. (1979) *The Politics of Organizational Change.* Westport, CT: Greenwood Press.

Mann, S. (1995) 'Politics and power in organizations: why women lose out', *Leadership and Organization Development Journal*, 16(2): 9–15.

Mann, S. (1999) *Hiding What We Feel, Faking What We Don't: Understanding the Role of Your Emotions at Work.* Shaftsbury, Dorset: Element Books.

Manning, T., Parker, R. and Pogson, G. (2006) 'A revised model of team roles and some research findings', *Industrial and Commercial Training*, 38(6): 287–96.

March, J.G. (1962) 'The business firm as a political coalition', *Journal of Politics*, 24(4): 662–78.

March, J.G. (1988) *Decisions and Organizations*. Oxford: Blackwell.

March, J. and Simon, H.A. (1958) *Organizations*. New York: Wiley.

March, J.G. and Olsen, J.P. (1976) *Ambiguity and Choice in Organizations*. Oslo: Universitetsforlaget.

Marchington, M. (1992) *Managing the Team: A Guide to Successful Employee Involvement*. Oxford: Blackwell.

Marchington, M. and Wilkinson, A. (2005) *Human Resource Management at Work*. London: Chartered Institute of Personnel and Development, (3rd edn).

Marcic, D. (1992) *Organizational Behavior: Experiences and Cases*. St Paul, MN: West Publishing, (3rd edn).

Marcic, D. (1995) *Organizational Behavior: Experiences and Cases*. St Paul, MN: West Publishing, (4th edn).

Margerison, C. and McCann, D. (1990) *Team Management*. London: W.H. Allen.

Marketing Week (2006) 'Net value judgements', 2 February, pp.20–21.

Martin, J. (1985) 'Can organization culture be managed?' in P.J. Frost, L.F. Moore and M.R. Louis (eds), *Organizational Culture*. Beverley Hills, CA: Sage Publications, pp.95–98.

Martin, J. (1992) *Cultures in Organizations: Three Perspectives*. Oxford: Oxford University Press.

Martin, J. (2001) *Organizational Culture: Mapping the Terrain*. London: Sage Publications.

Martin, J. (2005) *Organizational Behaviour and Management*. London: Thomson (3rd edn).

Martin, G., Reddington, M. and Kneafsey, M.B. (2008) *Web 2.0 and HR: A Discussion Paper*. London: Chartered Institute for Personnel and Development.

Maslach, C. and Leiter, M.P. (1999) *The Truth About Burnout*. New York: Jossey-Bass.

Maslow, A. (1943) 'A theory of human motivation', *Psychological Review*, 50(4): 370–96.

Maslow, A. (1954) *Motivation and Personality*. New York: Harper & Row.

Maslow, A. (1971) *The Farther Reaches of Human Nature*. Harmondsworth: Penguin Books.

Mason, R.O. (2004) 'Lessons in organizational ethics from the Columbia disaster: can culture be lethal', *Organizational Dynamics*, 33(2): 128–42.

Mattos, M. (2007) 'The last word: McJob', *Shameless Magazine*, Fall, p.1.

Maule, J.A. and Hodgkinson, G., P. (2003) 'Re-appraising managers' perceptual errors: a behavioural decision-making perspective', *British Journal of Management*, 14(1): 33–37.

Maurer, S.D., Sue-Chan, C. and Latham, G.P. (1999) 'The situational interview', in Robert W. Eder and Michael M. Harris (eds), *The Employment Interview Handbook*. Thousand Oaks, CA: Sage Publications, pp.159–77.

Mayes, B.T. and Allen, R.W. (1977) 'Toward a definition of organizational politics', *Academy of Management Review*, 2(4): 672–78.

Mayo, E. (1933) *The Human Problems of an Industrial Civilization*. New York: Macmillan.

Mayo, E. (1945) *The Social Problems of an Industrial Civilization*. Cambridge, MA: Harvard University Press.

McAuley, J., Duberley, J. and Johnson, P. (2007) *Organization Theory: Challenges and Perspectives*. Harlow: Financial Times Prentice Hall.

McCaffrey, D.P., Faerman, S.R. and Hart, D.W. (1995) 'The appeal and difficulties of participative systems', *Organization Science*, 6(6): 603–27.

McCall, A. (2008) 'How well does your employer scrub up?' *The Sunday Times 100 Best Companies to Work For*, 9 March, pp.1–88.

McCarty, J. (2004) *Bullets Over Hollywood: The American Gangster Picture from the Silents to 'The Sopranos'*. Cambridge, MA: Da Capo Press.

McCauley, C. (1989) 'The nature of social influence in groupthink: compliance and internationalization', *Journal of Personality and Social Psychology*, 57(2): 250–60.

McClelland, D.C. (1961) *The Achieving Society*. Princeton, NJ: Van Nostrand Reinhold.

McClelland, D.C. and Boyatzis, R.E. (1982) 'Leadership motive pattern and long term success in management', *Journal of Applied Psychology*, 67(6): 737–43.

McClelland, D.C., Atkinson, J.W., Clark, R.A. and Lowell, E.L. (1976) *The Achievement Motive*. New York: Irvington, (2nd edn).

McDonald, B.A. (1981) 'Analytical or creative?: a problem-solving comparison', in J.E. Jones and Jeffrey W. Pfeffer (eds), *The 1981 Annual Handbook for Group Facilitators*. San Diego, CA: University Associates, pp.24–26.

McGahan, A.M. (2007) 'Academic research that matters to managers: on zebras, dogs, lemmings, hammers, and turnips', *Academy of Management Journal*, 50(4): 748–53.

McGee, L. (2006) 'Interview for engagement', *People Management*, 12(15): 40–41.

McGrath, J.E. (1984) *Groups: Interaction and Performance*. Upper Saddle River, NJ: Prentice Hall.

McGregor, D.M. (1960) *The Human Side of Enterprise*. New York: McGraw-Hill.

McKeown, M. (2008) 'Max headroom', *People Management*, 14(4): 28–32.

McKinlay, A. and Quinn, B. (1999) 'Management technology and work in commercial broadcasting', *New Technology, Work and Employment*, 14(1): 2–17.

McKinley, A. and Taylor, P. (2000) *Inside the Factory of the Future: Work, Power and Authority in Microelectronics*. London: Routledge.

McLeod, P.L., Baron, R.S., Marti, M.W. and Yoon, K. (1997) 'The eyes have it', *Journal of Applied Psychology*, 82(5): 706–18.

McLoughlin, I. (1999) *Creative Technological Change: The Shaping of Technology and Organizations*. London: Routledge.

McLoughlin, I. and Clark, J. (1994) *Technological Change at Work*. Buckingham: Open University Press, (2nd edn).

McLoughlin, I. and Harris, M. (eds) (1997) *Innovation, Organizational Change and Technology*, London: International Thomson.

McNabb, R. and Whitfield, K. (1999) 'The distribution of employee participation schemes at the workplace', *International Journal of Human Resource Management*, 10(1): 122–36.

McNeill, D. (2000) *The Face*. London: Penguin Books.

McRae, R.R. (1992) 'The five-factor model: issues and applications', *Journal of Personality and Social Psychology*, 60(2): special issue.

Mead, G.H. (1934) *Mind, Self and Society*. Chicago, IL: University of Chicago Press.

Medvec, V.H., Madey, S.F. and Gilovich, T. (1995) 'When less is more: counterfactual thinking and satisfaction among Olympic medallists', *Journal of Personality and Social Psychology*, 69(4): 603–10.

Meek, V.L. (1988) 'Organization culture: origins and weaknesses', *Organization Studies*, 9(4): 453–73.

Meier, K.J. and Bohte, J. (2000) 'Ode to Luther Gulick: span of control and organizational performance', *Administration and Society*, 32(2): 115–37.

Merkle, J. (1980) *Management and Ideology*. Berkeley, CA: University of California Press.

Merton, R.K. (1939/1940) 'Bureaucratic structure and personality', *Social Forces*, 18(1/4): 560–68.

Metcalfe, B.-A. and Metcalfe, J.-A. (2002) 'The great and the good', *People Management*, 8(11): 32–34.

Metcalfe, B.-A. and Metcalfe, J.-A. (2003) 'Under the influence', *People Management*, 9(5): 32–35.

Meyerson, D.E. (2001a) 'Radical change, the quiet way', *Harvard Business Review*, 79(9): 92–100.

Meyerson, D.E. (2001b) *Tempered Radicals: How People Use Difference to Inspire Change at Work*. Boston, MA: Harvard Business School Press.

Meyerson, D. and Martin, J. (1987) 'Culture change: an integration of three different views', *Journal of Management Studies*, 24(6): 623–47.

Mezias, J.M. and Starbuck, W.H. (2003) 'Studying the accuracy of managers' perceptions: a research odyssey', *British Journal of Management*, 14(1): 3–17.

Milanovich, D.M., Driskell, J.E., Stout, R.J. and Salas, E. (1998) 'Status and cockpit dynamics: a review and empirical study', *Group Dynamics: Theory, Research and Practice*, 2(3): 155–67.

Milgram, S. (1973 and 2005) *Obedience to Authority*. London: Tavistock Publications and Pinter & Martin.

Milkman, R. (1997) *Farewell to the Factory: Autoworkers in the Late Twentieth Century*. Berkeley, CA: University of California Press.

Milkman, R. (1998) 'The new American workplace: high road or low road?' in P. Thompson and C. Warhurst (eds), *Workplaces of the Future*. Basingstoke: Macmillan, pp.25–39.

Millard, R. (2006) 'Drawing back from extreme jobs', *The Sunday Times*, News Review, 3 December, p.9.

Miller, D. (1994) 'What happens after success: the perils of excellence', *Journal of Management Studies*, 31(3): 325–58.

Miller, E.J. and Rice, A.K. (1967) *Systems of Organization: The Control of Task and Sentient Boundaries*. London: Tavistock Publications.

Miller, R. and Stewart, J. (1999) 'Opened university', *People Management*, 5(12): 42–46.

Mills, C.W. (1951) *White Collar: The American Middle Classes*. New York: Oxford University Press.

Mintzberg, H. (1973) *The Nature of Managerial Work*. London: HarperCollins.

Mintzberg, H. (1977) 'The manager's job: folklore and fact', *Harvard Business Review*, 55(44): 49–61.

Mintzberg, H. (1979) *The Structure of Organizations*. Englewood Cliffs, NJ: Prentice Hall.

Mintzberg, H. (1983) *Power In and Around Organizations*. Englewood Cliffs, NJ: Prentice Hall.

Mintzberg, H.J. (1989) *Mintzberg on Management: Inside Our Strange World of Organizations*. New York: The Free Press.

Mitchell, C. (2009) *Doing Visual Research*. London: Sage Publications.

Mitchell, W. (1999) 'Alliances: achieving long term value and short term goals', *Financial Times, Mastering Strategy Supplement*, 18 October, pp.6–7.

Mohr, L.B. (1982) *Explaining Organizational Behaviour: The Limits and Possibilities of Theory and Research*. San Francisco, CA: Jossey-Bass.

Mohrman, S.A., Cohen, S.G. and Mohrman, A.M. (1995) *Designing Team-Based Organizations*. San Francisco, CA: Jossey-Bass.

Mone, M. (2009) 'Has it damaged me?: probably', *The Times*, Times 2, 15 January, pp.7–8.

Montoya, M.M., Massey, A.P., Hung, Y.C. and Crisp, C.B. (2009) 'Can you hear me now?: Communication in virtual product development teams', *Journal of Product Innovation Management*, 26(2): 139–55.

Morehead, A., Steele, M., Alexander, M., Stephen, K. and Dufflin, L. (1997) *Changes at Work: The 1995 Australian Workplace Industrial Relations Survey*. Melbourne: Longman.

Moorhead, G. and Montanari, J.R. (1986) 'An empirical investigation of the groupthink phenomenon', *Human Relations*, 39(5): 399–410.

Moorhead, G., Ference, R. and Neck, C.P. (1991) 'Group decision fiascos continue: Space Shuttle Challenger', *Human Relations*, 44(6): 539–50.

Moreland, R.L. and Levine, J.M. (1982) 'Socialization in small groups: temporal changes in individual-group relations', in L. Berkowicz (ed.), *Advances in Experimental and Social Psychology Volume 15*. New York: Academic Press, pp.137–92.

Morell, V. (2001) 'The pyramid builders', *National Geographic*, November, pp.78–99.

Moreno, J.L. (1953) *Who Shall Survive?* New York: Beacon Press, (2nd edn).

Morgan, G. (1989) *Creative Organization Theory*. London: Sage Publications.

Morgan, G. (2006) *Images of Organization*. London: Sage Publications, (3rd edn).

Morgan, G., Frost, J. and Pondy, L. (1983) 'Organization Symbolism', in L. Pondy, P. Frost, G. Morgan and T. Dandridge (eds), *Organization Symbolism*. Greenwich, CT: JAI Press, pp.55–65.

Morgan, N. (2001) 'How to overcome "change fatigue" ', *Harvard Management Update*: 1–3.

Morita, M. (2001) 'Have the seeds of Japanese teamworking taken root abroad?' *New Technology, Work and Employment*, 16(3): 178–90.

Morris, S. (1999) 'An Eastern art of healing that is heading West', *The Times*, 26 October, p.47.

Morse, G. (2006) 'High fidelity: Ivor Tiefenbrun on tapping talent', *Harvard Business Review*, 84(11): 28.

Moscovici, S. (1980) 'Towards a theory of conversion behaviour', in L. Berkowitz (ed.), *Advances in Experimental Social Psychology*, Vol.13. New York: Academic Press, pp.209–39.

Moscovici, S. (1984) 'The phenomenon of social representations', in R.M. Farr and S. Moscovici (eds), *Social Representations*. Cambridge: Cambridge University Press, pp.3–69.

Moutafi, J., Furnham, A. and Crump, J. (2007) 'Is managerial level related to personality?' *British Journal of Management*, 18(3): 272–80.

Mullen, B., Johnson, C. and Salas, E. (1991) 'Productivity loss in brainstorming groups, a meta-analytical integration', *Basic and Applied Social Psychology*, 12(1): 3–23.

Mullen, B., Anthony, T., Salas, E. and Driskell, J.E. (1994) 'Group cohesiveness and quality of decision-making: an integration of tests of the groupthink hypothesis', *Small Group Research*, 25(2): 189–204.

Murakami, T. (1997) 'The autonomy of teams in the car industry – a cross-national comparison', *Work, Employment and Society*, 11(4): 749–58.

Murray, S. (2007) 'In-house partners', *Financial Times*, Understanding the Culture of Collaboration supplement, 29 June, pp.13–14.

Myers, I.B. (1962) *The Myers-Briggs Type Indicator Manual*. Princeton, NJ: Educational Testing Service.

Myers, I.B. (1976) *Introduction to Type*. Gainesville, FL: Centre for Applications of Psychological Type, (2nd edn).

Myers, I.B. and McCaulley, M.H. (1985) *Manual: A Guide to the Development and Use of the Myers-Briggs Type Indicator*. Palo Alto, CA: Consulting Psychologists Press.

Nadler, D., Behan, M.A. and Nadler, B.A. (2006) *Building Better Boards*. San Francisco, CA: Jossey-Bass.

Naquin, C.E. and Tynan, R.O. (2003) 'The team halo effect: why teams are not blamed for their failures', *Journal of Applied Psychology*, 88(2): 332–40.

Narayanan, V.K. and Rath, R.N. (1993) *Organization Theory: A Strategic Approach*. Homewood IL: Richard D. Irwin.

Nardi, H. (2008) *The Greenwood Encyclopedia of Love, Courtship and Sexuality Through History*. Westport, CT: Greenwood Press, (6th edn).

National Transportation Safety Board (1994) *A Review of Flightcrew-Involved, Major Accidents of US Air Carriers, 1978 through 1990: Safety Study NTSB/SS-94/01*. Washington, DC: National Transportation Safety Board.

Nelson-Jones, R. (2000) *Introduction to Counselling Skills: Text and Actitivies*. London: Sage Publications.

Nemeth, C. (1986) 'Differential contributions of majority and minority influences', *Psychological Review*, 93(1): 23–32.

Nevis, E. (1983) 'Using an American perspective in understanding another culture: toward a hierarchy of needs for the People's Republic of China', *Journal of Applied Behavioral Science*, 19(3): 249–64.

Newing, R. (2007) 'The great enabler: trust', *Financial Times*, Understanding the Culture of Collaboration supplement, 29 June, pp.18–19.

Ng, K.Y. and Van Dyne, L. (2001) 'Individualism-collectivism as a boundary condition for effectiveness and minority influence in decision making', *Organization Behaviour and Human Decision Processes*, 84(2): 198–225.

Nicholson, N. (2003) 'How to motivate your problem people', *Harvard Business Review*, 81(1): 57–65.

Nohria, N., Groysberg, B. and Lee, L.-E. (2008) 'Employee motivation: a powerful new model', *Harvard Business Review*, 86(7/8): 78–84.

Nonaka, I. and Takeuchi, H. (1995) *The Knowledge Creating Company*. New York: Oxford University Press.

Nonaka, I., Umemoto, K. and Sasaki, K. (1999) 'Three tales of knowledge-creating companies', in Georg von Krogh, Johan Roos and Dirk Kleine (eds), *Knowing in Firms: Understanding, Managing and Measuring Knowledge*. London: Sage Publications, pp.146–72.

Noon, M. and Blyton, P. (2007) *The Realities of Work*. Basingstoke: Palgrave, (3rd edn).

Norstedt, J.P. and Aguren, S. (1973) *Saab-Scania Report*. Stockholm: Swedish Employers' Confedertion.

Novak, S. and Fine, C.H. (1996) *Culture Clash: The Corporate Socialization Process meets Non-Congruent Organization Subcultures*. Cambridge, MA: Sloan School of Management, Massachusetts Institute of Technology.

Nunamaker, J.F., Reinig, B.A. and Briggs, R.O. (2009) 'Principles for effective virtual teamwork', *Communications of the ACM*, 52(4): 113–17.

Oakley, A. (1972) *Sex, Gender and Society*. London: Temple Smith.

Oakley, J. (2000) 'Gender-based barriers to senior management promotions: understanding the scarcity of female CEOs', *Journal of Business Ethics*, 27(4): 323–34.

O'Connor, E. (1999) 'Minding the workers: the meaning of "human" and "human relations" of Elton Mayo', *Organization*, 6(2): 223–46.

Ogbonna, E. (1993) 'Managing organizational culture: fantasy or reality ?' *Human Resource Management Journal*, 3(2): 42–54.

Ogbonna, E. and Harris, L.C. (2002) 'Organizational culture: a ten year, two-phase study of change in the UK food retailing sector', *Journal of Management Studies*, 39(5): 673–706.

Ogburn, W.F. (1922) *Social Change: With Respect to Culture and Original Nature*. New York: B.W. Huebsch.

O'Hanlon, J. (2007) 'Innocent Drinks', *ExecDigital*, from http://www.execdigital.co.uk/Innocent-Drinks_3545.aspx, accessed 18 June 2009.

Ohmae, K. (2005) *The Next Global Stage: Challenges and Opportunities in our Borderless World*. Philadelphia, PA: Wharton School Publishing.

O'Leary-Kelly, A.M., Griffin, R.W. and Glew, D.J. (1996) 'Organization-motivated aggression: a research framework', *Academy of Management Review*, 21(1): 225–53.

Oliver, N., Delbridge, R., Jones, D. and Lowe, J. (1994) 'World class manufacturing: further evidence in the lean production debate', *British Journal of Management*, 15(2): 53–63.

Olsen, J.P. (2006) 'Maybe it's time to rediscover bureaucracy', *Journal of Public Administration Research and Theory*, 16(1): 1–24.

O'Reilly, C.A. (1989) 'Corporations, culture and commitment: motivation and social control in organizations', *California Management Review*, 31(4): 9–25.

Oswick, C. and Grant, D. (eds) (1996) *Organization Development: Metaphorical Explorations*, London: Pitman.

Ouchi, W. (1981) *Theory Z*. Reading, MA: Addison-Wesley.

Ouchi, W.G. and Johnson, A.M. (1978) 'Type Z organizations: stability in the midst of mobility', *Academy of Management Review*, 3(2): 305–14.

Overell, S. (2002) 'The workplace story', *Personnel Today*, 30 April, p.15.

Overell, S. (2005) 'Getting back to the coalface', *Personnel Today*, 15 March, p.11.

Oxman, A.D., Sackett, D.L., Chalmers, I. and Prescott, T.E. (2005) 'A surrealistic mega-analysis of redisorganization theories', *Journal of the Royal Society of Medicine*, 98(12): 563–68.

Palmer, I. and Hardy, C. (2000) *Thinking About Management: Implications of Organizational Debates for Practice*. London: Sage Publications.

Palmer, I., Dunford, R. and Akin, G. (2009) *Managing Organizational Change: A Multiple Perspectives Approach*. Boston, MA: McGraw Hill International, (2nd edn).

Pardi, T. (2007) 'Redefining the Toyota Production System: the European side of the story', *New Technology, Work and Employment*, 22(1): 2–20.

Parker, G.M. (1990) *Team Players and Teamwork: The New Competitive Business Strategy*. Oxford: Jossey-Bass.

Parker, M. (2000) *Organizational Culture and Identity: Unity and Division at Work*. London: Sage Publications.

Parker, M. and Slaughter, J. (1988a) *Choosing Sides: Unions and the Team Concept*. Boston, MA: South End Press.

Parker, M. and Slaughter, J. (1988b) 'Management by stress', *Technology Review*, 91(7): 36–44.

Parkinson, M. (1999) *Using Psychology in Business*. Aldershot: Gower.

Parry, R.L. (2003) 'Teeth clean? Nose hair cut? OK, now go get some votes', *The Times*, 31 October, p.23.

Parry, K.W. and Bryman, A. (2006) 'Leadership in organizations', in Stewart R. Clegg, Cynthia Hardy, Tom Lawrence and Walter R. Nord (eds), *The Sage Handbook of Organization Studies*. London: Sage Publications, (2nd edn).

Pascale, R.T. (1985) 'The paradox of organization culture: reconciling ourselves to socialization', *California Management Review*, 27(2): 26–41.

Pascale, R.T. and Athos, A.G. (1982) *The Art of Japanese Management*. Harmondsworth: Penguin Books.

Pascale, R., Millemann, M. and Gioja, L. (1997) 'Changing the way we change', *Harvard Business Review*, 75(3): 127–39.

Patten, S. (1999) 'Incentives prove key method of keeping staff', *The Times*, 12 October, p.38.

Patterson, M.G., West, M.A., Lawthom, R. and Nickell, S. (1997) *Impact of People Management Practices on Business Performance*. London: Institute of Personnel and Development.

Paulus, P.B. and van der Zee, K. (2004) 'Should there be romance between teams and groups?' *Journal of Occupational and Organizational Psychology*, 77(4): 474–80.

Paulus, P.B., Larey, T.S. and Dzindolet, M.T. (2001) 'Creativity in groups and teams', in M.E. Turner (ed.), *Groups at Work: Theory and Research*. Mahwah, NJ: Lawrence Erlbaum Associates.

Paulus, P.B., Dugosh, K.L., Dzindolet, M.T., Coskun, H. and Putman, V.L. (2002) 'Social and cognitive influences in group brainstorming: predicting production gains and losses', in, *European Review of Social Psychology: Volume 12*. Chichester: Wiley, pp.299–325.

Pearce, C.L., Gallagher, C.A. and Ensley, M.D. (2002) 'Confidence at the group level of analysis: a longitudinal investigation of the relationship between potency and team effectiveness', *Journal of Occupational and Organizational Psychology*, 75(1): 115–20.

Pease, A. (1985) *Body Language: How to Read Others' Thoughts by Their Gestures*. Avalon Beach, NSW Australia: Camel Publishing.

Pease, A. (1997) *Body Language: How to Read Others' Thoughts by Their Gestures*. London: Sheldon Press, (3rd edn).

Pedler, M., Burgoyne, J. and Boydell, T. (1997) *The Learning Company: A Strategy for Sustainable Development*. London: McGraw-Hill, (2nd edn).

Peek, L., Coates, S. and Philp, C. (2003) 'Unions accuse BT of exporting call centre work', *The Times*, 8 March, p.5.

Pennington, D.C. (2002) *The Social Psychology of Behaviour in Small Groups*. Hove, East Sussex: Psychology Press/Taylor & Francis.

Perrewé, P.L. and Nelson, D.L. (2004) 'Gender and career success: the facilitative role of political skill', *Organizational Dynamics*, 33(4): 366–78.

Perrow, C. (1970) *Organizational Analysis: A Sociological View*. Belmont, CA: Wadsworth.

Persaud, J. (2004) 'Higher return', *People Management*, 10(7): 40–41.

Personnel Today (2003) 'Burger chain cheesed off by McJob definition', 19 November, p.1.

Personnel Today (2000) 'Taxing message behind IR jargon', 18 April, p.68.

Personnel Today (2006) 'Will L'Oreal's Body Shop deal be worth it?' 28 March, p.4.

Personnel Today (2007) 'Virtually on strike', 2 October, p.3.

Personnel Today (2008) 'McDonald's HR team take credit for food chain success', 19 August, p.4.

Peters, T. (1987) *Thriving on Chaos: Handbook for a Management Revolution*. London: Macmillan.

Peters, T.J. and Waterman, R.H. (1982) *In Search of Excellence: Lessons from America's Best Run Companies*. New York: Harper & Row.

Pettigrew, A.M. (1973) *The Politics of Organizational Decision-Making*. London: Tavistock Publications.

Pettigrew, A.M. (1985) *The Awakening Giant: Continuity and Change in ICI*. Oxford: Basil Blackwell.

Pettigrew, A.M. (1987) 'Context and action in the transformation of the firm', *Journal of Management Studies*, 24(6): 649–70.

Pettigrew, A.M. (ed.) (1987) *The Management of Strategic Change*, Oxford: Basil Blackwell.

Pettigrew, A.M. (1998) 'Success and failure in corporate transformation initiatives', in R.D. Galliers and W.R.J. Baets (eds), *Information Technology and Organizational Transformation*. Chichester: Wiley, pp.271–89.

Pettigrew, A.M. (1999) 'Organizing to improve company performance', *Hot Topics (Warwick University Business School)*, 1(5).

Pettigrew, A.M. and McNulty, T. (1995) 'Power and influence in and around the boardroom', *Human Relations*, 48(8): 845–73.

Pettigrew, A.M. and Whittington, R. (2001) 'How to "join up" change', *People Management*, 7(20): 52–54.

Pfeffer, J. (1981) *Power in Organizations*. London: HarperCollins.

Pfeffer, J. (1992a) 'Understanding power in organizations', *California Management Review*, 34(2): 29–50.

Pfeffer, J. (1992b) *Managing With Power: Politics and Influence in Organizations*. Boston, MA: Harvard Business School Press, (2nd edn).

Pfeffer, J. (1996) *Competitive Advantage Through People: Unleashing the Power of the Work Force*. Boston, MA: Harvard Business School Press.

Pfeffer, J. (1998) *The Human Equation: Building Profits by Putting People First*. Boston, MA: Harvard Business School Press.

Pfeffer, J. and Salancik, G.R. (1978) *The External Control of Organizations: A Resource Dependence Perspective*. New York: Harper & Row.

Pfeffer, J. and Sutton, R.I. (2006) *Hard Facts, Dangerous Half-Truths, and Total Nonsense: Profiting from Evidence-Based Management*. Boston, MA: Harvard Business School Press.

Phillips, N. (1995) 'Telling organizational tales: on the role of narrative fiction in the study of organization', *Organization Studies*, 16(4): 625–49.

Philp, C. (2008) 'New-look Hillary puts the bad hair days behind her', *The Times*, 8 February, p.37.

Pickard, J. (2007) 'Tried and tested', *People Management*, 13(22): 32–35.

Pinder, C.C. (2008) *Work Motivation in Organizational Behaviour*. Hove, East Sussex: Psychology Press/Taylor & Francis, (2nd edn).

Pinker, S. (1997) *How the Mind Works*. London: Penguin Books.

Pinker, S. (2002) *The Blank Slate: The Modern Denial of Human Nature*. London: Allen Lane The Penguin Press.

Pinker, S. (2008) *The Sexual Paradox: Troubled Boys, Gifted Girls, and the Real Difference Between the Sexes*. London: Atlantic Books.

Pisano, G. and Verganti, R. (2008) 'Which kind of collaboration is right for you?', *Harvard Business Review*, 86(12): 78–86.

Porter, M. and Ketels, C.H.M. (2003) *UK Competitiveness: Moving to the Next Stage: Economics Paper 3*. London: Department of Trade and Industry.

Power, S.J. and Lundsten, L.L. (2005) 'Managerial and other white-collar employees' perceptions of ethical issues in their workplace', *Journal of Business Ethics*, 60(2): 185–93.

Preece, D., Steven, G. and Steven, V. (1999) *Work, Change and Competition: Managing for Bass*. London: Routledge.

Prescott, B.D. (1980) *Effective Decision Making: A Self-Development Programme*. Aldershot: Gower Publishing.

Pringle, R. (1989) *Secretaries Talk: Sexuality, Power and Work*. London: Verso.

Procter, S. and Currie, G. (2004) 'Target-based teamworking: groups, work and interdependence in the UK civil service', *Human Relations*, 57(2): 1547–72.

Proctor, S. and Burridge, M. (2008) 'Teamworking and performance: the extent and intensity of teamworking in the 1998 UK Workplace Employee Relations Survey (WERS98)', *The International Journal of Human Resource Management*, 19(1): 153–68.

Prosser, J. (ed.) (1998) *Image-Based Research: A Sourcebook for Qualitative Researchers*, London: Falmer Press, Taylor & Francis.

Pruitt, S. and Barrett, T. (1991) 'Corporate virtual workspace', in M. Benedid (ed.), *Cyberspace: First Steps*. Boston, MA: MIT Press, pp.383–409.

Psoinos, A. and Smithson, S. (2002) 'Employee empowerment in manufacturing: a study of organizations in the UK', *New Technology, Work and Employment*, 17(2): 132–48.

Pugh, D.S. (ed.) (1971) *Organization Theory: Selected Readings*, Harmondsworth: Penguin Books.

Pugh, D.S. and Hickson, D.J. (1976) *Organization Structure in its Context: The Aston Programme 1*. Farnborough: Gower.

Purcell, J., Kinnie, N., Hutchinson, S. and Rayton, B. (2000) 'Inside the box', *People Management*, 6(21): 30–38.

Purcell, J., Kinnie, N., Hutchinson, S., Rayton, B. and Stuart, J. (2003) *Understanding the People and Performance Link: Unlocking the Black Box*. London: Chartered Institute of Personnel and Development.

Quah, D.T. (1997) 'Weightless economy packs a heavy punch', *Independent on Sunday*, 18 May, p.4.

Rafaeli, A. (1989) 'When cashiers meet customers: an analysis of supermarket cashiers', *Academy of Management Journal*, 32(2): 245–73.

Rafaeli, A. and Sutton, R.I. (1987) 'The expression of emotion in organizational life', in L.L. Cummings and B.M. Staw (eds), *Research in Organizational Behaviour Volume 11*. Greenwich, CT: JAI Press, pp.1–42.

Rajan, A., Lank, E. and Chapple, K. (1999) *Good Practices in Knowledge Creation and Exchange*. London: Focus/London Training and Enterprise Council.

Rakos, R.F. and Grodek, M.V. (1984), 'An empirical evaluation of a behavioural self-management course in a college setting', *Teaching of Psychology*, October, pp.157–62.

Ray, C.A. (1986) 'Corporate culture; the last frontier of control?' *Journal of Management Studies*, 23(3): 287–97.

Reade, Q. (2003) 'Graduates put enjoyment at top of ideal job wish list', *Personnel Today*, 7 January, p.8.

Redman, T. and Wilkinson, A. (2001) *Contemporary Human Resource Management: Text and Cases*. Harlow: Financial Times Prentice Hall.

Rees, D. (2004) *Women in the Boardroom: A Bird's Eye View*. London: Chartered Institute of Personnel and Development.

Reeves, B., Malone, T.W. and O'Driscoll, T. (2008) 'Leadership's online labs', *Harvard Business Review*, 86(5): 58–66.

Reich, R. (1993) *The Work of Nations*. London: Simon & Schuster.

Renard, M.K. (2008) 'It's all about money: Chris and Pat compare salaries', *Journal of Management Education*, 32(2): 248–61.

Riach, K. and Wilson, F. (2007) 'Don't screw the crew: exploring the rules of engagement in organizational romance', *British Journal of Management*, 18(1): 79–92.

Rice, A.K. (1958) *Productivity and Social Organization*. London: Tavistock Publications.

Rice, A.K. (1963) *The Enterprise and its Environment*. London: Tavistock Publications.

Richards, J. (2008) 'Because I need somewhere to vent: the expression of conflict through work blogs', *New Technology and Employment*, 23(1–2): 95–110.

Riley, P. (1983) 'A structuralist account of political cultures', *Administrative Science Quarterly*, 28(3): 414–37.

Ritzer, G. (1995) *Expressing America: A Critique of the Global Credit Card Society*. Thousand Oaks, CA: Pine Forge Press.

Ritzer, G. (ed.) (1998) *The McDonaldization Thesis*, London: Sage Publications.

Ritzer, G. (2004) *The McDonaldization of Society: An Investigation into the Changing Character of Contemporary Social Life*. Thousand Oaks, CA: Pine Forge Press.

Ritzer, G. (ed.) (2006) *McDonaldization: The Reader*, Thousand Oaks, CA: Pine Forge Press, (2nd edn).

Ritzer, G. (2007) *The McDonaldization of Society: An Investigation into the Changing Character of Contemporary Social Life*. Thousand Oaks, CA: Pine Forge Press, (5th revised edn).

Rivard, S., Bennoit, A.A., Patry, M., Pare, G. and Smith, H.A. (2004) *Information Technology and Organizational Transformation*. Oxford: Elsevier/Butterworth-Heinemann.

Robbins, S.P. (1974) *Managing Organizational Conflict: A Non-traditional Approach*. Englewood Cliffs, NJ: Prentice Hall.

Robbins, S.P. (1990) *Organization Theory*. Englewood Cliffs, NJ: Prentice Hall.

Robbins, S.P. (1998) *Organizational Behaviour: Concepts, Controversies and Applications*. Upper Saddle River, NJ: Pearson Educational Inc, (8th edn).

Robbins, S.P. and Judge, T.A. (2008) *Organizational Behaviour*. Upper Saddle River, NJ: Pearson Education, (12th edn).

Roberts, J. (2004) *The Modern Firm: Organizational Design for Performance and Growth*. Oxford: Oxford University Press.

Roberts, D. (2009) 'Innocent shows who is really worldly wise', from www.guardian.co.uk/business/2009/apr/07/innocent-smoothies, accessed May 2009.

Robertson, I.T. (1994) 'Personality and personnel selection', in Cary L. Cooper and D.M. Rousseau (eds), *Trends in Organizational Behaviour*. London: John Wiley.

Robertson, I. (2001) 'Undue diligence', *People Management*, 7(23): 42–43.

Robinson, S.L. and O'Leary-Kelly, A.M. (1998) 'Monkey see, monkey do: the influence of work groups on the antisocial behaviour of employees', *Academy of Management Journal*, 41(6): 658–72.

Roethlisberger, F.J. (1977) *The Elusive Phenomenon: An Autobiographical Account of My Work in the Field of Organizational Behaviour at the Harvard Business School*. Boston, MA: Harvard University Press.

Roethlisberger, F.J. and Dickson, W.J. (1939) *Management and the Worker*. Cambridge, MA: Harvard University Press.

Rogelberg, S.G., Barnes-Farrell, J.L. and Lowe, C.A. (1992) 'The stepladder technique: an alternative group structure facilitating effective group decision making', *Journal of Applied Psychology*, 77(5): 337–58.

Rogers, C.R. (1947) 'Some observations on the organization of personality', *American Psychologist*, 2(9): 358–68.

Rogers, E. (1995) *The Diffusion of Innovation*. New York: The Free Press, (4th edn).

Rogers, C.R. and Roethlisberger, F.J. (1952) 'Barriers and gateways to communication', *Harvard Business Review*, 30(4): 46–52.

Rollinson, D. (2008) *Organizational Behaviour and Analysis: An Integrated Approach*. Harlow: Financial Times Prentice Hall, (4th edn).

Rose, M. (1988) *Industrial Behaviour and Control*. Harmondsworth: Penguin Books.

Rose, N. (1989) *Governing the Soul*. London: Routledge.

Rose, N. (1990) *Governing the Soul: The Shaping of the Private Self*. London: Routledge.

Rosenfeld, P., Giacalone, R.A. and Riordan, C.A. (2001) *Impression Management: Building and Enhancing Reputations at Work*. London: Thomson Learning.

Rosenzweig, P. (2007) *The Halo Effect: And the Eight Other Business Delusions That Deceive Managers*. Glencoe, IL: The Free Press.

Ross, L. (1977) 'The intuitive psychologist and his shortcomings: distortions in the attribution process', in L. Berkowitz (ed.), *Advances in Experimental Social Psychology*. New York: Academic Press, pp.173–220.

Ross, A. (2004) *No Collar: The Humane Workplace and its Hidden Cost*. Philadelphia, PA: Temple University Press.

Ross, J. and Staw, B.M. (1993) 'Organizational escalation and exit: lessons from the Shoreham nuclear power plant', *Academy of Management Journal*, 36(4): 701–32.

Rosser, M.H. (2007) 'The magic of leadership: an exploration of *Harry Potter and the Goblet of Fire*', *Advances in Developing Human Resources*, 9(2): 236–50.

Rost, J.C. (1991) *Leadership for the Twenty-First Century*. Westport, CT: Praeger/Greenwood Publishing.

Rothlin, P. and Werder, P.R. (2008) *Boreout!: Overcoming Workplace Demotivation*. London: Kogan Page.

Rothwell, J.D. (1992) *In Mixed Company: Small Group Communication*. Fort Worth, Texas: Harcourt, Brace Jovanovich.

Rotter, J.B. (1966) 'Generalized expectations for internal versus external control of reinforcement', *Psychological Monographs*, 80(609; whole issue): 1–28.

Rotundo, M. and Xie, J.L. (2008) 'Understanding the domain of counterproductive work behaviour in China', *International Journal of Human Resource Management*, 19(5): 856–77.

Rousseau, D.M. (1999) 'Why workers still identify with organizations', *Journal of Organizational Behaviour*, 19(3): 217–33.

Rousseau, D.M. (2006) 'Is there such a thing as "evidence-based management"?' *Academy of Management Review*, 31(2): 256–69.

Roy, D.F. (1960) 'Banana time: job satisfaction and informal interaction', *Human Organization*, 18(4): 158–68.

Rubery, J., Cooke, F.L., Earnshaw, J. and Marchington, M. (2003) 'Inter-organizational relations and employment in a multi-employer environment', *British Journal of Industrial Relations*, 41(2): 265–89.

Ruble, T.T. and Thomas, K. (1976) 'Support for a two-dimensional model of conflict behaviour', *Organizational Behaviour and Human Performance*, 16(1): 143–55.

Ruigrok, W., Pettigrew, A.M., Peck, S. and Whittington, R. (1999) 'Corporate restructuring and new forms of organizing in Europe', *Management International Review*, 39(2): 41–64.

Rushe, D. (2006) 'Alpha males can make and break a business', *The Sunday Times*, Business Section, 3 September, p.11.

Ryan, R.M. and Connell, J.P. (1989) 'Perceived locus of causality and internalization', *Journal of Personality and Social Psychology*, 57(5): 749–61.

Ryan, M.K. and Haslam, S.A. (2005) 'The glass cliff: evidence that women are over-represented in precarious leadership positions', *British Journal of Management*, 16(2): 81–90.

Ryan, M.K. and Haslam, S.A. (2007) 'The glass cliff: exploring the dynamics surrounding the appointment of women to precarious leadership positions', *Academy of Management Review*, 32(2): 549–72.

Sabel, C. (1991) 'Moebius-strip organizations and open labour markets: some consequences of the reintegration of conception and execution in a volatile economy', in P. Bourdeu and C. Sabel (eds), *Social Theory for a Changing Society*. London: Sage Publications, pp.23–61.

Sagie, A., Stahevsky, S. and Koslowsky, M. (2004) *Misbehaviour and Dysfunctional Attitudes in Organizations*. Basingstoke: Palgrave.

Salancik, G.R. and Pfeffer, J. (1974) 'The bases and use of power in organizational decision-making', *Administrative Science Quarterly*, 19(4): 453–73.

Salancik, G.R. and Pfeffer, J. (1977) 'Who gets power – and how they hold on to it: a strategic contingency model of power', *Organizational Dynamics*, 5(3): 2–21.

Salovey, P. and Mayer, J.D. (1990) 'Emotional intelligence', *Imagination, Cognition and Personality*, 9: 185–211.

Samaras, J.T. (1989) *Management Applications: Exercises, Cases and Readings*. Englewood Cliffs, NJ: Prentice Hall.

Samuel, H. (2006) 'Bureaucrats look to Kafka', *The Daily Telegraph*, 15 April, p.17.

Sashkin, M. and Morris, W.C. (1987) 'Decision Types', *Experiencing Management*. Reading, MA: Addison Wesley Longman, pp. 73–74.

Saucer, P.J. (2003) 'Open-door management', *INC Magazine*, June: 44.

Savage, G.T., Blair, J.D. and Soreson, R.L. (1989) 'Consider both relationships and substance when negotiating strategy', *Academy of Management Executive*, 3(1): 37–48.

Scahill, J. (2007) *Blackwater: The Rise of the World's Most Powerful Mercenary Army*. New York: Nation Books.

Scarbrough, H. (1999) 'System error', *People Management*, 8 April, pp.68–74.

Scarbrough, H. and Swan, J. (1999) *Case Studies in Knowledge Management*. London: Institute of Personnel and Development.

Schein, E.H. (1983) 'The role of the founder in creating organization culture', *Organization Dynamics*, 12(1): 13–28.

Schein, E.H. (1984) 'Coming to a new awareness of organizational culture', *Sloan Management Review*, 25(2): 3–16.

Schein, E.H. (2004) *Organizational Culture and Leadership*. San Francisco, CA: Jossey-Bass, (3rd edn).

Schilling, M.A. and Steensma, H.K. (2001) 'The use of modular organizational forms: An industry level analysis', *Academy of Management Journal*, 44(6): 1149–69.

Schilt, W.K. (1986) 'An examination of individual differences as moderators of upward influence activity in strategic decisions', *Human Relations*, 39(10): 933–53.

Schmitt, N. and Chan, D. (1998) *Personnel Selection: A Theoretical Approach*. Thousand Oaks, CA: Sage Publications.

Scholz, C. (1987) 'Organization culture and strategy – the problem of strategy fit', *Long Range Planning*, 20(4): 78–87.

Schön, D.A. (1983) *The Reflective Practitioner*. New York: Basic Books.

Schuler, R. and Jackson, S. (2001) 'HR issues and activities in mergers and acquisitions', *European Journal of Management*, 19(3): 239–53.

Schuler, R. and Jackson, S. (2001) 'Seeking an edge in mergers', *Financial Times, Mastering People Management*, 22 October, pp.6, 8 and 10.

Schultz, M. (1995) *Studying Organizational Cultures: Diagnosis and Understanding*. Berlin: De Gruyter.

Sellers, P. (2003) 'Power: do women really want it?', *Fortune*, 13 October, pp.58–65.

Semler, R. (1993) *Maverick*. London: Century.

Senge, P. (1990) *The 5th Discipline: The Art and Practice of the Learning Organization*. New York: Doubleday Currency.

Senge, P., Kleiner, A., Roberts, C., Ross, R., Roth, G., and Smith, B. (1991) *The Dance of Change: The Challenges of Sustaining Momentum in Learning Organizations*. London: Nicholas Brealey.

Sewell, G. (1998) 'The discipline of teams: the control of team-based inductrial work through electronic and peer surveillance', *Administrative Science Quarterly*, 43(1): 397–429.

Sewell, G. and Wilkinson, B. (1992) 'Someone to watch over me: surveillance, discipline and just-in-time labour processes', *Sociology*, 26(2): 271–91.

Shankland, S. (2006) 'IBM to give birth to "2nd Life" business group', CNET News, from http://news.cnet.com/2100-1014_3-6143175.html, accessed 12 December.

Shannon, C.E. and Weaver, W. (1949) *The Mathematical Theory of Communication*. Urbana, IL: University of Illinois Press.

Shapiro, B.P. (1977) 'Can marketing and manufacturing coexist?', *Harvard Business Review*, 55(5): 104–14.

Shapiro, D.L., Furst, S.A., Speitzer, G.M. and Von Glinow, M.A. (2002) 'Transnational teams in the electronic age: are teams identity and high performance at risk', *Journal of Organizational Behaviour*, 23(4): 455–67.

Sharpe, E.K. (2005) 'Going above and beyond: the emotional labour of adventure guides', *Journal of Leisure Research*, 37(1): 29–50.

Shaw, M.E. (1976) *Group Dynamics*. New York: McGraw-Hill, (2nd edn).

Shaw, M.E. (1978) 'Communication networks fourteen years later', in L. Berkowitz (ed.), *Group Processes*. New York: Academic Press, pp.351–61.

Sheldon, W. (1942) *The Varieties of Temperament: A Psychology of Constitutional Differences*. New York: Harper & Row.

Sherif, M. (1936) *The Psychology of Social Norms*. New York: Harper & Row.

Shin, Y. (2005) 'Conflict resolution in virtual teams', *Organizational Dynamics*, 34(4): 331–45.

Siegele, L. (2008) 'Let it rise: a special report on corporate IT', *The Economist*, 25 October, pp.1–20.

Simon, H. (1957) *Administrative Behaviour*. New York: Macmillan, (2nd edn).

Simon, H. (1960) *The New Science of Management Decision*. New York: Harper & Row.

Simon, H.A. (1979) 'Rational decision making in business organizations', *American Economic Review*, 69(4): 493–513.

Simon, H. (1986) 'Rationality in psychology and economics', *Journal of Business*, 59(4): 209–24.

Sims, H.P. and Lorenzi, P. (1992) *The New Leadership Paradigm*. Newbury Park, CA: Sage Publications.

Sinclair, A. (1992) 'The tyranny of team ideology', *Organization Studies*, 13(4): 611–26.

Singh, V. and Vinnicombe, S. (2005), *The Female FTSE Report 2005*, Cranfield: Cranfield University School of Management.

Singh, V. and Vinnicombe, S. (2008) *The Female FTSE Report 2008*. Cranfield: Cranfield University School of Management.

Singh, V., Kumra, S. and Vinnicombe, S. (2002) 'Gender and impression management: playing the promotion game', *Journal of Business Ethics*, 37(1): 77–89.

Sirkin, H.L., Hemerling, J.W. and Bhattacharya, A.K. (2008) *Globality: Competing with Everyone from Everywhere for Everything*. New York and Boston: Business Plus.

Sitkin, S.B. and Pablo, A.L. (1992) 'Reconceptualizing the determinants of risk behaviour', *Academy of Management Review*, 17(1): 9–38.

Slocum, J.W. and Hellriegel, D. (2009) *Principles of Organizational Behaviour*. London: South-Western Cengage Learning, (12th edn).

Sloman, M. (2002) 'Ground force', *People Management*, 8(13): 42–46.

Slovic, P. and Lichtenstein, S. (1971) 'Comparison of Bayesian and regression approaches in the study of information processing and judgement', *Organizational Behaviour and Human Decision Processes*, 6(6): 649–744.

Smircich, L. (1983) 'Concepts of culture and organization analysis', *Administrative Science Quarterly*, 28(3): 339–58.

Smircich, L. and Morgan, G. (1982) 'Leadership: the management of meaning', *Journal of Applied Behavioural Science*, 18(2): 257–73.

Smircich, L. and Stubbart, C. (1985) 'Strategic management in an enacted world', *Academy of Management Review*, 10(4): 724–35.

Smith, W.P. (1987) 'Conflict and negotiation: trends and emerging issues', *Journal of Applied Social Psychology*, 17(7): 631–77.

Snowden, D.J. and Boone, M.E. (2007) 'A leader's framework for decision making', *Harvard Business Review*, 85(11): 69–76.

Snyder, M. (1987) *Public Appearance and Private Realities: The Psychology of Self-Monitoring*. New York: W.H. Freeman.

Sonnenfeld, J. (1985) 'Shedding light on the Hawthorne Studies', *Journal of Occupational Behaviour*, 6(2): 111–30.

Sonsino, S. (2007) 'It's the fault that counts', *People Management*, 13(1): 37–38.

Sørensen, C. (2004) *The Future Role of Trust in Work: The Key Success Factor for Mobile Technology*. Reading: Microsoft Corporation.

Sorge, A. and Warner, M. (eds) (1997) *The Handbook of Organizational Behaviour*. London: International Thomson Business Press.

Spear, S. and Bowen, H.K. (1999) 'Decoding the DNA of the Toyota production system', *Harvard Business Review*, 77(5): 97–106.

Spencer, J. and Pruss, A. (1992) *Managing Your Team*. London: Piatkus.

Spinney, L. (2000) 'Blind to change', *New Scientist*, 18 November, pp.27–32.

Stace, D. and Dunphy, D. (2001) *Beyond the Boundaries: Leading and Re-creating the Successful Enterprise*. Sydney: McGraw-Hill.

Stanton, N.A., Ashleigh, M.J., Roberts, A.D. and Xu, F. (2001) 'Testing Hollnagel's contextual control model: assessing team behaviour in a human supervisory control task', *International Journal of Cognitive Ergonomics*, 5(2): 111–23.

Staw, B.M. (1976) 'Knee deep in the big muddy: a study of escalating commitment to a chosen course of action', *Organizational Behaviour and Human Performance*, 16(1): 27–44.

Staw, B.M. (1981) 'The escalation of commitment to a course of action', *Academy of Management Review*, 6(4): 569–78.

Steers, R.M., Mowday, R.T. and Shapiro, D.L. (2004) 'The future of work motivation theory', *Academy of Management Review*, 29(3): 379–87.

Steijn, B. (2001) 'Work systems, quality of working life and attitudes of workers: an empirical study towards the effects of team and non-teamwork', *New Technology, Work and Employment*, 16(3): 191–203.

Steiner, I. (1972) *Group Process and Productivity*. New York: Academic Press.

Steiner, I. and Rajaratnam, N.A. (1961) 'A model for the comparison of individual and group performance scores', *Behavioural Science*, 6(2): 142–47.

Steiner, R. (1999) 'Pinstripes put Roddick on the right scent', *The Sunday Times*, 24 October, p.3.15.

Stern, S. and Wiggins, J. (2007) 'New definition would be just the job for McDonald's', *Financial Times*, 20 March, p.1.

Sternberg, R.J. (1988) *The Triarchic Mind: A New Theory of Human Intelligence*. New York: Viking.

Sternberg, R.J. (1999) 'Survival of the fit test', *People Management*, 4(24): 29–31.

Sternberg, R.J. and Soriano, L.J. (1984) 'Styles of conflict resolution', *Journal of Personality and Social Psychology*, 47(1): 115–26.

Stogdill, R.M. (1948) 'Personal factors associated with leadership', *Journal of Psychology*, 25: 35–71.

Stogdill, R.M. (1950) 'Leadership, membership and organization', *Psychological Bulletin*, 47(1): 1–14.

Stogdill, R.M. (1974) *Handbook of Leadership: A Survey of Theory and Research*. New York: The Free Press.

Stogdill, R.M. and Coons, A.E. (eds) (1951) *Leader Behaviour: Its Description and Measurement, Research Monograph No.88*, Columbus, OH: Ohio State University Bureau of Business Research.

Stoner, J.A.F. (1961) 'Unpublished Master's degree thesis: A comparison of individual and group decisions involving risk'. Massachusetts Institute of Technology, Boston, MA.

Stopford, J.M. and Wells, L.T. (1972) *Managing the Multinational Enterprise: Organization of the Firm and Ownership of Subsidiaries*. London: Longman.

Story, J. (2001) 'When internal boundaries become network relationships', *Financial Times, Mastering People Supplement*, 12 November, pp.6 and 8.

Stredwick, J. and Ellis, S. (1998) *Flexible Working Practices: Techniques and Innovations*. London: Institute of Personnel and Development.

Stuster, J. (1996) *Bold Endeavours: Lessons from Polar and Space Exploration*. Annapolis, MD: Naval Institute Press.

Suchman, L. (1996) 'Supporting articulation work', in R. Kling (ed.), *Computerization and Controversy*. San Diego, CA: Academic Press, pp.407–23.

Sundstrom, E. and Altman, I. (1989) 'Physical environments and work group effectiveness', in L.L. Cummings and B. Staw (eds), *Research in Organizational Behaviour: Volume 11*. Greenwich, CT: JAI Press, pp.175–209.

Sundstrom, E., de Meuse, K.P. and Futrell, D. (1990) 'Work teams: applications and effectiveness', *American Psychologist*, 45(2): 120–33.

Sweeney, P.D., McFarlin, D.B. and Inderrieden, E.J. (1990) 'Using relative deprivation theory to explain satisfaction with income and pay level: a multistudy examination', *Academy of Management Journal*, 33(2): 423–36.

Sweney, M. (2009a) 'Virgin ad prompts complaints of sexism', from http://www.guardian.co.uk/media/2009/feb/09/virgin-atlantic-ad-sexistofeom, accessed 21 April 2009.

Sweney, M. (2009b) 'Virgin ad not sexist, rules ASA', from http://www.guardian.co.uk/media/2009/feb/09/virgin-atlantic-ad-notsexist-rules-asa, accessed 21 April 2009.

Syedain, H. (2007) 'Topped with satisfaction', *People Management*, 13(14): 30–33.

Syedain, H. (2008a) 'Out of this world', *People Management*, 14(8): 20–24.

Syedain, H. (2008b) 'Keyboard directors', *People Management*, 14(12): 34–36.

Taffinder, P. (1998) 'Conflict is not always a bad thing', *Personnel Today*, 10 September, p.19.

Taggert, W.M. and Silbey, V. (1986) *Informational Systems: People and Computers in Organizations*. Boston, MA: Allyn & Bacon.

Taher, A. (2009) 'Number's up for "unlucky" eight', *The Sunday Times*, 11 January, p.7.

Tajfel, H. and Turner, J.C. (1986) 'The social identity theory of inter-group behaviour', in S. Worchel and W.G. Austin (eds), *Psychology of Inter-group Relations*. Chicago, IL: Nelson-Hall, (2nd edn.), pp.7–24.

Takeuchi, H., Osono, E. and Shimuzu, N. (2008) 'The contradictions that drive Toyota's success', *Harvard Business Review*, 86(6): 96–104.

Tannen, D. (1990) *You Just Don't Understand: Women and Men in Conversation*. New York: William Morrow.

Tannen, D. (1995) 'The power of talk: who gets heard and why', *Harvard Business Review*, 73(5): 138–48.

Tannenbaum, R. and Schmidt, W.H. (1958) 'How to choose a leadership pattern', *Harvard Business Review*, 36(2): 95–102 (reprinted in May–June 1973).

Tarnow, E. (2000) 'Self-destructive obedience in the airplane cockpit and the concept of obedience optimization', in T. Blass (ed.), *Obedience to Authority: Current Perspectives on the Milgram Paradigm*. Mahwah, NJ: Erlbaum, pp.111–24.

Taylor, A. (2004) 'GM gets its act together finally', *Fortune*, 5 April, pp.136–46.

Taylor, D.W., Berry, P.C. and Block, C.H. (1958) 'Does group participation when using brainstorming techniques facilitate or inhibit creative thinking?' *Administrative Science Quarterly*, 3(1): 23–47.

Taylor, F.W. (1911) *Principles of Scientific Management*. New York: Harper.

Taylor, P. and Bain, P. (1999) 'An assembly line in the head: work and employee relations in a call centre', *Industrial Relations Journal*, 30(2): 101–17.

Taylor, P. and Parker, A. (2008) 'Android is set to take on smartphone market', *Financial Times*, 23 September, p.30.

Taylor, S. (1998) 'Emotional labour and the new workplace', in P. Thompson and C. Warhurst (eds), *Workplaces of the Future*. Basingstoke: Macmillan, pp.84–103.

Taylor, S. and Tyler, M. (2000) 'Emotional labour and sexual difference in the airline industry', *Work, Employment and Society*, 14(1): 77–95.

Tehrani, N. and Ayling, L. (2008) *Stress at Work*. London: Chartered Institute of Personnel and Development.

Thatcher, M. (1996) 'Allowing everyone to have their say', *People Management*, 21 March, pp.28–30.

The Daily Telegraph (2004) 'Cost of fat air passengers takes off', 6 November, p.10.

The Daily Telegraph (2006) 'Google: cyber saints or sinners?' 4 February, p.32.

The Economist (1994) 'The celling out of America', 17 December, pp.71–72.

The Economist (1999a) 'The Exxon Valdez: stains that remain', 20 March, p.63.

The Economist (1999b) 'All over in a flash', 9 October, p.142.

The Economist (1999c) 'Rethinking thinking', 18 December, pp.77–79.

The Economist (2000) 'The land of disappointments', 4 March, pp.115–17.

The Economist (2001a) 'A long march; special report on mass customization', 14 July, p.81.

The Economist (2001b) 'Of high priests and pragmatists', 23 June, p.16.

The Economist (2002a) 'No small matter', 2 March, pp.68–69.

The Economist (2002b) 'Washington's mega-merger', 23 November, pp.51–53.

The Economist (2002c) 'Incredible shrinking plants', 23 February, pp.99–101.

The Economist (2004a) 'Be prepared', *Supplement: Living Dangerously: A Survey of Risk*, 24 January, p.20.

The Economist (2004b) 'I understand, up to a point', 4 September, p.44.

The Economist (2005a) 'Boeing gets back on track', 4 June, pp.71–72.

The Economist (2005b) 'Imagining something much worse than London', 16 July, pp.40–41.

The Economist (2006a) 'Light up', 11 February, p.72.

The Economist (2006b) 'A survey of France: insiders and outsiders', 28 October, pp.5–6.

The Economist (2006c) 'Take a deep breath: A survey of the company', 21 January, pp.5, 6 and 8.

The Economist (2006d) 'In tandem', 1 April, pp.69–71.

The Economist (2006e) 'Headless', 5 October, p.76.

The Economist (2006f) 'Allergic reactions', 1 April, p.58.

The Economist (2006g) 'The airliner that fell to earth', 7 October, pp.81–82.

The Economist (2006h) 'Open, but not as usual', 18 March, pp.73–75.

The Economist (2007a) 'Inside the Googleplex', 1 September, pp.52–54.

The Economist (2007b) 'Cosmic mood swings', 30 June, pp.93–94.

The Economist (2007c) 'Far away yet strangely personal', 25 August, pp.63–64.

The Economist (2007d) 'External affairs', 28 July, pp.69–70.

The Economist (2007e) 'Opposite headings', 8 December, pp.76–77.

The Economist (2007f) 'Barrelling along', 29 September, pp.80–81.

The Economist (2007g) 'Odd couple', 5 May, pp.71–72.

The Economist (2007h) 'Knocking heads together', 3 February, p.64.

The Economist (2008a) 'Debating the debates', Lexington, 11 October, p.62.

The Economist (2008b) 'The last word', 18 October, p.62.

The Economist (2008c) 'Technology Quarterly: Software that makes software better', 6 March, pp.22–24.

The Economist (2008d) 'If looks could kill', 25 October, pp.97–98.

The Economist (2008e) 'The good, the bad and the inevitable – the electronic bureaucrat: a special report on technology and government', 16 February, pp.6–9.

The Economist (2008f) 'Operating profit', 16 August, pp.74–76.

The Economist (2008g) 'Striking differences', 13 September, pp.80–82.

The Economist (2008h) 'So much for scare stories', 7 June, p.43.

The Economist (2008i) 'The un-iPhone', 27 September, p.84.

The Economist (2008j) 'Following the crowd', 6 September, pp.8–10.

The Economist (2008k) 'Unanswered questions', 20 March, p.74.

The Economist (2008l) 'Polyclinics in the NHS: the latest new thing', 1 March, pp.36–37.

The Economist (2008m) 'Unnecessary treatment', 24 May, p.48.

The Economist (2008n) 'Losing face', 8 November, p.82.

The Economist (2008o) 'On strike, virtually', 15 March, p.91.

The Times 100 website (2007) 'In the news, McJobs – an outdated definition', 4 June.

The Times Magazine (1999) 'Someone is watching you – and it could be your boss', 6 November, pp.26–30.

Theobald, N.A. and Nicholson-Crotty, S. (2005) 'The many faces of span of control: Organization structure across multiple goals', *Administration and Society*, 36(6): 648–60.

Thomas, A.B. (2003) *Controversies in Management*. London: Routledge, (2nd edn).

Thomas, H. (1974) 'Finding a better way', *Guardian*, 17 January, p.12.

Thomas, K.W. (1976) 'Conflict and conflict management', in M.D. Dunette (ed.), *Handbook of Industrial and Organizational Psychology*. Chicago, IL: Rand McNally, pp.889–935.

Thomas, K.W. (1977) 'Towards multi-dimensional values in teaching: the example of conflict behaviours', *Academy of Management Review*, 2(3): 484–528.

Thompson, J.D. (1967) *Organizations in Action*. New York: McGraw-Hill.

Thompson, J. and McGivern, J. (1996) 'Parody, process and practice', *Management Learning*, 27(1): 21–35.

Thompson, J. and Tuden, A. (1959) 'Strategies, structures and processes of organizational decisions', in J.D. Thompson, P.B. Hammond, R.W. Hawkes, B.H. Junker and A. Tuden (eds), *Comparative Studies in Administration*. Pittsburgh, PA: University of Pittsburgh Press, pp.195–216.

Thompson, P. (1983) *The Nature of Work: An Introduction to the Debates in the Labour Process*. London: Macmillan.

Thompson, P. and Ackroyd, S. (1995) 'All quiet on the workplace front?: a critique of recent trends in British industrial sociology', *Sociology*, 29(4): 610–33.

Thompson, P. and Davidson, J.O. (1995) 'The continuity of discontinuity: a managerial rhetoric in turbulent times', *Personnel Review*, 24(4): 17–33.

Thompson, P. and McHugh, D. (2002) *Work Organization: A Critical Introduction*. Basingstoke: Palgrave, (3rd edn).

Thompson, P. and Warhurst, C. (eds) (1998) *Workplaces of the Future*, Basingstoke: Macmillan.

Thompson, W.E. (1983) 'Hanging tongues: a sociological encounter with the assembly line', *Qualitative Sociology*, 6(3): 215–37.

Thomson, R. (2006) *Divided Kingdom*. London: Bloomsbury Press.

Thorne, M. (1999) *Eight Minutes Idle*. London: Phoenix/Orion Books.

Tichy, N.M. (2001) 'No ordinary boot camp', *Harvard Business Review*, 79(1): 63–70.

Tichy, N.M. and Devanna, M.A. (1986) *The Transformational Leader*. New York: Wiley.

Tichy, N. and Fombrun, C. (1979) 'Network analysis on organizational settings', *Human Relations*, 32(11): 923–65.

Timmins, N. (2007) 'When all else fails, reorganize. But do the sums first', *Financial Times*, 18 April, p.15.

Tjosvold, D. (2008) 'The conflict-positive organization: it depends on us', *Journal of Organizational Behaviour*, 29(1): 19–28.

Toffler, A. (1970) *Future Shock*. London: Pan Books.

Tompkins, P.K. and Cheney, G. (1985) 'Communication and unobtrusive control in contemporary organizations', in R.D. McPhee and P.K. Tompkins (eds), *Organizational Communication: Traditional Themes and New Directions*. Beverley Hills, CA: Sage Publications, pp.179–210.

TOP Politics Group (2009) 'Organizational architecture', from http://top.xwiki.com/xwiki/bin/view/Main/Organizational_Architecture, accessed 27 January.

Toplis, J., Dulewicz, V. and Fletcher, C. (2005) *Psychological Testing: A Manager's Guide*. London: Chartered Institute of Personnel and Development, (4th edn).

Torrington, D. and Hall, L. (1998) *Human Resource Management*. London: Prentice Hall, (4th edn).

Townend, A.M., DeMarie, S.M. and Hendrickson, A.R. (1998) 'Virtual teams: technology and the workplace of the future', *Academy of Management Executive*, 12(3): 17–20.

Townsend, K. (2005) 'Electronic surveillance and cohesive teams: room for resistance in an Australian call centre ?' *New Technology, Work and Employment*, 20(1): 47–59.

Training (1996) 'What self-managing teams manage', *1996 Industry Report*, 33(10).

Trice, H.M. and Beyer, J.M. (1984) 'Studying organization cultures through rites and ceremonials', *Academy of Management Review*, 9(4): 653–69.

Trice, H.M. and Beyer, J.M. (1993) *The Cultures of Work Organizations*. Englewood Cliffs, NJ: Prentice Hall.

Triplett, N. (1898) 'The dynamogenic factors in pacemaking and competition', *American Journal of Psychology*, 9: 507–33.

Trist, E.L. and Bamforth, K.W. (1951) 'Some social and psychological consequences of the longwall method of coal-getting', *Human Relations*, 4(1): 3–38.

Trist, E.L., Higgin, G.W., Murray, H. and Pollock, A.B. (1963) *Organizational Choice*. London: Tavistock Publications.

Trompenaars, F. and Woolliams, P. (2002) 'Model Behaviour', *People Management*, 8(24): 30–55.

Tryhorn, C. and Sweney, M. (2009) 'Smoothie operators Innocent tread familiar path to lucrative deal', from www.guardian.co.uk/business/2009/apr/07/innocent-smoothies-coca-cola, accessed May 2009.

Tuckman, B.W. (1965) 'Development sequences in small groups', *Psychological Bulletin*, 3(6): 384–99.

Tuckman, B.W. and Jensen, M.A.C. (1977) 'Stages of small group development revisited', *Group and Organizational Studies*, 2(4): 419–27.

Turner, A.N. and Lawrence, P.R. (1965) *Industrial Jobs and the Worker: An Investigation of Response to Task Attributes*. Boston, MA: Division of Research, Harvard Business School.

Turner, M.E. and Pratkanis, A.R. (1998) 'Twenty-five years of groupthink theory and research: lessons from the evaluation of theory', *Organizational Behaviour and Human Decision Processes*, 73(2–3): 105–15.

Turniansky, B. and Hare, A.P. (1998) *Individuals and Groups in Organizations: A Social Psychological Approach*. London: Sage Publications.

University of Michigan (2003) 'World Values Survey', from http://wvs.isr.umich.ed.

Ury, W. (1991) *Getting Past No: Negotiating With Difficult People*. New York: Bantam Books.

Ury, W. and Patton, B. (1997) *Getting to Yes: Negotiating An Agreement Without Giving In*. London: Arrow Books, (2nd edn).

Uzzi, B. and Dunlap, S. (2005) 'How to build your network', *Harvard Business Review*, 83(12): 53–80.

Vaill, P.B. (1982) 'The purposing of high-performing systems', *Organizational Dynamics*, 11(2): 23–39.

Valmet Automotive Newsletter (2005) 'The production of the new Porsche Boxster started', March, p.2.

van den Broek, D., Callaghan, G. and Thompson, P. (2002) 'Teams without teamwork: explaining the call centre paradox', paper presented at the 6th International Workshop on Teambuilding, Malmo University, Sweden.

Vanhoegaerden, J. (1999/2000) 'Sense and sensitivity', *Directions: The Ashridge Journal* (Ashridge corporate website, August).

van Maanen, J. (1991) 'The smile factory: work at Disneyland', in P. Frost, L. Moore, M. Louis, C. Lundberg and J. Martin (eds), *Reframing Organizational Culture*. Newbury Park, CA: Sage Publications, pp.31–54.

van Maanen, J. and Schein, E.H. (1979) 'Toward a theory of organization socialization', *Research in Organization Behaviour*, 1: 209–64.

van Maanen, J. and Barley, S. (1984) 'Occupational communities: culture and control in organizations', in B. Staw and L.L. Cummings (eds), *Research in Organizational Behaviour* Vol.6. Greenwich, CT: JAI Press, pp.287–366.

van Maanen, J. and Kunda, G. (1989) 'Real feelings: emotional expression and organization culture', in L.L. Cummings and B.M. Staw (eds), *Research in Organizational Behaviour*. Greenwich, CT: JAI Press, pp.43–103.

Velasquez, M., Moberg, D.J. and Cavanagh, G.F. (1983) 'Organizational statesmanship and dirty politics: ethical guidelines for the organizational politician, *Organizational Dynamics*, 12(2): 65–80.

Veloutsou, C.A. and Panigyrakis, G.G. (2001) 'Brand teams and brand management structure in pharmaceutical and other fast-moving consumer good companies', *Journal of Strategic Marketing*, 9(3): 233–51.

Venkatesh, S.A. and Levitt, S.D. (2000) 'Are we a family or a business?: history and disjuncture in the urban American street gang', *Theory and Society*, 29(4): 427–62.

Venkatesh, S.A. and Levitt, S.D. (2001) 'Growing up in the projects: the economic lives of a cohort of men who came of age in Chicago public housing', *American Economic Review*, 91(2): 79–84.

Venkatraman, N. and Henderson, J.C. (1998) 'Real strategies for virtual organizing', *Sloan Management Review*, 40(1): 33–48.

Vermeir, I. and Van Kenhove, P. (2008) 'Gender differences in double standards', *Journal of Business Ethics*, 81(1): 281–95.

Vickerstaff, S. (ed.) (1992) *Human Resource Management in Europe: Text and Cases*, London: Chapman and Hall.

Vinnicombe, S. and Bank, J. (2002) *Women With Attitude: Lessons for Career Management*. London: Routledge.

Viteles, M.S. (1950) 'Man and machine relationship: the problem of boredom', in R.B. Ross (ed.), *Proceedings of the Annual Fall Conference of the Society for Advancement of Management*. New York: Society for the Advancement of Management, pp.129–38.

von Oech, R. (1998) *A Whack on the Side of the Head*. London: Angus & Robertson Publishers.

Vroom, V.H. (1964) *Work and Motivation*. New York: John Wiley.

Vroom, V.H. (1973) 'A new look at managerial decision making', *Organizational Dynamics*, 1(4): 66–80.

Vroom, V.H. (2000) 'Leadership and the decision making process', *Organizational Dynamics*, 28(4): 82–94.

Vroom, V.H. and Yetton, P.W. (1973) *Leadership and Decision Making*. Pittsburgh, PA: University of Pittsburgh Press.

Vroom, V.H. and Jago, A.G. (1988) *The New Leadership: Managing Participation in Organizations*. Englewood Cliffs, NJ: Prentice Hall.

Walker, C.R. (1950) 'The problem of the repetitive job', *Harvard Business Review*, 28(3): 54–58.

Walker, C.R. and Guest, R.H. (1952) *The Man on the Assembly Line*. Cambridge, MA: Harvard University Press.

Wall, T. and Wood, S. (2002) 'Delegation's a powerful tool', *Professional Manager*, 11(6): 37.

Wallace, P. (2001) *The Psychology of the Internet*. Cambridge: Cambridge University Press, (2nd edn).

Wallace, T. (2008) 'Cycles of production: from assembly lines to cells to assembly lines in the Volvo Cab Plant', *New Technology, Work and Employment*, 23(1–2): 111–24.

Wallach, M.A., Kogan, N. and Bem, D.J. (1962) 'Group influences on individual risk taking', *Journal of Abnormal and Social Psychology*, 65(2): 75–86.

Wallach, M.A., Kogan, N. and Bem, D.J. (1964) 'Diffusion of responsibility and level of risk taking in groups', *Journal of Abnormal and Social Psychology*, 68(3): 263–74.

Walters, C.C. and Grusek, J.E. (1977) *Punishment*. San Francisco, CA: Freeman.

Walton, R.E. (1975) 'The diffusion of new work structures: explaining why success didn't take', *Organizational Dynamics*, 3(3): 3–22.

Walton, R.E. and McKersie, R.B. (1965) *A Behavioural Theory of Labour Relations*. New York: McGraw Hill.

Walton, R.E. and Susman, G.I. (1987) 'People policies for the new machines', *Harvard Business Review*, 65(2): 98–106.

Warhurst, C. and Thompson, P. (1998) 'Hands, hearts and minds: changing work and workers at the end of the century', in P. Thompson and C. Warhurst (eds), *Workplaces of the Future*. London: Macmillan Business, pp.1–24.

Warner, M. (2000) 'Introduction', in M. Warner (ed.), *International Encyclopedia of Business and Management*. London: Thomson Learning, (2nd edn.) pp.ix–xiv.

Warner, M. and Witzel, M. (2004) *Managing in Virtual Organizations*. London: International Thomson Business Press.

Warren, S. (2009) 'Visual methods in organizational research', in David A. Buchanan and Alan Bryman (eds), *The Sage Handbook of Organizational Research Methods*. London: Sage Publications.

Warrick, D.D. (1984) *MODMAN: Managing Organizational Change and Development*. New York: Science Research Associates Inc.

Watson, T.J. (1994) *In Search of Management: Culture, Chaos and Control in Management Work*. London: Routledge.

Watson, T.J. (2002) *Organizing and Managing Work*. Harlow: Financial Times Prentice Hall.

Webb, M.S. (2006) 'Why boys get better gifts – and higher salaries', *The Sunday Times*, Money, 1 January, p.3.9.

Weber, M. (1924) 'Zur Psychophysik der industriellen Arbeit (first written in 1908/09)', in M. Weber (ed.), *Gesammelte Aussatze zur Sociologie und Sozialpolitik von Max Weber*. Tubingen: J.C.B. Mohr, pp.61–255.

Weber, M. (1947) *The Theory of Social and Economic Organization* (A.M. Henderson and T. Parsons, Trans.) Oxford: Oxford University Press.

Weber, C.E. (1984) 'Strategic thinking – dealing with uncertainty', *Long Range Planning*, 7(5): 60–70.

Weick, K.E. (1977) 'Organizational design: organizations as self-designing systems', *Organizational Dynamics*, 6(2): 30–46.

Weick, K.E. (1979) *The Social Psychology of Organizing*. Boston, MA: Addison-Wesley.

Weick, K.E. (1990) 'The vulnerable system: an analysis of the Tenerife air disaster', *Journal of Management*, 16(3): 571–93.

Weick, K.E. (1995) *Sensemaking in Organizations*. London: Sage Publications.

Weick, K.E. (2003) 'Enacting an environment: the infrastructure of organizing', in Westwood. R. and S. Clegg (eds), *Debating Organization*. Oxford: Blackwell, pp.184–94.

Weick, K.E. and Westley, F. (1996) 'Organizational learning: affirming an oxymoron', in S.R. Clegg, C. Hardy and W.R. Nord (eds), *Handbook of Organization Studies*. London: Sage Publications, pp.440–58.

Weiner, E.L., Kanki, B.G. and Helmreich, R.L. (eds) (1993) *Cockpit Resource Management*, New York: Academic Press.

Weiss, H.M. (1990) 'Learning theory and industrial and organizational psychology', in M.D. Dunnette and L.M. Hough (eds), *Handbook of Industrial and Organizational Psychology*. Palo Alto, CA: Consulting Psychologists Press, pp.75–169.

Weiss, J. and Hughes, J. (2005) 'Want collaboration?: accept – and actively manage – conflict', *Harvard Business Review*, 83(3): 93–101.

Weitzman, M. (2008) 'Boeing counts the cost of strike action', *Financial Times*, 29 October, p.27.

West, M.A. (ed.) (1998) *Handbook of Work Group Psychology*, Chichester: Wiley.

West, M. and Johnson, R. (2002) 'A matter of life and death', *People Management*, 8(4): 30–36.

West, M.A., Borrill, C.S. and Unsworth, K.L. (1998) 'Team effectiveness in organizations', in C.L. Cooper and I.T. Robertson (eds), *International Review of Industrial and Organizational Psychology 1998*: Vol. 13. Chichester: Wiley.

West, M.A., Borrill, C., Dawson, J., Scully, J., Carter, M., Anelay, S., Patterson, M. and Waring, J. (2002) 'The link between the management of employees and patient mortality in acute hospitals', *International Journal of Human Resource Management*, 13(8): 1299–310.

Westenholz, A. (2003) 'Organizational citizens – unionized wage earners, participative management and beyond', in B. Czarniawska and G. Sevón (eds), *The Northern Lights – Organization Theory in Scandinavia*. Copenhagen: Copenhagen Business School Press.

Western, S. (2007) *Leadership: A Critical Text*. London: Sage Publications.

Westwood, A. (2002) *Is New Work Good Work*. London: The Work Foundation.

Westwood, R. and Clegg, S.R. (2003) 'Organization-environment', in R. Westwood and S.R. Clegg (eds), *Debating Organization*. Oxford: Blackwell, pp.183–84.

Wharton, A. (1993) 'The affective consequences of service work: managing emotions on the job', *Work and Occupations*, 20(2): 205–32.

Wheelan, S.A. (1999) *Creating Effective Work Teams*. London: Sage Publications.

Whetten, D., Cameron, K. and Woods, M. (1996) *Effective Conflict Management*. London: HarperCollins.

Whetten, D., Cameron, K. and Woods, M. (2000) *Developing Management Skills for Europe*. Harlow: Financial Times Prentice Hall, (2nd edn).

White, R.W. (1959) 'Motivation reconsidered: the concept of competence', *Psychological Review*, 66(5): 297–333.

White, R. and Lippitt, R. (1960) *Autocracy and Democracy*. New York: Harper & Row.

White, M., Hill, S., Mills, C. and Smeaton, D. (2004) *Managing to Change?: British Workplaces and the Future of Work*. London: Palgrave Macmillan.

Whitehead, M. (1999) 'Watch your workloads', *People Management*, 5(14): 12–13.

Whittell, G. (1999) 'Exxon challenges payout a decade after Valdez spill', *The Times*, 25 March, p.20.

Whittington, R. and Mayer, M. (2002) *Organizing for Success in the Twenty-First Century: A Starting Point for Change*. London: Chartered Institute of Personnel and Development.

Whittington, R., Mayer, M. and Smith, A. (2002) 'Restructuring roulette', *Financial Times Mastering Leadership Supplement*, 8 November, p.6 and 8.

Whittington, R., Pettigrew, A., Peck, S., Fenton, E. and Conyon, M. (1999a) 'Change and complementarities in the new competitive landscape: a European panel study, 1992–1996', *Organizational Science*, 10(5): 583–600.

Whittington, R., Pettigrew, A. and Ruigrok, W. (1999b) 'New notions of organizational "fit"', *Financial Times Mastering Strategy Supplement*, 29 November, p.8 and 10.

Whyte, W.F. (1948) *Human Relations in the Restaurant Industry*. New York: McGraw-Hill.

Whyte, W.H. (1955) *The Organization Man*. Harmondsworth: Penguin Books.

Whyte, G. (1986) 'Escalation of commitment to a course of action: a reinterpretation', *Academy of Management Review*, 11(2): 311–21.

Whyte, G. (1993) 'Escalating commitment in the individual and group decision making: a prospect theory approach', *Organizational Behaviour and Human Decision Processes*, 54(3): 430–55.

Wickens, P. (1999) 'Values added', *People Management*, 5(10): 33–37.

Wiener, N. (1954) *The Human Use of Human Beings: Cybernetics and Society*. New York: Avon Books.

Wiggins, J. (2007) 'Coke develops thirst for sustainability', *Financial Times*, 2 July, p.26.

Williams, C. (2003) 'Sky service: the demands of emotional labour in the airline industry', *Gender, Work and Organization*, 10(5): 513–50.

Williams, C.L., Giuffre, P.A. and Dellinger, K. (1999) 'Organizational control, sexual harassment and the pursuit of pleasure', in Annual Reviews Inc (ed.), *Annual Review of Sociology: Volume 25*. Palo Alto, CA: pp.73–93.

Williams, K., Harkins, S. and Latane, L. (1981) 'Identifiability and social loafing: two cheering experiments', *Journal of Personality and Social Psychology*, 40(2): 303–11.

Williams, L.A. and Kessler, R.R. (2000) 'All I really need to know about pair programming, I learned in kindergarten', *Communications of the ACM*, 43(5): 108–14.

Williamson, O.E. (1975) *Markets and Hierarchies: Analysis and Antitrust Implications, A Study in the Economics of Internal Organizations*. London: Macmillan.

Willmott, H. (1993) 'Strength is ignorance; slavery is freedom; managing culture in modern organizations', *Journal of Management Studies*, 30(4): 515–52.

Willmott, H. (2005) 'Studying managerial work: a critique and a proposal', in C. Grey and H. Willmott (eds), *Critical Management Studies: A Reader*. Oxford: Oxford University Press, pp.324–47.

Wilson, F. (2002) *Organizational Behaviour and Gender*. Aldershot: Ashgate, (2nd edn).

Wilson, F. (2004) *Organizational Behaviour and Work: A Critical Introduction*. Oxford: Oxford University Press, (2nd edn).

Winner, L. (1977) *Autonomous Technology: Technics-Out-Of-Control as a Theme in Political Thought*. Cambridge, MA: MIT Press.

Winner, D. (2001) *Brilliant Orange: The Neurotic Genius of Dutch Football*. London: Bloomsbury Press.

Witzel, M. (2007) 'Types of collaboration: the right vehicle', *Financial Times*, Understanding the Culture of Collaboration supplement, 29 June, p.4.

Wolff, S.B. (2009) *OB in Action: Cases and Exercises*. Boston, MA: Houghton Mifflin (8th edn).

Wolfinger, R.E. (1971) 'Nondecisions and the study of local politics', *American Political Science Review*, 65(4): 1063–80.

Womack, J.P., Jones, D.T. and Roos, D. (1990) *The Machine that Changed the World: The Triumph of Lean Production*. New York: Macmillan.

Wood, J. (1995) 'Mastering management: organizational behaviour', *Financial Times Mastering Management Supplement (part 2 of 20)*.

Wood, W.S. (2001) 'Can we go to Mars without going crazy?' *Discover Magazine*, 5 May, from http://discovermagazine.com/2001/may/cover, accessed May 2009.

Wood, S. (2003) 'Human resource practices showing their promise', *Social Sciences*, 53: 6.

Wood, W., Lundgren, S., Ouellette, J.A., Busceme, S. and Blackstone, T. (1994) 'Minority influence: a meta-analytical review of social influence processes', *Psychological Bulletin*, 115(3): 323–45.

Woodcock, M. (1989) *Team Development Manual*. Aldershot: Gower.

Woodman, P. and Cook, P. (2005) *Bullying at Work: The Experience of Managers*. London: Chartered Management Institute.

Woodruffe, C. (2001) 'Promotional intelligence', *People Management*, 7(1): 26–29.

Woodward, J. (1958) *Management and Technology*. London: HMSO.

Woodward, J. (1965) *Industrial Organization: Theory and Practice*. Oxford: Oxford University Press.

Wooldridge, A. (2006) 'The battle for brainpower', *The Economist*, Survey of Talent supplement, pp.3–6.

Worral, L. and Cooper, C. (2006) 'Short changed', *People Management*, 12(13): 36–38.

Wuchty, S., Jones, B.F. and Uzzi, B. (2007) 'The increasing dominance of teams in production of knowledge', *Science*, 316(5827): 1036–39.

Wyke, N. (2002) 'Cool centres welcome call of excellence', *The Times Agile Business Supplement*, 25 April, p.8.

Yates, S. (1985) *The Politics of Management*. San Francisco, CA: Jossey-Bass.

Yerkes, R.M. and Dodson, J.D. (1908) 'The relationship of strength of stimulus to rapidity of habit-formation', *Journal of Comparative Neurology and Psychology*, 18(5): 459–82.

Yetton, P.W. and Bottger, P.C. (1982) 'Individual versus group problem-solving: an empirical test of a best-member strategy', *Organizational Behaviour and Human Performance*, 29(3): 307–21.

York, P. (1999) 'The gender agenda', *Management Today*, October, pp.56–63.

Yukl, G. (2000) 'Using power effectively', in E.A. Locke (ed.), *The Blackwell Handbook of Principles of Organizational Behaviour*. Oxford: Blackwell Business, pp.241–56.

Yukl, G. (2005) *Leadership in Organizations*. Thousand Oaks, CA: Prentice Hall, (6th edn).

Yukl, G. and Falbe, C.M. (1990) 'Influencing tactics in upward, downward and lateral influencing attempts', *Journal of Applied Psychology*, 75(2): 132–40.

Zajonc, R.B. (1965) 'Social facilitation', *Science*, 149(3681): 269–74.

Zajonc, R.B. (1980) 'Compresence', in P.B. Paulus (ed.), *Psychology of Group Influence*. Hillsdale, NJ: Erlbaum, pp.35–60.

Zaleznik, A. (1977) 'Managers and leaders: are they different ?' *Harvard Business Review*, 15(3): 67–84.

Zaleznik, A. (1993) 'The mythological structure of organizations and its impact', in L. Hirschhorn and C.K. Barnett (eds), *The Psychodynamics of Organizations*. Philadelphia, PA: Temple University Press, pp.179–89.

Zaleznik, A. and Kets de Vries, M. (1975) *Power and the Corporate Mind*. Boston, MA: Houghton Mifflin.

Zalkind, S.S. and Costello, T.W. (1962) 'Perception: some recent research and implications for administration', *Administrative Science Quarterly*, 7(2): 218–35.

Zaniello, T. (2003) *Working Stiffs, Union Maids, Reds, and Riffraff: An Expanded Guide to Films About Labor*. Ithaca and London: ILR Press/Cornell University Press.

Zaniello, T. (2007) *The Cinema of Globalization: A Guide to Films About The New Economic Order*. Ithaca and London: ILR Press/Cornell University Press.

Zeleny, L.D. (1947) 'Selection of compatible flying partners', *American Journal of Sociology*, 51(5): 424–31.

Zenger, T. (2002) 'Crafting internal bids: complementarities, common change initiatives, and the team-based organization', *International Journal of Economics and Business*, 9(1): 79–95.

Ziegler, M. (2003) 'Storybook solution', *Professional Manager*, May, pp.26–27.

Zimbalist, A.S. (1979) *Case Studies on the Labour Process*. London: Monthly Review Press.

Zimbardo, P.G. (2007) *The Lucifer Effect: How Good People Turn Evil*. London: Rider & Co.

Zuboff, S. (1988) *In the Age of the Smart Machine: The Future of Work and Power*. Oxford: Heinemann Professional Publishing.

Name Index

Subject Index

A, personality type 180–1
abilities 28–9, 83, 600
aboriginal culture and communication 213–14
abrasive leadership 608
acceptance 707, 276, 567, 642
accommodating in conflict resolution 672, 673
accountability 464, 570
accounting 223
achievement, needs for (nAch) 188–9, 712
acquisition needs 267
acting 686
action-centred abilities 83
action research 579
action teams 390, 393–4, 439
actions
    distortion of 374
    information–perception–actions link 244
active skin 70
activities 315, 316, 336
ad hoc organizations 566
adaptation 41, 118, 127
adapter traits 179
adaptive reorganizations 562
additive tasks 304
adherence to values 109
adhocracy 566
adjourning 317, 318
adjustment, incremental 574
ADR (alternative dispute resolution) 675
advancement, organizational currencies 697
advice teams 390, 392–3
advocacy, inquiry versus 648–9
aesthetic needs 268–9
affiliation, needs for (nAff) 268, 270, 712
affluence, corporate social responsibilities as result of 61–2
age discrimination 42, 43, 252–3
aggregates 301–2
aggressive goal behaviour 122
aggressiveness indices 22

agreeableness 179, 180
agreement, change resistance management by 572
Airbus 495
Alessi 547
alienation 86, 679
alliances 705
alpha males and alpha females 603
alternative dispute resolution (ADR) 675
alternative organizational lifestyles 608
altruism 266, 543
Amazon.com 108–9, 144, 419, 462, 542
American Express 264
Android 542
anger 567, 608
anonymity 376
antagonisms, structural 679
anticipatory strategies 49
anxiety 219
AOL 79
Apache 547
appearance discrimination 252–3
Apple 117, 540, 542
apprising 708
appropriate behaviour
    women and organizational politics 719
arbitration 674–5
architectural leadership 617–18
artefacts 101–3
ASEAN (Association of South East Asian Nations) 39
assembly lines 431–6
assertiveness 125, 126
assessment centres 194
assistance, organizational currencies 697
Association of South East Asian Nations (ASEAN) 39
assumptions 106–7, 249–51, 715
asthenization 300
asynchronous communications 345
attention, selective 238, 240
attractiveness 252–3, 472, 706
attributions 14, 251–2

attunement 203
authoritarian leadership 342
authoritative leadership 607, 614
authority 127, 464, 489, 490, 602, 638, 665–6, 668, 707
autocratic leadership 343, 607
autocratic management 616
autonomous teamwork 392
autonomous work groups 86, 400, 402–3
autonomy 281, 282, 389–92
avoiding conflict resolution 672, 673
ayurveda principle 172

B, personality type 180–1
bait-and-switch technique 706
balanced scorecard 15
bank examiner scheme 707
Barclays Bank 156–7
bargaining 567, 674, 694
basic assumptions 106–7
Bath People and Performance Model 28–30
battles tasks 298
Bay of Pigs 644, 648–9
behaviour
    aggressive 22
    ethical 51–6
    human 265–6
    manipulation 223
    modification 27, 146, 149–50, 154–6
    non-observable 700
    observable 700
behavioural modelling 151–2
behavioural sciences 7
behavioural self-management (BSM) 155
behavioural theory of decision-making 632
behaviourism 138, 141–7, 149–50
beliefs, differentiation and 715
benevolent authoritative leadership 607
best case, worst case possibilities 46
best-known-way-at-present 430
best practices 585–7
Bethlehem Iron Company 425–6